Finite Mathematics With Applications

For Business And Social Sciences

Finite Mathematics With Applications

For Business And Social Sciences

John Wiley & Sons, Inc.
New York London
Sydney Toronto

Abe Mizrahi
Indiana University Northwest

Michael Sullivan
Chicago State University

To our parents with gratitude

This book was set in Optima
by Progressive Typographers,
Inc., and printed and bound
by Halliday Lithographers, Inc.
The text and cover were designed by Jerome Wilke; the
drawings were done by the
Wiley Illustration Department;
the editor was Beverly D.
Nerenberg; Robert S. Kamen
supervised production.

Library of Congress Cataloging in Publication Data:

Mizrahi, Abe.
  Finite mathematics with applications for business
and social sciences.

  Includes bibliographies.
  1. Business mathematics.   2. Social sciences—
Methodology.   3. Mathematics—1961–
I. Sullivan, Michael, 1942–   joint author.
II. Title.

HF5695.M66   513'.93   72-5578
ISBN 0-471-61185-9

Printed in the United States of America

10 9 8 7 6 5 4 3

Several years ago we felt a pressing need for an elementary textbook that could be used in the course now generally referred to as *Finite Mathematics*. Our objective was to write a textbook that would provide a motivating study for students whose mathematical background is minimal.

In fulfilling this need we present various topics in mathematics by first introducing problems through real-life situations and continue by developing the necessary mathematics to handle similar situations. That is to say, we utilize mathematical models and, to emphasize the relevant character of these models, cite many references to current applications in the social sciences, business, and life sciences.

Throughout the book we have attempted to minimize abstraction and sophisticated mathematical theory but not at the expense of sacrificing an understanding of the basic concepts that underlie the use of mathematics. A student who masters the material found here will be well prepared to engage in a deeper study of the mathematics and applications given.

This book is truly a collaborative effort and the order of authorship signifies alphabetical precedence. We assume equal responsibility for the book's strengths and weaknesses and welcome comments and suggestions for its improvement.

ORGANIZATION

This book touches on many topics in mathematics. The first chapter on logic, although not absolutely essential for the ensuing study of finite mathematics, will help the student reason clearly and precisely. Chapter 2 forms the basis for the subsequent study of probability in Chapter 3 by introducing properties of sets and counting principles. Chapter 4 gives a brief but important introduction to mathematical models. Chapter 5, which may be omitted if the preparation of the student in high school algebra is sound, discusses the straight line and linear inequalities. However, the topics found in Chapter 5 are essential for the ensuing study of linear programming in Chapter 6.

Chapter 7 discusses various topics in matrix algebra including addition and multiplication of matrices as well as systems of equations and the inverse of a matrix. Applications to cryptography, demography, and accounting are included in a separate section and may be omitted without a loss of continuity.

Chapter 8 continues the study of linear programming and introduces the simplex method. Chapter 9 covers applications of matrices to directed graphs. Included here are applications to social psychology (dominance, communication, and detection of cliques) and business (identification of liaison officials). This chapter only requires a knowledge of Sections 7.1 to 7.3 of Chapter 7.

Chapter 10 discusses various applications in probability theory that use Markov chain models. Included here are applications in business and genetics. Chapter 11 gives a survey of game theory and some of its applications to business situations.

Chapter 12, statistics, may be covered any time after Chapter 3. Chapter 13 is independent of all chapters and may be covered at any time.

The following diagram illustrates the dependence/independence of the chapters and summarizes the preceding discussion.

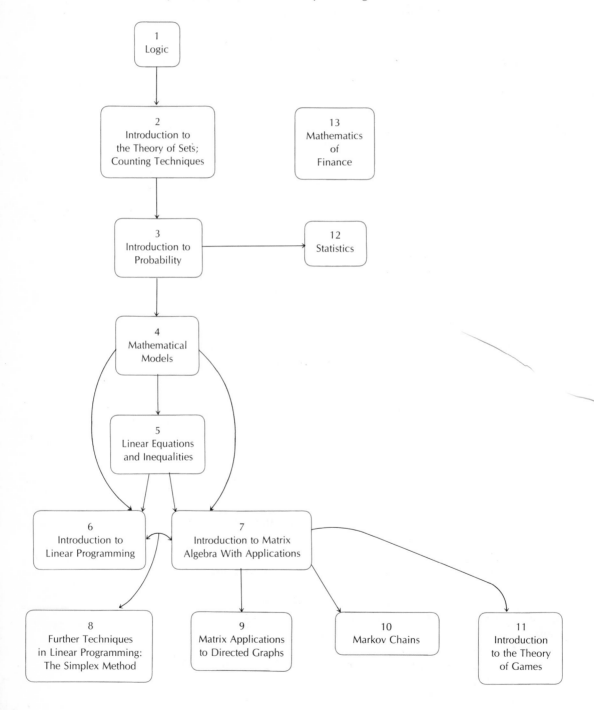

Since credit hours for this type of course vary, we suggest possible plans in the table below.

Time	Sections To Be Covered
3 Semester hours	Chapters 1, 2, 3, 4, 5, 6 or Chapters 2, 3, 4, 5, 6, 7.1–7.3, 9 or Chapters 2, 3, 4, 5, 6, 7.1–7.3, 11 or Chapters 2, 3, 4, 5, 6, 7, 10 or Chapters 2, 3, 4, 5, 6, 12 or Chapters 2, 3, 4, 5, 6, 13 or Chapters 3, 4, 6, 7, 9, 11, 12
5 Semester hours	Chapters 1–11 inclusive or Chapters 2–12 inclusive
6 Semester hours	Entire text

Answers to approximately fifty percent of the problems are given in the back of the book. Worked out solutions to many of the exercises and answers to all problems are available in a Solutions Manual. Problems with asterisks are to be considered as more challenging.

Following each chapter a review of important terms and additional problems are given. Supplementary reading material is listed at the end of most chapters. Finally, the text contains all tables required in the exercises.

ACKNOWLEDGMENTS

It is not possible to list here all the individuals who encouraged and assisted us in this project. We are indebted to our colleagues and to all our students who helped make this project a reality.

We are singularly thankful for the efforts of Daniel P. Maki, Professor of Mathematics at Indiana University in Bloomington, whose constructive criticisms and helpful suggestions played a major role in final revisions.

We are also thankful to these reviewers for their suggestions on improving the manuscript: Edith Ainsworth, Professor of Mathematics at the University of Alabama; Orie Eigsti, Professor of Botany at Chicago State University; Leon Luey, Professor of Mathematics, City College of San Francisco; George Mandler, Professor of Psychology, University of California at San Diego; Carletta Miller, Professor of Mathematics at Texas A. & I. University; Gary P. Moran, Professor of Psychology at Indiana University Northwest; Victor Okkerrse, Professor of Mathematics, Fresno City College; Frank Olson, Professor of Mathematics, Fredonia State College; and Jay Welch, Professor of Mathematics, San Jacinto Junior College.

We also appreciate the patience and skill of Ruth Flessor and Tedgena

Benedyk who, laboring under the handicap of our handwritten corrections, typed the final draft.

Finally, we are indebted to the skill exhibited by the many people at John Wiley and Sons whose talent played a significant role in the final appearance of this book. In particular, we wish to thank Mr. Frederick Corey, Mathematics Editor, for his valuable advice and assistance.

Gary, Indiana
Chicago, Illinois
July, 1972

Abe Mizrahi
Michael Sullivan

1 Logic

2 Introduction to the Theory of Sets; Counting Techniques

3 Introduction to Probability

4 Mathematical Models

5 Linear Equations and Inequalities

Logic Chapter 1

In this chapter, we shall survey many of the more fundamental concepts found in the area of mathematics called *logic*. There are several reasons for studying logic. Two of the more important ones are (1) to gain proficiency in correct mathematical reasoning and (2) to apply the tool of logic to practical situations.

In mathematics, the words "not," "or," "if . . . , then . . . ," "if and only if," and so on are used extensively. A knowledge of the exact meaning of these words is necessary before we can make precise the laws of inference and deduction that are constantly used in mathematics. Our subsequent study of logic will enable us to gain a basic understanding of what constitutes a mathematical argument. This will eliminate common errors made in mathematical, as well as nonmathematical arguments.

Second, we shall use the concepts of logic to study practical applications in the area of elementary electrical circuits and life insurance.

We hope this chapter offers some vindication of the usefulness of logic in uncovering ambiguities and non sequiturs. Furthermore, we hope this chapter offers evidence in favor of Church's remark that ". . . the value of logic . . . is not that it supports a particular system, but that the process of logical organization of any system (empiricist or otherwise) serves to test its internal consistency, to verify its logical adequacy to its declared purpose, and to isolate and clarify the assumptions on which it rests."[1]

---

[1]Church, A., *Introduction to Mathematical Logic,* Vol. 1, Princeton, N.J.: Princeton University Press, 1956, p. 55.

1.2
PROPOSITIONS

Before embarking on our study, let us consider the development of language. Any developed language, such as English, is composed of various words and phrases with a distinct function. These special words and phrases have a bearing on the truth or falsity of the assertion in which they occur.

English sentences are usually classified as belonging to one of four categories: (1) declarative, (2) interrogative, (3) exclamatory, and (4) imperative. We assume that the student can easily recognize in which category a particular sentence belongs. This ability on the part of the student is required since our study will deal mainly with *declarative sentences*.

1.2.1
Definition

A *proposition* **is a declarative sentence that can be meaningfully classified as either true or false.**

1.2.1
Example

The price of corn in Chicago rose on June 16, 1969.
    This is a proposition, although few of us can say whether it is true or false.

1.2.2
Example

The earth is round.
    This sentence records a possible fact about reality and is a proposition. Some people would classify this proposition as "true" and others as "false," depending on their interpretation of the word *round*. Thus, we see that the classification of propositions as "true" or "false" is an idealization. Actually, the *truth-values of propositions fluctuate as we sharpen our interpretation of the words they contain.*

1.2.3
Example

What is the exchange rate from United States dollars to German marks?
    This is not a proposition—it is a question.

1.2.4
Example

The prices of most stocks on the New York Stock Exchange rose during the period 1929 to 1931.
    Although we know this to be a false statement, it is a proposition.
    We conclude that the classification of propositions into the two categories, true and false, rests on the tacit and ideal assumption that the meanings of the words assumed in the propositions are perfectly clear. We shall see that this idealism can be avoided when we encounter propositions in mathematics by initiating the study of logic.

1.2.5
Example

Consider the proposition "Jones is handsome and Smith is selfish." This sentence is obtained by joining the two propositions "Jones is handsome" "Smith is selfish" by the word "and."

1.2.2
Definition

The combination of two or more propositions is called a *compound proposition.* **The words used to combine the propositions of a compound proposition are called** *connectives.*

Some examples of connectives are: *not, or, and, if . . . then, if and only if.*

Let p and q denote any propositions. The compound proposition "p and q" is called the *conjunction of p and q,* **and is denoted symbolically by**

$$p \land q$$

We define the statement $p \land q$ to be true when both p and q are true and to be false otherwise.

Consider the two statements

    p: Washington D.C. is the capital of the United States.
    q: Hawaii is the fiftieth state of the United States.

The conjunction of p and q is

    $p \land q$: Washington D.C. is the capital of the United States and Hawaii is the fiftieth state of the United States.

Since both p and q are true statements, we conclude that the compound statement $p \land q$ is true.

Consider the two statements

    p: Washington D.C. is the capital of the United States.
    q: Vermont is the largest of the fifty states.

The compound proposition $p \land q$ is

    $p \land q$: Washington D.C. is the capital of the United States and Vermont is the largest of the fifty states.

Since the statement q is false, the compound statement $p \land q$ is false—even though p is true.

Let p and q be any propositions. The compound proposition "p or q" is called the *inclusive disjunction of p and q* **and is denoted symbolically by**

$$p \lor q$$

We define the compound proposition $p \lor q$ to be true if both p and q are true, if p is true and q is false, or if p is false and q is true. The compound proposition $p \lor q$ is false if both p and q are false.

Consider the propositions

    p: XYZ Company is the largest producer of nails in the world.
    q: Mines Ltd. has three uranium mines in Nevada.

The compound proposition $p \lor q$ is

> $p \lor q$: XYZ Company is the largest producer of nails in the world or Mines Ltd. has three uranium mines in Nevada.

1.2.5
Definition

Let p and q be any propositions. The *exclusive disjunction of p and q*, **read as "p or q," is denoted symbolically by**

$$p \veebar q$$

We define the compound proposition $p \veebar q$ to be true whenever p is true and q is false, and whenever p is false and q is true. The compound proposition $p \veebar q$ is false whenever p is false and q is false or whenever p is true and q is true.

Thus, in the English language, "or" is a connective that can be used in two different ways. The correct meaning is usually apparent from the context in which it is used. However, to remain precise, we shall distinguish between the two meanings of "or."

1.2.8
Example

Consider the propositions

> p: XYZ Company earned $3.20 per share in 1970.
> q: XYZ Company paid a dividend of $1.20 per share in 1970.

The inclusive disjunction of p and q is

> $p \lor q$: XYZ Company earned $3.20 per share in 1970 or XYZ Company paid a dividend of $1.20 per share in 1970 or both.

The exclusive disjunction of p and q is

> $p \veebar q$: XYZ Company earned $3.20 per share in 1970 or XYZ Company paid a dividend of $1.20 per share in 1970, but *not* both.

1.2.9
Example

Consider the compound proposition

> p: This weekend I will date Caryl or Mary.

The use of the connective "or" is not clear here. If the "or" means inclusive disjunction, then at least one and possibly both girls will be dated. If the "or" means exclusive disjunction then only one girl will be dated.

1.2.6
Definition

If p is any proposition, the *negation of p*, **denoted by**

$$\sim p$$

and read as "not p" is that proposition for which

> **1. If p is true, then $\sim p$ is false.**
> **2. If p is false, then $\sim p$ is true.**

Implied in this definition is the *law of contradiction* from classical logic which states that a proposition p and its negation $\sim p$ cannot both be true.

Consider the proposition

p: One share of XYZ Company is worth $85.

The negation of p is

$\sim p$: One share of XYZ Company is not worth $85.

The statement "one share of XYZ Company is worth $80" is *not* a correct negation of p.

A *quantifier* is a word or phrasing telling how many (*quant*). The quantifiers "each," "every," "any," and "all" are interchangeable.

The following propositions have the same meaning.

p: All men are intelligent.
q: Every man is intelligent.
r: Each man is intelligent.
s: Any man is intelligent.

The quantifiers "some" and "there exists" are interchangeable.

The negation of the proposition.

p: All men are intelligent

is

$\sim p$: Some men are not intelligent.
$\sim p$: There exists a man who is not intelligent.

The negation of

p: There is a man who is not intelligent.
p: Some men are not intelligent

is

$\sim p$: All men are intelligent.

1. Determine which of the following are propositions.
   (a) The cost of shell egg futures was up on June 18, 1970.
   (b) The gross national product exceeded one billion dollars in 1935.
   (c) What a portfolio!
   (d) Why did you buy XYZ Company stock?
   (e) The earnings of XYZ Company doubled last year.
   (f) Where is the new mine of Mines Ltd?

(g) Jones is guilty of murder in the first degree.
2. Negate the following propositions.
    (a) A fox is an animal.
    (b) The outlook for bonds is not good.
    (c) I am buying stocks and bonds.
    (d) Mike is selling his apartment building and his business.
    (e) No one wants to buy my house.
    (f) Everyone has at least one television set.
    (g) Some people have no car.
    (h) Jones is permitted not to see that all votes are not counted.
3. Let p denote "John is an economics major" and let q denote "John is a sociology minor." State the following compound propositions as simple sentences.
    (a) $p \lor q$
    (b) $p \underline{\lor} q$
    (c) $p \land q$
    (d) $\sim p$
    (e) $\sim p \lor \sim q$
    (f) $\sim(\sim q)$
    (g) $\sim p \lor q$

1.3
TRUTH TABLES

For a given proposition p we are interested in determining whether the proposition is true or false; that is, we seek the *truth value* of p. First let us denote "true" by "T" and "false" by "F." We can determine the truth value by a truth table that spells out the truth value of a compound proposition for all the possible truth-value cases.

For example, consider the conjunction of any two propositions p and q. Recall that $p \land q$ is false if either p is false or q is false, or if both p and q are false. There are four truth-value possibilities for the compound statement.

1. p is true and q is true.
2. p is true and q is false.
3. p is false and q is true.
4. p is false and q is false.

The four truth-value cases for $p \land q$ are gathered together in Figure 1.1. For convenience, the possibilities for p and for q will always be listed in this order:

	p	q	$p \land q$
Case 1	T	T	T
Case 2	T	F	F
Case 3	F	T	F
Case 4	F	F	F

Figure 1.1

p	$\sim p$
T	F
F	T

Figure 1.2

The truth values of $\sim p$ are given in Figure 1.2.

Using the previous definitions of inclusive disjunction and exclusive disjunction, Figure 1.3 provides the truth tables for $p \vee q$ and $p \underline{\vee} q$.

p	q	$p \vee q$	$p \underline{\vee} q$
T	T	T	F
T	F	T	T
F	T	T	T
F	F	F	F

Figure 1.3

In addition to using the connectives $\vee$, $\wedge$, $\underline{\vee}$ separately to form compound propositions, we can use them together to form more complex assertions. Let us denote by $P(p,q, \ldots)$ a compound proposition, where $p, q, \ldots$ are the components making the compound proposition. The truth value of a compound proposition depends exclusively on the truth values of its components, that is, the truth value of a compound proposition is known once the truth values of its components are known. Truth tables will be used to demonstrate this relationship.

For example, the truth table for $(p \vee q) \underline{\vee} (\sim p)$, which involves two components p and q, is given in Figure 1.4.

p	q	$p \vee q$	$\sim p$	$(p \vee q) \underline{\vee} (\sim p)$
T	T	T	F	T
T	F	T	F	T
F	T	T	T	F
F	F	F	T	T

Figure 1.4

Observe that the first columns of the table are for the component propositions $p, q, \ldots$ and that there are enough rows in the table to allow for all possible combinations of T and F (for two components p and q, 4 rows are necessary; for three p, q, and r, 8 are necessary; and for n, 2^n rows will be necessary).

Observing Figure 1.4 we notice that there are five columns, in which each column corresponds to a "stage" in constructing the compound proposition. Notice that each stage depends on its predecessors. In essence, the first two columns and the last one are of interest to us and the other middle two are just intermediate ones leading to the final stage. Hence, let us analyze the compound proposition to observe carefully these stages.

First construct the following table.

p	q	$p \vee q$	$\sim p$	$(p \vee q) \veebar (\sim p)$
T	T			
T	F			
F	T			
F	F			

Observe that the compound proposition is written on the top row to the right of its components and that there is a column under each component or connective. Truth values are then entered in the truth table in various steps as in stages 1 to 3.

p	q	$p \vee q$	$\sim p$	$(p \vee q) \veebar (\sim p)$
T	T	T		
T	F	T		
F	T	T		
F	F	F		

Stage 1

p	q	$p \vee q$	$\sim p$	$(p \vee q) \veebar (\sim p$
T	T	T	F	
T	F	T	F	
F	T	T	T	
F	F	F	T	

Stage 2

p	q	$p \vee q$	$\sim p$	$(p \vee q) \veebar (\sim p)$
T	T	T	F	T
T	F	T	F	T
F	T	T	T	F
F	F	F	T	T

Stage 3

The truth table of the compound proposition then consists of the original columns under p and q and the fifth column entered into the table, namely the last stage.

Determine the truth table $(p \lor {\sim}q) \land p$. Notice that the component parts of this proposition are p, ${\sim}q$, and $p \lor {\sim}q$. See Figure 1.5 for the truth table.

p	q	${\sim}q$	$p \lor {\sim}q$	$(p \lor {\sim}q) \land p$
T	T	F	T	T
T	F	T	T	T
F	T	F	F	F
F	F	T	T	F

Figure 1.5

Determine the truth table for the compound proposition $(p \lor {\sim}q) \land {\sim}p$. The component parts of this proposition are p, ${\sim}q$, $p \lor {\sim}q$, and ${\sim}p$. See Figure 1.6.

p	q	${\sim}q$	$p \lor {\sim}q$	${\sim}p$	$(p \lor {\sim}q) \land {\sim}p$
T	T	F	T	F	F
T	F	T	T	F	F
F	T	F	F	T	F
F	F	T	T	T	T

Figure 1.6

Determine the truth table for ${\sim}(p \lor q) \lor ({\sim}p \land {\sim}q)$. (It is understood that the first negation symbol only negates $p \lor q$ and is not intended to negate the entire expression.) See Figure 1.7.

p	q	${\sim}p$	${\sim}q$	$p \lor q$	${\sim}(p \lor q)$	$({\sim}p \land {\sim}q)$	${\sim}(p \lor q) \lor ({\sim}p \land {\sim}q)$
T	T	F	F	T	F	F	F
T	F	F	T	T	F	F	F
F	T	T	F	T	F	F	F
F	F	T	T	F	T	T	T

Figure 1.7

The following is an example of a truth table involving three components, p, q, and r.

1.3 4
Example

Determine the truth table of $p \wedge (q \vee r)$. See Figure 1.8.

p	q	r	$q \vee r$	$p \wedge (q \vee r)$
T	T	T	T	T
T	T	F	T	T
T	F	T	T	T
T	F	F	F	F
F	T	T	T	F
F	T	F	T	F
F	F	T	T	F
F	F	F	F	F

Figure 1.8

1.3.1
Exercise

Construct a truth table for the following compound propositions

1. $p \vee \sim q$
2. $\sim p \vee \sim q$
3. $\sim p \wedge \sim q$
4. $\sim p \wedge q$
5. $\sim (\sim p \wedge q)$
6. $(p \vee \sim q) \wedge \sim p$
7. $\sim (\sim p \vee \sim q)$
8. $(p \vee \sim q) \wedge (q \wedge \sim p)$
9. $(p \vee \sim q) \wedge p$
10. $p \wedge (q \vee \sim q)$
11. $(p \veebar q) \wedge (p \wedge \sim q)$
12. $(p \wedge \sim q) \vee (q \wedge \sim p)$
13. $(p \wedge q) \vee (\sim p \wedge \sim q)$
14. $(p \wedge q) \vee (p \wedge r)$
15. $(p \wedge \sim q) \veebar r$
16. $(\sim p \vee q) \wedge \sim r$

Very often two propositions stated differently have the same meaning. For example, in law to say that "Jones has a duty to Smith to paint his house" is the same as saying that "it ought to be the case Jones does paint the house for Smith."

1.3.1
Definition

If two propositions a and b have the same truth values in every possible case, the propositions are called *logically equivalent.* **This situation is denoted by $a \equiv b$.**

$\sim(p \wedge q)$ is logically equivalent to $\sim p \vee \sim q$.

1	2	3	4	5	6	7
p	q	$p \wedge q$	$\sim(p \wedge q)$	$\sim p$	$\sim q$	$\sim p \vee \sim q$
T	T	T	F	F	F	F
T	F	F	T	F	T	T
F	T	F	T	T	F	T
F	F	F	T	T	T	T

Figure 1.9

Notice that the entries in columns 4 and 7 of Figure 1.9 are the same. Hence, the two propositions are logically equivalent.

Show that $\sim p \wedge \sim q$ is logically equivalent to $\sim(p \vee q)$. First, construct the truth table as in Figure 1.10.

p	q	$p \vee q$	$\sim p$	$\sim q$	$\sim p \wedge \sim q$	$\sim(p \vee q)$
T	T	T	F	F	F	F
T	F	T	F	T	F	F
F	T	T	T	F	F	F
F	F	F	T	T	T	T

Figure 1.10

Because the entries in the last two columns are the same, the two propositions are logically equivalent.

Now that the idea of logically equivalent propositions has been introduced, we can discuss various identities or properties that will be used later in this chapter. That is, certain combinations of statements and connectives will turn out to have the *same* truth values as other combinations of statements and connectives.

Idempotent Laws

For any proposition p,

$$p \wedge p \equiv p \qquad p \vee p \equiv p$$

Thus, $p \wedge p \equiv p$ means that the compound statement p *and* p is logically equivalent to p. Similarly, p *or* p is logically equivalent to p.

Associative Laws

For any three propositions p, q, r,

$$(p \wedge q) \wedge r \equiv p \wedge (q \wedge r) \qquad (p \vee q) \vee r \equiv p \vee (q \vee r)$$

Thus, $(p \wedge q) \wedge r \equiv p \wedge (q \wedge r)$ means that given a compound statement composed of three propositions connected by *and*, changing the position of parentheses does not change the statement. (Similarly with *or*.)

Commutative Laws

For any two propositions p and q,

$$p \wedge q \equiv q \wedge p \qquad p \vee q \equiv q \vee p$$

Thus, $p \wedge q \equiv q \wedge p$ means that the compound proposition p *and* q is equivalent to the compound proposition q *and* p. The cummutative law tells us that when two propositions are compounded by using the connectives *or* or *and*, the order in which the propositions appear does not affect the truth value of the compound proposition.

For example, for the two statements

p: Jones is handsome
q: Jones is intelligent

the truth values of the compound propositions

$p \wedge q$: Jones is handsome and Jones is intelligent
$q \wedge p$: Jones is intelligent and Jones is handsome

are the same.

Of course, the same remarks are also valid for the connective *or*.

Distributive Laws

For any three propositions p, q, r,

$$p \vee (q \wedge r) \equiv (p \vee q) \wedge (p \vee r)$$
$$p \wedge (r \vee q) \equiv (p \wedge r) \vee (p \wedge q)$$

Thus, $p \vee (q \wedge r) \equiv (p \vee q) \wedge (p \vee r)$ means that p *or* (q *and* r) is the same as (p *or* q) *and* (p *or* r). Also, $p \wedge (r \vee q) \equiv (p \wedge r) \vee (p \wedge q)$ means that the compound proposition p *and* (r *or* q) is equivalent to the compound proposition (p *and* r) *or* (p *and* q).

For example, consider the three propositions

p: Jones is handsome
q: Jones is intelligent
r: Jones is humble

The significance of the first distributive law, namely,

$$p \lor (q \land r) \equiv (p \lor q) \land (p \lor r)$$

is that the two statements

1. Jones is handsome or (Jones is intelligent and humble) is equivalent to
2. (Jones is handsome or Jones is intelligent) and (Jones is handsome or humble)

De Morgan's Laws

For any two propositions p and q,

$$\sim(p \lor q) \equiv \sim p \land \sim q \qquad \sim(p \land q) \equiv \sim p \lor \sim q$$

That is, the negation of p or q is logically equivalent to the negation of p and the negation of q. Moreover, the negation of p and q is logically equivalent to the negation of p or the negation of q.

Notice that Figures 1.9 and 1.10 are the truth tables for De Morgan's Laws.

Absorption Laws

For any two propositions p and q,

$$p \lor (p \land q) \equiv p \qquad p \land (p \lor q) \equiv p$$

Thus, $p \lor (p \land q) \equiv p$ means that p or (p and q) is logically equivalent to p. Also, $p \land (p \lor q) \equiv p$ means that p and (p or q) is logically equivalent to p.

Prove the distributive law, $p \lor (q \land r) \equiv (p \lor q) \land (p \lor r)$.

1.3.7
Example

p	q	r	q ∧ r	p ∨ q	p ∨ r	p ∨ (q ∧ r)	(p ∨ q) ∧ (p ∨ r)
T	T	T	T	T	T	T	T
T	T	F	F	T	T	T	T
T	F	T	F	T	T	T	T
T	F	F	F	T	T	T	T
F	T	T	T	T	T	T	T
F	T	F	F	T	F	F	F
F	F	T	F	F	T	F	F
F	F	F	F	F	F	F	F

Figure 1.11

Since the entries in the last two columns of Figure 1.11 are the same, the two propositions are logically equivalent.

1.3.8
Example

Prove the idempotent law, $p \land p \equiv p$. See the truth table in Figure 1.12.

p	$p \land p$
T	T
F	F

Figure 1.12

The rest of the laws are left as exercises for the reader.

1.3.2
Exercise

1. Construct truth tables for:
    (a) the idempotent laws
    (b) the commutative laws
    (c) the associative laws
    (d) the distributive laws
    (e) the absorption laws
2. Show that the following propositions are logically equivalent:
    (a) $p \land (\sim q \lor q)$ and p
    (b) $p \lor (q \land \sim q)$ and p
    (c) $\sim(\sim p)$ and p
3. Construct truth tables for the following:
    (a) $p \land (q \land \sim p)$
    (b) $(p \land q) \lor p$
    (c) $\{(p \land q) \lor (\sim p \land \sim q)\} \land p$
    (d) $(\sim p \land \sim q \land r) \lor (p \land q \land r)$
4. For the propositions

    p: Smith is an exconvict
    q: Smith is rehabititated,

    give examples, using English sentences, of
    (a) idempotent laws
    (b) commutative laws
    (c) De Morgan's laws

1.4
IMPLICATIONS

Consider the following compound proposition: "If I get an A in math, then I will continue to study." The above sentence states a condition under which I shall continue to study.

Another example of such a proposition is: "If today is Sunday, then tomorrow is Monday."

Such propositions occur quite frequently in mathematics, and an understanding of their nature is extremely important.

1.4.1
Definition

If p and q are any two propositions, then we call the proposition:

"if p, then q"

an *implication* **and the connective "if — then —"** the *conditional connective.*

We denote the conditional connective symbolically by $\Rightarrow$ and the implication by $p \Rightarrow q$ (read as: "If p, then q"). In the above, p is called the *hypothesis* **and q the** *conclusion.* **The conditional $p \Rightarrow q$ can also be read as follows:**

1. p **implies** q
2. p **is sufficient for** q
3. p **only if** q
4. q **is necessary for** p

The truth table for implication is given in Figure 1.13.

p	q	$p \Rightarrow q$
T	T	T
T	F	F
F	T	T
F	F	T

Figure 1.13

We shall say that a compound proposition has been expressed symbolically if each component sentence has been replaced by an appropriate symbol.

For example, denoting "I study" and "I shall pass" by "a" and "b" respectively, then the proposition, "If I study, then I shall pass," is expressed or written as $a \Rightarrow b$. This proposition can also be read as "A sufficient condition for passing is to study."

To understand "implication" better, look at an implication as if it is a conditional promise. If the promise is broken the implication is false — otherwise it is true. For this reason the only circumstances under which the implication $p \Rightarrow q$ is false is when p is true and q is false.

1.4.1
Example

Consider the implication
"If you are guilty, then you will go to jail." If you are guilty and you do go to jail, the promise is not broken. Hence, the implication is true. If you are

guilty and you do not go to jail, the promise is broken. Hence, the implication is false. If you are not guilty, the promise is not tested and therefore it is not broken; hence, the implication is true.

The word "then" in an implication merely serves to separate the conclusion from the hypothesis—it could be, and usually is, omitted.

The implication $p \Rightarrow q$ is, in essence, a part of the language we developed thus far. If we construct the truth table of $\sim p \lor q$, we will find out that $\sim p \lor q$ is logically equivalent to $p \Rightarrow q$, that is,

$$\sim p \lor q \equiv p \Rightarrow q$$

See Figure 1.14.

p	q	$\sim p$	$\sim p \lor q$	$p \Rightarrow q$
T	T	F	T	T
T	F	F	F	F
F	T	T	T	T
F	F	T	T	T

Figure 1.14

Suppose we start with the implication $p \Rightarrow q$ and then interchange the roles of p and q, obtaining the implication, "If q, then p."

1.4.2
Definition
The implication "If q, then p" is called the *converse* **of the implication "If p, then q."**

1.4.2
Example
If we let p and q stand for propositions, then $q \Rightarrow p$ is the converse of $p \Rightarrow q$.

Now let us consider simultaneously the truth tables for the implication $p \Rightarrow q$ and its converse $q \Rightarrow p$. See Figure 1.15.

p	q	$p \Rightarrow q$	$q \Rightarrow p$
T	T	T	T
T	F	F	T
F	T	T	F
F	F	T	T

Figure 1.15

Notice that $p \Rightarrow q$ and $q \Rightarrow p$ are not equivalent. That is, the fact that an implication is true tells us nothing about the truth of its converse. To show that this is so, consider the following example.

Consider the statements

> p: "you are a murderer"
> q: "you are in jail"

The implication $p \Rightarrow q$ states that

> "if you are a murderer, then you are in jail."

The converse of this implication, namely, $q \Rightarrow p$, states that

> "if you are in jail, then you are a murderer."

Clearly, to say that all murderers are in jail is not the same as saying that everyone who is in jail is a murderer.

This example illustrates that the truth of an implication does not imply the truth of its converse. Many of the most common fallacies in thinking arise from a confusion of an implication and its converse.

The implication "if not q, then not p," written as $\sim q \Rightarrow \sim p$, is called the *contrapositive* **of the implication $p \Rightarrow q$.**

Consider the statement

> p: you are a murderer
> q: you are in jail

The implication $p \Rightarrow q$ states "if you are a murderer, then you are in jail." The contrapositive of $p \Rightarrow q$, namely, $\sim q \Rightarrow \sim p$, is "if you are not in jail, then you are not a murderer."

The implication "if not p, then not q," written as $\sim p \Rightarrow \sim q$, is called the *inverse* **of the implication "if p, then q."**

Consider the statements

> p: you are a murderer
> q: you are in jail

The implication $p \Rightarrow q$ states "if you are a murderer, then you are in jail." The inverse of $p \Rightarrow q$, namely, $\sim p \Rightarrow \sim q$, is "if you are not a murderer, then you are not in jail."

The truth table for $p \Rightarrow q$, $q \Rightarrow p$, $\sim p \Rightarrow \sim q$, and $\sim q \Rightarrow \sim p$ is given in Figure 1.16.

State-ments		Impli-cation	Con-verse			Inverse	Contra-positive
p	q	$p \Rightarrow q$	$q \Rightarrow p$	$\sim p$	$\sim q$	$\sim p \Rightarrow \sim q$	$\sim q \Rightarrow \sim p$
T	T	T	T	F	F	T	T
T	F	F	T	F	T	T	F
F	T	T	F	T	F	F	T
F	F	T	T	T	T	T	T

Figure 1.16

Notice that the entries under Implication and Contrapositive are the same; also the entries under Converse and Inverse are the same; hence we conclude that

$$p \Rightarrow q \equiv \sim q \Rightarrow \sim p \qquad q \Rightarrow p \equiv \sim p \Rightarrow \sim q$$

Thus, we have shown that an implication and its contrapositive are logically equivalent. Also, the converse and inverse of an implication are logically equivalent.

Write the converse, contrapositive, and inverse of

1. (a) $\sim p \Rightarrow q$ (b) $\sim p \Rightarrow \sim q$ (c) $\sim q \Rightarrow \sim p$ (d) $p \Rightarrow \sim q$
2. If it is raining, the grass is wet.
3. It is raining if it is cloudy.
4. It is raining or it is cloudy.
5. If it is not cloudy then it is not raining.
6. A necessary condition for rain is that it be cloudy.
7. A sufficient condition for rain is that it be cloudy.
8. Rain is necessary for it to be cloudy.
9. Give a verbal sentence which describes
      (a) $p \Rightarrow q$ (b) $q \Rightarrow p$ (c) $\sim p \Rightarrow q$
using:

   p: Jack studies psychology
   q: Mary studies sociology

Consider the statement "q, only if p." This in general can be reworded in the form

   "If q, then p."

For example, consider the propositions

p: The youth is handsome
q: The youth is intelligent

The compound proposition "The youth is intelligent only if the youth is handsome" means that the only time the youth is intelligent is when the youth is handsome. Another way of saying this is to say that if the youth is intelligent then the youth is handsome. Thus, it should be clear that

only if p, then q or q only if p

and

if q, then p

are equivalent. However, it is already known that

if q, then p
if not p, then not q

are equivalent.
  Hence, the three compound statements

only if p, then q
if q, then p
if not p, then not q

are equivalent to each other.
  Thus we have another rule for forming the converse of the implication "if p then q." That is, to form the converse of "if p, then q," replace "if" by "only if."

The connective if and only if **is called the** biconditional connective **and is denoted by** $\Leftrightarrow$. **If** p **and** q **are two propositions for which**

$$p \Rightarrow q \text{ and } q \Rightarrow p \qquad (1.5.1)$$

then we say p if and only if q **and we write**

$$p \Leftrightarrow q \qquad (1.5.2)$$

1.5.1
Definition

  The statement $\Leftrightarrow$ may be read as "p if and only if q," or as "p is equivalent to q," or as "p implies q, and q implies p," or as "p is necessary and sufficient for q." An abbreviation for $p \Leftrightarrow q$ is "p iff q," read as "p if and only if q."
  We can restate Definition 1.5.1 by using the truth table in Figure 1.17.

Let p and q denote the statements

p: Smith is a murderer
q: Smith is in jail

1.5.1
Example

Then "a necessary condition for Smith to be in jail is that Smith be a murderer" is equivalent to

p	q	$p \Rightarrow q$	$q \Rightarrow p$	$(p \Rightarrow q) \wedge (q \Rightarrow p)$	$p \Leftrightarrow q$
T	T	T	T	T	T
T	F	F	T	F	F
F	T	T	F	F	F
F	F	T	T	T	T

Figure 1.17

"if Smith is in jail, then Smith is a murderer"

Also, "a sufficient condition for Smith to be in jail is that Smith be a murderer" is equivalent to

"if Smith is a murderer, then Smith is in jail."

Notice that the statements "if Smith is a murderer, Smith is in jail," "if Smith is not in jail, then Smith is not a murderer," and "only if Smith is in jail is Smith a murderer" are equivalent.

Also, assuming the two implications $p \Rightarrow q$ and $q \Rightarrow p$, are both correct from a practical point of view, then we conclude that a necessary and sufficient condition for Smith to be in jail is that Smith is a murderer. In this case, we say

"Smith is in jail if and only if Smith is a murderer."

The truth table for the biconditional connective $\Leftrightarrow$ for two statements p and q is illustrated by the truth table given previously in Figure 1.17. The biconditional connective $p \Leftrightarrow q$ is true whenever $p \equiv q$ and is false otherwise.

**1.5
Exercise**

1. Construct a truth table for each of the following:
   (a) $\sim p \vee (p \wedge q)$
   (b) $\sim p \wedge (p \vee q)$
   (c) $p \vee (\sim p \wedge q)$
   (d) $(p \vee q) \wedge \sim q$
   (e) $\sim p \Rightarrow q$
   (f) $(p \vee q) \Rightarrow p$
   (g) $\sim p \vee p$
   (h) $p \wedge \sim p$
   (i) $p \wedge (p \Rightarrow q)$
2. Prove that the following only have truth value T.
   (a) $p \wedge (q \wedge r) \Leftrightarrow (p \wedge q) \wedge r$
   (b) $p \wedge (p \vee q) \Leftrightarrow p$
   (c) $p \vee (p \wedge q) \Leftrightarrow p$
3. Let p be "The examination is hard" and q be "The grades are low." Write symbolically each of the following sentences:
   (a) If the examination is hard, the grades are low.

(b) The examination is not hard nor are the grades low.
(c) The grades are not low, and the examination is not hard.
(d) The examination is not hard and the grades are low.
(e) The grades are low only if the examination is hard.

In Section 1.3 we saw how it is possible to obtain compound propositions from simple propositions by using connectives. By using symbols of grouping, such as parentheses and brackets, we can form more complicated propositions. We denote by $P(p,q, \ldots)$ a compound proposition, where $p,q, \ldots$ are components making the compound propositions. Some examples of such propositions are

$$\sim(p \wedge q), \qquad \sim p \wedge \sim q, \qquad p \wedge \sim q, \qquad (p \wedge \sim q) \vee (\sim p \wedge q)$$

Ordinarily when we write a compound proposition, we cannot be certain of the truth of that proposition unless we know the truth or falsity of the component propositions. There are certain compound propositions that are true regardless of the truth or falsity of the component propositions. Compound propositions which have this characteristic are called *tautologies*.

A *tautology* is a compound proposition $P(p,q, \ldots)$ that is always true.

Examples of tautologies are

$$p \vee \sim p, \qquad p \Rightarrow (p \vee q)$$

Figures 1.18 and 1.19 show the truth tables of these tautologies.

p	$\sim p$	$p \vee \sim p$
T	F	T
F	T	T

Figure 1.18

p	q	$p \vee q$	$p \Rightarrow (p \vee q)$
T	T	T	T
T	F	T	T
F	T	T	T
F	F	F	T

Figure 1.19

Let $P(p,q \ . \ . \ .)$ represent a compound composition. Now if we substitute for p a proposition h that is logically equivalent to p, we obtain a compound proposition $P(h,q, \ . \ . \ .)$, which is logically equivalent to $P(p,q, \ . \ . \ .)$. This is a reasonable assumption since the truth of $P(p,q, \ . \ . \ .)$ depends on the truth of the component propositions $p,q, \ . \ . \ .$ and "h is true whenever p is true" and "h is false whenever p is false." This leads us to assert the law of substitution.

Law of Substitution

If $h \equiv p$ and we substitute h for p in the compound proposition $P(p,q, \ . \ . \ .)$, then

$$P(p,q, \ . \ . \ .) \equiv P(h,q, \ . \ . \ .)$$

This principle can be used to obtain new tautologies. If we have a tautology and substitute for some of the component propositions other propositions that are logically equivalent to them, we obtain a *new* tautology.

1.6.2
Definition

It is our desire to use some of the concepts introduced thus far in checking the validity of *arguments.* **By** *argument* **we mean the assertion that a certain statement (called the** *conclusion*) **follows from certain other statements (called** *premises.*) **An argument is** *valid* **if and only if the conjunction of the premises implies (yields, has as a consequence) the conclusion; if an argument is false (that is, not valid), it is called a** *fallacy.*

Valid arguments give rise to what are called *valid conclusions.* Valid arguments together with a true premise give rise to *true conclusions.* A valid argument does not necessarily lead to a true conclusion.

It is important to realize that the truth of the conclusion is irrelevant as a test for the validity of the argument. A true conclusion does not necessarily mean a valid argument has been given. For example, sometimes students will do a problem and make several errors but accidentally arrive at the right answer. This is an example of an invalid argument giving rise to a true conclusion.

We are now in a position to discuss how to determine whether a given implication is true or false. Until this time, we were concerned with the various truth values that could be assigned to the implication.

if p, then q

for all possible truth values of p and of q.

Now we shall discuss how to demonstrate that a statement q is true whenever p is true. This will then show that the implication $p \Rightarrow q$ is true. Of course, if q is false whenever p is true, then the implication $p \Rightarrow q$ is false.

We shall limit our discussion to two types: direct proof and indirect proof.

In a *direct proof* one goes through a chain of propositions, beginning with the given propositions and leading to the desired conclusion.

Suppose it is true that

> Either John obeys the law or John is punished

and

> John was not punished.

We would like to prove that

> John obeyed the law.

A valid argument in the form of a direct proof can be given as follows. Let p and q denote the propositions

> p: John obeys the law
> q: John is punished

We can write the premise as

$$p \vee q \text{ and } \sim q$$

Since $\sim q$ is true and since $p \vee q$ is true, then q is false and either p is true or q is true. Thus, p must be true.

More examples of direct proof are given later, but before we look at them, let us discuss two laws of logic that are quite useful in a direct proof.

Law of Detachment

If the implication

$$p \Rightarrow q$$

is true, and if p is true, then q must be true.
    See Figure 1.13 for an illustration of this law.

Law of Syllogisms

Let p,q,r be three propositions. If

$$p \Rightarrow q \text{ and } q \Rightarrow r$$

are both true, then

$$p \Rightarrow r$$

is true.
    Figure 1.20 illustrates this law.

Suppose it is true that

> It is snowing

and

> if it is warm, then it is not snowing.

p	q	r	$p \Rightarrow q$	$q \Rightarrow r$	$p \Rightarrow r$	$(p \Rightarrow q) \wedge (q \Rightarrow r)$	$(p \Rightarrow q \wedge q \Rightarrow r) \Rightarrow (p \Rightarrow r)$
T	T	T	T	T	T	T	T
T	T	F	T	F	F	F	T
T	F	T	F	T	T	F	T
T	F	F	F	T	F	F	T
F	T	T	T	T	T	T	T
F	T	F	T	F	T	F	T
F	F	T	T	T	T	T	T
F	F	F	T	T	T	T	T

Figure 1.20

and

> if it is not warm, then I cannot go swimming.

We want to prove that

> I cannot go swimming.

is a true statement.

A valid argument for this is given as a direct proof below.
Let p, q, r represent the statements

> p: it is snowing
> q: it is warm
> r: I can go swimming

Our premise is that the propositions

$$p, \quad q \Rightarrow \sim p, \quad \sim q \Rightarrow \sim r$$

are true. We want to prove that

$$\sim r$$

is true.

Since $q \to \sim p$ is true, its contrapositive

$$p \Rightarrow \sim q$$

is also true. Using the law of syllogisms, we see that

$$p \Rightarrow \sim r$$

since $p \Rightarrow \sim q$ and $\sim q \Rightarrow \sim r$. But we know p is true. By the law of detachment, $\sim r$ is true.

1.6.3
Example

Suppose it is true that

> if Dan comes, so will Bill

and

if Sandy does not come, then Bill will not come.

We want to show that

If Dan comes, then Sandy will come.

Let p,q,r denote the propositions

p: Dan is coming
q: Bill will come
r: Sandy is coming

Then we know that

$$p \Rightarrow q, \qquad \sim r \Rightarrow \sim q$$

Since $\sim r \Rightarrow \sim q$ is true, then $q \Rightarrow r$ is also true. Thus,

$$p \Rightarrow q, \qquad q \Rightarrow r$$

By the law of syllogisms, it is true that

$$p \Rightarrow r$$

That is, if Dan comes, then Sandy will come.

Suppose it is true that

1.6.4
Example

if I enjoy studying, then I will study

and

I will do my homework or I will not study

and

I will not do my homework

We want to show that

I do not enjoy studying.

Let p,q,r denote the three propositions

p: I enjoy studying
q: I will study
r: I will do my homework

Then we know that

$$\sim r, \qquad r \vee \sim q, \qquad p \Rightarrow q$$

are true. We want to prove that $\sim p$ is true.

Since $\sim r$ is true, then r is false. Also, either r or $\sim q$ is true. Thus, $\sim q$ is true. Since $p \Rightarrow q$, we have

$$\sim q \Rightarrow \sim p$$

is true. Hence, $\sim p$ must be true.

The above are all examples of proving statements by means of a direct proof. Notice that this technique is essentially one of proceeding by means of the laws of logic from the premise to the desired conclusion.

Suppose we want to show that in an implication $p \Rightarrow q$, the conclusion q is true whenever p is true. To prove that q is true by the method of an *indirect proof*, it is necessary to show that $\sim q$ is a false statement. This can be done by assuming that $\sim q$ is true and that this assumption, when combined with other statements of the premise, leads to a logical contradiction.

The following two examples illustrate indirect proof.

1.6.5
Example

Prove the result of Example 1.6.1 using an indirect proof.

Since we wish to prove that p is true, we shall make the assumption that p is false or that $\sim p$ is true, hoping that this leads to a contradiction — since, if it does, then p must be true.

We know that

$$\sim p, \qquad \sim q, \qquad p \vee q$$

are true. Thus, either p is true or q is true. But both p and q are false. This is impossible. Thus, we have reached a contradiction — which means that p must be true.

1.6.6
Example

Suppose that it is true that

 if I am lazy, then I do not study

and

 I study or I enjoy myself

and

 I do not enjoy myself.

Prove that

 I am not lazy.

Let p,q,r be the statements

 p: I am lazy
 q: I study
 r: I enjoy myself

Then, we know that

$$\sim r, \qquad p \Rightarrow \sim q, \qquad q \vee r$$

are true.

We want to show that $\sim p$ is true.

If we use an indirect proof, then we assume that p is true. Since p is true and $p \rightarrow \sim q$ is true, then $\sim q$ is true. Thus, q is false. Also, r is false. But either q or r is true. This is impossible. This contradiction means that the assumption that p is true is a false one. Thus, $\sim p$ is true.

Prove the following first by using a direct proof and then by an indirect proof.

1.6
Exercise

1. When it rains, John does not go to school. John is going to school. Show that it is not raining.
2. If I do not go to work, I will go fishing. I will not go fishing. Show that I shall go to work.
3. If Smith is elected president, Kuntz will be elected secretary. If Kuntz is elected secretary, then Brown will not be elected treasurer. Smith is elected president. Show that Brown is not elected treasurer.
4. Using reasons for logic, give a valid argument (either direct or indirect) to answer the question: Does Danny cry? Either Katy is a good girl or Mike is a good boy. If Danny cries, then Katy is not a good girl. Mike is not a good boy.

By a switching network we mean a collection of wires capable of carrying an electric current and various switches each capable of creating a gap in the wire.

1.7
APPLICATION
TO SWITCHING
NETWORKS

The simplest kind of network is a single wire—capable of transmitting currents from one end A to the other end B. See Figure 1.21(a). If we add a switch to this wire, we obtain the network of Figure 1.21(b).

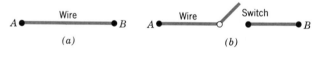

Figure 1.21

Now this switch admits only two possibilities—it is either open (O), in which case current does not flow; or else it is closed (C), in which case current will flow. Thus, we have a situation very much like the one we had with propositions. That is, a proposition is either true (T) or false (F); a switch is either closed (C) or open (O).

Let us now represent switches by p, q, and so on and let us analyze some very elementary networks.

Consider the network of Figure 1.22.

Figure 1.22

This network has two switches p and q placed in *parallel*. Suppose the question is asked — When does current flow from A to B? It is clear that if either p or q or both are closed, then current flows from A to B; but if p and q are both open, then current does not flow. That is,

1	2	3
p	q	
C	C	C
C	O	C
O	C	C
O	O	O

Figure 1.23

The values given in column 3 of Figure 1.23 are merely the inclusive disjunction $p \vee q$. Thus, the truth values of $p \vee q$ will tell us whether current flows in a *parallel network*.

Another network commonly encountered is the *series network*. See Figure 1.24.

Figure 1.24

Here we discover that current flows from A to B only if both p and q are closed and current will not flow if either p or q or both are open. See Figure 1.25.

1	2	3
p	q	
C	C	C
C	O	O
O	C	O
O	O	O

Figure 1.25

The values in column 3 are those of the conjunction of p and q, namely, $p \wedge q$. That is, for a series network, if $p \wedge q$ is true, current flows; whereas if $p \wedge q$ is false, current does not flow.

Next, let us interpret the network in Figure 1.26.

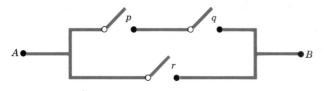

Figure 1.26

The question is asked "When does current flow from A to B?"

To answer this, we want to find the truth value of $r \vee (p \wedge q)$, since p and q are in series $(p \wedge q)$ and r is in parallel with $p \wedge q$. The answer is given in Figure 1.27.

1	2	3	4	5
p	q	r	$p \wedge q$	$r \vee (p \wedge q)$
C	C	C	C	C
C	C	O	C	C
C	O	C	O	C
C	O	O	O	O
O	C	C	O	C
O	C	O	O	O
O	O	C	O	C
O	O	O	O	O

Figure 1.27

Thus, by looking at column 5, we see that current flows from A to B only under the following conditions:

1. p closed, q closed, r closed
2. p closed, q closed, r open
3. p closed, q open, r closed
4. p open, q closed, r closed
5. p open, q open, r closed

In the above problem, suppose we had demanded that whenever p was closed, r was open and whenever p was open, r was closed. This means that

$$r \equiv \sim p$$

Under these circumstances, current flows from A to B depending on the truth value of

$$\sim p \vee (p \wedge q)$$

Instead of constructing a truth table to get the answer, let us use some of the laws developed earlier in this section to simplify the compound statement $\sim p \lor (p \land q)$. Then using the distributive law

$$\sim p \lor (p \land q) \equiv (\sim p \lor p) \land (\sim p \lor q)$$

Since $\sim p \lor p$ is always closed, the above reduces to

$$\sim p \lor (p \land q) \equiv \sim p \lor q$$

In other words, the network of Figure 1.26 with $r \equiv \sim p$, is equivalent to the network given in Figure 1.28.

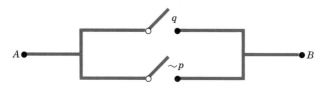

Figure 1.28

1.7.1
Example

For the network of Figure 1.29, determine when the current flows from A to B. Also, write a network equivalent to it with less switches in it.

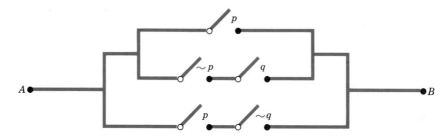

Figure 1.29

Here current flows from A to B whenever the truth value of

$$(p \land \sim q) \lor [p \lor (\sim p \land q)]$$

is C.
Let us first simplify the expression in the brackets. Thus

$$p \lor (\sim p \land q) \equiv (p \lor \sim p) \land (p \lor q) \equiv p \lor q$$

Then, using this fact, we have

$$
\begin{aligned}
(p \land \sim q) \lor [p \lor (\sim p \land q)] &\equiv (p \land \sim q) \lor (p \lor q) \\
&\equiv [(p \land \sim q) \lor p] \lor q \\
&\equiv p \lor q
\end{aligned}
$$

Thus, the complicated network of Figure 1.29 is equivalent to a network of two switches p and q placed in parallel. Also, current flows from A to B in the network of Figure 1.29, if

1. p is closed, q is closed
2. p is open, q is closed
3. p is closed, q is open

A network in which current always flows no matter what position the switches are in is a tautology; a network in which current never flows is the negation of a tautology.

1. Determine when current flows from A to B in the following circuits by using a truth table.

1.7
Exercise

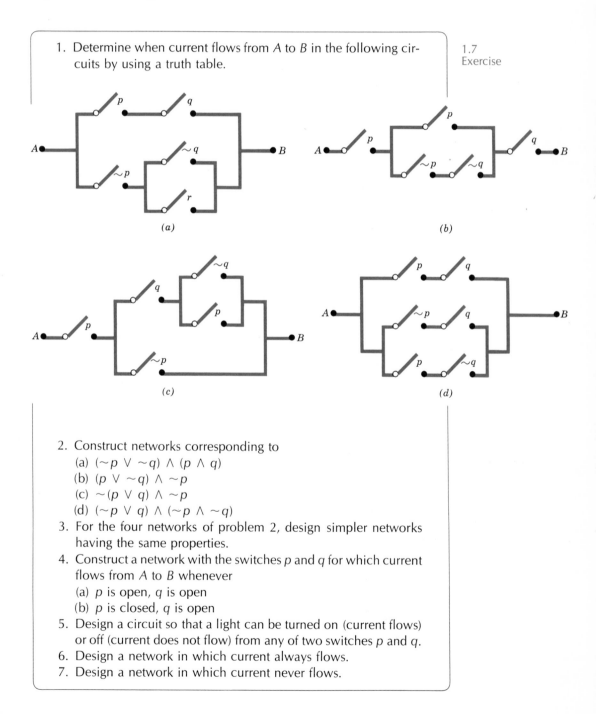

(a)

(b)

(c)

(d)

2. Construct networks corresponding to
   (a) $(\sim p \lor \sim q) \land (p \land q)$
   (b) $(p \lor \sim q) \land \sim p$
   (c) $\sim(p \lor q) \land \sim p$
   (d) $(\sim p \lor q) \land (\sim p \land \sim q)$
3. For the four networks of problem 2, design simpler networks having the same properties.
4. Construct a network with the switches p and q for which current flows from A to B whenever
   (a) p is open, q is open
   (b) p is closed, q is open
5. Design a circuit so that a light can be turned on (current flows) or off (current does not flow) from any of two switches p and q.
6. Design a network in which current always flows.
7. Design a network in which current never flows.

The following problem was first studied by Mr. Edmund C. Berkeley in 1936 and was solved by the use of principles of logic. His employer, the Prudential Life Insurance Company, had the procedure that when any policyholder requested a change in the schedule of premium payments, one of two rules was involved as company policy. The question was raised as to whether these two rules were logically equivalent. That is, did both rules give rise to the same payment arrangements or did the use of one rule over the other give different payment arrangements?

Mr. Berkeley was of the opinion that the two rules, in some instances, gave different directions to the policyholder. An example of a typical clause found in one of the rules was: If a policyholder was making premium payments several times a year with one of the payments falling due on the policy anniversary and if he requested the schedule be changed to one annual payment on the anniversary date, and if his payments were in full up to a date not the anniversary date and if he made this request more than two months after the issue date and if his request also came within two months after the policy anniversary date, then a certain action was to be taken!

Mr. Berkeley replaced this complicated part of one of the rules by the compound proposition

$$p \wedge q \wedge r \wedge s \wedge t \Rightarrow A$$

where p, q, r, s, t are the five statements and A is the action called for. By doing the same with all parts of both rules and by using the laws of logic, Mr. Berkeley was able to demonstrate an inconsistency of application of one rule over the other. In fact, there turned out to be four situations in which contradictory actions occurred.

As a result of Mr. Berkeley's effort, Prudential replaced the two cumbersome rules by a simple one.

Since this incident, similar situations involving a maze of if's, and's, but's, and implications, particularly in the areas of legal contracts between corporations, have been checked for accuracy and consistency (to eliminate loopholes, etc.) by the use of logic.

proposition	**De Morgan's laws**
connective	**absorption laws**
conjunction ($\wedge$)	**idempotent laws**
inclusive disjunction ($\vee$)	**implication** ($\Rightarrow$)
exclusive disjunction ($\underline{\vee}$)	**conditional connective** ($\Rightarrow$)
negation	**sufficient condition**
law of contradiction	**necessary condition**
quantifier	**converse**
truth value	**inverse**
logically equivalent ($\equiv$)	**contrapositive**
commutative laws	**biconditional connective** ($\Leftrightarrow$)
associative laws	**tautology**
distributive laws	**law of substitution**

[2]Pfeiffer, John E., "Symbolic Logic," *Scientific American*, December 1950.

argument
fallacy
direct proof
law of detachment
law of syllogisms

indirect proof
circuit
series
parallel

Circle each correct answer; some questions have more than one correct answer.

1. Which of the following negate the statement

p: All people are rich

   a. Some people are rich
   b. Some people are poor
   c. Some people are not rich
   d. No person is rich

2. Which of the following negate the statement

p: it is either hot or humid

   a. It is neither hot nor humid
   b. Either it is not hot or it is not humid
   c. It is not hot and it is not humid
   d. It is hot, but not humid

3. Which of the following statements are logically equivalent to

$$(\sim p \vee q) \wedge r$$

   a. $(p \Rightarrow q) \wedge r$
   b. $\sim p \vee (q \wedge r)$
   c. $(\sim p \Rightarrow q) \wedge r$
   d. $(\sim p \vee r) \wedge (q \wedge r)$

4. Which of the following statements are logically equivalent to

$$p \wedge \sim q$$

   a. $\sim q \wedge p$
   b. $p \vee q$
   c. $\sim p \vee q$
   d. $q \Rightarrow \sim p$

5. Which of the following are true.
   a. $(p \vee \sim q) \wedge (p \Leftrightarrow q)$
   b. $(p \text{ only if } q) \Leftrightarrow (q \Rightarrow p)$
   c. $(p \text{ only if } q) \Leftrightarrow (p \Rightarrow q)$
   d. p is sufficient for q means $q \Rightarrow p$

1. Negate the propositions
   a. Some people are rich.
   b. Danny is not tall and Mary is short.
   c. Neither Mike nor Katy are big.

2. Construct truth tables for each of the compound propositions.
   a. $(p \wedge q) \vee \sim p$
   b. $\sim p \vee (p \vee \sim q)$
   c. $\sim p \Rightarrow (p \vee q)$
3. Let "p" stand for "I will pass the course" and "q" for "I will do homework regularly." Put the following statements into symbolic form.
   a. I will pass the course, if I do homework regularly.
   b. Passing this course is a sufficient condition for me to do homework regularly.
   c. I will pass this course if and only if I do homework regularly.
4. Write the converse, contrapositive, and inverse of the statement

   "if it is not sunny, it is cold"

5. Prove the following by the use of direct proof.
   If I do not go to paint, I will go bowling. I will not go bowling. Show that I will go to paint.
6. Using reasons from logic, give a valid argument to answer the question: Is Katy a good girl?
   Given that (1) Mike is a bad boy or Danny is crying; (2) If Katy is a good girl, then Mike is not a bad boy; (3) Danny is not crying.
7. Determine whether the following are logically equivalent.

   $\sim p \vee q$ $\qquad\qquad\qquad\qquad$ $p \Rightarrow q$

8. Determine whether the two statements

   $(p \Rightarrow q) \wedge (\sim q \vee p)$ $\qquad\qquad$ $p \Leftrightarrow q$

   are logically equivalent.

Additional Reading

Church, A., *Introduction to Mathematical Logic,* Vol. 1, Princeton, N.J.: Princeton University Press, 1956.

Copi, Irving, M., *Introduction to Logic,* Macmillan, 3rd edition, 1968.

Hohfeld, W. N., *Fundamental Legal Conceptions as Applied in Judicial Reasoning and Other Essays,* Walter Wheeler Cook, Ed., New Haven: Yale University Press, 1919.

Hohn, Franz, "Some Mathematical Aspects of Switching," *The American Mathematical Monthly,* **62** (1955), pp. 75–90.

Pfeiffer, John E., "Symbolic Logic," *Scientific American,* December 1950.

Introduction to the
Theory of Sets; Counting Techniques Chapter 2

In this chapter, we shall give a brief introduction to that area of mathematics commonly referred to as *set theory*. A knowledge of sets and some of their properties, will be useful to us in two ways: (1) to develop knowledge of mathematical language and notational usage which will be employed in many later chapters and (2) to study the nature of counting and some of the applications to various practical situations.

The applications studied in this chapter are in the areas of survey analysis and permutations and combinations. For example, in the section dealing with applications of the techniques of counting, we shall solve problems involving the compilation of data and we shall determine ways to find out whether such data can be accurate from a logical point of view. In the section on permutations and combinations, such questions as "In how many ways can five people be seated in a nine-passenger station wagon" and "How many different outcomes are possible when a committee of seven people vote" are answered. Further use for the applications presented in this chapter will be found in subsequent chapters.

There are many examples of sets of which the student is already aware. For example, a student may speak of being a member of a certain class, say Mathematics 101. In this case, Mathematics 101 is a set and a student enrolled in this course is an element of the set. A student *not* enrolled in Mathematics 101 is *not* a member of the set. If no students register for this course, Mathematics 101, then the set is called an *empty set,* that is, a set having *no* elements.

A *set S* is a collection of objects, considered as a whole. The objects of a set S are called *elements of S* or *members of S*. A set that has no elements is called the *empty set*, or *null set*, or *vacuous set*, and is denoted by the symbol $\varnothing$.

Suppose S is a set and a is an element of the set S. Then we write

$$a \in S$$

read as "a is an element of S" or "a is in S." If a is *not* an element of the set S, then we write

$$a \notin S$$

read as "a is not an element of S" or "a is not in S."

Ordinarily, a set S can be written in one of two ways. These two ways of writing sets are illustrated by the following examples.

**2.2.1
Example**

Consider the set D of digits. The elements of the set D are

$$0, 1, 2, 3, 4, 5, 6, 7, 8, 9$$

In this case, we write

$$D = \{0, 1, 2, 3, 4, 5, 6, 7, 8, 9\}$$

read as "D is the set consisting of the elements 0, 1, 2, 3, 4, 5, 6, 7, 8, 9." Here, we are actually *listing* or *displaying* the elements of the set D.

Another way of writing this same set D of digits is to write

$$D = \{x|x \text{ is a digit}\}$$

read as "D is the set of all x such that x is a digit."

Here we describe the set D by giving a property that every element of D has and that no element not in D can have, namely the property of being a digit. This way of writing a set is called *set-builder notation*.

Of course, when it is possible, either of the above two methods of describing a set and its elements may be used. Sometimes, however, it is impossible to list all elements of a set because of the nature of the set. Examples of such occurrences will appear quite often as we pursue our study of elementary mathematics.

**2.2.2
Example**

Consider the set W, whose elements are the days in a week. Here we may actually list the elements of W by writing

$$W = \{\text{Monday, Tuesday, Wednesday, Thursday, Friday, Saturday, Sunday}\}$$

In set-builder notation, W is written as

$$W = \{x|x \text{ is a day of the week}\}$$

It is important for the student to notice that elements of a set are *not* repeated. A given element is entered as a member of a set only once; there is never a duplication of an element in a set.

Thus, we would never write

$$\{3, 2, 2\}$$

but instead we would write

$$\{3, 2\}$$

Also, because a set is a collection of objects considered as a whole, when considering a set, the order in which the elements of a set are listed does not make any difference. Thus, the three sets

$$\{2, 3, 4\}, \quad \{2, 4, 3\}, \quad \{3, 4, 2\}$$

are representations of the *same* set. The *elements* of a set distinguish sets—*not the order* in which the elements are written.

Let us agree, henceforth, to adopt the convention that upper case letters such as *A*, *B*, and so on will represent sets and lower case letters, *a*, *b*, . . . *x*, *y*, and so on will represent elements of sets.

Write each of the following sets in two ways.

1. The set *A* of digits from 6 to 9 inclusive.
2. The set *B* of vowels in the alphabet.
3. The set *C* of digits in your age (in years).

In the following problems, replace the asterisk by either $\in$ or $\notin$, whichever is correct.

4. 3 * $\{2, 3, 7\}$
5. 0 * $\{1, 3\}$
6. 1/2 * $\{x | x$ is a digit$\}$
7. 10 * $\{x | x$ is a digit$\}$
8. 4 * $\{2, 1, 6\}$
9. Find a set whose elements cannot be easily listed, but that can be readily described using the set-builder notation.
10. Find a set whose elements can be easily listed, but that cannot be readily described by using set-builder notation.

2.2
Exercise

When we see two people, we can usually relate them in many ways. We say that they have the same color eyes, or that one is taller than the other, or that one is heavier than the other.

2.3
RELATIONS
BETWEEN SETS

We shall discuss *four* ways of relating two sets. If we look at the sets

$$A = \{1, 2\}, \quad B = \{1, 2, 3\}$$

we notice that the elements of the set *A* are also elements of the set *B*. This is one way of comparing two sets.

Consider the following two sets.

$$A = \{1, 2\}, \quad B = \{4, 5\}$$

If we look at these two sets, we notice that each of these sets possesses the same number of elements. This is easily seen by "matching" or "corresponding" elements of these sets. If we use a double arrow "↔" to denote this "match," then

$$1 \leftrightarrow 4, \qquad 2 \leftrightarrow 5 \qquad \text{or} \qquad 1 \leftrightarrow 5, \qquad 2 \leftrightarrow 4$$

Here we would say that the sets A and B are *equivalent*.

These *relations between sets* are defined more carefully below.

2.3.1
Definition

Let A and B be two nonempty sets. We say that A *is equal to* B, **written as**

$$A = B$$

if and only if A and B have the same elements.

If two sets A and B are *not* equal, we write

$$A \neq B$$

2.3.2
Definition

Let A and B be two nonempty sets. We say that A *is equivalent to* B, **written as**

$$A \sim B$$

if and only if there can be found a one-to-one correspondence between the elements of A and B. By one-to-one correspondence we mean that for each element in A, there can be matched one element in B; and each element in B can be matched to exactly one element in A.

If two sets A and B are *not* equivalent, we write

$$A \nsim B$$

There is a relationship between the concept of equality and that of equivalence.

If two sets A and B are equal, so that they have the *same* elements, it is easy to see that A and B must also be equivalent.

The necessary one-to-one correspondence is found merely by associating or matching that element in A with the identical element of B. Since the elements of A and B are the same, the elements of the two sets A and B are in one-to-one correspondence, and hence are equivalent.

Suppose we consider the converse. That is, suppose two sets A and B are equivalent. Are they then equal? Or can two sets be equivalent without being equal? The following example gives us the answer.

2.3.1
Example

Let the two sets A and B be given by

$$A = \{1, 2, 3\}, \qquad B = \{7, 8, 9\}$$

Clearly, A is not equal to B. However, since we can match the elements of A and B by

$$1 \leftrightarrow 7, \quad 2 \leftrightarrow 8, \quad 3 \leftrightarrow 9$$

it is seen that A is equivalent to B.

The following result has thus been established.

If two sets A and B are equal, then A and B are equivalent. The converse is *not* true. Thus, two sets A and B may be equivalent, and yet be unequal.

Let A and B be two nonempty sets. We shall say that A *is a subset of B or* **that** A *is contained in B* **or that** B *contains A,* **written as**
2.3.3
Definition

$$A \subseteq B \text{ or } B \supseteq A$$

if and only if every element of A is also an element of B.

If a set A is not a subset of a set B, we write

$$A \nsubseteq B$$

The definition that A is a subset of B could have been given equivalently as "there are no elements in set A that are not also elements in set B." Of course, $A \subseteq B$ if and only if whenever $x \in A$, then $x \in B$ for all x. This latter way of interpreting the meaning of $A \subseteq B$ is useful for obtaining various laws that sets obey.

Let A and B be two nonempty sets. We shall say that A *is a proper subset of B or that* A *is properly contained in B* **or that** B *properly contains A,* **written as**
2.3.4
Definition

$$A \subset B \text{ or } B \supset A$$

if and only if every element of the set A is also an element of set B, but there is at least one element in set B that is *not* in set A.

The student should notice that A is a proper subset of B means that there are *no* elements of A that are not also elements of B, but there is at least one element of B which is not in A.

If a set A is *not* a proper subset of a set B, we write

$$A \not\subset B$$

The following example illustrates the uses of the four relations of $=$, $\sim$, $\subseteq$, and $\subset$ just defined.

Consider three sets A, B, and C given by
2.3.2
Example

$$A = \{1, 2, 3\}, \quad B = \{1, 2, 3, 4, 5\}, \quad C = \{1, 2, 3\}$$

Below are some of the relations between pairs of these sets:

(a) $A = C$
(b) $A \sim C$
(c) $A \subseteq B$
(d) $A \subset B$
(e) $B \supset C$
(f) $A \subseteq C$
(g) $C \subseteq A$

In comparing the two definitions given above of "subset" and "proper subset," the student should notice that if a set A is a subset of a set B, then either A is a proper subset of B or else A equals B. That is,

$$A \subseteq B \text{ if and only if either } A \subset B \text{ or } A = B.$$

Also, if A is a proper subset of B, we can infer that A is a subset of B, but A does not equal B. That is,

$$A \subset B \text{ if and only if } A \subseteq B \text{ and } A \neq B$$

The distinction that is made between "subset" and "proper subset" is rather subtle and is quite important. Let us try to describe this distinction further by using some familiar everyday examples.

We often hear "my weight *does not exceed* 200 pounds." What this means is the weight in question equals 200 pounds or is less than 200 pounds. If A is a subset of B, then A equals B or A is a proper subset of B. If one's weight is less than 200 pounds, then his weight does not exceed 200 pounds and does not equal 200 pounds. Thus, if A is a proper subset of B, we know that A is a subset of B, but $A \neq B$.

We can think of the relation $\subset$ as a refinement of the relation $\subseteq$. On the other hand, the relation $\subseteq$ is an extension of $\subset$, in the sense that $\subseteq$ may include equality whereas with $\subset$, equality cannot be included.

Because of the way the relation $\subseteq$ (is a subset of) has been defined, it is easy to see that for any set A

$$\varnothing \subseteq A$$

The reason for this is that there is no element of the set $\varnothing$ which is not also in A since the empty set $\varnothing$ has no elements.

Also, if A is any nonempty set, that is, any set having at least one element, then

$$\varnothing \subset A$$

The following proposition shows a property that the relation "$\subseteq$" (is a subset of) obeys.

Theorem 2.3.1 Antisymmetric Law

This law states that if a set A is a subset of a set B and if the set B is a subset of set A, then the two sets A and B are equal. That is

if $A \subseteq B$ and if $B \subseteq A$, then $A = B$

Proof

If $A \subseteq B$, then every element in set A must be in set B. Since $B \subseteq A$, then every element in set B must be in set A. This means that A and B have the *same* elements. That is

$$A = B$$

As we shall see later in the chapter, the antisymmetric law is *very* important for showing the equality of two sets. To actually prove that two sets A and B are equal, first show that any element in set A is in set B (so that $A \subseteq B$), then show that any element in set B must be in set A (so that $B \subseteq A$.) Once this has been done, the equality of A and B is a consequence of the antisymmetric law.

Thus far we have talked about comparing pairs of sets by means of the relations $\subset$ and $\subseteq$. We have said A is a subset of B, or A equals B, or B is a subset of A. For some pairs of sets, none of these relations can be used for comparison. This situation is illustrated by the following example.

Consider two sets A and B whose elements are

2.3.3
Example

$$A = \{1, 2, 3\} \qquad B = \{3, 4\}$$

Notice that not every element in A is in B. Thus

$$A \nsubseteq B$$

Also, notice that not every element in B is in A. Then

$$B \nsubseteq A$$

Finally, A and B are *not* equal. They have different elements. Thus

$$A \neq B$$

This is, the sets A and B given in Example 2.3.3 are *not comparable*.

Thus, at times, we cannot say about any two sets C and D that either (1) C is a subset of D, or (2) C is equal to D, or (3) D is a subset of C. When we can say one of the above three about two sets C and D, then C and D are said to be *comparable*.

The *universal set U* is defined as that set consisting of all elements under consideration.

2.3.5
Definition

Thus, if A is any set and if U is the universal set, then every element in A must be in U (since U consists of all elements under consideration). Hence we may write

$$A \subseteq U$$

for *any* set A.

2.3
Exercise

Replace the asterisk by those relations $=, \sim, \subset, \subseteq, \supset, \supseteq$ that give a true statement or by *none of these* if none of these relations holds.

1. $\{1, 3, 7\} * \{1, 3\}$
2. $\{4, 9\} * \{9, 10, 4\}$
3. $\{5, 7\} * \{5, 8\}$
4. $\{0, 1, 4\} * \{0, 5, 8, 9\}$
5. $\varnothing * \{1, 3\}$
6. $\{0\} * \{1, 3\}$
7. $\{5, 8, 9, 15\} * \{9\}$
8. $\{2, 3\} * \{2, 3, 6, 8, 0\}$
9. $\{2, 3\} * \{2, 3\}$
10. If $A \subseteq B$ and $B \subseteq C$, what do you conclude? Why?
11. Give two sets that are not comparable.
12. Write down all possible subsets of (a) the set $\{a, b, c, d\}$ and (b) the set $\{a, b, c\}$.
13. If the universal set is the set of people, let A denote the subset of fat people, let B denote the subset of bald people, and let C denote the subset of bald and fat people. Write down several correct relations involving A, B, and C.

2.4
OPERATIONS
WITH SETS;
VENN DIAGRAMS

In the last section, we discussed relations between sets. In this section, we shall introduce operations that are performed on sets. The student is already familiar with many operations that are performed on numbers. For example, we speak of "taking the square root of a number" or "squaring a number." These are examples of *unary operations,* since they are operations performed on only *one* number. Also, we speak of "adding two numbers" or "multiplying two numbers." These are examples of *binary* operations, since they involve *two* numbers.

2.4.1
Definition

Let A and B be any two sets. The *union of A with B,* **written as**

$$A \cup B$$

is defined to be that set consisting of those elements either in A or in B or in both A and B. That is, using set-builder notation,

$$A \cup B = \{x | x \in A \text{ or } x \in B\}$$

The student should notice the similarity between the concept of the union of two sets and the inclusive disjunction of two statements from Chapter 1. Thus, we can write

$$A \cup B = \{x | x \in A \lor x \in B\}$$

2.4.2
Definition

Let A and B be any two sets. The *intersection of A with B,* **written as,**

$$A \cap B$$

is defined as the set consisting of those elements that are *both* **in** *A* **and in** *B*.
Thus

$$A \cap B = \{x | x \in A \text{ and } x \in B\}$$

Notice that the definition of the intersection of two sets is based on the definition of the conjunction of two statements. That is

$$A \cap B = \{x | x \in A \wedge x \in B\}$$

The student should recognize that to find the intersection of two sets *A* and *B* means to find the elements *common* to *A* and *B*.

If two sets *A* **and** *B* **have no elements in common, that is, if**

$$A \cap B = \emptyset$$

then *A* **and** *B* **are called** *disjoint sets.*

2.4.3
Definition

A *Venn diagram* is a pictoral representation of relationships involving sets. Usually, sets are represented by interlocking circles, each of which is enclosed in a rectangle that represents the universal set *U*.

Use a Venn diagram to illustrate (a) *A* ∩ *B*, (b) *A* ∪ *B*. Since *A* ∩ *B* consists of those elements both in *A* and in *B*, it is seen that the shaded region of Figure 2.1(a) is *A* ∩ *B*. Since *A* ∪ *B* consists of elements either in *A* or in *B*, the shaded region of Figure 2.1(b) is *A* ∪ *B*.

2.4.1
Example

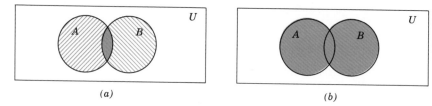

(a)   (b)

Figure 2.1

Venn diagrams are very useful for illustrating and motivating properties of sets. However, they are not intended to be a substitute for logical proofs.

Consider the three sets

$$A = \{1, 3, 5\}, \qquad B = \{3, 4, 5, 6\}, \qquad C = \{6, 7\}$$

Then

2.4.2
Example

$$A \cup B = \{1, 3, 5\} \cup \{3, 4, 5, 6\} = \{1, 3, 4, 5, 6\}$$
$$A \cap B = \{1, 3, 5\} \cap \{3, 4, 5, 6\} = \{3, 5\}$$
$$A \cap C = \{1, 3, 5\} \cap \{6, 7\} = \emptyset$$

Here *A* and *C* are disjoint sets.

The next result gives us a relationship between the operations of union and intersection. This theorem says that the intersection of two sets is always a subset of the union of the two sets. That is, every element of the intersection is also an element of the union. Figure 2.1 serves as motivation for this result.

Theorem 2.4.1
For any two sets A and B, we have

$$A \cap B \subseteq A \cup B$$

Proof
If $x \in A \cap B$, then $x \in A$ and $x \in B$. But if $x \in A$ and $x \in B$, then $x \in A$ or $x \in B$. This says that $x \in A \cup B$. Hence, any element in $A \cap B$ is in $A \cup B$. That is, $A \cap B \subseteq A \cup B$.

Theorem 2.4.2
If A and B are two sets, and if

$$A \cup B = \emptyset$$

then

$$A = \emptyset \text{ and } B = \emptyset$$

Proof
If $A \cup B = \emptyset$, then there are *no* elements either in A or in B. This says that A has no elements and B has no elements. Hence, $A = \emptyset$ and $B = \emptyset$.

The following theorem states that the intersection of a set A with any other set is a subset of the set A. It further says that a set A is always a subset of the union of A with any set. Thus, every element both in a set A and in some other set is also in A. Finally, every element in a set A is also in either A or any other set.

Although these statements are intuitively obvious, we shall give a formal proof of their validity.

Theorem 2.4.3
Let A and B be two sets. Then

$$A \cap B \subseteq A, \qquad A \subseteq A \cup B$$

Proof
Let $x \in A \cap B$. Then $x \in A$ and $x \in B$ so that $x \in A$. Hence, any element in $A \cap B$ must be in A. That is

$$A \cap B \subseteq A$$

The proof that $A \subseteq A \cup B$ is left to the student.

In Theorem 2.4.4, we state some further facts about sets. This one says that if a set A is a subset of a set B, the intersection of A and B (those elements in both A and B) is A and the union of A and B is B.

Theorem 2.4.4
Let A and B be any two sets. If

$$A \subseteq B$$

then

$$A \cap B = A, \qquad A \cup B = B \qquad\qquad (2.4.1)$$

Proof
By Theorem 2.4.3, we know that

$$A \cap B \subseteq A \qquad\qquad (2.4.2)$$

Now, let $x \in A$. Then $x \in A$ and $x \in B$, since every element in A must be in B. This says that $x \in A \cap B$. Thus, every element in A is in $A \cap B$. Hence

$$A \subseteq A \cap B \qquad\qquad (2.4.3)$$

If we apply the antisymmetric law to equations 2.4.2 and 2.4.3, we see that

$$A = A \cap B$$

The proof of the other relation in (2.4.1) is similar.

Next, we shall define a third binary operation involving sets. This one is quite similar to the concept of subtraction of numbers.

Let A and B be any two sets. The *relative complement of A with respect to B,* **written as,**

$$B - A$$

is defined as that set consisting of elements that are in B, but not in A. Thus, in set-builder notation,

$$B - A = \{x | x \in B \text{ and } x \notin A\} \qquad\qquad (2.4.4)$$

2.4.4
Definition

Sometimes the relative complement of A with respect to B is called the *difference $B - A$.*

Thus, to find the relative complement of a set A with respect to a set B, merely write down the elements of set B and delete from it those elements that are in A.

Figure 2.2 illustrates the concept of relative complement.

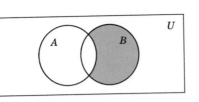

Figure 2.2

2.4.3
Example

If $A = \{1, 3, 5\}$, $B = \{1, 2\}$, then

$$B - A = \{2\}$$

and

$$A - B = \{3, 5\}$$

The above shows that the relative complement of B with respect to A is not always the same as the relative complement of A with respect to B. In other words

$$B - A \neq A - B$$

Thus far, three operations involving sets have been introduced. These three operations of union $\cup$, intersection $\cap$, and difference $-$, are examples of binary operations.

We are now ready to introduce an operation on sets involving one set— that is, a *unary* operation.

2.4.5
Definition

Let A be any set. The absolute complement of A, written as

$$\bar{A} \text{ (or } A', \text{ or } -A)$$

is defined as the set consisting of elements in the universe U which are not in A. Thus

$$\bar{A} = \{x | x \notin A\}$$

See Figure 2.3 for an illustration of absolute complement.

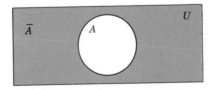

Figure 2.3

It is noted that taking the absolute complement of A is the same as finding the relative complement of A with respect to the universal set U. That is

$$\bar{A} = U - A$$

From equation 2.4.4 and Definition 2.4.5, we can conclude

$$B - A = B \cap \bar{A}$$

This relationship is very important and will be used extensively in Section 2.6. See Figure 2.4 for an illustration of $B \cap \bar{A}$ and compare it with Figure 2.2.

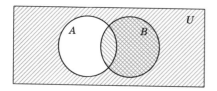

Figure 2.4

If $U =$ universal set $= \{0, 1, 2, 3, 4\}$ and if $A = \{0, 1, 2\}$, then

2.4.4
Example

$$\bar{A} = \{3, 4\}$$

Also, we see that

$$U - A = \{0, 1, 2, 3, 4\} - \{0, 1, 2\} = \{3, 4\}$$

Use a Venn diagram to illustrate that

2.4.5
Example

$$\bar{A} \cap \bar{B} = \overline{A \cup B}$$

First, let us draw two diagrams. See Figure 2.5.

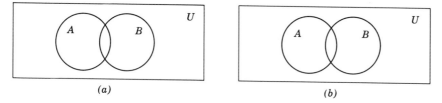

(a)   (b)

Figure 2.5

The diagram on the left we will use for $\bar{A} \cap \bar{B}$; the one on the right for $A \cup B$. Then

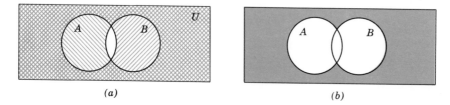

(a)   (b)

Figure 2.6

Thus, in Figure 2.6(a) $\bar{A} \cap \bar{B}$ is represented by the cross-hatched region and in Figure 2.6(b) $\overline{A \cup B}$ is represented by the shaded region. Since these regions correspond, this illustrates that the two sets $\bar{A} \cap \bar{B}$ and $\overline{A \cup B}$ are equal.

2.4.6
Example

Use a Venn diagram to illustrate

$$A \cup B = (A \cap \bar{B}) \cup (A \cap B) \cup (\bar{A} \cap B)$$

First, we construct Figure 2.7.

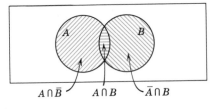

Figure 2.7

Now, shade the regions $A \cap \bar{B}$, $A \cap B$, and $\bar{A} \cap B$. See Figure 2.8.

$A \cap \bar{B}$ $A \cap B$ $\bar{A} \cap B$

Figure 2.8

Clearly, the region shaded above is the set $A \cup B$.

2.4.7
Example

Use a Venn diagram to illustrate

$$(A \cup B) \cap C$$

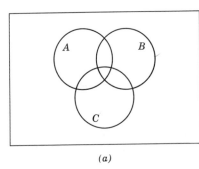

(a)   (b)

Figure 2.9

First we construct Figure 2.9(a). Then we shade $A \cup B$ and C as in (b). The cross-hatched region is the set $(A \cup B) \cap C$.

Find the most general conditions on two sets A and B so that

$$A \cup B = B$$

Here it is known that the elements of $A \cup B$ and those of B are the same. But the elements of $A \cup B$ consist of all elements either in A or in B. Now, if we demand that elements either in A or B are the same as those in B, we must have every element in A also in B. For, if A had elements not found in B, then $A \cup B$ would contain elements not found in B and hence $A \cup B$ and B would not be equal. Thus, if $A \cup B = B$, then $A \subseteq B$.

2.4.8
Example

For a general nonempty set A, find the most general conditions on a set X so that

2.4.9
Example

$$X \cup A = U$$

Here we want to find a set X so that the union of X with A is the universal set. We can rephrase the question as follows: What elements must set X have if those elements either in X or in A are all elements under consideration. It is clear now that X must at least have those elements *not* in A. Because if X did not have an element found in $\bar{A}$, then $X \cup A$ could not be the universal set. However, it does no harm for X to contain elements besides those found in $\bar{A}$. We can state these conditions on X by writing

$$\bar{A} \subseteq X$$

If $U =$ universal set $= \{1, 2, 3, 4\}$ and if A and B are two nonempty sets, find all possibilities for A if

2.4.10
Example

$$A \cap B = \{3\} \quad \text{and} \quad B = \{2, 3\}$$

Here, because $A \cap B \subseteq A$, we know that the element 3 must be in set A. Since $B = \{2, 3\}$, then if 2 were an element of A, we would have to have 2 in their intersection. Since $2 \notin A \cap B$, then $2 \notin A$. Thus, the only possible elements for A to have are

$$A = \{3\}, \quad A = \{1, 3\}, \quad A = \{3, 4\}, \quad A = \{1, 3, 4\}$$

---

1. If A is any set and U is the universal set, evaluate the following:
   (a) $A \cup \varnothing$ (c) $A \cup U$
   (b) $A \cap \varnothing$ (d) $A \cap U$
2. If $U =$ universal set $= \{x | x$ is a digit$\}$ and if $A = \{0, 1, 5, 7\}$, $B = \{2, 3, 5, 8\}$, $C = \{5, 6, 9\}$, find
   (a) $A \cup B$ (e) $\bar{A} - \bar{B}$

2.4
Exercise

(b) $B \cap C$

(f) $A \cup (B \cap A)$

(c) $A - B$

(g) $(C - A) \cap (\bar{A})$

(d) $\overline{A - B}$

(h) $(A - B) \cup (B - C)$

3. If $U =$ universal set $= \{1, 2, 3, 4, 5\}$ and if $A = \{3, 5\}$, $B = \{1, 2, 3\}$, $C = \{2, 3, 4\}$, find

(a) $\bar{A} - \bar{C}$

(e) $\overline{A - C}$

(b) $(A \cup B) \cap C$

(f) $\overline{A \cup B}$

(c) $A \cup (B \cap C)$

(g) $\bar{A} \cap \bar{B}$

(d) $(A \cup B) \cap (A \cup C)$

4. Consider the sets

$A = \{x | x$ is a customer of IBM$\}$
$B = \{x | x$ is a secretary employed by IBM$\}$
$C = \{x | x$ is a computer operator at IBM$\}$
$D = \{x | x$ is a stockholder of IBM$\}$
$E = \{x | x$ is a member of Board of Directors of IBM$\}$

Describe the sets

(a) $A \cap E$

(c) $B \cap D$

(b) $A \cup D$

(d) $C \cap E$

5. Use Venn diagrams to illustrate the following.

(a) $\bar{A} \cap B$

(e) $(A \cup B) \cap (A \cup C)$

(b) $(\bar{A} \cap \bar{B}) \cup C$

(f) $A \cup (B \cap C)$

(c) $A \cap (A \cup B)$

(g) $A = (A \cap B) \cup (A \cap \bar{B})$

(d) $A \cup (A \cap B)$

(h) $B = (A \cap B) \cup (\bar{A} \cap B)$

6. Use Venn diagrams to illustrate the following.

(a) $A \cap (B \cup C) = (A \cap B) \cup (A \cap C)$ (distributive law)

(b) $A \cap (A \cup B) = A$ (absorption law)

(c) $\overline{A \cap B} = \bar{A} \cup \bar{B}$ (De Morgan's law)

(d) $A \cup A = A$ (idempotent law)

(e) $(A \cup B) \cup C = A \cup (B \cup C)$ (associative law)

7. If $A = \{1, 2, 3\}$, $B = \{3, 4, 5, 6\}$, $C = \{3, 5, 7\}$, find

(a) $A \cup B$

(e) $A \cap C$

(b) $A \cup C$

(f) $B \cap C$

(c) $(A \cup B) \cap C$

(g) $(A \cap B) \cap C$

(d) $A \cap B$

(h) $(A \cap B) \cup C$

8. If $A = \{1, 3, 5, 7\}$, $B = \{2, 4\}$, $C = \{1, 2, 3\}$, $U =$ universal set $= \{1, 2, 3, 4, 5, 7\}$, find

(a) $\bar{A} \cup \bar{B}$

(f) $\overline{C \cup B}$

(b) $\overline{A \cap B}$

(g) $\overline{C \cap A}$

(c) $\bar{A} \cap \bar{B}$

(h) $C - A$

(d) $\overline{A \cup B}$

(i) $A - C$

(e) $\overline{U \cap B}$

*9. Find the most general condition on the sets A and B so that

(a) $A - B = B - A$

(d) $A - B = B$

(b) $A \cap B = A \cup B$

(e) $A \cap B = A$

(c) $A - B = A$

*10. Find the most general conditions on a set X so that for a given nonempty set A, we have

* Indicates a challenging problem.

(a) $A \cup X = X \cup A$　　(d) $\bar{X} = \varnothing$
(b) $\bar{X} = A$　　(e) $X \cap A = \varnothing$
(c) $\bar{X} = U$　　(f) $X \cap A = U$
*11. If $U =$ universal set $= \{1, 2, 3, 4, 5, 6\}$, $C = \{1, 3\}$, and A and B are nonempty, find all possibilities for A in each of the following.
　(a) $A \cup B = U$ and $A \cap B = \{3\}$ and $B = \{2, 3, 4\}$
　(b) $A \cap B = \varnothing$ and $A \cup B = \{1, 2, 3, 4, 5\}$ and $B \cup C = \{1, 2, 3\}$
*12. Prove that $A \subseteq A \cup B$ for any two sets A and B.
*13. Prove that if $A \subseteq B$, then $A \cup B = B$.
*14. Prove that if $A \subset B$, then $\bar{B} \subset \bar{A}$.

The idea of counting is really one of comparison. That is, when one counts one generally takes the objects to be counted and matches each of these objects exactly once to the counting numbers 1, 2, 3, and so on until *no* objects remain.

Even before numbers had names and symbols assigned to them, this method of counting was used. Early cavemen determined how many of their herd of cattle did not return from pasture by using rocks. As each cow left, a rock was placed aside. As each cow returned, a rock was removed from the pile. If rocks remained after all the cows returned, it was then known that some cows were missing.

It is rather important to realize that cavemen were able to do this without developing a language or symbolism for numbers. We have a highly developed language and symbolism for numbers. There is no question of understanding what is meant by the symbol 2316 or two thousand three hundred sixteen.

Consider the set L of letters in the alphabet

$$L = \{a, b, c, d, e, f, \ldots, x, y, z\}$$

Also, consider the set

$$\{1, 2, 3, 4, 5, \ldots, 24, 25, 26\}$$

Clearly, these two sets are equivalent, that is, we can match up their elements in a one-to-one correspondence. Because of this, we say that the set L has 26 elements or that the *cardinal number* of the set L is 26 and we write $c(L) = 26$.

The empty set $\varnothing$ has no elements and its cardinal number is defined to be zero so that

$$c(\varnothing) = 0$$

A set A is said to have n members or have *cardinal number n* **provided**

$$A \sim \{1, 2, 3, \ldots, n-1, n\}$$

and we write

$$c(A) = n$$

where $n \geqq 1$ is a positive integer.

Sets obeying the conditions of Definition 2.5.1 are called *finite sets* and the area of mathematics that deals with a study of finite sets is called *finite mathematics*. We shall mainly be concerned with such sets and this is the reason for the title given the text.

2.5.2
Example

A survey of a group of people indicated there were 25 with brown eyes and 15 with black hair. If 10 people had both brown eyes and black hair and 23 people had neither, how many people were interviewed?

If we let A denote the set of persons with brown eyes and B the set of persons with black hair, then the data given tells us

$$c(A) = 25, \qquad c(B) = 15, \qquad c(A \cap B) = 10$$

Now, the number of persons with either brown eyes or black hair cannot be $c(A) + c(B)$, since those with both would be counted twice. The correct procedure then would be to subtract off those with both. That is,

$$\cdot \quad c(A \cup B) = c(A) + c(B) - c(A \cap B) = 25 + 15 - 10 = 30$$

Clearly, the sum of those people found either in A or in B and those found neither in A nor in B is the total interviewed. Thus, the number of people interviewed is

$$30 + 23 = 53$$

See Figure 2.10.

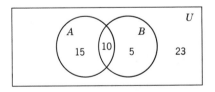

Figure 2.10

This example leads us to formulate the following important result.

Theorem 2.5.1
Let A and B be two finite sets. Then

$$c(A \cup B) = c(A) + c(B) - c(A \cap B)$$

The next section will give us a way of handling problems in which more than two sets are needed.

1. What are the cardinal numbers of the following sets?
   (a) Set D of digits $= \{0, 1, 2, 3, 4, 5, 6, 7, 8, 9\}$
   (b) $A = \{1, 3, 5, 7\}$
   (c) $A = \{0, 1, 2\}$
2. For the two sets $A = \{1, 2, 3, 5\}$ and $B = \{4, 6, 8\}$, find the cardinal number of
   (a) A (d) $A \cup B$
   (b) B (e) $A - B$
   (c) $A \cap B$ (f) $B - A$
3. For the sets $A = \{1, 3, 6, 8\}$, $B = \{8\}$, and $C = \{8, 10\}$, find the cardinal number of the following.
   (a) $A \cup (B \cap C)$ (d) $A \cup (B \cup C)$
   (b) $A \cap (B \cap C)$ (e) $(A \cap B) \cup C$
   (c) $A - (B \cup C)$ (f) $A - (B \cap C)$
4. If $c(A) = m$ and $c(B) = n$ and $c(A \cup B) = m + n$, what is $c(A \cap B)$?
5. If $c(A) = m$, $c(B) = n$, and $c(A \cup B) = r$, where r is less than $m + n$, explain how to determine the cardinal number of $A \cap B$.
6. If $c(A) = 10$, $c(A \cup B) = 29$, and $c(A \cap B) = 5$, what is $c(B)$?
7. If $c(A) = c(B)$, $c(A \cup B) = 16$, and $c(A \cap B) = 6$, find $c(B)$.
8. Motors Incorporated in one day manufactured 325 cars with automatic transmissions, 216 with power steering, and 89 with both these options. How many cars were manufactured if every car has at least one option?
*9. Show that the union of two finite sets A and B is also a finite set. (Hint: let $A = \{a_1, a_2, \ldots, a_n\}$ and $B = \{b_1, b_2, \ldots, b_m\}$. Then $A \cup B \sim C$, where $c(C) \leq m + n$).
10. In 1948, according to a study made by Berelsa, Lazarfeld, and McPhee, the influence of religion and age on voting in Elmira, New York was given by the following table.

	Age		
	Below 35	35–54	Over 54
Protestant voting Republican	82	152	111
Protestant voting Democratic	42	33	15
Catholic voting Republican	27	33	7
Catholic voting Democratic	44	47	33

Find
  (a) The number of voters who are Catholic or Republican or both.
  (b) The number of voters who are Catholic or over 54 or both.
  (c) The number of Democratic voters below 35 or over 54.

2.6
**APPLICATION OF
THE TECHNIQUES
OF COUNTING TO
SURVEY ANALYSIS**

Venn diagrams are very useful for depicting certain practical results. The following examples illustrate how Venn diagrams can be used to solve some practical problems in survey analysis.

2.6.1
Example

In a survey of 75 consumers, 12 indicated they would be buying a new car, 18 said they would buy a new refrigerator, and 24 said they would buy a new stove. Of these, 6 were buying both a car and a refrigerator, 4 were buying a car and a stove, and 10 were buying a stove and refrigerator. One person indicated he would buy all three items.
  (a) How many are buying none of these items?
  (b) How many are buying only a car?
  (c) How many are buying only a stove?
  (d) How many are buying only a refrigerator?
Denote the set of people buying cars, refrigerators, and stoves, by C, R, and S, respectively. Then we know from the data given that

$$c(C) = 12, \quad c(R) = 18, \quad c(S) = 24$$
$$c(C \cap R) = 6, \quad c(C \cap S) = 4, \quad c(S \cap R) = 10$$
$$c(C \cap R \cap S) = 1$$

We use the information given above in the reverse order. Thus, beginning with the fact that $c(C \cap R \cap S) = 1$, we place a 1 in that set. See Figure 2.11(a). Now $c(C \cap R) = 6$, $c(C \cap S) = 4$, and $c(S \cap R) = 10$. Thus, we place $6 - 1 = 5$ in the proper region (giving a total of 6 in the set $C \cap R$). Similarly, we place 3 and 9 in the proper regions for the sets $C \cap S$ and $S \cap R$. See Figure 2.11(b). Now, $c(C) = 12$ and 9 of these 12 are already accounted for. Also, $c(R) = 18$ with 15 accounted for and $c(S) = 24$ with

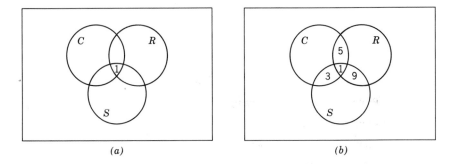

(a)   (b)

Figure 2.11

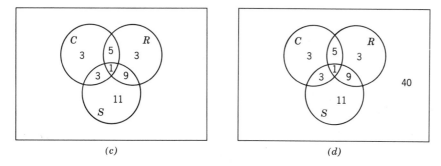

(c)

(d)

Figure 2.11 (*Continued*)

13 accounted for. See Figure 2.11(c) Finally, the number in $\overline{C \cup R \cup S}$ is the total of 75 less those accounted for in C, R, and S, namely $3 + 5 + 1 + 3 + 3 + 9 + 11 = 35$. Thus

$$c(\overline{C \cup R \cup S}) = 75 - 35 = 40$$

See Figure 2.11(d). From this figure, it is easy to see that 40 are buying none of the items, 3 are only buying cars, 3 are only buying refrigerators, and 11 are only buying stoves.

In a survey of 10,281 people restricted to ones who were either black or married or male, the following data was obtained:

2.6.2
Example

Black: 3490
Male: 5822
Married: 4722
Black males: 1745
Married males: 859
Married blacks: 1341
Black married males: 239

The data is not valid. Why?
Just as in the previous example, denote the set of people who were black

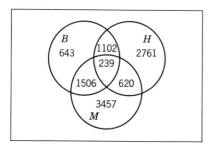

Figure 2.12

by B, married by H, and male by M. Then we know that

$$c(B) = 3490, \qquad c(M) = 5822, \qquad c(H) = 4722$$
$$c(B \cap M) = 1745, \qquad c(H \cap M) = 859$$
$$c(H \cap B) = 1341, \qquad c(H \cap M \cap B) = 239$$

Since $H \cap M \cap B \neq \varnothing$, we shall use the situation depicted in Figure 2.12. This means that

$$239 + 1102 + 620 + 1506 + 3457 + 643 + 2761 = 10{,}328$$

people were interviewed. However, it is given that only 10,281 were interviewed. This means the data is suspect.

1. Blood is classified as being either Rh positive or Rh negative and according to type. If blood contains an A antigen, it is type A; if it has a B antigen, it is type B; if it has both A and B antigen, it is type AB; and if it has neither antigen, it is type O. Use a Venn diagram to illustrate these possibilities. How many different possibilities are there?
2. In a survey of 75 college students, it was found that of the three weekly news magazines "Time," "Newsweek," and "U.S. News and World Report,"
   (a) 23 read "Time."
   (b) 18 read "Newsweek."
   (c) 14 read "U.S. News and World Report."
   (d) 10 read "Time and Newsweek."
   (e) 9 read "Time" and "U.S. News and World Report."
   (f) 8 read "Newsweek" and "U.S. News and World Report."
   (g) 5 read all three.
      (i) How many read none of these three magazines?
      (ii) How many read Time alone?
      (iii) How many read Newsweek alone?
      (iv) How many read U.S. News and World Report alone?
      (v) How many read neither Time nor Newsweek?
      (vi) How many read Time or Newsweek or both?
3. A staff member at a large engineering school was presenting data to show that the students there received a liberal education as well as a scientific one. "Look at our record," he said. "Out of one senior class of 500 students, 281 are taking English, 196 are taking English and History, 87 are taking History and a foreign language, 143 are taking a foreign language and English, and 36 are taking all of these. He was fired. Why?
4. Of the cars sold during the month of July, 90 had air conditioning, 100 had automatic transmissions, and 75 had power steering. Five cars had all three of these extras. Twenty cars had none of these extras. Twenty cars had only air conditioning; 60 cars had only automatic transmissions; and 30 had

only power steering. Ten cars had both automatic transmission and power steering.

(a) How many cars had both power steering and air conditioning?
(b) How many had both automatic transmission and air conditioning?
(c) How many had neither power steering nor automatic transmission?
(d) How many cars were sold in July?
(e) How many had automatic transmission or air conditioning or both?

*5. A survey of 52 families from the inner-city area of Chicago indicated that there was a total of 241 children below the age of 18. Of these, 109 were male, 132 were below the age of 11, 143 had police records, and 69 males were of age under 11. If 45 females under 11 had police records and 30 males under 11 had police records, how many children over 11 and under 18 had police records?

Before discussing the nature of permutations and combinations, we shall introduce a useful shorthand notation—the *factorial symbol*.

**2.7
PERMUTATIONS
AND
COMBINATIONS**

Let $n \geq 0$ be an integer. The symbol $n!$, read as "n factorial," means

2.7.1
Definition

$$0! = 1, \qquad 1! = 1, \qquad n! = n(n-1)(n-2) \cdots (3)(2)(1)$$

Thus, for example,

$$4! = (4)(3)(2)(1) = 24 \qquad 2! = (2)(1) = 2$$

A useful formula is

$$(n + 1)! = (n + 1) \cdot n!$$

Now, consider the following situation. In traveling from New York to Los Angeles, Mr. Williams wishes to stop over in Chicago. If he has 5 dif-

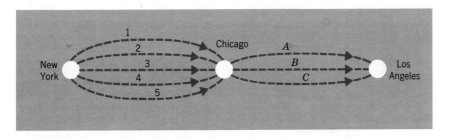

Figure 2.13

ferent routes to choose from in going from New York to Chicago and has 3 routes to choose from in going from Chicago to Los Angeles, in how many ways can Mr. Williams travel from New York to Los Angeles?

To solve this problem, we notice that corresponding to each of the 5 routes from New York to Chicago there are 3 routes from Chicago to Los Angeles. Thus, in all, there are $5 \cdot 3 = 15$ different routes (see Figure 2.13). These 15 different routes can be enumerated as

1A, 1B, 1C   2A, 2B, 2C   3A, 3B, 3C   4A, 4B, 4C   5A, 5B, 5C

This same problem can also be interpreted by using a *tree diagram* (see Figure 2.14).

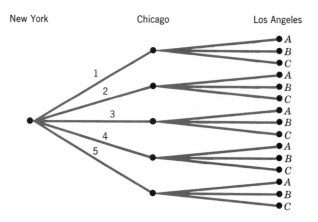

Figure 2.14

Of course, it is easy to see that there is a total of 15 different routes.

In general, we are led to the principle in Theorem 2.7.1.

Theorem 2.7.1 Fundamental Principle of Counting

If we can perform a first task in p different ways, a second task in q different ways, a third task in r different ways, . . . , then the total act of performing the first task followed by performing the second task, and so on, can be done in $p \cdot q \cdot r$ . . . ways.

2.7.1
Example

In a city election, there are 4 candidates for mayor, 3 candidates for vice-mayor, 6 candidates for treasurer, and 2 for secretary. In how many ways can these 4 offices be filled?

Again, we reason as follows. Corresponding to each of the 4 possible mayors, there are 3 vice-mayors. These 2 offices can be filled in $4 \cdot 3 = 12$ different ways. Also, corresponding to each of these 12 possibilities, we have 6 different choices for treasurer—giving $12 \cdot 6 = 72$ different possibilities. Finally, to each of these 72 possibilities there can correspond 2 choices for secretary. Thus, all told, these offices can be filled in 144 different ways. That is, $4 \cdot 3 \cdot 6 \cdot 2 = 144$ different ways (see Figure 2.15). Figure 2.15 is sometimes referred to as a *decision tree*.

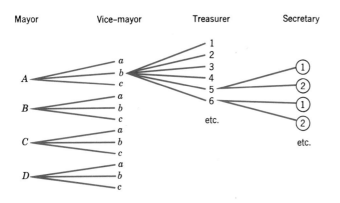

Figure 2.15

From how many different batting orders must the manager of a baseball team (nine men) select? If he adheres to the rule that the pitcher always bats last and his star home run hitter is always clean-up (fourth), then from how many possibilities must he select?

2.7.2
Example

In the first slot, any of the nine players can be chosen. In the second slot, any one of the remaining eight can be chosen; and so on, so that there are

$$9 \cdot 8 \cdot 7 \cdot 6 \cdot 5 \cdot 4 \cdot 3 \cdot 2 \cdot 1 = 9! = 362,880$$

possible batting orders.

For the second problem, the first position can be filled in any one of seven ways, the second in any six ways, the third in any of five ways, the fourth has been designated, the fifth in any of four ways, . . . , so that here there are

$$7 \cdot 6 \cdot 5 \cdot 4 \cdot 3 \cdot 2 \cdot 1 = 7! = 5040$$

different batting orders of nine men after two have been designated.

Consider a set A that has n elements. How many subsets does A have? (Remember that A and $\varnothing$ are both subsets of A.)

2.7.3
Example

If n is very small, it is easy enough to list all the subsets and proceed to count them. However, this will not do if n is large, nor does it give us a formula to use to calculate this quantity. Thus, we attack the problem by considering an arbitrary subset X of A.

Any element of the set A is either in X or not in X—that is, there are two choices for each element. Since there are n such elements, each giving rise to two choices, we have altogether

$$2 \cdot 2 \cdot 2 \cdots 2 = 2^n$$

possible subsets of A.

Thus, the set $S = \{a, b, c, d\}$ has $2^4 = 2 \cdot 2 \cdot 2 \cdot 2 = 16$ subsets. These are

$\varnothing, \{a\}, \{b\}, \{c\}, \{d\}, \{a, b\}, \{a, c\}, \{a, d\}, \{b, c\}, \{b, d\}, \{c, d\}, \{a, b, c\},$
$\{a, b, d\}, \{b, c, d\}, \{a, c, d\}, \{a, b, c, d\}.$

**2.7.4
Example**

Suppose there are six candidates vying for three positions on the Board of Directors of XYZ company. The rules stipulate that the three obtaining the highest number of votes of the stockholders will be elected. How many possibilities are there for election to the Board?

Here any one of the six candidates might have the highest number of votes. Once this happened, any one of the five remaining could be next, and finally any one of the remaining four could be third. Thus, there are

$$6 \cdot 5 \cdot 4 = 120$$

possibilities. See Figure 2.16 for a partial illustration of this problem.

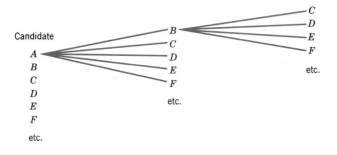

Figure 2.16

In Example 2.7.4, we asked in how many ways it was possible to fill three positions from a choice of six candidates. It is pointed out that the three positions are ordered and no replacements are allowed so that once a man has been chosen to fill a position, he cannot fill another one. Also, notice that the six candidates were individual, that is, distinct things. We now can give the following definition.

**2.7.2
Definition**

The number of *permutations of n different things taken r at a time,* **denoted by** $P(n,r)$, **means the number of all possible different arrangements of** *r* **things chosen from** *n* **different things.**

In Example 2.7.4, we asked for the number of permutations of six things taken three at a time, namely $P(6,3)$.

Let us obtain a general formula for $P(n,r)$. We wish to find the number of all possible different arrangements of *r* quantities that are chosen from *n* different quantities. The first entry can be filled by any one of the *n* possibilities, the second by any one of the remaining $(n - 1)$, the third by any one of the now remaining $(n - 2)$, . . . , the rth place (the last one), can be filled by any one of $(n - r + 1)$ things. Thus, the number of possibilities is

$$P(n,r) = n(n - 1) \cdot \cdot \cdot (n - r + 1)$$

Notice that $P(n,r)$ is the product of the r consecutive integers from $n - r + 1$ to n inclusive.

2.7.5
Example

A station wagon has nine seats in it. In how many different ways can five people be seated?

The first person can choose any one of the nine seats. The second person can then choose from any of the eight seats left. The third from seven seats, the fourth from six, and the fifth person from five seats. Thus, in all, there are

$$9 \cdot 8 \cdot 7 \cdot 6 \cdot 5 = 15,120$$

different seating arrangements.

If we recognize that Example 2.7.5 is asking for the number of permutations of 9 people taken 5 at a time, we see the answer is

$$P(9,5) = 9 \cdot 8 \cdot 7 \cdot 6 \cdot 5 = 15,120$$

Suppose, in the above example, there were nine people to be seated in the nine passenger station wagon. In this case, the number of possible arrangements is

$$P(9,9) = 9 \cdot 8 \cdot 7 \cdot 6 \cdot 5 \cdot 4 \cdot 3 \cdot 2 \cdot 1 = 9! = 362,880$$

In general, the number of permutations of n different objects taken n at a time is

$$P(n,n) = n!$$

In the above example, it is assumed the n objects are all different. However, we might ask about the number of permutations of n objects taken n at a time in which some of them are alike.

2.7.6
Example

How many different words (real or imaginary) can be formed from the word

seven

The word contains five letters and, if none were the same, the answer would be $P(5,5) = 5!$ different words. However, there are two e's which we cannot distinguish and so, 5! must be too large. Let P denote the number of permutations of the word *seven*. If we think of the e's as different letters, then the number of permutations of *seven* becomes 2!P. But in this case we have treated all the letters as distinct so that there would be 5! permutations.

Thus,

$$2!P = 5!$$
$$P = \frac{5!}{2!} = 5 \cdot 4 \cdot 3 = 60$$

different words that can be formed from the word *seven*.

As another example, how many different words (real or imaginary) can be formed from the word

mississippi

The word contains 11 letters and, if none were the same, the answer would be $P(11,11) = 11!$ different words. However, the fact that there are four i's, four s's, and two p's tells us that 11! must be too large—since we cannot distinguish one i from another. If P denotes the number of permutations and if we think of the i's as being distinct, there are $4!P$ permutations of mississippi treating the s's and p's as alike letters. If we think of the s's as distinct also, there will be $4!(4!P)$ permutations of mississippi with the p's alike. Finally, treating the p's as different letters, there are $2!4!4!P$ permutations of mississippi in which now we have treated every letter as distinct. But with every letter treated as distinct mississippi has 11! permutations. Thus,

$$2!4!4!P = 11!$$

or

$$P = \frac{11!}{2!4!4!} = \frac{39,916,800}{1,152} = 34,650$$

2.7.7
Example How many different vertical arrangements are possible for ten flags if two are white, three are red, and five are blue.

Here we want the different arrangements of ten objects, not all different. Thus, following the argument above, we have

$$\frac{10!}{2!3!5!} = \frac{10 \cdot 9 \cdot 8 \cdot 7 \cdot 6}{2 \cdot 3 \cdot 2} = 2520$$

different arrangements.

Up to this point, we have been very concerned with the order in which n objects can be rearranged. However, in many cases, order is not important. For example, in a draw poker hand, the order in which one receives his cards is not important at all—rather it is what cards are received that is important. That is, with poker hands, we are concerned with the *combination* of the cards—not the particular order of the cards.

2.7.3
Definition **The number of** *combinations of n different things taken r at a time* **denoted by** $C(n,r)$**, is defined to be the number of all possible selections of r objects chosen from n objects, neglecting the order of selection.**

Suppose we have n different objects from which we have chosen r objects. We can rearrange the order of these r objects in $r!$ ways. If $C(n,r)$ denotes the number of combinations of n things taken r at a time, we can form

$$r! \cdot C(n,r)$$

different arrangements. But this is just the number of permutations of n things taken r at a time. Hence,

$$r!C(n,r) = P(n,r)$$

$$C(n,r) = \frac{P(n,r)}{r!}$$

The reader should convince himself that

$$C(n,r) = \frac{n!}{(n-r)!r!}$$

Sometimes the notation $\binom{n}{r}$, read as "n things taken r at a time" is used in place of $C(n,r)$. Here, $\binom{n}{r}$ is called the *binomial coefficient*. The display of $\binom{n}{r}$ for $n = 0$ to $n = 6$ is given in Figure 2.17. This display is called a *Pascal triangle*.

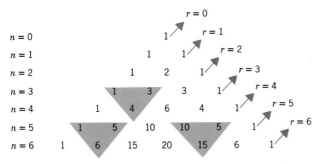

Figure 2.17

For example, $\binom{5}{2} = 10$, is in the row marked $n = 5$ and on the diagonal marked $r = 2$.

Notice that successive entries can be obtained by adding the two nearest entries in the row above it. The shaded triangles in Figure 2.17 illustrate this. For example, $10 + 5 = 15$, etc.

2.7.8
Example

From a deck of 52 cards, a hand of 5 cards is dealt. How many different hands are possible?

If the order of reception of the cards is considered, there are

$$52 \cdot 51 \cdot 50 \cdot 49 \cdot 48$$

different hands. But order is not important. Thus, since corresponding to each hand of five cards there are 5! different arrangements, we see that the number of different hands without regard to order is

$$\frac{52 \cdot 51 \cdot 50 \cdot 49 \cdot 48}{5!} = 2,598,960$$

Of course, we can also arrive at this result by recognizing that the number of different hands is C(52,5).

To further emphasize the difference between permutations and combinations, suppose we have four letters a, b, c, d and wish to choose two of them without repeating any letter more than once.

If order is important, then we have $P(4,2) = 4 \cdot 3 = 12$ possible arrangements, namely,

ab, ac, ad   bc, bd, cd   ba, ca, da   cb, db, dc

If order is not a consideration, we have $C(4,2) = 6$ selections, namely,

ab, ac, ad, bc, bd, cd

2.7.9
Example

A sociologist needs a sample of 12 welfare recipients located in a large metropolitan area. He divides the city into 4 areas—northwest, northeast, southwest, southeast. Each section contains 25 welfare recipients. He may select the 12 recipients in any way he wants—all from the same area, 2 from the southwest area and 10 from the northwest area, and so on. How many different groups of 12 recipients are there?

Since order of selection is not important, and since the selection is of 12 things from a possible $4 \cdot 25 = 100$ things, there are C(100,12) different groups. That is

$$C(100,12) = \frac{100!}{12!88!}$$

2.7.10
Example

A fraternity house has three bedrooms and ten students. One bedroom has three beds, the second has two beds, and the third has five beds. In how many different ways can the students be assigned bedrooms?

First of all, there are ten beds. There are $\binom{10}{3}$ ways of assigning the beds in the first bedroom. For the seven remaining students, we can assign the beds in the second bedroom in $\binom{7}{2}$ ways. Finally, the remaining five students can be assigned the five remaining beds in $\binom{5}{5}$ ways. In total, by the fundamental principle of counting, there are

$$\binom{10}{3} \cdot \binom{7}{2} \cdot \binom{5}{5} = \frac{10!}{3!7!} \cdot \frac{7!}{2!5!} \cdot \frac{5!}{0!5!} = \frac{10!}{2!3!5!} = 2520$$

different ways.

Notice that in the above example, the number of different ways the 10 beds can be assigned is $10!/2!3!5!$, in which each bedroom has 2 beds, 3 beds, and 5 beds. This problem is an example of the *multinomial theorem*. Sometimes $10!/2!3!5!$ is written using the notation $\binom{10}{2,\ 3,\ 5}$. Of course, the number of total beds must be the same as the number of students in order to use this result.

This example from the field of political science is sometimes referred to as the "voting paradox." Suppose three voters are to vote on three proposals (or candidates) A, B, and C and they are to list their order of preference. Then there are six possible orderings.

2.7.11
Example
Voting Paradox

ABC, ACB, BAC, BCA, CAB, CBA

In how many different ways can the three voters select their choices of ordering?

To answer the question, we consider three possibilities:

(a) All three voters select the same ordering.
(b) Two of the voters choose the same ordering and the other one selects one of the other five remaining orderings.
(c) Each of the three voters selects a different ordering.

For (a), it is clear that there are 6 ways in which all three voters select the same orderings. For (b), we see that there are 6 choices for a given pair of voters to agree on, leaving 5 choices for the third voter to choose or $6 \cdot 5 = 30$ ways for a given pair of voters to agree and the third disagree. However, there are 3 possible pairs of voters. Thus, there are

$$3 \cdot 6 \cdot 5 = 90$$

ways for any pair of voters to agree on an ordering while the third disagrees. Finally, for (c), if all three are to choose a different ordering, there are 6 orderings for the first voter to choose from, leaving only 5 for the second, and 4 for the third. Thus for (3) there are

$$6 \cdot 5 \cdot 4 = 120$$

ways for each of the three voters to choose a different ordering.

If either (a) or (b) is the result of the vote, these $90 + 6 = 96$ possibilities clearly indicate a majority opinion as to which order is preferred. In (c), 30 of the 120 possible no-majority outcomes result in a paradox. For example, suppose the voting resulted in

ABC, BCA, CAB

Notice that two voters prefer A to B, and two voters prefer B to C, indicating the majority decision is ABC. However, C is preferred to A by two

	Case 1	Case 2	Case 3	Case 4
Assumption	Without replacement and with regard to order	Without replacement and without regard to order	With replacement and with regard to order	With replacement and without regard to order
Selections by name	(Mike, Katy), (Mike, Danny), (Mike, Tammie), (Mike, Jack), (Katy, Mike), (Katy, Danny), (Katy, Tammie), (Katy, Jack), (Danny, Mike), (Danny, Katy), (Danny, Tammie), (Danny, Jack), (Tammie, Mike), (Tammie, Katy), (Tammie, Danny), (Tammie, Jack), (Jack, Mike), (Jack, Katy), (Jack, Danny), (Jack, Tammie)	(Mike, Katy), (Mike, Danny), (Mike, Tammie), (Mike, Jack), (Katy, Danny), (Katy, Tammie), (Katy, Jack), (Danny, Tammie), (Danny, Jack), (Tammie, Jack)	(Mike, Mike), (Mike, Katy), (Mike, Danny), (Mike, Tammie), (Mike, Jack) (Katy, Mike), (Katy, Katy), (Katy, Danny), (Katy, Tammie), (Katy, Jack) (Danny, Mike), (Danny, Katy), (Danny, Danny), (Danny, Tammie), (Danny, Jack) (Tammie, Mike), (Tammie, Katy), (Tammie, Danny), (Tammie, Tammie), (Tammie, Jack) (Jack, Mike), (Jack, Katy), (Jack, Danny), (Jack, Tammie), (Jack, Jack)	(Mike, Mike), (Mike, Katy), (Mike, Danny), (Mike, Tammie), (Mike, Jack) (Katy, Katy), (Katy, Danny), (Katy, Tammie), (Katy, Jack) (Danny, Danny), (Danny, Tammie), (Danny, Jack) (Tammie, Tammie), (Tammie, Jack) (Jack, Jack)
Number of selections	20	10	25	15
Rule	permutation $P(5,2) = 5 \cdot 4 = 20$	combination $C(5,2) = \dfrac{5 \cdot 4}{2} = 10$	principle of counting $5 \cdot 5 = 25$	$5 + 4 + 3 + 2 + 1 = 15$

voters. Thus, this decision cannot be the majority. Similarly, the other two choices cannot be the majority choice. This paradox is what is called the "voters paradox."

We close this section with an example that illustrates the difference between a permutation and a combination.

Consider a set of five students {Mike, Katy, Danny, Tammie, Jack}. In how many ways can two students be chosen from this set?

2.7.12
Example

As stated, the solution will depend on how the question is interpreted. For example, is the selection (Mike, Katy) different from (Katy, Mike)? Also, is it possible to select Danny twice as in (Danny, Danny)? Usually, the setting of the problem and the practical considerations of the problem, will answer these questions and lead us to the correct answers.

The table on page 66 lists the four cases and the assumptions of each case.

2.7
Exercise

1. Find the value of
   - (a) $P(6,4)$
   - (b) $P(7,2)$
   - (c) $P(5,1)$
   - (d) $P(5,4)$
   - (e) $P(8,7)$
   - (f) $P(6,6)$
2. Find the value of
   - (a) $C(6,4)$
   - (b) $C(7,2)$
   - (c) $C(5,1)$
   - (d) $C(5,4)$
   - (e) $C(8,7)$
   - (f) $C(8,8)$
3. Find x if
   - (a) $P(x,3) = 60$
   - (b) $C(x,2) = 10$
   - (c) $P(6,x) = 30$
   - (d) $C(7,x) = 35$
4. Find x and y if
   - (a) $P(x,y) = 120$ $C(x,y) = 5$
   - (b) $P(x,y) = 210$ $C(x,y) = 35$
5. Show that

$$P(n,r) = \frac{n!}{(n-r)!}$$

6. Interpret the meaning of $C(n,0)$ and $C(n,n)$. Can you now justify our definition of $0!$
7. A woman has four blouses and five skirts. How many different outfits can she wear?
8. Show that

$$C(n,r) = \frac{n!}{(n-r)!r!}$$

9. Write down entries in the Pascal triangle for $n = 7, 8, 9, 10$.
10. Show that

$$C(n,r) = C(n,n-r)$$

This fact should be checked by referring to the Pascal triangle.

11. XYZ Company wants to build a complex consisting of a factory, office building, and warehouse. If the building contractor has three different kinds of factories, two different office buildings, and four different warehouses, how many models must he build to show all possibilities to XYZ Company.

12. Cars Incorporated has three different car models and six color schemes. If you are one of the dealers, how many cars must you display to show each possibility.

13. How many different words (real or imaginary) can be formed from the word *economic?*

14. You are to set up a code of two digit words using the digits 1, 2, 3, 4 without using any digit more than once. What is the maximum number of words in such a language? If the words 12 and 21, for example, designate, the same word, how many words are possible?

15. A basketball team has six men who play at guard (two of five starting positions). How many different teams are possible? The remaining three positions are assumed filled and further assume that it is not possible to distinguish a left guard from a right guard.

16. On a basketball team of twelve men, two play only at center, three play only at guard, and the rest play at forward (5 men on a team; 2 forwards, 2 guards and 1 center). How many different teams are possible? Assume it is not possible to distinguish left and right guards and left and right forwards.

17. The Student Affairs Committee has three faculty, two administration, and five students on it. In how many ways can a subcommittee of one faculty, one administration, and two students be formed?

18. Of 1352 stocks traded one day in the New York Stock Exchange, 641 advanced, 234 declined, and the remainder were unchanged. In how many ways can this happen?

19. A mathematics department is allowed to tenure 4 of 17 eligible teachers. In how many ways can the selection for tenure be made?

20. How many different hands are possible in a bridge game? A bridge hand consists of 13 cards dealt from a deck of 52 cards.

21. On a mathematics test there are 10 multiple-choice questions with 4 possible answers and 15 true-false questions. In how many possible ways can the 25 questions be answered?

22. Colleen's Ice Cream Parlor offers 31 different flavors to choose from, and specializes in double dip cones. How many different cones are there to choose from if you may select the same flavor for each dip? How many different cones are there to choose from if you cannot repeat any flavor. Assume that a cone with vanilla on top of chocolate is different than a cone with chocolate on top of vanilla. How many are there if you consider any cone having chocolate on top and vanilla on the bottom the same as having vanilla on top and chocolate on the bottom?

23. The United States Senate has 100 members. Suppose it is de-
    sired to place each senator on exactly 1 of 7 possible com-
    mittees. The first committee has 22 members, the second 13,
    the third 10, the fourth 5, the fifth 16, the sixth and seventh
    17 apiece. In how many ways can these committees be
    formed?
24. In how many ways can ten children be placed on three teams
    of 3, 3, and 4 members?

empty set ($\varnothing$)	disjoint
null set ($\varnothing$)	relative complement
element	difference
set-builder notation	absolute complement
equivalent sets	cardinal number
equal sets	finite sets
one-to-one correspondence	Venn diagram
subset ($\subseteq$)	factorial
proper subset ($\subset$)	tree diagram
Antisymmetric law	fundamental principle of counting
comparable sets	permutation
universal set (U)	combination
operation	Pascal triangle
union ($\cup$)	
intersection ($\cap$)	

Circle each correct answer or answers. Some questions have more than
one correct answer. Replace the asterisk $*$ by all correct symbols.

a.   b.   c.   d.   e.   f.   g.

$\in$ $\notin$ $\subset$ $\subseteq$ $\sim$ $=$ none of these

	a	b	c	d	e	f	g	
1.	a	b	c	d	e	f	g	1. $0 * \varnothing$
2.	a	b	c	d	e	f	g	2. $\{0\} * \{1, 0, 3\}$
3.	a	b	c	d	e	f	g	3. $\{5, 6\} \cap \{2, 6\} * \{8\}$
4.	a	b	c	d	e	f	g	4. $\{2, 3\} \cup \{3, 4\} * \{3\}$
5.	a	b	c	d	e	f	g	5. $\{8, 9\} * \{9, 10, 11\}$
6.	a	b	c	d	e	f	g	6. $1 * \{1, 3, 5\} - \{3, 4\}$
7.	a	b	c	d	e	f	g	7. $5 * \{0, 5\}$
8.	a	b	c	d	e	f	g	8. $\varnothing * \{1, 2, 3\}$
9.	a	b	c	d	e	f	g	9. $\varnothing * \{1, 2\} \cap \{3, 4, 5\}$
10.	a	b	c	d	e	f	g	10. $\{2, 3\} * \{3, 4\}$
11.	a	b	c	d	e	f	g	11. $\{1, 2\} * \{1\} \cup \{3\}$
12.	a	b	c	d	e	f	g	12. $5 * \{1\} \cup \{2, 3\}$
13.	a	b	c	d	e	f	g	13. $\{4, 5\} - \{5, 6\} * \{4, 5\}$
14.	a	b	c	d	e	f	g	14. $\{6, 8\} * \{8, 9, 10\}$
15.	a	b	c	d	e	f	g	15. $\{6, 7, 8\} - \{8\} * \{6\}$
16.	a	b	c	d	e	f	g	16. $4 * \{6, 8\} \cap \{4, 8\}$

1. For the sets

$$A = \{1, 3, 5, 6, 8\}, \qquad B = \{2, 3, 6, 7\}, \qquad C = \{6, 8, 9\}$$

find
a. $(A \cap B) \cup C$
b. $(A - B) \cap C$
c. $(A \cup B) \cap B$

2. For the sets, U = universal set = $\{1, 2, 3, 4, 5, 6, 7\}$

$$A = \{1, 3, 5, 6\}, \qquad B = \{2, 3, 6, 7\}, \qquad C = \{4, 6, 7\}$$

find
a. $\overline{A - B}$
b. $(B \cap C) \cap A$
c. $\overline{B} \cup \overline{A}$

3. If U = universal set = $\{1, 2, 3, 4, 5\}$, find all sets A for which $A \cap B = \{1\}$, $B = \{1, 4, 5\}$.

4. If U = universal set = $\{1, 2, 3, 4, 5, 6\}$ and if $A = \{1, 3, 4\}$, $B = \{2, 4, 6\}$, $C = \{3, 4, 5\}$, find
a. $(A - B) \cup C$
b. $A \cap \overline{B}$
c. $(A - C) - B$
d. $(A \cap B) \cap \overline{C}$

5. If A and B are sets and if $c(A) = 14$, $c(A \cup B) = 33$, $c(B) = 12$, find $c(A \cap B)$.

6. During June, Colleen's Motors sold 75 cars with air conditioning, 95 with power steering, and 100 with automatic transmission. Twenty cars had all 3 options, 10 cars had none of these options, and 10 cars were sold that had only air conditioning. In addition, 50 cars had both automatic transmission and power steering and 60 cars had both automatic transmission and air conditioning.
a. How many cars were sold in June?
b. How many cars had only power steering?

7. In a survey of 125 college students, it was found that of three newspapers, the Wall Street Journal, N.Y. Times, and Chicago Tribune

> 60 read the Tribune,
> 40 read the Times,
> 15 read the Journal,
> 25 read the Tribune and Times,
> 8 read the Times and Journal,
> 3 read the Tribune and Journal,
> 1 read all three.

a. How many read none of these papers?
b. How many read only the Tribune?
c. How many read neither the Tribune nor the Times?
d. How many read the Tribune if and only if they read the Journal?

8. You are to set up a code of three-digit words using the digits 1, 2, 3, 4, 5, 6 without using any digit more than once in the same word. What

is the maximum number of words in such a language? If the words 124, 142, etc. designate the same word, how many different words are possible?

9. Five people are to line up for a group photograph. If two of them cannot stand each other and refuse to stand next to each other, in how many ways can the photograph be taken?

10. A small town consists of a north side and a south side. The north side has 16 houses and the south side has 10 houses. A poll taker is asked to visit 4 houses on the north side and 3 on the south side. In how many ways can this be done?

11. The figure below indicates a route between two houses *A* and *B* of a city in which the lines are streets. A person at *A* wishes to reach *B* and he can only travel in two directions, to the right and up. How many different paths are there from *A* to *B*?

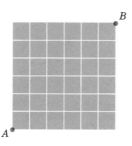

Below are seven problems concerning counting; worked-out solutions are found in the Answers.   Part C

1. In how many ways can we choose 3 words, one each from 5 three-letter words, 6 four-letter words, and 8 five-letter words?

2. A bookstore has 6 copies of Hemingway's novel "The Sun Also Rises," 3 copies of his novel "A Farewell to Arms," and 4 copies of his novel "For Whom the Bells Toll." In addition, the bookstore has 5 copies of a combined edition of "The Sun Also Rises" and "A Farewell to Arms," and 7 copies of a combined edition of "A Farewell to Arms" and "For Whom the Bells Toll." In how many ways can we purchase a selection one each of the 3 novels?

3. A newborn child can be given 1, 2, or 3 names. In how many ways can a child be named if we can choose from 100 names?

4. In how many ways can 5 girls and 3 boys be divided into 2 teams of 4 if each team is to include at least 1 boy?

5. A meeting is to be addressed by 5 speakers, A, B, C, D, E. In how many ways can the speakers be ordered if B must not precede A?

6. What is the answer to the preceding problem if B is to speak immediately after A?

7. An automobile license number contains 1 or 2 letters followed by a 4-digit number. Compute the maximal number of different licenses.

Additional Reading

Arrow, Kenneth, J., *Social Choice and Individual Values* (New York: Wiley, 1951).

Benson, Oliver, "The Use of Mathematics in the Study of Political Science," paper presented to a symposium sponsored by The American Academy on Political and Social Science, Philadelphia, June 1963.

Black, Duncan, *The Theory of Committees and Elections* (Cambridge: Cambridge University Press, 1958).

Cohen, Paul, and Hirsh, Ruben, "Non-Cantorian Set Theory," *Scientific American*, December 1967.

Mizrahi, A., and Sullivan, M., *Topics in Elementary Mathematics*, Holt, Rinehart, and Winston, New York, 1971, Chapters 2–3.

Riker, William H., "Voting and the Summations of Preferences," *American Political Science Review*, Vol. 55 (1961), pp. 900–911.

Slapley, L. S., and Shubik, M., "A Method for Evaluating the Distribution of Power in a Committee System," *The American Political Science Review*, Vol. 48 (1954), pp. 787ff.

Introduction to Probability Chapter 3

Probability theory is a part of mathematics which is useful for discovering and investigating the *regular* features of *random events*. Although it is not really possible to give a precise and simple definition of what is meant by the words "random" and "regular," our hope is that the explanation and the examples given below will make the understanding of these concepts easier.

It is convenient to regard certain phenomena in the real world as *chance phenomena*. By this we mean a phenomenon that does not always produce the same observed outcome and for which the outcome of any given observation of the phenomena may not be predictable, but which has a certain "long-range" behavior known as *statistical regularity*.

In some cases, we know the phenomenon under investigation sufficiently well to feel justified in making *exact* predictions with respect to the result of each individual observation. Thus, if one wants to know the time and place of a solar eclipse, we do not hesitate to predict, based on astronomical data, the exact answer to such a question.

However, in many cases our knowledge is not precise enough to allow exact predictions in particular situations. Some examples of such cases, called *random events,* are:

(a) Tossing a fair coin gives a result that is either a head or a tail. For any one throw, we cannot predict the result, although it is obvious that it is determined by definite causes (such as the initial velocity of the coin, the initial angle of throw, the surface on which the coin rests). Even though some of these causes can be controlled, we cannot predetermine the result of any particular toss. Thus, the result of tossing a coin is a *random event*.

(b) In a series of throws with an ordinary die, each throw yields as its result one of the numbers 1, 2, 3, 4, 5, or 6. Thus, the result of throwing a die is a *random event*.

(c) The sex of a newborn baby is either male or female. However, the sex of a newborn baby cannot be predicted in any particular case. This, too, is an example of a *random event*.

(d) Suppose that a box contains several objects (some of which are of perfect quality and some are defects). Pick up an object. Since it is not possible to know ahead of time whether the object is perfect or defective, the result of picking up an object in this manner is a *random event*.

The above examples demonstrate that in studying a sequence of random experiments, it is not possible to forecast individual results. These are subject to irregular, random fluctuations which cannot be exactly predicted. However, if the number of observations is large, that is, if we deal with a *mass phenomenon*, some regularity appears.

In example (a), we cannot predict the result of any particular toss. However, if we perform a long sequence of tosses, we notice that the number of times heads occurs is approximately equal to the number of times tails appears. That is, it seems *reasonable* to say that in any toss of this fair coin, a head or a tail is *equally likely* to occur. As a result, we might *assign a probability* of 1/2 for obtaining a head (or tail) on a particular toss.

The student should test this result for himself by flipping a coin 25 times, 50 times, and 100 times, noting the results. Of interest is the fact that K. Pearson, in tossing a coin 24,000 times, obtained heads 12,012 times.

For example (b) the appearance of any particular face is a random event. If, however, we perform a long series of tosses, any face is as *equally likely* to occur as any other, provided the die is fair. Here, we might *assign a probability* of 1/6 for obtaining a particular face.

For example (c), our intuition tells us that a boy baby and a girl baby are equally likely to occur. If we follow this reasoning, we might *assign a probability* of 1/2 to having a boy baby. However, were we to consult the data found in Figure 3.1, we would see that it might be more accurate to *assign a probability* of .512 to having a boy baby.

Year of Birth	Number of Births		Total Number of Births $b+g$	Ratio of Births	
	Boys b	Girls g		$\dfrac{b}{b+g}$	$\dfrac{g}{b+g}$
1950	1,863,000	1,768,000	3,631,000	.513	.487
1951	1,960,000	1,863,000	3,823,000	.513	.487
1952	2,005,000	1,908,000	3,913,000	.512	.488
1953	2,034,000	1,931,000	3,965,000	.513	.487
1954	2,090,000	1,988,000	4,078,000	.512	.488
1955	2,103,000	2,001,000	4,104,000	.512	.488
1956	2,162,000	2,056,000	4,218,000	.513	.487
1957	2,207,000	2,101,000	4,308,000	.512	.488
1958	2,179,000	2,076,000	4,255,000	.512	.488
1959	2,174,000	2,071,000	4,245,000	.512	.488
1960	2,180,000	2,078,000	4,258,000	.512	.488
Total	22,957,000	21,841,000	44,798,000	.512	.488

Figure 3.1 *Births of boys and girls (United States Census 1950–1960)*

The examples below illustrate some of the kinds of problems we shall encounter and solve in this chapter.

A fair die with six faces is thrown. With what probability will the face five occur?

3.1.1
Example

A fair coin is tossed. If it comes up heads (H) a fair die is rolled and the experiment is finished. If the coin comes up tails (T) the coin is tossed again and the experiment is finished. With what probability will the situation heads first, five second, occur?

3.1.2
Example

A room contains 50 people. With that probability will at least two of them have the same birthday?

3.1.3
Example

A factory produces light bulbs of which 80 percent are not defective. A sample of six bulbs is taken. With what probability will three or more of them be defective?

3.1.4
Example

Two dice each with six faces are rolled. With what probability will their total be 11, if they are fair? If one is "loaded" in a certain way, what is the probability of an 11?

3.1.5
Example

A group of 1200 people includes 50 cancer-ridden people and 500 females. Furthermore, suppose 35 females have cancer. With what probability will a person chosen at random be both cancer-ridden and female?

3.1.6
Example

Other questions that can be answered by using probability theory are given below. The student will not be equipped with enough theory in this chapter to solve such problems. They are listed merely as illustrations of the power of the probability theory. The interested reader should consult the bibliography found at the end of this chapter if he wishes to pursue a deeper study of probability theory.

Consider a telephone exchange with a finite number of lines. Suppose that the exchange is constructed in such a way that an incoming call that finds all the lines busy does not wait, but is lost. This is called an exchange without waiting lines. The most important problem to be solved *before* the exchange is constructed is to determine, for any time t, the probability of finding all the lines busy at time t.

3.1.7
Example
Queuing Theory

People arrive at random times at a ticket counter to be served by an attendant, lining up on que if others are waiting. Given information about the rate of arrival and the length of time an attendant requires to serve each customer, how much of the time is the attendant idle? How much of the time is the line more than 15 persons long? What would be the effect of adding another attendant? If the people are not allowed to wait in line but must go else-where, what percentage of arrivals go unanswered? The same questions can be asked about gas stations, booths in toll roads, hospital beds, and so on.

3.1.8
Example

The following problem occurs quite often in physics and biology and was formulated by Galton in 1874 in his study of the disappearance of family lines. Given that a man of a known family has a probability of

$$p_0, p_1, p_2, \cdots$$

of producing zero, one, two male offsprings, what is the probability that the family will eventually die out?

3.1.9
Example
Spread of
Epidemics

Suppose that an infectious disease is spread by contact, that a susceptible person has a chance of catching it with each contact with an infected person, but that one becomes immune after having had the disease and can no longer transmit it. Some of the questions we would like answered are: How many susceptibles will be left when the number of infected is zero? How long will the epidemic last? For a given community, what is the proba-bility that the disease will die out?

3.1
Exercise

1. Consult the United States census from 1960–1970 and con-struct a table similar to Figure 3.1. What probability would you assign to the birth of a boy baby based on this data?
2. Pick a page at random in your telephone directory and list the last digit of every number. Are all digits used equally often?
3. Toss a die six times and record the face shown. Denote this number by x (x can take the values 1, 2, 3, 4, 5, 6). Repeat the experiment 20 more times and tabulate the results. Do you ob-serve any regularity?
4. Suppose a needle is dropped at random onto a floor that is marked with parallel lines 6 inches apart. Suppose the needle is 4 inches long. With what probability does the needle fall between the two lines? Perform the experiment 20 times and record the number of times the needle rests completely within the two lines. This is a version of the Buffon needle problem. An

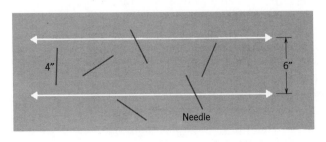

Figure 3.2

illustration is provided in Figure 3.2. and a solution may be found in *Mathematics in the Modern World.*[1]

5. Conduct the following experiment with your classmates. Assume that you have $90 and your classmate has $10. Flip a fair coin. If you lose you give him a dollar and if you win he gives you a dollar. The play ends when one of the players losses all his money. Can you guess how *long* the game will last? Can you guess who has the better chance of winning? A solution can be found in Chapter 10.

6. Conduct the following experiment in your classes. Find out how many students would bet that no two students had the same birthday. List the birthdays of each student and verify whether any two have the same birthday. Would you have won or lost the bet? See Section 3.3 for a table that provides a rationale for betting one way or the other.

7. (Chevalier de Mere's problem) Which of the following random events do you think is more likely to occur (a) to obtain at least one ace (face is one) in a simultaneous throw of four fair dice or (b) to obtain at least one double ace in a series of 24 throws of a pair of fair dice. See Problem 14 in Exercise 3.7.

8. Pick an editorial from your daily newspaper which contains at least 1000 words. List the number of times each letter of the alphabet is used. Based on this, what probability might you assign to the occurrence of a letter in an editorial?

In studying probability we shall be concerned with experiments, real or conceptual, and their outcomes. In this study we try to formulate in a precise manner a mathematical theory that closely resembles the experiment in question. The first stage of development of a mathematical theory is the building of what is termed a *mathematical model*. This model is then used as a predictor of outcomes of the experiment. The purpose of this section is to learn how a probabilistic model can be constructed.

3.2
SAMPLE SPACES
AND ASSIGNMENT
OF PROBABILITIES

One way of formulating the notion of an experiment is to write down the associated *sample space;* that is, write down all outcomes that can occur as a result of the experiment.

For example, if the experiment consists of flipping a coin, we would ordinarily agree that the only possible outcomes are "heads" and "tails." If we denote these outcomes by H and T, respectively, a sample space for the experiment is the set $\{H, T\}$.

Consider an experiment in which, for the sake of simplicity, one die is green and the other is red. When the two dice are rolled, the set of outcomes consists of all the different ways that the dice may come to rest. This is referred

3.2.1
Example

---

[1] *Mathematics in the Modern World,* Readings from *Scientific American,* W. H. Freeman and Company, San Francisco, 1968, pp. 169ff.

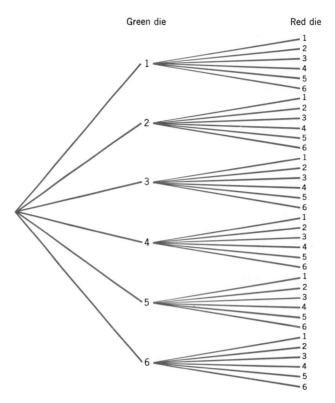

Figure 3.3

to as a set of all *logical possibilities*. This experiment can be displayed in two
different ways. One way is to use a tree diagram. See Figure 3.3.

The other way is to let g and r denote, respectively, the number that comes
up on the green die and the red die. Then an *outcome* can be represented by
an ordered pair (g, r) where both g and r can assume all values of a set S

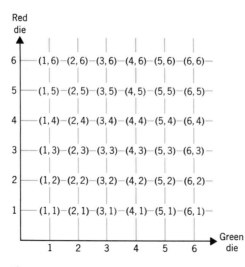

Figure 3.4

whose members are 1, 2, 3, 4, 5, 6. Thus, a sample space S of this experiment is the set

$$S = \{(g,r)|1 \leqq g \leqq 6, 1 \leqq r \leqq 6\}$$

Also, notice that the number of elements in S is 36, which is found by applying the fundamental principle of counting, namely, $6 \cdot 6 = 36$. Figure 3.4 illustrates a graphical representation for S.

In the above example, we touched on some fundamental concepts. Let us now introduce them precisely as definitions.

A *sample space S*, associated with a real or conceptual experiment, is the set of all logical possibilities that can occur as a result of the experiment. Each element of a sample space S is called an *outcome*.

3.2.1
Definition

The theory of probability begins as soon as a sample space has been specified. The sample space of an experiment plays the same role as the universal set in set theory for all questions concerning the experiment.

In this chapter, we shall confine our attention to those cases for which the sample space is finite, that is, to those situations in which it is possible to have only a finite number of outcomes.

The reader should notice that in our definition we say *a* sample space, rather than *the* sample space, since an experiment can be described in many different ways. In general, it is a safe guide to include as much detail as possible in the description of the outcomes of the experiment in order to answer all pertinent questions concerning the result of the experiment.

Consider the set of all families with three children. Describe the sample space for the experiment of drawing one family from the set of all possible three-child families.

3.2.2
Example

One way of describing the sample space is by denoting the number of girls in the family. The only possibilities are members of the set

$$\{0, 1, 2, 3\}$$

That is, a three-child family can have 0 girls, 1 girl, 2 girls, or 3 girls.

This sample space has four outcomes. A disadvantage of describing the experiment using this sample space is that a question such as "Was the second child a girl" cannot be answered. Thus, this method of classifying the outcomes may be too coarse since it may not provide enough wanted information.

Another way is by first defining B and G as "Boy" and "Girl," respectively. Then the sample space might be given as

$$\{BBB, BBG, BGG, GGG, GBG, GGB, GBB, BGB\} \qquad (3.2.1)$$

where BBB means first born is a boy, second born is a boy, third born is a boy, and so on. This can be depicted by the use of the tree diagram in Figure 3.5. Notice that the experiment has 8 possible outcomes.

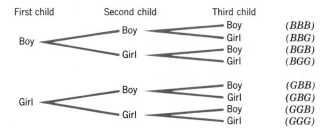

First child   Second child   Third child

Boy — Boy — Boy   (*BBB*)
                Girl   (*BBG*)
       Girl — Boy   (*BGB*)
                Girl   (*BGG*)

Girl — Boy — Boy   (*GBB*)
                Girl   (*GBG*)
       Girl — Boy   (*GGB*)
                Girl   (*GGG*)

Figure 3.5

The advantage of this classification of the sample space is that each outcome of the experiment corresponds to exactly one element in the sample space.

3.2.2
Definition

An *event* **is a subset of the sample space. If an event has exactly one element, that is, consists of only one outcome, it is called a** *simple event.*

Every event can be written as the union of simple events. For example, a sample space of Example 3.2.2 is given in (3.2.1). The event E that the family consists of exactly two boys is

$$E = \{BBG, GBB, BGB\}$$

The event E is the union of the three simple events $\{BBG\}, \{BGB\}, \{GBB\}$. That is

$$E = \{BBG\} \cup \{BGB\} \cup \{GBB\}$$

Since a sample space S is also an event, we can express a sample space S as the union of simple events. Thus, if the sample space S consists of n outcomes,

$$S = \{e_1, e_2, \ldots, e_n\}$$

then

$$S = \{e_1\} \cup \{e_2\} \cup \ldots \cup \{e_n\}$$

3.2.3
Example

In the two-dice experiment of Example 3.2.1, involving a green and red die, let A be the event that the green die registers less than or equal to 3 and the red die is 5 and let B be the event that the green die is 2 and the red die is 5 or 6. Describe the event A *or* B.
    Here

$$A = \{(g, r) | g \leq 3, r = 5\}, \qquad B = \{(g, r) | g = 2, r = 5, 6\}$$

Clearly, A has three members and B has two members. The event A *or* B is merely the union of A with B. Thus

$$A \cup B = \{(1, 5), (2, 5), (3, 5), (2, 6)\}$$

That is, the event A *or* B has four members. Of course, the event A *and* B, namely, $A \cap B$, has one member.

We are now in a position to formulate a definition for the probability of a simple event of a sample space.

Let S denote a sample space. To each simple event $\{e\}$ of S, we assign a real number, $P(\{e\})$, called the *probability of the simple event* $\{e\}$ **which has the two properties:**
> **(I)** $P(\{e\}) \geqslant 0$, **for all simple events $\{e\}$ in S**
> **(II) The sum of the probabilities of all the simple events of S equals one.**

3.2.3
Definition

If the sample space S is given by

$$S = \{e_1, e_2, \ldots e_n\}$$

then

> (I) $P(\{e_1\}) \geqslant 0, \quad P(\{e_2\}) \geqslant 0, \ldots, P(\{e_n\}) \geqslant 0$
> (II) $P(\{e_1\}) + P(\{e_2\}) + \cdots + P(\{e_n\}) = 1$

The real number assigned to the simple event $\{e\}$ is *completely arbitrary* within the framework of the above restrictions. For example, let a die be thrown. A sample space S is then

$$S = \{1, 2, 3, 4, 5, 6\}$$

There are six simple events in S: $\{1\}, \{2\}, \{3\}, \{4\}, \{5\}, \{6\}$. Any of the following assignments of probabilities are acceptable.

(I)

$$P(\{1\}) = 1/6, \quad P(\{2\}) = 1/6, \quad P(\{3\}) = 1/6$$
$$P(\{4\}) = 1/6, \quad P(\{5\}) = 1/6, \quad P(\{6\}) = 1/6$$

This choice is in agreement with the above definition since the probability of each simple event is nonnegative and their sum is one. This is an example of a "fair" die in which each simple event is equally likely to occur.

(II)

$$P(\{1\}) = 0, \quad P(\{2\}) = 0, \quad P(\{3\}) = 1/3$$
$$P(\{4\}) = 2/3, \quad P(\{5\}) = 0, \quad P(\{6\}) = 0$$

This choice is also acceptable even though it is unnatural. Implied here is the existence of a "loaded" die in which only a 3 or a 4 appears and a four is twice as likely to occur as a 3.

A coin is weighted so that heads $\{H\}$ is five times more likely to occur than tails $\{T\}$. What probability should we assign to heads? to tails?

3.2.4
Example

Let x denote the probability that tails occurs.
Then, $P(\{T\}) = x$ and

$$P(\{H\}) = 5x$$

From our definition of probability, we must have

$$P(\{H\}) + P(\{T\}) = 5x + x = 1$$

Then

$$x = 1/6$$

Thus, we would assign

$$P(\{H\}) = 5/6 \qquad P(\{T\}) = 1/6$$

Suppose probabilities have been assigned to each simple event of S. We now raise the question: What is the probability of an event? Let S be a sample space and let E be any event of S. It is clear that either $E = \varnothing$ or E is a simple event or E is the union of two or more simple events.

3.2.4
Definition

If $E = \varnothing$, we define the *probability of $\varnothing$* **to be**

$$P(\varnothing) = 0$$

In this case, the event $E = \varnothing$ is said to be *impossible*.
If E is simple, Definition 3.2.3 is applicable.
If E is the union of r simple events $\{e_{i_1}\}, \{e_{i_2}\}, \ldots, \{e_{i_r}\}$, we define the *probability of E* **to be**

$$P(E) = P(\{e_{i_1}\}) + P(\{e_{i_2}\}) + \cdots + P(\{e_{i_r}\})$$

In particular, if the sample space S given by

$$S = \{e_1, e_2, \ldots, e_n\}$$

we see from Definitions 3.2.3 and 3.2.4 that

$$P(S) = P(\{e_1\}) + \cdots + P(\{e_n\}) = 1$$

Thus, the probability of S, the sample space, is one.

3.2.5
Example

Let two coins be tossed. A sample space S is

$$S = \{HH, TH, HT, TT\}$$

This can be depicted in two ways. See Figure 3.6.
Let E be the event that they are both heads or both tails. Compute the probability for event E with the following two assignments of probabilities:

(a) $P(\{HH\}) = P(\{TT\}) = P(\{HT\}) = P(\{TH\}) = 1/4$
(b) $P(\{HH\}) = 1/3, P(\{TT\}) = 1/4, P(\{TH\}) = 1/6, P(\{HT\}) = 1/4$

Here the event E is $\{HH, TT\}$ and from Definition 3.2.4, we have

(a) $P(E) = P(\{HH\}) + P(\{TT\}) = 1/4 + 1/4 = 1/2$
(b) $P(E) = P(\{HH\}) + P(\{TT\}) = 1/3 + 1/4 = 7/12$

The fact that we have obtained different probabilities for the same event is not unexpected since it stems from our original assignment of probabilities to the simple events of the experiment. Any assignment that conforms to the restrictions given in Definition 3.2.3 is mathematically correct. The question of which assignment should be made is not a mathematical question, but is

(a) Describe the sample space.

(b) If $P(\{1\})$ is the probability for face one to show, find $P(\{1\}), P(\{2\}), P(\{3\}), P(\{4\}), P(\{5\}),$ and $P(\{6\})$.

(c) Let A be the event "even numbered face."

  B be the event "odd numbered face."

  C be the event "prime number as face." (2, 3, 5 are prime).

  Find $P(A), P(B), P(C), P(A \cup B), P(A \cup \bar{C})$.

9. A red die and green die are tossed. If r denotes the result on the red die and g the result on the green die, give verbal descriptions of the following algebraically described events:

(a) $r = 3g$ (d) $r + g = 8$

(b) $r - g = 1$ (e) $g = r^2$

(c) $r \leqq g$ (f) $r = g$

Graph each of these events using Figure 3.4 as a backdrop.

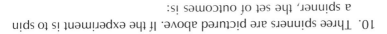
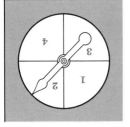

10. Three spinners are pictured above. If the experiment is to spin a spinner, the set of outcomes is:

Spinner 1: {red, green}

Spinner 2: {A, B, C}

Spinner 3: {1, 2, 3, 4}

Draw tree diagrams to find the number of possible outcomes when the experiment is

(a) First spinner 1 is spun and then spinner 2.

(b) Spinners 3, 2, and 1 are spun in this order.

(c) Spinner 1 is spun two times and the spinners 3 and 2 each one time in this order.

11. In Example 3.2.5, if the events E, F, G are

(a) E: "at least one head"

(b) F: "exactly one tail"

(c) G: "tails on both tosses"

find $P(E), P(F), P(G)$, for the two given assignments of probabilities.

12. A high school senior applies for admission to Midwest University and Western University. Let the event of his admission to Midwest be denoted by A, and that of his admission to Western be denoted by B. Using only the symbols $\cap, -, \cup, A$, and B, write expressions for the following simple events or events:

senator, congressman) if two people, a Democrat and a Republican are for each office.

2. Below are described certain experiments. Find the number of simple events in each sample space associated with the experiment.

   (a) A poker hand (five cards) is dealt from an ordinary deck of cards (52 cards).

   (b) A committee of five people is chosen at random from a group of six men and five women.

   (c) Three coins are tossed once.

   (d) Three dice are tossed once.

3. Construct probabilistic models for the experiments in problems 1(a), 1(c), 1(d), 1(e), 1(f), 1(g), 1(h), 2(a), 2(b), 2(c), and 2(d). You may assign any valid probabilities.

4. A sociologist noted two major rival street gangs, G and H. In addition there are four minor street gangs, a, b, c, d, who always ally themselves with one of the two major gangs on issues. Peace will prevail in the neighborhood if a major street gang is backed by two smaller ones. Construct the sample space and the events that maintain peace.

5. In a T-maze an animal may turn either to the right (R) or to the left (L). His behavior in making such "choices" is studied. Suppose a rat runs a T-maze three times. List the set of all possible outcomes and assign valid probabilities to each simple event. Find the probability of each of the events:

   (a) E: run to the right two consecutive times.

   (b) F: never run to the right.

   (c) G: run to the left on the first trial.

   (d) H: run to the right on the second trial.

6. Let $S = \{e_1, e_2, e_3, e_4, e_5, e_6, e_7\}$ be a given sample space. Let the probabilities assigned to the simple events be given as follows:

$$P(\{e_1\}) = P(\{e_2\}) = P(\{e_6\})$$
$$P(\{e_3\}) = 2P(\{e_4\}) = \tfrac{1}{2}P(\{e_1\})$$
$$P(\{e_5\}) = \tfrac{1}{2}P(\{e_7\}) = \tfrac{1}{4}P(\{e_1\})$$

   (a) Find $P(\{e_1\})$, $P(\{e_2\})$, $P(\{e_3\})$, $P(\{e_4\})$, $P(\{e_5\})$, $P(\{e_6\})$, $P(\{e_7\})$.

   (b) If $A = \{e_1, e_2\}$, $B = \{e_2, e_3, e_4\}$, $C = \{e_5, e_6, e_7\}$, $D = \{e_1, e_5, e_6\}$. Find $P(A)$, $P(B)$, $P(C)$, $P(D)$, $P(A \cup B)$, $P(A \cap D)$, $P(D \cup B)$, $P(A \cup \bar{B})$.

7. Three cars C_1, C_2, C_3, are in a race. If the probability of C_1 winning is p, that is, $P(C_1) = p$ and $P(C_1) = \tfrac{2}{3}P(C_2)$ and $P(C_3) = \tfrac{1}{3}P(C_2)$. Find $P(C_1)$, $P(C_2)$, and $P(C_3)$. Find $P(C_1 \cup C_2)$, $P(C_1 \cup C_3)$.

8. Consider an experiment with a loaded die such that the probability of any of the faces appearing in a toss is equal to that face times the probability that a one will occur. That is, $P(\{6\}) = 6 \cdot P(\{1\})$, $P(\{5\}) = 5 \cdot P(\{1\})$, and so on.

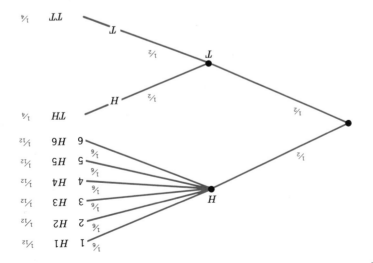

Figure 3.7

To each of these eight possible outcomes we assign the probability to be, respectively,

$$P:\ 1/12,\ 1/12,\ 1/12,\ 1/12,\ 1/12,\ 1/12,\ 1/4,\ 1/4$$

The above discussion constitutes a model, called a *probabilistic* or *stochastic model*, for the experiment.

For this model, let E be the event

$$E = \{H2,\ H4,\ TH\}$$

The probability of the event E, by Definition 3.2.4, is

$$P(E) = P(\{H2\}) + P(\{H4\}) + P(\{TH\})$$
$$= 1/12 + 1/12 + 1/4 = 5/12$$

3.2
Exercise

1. Below are described certain experiments. List the elements in each sample space and find the number of simple events in each sample space associated with the experiment.

(a) Tossing a coin 5 times.

(b) Tossing a coin until a head appears. (This is an example of an infinite sample space.)

(c) Five coins tossed once. (Compare your answer to the answer found in 1(a).

(d) A box contains five balls numbered 1, 2, 3, 4, 5. A ball is drawn at random.

(e) The same as in (d), except the ball is replaced and a second drawing is made.

(f) Tossing two dice and then a coin.

(g) Tossing a die and two coins.

(h) The vote of a single voter for three offices (President,

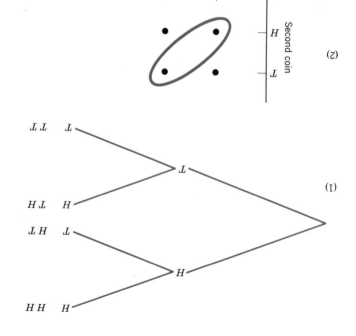

E = same result on both tosses = {HH, TT}

Figure 3.6

one that depends on the real world situation to which the theory is applied. In this example the coins were fair in case (a) and were loaded in case (b). Now that we have introduced the concepts of sample space, event, and probability of events, we introduce the idea of a probabilistic model.

To construct a probabilistic model we need to do the following:

(a) List all possible outcomes of the experiment under investigation, that is, give a sample space or, if this is not easy to do, determine the number of simple events in the sample space.

(b) Assign to each outcome a probability $P(\{e\})$ such that Definition 3.2.3 is satisfied.

Consider the following experiment.

3.2.6 Example

A fair coin is tossed. If it comes up H (heads), a fair die is rolled and the experiment is finished; if it comes up T (tails) the coin is tossed again. Describe a probabilistic model for this experiment.

First, all the possible outcomes of this experiment are

$$S: H1, H2, H3, H4, H5, H6, TT, \text{ and } TH$$

where $H1$ indicates head for the coin and the 1 for die, and so on. See Figure 3.7.

(a) that he will be rejected by Midwest
(b) that he will be rejected by Western
(c) that he will be rejected by both
(d) that he will be rejected by at least one
(e) that he will be rejected by exactly one
(f) that he will be accepted by both
(g) that he will be accepted by at least one
(h) that he will be accepted by exactly one

In this section, we shall state and prove results involving the probability of an event after the probabilistic model has been determined. The main tool we shall employ is that of set theory.

Two or more events of a sample space S are said to be *mutually exclusive* **if and only if they have no simple events in common.**

That is, if we treat the events as sets, they are disjoint.

The following result gives us a way of computing probabilities for mutually exclusive events.

Theorem 3.3.1

Let E and F be two events of a sample space S. If E and F are mutually exclusive, that is, if $E \cap F = \emptyset$, then the probability of the event "E or F" is the sum of their probabilities, namely,

$$P(E \cup F) = P(E) + P(F)$$

Since E and F can be written as a union of simple events in which no simple event of E appears in F and no simple event of F appears in E the result follows.

The probability of any simple event of a sample space S is nonnegative. Furthermore, since any event E of S is the union of simple events in S, and since $P(S) = 1$, it is easy to see that

$$0 \leqslant P(E) \leqslant 1$$

To summarize, the probability of an event E of a sample space S has the following three properties:

    I: *Positiveness:* $0 \leqslant P(E) \leqslant 1$ for every event E of S
    II: *Certainty:* $P(S) = 1$
    III: *Union:* $P(E \cup F) = P(E) + P(F)$ for any two events E and F of S for which $E \cap F = \emptyset$.

Let E be an event of a sample space. The complement of E is then the event "not E" in S. The next theorem gives a relationship between their probabilities.

Theorem 3.3.2

Let E be an event of a sample space S.

$$P(\bar{E}) = 1 - P(E)$$

where $\bar{E}$ is the complement of E.

Proof

We know that

$$S = E \cup \bar{E}, \qquad E \cap \bar{E} = \varnothing$$
$$P(S) = P(E) + P(\bar{E})$$

Now, apply Property II, setting $P(S) = 1$. Then

$$P(\bar{E}) = 1 - P(E)$$

This theorem gives us a tool for finding the probability that an event does not occur if we know the probability that it does occur. Thus, the probability $P(\bar{E})$ that E does not occur is obtained by subtracting from 1 the probability $P(E)$ that E does occur.

3.3.1
Example

In a study of women over 40 who smoke cigarettes, it is reasonable to assign a probability of .756 that such a person will have cancer. The probability that such a woman will not have cancer is

$$1 - .756 = .244$$

3.3.2
Example

In an experiment using two fair dice find
(a) The probability that the sum of the faces is less than or equal to 7.
(b) The probability that the sum of the faces is greater than 7.
The number of simple events in the event E described in (a) is 21. The number of simple events of the sample space S is 36. Thus, because the dice are fair,

$$P(E) = 21/36 = 7/12$$

For (b), we need to find $P(\bar{E})$. Clearly,

$$P(\bar{E}) = 1 - P(E) = 1 - 7/12 = 5/12$$

That is, the probability that the sum of the faces is greater than 7 is 5/12.

3.3.3
Example
Birthday problem

An interesting problem in which Theorem 3.3.2 is used is the so-called *birthday problem*. In general, the problem is to find the probability that in a group with r people there are at least two people having the same birthday (the same month and day of the year).

To solve the problem, let us first determine the number of simple events in the sample space. There are 365 possibilities for each person's birthday. Since there are r people in the group, there are 365^r possibilities for the birthdays. For, if there is one person in the group, there are 365 days on which his birthday can fall. For 2 people there are $(365)(365) = 365^2$ days. In general using the fundamental principle of counting, for r people there are 365^r possibilities.

Next, we assume each simple event is equally likely to occur so that we assign the probability $1/365^r$ to each simple event.

Let E be the event

E: "no two people have the same birthday"

Notice that the event $\bar{E}$ is that at least two people have the same birthday. To find the probability of E, we proceed as follows. Choose one person at random. There are 365 possibilities for his birthday. Choose a second person. There are 364 possibilities for his birthday if no two people are to have the same birthday. Choose a third person. There are 363 possibilities left for his birthday. Finally, we arrive at the r person. There are $365 - (r - 1)$ possibilities left for his birthday. By the fundamental principle of counting, the total number of possibilities is $365 \cdot 364 \cdot 363 \cdots (365 - r + 1)$.

Hence, the probability of event E is

$$P(E) = \frac{365 \cdot 364 \cdot 363 \cdots (365 - r + 1)}{365^r}$$

The probability of two or more people having the same birthday is then $P(\bar{E}) = 1 - P(E)$.

Figure 3.8 gives the probability for two or more people having the same birthday for some values of r. Notice that the probability is better than 1/2 for any group of people whose number exceeds 22.

	Number of People															
	5	10	15	20	21	22	23	24	25	30	40	50	60	70	80	90
Probability that two or more have same birthday	.027	.117	.253	.411	.444	.476	.507	.538	.569	.706	.891	.970	.994	.99916	.99991	.99999

Figure 3.8

The following result gives us a technique for finding the probability of the union of two events when they are not disjoint. The student should compare this result with that of Theorem 2.5.1. in Section 2.5.

Theorem 3.3.3
For any two events E and F of a sample space S

$$P(E \cup F) = P(E) + P(F) - P(E \cap F)$$

Proof

From Example 2.4.6 of Chapter 2, we have

$$E \cup F = (E \cap \bar{F}) \cup (E \cap F) \cup (\bar{E} \cap F)$$

Since $E \cap \bar{F}$, $E \cap F$, and $\bar{E} \cap F$ are pair-wise disjoint, we can use Property III to write

$$P(E \cup F) = P(E \cap \bar{F}) + P(E \cap F) + P(\bar{E} \cap F) \qquad (3.3.1)$$

From Exercise 2.4, Problems 5g, 5h, we have

$$E = (E \cap F) \cup (E \cap \bar{F})$$
$$F = (E \cap F) \cup (\bar{E} \cap F)$$

Since $E \cap F$ and $E \cap \bar{F}$ are disjoint and $E \cap F$ and $\bar{E} \cap F$ are disjoint, we have

$$P(E) = P(E \cap F) + P(E \cap \bar{F})$$
$$P(F) = P(E \cap F) + P(\bar{E} \cap F) \qquad (3.3.2)$$

From (3.3.1) and (3.3.2), we obtain

$$P(E \cup F) = P(E) + P(F) - P(E \cap F)$$

3.3.4
Example   Consider the two events

E: A male over 40 has a heart attack
F: A male over 40 is bald

Because of recent studies, we might assign

$$P(E) = .56 \qquad P(F) = .63$$

The probability that a male over 40 both has a heart attack and is bald is .33. What is the probability that a male over 40 has a heart attack or is bald?

Here we are looking for the probability of $E \cup F$. From Theorem 3.3.3, we know

$$P(E \cup F) = P(E) + P(F) - P(E \cap F)$$
$$= .56 + .63 - .33 = .86$$

3.3.5
Example   In an experiment with two fair dice, consider the events

E: "the sum of the faces is 8"
F: "doubles are thrown"

What is the probability of obtaining either E or F?

Here

$$E = \{(2, 6), (3, 5), (4, 4), (5, 3), (6, 2)\}$$
$$F = \{(1, 1), (2, 2), (3, 3), (4, 4), (5, 5), (6, 6)\}$$
$$E \cap F = \{(4, 4)\}$$

Also

$$P(E) = 5/36, \qquad P(F) = 6/36, \qquad P(E \cap F) = 1/36$$

Thus, the probability of E or F is

$$P(E \cup F) = 5/36 + 6/36 - 1/36 = 10/36 = 5/18$$

We conclude this section with a brief discussion of the relation between the probability of an event and the "odds" of this event occurring.

Let E be an event of a sample space S. We say that *odds for E are a to b if* **and only if**

$$P(E) = \frac{a}{a + b}$$

Using this condition the odds for E are $P(E)/P(\bar{E})$.

Let E be the event "Cubs win the pennant" and let us say that the odds for E are 12 to 5. Then

$$P(E) = \frac{12}{12 + 5} = \frac{12}{17}$$

If, on the other hand, we are given the probability of an event, the odds for or against this particular event can be determined from the given probability.

Let E be the event "White Sox win the pennant" and let

$$P(E) = .05$$

The odds for E are merely the ratio of $P(E)$ to $P(\bar{E})$. Thus, since $P(\bar{E}) = .95$, the odds for E are .05 to .95 or 1 to 19. A fair bet would be $19 for one who thinks they cannot win and $1 for anyone who thinks the Sox can win.

1. A die is rolled. Let E be the event "die shows 4," and F be the event "die shows even number." Are events E and F mutually exclusive?
2. The Chicago Black Hawks hockey team has a probability for winning of .6 and a probability for losing of .25. What is the probability for a tie?
3. An experiment has four mutually exclusive events A, B, C, and D. State for each of the following why it is not permissible to assign the following probabilities.
   (a) $P(A) = .7 \quad P(B) = .0 \quad P(C) = .4 \quad P(D) = .0$
   (b) $P(A) = .3 \quad P(B) = .4 \quad P(C) = .1 \quad P(D) = .1$
   (c) $P(A \cup B) = .5 \quad P(A) = .3 \quad P(B) = .4$
   (d) $P(A) = -.5 \quad P(B) = .5 \quad P(C) = .2 \quad P(D) = .8$
4. Use Figure 3.8 to find the approximate probability that two or more United States Senators have the same birthday. What is

the probability that two or more members of the House of Representatives have the same birthday?

5. Suppose E is the event "at least two people have birthdays in the same month," (disregarding the day and year). Find the probability of event E for a group of two people; for a group of three people; for a group of four people.

6. What are the odds that two United States presidents will have the same birthday? Consult the World Almanac and use Figure 3.8.

7. The daily death toll in a certain war is 30. What is the probability that at least two of the dead will have the same birthday?

8. A student needs to pass both mathematics and English in order to graduate. He estimates his probability of passing Mathematics at .4 and English at .6, and he estimates his probability of passing at least one of them at .8. What is his probability of passing both courses?

9. After mid-term exams, the student in Problem 8 reassesses his probability of passing Mathematics to .7. He feels his probability of passing at least one of these courses is still .8, but he has only a probability of .1 of passing both courses. If his probability of passing English is less than .4, he will drop English. Should he drop English? Why?

10. If two fair dice are thrown, what are the odds of obtaining a 7? An 11? A 7 or 11?

11. If the odds for event A are 1 to 5 and for event B are 1 to 3, what are the odds for the event A or B if the event A and B is impossible?

12. Using Definition 3.3.2 show that the odds for the event E are $P(E)/P(\bar{E})$.

13. In a track contest, the odds that A will win are 1 to 2 and the odds that B will win are 2 to 3. Find the probability and the odds that A or B wins the race, assuming a tie is impossible.

14. It has been estimated that in 70 percent of the fatal accidents involving two cars, at least one of the drivers is drunk. If you hear of a two-car fatal accident, what odds should you give a friend that at least one of the drivers is drunk?

15. If A and B represent two mutually exclusive events such that $P(A) = .35$, $P(B) = .50$ find each of the following:
(a) $P(\overline{A \cup B})$ (d) $P(\bar{A})$
(b) $P(A \cup B)$ (e) $P(A \cap B)$
(c) $P(\bar{B})$

16. Let A and B be events of a sample space S and let $P(A) = .5$, $P(B) = .3$, and $P(A \cap B) = .1$. Find the probabilities for each of the following events:
(a) A and B (c) B but not A
(b) A but not B (d) neither A nor B

*17. If $A \subseteq B$, show that $P(A) \leq P(B)$. Hint: Decompose B into two parts, those that are in A and those that are only in B, but not in A, that is $B = A \cup (B - A)$.

*18. Generalize Theorem 3.3.3 by showing that the probability of the occurrence of at least one among three events A, B, C is given by

$$P(A \cup B \cup C) = P(A) + P(B) + P(C)$$
$$-P(A \cap B) - P(A \cap C) - P(B \cap C)$$
$$+P(A \cap B \cap C)$$

Thus far we have seen that in some cases it is reasonable to assign the same probability to each simple event of the sample space. In this section, we shall restrict our study to sample spaces in which each simple event is equally likely. That is, the *same* probability is assigned to each simple event of the sample space. For example, if a sample space S has n simple events, the probability assigned to any one of them is $1/n$.

3.4
PROBABILITY
FOR EQUALLY
LIKELY EVENTS

Theorem 3.4.1
Let a sample space S be given by

$$S = \{e_1, e_2, \ldots, e_n\}$$

Suppose each of the simple events $\{e_1\}, \ldots, \{e_n\}$ are equally likely to occur. If E is the union of m of these n simple events, then

$$P(E) = m/n$$

Proof
Since the simple events $\{e_1\}, \ldots, \{e_n\}$ are equally likely, we know that

$$P(\{e_1\}) = \cdots = P(\{e_n\}) \qquad (3.4.1)$$

Since

$$S = \{e_1\} \cup \cdots \cup \{e_n\}$$

then from Definition 3.2.3 we have

$$P(S) = P(\{e_1\}) + \cdots + P(\{e_n\}) = 1 \qquad (3.4.2)$$

To satisfy both (3.4.1) and (3.4.2) we must have

$$P(\{e_1\}) = P(\{e_2\}) = \cdots = P(\{e_n\}) = 1/n$$

Now, for the event E of S, in which the m events have been reordered for convenience, we have

$$E = \{e_1\} \cup \cdots \cup \{e_m\}$$

Thus

$$P(E) = P(\{e_1\}) + \cdots + P(\{e_m\}) = \underbrace{1/n + \cdots + 1/n}_{m \text{ times}} = m/n$$

Theorem 3.4.1 is sometimes stated in the following way.

If an experiment has n **equally likely outcomes among which the event** E **occurs** m **times, then the probability of event** E, **written as** $P(E)$, **is** m/n. **That is**

$$P(E) = \frac{\text{number of possible ways that the event } E \text{ can take place}}{\text{number of all logical possibilities}} = \frac{m}{n}$$

If the fact that the event E **has occurred, is termed a** *success*, **then**

$$P(E) = \frac{\text{number of successes}}{\text{number of all logical possibilities}} = \frac{m}{n} \qquad (3.4.3)$$

Event E not occurring is referred to as a *failure*.

Often Theorem 3.4.1 is used to define *probability*. Had we decided to define the probability of an event by using Theorem 3.4.1, the properties I, II, and III previously stated would still be valid.

For, suppose an experiment resulted in no successes at all. By Theorem 3.4.1, we have

$$P(\text{success}) = \frac{0}{n} = 0 \qquad (3.4.4)$$

If the experiment resulted in all events in the sample space being successes, we then have

$$P(\text{success}) = m/n = n/n = 1$$

From this result and (3.4.4) we see that

$$0 \leq P(\text{success}) \leq 1$$

Suppose E is an event with m successes in a sample space S of n elements. Then

$$P(E) = m/n$$

Now $\bar{E}$ contains $n - m$ elements. Hence

$$\begin{aligned}
P(\bar{E}) &= (n - m)/n \\
&= n/n - m/n \\
&= 1 - m/n \\
&= 1 - P(E)
\end{aligned}$$

3.4.1
Example

In a two-dice experiment, we present the following in terms of events:

(a) The sum of the faces is 3.
(b) The sum of the faces is 7.
(c) The sum of the faces is 7 or 3.
(d) The sum of the faces is 7 and 3.

Find the probability of these events assuming the dice are fair. Now

(a) The sum of the faces is 3 if and only if the outcome is the event $A = \{(1, 2), (2, 1)\}$. The probability of the simple event $\{(1, 2)\}$ is 1/36 and the probability of the simple event $\{(2, 1)\}$ is 1/36. Thus

$$P(A) = 2/36 = 1/18$$

(b) The sum of the faces is 7 if and only if the outcome is a member of the event $B = \{(1, 6), (2, 5), (3, 4), (4, 3), (5, 2), (6, 1)\}$. Again,

$$P(B) = 6/36 = 1/6$$

(c) The sum of the faces is 7 or 3 if and only if the outcome is a member of $A \cup B$.

$$A \cup B = \{(2, 1), (1, 2), (1, 6), (2, 5), (3, 4), (4, 3), (5, 2), (6, 1)\}$$

Thus

$$P(A \cup B) = 8/36 = 2/9$$

(d) The sum of the faces is 3 and 7 if and only if the outcome is a member of $A \cap B$. Since $A \cap B = \varnothing$, the event is impossible.

A box contains 41 light bulbs of which 5 are defective. All bulbs look alike and have equal probability of being chosen. Three light bulbs are picked at random. What is the probability that all 3 are nondefective? What is the probability that all 3 are defective? What is the probability that at least 2 are defective?

3.4.2
Example

Let A be the event "3 light bulbs selected are nondefective." The number of elements in the event A is the number of combinations of 36 nondefective light bulbs taken 3 at a time. That is

$$\binom{36}{3} = \frac{36!}{3!(36 - 3)!} = \frac{36!}{3!33!}$$

The number of elements in the sample space S is equal to the number of combinations of 41 light bulbs taken 3 at a time, namely,

$$\binom{41}{3} = \frac{41!}{3!38!}$$

Using (3.4.3), the probability $P(A)$ is then

$$P(A) = \frac{\binom{36}{3}}{\binom{41}{3}} = \frac{\dfrac{36!}{3!33!}}{\dfrac{41!}{3!38!}} = .6698$$

Define B as the event "3 bulbs are defective." Then B can occur in $\binom{5}{3}$ ways, that is, the number of ways in which 3 defective bulbs can be chosen from 5 defective ones. The probability $P(B)$ is

$$P(B) = \frac{\binom{5}{3}}{\binom{41}{3}} = \frac{\frac{5!}{3!2!}}{\frac{41!}{38!3!}} = .000938$$

What is the probability of the event C "at least 2 are defective"?

The event C is equivalent to asking for the probability of selecting either two or three defective bulbs. Thus

$$P(C) = \frac{\binom{5}{2}\binom{36}{1}}{\binom{41}{3}} + P(B) = .0338 + .000938$$

$$= .0347$$

3.4.3
Example

Find the probability of obtaining (a) a straight and (b) a flush in a poker hand. (A poker hand is a set of 5 cards chosen at random from a deck of 52 cards.)

(a) A straight consists of five consecutive cards not all of the same suit. The sample space contains $\binom{52}{5}$ simple events, each equally likely to occur. Now, for the straight 4, 5, 6, 7, 8, the 4 can be drawn in 4 different ways, as can the 5, the 6, the 7, and the 8 for a total of 4^5 ways. There are a total of 10 different kinds of straights (A, 2, 3, 4, 5), (2, 3, 4, 5, 6), . . . , (9, 10, J, Q, K), and (10, J, Q, K, A). Thus, all told there are $10 \cdot 4^5$ straights. However, among these are the straight flushes (36) and the four Royal flushes which as stronger hands should not be included in the straight category. Thus, there are

$$10 \cdot 4^5 - 36 - 4 = 10{,}240 - 40 = 10{,}200$$

straights. The probability of drawing a straight is then

$$\frac{10{,}200}{\binom{52}{5}} = .0039$$

(b) A flush consists of five cards in a single suit, excluding a straight flush or Royal flush. The number of ways of obtaining a flush in a given suit is $\binom{13}{5} = 1287$ and there are four different suits for a total of $4(1287) = 5148$ flushes. However, straight flushes (36) and the four Royal flushes, each being stronger than a regular flush, should not be included in the flush category. Thus, there are

$$5148 - 36 - 4 = 5108$$

flushes. The probability for a flush is then

$$\frac{5108}{\binom{52}{5}} = .0020$$

1. In a throw of two fair dice, what is the probability that the numbers on their upper faces add up to 3? to 4? to 11?
2. If a fair die is thrown, what is the probability that the upper face shows more than 3? Less than 3? An even number? An odd number?
3. When two fair coins are tossed, what is the probability that both show heads? That they show one head and one tail?
4. In a throw of two fair dice what is the probability that the number on one die is double the number on the other?
5. In a throw of two fair dice what is the probability that one die gives a 5 and the other die a number less than 5?
6. Select a number from 1 to 15. Any one number is as likely to be selected as another. What is the probability that the number selected is:
   (a) Even.
   (b) Divisible by 5.
   (c) A prime number (1 is not prime).
   (d) Even or prime number.
   (e) Even, divisible by 5, a prime number and less than or equal to 3.
7. Two dice are thrown. Let A be the event that the sum of the faces is odd, B be the event that at least one ace appears. Describe the events $A \cap B$, $A \cup B$, and $A \cap \bar{B}$ and find their probability.
8. Through observation it has been determined that the probability for a given number of people waiting in line at a particular checkout register of a supermarket is:

Number waiting in line	0	1	2	3	4 or more
Probability		.10	.15	.20	.24	.31

   Find the probability of
   (a) At most two people in line.
   (b) At least two people in line.
   (c) At least one person in line.
9. In an election two amendments are proposed. The results indicated that of 1000 people eligible to cast a ballot, 480 voted in favor of Amendment I, 390 approved of Amendment II, 120 voted for both, and 100 approved of neither. If an eligible voter is selected at random (that is, any one is as likely to be chosen as another), compute the following probabilities:
   (a) He will be in favor of I, but not II.
   (b) He will be in favor of II, but not I.
   (c) He voted no for both.
   (d) He did not vote at all.

10. In a game of bridge, find the probability that a hand of 13 cards consists of 5 spades, 4 hearts, 3 diamonds, and 1 club.
11. Find the probability of obtaining each of the following poker hands.
    (a) Royal flush (ten, jack, queen, king, ace in a single suit).
    (b) Straight flush (five in a sequence in a single suit, but not a royal flush).
    *(c) Four of a kind (four cards of the same face value).
    *(d) Full house (one pair and one triple of the same face value).
    *(e) Straight or better.

3.5
MATHEMATICAL
EXPECTATION

An important concept, which had its origin in gambling and to which probability can be applied, is *expected value*. Gamblers, for instance, are quite concerned with the *expectation*, or *expected value* of a game. Suppose, for example, 1000 tickets are sold for $1 each to raffle off a television set worth $300. Out of the 1000 tickets, one ticket is worth $300 and the remaining 999 are worth $0. Thus the *expected (average) value* of a ticket is

$$E = \frac{\$300 + \$0 + \cdots + \$0}{1000} = \$300 \cdot \frac{1}{1000}$$

$$+ \$0 \cdot \frac{1}{1000} + \cdots + \$0 \cdot \frac{1}{1000} = \frac{\$300}{1000} = \$.30$$

As another example of expectation, suppose that you are to receive $3.00 each time you obtain two heads on a single toss of two coins and $0 otherwise. Then the *expected value*, which we will denote by E, is

$$E = \$3.00 \cdot 1/4 + \$0 \cdot 3/4 = \$0.75$$

This means that you should be willing to pay $0.75 each time you toss the coins if the game is to be a fair one. We arrive at the expected value E by multiplying the amount earned for a given result of the toss times the probability for that toss to occur and adding all possibilities.

Another example is a game consisting of flipping a coin in which if a head shows, the player losses $1, but if a tail shows he wins $2. Thus half of the time he loses a dollar and the other half he will win two dollars. The expected value E of the game is

$$E = 2 \cdot 1/2 + (-1) \cdot 1/2 = 1/2 = .50$$

Thus the player is expected to win $.50 each time he plays.

The examples mentioned thus far lead us to the following definition.

3.5.1
Definition

If an experiment has outcomes that can be assigned the numbers m_1, $m_2, \ldots, m_n$ occurring with probabilities $p_1, p_2, \ldots, p_n$, respectively, then the *expected value* **is given by**

$$E = m_1 \cdot p_1 + m_2 \cdot p_2 + \cdots + m_n \cdot p_n$$

The term *expected value* is not to be interpreted as the value that will necessarily occur on a single trial.

In gambling, for instance, E is interpreted as the average winning expected for the player in the long run. If E is positive we say that the game is *favorable to the player*; if $E = 0$, we say the game is *fair*; and if E is negative we say the game is *unfavorable to the player*.

Consider the experiment of rolling a fair die. The player recovers an amount of dollars equal to the number of dots on the face that turns up, except when face 5 or 6 turns up, in which case he will lose $5 or $6, respectively. What is the expected value of the game?

3.5.1 Example

Since all faces are equally likely to occur, we assign a probability of 1/6 to each of them. From Definition 3.5.1, we have

$$E = 1 \cdot 1/6 + 2 \cdot 1/6 + 3 \cdot 1/6 + 4 \cdot 1/6 + (-5) \cdot 1/6 + (-6) \cdot 1/6$$
$$= -1/6 = -.17$$

The player would expect to lose $.17 on each throw. This means that if the player began with $100, and played 10 times, he would *expect* to lose $10 \cdot 1/6 = \$1.67$, leaving him with $98.33. Actually, the player could have anywhere from $40 to $140 after 10 throws since he could throw 10 consecutive 6's and lose $60 or 10 consecutive 4's and win $40. But he would *expect* to lose $1.67 after 10 throws.

An oil company is bidding on two contracts for oil drilling in two different areas, I and II. It is estimated that a profit of $300,000 would be realized from the first field and $400,000 from the second field. Legal and other costs of bidding for the first oil field is $2500 and for the second, $5000. The probability of discovering oil in the first field is .60 and in the second, .70. The question is which oil field should the company bid for, that is, for which oil field is the expectation larger?

3.5.2 Example

In the first field, the company expects to discover oil .6 of the time at a gain of $300,000 and thus not to discover oil .4 of the time at a loss of $2500. The expectation E_I is

$$E_I = (\$300,000)(.6) + (-\$2,500)(.4) = \$179,000$$

Similarly, for the second field, the expectation E_{II} is

$$E_{II} = (\$400,000)(.7) + (-\$5,000)(.3) = \$278,500$$

Since the expected value for the second field exceeds that for the first, the oil company should bid on the second field.

A laboratory contains 10 electronic microscopes of which 2 are defective. If all microscopes are equally likely to be chosen and if 4 are chosen, what is the expected number of defective microscopes?

3.5.3 Example

The sample of 4 microscopes can contain 0, 1, or 2 defective micro-scopes. The probability p_0 that none in the sample is defective is

$$p_0 = \frac{\binom{2}{0}\binom{8}{4}}{\binom{10}{4}} = \frac{1}{3}$$

Similarly, the probabilities P_1 and P_2 for 1 or 2 defective microscopes is

$$p_1 = \frac{\binom{2}{1}\binom{8}{3}}{\binom{10}{4}} = \frac{8}{15}, \quad p_2 = \frac{\binom{2}{2}\binom{8}{2}}{\binom{10}{4}} = \frac{2}{15}$$

The expected value E is

$$E = 0 \cdot p_0 + 1 \cdot p_1 + 2 \cdot p_2 = \frac{8}{15} + \frac{4}{15} = \frac{4}{5}$$

Of course, we cannot have 4/5 of a defective microscope. However, we can interpret this to mean that in the long run such a sample will contain a defective microscope 4/5 or 80 percent of the time.

1. In a toss of a fair coin 3 times, a player wins $3 if 3 tails occur, $2 if 2 tails occurs and he loses $3 if no tails occur. If one tail occurs, no one wins.
   (a) What is the expected value of the game?
   (b) Is the game fair?
   (c) If the answer to (b) is no, how much should the player win or lose for a toss of exactly one tail to make the game fair?

*2. A coin weighted so that $P(H) = 1/4$ and $P(T) = 3/4$, is tossed until a head or 4 tails occur. Find the expected number of tosses of the coin.

3. In roulette, there are 38 equally likely possibilities: the numbers 1 to 36, 0, and 00 (double zero). What is the expected value for a gambler who bets $1.00 on number 15 if he wins $35 each time the number 15 turns up and loses $1 if any other number turns up? If he plays the number 15 for 200 consecutive times, what is his total expected gain?

4. A player rolls a fair die and receives a number of dollars equal to the number of dots appearing on the face of the die. What is the most the player should be willing to pay in order to play the game?

5. Assume that the odds for a certain race horse to win are 7 to 5. If a man receives $5 when the horse wins, how much should he pay when the horse loses to make the game fair?

6. A true-false test of 30 questions is scored according to the number of correct answers minus the number wrong. Find the

expected number of correct answers of a student who just guesses on each question. What will his score be?

7. A company operating a chain of supermarkets plans to open a new store in one of two locations. They conducted a survey of the two locations and estimated that the first location will show an annual profit of $15,000 if it is successful and a $3000 loss otherwise. For the second location, the estimated annual profit if successful, is $20,000 and is a $6000 loss otherwise. The probability of success at each location is 1/2. What location should the management decide on in order to maximize its profit?

8. For Problem 7 assume probability of success at the first location is 2/3 and the second location is 1/3. What location should be chosen?

*9. A box contains 3 defective bulbs and 9 good bulbs. If 5 bulbs are drawn from the box without replacement, what is the expected number of defective bulbs.

*10. Prove that if each outcome of an experiment with expected value E is multiplied by a constant c, the expected value of the new experiment is $c \cdot E$. Similarly, if to each outcome, we add the same constant k, the expected value of the new game is $E + k$.

The student will recall that in Chapter 2 we introduced the concepts of absolute and relative complement for sets. By absolute complement we mean the complement of a set A *relative to the universal set U*. By relative complement we mean the complement of a set A *relative to another set B*.

3.6
CONDITIONAL
PROBABILITY

In a similar way we would like to introduce a concept known as *conditional probability*. Recall that whenever we compute the probability of an event we do it relative to the entire sample space in question. Thus, when we ask for the probability $P(E)$ of the event E, this probability $P(E)$ represents an appraisal of the likelihood that a chance experiment will produce an outcome in the set E relative to a sample space S.

However, sometimes we would like to compute the probability of an event E of a sample space relative to another event F of the same sample space. That is, if we have *prior* information that the outcome must be in a set F, this information should be used to reappraise the likelihood that the outcome will also be in E. This reappraised probability is denoted by $P(E|F)$, and is read as the *conditional probability of E given F*.

Let us discuss some examples to illustrate the above and then state a formal definition.

Consider the experiment of flipping two fair coins. As we have previously seen, the sample space S is

3.6.1
Example

$$S = \{HH, HT, TH, TT\}$$

Figure 3.9 illustrates the sample space and, for convenience, the probability of each event.

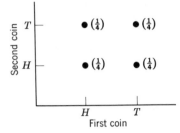

Figure 3.9

Suppose the experiment is performed by another person and we have no knowledge of the result, but we are informed that at least one tail was tossed. This information means the outcome HH could not have occurred. But the remaining outcomes HT, TH, TT are still possible. How does this alter the probabilities of the remaining outcomes?

For instance, we might be interested in calculating the probability of the event $\{TT\}$. The three simple events $\{TH\}$, $\{HT\}$, $\{TT\}$ were each assigned the probability (1/4) *before* we knew the information that at least one tail occurred so it is not reasonable to assign them this same probability now. Since only three outcomes are now possible, we assign to each of them the probability 1/3. See Figure 3.10.

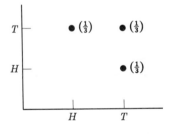

Figure 3.10

3.6.2
Example

Consider the experiment of drawing a single card from a deck of 52 playing cards. We are interested in the event E consisting of the outcome, a black ace is drawn. Since we may assume that there are 52 equally likely possible outcomes, we have

$$P(E) = 2/52$$

However, suppose a card is drawn and we are informed that it is a spade. How should this information be used to *reappraise* the likelihood of the event E?

Clearly, since the event F "a spade has been drawn" has occurred, the event "not spade" is no longer possible. Hence, the sample space has changed from 52 playing cards to 13 spade cards. Therefore, we must compute the probability of event E relative to the new sample space F. This probability is denoted by $P(E|F)$ and has the value

$$P(E|F) = 1/13$$

Let us analyze this situation more carefully. The event E is "a black ace is drawn." We have computed the probability of event E knowing event F has occurred. This means we are computing a probability relative to a *new* sample space F. That is, F is treated as the universal set. Thus, we can only con-

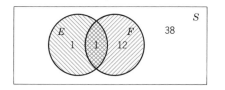

Figure 3.11

sider that part of E that is included in F; that is, we consider $E \cap F$. See Figure 3.11. Thus, the probability of E given F is the ratio of the number of entries in $E \cap F$ to those in F. Since $P(E \cap F) = 1/52$ and $P(F) = 13/52$, then

$$P(E|F) = \frac{1/52}{13/52} = \frac{1}{13}$$

Let E, F be events of a sample space S and suppose $P(F) > 0$. The *conditional probability of event E assuming the event F,* **denoted by $P(E|F)$, is defined as**

3.6.1
Definition

$$P(E|F) = \frac{P(E \cap F)}{P(F)}$$

Suppose a population of 1000 people includes 70 cancer-ridden people and 520 females. Let E be the event "a person has cancer." Let F be the event "a person is female." Then

3.6.3
Example

$$P(E) = \frac{70}{1000} = .07, \qquad P(F) = \frac{520}{1000} = .52$$

Instead of studying the entire population, we may want to investigate the female subpopulation and ask for the probability that a female chosen at random also be sick of cancer. If there are 40 females who have cancer, the ration 40/520 represents the conditional probability of the event E (cancerous) assuming the event F (the person chosen is female). In symbols, we would write

$$P(E|F) = \frac{40}{520} = \frac{1}{13}$$

Thus, from Example 3.6.3 and using Definition 3.6.1, we see that

$$P(E \cap F) = \frac{40}{1000}, \qquad P(F) = \frac{520}{1000}$$

$$P(E|F) = \frac{40/1000}{520/1000} = \frac{40}{520} = \frac{1}{13}$$

Figure 3.12 illustrates that in computing $P(E|F)$ we form the ratio of those entries in E and in F with those that are in F.

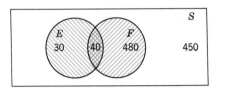

Figure 3.12

In Definition 3.6.1 if we replace F by S, the sample space, we get

$$P(E|S) = \frac{P(E \cap S)}{P(S)}$$

But $E \cap S = E$ and $P(S) = 1$. This reduces to

$$P(E|S) = P(E)$$

as expected.

The symbol $P(E|F)$ is sometimes read as "the probability of E given F."

**3.6.4
Example**

In Example 3.2.2, we considered a three-child family. The sample space S is

$$S = \{BBB, BBG, BGG, GGG, GGB, GBB, BGB, GBG\}$$

We assume each simple event is equally likely, so that each is assigned a probability of 1/8. Let E be the event "the family has three boys" and let F be the event "the first child is a boy." What is the probability that the family has three boys, given that the first born is a boy?

Here we want to find $P(E|F)$. The events E and F are

$$E = \{BBB\}, \qquad F = \{BBB, BBG, BGB, BGG\}$$

Clearly, $E \cap F = \{BBB\}$ and

$$P(E \cap F) = 1/8, \qquad P(F) = 1/2$$

Thus

$$P(E|F) = \frac{P(E \cap F)}{P(F)} = \frac{1/8}{1/2} = \frac{1}{4}$$

Thus, in 1/4 of three-child families in which the first born is a boy, the family will consist of three boys.

**3.6.5
Example**

Motors Incorporated has two plants to manufacture cars. Plant I manufactures 80 percent of the cars and Plant II manufactures 20 percent. At plant I,

85 out of every 100 cars are rated standard quality or better. At plant II only 65 out of every 100 cars are rated standard quality or better. We would like to find the answer to the following questions.

(1) What is the probability that a customer obtains a standard quality car, if he buys a car from Motors Inc.?

(2) What is the probability that the car came from Plant I if it is known that the car is of standard quality?

Let

A: "The car purchased is of standard quality."
B: "The car is of standard quality and came from Plant I."
C: "The car is of standard quality and came from Plant II."
D: "The car came from plant I."

As a preliminary step, we make the following computations.

The percentage of cars manufactured in Plant I that are of standard quality is just 85 percent of 80 percent which is equal to 68 percent. Similarly the percentage of cars manufactured in Plant II that are of standard quality is just 65 percent of 20 percent which is equal to 13 percent. Thus, a total of 81 percent of the cars are of standard quality.

To answer (1), we then have

$$P(B) = .68 \qquad P(C) = .13$$

Since $B \cap C = \emptyset$,

$$P(A) = P(B \cup C) = P(B) + P(C) = .68 + .13 = .81$$

To answer (2), we need to compute $P(D|A)$. Since $D \cap A = B$, we have

$$P(D|A) = \frac{P(D \cap A)}{P(A)} = \frac{P(B)}{P(A)} = \frac{.68}{.81} = .8395$$

---

1. For a 3-child family, find the probability of exactly 2 girls, given that the first born is a girl.

*2. In the population of a certain town 5 percent of males, and 1 percent of females are sick with cancer. Assume male and female each comprise 50 percent of the population. A researcher studying cancer selects a person with cancer. What is the probability that the persons so selected is (a) male? (b) female?

*3. Of the freshman in a certain college, it is known that 40 percent attended private secondary schools and 60 percent attended public schools. The registrar reports that 30 percent of all students who attended private schools maintain A averages in their freshman year and that 24 percent of the freshman had an A average. At the end of the year, one student is chosen at random from the freshman class and he has an A average. What is the conditional probability that the student attended private schools? Hint: use a Venn diagram.

3.6
Exercise

4. In a small town, it is known that 25 percent of the families have no children, 25 percent have 1 child, 18 percent have 2 children, 16 percent have 3 children, 8 percent have 4 children, and 8 percent have 5 or more children. Find the probability that a family has more than 2 children if it is known that it has at least 1 child. Hint: use a Venn diagram.

5. A pair of fair dice is thrown and we are told that the total appearing on the dice is even. Knowing this, what is the probability that the total exceeds 5?

*6. In a sample of people it is found that 35 percent of the men and 70 percent of the women are under 160 pounds. Assume that 50 percent of the sample are men. If a person is selected at random and this person is under 160 pounds, what is the probability that this person is a woman?

*7. If the probability that a married man will vote in a given election is .50, the probability that a married woman will vote in the election is .60, and the probability that a woman will vote in the election given that her husband votes is .90, find
   (a) The probability that a husband and wife will both vote in the elections.
   (b) The probability that a married man will vote in the election given that at least one member of the married couple will vote.

8. If E and F are two events with $P(E) > 0$, $P(F) > 0$, show that

$$P(F) \cdot P(E|F) = P(E) \cdot P(F|E)$$

9. A fair coin is tossed 4 successive times. Find the probability of obtaining 4 heads. Does the probability change if we are told that the second throw resulted in a head?

10. In a rural area in the north, registered Republicans outnumber registered Democrats by 3 to 1. In a recent election, all Democrats voted for the Democratic candidate and enough Republicans also voted for the Democratic candidate so that he won by a ratio of 5 to 4. If a voter is selected at random, what is the probability he is Republican? What is the probability he is Republican if it is known he voted for the Democratic candidate?

3.7
INDEPENDENT
EVENTS

One of the more important concepts in probability is that of independence. In this section we shall define what is meant by two events being *independent*. First, however, we shall try to develop an intuitive idea of the meaning of independent events.

3.7.1
Example

Consider a group of 36 students. Suppose that E and F are two properties that each student either has or does not have. For example, the events E and F might be

E: "student has blue eyes"
F: "student is a male"

With regard to these two properties, suppose it is found that the 36 students are distributed as follows

	Blue Eyes E	Not Blue Eyes Ē	Total
Male F	6	6	12
Female F̄	12	12	24
Total	18	18	36

If we choose a student at random, the probabilities corresponding to the events E and F are

$$P(E) = \frac{18}{36} = \frac{1}{2}$$

$$P(F) = \frac{12}{36} = \frac{1}{3}$$

$$P(E \cap F) = \frac{6}{36} = \frac{1}{6}$$

$$P(E|F) = \frac{P(E \cap F)}{P(F)} = \frac{1/6}{1/3} = \frac{1}{2} = P(E)$$

In this example, the probability of E given F equals the probability of E. This situation can be described by saying that the information that the event F has occurred does not affect a change in the probability of the event E. If this is the case, we say that E is independent of F.

Let E and F be two events of a sample space S with $P(F) > 0$**. The** event E is independent of the event F **if and only if**

$$P(E|F) = P(E)$$

3.7.1
Definition

In Exercise 3.6, Problem 8, it was shown that

$$P(F)P(E|F) = P(E)P(F|E) \tag{3.7.1}$$

provided $P(E) > 0$ and $P(F) > 0$. If E is independent of F, then we know that $P(E|F) = P(E)$. Substituting this into (3.7.1), we find that

$$P(F|E) = P(F)$$

That is, the event F is independent of E.
Thus, if two events E and F have positive probabilities and if the event E is

independent of F, **then** F **is also independent of** E. **In this case,** E **and** F **are called** *independent events.*

This leads us to the following Theorem on *independent events.*

Theorem 3.7.1
Two events E **and** F **of a sample space** S **are independent events if and only if**

$$P(E \cap F) = P(E) \cdot P(F)$$

That is, the probability of E **and** F **is equal to the product of the probability of** E **and the probability of** F.

Proof
If E, F are independent, then

$$P(E|F) = \frac{P(E \cap F)}{P(F)} \text{ and } P(E \mid F) = P(E)$$

Thus,

$$\frac{P(E \cap F)}{P(F)} = P(E)$$

Conversely, if $P(E \cap F) = P(E) \cdot P(F)$, then

$$P(E|F) = \frac{P(E \cap F)}{P(F)} = \frac{P(E) \cdot P(F)}{P(F)} = P(E)$$

That is, E and F are independent events.

3.7.2
Example
Suppose a red die and a green die are thrown. Let event E be "throw a 5 with the red die" and event F be "throw a 6 with the green die."
In this experiment, the events E and F are

$$E = \{(5, 1), (5, 2), (5, 3), (5, 4), (5, 5), (5, 6)\}$$
$$F = \{(1, 6), (2, 6), (3, 6), (4, 6), (5, 6), (6, 6)\}$$

Thus

$$P(E) = 1/6$$
$$P(F) = 1/6$$

Also, the event E and F is

$$E \cap F = \{(5, 6)\}$$

Then

$$P(E \cap F) = 1/36$$

Thus, E and F are independent events since $P(E \cap F) = P(E) \cdot P(F)$.

3.7.3
Example
In Exercise 3.2, Problem 5, show that the events E and G are not independent, but that the events G and H are independent.

The events E and G are

$$E = \{RRL, LRR, RRR\}$$
$$G = \{LLL, LLR, LRL, LRR\}$$

The sample space S has eight elements so that

$$P(E) = 3/8, \qquad P(G) = 1/2$$

Also, the event E and G is

$$E \cap G = \{LRR\}$$

and

$$P(E \cap G) = 1/8$$

Since $P(E \cap G) \neq P(E) \cdot P(G)$, the events E and G of Problem 5, Exercise 3.2 are not independent. Thus running to the right two consecutive times and running to the left on the first trial are dependent.

Next, the event H is

$$H = \{RRL, RRR, LRL, LRR\}$$

and

$$P(H) = 1/2$$

The event G and H and its probability are

$$G \cap H = \{LRL, LRR\}, \qquad P(G \cap H) = 1/4$$

Since $P(G \cap H) = P(G) \cdot P(H)$, the events G and H are independent. Thus running to the left on the first trial and running to the right on the second trial are independent events.

The above example illustrates that the question of whether two events are independent can be answered only by showing that Theorem 3.7.1 is or is not satisfied. Although we may often suspect two events E and F to be independent, our intuition must be checked by computing $P(E)$, $P(F)$, and $P(E \cap F)$ and determining whether $P(E \cap F) = P(E) \cdot P(F)$.

However, sometimes in constructing a probabilistic model for an experiment an assumption of independence is made. The following example illustrates such a situation.

In a group of seeds, 1/4 of which should produce white plants, the best germination that can be obtained is 75 percent. If one seed is planted, what is the probability that it will grow into a white plant?

**3.7.4
Example**

Let G and W be the events

G: the event that the plant will grow
W: the event that the seed will produce a white plant

Assume that W does not depend on G and vice versa, so that W and G are independent events.

Then, the probability that the plant grows and is white, namely, $P(W \cap G)$ is

$$P(W \cap G) = P(W) \cdot P(G) = \frac{1}{4} \cdot \frac{3}{4} = \frac{3}{16}$$

Thus, 3 out of 16 times, a white plant will grow.

There is a danger that mutually exclusive events and independent events may be confused. A source of this confusion is the common expression "have nothing to do with each other." This expression provides a description of independence when applied to everyday events; but when it is applied to sets, it suggests nonoverlapping. Nonoverlapping sets are mutually exclusive but are not necessarily independent. See Problem 5 in Exercise 3.7.

3.7
Exercise

1. If A and B are independent events, find $P(B)$ if $P(A) = 1/4$ and $P(A \cup B) = 1/3$.
2. In Problem 5, Exercise 3.2, are the two events E and F independent?
3. For a three-child family, let E be the event "the family has at most one boy" and F be the event "the family has children of both sexes." Are E and F independent events?
4. For a two-child family, are the events E and F as defined in Problem 3 independent?
5. Give an example of two events that are
   (a) independent, but not mutually exclusive (disjoint)
   (b) not independent but mutually exclusive (disjoint)
   (c) not independent and not mutually exclusive (disjoint)
6. Show that whenever two events are both independent and mutually exclusive, then at least one of them is impossible.
7. A die is loaded so that
   $$P\{1\} = P\{2\} = P\{3\} = 1/4$$
   $$P\{4\} = P\{5\} = P\{6\} = 1/12$$
   If $A = \{1, 2\}$, $B = \{2, 3\}$, $C = \{1, 3\}$, show that any pair of these events is independent.
8. Consider the experiment of three throws of a fair coin. Define the events E and F to be

   E: "a head turns up on the first throw"
   F: "a tail turns up on the second throw"

   Show that E and F are independent events.
9. In a survey of 100 people, categorized as drinkers or nondrinkers, with or without a liver ailment, the following data was obtained

	F Liver Ailment	$\bar{F}$ No Liver Ailment
Drinkers E	52	18
Nondrinkers $\bar{E}$	8	22

(a) Are the events E and F independent?

(b) Are the events $\bar{E}$ and $\bar{F}$ independent?

(c) Are the events E and $\bar{F}$ independent?

10. Let E be any event. If F is an impossible event, show that E and F are independent.

*11. Show that if E and F are independent events so are $\bar{E}$ and $\bar{F}$. (Hint: use DeMorgan's law).

*12. Show that if E and F are independent events and if $P(E) \neq 0$, $P(F) \neq 0$, then E and F are not mutually exclusive.

*13. Three events E, F, G are *independent* if any two of them are independent and

$$P(E \cap F \cap G) = P(E) \cdot P(F) \cdot P(G)$$

Use this definition to determine whether the events

E: "the first die shows a six"

F: "the second die shows a three"

G: "the sum on the two dice is seven"

for the experiment of tossing two fair dice are independent.

*14. Solve Problem 7 in Exercise 3.1. Hint:

(a) $P(\text{no ones are obtained}) = 5^4/6^4 = 625/1296 = .4823$

(b) The probability of not obtaining a double ace on any given toss is 35/36. Thus $P(\text{no double aces are obtained}) = (35/36)^{24} = .512$

*15. *The blood testing problem*.[2] A group of 1000 people are subject to a blood test which can be administered in two ways: (i) each person can be tested separately (in this case 1000 tests are required) or (ii) the blood samples of 30 people can be pooled and analyzed together. If we use the second way and the test is negative, then one test suffices for 30 people. If the test is positive, each of the 30 persons can then be tested separately, and, in all, $30 + 1$ tests are required for the 30 people.

Assume the probability p that the test is positive, is the same for all people and that the people to be tested are independent.

(a) What is the probability that the test for a pooled sample of 30 people will be positive?

(b) What is the expected number of tests necessary under plan (ii)?

3.8
BAYES' FORMULA

In this section, we consider experiments whose sample space can be divided or partitioned into two (or more) mutually exclusive events. This study involves a further application of conditional probabilities and leads us to the famous formula of Thomas Bayes which was first published in 1763.

We begin by considering the following example.

[2] Feller, William, *An Introduction to Probability Theory and Its Applications,* third edition, John Wiley, New York, 1968, pp. 239–240.

3.8.1
Example

Given two urns, I and II, suppose Urn I contains 4 black and 7 white balls. Urn II contains 3 black, 1 white, and 4 yellow balls. We select an urn at random and then draw a ball. What is the probability that we obtain a black ball?

Let U_I and U_{II} stand for the events "Urn I is chosen" and "Urn II is chosen," respectively. Similarly, let B, W, Y stand for the event that a black, white, or yellow ball is chosen," respectively.

$$P(U_I) = P(U_{II}) = 1/2$$
$$P(B|U_I) = 4/11, \qquad P(B|U_{II}) = 3/8$$

But using the result of Problem 5(g) in Exercise 2.4, the event B can be written as

$$B = (B \cap U_I) \cup (B \cap U_{II})$$

Since $B \cap U_I$ and $B \cap U_{II}$ are disjoint, we add their probabilities. Then

$$P(B) = P(B \cap U_I) + P(B \cap U_{II})$$

Using the definition of conditional probability, we have

$$P(B|U_I) = \frac{P(B \cap U_I)}{P(U_I)} \qquad P(B|U_{II}) = \frac{P(B \cap U_{II})}{P(U_{II})}$$

Thus,

$$P(B) = P(U_I) \cdot P(B|U_I) + P(U_{II}) \cdot P(B|U_{II})$$
$$= \frac{1}{2} \cdot \frac{4}{11} + \frac{1}{2} \cdot \frac{3}{8} = \frac{65}{176} = .369$$

A solution to Example 3.8.1 can be depicted using a tree diagram. See Figure 3.13.

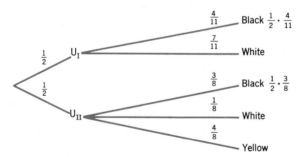

Figure 3.13

Suppose A_1 and A_2 are two nonempty, mutually exclusive events of a sample space S whose union is S; that is,

$$A_1 \neq \varnothing, \qquad A_2 \neq \varnothing, \qquad A_1 \cap A_2 = \varnothing, \qquad S = A_1 \cup A_2$$

Here we say A_1 and A_2 form a *partition* of S. See Figure 3.14.

Let E be any event in S. Using the result of Problem 5(g) in Exercise 2.4 we have

$$E = (E \cap A_1) \cup (E \cap A_2)$$

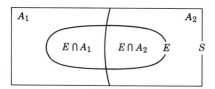

Figure 3.14

Now, $E \cap A_1$ and $E \cap A_2$ are disjoint. For,

$$(E \cap A_1) \cap (E \cap A_2) = (E \cap E) \cap (A_1 \cap A_2) = E \cap \emptyset = \emptyset$$

since A_1 and A_2 are disjoint. Using the definition for conditional probability, the probability for E is then

$$P(E) = P(E \cap A_1) + P(E \cap A_2)$$
$$= P(A_1) \cdot P(E|A_1) + P(A_2) \cdot P(E|A_2) \qquad (3.8.1)$$

The above formula is used to find the probability of an event E of a sample space when the sample space is partitioned into two sets A_1 and A_2.

Of the applicants to a medical school, it is felt that 80 percent are eligible to enter and 20 percent are not. To aid in the selection process, an admission test is administered which is designed so that an eligible candidate will pass 90 percent of the time while an ineligible candidate will pass 30 percent of the time. What is the probability that an applicant for admission will pass the admissions test?

3.8.2 Example

Here the sample space S consists of the applicants for admission and S can be partitioned into the two events

A_1: eligible applicant A_2: ineligible applicant

which are disjoint and whose union is S. The event E is

E: applicant passes admissions test

Now

$$P(A_1) = .8 \qquad P(A_2) = .2$$
$$P(E|A_1) = .9 \qquad P(E|A_2) = .3$$

Using the formula (3.8.1), we have

$$P(E) = P(E|A_1) \cdot P(A_1) + P(E|A_2) \cdot P(A_2) = (.9)(.8) + (.3)(.2)$$
$$= .72 + .06 = .78$$

If we partition a sample space S into three sets A_1, A_2, A_3 so that

$$S = A_1 \cup A_2 \cup A_3, \qquad A_1 \cap A_2 = \emptyset, \qquad A_2 \cap A_3 = \emptyset$$
$$A_1 \cap A_3 = \emptyset, \qquad A_1 \neq \emptyset, \qquad A_2 \neq \emptyset, \qquad A_3 \neq \emptyset$$

then by an extension of Problem 5(g), Exercise 2.4, any event E in S can be expressed by

$$E = (E \cap A_1) \cup (E \cap A_2) \cup (E \cap A_3)$$

The probability of event E is

$$\begin{aligned} P(E) &= P(E \cap A_1) + P(E \cap A_2) + P(E \cap A_3) \\ &= P(A_1) \cdot P(E|A_1) + P(A_2) \cdot P(E|A_2) + P(A_3) \cdot P(E|A_3) \end{aligned}$$
(3.8.2)

since $E \cap A_1$, $E \cap A_2$, and $E \cap A_3$ are disjoint. See Figure 3.15.

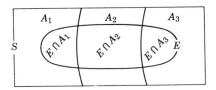

Figure 3.15

This formula is useful for finding the probability of an event E of a sample space when the sample space is partitioned into three sets A_1, A_2, and A_3.

**3.8.3
Example** Three machines I, II, and III manufacture, respectively, .4, .5, and .1 of the total production. The percentage of defective items produced by I, II, and III is 2, 4, and 1 percent, respectively. For an item chosen at random, what is the probability it is defective?

In this example, the sample space S is partitioned into three events A_1, A_2, and A_3, defined by

A_1: item produced by machine I
A_2: item produced by machine II
A_3: item produced by machine III

Clearly the events A_1, A_2, A_3 are mutually exclusive and their union is S. Define the event E in S to be

E: item is defective

Now

$$\begin{aligned} P(A_1) &= .4, & P(A_2) &= .5, & P(A_3) &= .1 \\ P(E|A_1) &= .02, & P(E|A_2) &= .04, & P(E|A_3) &= .01 \end{aligned}$$

Thus, using formula (3.8.2), we see that

$$\begin{aligned} P(E) &= (.4)(.02) + (.5)(.04) + (.1)(.01) \\ &= .008 + .020 + .001 = .029 \end{aligned}$$

Figure 3.16 gives a tree diagram solution to this problem.

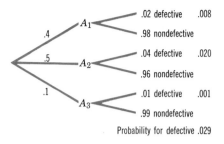

.02 defective   .008
.98 nondefective
.04 defective   .020
.96 nondefective
.01 defective   .001
.99 nondefective
Probability for defective .029

Figure 3.16

To generalize formulas (3.8.1) and (3.8.2) to a sample space S partitioned into n sets, we proceed as follows.

Let S be a sample space and let $A_1, A_2, A_3 \ldots A_n$ be n events which form a *partition* of the set S (that is, they are mutually exclusive, nonempty, and their union is S). Let E be any event in S. Then

$$E = (E \cap A_1) \cup (E \cap A_2) \cup \cdots \cup (E \cap A_n)$$

Clearly, $E \cap A_1$, $E \cap A_2$, $\ldots$, $E \cap A_n$ are mutually exclusive events. Hence

$$P(E) = P(E \cap A_1) + P(E \cap A_2) + \cdots + P(E \cap A_n) \qquad (3.8.3)$$

In (3.8.3) replace $P(E \cap A_1)$, $P(E \cap A_2)$, $\ldots$, $P(E \cap A_n)$ using the definition of conditional probability. Then we obtain the formula

$$\boxed{\begin{aligned} P(E) = P(A_1) \cdot P(E|A_1) + P(A_2) \cdot P(E|A_2) \\ + \cdots + P(A_n) \cdot P(E|A_n) \end{aligned}} \qquad (3.8.4)$$

In Example 3.8.2, suppose an applicant passes the admissions test. What is the probability that he was among those eligible; that is, what is the probability $P(A_1|E)$?

3.8.4
Example

Here, by the definition of conditional probability

$$P(A_1|E) = \frac{P(A_1 \cap E)}{P(E)} = \frac{P(A_1) \cdot P(E|A_1)}{P(E)}$$

But $P(E)$ is given by (3.8.4) when $n = 2$ or by (3.8.1). Thus

$$P(A_1|E) = \frac{P(A_1) \cdot P(E|A_1)}{P(A_1) \cdot P(E|A_1) + P(A_2) \cdot P(E|A_2)} \qquad (3.8.5)$$

Using the information supplied in Example 3.8.2, we find

$$P(A_1|E) = \frac{(.8)(.9)}{.78} = \frac{.72}{.78} = .923$$

Thus, the admissions test is a reasonably effective device. Less than 8 percent of the students passing the test are ineligible.

Equation (3.8.5) is known as *Bayes' formula* for the special case when the sample space is partitioned into two sets A_1 and A_2. The general formula is given in Theorem 3.8.1.

Theorem 3.8.1 Bayes' Formula
Let S be a sample space partitioned into n events $A_1, \ldots , A_n$. Let E be any event of S for which $P(E) > 0$. The probability for the event $A_j, j = 1, 2, \ldots , n$, given the event E, is

$$P(A_j|E) = \frac{P(A_j) \cdot P(E|A_j)}{P(A_1) \cdot P(E|A_1) + P(A_2) \cdot P(E|A_2) + \cdots + P(A_n) \cdot P(E|A_n)}$$
(3.8.6)

The proof is left as an exercise.
The following example will illustrate a use for Bayes' formula when the sample space S is partitioned into three mutually exclusive events.

3.8.5
Example

Motors Incorporated has three plants, I, II, and III. Plant I produces 35 percent of the car output, plant II produces 20 percent, and plant III produces the remaining 45 percent. One percent of the output of plant I is defective, as is 1.8 percent of II, and 2 percent of III. The annual total output of Motor Incorporated is 1,000,000 cars. A car is chosen at random from the annual output and it is found to be defective. What is the probability that it came from plant I? II? III?

To answer these questions let us define the following events.

E: "car is defective"
A_1: "car produced by plant I"
A_2: "car produced by plant II"
A_3: "car produced by plant III"

Also, $P(A_1|E)$ indicates the probability that a car is produced by plant I, given that it was defective. $P(A_2|E)$ and $P(A_3|E)$ are similarly defined. To find these, we proceed as follows.

From the data given in the problem, we can determine the following.

$$\begin{array}{ll} P(A_1) = .35 & P(E|A_1) = .010 \\ P(A_2) = .20 & P(E|A_2) = .018 \\ P(A_3) = .45 & P(E|A_3) = .020 \end{array}$$
(3.8.7)

Now

$A_1 \cap E$ is the event "produced by plant I and is defective"
$A_2 \cap E$ is the event "produced by plant II and is defective"
$A_3 \cap E$ is the event "produced by plant III and is defective"

From the definition of conditional probability, we find

$$\begin{array}{l} P(A_1 \cap E) = P(A_1) \cdot P(E|A_1) = (.35) \cdot (.010) = .0035 \\ P(A_2 \cap E) = P(A_2) \cdot P(E|A_2) = (.20) \cdot (.018) = .0036 \\ P(A_3 \cap E) = P(A_3) \cdot P(E|A_3) = (.45) \cdot (.020) = .0090 \end{array}$$

Since $E = (A_1 \cap E) \cup (A_2 \cap E) \cup (A_3 \cap E)$, we have

$$P(E) = P(A_1 \cap E) + P(A_2 \cap E) + P(A_3 \cap E)$$
$$= .0035 + .0036 + .0090$$
$$= .0161$$

Thus, the probability that a defective car is chosen is .0161.

Given that the car chosen is defective, the probability that it came from Plant I is $P(A_1|E)$. To compute $P(A_1|E), P(A_2|E), P(A_3|E)$, we use Bayes' formula.

$$P(A_1|E) = \frac{P(A_1) \cdot P(E|A_1)}{P(A_1) \cdot P(E|A_1) + P(A_2) \cdot P(E|A_2) + P(A_3) \cdot P(E|A_3)}$$

$$= \frac{P(A_1) \cdot P(E|A_1)}{P(E)} = \frac{(.35)(.01)}{.0161} = .217$$

$$P(A_2|E) = \frac{P(A_2) \cdot P(E|A_2)}{P(E)} = \frac{.0036}{.0161} = \frac{36}{161} = .224 \qquad (3.8.8)$$

$$P(A_3|E) = \frac{P(A_3) \cdot P(E|A_3)}{P(E)} = \frac{.0090}{.0161} = \frac{90}{161} = .559$$

Compare the probabilities found in (3.8.7) with those in (3.8.8). The probabilities $P(E|A_1)$, $P(E|A_2)$, and $P(E|A_3)$ are probabilities of a defective car being produced by one of the plants *before* it is chosen and examined. This is what we refer to as a *priori probability* that is, "before the fact" probability. The probabilities $P(A_1|E)$, $P(A_2|E)$, $P(A_3|E)$ are probabilities of a defective car being produced by one of the plants *after* we have examined and found it to be defective. This is referred as a *posteriori probability* or "after the fact" probability. Thus, Bayes' formula gives us a technique for computing a *posteriori probabilities*.

For example, before a car is chosen, the probability of choosing a defective car assuming it was from plant I is .01. After it is known that a defective car was chosen, the probability that it came from plant I is .217.

A particular case of Bayes' formula when the probability of each event of the partition is equally likely is given below. If

$$P(A_1) = P(A_2) = \cdots = P(A_n)$$

we obtain

$$P(A_j|E) = \frac{P(E|A_j)}{P(E|A_1) + P(E|A_2) + \cdots + P(E|A_n)} \qquad (3.8.9)$$

In Example 3.8.5 let us assume that $P(A_1) = P(A_2) = P(A_3)$, so that the three plants' share of the total production is the same. In this case, we can use equation 3.8.9 to obtain the probability that a car is produced at Plant I, given that it was defective. Thus

$$P(A_1|E) = \frac{P(E|A_1)}{P(E|A_1) + P(E|A_2) + P(E|A_3)}$$

$$= \frac{.010}{.010 + .018 + .02\bar{0}}$$

$$= \frac{.010}{.048} = \frac{5}{24} = .208$$

3.8.6
Example

The residents of a community are examined for cancer. The examination results are classified as positive (+) if a malignancy is suspected and as negative (−) if there are no indications of a malignancy. If a person has cancer, the probability of a suspected malignancy is .98; and the probability of reporting cancer where none existed is .15. If 5 percent of the community has cancer, what is the probability of a person not having cancer if the examination is positive?

Let us define the following events.

A_1: person has cancer
A_2: person does not have cancer
E: examination is positive

We want to know the probability of a person not having cancer, if it is known that the examination is positive; that is, we wish to find $P(A_2|E)$. Now

$$P(A_1) = .05, \quad P(A_2) = .95$$
$$P(E|A_1) = .98, \quad P(E|A_2) = .15$$

Using Bayes' formula we get

$$P(A_2|E) = \frac{P(A_2)P(E|A_2)}{P(A_1)P(E|A_1) + P(A_2)P(E|A_2)}$$

$$= \frac{(.95)(.15)}{(.05)(.98) + (.95)(.15)} = .744$$

Thus, even if the examination is positive, the person examined is more likely not to have cancer than to have cancer. The reason is that it is better for a healthy person to be examined more thoroughly than for someone with cancer to go undetected.

3.8.
Exercise

1. In Example 3.8.2, find $P(A_2|E)$.
2. In Example 3.8.3, suppose it is known that a defective item was produced. Find the probability it came from machine I; from machine II; from machine III.
3. In Example 3.8.5, suppose $P(A_1) = P(A_2) = P(A_3) = 1/3$. Find $P(A_2|E)$ and $P(A_3|E)$.
4. In Example 3.8.6, compute $P(A_1|E)$.
5. Three urns contain colored balls as follows:

Urn	Red (R)	White (W)	Blue (B)
I	5	6	3
II	3	4	5
III	7	5	4

One urn is chosen at random and a ball is withdrawn. The ball is red. What is the probability that it came from Urn I? from Urn II? from Urn III? Hint: Define the following events.

E: "Ball selected is red"
U_I: "Urn I selected"
U_{II}: "Urn II selected"
U_{III}: "Urn III selected"

Notice that $P(U_I) = P(U_{II}) = P(U_{III}) = 1/3$.
Also, the conditional probabilities are

$$P(E|U_I) = \frac{5}{14}, \qquad P(E|U_{II}) = \frac{3}{12} = \frac{1}{4}, \qquad P(E|U_{III}) = \frac{7}{16}$$

Determine $P(U_I|E)$, $P(U_{II}|E)$, $P(U_{III}|E)$, by using Bayes' formula.

6. Suppose that if a person with cholera is given a chest X ray, the probability that his condition will be detected is .90. If a person without cholera is given a chest X ray, the probability that he will be diagnosed incorrectly as having cholera is .3. Suppose, further, that 11 percent of the adult residents of a certain city have cholera. If one of these persons is diagnosed as having cholera based on the X ray, what is the probability that he actually has cholera? Interpret your result.

7. Cars are being produced by two factories I and II, but I produces twice as many cars as II in a given time. Factory I is known to produce 2 percent defective and II produces 1 percent defective. A car is examined and found to be defective. What are the *a priori* and *a posteriori* probabilities that the car was produced by I?

8. An absent-minded nurse is supposed to give Mr. Brown a pill each day. The probability that she will forget to give the pill is 2/3. If he receives the pill, the probability that Brown will die is 1/3. If he does not get his pill, the probability that he will die is 3/4. Mr. Brown died. What is the probability that the nurse forgot to give Brown the pill?

9. An oil well is to be drilled in a certain location. The soil there is either rock (probability .53), clay (probability .21), or sand. If it is rock, a geological test gives a positive result with 35 percent accuracy; if it is clay, this test gives a positive result with 48 percent accuracy; and if it is sand, the test gives a positive result with 75 percent accuracy. Given that the test is positive, what is the probability the soil is rock? What is the probability the soil is clay? What is the probability the soil is sand?

10. Prove Theorem 3.8.1.

By *finite stochastic processes* we mean a sequence of experiments that can be subjected to a probabilistic analysis. Each experiment has a given number of outcomes with given probabilities. The outcome of each particular experiment will depend on some chance (stochastic) element.

We shall limit ourselves to those processes for which the mathematical background needed to study them is not so extensive. Furthermore, we shall

3.9
BERNOULLI
TRIALS

make enough assumptions so that the work will be easier and at the same time applicable to practical problems. For these reasons we only concern ourselves with two types of finite stochastic processes, the Bernoulli trial and the Markov chain. In each process the number of outcomes of each experiment is finite. This section will cover various aspects of Bernoulli trials; Chapter 10 will deal with Markov chains.

Finite stochastic processes in general, and Bernoulli trials in particular, can often be described by the use of a tree diagram. Example 3.8.1 is an illustration of a stochastic process. There we found that the probability of drawing a black ball is

$$P(B) = \frac{1}{2} \cdot \frac{4}{11} + \frac{1}{2} \cdot \frac{3}{8} = \frac{65}{176}$$

The tree diagram describing this experiment is given in Figure 3.17.

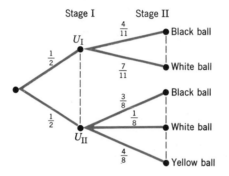

Figure 3.17

Notice that this tree diagram has two *stages*. Corresponding to Stage I, there are two branches, and to Stage II, there are five *branches*. The combination of stages with branches is called a *path*. In Figure 3.17 there are two paths that give the outcome that a black ball is drawn; two paths giving the outcome that a white ball is chosen; and one path giving the outcome a yellow ball is chosen.

To obtain a black ball, there are two paths: along the first path, the probabilities are 1/2 and 4/11 and along the second, the probabilities are 1/2 and 3/8. By multiplying the probabilities along each path and adding these products for all paths that give the same outcome, we obtain the probability for this outcome. Thus, in the example above,

$$P(B) = \frac{1}{2} \cdot \frac{4}{11} + \frac{1}{2} \cdot \frac{3}{8} = \frac{65}{176}$$
$$P(W) = \frac{1}{2} \cdot \frac{7}{11} + \frac{1}{2} \cdot \frac{1}{8} = \frac{67}{176}$$

Notice that the sum of the probabilities for each branch of every stage is always one—as it must be. That is, $1/2 + 1/2 = 1$, $4/11 + 7/11 = 1$, $3/8 + 1/8 + 4/8 = 1$.

As an example of a Bernoulli trial consider an experiment performed three times with two possible outcomes A and B with probabilities P_A and P_B, respectively. The tree diagram in Figure 3.18 represents this particular process.

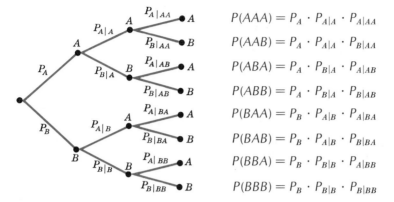

$$P(AAA) = P_A \cdot P_{A|A} \cdot P_{A|AA}$$

$$P(AAB) = P_A \cdot P_{A|A} \cdot P_{B|AA}$$

$$P(ABA) = P_A \cdot P_{B|A} \cdot P_{A|AB}$$

$$P(ABB) = P_A \cdot P_{B|A} \cdot P_{B|AB}$$

$$P(BAA) = P_B \cdot P_{A|B} \cdot P_{A|BA}$$

$$P(BAB) = P_B \cdot P_{A|B} \cdot P_{B|BA}$$

$$P(BBA) = P_B \cdot P_{B|B} \cdot P_{A|BB}$$

$$P(BBB) = P_B \cdot P_{B|B} \cdot P_{B|BB}$$

Figure 3.18

In assigning probabilities to branches in the second stage, we used the notation $P_{A|A}$, $P_{A|B}$, $P_{B|A}$, $P_{B|B}$ to indicate that these are conditional probabilities for the outcome on a particular branch given the outcome on the previous branch. $P_{A|B}$ is the probability of getting A in the second trial knowing that B was the outcome of the first trial. Furthermore, the probabilities must add up to 1 at each branch of every stage. Thus, for the first trial,

$$P_A + P_B = 1, \qquad P_{A|A} + P_{B|A} = 1, \qquad P_{A|B} + P_{B|B} = 1$$

Of interest is the fact that

$$P_A \cdot P_{A|A} + P_A \cdot P_{B|A} + P_{A|B} \cdot P_B + P_B \cdot P_{B|B}$$
$$= P_A(P_{A|A} + P_{B|A}) + P_B(P_{A|B} + P_{B|B})$$
$$= P_A + P_B$$
$$= 1$$

Consider a sequence of trials, each of which consists of repetition of a single experiment, so that the outcome of one experiment does not affect the outcome of any other one. That is, we assume the trials to be independent. Furthermore, assume that there are only two possible outcomes for each trial and label them "S" for *success* and "F" for *failure*. This is a rather simple experiment and it may be classified completely in terms of a single number p, which is the same throughout the process and where

$$p = P(S)$$

Since the probability of success is p, then the probability of failure is $1 - p$ and we write

$$q = 1 - p = P(F)$$

There are some obvious uses for this kind of experiment which has only two outcomes S and F. For example, in running a subject through a T-maze, we may label a turn to the right by S and a turn to the left by F. In asking a question in a poll, we may designate the answer "yes" by an S and any other answer ("no," "don't know") by an F. In determining cancerous tumors, a benign tumor can be labeled with an S and a malignant tumor with an F.

3.9.1
Definition **A finite stochastic process for which the trials are independent and for which any trial has only two possible outcomes is termed a** *Bernoulli process* **or** *Bernoulli trial.*

Consider a Bernoulli trial that consists of six stages or six trials. One path or one particular outcome might appear as *FSSSFS*. Since we are assuming that the trials are independent, we get the probability for this particular outcome to be,

$$q \cdot p \cdot p \cdot p \cdot q \cdot p = q \cdot p^3 \cdot q \cdot p = q^2 \cdot p^4$$

The probability for a different outcome like *SFSFSS* is also equal to $q^2 p^4$. The same is true for any outcome that has *exactly* the same number of S's and F's regardless of their order. To analyze these trials in a systematic way, let us consider tree diagrams for the cases of 2 and 3 trials. See Figure 3.19.

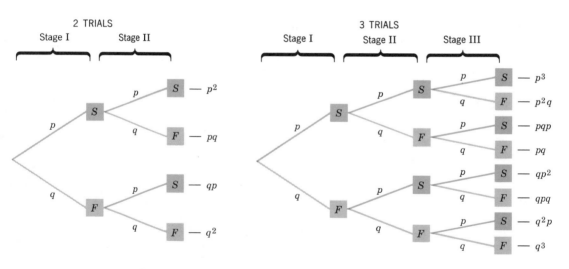

Figure 3.19

Several observations should be made with regard to the above two tree diagrams. First, notice that if we sum the probabilities at the conclusion of the last trial of each experiment we find that

$$p^2 + pq + qp + q^2 = p^2 + 2pq + q^2 = (p + q)^2$$
$$p^3 + p^2q + pqp + pq^2 + qp^2 + qpq + q^2p + q^3 = p^3 + 3p^2q + 3pq^2 + q^3 = (p + q)^3$$

In general with an experiment involving n trials the sum of the probabilities after the nth trial is $(p + q)^n$.

Second, notice that in a sequence of n independent trials with two outcomes, any sequence that contains k successes and $n - k$ failures has probability $p^k q^{n-k}$. To find the probability of obtaining exactly k successes in n trials, we must find the number of sequences having k successes. This number is obtained by noting that the k successes can appear in any k of the n trials; thus, the number of such sequences must be equal to the number of combinations of k objects that can be taken from a set of n objects, or $\binom{n}{k}$. If we multiply this number by the probability for obtaining this sequence, we obtain the result in Theorem 3.9.1.

Theorem 3.9.1
In a Bernoulli trial the probability of exactly k successes in n trials is given by

$$b(n,k;p) = \binom{n}{k} p^k \cdot q^{n-k} = \frac{n!}{k!(n-k)!} p^k \cdot q^{n-k}$$

in which $p + q = 1$.

A common model for the above result is a coin-flipping experiment:
  (a) there are exactly two possible mutually exclusive outcomes on each trial or toss (heads or tails).
  (b) the outcome on any trial (toss) is independent of the outcome on any other trial (toss).
  (c) the probability of a particular outcome (say H) remains constant from trial to trial (toss to toss); for example, on any toss the probability of H is always 1/2.

3.9.1
Example

We would like to compute the probability of obtaining exactly one tail in six tosses of a fair coin.

  Let S denote the simple event "tail shows."
  Let F denote the simple event "head shows."

Using Theorem 3.9.1 in which $k = 1$, $n = 6$, and $p = 1/2 = P(S)$, we obtain

$$P(\text{one success}) = b\left(6, 1; \frac{1}{2}\right) = \binom{6}{1}\left(\frac{1}{2}\right)^1\left(\frac{1}{2}\right)^{6-1} = .09375$$

A machine produces light bulbs to meet certain specifications and 80 percent of the bulbs produced meet these specifications. A sample of 6 bulbs is taken from the machine's production. What is the probability that 3 or more of them fail to meet the specifications?

3.9.2
Example

  In this example, as in many other applications, it is necessary to compute the probability not of exactly k successes, but of *at least* or *at most* k successes. To obtain such probabilities we have to compute all the individual probabilities and add them. Of course this is a cumbersome task and to avoid this situation tables of the binomial probabilities are found in most books on probability. See Table 9 in Appendix 1.

In this example we are looking for the probability of the event A "at least three fail to meet specifications." But this event is just the union of the mutually exclusive events "exactly 3 failures," "exactly 4 failures," "exactly 5 failures," and "exactly 6 failures." Hence using Theorem 3.9.1 for $n = 6$, $k = 3, 2, 1$, and 0, since the probability of exactly 3 failures is the same as that of exactly 2 successes, and so on, we have

$$q = P(\text{failure}) = .20, \ p = P(\text{success}) = .80$$

$$P(\text{exactly 3 failures}) = b(6, 3; .80) = \binom{6}{3} (.8)^3 (.2)^3 = .0819$$

$$P(\text{exactly 4 failures}) = b(6, 2; .80) = \binom{6}{2} (.8)^2 (.2)^4 = .0154$$

$$P(\text{exactly 5 failures}) = b(6, 1; .80) = \binom{6}{1} (.8)^1 (.2)^5 = .0015$$

$$P(\text{exactly 6 failures}) = b(6, 0; .80) = \binom{6}{0} (.8)^0 (.2)^6 = .0001$$

Therefore

$$P(\text{at least 3 failures}) = P(A) = .0819 + .0154 + .0015 + .0001 = .0989$$

Let us define the event E to be "less than 3 failures." Clearly $\bar{E} = A$. But

$$P(E) = P(\text{exactly 2 failures}) + P(\text{exactly 1 failure}) + P(\text{exactly 0 failures})$$
$$= b(6, 4; .80) + b(6, 5; .80) + b(6, 6; .80)$$
$$= .2458 + .3932 + .2621 = .9011$$

Notice that

$$1 - P(E) = P(A)$$

as expected.

3.9.3
Example
Testing sera
or vaccines[3]

Suppose that the normal rate of infection of a certain disease in cattle is 25 percent. To test a newly discovered serum, n healthy animals are injected with it. How are we to evaluate the result of the experiment?

For an absolutely worthless serum the probability that exactly k of the n test animals remain free from infection may be equated to $b(k, n; 0.75)$. For $k = n = 10$ this probability is about 0.056. Thus, if out of 10 test animals none catches infection, this may be taken as an indication that the serum has had an effect, although it is not conclusive proof. Notice that, without serum, the probability that out of 17 animals at most 1 catches infection is about 0.0501, $[b(17, 0; .25) + b(17, 1; .25)]$. Therefore there is *stronger evidence* in favor of the serum if out of 17 test animals at most 1 gets infected than if out of 10 all remain healthy. For $n = 23$ the probability of at most 2 animals catching infection is about 0.0492, and thus at most 2 failures out of 23 is again better evidence for the serum than at most 1 out of 17 or 0 out of 10.

[3] P. V. Sukhatme and V. G. Panse, "Size of experiments for testing sera or vaccines," *Indiana Journal of Veterinary Science and Animal Husbandry*, Vol. 13 (1943), pp. 75–82.

A man claims to be able to distinguish between two kinds of wines with 90 percent accuracy and presents his claim to an agency interested in promoting the consumptions of one of the two kinds of wines. To check his claim the following experiment is conducted: The man is to taste the two types of wines and distinguish between them. This is to be done 9 times with a 3-minute break after each taste. It is agreed that if the man is correct at least 6 out of the 9 times he is to be hired.

The main questions to be asked, on the one hand, is whether the above procedure gives sufficient protection to the hiring agency against a fraudulent claim and, on the other hand, whether the man is given sufficient chance to be hired if he is really a wine connoisseur.

To answer the first question, let us assume that the man made a fraudulent claim. Then he will have to guess in each trial and so has probability 1/2 of identifying the wine correctly. Let k be the number of correct identifications. Let us compute the binomial probability for $k = 6, 7, 8, 9$, to study the likelihood of the man being hired while making fraudulent claims. Now

$$b\left(9, 6; \frac{1}{2}\right) + b\left(9, 7; \frac{1}{2}\right) + b\left(9, 8; \frac{1}{2}\right) + b\left(9, 9; \frac{1}{2}\right)$$

$$= \binom{9}{6} \cdot \left(\frac{1}{2}\right)^6 \cdot \left(\frac{1}{2}\right)^3 + \binom{9}{7} \cdot \left(\frac{1}{2}\right)^7 \cdot \left(\frac{1}{2}\right)^2 + \binom{9}{8} \cdot \left(\frac{1}{2}\right)^8 \cdot \left(\frac{1}{2}\right)$$

$$+ \binom{9}{9} \cdot \left(\frac{1}{2}\right)^9 = .164 + .070 + .018 + .002 = .254$$

Thus there is a likelihood of the fraudulent claim passing of .254.

To answer the second question in the case where the claim is not fraudulent, we would like to find the sum of the probabilities $b(n, k; .90)$ for $k = 6, 7, 8, 9$. Then

$$b(9, 6; .90) + b(9, 7; .90) + b(9, 8; .90) + b(9, 9; .90)$$
$$= .045 + .172 + .387 + .387 = .991$$

We notice that the test is fair to the man since it practically assures him the position. Furthermore, the company should like the test because it assures them that they are picking the right person.

The student should administer a similar test in such a way that the answer to the first question is approximately .002 and the answer to the second part is approximately .500 and give interpretations to such a test.

In Section 3.5, the expected value of an event is introduced and discussed. Suppose the event is a success in a Bernoulli trial. What is the expected value of the event?

If there are n trials and p is the probability for success, then for any single trial, the expected value E is

$$E = 1 \cdot p + 0 \cdot (1 - p) = p$$

For n such trials, the expected value is

$$E = n \cdot p$$

Thus, we have the following theorem.

Theorem 3.9.2

In a Bernoulli process with n trials, the expected value E for a success is

$$E = np$$

where p is the probability for success.

To illustrate the usefulness of this result, we compute the expected value for obtaining tails by flipping a coin 5 times without using Theorem 3.9.2.

3.9.5
Example

In the case of a flip of a single fair coin 5 times, there are 6 possible outcomes: 0 tails, 1 tail, 2 tails, 3 tails, 4 tails, or 5 tails, each with the respective probabilities

$$\binom{5}{0}\left(\frac{1}{2}\right)^5, \binom{5}{1}\left(\frac{1}{2}\right)^5, \binom{5}{2}\left(\frac{1}{2}\right)^5, \binom{5}{3}\left(\frac{1}{2}\right)^5, \binom{5}{4}\left(\frac{1}{2}\right)^5, \binom{5}{5}\left(\frac{1}{2}\right)^5$$

Thus, the expectation E for a tail is

$$E = 0 \cdot \binom{5}{0}\left(\frac{1}{2}\right)^5 + 1 \cdot \binom{5}{1}\left(\frac{1}{2}\right)^5 + 2 \cdot \binom{5}{2}\left(\frac{1}{2}\right)^5$$

$$+ 3 \cdot \binom{5}{3}\left(\frac{1}{2}\right)^5 + 4 \cdot \binom{5}{4}\left(\frac{1}{2}\right)^5 + 5 \cdot \binom{5}{5}\left(\frac{1}{2}\right)^5 = \frac{5}{2}$$

Clearly, using Theorem 3.9.2 is much easier, since for $n = 5$ and $p = 1/2$, we obtain $E = 5 \cdot 1/2 = 5/2$.

3.9
Exercise

1. What is the probability of obtaining exactly two sevens in five rolls of two fair dice?
2. A fair coin is tossed six times (or six coins are tossed simultaneously).
   (a) What is the probability of obtaining exactly two heads?
   (b) What is the probability of obtaining exactly two heads, if it is known that at least one head appeared?
3. Assuming all sex distributions to be equally probable, what is the probability that a family with exactly six children will have three boys and three girls?
4. An experiment is performed four times, with two possible outcomes F (failure) and S (success) with probabilities 1/4 and 3/4, respectively.
   (a) Draw the tree diagram describing the experiment.
   (b) Calculate the probability of exactly two successes and two failures by using (a).
   (c) Verify (b) by using the binomial theorem and Table 9 in Appendix 1.
5. What is the probability that in a family of seven children
   (a) four will be girls?
   (b) at least two are girls?
   (c) at least two and not more than four are girls?

6. For a baseball player with a .250 batting average, what is the probability he will have at least two hits in four times at bat? Of at least one hit in the four times?

7. If the probability of hitting a target is 1/5 and 10 shots are fired independently, what is the probability of the target being hit at least twice?

8. Find the expected value of the face 5 appearing in a sequence of 2000 throws of a pair of fair dice.

9. Opinion polls based on small samples often yield misleading results. Suppose 65 percent of the people in a city are opposed to the war in Vietnam and the others favor it. If 7 people are asked for their opinion on the war, what is the probability that a majority of them will favor it?

10. A supposed coffee connoisseur claims he can distinguish between a cup of instant coffee and a cup of percolator coffee 75 percent of the time. You give him 6 cups of coffee and tell him that you will grant his claim if he correctly identifies at least 5 of the 6 cups.

    (a) What are his chances of having his claim granted, if he is in fact only guessing?

    (b) What are his chances of having his claim rejected, when in fact he really does have the ability he claims?

*11. How many times should a fair coin be flipped in order to have the probability of at least 1 head appearing be greater than .98?

*12. What is the probability that the birthdays of 6 people fall in 2 calendar months leaving exactly 10 months free? (Assume independence and equal probabilities for all months.)

*13. A book of 500 pages contains 500 misprints. Estimate the chance that a given page contains at least 3 misprints.

*14. In n Bernoulli trials with $p = 1/3$, for what least value of n does the probability of exactly 2 successes have its only maximum value?

*15. Prove the identity

$$b(n,k;p) = b(n, n - k; 1 - p)$$

How is this fact used in Table 9 of Appendix 1?

*16.[4] A man has 10 keys of which only 1 fits his door. He tries them successively (without replacement). Find the probability that a key fits with exactly 5 tries.

*17.[4] An elevator starts with 5 passengers and stops at 8 floors. Find the probability that no 2 passengers leave at the same floor. Assume that all arrangements of discharging the passengers have the same probability.

---

[4]Op. Cit., Feller.

probabilistic models
logical possibilities
outcome
sample space
event
simple event
mutually exclusive
odds
equally likely
success

failure
conditional probability
independent events
Bayes' formula
expected value
finite stochastic process
Bernoulli trials
a priori
a posteriori

Exercises

1. A survey of families with two children is made and the sexes of the children are recorded. Describe the sample space and draw a tree diagram of this random experiment.

2. A fair coin is tossed three times.
   a. Construct a stochastic model corresponding to this experiment.
   b. Find the probabilities of the following events:
   (i) the first toss is T
   (ii) the first toss is H
   (iii) either the first toss is T or the third toss is H
   (iv) at least one of the tosses is H
   (v) there are at least two T's
   (vi) no tosses are H

3. Below is a set of 20 chips labeled by ordered pairs of numbers. Let "a" denote the first component and "b" the second component of an ordered pair. One chip is drawn at random. Find the probability that it belongs to the subset described by:

$$(1,1)\ (1,2)\ (1,3)\ (1,4)\ (1,5)$$
$$(2,1)\ (2,2)\ (2,3)\ (2,4)\ (2,5)$$
$$(3,1)\ (3,2)\ (3,3)\ (3,4)\ (3,5)$$
$$(4,1)\ (4,2)\ (4,3)\ (4,4)\ (4,5)$$

   a. $a = 4$
   b. $a < 4$
   c. $a = 2$ and $b = 4$
   d. $a = 2$ or $b = 4$

   e. $a \neq 2$ and $b \neq 4$
   f. $a + b = 4$
   g. $a + b < 4$
   h. $a = b$

4. Jones lives at O. (See figure below.) He has 5 gas stations located 4 blocks away (dots). Each afternoon he checks on one of his gas stations. He starts at O. At each intersection he flips a fair coin. If it shows heads he will head North (N) otherwise he will head towards the East (E). What is the probability that he will end up at gas station G before coming to one of the other stations?

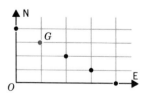

5. Consider the experiment of spinning the spinner in the figure below three times. (Assume the spinner cannot fall on a line.)

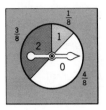

a. Are all outcomes equally likely?
b. If not, which of the outcomes has the highest probability?
c. Let F be the event "each digit will occur exactly once." Find $P(F)$.

6. If E and F are events with $P(E \cup F) = 5/8$, $P(E \cap F) = 1/3$, $P(E) = 1/2$ find:
a. $P(E)$
b. $P(F)$
c. $P(\bar{F})$

7. If E and F represent mutually exclusive events, $P(E) = 0.30$, and $P(F) = 0.45$, find each of the following probabilities:

a. $P(\bar{E})$ e. $P(\overline{E \cap F})$
b. $P(\bar{F})$ f. $P(\overline{E \cup F})$
c. $P(E \cap F)$ g. $P(\bar{E} \cup \bar{F})$
d. $P(E \cup F)$ h. $P(\bar{E} \cap \bar{F})$

8. Three envelopes are addressed for three secret letters written in invisible ink. A secretary randomly places each of the letters in an envelope and mails them. What is the probability that at least one person receives the correct letter?

9. What are the odds in favor of a five, when a fair die is thrown?

10. A man is willing to give $7:6$ odds that the Bears will win the NFL title. What is the probability of the Bears winning?

*11. Show that if E and F are independent events then:
a. E and F are independent
b. $\bar{E}$ and F are independent

12. A biased coin is such that the probability of heads (H) is 1/4 and the probability of tails (T) is 3/4. Show that in flipping this coin twice the events,
E: A head turns up in the first throw
F: A tail turns up in the second throw
are independent.

13. The record in the Dean of Students of Midwestern University shows that 38 percent of the students failed mathematics, 27 percent of the students failed physics, and 9 percent of the students failed mathematics and physics. A student is selected at random.
a. If he failed physics, what is the probability that he failed mathematics?
b. If he failed mathematics, what is the probability that he failed physics?
c. What is the probability that he failed mathematics or physics?

14. The table below indicates a survey conducted by a deodorant producer.

	Like the deodorant	Did not like the deodorant	No opinion
Group I	180	60	20
Group II	110	85	12
Group III	55	65	7

Let E be the event—customer likes the deodorant.
Let F be the event—customer does not like the deodorant.
Let G be the event—customer is from Group I.
Let H be the event—customer is from Group II.
Let K be the event—customer is from Group III.

Find: (a) $P(E|G)$ (e) $P(F|G)$
       (b) $P(G|E)$ (f) $P(G|F)$
       (c) $P(H|E)$ (g) $P(H|F)$
       (d) $P(K|E)$ (h) $P(K|F)$

15. In a factory, three machines A_1, A_2, A_3 produce respectively 55, 30, and 15 percent of total production. The percentage of defective output of these machines are 1, 2, and 3 percent, respectively. An item is chosen at random and it is defective. What is the probability it came from machine A_1? A_2? A_3? *Hint:* Use Bayes' formula.

16. A lung cancer test has been found to have the following reliability. The test can detect 85 percent of the people who have cancer and does not detect 15 percent of these people. Among the noncancerous group it detects 92 percent of not having cancer, whereas 8 percent of this group are detected erroneously as having lung cancer. Statistics show that about 1.8 percent of the population have cancer. Suppose an individual is given the test for lung cancer and it shows that he has the disease. What is the probability that he actually has cancer. Use Bayes' formula.

17. The figure below shows a spinning game for which a person pays $0.30 to purchase an opportunity to spin the dial. Each number on the table indicates the amount of payoff and its corresponding probability. Find the expected value of this game. Is the game fair?

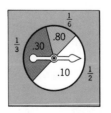

18. Consider the three urns in the figure below. The game is played in two stages. The first stage is to choose a ball from urn A. If the result is a ball marked I then we go to urn I, and we select a ball from there. The number drawn on the second stage is the gain. Find the expected value of this game.

19. What is the expected number of tails that will turn up if a coin is tossed 582 times?

20. Find the probability of throwing an 11 at least 3 times in 5 throws of a fair pair of dice.

21. A management believes that 1 out of 6 people watching a television advertisement about their new product will purchase the product. Five persons who watched the advertisement are picked at random. What

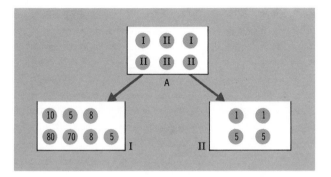

is the probability that 0, 1, 2, 3, 4, or 5 persons will purchase the product?

22. Suppose that the probability of a player hitting a home run is 1/3. In 5 tries what is the probability that he hits at least 1 home run?

23. In a 12-item true-false examination,
    a. What is the probability that a student will obtain all correct answers by chance if he is unprepared?
    b. If 7 correct answers constitute a passing grade, what is the probability that he will pass?
    c. What are the odds against his passing?

Additional Reading

Bush, R. R., and W. K. Estes, *Studies in Mathematical Learning Theory,* Stanford University Press, 1959.

Feller, W. *An Introduction to Probability Theory and its Applications,* Wiley, New York, 1968.

Goldberg, S., *Probability: An Introduction,* Prentice-Hall, Inc., Englewood Cliffs, New Jersey, 1960.

"Mathematics in the Modern World, readings from *Scientific American,* W. H. Freeman and Company, San Francisco, 1968.

Schlafer, R., *Probability and Statistics for Business Decisions,* McGraw-Hill, New York, 1959.

Weaver, Warren, *Lady Luck,* Anchor Books, New York, 1963.

Mathematical Models Chapter 4

Sooner or later, any study involving empirical data and practical needs will lead to the mathematical concept of a *function*. We shall not attempt a rigorous definition of function here but instead we shall describe a function very intuitively and rely on examples to give the reader an understanding of functions.

Very simply, a *function f* is a rule or law that associates or corresponds to one or more given numbers $x, y, : \ldots$ a single number $f(x, y, \ldots)$.

For example, the function f that associates the square of a number to a given number x is

$$f(x) = x^2 \qquad (4.1.1)$$

The function f that associates the product of two numbers to two given numbers x and y is

$$f(x, y) = x \cdot y \qquad (4.1.2)$$

The function f in (4.1.1) is called a function of *one variable*, whereas the function f in (4.1.2) is a function of *two variables*.

The number of permutations of n different things taken r at a time

$$P(n, r) = n(n - 1) \cdots (n - r + 1)$$

is an example of a function f of the two variables n and r. So is the number of combinations of n different things taken r at a time

$$C(n, r) = \frac{n!}{n!(n-r)!}$$

The number associated to a function of one or more variables is called the *dependent variable* since it depends for its value on the value(s) of the other variable(s).

4.1.1 Example   For the function

$$f(x) = 2x^2 + 5$$

find the value of the dependent variable when the variable x equals 4. Here, the value of the dependent variable is

$$f(4) = 2(4)^2 + 5 = 2 \cdot 16 + 5 = 32 + 5 = 37$$

4.1.2 Example   For the function

$$f(x, y) = x^2 + y$$

find $f(-3, 4)$.
Here for $x = -3$ and $y = 4$, we find

$$f(-3, 4) = (-3)^2 + 4 = 9 + 4 = 13$$

4.1.3 Example   If a ball is dropped from a height 96 feet above the ground, how far will it have fallen after 2 seconds? How long will it take before the ball strikes the ground?

It has been determined through experimentation that the distance s a ball falls is given by the function or formula

$$s = \tfrac{1}{2}gt^2$$

where t is the time measured in seconds, $g = 32$ ft/sec^2 is a constant, and s is measured in feet.

After 2 seconds ($t = 2$), we see that the distance s in feet that the ball has fallen is

$$s = 16(2)^2 = 16 \cdot 4 = 64$$

Thus, after 2 seconds, the ball has fallen 64 feet or is 32 feet from the ground.

Now, the ball will strike the ground when it has fallen 96 feet. Thus, the time t needed for this is found by solving

$$96 = 16 \cdot t^2$$

It is easily seen that

$$t^2 = 6$$

Mathematically, this equation has two solutions.

$$t = \sqrt{6} = 2.4 \quad \text{or} \quad t = -\sqrt{6} = -2.4$$

Physically, only positive time is meaningful. Thus, it will take the ball about 2.4 seconds before it strikes the ground.

The preceding example gives us a mathematical interpretation of a physical event. The function

$$s = f(t) = \tfrac{1}{2}gt^2$$

is an interpretation of the distance a ball would fall in t seconds.

In Chapter 3 we encountered situations in which it was not possible to predict in an exact way the outcome of an experiment. For example, in tossing a coin we cannot predict with any certainty whether a head or a tail will occur. This uncertainty required us to construct what we called a *probabilistic model* in order to answer questions about this kind of real world situation.

In Example 4.1.3, we have the real world situation of a falling body. In this case the factors to be eliminated (such as the effect of air resistance), as well as those that have considerable effect on the motion (such as gravity) can be identified. Having made appropriate assumptions, an analysis of the physical laws governing the motion of the body leads to a description (namely, $s = \tfrac{1}{2}gt^2$) of the situation that predicts *in an exact way* the behavior of the body. This is an example of a *deterministic model*.

Mathematical models are thus of two types: *probabilistic* **and** *deterministic*. **A** *probabilistic* *model* **is one that deals with situations that are random in character. A** *deterministic* *model* **is one that, based on certain assumptions and laws, will predict exactly the outcome of a situation.**

The examples found in this chapter are of deterministic models. For examples of probabilistic models the reader is referred to Chapter 3.

4.1.1
Definition

How does one go about constructing a mathematical model? Once constructed, how can we be sure the model gives an accurate interpretation? How do we test models?

Many times the answers will depend on both the degree of accuracy wanted and on the degree of difficulty of a particular model. That is, a given physical event can sometimes be interpreted mathematically in more than one way, with one way giving more accurate results, but at the same time requiring more involved computation or deeper mathematical principles.

Other times, two different models for the same physical event may not be so easy to distinguish between. In these cases individual biases or historical bases may decide the "better" model.

Let us follow the historical development of a model from the field of astronomy. Early astronomers were concerned with explaining the behavior of the sun, moon, and planets. They watched both the sun and moon rise in the east and set in the west and concluded that both the sun and moon revolved about the earth in a circular orbit. This circular orbiting of the sun and moon about the earth is an interpretation of a physical event—a model. Through the use of this model, various conclusions, many of them valid, most of them false and contradictory, were arrived at.

Because of the many contradictions that arose, the model went through various changes and refinements. Finally, the famous astronomer Kepler proposed a model for planetary motion in which the planets moved about the sun in an elliptical path with the sun fixed at a focus of the ellipse. See Figure 4.1.

The model in Figure 4.1 led to results that closely agreed with observa-

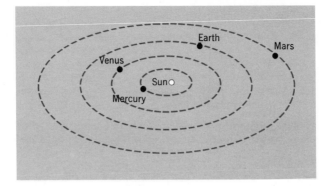

Figure 4.1

tions. Thus, a "better" (more accurate) model for explaining planetary motion had been discovered.

Later Newton's gravity principle was able to verify mathematically what Kepler had devised from observation. Thus, this Kepler model for planetary motion was accepted as being an accurate predictor of planetary behavior.

Still, slight discrepancies with observed fact occurred with the Kepler model. For example, slight aberrations in the orbit of Mercury were observed, but could not be explained by the Keplerian model. Einstein refined the Keplerian model so that the Mercury aberration was taken in account. Thus, the construction of a model is often an on-going process of continual refinements.

The above account answers in part the question of accuracy of models. The following example from the field of biology shows how a model can be constructed.

4.1.4
Example

Biologists are often concerned with the study of the reproduction of cells. They want to know how long it takes for an initial number of cells to grow to a given prescribed number of cells and they want to know what the rate of growth is for such cells.

To obtain the answers, a model is constructed to accurately describe the situation of cell growth. In the laboratory, a culture that contains cells of the type to be studied is observed. Cells multiply by dividing: each cell grows for a certain period of time and then divides into two separate parts. Each of these parts, in turn, grows and eventually divides into two parts. After observing this process for a long time, it can be determined that the time needed for a cell to grow and split into two separate parts is always about the same. Suppose t_0 seconds is the average time required for a single cell to grow and divide into two parts.

For the construction of the model, we *assume* that t_0 seconds is the exact time required for every cell of this type to grow and divide into two parts. Once we have made this assumption, we begin to build our model.

Suppose the function f is the law that relates time t to the number of cells N. That is

$$N = f(t)$$

If we can find out what the function f is, we have our model.

Now, if we start with a culture containing N_0 cells, we know that at time $t = 0$, there are N_0 cells. That is

$$N_0 = f(0)$$

After t_0 seconds, each cell has divided into two. Thus, after t_0 seconds there are $2N_0$ cells or

$$2N_0 = f(t_0)$$

After an additional t_0 seconds, the cells have divided again giving $4N_0$ cells after $2t_0$ seconds. That is

$$4N_0 = f(2t_0)$$

Continuing in this way, we obtain

$$8N_0 = f(3t_0) \text{ or } 2^3N_0 = f(3t_0)$$
$$16N_0 = f(4t_0) \text{ or } 2^4N_0 = f(4t_0)$$
$$\cdots$$

$$2^kN_0 = f(kt_0)$$

This formula is proper for integral multiples of t_0. To obtain a formula for any time t, we set $t = kt_0$. Then, since $k = t/t_0$, we have

$$f(t) = 2^{t/t_0} N_0$$

Thus, our model for cell division is that for an initial number N_0 of cells, which divide in two every t_0 seconds, there will be

$$2^{t/t_0} N_0$$

cells after t seconds.

Mitosis, or divisions of cells, is a universal process in the growth of living things such as amoeba, plants, and human skin cells. One of the few exceptions are human nerve cells. Of course, the above model is based on an ideal situation in which no cells die and no by-products are produced. In actuality, cells do die and by-products are produced so that after a period of time the growth rate is effectively reduced to almost zero instead of doubling. However, the above model accurately reflects what happens during the growth stage of mitosis.

The following model is from the field of social psychology.

In an organizational chart or in the Army, one person gives assignments or orders to others who, in turn, give orders to others, and so on. Such an organizational structure is termed a *command structure* or a *superior-subordinate structure* or a *hierarchy*.

4.1.5
Example

A typical internal organizational chart for a small college or university is given in Figure 4.2.

If we denote direct influence by a 1 and no influence or indirect influence by a 0 (we also use a 0 to denote influence on oneself), we can write the chart given in Figure 4.3.

Observe that the sum of the entries in a given row gives the total number of people influenced by that person; similarly, the sum of the entries in a given column provides the total number of people who influence that person. Thus, in the above example, the president directly influences four people,

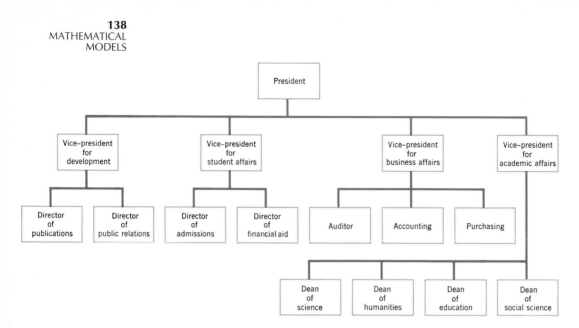

Figure 4.2

but he is directly influenced by no one. He also has two-stage influence over each director, the auditor, accountant, and so on.

In hierarchical structure, it is customary to speak of a *level of subordinacy*. This is defined to be the *smallest* number of stages from the superior to the subordinate.

For example, in Figure 4.4, each vice-president has a level of subordinacy of 1 with respect to the president; secretary k also has a level of subordinacy of 1 with respect to the president, while secretary i has a level of subordinacy of 2 with respect to the president.

	1	2	3	4	5	6	7	8	9	10	11	12	13	14	15	16	
1. President	0	1	1	1	1	0	0	0	0	0	0	0	0	0	0	0	1
2. V. P. Development	0	0	0	0	0	1	1	0	0	0	0	0	0	0	0	0	2
3. V. P. Stud. Aff.	0	0	0	0	0	0	0	1	1	0	0	0	0	0	0	0	3
4. V. P. Bus. Aff.	0	0	0	0	0	0	0	0	0	1	1	1	0	0	0	0	4
5. V. P. Acad. Aff.	0	0	0	0	0	0	0	0	0	0	0	0	1	1	1	1	5
6. Dir. of Publications	0	0	0	0	0	0	0	0	0	0	0	0	0	0	0	0	6
7. Dir. of Pub. Rel.	0	0	0	0	0	0	0	0	0	0	0	0	0	0	0	0	7
8. Dir. of Admiss.	0	0	0	0	0	0	0	0	0	0	0	0	0	0	0	0	8
9. Dir. of Fin. Aid	0	0	0	0	0	0	0	0	0	0	0	0	0	0	0	0	9
10. Auditor	0	0	0	0	0	0	0	0	0	0	0	0	0	0	0	0	10
11. Accounting	0	0	0	0	0	0	0	0	0	0	0	0	0	0	0	0	11
12. Purchasing	0	0	0	0	0	0	0	0	0	0	0	0	0	0	0	0	12
13. Dean of Science	0	0	0	0	0	0	0	0	0	0	0	0	0	0	0	0	13
14. Dean of Humanities	0	0	0	0	0	0	0	0	0	0	0	0	0	0	0	0	14
15. Dean of Educ.	0	0	0	0	0	0	0	0	0	0	0	0	0	0	0	0	15
16. Dean of Soc. Sc.	0	0	0	0	0	0	0	0	0	0	0	0	0	0	0	0	16

Figure 4.3

Next we wish to develop a measure for the status of each person in a hierarchical organization. If p is a person in such an organization, we shall denote his *measure of status* by the function $m(p)$ and we shall require the measure to have the following properties:

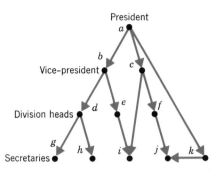

Figure 4.4

1. $m(p)$ is always a nonnegative whole number.
2. If p has no subordinates, then $m(p) = 0$.
3. If, without otherwise changing the structure, a new subordinate is added to p, then $m(p)$ will increase.
4. If, without otherwise changing the structure, a subordinate to p is moved to a lower level relative to p, then $m(p)$ will increase.

Harary[1] proposed the following formula for measuring the status of each person in a hierarchical organization.

If a person p has n_k subordinates in the kth stage relative to p, the Harary measure of status $m(p)$ is

$$m(p) = 1 \cdot n_1 + 2 \cdot n_2 + 3 \cdot n_3 + \cdots + k \cdot n_k$$

For example, in the organization of Figure 4.4, the Harary measure of each person is

$$m(a) = 1 \cdot 3 + 2 \cdot 5 + 3 \cdot 2 = 3 + 10 + 6 = 19$$
$$m(b) = 1 \cdot 2 + 2 \cdot 3 = 8$$
$$m(c) = 1 \cdot 2 + 2 \cdot 1 = 4$$
$$m(d) = 1 \cdot 2 = 2$$
$$m(e) = 1 \cdot 1 = 1 \qquad\qquad (4.1.3)$$
$$m(f) = 1 \cdot 1 = 1$$
$$m(g) = 0, \qquad m(h) = 0, \qquad m(i) = 0, \qquad m(j) = 0$$
$$m(k) = 1 \cdot 1 = 1$$

It is very important to notice that once a subordinate has been counted in the Harary measure, that person should not be counted again.

Although at first glance this measure appears to be a good model for measuring status, it does present certain difficulties as demonstrated in the organization of Figure 4.5.

The Harary measures for a and b are

$$m(a) = 1 \cdot 2 + 2 \cdot 4 + 3 \cdot 1 = 13$$
$$m(b) = 1 \cdot 2 + 2 \cdot 1 + 3 \cdot 1 + 4 \cdot 2 = 15$$

The Harary measure of status gives more status to b than to a, even though b is a subordinate of a.

To refine our model, we need to reexamine the way in which "level" is

[1] Harary, F. "A Criterion for Unanimity in French's Theory of Social Power," *Studies in Social Power*, D. Cartwright, Ed. (Ann Arbor, Mich.: Institute for Social Research, 1959).

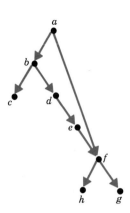

Figure 4.5

used. Instead of defining level of subordinate as the *smallest* number of stages from superior to subordinate we shall define it as the *largest* number of stages from superior to subordinate. Using this definition, the Harary measures of a and b are

$$m(a) = 1 \cdot 1 + 2 \cdot 2 + 3 \cdot 1 + 4 \cdot 1 + 5 \cdot 2 = 22$$
$$m(b) = 1 \cdot 2 + 2 \cdot 1 + 3 \cdot 1 + 4 \cdot 2 = 15$$

The next example is a model for computing distance between points.

4.1.6
Example

In high school geometry, we use the Pythagorean theorem as a model for computing distance. For example, if a man walks three blocks west and four blocks south, the shortest straight line distance from where he starts to where he ends up is

$$\sqrt{3^2 + 4^2} = \sqrt{9 + 16} = \sqrt{25} = 5$$

blocks. See Figure 4.6.

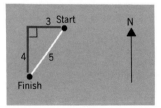

Figure 4.6

This model is perfectly accurate—provided the distances are small, that is, provided the spherical surface of the earth can be approximated well by a flat surface. However, once distances become large, this physical approximation is no longer accurate and, hence, the model is no longer accurate. Thus, if one travels 3000 miles west and then 4000 miles south, on the earth's surface, the shortest distance from start to finish is *not* 5000 miles but 4740 miles. See Figure 4.7.

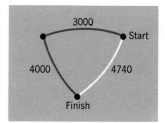

Figure 4.7

The result 4740 miles is obtained using spherical trigonometry, as opposed to plane trigonometry. Also, notice that the path is depicted as part of a circle, since we know the earth is roughly spherical. It is interesting to note that a slightly different answer is obtained if we use the circumference of the earth measured through the two poles rather than the circumference measured around the equator. This is because the earth is pear-shaped and not exactly spherical.

Next, we shall construct a model involving transportation of items. As we shall see in Chapter 6, this model can be used to solve many practical problems from business, geography, and health sciences.

Mary's File Cabinet House is a retailer of filing cabinets, having three stores at which the cabinets are sold and two warehouses in which they are stored. The company has solid information going back several years about the cost of shipping cabinets between each warehouse and each store and about the number of files stored in each warehouse and the number needed by each store. However, the company wants to know how many files should be stored in each warehouse so that each store can be sufficiently stocked, and at the same time keeping the shipping costs at a minimum.

4.1.7
Example

To solve the problem, the company sets the stock needed at store 1 to be S_1, store 2 to be S_2, and store 3 to be S_3. Similarly, the files kept at warehouse 1 is W_1 and warehouse 2 is W_2. Finally, the cost of shipping from warehouse 1 to store 1 will be C_{11}, from warehouse 2 to store 1 is C_{21}, and so on.

If the number of files shipped from warehouse 1 to store 1 is N_{11}, from warehouse 1 to store 2 is N_{12}, and so on, we can write a mathematical description of the above situation. Keep in mind that many variables have not been considered in this setup. The company assumes the other parameters involved are of little significance.

Now, store 1 must receive at least S_1 files. Thus, the number of files shipped to store 1 from warehouse 1 and warehouse 2 must exceed S_1. That is

$$N_{11} + N_{21} \geqq S_1$$

Similarly

$$N_{12} + N_{22} \geqq S_2$$
$$N_{13} + N_{23} \geqq S_3$$

Also, the number shipped from warehouse 1 cannot exceed the number stored in warehouse 1. That is

$$N_{11} + N_{12} + N_{13} \leqq W_1$$
$$N_{21} + N_{22} + N_{23} \leqq W_2$$

Finally, the cost function C of shipping is the sum of the number from warehouse 1 to store 1 times the cost C_{11}, the number from warehouse 1 to store 2 times the cost C_{12}, and so on. That is

$$C = N_{11} \cdot C_{11} + N_{12} \cdot C_{12} + N_{13} \cdot C_{13} + N_{21} \cdot C_{21} + N_{22} \cdot C_{22} + N_{23} \cdot C_{23}$$

Our problem then is to find the numbers $N_{11}, N_{12}, N_{13}, N_{21}, N_{22}, N_{23}$ so that the cost function C is as small as possible.

As stated, the above is called the *transportation problem*. Techniques for solving this and other related problems are considered in Chapter 6.

Our final example is a model from the field of economics.

4.1.8
Example

An elementary model of the dynamics of national income and how it varies with time can be constructed as follows. National income consists of three components; (1) consumer expenditures (amount spent on consumer goods), (2) government expenditures (the amount spent by the government), (3) induced private investments (the amount invested for capital improvements such as increasing factory space, machinery, and so on). We shall symbolize the above concepts as follows:

$Y(t)$: national income in the year t
$C(t)$: consumer expenditure in the year t
$G(t)$: government expenditure in the year t
$I(t)$: induced private investment in the year t

where it is assumed that the same fiscal year is used to measure each component.

Our assumption is that total national income in year t is the sum of consumer expenditure, government expenditure, and induced private investment. Thus

$$Y(t) = C(t) + G(t) + I(t) \tag{4.1.4}$$

Further assumptions made by economists are that

(a) The consumer expenditure is proportional to the national income of the previous year, that is,

$$C(t) = aY(t-1) \tag{4.1.5}$$

where the factor of proportionability, a, is called the *marginal propensity to consume*.

(b) Induced private investment in year t is proportional to the increase in consumption in year t over what it was in the preceding year, that is,

$$I(t) = b \cdot [C(t) - C(t-1)] \tag{4.1.6}$$

where b is positive and is called the *relation*.

Assumption (b) is sometimes called the *acceleration principle*.

(c) Government expenditure remains constant, that is, it is the same each year. Since government expenditure does not depend on t, we shall set

$$G(t) = G \qquad (4.1.7)$$

If we substitute (4.1.5), (4.1.6), and (4.1.7) into (4.1.4), the new formula for total national income is

$$
\begin{aligned}
Y(t) &= aY(t-1) + b[C(t) - C(t-1)] + G \\
&= aY(t-1) + b[aY(t-1) - aY(t-2)] + G \qquad (4.1.8) \\
&= a(1+b)Y(t-1) - abY(t-2) + G
\end{aligned}
$$

An equation of the form (4.1.8) is called a *difference equation of the second order.*

The above examples illustrate that mathematics cannot deal directly with real-world situations. In order to use mathematics to solve problems in real world, it is necessary to construct a mathematical model in which real life objects are represented by mathematical objects.

Jchn Synge[2] in 1961 described the modeling process as consisting of three stages:

(1) a dive from the world of reality into the world of mathematics
(2) a swim in the world of mathematics
(3) a climb from the world of mathematics back into the world of reality, carrying a prediction in our teeth.

The modeling process can be more concisely defined by using a flow chart, such as computer programmers use. See Figure 4.8.

To summarize, the flow chart in Figure 4.8 consists of the following steps:

(1) Remove from the original setting only the bare features of the real-world problem. This requires due examination of the original setting to gain direction in determining that which is fundamental. The result of such an effort is a simplified, idealized physical model of the original problem.
(2) Make this idealized model the subject of mathematical investigation by direct translation to mathematical terms. Essentially, this translation is a mathematical model of the idealized physical model of the original problem.
(3) Through manipulative computation obtain a solution for the mathematical model. In this stage there is no reference to the original setting or to the idealized physical model.
(4) Interpret the solution in terms of the idealized physical model.
(5) Finally, interpret the solution in terms of the original setting.

The validity of the results must be verified and depends upon the extent to which the models include all of the known pertinent facts.

Throughout this course in finite mathematics, applications, illustrations, examples, and problems of real-world situations will be solved or explained through the use of a model developed for this purpose. It is very important to remember that solutions or explanations given are in actuality solutions or explanations of a mathematical model, which is merely an interpretation of the real-world situation and may only approximate reality.

---

[2] Synge, John, "Mathematical Education Notes," *American Mathematical Monthly* 68 (October 1961), p. 799.

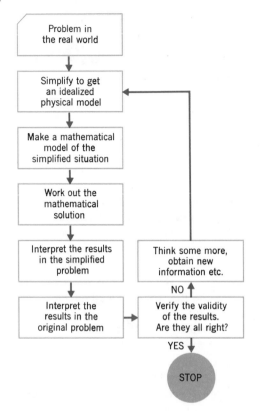

Figure 4.8

1. For the function $f(x) = 2x + 1$, find
   (a) $f(-2)$ (c) $f(12)$
   (b) $f(3)$ (d) $f(0)$
2. For the function $f(x) = 2x^3 + 1$, find
   (a) $f(1)$ (c) $f(h + 1)$
   (b) $f(h)$ (d) $f(2)$
3. For the function $f(x, y) = x^2y + x$, find
   (a) $f(-2, 3)$ (c) $f(x + 1, 0)$
   (b) $f(3, -2)$ (d) $f(0, 0)$
4. If a ball is dropped from a height of 128 feet, how long will it take for it to strike the ground? How far did it go in half this time?
5. Find the Harary measure of status for each person in the following organization using each definition of level of subordinacy.

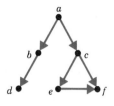

6. Find the Harary measure of status for each person in the organization given in Figure 4.4 using the largest number of stages as a definition of level. Compare and interpret these results with those given in (4.1.3).

7. The president of a small company with eight employees wants to organize his company so that his measure of status is the largest possible. What organization should he have? What organization gives him least status while keeping each employee a subordinate? (Use both definitions for level of subordinacy.)

8. Construct a model for cell growth if each cell in a culture divides into two parts every 5 seconds. If you begin with 1000 such cells, how many are there after 2 minutes? After one hour? Assume the growth stage lasts this long.

9. Construct a model for material decay if 1/2 of the original amount remains after a period of 2 years. If you start with 1 ton of such a material, how much remains after 50 years? After 200 years?

10. A radioactive substance has a half-life of 8 years. That is, if we start with a given amount of the radioactive substance, then after 8 years only 1/2 of the original amount is left; 8 years later 1/2 of the amount left after 8 years remains, and so on.
    (a) How long does it take for 3/4 of the substance to decay?
    (b) After 28 years, how much is left?
    (c) Assume even minute quantities of this substance will have the same half-life, how long does it take for the substance to disappear completely?

function
variable
dependent variable
probabilistic model
deterministic model
mitosis
command structure

hierarchy
superior-subordinate structure
level of subordinacy
measure of status
transportation problem
modeling process

Additional Reading

Kemeny, J. C. and Snell, J. L. *Mathematical Models in the Social Sciences,* Blaisdell Publishing Company, Waltham, Massachusetts, 1962.

Maki, Daniel P. and Thompson, Maynard, *Mathematical Models and Applications,* Indiana University, Bloomington, Indiana, 1972.

Linear Equations and Inequalities Chapter 5

A *real line* is a collection of points so that there is a one-to-one correspondence between the set $R\#$ of real numbers[1] and this collection of
points. If P denotes a point on a real line and if x is the real number associated to P, then x is called the *coordinate of P.*

There are many ways a one-to-one correspondence between real
numbers x and points P on the real line can be established. One way is to
pick a point O, called the *origin O*, and associate to O the real number
$x = 0$. Then, we establish a *unit of measurement* or *scale*, which may be one
inch, one foot, one light-year, and so on, depending on our needs. To that
point one unit to the right of the origin O, we associate the real number
$x = 1$; to that point one unit to the left of O, we associate the real number
$x = -1$. Continuing in this way, we obtain a coordinatization of the real
line. See Figure 5.1.

5.1
COORDINATE
SYSTEMS

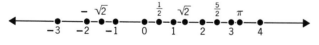

Figure 5.1

Suppose we have two real lines that are mutually perpendicular. Call the
horizontal line the *x-axis* and the vertical line the *y-axis*. Coordinatize each

---

[1]Students may wish to consult the Appendix for a brief review of the properties of real numbers.

of these lines as described earlier using their point of intersection as the origin O and using the same scale for each. It is not essential to always use the same scale. In fact, for most of our applications, a different scale will be used. If we follow the usual convention that points on the x-axis to the right of O are associated with positive real numbers, those to the left of O to negative numbers, those on the y-axis above O to positive numbers, and those on the y-axis below O to negative real numbers, we obtain Figure 5.2.

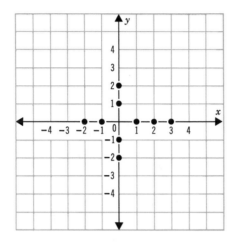

Figure 5.2

Now any point P in the plane can be located by using an ordered pair (x, y) of real numbers by the following method. Let x denote the signed distance of P from the y-axis (signed in the sense that if P is to the right of the y-axis, then $x > 0$ and if P is to the left of the y-axis, then $x < 0$). Let y denote the signed distance of P from the x-axis. Then, the ordered pair (x, y) gives us enough information to locate the point P. By following this procedure, we can assign ordered pairs of real numbers to every point P. In this way, we can *coordinatize the plane.* See Figure 5.3.

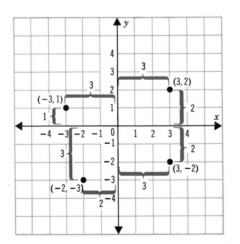

Figure 5.3

If (x, y) is the coordinate of a point P, then x is called the *abscissa of P* and y is the *ordinate of P*. For example, the coordinate of the origin O is $(0, 0)$. The abscissa of any point on the y-axis is zero.

The type of coordinate system introduced above is a *rectangular coordinate system*. Notice that it divides the plane into four sections. These sections are called *quadrants* and are depicted in Figure 5.4.

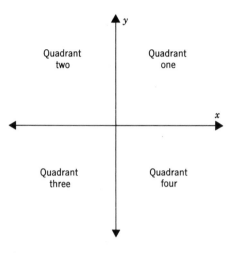

Figure 5.4

Notice that in Quadrant one, both the abscissa x and the ordinate y of all points P are positive.

The most important use of the preceding discussion will be for *graphing*. If $y = f(x)$ is a function, the set of all ordered pairs (x, y) for which $y = f(x)$ is called the *graph of the function f*.

Graph the function f defined by

$$f : y = x$$

5.1.1
Example

Here, we wish to locate all points (x, y) for which the abscissa x and ordinate y are equal. Some of these points are

$$(0, 0), (.1, .1), (1, 1), (1.5, 1.5), (-2, -2), (-.2, -.2), (8, 8)$$

The graph of f is given in Figure 5.5.

Graph the function f given by

$$f : y = 2x + 5$$

5.1.2
Example

Here, we want to find all points (x, y) for which the ordinate y equals twice the abscissa x plus 5. To locate some of these points (and thus to get an idea of the pattern of the graph), let us assign some values to x and find corresponding values for y. Thus:

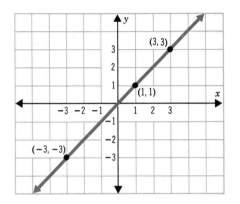

Figure 5.5

$$\text{if } x = 0, \qquad y = 2 \cdot 0 + 5 = 5$$
$$\text{if } x = 1, \qquad y = 2 \cdot 1 + 5 = 7$$
$$\text{if } x = -5, \quad y = 2 \cdot (-5) + 5 = -5$$
$$\text{if } x = 10, \qquad y = 2 \cdot (10) + 5 = 25$$

Graphing these points, we obtain Figure 5.6.

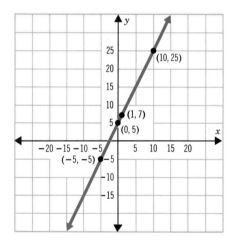

Figure 5.6

5.1
Exercise

1. Locate the following points in a rectangular coordinate system.
   - (a) $(3, -2)$
   - (b) $(-6, 5)$
   - (c) $(0, 5)$
   - (d) $(6, 0)$
   - (e) $(-3, -5)$
   - (f) $(4, 5)$
2. Label the points in Figure 5.7.

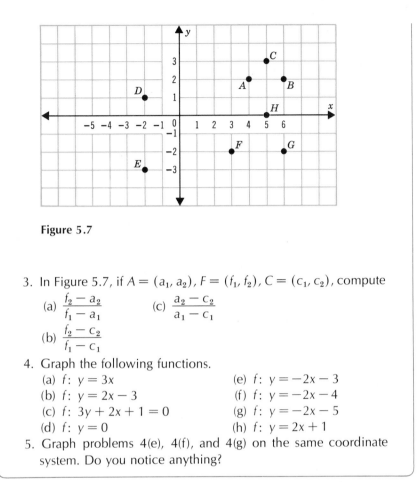

Figure 5.7

3. In Figure 5.7, if $A = (a_1, a_2)$, $F = (f_1, f_2)$, $C = (c_1, c_2)$, compute

   (a) $\dfrac{f_2 - a_2}{f_1 - a_1}$ (c) $\dfrac{a_2 - c_2}{a_1 - c_1}$

   (b) $\dfrac{f_2 - c_2}{f_1 - c_1}$

4. Graph the following functions.
   (a) $f: y = 3x$ (e) $f: y = -2x - 3$
   (b) $f: y = 2x - 3$ (f) $f: y = -2x - 4$
   (c) $f: 3y + 2x + 1 = 0$ (g) $f: y = -2x - 5$
   (d) $f: y = 0$ (h) $f: y = 2x + 1$
5. Graph problems 4(e), 4(f), and 4(g) on the same coordinate system. Do you notice anything?

In this section, we shall study a certain type of function f, the *linear function*, and its graph, the *straight line*. The information found in this section is of fundamental importance for the study of linear programming in Chapter 6.
   We begin by recalling a result from plane geometry.
   If P *and* Q *are two distinct points, there is one and only one line* L *containing* P *and* Q. *See Figure 5.8.*

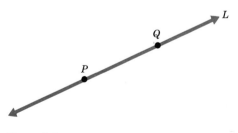

Figure 5.8

If we coordinatize the plane so that P and Q are both represented by ordered pairs of real numbers, the following definition can be given.

5.2.1
Definition

Let P and Q be two distinct points with coordinates (x_1, y_1) and (x_2, y_2), respectively. The *slope m of the line L* **containing P and Q is defined by the formula**

$$m = \frac{y_2 - y_1}{x_2 - x_1} \quad \text{if } x_1 \neq x_2$$

If $x_1 = x_2$, the slope m of L is said to be *undefined.*

In words, the slope m of the line L measures the ratio of the difference of the ordinates of P and Q to the difference of the abscissas of P and Q. Since

$$\frac{y_2 - y_1}{x_2 - x_1} = \frac{y_1 - y_2}{x_1 - x_2}$$

it will not matter which point is taken first in computing the slope m.

Geometrically, the slope m measures the "rise over run" of a line L. See Figure 5.9.

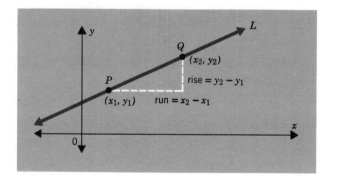

Figure 5.9

To get a better idea of the meaning of the slope of a line L, consider the following examples.

5.2.1
Example

Compute the slope of the line containing the following pairs of points. Graph each line so determined.

(a) $P = (2, 3)$, $Q_1 = (-1, -2)$
(b) $P = (2, 3)$, $Q_2 = (3, -1)$
(c) $P = (2, 3)$, $Q_3 = (5, 3)$
(d) $P = (2, 3)$, $Q_4 = (2, 5)$

Let m_1, m_2, m_3, m_4, denote the slopes of the lines L_1, L_2, L_3, L_4 given by the points P, Q_1; P, Q_2; P, Q_3; P, Q_4, respectively. Then

$$m_1 = \frac{-2-3}{-1-2} = \frac{-5}{-3} = \frac{5}{3}$$

$$m_2 = \frac{-1-3}{3-2} = \frac{-4}{1} = -4$$

$$m_3 = \frac{3-3}{5-2} = \frac{0}{3} = 0$$

$$m_4 \qquad \text{is undefined}$$

The graph of these lines is given in Figure 5.10.

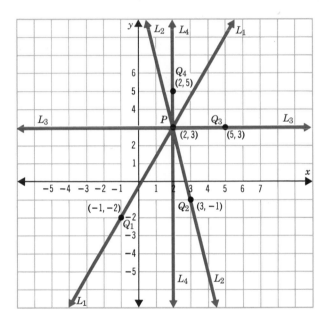

Figure 5.10

As the illustration indicates, when the slope m of a line is positive, the line *slants upward* from left to right (L_1); when the slope m is negative the line *slants downward* from left to right (L_2); when the slope $m = 0$, the line is horizontal (L_3); and when the slope m is undefined, the line is vertical (L_4).

We can also recognize something else regarding the slope of a line. Since slopes measure rise over run of two points on a line and since a line has a constant or never-changing rise over run, it can be concluded that the slope of a line L will be the same no matter what two distinct points on L are used. That this is indeed the case is easily vertified by using the notion of similar triangles.

Let L be a line joining P and Q and let X and Y be any other distinct points on L. Construct the triangles depicted in Figure 5.11. Since $\triangle PQA$ is

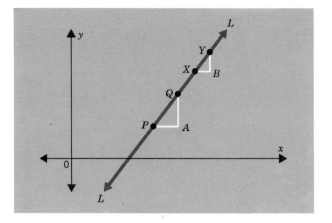

Figure 5.11

similar to $\triangle XYB$ (why?), it follows that corresponding sides are in proportion. That is

$$\frac{AQ}{BY} = \frac{AP}{BX}$$

Or

$$\frac{AQ}{AP} = \frac{BY}{BX} \qquad (5.2.1)$$

But the slope m of L is

$$m = \frac{AQ}{AP}$$

By (5.2.1), we see that

$$m = \frac{BY}{BX}$$

Thus, since X, Y were arbitrary, we see that *the slope m of a line L is the same no matter what points on L are used to compute m.*

With this fact, we can now proceed to find out what relationship exists between the abscissa x and ordinate y of a point $P = (x, y)$ on a given line L — that is, we can ask which functions $y = f(x)$ give a straight line.

We begin by answering an easier question. What property will every point $P = (x, y)$ on a vertical line L have? For a vertical line L, the abscissa x of every point on L is the same, while the ordinate y varies. Thus we have Theorem 5.2.1.

Theorem 5.2.1
A vertical line is represented by

$$x = a$$

where a is fixed.

Notice that the slope m of a vertical line is undefined.

Graph all points (x, y) that obey

$$x = 3$$

By Theorem 5.2.1, this is a vertical line and its graph is given in Figure 5.12.

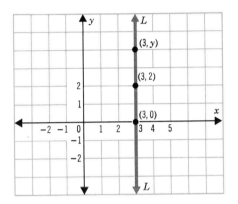

Figure 5.12

Next, consider the question of nonvertical lines. Suppose $P_1 = (x_1, y_1)$ and $P_2 = (x_2, y_2)$ are two distinct points on a line L. (Since L is assumed to be nonvertical, we know that $x_1 \neq x_2$.) Suppose $P(x, y)$ is *any* point on L. Then, since the slope m on L is the same no matter what two points are used, we can compute m by using P_1, P_2 and by using P_1, P. Then

$$m = \frac{y_2 - y_1}{x_2 - x_1}, \qquad m = \frac{y - y_1}{x - x_1}$$

Setting the values of m equal gives

$$\frac{y_2 - y_1}{x_2 - x_1} = \frac{y - y_1}{x - x_1}$$

Or, simplifying,

$$y - y_1 = \left(\frac{y_2 - y_1}{x_2 - x_1}\right)(x - x_1)$$

Theorem 5.2.2
The function f that defines a nonvertical line L passing through $P_1 = (x_1, y_1)$, $P_2 = (x_2, y_2)$ is

$$f: \quad y = y_1 + \frac{(y_2 - y_1)}{(x_2 - x_1)}(x - x_1)$$

This is sometimes called the *two-point form* of a line L.

Corollary

The function f that defines a nonvertical line L of slope m and passing through the point (x_1, y_1) is

$$f: y = y_1 + m(x - x_1) \tag{5.2.2}$$

This is sometimes called the *point-slope form of a line L.*
The proof is evident since the slope m of a nonvertical line L is

$$m = \frac{(y_2 - y_1)}{(x_2 - x_1)} \quad x_1 \neq x_2$$

5.2.3 Find the function f that defines that line L passing through the points $(2, 3)$
Example and $(-4, 5)$. Graph the line L.
Here, since two points are given, we use the two point form to find f. Thus

$$f: y = 3 + \frac{(5 - 3)}{(-4 - 2)}(x - 2)$$

or

$$f: y = 3 + \frac{2}{-6}(x - 2) \text{ or } y = -\frac{1}{3}x + \frac{11}{3}$$

Simplifying gives

$$f: x + 3y - 11 = 0$$

The graph of f is given in Figure 5.13.

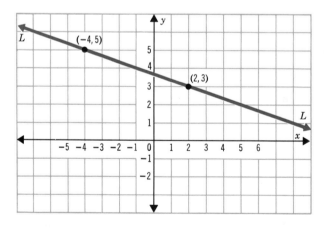

Figure 5.13

Usually, the function f defining a line L is called the *equation of the line L.*

5.2.4 Find the equation of the line L with slope 4 and passing through the point
Example $(1, 2)$.

Since we know the slope m and a point P, we use the point-slope form of a line. Then by (5.2.2), we have

$$y = 2 + 4(x - 1)$$

Or

$$4x - y - 2 = 0$$

Now to graph this line L, we need to know two points. To find another point on L, we assign an arbitrary value to x, say $x = 0$. Then when $x = 0$, $y = -2 + 4(0) = -2$. Thus, $(0, -2)$ is also on L. The graph of L is given in Figure 5.14.

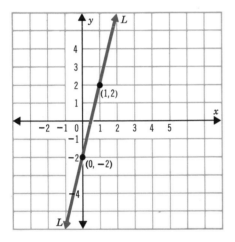

Figure 5.14

The fact that the slope $m = 4 > 0$ agrees with the fact that L moves upward from left to right.

In Example 5.2.4, we needed to find another point on L and set $x = 0$ to find the point on the x-axis. Those points on a line L at which the axes are crossed are of special importance.

Those points, if there are any, at which the graph of a line L crosses the axes are called *intercepts*. **The** *x-intercept* **is the abscissa of the point at which the line crosses the x-axis and the** *y-intercept* **is the ordinate of the point at which the y-axis is crossed.**

5.2.2
Definition

See Figure 5.15.

If we know the slope m of a line L and if we know its y-intercept is b, then we know both the slope m of L and a point of L, namely, $(0, b)$, and can find the equation of L by using the point-slope form. Then, we obtain

$$y - b = m(x - 0)$$

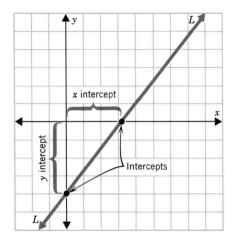

Figure 5.15

or

$$y = mx + b$$

Theorem 5.2.3
The equation of a line L with slope m and y-intercept b is

$$y = mx + b \qquad (5.2.3)$$

This is called the *slope-intercept form of a line L.*

5.2.5
Example

For the line

$$y = -3x + 6$$

the slope is -3 and the y-intercept is 6. Its graph is given in Figure 5.16.
Sometimes it is more convenient to write the equation of a line L in the *general form,* namely,

$$Ax + By + C = 0$$

where A, B, and C are three real numbers with either $A \neq 0$ or $B \neq 0$.

5.2.6
Example

Find the slope m and y-intercept b of the line L given by

$$2x + 4y - 8 = 0 \qquad (5.2.4)$$

Graph the line.
Here, we wish to transform (5.2.4) so that it looks like (5.2.3). To do this, solve (5.2.4) for y. Then

$$4y = -2x + 8$$
$$y = -\tfrac{1}{2}x + 2$$

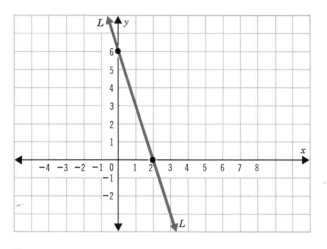

Figure 5.16

Comparing this to $y = mx + b$, we see that

$$m = -\tfrac{1}{2}, \qquad b = 2$$

Thus, the line L given by (5.2.4) has slope $m = -1/2$ and y-intercept $b = 2$.

To graph L, we need one other point on L [since we only know that $(0, 2)$ is on L]. The x-intercept of L can be formed by setting $y = 0$ and finding x. Then, $x = 4$.

Thus, the x-intercept is 4 and $(4, 0)$ is on L. See Figure 5.17.

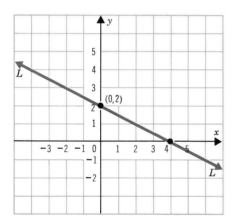

Figure 5.17

The theorems given earlier can be used either to find the equation of a line L when information is known about L (such as its slope m, etc.) or to find out information about L when its equation is known.

1. Find the slope m of the lines joining the following pairs of points.
   (a) $P_1 = (2, 3)$, $P_2 = (0, 1)$
   (b) $P_1 = (1, 1)$, $P_2 = (5, -6)$
   (c) $P_1 = (-3, 0)$, $P_2 = (-5, -4)$
   (d) $P_1 = (4, -3)$, $P_2 = (0, 0)$
   (e) $P_1 = (.1, .3)$, $P_2 = (1.5, 4.0)$
   (f) $P_1 = (-3, -2)$, $P_2 = (6, -2)$

2. Find the equations of the lines passing through the points given in Problem 1. Graph these lines.

3. Find the equations of the lines with the properties
   (a) slope $m = 1/2$, passing through $(-2, 3)$
   (b) slope $m = 0$, passing through $(-2, 0)$
   (c) slope $m = -3$, passing through $(0, 0)$
   (d) passing through the points $(0, 3)$ and $(1, 1)$
   (e) slope $m = 2$, y-intercept $= 3$
   (f) slope $m = 3$, x-intercept $= 1/2$
   (g) x-intercept $= -3$, y-intercept $= -1/2$
   Graph each line.

4. Copy and complete each of the values of the given equations.

   (a) $y = x - 3$ 　　　　　　(b) $y = \frac{1}{2}x - \dfrac{1}{17}$

x	0	.1	$-\frac{1}{2}$		5	
y			3	.2		-6

x		.2		-3	0		$\frac{3}{2}$		18
y	0		4			$\frac{1}{2}$		1	

   (c) $2x - y = 6$

x	$\frac{1}{2}$			.2		-4
y		2	.3		-3	

5. Find the slope m, and y-intercept of the following lines. Graph each line.
   (a) $3x - 2y = 6$ 　　　　　　(e) $y = 5$
   (b) $x + y = 0$ 　　　　　　(f) $2x - 2y = 1$
   (c) $2x + 5y = 10$ 　　　　　(g) $y = x$
   (d) $x = 2$ 　　　　　　　　(h) $-2x + y = 6$

6. The annual sales of Motors Incorporated for the past five years are

Years	Units Sold (in thousands)
1967	2200
1968	2800
1969	3100
1970	3200
1971	3400

(a) Graph this information using the x-axis for years and the y-axis for units sold. (For convenience, use a different scale on the axes.)
(b) Draw a line L that passes through two of the points and comes close to passing through the remaining points.
(c) Find the equation of the line L.
(d) Using the equation of the line, what is your estimate for units sold in 1972?

Let L and M be two lines. There are three possibilities for these two lines L and M.

5.3
INTERSECTING
LINES

(a) Either all the points on L are the same as the points on M.
(b) Or L and M have exactly one point in common.
(c) Or L and M have no points in common.

For the first possibility, the lines L and M are called *identical*. In this case, their slopes and their intercepts will be the same. Henceforth, we assume the lines L and M are distinct.

Let L and M be two (distinct) lines. If L and M have exactly one point P in common, then L and M are said to *intersect* **and the common point P is called the** *point of intersection.* **If L and M have no points in common, they are said to be** *parallel.*

5.3.1
Definition

First, we shall discuss the case in which L and M are *parallel*. If L and M are two lines with no points in common, then the rise over run of each must be the same. Otherwise, they would eventually meet. Thus

Two lines L and M are parallel if and only if their slopes are equal.

The two lines

5.3.1
Example

$$L:\ 2x + 3y - 4 = 0, \qquad M:\ 4x + 6y - 12 = 0$$

are parallel.
The slope m_L of L and the slope m_M of M are

$$m_L = -\frac{2}{3}, \ m_M = -\frac{2}{3}$$

Their graphs are given in Figure 5.18.
Next, suppose we have two lines L and M which intersect. There is a point (x, y) that is on both L and M. This means that some value of x and some value of y will satisfy the equation of L *and* the equation of M. The next ex-

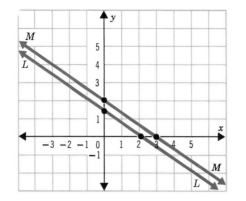

Figure 5.18

ample shows how this fact is used to find the common point of two inter-secting lines.

Find the point P of intersection of the two lines.

$$L: x + y - 5 = 0, \qquad M: 2x + y - 6 = 0$$

Let the coordinates of the point P of intersection of L and M be (x_0, y_0). Since (x_0, y_0) is on both L and M, then

$$x_0 + y_0 - 5 = 0, \qquad 2x_0 + y_0 - 6 = 0$$

Thus

$$y_0 = 5 - x_0, \qquad y_0 = -2x_0 + 6$$

Setting these equal, we obtain

$$5 - x_0 = 6 - 2x_0$$
$$x_0 = 1$$

If $x_0 = 1$, then $y_0 = 5 - x_0 = 4$. Thus, the point P of intersection of L and M is $(1, 4)$. To check this result, we see if $(1, 4)$ is on both L and M. Since

$$1 + 4 - 5 = 0, \qquad 2 \cdot 1 + 4 - 6 = 0$$

$(1, 4)$ is the point of intersection

The graph of Example 5.3.2 is given by Figure 5.19.

The technique given in the previous example for finding the point P of in-tersection of two lines is sometimes called the "substitution technique," since the value for y in one equation is substituted for the value of y in the other equation.

This technique can also be used to solve a *system of two linear equations in two unknowns*. A *system of two linear equations in two unknowns* x and y

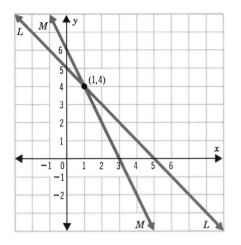

Figure 5.19

is of the form

$$L: Ax + By + C = 0$$
$$M: A_1x + B_1y + C_1 = 0$$

in which A, B, C, A_1, B_1, C_1 are real numbers.

A *solution* (x, y) of such a system is an ordered pair of real numbers that satisfies both equations. Finding the solution (x, y) of a system of two linear equations in two unknowns is the same as finding the point P of intersection of the two lines determined by the equation. Of course, if the equations of a system represent parallel lines, there will be no solution; if the equation represents identical lines, any point P on one of the lines will be a solution (in this case there is an infinite number of solutions).

Find the solution, if there is one, of the system of two linear equations in two unknowns.

5.3.3
Example

$$2x + y + 6 = 0$$
$$4x + 2y + 8 = 0$$

If we treat these equations as lines, we can place them in slope-intercept form as

$$y = -2x - 6$$
$$y = -2x - 4$$

Notice that each of these lines has a slope of -2. Since their y-intercepts are different (one is -6, the other -4), these equations represent two parallel lines. Hence, there are no values (x, y) that satisfy both equations. That is, the system has no solution. See Figure 5.20.

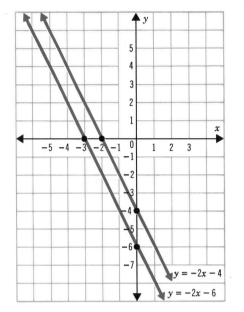

Figure 5.20

5.3.4
Example

Nutt's Nuts, a store that specializes in selling nuts, sells cashews for $1.50 per pound and peanuts for $0.80 per pound. At the end of the month it is found that the peanuts are not selling well. In order to sell 30 pounds of peanuts more quickly, Mr. Nutt decides to mix the 30 pounds of peanuts with some cashews and sell the mixture of peanuts and cashews for $1.00 a pound. How many pounds of cashews should be mixed with the peanuts so that his profits remain the same?

Here, there are two unknowns: the number of pounds of cashews (call this x) and the number of pounds of the mixture (call this y). Then, we know that the number of pounds of cashews plus 30 pounds of peanuts equals the number of pounds of the mixture. That is

$$y = x + 30$$

Also, in order to keep profits the same, we must have

(pounds of cashews) · (price per pound) + (pounds of peanuts) · (price per pound) = (pounds of mixture) · (price per pound)

That is

$$(1.50)x + (0.80)(30) = (1.00)y$$

Thus, we have a system of two linear equations in two unknowns to solve, namely,

$$y = x + 30$$
$$y = \tfrac{3}{2}x + 24$$

Here

$$\tfrac{3}{2}x + 24 = x + 30, \qquad \text{or} \qquad x = 12$$

Thus, the owner should mix 12 pounds of cashews with 30 pounds of peanuts. See Figure 5.21.

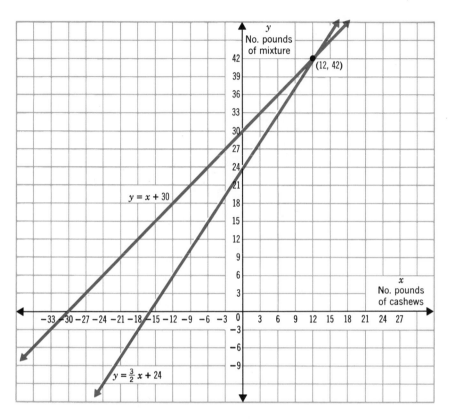

Figure 5.21

Thus far, we have discussed the meaning of *two* lines having a single point in common. It is conceivable that *three* distinct lines could have exactly one point in common.

Three distinct lines L, M, **and** N **having a single point** P **in common are said to be** *concurrent* **and the point** P **is called the** *point of concurrency*.

5.3.2
Definition

See Figure 5.22.

To test whether three lines L, M, and N are concurrent, merely find the points of intersection of L and M. If the point of intersection of L and M is also on the line N, the three lines are concurrent. Otherwise, they are not concurrent.

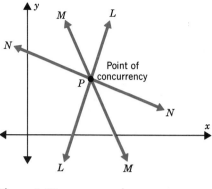

Figure 5.22

5.3.5
Example
Determine whether the lines

$$L: 9x + 2y - 10 = 0$$
$$M: 2x + y - 2 = 0$$
$$N: x + 3y = 0$$

are concurrent.

Here, we place the lines L and M in slope-intercept form. Then

$$L: y = -9/2 \times +5$$
$$M: y = -2x + 2$$

The point P of intersection of L and M is found to be

$$P: x = \frac{6}{5}, \qquad y = -\frac{2}{5}$$

To see if $P(6/5, -2/5)$ is on the line N, we test

$$\frac{6}{5} + 3\left(-\frac{2}{5}\right) = \frac{6}{5} - \frac{6}{5} = 0$$

Thus, $(6/5, -2/5)$ is also on N and L, M, and N are concurrent. See Figure 5.23.

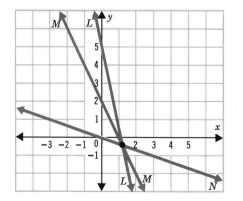

Figure 5.23

A *system of three linear equations in two unknowns* is of the form

$$A_1x + B_1y + C_1 = 0$$
$$A_2x + B_2y + C_2 = 0$$
$$A_3x + B_3y + C_3 = 0$$

in which A_1, A_2, A_3, B_1, B_2, B_3, C_1, C_2, C_3 are real numbers. A *solution* of this system is an ordered pair (x, y) that obeys all three equations.

To find the solution (if there is one) of a system of three equations in two unknowns, merely treat each equation as a line and determine if the three lines given in the system have a point in common. If they do, this point is the solution of the system; if they do not have a point in common, the system has no solution.

5.3
Exercise

1. Determine whether the following lines are identical, parallel, or intersecting. If they intersect, find the point P of intersection. Graph each pair of lines.

(a) L: $2x - 3y + 6 = 0$
    M: $4x - 6y + 7 = 0$

(b) L: $-2x + 3y + 6 = 0$
    M: $4x - 6y - 12 = 0$

(c) L: $3x - 3y + 10 = 0$
    M: $x + y - 2 = 0$

(d) L: $4x - y + 2 = 0$
    M: $3x + 2y = 0$

(e) L: $2x + 3y - 5 = 0$
    M: $5x - 6y + 1 = 0$

(f) L: $2x - 5y - 1 = 0$
    M: $x - 2y - 1 = 0$

2. Are the following lines concurrent? If they are, find the point of concurrency. Graph all lines.

(a) L: $3x - 2y - 5 = 0$
    M: $x + 3y - 9 = 0$
    N: $3x - y - 7 = 0$

(b) L: $2x - y + 5 = 0$
    M: $3x - y + 5 = 0$
    N: $3x + 2y - 10 = 0$

(c) L: $x - y + 2 = 0$
    M: $x - y + 3 = 0$
    N: $2x - y + 2 = 0$

(d) L: $-x + y - 3 = 0$
    M: $3x - 2y = 0$
    N: $3x - 3y + 5 = 0$

(e) L: $2x - 3y + 1 = 0$
    M: $4x + 2y - 5 = 0$
    N: $x - y = 0$

3. Sweet Delight Candys, Inc. sells boxes of candy consisting of creams and caramels. Each box sells for $4.00 and holds 50 pieces of candy (all pieces are of the same size). If the caramels cost $.05 to produce and the creams cost $.10 to produce, how many caramels and creams should be in each box for no profit or loss? Would you increase or decrease the number of caramels in order to obtain a profit?

4. Mr. Nicholson has just retired and needs $4000 per year in income to live on. He has $50,000 to invest and can invest in AAA bonds at 9 percent annual interest or in Savings and Loan Certificates at 7 percent interest per year. How much money should be invested in each so that he realizes exactly $4000 in income per year?

5. Mr. Nicholson finds after one year that because of inflation he now needs $4200 per year to live on. How should he transfer

his funds to achieve this amount? (Use the same data as in Problem 4.)

6. Mr. Nutt, owner of Nutt's Nuts, regularly sells cashews for $1.50 per pound, pecans for $1.80 per pound, and peanuts for $0.80 per pound. How many pounds of cashews and pecans should be mixed with 40 pounds of peanuts to obtain a mixture of 100 pounds that will sell at $1.25 a pound so that the profit or loss is unchanged?

7. Mike has $1.65 in his piggy bank. He knows he only placed nickels and quarters in the bank and he knows that, in all, he put 13 coins in the bank. Can he find out how many nickels he has without breaking his bank?

8. A coffee manufacturer wants to market a new blend of coffee that will cost $.90 per pound, by mixing $.75 per pound coffee and $1 per pound coffee. What amounts of the $.75 per pound coffee and $1 per pound coffee should be blended to obtain the desired mixture? Hint: Assume the total weight of the desired blend is 100 pounds.

9. One solution is 15 percent acid and another is 5 percent acid. How many cubic centimeters of each should be mixed to obtain 100 c.c. of a solution that is 8 percent acid?

10. A bank loaned $10,000, some at an annual rate of 8 percent and some at an annual rate of 18 percent. If the income from these loans was $1000, how much was loaned at 8 percent? How much at 18 percent?

11. The Star Theatre wants to know whether the majority of its patrons are adults or children. During a week in July, 5200 tickets were sold and the receipts totaled $11,875. The adult admission is $2.75 and the children's admission is $1.50. How many adult patrons were there?

12. After one hour of a car ride, 1/3 of the total distance is covered. One hour later, the car is 18 miles past the halfway point. What is the speed of the car (assumed constant for the trip) and what is the total distance to be covered? How long will the trip take? (Hint: distance = speed · time.)

**5.4
BREAK-EVEN
ANALYSIS**

In many businesses, the cost of production C can be expressed as a linear function of the number x of items produced. Similarly, the amount A obtained from sales can also be given as a linear function of the number x of items produced. It is clear that when the cost of production C exceeds the amount A from sales, the business is operating at a loss; if the amount A exceeds the cost C, then there is a profit; when the amount A and the cost C are equal, there is no profit or loss—this value is usually referred to as the *break-even point.*

**5.4.1
Example**

Sweet Delight Candies, Inc. has a daily overhead from salaries and building operation of $300. Each pound of candy produced costs $1 and is sold for

$2 per pound. What is the break-even point—that is, how many pounds of candy must be sold daily to guarantee no loss and no profit?

Here the cost of production C is the overhead cost plus the cost of producing x pounds of candy at $1 per pound. Thus

$$C = \$1 \cdot x + \$300$$

The amount A gained from the sale of x pounds of candy at $2 per pound is

$$A = \$2 \cdot x$$

The break-even point is that point at which these two lines meet. Thus, setting $A = C$, we find

$$x + 300 = 2x \qquad \text{or} \qquad x = 300$$

That is, 300 pounds of candy must be sold in order to break-even. See Figure 5.24 for a graphical interpretation.

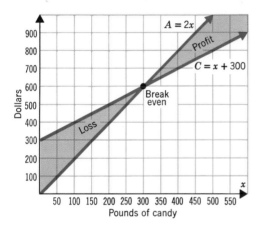

Figure 5.24

After a negotiation with employees of Sweet Delight Candies and an increase in the price of chocolate, the daily cost of production C for each pound x of candy is

5.4.2
Example

$$C = \$1.05x + \$330$$

(a) If each pound is sold for $2, how many must be sold daily to break even?
(b) If the selling is increased to $2.25 per pound, what is the break even point? (c) If it is known that at least 325 pounds of candy can be sold daily, what price should be charged per pound to guarantee no loss?

(a) If each pound is sold for $2, the amount A from sales is

$$A = \$2x$$

where x represents the number of pounds sold. The break-even point obeys

$$2x = 1.05x + 330$$
$$0.95x = 330$$

$$x = \frac{33000}{95} = 347.37$$

Thus, if 347 pounds are sold, a loss is incurred; if 348 pounds are sold, a profit results.

(b) If the selling price is increased to $2.25 per pound, the amount A from sales is

$$A = \$2.25x$$

The break-even point obeys

$$2.25x = 1.05x + 330$$
$$1.2x = 330$$
$$x = \frac{3300}{12} = 275$$

With the new selling price, the break-even point is 275 pounds.

(c) If we know at least 325 pounds will be sold daily, the price per pound p needed to guarantee no loss (that is, to guarantee at worst a break-even point) obeys

$$325p = (1.05)(325) + 330$$
$$325p = 671.25$$
$$p = \$2.07$$

We should charge approximately $2.07 per pound to guarantee at worst break even if at least 325 pounds will be sold.

5.4.3
Example

A producer sells items for $0.30 each. If his cost for production is

$$C = \$0.15x + \$105$$

where x is the number of items sold, find his break-even point. If he can change his cost to

$$C = \$.12x + \$110$$

would it be to his advantage to do so?

First, the amount A received is

$$A = \$.3x$$

The break-even point obeys

$$0.3x = 0.15x + 105$$
$$0.15x = 105$$
$$x = 700$$

Thus, for the first cost function, the break-even point is 700 items.

To determine the answer to the second part, we turn to the graph in Figure 5.25. Notice that the break-even point caused by the new cost function is $x = 611.11$. The old break-even point was $x = 700$. Thus, the new cost function will require less items to be sold in order to break-even. All other things being equal, management should change over to the new cost function.

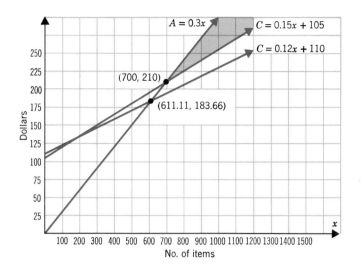

Figure 5.25

The supply function in economics is used to specify the amount of a particular commodity that sellers have available to offer in the market at various prices. The demand function specifies the amount of a particular commodity that buyers are willing to purchase at various prices. Let S denote the supply at price p and D denote the amount demanded at price p.

It is well known that an increase in price causes an increase in the supply but a decrease in demand; on the other hand, a decrease in price brings

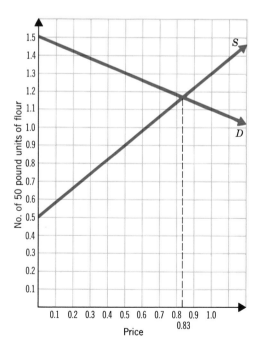

Figure 5.26

about a decrease in supply and an increase in demand. The market price is defined as the price at which supply and demand are equal.

5.4.4
Example

The supply and demand functions for flour during the period 1920 to 1935 were estimated as being given by the equations

$$S = 0.8p + 0.5, \qquad D = -0.4p + 1.5$$

where p is measured in dollars and S and D are measured in 50 pound units of flour. Find the market price and graph the supply and demand functions.

The market price is the point of intersection of the two lines. Thus, the market price p is the solution of

$$0.8p + 0.5 = -0.4p + 1.5$$
$$1.2p = 1$$
$$p = 0.83$$

The graphs are given in Figure 5.26.

5.4
Exercise

1. Find the break-even point for the cost of production C and the amount A received for each of the following and graph each result.
   (a) $C = \$10x + \$600, \qquad A = \$30x$
   (b) $C = \$5x + \$200, \qquad A = \$8$
   (c) $C = \$0.2x + \$50, \qquad A = \$0.3x$
   (d) $C = \$1800x + \$3000, \qquad A = \$2500x$
2. A manufacturer produces items at a daily cost to him of $0.75 per item and sells them for $1 per item. His daily operational overhead is $300. What is his break-even point? Graph your result.
3. If the manufacturer of Problem 2 is able to reduce his cost per item to $0.65 but with an increase to $350 in operational overhead, is it to his advantage to do so? Graph your result.
4. The supply and demand functions for sugar from 1890 to 1915 were estimated by H. Schulz[3] to be given by

$$S = 0.7p + 0.4, \qquad D = -0.5p + 1.6$$

Find the market price. What quantity of supply is demanded at this market price? Graph both the supply function and demand function. Interpret the point of intersection of the two lines.

5.5
LINEAR
INEQUALITIES

We have already discussed linear equations or linear equalities, namely, equations of the form

$$Ax + By + C = 0 \qquad (5.5.1)$$

---

[3] H. Schulz, *Statistical Laws of Demand and Supply with Special Applications to Sugar*, Univ. of Chicago Press, Chicago, 1928.

where A, B, C are real numbers. If we replace the equal sign in (5.5.1) by either $>$, $<$, $\geqq$, or $\leqq$[4] we obtain a *linear inequality*.

Thus,

$$2x + 3y - 6 \geqq 0, \qquad 3x - 4y + 7 < 0$$

are examples of linear inequalities. The following example will indicate a technique for graphing linear inequalities.

Graph the set of points (x, y) obeying

$$2x + 3y - 6 \geqq 0 \qquad\qquad (5.5.2)$$

5.5.1
Example

First, we shall find the graph of the line

$$L: 2x + 3y - 6 = 0 \qquad\qquad (5.5.3)$$

Since any point on the line L of (5.5.3) will obey (5.5.2), these points are in the set of points obeying (5.5.2). [If the $\geqq$ in (5.5.2) were replaced by $>$, the points on the line L would *not* be in the set of points obeying (5.5.2).] See Figure 5.27.

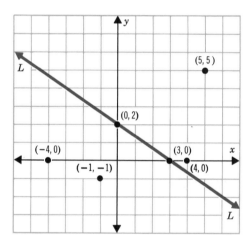

Figure 5.27

Let us begin to test a few points, such as $(-1, -1)$, $(5, 5)$ $(4, 0)$, $(-4, 0)$. Now

$$(-1, -1): \ 2(-1) + 3(-1) - 6 = -2 - 3 - 6 = -11 < 0$$

Thus, $(-1, -1)$ is not part of the graph. Next

$$(5, 5): \ 2(5) + 3(5) - 6 = 25 - 6 = 19 > 0$$

Thus, $(5, 5)$ is part of the graph. Also

$$(4, 0): \ 2(4) + 3(0) - 6 = 8 - 6 = 2 > 0$$
$$(-4, 0): \ 2(-4) + 3(0) - 6 = -8 - 6 = -14 < 0$$

[4] A quick review of the definition of these symbols is found in the Appendix.

Thus, (4, 0) is on the graph but (−4, 0) is not. Notice that the two points (4, 0) and (5, 5) that are on the graph both lie on one side of *L* and the points (−4, 0) and (−1, −1) (not on the graph) lie on the other side of *L*. This is not an accident. The graph of (5.5.2) is the shaded region of Figure 5.28.

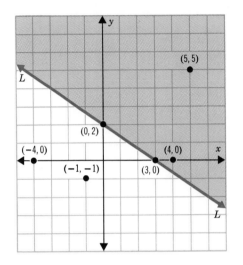

Figure 5.28

The following rules should be used to graph linear inequalities:

1. Graph the corresponding linear equality, a line *L*.
2. Find *one* point not on the line *L* that obeys the linear inequality.
3. All other points obeying the linear inequality will lie on the same side of *L* as the one found in the previous rule.

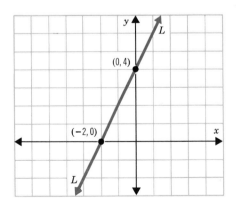

Figure 5.29

Graph the linear inequality

$$2x - y + 4 < 0$$

The corresponding linear equation is the line

$$L: 2x - y + 4 = 0$$

For its graph, see Figure 5.29.

We select two points on either side of L to be tested, for example $(0, 0)$ and $(-5, 0)$. Then

$$(0, 0): 2(0) - 0 + 4 = 4 > 0$$
$$(-5, 0): 2(-5) - 0 + 4 = -10 + 4 = -6 < 0$$

Thus $(0, 0)$ is not on the graph, but $(-5, 0)$ is. All points on the same side of L as $(-5, 0)$ are on the graph.

Since no point on L can be on the graph (why?), the graph is the shaded region of Figure 5.30 in which the line L is dotted to indicate it is not part of the graph.

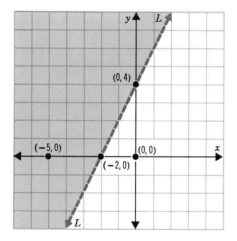

Figure 5.30

The set of points belonging to the graph of a linear inequality is sometimes called a *half-plane*.

Recall that a system of two distinct linear equations in two unknowns either has no solution (if the lines are parallel) or one solution (if they intersect). A system of two distinct linear inequalities in two unknowns, as will be seen, will have a certain region of the x, y plane as a solution.

That this is the case can be seen by considering two linear inequalities. Let L and M be the lines corresponding to these linear inequalities. Suppose L and M intersect. See Figure 5.31.

The two lines L and M divide the plane into four regions a, b, c, and d. One of these regions is the solution of the system. If the lines L and M are

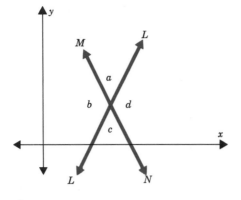

Figure 5.31

parallel, the system of linear inequalities may or may not have a solution. Examples of such situations are given below.

5.5.3
Example

Graph the system

$$2x - y + 4 < 0$$
$$x + y + 1 \geqq 0 \qquad (5.5.4)$$

The lines corresponding to each of these linear inequalities are

$$L: 2x - y + 4 = 0$$
$$M: x + y + 1 = 0$$

The graphs of L and M are given in Figure 5.32.

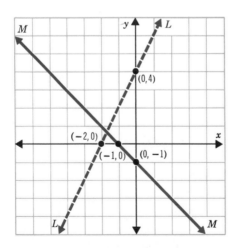

Figure 5.32

Now if we graph each linear inequality of (5.5.4) as a separate problem and then find the intersection of the two resulting half-planes, we will have the solution of the system. Thus, we obtain Figure 5.33.

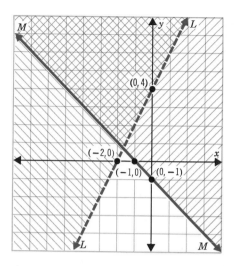

Figure 5.33

The checkered region is the solution. The fact that L is dotted indicates points on L are not part of the solution; M is drawn in full since its points are to be included.

It should be pointed out that the checkered region is merely the intersection of the sets $A = \{(x, y)|2x - y + 4 < 0\}$ and $B = \{(x, y)|x + y - 1 \geq 0\}$. It is usually easier, however, to express the solution graphically than to attempt to write it as a single set. As it turns out, we will not need to write out the solution as a single set.

Graph the system

$$2x - y + 4 < 0$$
$$2x - y + 2 \leq 0$$

5.5.4
Example

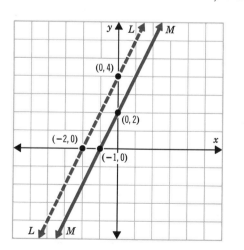

Figure 5.34

The lines corresponding to each of these linear inequalities are

$$L: \ 2x - y + 4 = 0$$
$$M: \ 2x - y + 2 = 0$$

These lines are parallel. Their graphs are given in Figure 5.34.
The graphs of the two linear inequalities are given in Figure 5.35.

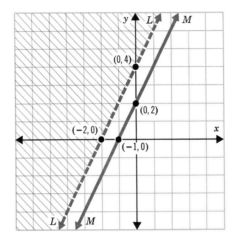

Figure 5.35

The solution is given by the checkered region in Figure 5.35. Notice that the solution of the system is the same as that of the single linear inequality $2x - y + 4 < 0$.

The graph of the system

$$2x - y + 4 > 0$$
$$2x - y + 2 \leqq 0$$

is given in Figure 5.36.

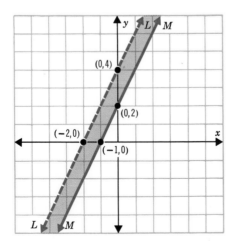

Figure 5.36

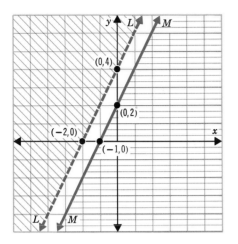

Figure 5.37

Such a region is sometimes referred to as a *strip*.
The system

$$2x - y + 4 < 0$$
$$2x - y + 2 \geqq 0$$

has no solution, as Figure 5.37 indicates.

Thus far we have only considered systems of two linear equations in two unknowns. The next example is of a system of four equations in two unknowns. As we shall see, the technique for graphing such systems is the same as that used for two equations in two unknowns.

Graph the system

$$x + y - 2 \geqq 0$$
$$2x + y - 3 > 0$$
$$x \geqq 0$$
$$y \geqq 0$$

5.5.5
Example

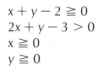

Figure 5.38

Again, we first look at the graphs of the four lines

$$L_1: x + y - 2 = 0$$
$$L_2: 2x + y - 3 = 0$$
$$L_3: x = 0$$
$$L_4: y = 0$$

Figure 5.38 gives the graph of L_1, L_2, L_3, and L_4. Notice that L_3 and L_4 are the y-axis and x-axis, respectively.

The graph of the system in Example 5.5.5 will be the intersection of the four regions determined by each of the four inequalities. The shaded region in Figure 5.39 gives the graph of the system in Example 5.5.5.

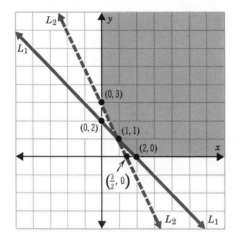

Figure 5.39

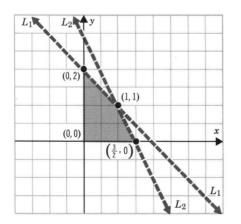

Figure 5.40

Graph the system

$$x + y - 2 < 0$$
$$2x + y - 3 < 0$$
$$x \geqq 0$$
$$y \geqq 0$$

Since the lines associated with these linear inequalities are the same as those of the previous example, we proceed directly to the graph. See Figure 5.40.

The region determined by the four linear inequalities in Example 5.5.6 is a quadrilateral whose vertices are the points $(0, 0)$, $(0, 2)$, $(1, 1)$, and $(3/2, 0)$.

1. Graph the regions
   (a) $2x + y + 5 > 0$
   (b) $3x + 4y - 12 \leqq 0$
   (c) $x \geqq 0$
   (d) $x < 0, \quad y > 0$
   (e) $x - 5 < 0$
   (f) $2x + 3y - 4 \geqq 0$
2. Graph the following systems of inequalities.
   (a) $5x - 12y - 60 > 0, \quad x - y + 2 < 0$
   (b) $3x - 4y < 0, \quad x + y \geqq 0$
   (c) $2x + 2y - 5 > 0, \quad x + y - 2 < 0$
   (d) $3x - y \leqq 0, \quad 3x - y > 0$
   (e) $x - y + 2 > 0, \quad 2x - 2y + 5 \leqq 0$
   (f) $2x - y + 4 \leqq 0, \quad x \geqq 0, \quad y \geqq 0$
   (g) $2x - y \leqq 0, \quad x + y - 8 < 0, \quad x \geqq 0, \quad y \geqq 0$
   (h) $x + 2y - 4 \geqq 0, \quad x + y \leqq 12, \quad x \geqq 0, \quad y \geqq 0$
   (i) $2x - y - 4 > 0, \quad x - 2y - 10 < 0,$
       $x \geqq 0, \quad y \geqq 0, \quad x + y - 2 < 0$
   (j) $x + 3y - 12 \leqq 0, \quad 3x + 2y - 6 < 0,$
       $x \geqq 0, \quad y \geqq 0$
   (k) $3x + 4y - 12 \leqq 0, \quad x - y + 2 > 0,$
       $x \geqq 0, \quad y \geqq 0$

real line
coordinate
origin
scale
unit of measurement
abscissa
ordinate
rectangular coordinate system
quadrant
graph of a function
linear function
straight line

vertical line
slope of a line
two-point form
point-slope form
intercepts
slope-intercept form
general form
intersecting lines
parallel lines
**system of two linear equations in
    two unknowns**
solution of a system

concurrent lines
system of three linear equations
  in two unknowns
break-even point

supply and demand
linear inequality
half-plane

Exercises

1. Graph the functions
   a. $f: y = -2x + 3$
   b. $f: y = 6x - 2$
   c. $f: 2y = 3x + 5$

2. Find the equations of the lines passing through the points:
   a. $P_1 = (1,2)$, $P_2 = (-3,4)$
   b. $P_1 = (0,0)$, $P_2 = (-2,3)$
   c. $P_1 = (-1,-1)$, $P_2 = (2,2)$

3. Find the slope and y-intercept of the following lines. Graph each line.
   a. $3x - 4y + 12 = 0$
   b. $-9x - 3y + 5 = 0$
   c. $4x + 2y - 9 = 0$

4. Determine whether the following lines are identical, parallel, or intersect. If they intersect, find the point of intersection. Graph each pair of lines.
   a. $3x - 4y + 12 = 0$
      $6x - 8y + \quad 9 = 0$
   b. $\quad x - \quad y + \quad 2 = 0$
      $3x - 4y + 12 = 0$
   c. $\quad x - \quad y \quad\quad = 0$
      $2x + 3y + 6 = 0$

5. Mr. Byrd has just retired and finds that he and his wife need $5000 per year to live on. Fortunately, he has a nest egg of $70,000 which he can invest in somewhat risky A-rated bonds at 9 percent interest per year or in a well-known bank at 4 percent per year. How much money should he invest in each so that he realizes exactly $5000 in income each year?

6. One solution is 20 percent acid and another 12 percent acid. How many cubic centimeters of each should be mixed to obtain 100cc of a solution which is 15 percent acid?

7. Find the break-even point for the cost of production (C) and the amount (A) received if:
   a. $C = \$5x + \$30$, $A = \$10x$
   b. $C = \$100x + \$500$, $A = \$300x$
   c. $C = \$15x + \$35$, $A = \$25x$

8. Graph the following systems of inequalities.
   a. $2x - 3y + 6 \geq 0$, $x \geq 0$, $y \geq 0$
   b. $y + 3x \geq 2$, $x \geq 0$, $y \geq 0$
   c. $y + 2x \geq 4$, $x + 2y \geq 4$, $x \geq 0$, $y \geq 0$
   d. $y + 2x \leq 4$, $x + 2y \leq 4$, $x \geq 0$, $y \geq 0$

Introduction to Linear Programming Chapter 6

The flow of resources in a production process or between sectors of the economy involves complex interrelationships between numerous activities. Differences may exist between the processes involved as well as between the goals to be achieved. Nevertheless, in many cases there are essential similarities in the operation of seemingly very different systems.

In order to analyze such systems, it is necessary to construct a statement of the working parts of the system (such as capital, raw materials, and man power) and the goal or objective to be achieved (such as minimum cost or maximum profit). If the system can be represented mathematically (that is, if a *model* for the system can be found) and if the goal can be similarly quantified, it may be possible to devise a computational scheme for determining the *best* program or schedule of actions among alternatives to achieve the goal. Such schemes are called *mathematical programs*.

If the system to be analyzed can be represented by a model consisting of linear inequalities, and if the goal or objective can be expressed as the minimization or maximization of a linear expression, the analysis of the structure is known as a *linear program*. A large class of business, economic, and engineering problems can be represented by a linear system. Other times, a linear system constitutes a good approximation of the conditions of the problem. Of course, for any particular application, one must determine whether a linear system constitutes a "good enough" approximation. We shall not concern ourselves here with whether a given approximation is "good enough," but rather we shall give the student an introduction to the technique of solving *linear programming problems*.

Historically, linear programs for the solution of problems involving resource allocation were first developed during World War II by the United States Air Force. Among those who worked on such problems for the Air Force was George Dantzig who later gave a general formulation of the linear programming problem and offered a method for solving it. His technique, called the *simplex method,* is studied in Chapter 8.

Before studying ways to solve a linear programming problem, we shall give several examples of the types of systems that can be solved using a linear program model.

6.1.1
Example

A producer of chicken feed is required by the United States Department of Agriculture to furnish a certain amount of nutritional elements (such as vitamins and minerals) per hundred pounds of feed. These elements are found in known proportions in various grains and concentrated supplements whose cost is known. What proportions of these grains and concentrated supplements should be mixed so that the desired amount of nutritional elements is found in the feed and at the same time the producer's cost for these elements is least.

Problems like Example 6.1.1 are called *diet* or *mixture problems.*

6.1.2
Example

A manufacturer has several production facilities and a number of warehouses. Each production facility can ship goods to any of the warehouses requiring goods. Shipments must be such that each warehouse receives at least as much as its requirements, possibly from more than one source. There is a known cost per unit shipped along each route from production facility to warehouse. The manufacturer wishes to devise a shipping scheme that satisfies the requirements of the warehouses at lowest possible total transportation cost.

Problems like Example 6.1.2 are called *transportation problems.*

6.1.3
Example

A company manufactures several different products. In making each product, a certain amount of manpower, skilled and nonskilled, and a known amount of raw material are used. The company sells each product for a known profit. How much of each product should be manufactured in order to maximize profits?

Each of the above examples has certain similarities. All require a linear function (called the *objective function*) to be minimized or maximized. All require this objective function to occur under given conditions or restraints that can be expressed by linear inequalities. Problems with these two characteristics can usually be solved by using a *linear program.*

The importance of linear programming should be quite clear. When many alternative actions are possible, a guessing technique (sometimes referred to as intuition or as a "by the seat of the pants approach") may not give the best solution. The difference between the intuition solution and a linear programming solution could be millions of dollars.

185
A GRAPHICAL
SOLUTION
TO LINEAR
PROGRAMMING
PROBLEMS

The next section provides a way of solving certain kinds of linear programming problems by graphical methods. Although such kinds of problems are too simple to be realistic, they are instructional. Chapter 8 discusses a technique called the *simplex method* for solving more complicated linear programming problems. It is this method that is adaptable to computer systems for relatively fast solutions.

6.2
A GRAPHICAL
SOLUTION TO
LINEAR
PROGRAMMING
PROBLEMS

If we restrict ourselves to a linear programming problem in two variables it is possible to represent and solve the problem graphically. Although problems in two variables are too simplistic to be of much practical interest, considerations of simple problems will nevertheless illuminate the nature of linear programming problems in general.

The problem consists of two sorts of expressions: (1) a linear objective function which is to be minimized (or maximized) and (2) a set of linear inequalities which must be simultaneously satisfied.

Let us first consider the objective function. It is an expression of the form

$$f = Ax + By \qquad (6.2.1)$$

where A and B are given real numbers. If we fix f at some value, this expression describes a line in the plane. Consider a change in the value of f. Then the expression (6.2.1) describes another line that is *parallel to the first*. If we let f vary through all possible real values, the expression (6.2.1) represents a family of straight lines all with the same slope $(-A/B)$.

In a certain linear programming problem, the linear objective function is given by the expression

$$f = x + 2y$$

Graph the above linear function for $f = 0$, $f = 1$, $f = 2$, $f = 6$.

If we rewrite this linear function in point-slope form we obtain

$$y = -\frac{1}{2}x + \frac{f}{2}$$

Notice that no matter what value is assigned to f, the slope of the linear objective function is $-1/2$. Figure 6.1 gives the graph. It should be clear that the possible values that f can take on are unlimited in the absence of some restrictions.

A linear programming problem consists of minimizing (or maximizing) an objective function

$$f = Ax + By$$

in which A and B are given real numbers, subject to certain conditions or constraints expressible as linear inequalities in x and y.

If we graph the linear inequalities (the constraints of the linear programming problem), we obtain a set of points called a *polyhedral set*. This polyhedral set of points is *convex*; that is, it has the property that the line

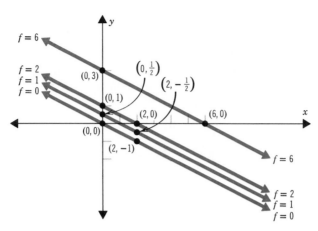

Figure 6.1

segment that joins any pair of points in the set lies entirely in the set. See Figure 6.2.

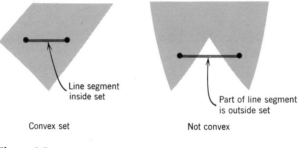

Figure 6.2

Fortunately, the set resulting from the constraints of a linear programming problem always results in a polyhedral convex set. It is this fact and the fact that the intersection of a finite number of convex sets is a convex set that allows us to solve linear programming problems the way we do.

Any point (x,y) in the polyhedral convex set of the constraints of the linear programming problem is called a *feasible solution*. If no such point exists, the linear programming problem has no solution.

In a linear programming problem, we want to find that feasible solution which minimizes (or maximizes) the objective function. If none of the possible feasible solutions minimize (or maximize) the objective function, then the linear programming problem has no solution.

6.2.2
Example

A linear programming problem consists of minimizing the objective function

$$f = x + 2y$$

subject to the condition that

187
A GRAPHICAL
SOLUTION
TO LINEAR
PROGRAMMING
PROBLEMS

$$x + y \geqq 1$$

First, we graph the condition $x + y \geqq 1$. See Figure 6.3.

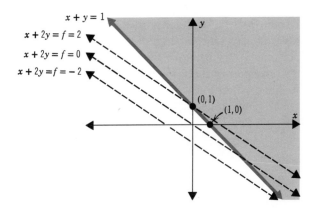

Figure 6.3

Notice that any value of (x,y) in the shaded region including the points on the line $x + y = 1$, is a feasible solution. However, since none of these values make f smallest, the linear programming problem has no solution. This can be verified by noticing that for any value of f, no matter how small, the objective function will pass through the shaded region.

A linear programming problem consists of minimizing the objective function

6.2.3
Example

$$f = x + 2y \qquad (6.2.2)$$

subject to the conditions

$$x + y \geqq 1, \qquad x \geqq 0, \qquad y \geqq 0$$

Again we graph the constraints. See Figure 6.4.

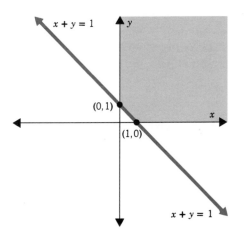

Figure 6.4

The shaded region of Figure 6.4 shows the polyhedral convex set of feasible solutions. To see if there is a value that makes f smallest, we graph the line (6.2.2) and move it parallel to itself. This allows us to observe all solutions of the objective functions. If part of the line (6.2.2) lies within the shaded region we have some *feasible* solutions; that is, some solutions of the objective equation which also satisfy the set of restrictions. Since we want a minimum solution for f we try to move $f = x + 2y$ down as far as is possible while keeping some part of the line within the feasible region. The "best" solution is obtained when the line just touches one corner or *vertex* of the feasible region. This situation is shown in Figure 6.5. The "best" solution is $x = 1$, $y = 0$, and $f = 1$. There is no other feasible solution for which f is smaller.

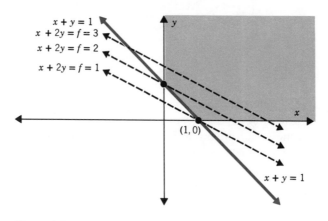

Figure 6.5

Notice that the solution which minimizes f is unique. This is not an unusual situation. If there is a solution minimizing (or maximizing) the objective function and satisfying the restrictions of the problem, it is *usually* unique and is located at a vertex of the polyhedral convex set of feasible solutions.

However, it is possible to have a nonunique solution. This may occur when the slope of the objective function is the same as the slope of one side of the set of feasible solutions. The following example illustrates this possibility.

6.2.4
Example

A linear programming problem consists of minimizing the objective function

$$f = x + 2y \tag{6.2.3}$$

subject to the conditions

$$x + y \geqq 1, \qquad x \geqq 0, \qquad y \geqq 0, \qquad 2x + 4y \geqq 3 \tag{6.2.4}$$

Again, we first graph the constraints of (6.2.4). See Figure 6.6. The shaded region of Figure 6.6 shows the polyhedral convex set of feasible solutions.

189
A GRAPHICAL
SOLUTION
TO LINEAR
PROGRAMMING
PROBLEMS

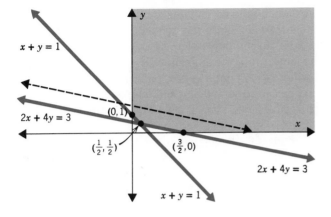

Figure 6.6

If we graph the objective function (6.2.3) and move it down, we see that a minimum is reached when $f = 3/2$. However, any point on the line $2x + 4y = 3$ between $(1/2, 1/2)$ and $(3/2, 0)$ will minimize the objective function. Notice that the points $(3/2, 0)$ and $(1/2, 1/2)$ are at vertices of the polyhedral convex set of feasible solutions. Of course, the reason any point on $2x + 4y = 3$ minimizes the objective function $f = x + 2y$ is that these two lines are parallel (both have slope $-1/2$).

In each example so far that had a solution, *at least one* feasible solution which minimized the objective function is found at a vertex of the set of feasible solutions. We state the following general result and give a sketch of the proof.

If a linear programming problem has a unique solution, it is located at a vertex of the polyhedral convex set of feasible solutions; if a linear programming problem has multiple solutions, at least one of them is located at a vertex of the polyhedral convex set of feasible solutions.

Even though it is beyond the scope of this book to give a rigorous mathematical proof of the above statement, it is possible to sketch the general idea that gives rise to this result. Consider Figure 6.7.

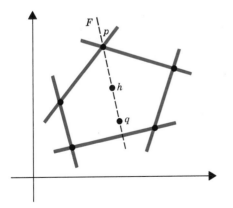

Figure 6.7

Let f be the objective function to be minimized over the polyhedral convex set in Figure 6.7. Let p be any point and denote by $f(p)$ the value of f at the point p. Suppose h lies in the polyhedral set of feasible solutions and suppose that $f(h)$ is the largest value f can assume. Then, $f(p) \leqq f(h)$. If h is a vertex, the result is verified. If h is not a vertex, pick another point q in the set of feasible solution "below" h such that p and h lie on the same straight line. Suppose that $f(p) < f(h)$. Since f is a straight line and since f increases from p to h, it has to increase from h to q and so $f(h) < f(q)$. But this contradicts the assumption that $f(h)$ is the largest value over the set of feasible solution. Thus we cannot have $f(p) < f(h)$ and we must have $f(p) = f(h)$. That is, the vertex p makes the objective function f a minimum.

Notice that the above law is valid whether the objective function is to be minimized or maximized. Also, the result is independent of the number of variables involved. Because of this, the solution of a linear programming problem involves finding the vertices of the polyhedral convex set of feasible solutions and then evaluating the objective function for these values. Fortunately, a technique better than graphing has been developed to find those vertices that minimize (or maximize) the objective function. This technique—the *simplex method*—is discussed later.

Finally, it is important to observe that the above law assumes the existence of a solution of the problem.

It is possible for the set of feasible solutions to be empty or to have only one point. The following example illustrates these possibilities.

**6.2.5
Example**

The constraints or restrictions of a linear programming problem consist of

$$x + y \geqq 1, \qquad x - y \geqq 1, \qquad 2x + y \leqq 2$$

Find the set of feasible solutions.

The set of feasible solutions consists of a single point $(1,0)$. See Figure 6.8.

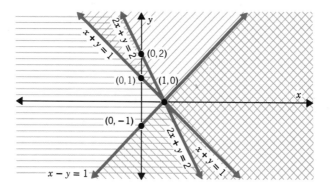

Figure 6.8

If we add the constraint

$$x - y \geqq 2$$

to the constraints of Example 6.2.5, there is no point in the set of feasible solutions. (The empty set is considered to be a convex set.)

Nutt's Nuts has 75 pounds of cashews and 120 pounds of peanuts. These
are to be mixed in 1-pound packages as follows: a low-grade mixture that
contains 4 ounces of cashews and 12 ounces of peanuts and a high-grade
mixture that contains 8 ounces of cashews and 8 ounces of peanuts. On the
low-grade mixture a profit of $0.25 a package is to be made, while the
high-grade mixture profit is to be $0.45 a package. How many packages
of each mixture should be made to obtain a maximum profit?

6.2.6
Example

First, we notice there are two variables. Let

$$x = \text{Number of packages of low-grade mixture}$$
$$y = \text{Number of packages of high-grade mixture}$$

The profit P is given by the linear function

$$P = (\$0.25)x + (\$0.45)y$$

The restrictions on x and y are that

$$x \geq 0, \qquad y \geq 0$$

since x and y stand for numbers of packages and negative numbers of packages are meaningless. Also, there is a limit to the number of pounds of
cashews and peanuts available. That is, the total number of pounds of
cashews cannot exceed 75 pounds (1200 ounces) and the number of
pounds of peanuts cannot exceed 120 pounds (1920 ounces). This means
that

$$4x + 8y \leq 1200$$
$$12x + 8y \leq 1920$$

The linear programming problem is to maximize the objective (profit)
function

$$P = \$0.25x + \$0.45y \tag{6.2.5}$$

subject to the conditions

$$x + 2y \leq 300, \qquad 3x + 2y \leq 480, \qquad x \geq 0, \qquad y \geq 0 \tag{6.2.6}$$

Now since we know the solution, if it exists, is found at a vertex, we
need only solve each pair of linear equations of (6.2.6) to find their point
of intersection. If we do this (using the methods developed in Chapter 5),
we find the vertices of the set of feasible solutions are

$$(0,0), \qquad (0,150), \qquad (160,0), \qquad (90,105)$$

See Figure 6.9 for the graph of the set of feasible solutions. It only remains
to test each of these values in the profit function (6.2.5). Then

$$P_1 = (\$0.25)(0) + (\$0.45)(0) = 0$$

Clearly, a profit of $0.00 is not a maximum. Next,

$$P_2 = (\$0.25)(0) + (\$0.45)(150) = \$67.50$$
$$P_3 = (\$0.25)(160) + (\$0.45)(0) = \$40.00$$
$$P_4 = (\$0.25)(90) + (\$0.45)(105) = \$69.75$$

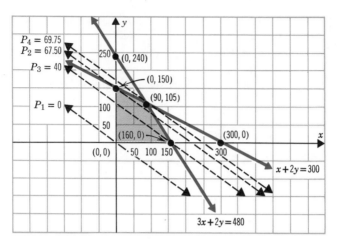

Figure 6.9

Thus, a maximum profit is obtained if 90 packages of low-grade mixture and 105 packages of high-grade mixture are made. The maximum profit obtainable under the conditions described is $69.75.

We now have a method for solving a linear programming problem provided it has a solution. We outline this procedure below.

1. **Find an expression for the objective function that is to be maximized or minimized.**
2. **List all the constraints.**
3. **Find the vertices of the polyhedral convex set of constraints.**
4. **Determine the value of the objective function at each vertex.**

6.2.7
Example

Mike's Famous Toy Trucks manufactures two kinds of toy trucks—a standard model and a deluxe model. In the manufacturing process, each standard model requires 2 hours of grinding and 2 hours of finishing, and each deluxe model needs 2 hours of grinding and 4 hours of finishing. The company has 2 grinders and 3 finishers, each of whom work 40 hours per week. Each standard model toy truck brings a profit of $3 and each deluxe model a profit of $4. Assuming every truck made will be sold, how many of each should be made to maximize profits?

First, let

$$x = \text{Number of standard models made}$$
$$y = \text{Number of deluxe models made}$$

The profit P is given by the linear function

$$P = \$3x + \$4y$$

To manufacture 1 standard model requires 2 grinding hours and to make 1 deluxe model requires 2 grinding hours. Thus, the number of grinding hours for x standard and y deluxe models is

193
A GRAPHICAL
SOLUTION
TO LINEAR
PROGRAMMING
PROBLEMS

$$2x + 2y$$

But there is at most 80 hours per week of grinding. This means we have the additional constraint

$$2x + 2y \leqq 80$$

associated with this problem. Similarly, we have the constraint

$$2x + 4y \leqq 120$$

for the finishing hours.

The linear programming problem is to maximize the objective (profit) function

$$P = 3x + 4y$$

subject to the conditions

$$2x + 2y \leqq 80, \qquad x \geqq 0$$
$$2x + 4y \leqq 120, \qquad y \geqq 0$$

The vertices of the polyhedral convex set of feasible solutions are

$$(0,0), \qquad (0,30), \qquad (40,0), \qquad (20,20)$$

See Figure 6.10.

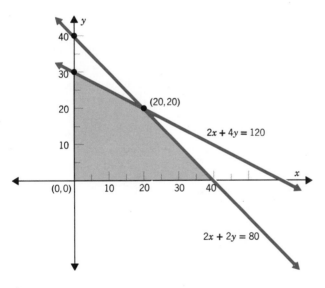

Figure 6.10

Testing each of these values, we see that

$$P_1 = 3(0) + 4(0) = \$0$$
$$P_2 = 3(0) + 4(30) = \$120$$
$$P_3 = 3(40) + 4(0) = \$120$$
$$P_4 = 3(20) + 4(20) = \$140$$

Thus, a maximum profit is obtained if 20 standard trucks and 20 deluxe trucks are manufactured. The maximum profit is $140.

The following example is taken from a paper by Robert E. Kohn.[1]

6.2.8
Example
An Application to
Pollution Control

In this paper, a linear programming model is proposed that can be useful in determining what air pollution controls should be adopted in an airshed. The methodology is based on the premise that air quality goals should be achieved at the least possible cost. Advantages of the model are its simplicity, its emphasis on economic efficiency, and its appropriateness for the kind of data that is already available.

To illustrate the model, consider a hypothetical airshed with a single industry, cement manufacturing. Annual production is 2,500,000 barrels of cement. Although the kilns are equipped with mechanical collectors for air pollution control, they are still emitting two pounds of dust for every barrel of cement produced. The industry can be required to replace the mechanical collectors with four-field electrostatic precipitators, which would reduce emissions to 0.5 pound of dust per barrel of cement or with five-field electrostatic precipitators, which would reduce emissions to 0.2 pound per barrel. If the capital and operating costs of the four-field precipitator are $0.14 per barrel of cement produced and of the five-field precipitator are $0.18 per barrel, what control methods should be required of this industry? Assume that, for this hypothetical airshed, it has been determined that particulate emissions (which now total 5,000,000 pounds per year) should be reduced by 4,200,000 pounds.

If C represents the cost of control, x the number of barrels of annual cement production subject to the four-field electrostatic precipitator, whose cost is $0.14 a barrel of cement produced, and with which the pollutant reduction is (2–0.5) or 1.5 pounds of particulates per barrel of cement produced, and y is the number of barrels of annual cement production subject to the five-field electrostatic precipitator control method, whose cost is $0.18 and with which the particulate reduction is (2–0.2) or 1.8 pounds per barrel of cement produced, then the model can be stated as follows:

Minimize

$$C = \$0.14x + \$0.18y$$

subject to

$$x + y \leq 2,500,000$$
$$1.5x + 1.8y \geq 4,200,000$$
$$x \geq 0, \qquad y \geq 0$$

The first equation states that our objective is to minimize air pollution control costs; the second that barrels of cement production subject to the two control methods cannot exceed the annual production; the third that the particulate reduction from the two methods must be greater than or equal to the particulate reduction target; while the final expression precludes a solution of the model with negative quantities of cement.

[1]R. E. Kohn, "A Mathematical Programming Model for Air Pollution Control," *School Science and Mathematics,* June 1969, pp. 487–499.

195
A GRAPHICAL
SOLUTION
TO LINEAR
PROGRAMMING
PROBLEMS

Figure 6.11 illustrates a graphic solution to the problem.

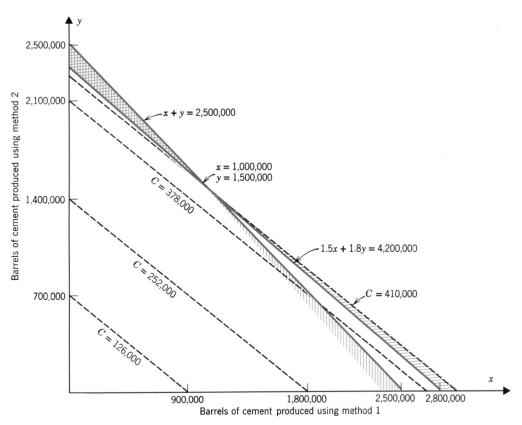

Figure 6.11

The least cost solution would be to install the four-field precipitator on kilns producing 1,000,000 ($x = 1,000,000$) and the five-field precipitator on kilns producing 1,500,000 barrels of cement ($y = 1,500,000$) at a cost of $C = \$410,000$.

A further analysis of this problem is found in Example 8.4.4.

The example concerns reclaimed land and its allocation into two major uses — agricultural and urban (or nonagricultural). The reclamation of land for urban purposes (x) costs \$400 per acre and for agricultural uses (y), \$300. The primal problem is that the reclamation agency wishes to minimize the total cost C of reclaiming the land

6.2.9
Example
An Application to
Urban Geography[2]

$$C = \$400x + \$300y$$

where x = the number of acres of urban land and y = the number of acres of agricultural land. Obviously this equation can be minimized by setting

[2] Maurice Yeates. *An Introduction to Quantitative Analysis in Economic Geography*, McGraw-Hill, New York, 1968.

both x and y at zero, that is, reclaiming nothing, but the problem is subject to a number of constraints derived from three different groups.

The first is an urban group which insists that at least 4000 acres of land be reclaimed for urban purposes. The second group is concerned with agriculture and says that at least 5000 acres of land must be reclaimed for agricultural uses. Finally, the third group is concerned only with reclamation and is quite disinterested in the use to which the land will be put. The third group, however, says that at least 10,000 acres of land must be reclaimed. The primal problem and the constraints can therefore be written in full as follows.

Minimize

$$C = \$400x + \$300y$$

subject to

$$x + 0 \cdot y \geqq 4000$$
$$0 \cdot x + y \geqq 5000$$
$$x + y \geqq 10,000$$

The graphic solution to this problem is presented in Figure 6.12.

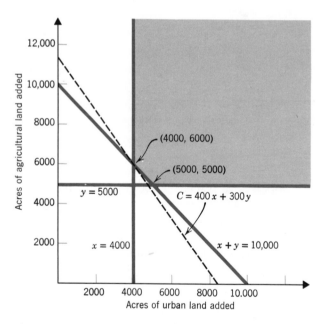

Figure 6.12

The combination of urban and agricultural land at the vertex (4000,6000) reveals that if 4000 acres are devoted to urban purposes and 6000 acres to agricultural purposes, the cost is a minimum and is

$$C = (\$400)(4000) + (\$300)(6000) = \$3,400,000$$

Solve each of the following linear programming problems by using graphing techniques.

1. Minimize the objective function

$$f = x + y$$

subject to the conditions

$$2x + y \geq 10, \qquad x + 2y \geq 10$$

2. Minimize the objective function

$$f = x + y$$

subject to the conditions

$$2x + y \leq 10, \qquad x + 2y \geq 10$$

3. Maximize the objective function

$$f = x - y$$

subject to the conditions

$$2x + y \geq 10, \qquad x + 2y \geq 10, \qquad x + y \leq 10$$

4. Maximize the objective function

$$f = x + 5y$$

subject to the conditions

$$x + y \geq 10, \qquad 2x + y \leq 10, \qquad x + 2y \leq 10$$

5. Maximize and minimize the objective function

$$f = 5x + 7y$$

subject to the conditions

$$x \geq 0, \qquad y \geq 0, \qquad 2x + 3y \leq 12, \qquad 3x + y \leq 12$$

6. Maximize and minimize the objective function

$$f = 5x + 7y$$

subject to the conditions

$$x \geq 0, \qquad y \geq 0, \qquad x + y \geq 2,$$
$$2x + 3y \leq 12, \qquad 3x + y \leq 12$$

7. Maximize and minimize the objective function

$$f = 5x + 7y$$

subject to the conditions

$$x \geq 0, \qquad y \geq 0, \qquad 2 \leq x + y \leq 8,$$
$$2x + y \leq 10, \qquad 3x + y \leq 12$$

8. Maximize and minimize the objective function

$$f = 5x + 7y$$

subject to the conditions

$$x \geq 0, \quad y \geq 0, \quad 2x + 3y \geq 6,$$
$$x + 3y \leq 21, \quad 2x + 3y \leq 24$$

9. Maximize and minimize the objective function

$$f = 5x - 7y$$

subject to the conditions of Problem 5.

10. Maximize and minimize the objective function

$$f = 5x - 7y$$

subject to the conditions of Problem 6.

11. Maximize and minimize the objective function

$$f = 5x - 7y$$

subject to the conditions of Problem 7.

12. Maximize and minimize the objective function

$$f = 5x - 7y$$

subject to the conditions of Problem 8.

13. In Example 6.2.6, if the profit on the low-grade mixture is $0.30 per package and the profit on the high-grade mixture is $0.40 per package, how many packages of each mixture should be made for a maximum profit?

14. A diet is to contain at least 400 units of vitamins, 500 units of minerals, and 1000 calories. There are available two foods F_1 and F_2 costing $0.05 per unit and $0.03 per unit, respectively. A unit of food F_1 contains 2 units of vitamins, 1 unit of minerals, and 2 calories; a unit of food F_2 contains 1 unit of vitamin, 2 units of mineral, and 4 calories. Find the minimum cost for a diet consisting of a mixture of these two foods which meets the minimal nutrition requirements.

15. Danny's Chicken Farm is a producer of frying chickens. In order to produce the best fryers possible, he supplements the regular chicken feed by 4 vitamins. The minimum amount required per 100 ounces of feed of each vitamin is Vitamin 1, 50 units; Vitamin 2, 100 units; Vitamin 3, 60 units; Vitamin 4, 180 units. Two kinds of supplement are available. Supplement I costs $0.03 per ounce and contains 5 units of Vitamin 1 per ounce, 25 units of Vitamin 2 per ounce, 10 units of Vitamin 3 per ounce, and 35 units of Vitamin 4 per ounce. Supplement II costs $0.04 per ounce and contains 25 units of Vitamin 1 per ounce, 10 units of Vitamin 2 per ounce, 10 units of Vitamin 3 per ounce, and 20 units of Vitamin 4 per ounce. How much of each supplement should he buy to add to each

100 ounces of feed in order to minimize his cost, but still have the desired vitamin amounts present?

16. Using the information supplied in Example 6.2.7, suppose the profit on each standard model is $4 and the profit on each deluxe model is $4. How many of each should be manufactured in order to maximize profit?

17. Using the information supplied in Example 6.2.7, suppose the profit on each standard model is $4 and on each deluxe model is $3. How many of each should be manufactured in order to maximize profits?

18. Mr. Thomas, who owns a 100-acre farm, wants to plant crop A and crop B. The seed and other costs for crop A amount to $10 per acre and for crop B amounts to $40 per acre. Expected profit from crop A is $40 per acre, and from crop B is $120 per acre. Labor for crop A is 2 man-days per acre and for crop B is 3 man-days per acre. If Mr. Thomas has a capital of $1100 and 160 man-days of labor to invest in his farm, how many acres of each crop should he plant to insure himself maximum profit? How much of his land must remain idle in order to maximize his profit?

*19. Maximize

$$f = 2x + y + 3z$$

subject to

$$x + 2y + z \leq 25$$
$$3x + 2y + 3z \leq 30$$
$$x \geq 0, \quad y \geq 0, \quad z \geq 0$$

Hint: Solve the constraints three at a time and find those points that are in the set of feasible solutions and test each of them in the objective function.

mathematical program

linear program

linear programming problem

objective function

polyhedral set

convex set

feasible solution

constraints

vertex

polyhedral convex set

1. Maximize and minimize the objective function

$$f = 15x + 20y$$

subject to the conditions

(a) $3x + 4y \leq 12$
$x \geq 0, \quad y \geq 0$

(b) $x + 2y \leq 40$
$x - 3y \geq 20$
$x \geq 0, \quad y \geq 0$

(c) $5x + 2y \leq 30$

$x + y \leq 9$

$x \geq 0, \qquad y \geq 0$

(d) $x + y \geq 5$

$x + y \leq 20$

$x \geq 0, \qquad y \geq 0$

2. Maximize and minimize the objective function

$$f = 15x - 20y$$

subject to the conditions of Problem 1.

3. Katy needs at least 60 units of carbohydrates, 45 units of protein and 30 units of at each month. From each pound of Food A, she receives 5 units of carbohydrates, 3 of protein and 4 of fat. Food B contains, respectively, 2, 2 and 1 units of carbohydrates, protein and fat per pound. If Food A costs $1.30 per pound and Food B costs $0.80 per pound, how many pounds of each food should Katy buy each month to keep costs at a minimum?

Introduction to Matrix Algebra
with Applications Chapter 7

There are many situations in both pure and applied mathematics in which we have to deal with rectangular arrays of numbers or functions. In fact in many branches of the physical, biological, and social sciences, it is necessary for scientists to express and use a set of numbers in a rectangular array.

7.1
PRELIMINARY
REMARKS

In this chapter we shall survey briefly a branch of mathematics called *linear algebra*. Linear algebra deals with generalizations of numbers, called *vectors and matrices*. These generalizations are made in such a way that most of the algebraic properties of the real numbers are retained.

Motors Incorporated produces three models of cars: a sedan, a hard top, and a convertible. If the company wishes to compare the units of raw material and the units of labor involved in one month's production of each of

7.1.1
Example

	Sedan Model	Hard-top Model	Convertible Model
Units of material	23	16	10
Units of labor	7	9	11

Figure 7.1

these models, a rectangular array could be used to present the data (see Figure 7.1). If the pattern in which the units and models are to be recorded is retained, this array may be presented simply by

$$A = \begin{pmatrix} 23 & 16 & 10 \\ 7 & 9 & 11 \end{pmatrix}$$

In this example, the array, called a *matrix,* has two rows (the units) and three columns (the models).

A *matrix A* **is a rectangular array of elements** a_{ij} **of the form**

$$A = \begin{pmatrix} a_{11} & a_{12} & \cdots & a_{1j} & \cdots & a_{1m} \\ a_{21} & a_{22} & \cdots & a_{2j} & \cdots & a_{2m} \\ \vdots & \vdots & & \vdots & & \vdots \\ a_{i1} & a_{i2} & \cdots & a_{ij} & \cdots & a_{im} \\ \vdots & \vdots & & \vdots & & \vdots \\ a_{n1} & a_{n2} & \cdots & a_{nj} & \cdots & a_{nm} \end{pmatrix}$$

jth column spanning the top; ith row labels the row with a_{ij} entries.

(7.1.1)

in which the a_{ij} **are** $n \cdot m$ **real numbers.**

Each element a_{ij} of the matrix A has two indices: the *row index, i,* and the *column index, j.* The elements $a_{i1}, a_{i2}, \ldots , a_{im}$ are the elements of the ith row, and the elements $a_{1j}, a_{2j}, \ldots , a_{nj}$ are the elements of the jth column.

For convenience, matrices will be denoted by capital letters and the elements (also called *entries* or *components*) will be denoted by small letters corresponding to the capital letter denoting the matrix. That is, the matrix A of (7.1.1) will be abbreviated by

$$A = (a_{ij}) \qquad i = 1, 2, \ldots , n; \qquad j = 1, 2, \ldots , m$$

which has n rows and m columns.

The following are all examples of matrices.

$$A = \begin{pmatrix} 1 & \frac{1}{2} \\ 0 & 2 \end{pmatrix} \qquad\qquad B = \begin{pmatrix} 2 \\ -5 \end{pmatrix}$$

$$C = \begin{pmatrix} 0.01 & 0.02 & 0.07 \\ 0.1 & 0.9 & 0 \end{pmatrix} \qquad D = (1.2 \quad 5)$$

The matrix A has two rows and two columns; the matrix B has two rows and one column; C has two rows and three columns; and matrix D has one row and two columns.

7.1.2 Definition

The *dimension of a matrix A* **is the number of rows and the number of columns of the matrix. If a matrix** A **has** n **rows and** m **columns, we denote the dimension of** A **by** $n \times m$**, read as** "n *by* m."

For a 2×3 matrix, it is important to remember that the first number 2 denotes the number of rows and the second number 3 is the number of columns. A matrix with 3 rows and 2 columns is of dimension 3×2.

Let $A = (a_{ij})$ be a matrix of dimension $n \times m$, $i = 1, \ldots, n$; $j = 1, \ldots, m$. The entries of A for which $i = j$, namely, a_{11}, a_{22}, a_{33}, a_{44}, and so on, form the *diagonal of A*.

7.1.3 Definition

If a matrix A **has the same number of rows as it has columns, it is called a** *square matrix*.

A square matrix of dimension $n \times n$ is of the form

$$A = (a_{ij}) = \begin{pmatrix} a_{11} & a_{12} & \cdots & a_{1n-1} & a_{1n} \\ a_{21} & a_{22} & \cdots & a_{2n-1} & a_{2n} \\ \cdot & \cdot & & \cdot & \cdot \\ \cdot & \cdot & & \cdot & \cdot \\ \cdot & \cdot & & \cdot & \cdot \\ a_{n-11} & a_{n-12} & \cdots & a_{n-1n-1} & a_{n-1n} \\ a_{n1} & a_{n2} & \cdots & a_{nn-1} & a_{nn} \end{pmatrix}$$

7.1.3 Example

In a psychological experiment in which information theory is applied to the study of response to stimulus presentation, the so-called "confusion matrix" is used. It is of the form given in Figure 7.2.

$$R = \text{Stimulus presentation} = \overset{\text{Response}}{\begin{pmatrix} 1 & \mu & \mu^2 & \cdots & \mu^{k-1} \\ \mu & 1 & \mu & \cdots & \mu^{k-2} \\ \mu^2 & \mu & 1 & \cdots & \mu^{k-3} \\ \cdot & \cdot & \cdot & \cdots & \cdot \\ \cdot & \cdot & \cdot & \cdots & \cdot \\ \cdot & \cdot & \cdot & \cdots & \cdot \\ \mu^{k-1} & \mu^{k-2} & \mu^{k-3} & \cdots & 1 \end{pmatrix}}$$

Figure 7.2

Figure 7.2 is a square matrix and the dimension of the matrix is $k \times k$. The 1's are the diagonal entries.

Notice that in this example all entries above the diagonal are the same as the entries below it. A matrix with this property is called a *symmetric matrix*. That is, a square matrix $A = (a_{ij})$ is *symmetric* if and only if $a_{ij} = a_{ji}$ for all i, j.

7.1.4
Definition **A** *row matrix* **is a matrix with one row of elements. A** *column matrix* **is a matrix with one column of elements.**

Row matrices and column matrices are usually referred to as *row vectors* and *column vectors,* respectively.

7.1.4
Example The matrices

$$A = (23 \quad 16 \quad 10) \qquad B = (7 \quad 9)$$

$$C = \begin{pmatrix} 23 \\ -1 \\ 7 \end{pmatrix} \qquad\qquad D = \begin{pmatrix} 16 \\ 9 \end{pmatrix} \qquad E = (10)$$

have the dimensions A: 1×3, B: 1×2, C: 3×1, D: 2×1, E: 1×1. Here, A, B, and E are row vectors and C, D, and E are column vectors.

The matrix $E = (10)$ is a 1×1 matrix and, as such, can be treated as merely a real number. That is, $E = (10) = 10$, the real number 10.

As with most mathematical quantities, we now want to ask about relationships between two matrices. We might ask, "When, if at all, are two matrices equal?"

Let us try to arrive at a sound definition for equality of matrices by requiring equal matrices to have certain desirable properties. First it would seem necessary that two equal matrices have the same dimension, that is, that they both be $n \times m$ matrices. Next, it would seem necessary that their entries be identical numbers. With these two restrictions, we will now define equality of matrices.

7.1.5
Definition **Two $n \times m$ matrices $A = (a_{ij})$ and $B = (b_{ij})$ are** *equal* **if and only if $a_{ij} = b_{ij}$, where $i = 1, 2, \ldots, n$ and $j = 1, 2, \ldots, m$. In this case, we write $A = B$, read as "matrix A is equal to matrix B."**

7.1.5
Example In order for the two matrices

$$A = \begin{pmatrix} p & q \\ 1 & 0 \end{pmatrix} \qquad \text{and} \qquad B = \begin{pmatrix} \frac{1}{2} & \frac{1}{2} \\ n & 0 \end{pmatrix}$$

to be equal, we must have $p = 1/2$, $q = 1/2$, and $n = 1$.

7.1.6
Example Let A and B be the two matrices given by

$$A = \begin{pmatrix} x + 2 \\ 3y - 7 \end{pmatrix} \qquad B = \begin{pmatrix} 4 - y \\ x - 3 \end{pmatrix}$$

Find x and y so that $A = B$.

It is important to recognize that both A and B are 2×1 matrices—or column vectors. Also, the entry $x + 2$ must be treated as a single number or entry.

Now, from Definition 7.1.5, $A = B$ if and only if

$$x + 2 = 4 - y \quad \text{and} \quad 3y - 7 = x - 3$$

Here we have two equations in two unknowns x and y. Solving them, we see that the solutions are

$$x = \frac{1}{2}, \quad y = \frac{3}{2}$$

We check this solution by substituting in A and B.

$$A = \begin{pmatrix} \frac{1}{2} + 2 \\ 3 \cdot \frac{3}{2} - 7 \end{pmatrix} = \begin{pmatrix} \frac{5}{2} \\ -\frac{5}{2} \end{pmatrix}, \, B = \begin{pmatrix} 4 - \frac{3}{2} \\ \frac{1}{2} - 3 \end{pmatrix} = \begin{pmatrix} \frac{5}{2} \\ -\frac{5}{2} \end{pmatrix}$$

Let A and B be two matrices given by

7.1.7
Example

$$A = \begin{pmatrix} x + y & 6 \\ 2x - 3 & 2 - y \end{pmatrix} \qquad B = \begin{pmatrix} 5 & 5x + 2 \\ y & x - y \end{pmatrix}$$

Find x and y so that A and B are equal.

A and B are both 2×2 matrices. Thus, $A = B$ if and only if

(a) $x + y = 5$ (c) $2x - 3 = y$

(b) $5x + 2 = 6$ (d) $2 - y = x - y$

Here we have four equations in the two unknowns x and y. From equation (d), we see that $x = 2$. Using this value in equation (a), we obtain $y = 3$. But $x = 2$, $y = 3$ do not satisfy either (c) or (d). Hence, there are *no* values for x and y satisfying all four equations. This means A and B can never be equal. That is,

$$A \neq B.$$

---

1. Find the dimension of the following matrices:

7.1
Exercise

(a) $A = \begin{pmatrix} 2 & 1 & -3 \\ 1 & 0 & -1 \end{pmatrix}$ (d) $A = \begin{pmatrix} 1 & 2 \\ 2 & 1 \\ 1 & 2 \end{pmatrix}$

(b) $A = \begin{pmatrix} 4 \\ 1 \end{pmatrix}$ (e) $A = \begin{pmatrix} 5 & -7 & 2 & 5 \\ 1 & -\frac{1}{2} & 6 & 4 \\ \frac{1}{3} \end{pmatrix}$

(c) $A = (2 \quad 1 \quad -3)$ (f) $A = (2)$

2. XYZ Company produces steel and aluminum nails. One week, 25 gross 1/2-inch steel nails and 45 gross 1-inch steel nails were

produced. Suppose, 13 gross 1/2-inch and 20 gross 1-inch aluminum nails and 35 gross 2-inch steel and 23 gross 2-inch aluminum nails were also made. Write a 2 × 3 matrix depicting this. Could you also write a 3 × 2 matrix for this situation?

3. Katy, Mike, and Danny go to the candy store. Katy buys 5 sticks of gum, 2 ice cream cones, and 10 jelly beans. Mike buys 2 sticks of gum, 15 jelly beans, and 2 candy bars. Danny buys 1 stick of gum, 1 ice cream cone, and 4 candy bars. Write a matrix depicting this situation.

4. Find x so that the matrices

$$A = \begin{pmatrix} x \\ 3 \end{pmatrix} \qquad\qquad B = \begin{pmatrix} 4 \\ 3 \end{pmatrix}$$

are equal.

5. Find x, y, and z so that the matrices

$$A = \begin{pmatrix} x+y & 2 \\ 4 & 0 \end{pmatrix} \qquad\qquad B = \begin{pmatrix} 6 & x-y \\ 4 & z \end{pmatrix}$$

are equal.

6. Find x and y so that the matrices

$$A = \begin{pmatrix} x-2y & 0 \\ -2 & 6 \end{pmatrix} \qquad\qquad B = \begin{pmatrix} 3 & 0 \\ -2 & x+y \end{pmatrix}$$

are equal.

7. Find x, y, and z so that the matrices

$$A = \begin{pmatrix} x-2 & 3 & 2z \\ 6y & x & 2y \end{pmatrix} \qquad B = \begin{pmatrix} y & z & 6 \\ 18z & y+2 & 6z \end{pmatrix}$$

are equal.

**7.2
ADDITION OF
MATRICES**

Thus far we have discussed the concept of equality of matrices. Can two matrices be added? And, if so, what is the rule or law for addition of matrices?

Let us return to Example 7.1.1. In that example, we recorded one month's production of Motors Incorporated with the matrix

$$A = \begin{pmatrix} 23 & 16 & 10 \\ 7 & 9 & 11 \end{pmatrix}$$

Suppose the next month's production is

$$B = \begin{pmatrix} 18 & 12 & 9 \\ 14 & 6 & 8 \end{pmatrix}$$

in which the pattern of recording units and models remains the same.

The total production for the two months can be displayed by the matrix

$$C = \begin{pmatrix} 41 & 28 & 19 \\ 21 & 15 & 19 \end{pmatrix}$$

since the number of units of material for sedan models is $41 = 23 + 18$; the number of units of material for hard-top models is $28 = 16 + 12$; and so on.

This leads us to define the sum $A + B$ of two matrices A and B as merely that matrix consisting of the sum of corresponding entries from A and B.

Let $A = (a_{ij})$ **and** $B = (b_{ij})$ **be two** $n \times m$ **matrices. The** *sum* $A + B$ **is de-fined as the** $n \times m$ **matrix** $(a_{ij} + b_{ij})$.

7.2.1
Definition

Notice that it is possible to add two matrices only if their dimensions are the same. Also, the dimension of the sum of two matrices is the same as that of the two original matrices.

Using the matrices given previously, we see that

$$A + B = \begin{pmatrix} 23 & 16 & 10 \\ 7 & 9 & 11 \end{pmatrix} + \begin{pmatrix} 18 & 12 & 9 \\ 14 & 6 & 8 \end{pmatrix}$$

$$= \begin{pmatrix} 23 + 18 & 16 + 12 & 10 + 9 \\ 7 + 14 & 9 + 6 & 11 + 8 \end{pmatrix}$$

$$= \begin{pmatrix} 41 & 28 & 19 \\ 21 & 15 & 19 \end{pmatrix} = C$$

The following pairs of matrices cannot be added since they are of different dimension

(a) $A = \begin{pmatrix} 1 & 2 \\ 7 & 2 \end{pmatrix}$, $\quad B = \begin{pmatrix} 1 \\ -3 \end{pmatrix}$

(b) $A = (2 \quad 3)$, $\quad B = (1 \quad 1 \quad 1)$

(c) $A = \begin{pmatrix} -1 & 7 & 0 \\ 2 & \frac{1}{2} & 0 \end{pmatrix}$, $\quad B = \begin{pmatrix} -1 & 2 \\ 3 & 0 \\ 1 & 5 \end{pmatrix}$

Now that we have a definition for adding two matrices, we would like to find out whether the usual rules for addition of numbers (i.e., commutative laws, associative laws) are also valid for matrix addition. Fortunately, it turns out that matrix addition and addition of numbers have the same properties.

Theorem 7.2.1

If A **and** B **are two matrices of the same dimension then**

$$A + B = B + A$$

That is, matrix addition is *commutative*.

Let

7.2.1
Example

$$A = \begin{pmatrix} 1 & 5 \\ 7 & -3 \end{pmatrix}, \quad B = \begin{pmatrix} 3 & -2 \\ 4 & 1 \end{pmatrix}$$

Then

$$A + B = \begin{pmatrix} 1 & 5 \\ 7 & -3 \end{pmatrix} + \begin{pmatrix} 3 & -2 \\ 4 & 1 \end{pmatrix} = \begin{pmatrix} 1+3 & 5+(-2) \\ 7+4 & -3+1 \end{pmatrix} = \begin{pmatrix} 4 & 3 \\ 11 & -2 \end{pmatrix}$$

$$B + A = \begin{pmatrix} 3 & -2 \\ 4 & 1 \end{pmatrix} + \begin{pmatrix} 1 & 5 \\ 7 & -3 \end{pmatrix} = \begin{pmatrix} 4 & 3 \\ 11 & -2 \end{pmatrix}$$

Theorem 7.2.2

If A, B, C, are three matrices of the same dimension, then

$$A + (B + C) = (A + B) + C$$

That is, matrix addition is *associative.*

Proof
Let

$$A = (a_{ij}), \qquad B = (b_{ij}), \qquad C = (c_{ij})$$

Then

$$\begin{aligned} A + [B + C] &= (a_{ij}) + [(b_{ij}) + (c_{ij})] = (a_{ij}) + [(b_{ij} + c_{ij})] \\ &= (a_{ij}) + (b_{ij} + c_{ij}) = (a_{ij} + b_{ij} + c_{ij}) \\ &= [(a_{ij} + b_{ij})] + (c_{ij}) = [(a_{ij}) + (b_{ij})] + (c_{ij}) \\ &= [A + B] + C \end{aligned}$$

In the proof, we used the fact that addition of real numbers is associative. Where?

The fact that addition of matrices is associative means that the notation $A + B + C$ is *not* ambiguous since $(A + B) + C = A + (B + C)$.

**7.2.2
Definition**

The matrix in which all entries are zero is called the *zero matrix* **and is denoted by the symbol θ.**

An important property of the zero matrix θ is that whenever it is added to a matrix A the result is A. In this case, the dimension of θ is the same as that of A.

Theorem 7.2.3

Let A be an $n \times m$ matrix. Then

$$A + \theta = A$$

Proof
Let $A = (a_{ij})$. Then

$$A + \theta = (a_{ij}) + (0) = (a_{ij} + 0) = (a_{ij}) = A$$

If

$$A = \begin{pmatrix} 3 & 4 & -\dfrac{1}{2} \\ \sqrt{2} & 0 & 3 \end{pmatrix}$$

$$A + \theta = \begin{pmatrix} 3 & 4 & -\dfrac{1}{2} \\ \sqrt{2} & 0 & 3 \end{pmatrix} + \begin{pmatrix} 0 & 0 & 0 \\ 0 & 0 & 0 \end{pmatrix}$$

$$= \begin{pmatrix} 3+0 & 4+0 & -\dfrac{1}{2}+0 \\ \sqrt{2}+0 & 0+0 & 3+0 \end{pmatrix} = \begin{pmatrix} 3 & 4 & -\dfrac{1}{2} \\ \sqrt{2} & 0 & 3 \end{pmatrix}$$

With the sum of two matrices having been defined, it is natural to ask about the *difference* of two matrices. As will be seen, subtracting matrices and subtracting numbers are much the same kind of process.

Let $A = (a_{ij})$ **and** $B = (b_{ij})$ **be two** $n \times m$ **matrices. The** *difference* $B - A$ **is defined as the** $n \times m$ **matrix** X **for which**

$$A + X = B$$

If

$$A = \begin{pmatrix} 2 & 3 & 4 \\ 1 & 0 & 2 \end{pmatrix}, \qquad B = \begin{pmatrix} -2 & 1 & -1 \\ 3 & 0 & 3 \end{pmatrix}$$

To find $X = B - A$, let

$$X = \begin{pmatrix} a & b & c \\ d & e & f \end{pmatrix}$$

Then

$$A + X = \begin{pmatrix} 2+a & 3+b & 4+c \\ 1+d & e & 2+f \end{pmatrix} = \begin{pmatrix} -2 & 1 & -1 \\ 3 & 0 & 3 \end{pmatrix}$$

That is

$2 + a = -2$	or	$a = -4$
$3 + b = 1$	or	$b = -2$
$4 + c = -1$	or	$c = -5$
$1 + d = 3$	or	$d = 2$
$e = 0$	or	$e = 0$
$2 + f = 3$	or	$f = 1$

Thus

$$X = B - A = \begin{pmatrix} -4 & -2 & -5 \\ 2 & 0 & 1 \end{pmatrix}$$

Notice that $B - A$ is nothing more than the matrix formed by subtracting the entries in A from the corresponding entries in B. That is

$$B - A = \begin{pmatrix} -2 & 1 & -1 \\ 3 & 0 & 3 \end{pmatrix} - \begin{pmatrix} 2 & 3 & 4 \\ 1 & 0 & 2 \end{pmatrix}$$

$$= \begin{pmatrix} -2-2 & 1-3 & -1-4 \\ 3-1 & 0-0 & 3-2 \end{pmatrix} = \begin{pmatrix} -4 & -2 & -5 \\ 2 & 0 & 1 \end{pmatrix}$$

7.2
Exercise

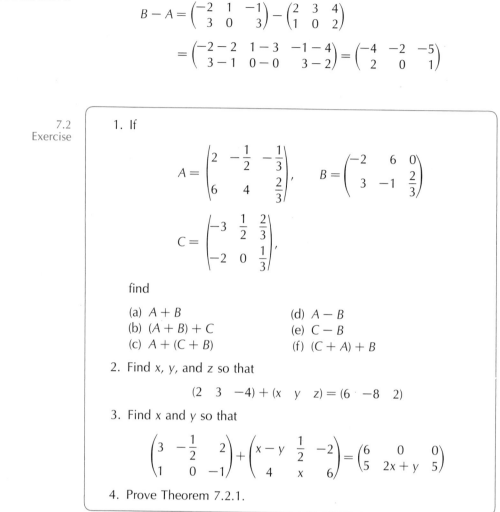

1. If

$$A = \begin{pmatrix} 2 & -\frac{1}{2} & -\frac{1}{3} \\ 6 & 4 & \frac{2}{3} \end{pmatrix}, \qquad B = \begin{pmatrix} -2 & 6 & 0 \\ 3 & -1 & \frac{2}{3} \end{pmatrix}$$

$$C = \begin{pmatrix} -3 & \frac{1}{2} & \frac{2}{3} \\ -2 & 0 & \frac{1}{3} \end{pmatrix},$$

find

(a) $A + B$ (d) $A - B$
(b) $(A + B) + C$ (e) $C - B$
(c) $A + (C + B)$ (f) $(C + A) + B$

2. Find x, y, and z so that

$$(2 \quad 3 \quad -4) + (x \quad y \quad z) = (6 \quad -8 \quad 2)$$

3. Find x and y so that

$$\begin{pmatrix} 3 & -\frac{1}{2} & 2 \\ 1 & 0 & -1 \end{pmatrix} + \begin{pmatrix} x-y & \frac{1}{2} & -2 \\ 4 & x & 6 \end{pmatrix} = \begin{pmatrix} 6 & 0 & 0 \\ 5 & 2x+y & 5 \end{pmatrix}$$

4. Prove Theorem 7.2.1.

7.3
MATRIX
MULTIPLICATION

As we shall see, there will be two kinds of multiplication involving matrices. We can multiply a real number and a matrix, *scalar multiplication*, and we can multiply two matrices, *matrix multiplication*.

Before defining what the meaning of scalar multiplication is, let us return to the production of Motors Incorporated during the month specified in Example 7.1.1. You may recall the matrix A describing this production is

$$A = \begin{pmatrix} 23 & 16 & 10 \\ 7 & 9 & 11 \end{pmatrix}$$

Let us assume that for 3 consecutive months, the monthly production remained the same. Then the total production for the 3 months is merely the sum of the matrix A 3 times. If we represent the total production by the matrix T, then

$$T = \begin{pmatrix} 23 & 16 & 10 \\ 7 & 9 & 11 \end{pmatrix} + \begin{pmatrix} 23 & 16 & 10 \\ 7 & 9 & 11 \end{pmatrix} + \begin{pmatrix} 23 & 16 & 10 \\ 7 & 9 & 11 \end{pmatrix}$$

$$= \begin{pmatrix} 23 + 23 + 23 & 16 + 16 + 16 & 10 + 10 + 10 \\ 7 + 7 + 7 & 9 + 9 + 9 & 11 + 11 + 11 \end{pmatrix}$$

$$= \begin{pmatrix} 3 \cdot 23 & 3 \cdot 16 & 3 \cdot 10 \\ 3 \cdot 7 & 3 \cdot 9 & 3 \cdot 11 \end{pmatrix} = \begin{pmatrix} 69 & 48 & 30 \\ 21 & 27 & 33 \end{pmatrix}$$

In other words, when we add the matrix A 3 times, we merely multiply each entry of A by 3. This leads to the following definition of scalar multiplication.

Let $A = (a_{ij})$ **be an** $n \times m$ **matrix and let** c **be a real number. The** *scalar product* cA **of the matrix** A **and the real number** c **(called the** *scalar***) is the** $n \times m$ **matrix** $cA = (ca_{ij})$**.**

7.3.1
Definition

Thus, when multiplying a scalar times a matrix, each entry of the matrix is multiplied by the scalar. Notice that the dimension of A and the dimension of the scalar product cA are the same.

Let

7.3.1
Example

$$A = \begin{pmatrix} -2 \\ 5 \\ -7 \end{pmatrix} \qquad B = \begin{pmatrix} 21 & 1 \\ 18 & 8 \end{pmatrix}$$

Then

$$3A = 3 \begin{pmatrix} 2 \\ 5 \\ -7 \end{pmatrix} = \begin{pmatrix} 3 \cdot 2 \\ 3 \cdot 5 \\ 3 \cdot -7 \end{pmatrix} = \begin{pmatrix} 6 \\ 15 \\ -21 \end{pmatrix}$$

and

$$\frac{1}{2}B = \frac{1}{2} \begin{pmatrix} 21 & 1 \\ 18 & 8 \end{pmatrix} = \begin{pmatrix} \frac{1}{2} \cdot 21 & \frac{1}{2} \cdot 1 \\ \frac{1}{2} \cdot 18 & \frac{1}{2} \cdot 8 \end{pmatrix} = \begin{pmatrix} \frac{21}{2} & \frac{1}{2} \\ 9 & 4 \end{pmatrix}$$

Let

7.3.2
Example

$$A = \begin{pmatrix} 3 & 1 \\ 4 & 0 \\ 2 & -3 \end{pmatrix} \qquad B = \begin{pmatrix} 2 & -3 \\ -1 & 1 \\ 1 & 0 \end{pmatrix}$$

Then

$$A - B = \begin{pmatrix} 1 & 4 \\ 5 & -1 \\ 1 & -3 \end{pmatrix}$$

Also

$$A + (-1) \cdot B = \begin{pmatrix} 3 & 1 \\ 4 & 0 \\ 2 & -3 \end{pmatrix} + \begin{pmatrix} -2 & 3 \\ 1 & -1 \\ -1 & 0 \end{pmatrix} = \begin{pmatrix} 1 & 4 \\ 5 & -1 \\ 1 & -3 \end{pmatrix}$$

The above example illustrates the following result.

$$A - B = A + (-1) \cdot B$$

In order to arrive at a definition for multiplying two matrices, we consider the following example.

7.3.3 Example Using the data of one month's production of Motors Incorporated from Example 7.1.1, we have Figure 7.3.

$$A = \begin{pmatrix} \overset{\text{sedan}}{23} & \overset{\text{hard-top}}{16} & \overset{\text{convertible}}{10} \\ 7 & 9 & 11 \end{pmatrix} \begin{array}{l} \text{units of material} \\ \text{units of labor} \end{array}$$

Figure 7.3

Suppose that in this month's production, the cost for each unit of material is \$45 and the cost for each unit of labor is \$60. What is the total cost to manufacture the sedans, the hard tops, and the convertibles?

We can represent the cost of units of material and the units of labor by the row vector

$$U = (45 \quad 60)$$

The total cost of units for sedans, hard tops, and convertibles will then be $U \cdot A$. Now $U \cdot A$ is computed as follows.

For sedans, the cost is 23 units of material at \$45 each plus 7 units of labor at \$60 each for a total cost of

$$23 \cdot 45 + 7 \cdot 60 = 1035 + 420 = 1455$$

Similarly, for hard tops, the total cost is

$$16 \cdot 45 + 9 \cdot 60 = 720 + 540 = 1260$$

Finally, for convertibles, the total cost is

$$10 \cdot 45 + 11 \cdot 60 = 450 + 660 = 1110$$

We can represent the total cost for sedans, hard tops, and convertibles by the matrix

$$(1455 \quad 1260 \quad 1110)$$

We arrived at the above matrix (row vector) by

$$U \cdot A = (45 \quad 60) \cdot \begin{pmatrix} 23 & 16 & 10 \\ 7 & 9 & 11 \end{pmatrix}$$
$$= (45 \cdot 23 + 60 \cdot 7 \quad 45 \cdot 16 + 60 \cdot 9 \quad 45 \cdot 10 + 60 \cdot 11)$$
$$= (1455 \quad 1260 \quad 1110)$$

In this example, notice that the number of columns of U is the same as the number of rows of A. Also, the number of rows of U is the same as the number of rows of the product $U \cdot A$ and the number of columns of A is the same as the number of columns of the product $U \cdot A$. With this in mind, we shall define the product of two matrices.

Let $A = (a_{ij})$ be a matrix of dimension $n \times m$ and let $B = (b_{jk})$ be a matrix of dimension $m \times p$. The *product* **$A \cdot B$ is the matrix $C = (c_{ik})$ of dimension $n \times p$ where the ikth entry of C is**

7.3.2
Definition

$$c_{ik} = a_{i1}b_{1k} + a_{i2}b_{2k} + a_{i3}b_{3k} + \cdots + a_{im}b_{mk}$$

The element in the ith row and kth column of C, namely, c_{ik}, is obtained by summing the products of the elements of the ith row of A and the corresponding elements of the kth column of B, taken in order.

The rule for multiplication of matrices is best illustrated by the following examples.

Let

7.3.4
Example

$$A = \begin{pmatrix} 1 & 3 & -2 \\ 4 & -1 & 5 \end{pmatrix}, \qquad B = \begin{pmatrix} 2 & -3 & 4 & 1 \\ -1 & 2 & 2 & 0 \\ 4 & 5 & 1 & 1 \end{pmatrix}$$

Here A is 2×3 and B is 3×4. The product $A \cdot B$ will be 2×4 and is

$$A \cdot B = \begin{pmatrix} 1 \cdot 2 + 3(-1) + (-2)4 & 1(-3) + 3 \cdot 2 + (-2)5 \\ 4 \cdot 2 + (-1)(-1) + 5 \cdot 4 & 4(-3) + (-1)2 + 5 \cdot 5 \end{pmatrix}$$
$$\begin{pmatrix} 1 \cdot 4 + 3 \cdot 2 + (-2)1 & 1 \cdot 1 + 3 \cdot 0 + (-2) \cdot 1 \\ 4 \cdot 4 + (-1)2 + 5 \cdot 1 & 4 \cdot 1 + (-1) \cdot 0 + 5 \cdot 1 \end{pmatrix}$$
$$= \begin{pmatrix} -9 & -7 & 8 & -1 \\ 29 & 11 & 19 & 9 \end{pmatrix}$$

Let

7.3.5
Example

$$A = \begin{pmatrix} 2 & -1 & 2 \\ 1 & 2 & -4 \\ 3 & -1 & 1 \end{pmatrix}, \qquad B = \begin{pmatrix} x \\ y \\ z \end{pmatrix}$$

Here A is 3×3 and B is 3×1. The product $A \cdot B$ is 3×1 and is

$$A \cdot B = \begin{pmatrix} 2 & -1 & 2 \\ 1 & 2 & -4 \\ 3 & -1 & 1 \end{pmatrix} \begin{pmatrix} x \\ y \\ z \end{pmatrix} = \begin{pmatrix} 2x - y + 2z \\ x + 2y - 4z \\ 3x - y + z \end{pmatrix}$$

If A is a matrix of dimension $n \times m$ (which has m columns) and B is a matrix of dimension $p \times q$ (which has p rows) and if $m \neq p$, there is *no* product $A \cdot B$ defined. That is, multiplication of matrices is possible only if the number of columns of the first equals the number of rows of the second. Otherwise, it is impossible.

If A is of dimension $n \times m$ and if B is of dimension $m \times p$, then the product $A \cdot B$ can be found and the product matrix is of dimension $n \times p$. Because of this requirement for multiplying matrices, it may be possible to find the product $A \cdot B$ of two matrices, although it is impossible to find $B \cdot A$. The matrices in Example 7.3.4 illustrate this.

We shall continue our study of scalar multiplication and matrix multiplication by listing some of the properties obeyed.

Theorem 7.3.1

Let k and h be two real numbers and let $A = (a_{ij})$ and $B = (b_{ij})$, $i = 1, \ldots, n, j = 1, \ldots, m$ be matrices of dimension $n \times m$. Then

(I) $\qquad\qquad\qquad k[hA] = [kh]A$

(II) $\qquad\qquad\qquad [k + h]A = kA + hA$

(III) $\qquad\qquad\qquad k[A + B] = kA + kB$

Proof

(I) Here

$$k[hA] = k[h(a_{ij})] = k[(ha_{ij})] = k(ha_{ij})$$
$$= (kha_{ij}) = [kh](a_{ij})$$

(II) For this property we have

$$[k + h]A = [k + h](a_{ij}) = ([k + h]a_{ij})$$
$$= (ka_{ij} + ha_{ij}) = (ka_{ij}) + (ha_{ij})$$
$$= k(a_{ij}) + h(a_{ij}) = kA + hA$$

(III) This is left for the student.

The three properties listed above in Theorem 7.3.1 are illustrated in the following example:

7.3.6
Example

Let

$$A = \begin{pmatrix} 2 & -3 & -1 \\ 5 & 6 & 4 \end{pmatrix}, \qquad B = \begin{pmatrix} -3 & 0 & 4 \\ 2 & -1 & 5 \end{pmatrix}$$

Then

(I)

$$5(2A) = 5 \begin{pmatrix} 4 & -6 & -2 \\ 10 & 12 & 8 \end{pmatrix} = \begin{pmatrix} 20 & -30 & -10 \\ 50 & 60 & 40 \end{pmatrix}$$

$$10A = \begin{pmatrix} 20 & -30 & -10 \\ 50 & 60 & 40 \end{pmatrix}$$

Also

(II)

$$(4 + 3)A = 7A = \begin{pmatrix} 14 & -21 & -7 \\ 35 & 42 & 28 \end{pmatrix}$$

$$4A + 3A = \begin{pmatrix} 8 & -12 & -4 \\ 20 & 24 & 16 \end{pmatrix} + \begin{pmatrix} 6 & -9 & -3 \\ 15 & 18 & 12 \end{pmatrix}$$

$$= \begin{pmatrix} 14 & -21 & -7 \\ 35 & 42 & 28 \end{pmatrix}$$

Finally

(III) $\quad 3(A + B) = 3 \begin{pmatrix} -1 & -3 & 3 \\ 7 & 5 & 9 \end{pmatrix} = \begin{pmatrix} -3 & -9 & 9 \\ 21 & 15 & 27 \end{pmatrix}$

$\quad 3A + 3B = \begin{pmatrix} 6 & -9 & -3 \\ 15 & 18 & 12 \end{pmatrix} + \begin{pmatrix} -9 & 0 & 12 \\ 6 & -3 & 15 \end{pmatrix} = \begin{pmatrix} -3 & -9 & 9 \\ 21 & 15 & 27 \end{pmatrix}$

Next, we list some properties of matrix multiplication. We agree to follow the notational convention that $A \cdot B = AB$.

Theorem 7.3.2
Let A be a matrix of dimension $n \times m$, let B be a matrix of dimension $m \times p$, and let C be a matrix of dimension $p \times q$. Then matrix multiplication is *associative.* **That is**

$$A(BC) = (AB)C$$

The resulting matrix ABC is of dimension $n \times q$.

Again, notice the limitations that are placed on the dimensions of the matrices in order for multiplication to be associative.

Theorem 7.3.3
Let A be a matrix of dimension $n \times m$. Let B and C be matrices of dimension $m \times p$. Then *matrix multiplication distributes over matrix addition.* **That is**

$$A(B + C) = AB + AC$$

The resulting matrix $AB + AC$ is of dimension $n \times p$.

Problems 5, 9, and 10 in Exercise 7.3 illustrate that multiplication of matrices is usually not commutative. The above theorems indicate that under certain conditions multiplication is associative and multiplication distributes over addition.

A special type of square matrix of great interest to us is the *identity matrix,* which is denoted by I_n and has the property that all its diagonal entries are 1's and all other entries are 0's. It is of the form

$$I_n = \begin{pmatrix} 1 & 0 & \cdots & 0 & 0 \\ 0 & 1 & \cdots & 0 & 0 \\ \cdot & \cdot & \cdot & & \cdot & \cdot \\ \cdot & \cdot & & \cdot & & \cdot \\ \cdot & \cdot & & & \cdot & \cdot \\ 0 & 0 & \cdots & 1 & 0 \\ 0 & 0 & \cdots & 0 & 1 \end{pmatrix}$$

where the subscript n denotes the fact that I_n is of dimension $n \times n$.

**7.3.7
Example** Let

$$A = \begin{pmatrix} 3 & 2 \\ -4 & \frac{1}{2} \end{pmatrix}, \qquad I_2 = \begin{pmatrix} 1 & 0 \\ 0 & 1 \end{pmatrix}$$

Then

$$AI_2 = \begin{pmatrix} 3 & 2 \\ -4 & \frac{1}{2} \end{pmatrix}\begin{pmatrix} 1 & 0 \\ 0 & 1 \end{pmatrix} = \begin{pmatrix} 3 & 2 \\ -4 & \frac{1}{2} \end{pmatrix} = A$$

Also

$$I_2 A = \begin{pmatrix} 1 & 0 \\ 0 & 1 \end{pmatrix}\begin{pmatrix} 3 & 2 \\ -4 & \frac{1}{2} \end{pmatrix} = \begin{pmatrix} 3 & 2 \\ -4 & \frac{1}{2} \end{pmatrix} = A$$

This example can be generalized by the following result.

Theorem 7.3.4
If A is a square matrix of dimension $n \times n$ and if I_n is an identity matrix of dimension $n \times n$, then

$$AI_n = I_n A = A$$

Thus far we have only considered identity matrices with regard to a *square* matrix A. The reason for this is illustrated in the following example.

**7.3.8
Example** Let

$$A = \begin{pmatrix} 1 & 2 \\ 3 & 2 \\ 1 & 1 \end{pmatrix}$$

Then

$$A \cdot \begin{pmatrix} 1 & 0 \\ 0 & 1 \end{pmatrix} = \begin{pmatrix} 1 & 2 \\ 3 & 2 \\ 1 & 1 \end{pmatrix}\begin{pmatrix} 1 & 0 \\ 0 & 1 \end{pmatrix} = \begin{pmatrix} 1 & 2 \\ 3 & 2 \\ 1 & 1 \end{pmatrix} = A$$

However, $\begin{pmatrix} 1 & 0 \\ 0 & 1 \end{pmatrix} \cdot A$ is *not* possible. Notice, though, that

$$\begin{pmatrix} 1 & 0 & 0 \\ 0 & 1 & 0 \\ 0 & 0 & 1 \end{pmatrix} \cdot A = \begin{pmatrix} 1 & 0 & 0 \\ 0 & 1 & 0 \\ 0 & 0 & 1 \end{pmatrix}\begin{pmatrix} 1 & 2 \\ 3 & 2 \\ 1 & 1 \end{pmatrix} = \begin{pmatrix} 1 & 2 \\ 3 & 2 \\ 1 & 1 \end{pmatrix} = A$$

That is, for nonsquare matrices, the identity matrix is *not* unique.

**7.3.3
Definition** **Let A be a matrix of dimension $n \times n$. A matrix B of dimension $n \times n$ is called an *inverse* of A if and only if $AB = I_n$. We denote the inverse of a matrix A, if it exists, by A^{-1}.**

Theorem 7.3.5
A square matrix A has at most one inverse. That is, the inverse of a matrix is _unique_ if it exists.

Proof
Suppose that we have two inverses B and C for a matrix A. Then

$$AB = BA = I_n \quad \text{and} \quad AC = CA = I_n$$

Multiplying both sides of $AC = I_n$ by B, we find

$$B(AC) = BI_n = B$$

Similarly, multiplying both sides of $BA = I_n$ by C, we obtain

$$(BA)C = I_n C = C$$

But

$$B(AC) = (BA)C$$

Thus

$$B = C$$

Not all matrices possess inverses. A nonsquare matrix, for example, does not have an inverse since the products AB and BA cannot be equal. Even if a matrix is square its inverse does not always exist. Consider the following example.

Does the matrix

7.3.9
Example

$$A = \begin{pmatrix} 0 & 1 \\ 0 & 0 \end{pmatrix}$$

have an inverse?
Suppose its inverse is

$$B = \begin{pmatrix} x & y \\ z & w \end{pmatrix}$$

Then, we must have

$$A \cdot B = I_2$$

That is

$$\begin{pmatrix} 0 & 1 \\ 0 & 0 \end{pmatrix}\begin{pmatrix} x & y \\ z & w \end{pmatrix} = \begin{pmatrix} 1 & 0 \\ 0 & 1 \end{pmatrix}$$

Performing the multiplication, we have,

$$\begin{pmatrix} z & w \\ 0 & 0 \end{pmatrix} = \begin{pmatrix} 1 & 0 \\ 0 & 1 \end{pmatrix}$$

These two matrices can never be equal. Hence, the matrix A in Example 7.3.9 has _no_ inverse.

218
INTRODUCTION TO
MATRIX ALGEBRA
WITH APPLICATIONS

7.3
Exercise

1. Perform the matrix multiplications:

(a) $\begin{pmatrix} 1 & -1 & 1 \\ 2 & 0 & 1 \\ 3 & -1 & 1 \end{pmatrix} \begin{pmatrix} 1 & 2 \\ -1 & 1 \\ 1 & 3 \end{pmatrix}$ (c) $\begin{pmatrix} d_1 & 0 & 0 \\ 0 & d_2 & 0 \\ 0 & 0 & d_3 \end{pmatrix} \begin{pmatrix} a_1 & a_2 \\ b_1 & b_2 \\ c_1 & c_2 \end{pmatrix}$

(b) $\begin{pmatrix} 1 & 0 & 0 \\ 0 & 1 & 0 \\ 0 & 0 & 1 \end{pmatrix} \begin{pmatrix} a_1 & a_2 & a_3 \\ b_1 & b_2 & b_3 \\ c_1 & c_2 & c_3 \end{pmatrix}$

2. Let

$$A = \begin{pmatrix} 1 & -1 & 1 \\ 20 & 1 & 0 \end{pmatrix} \qquad B = \begin{pmatrix} 1 & -1 & 0 \\ 0 & 1 & -1 \\ 1 & 1 & 1 \end{pmatrix} \qquad C = \begin{pmatrix} 1 & 0 \\ 0 & 1 \\ 1 & 1 \end{pmatrix}$$

Test the rule $(AB)C = A(BC)$.

3. If possible find a matrix A such that

$$A \cdot \begin{pmatrix} 0 & 1 \\ 2 & -1 \end{pmatrix} = \begin{pmatrix} 2 & 1 \\ -1 & 0 \end{pmatrix}$$

Hint: Let $A = \begin{pmatrix} a & b \\ c & d \end{pmatrix}$

4. For what values of x will

$$(x \quad 4 \quad 1) \cdot \begin{pmatrix} 2 & 1 & 0 \\ 1 & 0 & 2 \\ 0 & 2 & 4 \end{pmatrix} \cdot \begin{pmatrix} x \\ -7 \\ \dfrac{5}{4} \end{pmatrix} = 0$$

5. Let

$$A = \begin{pmatrix} 1 & -1 \\ 2 & 0 \end{pmatrix} \qquad B = \begin{pmatrix} 3 & 2 \\ -1 & 4 \end{pmatrix}$$

find AB and BA. Notice that $AB \neq BA$. Could this have been predicted?

6. Let

$$U = \begin{pmatrix} 2 \\ -1 \\ 3 \end{pmatrix}, \qquad V = \begin{pmatrix} 1 \\ 2 \\ 0 \\ 1 \end{pmatrix}, \qquad W = \begin{pmatrix} -3 \\ -7 \\ 0 \end{pmatrix}$$

Compute the following:
(a) $U + V$ (d) $U + V - W$
(b) $U - V$ (e) $2U - 7V$
(c) $\frac{1}{2}(U + V)$ (f) $\frac{1}{4}U - \frac{1}{4}V - \frac{1}{4}W$

7. Find a_1, a_2, a_3 which satisfy the following:

$$\begin{pmatrix} 2 \\ 1 \\ 0 \end{pmatrix} + \begin{pmatrix} a_1 \\ a_2 \\ a_3 \end{pmatrix} = \begin{pmatrix} 2 \\ -1 \\ 3 \end{pmatrix}$$

8. Consider the two column vectors

$$U = \begin{pmatrix} u_1 \\ u_2 \\ \cdot \\ \cdot \\ \cdot \\ u_n \end{pmatrix} \qquad V = \begin{pmatrix} v_1 \\ v_2 \\ \cdot \\ \cdot \\ \cdot \\ v_n \end{pmatrix}$$

Find the vector $\dfrac{1}{n}(U + V)$.

9. What must be true about a, b, c, and d if we demand $A \cdot B = B \cdot A$, for

$$A = \begin{pmatrix} a & b \\ c & d \end{pmatrix}, \qquad B = \begin{pmatrix} 1 & 1 \\ -1 & 1 \end{pmatrix}$$

Assume that

$$\begin{pmatrix} a & b \\ c & d \end{pmatrix} \neq \begin{pmatrix} 1 & 0 \\ 0 & 1 \end{pmatrix}$$

10. If $AB = BA$ the matrices A and B are said to be *commutative*. Show that for all values a, b, c, and d the matrices

$$A = \begin{pmatrix} a & b \\ -b & a \end{pmatrix} \qquad \text{and} \qquad B = \begin{pmatrix} c & d \\ -d & c \end{pmatrix}$$

are commutative.

11. Let

$$A = \begin{pmatrix} a & b \\ b & a \end{pmatrix}$$

Find a and b such that $A^2 + A = \theta$, where $A^2 = A \cdot A$.

12. Let

$$A = \begin{pmatrix} 1 & 2 & 5 \\ 2 & 4 & 10 \\ -1 & -2 & -5 \end{pmatrix}$$

Show that $A^2 = \theta$. Thus, the rule in the real number system that if $a^2 = 0$, then $a = 0$ will not hold for matrices.

13. For the matrix

$$A = \begin{pmatrix} a & 1 - a \\ 1 + a & -a \end{pmatrix}$$

show that $A^2 = A \cdot A = I_2$. A matrix A with this property is called *involutorial*.

14. Find the vector $(x_1 \quad x_2)$ such that

$$(x_1 \quad x_2) \begin{pmatrix} \dfrac{1}{2} & \dfrac{1}{2} \\ \dfrac{1}{4} & \dfrac{3}{4} \end{pmatrix} = (x_1 \quad x_2)$$

under the condition that $x_1 + x_2 = 1$.

Here the vector $(x_1 \quad x_2)$ is called a fixed vector of the matrix

$$\begin{pmatrix} \frac{1}{2} & \frac{1}{2} \\ \frac{1}{4} & \frac{3}{4} \end{pmatrix}$$

15. Let

$$A = \begin{pmatrix} 2 & 3 & 0 \\ 1 & 1 & 0 \\ 2 & 1 & 2 \end{pmatrix}$$

Compute $I_3 - A$, $\quad A - I_3$.

16. Prove III in Theorem 7.3.1.

17. Prove that if $AB = I_n$, then $BA = I_n$, where A and B are of dimension $n \times n$.

18. Mike went to a department store and purchased 6 pants, 8 shirts, and 2 jackets. Danny purchased 2 pants, 5 shirts and 3 jackets. If the pants are $5 each, the shirts $3 each and the jackets $9 each, use matrix multiplication to find the amounts spent by Mike and Danny.

19. Suppose a factory is asked to produce three types of products, which we will call P_1, P_2, P_3. Suppose the following purchasing order was received: $P_1 = 7, P_2 = 12, P_3 = 5$. Represent this order by a row vector and call it P.

$$P = (7 \quad 12 \quad 5)$$

To produce each of the products raw material of four kinds is needed. Call the raw material M_1, M_2, M_3, and M_4. The matrix below gives the amount of material needed corresponding to each product.

$$Q = \begin{matrix} & M_1 & M_2 & M_3 & M_4 \\ P_1 & 2 & 3 & 1 & 12 \\ P_2 & 7 & 9 & 5 & 20 \\ P_3 & 8 & 12 & 6 & 15 \end{matrix}$$

Suppose the cost for each of the materials M_1, M_2, M_3, and M_4 is 10, 12, 15, and 20 dollars, respectively. The cost column is

$$C = \begin{pmatrix} 10 \\ 12 \\ 15 \\ 20 \end{pmatrix}$$

Compute the following
(a) $P \cdot Q$ (c) $P \cdot Q \cdot C$
(b) $Q \cdot C$
Interpret each of these.

*20. For a square matrix A, it is always possible to find $A \cdot A = A^2$. It is also clear that we can compute

$$A^n = \underbrace{A \cdot A \cdots A}_{n \text{ times}}$$

Find A^2, A^3, A^4 for the following square matrices:

(a) $A = \begin{pmatrix} 1 & 0 \\ 3 & 2 \end{pmatrix}$

(d) $A = \begin{pmatrix} 1 & 0 \\ 0 & 1 \end{pmatrix}$

(b) $A = \begin{pmatrix} 3 & 1 \\ -2 & -1 \end{pmatrix}$

(e) $\begin{pmatrix} \dfrac{1}{2} & \dfrac{1}{2} \\ \dfrac{1}{4} & \dfrac{3}{4} \end{pmatrix}$

(c) $A = \begin{pmatrix} 0 & 1 & 1 \\ 0 & -1 & 2 \\ 6 & 3 & -2 \end{pmatrix}$

Can you guess what A^n looks like for 20(d)? for 20(e)?

To develop a procedure for determining solutions of a system of n linear equations in m unknowns and to obtain a technique for finding the inverse of a matrix, we need to be able to manipulate matrices. These manipulations are called *elementary (matrix) operations*.

**7.4
EQUIVALENT
MATRICES**

The elementary row or column operations are outlined as follows:

(I) The interchange of any two rows (or any two columns) of a matrix.

(II) The replacement of any row (or column) of a matrix by a nonzero scalar product of that same row (or column).

(III) The replacement of any row (or column of a matrix by the sum of that row (or column) and a scalar multiple of some other row (or column) of the matrix.

An example of each of these elementary operations is given below.

Consider the matrix

**7.4.1
Example**

$$A = \begin{pmatrix} 3 & 4 & -3 \\ 7 & -\dfrac{1}{2} & 0 \end{pmatrix}$$

(I) The matrix obtained by interchanging the first and second rows of A is

$$\begin{pmatrix} 7 & -\dfrac{1}{2} & 0 \\ 3 & 4 & -3 \end{pmatrix}$$

The matrix obtained by interchanging the first and third columns of A is

$$\begin{pmatrix} -3 & 4 & 3 \\ 0 & -\dfrac{1}{2} & 7 \end{pmatrix}$$

(II) The matrix obtained by replacing row 2 of A by a multiple of 5 is

$$\begin{pmatrix} 3 & 4 & -3 \\ 35 & -\dfrac{5}{2} & 0 \end{pmatrix}$$

We can also replace column 2 of A by 3 times column 2 obtaining

$$\begin{pmatrix} 3 & 12 & -3 \\ 7 & -\dfrac{3}{2} & 0 \end{pmatrix}$$

(III) The matrix obtained by adding 3 times row 1 to row 2 is

$$\begin{pmatrix} 3 & 4 & -3 \\ 7+3\cdot 3 & -\dfrac{1}{2}+3\cdot 4 & 0+3\cdot(-3) \end{pmatrix} = \begin{pmatrix} 3 & 4 & -3 \\ 16 & \dfrac{23}{2} & -9 \end{pmatrix}$$

The matrix obtained by adding 4 times column 2 to column 3 is

$$\begin{pmatrix} 3 & 4 & 4\cdot 4+(-3) \\ 7 & -\dfrac{1}{2} & 4\cdot\left(-\dfrac{1}{2}\right)+0 \end{pmatrix} = \begin{pmatrix} 3 & 4 & 13 \\ 7 & -\dfrac{1}{2} & -2 \end{pmatrix}$$

Of course, the matrix that is the result of such operations is not equal to the given matrix. However, we shall call such matrices *equivalent*.

**7.4.1
Definition**

Two matrices A and B are *equivalent,* **written as**

$$A \approx B$$

if and only if B can be obtained from A by using one or more elementary operations.

**7.4.2
Example**

For the matrix A

$$A = \begin{pmatrix} 1 & -1 & 2 \\ 0 & 5 & 3 \\ 2 & 4 & -2 \end{pmatrix}$$

find a matrix $B \approx A$ by multiplying the first row (r_1) of A by 2 and subtracting it from the third row (r_3) of A.

Here, the matrix B has the same first row as A and the same second row as A. However, the third row (r_3') of B is

$$r_3' = r_3 - 2r_1$$

The matrix B is

$$B = \begin{pmatrix} 1 & -1 & 2 \\ 0 & 5 & 3 \\ 0 & 6 & -6 \end{pmatrix}$$

Now what we want to do is find a matrix H (equivalent to a given matrix A) that has particular entries in it. This matrix is called the *reduced matrix of A*.

**7.4.2
Definition**

Let A be a given matrix of dimension $n \times m$. The *reduced matrix H* **(due to Hermite) is a matrix equivalent to A for which**

1. **The entries on the diagonal of H are either 0 or 1.**
2. **If there are k 1's on the diagonal of H, they are in the first k rows of H.**
3. **All the elements in the same column with a 1 on the diagonal are 0.**
4. **All the elements in the same row with a 0 on the diagonal are 0.**

For example, the matrix

$$\begin{pmatrix} 1 & 0 & 0 & 7 & 5 \\ 0 & 1 & 0 & 8 & 1 \\ 0 & 0 & 1 & 9 & 6 \\ 0 & 0 & 0 & 0 & 0 \\ 0 & 0 & 0 & 0 & 0 \end{pmatrix}$$

is a reduced matrix.

Find the reduced matrix H of

7.4.3
Example

$$A = \begin{pmatrix} 1 & -1 & 2 \\ 2 & -3 & 2 \\ 3 & -5 & 2 \end{pmatrix}$$

We begin by looking at the entry a_{11}. If $a_{11} \neq 1$, we perform an elementary operation in which $a_{11}' = 1$.

Now, with $a_{11} = 1$, we want to obtain an equivalent matrix in which all the entries in column 1 except a_{11}, are zero.

We can obtain such a matrix by

$$r_2' = r_2 - 2r_1$$
$$r_3' = r_3 - 3r_1$$

The new matrix is

$$\begin{pmatrix} 1 & -1 & 2 \\ 0 & -1 & -2 \\ 0 & -2 & -4 \end{pmatrix}$$

We want $a_{22} = 1$. By multiplying row 2 by (-1), we obtain

$$\begin{pmatrix} 1 & -1 & 2 \\ 0 & 1 & 2 \\ 0 & -2 & -4 \end{pmatrix}$$

Now column 2 should have zeros except for $a_{22} = 1$. This can be accomplished by applying the following row operations.

$$r_1' = r_1 + r_2$$
$$r_3' = r_3 + 2r_2$$

The new matrix is

$$\begin{pmatrix} 1 & 0 & 4 \\ 0 & 1 & 2 \\ 0 & 0 & 0 \end{pmatrix}$$

The matrix above is in reduced form since only 1's and 0's appear along the diagonal; whenever a 1 appears on the diagonal, the other entries in that column are 0's. Of course, the matrix A given in Example 7.4.3 is equivalent to the matrix given above.

7.4.4
Example

Find the reduced matrix H of

$$A = \begin{pmatrix} 1 & -1 & 2 & 2 \\ 2 & -3 & 2 & 1 \\ 3 & -5 & 2 & -3 \\ -4 & 12 & 8 & 10 \end{pmatrix}$$

As before, we perform elementary operations. If we perform

$$r_2' = r_2 - 2r_1, \qquad r_3' = r_3 - 3r_1, \qquad r_4' = r_4 + 4r_1$$

we obtain

$$\begin{pmatrix} 1 & -1 & 2 & 2 \\ 0 & -1 & -2 & -3 \\ 0 & -2 & -4 & -9 \\ 0 & 8 & 16 & 18 \end{pmatrix}$$

If we perform $r_2' = -r_2$, we obtain

$$\begin{pmatrix} 1 & -1 & 2 & 2 \\ 0 & 1 & 2 & 3 \\ 0 & -2 & -4 & -9 \\ 0 & 8 & 16 & 18 \end{pmatrix}$$

If we perform

$$r_1' = r_2 + r_1, \qquad r_3' = r_3 + 2r_2, \qquad r_4' = r_4 - 8r_2$$

we have

$$\begin{pmatrix} 1 & 0 & 4 & 5 \\ 0 & 1 & 2 & 3 \\ 0 & 0 & 0 & -3 \\ 0 & 0 & 0 & -6 \end{pmatrix}$$

Interchanging c_3 and c_4 gives

$$\begin{pmatrix} 1 & 0 & 5 & 4 \\ 0 & 1 & 3 & 2 \\ 0 & 0 & -3 & 0 \\ 0 & 0 & -6 & 0 \end{pmatrix}$$

If $c_3' = -(1/3)c_3$, then

$$\begin{pmatrix} 1 & 0 & -\dfrac{5}{3} & 4 \\ 0 & 1 & -1 & 2 \\ 0 & 0 & 1 & 0 \\ 0 & 0 & 2 & 0 \end{pmatrix}$$

Finally, if

$$r_1' = r_1 + \tfrac{5}{3}r_3, \qquad r_2' = r_2 + r_3, \qquad r_4' = r_4 - 2r_3,$$

we obtain

$$H = \begin{pmatrix} 1 & 0 & 0 & 4 \\ 0 & 1 & 0 & 2 \\ 0 & 0 & 1 & 0 \\ 0 & 0 & 0 & 0 \end{pmatrix}$$

Let H be a reduced matrix. If there are r 1's appearing along the diagonal of H, then r is called the *rank of H.*

For example, the matrix H in Example 7.4.3 is of rank 2. The matrix H of Example 7.4.4 is of rank 3.

We also use "rank" with regard to any matrix A. **A matrix A is of** *rank r* **if and only if its reduced matrix H is of rank r.**

This definition is possible because two equivalent matrices cannot have different ranks.

It should be clear that the rank r of a matrix A of dimension $n \times m$ can never exceed the smaller of n and m. That is

$$\text{rank } A \leqq \min(n,m)$$

1. Show that

   (a) $\begin{pmatrix} 3 & 2 & 1 \\ 2 & 1 & 0 \end{pmatrix} \approx \begin{pmatrix} 1 & 2 & 3 \\ 0 & 1 & 2 \end{pmatrix}$

   (b) $\begin{pmatrix} 3 & 2 & 1 \\ 2 & 1 & 0 \end{pmatrix} \approx \begin{pmatrix} 12 & 8 & 4 \\ 2 & 1 & 0 \end{pmatrix}$

   (c) $\begin{pmatrix} 3 & 2 & 1 \\ 2 & 1 & 0 \end{pmatrix} \approx \begin{pmatrix} 3 & 2 & 1 \\ 4 & 2 & 0 \end{pmatrix} \approx \begin{pmatrix} 3 & 2 & 1 \\ 1 & 0 & -1 \end{pmatrix}$

2. Find the reduced matrix of the following matrices in order to determine *rank*.

   (a) $\begin{pmatrix} 1 & 2 & 3 & 8 \\ 0 & 5 & -2 & 1 \\ -2 & 0 & -3 & 4 \\ 2 & 2 & 2 & 2 \end{pmatrix}$

   (e) $\begin{pmatrix} 2 & 4 & 5 & 2 \\ 3 & 4 & 5 & 4 \\ 4 & 4 & 5 & 3 \\ 1 & 4 & 5 & 1 \end{pmatrix}$

   (b) $\begin{pmatrix} 2 & 1 & -1 & 2 \\ 7 & 5 & 3 & 2 \end{pmatrix}$

   (f) $\begin{pmatrix} 1 & 0 & 1 & 0 \\ 1 & 1 & 0 & 0 \\ 0 & 1 & 1 & 1 \end{pmatrix}$

   (c) $(1 \quad 1 \quad 1)$

   (g) $\begin{pmatrix} 0 & 1 \\ 1 & 0 \end{pmatrix}$

   (d) $\begin{pmatrix} 1 \\ 1 \\ 1 \end{pmatrix}$

Now that we have introduced the concepts of elementary operations, equivalence of matrices, and rank of matrices we can discuss the problem of a solution to a system of m linear equations in n unknowns.

A system of m linear equations in the n unknowns $x_1, x_2, \ldots, x_n$ is of the form

$$
\begin{aligned}
a_{11}x_1 + a_{12}x_2 + \cdots + a_{1n}x_n &= b_1 \\
a_{21}x_1 + a_{22}x_2 + \cdots + a_{2n}x_n &= b_2 \\
a_{31}x_1 + a_{32}x_2 + \cdots + a_{3n}x_n &= b_3 \\
&\vdots \\
a_{i1}x_1 + a_{i2}x_2 + \cdots + a_{in}x_n &= b_i \\
&\vdots \\
a_{m1}x_1 + a_{m2}x_2 + \cdots + a_{mn}x_n &= b_m
\end{aligned}
\tag{7.5.1}
$$

where a_{ij} and b_{ij} are real numbers, $i = 1, 2, \ldots, m$, $j = 1, 2, \ldots, n$.

This is a system of *linear* equations because the unknowns $x_1, x_2, \ldots, x_n$ all appear to the power one and there are no products of unknowns. Keep in mind that the subscript on the x is meant only as a distinguishing symbol—it is *not* an exponent. Finally, if we count the number of equations in (7.5.1), we see that there are m of them, with a total of n unknowns $x_1, x_2, \ldots, x_n$.

**7.5.1
Definition** **By a *solution* of the system of equations (7.5.1) is meant any ordered n-tuple $(x_1, x_2, \ldots, x_n)$ of real numbers for which** each **of the m equations of the system is satisfied.**

For example, it can be verified that the ordered pair $(4/3, 2)$ is a solution to the system of two linear equations in the two unknowns x_1 and x_2.

$$
\begin{aligned}
3x_1 + 4x_2 &= 12 \\
3x_1 - 2x_2 &= 0
\end{aligned}
$$

For

$$
3 \cdot \frac{4}{3} + 4 \cdot 2 = 12
$$

$$
3 \cdot \frac{4}{3} - 2 \cdot 2 = 0
$$

Define X and B as the column vectors

$$
X = \begin{pmatrix} x_1 \\ \vdots \\ x_n \end{pmatrix} \qquad B = \begin{pmatrix} b_1 \\ \vdots \\ b_m \end{pmatrix}
$$

Let A denote the *coefficient matrix* of the system of equations (7.5.1), namely,

$$A = \begin{pmatrix} a_{11} & a_{12} & \cdots & a_{1n} \\ a_{21} & a_{22} & \cdots & a_{2n} \\ \cdot & \cdot & & \cdot \\ \cdot & \cdot & \cdots & \cdot \\ \cdot & \cdot & \cdots & \cdot \\ a_{m1} & a_{m2} & \cdots & a_{mn} \end{pmatrix}$$

Now the system of equations (7.5.1) can be written in matrix form as

$$AX = B$$

The *augmented* matrix of the system of linear equations (7.5.1) is the matrix $A|B$ formed by appending the column B to the coefficient matrix A.

7.5.2
Definition

Consider the following system of three equations in three unknowns

7.5.1
Example

$$\begin{aligned} x_1 + x_2 + x_3 &= 6 \\ 3x_1 + 2x_2 - x_3 &= 4 \\ 3x_1 + x_2 + 2x_3 &= 11 \end{aligned}$$

The matrix form of this system is:

$$\begin{pmatrix} 1 & 1 & 1 \\ 3 & 2 & -1 \\ 3 & 1 & 2 \end{pmatrix} \begin{pmatrix} x_1 \\ x_2 \\ x_3 \end{pmatrix} = \begin{pmatrix} 6 \\ 4 \\ 11 \end{pmatrix}$$

The coefficient matrix A is

$$A = \begin{pmatrix} 1 & 1 & 1 \\ 3 & 2 & -1 \\ 3 & 1 & 2 \end{pmatrix}$$

The augmented matrix $A|B$ is

$$A|B = \begin{pmatrix} 1 & 1 & 1 & | & 6 \\ 3 & 2 & -1 & | & 4 \\ 3 & 1 & 2 & | & 11 \end{pmatrix}$$

Notice that A is of dimension 3×3, while $A|B$ is of dimension 3×4.
Since

$$A = \begin{pmatrix} 1 & 1 & 1 \\ 3 & 2 & -1 \\ 3 & 1 & 1 \end{pmatrix} \approx \begin{pmatrix} 1 & 0 & 0 \\ 0 & 1 & 0 \\ 0 & 0 & 1 \end{pmatrix}$$

the rank of A is

$$\text{rank } A = 3$$

For the augmented matrix $A|B$, we have

$$A|B = \begin{pmatrix} 1 & 1 & 1 & | & 6 \\ 3 & 2 & -1 & | & 4 \\ 3 & 1 & 1 & | & 11 \end{pmatrix} \approx \begin{pmatrix} 1 & 0 & 0 & | & 0 \\ 0 & 1 & 0 & | & 0 \\ 0 & 0 & 1 & | & 0 \end{pmatrix}$$

Thus

$$\text{rank } A|B = 3$$

Since the augmented matrix $A|B$ of a system of equations is formed by adding one column to the coefficient matrix A of the system, it follows that

$$\text{rank } A \leqq \text{rank } A|B$$

The augmented matrix $A|B$ of a system of equations gives us all the essential information we need to know about the system — provided we remember which unknown is associated with which *column* and we remember the significance of the last *column*. If we perform only *row* operations on $A|B$, we obtain a system of equations having the same solutions as that of the original system — since *row* operations will not affect the significance we have placed on the *columns*. **Thus, when solving a system of equations, the only elementary operations permissible on** $A|B$ **are row operations.**

This technique for solving a system of equations is illustrated below.

7.5.2
Example

Find the solutions of

$$x_1 + x_2 + x_3 = 6$$
$$3x_1 + 2x_2 - x_3 = 4$$
$$3x_1 + x_2 + 2x_3 = 11$$

The augmented matrix $A|B$ of this system is

$$A|B = \begin{pmatrix} 1 & 1 & 1 & | & 6 \\ 3 & 2 & -1 & | & 4 \\ 3 & 1 & 2 & | & 11 \end{pmatrix}$$

Let us approach $A|B$ as if we were to obtain the reduced matrix — except that we cannot perform any column operations. Let

$$r_1' = -2r_1 + r_2$$

We obtain

$$\begin{pmatrix} 1 & 0 & -3 & | & -8 \\ 3 & 2 & -1 & | & 4 \\ 3 & 1 & 2 & | & 11 \end{pmatrix}$$

Perform the row operations

$$r_2' = -3r_1 + r_2$$
$$r_3' = -3r_1 + r_3$$

Then, we obtain

$$\begin{pmatrix} 1 & 0 & -3 & | & -8 \\ 0 & 2 & 8 & | & 28 \\ 0 & 1 & 11 & | & 35 \end{pmatrix}$$

If we let $r_2' = -\frac{1}{2}r_2$, we have

$$\begin{pmatrix} 1 & 0 & -3 & | & -8 \\ 0 & -1 & -4 & | & -14 \\ 0 & 1 & 11 & | & 35 \end{pmatrix}$$

If the row operation $r_3' = r_2 + r_3$ is performed, we have

$$\begin{pmatrix} 1 & 0 & -3 & | & -8 \\ 0 & -1 & -4 & | & -14 \\ 0 & 0 & 7 & | & 21 \end{pmatrix}$$

The system of equations is now

$$x_1 + 0 \cdot x_2 - 3x_3 = -8$$
$$0 \cdot x_1 - 1 \cdot x_2 - 4x_3 = -14$$
$$0 \cdot x_1 + 0 \cdot x_2 + 7x_3 = 21$$

Continuing, let

$$r_2' = -r_2$$
$$r_3' = \frac{1}{7}r_3$$

Then we obtain

$$\begin{pmatrix} 1 & 0 & -3 & | & -8 \\ 0 & 1 & 4 & | & 14 \\ 0 & 0 & 1 & | & 3 \end{pmatrix} \qquad \begin{matrix} x_1 + 0 \cdot x_2 - 3x_3 = -8 \\ 0 \cdot x_1 + 1 \cdot x_2 + 4x_3 = 14 \\ 0 \cdot x_1 + 0 \cdot x_2 + 1x_3 = 3 \end{matrix}$$

Finally

$$r_1' = r_1 + 3r_3$$
$$r_2' = r_2 - 4r_3$$

With these operations, we have

$$\begin{pmatrix} 1 & 0 & 0 & | & 1 \\ 0 & 1 & 0 & | & 2 \\ 0 & 0 & 1 & | & 3 \end{pmatrix} \qquad \begin{matrix} x_1 + 0 \cdot x_2 + 0 \cdot x_3 = 1 \\ 0 \cdot x_1 + 1 \cdot x_2 + 0 \cdot x_3 = 2 \\ 0 \cdot x_1 + 0 \cdot x_2 + 1 \cdot x_3 = 3 \end{matrix}$$

The solution set of the system of Example 7.5.2 is

$$x_1 = 1, \qquad x_2 = 2, \qquad x_3 = 3$$
$$\text{or } (1,2,3)$$

Suppose $A|B$ is the augmented matrix of a system of equations. To find the rank of $A|B$, either row or column operations are valid. To find the solution of the system, only row operations are valid.

Now some systems of equations will not have solutions. Other systems may have more than one set of solutions. If a system of equations has at least one set of solutions, it is called a *consistent system*; otherwise, it is said to be *inconsistent*.

The tests for whether a system of linear equations has a solution and the test for uniqueness are given below.

A system of equations $\qquad\qquad\qquad\qquad\qquad\qquad\qquad\qquad$ TEST I

$$AX = B$$

has at least one set of solutions if and only if

$$\text{rank } A = \text{rank } A|B$$

Otherwise, the system has no solution.

TEST II   A system of equations

$$AX = B$$

has exactly one set of solutions if and only if

rank A = rank $A|B \geqq$ number of unknowns

For the system of equations

$$AX = B$$

suppose

rank A = **rank** $A|B = r$

and

number of unknowns = m

If $m \leqq r$, the set of solutions is unique.
If $m > r$, there are infinitely many solutions.
The following examples illustrate these possibilities.

7.5.3   Consider the system of equations
Example

$$\begin{aligned}
x_1 + 2x_2 + x_3 &= 1 \\
2x_1 - x_2 + 2x_3 &= 2 \\
3x_1 + x_2 + 3x_3 &= 4
\end{aligned}$$

The coefficient matrix A and the augmented matrix $A|B$ are

$$A = \begin{pmatrix} 1 & 2 & 1 \\ 2 & -1 & 2 \\ 3 & 1 & 3 \end{pmatrix}, \qquad A|B = \begin{pmatrix} 1 & 2 & 1 & 1 \\ 2 & -1 & 2 & 2 \\ 3 & 1 & 3 & 4 \end{pmatrix}$$

The reader should verify that

rank $A = 2$,   rank $A|B = 3$

Thus, the system of Example 7.5.3 has no solution.
  Were we to approach this system as we did the one in Example 7.5.2, we would arrive at

$$\begin{pmatrix} 1 & 0 & 1 & 1 \\ 0 & 1 & 0 & 0 \\ 0 & 0 & 0 & 1 \end{pmatrix} \qquad \begin{aligned} x_1 + 0 \cdot x_2 + x_3 &= 1 \\ 0 \cdot x_1 + x_2 + 0 \cdot x_3 &= 0 \\ 0 \cdot x_1 + 0 \cdot x_2 + 0 \cdot x_3 &= 1 \end{aligned}$$

It is clear from the contradiction of the third equation $(0 = 1)$, that the system has no solution.

7.5.4   Consider the system
Example

$$\begin{aligned}
x_1 + 3x_2 + x_3 &= 6 \\
3x_1 - 2x_2 - 8x_3 &= 7 \\
4x_1 + 5x_2 - 6x_3 &= 17
\end{aligned}$$

The coefficient matrix A and the augmented matrix $A|B$ are

$$A = \begin{pmatrix} 1 & 3 & 1 \\ 3 & -2 & -8 \\ 4 & 5 & -6 \end{pmatrix}, \qquad A|B = \begin{pmatrix} 1 & 3 & 1 & 6 \\ 3 & -2 & -8 & 7 \\ 4 & 5 & -6 & 17 \end{pmatrix}$$

Here

$$\text{rank } A = 2, \qquad \text{rank } A|B = 2$$

Thus, the solution set of Example 7.5.4 exists. However

$$\text{number of unknowns} = 3$$

Thus, the solution is *not* unique.

By performing row operations on $A|B$, we obtain

$$\begin{pmatrix} 1 & 0 & -2 & 3 \\ 0 & 1 & 1 & 1 \\ 0 & 0 & 0 & 0 \end{pmatrix} \qquad \begin{matrix} x_1 + 0 \cdot x_2 - 2 \cdot x_3 = 3 \\ 0 \cdot x_1 + 1 \cdot x_2 + 1 \cdot x_3 = 1 \\ 0 \cdot x_1 + 0 \cdot x_2 + 0 \cdot x_3 = 0 \end{matrix}$$

There are infinitely many solutions since

$$x_1 = 3 + 2x_3 \qquad x_2 = 1 - x_3$$

and we can allow x_3 to take on any value.

Note: In Example 7.5.4

$$\text{number of unknowns} - \text{rank } A = 3 - 2 = 1$$

and we solved for two unknowns x_1 and x_2 in terms of the remaining unknown x_3. In general, if

$$\text{number of unknowns} - \text{rank } A = m - r$$

we can solve for r of the unknowns in terms of the remaining $m - r$ unknowns.

Consider the system

7.5.5
Example

$$\begin{matrix} x_1 + 3x_2 + 5x_3 + x_4 = 2 \\ 2x_1 + 3x_2 + 4x_3 + 2x_4 = 1 \\ x_1 + 2x_2 + 3x_3 + x_4 = 1 \end{matrix}$$

The coefficient matrix A and the augmented matrix $A|B$ are

$$A = \begin{pmatrix} 1 & 3 & 5 & 1 \\ 2 & 3 & 4 & 2 \\ 1 & 2 & 3 & 1 \end{pmatrix}, \qquad A|B = \begin{pmatrix} 1 & 3 & 5 & 1 & 2 \\ 2 & 3 & 4 & 2 & 1 \\ 1 & 2 & 3 & 1 & 1 \end{pmatrix}$$

Their ranks are

$$\text{rank } A = 2, \qquad \text{rank } A|B = 2$$

Since there are four unknowns, we know that this system has infinitely many solutions and that we can solve for two of the unknowns in terms of the remaining two. A solution is

$$x_1 = x_3 - x_4 + 1, \qquad x_2 = -2x_3 + 1$$

Here we treat x_3 and x_4 as *parameters*, that is, constants that may be changed at the option of the person handling the system. Of course, we could have written the solution in the form

$$x_3 = -\tfrac{1}{2}x_2 + \tfrac{1}{2}, \qquad x_4 = -x_1 - \tfrac{1}{2}x_2 + \tfrac{3}{2}$$

in which we have solved for x_3, x_4 in terms of x_1, x_2. In this case, x_1 and x_2 are now treated as parameters.

<table>
<tr><td>7.5.6
Example</td><td>In a chemistry laboratory one solution is 10 percent hydrochloric acid, a second solution contains 20 percent HCl and a third contains 40 percent HCl. How many liters of each should be mixed to obtain 100 liters of 25 percent HCl?</td></tr>
</table>

In a chemistry laboratory one solution is 10 percent hydrochloric acid, a second solution contains 20 percent HCl and a third contains 40 percent HCl. How many liters of each should be mixed to obtain 100 liters of 25 percent HCl?

First, let x_1, x_2, and x_3 represent the number of liters of 10, 20, and 40 percent solutions of HCl, respectively. Then

$$\begin{aligned} x_1 + x_2 + x_3 &= 100 \\ 0.1x_1 + 0.2x_2 + 0.4x_3 &= 25 \end{aligned}$$

since we want 100 liters in all and the amount of HCl obtained from each solution must sum to 25 percent of 100 or 25 liters. Thus, our problem reduces to two equations in three unknowns and so we can solve for any two in terms of the third.

If we decide that x_3 is to be the parameter, we have

$$\begin{aligned} x_1 + x_2 &= 100 - x_3 \\ x_1 + 2x_2 &= 250 - 4x_3 \end{aligned}$$

Thus

$$\begin{aligned} x_1 &= 2x_3 - 50 \\ x_2 &= -3x_3 + 150 \end{aligned}$$

where x_3 can represent any real number. Now the practical considerations of this problem lead us to the conditions that $x_1 \geqq 0$, $x_2 \geqq 0$, $x_3 \geqq 0$. Thus, we must have $x_3 \geqq 25$ and $x_3 \leqq 50$ since otherwise $x_1 < 0$ or $x_2 < 0$. Some

No. liters 10% Solution	No. liters 20% Solution	No. liters 40% Solution
10	60	30
12	57	31
16	51	33
20	45	35
25	37.5	37.5
26	36	38
30	30	40
36	21	43
38	18	44
46	6	48
50	0	50

Figure 7.4

possible solutions are listed in Figure 7.4. The final determination by the chemistry laboratory will more than likely be based on the amount and availability of one acid solution versus others.

We shall now discuss a technique for finding the inverse of a matrix. Recall that if A, B, and I_n are square matrices of dimension $n \times n$, then B is an inverse of A if and only if $AB = I_n$, where I_n is the identity matrix.

Suppose we want to find the inverse of a matrix A given by

$$A = \begin{pmatrix} -1 & -2 \\ 3 & 5 \end{pmatrix}$$

Let

$$X = \begin{pmatrix} x_1 & x_2 \\ x_3 & x_4 \end{pmatrix}$$

be an inverse of A, if such an inverse exists. Then

$$AX = I_2 \tag{7.5.2}$$

This matrix equation can be written as the following system of equations

$$\begin{aligned} -x_1 - 2x_3 &= 1, & -x_2 - 2x_4 &= 0 \\ 3x_1 + 5x_3 &= 0, & 3x_2 + 5x_4 &= 1 \end{aligned}$$

Solving these equations, using previous techniques, we find that

$$x_1 = 5, \quad x_2 = 2, \quad x_3 = -3, \quad x_4 = -1$$

Thus, the inverse of A is

$$A^{-1} = \begin{pmatrix} 5 & 2 \\ -3 & -1 \end{pmatrix}$$

Return to equation 7.5.2. If we treat this matrix equation in a way similar to the way we solved systems of equations, the coefficient matrix A is

$$A = \begin{pmatrix} -1 & -2 \\ 3 & 5 \end{pmatrix}$$

The augmented matrix $A|I_2$ will be

$$A|I_2 = \begin{pmatrix} -1 & -2 & | & 1 & 0 \\ 3 & 5 & | & 0 & 1 \end{pmatrix}$$

Performing only row operations on $A|I_2$, we obtain the following equivalent matrix

$$\begin{pmatrix} 1 & 0 & | & 5 & 2 \\ 0 & 1 & | & -3 & -1 \end{pmatrix}$$

Notice that the 2×2 matrix on the right-hand side of the above matrix is A^{-1}.

This example illustrates the following general principle:

Let A be a matrix of dimension $n \times n$ having an inverse. Let $A|I_n$ denote its augmented matrix. If $I_n|B$ is a matrix equivalent to $A|I_n$, then B is an inverse of A.

7.5.7
Example

Find the inverse of

$$A = \begin{pmatrix} 1 & 1 & 2 \\ 2 & 1 & 0 \\ 1 & 2 & 2 \end{pmatrix}$$

The augmented matrix $A\|I_3$ is

$$\begin{pmatrix} 1 & 1 & 2 & | & 1 & 0 & 0 \\ 2 & 1 & 0 & | & 0 & 1 & 0 \\ 1 & 2 & 2 & | & 0 & 0 & 1 \end{pmatrix}$$

Now

$$\begin{pmatrix} 1 & 1 & 2 & | & 1 & 0 & 0 \\ 2 & 1 & 0 & | & 0 & 1 & 0 \\ 1 & 2 & 2 & | & 0 & 0 & 1 \end{pmatrix} \approx \begin{pmatrix} 1 & 1 & 2 & | & 1 & 0 & 0 \\ 0 & -1 & -4 & | & -2 & 1 & 0 \\ 0 & 1 & 0 & | & -1 & 0 & 1 \end{pmatrix}$$

$$\approx \begin{pmatrix} 1 & 0 & 2 & | & 2 & 0 & -1 \\ 0 & 0 & -4 & | & -3 & 1 & 1 \\ 0 & 1 & 0 & | & -1 & 0 & 1 \end{pmatrix} \approx \begin{pmatrix} 1 & 0 & 2 & | & 2 & 0 & -1 \\ 0 & 1 & 0 & | & -1 & 0 & 1 \\ 0 & 0 & 1 & | & \frac{3}{4} & -\frac{1}{4} & -\frac{1}{4} \end{pmatrix}$$

$$\approx \begin{pmatrix} 1 & 0 & 0 & | & \frac{1}{2} & \frac{1}{2} & \frac{1}{2} \\ 0 & 1 & 0 & | & -1 & 0 & 1 \\ 0 & 0 & 1 & | & \frac{3}{4} & -\frac{1}{4} & -\frac{1}{4} \end{pmatrix}$$

Thus, the inverse of A is

$$A^{-1} = \begin{pmatrix} \frac{1}{2} & \frac{1}{2} & -\frac{1}{2} \\ -1 & 0 & 1 \\ \frac{3}{4} & -\frac{1}{4} & -\frac{1}{4} \end{pmatrix}$$

The student should verify that $AA^{-1} = I_3$.

The following result gives the condition under which a matrix A has an inverse. We omit the proof.

A matrix A of dimension $n \times n$ has an inverse A^{-1} if and only if the rank of $A = n$. Moreover, this inverse is unique.

A matrix A that has an inverse is said to be *nonsingular*.

An application of the use of inverse matrices to the solution of systems of equations in which the coefficient matrix is nonsingular is given below.

7.5.8
Example

Solve the system of equations

$$\begin{aligned} x_1 + x_2 + 2x_3 &= 1 \\ 2x_1 + x_2 \quad\quad &= 2 \\ x_1 + 2x_2 + 2x_3 &= 3 \end{aligned}$$

If we let

$$A = \begin{pmatrix} 1 & 1 & 2 \\ 2 & 1 & 0 \\ 1 & 2 & 2 \end{pmatrix}, \quad X = \begin{pmatrix} x_1 \\ x_2 \\ x_3 \end{pmatrix}, \quad B = \begin{pmatrix} 1 \\ 2 \\ 3 \end{pmatrix}$$

the above system can be written as

$$AX = B \qquad (7.5.3)$$

in which A is the coefficient matrix. Since A is nonsingular (see Example 7.5.7), its inverse A^{-1} exists. If we multiply equation 7.5.3 by A^{-1}, we obtain

$$A^{-1}(AX) = A^{-1}B$$
$$(A^{-1}A)X = A^{-1}B$$
$$I_3 X = A^{-1}B$$
$$X = A^{-1}B$$

$$X = \begin{pmatrix} \frac{1}{2} & \frac{1}{2} & -\frac{1}{2} \\ -1 & 0 & 1 \\ \frac{3}{4} & -\frac{1}{4} & -\frac{1}{4} \end{pmatrix} \begin{pmatrix} 1 \\ 2 \\ 3 \end{pmatrix}$$

$$= \begin{pmatrix} 0 \\ 2 \\ -\frac{1}{2} \end{pmatrix}$$

Thus the solution is

$$x_1 = 0, \qquad x_2 = 2, \qquad x_3 = -\tfrac{1}{2}$$

United States Oil is a producer of gasoline, oil, and natural gas. To produce the gasoline, oil, and natural gas, some of these products are used by the company. Suppose that to produce 1 unit of gasoline, the company uses 0 units of gasoline, 1 unit of oil, and 1 unit of natural gas. To produce 1 unit of oil, the company uses 0 unit of gasoline, 1/5 unit of oil, and 2/5 unit of natural gas. For 1 unit of natural gas, the company uses 1/5 unit of gasoline, 2/5 unit of oil, and 1/5 unit of natural gas. This data can be placed in a matrix C (for consumption) (see Figure 7.5).

7.5.9
Example

$$C = \begin{matrix} & \text{Gasoline} & \text{Oil} & \text{Natural Gas} \\ & \begin{pmatrix} 0 & 0 & \frac{1}{5} \\ 1 & \frac{1}{5} & \frac{2}{5} \\ 1 & \frac{2}{5} & \frac{1}{5} \end{pmatrix} & & \begin{matrix} \text{Gasoline used} \\ \text{Oil used} \\ \text{Natural gas used} \end{matrix} \end{matrix}$$

Figure 7.5

Let x, y, and z denote the daily production of units of gasoline, oil, and natural gas, respectively. The production matrix P is

$$P = \begin{pmatrix} x \\ y \\ z \end{pmatrix}$$

The product CP gives the amount of gasoline, oil, and natural gas used by the company. United States Oil has buyers for 100 units of gasoline, 100 units of oil, and 100 units of natural gas. How many units of each of these should be produced to meet the demand?

Let D denote the demand. Then

$$D = \begin{pmatrix} 100 \\ 100 \\ 100 \end{pmatrix}$$

To calculate the needed production, the amount used by the company for production must be subtracted from the amount produced. This amount is $P - CP$. Thus

$$P - CP = D, \qquad I_3 \cdot P - C \cdot P = D$$

Thus

$$(I_3 - C) \cdot P = D \qquad \text{or} \qquad P = (I_3 - C)^{-1} \cdot D$$

Then, computing these quantities, we obtain

$$P = \left[\begin{pmatrix} 1 & 0 & 0 \\ 0 & 1 & 0 \\ 0 & 0 & 1 \end{pmatrix} - \begin{pmatrix} 0 & 0 & \frac{1}{5} \\ 1 & \frac{1}{5} & \frac{2}{5} \\ 1 & \frac{2}{5} & \frac{1}{5} \end{pmatrix} \right]^{-1} \begin{pmatrix} 100 \\ 100 \\ 100 \end{pmatrix} = \begin{pmatrix} 300 \\ 1000 \\ 1000 \end{pmatrix}$$

The company must produce 300 units of gasoline, 1000 units of oil, and 1000 units of natural gas to meet the demand D.

Once a company has found its consumption matrix C, then production P needed for a demand D is

$$P = (I - C)^{-1} \cdot D$$

in which $(I - C)^{-1}$ is fixed, since consumption is fixed.

**7.5
Exercise**

1. Find solutions, if they exist, for the following.

(a) $2x_1 + 3x_2 - x_3 = 8$
$x_1 + x_2 + x_3 = 7$
$2x_2 - x_3 = 3$

(b) $2x_1 + 3x_2 = 8$
$2x_1 - x_2 = 12$

(c) $x_1 + x_2 - x_3 = 12$
$3x_1 - x_2 = 1$
$2x_1 - 3x_2 + 4x_3 = 3$

(d) $x_1 + x_2 = 7$
$x_2 - x_3 + x_4 = 5$
$x_1 - x_2 + x_3 + x_4 = 6$
$x_2 - x_4 = 10$

(e) $x_1 + 2x_2 - x_3 = 1$
$2x_1 - x_2 = -3$
$x_2 + 2x_3 = 5$

(f) $3x_1 - 4x_2 = 7$
$6x_1 - 8x_2 = 13$

(g) $x_1 + 2x_2 + 3x_3 - x_4 = 0$
$3x_1 - x_3 = 4$
$x_2 - x_3 - x_4 = 2$

(h) $2x_1 - 3x_2 + 4x_3 = 7$
$x_1 - 2x_2 + 3x_3 = 2$

(i) $x_1 + x_2 + x_3 + x_4 = 0$
$2x_1 - x_2 - x_3 + x_4 = 0$
$x_1 - x_2 - x_3 + x_4 = 0$
$x_1 + x_2 - x_3 - x_4 = 0$

2. Follow the directions of Problem 1, in which the left-hand side of problems (a), (b), (c), (d) remain the same and the right-hand side changes to

(a) 3
   7
   8

(b) 5
   7

(c) 0
   0
   0

(d) 0
   1
   0
   1

3. Find the inverse of each of the following matrices

(a) $\begin{pmatrix} 0 & 0 & 1 \\ 0 & 1 & 0 \\ 1 & 0 & 0 \end{pmatrix}$

(b) $\begin{pmatrix} -1 & 1 & 0 \\ 1 & 0 & 2 \\ 3 & 1 & 0 \end{pmatrix}$

(c) $\begin{pmatrix} 2 & 3 & -1 \\ 1 & 1 & 1 \\ 0 & 2 & -1 \end{pmatrix}$

(d) $\begin{pmatrix} 2 & 3 \\ 2 & -1 \end{pmatrix}$

(e) $\begin{pmatrix} 1 & 1 & -1 \\ 3 & -1 & 0 \\ 2 & -3 & 4 \end{pmatrix}$

(f) $\begin{pmatrix} 1 & 1 & 0 & 0 \\ 0 & 1 & -1 & 1 \\ 1 & -1 & 1 & 1 \\ 0 & 1 & 0 & -1 \end{pmatrix}$

(g) $\begin{pmatrix} 2 & 1 \\ 4 & 3 \end{pmatrix}$

(h) $\begin{pmatrix} 1 & 1 & -1 \\ 2 & 1 & 1 \\ 1 & 0 & 1 \end{pmatrix}$

(i) $\begin{pmatrix} 1 & 1 & 1 \\ 2 & 1 & 1 \\ 1 & 1 & 2 \end{pmatrix}$

*4. What is the necessary and sufficient condition for

$$A = \begin{pmatrix} a & b \\ c & d \end{pmatrix}$$

to have an inverse?

5. Find a matrix A such that

$$A \begin{pmatrix} 1 & 4 \\ 2 & 3 \end{pmatrix} = I_2$$

6. Find a matrix A such that

$$\begin{pmatrix} 1 & 2 \\ 3 & 4 \end{pmatrix} A = \begin{pmatrix} 9 & 1 \\ 0 & 7 \end{pmatrix}$$

7. Show that a solution to

$$\begin{pmatrix} 1 & 1 \\ 1 & 1 \end{pmatrix} \begin{pmatrix} x_1 \\ x_2 \end{pmatrix} = \begin{pmatrix} 1 \\ 1 \end{pmatrix}$$

is

$$\begin{pmatrix} x_1 \\ x_2 \end{pmatrix} = \begin{pmatrix} \frac{1}{2} \\ \frac{1}{2} \end{pmatrix}.$$

8. Show that

(a) $(A^{-1})^{-1} = A$ for $A = \begin{pmatrix} 3 & -2 \\ 2 & 4 \end{pmatrix}$

(b) $(AB)^{-1} = B^{-1}A^{-1}$ for $A = \begin{pmatrix} 3 & -2 \\ 2 & 4 \end{pmatrix}$, $B = \begin{pmatrix} 4 & -1 \\ 5 & 2 \end{pmatrix}$

9. An amount of \$5000 is put into three investments at rates of 6, 7, and 8 percent per annum, respectively. The total annual income is \$390. The income from the first two investments is \$60 less than the income from the third investment. Find the amount of each investment. Let x_1, x_2, and x_3 denote the amount invested at 6, 7, and 8 percent, respectively. Thus

$$0.06x_1 + 0.07x_2 + 0.08x_3 = 390$$
$$0.06x_1 + 0.07x_2 - 0.08x_3 = 60$$
$$x_1 + x_2 + x_3 = 5000$$

These three equations can be written in a matrix form as follows where

$$AX = B$$

$$A = \begin{pmatrix} 0.06 & 0.07 & 0.08 \\ 0.06 & 0.07 & -0.08 \\ 1 & 1 & 1 \end{pmatrix}, \quad X = \begin{pmatrix} x_1 \\ x_2 \\ x_3 \end{pmatrix}, \quad B = \begin{pmatrix} 390 \\ 60 \\ 5000 \end{pmatrix}$$

Find X.

10. If $A = \begin{pmatrix} 1 & 2 \\ 7 & 9 \end{pmatrix}$, find $(I_2 - A)^{-1}$.

11. A mixture consists of x gallons of milk and y grams of chocolate. A mixing machine will produce $3x + 7y$ grams of Grade A chocolate milk and $4x + 2y$ grams of Grade B chocolate milk. How much chocolate and milk is necessary to obtain 30 gallons Grade A and 40 gallons Grade B? How much chocolate and milk is needed if we want 20 gallons Grade A and 15 gallons Grade B?

Hint: If $\begin{pmatrix} x \\ y \end{pmatrix}$ denotes the unknown quantities, then the process can be interpreted by the matrix equation

$$\begin{pmatrix} 3 & 7 \\ 4 & 2 \end{pmatrix}\begin{pmatrix} x \\ y \end{pmatrix} = \begin{pmatrix} 30 \\ 40 \end{pmatrix}$$

12. Using the data given in Example 7.5.9, what should the production of United States Oil be if the demand D is for 500 units of gasoline, 1200 units of oil, and 1200 units of natural gas.

7.6 Cryptography

Our first application is to *cryptography,* the art of writing in or deciphering secret codes. We begin by giving examples of elementary codes.

A message can be encoded by associating each letter of the alphabet to some other letter of the alphabet according to a prescribed pattern. Thus, for example, we might have:

A B C D E F G H I J K L M N O P Q R S T U V W X Y Z
↓ ↓
C D E F G H I J K L M N O P Q R S T U V W X Y Z A B

With the above code, the word *BOMB* would become *DQOD*.

Another code is to associate numbers with the letters of the alphabet. Thus, for example, we might have

A B   C D ··· M N ··· W X Y Z
↓ ↓   ↓ ↓   ↓ ↓   ↓ ↓ ↓ ↓
26 25 24 23 ··· 14 13 ··· 4 3 2 1

In this code, the word *PEACE* looks like 11 22 26 24 22.

Both the above codes have one important feature in common. The association of letters with the coding symbols is made using a one-to-one correspondence so that no possible ambiguities can arise.

Suppose we want to encode the following message:

BEWARE THE IDES OF MARCH

We decide to divide the message into pairs of letters. The message becomes:

BE WA RE TH EI DE SO FM AR CH

(If there is a letter left over, we arbitrarily assign Z to the last position). Using the correspondence of letters to numbers given in Example 7.6.2, and writing each pair of letters as a column vector, we obtain

$$\binom{B}{E} = \binom{25}{22}, \quad \binom{W}{A} = \binom{4}{26}, \quad \binom{R}{E} = \binom{9}{22}, \quad \binom{T}{H} = \binom{7}{19}, \text{ etc.}$$

Next, we arbitrarily choose a 2×2 matrix A, which we know has an inverse (the reason for this is seen later). Furthermore, we choose a nonsingular matrix A in which both A and A^{-1} have integral values. Suppose we choose

$$A = \begin{pmatrix} 2 & 3 \\ 1 & 2 \end{pmatrix}$$

This is nonsingular and its inverse is

$$A^{-1} = \begin{pmatrix} 2 & -3 \\ -1 & 2 \end{pmatrix}$$

Now, we transform each of the column vectors representing the message by multiplying each of them on the left by the matrix A. Then

$$(1) \quad A \cdot \binom{B}{E} = A \cdot \binom{25}{22} = \binom{116}{69}$$

$$(2) \quad A \cdot \binom{W}{A} = A \cdot \binom{4}{26} = \binom{86}{56}$$

$$(3) \quad A \cdot \binom{R}{E} = A \cdot \binom{9}{22} = \binom{84}{53}, \text{ etc.}$$

The coded message is

$$116 \quad 69 \quad 86 \quad 56 \quad 84 \quad 53 \quad \text{etc.}$$

To decode or unscramble the above message, pair each number in a 2×1 column vector. Multiply each of these column vectors by A^{-1} on the left. Then

$$(1) \quad A^{-1} \binom{116}{69} = \binom{25}{22}$$

$$(2) \quad A^{-1} \binom{86}{56} = \binom{4}{26}$$

By reassigning letters to these numbers, we obtain the original message.

7.6.3
Example

The message to be encoded is

THE END IS NEAR

We agree to associate numbers to letters as follows:

$$
\begin{array}{ccccccc}
A & B & C & \cdots & X & Y & Z \\
\updownarrow & \updownarrow & \updownarrow & & \updownarrow & \updownarrow & \updownarrow \\
1 & 2 & 3 & \cdots & 24 & 25 & 26
\end{array}
$$

This time we divide the message into triplets of letters, obtaining

THE END ISN EAR

(If the message requires additional letters to complete the triplet, use Z or YZ).

Now we choose a 3×3 nonsingular matrix such as

$$A = \begin{pmatrix} 1 & 0 & 0 \\ 3 & 1 & 5 \\ -2 & 0 & 1 \end{pmatrix}$$

The inverse is

$$A^{-1} = \begin{pmatrix} 1 & 0 & 0 \\ -13 & 1 & -5 \\ 2 & 0 & 1 \end{pmatrix}$$

The encoded message is obtained by multiplying the matrix A times each column vector of the original message. Thus, we obtain

$$A \cdot \begin{pmatrix} T \\ H \\ E \end{pmatrix} = \begin{pmatrix} 1 & 0 & 0 \\ 3 & 1 & 5 \\ -2 & 0 & 1 \end{pmatrix} \cdot \begin{pmatrix} 20 \\ 8 \\ 5 \end{pmatrix} = \begin{pmatrix} 20 \\ 93 \\ -35 \end{pmatrix}$$

$$A \cdot \begin{pmatrix} E \\ N \\ D \end{pmatrix} = \begin{pmatrix} 1 & 0 & 0 \\ 3 & 1 & 5 \\ -2 & 0 & 1 \end{pmatrix} \cdot \begin{pmatrix} 5 \\ 14 \\ 4 \end{pmatrix} = \begin{pmatrix} 5 \\ 49 \\ -6 \end{pmatrix}$$

$$A \cdot \begin{pmatrix} I \\ S \\ N \end{pmatrix} = \begin{pmatrix} 1 & 0 & 0 \\ 3 & 1 & 5 \\ -2 & 0 & 1 \end{pmatrix} \cdot \begin{pmatrix} 9 \\ 19 \\ 14 \end{pmatrix} = \begin{pmatrix} 9 \\ 116 \\ -4 \end{pmatrix}$$

$$A \cdot \begin{pmatrix} E \\ A \\ R \end{pmatrix} = \begin{pmatrix} 1 & 0 & 0 \\ 3 & 1 & 5 \\ -2 & 0 & 1 \end{pmatrix} \cdot \begin{pmatrix} 5 \\ 1 \\ 18 \end{pmatrix} = \begin{pmatrix} 5 \\ 106 \\ 8 \end{pmatrix}$$

The coded message is

20   93   −35   5   49   −6   9   116   −4   5   106   8

Of course, to decode such a message, form 3×1 column vectors of these numbers and multiply on the left by A^{-1}.

---

1. Using the correspondence

$$A \leftrightarrow 1, \quad B \leftrightarrow 2, \ldots, \quad Y \leftrightarrow 25, \quad Z \leftrightarrow 26$$

and the matrices

(a) $A = \begin{pmatrix} 2 & 3 \\ 1 & 2 \end{pmatrix}$ 　　　(b) $A = \begin{pmatrix} 1 & 0 & 0 \\ 3 & 1 & 5 \\ -2 & 0 & 1 \end{pmatrix}$

Encode the following messages:
(a) MEET ME AT THE CASBAH.
(b) TOMORROW NEVER COMES.
(c) THE MISSION IS IMPOSSIBLE.

2. Using the correspondence given in Problem 1 and the matrix

$$A = \begin{pmatrix} 2 & 3 \\ 1 & 2 \end{pmatrix}$$

decode the following messages:
(a) 51   30   27   16   75   47   19   10   48   26
(b) 70   45   103   62   58   38   102   61   88   57

3. Using the correspondence given in Problem 1 and the matrix

$$A = \begin{pmatrix} 1 & 0 & 0 \\ 3 & 1 & 5 \\ -2 & 0 & 1 \end{pmatrix}$$

decode the message
25   195   −29   6   135   9   14   183   −2

Demography[1]

A further application of matrices can be made to demography, a science of vital statistics, which deals with birth rates, death rates, and population trends.

[1] Stone, Richard, "Mathematics in the Social Sciences," *Scientific American*, September, 1964.

To project population trends, three sets of data are needed: (1) the number of people living in different age categories on a given date, (2) the number of people surviving in these age categories over a time interval from that date, (3) the number of people born in the time interval to people in a given age category.

In order to simplify the data involved in such a study, (1) we shall assign daughters born according to the age category of their mother, and (2) we shall assume a constant pattern of birth and death for the time interval studied.

Based on the 1940 United States Census, we obtain the data matrix for the time interval 1940–1955. See Figure 7.6.

Age	No. Females Alive in 1940	Females Alive 15 Years Later (in 1955)	Daughters Born in 15-Year Interval (1940–1955)
0–14	14,459	16,428	4,651
15–29	15,264	14,258	10,403
30–44	11,346	14,836	1,374

Figure 7.6

The entries in column one represent the number of females alive in 1940 for the three age groups specified. The entries in column two represent the number of females that are alive in 1955 for each of the three age brackets. For example, the entry in row two, column two, 14,258 represents the survivors from the age group 0–14 alive in 1940 (14,459). Similarly, 14,836 represents the number of females alive in 1955 that survived from the 15,264 alive in 1940. The entries in column three represent the number of daughters born to females from the three age groups during the 15 year period 1940–1955.

Now, divide the number of daughters born in the 15-year interval (as shown in the third column) by the total number of females (as shown in the first column). The resulting ratios give the frequency for births in a given age group. These ratios are inserted in the first row of the frequency matrix shown in Figure 7.6. To obtain the second row, we need to know the survival frequency from the 0–14 age group to the 15–29 age group. Those females in the 0–14 age group (14,459) who survived 15 years later num-

$$
\begin{array}{c}
\begin{array}{ccc} 0\text{--}14 & 15\text{--}29 & 30\text{--}44 \end{array} \\
\begin{array}{l} \text{Frequency} \\ \text{for birth} \\ \text{Survival} \\ \text{frequency} \\ 0\text{--}14 \text{ to } 15\text{--}29 \\ \text{Survival} \\ \text{frequency} \\ 15\text{--}29 \text{ to } 30\text{--}44 \end{array}
\begin{pmatrix}
\dfrac{4651}{14459} & \dfrac{10403}{15264} & \dfrac{1374}{11346} \\[2ex]
\dfrac{14258}{14459} & 0 & 0 \\[2ex]
0 & \dfrac{14836}{15264} & 0
\end{pmatrix}
\end{array}
$$

Figure 7.7

ber 14,258. Thus, the ratio of survival is $14258 \div 14{,}459$. We use zeros for the remaining entries of row 2 since it is not possible to speak of a survival frequency in these age groups. Similarly, row 3 is obtained. See Figure 7.7.

The product of the frequency matrix F by the column matrix for females alive in 1940 gives the number of females alive in 1955. That is

$$
\underset{\text{Frequency matrix } F}{\begin{pmatrix} 0.32167 & 0.68154 & 0.12110 \\ 0.98610 & 0 & 0 \\ 0 & 0.97203 & 0 \end{pmatrix}} \underset{\text{Females (1940)}}{\begin{pmatrix} 14459 \\ 15264 \\ 11346 \end{pmatrix}} = \underset{\substack{\text{Females alive 15} \\ \text{years later (1955)}}}{\begin{pmatrix} 16428 \\ 14258 \\ 14836 \end{pmatrix}}
$$

Since this is in agreement with the information in Figure 7.6, it indicates that our frequency matrix F has been correctly calculated.

To obtain a projection for 1970, which is 15 years later than 1955, merely find the product of the square of the frequency matrix F times the column matrix for females in 1940. Thus

$$
F^2 \cdot \overset{\text{Females (1940)}}{\begin{pmatrix} 14459 \\ 15264 \\ 11346 \end{pmatrix}} = \begin{pmatrix} 0.77554 & 0.33694 & 0.03895 \\ 0.31719 & 0.67207 & 0.11942 \\ 0.95852 & 0 & 0 \end{pmatrix} \begin{pmatrix} 14459 \\ 15264 \\ 11346 \end{pmatrix} = \begin{pmatrix} 16{,}799 \\ 16{,}200 \\ 13{,}863 \end{pmatrix}
$$

To obtain a projection for 1985 (30 years past 1955), find the product of the cube of the frequency matrix times the column matrix for females in 1940. Then

$$
F^3 \cdot \overset{\text{Females (1940)}}{\begin{pmatrix} 14459 \\ 15264 \\ 11346 \end{pmatrix}} = \begin{pmatrix} 0.58172 & 0.56643 & 0.09392 \\ 0.76476 & 0.33226 & 0.03841 \\ 0.30832 & 0.65327 & 0.11608 \end{pmatrix} \begin{pmatrix} 14459 \\ 15264 \\ 11346 \end{pmatrix} = \begin{pmatrix} 18{,}123 \\ 16{,}565 \\ 15{,}747 \end{pmatrix}
$$

7.6.2
Exercise

1. Using the 1950 United States Census, and data from 1965, develop a projection for females in the 0–14, 15–29, and 30–44 age groups for the years 1980 and 1995.
2. Make the same sort of projection as in Problem 1 using data from the 1955 and the 1970 United States Census as a base. How does this projection compare with that found in the text for the year 1985?

Accounting

Consider a firm which has two types of departments, production and service. The production departments produce goods that can be sold in the market and the service departments provide services to the production departments.

The price of the final product must include direct costs (salaries, wages, costs of materials) and indirect costs (charges for the services the production departments receive from the service departments). Moreover, the service departments also provide services for the service departments themselves. For example, an accounting department usually provides accounting services for service departments as well as for the production departments. Thus the cost of services rendered by a service department must be determined in order to correctly assess the production departments. The total costs of a service department consist of its direct costs (salaries, wages, and materials) and its indirect costs (charges for the services it receives from the service departments). The nature of the problem and its solution are illustrated by the following example.

7.6.4 Example Consider a firm with two production departments P_1 and P_2 and three service departments S_1, S_2, and S_3. These five departments are shown in the column I of the table in Figure 7.8. The total monthly costs of these departments are unknown and are denoted by x_1, x_2, x_3, x_4, x_5. The direct monthly costs of the five departments are shown in the third column. The fourth, fifth, and sixth columns show the allocation of charges for the services of S_1, S_2, and S_3 to the various departments. Since the total cost of a department is the direct plus indirect costs, the first three rows of the table yield the total costs for the three service departments. Thus

$$x_1 = 600 + 0.25x_1 + 0.15x_2 + 0.15x_3$$
$$x_2 = 1100 + 0.35x_1 + 0.20x_2 + 0.25x_3 \qquad (7.6.1)$$
$$x_3 = 600 + 0.10x_1 + 0.10x_2 + 0.35x_3$$

Department	Total Costs	Direct Costs, dollars	Indirect Costs for Services from Departments S_1	S_2	S_3
S_1	x_1	600	$0.25x_1$	$0.15x_2$	$0.15x_3$
S_2	x_2	1100	$0.35x_1$	$0.20x_2$	$0.25x_3$
S_3	x_3	600	$0.10x_1$	$0.10x_2$	$0.35x_3$
P_1	x_4	2100	$0.15x_1$	$0.25x_2$	$0.15x_3$
P_2	x_5	1500	$0.15x_1$	$0.30x_2$	$0.10x_3$
Totals			x_1	x_2	x_3

Figure 7.8

Let X, C, and D denote the following matrices.

$$X = \begin{pmatrix} x_1 \\ x_2 \\ x_3 \end{pmatrix}, \quad C = \begin{pmatrix} 0.25 & 0.15 & 0.15 \\ 0.35 & 0.20 & 0.25 \\ 0.10 & 0.10 & 0.35 \end{pmatrix}, \quad D = \begin{pmatrix} 600 \\ 1100 \\ 600 \end{pmatrix}$$

Then the set of equations (7.6.1) can be written in matrix notation

$$X = D + C \cdot X$$

This is equivalent to:

$$(I_3 - C) \cdot X = D \tag{7.6.2}$$

The total costs of the three service departments can be obtained by solving the matrix equation (7.6.2) for X. The solution is

$$X = (I_3 - C)^{-1} \cdot D \tag{7.6.3}$$

Now

$$I_3 - C = \begin{pmatrix} 0.75 & -0.15 & -0.15 \\ -0.35 & 0.80 & -0.25 \\ -0.10 & -0.10 & 0.65 \end{pmatrix}$$

The student can verify that

$$(I_3 - C)^{-1} = \begin{pmatrix} 1.57 & 0.36 & 0.50 \\ 0.79 & 1.49 & 0.76 \\ 0.36 & 0.28 & 1.73 \end{pmatrix} \tag{7.6.4}$$

It is significant that the inverse of $(I_3 - C)$ exists, and that all of its entries are nonnegative. Because of this and the fact that the matrix D contains only nonnegative entries, the matrix X computed from (7.6.3) will also have only nonnegative entries. This means there is a meaningful solution to the accounting problem.

From equations (7.6.3) and (7.6.4) the matrix X is

$$X = \begin{pmatrix} 1638.00 \\ 2569.00 \\ 1562.00 \end{pmatrix}$$

Thus $x_1 = \$1638.00$, $x_2 = \$2569.00$, and $x_3 = \$1562.00$. All direct and indirect costs can now be determined by substituting these values in the table of Figure 7.8. See Figure 7.9.

Department	Total Costs, dollars	Direct Costs dollars	Indirect Costs for Services from Departments, dollars S_1	S_2	S_3
S_1	1629.15	600	409.50	385.35	234.30
S_2	2577.60	1100	573.30	513.80	390.50
S_3	1567.40	600	163.80	256.90	546.70
P_1	3222.25	2100	245.70	642.25	234.30
P_2	2672.60	1500	245.70	770.70	156.20

Figure 7.9 *Monthly costs corresponding to the information in Figure 7.8*

From Figure 7.9, we learn that department P_1 pays \$1122.25 for the services it receives from S_1, S_2, S_3, and P_2 pays \$1172.60 for the services it receives from these departments. The procedure we have followed charges the direct costs of the service departments to the production departments, and each production department is charged according to the services it utilizes. Furthermore, the total cost for P_1 and P_2 is \$5894.85, and this figure approximates the sum of the direct costs of the three service departments and the two production departments. The results are consistent with conventional accounting procedure. Discrepancies that occur are due to rounding off.

Finally, a comment should be made about the allocation of charges for services as shown in Figure 7.8. How is it determined that 25 percent of the total cost x_1 of S_1 should be charged to S_1, 35 percent to S_2, 10 percent to S_3, 15 percent to P_1, and 15 percent to P_2? There are two possible answers. First, it may be an arbitrary decision. Second, the services of each department may be measured in some suitable unit, and each department may be charged according to the number of these units of service it receives. If 20 percent of the accounting items concern a given department, that department is charged 20 percent of the total cost of the accounting department.

7.6.5
Example
Consider a firm for which the departments, direct costs, and allocations of indirect costs are those shown in the table of Figure 7.10. It should be observed that the total costs of the service departments S_1 and S_2 are allocated to these same two departments.

Department	Total Costs	Direct Costs, dollars	Indirect Costs for Services from Departments			
			S_1	S_2	S_3	S_4
S_1	x_1	1600	$0.35x_1$	$0.40x_2$	$0.15x_3$	$0.05x_4$
S_2	x_2	1000	$0.65x_1$	$0.60x_2$	$0.20x_3$	$0.10x_4$
S_3	x_3	800	0	0	$0.20x_3$	$0.05x_4$
S_4	x_4	1700	0	0	$0.15x_3$	$0.15x_4$
P_1	x_5	5000	0	0	$0.10x_3$	$0.20x_4$
P_2	x_6	4000	0	0	$0.10x_3$	$0.25x_4$
P_3	x_7	2500	0	0	$0.10x_3$	$0.20x_4$
Totals			x_1	x_2	x_3	x_4

Figure 7.10

Proceeding as in Example 7.6.4, we obtain the following equations for determining the total costs x_1, x_2, x_3, x_4 of the four service departments S_1, S_2, S_3, S_4.

$$x_1 = 1600 + 0.35x_1 + 0.40x_2 + 0.15x_3 + 0.05x_4$$
$$x_2 = 1000 + 0.65x_1 + 0.60x_2 + 0.20x_3 + 0.10x_4$$
$$x_3 = 800 + 0.20x_3 + 0.05x_4$$
$$x_4 = 1700 + 0.15x_3 + 0.15x_4$$

If we solve the last two of these four equations for x_3 and x_4, we find that $x_4 < 0$. Thus it is clear that no set x_1, x_2, x_3, x_4 of nonnegative numbers satisfies these equations. Clearly, a practical constraint for the x's is that they must be nonnegative. Therefore, the accounting problem specified by the data in the table in Figure 7.10 has no solution.

7.6.3
Exercise

1. Consider the accounting problem described by the data in the table in Figure 7.11. Determine whether this accounting problem has a solution. If it does, find the total costs.

Department	Total Costs	Direct Costs, dollars	Indirect Costs	
			S_1	S_2
S_1	x_1	2000	$1/9\ x_1$	$3/9\ x_2$
S_2	x_2	1000	$3/9\ x_1$	$1/9\ x_2$
P_1	x_3	2500	$1/9\ x_1$	$2/9\ x_2$
P_2	x_4	1500	$3/9\ x_1$	$1/9\ x_2$
P_3	x_5	3000	$1/9\ x_1$	$2/9\ x_2$
Totals			x_1	x_2

Figure 7.11

Make a table that corresponds to the one in Figure 7.9. Show that the total of the service charges allocated to P_1, P_2, P_3 is equal to the sum of the direct costs of the service departments S_1, S_2.

2. Midwestern University has a School of Arts and Sciences, a School of Education, and a School of Business. The direct costs (in thousands of dollars) of operating the three schools are shown in the third column of the table in Figure 7.12. The costs of operating the three schools are charged to the schools themselves (they provide services for one another) and to legislative appropriations, student fees, and endowment income. The Board of Trustees decides that the costs of the three schools shall be allocated as shown in the fourth, fifth, and sixth columns in the table in Figure 7.12. Observe that $x_4 + x_5 + x_6$ (the sum of the outside funds required to operate the three schools) is exactly equal to the sum of the direct costs of operating the

School	Total Costs	Direct Costs, thousands of dollars	Allocation of Costs		
			Arts and Sciences	Engineering	Fine Arts
Arts and Sciences x_1		3000	$0.05x_1$	$0.10x_2$	$0.15x_3$
Education x_2		3000	$0.06x_1$	$0.06x_2$	$0.15x_3$
Fine Arts Business x_3		1500	$0.05x_1$	$0.10x_2$	$0.15x_3$
Legislative appropriations x_4			$0.50x_1$	$0.55x_2$	$0.20x_3$
Student fees x_5			$0.25x_1$	$0.12x_2$	$0.15x_3$
Endowment x_6			$0.09x_1$	$0.07x_2$	$0.20x_3$
Totals			x_1	x_2	x_3

Figure 7.12

three schools. Determine whether this accounting problem has a solution, and if it does, find the total costs.

Exercises

1. Let A, B, C, be the following matrices:

$$A = \begin{pmatrix} -2 & 0 & 7 \\ 1 & 8 & 3 \\ 2 & 4 & 21 \end{pmatrix} \quad B = \begin{pmatrix} 1 & 3 & 9 \\ 2 & 7 & 5 \\ 3 & 6 & 8 \end{pmatrix} \quad C = \begin{pmatrix} 0 & 1 & 2 \\ 0 & 5 & 1 \\ 8 & 7 & 9 \end{pmatrix}$$

Find the following matrices:

a. $A + B$
b. $B + A$
c. $3(A + B)$
d. $3A + 3B$
e. $3A - 3B$

f. $2(5A)$
g. $\frac{3}{2} A$
h. $B - C$
i. $C - B$
j. $2A + \frac{1}{2}B - 3C$

k. AB
l. BA
m. $(B - A) \cdot C$

2. What must be true about x, y, z, w, if the matrices

$$A = \begin{pmatrix} x & y \\ z & w \end{pmatrix} \quad \text{and} \quad B = \begin{pmatrix} 1 & 1 \\ -1 & 1 \end{pmatrix}$$

are to commute? That is, $AB = BA$.

3. Let $t = (t_1 \quad t_2)$, with $t_1 + t_2 = 1$ and let $A = \begin{pmatrix} \dfrac{1}{4} & \dfrac{3}{4} \\ \dfrac{2}{3} & \dfrac{1}{3} \end{pmatrix}$. Find t such that $tA = t$.

4. Find the inverse of the matrices,

   a. $\begin{pmatrix} 3 & 0 \\ -2 & 1 \end{pmatrix}$ b. $\begin{pmatrix} 1 & 2 & 3 \\ 2 & 4 & 5 \\ 3 & 5 & 6 \end{pmatrix}$

5. Find the reduced matrix of the following matrices and determine their rank.

   a. $\begin{pmatrix} 2 & 0 & 1 \\ 3 & 7 & -1 \\ 1 & 0 & 2 \end{pmatrix}$ b. $\begin{pmatrix} 1 \\ 1 \\ 1 \end{pmatrix}$

6. Find the solution of

$$\begin{aligned} 2x_1 - x_2 + x_3 &= 1 \\ x_1 + x_2 - x_3 &= 2 \\ 3x_1 - x_2 + x_3 &= 0 \end{aligned}$$

   using the matrix technique introduced in this chapter.

7. Associate numbers to letters as follows:

```
1 2 3 4 5 6 7 8 9 10 11 12 13 14 15 16 17 18 19 20 21 22 23 24 25 26
↓ ↓ ↓ ↓ ↓ ↓ ↓ ↓ ↓ ↓  ↓  ↓  ↓  ↓  ↓  ↓  ↓  ↓  ↓  ↓  ↓  ↓  ↓  ↓  ↓  ↓
A B C D E F G H I J  K  L  M  N  O  P  Q  R  S  T  U  V  W  X  Y  Z
```

The matrix A used to encode a message has as inverse the matrix

$$A^{-1} = \begin{pmatrix} 2 & -3 \\ -1 & 2 \end{pmatrix}$$

Decode the message:

   11, 7, 84, 51, 51, 28, 66, 43, 44, 29, 107, 65, 64, 41

8. Associate numbers to letters as in Problem 7. Use the matrix

$$A = \begin{pmatrix} 1 & 0 & 0 \\ 3 & 1 & 5 \\ -2 & 0 & 1 \end{pmatrix} \quad \text{to encode the message, "IT'S OVER."}$$

Additional Reading

Gale, D., *The Theory of Linear Economic Models*, New York: McGraw-Hill, 1960.

Johnston, J., Price, G., and VanVleck, F., *Linear Equations and Matrices*, Reading, Mass.: Addison-Wesley, 1966.

Vazsonyi, A., "The Use of Mathematics in Production and Inventory Control," *Management Science*, **1** (1954), pp. 70–75.

The method introduced in Chapter 6 for solving a linear programming problem has several disadvantages. One of them is that as the number of variables increases it becomes cumbersome to find all the vertices of the polyhedral convex set of feasible solutions. Consequently, a method called the *simplex method* has been developed for solving linear programming problems in a manner suitable for computer programming.

8.1
THE PIVOT
OPERATION

However before we can introduce the simplex method for solving a linear programming problem, we need to discuss a procedure called the *pivot operation,* used to interchange rows and columns of matrices. The pivot operation will be fundamental for using the simplex method.

We shall illustrate the pivot operation by the following examples.

Consider the system of two equations in three unknowns

$$x = a + bz$$
$$y = c + dz$$
(8.1.1)

In (8.1.1), we have solved for x and y in terms of z. Suppose, however, we want to solve for z and y in terms of x. What form will the solution take?

We can ask the same question differently. If we have the matrix equation

$$\begin{pmatrix} x \\ y \end{pmatrix} = \begin{pmatrix} a & b \\ c & d \end{pmatrix} \begin{pmatrix} 1 \\ z \end{pmatrix}$$

find the matrix A so that

$$\begin{pmatrix} z \\ y \end{pmatrix} = A \begin{pmatrix} 1 \\ x \end{pmatrix}$$

252
FURTHER
TECHNIQUES
IN LINEAR
PROGRAMMING: THE
SIMPLEX METHOD

From (8.1.1), we have

$$z = -\frac{a}{b} + \frac{x}{b}$$

Substitute this value of z into the second equation of (8.1.1). Then

$$y = c + d\left[-\frac{a}{b} + \frac{x}{b}\right] = \frac{bc - ad}{b} + \frac{d}{b}x$$

Thus, the desired solution is

$$z = -\frac{a}{b} + \frac{x}{b}$$

$$y = \frac{bc - ad}{b} + \frac{d}{b}x$$

In matrix form, this is

$$\begin{pmatrix} z \\ y \end{pmatrix} = \begin{pmatrix} -\dfrac{a}{b} & \dfrac{1}{b} \\ \dfrac{bc - ad}{b} & \dfrac{d}{b} \end{pmatrix} \begin{pmatrix} 1 \\ x \end{pmatrix} \qquad (8.1.2)$$

Let us now review what happened. The original system (8.1.1) can be written in shorthand as

$$\begin{array}{cc} & \begin{array}{cc} 1 & z \end{array} \\ \begin{array}{c} x \\ y \end{array} & \begin{pmatrix} a & b \\ c & d \end{pmatrix} \end{array} \qquad (8.1.3)$$

The matrix in (8.1.2) can be written as

$$\begin{array}{cc} & \begin{array}{cc} 1 & x \end{array} \\ \begin{array}{c} z \\ y \end{array} & \begin{pmatrix} -\dfrac{a}{b} & \dfrac{1}{b} \\ \dfrac{bc - ad}{b} & \dfrac{d}{b} \end{pmatrix} \end{array}$$

In this new matrix, the roles x and z have been interchanged. In (8.1.3), the entry b belongs to the row *and* column of the two variables to be interchanged (x and z). This entry b is called the *pivot element*. The row containing the pivot element is called the *pivot row*; the column containing the pivot element is termed the *pivot column*.

The new matrix is obtained from the original matrix as follows.

1. If p is the pivot element, let a be any element *not* in the pivot row or pivot column. Replace a by the quantity

$$a \cdot p - \begin{pmatrix} \text{entry in} \\ p \text{ row} \\ a \text{ column} \end{pmatrix} \cdot \begin{pmatrix} \text{entry in} \\ a \text{ row} \\ p \text{ column} \end{pmatrix}$$

2. Change the sign of all elements in the pivot *row* except the pivot element.
3. Replace the pivot element by 1.
4. Divide each entry by the pivot element.

The scheme below illustrates how the above steps apply to a 2×2 matrix $\begin{pmatrix} a_{11} & a_{12} \\ a_{21} & a_{22} \end{pmatrix}$ in which a_{11} is the pivot element (indicated by the circle).

$$\begin{pmatrix} \textcircled{a_{11}} & a_{12} \\ a_{21} & a_{22} \end{pmatrix} \xrightarrow{\text{Step 1}} \begin{pmatrix} a_{11} & a_{12} \\ a_{21} & a_{11}a_{22} - a_{21}a_{12} \end{pmatrix}$$

$$\downarrow \text{Step 2}$$

$$\begin{pmatrix} a_{11} & -a_{12} \\ a_{21} & a_{11}a_{22} - a_{21}a_{12} \end{pmatrix}$$

$$\downarrow \text{Step 3}$$

$$\begin{pmatrix} 1 & -a_{12} \\ a_{21} & a_{11}a_{22} - a_{21}a_{22} \end{pmatrix}$$

$$\downarrow \text{Step 4}$$

$$\begin{pmatrix} \dfrac{1}{a_{11}} & \dfrac{-a_{12}}{a_{11}} \\ \dfrac{a_{21}}{a_{11}} & \dfrac{a_{11}a_{22} - a_{21}a_{12}}{a_{11}} \end{pmatrix}$$

The above rules can be used to interchange the variables in any system of linear equations.

For the system of equations

8.1.1
Example

$$x = 5 + 2z$$
$$y = 3 - 4z$$

find x and z in terms of y.

We first write the equations in matrix form as

$$\begin{array}{cc} & \begin{array}{cc} 1 & z \end{array} \\ \begin{array}{c} x \\ y \end{array} & \begin{pmatrix} 5 & 2 \\ 3 & -4 \end{pmatrix} \end{array}$$

Since we want to interchange z and y, the pivot element is -4. From step 1, we have

$$\begin{pmatrix} 5(-4) - 2 \cdot 3 & 2 \\ 3 & -4 \end{pmatrix} = \begin{pmatrix} -26 & 2 \\ 3 & -4 \end{pmatrix}$$

Applying step 2, we obtain

$$\begin{pmatrix} -26 & 2 \\ -3 & -4 \end{pmatrix}$$

From step 3, we have

$$\begin{pmatrix} -26 & 2 \\ -3 & 1 \end{pmatrix}$$

254
FURTHER
TECHNIQUES
IN LINEAR
PROGRAMMING: THE
SIMPLEX METHOD

Finally, applying step 4, we obtain

$$
\begin{array}{c}
\begin{array}{cc} 1 & y \end{array} \\
\begin{array}{c} x \\ z \end{array}
\begin{pmatrix}
\dfrac{26}{4} & -\dfrac{2}{4} \\[2mm]
\dfrac{3}{4} & -\dfrac{1}{4}
\end{pmatrix}
\end{array}
$$

Thus, the desired solution is

$$
x = \frac{26}{4} - \frac{2}{4}y
$$

$$
z = \frac{3}{4} - \frac{1}{4}y
$$

**8.1.2
Example**   For the system of equations

$$
x = 4 - 3u + 2v
$$

$$
y = 2 + u - v
$$

$$
z = -3 - u + 2v
$$

find x, u, and z, in terms of y and v.

The above equations in matrix form are

$$
\begin{array}{c}
\begin{array}{ccc} 1 & u & v \end{array} \\
\begin{array}{c} x \\ y \\ z \end{array}
\begin{pmatrix}
4 & -3 & 2 \\
2 & 1 & -1 \\
-3 & -1 & 2
\end{pmatrix}
\end{array}
$$

Since we want to interchange y and u, the pivot element is 1. Applying step 1, we obtain the matrix

$$
\begin{pmatrix}
4 \cdot 1 - 2 \cdot (-3) & -3 & 2 \cdot 1 - (-3)(-1) \\
2 & 1 & -1 \\
-3 \cdot 1 - 2 \cdot (-1) & -1 & 2 \cdot 1 - (-1)(-1)
\end{pmatrix}
=
\begin{pmatrix}
10 & -3 & -1 \\
2 & 1 & -1 \\
-1 & -1 & 1
\end{pmatrix}
$$

From step 2, we have

$$
\begin{pmatrix}
10 & -3 & -1 \\
-2 & 1 & 1 \\
-1 & -1 & 1
\end{pmatrix}
$$

Steps 3 and 4 are unnecessary since the pivot element is 1. Thus, the new matrix is

$$
\begin{array}{c}
\begin{array}{ccc} 1 & y & v \end{array} \\
\begin{array}{c} x \\ u \\ z \end{array}
\begin{pmatrix}
10 & -3 & -1 \\
-2 & 1 & 1 \\
-1 & -1 & 1
\end{pmatrix}
\end{array}
$$

The system of equations of Example 8.1.2 becomes

$$x = 10 - 3y - v$$
$$u = -2 + y + v$$
$$z = -1 - y + v$$

For the system of equations

$$x = 4 - 3u + 2v$$
$$y = 2 + u - v$$
$$z = -3 - u + 2v$$

find x, u, and v in terms of y and z.

Here we must apply the pivot operation twice since we are interchanging the roles of y and u and then of z and v. The interchange of y and u (see Example 8.1.2) gives

$$x = 10 - 3y - v$$
$$u = -2 + y + v$$
$$z = -1 - y + v$$

The matrix is

$$\begin{array}{c} \\ x \\ u \\ z \end{array} \begin{array}{ccc} 1 & y & v \\ \left(\begin{array}{ccc} 10 & -3 & -1 \\ -2 & 1 & 1 \\ -1 & -1 & 1 \end{array}\right) \end{array}$$

To interchange z and v, we use 1 as pivot element. By step 1, we obtain

$$\left(\begin{array}{ccc} 9 & -4 & -1 \\ -1 & 2 & 1 \\ -1 & -1 & 1 \end{array}\right)$$

From step 2, we have

$$\left(\begin{array}{ccc} 9 & -4 & -1 \\ -1 & 2 & 1 \\ 1 & 1 & 1 \end{array}\right)$$

Since the pivot element is 1, steps 3 and 4 are unnecessary. Thus, the new matrix is

$$\begin{array}{c} \\ x \\ u \\ v \end{array} \begin{array}{ccc} 1 & y & z \\ \left(\begin{array}{ccc} 9 & -4 & -1 \\ -1 & 2 & 1 \\ 1 & 1 & 1 \end{array}\right) \end{array}$$

The system of equations of Example 8.1.3 is transformed to

$$x = 9 - 4y - z$$
$$u = -1 + 2y + z$$
$$v = 1 + y + z$$

1. Find the new matrix obtained by performing a pivot operation on the following matrices in which the pivot element is circled.

(a) $\begin{pmatrix} 6 & -2 & 1 \\ 4 & 3 & ③ \end{pmatrix}$

(b) $\begin{pmatrix} 5 & 7 \\ 2 & ③ \end{pmatrix}$

(c) $\begin{pmatrix} -3 & -1 \\ -2 & ⊝ \\ 4 & 2 \end{pmatrix}$

(d) $\begin{pmatrix} 4 & 6 & 2 & 1 \\ 2 & 7 & ③ & 2 \\ 1 & 0 & -2 & 1 \end{pmatrix}$

(e) $\begin{pmatrix} 6 & 2 & 1 \\ 4 & 0 & ② \\ 1 & 1 & 1 \end{pmatrix}$

(f) $\begin{pmatrix} 2 & 4 & 8 & 1 \\ 3 & -1 & ② & 3 \end{pmatrix}$

(g) $\begin{pmatrix} 4 & -2 & ①② \\ 1 & -1 & -1 \\ 3 & 0 & 2 \end{pmatrix}$

2. For the system of equations

$$x = 3 - 2u + 4v$$
$$y = 6 - u + v$$

find x and v in terms of u and y.

3. For the system of equations

$$x = 3 - 2u + 4v - w$$
$$y = 6 - u + v + w$$

find x and w in terms of u, v, and y.

4. For the system of equations

$$x = 6 + 2u - v + w$$
$$y = -1 - u + v + 2w$$
$$z = 0 + u + v - w$$

find x, u, and v in terms of w, y, and z.

5. For the system of equations

$$x = 2 - u + v - 2w$$
$$y = 1 + u + 2v - w$$
$$z = 6 - u + 3v + 2w$$

find u, v, and z in terms of x, y, and w.

*6. For the system

$$x_1 = 1 - 2x_5 + x_6 - x_7$$
$$x_2 = 3 - 2x_5 - x_6 + 2x_7$$
$$x_3 = -2 + x_5 - 2x_6 - 2x_7$$
$$x_4 = 3 + 2x_5 + 2x_6 + x_7$$

find x_1, x_5, x_6, and x_7 in terms of x_2, x_3, and x_4.

As indicated in Section 6.2, a linear programming problem is characterized by a linear objective function, which is to be minimized or maximized subject to a collection of conditions or constraints. The constraints are expressed as linear inequalities.

8.2
THE SIMPLEX
METHOD FOR
MAXIMIZING A
LINEAR OBJECTIVE
FUNCTION

In Section 6.2, we learned a technique for solving a small class of linear programming problems. There we restricted our study to linear objective functions that depended on only *two* variables. Not only that, but the collection of restrictions placed on the linear objective function consisted of only three or four linear inequalities. In practice, the objective function will depend on more than two variables and the number of restrictions will be greater. This means that the graphing method used previously to solve linear programming problems cannot be used since it is too cumbersome and time-consuming to find all the extreme points of a system of linear inequalities in several variables and then to test each one to see which minimizes (or maximizes) the objective function.

The method introduced here to solve linear programming problems for maximizing linear objective functions with more than two variables or with restrictions involving a high number of linear inequalities is the *simplex method,* first introduced by G. Dantzig in 1947. The simplex method for solving linear programming problems is a technique which enables us to test the objective function at extreme points in stages, with each stage bringing us closer to the maximum values. This technique utilizes the pivot operation explained in Section 8.1.

We shall introduce the *simplex method* for solving linear programming problems by the following example.

A linear programming problem consists of maximizing the objective function

$$P = 0.25x + 0.45y \tag{8.2.1}$$

subject to the conditions

$$x + 2y \leq 300, \qquad 3x + 2y \leq 480, \qquad x \geq 0, \qquad y \geq 0 \tag{8.2.2}$$

The simplex method of solution requires that the constraints or conditions be expressed as linear equations *not* as linear inequalities. Thus, we must somehow rearrange the conditions (8.2.2) so that they become equalities. To do this, we use what are termed *slack variables.* That is, since,

$$x + 2y \leq 300$$

there is a nonnegative real number u so that

$$x + 2y + u = 300, \qquad u \geq 0$$

Here, u is a *slack variable.* Also, there is a nonnegative real number v so that

$$3x + 2y + v = 480, \qquad v \geq 0$$

Here, v is a *slack variable.* Now, the original linear programming problem can be restated as follows:

258
FURTHER
TECHNIQUES
IN LINEAR
PROGRAMMING: THE
SIMPLEX METHOD

Maximize

$$P = 0.25x + 0.45y$$

subject to the conditions

$$u = 300 - x - 2y, \qquad x \geq 0, \qquad y \geq 0$$
$$v = 480 - 3x - 2y, \qquad u \geq 0, \qquad v \geq 0$$

Notice that the two constraints are now expressed as linear equations (except, of course, for the nonnegative conditions) in which the slack variables u and v are expressed in terms of the variables x and y.

We can express the linear programming problem by the matrix

$$
\begin{array}{c}
 \\
P \\
u \\
v
\end{array}
\begin{array}{ccc}
1 & x & y \\
\left(\begin{array}{c} 0 \\ 300 \\ 480 \end{array}\right. & \begin{array}{c} 0.25 \\ -1 \\ -3 \end{array} & \left.\begin{array}{c} 0.45 \\ -2 \\ -2 \end{array}\right)
\end{array}
$$

Let us now develop the rationale for the selection of a pivot element. Keep in mind that P is to be *maximized*. This being the case, since the coefficient of y in the expression for P is larger than the coefficient of x, let us see what happens as we increase y and keep $x = 0$. It is clear that the value of y cannot be increased indefinitely, since for y large enough, the value of the slack variable u will become negative. The actual condition is

$$u = 300 - 2y, \qquad x = 0 \tag{8.2.3}$$

Clearly, the largest value y can attain for $x = 0$ is $y = 150$, since for $y > 150$, the value of u is negative. At the same time, we have the condition

$$v = 480 - 2y, \qquad x = 0$$

Here, the largest value of y for $x = 0$ is $y = 240$, since for $y > 240$, the value of v is negative. But neither u nor v can be negative. Thus the largest value we can have for y when $x = 0$ is $y = 150$. The origin of $y = 150$ is equation (8.2.3), which involves the variables u and y. It will be these two variables that we interchange the role of. Thus, our pivot element is -2 and our matrix is

$$
\begin{array}{c}
 \\
P \\
u \\
v
\end{array}
\begin{array}{ccc}
1 & x & y \\
\left(\begin{array}{c} 0 \\ 300 \\ 480 \end{array}\right. & \begin{array}{c} 0.25 \\ -1 \\ -3 \end{array} & \left.\begin{array}{c} 0.45 \\ \boxed{-2} \\ -2 \end{array}\right)
\end{array}
\tag{5.4.4}
$$

in which the pivot element -2 is circled.

Performing the pivot operation as explained in Section 8.1 we obtain the matrix

$$
\begin{array}{c}
 \\
P \\
y \\
v
\end{array}
\begin{array}{ccc}
1 & x & u \\
\left(\begin{array}{c} 67.5 \\ 150 \\ 180 \end{array}\right. & \begin{array}{c} 0.025 \\ -\frac{1}{2} \\ -2 \end{array} & \left.\begin{array}{c} -0.225 \\ -\frac{1}{2} \\ 1 \end{array}\right)
\end{array}
$$

Look at the P row. Since there is a positive entry in this row besides the positive entry in the first column, we have not yet found a maximal value.

259
THE SIMPLEX
METHOD FOR
MAXIMIZING A
LINEAR OBJECTIVE
FUNCTION

(Had only the first column entry been positive, then $P = 67.5$ would have been the maximum value.) However, we must now repeat the process, performing a pivot operation in the above matrix.

To find the pivot element, we proceed as before. Since P is to be maximized, and since in the P row, the coefficient of x (0.025) is larger than the coefficient of u (-0.225), let us increase x and set $u = 0$. The conditions are

$$y = 150 - \tfrac{1}{2}x, \qquad u = 0$$
$$v = 180 - 2x, \qquad u = 0$$

Thus, from the first of these, $x = 300$ and from the second $x = 90$. Since $x > 90$ will make $v < 0$, we will take $x = 90$, and since this came from the second equation, we will interchange the variables v and x. This means that -2 is the pivot element.

Again performing the pivot operation, we obtain

$$
\begin{array}{c}
\quad\quad 1 \quad\quad\quad v \quad\quad\quad u \\
\begin{array}{c} P \\ y \\ x \end{array}
\left(
\begin{array}{ccc}
69.75 & -0.0125 & -0.2125 \\
105 & 0.25 & -0.75 \\
90 & -\tfrac{1}{2} & 0.5
\end{array}
\right)
\end{array}
$$

Look at the P row. The only positive entry is in the first column. The simplex method tells us this positive entry 69.75 is the maximum for P. The simplex method also tells us that $y = 105$ and $x = 90$ (see the first column) gives us the maximum of $P = 69.75$.

As should be expected, this result checks with the result obtained by graphing in Example 6.2.6.

Let us review the simplex method for maximizing a linear objective function before we work another example. The technique can be summarized as follows:

1. **Introduce slack variables so that all the constraints (except the ones expressing nonnegativeness) are written as linear equations in which the slack variables are given in terms of the original variables.**
2. **Write the matrix representing the objective function and its constraints.**
3. **Pick a pivot element (as done in Example 8.2.1) and perform the pivot operation.**
4. **Look at the objective function row. If all entries except the entry in the first column are negative, the entry in the first column is the maximum. If other entries are also positive, repeat the process starting at step 3.**

A linear programming problem consists of maximizing

$$P = 5x + 7y$$

8.2.2
Example

subject to the conditions

$$2x + 3y \leq 12, \qquad 3x + y \leq 12, \qquad x \geq 0, \qquad y \geq 0$$

First, we introduce slack variables u and v so that the constraints become

$$2x + 3y + u = 12, \qquad x \geq 0, \qquad y \geq 0$$
$$3x + y + v = 12, \qquad u \geq 0, \qquad v \geq 0$$

260
FURTHER
TECHNIQUES
IN LINEAR
PROGRAMMING: THE
SIMPLEX METHOD

The linear programming problem is:

Maximize

$$P = 5x + 7y$$

subject to

$$u = 12 - 2x - 3y$$
$$v = 12 - 3x - y$$

The matrix representing the objective P and its constraints is

$$\begin{array}{c} \\ P \\ u \\ v \end{array} \begin{array}{ccc} 1 & x & y \\ \left(\begin{array}{ccc} 0 & 5 & 7 \\ 12 & -2 & -3 \\ 12 & -3 & -1 \end{array} \right) \end{array}$$

To find the pivot element, we notice the coefficient of y is 7 and of x is 5. Since we are to maximize P, we set $x = 0$ and increase y. The conditions then become

$$u = 12 - 3y, \qquad x = 0$$
$$v = 12 - y, \qquad x = 0$$

Since $u \geqq 0$, $v \geqq 0$, and the solutions for y are, respectively, $y = 4$ and $y = 12$, we must take $y = 4$. (If $y = 12$, then $u < 0$—contradicting the assumption $u \geqq 0$.) Now, $y = 4$ is obtained from $u = 12 - 3y$. Thus, we will interchange the roles of u and y and hence choose -3 as pivot element.

Performing the pivot operation on the matrix above with -3 as pivot element, we obtain

$$\begin{array}{c} \\ P \\ y \\ v \end{array} \begin{array}{ccc} 1 & x & u \\ \left(\begin{array}{ccc} 28 & \dfrac{1}{3} & -\dfrac{7}{3} \\ 4 & -\dfrac{2}{3} & -\dfrac{1}{3} \\ 8 & -\dfrac{7}{3} & \dfrac{1}{3} \end{array} \right) \end{array}$$

Since the objective row P has two positive elements in it, we are forced to repeat the process.

Our new pivot element is $-7/3$. For, the objective function P is

$$P = 28 + \tfrac{1}{3}x - \tfrac{7}{3}u$$

Since the coefficient of x (1/3) is larger than that of u ($-7/3$), we set $u = 0$ and increase x. This leads to the conditions

$$y = 4 - \tfrac{2}{3}x$$
$$v = 8 - \tfrac{7}{3}x$$

The largest values for x are $x = 6$ and $x = 24/7$, respectively. However, $x = 6$ makes $v < 0$, which is impossible. Thus, we take $x = 24/7$. Since this came from the equation involving v and x, we will interchange these variables. Hence, our pivot choice is $-7/3$.

261
THE SIMPLEX
METHOD FOR
MAXIMIZING A
LINEAR OBJECTIVE
FUNCTION

Performing the pivot operation on the matrix above with $-7/3$ as pivot element, we obtain

$$
\begin{array}{c}
 & 1 & v & u \\
P & \left(\begin{array}{ccc}
\dfrac{204}{7} & -\dfrac{1}{7} & -\dfrac{48}{21} \\[2mm]
y & \dfrac{12}{7} & \dfrac{2}{7} & -\dfrac{3}{7} \\[2mm]
x & \dfrac{24}{7} & -\dfrac{3}{7} & \dfrac{1}{7}
\end{array}\right)
\end{array}
$$

In the P row, all entries are negative except the one in the first column. Thus, the maximum value for P is $204/7$ and this is obtained for $x = 24/7$, $y = 12/7$.

Use the simplex method to solve the following linear programming problems.

1. Maximize the objective function

$$f = x + 5y$$

   subject to the conditions

   $$2x + y \leqq 10, \qquad x + 2y \leqq 10, \qquad x \geqq 0, \qquad y \geqq 0$$

2. Maximize the objective function

$$f = 5x + 7y$$

   subject to the conditions

   $$2x + y \leqq 12, \qquad x + 3y \leqq 12, \qquad x \geqq 0, \qquad y \geqq 0$$

3. Maximize the objective function

$$f = 5x + 7y$$

   subject to the conditions

   $$x + y \leqq 8, \qquad 2x + y \leqq 10, \qquad 3x + y \leqq 12,$$
   $$x \geqq 0, \qquad y \geqq 0$$

4. Maximize the objective function

$$f = 5x + 7y$$

   subject to the conditions

   $$2x + 3y \leqq 12, \qquad x + 2y \leqq 8, \qquad x \geqq 0, \qquad y \geqq 0$$

5. Maximize the objective function

$$f = 5x + 7y$$

   subject to the conditions

   $$x + y \leqq 7, \qquad 2x + y \leqq 9, \qquad 3x + y \leqq 12,$$
   $$x \geqq 0, \qquad y \geqq 0$$

262
FURTHER
TECHNIQUES
IN LINEAR
PROGRAMMING: THE
SIMPLEX METHOD

6. Maximize the objective function

$$f = 5x - 7y$$

subject to the conditions of Problem 2.

7. Maximize

$$f = 5x - 7y$$

subject to conditions of Problem 3.

8. Maximize

$$f = 5x - 7y$$

subject to conditions of Problem 4.

9. Maximize

$$f = 5x - 7y$$

subject to conditions of Problem 5.

8.3
THE SIMPLEX
METHOD FOR
MINIMIZING A
LINEAR OBJECTIVE
FUNCTION

The simplex method for minimizing linear objective functions is almost like the technique for maximizing linear objective functions discussed in Section 8.2. This is because the problem of minimizing an objective function f subject to certain conditions is equivalent to the problem of maximizing the objective function $(-f)$ subject to the *same* conditions. Thus, the technique to be followed is that of the previous section, with one exception. This exception is illustrated below.

8.3.1
Example

Minimize the objective function

$$f = x + 2y$$

subject to the conditions

$$x + y \geq 1, \qquad 2x + 4y \geq 3, \qquad x \geq 0, \qquad y \geq 0$$

First, we write the equivalent problem.
Maximize

$$-f = -x - 2y$$

subject to the conditions

$$x + y \geq 1, \qquad 2x + 4y \geq 3, \qquad x \geq 0, \qquad y \geq 0$$

Introducing the slack variables u and v, we have

$$x + y = 1 + u, \qquad 2x + 4y = 3 + v,$$

$$x \geq 0, \qquad y \geq 0, \qquad u \geq 0, \qquad v \geq 0$$

Solving for the slack variables u and v gives

$$u = -1 + x + y, \qquad v = -3 + 2x + 4y \qquad (8.3.1)$$

Notice that when x and y are both zero, the slack variables u and v are negative. This contradiction of the fact $u \geq 0$, $v \geq 0$, means we cannot set

263
THE SIMPLEX
METHOD FOR
MINIMIZING A
LINEAR OBJECTIVE
FUNCTION

up the matrix from these equations. We need to express every constraint equation so that the constant term is positive. Thus, in the first condition, if we solve for x in terms of u and y, we have

$$x = 1 + u - y$$

Substituting this into the expression for v gives

$$v = -3 + 2(1 + u - y) + 4y = -1 + 2u + 2y$$

Since the constant term is negative, this set will not do. Returning to the first condition of (8.3.1), solve for y in terms of x and u. Then

$$y = 1 + u - x \qquad (8.3.2)$$

Substituting this into the second condition, we have

$$v = -3 + 2x + 4(1 + u - x) = 1 + 4u - 2x \qquad (8.3.3)$$

Now both constraints (8.3.2) and (8.3.3) have positive constant terms. The objective function $-f$ must now be expressed in terms of u and x. Thus

$$-f = -x - 2y = -x - 2(1 + u - x) = -2 - 2u + x$$

The constraints are

$$y = 1 + u - x$$
$$v = 1 + 4u - 2x$$

The matrix of this linear program is

$$\begin{array}{c} \\ -f \\ y \\ v \end{array} \begin{array}{ccc} 1 & u & x \\ \left(\begin{array}{ccc} -2 & -2 & 1 \\ 1 & 1 & -1 \\ 1 & 4 & -2 \end{array}\right) \end{array}$$

Since the $-f$ now contains negative entries besides the one in the first column, we must perform a pivot operation. To find the pivot element, we proceed as in Section 8.2. Since the coefficient of x is larger than that of u in the $-f$ row, set $u = 0$ and increase x. This leads to the conditions

$$y = 1 - x, \qquad v = 1 - 2x$$

The largest values for x are 1 and 1/2, respectively. Since $x > 1/2$ makes $v < 0$, we take $x = 1/2$. Thus, we want to interchange v and x and so will choose -2 as pivot element. Performing the pivot operation gives

$$\begin{array}{c} \\ -f \\ y \\ x \end{array} \begin{array}{ccc} 1 & u & v \\ \left(\begin{array}{ccc} -\dfrac{3}{2} & 0 & -\dfrac{1}{2} \\ \dfrac{1}{2} & -1 & \dfrac{1}{2} \\ \dfrac{1}{2} & 2 & -\dfrac{1}{2} \end{array}\right) \end{array}$$

In the $-f$ row, no entry (except possibly the one in the first column) is positive. Hence, $-3/2$ is the maximum value of $-f$ and is attained at $x = 1/2$, $y = 1/2$. Thus, the minimum value of f is 3/2 attained at $x = 1/2$, $y = 1/2$.

264
FURTHER
TECHNIQUES
IN LINEAR
PROGRAMMING: THE
SIMPLEX METHOD

To summarize, if the objective function f of a linear programming problem is to be minimized,

1. **Change the problem to one of maximizing the objective function $-f$.**
2. **Introduce slack variables so that the constraints are linear equations.**
3. **Express each constraint equation so that the constant term is positive.**
4. **Proceed as in Section 8.2 to maximize $-f$.**

8.3.2
Example

Minimize the objective function

$$f = 6x + 8y + z$$

Subject to the conditions

$$3x + 5y + 3z \geq 20, \qquad x \geq 0$$
$$x + 3y + 2z \geq 9, \qquad y \geq 0 \qquad (8.3.4)$$
$$6x + 2y + 5z \geq 30, \qquad z \geq 0$$

The equivalent problem is to maximize

$$-f = -6x - 8y - z$$

subject to the conditions (8.3.4). Introducing slack variables u, v, and w, the linear inequalities (8.3.4) become

$$u = 3x + 5y + 3z - 20, \qquad x \geq 0, \qquad y \geq 0$$
$$v = x + 3y + 2z - 9, \qquad z \geq 0, \qquad u \geq 0 \qquad (8.3.5)$$
$$w = 6x + 2y + 5z - 30, \qquad v \geq 0, \qquad w \geq 0$$

Next, we have to solve each condition (except the nonnegative ones) for a variable that makes the constant term positive. Now, it is clear that if we solve for u, v, or w, the constant term is negative. We shall try x. Then, from the second equation in (8.3.5)

$$x = 9 - 3y - 2z + v$$

Substituting this value for x in the remaining two equations gives

$$u = 3(9 - 3y - 2z + v) + 5y + 3z - 20$$
$$= 7 - 4y - 3z + 3v$$
$$w = 6(9 - 3y - 2z + v) + 2y + 5z - 30$$
$$= 24 - 16y - 7z + 6v$$

Since each of these have positive constant terms, we can proceed. (If they did not, we would solve for a variable other than x). Now the objective function $-f$ must be expressed in terms of y, z, and v. Thus, the objective function $-f$ to be maximized is

$$-f = -6x - 8y - z = -6(9 - 3y - 2z + v) - 8y - z$$
$$= -54 + 10y + 11z - 6v$$

265
THE SIMPLEX
METHOD FOR
MINIMIZING A
LINEAR OBJECTIVE
FUNCTION

subject to

$$x = 9 - 3y - 2z + v$$

$$u = 7 - 4y - 3z + 3v$$

$$w = 24 - 16y - 7z + 6v$$

The matrix is

$$
\begin{array}{c c}
 & \begin{array}{cccc} 1 & y & z & v \end{array} \\
\begin{array}{c} -f \\ x \\ u \\ w \end{array} &
\left(\begin{array}{cccc}
-54 & 10 & 11 & -6 \\
9 & -3 & -2 & 1 \\
7 & -4 & -3 & 3 \\
24 & -16 & -7 & 6
\end{array}\right)
\end{array}
$$

Since we are to maximize $-f$ and since the coefficient of z is larger than that of either y or v, we set $y = v = 0$ and increase z. This gives the conditions

$$x = 9 - 2z$$

$$u = 7 - 3z$$

$$w = 24 - 7z$$

Since $x, u, w \geqq 0$, the largest value of z is $z = 7/3$. Thus, we will interchange u and z, using the pivot element -3. Applying the pivot operation with pivot element -3 to the matrix above, we obtain

$$
\begin{array}{c c}
 & \begin{array}{cccc} 1 & y & u & v \end{array} \\
\begin{array}{c} -f \\ \\ x \\ \\ z \\ \\ w \end{array} &
\left(\begin{array}{cccc}
-\dfrac{85}{3} & -\dfrac{14}{3} & -\dfrac{11}{3} & 5 \\[2mm]
\dfrac{13}{3} & -\dfrac{1}{3} & \dfrac{2}{3} & -1 \\[2mm]
\dfrac{7}{3} & -\dfrac{4}{3} & -\dfrac{1}{3} & 1 \\[2mm]
\dfrac{23}{3} & -\dfrac{20}{3} & \dfrac{7}{3} & -1
\end{array}\right)
\end{array}
$$

Since in the $-f$ row, the entry in the v column is positive, we must repeat the pivot operation. Since we are to maximize $-f$, we set $y = 0$, $u = 0$, and increase v. This gives

$$x = \frac{13}{3} - v$$

$$z = \frac{7}{3} + v$$

$$w = \frac{23}{3} - v$$

Since $x, z, w \geqq 0$, the largest value for v is $v = 13/3$ and this value is obtained from the equation involving x and v. The pivot element is -1. The

266
FURTHER
TECHNIQUES
IN LINEAR
PROGRAMMING: THE
SIMPLEX METHOD

new matrix is

$$
\begin{array}{c}
\\
-f \\
\\
v \\
\\
z \\
\\
w
\end{array}
\begin{array}{cccc}
1 & y & u & x \\
\left(-\dfrac{20}{3}\right. & -\dfrac{19}{3} & -\dfrac{1}{3} & -5 \\
\dfrac{13}{3} & -\dfrac{1}{3} & \dfrac{2}{3} & -1 \\
\dfrac{20}{3} & -\dfrac{5}{3} & \dfrac{1}{3} & -1 \\
\dfrac{10}{3} & -\dfrac{19}{3} & \dfrac{5}{3} & \left.1\right)
\end{array}
$$

Since all entries in the $-f$ row are negative, we have a maximum for $-f$ of $-20/3$ attained at $z = 20/3$, with $y = 0$, $x = 0$. (Here $v = 13/3$ and $w = 10/3$ are the values of the slack variables which make $-f$ a maximum). Thus, $f = 20/3$ is the minimum value of f and is attained at $x = 0$, $y = 0$, $z = 20/3$.

**8.3
Exercise**

Use the simplex method to solve the following linear programming problems.

1. Minimize

$$f = 6x + 3y$$

subject to the conditions

$$x + y \geq 4, \qquad 3x + 4y \geq 12, \qquad x \geq 0, \qquad y \geq 0$$

2. Minimize

$$f = 5x + 7y$$

subject to the conditions

$$x + 2y \geq 4, \qquad 2x + 3y \geq 6, \qquad x \geq 0, \qquad y \geq 0$$

3. Minimize

$$f = 2x + 3y + 4z$$

subject to the conditions

$$
\begin{aligned}
x - 2y - 2z &\geq -2, & x &\geq 0 \\
x + y + z &\geq 2, & y &\geq 0 \\
2x + z &\geq 3, & z &\geq 0
\end{aligned}
$$

4. Minimize

$$f = 2x + 3y$$

subject to the conditions

$$x + y \geq 3, \qquad 2x + 3y \geq 6, \qquad x \geq 0, \qquad y \geq 0$$

5. Minimize

$$f = 6x + 2y$$

subject to the conditions

$$x + 2y \geq 4, \qquad 3x + y \geq 6, \qquad x \geq 0, \qquad y \geq 0$$

6. Minimize

$$f = 3x + 4y$$

subject to the conditions

$$2x + 3y \geq 6, \qquad x + 4y \geq 4, \qquad 2x + y \geq 2,$$
$$x \geq 0, \qquad y \geq 0, \qquad z \geq 0$$

7. Minimize

$$f = 1 + 2x + 3y + 4z$$

subject to the conditions

$$3x - 2y + 2z \geq -2, \qquad x \geq 0$$
$$x + 2y + z \geq 2, \qquad y \geq 0$$
$$2x + 3y \geq 6, \qquad z \geq 0$$

8. Minimize

$$f = x + 2y + z$$

subject to the conditions

$$x - 3y + 4z \geq 12, \qquad x \geq 0$$
$$3x + y + 2z \geq 10, \qquad y \geq 0$$
$$x - y - z \leq -8, \qquad z \geq 0$$

In Section 6.1, we gave two examples of practical situations that lead to linear programming problems—the mixture problem and the transportation problem. In Section 6.2, it was seen that the problem of maximizing profit and minimizing cost are often problems of a linear programming nature. In this section, we shall give further examples of applications of linear programming.

The first example is typical of a *transportation problem*.

8.4
APPLICATIONS

The Red Tomato Company operates two plants for canning their tomatoes and has three warehouses for storing the finished products until they are purchased by retailers. The Company wants to arrange its shipments from the plants to the warehouses so that the requirements of the warehouses are met and so that shipping costs are kept at a minimum. The schedule in Figure 8.1 represents the per case shipping cost from plant to warehouse.

8.4.1
Example

268
FURTHER
TECHNIQUES
IN LINEAR
PROGRAMMING: THE
SIMPLEX METHOD

Warehouse		
A	B	C

Plant	I	\$0.25	\$0.17	\$0.18
	II	\$0.25	\$0.18	\$0.14

Figure 8.1

Each week, plant I can produce up to 850 cases and plant II can produce up to 650 cases of tomatoes. Also, each week warehouse A requires 300 cases, warehouse B, 400 cases, and warehouse C, 500 cases. If we represent the number of cases shipped from plant I to warehouse A by x_1, from plant I to warehouse B by x_2, and so on, the above data can be represented by the table in Figure 8.2.

		Warehouse			Total Available
		A	B	C	
Plant	I	x_1	x_2	x_3	850
	II	x_4	x_5	x_6	650
Total Demand		300	400	500	

Figure 8.2

The linear programming problem is stated as follows:
Minimize the cost function

$$C = 0.25x_1 + 0.17x_2 + 0.18x_3 + 0.25x_4 + 0.18x_5 + 0.14x_6 \quad (8.4.1)$$

subject to the conditions

$$x_1 + x_2 + x_3 \leq 850, \qquad x_1 \geq 0, \qquad x_2 \geq 0$$
$$x_4 + x_5 + x_6 \leq 650, \qquad x_3 \geq 0, \qquad x_4 \geq 0$$
$$x_1 + x_4 = 300, \qquad x_5 \geq 0, \qquad x_6 \geq 0 \qquad (8.4.2)$$
$$x_2 + x_5 = 400$$
$$x_3 + x_6 = 500$$

Before we begin to find a solution, notice that the linear objective function contains *six* variables. Also, the number of constraints is eleven.

The simplex method requires that the constraints of a linear programming problem be given as linear *equations*, not as linear *inequalities*. Thus, before proceeding further, we must change the inequalities of (8.4.2) to equalities. In order to do this, we introduce slack variables. For example, since

$$x_1 + x_2 + x_3 \leq 850$$

there is some nonnegative real number x_7, so that

$$x_1 + x_2 + x_3 + x_7 = 850, \qquad x_7 \geqq 0$$

Here x_7 is a slack variable. Similarly, there is a nonnegative integer x_8 so that

$$x_4 + x_5 + x_6 + x_8 = 650, \qquad x_8 \geqq 0$$

Thus, by introducing slack variables, the linear programming problem can be restated as:

Minimize the cost function

$$C = 0.25x_1 + 0.17x_2 + 0.18x_3 + 0.25x_4 + 0.18x_5 + 0.14x_6$$

subject to the conditions

$$
\begin{array}{lll}
x_1 + x_2 + x_3 + x_7 = 850, & x_1 \geqq 0, & x_2 \geqq 0 \\
x_4 + x_5 + x_6 + x_8 = 650, & x_3 \geqq 0, & x_4 \geqq 0 \\
x_1 + x_4 = 300, & x_5 \geqq 0, & x_6 \geqq 0 \qquad (8.4.3) \\
x_2 + x_5 = 400, & x_7 \geqq 0, & x_8 \geqq 0 \\
x_3 + x_6 = 500 & &
\end{array}
$$

Now the constraints have been expressed as linear equalities.

Physically, the two slack variables x_7 and x_8 can be interpreted as cases of tomatoes produced at plant I and plant II, respectively, but *not shipped* to any warehouse. It is clear that the shipping cost of not shipping is zero so that the slack variables introduced cannot affect the objective (cost) function to be minimized.

Now, the system of equations (8.4.3) is five equations in eight unknowns. In general, then, we can solve for five of these unknowns in terms of the remaining three. However, we must solve for those five that have a positive constant term. Either by using trial and error or by using the techniques introduced in Chapter 7, we can solve the system (8.4.3) as

$$
\begin{array}{l}
x_1 = 300 \qquad\ \ - x_4 \\
x_2 = 400 \qquad\qquad\ - x_5 \\
x_6 = 500 - x_3 \\
x_7 = 150 - x_3 + x_4 + x_5 \\
x_8 = 150 + x_3 - x_4 - x_5
\end{array}
$$

in which each constant term is positive. The cost function C then becomes

$$C = 213 + 0.04x_3 + 0.01x_5$$

The matrix representing the linear programming problem is

$$
\begin{array}{c c}
 & \begin{array}{cccc} 1 & x_3 & x_4 & x_5 \end{array} \\
\begin{array}{c} -C \\ x_1 \\ x_2 \\ x_6 \\ x_7 \\ x_8 \end{array} &
\left(\begin{array}{rrrr}
-213 & -0.04 & 0 & -0.01 \\
300 & 0 & -1 & 0 \\
400 & 0 & 0 & -1 \\
500 & -1 & 0 & 0 \\
150 & -1 & 1 & 1 \\
150 & 1 & -1 & -1
\end{array}\right)
\end{array}
$$

270
FURTHER
TECHNIQUES
IN LINEAR
PROGRAMMING: THE
SIMPLEX METHOD

in which $-C$ is to be maximized. Since every entry in the $-C$ row is negative or zero, we need go no further. The maximum value for $-C$ is -213. The minimum cost C is then $213. The values $x_1, x_2, x_3, x_4, x_5, x_6$, giving this minimum cost of $213 are

$$x_1 = 300, \qquad x_2 = 400, \qquad x_3 = 0$$
$$x_4 = 0, \qquad x_5 = 0, \qquad x_6 = 500$$

Note: Had we solved the system of equations (8.4.3) differently, a series of pivot operations would have eventually given us the matrix above.

8.4.2
Example

Mike's Famous Toy Trucks specializes in making four kinds of toy trucks: a delivery truck, a dump truck, a garbage truck, and a gasoline truck. Three machines—a metal casting machine, a paint spray machine, and a packaging machine—are used in the production of these trucks. The time, in hours, each machine works to make each type of truck and the profit for each truck are given in Figure 8.3.

	Metal Casting	Paint Spray	Packaging	Profit
Delivery truck	2	0.5	0.5	$0.50
Dump truck	2.5	1.5	0.5	$1.00
Garbage truck	2	2	1	$1.50
Gasoline truck	2.5	2.5	1.5	$2.00

Figure 8.3

The maximum time available per week for each machine is: metal casting 4000 hours; paint spray 1800 hours; and packaging 1000 hours. How many of each type truck maximizes profit? Assume every truck made is sold.

First let x_1, x_2, x_3, and x_4 denote the number of delivery trucks, dump trucks, garbage trucks, and gasoline trucks, respectively, to be made. If P denotes the profit to be maximized, we have the problem:
Maximize

$$P = 0.5x_1 + x_2 + 1.5x_3 + 2x_4$$

subject to the conditions

$$2x_1 + 2.5x_2 + 2x_3 + 2.5x_4 \leqq 4000, \qquad x_1 \geqq 0$$
$$0.5x_1 + 1.5x_2 + 2x_3 + 2.5x_4 \leqq 1800, \qquad x_2 \geqq 0$$
$$0.5x_1 + 0.5x_2 + x_3 + 1.5x_4 \leqq 1000, \qquad x_3 \geqq 0, \qquad x_4 \geqq 0$$

Introducing the slack variables x_5, x_6, x_7 and since this is a maximizing problem, solving for them, we have

$$x_5 = 4000 - 2x_1 - 2.5x_2 - 2x_3 - 2.5x_4$$
$$x_6 = 1800 - 0.5x_1 - 1.5x_2 - 2x_3 - 2.5x_4$$
$$x_7 = 1000 - 0.5x_1 - 0.5x_2 - x_3 - 1.5x_4$$

The matrix representing this problem is

$$
\begin{array}{c c c c c c}
 & 1 & x_1 & x_2 & x_3 & x_4 \\
P & 0 & 0.5 & 1 & 1.5 & 2 \\
x_5 & 4000 & -2 & -2.5 & -2 & -2.5 \\
x_6 & 1800 & -0.5 & -1.5 & -2 & -2.5 \\
x_7 & 1000 & -0.5 & -0.5 & -1 & -1.5
\end{array}
$$

To find the pivot element, notice that the coefficient of x_4 is largest. Setting $x_1 = x_2 = x_3 = 0$, we obtain

$$x_5 = 4000 - 2.5x_4$$

$$x_6 = 1800 - 2.5x_4$$

$$x_7 = 1000 - 1.5x_4$$

Since $x_5 \geq 0$, $x_6 \geq 0$, $x_7 \geq 0$, the largest possible value for x_4 is $x = 2000/3$. Thus, we interchange x_4 and x_7, using -1.5 as pivot element. The new matrix is

$$
\begin{array}{c c c c c c}
 & 1 & x_1 & x_2 & x_3 & x_7 \\
P & \dfrac{4000}{3} & -\dfrac{1}{6} & \dfrac{1}{3} & \dfrac{1}{6} & -\dfrac{4}{3} \\[2mm]
x_5 & \dfrac{7000}{3} & -\dfrac{7}{6} & -\dfrac{5}{3} & -\dfrac{1}{3} & \dfrac{5}{3} \\[2mm]
x_6 & \dfrac{400}{3} & \dfrac{1}{3} & -\dfrac{2}{3} & -\dfrac{1}{3} & \dfrac{5}{3} \\[2mm]
x_4 & \dfrac{2000}{3} & -\dfrac{1}{3} & -\dfrac{1}{3} & -\dfrac{2}{3} & -\dfrac{2}{3}
\end{array}
$$

The largest entry in the P row is $1/3$. Setting $x_1 = x_3 = x_7 = 0$, we obtain

$$x_5 = \frac{7000}{3} - \frac{5}{3}x_2$$

$$x_6 = \frac{400}{3} - \frac{2}{3}x_2$$

$$x_4 = \frac{2000}{3} - \frac{1}{3}x_2$$

The largest possible value for x_2 is $x_2 = 200$. Thus, we interchange x_2 and x_6, using $-2/3$ as pivot element. The new matrix is

$$
\begin{array}{c c c c c c}
 & 1 & x_1 & x_6 & x_3 & x_7 \\
P & 1400 & 0 & -\dfrac{1}{2} & 0 & -\dfrac{1}{2} \\[2mm]
x_5 & 2000 & -2 & \dfrac{5}{2} & \dfrac{1}{2} & -\dfrac{5}{2} \\[2mm]
x_6 & 200 & \dfrac{1}{2} & -\dfrac{3}{2} & -\dfrac{1}{2} & \dfrac{5}{2} \\[2mm]
x_4 & 600 & -\dfrac{1}{2} & \dfrac{1}{2} & -\dfrac{1}{2} & -\dfrac{3}{2}
\end{array}
$$

Since all the entries in the P row are nonpositive (except, of course, for the entry in the first column), we have reached a maximizing situation. The

272
FURTHER
TECHNIQUES
IN LINEAR
PROGRAMMING: THE
SIMPLEX METHOD

maximum profit P is \$1400 and is attained for

$$x_1 = 0, \qquad x_2 = 200, \qquad x_3 = 0, \qquad x_4 = 600$$

The practical considerations of this situation are that delivery trucks and garbage trucks are either too costly to produce or too little profit is being gained from their sale. Since the slack variable x_5 has a value of 2000 for maximum P and since x_5 represents the number of hours the metal casting machine is printing no truck (that is, the time the machine is idle), it may be possible to release this machine for other duties.

8.4.3
Example

Katy's Hand Made Dolls must decide how many of two types of dolls to produce in order to maximize profits. One type is a Crying Doll that requires 15 minutes in machine production and 1 3/4 hours in hand finishing; the other type is a Laughing and Crying Doll requiring 30 minutes for machine production and 3 hours in hand finishing. The profit on the Crying Doll is \$8 and on the Laughing and Crying Doll \$12. Machine production is limited to 10 hours per day and hand finishing is limited to 8 hours per day.

Let x represent the number of Crying Dolls and y the number of Laughing and Crying Dolls to be produced. Our problem is to maximize

$$P = 8x + 12y$$

subject to the conditions

$$\tfrac{1}{4}x + \tfrac{1}{2}y \leq 10, \qquad \tfrac{7}{4}x + 3y \leq 8, \qquad x \geq 0, \qquad y \geq 0$$

Introducing slack variables u and v and solving for them, we have

$$u = 10 - \tfrac{1}{4}x - \tfrac{1}{2}y, \qquad v = 8 - \tfrac{7}{4}x - 3y$$

The matrix representing this problem is

$$
\begin{array}{c}
 \\ P \\ u \\ v
\end{array}
\begin{array}{ccc}
1 & x & y \\
\left(\begin{array}{ccc}
0 & 8 & 12 \\
10 & -\dfrac{1}{4} & -\dfrac{1}{2} \\
8 & -\dfrac{7}{4} & -3
\end{array}\right)
\end{array}
$$

Since the coefficient of y is largest, we set $x = 0$. Then

$$u = 10 - \tfrac{1}{2}y, \qquad v = 8 - 3y$$

The largest possible value for y is $y = 8/3$. Thus, -3 is our pivot element. The new matrix is

$$
\begin{array}{c}
 \\ P \\ u \\ y
\end{array}
\begin{array}{ccc}
1 & x & v \\
\left(\begin{array}{ccc}
32 & 1 & -4 \\
\dfrac{26}{3} & \dfrac{1}{24} & \dfrac{1}{6} \\
\dfrac{8}{3} & -\dfrac{7}{12} & -\dfrac{1}{3}
\end{array}\right)
\end{array}
$$

The coefficient of x is larger, so we set $v = 0$. Then

$$u = \frac{26}{3} + \frac{1}{24}x, \quad y = \frac{8}{3} - \frac{7}{12}x$$

Clearly, $-7/12$ is the pivot element. The new matrix is

$$
\begin{array}{c}
 \\
P \\
u \\
x
\end{array}
\begin{array}{ccc}
1 & y & v \\
\left(\begin{array}{ccc}
\dfrac{256}{7} & -\dfrac{12}{7} & -\dfrac{32}{7} \\[2mm]
\dfrac{62}{7} & -\dfrac{1}{14} & \dfrac{1}{7} \\[2mm]
\dfrac{32}{7} & -\dfrac{12}{7} & -\dfrac{4}{7}
\end{array} \right)
\end{array}
$$

Thus, we can approximate the maximum profit at $P = \$32.00$ per day when 4 Crying Dolls are made and no Laughing and Crying Dolls are made.

The fact that the slack variable u, which is indicative of idle machine time, is positive indicatives that more help should be hired to reduce the time the machine is idle.

The approximate solution given to the problem in Example 8.4.3 illustrates a common situation in which only integers are really appropriate as an answer. One may come to the conclusion that the "best integer solution" is found nearest the fractional solution. Unfortunately, this is not the case. Thus, the solution $x = 4$, $y = 0$ is found by a trial-and-error method rather than a simplex method.

We refer the interested reader to consult recent publications on Integer Programming.

In Example 6.2.8, we considered an application to air pollution control. A more realistic continuation is given in Example 8.4.4.

Now consider a more realistic model. There are many pollution sources and not one, but five major pollutants. In the larger model, the required pollutant reductions in the Saint Louis airshed for the year 1970 are as follows:

**8.4.4
Example**

**Pollution
Control**

sulfur dioxide	485,000,000 pounds
carbon monoxide	1,300,000,000 pounds
hydrocarbons	280,000,000 pounds
nitrogen oxides	75,000,000 pounds
particulate matter	180,000,000 pounds

The model includes a wide variety of possible control methods. Among them are the installation of exhaust and crankcase devices on used as well as new automobiles, the substitution of natural gas for coal; the catalytic oxidation system to convert sulfur dioxide in the stacks of power plants to salable sulfuric acid, even the municipal collection of leaves as an alternative to burning.

The most contested control method in the Saint Louis airshed has been a restriction on the sulfur content of coal. Consider a particular category of traveling grate stoker that burns 3.1 percent sulfur coal. Let control

274
FURTHER
TECHNIQUES
IN LINEAR
PROGRAMMING: THE
SIMPLEX METHOD

method 3 be the substitution of 1.8 percent sulfur coal for the high sulfur coal in these stokers. The variable X_3 represents the number of tons of 3.1 percent sulfur coal replaced with low sulfur coal.

Total cost of this control method is

$$C = (\$2.50)X_3$$

where \$2.50 is an estimate of the incremental cost of the low sulfur coal.

Just as the barrels of cement controlled by any process were constrained in our simple example, so

$$X_3 \leqq 200{,}000$$

where 200,000 tons is the estimate of the quantity of coal that will be burned in this category of traveling grate stokers in 1970.

For every ton of 3.1 percent sulfur coal replaced by 1.8 percent sulfur coal, sulfur dioxide emissions are reduced.

[(0.031 sulfur content)
  (2000 pounds per ton of coal)(0.95 complete burning)(2)]
  − [(0.944)(0.018 sulfur content)(2000 pounds)(0.95)(2)] = 53.2 pounds

where the factor (2) doubles the weight of sulfur burned to get the weight of sulfur dioxide; where the factor (0.944) accounts for the higher BTU content of the low sulfur coal which permits 0.944 ton of it to replace one ton of the high sulfur coal; and where (0.95) incorporates an assumption of 95 percent complete burning. The two square bracketed terms represent emission of sulfur dioxide from 3.1 percent and 1.8 percent sulfur coal, respectively. Thus we have

$$(53.2)X_3 = \text{pounds of sulfur dioxide reduced}$$

The remaining pollutant reductions are

$$(0.2)X_3 = \text{pounds of carbon monoxide reduced}$$
$$(0.1)X_3 = \text{pounds of hydrocarbons reduced}$$
$$(1.1)X_3 = \text{pounds of nitrogen oxide reduced}$$
$$(12.2)X_3 = \text{pounds of particulates reduced}$$

The relatively high reduction in particulates reflects not only the fact that 0.944 ton of the 1.8 percent sulfur coal is burned in place of one whole ton but also the lower ash content of the substituted coal. (Reduction coefficients are not always positive; low sulfur coal in a pulverized coal boiler, having a high efficiency electrostatic precipitator, can cause an increase in particulate emissions. The presence of less sulfur dioxide in the flue gas reduces the chargeability of the particles so that the benefits of the lower ash and higher BTU content may be offset by the reduced efficiency of the electrostatic precipitator.)

Figure 8.4 illustrates the mathematical programming model for 1970. Notice that control methods X_1 and X_2 for the cement industry are included, as well as control method X_3. The dots represent the remaining 200 to 300 control methods.

The pollution reduction requirements mentioned above appear in the

Minimize $C = \$0.14X_1 + \$0.18X_2 + \$2.50X_3 + \cdots \cdots \cdots$
Subject to $\qquad X_1 + \qquad X_2 \qquad\qquad\qquad\qquad \leq \quad 2,500,000$
$\qquad\qquad\qquad\qquad\qquad X_3 + \cdots \cdots \cdots \leq \quad\quad 200,000$
$\qquad\qquad\qquad\qquad\qquad\qquad\qquad \cdots \cdots \cdots \leq \qquad \cdot$
$\qquad\qquad\qquad\qquad\qquad\qquad\qquad \cdots \cdots \cdots \leq \qquad \cdot$
$\qquad\qquad\qquad\qquad\qquad\qquad\qquad \cdots \cdots \cdots \leq \qquad \cdot$
$\qquad\qquad\qquad\qquad\qquad\qquad\qquad \cdots \cdots \cdots \leq \qquad \cdot$
$\qquad\qquad\qquad\qquad\quad 53.2X_3 + \cdots \cdots \cdots \geq 485,000,000$ pounds of sulfur dioxide
$\qquad\qquad\qquad\qquad\quad\;\, 0.2X_3 + \cdots \cdots \cdots \geq 1,300,000,000$ pounds of carbon monoxide
$\qquad\qquad\qquad\qquad\quad\;\, 0.1X_3 + \cdots \cdots \cdots \geq 280,000,000$ pounds of hydrocarbons
$\qquad\qquad\qquad\qquad\quad\;\, 1.1X_3 + \cdots \cdots \cdots \geq 75,000,000$ pounds of nitrogen oxides
$\qquad\quad 1.5X_1 + \quad 1.8X_2 + \quad 12.2X_3 + \cdots \cdots \cdots \geq 180,000,000$ pounds of particulates
$\qquad\qquad\quad X_1, \qquad\quad X_2, \qquad\quad X_3, \quad \cdots \cdots \cdots \geq 0$

Figure 8.4

model given in Figure 8.4. In summing the pollutant reductions contributed by the various control methods, we are assuming that all pounds of any pollutant are homogeneous, regardless of where or when they are emitted. This is a limitation of the model because it is dependent on a close correspondence between a pollutant reduction and a specific concentration measured in parts per million or micrograms per cubic meter of that pollutant in the ambient air.

However, where necessary, meteorological sophistication can be incorporated in the model by selective weighting of those sources that seem to have a greater or lesser proportional effect on air quality than others.

The solution of this model, which is obtained with a computer, gives the cost of achieving the required air pollution reduction. It also indicates which of the control methods should be used and which ones are inefficient. This should provide a useful guide for a community in selecting regulations that have sound economic justification.

8.4
Exercise

1. Minimize the cost of preparing the following mixture of foods if the mixture is made up of three foods I, II, III in which food I costs $2 per unit, food II costs $1 per unit, and food III costs $3 per unit. Also, each unit food I contains 2 ounces of protein and 4 ounces carbohydrate; each unit of food II has 3 ounces of protein and 2 ounces of carbohydrate; each unit of food III has 4 ounces of protein and 2 ounces of carbohydrate. The mixture must contain at least 20 ounces of protein and 15 ounces of carbohydrate.

2. Nutt's Nut Company has 500 pounds of cashews, 100 pounds of pecans and 50 pounds of peanuts on hand. They package three 5-pound cans of nuts consisting of

can I: 3 pounds cashews, 1 pound pecans, 1 pound peanuts
can II: 4 pounds cashews, 1/2 pound pecans, 1/2 pound peanuts
can III: 5 pounds cashews

276
FURTHER
TECHNIQUES
IN LINEAR
PROGRAMMING: THE
SIMPLEX METHOD

The selling price for each can is $5, $4, and $6, respectively. How many cans of each kind should be made to maximize revenue?

3. By hiring additional help, Katy's Hand Made Dolls finds that its Crying Dolls can be made with 15 minutes of machine production and 1 hour of hand finishing, and its Laughing and Crying Doll requires 30 minutes of machine production and 2 hours of hand finishing. The profit on the Crying Doll is $8; on the Laughing and Crying Doll, $12. Machine production is limited to 10 hours per day, while hand finishing is limited to 50 hours per day (about 6 full-time people). What number of each type doll will give a maximum profit?

CHAPTER
REVIEW

Important
Terms

pivot operation
pivot element
pivot row

pivot column
simplex method
slack variables

Exercises

1. Solve the system of equations

$$3x_1 + 5x_2 + x_3 \qquad\quad = 12$$
$$x_1 + 7x_2 \qquad + x_4 \quad = 8$$
$$x_1 + 2x_2 \qquad\quad - x_5 = 0$$

for x_1, x_2 and x_3 in terms of x_4 and x_5.

2. Maximize the objective function

$$f = 40x_1 + 60x_2 + 50x_3$$

subject to the constraints

$$x_1 + x_2 + x_3 \leqq 30$$
$$- x_1 + 2x_3 \leqq 0$$
$$x_1 + x_3 - x_2 \geqq 0$$
$$x_1 \geqq 0, \qquad x_2 \geqq 0, \qquad x_3 \geqq 0$$

3. Minimize the objective function

$$f = 5x_1 + 4x_2 + 3x_3$$

subject to the constraints

$$x_1 + x_2 + x_3 \leqq 30$$
$$- x_1 + 2x_3 \geqq 0$$
$$x_1 - x_2 + x_3 \geqq 0$$
$$x_1 + x_2 + x_3 \geqq 20$$
$$x_1 \geqq 0, \qquad x_2 \geqq 0, \qquad x_3 \geqq 0$$

Additional Reading

Dantzig, George B., *Linear Programming and Extensions,* Princeton University Press, Princeton, New Jersey, 1963.

Ferguson, C. E., *Microeconomic Theory,* Richard D. Irwin, Inc., Homewood, Illinois, 1969.

Samuelson, Paul, Robert Dorfman, and Robert Solow, *Linear Programming and Economic Analysis,* McGraw-Hill, New York, 1958.

Vazsonyi, Andrew, *Scientific Programming in Business and Industry,* John Wiley and Sons, New York, 1958.

Matrix Applications to
Directed Graphs Chapter 9

Many situations that occur in psychology, sociology, and business that are of a combinatorial nature can be interpreted by using techniques found in a relatively new area of mathematics called *graph theory*. In this chapter, we present a brief introduction and will explain some of the more elementary results of graph theory and their applications.

It is our intention to proceed only as far with a topic as is necessary to equip the reader with an introduction to the types of problems that can be considered and to some of the techniques used to solve them. The associated theory is demonstrated through examples. Our hope is that the presentation will stimulate interest in this new and growing field.

Before giving a formal definition of a graph, we point out that the term graph has two quite different meanings. One definition of a graph is the one we studied in Chapter 5 and used in Chapter 6 when we graphed straight lines and linear inequalities.

In this chapter a *graph* will mean a collection of points (called vertices) with one or more curves or lines (called *edges*) connecting a pair of points. Our main concern is not what the edge looks like but rather whether two vertices have an edge joining them or not. As we shall see, this will allow us to use graphs to interpret many situations.

For example, in team competition, two teams are pitted against one another. If eight teams *A, B, C, D, E, F, G, H* all belong to the same league, then after a few matches have taken place, we might have the situation that

A has played *D, G, H*
B has played *C, F*
C has played *B, G, H*
D has played *A*
E has not played
F has played *B*
G has played *A, C*
H has played *A, C*

We can illustrate this situation by a diagram in which the teams *A, B, C, D, E, F, G, H* are dots, and a line joining two dots indicates these two teams have played. Such a geometric design is called a *graph*. The points *A, B, C, D, E, F, G, H* are *vertices* and the arcs *AD, CB*, and so on are called *edges*. See Figure 9.1.

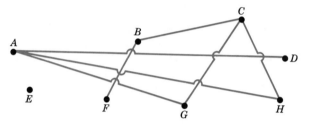

Figure 9.1

Notice that a "hook" is used to indicate that the line joining *B* and *F* does not meet the lines joining *AD, AH*, and *AG*.

9.1.1
Definition

A *graph* is a collection of a finite number of vertices $P_1, P_2, P_3, \ldots P_n$ together with a finite number of edges P_iP_j joining a pair of vertices P_i and P_j.

It is pointed out that a pair of vertices may have more than one edge joining them. Also, a vertex may have no edge joining it. (The team *E* in Figure 9.1 is an example of such a vertex.) An edge may join a vertex to itself. (Such an edge is called a *loop*.) Finally, it is understood that edges are not ordered, so that the edge P_iP_j and the edge P_jP_i are identical.

In depicting graphs we may denote the edges by either a line or an arc, whichever is more convenient.

Figure 9.2 illustrates some graphs. Notice that the graph (a) has an edge from vertex *A* back to *A*. This is a loop.

In Figure 9.2, (a) is a graph with two vertices *A* and *B* and two edges *AA* and *AB*; (b) is a graph with four vertices *A, B, C, D* and two edges *AB, AC*; (c) is a graph with four vertices *A, B, C, D* and five edges *AB, AC, AD, BC, BD*; and (d) is a graph with four vertices *A, B, C, D* and four edges *AC, AC, BC, BD*.

Let us return to the team competition depicted by the graph in Figure 9.1. This graph shows which teams have played by using an edge to join

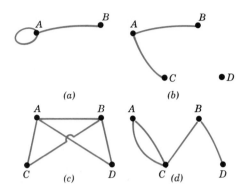

Figure 9.2

pairs of vertices. However, usually we are more interested in who won rather than who played. Thus, if we are told that

A won over G, H and lost to D
B won over C, F
C won over G and lost to B, H
D won over A
E has not played
F lost to B
G lost to A, C
H won over C and lost to A

we can use a directed edge with the arrow pointing toward the loser to illustrate this information. This is an example of what is called a *directed graph* or *digraph*. See Figure 9.3.

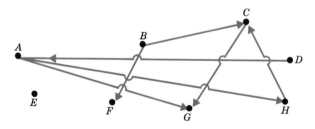

Figure 9.3

At this point let us define more precisely the ideas we have just presented.

A *directed graph* **or a** *digraph* **is a collection of a finite number of vertices**
$P_1, P_2, \ldots, P_n$ **together with a finite number of directed edges:** P_iP_j
in which $i \neq j$.

9.1.2
Definition

Notice that since the edges are now directed, the directed edge P_iP_j (depicted by an arrow from P_i pointing toward P_j) is different from the directed edge P_jP_i. Also, in a digraph, it is not possible to have a loop since we do not allow directed edges from a vertex back to itself.

Some examples of directed graphs are given in Figure 4.4 and 4.5 of Chapter 4 in which we describe organizational charts used in the Harary hierarchy model. Other illustrations of directed graphs are given in Figure 9.4.

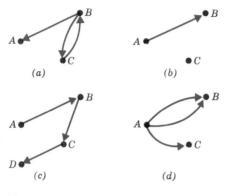

Figure 9.4

In Figure 9.4, (a) is a directed graph with vertices A, B, C and three directed edges BA, BC, CB; (b) is a directed graph with vertices A, B, C and one directed edge AB; (c) is a directed graph with vertices A, B, C, D and three directed edges AB, BC, CD; and (d) is a directed graph with vertices A, B, C and three directed edges AB, AB, AC.

Usually, we shall denote a directed edge AB by $A \rightarrow B$. Also, if AB and BA are two directed edges in a digraph, we will write $A \leftrightarrow B$.

In order to more easily visualize the information given in a digraph and to be in a position to draw conclusions about the situation depicted by a digraph, we use a matrix to represent the information given in a digraph. This will allow us to take full advantage of the computer for tedious computations.

To determine the matrix representative of a digraph, we use a square matrix in which the entry in row A column B is the number of directed edges from A to B. For example, the digraphs in Figure 9.4 have the matrix representations

$$
\begin{array}{c}
\begin{array}{ccc} A & B & C \end{array} \\
\begin{array}{c} A \\ B \\ C \end{array}\left(\begin{array}{ccc} 0 & 0 & 0 \\ 1 & 0 & 1 \\ 0 & 1 & 0 \end{array}\right) \\
\text{(a)}
\end{array}
\qquad
\begin{array}{c}
\begin{array}{ccc} A & B & C \end{array} \\
\begin{array}{c} A \\ B \\ C \end{array}\left(\begin{array}{ccc} 0 & 1 & 0 \\ 0 & 0 & 0 \\ 0 & 0 & 0 \end{array}\right) \\
\text{(b)}
\end{array}
$$

$$
\begin{array}{c}
\begin{array}{cccc} A & B & C & D \end{array} \\
\begin{array}{c} A \\ B \\ C \\ D \end{array}\left(\begin{array}{cccc} 0 & 1 & 0 & 0 \\ 0 & 0 & 1 & 0 \\ 0 & 0 & 0 & 1 \\ 0 & 0 & 0 & 0 \end{array}\right) \\
\text{(c)}
\end{array}
\qquad
\begin{array}{c}
\begin{array}{ccc} A & B & C \end{array} \\
\begin{array}{c} A \\ B \\ C \end{array}\left(\begin{array}{ccc} 0 & 2 & 1 \\ 0 & 0 & 0 \\ 0 & 0 & 0 \end{array}\right) \\
\text{(d)}
\end{array}
$$

Any organization (such as a highway system, a network for telephone communication, a political party) that can be *structured* in the sense that the components of the organization, the cities in a highway system, the homes in a telephone network, the people in a political party, are related in certain ways, can be depicted by a directed graph. In this chapter, we shall study four general types of organizational structures: dominance, perfect communication, business communication, and cliques.

Dominance

Here we study organizations of people in which we assume that for every pair of people one of them either dominates (has influence over) or is dominated by (is influenced by) the other. If we use a vertex to represent a person and an edge to represent dominance or influence so that AB or $A \rightarrow B$ means A has influence over B, then organizations with this property can be illustrated with a directed graph, called a *dominance digraph*.

Such a situation occurs in round-robin tournaments in which each team must play every other team once and no ties are allowed. This means, of course, that for every pair of teams, one wins and the other loses. For example, in Figure 9.5, we have a group of four teams A, B, C, D, in which

team A has won over B and C
team B has won over C, D
team C has won over D
team D has won over A

where $A \rightarrow B$ indicates A has won over B.

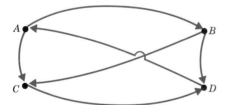

Figure 9.5

The matrix representation for this digraph is

$$
\begin{array}{c}
\\
A \\
B \\
C \\
D
\end{array}
\begin{array}{cccc}
A & B & C & D \\
\left(\begin{array}{cccc}
0 & 1 & 1 & 0 \\
0 & 0 & 1 & 1 \\
0 & 0 & 0 & 1 \\
1 & 0 & 0 & 0
\end{array} \right)
\end{array}
$$

Other situations that give rise to a *dominance digraph* occur in large groups in which an investigation of every pair of people reveals the dominant or influential one. For example, in a group of four people A, B, C, D, we might write all possible pairings and determine which in each pair is the dominant one. The following table illustrates this.

Pair	AB	AC	AD	BC	BD	CD
Dominant one	A	A	D	C	B	D

A dominance digraph can be used to represent this situation if by $A \rightarrow B$ we mean A dominates B in the pairing AB. See Figure 9.6.

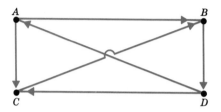

Figure 9.6

The matrix representation for the digraph in Figure 9.6 is

$$
\begin{array}{c}
\quad\; A \;\; B \;\; C \;\; D \\
\begin{array}{c} A \\ B \\ C \\ D \end{array}
\begin{pmatrix}
0 & 1 & 1 & 0 \\
0 & 0 & 0 & 1 \\
0 & 1 & 0 & 0 \\
1 & 0 & 1 & 0
\end{pmatrix}
\end{array}
$$

Every situation that gives rise to a dominance digraph has the property that for every pair of vertices either $A \rightarrow B$ or $B \rightarrow A$ but not both. This means the matrix representation of a dominance digraph has entries that are either 0's or 1's. Such matrices are called *incidence matrices*. Moreover, in a dominance digraph, if A dominates B, then B cannot dominate A. Thus, if $M = (a_{ij})$ is the incidence matrix for a dominance digraph, then $a_{ij} = 0$ implies $a_{ji} = 1$ and $a_{ij} = 1$ implies $a_{ji} = 0$, $i \neq j$. Such an incidence matrix is said to be *asymmetric*.

The matrix representation of a dominance digraph is always an asymmetric incidence matrix.

Perfect Communication

Here we study collections of towns connected by highways or collections of homes connected by telephone links. That is, we will study collections with the properties that

(1) If $A \rightarrow B$, then $B \rightarrow A$
(2) The edge $A \rightarrow B$ may occur more than once

Such situations occur in long distance telephone communications among cities in which we assume a city does not directly have a long distance line to itself and if city A is connected by a direct line to city B, then city B is also connected to city A. Of course, A and B may be connected by more than one line.

For example, suppose three cities *A, B, C,* have long distance telephone lines connected according to

  A is connected with *B* by two different lines
  B is connected to *C* by one line

If $A \leftrightarrow B$ denotes a telephone line between *A* and *B*, we can use a *perfect communication digraph* to represent this situation. See Figure 9.7.

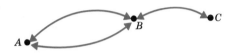

Figure 9.7

The matrix representation for the digraph in Figure 9.7 is

$$
\begin{array}{c}
 \\
A \\
B \\
C
\end{array}
\begin{array}{c}
\begin{array}{ccc} A & B & C \end{array} \\
\left(\begin{array}{ccc}
0 & 2 & 0 \\
2 & 0 & 1 \\
0 & 1 & 0
\end{array}\right)
\end{array}
$$

It is characteristic of a perfect communication digraph that its matrix representation is symmetric.

Business Communication

A special class of communication models used extensively in business are those models depicting a symmetric relationship.

The business communication digraph in Figure 9.8 illustrates a situation in which *A, B, C, D,* and *E* are officials of a business structure and the double arrow $\leftrightarrow$ indicates a communication relation between them. For example, $\leftrightarrow$ might mean memos are exchanged.

The matrix representation for the digraph in Figure 9.8 is

$$
\begin{array}{c}
 \\
A \\
B \\
C \\
D \\
E
\end{array}
\begin{array}{c}
\begin{array}{ccccc} A & B & C & D & E \end{array} \\
\left(\begin{array}{ccccc}
0 & 1 & 0 & 0 & 1 \\
1 & 0 & 1 & 0 & 0 \\
0 & 1 & 0 & 1 & 1 \\
0 & 0 & 1 & 0 & 0 \\
1 & 0 & 1 & 0 & 0
\end{array}\right)
\end{array}
$$

By definition, business communication digraphs have the properties that

(1) $A \rightarrow B$ if $B \rightarrow A$
(2) no pair of vertices is joined by more than one edge

It is characteristic of the matrix representing business communication digraphs that they are symmetric incidence matrices.

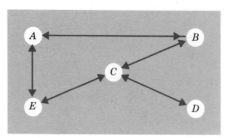

Figure 9.8

Cliques

In a group of people, relationships such as "is a friend of" or "communicates with" may exist. It is clear that in a large group, person A may be a friend of B, while B is not a friend of A. Also, A and C may have no communication between each other at all, while B and C may be mutual friends or have mutual communication. Any group of three or more people who are all mutual friends of each other is termed a *clique*.

For example, suppose that in a group of four people A, B, C, D, we find that A likes B, C; B likes C, D; C likes B, D; and D likes B, C. If we use the directed edge AB or A → B to denote A likes B, then this situation can be illustrated by the clique digraph in Figure 9.9.

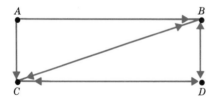

Figure 9.9

Notice that {B, C, D} form a clique since they are mutual friends. The matrix representation of the digraph in Figure 9.9 is

$$
\begin{array}{c}
 \\
A \\
B \\
C \\
D
\end{array}
\begin{array}{cccc}
A & B & C & D \\
\begin{pmatrix}
0 & 1 & 1 & 0 \\
0 & 0 & 1 & 1 \\
0 & 1 & 0 & 1 \\
0 & 1 & 1 & 0
\end{pmatrix}
\end{array}
$$

The matrix representation of any clique digraph is an incidence matrix.

9.1
Exercise

1. For the following matrices, find the corresponding directed graphs. List all the digraphs (i.e., dominance, perfect communication, business communication, clique) they could represent.

(a) $\begin{pmatrix} 0 & 0 & 1 \\ 1 & 0 & 1 \\ 0 & 0 & 0 \end{pmatrix}$ (d) $\begin{pmatrix} 0 & 1 & 1 & 1 \\ 0 & 0 & 1 & 1 \\ 0 & 0 & 0 & 1 \\ 0 & 0 & 0 & 0 \end{pmatrix}$

(b) $\begin{pmatrix} 0 & 1 & 0 \\ 1 & 0 & 1 \\ 0 & 1 & 0 \end{pmatrix}$ (e) $\begin{pmatrix} 0 & 1 & 0 & 0 \\ 1 & 0 & 1 & 0 \\ 0 & 0 & 0 & 0 \\ 1 & 0 & 1 & 0 \end{pmatrix}$

(c) $\begin{pmatrix} 0 & 1 \\ 1 & 0 \end{pmatrix}$ (f) $\begin{pmatrix} 0 & 2 & 1 & 0 \\ 2 & 0 & 0 & 0 \\ 1 & 0 & 0 & 1 \\ 0 & 0 & 1 & 0 \end{pmatrix}$

2. For the following digraphs, write the corresponding matrices. List all the digraphs they could represent.

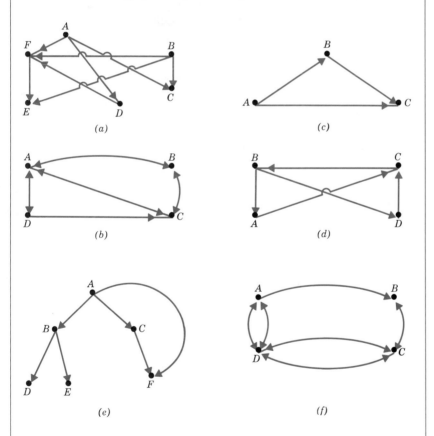

(a)   *(c)*

(b)   *(d)*

(e)   *(f)*

3. Four people A, B, C, D live in an apartment building. If A hears a piece of gossip, he will pass it on to B and D; B passes gossip on to C; C passes gossip on to A; D never gossips. Write a directed graph for this situation. What is the matrix representation? Is this situation an example of a dominance, communication, or clique digraph?

4. For the hierarchy structure given by the digraph of Figure 4.4 in Chapter 4, find the matrix representation. Is this situation an example of a dominance, perfect communication, business communication, or clique digraph?

9.2
DOMINANCE
MODEL

A common sociological relation is the dominance relation. In such a relation we assume that in every pair of people the first dominates or is dominated by the other person.

For example, suppose a sociologist wishes to determine the influence generated by each person in a street gang on the other members of the gang. As a first step, the sociologist might pair off the members of the gang and determine in each pair which one has influence over the other. Although there are obvious drawbacks to this procedure, it seems reasonable to assume that in every one-on-one situation, one person will have influence or will dominate the other. The results of this survey can be represented by a digraph in which $A \rightarrow B$ means B is influenced by A or that A dominates B. Notice that in this model, if A dominates B, then B cannot dominate A.

9.2.1
Example

A gang consisting of five members A, B, C, D, E is interviewed by a sociologist in the manner described above and the resulting dominance digraph is shown in Figure 9.10.

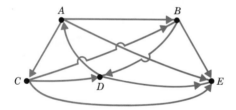

Figure 9.10

The incidence matrix for this situation is

$$M = \begin{array}{c} \\ A \\ B \\ C \\ D \\ E \end{array} \begin{array}{ccccc} A & B & C & D & E \\ \begin{pmatrix} 0 & 1 & 1 & 0 & 1 \\ 0 & 0 & 0 & 1 & 1 \\ 0 & 1 & 0 & 1 & 1 \\ 1 & 0 & 0 & 0 & 1 \\ 0 & 0 & 0 & 0 & 0 \end{pmatrix} \end{array}$$

We notice from either the digraph or the matrix that member A dominates $B, C,$ and E; B dominates D and E; C dominates $B, D,$ and E; D dominates A and E; and E dominates no one.

By adding the entries in a row, we obtain the number of one-stage dominance of a person. For example, A dominates three people in one stage; C

also dominates three people in one stage. Any person who dominates everyone in one stage is called a *consensus leader* of the group.

If there is no person that dominates everyone in one stage, as in our example, we look to find the person who dominates the most people in one stage, and call this individual a *leader*. In our example, there are two people A and C who dominate the most people in one stage. Which one should be designated as leader?

To answer this, we introduce the notion of *two-stage dominance*. Notice that A dominates B and B dominates D. Although A does not dominate D, however, since $A \rightarrow B$ and $B \rightarrow D$, we say that A has two-stage dominance or two-stage influence over D. In this case, we write $A \rightarrow B \rightarrow D$ to indicate A dominates D in two stages. Because of this concept, in the case of a tie for the most number of one-stage dominances, we agree that the person who dominates the most people in one or two stages will be designated as the *leader* of the group.

It is important to realize that there is no transitive property for dominance. Thus, if A dominates B and B dominates C, it may or may not follow that A dominates C.

But how can the number of two-stage dominances of one individual be determined? As we shall see, the square M^2 of the incidence matrix M plays a major role. For the incidence matrix of Example 9.2.1

$$M^2 = \begin{pmatrix} 0 & 1 & 0 & 2 & 2 \\ 1 & 0 & 0 & 0 & 1 \\ 1 & 0 & 0 & 1 & 2 \\ 0 & 1 & 1 & 0 & 1 \\ 0 & 0 & 0 & 0 & 0 \end{pmatrix}$$

How should the matrix M^2 be interpreted?

From the incidence matrix M, we see that A dominates C and C dominates B so that A has two-stage dominance over B as the matrix M^2 indicates. Similarly, C dominates D and D dominates A, so C has two-stage dominance over A as M^2 indicates. The entry "2" in row A column D indicates A has two-stage dominance over D in two ways, namely $A \rightarrow B \rightarrow D$ and $A \rightarrow C \rightarrow D$. Thus, *the square of an incidence matrix gives the number of two-stage dominances for each entry.*

If we add the matrices M and M^2, the total number of ways that people can be dominated by A in either one or two stages is the sum of the entries in row A, while the sum of the entries in column A gives the total number of ways people can dominate A in one or two stages.

$$M + M^2 = \begin{array}{c} \\ A \\ B \\ C \\ D \\ E \end{array} \begin{array}{c} \begin{array}{ccccc} A & B & C & D & E \end{array} \\ \begin{pmatrix} 0 & 2 & 1 & 2 & 3 \\ 1 & 0 & 0 & 1 & 2 \\ 1 & 1 & 0 & 2 & 3 \\ 1 & 1 & 1 & 0 & 2 \\ 0 & 0 & 0 & 0 & 0 \end{pmatrix} \end{array}$$

Thus, we see that A can dominate in 8 ways in one or two stages, B can dominate in 4 ways in one or two stages, C can dominate in 7 ways in one or two stages, and D can dominate in 5 ways in one or two stages.

E can dominate no one in one or two stages. Also A can be dominated in 3 ways in one or two stages, B can be dominated in 4 ways, C in 2 ways, D in 5 ways, and E in 10 ways, each in one or two stages.

In order to determine who is leader of the gang is (recall that A and C each had one- or two-stage dominance over the most people), we might call A the leader since he dominates the most people in one or two stages.

If we cube the incidence matrix M, obtaining the matrix M^3, namely,

$$M^3 = \begin{pmatrix} 2 & 0 & 0 & 1 & 3 \\ 0 & 1 & 1 & 0 & 1 \\ 1 & 1 & 1 & 0 & 2 \\ 0 & 1 & 0 & 2 & 2 \\ 0 & 0 & 0 & 0 & 0 \end{pmatrix}$$

we have the number of three-stage dominances in the group. The matrix M^4 gives the number of four-stage dominances, and so on.

In general, we state the following result:

Theorem 9.2.1

In an incidence matrix M of dimension $n \times n$, suppose the kth power of M is:

$$M^k = (a_{ij}) = \begin{matrix} & \begin{matrix} 1 & 2 & \cdots & n \end{matrix} \\ \begin{matrix} 1 \\ 2 \\ \cdot \\ \cdot \\ \cdot \\ n \end{matrix} & \begin{pmatrix} a_{11} & a_{12} & \cdots & a_{1n} \\ a_{21} & a_{22} & \cdots & a_{2n} \\ \cdot & \cdot & & \cdot \\ \cdot & \cdot & & \cdot \\ \cdot & \cdot & & \cdot \\ a_{n1} & a_{n2} & \cdots & a_{nn} \end{pmatrix} \end{matrix}$$

Then the entry in row i column j, a_{ij} is the number of k-stage dominances of person i over person j.

For example, the matrix M^3 above indicates that person A has three-stage dominance over person E in exactly 3 ways, namely, $A \rightarrow B \rightarrow D \rightarrow E$, $A \rightarrow C \rightarrow B \rightarrow E$ and $A \rightarrow C \rightarrow B \rightarrow E$. Notice that $A \rightarrow B \rightarrow E \rightarrow E$ is not a three-stage dominance.

Theorem 9.2.2

Let M be an incidence matrix of dimension $n \times n$. The entries in the matrix

$$M + M^2 + \cdots\cdots + M^k$$

give the total number of ways each person can dominate in one, two, . . . , up to k stages.

9.2.2
Example

In a group of three people A, B, C suppose we know that B dominates A, A dominates C, and C dominates B. Find a digraph illustrating this situation. Write the incidence matrix and find the number of two-stage influences. Find the leader. Is there a consensus leader? Find the total number of ways to dominate each person in one or two stages.

The digraph is given in Figure 9.11.

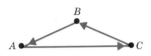

Figure 9.11

The incidence matrix M is

$$M = \begin{matrix} & \begin{matrix} A & B & C \end{matrix} \\ \begin{matrix} A \\ B \\ C \end{matrix} & \begin{pmatrix} 0 & 0 & 1 \\ 1 & 0 & 0 \\ 0 & 1 & 0 \end{pmatrix} \end{matrix}$$

Since no row of M has entries whose sum is 2, there is no consensus leader. Also, the square of M is

$$M^2 = \begin{matrix} & \begin{matrix} A & B & C \end{matrix} \\ \begin{matrix} A \\ B \\ C \end{matrix} & \begin{pmatrix} 0 & 1 & 0 \\ 0 & 0 & 1 \\ 1 & 0 & 0 \end{pmatrix} \end{matrix}$$

The sum $M + M^2$ is

$$M + M^2 = \begin{matrix} & \begin{matrix} A & B & C \end{matrix} \\ \begin{matrix} A \\ B \\ C \end{matrix} & \begin{pmatrix} 0 & 1 & 1 \\ 1 & 0 & 1 \\ 1 & 1 & 0 \end{pmatrix} \end{matrix}$$

A is a leader since A dominates two people in one or two stages; similarly, B and C also dominate two people in one or two stages. Here we have an example of the paradoxical situation of 3 people all of whom could be designated as leaders.

Let us turn to a somewhat similar application of dominance—to tournaments. A tournament consists of teams $A, B, C, \ldots$ in which every pair of teams plays each other once, and one of the teams wins while the other loses (no ties are allowed). If A wins over B, we will write $A \rightarrow B$. Thus, tournaments can be represented by dominance digraphs.

A tournament involving 5 teams A, B, C, D, E ended up as

9.2.3
Example

$$A \rightarrow B, A \rightarrow C, B \rightarrow C, B \rightarrow D, B \rightarrow E,$$
$$C \rightarrow D, D \rightarrow A, E \rightarrow A, E \rightarrow C, E \rightarrow D$$

Draw a digraph for this situation. Find the incidence matrix. Who should be declared winner of the tournament?

The digraph is given in Figure 9.12.

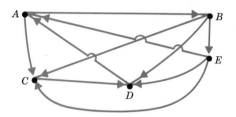

Figure 9.12

The incidence matrix is

$$
M = \begin{array}{c} \\ A \\ B \\ C \\ D \\ E \end{array}
\begin{array}{c} \begin{array}{ccccc} A & B & C & D & E \end{array} \\
\begin{pmatrix}
0 & 1 & 1 & 0 & 0 \\
0 & 0 & 1 & 1 & 1 \\
0 & 0 & 0 & 1 & 0 \\
1 & 0 & 0 & 0 & 0 \\
1 & 0 & 1 & 1 & 0
\end{pmatrix}
\end{array}
$$

The number of games each team won is the sum of the entries of their row. Thus, team A won 2 games, B won 3, C won 1, D won 1, and E won 3. However, there is a tie for first between teams B and E and so there is no clear winner.

To see which team should be declared the winner, we might look at the matrix M^2 to determine the number of two-stage wins for each team. Now

$$
M^2 = \begin{array}{c} \\ A \\ B \\ C \\ D \\ E \end{array}
\begin{array}{c} \begin{array}{ccccc} A & B & C & D & E \end{array} \\
\begin{pmatrix}
0 & 0 & 1 & 2 & 1 & 4 \\
2 & 0 & 1 & 2 & 0 & 5 \\
1 & 0 & 0 & 0 & 0 & 1 \\
0 & 1 & 1 & 0 & 0 & 2 \\
1 & 1 & 1 & 1 & 0 & 4
\end{pmatrix}
\end{array}
$$

Thus, team B has a total of 5 two-stage wins, while team E has a total of 4 two-stage wins. Also, team A has a total of 4 two-stage wins while team D has only 2. Thus, we might award the top prize to team B, followed by team E, team A, team D and lastly, team C.

Another situation that leads to a dominance digraph is the notion of a "paired comparison." In making paired-comparisons, a person is asked to select her favorite flavor of ice cream or favorite color etc., through a pairing of all flavors or colors and selecting the one he favors better of the two. Since in every pair, one is chosen over the other and this is done for all possible pairs, this situation can be depicted as a dominance digraph. See problem 6.

With regard to dominance digraphs, the following result is quite interesting.
In a dominance digraph, the person who dominates the most people in one stage will also dominate everyone in one or two stages.

1. Which of the following matrices can be interpreted as dominance matrices? For those that can be, find the two-stage dominances and find the total number each person dominates in one or two stages.

(a)
$$M = \begin{pmatrix} 0 & 1 & 1 \\ 0 & 0 & 0 \\ 0 & 1 & 1 \end{pmatrix}$$

(d)
$$M = \begin{pmatrix} 0 & 0 & 0 \\ 1 & 0 & 1 \\ 1 & 0 & 0 \end{pmatrix}$$

(b)
$$M = \begin{pmatrix} 0 & 1 \\ 1 & 0 \end{pmatrix}$$

(e)
$$M = \begin{pmatrix} 0 & 0 & 1 \\ 1 & 0 & 0 \\ 0 & 1 & 0 \end{pmatrix}$$

(c)
$$M = \begin{pmatrix} 0 & 1 & 1 & 0 \\ 0 & 0 & 1 & 0 \\ 0 & 0 & 1 & 1 \\ 1 & 1 & 0 & 0 \end{pmatrix}$$

2. For the dominance matrix

$$M = \begin{array}{c} \\ A \\ B \\ C \\ D \end{array} \begin{array}{cccc} A & B & C & D \\ \begin{pmatrix} 0 & 1 & 0 & 0 \\ 0 & 0 & 1 & 1 \\ 1 & 0 & 0 & 0 \\ 1 & 0 & 1 & 0 \end{pmatrix} \end{array}$$

find the two-stage dominances. What total do A and C dominate in one or two stages? What total are dominated by D in two stages?

3. For the dominance matrix

$$M = \begin{array}{c} \\ A \\ B \\ C \end{array} \begin{array}{ccc} A & B & C \\ \begin{pmatrix} 0 & 1 & 1 \\ 0 & 0 & 1 \\ 0 & 0 & 0 \end{pmatrix} \end{array}$$

find the two-stage dominances and interpret your answer. Interpret $M + M^2$.

4. For the dominance digraph

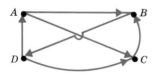

write the incidence matrix. Find the two-stage dominances. What total number are dominated in one or two stages by A, B, and C?

5. In a basketball tournament composed of seven teams, the final standing showed that

	Won	Lost
Team A	4	2
B	4	2
C	4	2
D	3	3
E	3	3
F	2	4
G	1	5

It is known that

A beat D, E, F, G
B beat A, C, D, F
C beat A, E, F, G
D beat C, F, G
E beat B, D, G
F beat E, G
G beat B

Who should be declared the winner?

6. In trying to determine the flavor of ice cream Mr. Polansky likes best, a survey team decides to use paired comparisons. The questionnaire establishes that Mr. Polansky would choose Vanilla over Neapolitan, Pecan, Fudge Ripple and Cherry. Chocolate was preferred over Vanilla, Strawberry, Neapolitan, and Fudge Ripple. Strawberry was chosen over Vanilla, Pecan, Fudge Ripple and Cherry. Pecan won out over Chocolate, Neapolitan, and Cherry. Fudge Ripple was preferred to Pecan and Cherry and, finally, Cherry was chosen over Chocolate. What flavor does Mr. Polansky like best?

*7. It has been established among the countries in Southeast Asia that the following relationships exist. In a war between any two, say A and B, either A defeats B or B defeats A. Prove that there is a strongest country, S, in the sense that either S can defeat any other country X or S can defeat a country Y which can defeat X. Also show that there is a weakest country W in the sense that if X is any other country, then either X can defeat W or X can defeat a country Y which can defeat W.

*8. In a closed community, suppose
   (a) no one hates himself
   (b) given any two people A and B, either A hates B or B hates A but not both.
   Prove that there is a person P in this community such that if X is any other person, then either X hates P, or X hates Y who hates P.

In a perfect communication model, we assume the existence of a group of cities A, B, C . . . and a mode of communication between them such as highways or long distance telephone lines. In such a model, if city A communicates with city B, then by necessity, city B communicates with city A. Two cities may or may not communicate with each other, but there may be more than one line connecting two cities. Common models for such situations are highway networks between cities and telephone links. A communication relation between two cities will be denoted by a double arrow. Thus, the double arrow between A and B, namely, $A \leftrightarrow B$, indicates that city A communicates with B and vice versa. The matrix representation for such a situation will be a *symmetric* matrix. However, it will not usually be an incidence matrix since we allow for more than one edge connecting two vertices. The following example illustrates this.

Connecting four cities, there exist direct telephone lines as depicted in the directed graph in Figure 9.13.

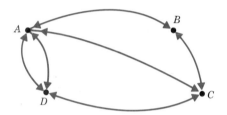

Figure 9.13

The number of lines directly connecting A with B is one, directly connecting A with C is one, directly connecting A with D is two, and one line connects B with C and D with C. We can represent the digraph of direct connections by the matrix

$$\begin{array}{cccc} & A & B & C & D \\ \begin{matrix} A \\ B \\ C \\ D \end{matrix} & \begin{pmatrix} 0 & 1 & 1 & 2 \\ 1 & 0 & 1 & 0 \\ 1 & 1 & 0 & 1 \\ 2 & 0 & 1 & 0 \end{pmatrix} \end{array}$$

in which a zero is used for convenience to denote the number of connection of a city with itself.

The significance of the matrix M^2 is that it tells the number of lines of communication between two cites, passing through exactly one other city.

Now

$$M^2 = \begin{pmatrix} 6 & 1 & 3 & 1 \\ 1 & 2 & 1 & 3 \\ 3 & 1 & 3 & 2 \\ 1 & 3 & 2 & 5 \end{pmatrix}$$

The entries given in M^2 can be verified by looking at Figure 9.13.

Thus the matrix M^2 tells us that there are three different ways that A can communicate with C in two stages, and certainly this is not immediately obvious from Figure 9.13. The ways are $A \to B \to C$, $A \to D \to C$, $A \to D \to C$.

The matrix M^3 gives the number of lines of communication between two cities, passing through exactly two other cities.

9.3.2
Example

A perfect communication matrix showing telephone lines connecting the homes of three people is

$$M = \begin{matrix} & \begin{matrix} A & B & C \end{matrix} \\ \begin{matrix} A \\ B \\ C \end{matrix} & \begin{pmatrix} 0 & 1 & 1 \\ 1 & 0 & 1 \\ 1 & 1 & 0 \end{pmatrix} \end{matrix}$$

The square of the matrix M is

$$M^2 = \begin{matrix} & \begin{matrix} A & B & C \end{matrix} \\ \begin{matrix} A \\ B \\ C \end{matrix} & \begin{pmatrix} 2 & 1 & 1 \\ 1 & 2 & 1 \\ 1 & 1 & 2 \end{pmatrix} \end{matrix}$$

This matrix illustrates the number of two-stage communication lines between pairs of homes in the group. The 2's on the diagonal indicate that there are two ways (in this case through B and through C) for A to get information back to himself through one other person. The 1's indicate the number of ways, for example, B can communicate with A through one other person (in this case C).

The matrix M^3 will give the number of three-stage communication lines between pairs of homes. The values along the diagonal are of importance since they give the number of ways a person in one home can get information back to himself through two other homes (feedback information). In this example, we see that A has two ways of obtaining feedback information, namely $A \to B \to C \to A$ or $A \to C \to B \to A$.

$$M^3 = \begin{matrix} & \begin{matrix} A & B & C \end{matrix} \\ \begin{matrix} A \\ B \\ C \end{matrix} & \begin{pmatrix} 2 & 3 & 3 \\ 3 & 2 & 3 \\ 3 & 3 & 2 \end{pmatrix} \end{matrix}$$

To find out how many ways A can obtain two-stage or three-stage feedback, we need only look at the value in the diagonal of $M + M^2 + M^3$.

$$M + M^2 + M^3 = \begin{matrix} & \begin{matrix} A & B & C \end{matrix} \\ \begin{matrix} A \\ B \\ C \end{matrix} & \begin{pmatrix} 4 & 5 & 5 \\ 5 & 4 & 5 \\ 5 & 5 & 4 \end{pmatrix} \end{matrix}$$

Thus, A has 4 such ways to get feedback. The 5's in row A column B indicate the total number of ways for A to communicate with B using one stage, two stages, or three stages.

9.3
Exercise

1. Which of the following matrices can be interpreted as perfect communication matrices? For those that are, find the two-stage communication lines.

(a)
$$M = \begin{pmatrix} 1 & 1 & 1 \\ 1 & 1 & 1 \\ 1 & 1 & 1 \end{pmatrix}$$

(c)
$$M = \begin{pmatrix} 0 & 0 & 1 \\ 1 & 0 & 1 \\ 1 & 1 & 0 \end{pmatrix}$$

(b)
$$M = \begin{pmatrix} 0 & 1 & 1 & 0 \\ 1 & 0 & 0 & 1 \\ 1 & 0 & 0 & 0 \\ 0 & 1 & 0 & 0 \end{pmatrix}$$

(d)
$$M = \begin{pmatrix} 0 & 1 & 0 \\ 1 & 0 & 1 \\ 0 & 1 & 0 \end{pmatrix}$$

2. For the communication network between three cities of the digraph below, write a matrix M describing the number of lines connecting two cities without passing through another city.

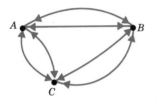

Also, find M^2 and interpret this result.

3. For the data in Problem 2, find the number of ways that city A can communicate with itself through one other city. What are the total number of ways city A can communicate with city C using no other cities or one other city?

4. Write a communication matrix for the group Mike, Danny, and Katy if

(a) Katy communicates with Mike and Danny.
(b) Mike communicates with Danny.

Find the total number of ways Katy can communicate with Mike through no other person or one other person. In how many ways can Mike get one-stage feedback information?

We will discuss in this section a special class of business communication models dealing with relations that arise in the world of business.

Consider a mode of communication among a finite number of officials $A, B, C, \ldots$ in a business structure that obeys the assumptions:

9.4
BUSINESS
COMMUNICATION
MODEL[1]

(1) If official A communicates with B, then by necessity B communicates with A. We will use $A \leftrightarrow B$ to indicate this.
(2) No official communicates with himself.
(3) Two officials may or may not communicate at all.
(4) The matrix representation is always an incidence matrix.

Assumption (4) makes the business communication model different from the perfect communication model discussed in Section 9.3.

[1] Harrary, F. and L. C. Ross, "Identification of the liaison persons of an organization using the structure matrix," *Management Science* **1** (1955).

Of course, even though we are confining ourselves to a business situation, similar situations arise in the areas of mutual influence, two-way communication, and reciprocated sociometric choice.

9.4.1
Example

Figure 9.14 depicts the internal communication digraph as it exists in an organization headed by five officials, which we will denote by *A, B, C, D,* and *E.*

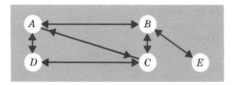

Figure 9.14

The double arrow from *A* to *B,* for example, denotes a communication relation between *A* and *B.* No arrow indicates no such relation between two officials. For instance, there exists no arrow between *B* and *D.* However, we can reach *D* from *B* if we go through *C;* that is, there is a *path* from *B* to *D,* namely, $B \rightarrow C \rightarrow D.$ We can use the path $A \rightarrow B \rightarrow E$ to go from *A* to *E.* In general, a *path* joining two people P_1 and P_2 is a collection of arrows and vertices of the form

$$P_1 \rightarrow P_3 \rightarrow P_4 \rightarrow P_5 \rightarrow \cdots \rightarrow P_2$$

in which no person is repeated.

For example, in Figure 9.14

$$A \rightarrow B \rightarrow C \rightarrow A \rightarrow D$$

is not a path from *A* to *D* since *A* has been repeated. Another example from Figure 9.14 that is not a path is

$$E \rightarrow B \rightarrow C \rightarrow B \rightarrow A$$

since *B* is repeated. However, $E \rightarrow B \rightarrow A$ is a path from *E* to *A.*

9.4.1
Definition

A digraph is said to be *connected* **if there is a path between every two officials.**

Figure 9.14 is an example of a connected digraph; Figure 9.15 is a *disconnected graph.* We obtain this by simply deleting *B* and all arrows connected to *B* from Figure 9.14.

A *liaison official* in a connected digraph is an official whose removal from the digraph results in a disconnected graph. Officials in an organization which appear as liaison officials in the digraph of the organization structure may be viewed as having special static and dynamic properties.

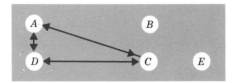

Figure 9.15

From the static point of view, a liaison official is crucial because his re-moval destroys the connected unity of the organization. This is why an organization is most vulnerable at such official positions. From the dynamic point of view, a liaison official is crucial because he cannot be replaced by some other official. For example, if a liaison official is a "bottleneck," the organization will suffer; if he is very efficient, the organization operates very well.

If we follow the convention adopted thus far to construct the matrix representation of the digraph in Figure 9.14, we will obtain the incidence matrix

$$
M = \begin{matrix} & \begin{matrix} A & B & C & D & E \end{matrix} \\ \begin{matrix} A \\ B \\ C \\ D \\ E \end{matrix} & \begin{pmatrix} 0 & 1 & 1 & 1 & 0 \\ 1 & 0 & 1 & 0 & 1 \\ 1 & 1 & 0 & 1 & 0 \\ 1 & 0 & 1 & 0 & 0 \\ 0 & 1 & 0 & 0 & 0 \end{pmatrix} \end{matrix} \qquad (9.4.1)
$$

The zeros along the diagonal indicate that no official can communicate with himself.

From Theorem 9.2.1, we know that a nonzero entry in row i, column j of the kth power of the incidence matrix M implies that we can go from person P_i to person P_j using at most k stages. However, as we have seen, this connection from P_i to P_j may not be a path. But if we eliminate all repeated vertices from this connection, we then have a path from P_i to P_j.

Recall that the square of the incidence matrix M gives the number of two-stage connections between vertices. Clearly, in a connected digraph, every official must have two-way communication with at least one other person so that he will be able to get feedback in two stages. That is, the diagonal entries of M^2 will be nonzero for a business communication di-graph. For example, for the digraph of Figure 9.14, the square of the inci-dence matrix M is

$$
M^2 = \begin{matrix} & \begin{matrix} A & B & C & D & E \end{matrix} \\ \begin{matrix} A \\ B \\ C \\ D \\ E \end{matrix} & \begin{pmatrix} 3 & 1 & 2 & 1 & 1 \\ 1 & 3 & 1 & 2 & 0 \\ 2 & 1 & 3 & 1 & 1 \\ 1 & 2 & 1 & 2 & 0 \\ 1 & 0 & 1 & 0 & 1 \end{pmatrix} \end{matrix}
$$

Referring to Theorem 9.2.2 and applying this result to business com-munication digraphs, we can state the following result, which serves as a test for determining whether a graph is connected or disconnected.

Theorem 9.4.1

The graph of a relation obeying properties (1), (2), (3), and (4) involving n officials is disconnected if and only if the corresponding incidence matrix M of the graph has the property that

$$M + M^2 + M^3 + \cdots + M^{n-1}$$

has one or more zero entries.

9.4.2
Example

Determine whether the graph in Figure 9.14 is connected.

First of all, there are 5 officials in the organization so we must find

$$M + M^2 + M^3 + M^4$$

where M is given in (9.4.1). A little computation with the assistance of a computer yields

$$M + M^2 + M^3 + M^4 = \begin{pmatrix} 23 & 18 & 23 & 16 & 8 \\ 18 & 20 & 18 & 16 & 6 \\ 23 & 18 & 23 & 16 & 8 \\ 16 & 16 & 16 & 14 & 4 \\ 8 & 6 & 8 & 4 & 4 \end{pmatrix}$$

Since no zero entry appears, the graph in Figure 9.14 is connected as we expected.

9.4.3
Example

Determine whether the graph in Figure 9.15 is connected.

The incidence matrix N for the graph in Figure 9.15 is

$$N = \begin{matrix} & \begin{matrix} A & C & D & E \end{matrix} \\ \begin{matrix} A \\ C \\ D \\ E \end{matrix} & \begin{pmatrix} 0 & 1 & 1 & 0 \\ 1 & 0 & 1 & 0 \\ 1 & 1 & 0 & 0 \\ 0 & 0 & 0 & 0 \end{pmatrix} \end{matrix}$$

Since the graph contains 4 officials, we look at the matrix $N + N^2 + N^3$. It is easy to verify that this matrix contains zero entries. Thus, the graph in Figure 9.15 is disconnected as we expected.

Recall that a liaison official is a person that, if removed, causes a connected digraph to become a disconnected graph. Let us then see how the theorem above helps us to determine whether an official is a liaison person.

To determine whether a person P from among n officials is a liaison official, delete from the incidence matrix M the column and the row corresponding to P. Call the deleted matrix N. Then the graph obtained by deleting P is disconnected if

$$N + N^2 + N^3 + \cdots + N^{n-2}$$

contains zero entries. In this case, P is a liaison official.

For the graph of Figure 9.15, with five officials the person E is not liaison official, since if he is removed we still have a connected graph. Let us verify this by using Theorem 9.4.1. Delete from the incidence matrix M in (9.4.1) the row and the column corresponding to E. We get the deleted matrix

$$N = \begin{array}{c} \\ A \\ B \\ C \\ D \end{array} \begin{array}{c} \begin{array}{cccc} A & B & C & D \end{array} \\ \begin{pmatrix} 0 & 1 & 1 & 1 \\ 1 & 0 & 1 & 0 \\ 1 & 1 & 0 & 1 \\ 1 & 0 & 1 & 0 \end{pmatrix} \end{array}$$

The reader should verify that $N + N^2 + N^3$ contains nonzero entries, thus showing that E is not a liaison official.

---

1. For the business communication digraph below, answer the following questions.
   (a) Construct the incidence matrix corresponding to the digraph.
   (b) Is the graph disconnected?
   (c) Which officials are liaison officials?

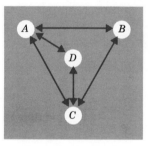

2. (a) Give the digraph corresponding to the following business communication matrix

$$M = \begin{pmatrix} 0 & 1 & 0 & 1 \\ 1 & 0 & 1 & 0 \\ 0 & 1 & 0 & 1 \\ 1 & 0 & 1 & 0 \end{pmatrix}$$

   (b) Which of the persons are liaison officials?
3. For the business communication digraph below, answer the same questions as in Problem 1.

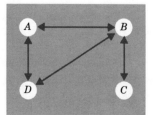

4. In what way is the digraph below different from the one in Problem 3 above?

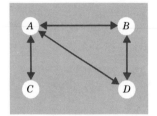

5. Write the incidence matrix for the business communication digraph below and from the graph find all liaison officials.

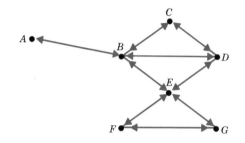

6. Consider five housewives A, B, C, D, E some of whom gossip with each other. The incidence matrix representing this situation is where the entry 1 means gossiping takes place and 0 means it does not.

$$
\begin{array}{c c}
& \begin{array}{c c c c c} A & B & C & D & E \end{array} \\
\begin{array}{c} A \\ B \\ C \\ D \\ E \end{array} &
\begin{pmatrix}
0 & 1 & 0 & 1 & 1 \\
1 & 0 & 0 & 1 & 0 \\
0 & 0 & 0 & 1 & 1 \\
1 & 1 & 1 & 0 & 1 \\
1 & 0 & 1 & 1 & 0
\end{pmatrix}
\end{array}
$$

If housewife E moves out of the neighborhood, is it possible for a rumor to spread among the remaining four housewives?

9.5
CLIQUE MODEL[2]

Thus far, we have discussed several digraphs used in social science and business applications, two of which are the dominance digraph and the business communication digraph. Recall that in a dominance digraph, we assume that for every pair of people one always dominates the other so that the incidence matrix representation is *asymmetric*. That is, if A dominates B, then B cannot dominate A. In a business communication matrix,

[2] Luce, R. Duncan, and Albert D. Perry, "A Method of Matrix Analysis of Group Structure," *Psychometrika* **14** (1949), pp. 94–116.

we assume that if *A* communicates with *B*, then *B* communicates with *A* so that the incidence matrix representation is *symmetric*. In this section, we shall discuss social situations in which the matrix representations are incidence matrices, but are not necessarily asymmetric or symmetric. The relationship of friendship is one that is usually neither symmetric nor asymmetric.

For example, in a group of five people consisting of the set {*A, B, C, D, E*} the relationship "is friendly to," might result in the following situation:

A is friendly to *B, C, D, E*
B is friendly to *A, C, D*
C is friendly to *A, B, D, E*
D is friendly to *B, C, E*
E is friendly to *A, B, C, D*

The digraph representing this situation is given in Figure 9.16, in which an arrow → denotes the relation "is friendly to" and a double arrow ↔ denotes mutual friends.

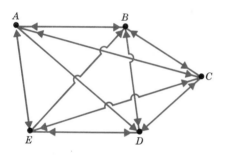

Figure 9.16

In analyzing the digraph in Figure 9.16, we find that certain subsets of the group are mutual friends. For example {*A, B, C*} are mutual friends as are {*C, D, E*}, {*B, C, D*}, {*A, C, E*}. Each of these is an example of a *clique*.

A *clique* is the largest collection of three or more individuals with the property that any two of them are mutual friends.

9.5.1
Definition

Thus, even though two people are mutual friends, they do not form a clique since every clique must have at least three members. Furthermore, if three people are mutual friends and if each one is a mutual friend of a fourth person, the three do not form a clique since they do not form the *largest* collection of mutual friends.

If the number of individuals in the group to be analyzed is large, then it is difficult to find cliques by inspection. Therefore, we shall find cliques using matrix techniques and let computers do any necessary calculations.

Using the procedure of the previous sections, the incidence matrix *M* of the group structure given in Figure 9.16 is

$$
M = \begin{array}{c} \\ A \\ B \\ C \\ D \\ E \end{array}
\begin{array}{c}
\begin{array}{ccccc} A & B & C & D & E \end{array} \\
\begin{pmatrix}
0 & 1 & 1 & 1 & 1 \\
1 & 0 & 1 & 1 & 0 \\
1 & 1 & 0 & 1 & 1 \\
0 & 1 & 1 & 0 & 1 \\
1 & 1 & 1 & 1 & 0
\end{pmatrix}
\end{array}
$$

This incidence matrix M is not asymmetric nor is it symmetric. However, if we limit ourselves to the pairs connected by a double arrow, $\leftrightarrow$, namely

$$A \leftrightarrow B, A \leftrightarrow C, A \leftrightarrow E, C \leftrightarrow E$$
$$B \leftrightarrow C, B \leftrightarrow D, C \leftrightarrow D, D \leftrightarrow E$$

the resulting matrix representing this situation, denoted by S, is

$$
S = \begin{array}{c} \\ A \\ B \\ C \\ D \\ E \end{array}
\begin{array}{c}
\begin{array}{ccccc} A & B & C & D & E \end{array} \\
\begin{pmatrix}
0 & 1 & 1 & 0 & 1 \\
1 & 0 & 1 & 1 & 0 \\
1 & 1 & 0 & 1 & 1 \\
0 & 1 & 1 & 0 & 1 \\
1 & 0 & 1 & 1 & 0
\end{pmatrix}
\end{array}
$$

Clearly, the matrix S is a symmetric matrix.

In general, the matrix S obtained from M by eliminating unidirectional arrows is called the *symmetric matrix S associated with the matrix M*. That is, if two people are mutual friends, the entry 1 appears in their respective row and column in S; otherwise, a 0 appears.

To find cliques in a group, we examine the entries in the matrix S^3. The reason for this is that the entries along the diagonal of S^3 give the number of three-stage relations between a person and himself. Since a person cannot be a friend to himself, a nonzero diagonal entry means a relationship from a person back to himself through two others.

We proceed to state without proof a result we will use to determine cliques in a group.

Theorem 9.5.1

Let M be the incidence matrix representation of a clique digraph and let $S = (s_{ij})$ be the symmetric matrix associated to M. Let $s_{ij}^{(3)}$ denote the entry in row i column j of matrix S^3.

1. If $s_{ii}^{(3)}$ is positive, the person P_i belongs to at least one clique.
2. If $s_{ii}^{(3)} = 0$, the person P_i belongs to no clique.

9.5.1
Example

Consider a group of four people $\{A, B, C, D\}$ whose incidence matrix is

$$
M = \begin{array}{c} \\ A \\ B \\ C \\ D \end{array}
\begin{array}{c}
\begin{array}{cccc} A & B & C & D \end{array} \\
\begin{pmatrix}
0 & 1 & 0 & 0 \\
1 & 0 & 1 & 0 \\
1 & 0 & 0 & 1 \\
0 & 0 & 1 & 0
\end{pmatrix}
\end{array}
$$

Analyze the group structure.

Here, of course, A is friendly to B, B is friendly to A and C, C is friendly to A and D, and D is friendly to C. The symmetric matrix S associated with M is

$$S = \begin{array}{c} \\ A \\ B \\ C \\ D \end{array} \begin{array}{cccc} A & B & C & D \\ \begin{pmatrix} 0 & 1 & 0 & 0 \\ 1 & 0 & 0 & 0 \\ 0 & 0 & 0 & 1 \\ 0 & 0 & 1 & 0 \end{pmatrix} \end{array}$$

The cube of S is

$$S^3 = \begin{array}{c} \\ A \\ B \\ C \\ D \end{array} \begin{array}{cccc} A & B & C & D \\ \begin{pmatrix} 0 & 1 & 0 & 0 \\ 1 & 0 & 0 & 0 \\ 0 & 0 & 0 & 1 \\ 0 & 0 & 1 & 0 \end{pmatrix} \end{array}$$

Since the diagonal entries are zero, this group contains no clique.

The reader should verify that $\{B, C, D\}$ in Figure 9.9 form a clique by using Theorem 9.5.1.

The next result gives us some information regarding the size and number of cliques in a group.

Theorem 9.5.2

Let M be the incidence matrix representation of a clique digraph and let $S = (s_{ij})$ be the symmetric matrix associated with M. An individual is a member of exactly one clique with k members if and only if his diagonal entry in S^3 equals $(k - 1) \cdot (k - 2)$. That is

$$s_{ii}^{(3)} = (k - 1) \cdot (k - 2)$$

For example, in a group of four people, a clique of either 3 or 4 members can result. In this case, a person will belong to exactly one clique provided his diagonal entry in S^3 is $(3 - 1) \cdot (3 - 2) = 2$ or $(4 - 1) \cdot (4 - 2) = 6$. If his diagonal entry is 2, he belongs to one clique of 3 members. If his diagonal entry is 6, he belongs to one clique of 4 members. If his diagonal entry is 0, he belongs to no clique. If his diagonal entry is neither 0, 2, nor 6, he belongs to more than one clique.

In a group of five people, the only possible sizes for a clique are 3, 4, or 5 members. In this case, a person belongs to exactly one clique provided his diagonal entry in S^3 is either

$$(3 - 1)(3 - 2) = 2$$
$$(4 - 1)(4 - 2) = 6$$
$$(5 - 1)(5 - 2) = 12$$

If his diagonal entry is 2, he belongs to one clique of 3 members. If his diagonal entry is 6, he belongs to one clique of 4 members. If it is 12, he belongs to one clique of 5 members. If his diagonal entry is 0, he belongs to no clique. If his diagonal entry is neither 0, 2, 6, nor 12, he belongs to more than one clique.

9.5.2
Example
Analyze the group structure given by the digraph in Figure 9.16. The incidence matrix M and the symmetric matrix S associated to M were given earlier. The cube of S is

$$
S^3 = \begin{array}{c c} & \begin{array}{c c c c c} A & B & C & D & E \end{array} \\ \begin{array}{c} A \\ B \\ C \\ D \\ E \end{array} & \left(\begin{array}{c c c c c} 4 & 8 & 8 & 4 & 8 \\ 8 & 4 & 8 & 8 & 4 \\ 8 & 8 & 8 & 8 & 4 \\ 4 & 8 & 8 & 4 & 8 \\ 8 & 4 & 8 & 8 & 4 \end{array}\right) \end{array}
$$

Clearly, each person in the group belongs to at least one clique since their diagonal entries are positive. Our problem is to determine the composition and number of cliques. Since none of the diagonal entries equals 2, 6, or 12, each person must belong to more than one clique.

To determine how many cliques each person belongs to, we proceed as follows:

Consider person A whose diagonal entry in S^3 is 4. Using only addition and the numbers 2, 6, and 12, how can a 4 be arrived at? Clearly, the only possible way is $2 + 2 = 4$. This means person A belongs to exactly 2 cliques, each containing 3 persons. Similarly, persons B, D, and E belong to 2 cliques, each containing 3 persons.

The diagonal entry 8 in S^3 can only be obtained from 2, 6, and 12 by $2 + 2 + 2 + 2$ or $2 + 6$. Thus person C belongs to 4 cliques of 3 persons each $(2 + 2 + 2 + 2)$ or else to 2 cliques one containing 3 persons and the other containing 4 persons. Since no one else in the group belongs to a clique of 4 people, person C must belong to 4 cliques of 3 persons each.

Consulting the matrix S, we can determine the composition of the 4 cliques. They are: $\{A, B, C\}$, $\{A, C, E\}$, $\{B, C, D\}$, and $\{C, D, E\}$.

9.5.3
Example
Consider a group of ten people and let the relationship be one of friendship. The matrix M which describes the friendship relationship is given by

$$
M = \begin{array}{c c} & \begin{array}{c c c c c c c c c c} 1 & 2 & 3 & 4 & 5 & 6 & 7 & 8 & 9 & 10 \end{array} \\ \begin{array}{c} 1 \\ 2 \\ 3 \\ 4 \\ 5 \\ 6 \\ 7 \\ 8 \\ 9 \\ 10 \end{array} & \left(\begin{array}{c c c c c c c c c c} 0 & 0 & 1 & 1 & 1 & 0 & 0 & 0 & 0 & 1 \\ 0 & 0 & 0 & 0 & 0 & 1 & 0 & 0 & 1 & 0 \\ 1 & 0 & 0 & 1 & 0 & 0 & 0 & 0 & 0 & 0 \\ 1 & 0 & 1 & 0 & 0 & 1 & 0 & 0 & 1 & 1 \\ 1 & 0 & 0 & 0 & 0 & 0 & 0 & 0 & 0 & 0 \\ 0 & 1 & 0 & 0 & 0 & 0 & 1 & 0 & 0 & 0 \\ 0 & 1 & 0 & 0 & 0 & 1 & 0 & 0 & 0 & 0 \\ 0 & 0 & 0 & 0 & 1 & 0 & 0 & 0 & 1 & 0 \\ 0 & 0 & 0 & 1 & 1 & 0 & 0 & 1 & 0 & 0 \\ 1 & 0 & 1 & 0 & 0 & 0 & 1 & 0 & 0 & 0 \end{array}\right) \end{array}
$$

Analyze the group structure.

The symmetric matrix S associated with M is

$$
S = \begin{array}{c}
\\
1 \\ 2 \\ 3 \\ 4 \\ 5 \\ 6 \\ 7 \\ 8 \\ 9 \\ 10
\end{array}
\begin{array}{c}
\begin{array}{cccccccccc}
1 & 2 & 3 & 4 & 5 & 6 & 7 & 8 & 9 & 10
\end{array} \\
\left(\begin{array}{cccccccccc}
0 & 0 & 1 & 1 & 1 & 0 & 0 & 0 & 0 & 1 \\
0 & 0 & 0 & 0 & 0 & 1 & 0 & 0 & 0 & 0 \\
1 & 0 & 0 & 1 & 0 & 0 & 0 & 0 & 0 & 0 \\
1 & 0 & 1 & 0 & 0 & 0 & 0 & 0 & 1 & 0 \\
1 & 0 & 0 & 0 & 0 & 0 & 0 & 0 & 0 & 0 \\
0 & 1 & 0 & 0 & 0 & 0 & 1 & 0 & 0 & 0 \\
0 & 0 & 0 & 0 & 0 & 1 & 0 & 0 & 0 & 0 \\
0 & 0 & 0 & 0 & 0 & 0 & 0 & 0 & 1 & 0 \\
0 & 0 & 0 & 1 & 0 & 0 & 0 & 1 & 0 & 0 \\
1 & 0 & 0 & 0 & 0 & 0 & 0 & 0 & 0 & 0
\end{array}\right)
\end{array}
$$

Next, using a computer, we find the matrix S^3 to be

$$
S^3 = \begin{array}{c}
\\
1 \\ 2 \\ 3 \\ 4 \\ 5 \\ 6 \\ 7 \\ 8 \\ 9 \\ 10
\end{array}
\begin{array}{c}
\begin{array}{cccccccccc}
1 & 2 & 3 & 4 & 5 & 6 & 7 & 8 & 9 & 10
\end{array} \\
\left(\begin{array}{cccccccccc}
2 & 0 & 5 & 6 & 4 & 0 & 0 & 1 & 1 & 4 \\
0 & 0 & 0 & 0 & 0 & 2 & 0 & 0 & 0 & 0 \\
5 & 0 & 2 & 4 & 1 & 0 & 0 & 1 & 1 & 1 \\
6 & 0 & 4 & 2 & 1 & 0 & 0 & 0 & 4 & 1 \\
4 & 0 & 1 & 1 & 0 & 0 & 0 & 0 & 1 & 0 \\
0 & 2 & 0 & 0 & 0 & 0 & 2 & 0 & 0 & 0 \\
0 & 0 & 0 & 0 & 0 & 2 & 0 & 0 & 0 & 0 \\
1 & 0 & 1 & 0 & 0 & 0 & 0 & 0 & 2 & 0 \\
1 & 0 & 1 & 4 & 1 & 0 & 0 & 2 & 0 & 1 \\
4 & 0 & 1 & 1 & 0 & 0 & 0 & 0 & 1 & 0
\end{array}\right)
\end{array}
$$

By consulting the diagonal of S^3, we determine that persons 2, 5, 6, 7, 8, 9, and 10 belong to no clique since a zero appears in their respective row and column. Those people whose main diagonal entries are nonzero, namely persons 1, 3, and 4, belong to at least one clique.

To find the composition and number of the cliques, we compute the values of $(k-1) \cdot (k-2)$ for $k = 3, 4, 5, 6, 7, 8, 9, 10$.

No. of members of clique	$(k-1)(k-2)$
3	2
4	6
5	12
6	20
7	30
8	42
9	56
10	72

The entry 2 in row 1 column 1, row 3 column 3, and row 4 column 4 tells us that these three belong to exactly one clique.

1. Analyze the structure of the clique whose incidence matrix is

$$
\begin{array}{c c c c c c}
 & A & B & C & D & E \\
A & 0 & 0 & 1 & 1 & 1 \\
B & 1 & 0 & 1 & 1 & 1 \\
C & 1 & 1 & 0 & 1 & 1 \\
D & 1 & 1 & 1 & 0 & 1 \\
E & 0 & 1 & 1 & 1 & 0
\end{array}
$$

2. Analyze the structure of the clique whose incidence matrix is

$$
\begin{array}{c c c c c c c}
 & 1 & 2 & 3 & 4 & 5 & 6 \\
1 & 0 & 1 & 1 & 1 & 1 & 0 \\
2 & 1 & 0 & 1 & 1 & 1 & 1 \\
3 & 1 & 1 & 0 & 1 & 1 & 1 \\
4 & 1 & 1 & 1 & 0 & 1 & 1 \\
5 & 1 & 0 & 0 & 0 & 0 & 0 \\
6 & 0 & 1 & 0 & 1 & 1 & 0
\end{array}
$$

3. Analyze the structure of the clique whose incidence matrix is

$$
\begin{array}{c c c c c c c c}
 & & 1 & 2 & 3 & 4 & 5 & 6 & 7 \\
 & 1 & 0 & 1 & 1 & 0 & 1 & 0 & 1 \\
 & 2 & 1 & 0 & 1 & 0 & 0 & 0 & 0 \\
 & 3 & 1 & 1 & 0 & 1 & 1 & 0 & 0 \\
M = & 4 & 0 & 0 & 1 & 0 & 1 & 1 & 1 \\
 & 5 & 1 & 0 & 1 & 1 & 0 & 1 & 1 \\
 & 6 & 0 & 0 & 1 & 1 & 1 & 0 & 1 \\
 & 7 & 1 & 1 & 0 & 1 & 1 & 1 & 0
\end{array}
$$

The cube of the associated matrix S of M is

$$
\begin{array}{c c c c c c c c}
 & & 1 & 2 & 3 & 4 & 5 & 6 & 7 \\
 & 1 & 2 & 4 & 8 & 4 & 4 & 4 & 8 \\
 & 2 & 4 & 2 & 5 & 3 & 3 & 3 & 3 \\
 & 3 & 8 & 5 & 4 & 10 & 10 & 5 & 5 \\
S^3 = & 4 & 4 & 3 & 10 & 8 & 9 & 9 & 11 \\
 & 5 & 4 & 3 & 10 & 9 & 8 & 9 & 11 \\
 & 6 & 4 & 3 & 5 & 9 & 9 & 6 & 8 \\
 & 7 & 8 & 3 & 5 & 11 & 11 & 8 & 6
\end{array}
$$

4. Analyze the structure of the clique whose incidence matrix is

$$
\begin{array}{c c c c c c c c c c c}
 & & 1 & 2 & 3 & 4 & 5 & 6 & 7 & 8 & 9 & 10 \\
 & 1 & 0 & 1 & 0 & 1 & 0 & 0 & 1 & 1 & 0 & 1 \\
 & 2 & 1 & 0 & 0 & 1 & 1 & 0 & 1 & 1 & 1 & 1 \\
 & 3 & 1 & 0 & 0 & 0 & 0 & 0 & 0 & 1 & 0 & 0 \\
 & 4 & 1 & 1 & 0 & 0 & 0 & 0 & 1 & 0 & 1 & 1 \\
M = & 5 & 0 & 0 & 0 & 0 & 0 & 1 & 0 & 0 & 0 & 0 \\
 & 6 & 0 & 0 & 0 & 0 & 1 & 0 & 0 & 0 & 0 & 0 \\
 & 7 & 1 & 1 & 0 & 1 & 0 & 0 & 0 & 1 & 0 & 0 \\
 & 8 & 1 & 1 & 0 & 1 & 0 & 0 & 1 & 0 & 1 & 0 \\
 & 9 & 0 & 0 & 0 & 0 & 0 & 0 & 0 & 0 & 0 & 0 \\
 & 10 & 1 & 1 & 0 & 1 & 1 & 0 & 0 & 0 & 0 & 0
\end{array}
$$

The cube of the associated matrix S of M is

$$
S^3 = \begin{array}{c@{\;}c}
 & \begin{array}{cccccccccc} 1 & 2 & 3 & 4 & 5 & 6 & 7 & 8 & 9 & 10 \end{array} \\
\begin{array}{c} 1 \\ 2 \\ 3 \\ 4 \\ 5 \\ 6 \\ 7 \\ 8 \\ 9 \\ 10 \end{array} &
\left(\begin{array}{cccccccccc}
14 & 15 & 0 & 14 & 0 & 0 & 14 & 12 & 0 & 12 \\
15 & 14 & 0 & 14 & 0 & 0 & 14 & 12 & 0 & 12 \\
0 & 0 & 0 & 0 & 0 & 0 & 0 & 0 & 0 & 0 \\
14 & 14 & 0 & 10 & 0 & 0 & 13 & 8 & 0 & 10 \\
0 & 0 & 0 & 0 & 0 & 1 & 0 & 0 & 0 & 0 \\
0 & 0 & 0 & 0 & 1 & 0 & 0 & 0 & 0 & 0 \\
14 & 14 & 0 & 13 & 0 & 0 & 10 & 10 & 0 & 8 \\
12 & 12 & 0 & 8 & 0 & 0 & 10 & 6 & 0 & 7 \\
0 & 0 & 0 & 0 & 0 & 0 & 0 & 0 & 0 & 0 \\
12 & 12 & 0 & 10 & 0 & 0 & 8 & 7 & 0 & 6
\end{array}\right)
\end{array}
$$

CHAPTER
REVIEW

Important
Terms

Important Terms

graph	**two-stage dominance**
vertices	**leader**
edges	**consensus leader**
directed graph	**k-stage dominance**
digraph	**perfect communication matrix**
dominance digraph	**feedback information**
perfect communication digraph	**path**
business communication digraph	**connected digraph**
clique digraph	**disconnected graph**
incidence matrix	**liaison official**
one-stage dominance	

Exercises

1. For the matrices below find the corresponding directed graph. Determine which are incidence matrices and list all the models they could represent.

a. $\begin{pmatrix} 0 & 1 & 0 \\ 0 & 0 & 1 \\ 0 & 1 & 0 \end{pmatrix}$ b. $\begin{pmatrix} 0 & 1 & 2 \\ 1 & 0 & 0 \\ 2 & 0 & 0 \end{pmatrix}$ c. $\begin{pmatrix} 0 & 1 & 1 \\ 0 & 0 & 0 \\ 0 & 1 & 0 \end{pmatrix}$

2. For those that are dominance situations in Problem 1, find the two-stage dominance relations and find the number of people each person dominates in one or two stages.

3. In a five-team round-robin tournament, the final standings were

		Won	Lost
Team	A	3	1
	B	3	1
	C	2	2
	D	2	2
	E	0	4

If

$$A \text{ beat } B, C, E$$
$$B \text{ beat } C, D, E$$
$$C \text{ beat } D, E$$
$$D \text{ beat } A, E$$
$$E \text{ beat no one}$$

who should be declared the winner? Give reasons!

4. How many ways can city A communicate with city B through one other city for the situation below. Give reasons!

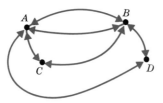

5. Which are liaison officials for the business situation

$$M = \begin{array}{c} \\ A \\ B \\ C \\ D \end{array} \begin{array}{cccc} A & B & C & D \\ \begin{pmatrix} 0 & 1 & 0 & 1 \\ 1 & 0 & 1 & 0 \\ 0 & 1 & 0 & 1 \\ 1 & 0 & 1 & 0 \end{pmatrix} \end{array}$$

6. For the communication network

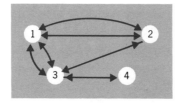

write the matrix A describing the numbers of lines connecting two cities without passing through another city.

7. Analyze the group structure of the matrix M, whose entries are

$$M = \begin{pmatrix} 0 & 1 & 1 & 1 \\ 1 & 0 & 0 & 1 \\ 1 & 0 & 0 & 1 \\ 1 & 1 & 1 & 0 \end{pmatrix}$$

a. Find S and S^3.
b. Find all cliques, if there are any.

Additional Reading

Bavelas, A., "A Mathematical Model for Group Structure," *Applied Anthropology,* 1948, Chapter 7, pp. 16–30.

Festinger, L., "The Analysis of Sociograms Using Matrix Algebra," *Human Relations,* 1949, **2,** pp. 153–158.

Forsyth, E., and Katz, L., "A Matrix Approach to the Analysis of Sociometric Data: Preliminary Report," *Sociometry,* 1946, **9,** pp. 340–347.

Markov Chains Chapter 10

In Chapter 3 we were introduced to one kind of stochastic process, the Bernoulli trial. In discussing Bernoulli trials, we made the assumption that the outcome of each experiment is *independent* of the outcome of any previous experiment.

It is our purpose here to discuss another type of stochastic process, called a *Markov chain*. A Markov chain is a theory that can be used to characterize a series of experiments, in which the result of each experiment will depend only on the result of the immediately preceding experiment and not on other prior experiments.

This type of process has proven to have application to many of the sciences as we will illustrate in our examples and exercises. Let us discuss one such application and then introduce some of its theory.

Consider the maze consisting of four connecting compartments given in Figure 10.1. Each compartment is numbered 1, 2, 3, 4 for convenience and

1 Red	2 Green
Blue 3	White 4

Figure 10.1

each compartment contains pulsating lights of different colors. The experiment consists of releasing a mouse in a particular compartment and observing his behavior.

The system is composed of the mouse and the maze. The experiment begins when the mouse is placed in a compartment; this is called the *initial state*. Then, we assign an initial probability to each possible initial state. For example, in our experiment, if we decide the selection of the initial state should be made in an equally likely way, the *initial probability distribution* would be the vector $A^{(0)} = (1/4 \quad 1/4 \quad 1/4 \quad 1/4)$. If we decide to always begin the experiment by placing the mouse in compartment 1, the initial probability distribution is $A^{(0)} = (1 \quad 0 \quad 0 \quad 0)$.

The experiment consists of observing at regular fixed intervals of time the position and movement of the mouse. For example, if the mouse is placed initially in compartment 1, after a fixed time he may be in state 1, state 2, or state 3. He could not have moved to state 4 since the maze does not contain a passage from 1 to 4 and we assume an observation is made whenever a movement occurs or after a fixed time interval, whichever comes first.

Since it is not possible to determine exactly the movement of the mouse (because it is random in character), we will use probabilistic terms to describe it. The mouse's behavior at a specific instant of time will depend on where it is and how it arrived there. For example, due to the pulsating lights, the probability p_{12} that the mouse moves from state 1 to state 2 might be $p_{12} = 1/2$, while the probabilities of moving from state 1 to either 1 or 3 might be $p_{11} = p_{13} = 1/4$ each. We make the assumption that the state of the mouse on a given observation depends only on the state occupied in the preceding observation. (This is equivalent to the assumption that the mouse has no memory.)

At a given observation, the mouse can be in any of four states. Suppose we assign probabilities for moving from one state to another. We can then conveniently display these probabilities in a matrix, called the *transition matrix*. Thus, if p_{ij} is the probability of moving from state i to state j, then $P = (p_{ij})$ is the *transition matrix* for the experiment.

In our example, there are four states so that the transition matrix $P = (p_{ij})$ is a 4×4 matrix.

In general, a *Markov chain* **is a sequence of n experiments in which each experiment has m possible outcomes $E_1, E_2, \ldots, E_m$ and the probability that a particular outcome occurs depends only on the probability of the outcome of the preceding experiment.**

Suppose then, that we are given a sequence of experiments and as a result of each experiment there can be only one outcome out of a finite number of m mutually exclusive events. Let us call this outcome a *state* and denote all the possible states by $E_1, E_2, E_3, \ldots, E_m$. Of course, any one of these states can occur in any one of the n trials of the experiment. We shall use the notation $E_j^{(n)}$ for $1 \leq j \leq m$ to indicate that the experiment is in the state E_j in the nth trial. The *transition probability*, denoted by p_{ij}, is the probability that the experiment moves into the state E_j from the state E_i. That is, p_{ij} is a conditional probability, which can be expressed as

$$p_{ij} = P(E_j|E_i)$$

The subscripts i and j of p_{ij} can assume any integer between 1 and m. If we let the first subscript stand for a row and the second for a column, the transition probabilities can be arranged in a *matrix P of transition probabilities,* with all entries being nonnegative and less than or equal to one. That is

$$P = \begin{pmatrix} p_{11} & p_{12} & \cdots & p_{1m} \\ p_{21} & p_{22} & \cdots & p_{2m} \\ \cdot & \cdot & & \cdot \\ \cdot & \cdot & & \cdot \\ \cdot & \cdot & & \cdot \\ p_{m1} & p_{m2} & \cdots & p_{mm} \end{pmatrix}$$

Each entry of P represents the transition probability for moving from one state to another. The entry p_{24} for instance, stands for the probability of moving from the state E_2 to the state E_4; whereas, p_{42} represents the probability of moving from state E_4 to the state E_2. Since the probability for a subsequent state depends only on the preceding state, once the transition matrix P is determined, the probability of the outcomes for all successive stages can be found provided the *initial probability distribution $A^{(0)}$* is known. Of course, $A^{(0)}$ is a row vector of the form

$$A^{(0)} = (p_1^{(0)} \quad p_2^{(0)} \quad \cdots \quad p_m^{(0)})$$

This is the probability of being in a particular state when the experiment begins.

It should be clear that a transition matrix P is a square matrix whose entries are always nonnegative in which the sum of the entries in every row is one. On the other hand, the initial probability distribution is a row vector, whose entries are nonnegative in which the sum of the entries is one. In general, any matrix M whose entries are nonnegative in which the sum of the entries in every row is one is called a *stochastic matrix* or a *probability matrix.* Thus, a transition matrix is a square stochastic matrix while an initial probability distribution is a stochastic row vector.

Return to the maze of Example 10.1.1. Suppose we assign the following transition probabilities:

10.1.2
Example

$$\text{From 1 to} \begin{cases} 1 & 2 & 3 & 4 \\ \dfrac{1}{3} & \dfrac{1}{3} & \dfrac{1}{3} & 0 \end{cases}$$

$$\text{From 2 to} \begin{cases} 1 & 2 & 3 & 4 \\ \dfrac{1}{3} & \dfrac{1}{3} & 0 & \dfrac{1}{3} \end{cases}$$

$$\text{From 3 to} \begin{cases} 1 & 2 & 3 & 4 \\ \dfrac{1}{3} & 0 & \dfrac{1}{3} & \dfrac{1}{3} \end{cases}$$

$$\text{From 4 to} \begin{Bmatrix} 1 & 2 & 3 & 4 \\ 0 & \dfrac{1}{3} & \dfrac{1}{3} & \dfrac{1}{3} \end{Bmatrix}$$

Find the transition matrix P. If the initial placement of the mouse is in compartment 4, find the initial probability distribution. What are the probabilities of being in each compartment after two observations?

First, the transition matrix P is

$$P = (p_{ij}) = \begin{array}{c} \\ 1 \\ 2 \\ 3 \\ 4 \end{array} \begin{pmatrix} \dfrac{1}{3} & \dfrac{1}{3} & \dfrac{1}{3} & 0 \\ \dfrac{1}{3} & \dfrac{1}{3} & 0 & \dfrac{1}{3} \\ \dfrac{1}{3} & 0 & \dfrac{1}{3} & \dfrac{1}{3} \\ 0 & \dfrac{1}{3} & \dfrac{1}{3} & \dfrac{1}{3} \end{pmatrix}$$

Next, since the initial placement of the mouse is in compartment 4, the initial probability distribution is

$$A^{(0)} = (p_1^{(0)} \quad p_2^{(0)} \quad p_3^{(0)} \quad p_4^{(0)}) = (0 \quad 0 \quad 0 \quad 1)$$

To answer the last question, we use a tree diagram. See Figure 10.2.

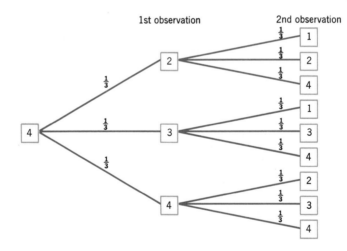

Figure 10.2

The numbers in each square refer to the compartment occupied. For this tree diagram we deduce, for example, that the mouse will be in state 1 after two observations with probability

$$p_{41}^{(2)} = \frac{1}{3} \cdot \frac{1}{3} + \frac{1}{3} \cdot \frac{1}{3} = \frac{2}{9}$$

Similarly

$$p_{42}^{(2)} = \frac{1}{3} \cdot \frac{1}{3} + \frac{1}{3} \cdot \frac{1}{3} = \frac{2}{9}$$

$$p_{43}^{(2)} = \frac{1}{3} \cdot \frac{1}{3} + \frac{1}{3} \cdot \frac{1}{3} = \frac{2}{9}$$

$$p_{44}^{(2)} = \frac{1}{3} \cdot \frac{1}{3} + \frac{1}{3} \cdot \frac{1}{3} + \frac{1}{3} \cdot \frac{1}{3} = \frac{1}{3} \tag{10.1.1}$$

The technique used above to compute the probabilities of being in a given state after k observations is cumbersome and tedious. A fundamental property of Markov chains is the availability of the following straightforward technique.

Theorem 10.1.1
In a Markov chain the probability distribution after k observations is

$$A^{(k)} = A^{(0)}P^k$$

where P^k is the kth power of the transition matrix P and $A^{(0)}$ is the initial probability distribution.

In the example above, to find the probability distribution after two observations, we square the transition matrix P obtaining

$$P^2 = \begin{pmatrix} \frac{1}{3} & \frac{2}{9} & \frac{2}{9} & \frac{2}{9} \\ \frac{2}{9} & \frac{1}{3} & \frac{2}{9} & \frac{2}{9} \\ \frac{2}{9} & \frac{2}{9} & \frac{1}{3} & \frac{2}{9} \\ \frac{2}{9} & \frac{2}{9} & \frac{2}{9} & \frac{1}{3} \end{pmatrix}$$

Notice that the result in (10.1.1) appears in row 4 of P^2. Now the probability distribution after two observations, namely, $A^{(2)}$ is

$$A^{(2)} = A^{(0)}P^2 = \begin{pmatrix} \frac{2}{9} & \frac{2}{9} & \frac{2}{9} & \frac{1}{3} \end{pmatrix}$$

which agrees with our previous result.

In the latest United States census the following figures were obtained with regard to the city of Miller. Each year 7 percent of city residents move to the suburbs and 1 percent of the people in the suburbs move to the city. Assuming that the total number of people remains constant, determine the probability distribution of city and suburb residents after 5 years, that is, after 5 observations, if the initial probability distribution is that 85 percent are city residents and 15 percent are suburban residents.

10.1.3
Example

The percent of movement can be taken as the probability for such movement. Now, this problem can be expressed as a sequence of experiments in which each experiment measures the ratio of people in the city to people in the suburbs. After n years, based on the given probabilities for movement, let p_n represent this ratio. The ratio p_{n+1} after $n + 1$ years will depend for its value only on the value of p_n, and not on any values preceding p_n. Thus, we have an experiment which can be represented as a *Markov chain*.

The initial probability distribution for this system is

$$\begin{array}{cc} \text{City} & \text{Suburbs} \\ A^{(0)} = (.85 & .15 \ ) \end{array}$$

The transition matrix P is

$$P = \begin{array}{c} \\ \text{City} \\ \text{Suburbs} \end{array} \begin{array}{cc} \text{City} & \text{Suburbs} \\ \begin{pmatrix} .93 & .07 \\ .01 & .99 \end{pmatrix} \end{array}$$

To find the probability distribution after 5 years, we need to compute P^5. A little effort yields

$$P^5 = \begin{pmatrix} .7017 & .2983 \\ .0426 & .9574 \end{pmatrix}$$

Using Theorem 10.1.1, the probability distribution after 5 years is

$$A^{(5)} = A^{(0)}P^5 = (.6028 \quad .3972)$$

Thus, after 5 years 60.28 percent of the residents live in the city and 39.72 percent live in the suburbs.

This example leads us to inquire whether the situation in Miller ever stabilizes; that is, after a certain number of years is an equilibrium reached? Also, does the equilibrium state depend on the initial state or are they independent? This type of problem is dealt with in the following section.

**10.1
Exercise**

1. Verify which of the following matrices are stochastic matrices.

(a) $\begin{pmatrix} 1 & 0 & 0 \\ 0 & 1 & 0 \\ 0 & 0 & 1 \end{pmatrix}$

(b) $\begin{pmatrix} 0 & 1 \\ 1 & 0 \end{pmatrix}$

(c) $\begin{pmatrix} 1 & \frac{1}{2} & \frac{1}{3} & \frac{1}{4} \\ 0 & 1 & 0 & 0 \\ 0 & \frac{1}{2} & \frac{1}{2} & \frac{1}{2} \\ 1 & 0 & 0 & 0 \end{pmatrix}$

(d) $\begin{pmatrix} 0 & 1 & 0 \\ 0 & \frac{1}{2} & \frac{1}{2} \end{pmatrix}$

(e) $\begin{pmatrix} -\frac{1}{2} & \frac{1}{2} & \frac{1}{2} \\ 0 & 1 & 0 \\ \frac{1}{3} & \frac{1}{3} & \frac{1}{3} \end{pmatrix}$

(f) $\begin{pmatrix} \frac{1}{4} & \frac{1}{4} & \frac{1}{4} & \frac{1}{4} \end{pmatrix}$

(g) $(0 \quad 0 \quad 1)$

2. The row vector $u = (1 \quad 2 \quad 3)$ is not a stochastic vector. However, if we divide u by 6 (which is the sum of the entries in the row vector) we get $(1/6 \quad 2/6 \quad 3/6)$, which is a stochastic vector. Do the same for $(3 \quad 1 \quad 2 \quad 4)$.

3. In the maze of Example 10.1.1, if the initial probability distribution is $A^{(0)} = (1/2 \quad 0 \quad 1/2 \quad 0)$, find the probability distribution after two observations.

4. In Example 10.1.2, if the initial probability distribution for Miller is $A^{(0)} = (.7 \quad .3)$, what is the probability distribution after five years?

5. Consider the maze with nine compartments in the figure below. The system consists of the maze and a mouse. Let us also assume that the following learning pattern exists: If the mouse is in cells 1, 2, 3, 4, or 5, it moves with equal probability to any cell that the maze permits; if it is in cell 8, it moves directly to cell 9; if it is in cells 6, 7, or 9, it remains there.

   (a) Explain why the above experiment is a Markov chain.

   (b) Construct the transition matrix P.

1	2	3
4	5	6
7	8	9

6. A company is promoting a certain product, say, brand X wine. The result of this is that 75 percent of the people drinking brand X wine over a period of one month, continue to drink it the next month; of those people drinking other brands of wine in a period of one month, 35 percent change over to the promoted wine the next month. We would like to know what fraction of wine drinkers will drink brand X wine after two months if 50 percent drink brand X wine now.

7. A professor either walks or drives to a university. He never drives two days in a row, but if he walks one day, he is just as likely to walk the next day as to drive his car. Show that this forms a Markov chain and give the transition matrix.

*8. If A is a transition matrix, what about A^2? A^3? What do you conjecture about A^n?

*9. Let

$$A = \begin{pmatrix} a_{11} & a_{12} \\ a_{21} & a_{22} \end{pmatrix}$$

be a transition matrix and

$$u = (u_1 \quad u_2)$$

be a stochastic row vector. Prove that uA is a stochastic vector.

*10. Let A and B be two stochastic matrices for which AB is defined. Prove that AB is stochastic.

Another fundamental property of a Markov chain is that sometimes one can obtain the transition probabilities after a large number of observations in a straightforward manner. When this is possible, questions involving the nature of long-run probability distributions can be answered with relative ease. In this section, we investigate the condition under which a Markov chain leads to an equilibrium or steady-state situation and give techniques for finding this equilibrium distribution.

We begin the discussion by referring to Problem 6 in Exercise 10.1.1. The transition matrix is

$$P = \begin{array}{c} \\ \text{Brand X } E_1 \\ \text{Other Brands } E_2 \end{array} \begin{pmatrix} \overset{\displaystyle E_1}{.75} & \overset{\displaystyle E_2}{.25} \\ .35 & .65 \end{pmatrix}$$

$$\begin{array}{cc} \text{Brand X} & \text{Other Brands} \end{array}$$

The tree diagram depicting this experiment is given in Figure 10.3.

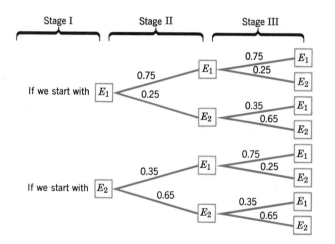

Figure 10.3

The probability $p_{11}^{(2)}$ of proceeding from E_1 to E_1 in two stages is

$$p_{11}^{(2)} = (.75)(.75) + (.25)(.35) = \frac{3}{4} \cdot \frac{3}{4} + \frac{1}{4} \cdot \frac{35}{100} = \frac{52}{80} = .65$$

The probability $p_{12}^{(2)}$ from E_1 to E_2 in two stages is

$$p_{12}^{(2)} = (.75)(.25) + (.25)(.65) = \frac{3}{4} \cdot \frac{1}{4} + \frac{1}{4} \cdot \frac{65}{100} = \frac{28}{80} = .35$$

The probability $p_{21}^{(2)}$ from E_2 to E_1 in two stages is

$$p_{11}^{(2)} = (.35)(.75) + (.65)(.35) = \frac{35}{100} \cdot \frac{3}{4} + \frac{65}{100} \cdot \frac{35}{100} = \frac{49}{100} = .49$$

The probability $p_{22}^{(2)}$ from E_2 to E_2 in two stages is

$$p_{22}^{(2)} = (.35)(.25) + (.65)(.65) = \frac{35}{100} \cdot \frac{1}{4} + \frac{65}{100} \cdot \frac{65}{100} = \frac{51}{100} = .51$$

If we square the matrix P we obtain

$$P^2 = \begin{pmatrix} (.75)(.75) + (.25)(.35) & (.75)(.25) + (.25)(.65) \\ (.35)(.75) + (.65)(.35) & (.35)(.25) + (.65)(.65) \end{pmatrix}$$

$$= \begin{pmatrix} \dfrac{52}{80} & \dfrac{28}{80} \\ \dfrac{49}{100} & \dfrac{51}{100} \end{pmatrix} = \begin{pmatrix} .65 & .35 \\ .49 & .51 \end{pmatrix} = \begin{pmatrix} p_{11}^{(2)} & p_{12}^{(2)} \\ p_{21}^{(2)} & p_{22}^{(2)} \end{pmatrix}$$

Thus, the *square* of the transition matrix gives the probabilities for moving from one state to another state in *two* stages. To see that this is true, recall that the entries of P stand for the transition probabilities of passing from state E_i to E_j in *one* step. However, we would like to find the probability of passing from the state E_i to the state E_j in exactly n steps. For $n = 1$, the original matrix P is the answer; for $n = 2$, we square the matrix P, obtaining

$$P^2 = \begin{pmatrix} p_{11} \cdot p_{11} + p_{12} \cdot p_{21} & p_{11} \cdot p_{12} + p_{12} \cdot p_{22} \\ p_{21} \cdot p_{11} + p_{22} \cdot p_{21} & p_{21} \cdot p_{12} + p_{22} \cdot p_{22} \end{pmatrix}$$

$$= \begin{pmatrix} p_{11}^{(2)} & p_{12}^{(2)} \\ p_{21}^{(2)} & p_{22}^{(2)} \end{pmatrix}$$

We observe that the entries in P^2 are the probabilities that an experiment that is in the state E_i will pass to the state E_j after the second trial. For instance

$$p_{11}^{(2)} = p_{11} \cdot p_{11} + p_{12} \cdot p_{21}$$

is the probability of starting in state E_1 and then passing to state E_1 or to state E_2 and finally passing back to state E_1. See Figure 10.4.

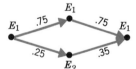

Figure 10.4

A similar interpretation can be given to the other entries of P^2. It seems then that the answer to the question as to what are the probabilities of a state E_i passing to a state E_j in two steps can be found in the entries of P^2. Similarly, to pass from E_i to E_j in n steps, the answer will be given by the entries of P^n.

Theorem 10.2.1
If P is the transition matrix of a Markov chain, then the entries $p_{ij}^{(n)}$ of P^n (nth power of P) give the probability for passing from state E_i to state E_j in n stages, for any i or j.

In studying Markov chains, one question of particular interest is whether after a given number of stages of a Markov process, the transition matrix approaches a steady or equilibrium state. We shall find out that under certain conditions an equilibrium state is attained, is unique, and depends only on the transition matrix and not on the initial probability distribution of the states, that is, the distribution when the process begins.

10.2.1
Example

For the information supplied in Problem 6 of Exercise 10.1, in the long run what will be the distribution of the wine drinkers?

Some of the various powers of the transition matrix P are

$$P = \begin{pmatrix} 0.7500 & 0.2500 \\ 0.3500 & 0.6500 \end{pmatrix} \qquad P^7 = \begin{pmatrix} 0.5840 & 0.4159 \\ 0.5823 & 0.4176 \end{pmatrix}$$

$$P^2 = \begin{pmatrix} 0.6500 & 0.3500 \\ 0.4900 & 0.5100 \end{pmatrix} \qquad P^8 = \begin{pmatrix} 0.5836 & 0.4163 \\ 0.5829 & 0.4170 \end{pmatrix}$$

$$P^3 = \begin{pmatrix} 0.6100 & 0.3900 \\ 0.5460 & 0.4540 \end{pmatrix} \qquad P^9 = \begin{pmatrix} 0.5834 & 0.4165 \\ 0.5831 & 0.4168 \end{pmatrix}$$

$$P^4 = \begin{pmatrix} 0.5940 & 0.4060 \\ 0.5683 & 0.4316 \end{pmatrix} \qquad P^{10} = \begin{pmatrix} 0.5833 & 0.4166 \\ 0.5832 & 0.4167 \end{pmatrix}$$

$$P^5 = \begin{pmatrix} 0.5876 & 0.4124 \\ 0.5773 & 0.4226 \end{pmatrix} \qquad P^{11} = \begin{pmatrix} 0.5833 & 0.4166 \\ 0.5833 & 0.4166 \end{pmatrix}$$

$$P^6 = \begin{pmatrix} 0.5850 & 0.4149 \\ 0.5809 & 0.4190 \end{pmatrix} \qquad P^{12} = \begin{pmatrix} 0.5833 & 0.4166 \\ 0.5833 & 0.4166 \end{pmatrix}$$

Notice an interesting fact about P^n. The entries in P^n stay the same after P^{11}. Thus as we increase n, the matrix P reaches a point of equilibrium where its entries are stabilized. The entries, of course, as stated earlier are the probabilities that the process moves from one state to another in n steps.

We do not always have to raise the transition matrix P to a certain nth power to obtain these probabilities. In some cases we can take a short cut. Once again let us return to Example 10.2.1 and perform the following computation.

$$(.5833 \quad .4166) \begin{pmatrix} .75 & .25 \\ .35 & .65 \end{pmatrix} = (.5833 \quad .4166)$$

Thus, the product of a row vector (taken from the matrix P^{12}) and the original matrix P results in the same row vector. Such a vector is called a *fixed vector* and shows the *equilibrium state* behavior of the process.

10.2.1
Definition

A probability row vector t, satisfying the equation

$$tP = t \tag{10.2.1}$$

is called a *fixed probability vector for the transition matrix P.*

Equation (10.2.1) tells us that the distribution of states tends toward or approaches the value **t**, which is independent of the original distribution.

Hence, **t** is sometimes called the *equilibrium distribution* since once this distribution is reached it will be maintained. In the previous example, the fixed vector **t** was obtained after raising the transition matrix to the 12th power. It should be noted that n need not be 12 in all cases and, in fact, it may happen that no finite value of n gives the fixed vector **t** as the rows of P^n.

The reader is warned that the equilibrium distribution is not usually reached by looking at a few powers of P. The fixed probability vector **t** is most easily found by using the method described below.

Find the fixed probability vector for Example 10.1.1.

**10.2.2
Example**

Let $\mathbf{t} = (t_1 \quad t_2)$ be the desired fixed probability vector such that $t_1 + t_2 = 1$. Then

$$(t_1 \quad t_2) \begin{pmatrix} .93 & .07 \\ .01 & .99 \end{pmatrix} = (t_1 \quad t_2)$$

Or

$$(.93t_1 + .01t_2 \quad .07t_1 + .99t_2) = (t_1 \quad t_2)$$
$$.93t_1 + .01t_2 = t_1$$
$$.07t_1 + .99t_2 = t_2$$
$$t_1 = \frac{1}{8}, \qquad t_2 = \frac{7}{8}$$

In obtaining the fixed probability vector $(1/8 \quad 7/8)$, we learn that in the long run 1/8 of the population will move to the city from the suburb and 7/8 will move to the suburb from the city.

Find the fixed probability vector **t** of the transition matrix

**10.2.3
Example**

$$P = \begin{pmatrix} \frac{1}{2} & 0 & \frac{1}{2} \\ 0 & 1 & 0 \\ \frac{1}{3} & \frac{1}{3} & \frac{1}{3} \end{pmatrix}$$

Let $(t_1 \quad t_2 \quad t_3)$ be the fixed vector such that $t_1 + t_2 + t_3 = 1$. Then

$$(t_1 \quad t_2 \quad t_3) \begin{pmatrix} \frac{1}{2} & 0 & \frac{1}{2} \\ 0 & 1 & 0 \\ \frac{1}{3} & \frac{1}{3} & \frac{1}{3} \end{pmatrix} = (t_1 \quad t_2 \quad t_3)$$

Or

$$(t_1 \quad t_2 \quad t_3) = (0 \quad 1 \quad 0)$$

Up until now, we have only discussed a way for finding the equilibrium state of a Markov chain, but we have not indicated how one tells which Markov chains have equilibrium states and which do not. Thus, at this point, we consider a particularly nice kind of Markov chain, one whose long-run behavior is very regular.

10.2.2
Definition **A transition matrix P of a Markov chain is said to be** *regular* **if for some power of P, all of the entries are positive.**

10.2.4
Example The transition matrix $P = \begin{pmatrix} \frac{1}{2} & \frac{1}{2} \\ 1 & 0 \end{pmatrix}$ is regular since the square of P, namely,

$$P^2 = \begin{pmatrix} \frac{3}{4} & \frac{3}{4} \\ \frac{1}{2} & \frac{1}{2} \end{pmatrix}$$

has only positive entries.

10.2.5
Example The matrix $P = \begin{pmatrix} 1 & 0 \\ \frac{3}{4} & \frac{1}{4} \end{pmatrix}$ is not regular since every power of P will always have $p_{12} = 0$.

The identity matrix is another example of a transition matrix that is not regular.

A Markov chain that has a regular matrix must, as a result, have the property that all possible states or outcomes will, sooner or later, occur. From the above example and Definition 10.2.2 we conjecture the following theorem about regular transition matrices.

Theorem 10.2.2

Let P be a regular transition matrix. Then

(a) P has a unique, fixed probability vector t, whose entries are all positive.
(b) The matrices P^n approach a matrix T, as n gets large. That is

$$P^n \rightarrow T \qquad \text{(as } n \text{ gets very large)}$$

and the rows of T are all identical and equal to the fixed probability vector t.
(c) If q is any probability row vector, then

$$qP^n \rightarrow t \qquad \text{(as } n \text{ gets very large)}$$

Models using Markov chains equip the researcher with a technique for finding the long-run behavior that is typical of many sequential experiments. The researcher hopes that no matter how the process begins it will settle down to some stable and hopefully predictable behavior. Such stable long-run behaviors that are independent of the initial state are not always possible. However, as the above theorem points out, when the Markov chain is regular, stable long-run behaviors result and can be predicted.

In the maze experiment of Example 10.1.1, near the beginning of the experiment the mouse might exhibit a preference for compartments as a result of having been released in a particular compartment. However, as the number of observations becomes large it sometimes happens that the transition probabilities stabilize at values that are independent of the compartment in which the mouse was first released.

Consider a certain community in a well-defined area with three types of grocery stores; for simplicity we shall call them I, II, and III. Within this community (we assume that the population is fixed) there always exists a shift of customers from one grocery store to another. A study was made on January 1 and it was found that 1/4 shopped at store I, 1/3 at store II, and 5/12 at store III. Each month store I retains 90 percent of its customers and loses 10 percent of them to store II. Store II retains 5 percent of its customers and loses 85 percent of them to store I and 10 percent of them to store III. Store III retains 40 percent of its customers and loses 50 percent of them to store I and 10 percent to store II. The transition matrix P is

$$P = \begin{matrix} I \\ II \\ III \end{matrix} \begin{pmatrix} .90 & .10 & 0 \\ .85 & .05 & .10 \\ .50 & .10 & .40 \end{pmatrix}$$

We would like to answer the following questions.

(a) What proportion of customers will each store retain by February 1? (b) by March 1? (c) Assuming the same pattern continues, what will be the *long-run distribution* of customers among the three stores?

(a) To answer the first question, we note that the initial probability distribution is $A^{(0)} = (1/4 \quad 1/3 \quad 5/12)$. Thus, by February 1, the probability distribution is

$$A^{(1)} = A^{(0)}P = \begin{pmatrix} \frac{1}{4} & \frac{1}{3} & \frac{5}{12} \end{pmatrix} \begin{pmatrix} .90 & .10 & .00 \\ .85 & .05 & .10 \\ .50 & .10 & .40 \end{pmatrix} = (.7166 \quad .0832 \quad .1999)$$

(b) To find the probability distribution after two months (March 1), we compute $A^{(2)}$. Then

$$A^{(2)} = A^{(0)}P^2 = \begin{pmatrix} \frac{1}{4} & \frac{1}{3} & \frac{5}{12} \end{pmatrix} \begin{pmatrix} .895 & .095 & .010 \\ .857 & .098 & .045 \\ .735 & .095 & .170 \end{pmatrix} = (.8155 \quad .0956 \quad .0882)$$

(c) To find the long-run distribution let us determine the fixed probability vector of the regular transition matrix P. Let $\mathbf{t} = (t_1 \quad t_2 \quad t_3)$ where $t_1 + t_2 + t_3 = 1$. Then

$$(t_1 \quad t_2 \quad t_3) \cdot \begin{pmatrix} .9 & .10 & .00 \\ .85 & .05 & .10 \\ .50 & .10 & .40 \end{pmatrix} = (t_1 \quad t_2 \quad t_3)$$

$$(t_1 \quad t_2 \quad t_3) = (.8888 \quad .0952 \quad .0158) \tag{10.2.2}$$

Thus in the long run store I will have about 89 percent of all customers, store II 9.5 percent, and store III 1.5 percent.

This example is based on an article by S. J. Prais, Department of Applied Economics, University of Cambridge.

In the example the following assumptions are made:

(1) Class is treated as if it related only to the male side of the family line. This is largely because in these studies social class is measured by the occupation of the father.

(2) The influence of one's ancestors in determining one's class is transmitted entirely through one's father so that if the influence of one's father has been taken into account, then the total influence of one's ancestors is accounted for.

Consider the following social transition matrix in England.

The Social Transition Matrix in England, 1949.

	1	2	3	4	5	6	7
1. Professional and high administrative	0.388	0.146	0.202	0.062	0.140	0.047	0.015
2. Managerial and executive	0.107	0.267	0.227	0.120	0.206	0.053	0.020
3. Higher grade supervisory and nonmanual	0.035	0.101	0.188	0.191	0.357	0.067	0.061
4. Lower grade supervisory and nonmanual	0.021	0.039	0.112	0.212	0.430	0.124	0.062
5. Skilled manual and routine nonmanual	0.009	0.024	0.075	0.123	0.473	0.171	0.125
6. Semi-skilled manual	0.000	0.013	0.041	0.088	0.391	0.312	0.155
7. Unskilled manual	0.000	0.008	0.036	0.083	0.364	0.235	0.274

$$(10.2.3)$$

The element in the ith row and jth column of this matrix, denoted by p_{ij}, gives the proportion of fathers in the ith social class whose sons move into the jth social class. Furthermore, if it is supposed that there is uncertainty in the tracing of a family line through time, the p_{ij} represents the probability of transition by a family from class i into class j in the interval of one generation. Thus, for example, p_{42} indicates that .039 sons of fathers in class 4 (lower grade supervisory and nonmanual) move into class 2 (managerial and executive). The equilibrium probability vector for the matrix in (10.2.3) was found by Mr. Prais to be (0.23 .042 .088 0.127 .409 .182 .129). Mr. Prais compared the above result with the actual data and obtained the following interesting figures. See Figure 10.5. The equilibrium distribution so defined thus depends only on the structural propensities of the society and not on the distribution of the population among the classes found at any instant.

The equilibrium distribution is also independent of the unit of time in which the elements of P are measured. Suppose, for example, that observations were taken showing the relationship between the social statuses of grandson and grandfather. Every element of the transition matrix would then be different since it would refer to a transition during a period of two generations instead of one generation. However, the equilibrium distribution corresponding to such a matrix would be unchanged. For, if the matrix relating the statuses of sons to fathers is P, that relating those of grandsons to grandfathers will be P^2 (provided, of course, that nothing

Class	Actual Distributions of		Equilibrium Distribution (3)
	Fathers (1)	Sons (2)	
1. Professional	0.037	0.029	0.023
2. Managerial	0.043	0.046	0.042
3. Higher grade nonmanual . .	0.098	0.094	0.088
4. Lower grade nonmanual. . .	0.148	0.131	0.127
5. Skilled manual	0.432	0.409	0.409
6. Semi-skilled manual . . .	0.131	0.170	0.182
7. Unskilled manual . . .	0.111	0.121	0.129

Figure 10.5 *Actual and equilibrium distributions of the social classes in England*

has happened to change the characteristics of the society in the period considered) and when these matrices are raised to the nth power, they obviously tend to the same value as n gets very large.

We would like to compute the average number of periods spent in a social class. Let s_j be the number of families in class j in the current generation. Of these, the number $s_j \cdot p_{jj}$ is the expected number found in the jth class in the next generation; the number $s_j \cdot p_{jj}^2$ is the expected number in the jth class in the third generation; and so on. Hence the total time $\mathbf{t}$ spent in the jth class by the s_j families at present in that class is expected to be

$$\mathbf{t} = s_j + s_j \cdot p_{jj} + s_j \cdot p_{jj}^2 + \cdots$$

dividing by s_j there results the average time t_j spent by a family in that class. That is

$$t_j = 1 + p_{jj} + p_{jj}^2 + \cdots$$

Since the jth class is an arbitrary class, the general formula is

$$T = I + P + P^2 + \cdots = I/(I - P) = (I - P)^{-1}$$

where T is the given average time, P is the social transition matrix, and I is the corresponding identity matrix.

10.2.8
Example
The Spread of Rumor

Assume that a given item of information is passed to A and that he in turn passes it to B, B to C, and so on, each time to a new individual, and with probability p that the information is passed on as being false so that $1 - p$ is the probability the information is passed on as being true. With what probability does the nth individual receive the information as being true?

Although it is not intuitively obvious, the answer is independent of p. This situation is another example of a Markov chain model. The model of this problem has the transition matrix

$$P = \begin{matrix} & \begin{matrix} \text{False} & \text{True} \end{matrix} \\ \begin{matrix} \text{False} \\ \text{True} \end{matrix} & \begin{pmatrix} 1 - p & p \\ p & 1 - p \end{pmatrix} \end{matrix}$$

where $1 - p$ represents probability that the information is passed on as being false and p that it is passed on as being true. Then the probability that the nth person will receive the information in one state or the other is given by successive powers of the matrix P, that is, by the matrix P^n. In fact, the answer in this case rapidly approaches $t_1 = 1/2$, $t_2 = 1/2$, after any considerable number of people are involved. This can easily be shown by verifying that the fixed probability vector of P is $(1/2 \quad 1/2)$.

If we interpret the above situation as successive voting situations in Congress and substitute the probability of a member changing his mind for that of spreading the rumor, we arrive at a possible model for explanation of the standard parliamentary device of minority delaying actions.

10.2
Exercise

1. Which of the following matrices are regular?

   (a) $\begin{pmatrix} \frac{1}{2} & \frac{1}{2} \\ 1 & 0 \end{pmatrix}$

   (d) $\begin{pmatrix} \frac{1}{4} & \frac{3}{4} & 0 \\ \frac{1}{2} & 0 & \frac{1}{2} \\ 0 & 1 & 0 \end{pmatrix}$

   (b) $\begin{pmatrix} \frac{1}{2} & \frac{1}{2} \\ 0 & 1 \end{pmatrix}$

   (e) $\begin{pmatrix} 0 & 1 \\ \frac{1}{4} & \frac{3}{4} \end{pmatrix}$

   (c) $\begin{pmatrix} 1 & 0 & 0 \\ \frac{1}{4} & \frac{1}{2} & \frac{1}{4} \\ 0 & 1 & 0 \end{pmatrix}$

   For those that are regular matrices, find the fixed probability vector.

2. Verify equation 10.2.2.

3. A grocer stocks his store with three types of detergents A, B, C. When brand A is sold out the probability is .7 that he stocks up with brand A again. When he sells out brand B the probability is .8 that he will stock up again with brand B. Finally when he sells out brand C the probability is .6 that he will stock up with brand C again. When he switches to another detergent he does so with equal probability for the remaining two brands. Find the transition matrix. In the long run how does he stock up with detergents?

4. A housewife buys three kinds of cereal: A, B, C. She never buys the same cereal on successive weeks. If she buys cereal A, then the next week she buys cereal B. However, if she buys either B or C, then the next week she is three times as likely to buy A as the other brands. Find the transition matrix. In the long run, how often does she buy each of the three brands?

5. In England, of the sons of members of the conservative party, 70 percent vote conservative and the rest vote labor. Of the sons of laborites, 50 percent vote labor, 40 percent vote conservative, and 10 percent vote socialist. Of the sons of socialists, 40 percent vote socialist, 40 percent vote labor, and 20 percent vote conservative. What is the probability that the

grandson of a laborite will vote socialist? What is the long-range voting pattern for each party?

6. If (1/3   0   1/3   1/3) is a fixed probability vector of a matrix P, can P be regular?

We have already seen examples of transition matrices in our presentation of Markov chains in which there are states that are impossible to leave. Such states are called *absorbing*. For instance, in Problem 5 Exercise 10.1, the cell 9 is absorbing since once cell 9 is reached the probability of leaving it and passing to some different cell is 0. Similarly, cell 6 is an absorbing state since it is impossible to leave cell 6.

10.3
ABSORBING
MARKOV CHAINS

In a Markov chain, if p_{ij} denotes the probability of going from state E_i to state E_j, then E_i is called an *absorbing* state if and only if $p_{ii} = 1$. A Markov chain is said to be an *absorbing chain* if and only if it contains at least one absorbing state and it is possible to go from *any* nonabsorbing state to an absorbing state in one or more stages.

10.3.1
Definition

Thus, an absorbing state will capture the process and will not allow any state to pass from it. For example, the Markov chain of Problem 5, Exercise 10.1 is an absorbing Markov chains.

The matrix

$$\begin{array}{c} \\ E_1 \\ E_2 \\ E_3 \end{array} \begin{array}{c} \begin{array}{ccc} E_1 & E_2 & E_3 \end{array} \\ \begin{pmatrix} 1 & 0 & 0 \\ 0 & \dfrac{1}{4} & \dfrac{3}{4} \\ 0 & \dfrac{1}{3} & \dfrac{2}{3} \end{pmatrix} \end{array}$$

is an example of a nonabsorbing matrix, since it is impossible to go from the nonabsorbing state E_2 to the absorbing state E_1.

Consider the following two-person game. Player I has \$3 and player II has \$2. They flip a fair coin; if it is a head, player I pays player II \$1 and if it is a tail, player II pays player I \$1. The total amount of money in the game is, of course, \$5. Throughout the game each player can increase or decrease the amount of money available to him. We would like to know how long the game will last, that is, how long it will take for one of the players to go broke or win all the money. (The above game can easily be generalized by assuming that player I has M dollars and player II has N dollars.)

10.3.1
Example
Random Walk;
Gambler's Ruin
Problem

In this experiment, how much money a player has after any given flip of the coin depends only on how much he had after the previous flip and will not depend (directly) on how much he had in the preceding stages of the game. This experiment can thus be represented by a *Markov chain*.

For the *Gambler's Ruin* problem, the game need not be one of flipping a coin. That is, the probability that player I wins may not equal the probability that player II wins. Also, the questions can be raised as to what happens if the stakes are doubled, how long can the game be expected to last, and so on.

The coin being flipped is fair so that a probability of 1/2 is assigned to each event. The states at each step are the amounts of money each player has at each stage of the game. Thus a player can have $0 to $5 at any stage. Each player can increase or decrease the amount of money he has by only $1 at a time.

The transition matrix P is then of the following form.

$$
P = \begin{array}{c@{\quad}c}
 & \begin{array}{cccccc} 0 & 1 & 2 & 3 & 4 & 5 \end{array} \\
\begin{array}{c} 0 \\ 1 \\ 2 \\ 3 \\ 4 \\ 5 \end{array} &
\left(\begin{array}{cccccc}
1 & 0 & 0 & 0 & 0 & 0 \\
\frac{1}{2} & 0 & \frac{1}{2} & 0 & 0 & 0 \\
0 & \frac{1}{2} & 0 & \frac{1}{2} & 0 & 0 \\
0 & 0 & \frac{1}{2} & 0 & \frac{1}{2} & 0 \\
0 & 0 & 0 & \frac{1}{2} & 0 & \frac{1}{2} \\
0 & 0 & 0 & 0 & 0 & 1
\end{array}\right)
\end{array}
$$

Notice that p_{00} is the probability of having $0 given that a player has started with $0. This is a sure event, since once a player is in state 0 he stays there forever (he is broke). Similarly p_{55} represents the probability of having $5 given a player started with $5 which is again a sure event (the player has won all the money).

With regard to the Random Walk; Gambler's Ruin problem given above, the following questions are of interest:

(a) Given that one gambler is in a nonabsorbing state, what is the expected number of times that he will hold between $1 and $4 inclusive before the termination of the game. That is, on the average, how many times will the process be in nonabsorbing states?
(b) What is the expected length of the process (game)?
(c) What is the probability that an absorbing state is reached (that is, that one gambler will eventually be wiped out)?

To answer the above questions let us look at the transition matrix P. Rearrange this matrix so that the two absorbing states will appear in the 1st two rows. Then

$$
P = \begin{array}{c@{\quad}c}
 & \begin{array}{cccccc} 0 & 5 & 1 & 2 & 3 & 4 \end{array} \\
\begin{array}{c} 0 \\ 5 \\ 1 \\ 2 \\ 3 \\ 4 \end{array} &
\left(\begin{array}{cc|cccc}
1 & 0 & 0 & 0 & 0 & 0 \\
0 & 1 & 0 & 0 & 0 & 0 \\ \hline
1/2 & 0 & 0 & 1/2 & 0 & 0 \\
0 & 0 & 1/2 & 0 & 1/2 & 0 \\
0 & 0 & 0 & 1/2 & 0 & 1/2 \\
0 & 1/2 & 0 & 0 & 1/2 & 0
\end{array}\right)
\end{array}
$$

If we let I_2, θ, S, Q denote the matrices

$$I_2 = \begin{pmatrix} 1 & 0 \\ 0 & 1 \end{pmatrix} \qquad \theta = \begin{pmatrix} 0 & 0 & 0 & 0 \\ 0 & 0 & 0 & 0 \end{pmatrix}$$

$$S = \begin{pmatrix} \frac{1}{2} & 0 \\ 0 & 0 \\ 0 & 0 \\ 0 & \frac{1}{2} \end{pmatrix} \qquad Q = \begin{pmatrix} 0 & \frac{1}{2} & 0 & 0 \\ \frac{1}{2} & 0 & \frac{1}{2} & 0 \\ 0 & \frac{1}{2} & 0 & \frac{1}{2} \\ 0 & 0 & \frac{1}{2} & 0 \end{pmatrix}$$

we can rewrite the matrix P in shorthand notation as

$$P = \begin{pmatrix} I_2 & \theta \\ S & Q \end{pmatrix}$$

It is important to note the above technique can be applied to any matrix representing an absorbing Markov chain. If r of the states are absorbing, the transition matrix P can be written as

$$P = \begin{pmatrix} I_r & \theta \\ S & Q \end{pmatrix}$$

in which I_r is the $r \times r$ identity matrix, θ is the zero matrix of dimension $r \times s$, S is of dimension $s \times r$, and Q is of dimension $s \times s$.

In order to answer the questions raised about the data of Example 10.3.1, we need the following result, which is stated without proof.

Theorem 10.3.1

For an absorbing Markov chain whose transition matrix P is of the form

$$P = \begin{pmatrix} I_r & \theta \\ S & Q \end{pmatrix}$$

where S is of dimension $s \times r$ and Q is of dimension $s \times s$, define the matrix T as

$$T = (I_s - Q)^{-1} \tag{10.3.1}$$

The entries of T give the expected number of times the process is in each nonabsorbing state, provided the process began in a nonabsorbing state.

The matrix T given in (10.3.1) is called the *fundamental matrix* of an absorbing Markov chain.

Returning to the Gambler's Ruin problem, the fundamental matrix T is

$$T = \left[\begin{pmatrix} 1 & 0 & 0 & 0 \\ 0 & 1 & 0 & 0 \\ 0 & 0 & 1 & 0 \\ 0 & 0 & 0 & 1 \end{pmatrix} - \begin{pmatrix} 0 & \frac{1}{2} & 0 & 0 \\ \frac{1}{2} & 0 & \frac{1}{2} & 0 \\ 0 & \frac{1}{2} & 0 & \frac{1}{2} \\ 0 & 0 & \frac{1}{2} & 0 \end{pmatrix} \right]^{-1} = \begin{array}{c} \\ 1 \\ 2 \\ 3 \\ 4 \end{array} \begin{array}{cccc} 1 & 2 & 3 & 4 \\ \begin{pmatrix} 1.6 & 1.2 & .8 & .4 \\ 1.2 & 2.4 & 1.6 & .8 \\ .8 & 1.6 & 2.4 & 1.2 \\ .4 & .8 & 1.2 & 1.6 \end{pmatrix} \end{array}$$

The entry .8 in row 3, column 1 indicates that .8 is the expected number of times the player will have $1 if he started with $3. In the fundamental matrix T, the columns indicate present money, while the rows indicate money started with.

To answer the second question, we again look at the fundamental matrix T. The expected number of games before absorption (when one of the players wins or loses all the money) can be found by adding the entries in each row of T. Thus, if a player starts with $3, the expected number of games before absorption is

$$.8 + 1.6 + 2.4 + 1.2 = 6.0$$

If a player starts with $1, the expected number of games before absorption is

$$1.6 + 1.2 + .8 + .4 = 5.0$$

To answer the third question, we find the product of the matrices T and S. Then

$$T \cdot S = \begin{pmatrix} 1.6 & 1.2 & .8 & .4 \\ 1.2 & 2.4 & 1.6 & .8 \\ .8 & 1.6 & 2.4 & 1.2 \\ .4 & .8 & 1.2 & 1.6 \end{pmatrix} \cdot \begin{pmatrix} \frac{1}{2} & 0 \\ 0 & 0 \\ 0 & 0 \\ 0 & \frac{1}{2} \end{pmatrix} = \begin{array}{c} \\ 1 \\ 2 \\ 3 \\ 4 \end{array}\begin{pmatrix} 0 & 5 \\ .8 & .2 \\ .6 & .4 \\ .4 & .6 \\ .2 & .8 \end{pmatrix}$$

The entry in row 3, column 2 indicates the probability is .6 that the player starting with $3 will win all the money. The entry in row 2 column 1 indicates the probability is .6 that a player starting with $2 will lose all his money.

The above techniques, of course, are applicable in general to any transition matrix P of an absorbing Markov chain. Also, the similarity between the fundamental matrix T of an absorbing Markov chain and the matrix T of Example 10.2.7, which gives the average time spent in a social class should be noticed.

In the Gambler's Ruin problem, we assumed player I started with $3

Probability that Player I wins	Amount of units Player I starts with	Amount of units Player II starts with	Probability that Player I goes broke	Expected length of game	Expected gain of Player I
.50	9	1	.1	9	0
.50	90	10	.1	900	0
.50	900	100	.1	90,000	0
.50	8000	2000	.2	16,000,000	0
.45	9	1	.210	11	−1.1
.45	90	10	.866	765.6	−76.6
.45	99	1	.182	171.8	−17.2
.40	90	10	.983	441.3	−88.3
.40	99	1	.333	161.7	−32.3

Figure 10.6

and player II with $2. Furthermore, we assumed the probability of Player I winning $1 was .5. Figure 10.6 gives probabilities for ruin and expected length for other kinds of betting situations for which the bet is one unit.

Suppose, for example, that Player I starts with $90 and Player II with $10, with Player I having a probability of .45 of winning (the game being unfavorable to Player I). If at each trial, the stake is $1, Figure 10.6 shows that the probability is .866 that Player I is ruined. If the same game is played for a stake of $10, the probability that Player I is ruined drops to .210. Thus, the effect of raising the stakes even in unfavorable games is very pronounced.

10.3
Exercise

1. State which of the following matrices are absorbing Markov chains.

   (a) $\begin{pmatrix} 0 & 1 & 0 & 0 \\ 1 & 0 & 0 & 0 \\ 0 & 0 & 1 & 0 \\ \frac{1}{4} & 0 & \frac{3}{4} & 0 \end{pmatrix}$

   (b) $\begin{pmatrix} 1 & 0 & 0 \\ \frac{1}{8} & \frac{5}{8} & \frac{2}{8} \\ 0 & 0 & 1 \end{pmatrix}$

   (c) $\begin{pmatrix} 0 & 0 & 1 \\ 1 & 0 & 0 \\ 0 & 1 & 0 \end{pmatrix}$

   (d) $\begin{pmatrix} 0 & 1 \\ \frac{1}{4} & \frac{3}{4} \end{pmatrix}$

   (e) $\begin{pmatrix} \frac{1}{3} & \frac{1}{3} & 0 & \frac{1}{3} \\ 0 & \frac{1}{4} & \frac{2}{4} & \frac{1}{4} \\ 0 & 0 & 1 & 0 \\ 0 & \frac{1}{2} & 0 & \frac{1}{2} \end{pmatrix}$

2. Find the fundamental matrix T for the absorbing Markov chains 1(b) and 1(e). For these chains, answer the three questions raised in the Random Walk; Gambler's Ruin example.

10.4
AN APPLICATION
OF MARKOV
CHAINS TO
GENETICS

Most of this section is based on the work of G. Mendel (1822–1884).

The Mendelian theory of genetics states that many traits of an offspring are determined by the genes of the parents. Each parent has a pair of genes and the basic assumption of Mendel's theory is that the offspring inherits one gene from each parent in a random, independent way.

In the most simple cases genes are of two types: *dominant,* denoted by *A* and *recessive,* denoted by *a*. There are four possible pairing of the two types of genes: *AA, Aa, aA,* and *aa.* However, genetically the two genotypes *Aa* and *aA* are the same. An individual having the genotype *AA* is called *dominant* or *homozygous;* an individual with the genotype *Aa* is called *hybrid* or *heterozygous;* and one with the genotype *aa* is called *recessive.*

Let us consider some of the possibilities. If both parents are dominant (homozygous), their offspring must be dominant (homozygous); if both parents are recessive, their offspring are recessive; and if one parent is dominant (homozygous) and one recessive, their offspring is hybrid (heterozygous).

If one parent is dominant (*AA*) and the other is hybrid (*Aa*), the offspring must get a dominant gene *A* from the dominant parent and either a dominant gene *A* or a recessive gene *a* from the hybrid parent. In this case, the probability is 1/2 the offspring will be dominant (*AA*) and the probability is 1/2 the offspring will be hybrid (*Aa*).

Similarly, if one parent is recessive (*aa*) and the other is hybrid (*Aa*), the probability is 1/2 the offspring will be recessive (*aa*) and the probability is 1/2 the offspring will be hybrid (*Aa*).

If both parents are hybrid (heterozygous), the offspring has equal probability of getting a dominant gene or recessive gene from each parent. Thus, the probability the offspring is dominant (homozygous) is 1/4, recessive 1/4, and hybrid (heterozygous) 1/2. See Figure 10.7.

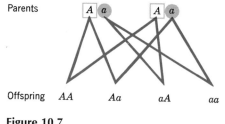

Parents

Offspring   *AA*   *Aa*   *aA*   *aa*

Figure 10.7

10.4.1
Example

Suppose we start with one parent whose genotype is unknown and another whose genotype is known, say hybrid (heterozygous). Their offspring is mated with a person whose genotype is hybrid (heterozygous). This mating procedure is continued. In the long run what is the genotype of the offspring?

Since the genotype of an offspring depends solely on the genotype of the parents, such a mating process is an example of a Markov chain. Label the possible states in the process by *D* (dominant), *H* (hybrid), and *R* (recessive). The transition matrix *P* is:

$$P = \begin{array}{c} \\ D \\ H \\ R \end{array} \begin{array}{ccc} D & H & R \\ \begin{pmatrix} \frac{1}{2} & \frac{1}{2} & 0 \\ \frac{1}{4} & \frac{1}{2} & \frac{1}{4} \\ 0 & \frac{1}{2} & \frac{1}{2} \end{pmatrix} \end{array} \qquad (10.4.1)$$

The entries of *P* are obtained as follows: the first row (1/2 1/2 0) of *P* gives the probabilities that the offspring be *D, H, R*, respectively, when the unknown parent is dominant (*AA*); the second row (1/4 1/2 1/4) of *P* gives the probabilities for the offspring to be *D, H, R* respectively, when the unknown parent is hybrid (*Aa*); the third row (0 1/2 1/2) of *P* gives probabilities for the offspring to be *D, H, R* respectively when the unknown parent is recessive (*aa*).

Now P is regular since the entries of P^2 are all positive.

$$P^2 = \begin{pmatrix} \dfrac{3}{8} & \dfrac{1}{2} & \dfrac{1}{8} \\ \dfrac{1}{4} & \dfrac{1}{2} & \dfrac{1}{4} \\ \dfrac{1}{8} & \dfrac{1}{2} & \dfrac{3}{8} \end{pmatrix}$$

The fixed probability vector of P is found to be

$$\mathbf{t} = \left(\frac{1}{4} \quad \frac{1}{2} \quad \frac{1}{4} \right) \tag{10.4.2}$$

Thus, in the long run, no matter what the genotype of the unknown parent, the probabilities for the genotype of the offspring to be dominant (homozygous) is 1/4, to be hybrid (heterozygous) is 1/2, and to be recessive is 1/4.

In the so called brother-sister mating problem, two individuals are mated, and from among their direct descendants two individuals of opposite sex are selected at random. These are mated, and the process continues indefinitely. With three possible genotypes AA, Aa, aa for each parent, we have to distinguish six combinations of offspring as follows:

$$E_1 : AA \times AA \qquad E_2 : AA \times Aa \qquad E_3 : Aa \times Aa$$
$$E_4 : Aa \times aa \qquad E_5 : aa \times aa \qquad E_6 : AA \times aa$$

10.4.2
Example
Brother-Sister
Mating Problem

where, for example, $E_4 : Aa \times aa$ indicates the mating of a hybrid (Aa) with a recessive (aa). The transition matrix for this experiment is:

$$
\begin{array}{c}
 \\ E_1 \\ E_2 \\ E_3 \\ E_4 \\ E_5 \\ E_6
\end{array}
\begin{array}{c}
\begin{array}{cccccc} E_1 & E_2 & E_3 & E_4 & E_5 & E_6 \end{array} \\
\begin{pmatrix}
1 & 0 & 0 & 0 & 0 & 0 \\
\dfrac{1}{4} & \dfrac{1}{2} & \dfrac{1}{4} & 0 & 0 & 0 \\
\dfrac{1}{16} & \dfrac{1}{4} & \dfrac{1}{4} & \dfrac{1}{4} & \dfrac{1}{16} & \dfrac{1}{8} \\
0 & 0 & \dfrac{1}{4} & \dfrac{1}{2} & \dfrac{1}{4} & 0 \\
0 & 0 & 0 & 0 & 1 & 0 \\
0 & 0 & 1 & 0 & 0 & 0
\end{pmatrix}
\end{array} \tag{10.4.3}
$$

We obtain the entries in (10.4.3) using the following reasoning. States E_1 and E_5 both have 1 on the diagonal and zero for all other elements in the same row, since crossing two dominants (homozygous) always yields a dominant (homozygous), and likewise crossing two recessive always yields a recessive. When the process is in one of the other states, say E_2, we have AA crossed with Aa. The probability of a dominant (homozygous) offspring or a hybrid (heterozygous) offspring is 1/2. To pass from E_2 to E_1 for example, the probability is 1/4; from E_2 to E_2 it is 1/2, from E_2 to E_3 it is 1/4, and from E_2 to E_4, E_5, or E_6 it is 0.

The process described above is an example of an absorbing Markov chain. The states E_1 and E_5 are absorbing states.

Let us perform the same calculations for the transition matrix P in (10.4.3) as we did for the Gambler's Ruin example of Section 10.3.

The transition matrix P is rewritten as follows.

$$
P = \begin{array}{c}
\\
E_1 \\
E_5 \\
E_2 \\
E_3 \\
E_4 \\
E_6
\end{array}
\begin{array}{c}
\begin{array}{cccccc}
E_1 & E_5 & E_2 & E_3 & E_4 & E_6
\end{array} \\
\left(\begin{array}{cccccc}
1 & 0 & 0 & 0 & 0 & 0 \\
0 & 1 & 0 & 0 & 0 & 0 \\
\frac{1}{4} & 0 & \frac{1}{2} & \frac{1}{4} & 0 & 0 \\
\frac{1}{16} & \frac{1}{16} & \frac{1}{4} & \frac{1}{4} & \frac{1}{4} & \frac{1}{8} \\
0 & \frac{1}{4} & 0 & \frac{1}{4} & \frac{1}{2} & 0 \\
0 & 0 & 0 & 1 & 0 & 0
\end{array}\right)
\end{array}
= \left(\begin{array}{c|c} I_2 & \theta \\ \hline S & Q \end{array}\right)
$$

where the matrices I_2, θ, S, and Q are

$$
I_2 = \begin{pmatrix} 1 & 0 \\ 0 & 1 \end{pmatrix}
\qquad
\theta = \begin{pmatrix} 0 & 0 & 0 & 0 \\ 0 & 0 & 0 & 0 \end{pmatrix}
$$

$$
S = \begin{pmatrix}
\frac{1}{4} & 0 \\
\frac{1}{16} & \frac{1}{16} \\
0 & \frac{1}{4} \\
0 & 0
\end{pmatrix}
\qquad
Q = \begin{pmatrix}
\frac{1}{2} & \frac{1}{4} & 0 & 0 \\
\frac{1}{4} & \frac{1}{4} & \frac{1}{4} & \frac{1}{8} \\
0 & \frac{1}{4} & \frac{1}{2} & 0 \\
0 & 1 & 0 & 0
\end{pmatrix}
$$

The fundamental matrix T is:

$$
T = (I_4 - Q)^{-1} =
\begin{array}{c}
\\
E_2 \\
E_3 \\
E_4 \\
E_6
\end{array}
\begin{array}{c}
\begin{array}{cccc}
E_2 & E_3 & E_4 & E_6
\end{array} \\
\left(\begin{array}{cccc}
\frac{8}{3} & \frac{4}{3} & \frac{2}{3} & \frac{1}{6} \\
\frac{4}{3} & \frac{8}{3} & \frac{4}{3} & \frac{1}{3} \\
\frac{2}{3} & \frac{4}{3} & \frac{8}{3} & \frac{1}{6} \\
\frac{4}{3} & \frac{8}{3} & \frac{4}{3} & \frac{4}{3}
\end{array}\right)
\end{array}
$$

The product of the fundamental matrix and S is:

$$
T \cdot S =
\begin{pmatrix}
\frac{8}{3} & \frac{4}{3} & \frac{2}{3} & \frac{1}{6} \\
\frac{4}{3} & \frac{8}{3} & \frac{4}{3} & \frac{1}{3} \\
\frac{2}{3} & \frac{4}{3} & \frac{8}{3} & \frac{1}{6} \\
\frac{4}{3} & \frac{8}{3} & \frac{4}{3} & \frac{4}{3}
\end{pmatrix}
\begin{pmatrix}
\frac{1}{4} & 0 \\
\frac{1}{16} & \frac{1}{16} \\
0 & \frac{1}{4} \\
0 & 0
\end{pmatrix}
=
\begin{array}{c}
\\
E_2 \\
E_3 \\
E_4 \\
E_6
\end{array}
\begin{array}{c}
\begin{array}{cc}
E_1 & E_5
\end{array} \\
\left(\begin{array}{cc}
\frac{3}{4} & \frac{1}{4} \\
\frac{1}{2} & \frac{1}{2} \\
\frac{1}{4} & \frac{3}{4} \\
\frac{1}{2} & \frac{1}{2}
\end{array}\right)
\end{array}
$$

Genetically, the matrix $T \cdot S$ can be interpreted to say that after a large number of inbred matings, a person is either in state E_1 or state E_5. That is, only pure genotypes remain, while the mixed genotype (hybrid heterozygous) will disappear. Notice also that if one starts in the state $E_4 : Aa \times aa$ which has 3 recessive genes and 1 dominant gene, the probability for ending up in the state $E_1 : AA \times AA$ is 1/4, which is the ratio of dominant genes to total genes.

From the fundamental matrix, we can find the expected number of generations needed to pass from a nonabsorbing state to either absorbing state. Thus, the expected number of generations needed to pass from E_3 to either E_1 or E_5 is:

$$\frac{4}{3} + \frac{8}{3} + \frac{4}{3} + \frac{1}{3} = \frac{17}{3} = 5\frac{2}{3}$$

Finally, consider a genetic experiment in which a large population is randomly mated. We assume that males and females have the same proportion of each genotype and that male and female offspring are equally likely to occur. It would seem a logical conclusion of Mendel's law that after a large number of matings, the recessive genotype must disappear. However, the mere fact that recessive genotypes continue to exist implies that this is not the case. This seeming discrepancy in the theory was resolved by the famous mathematician, G. H. Hardy,[1] early in the twentieth century, who proved that the proportion of genotypes in a population stabilizes after one generation.

---

1. Prove that the fixed probability vector for the transition matrix P of (10.4.1) is given by (10.4.2).
2. In Example 10.4.1, suppose the known genotype is dominant (homozygous) and each offspring is mated with a person having a dominant (homozygous) genotype.
   (a) Find the transition matrix P.
   (b) Find the fixed probability vector. Interpret the answer.
   (c) Find the fundamental matrix T.
   (d) What is the number of generations needed to pass from each nonabsorbing stage?
3. Answer the same questions given in Problem 2 if the known genotype is recessive.

10.4
Exercise

Markov chain
initial state
initial probability distribution

transition matrix
transition probability
stochastic matrix

CHAPTER REVIEW

Important Terms

regular Markov chain
fixed probability vector
equilibrium state
equilibrium distribution

absorbing state
absorbing Markov chain
fundamental matrix

Exercises   1. Find the fixed probability vector of

a. $\begin{pmatrix} \dfrac{1}{4} & \dfrac{3}{4} \\[2mm] \dfrac{1}{2} & \dfrac{1}{2} \end{pmatrix}$

b. $\begin{pmatrix} \dfrac{1}{3} & \dfrac{2}{3} \\[2mm] \dfrac{2}{3} & \dfrac{1}{3} \end{pmatrix}$

2. Define and explain in words the meaning of a *regular* stochastic matrix. Give an example of such a matrix and of a matrix that is not regular.

3. Three beer distributors A, B, and C each presently hold 1/3 of the beer market. Each wants to increase his share of the market and to do so, each introduces a new brand. During the next year, it is learned that
   a. A keeps 50 percent of his business, and loses 20 percent to B and 30 percent to C.
   b. B keeps 40 percent of his business and loses 40 percent to A and 20 percent to C.
   c. C keeps 25 percent of his business and loses 50 percent to A and 25 percent to B.
   Assuming this trend continues, after two years what share of the market does each distributor have? In the long-run, what is each distributor's share?

4. If the current share of the market for the beer distributors A, B, and C in Problem 3 is A: 25 percent, B: 25 percent, C: 50 percent, and the market trend is the same, answer the same questions.

5. A representative of a book publishing company has to cover three universities, U_1, U_2, and U_3. He never sells in the same university on successive months. If he sells in University U_1, then the next month he sells in U_2. However, if he sells in either U_2 or U_3, then the next month he is three times as likely to sell in U_1 as in the other university. In the long run how often does he sell in each of the universities?

6. Assume that the probability of a fat father having a fat son is .7 and that of a skinny father having a skinny son is .4. What is the probability of a fat father being the great grandfather of a fat great grandson? In the long run what will be the distribution? Does it depend on the initial physical state of the fathers?

7. Suppose a man has $2 which he is going to bet, $1 at a time, until he either loses all his money or he wins $5. Assume he wins with a probability of .45 and he loses with a probability of .55. Construct the transition probability for this game and answer the questions as stated on p. 332 of the text. Hint: The fundamental matrix T of the transition matrix P is

$$T = \begin{pmatrix} 1.584282 & 1.062331 & 0.6352810 & 0.2858764 \\ 1.298405 & 2.360736 & 1.411736 & 0.6352811 \\ 0.9489998 & 1.725454 & 2.360736 & 1.062331 \\ 0.5219499 & 0.9490000 & 1.298405 & 1.584281 \end{pmatrix}$$

Additional Reading

Dahlberg, G., *Mathematical Methods for Population Genetics*, Wiley-Interscience, New York, 1948.

Introduction to the Theory of Games Chapter 11

Game theory, as a branch of mathematics, is a relatively new field concerned with the analysis of human behavior in conflicts of interest. In other words, game theory gives mathematical expression to the strategies of opposing players and offers techniques for choosing the best possible strategy. In most parlor games, it is relatively easy to define winning and losing and, on this basis, to quantify the best strategy for each player. However, game theory is not merely a tool for the gambler so that he can take advantage of the odds, nor is it merely a method for winning games like ticktacktoe, matching pennies, or the Italian game called *morra*.

Gottfried Leibnitz (1646–1716) is generally recognized as being the first to see the relationship between games of strategy and the theory of social behavior. For example, when union and management sit down at the bargaining table to discuss contracts, each has definite strategies open to him. Each will bluff, persuade, and try to discover the other's strategy while at the same time trying to prevent the discovery of his own. If enough information is known, results from the theory of games can determine what is the best possible rational behavior or the best possible strategy for each player. Another application of game theory can be made to politics. If two people are vying for the same political office, each has open to him various campaign strategies. If it is possible to determine the impact of alternate strategies on the voters, the theory of games can be used to find the best strategy which is usually the one that gains the most votes, while losing the least votes. Thus, game theory can be used in certain situations of conflict to indicate how people should behave to achieve certain goals. Of course, game theory does not tell us how people behave. Game theory is the study, then, of rational behavior in conflict situations.

Some of the practical situations in which game theory can be used are illustrated in the following examples, many of which are solved later in the chapter.

The first example is usually referred to as a "business game." By this we mean a simplified representation of the profits and losses of two commercial rivals engaged in competition with each other. Each businessman has certain information at his disposal and based on this information will make decisions of strategy in a series of stages whose duration may be measured in days, months, or even years. The intention is that the strategy employed will maximize his own profits or minimize his rival's profits.

**11.1.1
Example
Business
Game**

Two franchising firms Alpha Products and Omega Industries are each planning to add an outlet in a certain city. It is possible for the site to be located either in the center of the city or in a large suburb of the city. If both firms decide to build in the center of the city, Alpha Products will show an annual profit of $1000 more than the profit of Omega Industries. If both firms decide to locate their outlet in the suburb, then it is determined that Alpha Products' profit will be $2000 less than the profit of Omega Industries. If Alpha locates in the suburb and Omega in the city, then Alpha shows a profit of $4000 more than does Omega. Finally if Alpha locates in the city and Omega in the suburb, then Alpha has a profit of $3000 less than Omega's. Is there a best site for each firm to locate its franchise? The best site is the one that produces the most competition against the other firm instead of the one that produces the highest gross sales. Of course, the term "best" is very relative here and someone else may well have a different interpretation of what constitutes the best site.

**11.1.2
Example**

In Arthur Conan Doyle's story "The Final Problem," Professor Moriarty is in pursuit of Sherlock Holmes. Holmes has planned to take a train from London to Dover and then make an escape to the Continent. As the Dover train is pulling out of Victoria station in London, Moriarty appears and the two men see each other. Moriarty, left behind in the station, charters a train to continue the chase. Holmes, meanwhile, must decide whether to get off at Canterbury, the only stop between London and Dover, or to stay on the train to Dover. Also, Moriarty must decide what to do. If both men go to the same place, it is assumed that this meeting will result in the death of Sherlock Holmes. If Holmes goes to Dover and Moriarty gets off at Canterbury, then Holmes is able to make his way to the Continent. If Holmes gets off at Canterbury and Moriarty goes to Dover, the game is declared a draw. Does the game favor Holmes or Moriarty?

Situations similar to the one described below are analyzed in that branch of Operations Research which deals with military tactics.

**11.1.3
Example**

General White's army and the enemy are each trying to occupy three hills. General White has three regiments and the enemy has two regiments. A hill is occupied when one force has more regiments present than the other force; if both try to occupy a hill with the same number of regiments, a draw results. How should the troops be deployed to gain maximum advantage?

The following example from political science has received considerable attention in many articles. Although the situation described is hypothetical, many practical applications give rise to similar situations.

Two prisoners, who have committed a crime together, are separated for questioning by the District Attorney who claims to have enough evidence to convict them. Each has the choice of squealing or not squealing on each other. If only one of them confesses, he will receive a suspended sentence, while the other will be sentenced to 10 years in jail. If both confess, however, they will each get 6 years in jail. If neither confesses, each will receive a sentence of 2 years. We assume the prisoners cannot communicate with each other. What should the prisoners do?

11.1.4
Example
The Prisoner's
Dilemma

The remainder of this chapter deals with techniques for solving problems like those illustrated above.

Any conflict or competition between *two* people is called a *two-person game*. Let us consider some examples of two-person games.

11.2
TWO-PERSON
ZERO-SUM MATRIX
GAMES

In a game similar to "matching pennies," Player I picks heads or tails and Player II attempts to guess the choice. Player I will pay Player II $3 if both choose heads; Player I will pay Player II $2 if both choose tails. If Player II guesses incorrectly, he will pay Player I $5.

11.2.1
Example

We use this example to illustrate some terminology. First, since two players are involved, this is a two-person game. Next, notice that no matter what outcome occurs (*HH,HT,TH,TT*), whatever is lost (or gained) by Player I is gained (or lost) by Player II. Such games are called *two-person zero-sum games*. *Nonzero-sum games* are introduced in Section 11.6.

If we denote the gains of Player I by positive entries and his losses by negative entries, we can display this game in a 2×2 matrix as

$$\begin{array}{cc} & \begin{array}{cc} H & T \end{array} \\ \begin{array}{c} H \\ T \end{array} & \begin{pmatrix} -3 & 5 \\ 5 & -2 \end{pmatrix} \end{array}$$

Each entry a_{ij} of a matrix game is termed a *payoff* and the matrix is called the *game matrix* or the *payoff matrix*.

Conversely, any $m \times n$ matrix $A = (a_{ij})$ can be regarded as the game matrix for a two-person zero-sum game in which Player I chooses any one of the m rows of A and simultaneously Player II chooses any one of the n columns of A. The entry in the row and column chosen is the payoff.

We will assume that the game is played repeatedly, and that the problem facing each player is what choice he should make so that he gains the most benefit. Thus, Player I wishes to maximize his winnings and Player II wishes to minimize his losses. By a *strategy* of Player I for a given matrix game A, we mean the decision by I to select rows of A in some manner.

11.2.2
Example

Consider a two-person zero-sum game given by the matrix

$$\begin{pmatrix} 3 & 6 \\ -2 & -3 \end{pmatrix}$$

in which the entries denote the winnings of Player I. The game consists of Player I choosing a row and Player II simultaneously choosing a column with the intersection of row and column giving the payoff for this play in the game. For example, if Player I chooses row one and Player II chooses column two, then Player I wins $6; if Player I chooses row two and Player II chooses column one, then Player I loses $2.

It is immediately evident from the matrix that this particular game is biased in favor of Player I. For, Player I will always choose row 1 since he cannot lose by doing so. Similarly, Player II, recognizing that Player I will choose row 1 will always choose column 1, since his losses are then minimized.

Thus, the *best strategy* for Player I is row 1 and the *best strategy* for Player II is column 1. When both players employ their best strategy, the result is that Player I wins $3. This amount is called the *value* of the game. Notice that the payoff $3 is the minimum of the entries in its row and is the maximum of the entries in its column.

11.2.1
Definition

A game defined by a matrix is said to be *strictly determined* **if and only if there is an entry of the matrix that is the smallest element in its row and is also the largest element in its column. This entry is then called a** *saddle point* **and is the** *value* **of the game.**

If a game has a positive value, the game favors Player I. If a game has a negative value, the game favors Player II. Any game whose value is zero is a *fair game*.

If a matrix game has a saddle point, it can be shown that the row containing the saddle point is the best strategy for Player I and the column containing the saddle point is the best strategy for Player II. This is why such games are called strictly determined games. Such games are also called games of *pure strategy*.

Of course, a matrix may have more than one saddle point, in which case each player has available to him more than one best strategy. However, the value of the game is always the same no matter how many saddle points the matrix may have. See Problem 4(i) in Exercise 11.2.

11.2.3
Example

Determine whether the game defined by the matrix

$$\begin{pmatrix} 3 & 0 & -2 & -1 \\ 2 & -3 & 0 & -1 \\ 4 & 2 & 1 & 0 \end{pmatrix}$$

is strictly determined.

First, we look at each row and find the smallest entry in each row.

These are:

row one: -2; row two: -3; row three: 0

Next, we check to see if any of the above elements are also the largest in their column. The element -2 in row one is not the largest entry in column three; the element -3 in row two is not the largest entry in column two; however, the element 0 in row three is the largest entry in its column. Thus, this game is strictly determined. Its value is 0 so the game is fair.

The game of Example 11.2.3 is represented by a 3×4 matrix. This means that Player I has 3 strategies open to him, while Player II can choose from 4 strategies.

In Example 11.1.1, a "business game" between Alpha Products and Omega Industries is described. If we assign rows as Alpha strategies and columns as Omega strategies and if we use positive entries to denote the gain of Alpha over that of Omega and negative entries for the gain of Omega over Alpha, then the matrix game for this situation is

$$
\begin{array}{cc}
 & \text{Omega} \\
 & \text{City} \quad \text{Suburb} \\
\text{Alpha} \quad \begin{array}{c} \text{City} \\ \text{Suburb} \end{array} & \left(\begin{array}{cc} 1 & -3 \\ 4 & -2 \end{array} \right)
\end{array}
$$

11.2.4
Example

where the entries are in thousands of dollars.

This game is strictly determined and the saddle point is -2, which is the value of the game. Thus, if both firms locate in the suburb, this results in the best competition. This is so since Omega will always choose to locate in the suburb, guaranteeing a larger profit than Alpha. This being the case, Alpha, in order to minimize this larger profit of Omega, must always choose the suburb. Of course, the game is not fair since it is favorable to Omega.

Write the matrix game that corresponds to each of the following two-person conflict situations.

1. Tami and Laura simultaneously each show one or two fingers. If they show the same number of fingers, Tami pays Laura one dime. If they show different numbers of fingers, Laura pays Tami one dime.
2. Tami and Laura simultaneously each show one or two fingers. If the total number of fingers shown is even, Tami pays Laura that number of dimes. If the total number of fingers shown is odd, Laura pays Tami that number of dimes.
3. Tami and Laura simultaneously and independently each write down one of the numbers 1, 4, or 7. If the sum of the numbers is even, Tami pays Laura that number of dimes. If the sum of the numbers is odd, Laura pays Tami that number of dimes.

11.2
Exercise

4. Determine which of the following two-person, zero-sum games are strictly determined. For those that are, find the value of the game. All entries are the winnings of Player I , who plays rows.

(a) $\begin{pmatrix} -1 & 2 \\ -3 & 6 \end{pmatrix}$

(f) $\begin{pmatrix} 4 & 0 \\ 0 & -1 \end{pmatrix}$

(b) $\begin{pmatrix} 4 & 2 \\ 3 & 1 \end{pmatrix}$

(g) $\begin{pmatrix} -6 & -1 \\ 0 & 0 \end{pmatrix}$

(c) $\begin{pmatrix} 2 & 0 & -1 \\ 3 & 6 & 0 \\ 1 & 3 & 7 \end{pmatrix}$

(h) $\begin{pmatrix} 2 & 3 & -2 \\ -2 & 0 & 4 \\ 0 & -3 & -2 \end{pmatrix}$

(d) $\begin{pmatrix} 1 & 0 & 3 \\ -1 & 2 & 1 \end{pmatrix}$

(i) $\begin{pmatrix} 1 & -3 & -2 \\ 2 & 5 & 4 \\ 2 & 3 & 2 \end{pmatrix}$

(e) $\begin{pmatrix} 6 & 4 & -2 & 0 \\ -1 & 7 & 5 & 2 \\ 1 & 0 & 4 & 4 \end{pmatrix}$

5. For what values of a is the matrix
$$\begin{pmatrix} a & 8 & 3 \\ 0 & a & -9 \\ -5 & 5 & a \end{pmatrix}$$
strictly determined.

6. Show that the matrix
$$\begin{pmatrix} a & a \\ b & c \end{pmatrix}$$
is strictly determined for any choice of a, b, or c.

*7. Find necessary and sufficient conditions for the matrix
$$\begin{pmatrix} a & 0 \\ 0 & b \end{pmatrix}$$
to be strictly determined.

11.3
MIXED STRATEGIES

11.3.1
Example

Consider a two-person zero-sum game given by the matrix

$$\begin{pmatrix} 6 & 0 \\ -2 & 3 \end{pmatrix}$$

in which the entries denote the winnings of Player I. Is this game strictly determined? If so, find its value.

Again, we find that the smallest entry in each row is

row one: 0; row two: −2

Now the entry 0 in row one is not the largest element in its column; similarly, the entry −2 in row two is not the largest element in its column. Thus, this game is not strictly determined.

At this stage, we would like to stress the point that a matrix game is not usually played just once. With this in mind, Player I might decide to always play row one since he may win $6 at best and win $0 at worst. Does this mean he should always employ this strategy? If he does, Player II would catch on and begin to choose column two since this strategy limits his losses to $0. However, after awhile Player I would probably start choosing row two to obtain a payoff of $3. Thus, in a nonstrictly determined game it would be advisable for the players to *mix* their strategies rather than to use the same one all the time. That is, a random selection is desirable. Indeed, to make certain that the other player does not discover the pattern of moves, it is best not to have any pattern at all. For instance Player I may elect to play row one 40 percent of the time (that is, with probability .4) while Player II elects to play column two 80 percent of the time (that is, with probability .8). This idea of mixing strategies is important and useful in game theory. Games in which each player's strategies are *mixed* are termed *mixed-strategy games.*

Suppose we know the probability for each player to choose a certain strategy. What meaning can be given to the term "payoff of a game" if mixed strategies are used? Since the payoff has been defined for a pair of pure strategies and in a mixed strategy situation we do not know which strategy is being used, it is not possible to define a payoff for a single game. However, in the long-run we do know how often each strategy is being used and we can use this information to compute the *expected payoff* of the game.

For Example 11.3.1, if Player I chooses row one 50 percent of the time and row two 50 percent of the time and if Player II chooses column one 30 percent of the time and column two 70 percent of the time, the expected payoff of the game can be computed. For example, the strategy of row one, column one is chosen $(.5)(.3) = .15$ of the time. This strategy has a payoff of $6 so that the expected payoff will be $(\$6)(.15) = \$.90$. Figure 11.1 summarizes the entire process.

Strategy	Payoff	Probability	Expected Payoff
row one — column one	6	.15	$.90
row two — column one	−2	.15	−0.30
row one — column two	0	.35	.00
row two — column two	3	.35	1.05
	Total	1.00	$1.65

Figure 11.1

Thus, the expected payoff E of this game when the given strategies are employed is $1.65, which makes the game favorable to Player I.

If we look very carefully at the above derivation, we get a clue as to how the expected payoff of a game that is not strictly determined should be defined.

Let us consider a game defined by the 2×2 matrix.

$$A = \begin{pmatrix} a_{11} & a_{12} \\ a_{21} & a_{22} \end{pmatrix}$$

Let the strategy for Player I who plays rows be denoted by the row vector $P = (p_1 \quad p_2)$ and the strategy for Player II who plays columns be denoted by the column vector $Q = \begin{pmatrix} q_1 \\ q_2 \end{pmatrix}$. Now the probability that Player I wins the amount a_{11} is $p_1 q_1$. Similarly the probabilities that he wins a_{12}, a_{21}, and a_{22} are $p_1 q_2$, $p_2 q_1$, and $p_2 q_2$ respectively. If we denote by $E(P,Q)$ the expectation of Player I, that is the expected value of the amount I wins when Player I uses strategy P and Player II uses strategy Q, then

$$E(P,Q) = p_1 q_1 a_{11} + p_1 q_2 a_{12} + p_2 q_1 a_{21} + p_2 q_2 a_{22}$$

Using matrix notation the above can be expressed as

$$E(P,Q) = PAQ$$

In general, if A is an $m \times n$ matrix game, we are led to the following definition.

11.3.1
Definition

The *expected payoff* E **of a two-person zero-sum game, defined by the matrix A in which the row vector P and column vector Q define the respective strategy probabilities of Player I and Player II is**

$$E = PAQ$$

If a matrix game $A = (a_{ij})$ of dimension $m \times n$ is strictly determined, then one of the entries is a saddle point. This saddle point can always be placed in the first row and first column by simply rearranging and renumbering the rows and columns of A. The value of the game is then a_{11} and P and Q are vectors of the form

$$P = (1 \quad 0 \quad 0 \quad 0 \quad 0 \quad \cdot \quad \cdot \quad \cdot \quad \cdot \quad 0)$$

and

$$Q = \begin{pmatrix} 1 \\ 0 \\ \cdot \\ \cdot \\ \cdot \\ \cdot \\ 0 \end{pmatrix}$$

where P is of dimension $1 \times m$ and Q is of dimension $n \times 1$.

11.3.2
Example

Find the expected payoff of the matrix game

$$\begin{pmatrix} 3 & -1 \\ -2 & 1 \\ 1 & 0 \end{pmatrix}$$

if Player I and Player II decide on the strategies

$$P = \begin{pmatrix} \frac{1}{3} & \frac{1}{3} & \frac{1}{3} \end{pmatrix}, \qquad Q = \begin{pmatrix} \frac{1}{3} \\ \frac{2}{3} \end{pmatrix}$$

The expected payoff E of this game is

$$E = P \cdot \begin{pmatrix} 3 & -1 \\ -2 & 1 \\ 1 & 0 \end{pmatrix} \cdot Q = \begin{pmatrix} \frac{1}{3} & \frac{1}{3} & \frac{1}{3} \end{pmatrix} \begin{pmatrix} 3 & -1 \\ -2 & 1 \\ 1 & 0 \end{pmatrix} \begin{pmatrix} \frac{1}{3} \\ \frac{2}{3} \end{pmatrix}$$

$$= \begin{pmatrix} \frac{2}{3} & 0 \end{pmatrix} \begin{pmatrix} \frac{1}{3} \\ \frac{2}{3} \end{pmatrix} = \frac{2}{9}$$

Thus, the game is biased in favor of Player I and has an expected payoff of 2/9.

Most games are not strictly determined. That is, most games do not give rise to best pure strategies for each player. Examples of not strictly determined games are matching pennies (see Example 11.2.1), bridge, poker, and so on. In Sections 11.4 and 11.5, we shall discuss techniques for finding optimal strategies for games that are not strictly determined.

1. For the game of Example 11.3.1, find the expected payoff E if Player I chooses row one 30 percent of the time and Player II chooses column one 40 percent of the time.
2. Find the expected payoff of the game

$$\begin{pmatrix} 4 & 0 \\ 2 & 3 \end{pmatrix}$$

for the strategies

(a) $P = \begin{pmatrix} \frac{1}{2} & \frac{1}{2} \end{pmatrix} \qquad Q = \begin{pmatrix} \frac{1}{2} \\ \frac{1}{2} \end{pmatrix}$

(b) $P = \begin{pmatrix} \frac{1}{2} & \frac{1}{2} \end{pmatrix} \qquad Q = \begin{pmatrix} \frac{3}{4} \\ \frac{1}{4} \end{pmatrix}$

(c) $P = \begin{pmatrix} \frac{1}{4} & \frac{3}{4} \end{pmatrix} \qquad Q = \begin{pmatrix} \frac{1}{2} \\ \frac{1}{2} \end{pmatrix}$

(d) $P = \begin{pmatrix} 0 & 1 \end{pmatrix} \qquad Q = \begin{pmatrix} 0 \\ 1 \end{pmatrix}$

11.3
Exercise

3. Find the expected payoff of each of the following games for the strategies given

(a) $\begin{pmatrix} 4 & 0 \\ -3 & 6 \end{pmatrix}$ $P = \begin{pmatrix} \frac{2}{3} & \frac{1}{3} \end{pmatrix}$ $Q = \begin{pmatrix} \frac{1}{3} \\ \frac{2}{3} \end{pmatrix}$

(b) $\begin{pmatrix} 1 & 0 & 0 \\ 0 & 1 & 0 \\ 0 & 0 & 1 \end{pmatrix}$ $P = \begin{pmatrix} \frac{1}{3} & \frac{1}{3} & \frac{1}{3} \end{pmatrix}$ $Q = \begin{pmatrix} \frac{1}{3} \\ \frac{1}{3} \\ \frac{1}{3} \end{pmatrix}$

(c) $\begin{pmatrix} 4 & -1 & 0 \\ 2 & 3 & 1 \end{pmatrix}$ $P = \begin{pmatrix} \frac{1}{3} & \frac{2}{3} \end{pmatrix}$ $Q = \begin{pmatrix} \frac{2}{3} \\ \frac{1}{6} \\ \frac{1}{6} \end{pmatrix}$

*4. Show that in a 2 × 2 game

$$\begin{pmatrix} a_{11} & a_{12} \\ a_{21} & a_{22} \end{pmatrix}$$

the only not strictly determined games are those for which either

(a) $a_{11} > a_{12}, a_{11} > a_{21}, a_{21} < a_{22}, a_{12} < a_{22}$

or

(b) $a_{11} < a_{12}, a_{11} < a_{21}, a_{11} > a_{22}, a_{12} > a_{22}$

and all others are strictly determined.

**11.4
DETERMINATION
OF OPTIMAL
STRATEGY IN
TWO-PERSON
ZERO-SUM GAMES
WITH 2 × 2
MATRICES**

We have already seen that the best strategy for two-person zero-sum games that are strictly determined is found in the row and column containing the saddle point. Suppose the game is not strictly determined so that the conditions given in Problem 4, Exercise 11.3 are satisfied.

In 1927, John von Neumann, along with E. Borel, initiated research in the theory of games and proved that even in non-strictly determined games there is a single course of action that represents the best strategy. In practice, this means that a player in a game, in order to avoid always using a single strategy, may instead choose it randomly according to a fixed probability. This has the effect of making it impossible for his opponent to know what the player will do since even he will not know until the final moment. That is, by selecting a strategy randomly according to the laws of probability, the actual strategy chosen at any one time cannot even be known to the one choosing it.

For example, in the Italian game of *morra*, each player shows one, two, or three fingers and simultaneously calls out his guess as to what the sum

351
DETERMINATION
OF OPTIMAL
STRATEGY IN
TWO-PERSON
ZERO-SUM GAMES
WITH 2 × 2
MATRICES

of his and his opponent's fingers is. It can be shown that if he guesses four fingers each time and varies his own moves so that every 12 times he shows one finger five times, two fingers four times, and three fingers three times, he will, at worst, break even (in the long run).

Consider now a two-person zero-sum game given by the 2 × 2 matrix

$$A = \begin{pmatrix} a_{11} & a_{12} \\ a_{21} & a_{22} \end{pmatrix}$$

in which Player I chooses row strategies and Player II chooses column strategies.

It can be shown that the optimal strategy for Player I is given by $P = (p_1 \quad p_2)$ where

$$p_1 = \frac{a_{22} - a_{21}}{a_{11} + a_{22} - a_{12} - a_{21}}, \qquad p_2 = \frac{a_{11} - a_{12}}{a_{11} + a_{22} - a_{12} - a_{21}} \qquad (11.4.1)$$

with $a_{11} + a_{22} - a_{12} - a_{21} \neq 0$. Notice that $p_1 + p_2 = 1$, as must be the case. Similarly, the optimal strategy for Player II is given by $Q = \begin{pmatrix} q_1 \\ q_2 \end{pmatrix}$ where

$$q_1 = \frac{a_{22} - a_{12}}{a_{11} + a_{22} - a_{12} - a_{21}}, \qquad q_2 = \frac{a_{11} - a_{21}}{a_{11} + a_{22} - a_{12} - a_{21}} \qquad (11.4.2)$$

with $a_{11} + a_{22} - a_{12} - a_{21} \neq 0$. Again, $q_1 + q_2 = 1$. The expected payoff E of the game corresponding to these optimal strategies is

$$E = PAQ = \frac{a_{11} \cdot a_{22} - a_{12} \cdot a_{21}}{a_{11} + a_{22} - a_{12} - a_{21}}$$

When optimal strategies are used, the expected payoff E of the game is called the *value* V of the game.

For the matrix of Example 11.2.1,

11.4.1
Example

$$\begin{pmatrix} -3 & 5 \\ 5 & -2 \end{pmatrix}$$

determine the optimal strategies and the value of the game.

Here, using the above formulas,

$$p_1 = \frac{-2 - 5}{-3 + (-2) - 5 - 5} = \frac{7}{15}, \qquad p_2 = \frac{-3 - 5}{-3 + (-2) - 5 - 5} = \frac{8}{15}$$

Thus, Player I's optimal strategy is to select row one with probability 7/15 and row two with probability 8/15. Also

$$q_1 = \frac{-2 - 5}{-3 + (-2) - 5 - 5} = \frac{7}{15}, \qquad q_2 = \frac{-3 - 5}{-3 + (-2) - 5 - 5} = \frac{8}{15}$$

Player II's optimal strategy is to select column one with probability 7/15 and column two with probability 8/15. The value V of the game is

$$V = \frac{(-3)(-2) - (5)(5)}{-15} = \frac{-19}{-15} = \frac{19}{15}$$

Thus, in the long run, the game is favorable to Player I.

11.4.2 Example Find optimal strategies and the value of the game given in Example 11.3.1. The matrix A is

$$A = \begin{pmatrix} 6 & 0 \\ -2 & 3 \end{pmatrix}$$

Player I's optimal strategy is

$$p_1 = \frac{3 - (-2)}{6 + 3 - (-2) - 0} = \frac{5}{11}, \qquad p_2 = \frac{6 - 0}{11} = \frac{6}{11}$$

Player II's optimal strategy is

$$q_1 = \frac{3 - 0}{11} = \frac{3}{11}, \qquad q_2 = \frac{6 - (-2)}{11} = \frac{8}{11}$$

The value V of the game is

$$V = \frac{(6)(3) - (-2)(0)}{11} = \frac{18}{11} = \$1.64$$

Thus, the game favors Player I whose optimal strategy is (5/11 6/11).

11.4.3 Example In a presidential campaign, there are two candidates, a democrat (D) and a republican (R) and two issues, domestic issues and foreign issues. The units assigned to each candidates strategy are given in Figure 11.2.

		Republican	
		Domestic	Foreign
Democrat	Domestic	4	−2
	Foreign	−1	3

Figure 11.2

We assume that positive entries indicate a strength for the democratic candidate, while negative entries indicate a weakness. We also assume that a strength of one candidate equals a weakness of the other so that the game is zero-sum. The question is what is the best strategy for each candidate? What is the value of the game?

Notice first that this game is not strictly determined. If D chooses to always play his strongest hand (foreign issues), then R will counter with

353
DETERMINATION
OF OPTIMAL
STRATEGY IN
TWO-PERSON
ZERO-SUM GAMES
WITH 2×2
MATRICES

domestic issues in which case D would also talk about domestic issues in which case, etc., etc. There is no *single* strategy either can use.

Using the formulas given previously, we compute that the optimal strategy for the democrat is

$$p_1 = \frac{3 - (-1)}{4 + 3 - (-1) - (-2)} = \frac{4}{10} = .4, \qquad p_2 = \frac{4 - (-2)}{10} = .6$$

The optimal strategy for the republican is

$$q_1 = \frac{3 - (-2)}{10} = .5, \qquad q_2 = \frac{4 - (-1)}{10} = .5$$

Thus the best strategy for the democrat is to spend 40 percent of his time on domestic issues and 60 percent on foreign issues, while the republican should divide his time evenly between the two issues.

The value of the game is

$$V = \frac{3 \cdot 4 - (-1)(-2)}{10} = \frac{10}{10} = 1.0$$

Thus, no matter what the republican does, the democrat gains at least 1.0 units by employing his best strategy.

In a naval battle, attacking bomber planes are trying to sink ships in a fleet protected by an aircraft carrier with fighter planes. The bombers can attack either "high" or "low," with a low attack giving more accurate results. Similarly, the aircraft carrier can send its fighters at high altitudes or low altitudes to search for the bombers. If the bombers avoid the fighters, credit the bombers with 8 points, and if the bombers and fighters meet, credit the bombers with -2 points. Also, credit the bombers with 3 additional points for flying low, (since this results in more accurate bombing). Find optimal strategies for the bombers and the fighters. What is the value of the game?

11.4.4 Example

First, we must set up the game matrix. Designate the bombers as playing rows and the fighters as playing columns. Also, each entry of the matrix will denote winnings of the bombers. Then the game matrix is

$$\begin{array}{cc} & \text{Fighters} \\ & \begin{array}{cc} \text{Low} & \text{High} \end{array} \\ \text{Bombers} \begin{array}{c} \text{Low} \\ \text{High} \end{array} & \begin{pmatrix} 1 & 11 \\ 8 & -2 \end{pmatrix} \end{array}$$

The reason for a 1 in row one, column one is that -2 points are credited for the planes meeting, but 3 additional points are credited to the bombers for a low flight.

Next, using the formulas (11.4.1) and (11.4.2), the optimal strategies for the bombers $(p_1 \quad p_2)$ and for the fighters $(q_1 \quad q_2)$ are

$$p_1 = \frac{-10}{-20} = \frac{1}{2}, \qquad p_2 = \frac{-10}{-20} = \frac{1}{2}$$

$$q_1 = \frac{-13}{-20} = \frac{13}{20}, \qquad q_2 = \frac{-7}{-20} = \frac{7}{20}$$

The value V of the game is

$$V = \frac{-2 - 88}{-20} = \frac{-90}{-20} = 4.5$$

Thus, the game is favorable to the bombers if both players employ their optimal strategies.

The bombers can decide whether to fly high or low by flipping a fair coin and flying high whenever heads appears. The fighters can decide whether to fly high or low by using an urn with 13 black balls and 7 white balls. Each day, a ball should be selected at random and then replaced. If the ball is black, they will go low; if it is white, they go high.

11.4.5
Example

Let us return to Example 11.1.2, in which Sherlock Holmes and Professor Moriarty are engaged in a battle of wits. Let us assume that Holmes plays rows and that all entries denote "winnings" for him. If Moriarty and Holmes meet, Holmes is killed. Thus we assign a payoff of -100 for this occurrence. If Holmes goes to Dover and Moriarty gets off at Canterbury, then Holmes has "won." However, since death is a much worse defeat than getting away is a victory, we assign a payoff of 50 for this case. The other possibility determines no clear advantage to either player so that we assign a payoff of 0 for this situation. The game matrix is

$$
\begin{array}{cc}
 & \text{Moriarty} \\
 & \begin{array}{cc} \text{Dover} & \text{Canterbury} \end{array} \\
\text{Holmes} \begin{array}{c} \text{Dover} \\ \text{Canterbury} \end{array} & \begin{pmatrix} -100 & 50 \\ 0 & -100 \end{pmatrix}
\end{array}
$$

Next, to see which person the game favors, we must determine the value of the game when each player uses his optimal strategy. The optimal strategy for Holmes is

$$p_1 = \frac{-100}{-250} = .4, \qquad p_2 = \frac{-150}{-250} = .6$$

The optimal strategy for Moriarty is

$$q_1 = \frac{-150}{-250} = .6, \qquad q_2 = \frac{-100}{-250} = .4$$

The value of the game is

$$V = \frac{(-100)(-100)}{-250} = -40$$

Thus, the game favors Professor Moriarty. Of course, these results are for repeated plays of the game. In reality, the game would only be played once. Also, even though our results indicate the game does not favor Holmes, in Arthur Conan Doyle's story, the hero Holmes successfully escaped to the Continent.

1. Find the optimal strategies for each player and find the value of the following 2×2 games.

(a) $\begin{pmatrix} 1 & 2 \\ 4 & 1 \end{pmatrix}$

(d) $\begin{pmatrix} 2 & 4 \\ 3 & -2 \end{pmatrix}$

(b) $\begin{pmatrix} -3 & 2 \\ 1 & 0 \end{pmatrix}$

(e) $\begin{pmatrix} 3 & -2 \\ -1 & 2 \end{pmatrix}$

(c) $\begin{pmatrix} 2 & -1 \\ -1 & 4 \end{pmatrix}$

(f) $\begin{pmatrix} 5 & 4 \\ -3 & 7 \end{pmatrix}$

2. In Example 11.4.3, suppose the candidates are assigned the following weights for each issue:

		Republican	
		Domestic	Foreign
Democrat	Domestic	4	−1
	Foreign	0	3

What is each candidates best strategy? What is the value of the game and whom does it favor?

3. For the situation described in Example 11.4.4, credit the bomber with 4 points for avoiding the fighters and with −6 points for meeting the fighters. Also, grant the bombers two additional points for flying low. What are the optimal strategies and the value of the game? Give instructions to the fighters and bombers as to how they decide whether to fly high or low.

4. A spy can leave an airport through two exits, one a relatively deserted exit and the other an exit heavily used by the public. His opponent, having been notified of the spy's presence in the airport, must guess which exit he will use. If the spy and opponent meet at the deserted exit, the spy will be killed; if the two meet at the heavily used exit, the spy will be arrested. Assign a payoff of 30 points to the spy if he avoids his opponent by using the deserted exit and of 10 points to the spy if he avoids his opponent by using the busy exit. Assign a payoff of −100 points to the spy if he is killed and −2 points if he is arrested. What are the optimal strategies and the value of the game?

5. In Example 11.4.5, what is the probability that Holmes loses?

*6. In a matrix game, $\begin{pmatrix} a_{11} & a_{12} \\ a_{21} & a_{22} \end{pmatrix}$, what can be said if $a_{11} + a_{22} - a_{12} - a_{21} = 0$?

11.5
DETERMINATION
OF OPTIMAL
STRATEGY IN
OTHER
TWO-PERSON
ZERO-SUM GAMES
USING GEOMETRIC
METHODS

Thus far we have only discussed how to find optimal strategies for two-person zero-sum games which can be represented by a 2 × 2 matrix. In the remainder of this section, we shall give techniques for finding optimal strategies when the matrix is not 2 × 2.

We begin with the following definition.

11.5.1
Definition

If a matrix A contains a row r^* whose entries are all less than or equal to the corresponding entries in some other row r, then row r is said to *dominate* **row r^* and r^* is said to be** *recessive.*

11.5.1
Example

In the matrix

$$A = \begin{pmatrix} -6 & -3 & 2 & 2 \\ -2 & 0 & 3 & 2 \\ 5 & -2 & 4 & 0 \end{pmatrix}$$

row one is dominated by row two since each entry in row one is less than or equal to its corresponding entry in row two; that is

$$-6 < -2, \qquad -3 < 0, \qquad 2 < 3, \qquad 2 = 2$$

If the matrix A of Example 11.5.1 were a game in which the entries represent winnings for Player I and if Player I chooses rows, it is clear that Player I would always choose row two over row one, since the values in row two always give greater benefit to him than those in row one. Thus, as far as the matrix representation of this game is concerned, we could represent it by the *reduced matrix*

$$\begin{pmatrix} -2 & 0 & 3 & 2 \\ 5 & -2 & 4 & 0 \end{pmatrix}$$

in which row one of matrix A is eliminated since it would never have been chosen.

11.5.2
Definition

If a matrix A contains a column c^* whose entries are all greater than or equal to the corresponding entries in some other column c, then column c is said to *dominate* **column c^* and c^* is said to be** *recessive.*

11.5.2
Example

In the matrix

$$A = \begin{pmatrix} -6 & 2 & 4 \\ 4 & 4 & 2 \\ 1 & 3 & -1 \end{pmatrix}$$

column one dominates column two since each entry in column two is greater than or equal to its corresponding entry in column one; that is

$$2 > -6, \qquad 4 = 4, \qquad 3 > 1$$

If the matrix A in Example 11.5.2 is a matrix game in which the entries denote winnings for Player I and if Player II chooses columns, it is clear

357
DETERMINATION
OF OPTIMAL
STRATEGY IN
OTHER TWO-PERSON
ZERO-SUM GAMES
USING GEOMETRIC
METHODS

that Player II would always prefer column one over column two since the smaller entries indicate lower losses to Player II. For this reason, column two can be eliminated from the matrix A and instead the reduced matrix

$$\begin{pmatrix} -6 & 4 \\ 4 & 2 \\ 1 & -1 \end{pmatrix}$$

will be used.

It is important to remember that when reducing a game matrix, *recessive rows* have entries *smaller* than those in another row and *recessive columns* have entries *larger* than those in another column.

By eliminating recessive rows and columns, find the reduced form of the matrix

**11.5.3
Example**

$$A = \begin{pmatrix} -6 & -4 & 2 \\ 2 & -1 & 2 \\ -3 & 4 & 4 \end{pmatrix}$$

First we look at the rows of the matrix A. Notice that each entry in row three is greater than or equal to each entry in row one. Thus, row one is recessive and can be eliminated. The new matrix is

$$\begin{pmatrix} 2 & -1 & 2 \\ -3 & 4 & 4 \end{pmatrix}$$

Neither row one nor row two in the new matrix is recessive so we consider the columns. Notice that the entries of column three are greater than or equal to the corresponding entries in either column one or column two. Thus, column three is recessive. The reduced matrix is

$$\begin{pmatrix} 2 & -1 \\ -3 & 4 \end{pmatrix}$$

The above example shows how a 3×3 matrix game can sometimes be reduced to a 2×2 matrix by eliminating recessive rows and recessive columns.

Find optimal strategies for each player and find the value of the two-person, zero-sum game

**11.5.4
Example**

$$\begin{pmatrix} -6 & -4 & 2 \\ 2 & -1 & 2 \\ -3 & 4 & 4 \end{pmatrix}$$

in which the entries denote the winnings of Player I whose chooses rows and in which each player has three possible strategies.

By eliminating recessive rows and columns, this matrix reduces to

$$\begin{pmatrix} 2 & -1 \\ -3 & 4 \end{pmatrix}$$

Using the formulas of Section 11.4, we find that the optimal strategy for Player I is

$$p_1 = \frac{7}{10}, \qquad p_2 = \frac{3}{10}$$

The optimal strategy for Player II is

$$q_1 = \frac{5}{10}, \qquad q_2 = \frac{5}{10}$$

The value of the game is

$$V = \frac{5}{10}$$

Thus the game given in Example 11.5.4 is favorable to Player I and his best strategy is to choose row two 70 percent of the time and row three 30 percent of the time (row one is recessive).

Suppose we now consider two-person zero-sum games whose matrix representations are $2 \times m$ or $m \times 2$ ($m > 2$) matrices that are not strictly determined and that contain no recessive rows or columns. For a $2 \times m$ matrix game, Player I has two strategies and Player II has m strategies; for an $m \times 2$ matrix game, Player I has m strategies and Player II has 2 strategies.

We begin with the following example to illustrate how to find optimal strategies.

11.5.5
Example
Find the optimal strategy for each player in the 2×3 game

$$\begin{pmatrix} 4 & -1 & 0 \\ -1 & 4 & 2 \end{pmatrix}$$

in which entries denote winnings for Player I. What is the value of this game?

In the above game, Player I has two strategies and Player II has three strategies. Suppose p is the probability that Player I plays row one. Then $1 - p$ is the probability that row two is played. Now let us compute the expected earnings of Player I in terms of p.

If Player II elects to play column one, then the expected earnings E_1 of Player I are equal to $4p - 1 \cdot (1 - p)$ or

$$\text{①} \, E_1 = 5p - 1$$

Similarly, if Player II selects column two and column three, the expected earnings for Player I are, respectively,

$$\text{②} \, E_1 = 4 - 5p, \qquad \text{③} \, E_1 = 2 - 2p$$

Next, we graph each of these three straight lines measuring E_1 along the y-axis and p along the x-axis and compare them. If Player II is restricted to these three strategies (the lines) then the worst that can happen to the row player is that his earnings are on the heavy line in Figure 11.3. Since the row player wishes to maximize his earnings he should choose p so that the corresponding earnings are at the highest point. Observing the graph,

359
DETERMINATION
OF OPTIMAL
STRATEGY IN
OTHER TWO-PERSON
ZERO-SUM GAMES
USING GEOMETRIC
METHODS

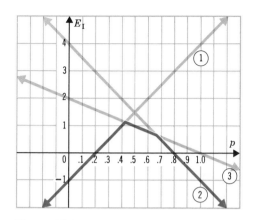

Figure 11.3

we see that the highest point occurs at the intersection of the lines

$$① E_1 = 5p - 1, \qquad ③ E_1 = 2 - 2p$$

Their intersection is the point

$$p = \frac{3}{7}, \qquad E_I = \frac{8}{7}$$

Thus, the optimal strategy for Player I is to choose row one 3/7 of the time and row two 4/7 of the time. The value of this game in this case is 8/7.

To find the optimal strategy for Player II, notice that Player I's optimal strategy comes from earnings calculated by using columns one and three of the matrix game. The matrix which results by eliminating column two from the matrix in Example 11.5.5 is

$$\begin{pmatrix} 4 & 0 \\ -1 & 2 \end{pmatrix}$$

The optimal strategy for Player II can now be found by the formula given in Section 11.4. It is

$$q_1 = \frac{2}{7}, \qquad q_2 = 0, \qquad q_3 = \frac{5}{7}$$

Thus, Player II's strategy is to play column one 2/7 of the time, column two 0 times (this is the column eliminated), and column three 5/7 of the time.

Find the optimal strategy for each player in the 5 × 2 matrix game

11.5.6
Example

$$\begin{pmatrix} -2 & 2 \\ -1 & 1 \\ 2 & 0 \\ 3 & -1 \\ 4 & -2 \end{pmatrix}$$

in which the entries denote winnings for Player I. What is the value of this game?

Here Player II has two strategies. Let q be the probability that he chooses column one so that $1 - q$ is the probability that column two is chosen. Player I's earnings E_I are then, respectively,

①$E_1 = -2q + 2(1 - q)$,   ②$E_1 = -q + (1 - q)$,   ③$E_1 = 2q$,
    ④$E_1 = 3q - (1 - q)$,   ⑤$E_1 = 4q - 2(1 - q)$

①$E_1 = -4q + 2$,   ②$E_1 = -2q + 1$,   ③$E_1 = 2q$,
    ④$E_1 = 4q - 1$,   ⑤$E_1 = 6q - 2$

Again we graph these five linear equalities. See Figure 11.4.

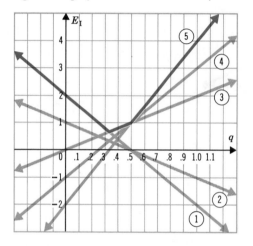

Figure 11.4

Now Player II wants the earnings of Player I to be as small as possible. This occurs at the intersection of ① and ③. This point is $q = 1/3$, $E_I = 2/3$. Thus, the optimal strategy for Player II is to choose column one 1/3 of the time and column two 2/3 of the time. The value of the game is 2/3 and it is favorable to Player I.

Now, to find Player I's optimal strategy, we notice that Player II's optimal strategy comes from lines ① and ③. If we eliminate rows two, four, five, and six from the matrix in Example 11.5.6, we obtain the matrix

$$\begin{pmatrix} -2 & 2 \\ 2 & 0 \end{pmatrix}$$

Applying the formula from Section 11.4, Player I's optimal strategy is

$$p_1 = \frac{-2}{-6} = \frac{1}{3}, \qquad p_3 = \frac{-4}{-6} = \frac{2}{3}$$

**11.5.7
Example
Cultural
Anthropology**   In 1960, Davenport[1] published an analysis of the behavior of Jamaican fishermen. Each fishing crew is confronted with a three-choice decision

[1]E. Davenport, "Jamaican Fishing: A Game Theory Analysis in Papers on Caribbean Anthropology," Yale University Publication in Anthropology Nos. 57–64, 1960.

361
DETERMINATION
OF OPTIMAL
STRATEGY IN
OTHER TWO-PERSON
ZERO-SUM GAMES
USING GEOMETRIC
METHODS

of fishing in the inside banks, the outside banks, or a combination of inside-outside banks. Fairly reliable estimates can be made of the quantity and quality of fish caught in these three areas under the two conditions that current is present or not present.

If we take the village as a whole as one player and the environment as another player we have the components for a two-person zero-sum game, in which the village has three strategies (inside, inside-outside, outside) and the environment has two strategies (current, no current). Davenport computed an estimate of income claimed by the fisherman using each of the alternations. This estimate is given in matrix form by

$$
\begin{array}{c}
 & \text{Environment} \\
 & \text{current} \quad \text{no current} \\
\text{Village} \begin{array}{l} \text{Inside} \\ \text{Inside-outside} \\ \text{Outside} \end{array}
\left(
\begin{array}{cc}
17.3 & 11.5 \\
5.2 & 17.0 \\
-4.4 & 20.6
\end{array}
\right)
\end{array}
$$

Here, the environment has two strategies; let q be the probability of current so that $1 - q$ is the probability of no current. If E_I represents the villagers' expected earnings, then

① $E_1 = 17.3q + 11.5(1 - q)$,　② $E_1 = 5.2q + 17(1 - q)$,
　　　　　　　　　　　　　　　　　　③ $E_1 = -4.4q + 20.6(1 - q)$

① $E_1 = 5.8q + 11.5$,　② $E_1 = -11.8q + 17$,　③ $E_1 = -25q + 20.6$

Figure 11.5 shows that the optimal strategy comes from the intersection of lines ① and ②.

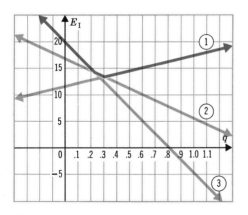

Figure 11.5

Computing this intersection we obtain

$$q = .31 \qquad 1 - q = .69$$

To obtain the optimal strategy of the village we must note that the optimal strategy of the environment comes from lines ① and ②. If we eliminate row three from the matrix in Example 11.5.7 we find

$$\begin{pmatrix} 17.3 & 11.5 \\ 5.2 & 17.0 \end{pmatrix}$$

Applying previous formulas, the villager's optimal strategy is

$$p_1 = \frac{17.0 - 5.2}{34.3 - 16.7} = \frac{11.8}{17.6} = .67 \qquad p_2 = \frac{5.8}{17.6} = .33$$

Figure 11.6 compares the observed frequency of strategy usage as compared with the optimal usuage as predicted by the game.

	Observed	Predicted
Outside	0	0
Inside	.69	.67
Inside-outside	.39	.33
Current	.25	.31
No current	.75	.69

Figure 11.6

11.5.8
Example
Simplified Investment
Problem

The following is an example from a paper by J. D. Williams.[2] An investor plans to invest $10,000 during a period of international uncertainty as to whether there will be peace, a continuation of the cold war, or an actual war. His investment can be made in government bonds, armament stocks, or industrial stocks. The game is a struggle between the investor and nature. The matrix below gives the rates of interest for each player's strategy.

$$\begin{array}{cc} & \begin{array}{ccc} \text{Hot war} & \text{Cold war} & \text{Peace} \end{array} \\ \begin{array}{c} \text{Government bonds} \\ \text{Investor} \quad \text{Armament stocks} \\ \text{Industrial stocks} \end{array} & \begin{pmatrix} 2 & 3 & 3.2 \\ 18 & 6 & -2 \\ 2 & 7 & 12 \end{pmatrix} \end{array}$$

Calculate the investor's optimal strategy.

First we look at the matrix to see if there is any row dominance or column dominance. Notice that row three dominates row one so that the reduced matrix for this game is

$$\begin{array}{cc} & \begin{array}{ccc} \text{Hot war} & \text{Cold war} & \text{Peace} \end{array} \\ \begin{array}{c} \text{Armament stock} \\ \text{Industrial stock} \end{array} & \begin{pmatrix} 18 & 6 & -2 \\ 2 & 7 & 12 \end{pmatrix} \end{array}$$

This is a 2×3 matrix that can be solved by the graphing method. The optimal strategy for the investor is

$$p_1 = 0, \qquad p_2 = \frac{5}{17}, \qquad p_3 = \frac{12}{17}$$

The value of the game is

$$V = 6.7$$

Thus the investor is assured of a return of at least 6.7 percent when he invests $5/17 = .29$ percent in armament stocks and $12/17 = .71$ percent in

J. D. William, *La Strategie dans les actions humaines*, Dunod, Paris, 1956.

363
DETERMINATION
OF OPTIMAL
STRATEGY IN
OTHER TWO-PERSON
ZERO-SUM GAMES
USING GEOMETRIC
METHODS

industrial stocks. In the event of a hot war the return is

$$18\left(\frac{5}{17}\right) + 2\left(\frac{12}{17}\right) = 6.7 \text{ percent}$$

In the event of a cold war the return is

$$6\left(\frac{5}{17}\right) + 7\left(\frac{12}{17}\right) = 6.7 \text{ percent}$$

In the event of peace the return is

$$(-2)\left(\frac{5}{17}\right) + 12\left(\frac{12}{17}\right) = 7.9 \text{ percent}$$

Return to Example 11.1.3 in which General White must decide how to best display his three regiments. We shall denote the three strategies available to General White as follows:

**11.5.9
Example
Military Game**

  3: All three regiments used together to attack one hill.
 2,1: Two regiments used together and one used by itself to attack two hills.
1,1,1: All three regiments used separately to attack three hills.

White's opponent has two strategies available, namely:

  2: The two regiments used together to defend one hill.
 1,1: The two regiments used separately to defend two of the hills.

Furthermore, White will play rows and the entries will denote White's expected winnings based on the rule that when White takes a hill, he earns one point, when a draw results, he earns zero points, and when he is defeated he loses one point. Also, for each division that is overpowered, one point is earned.

 Figure 11.7 shows the points won (or lost) by General White for all pos-

	200	020	002	110	101	011
300	3	0	0	1	1	−1
030	0	3	0	1	−1	1
003	0	0	3	−1	1	1
210	1	−1	1	2	2	0
201	1	1	−1	2	2	0
120	−1	1	1	2	0	2
021	1	1	−1	2	0	2
102	−1	1	1	0	2	2
012	1	−1	1	0	2	2
111	0	0	0	1	1	1

Figure 11.7

sible deployments of his regiments. Notice that the order of deployment is quite important.

For example, if White deploys his regiments as 3,0,0 and his opponent uses the deployment 2,0,0, then White captures hill I, winning one point, and overpowers two regiments, winning two points for a total score of three points. If White uses 0,2,1 and his opponent uses 0,1,1, then hill I is a standoff, White wins hill II and overpowers one regiment, and hill III is a draw. Here White has a total score of two points.

To determine the game matrix, we proceed as follows: If White uses a 3 deployment and his enemy uses a 2 deployment, then White expects to score 3 points 1/3 of the time and score 0 points 2/3 of the time. We assign an expected payoff to White of $3 \cdot 1/3 + 0 \cdot 2/3 = 1$ point in this case. If White uses a 2,1 deployment and his enemy used a 1,1 deployment, then White expects to gain 2 points 2/3 of the time and 0 points 1/3 of the time for an expected payoff of 4/3 points. The game matrix can be written as

$$
\begin{array}{cc}
 & \text{Enemy} \\
 & \begin{array}{cc} 2 & 1,1 \end{array} \\
\text{White} \quad \begin{array}{c} 3 \\ 2,1 \\ 1,1,1 \end{array} & \begin{pmatrix} 1 & \frac{1}{3} \\ \frac{1}{3} & \frac{4}{3} \\ 0 & 1 \end{pmatrix}
\end{array}
$$

Notice that the matrix above can be reduced since row 2 dominates row 3. The reduced matrix is

$$
\begin{array}{cc}
 & \text{Enemy} \\
 & \begin{array}{cc} 2 & 1,1 \end{array} \\
\text{White} \quad \begin{array}{c} 3 \\ 2,1 \end{array} & \begin{pmatrix} 1 & \frac{1}{3} \\ \frac{1}{3} & \frac{4}{3} \end{pmatrix}
\end{array}
$$

This matrix is not strictly determined. The optimal (mixed) strategy for General White is

$$
p_1 = \frac{1}{\frac{7}{3} - \frac{2}{3}} = .6 \qquad p_2 = \frac{\frac{2}{3}}{\frac{5}{3}} = .4 \qquad p_3 = 0
$$

The optimal strategy for the enemy is

$$
q_1 = \frac{1}{\frac{5}{3}} = .6 \qquad q_2 = \frac{\frac{2}{3}}{\frac{5}{3}} = .4
$$

The value of the game is

$$
V = \frac{\frac{4}{3} - \frac{1}{9}}{\frac{5}{3}} = \frac{\frac{11}{9}}{\frac{5}{3}} = \frac{11}{15}
$$

The game is favorable to General White who should deploy his troops in a 3 strategy 60 percent of the time and in a 2,1 strategy 40 percent of

365
DETERMINATION
OF OPTIMAL
STRATEGY IN
OTHER TWO-PERSON
ZERO-SUM GAMES
USING GEOMETRIC
METHODS

the time. Since no one hill is more likely to be chosen for attack than any other, it follows that each hill should be attacked by all three regiments 20 percent of the time. Furthermore, for the 2,1 deployment, each possible selection of the hills to receive 0,1, or 2 regiments (6 in all) will be used $40/6 = 6.67$ percent of the time.

1. Find the optimal strategies for each player in the following games in which Player I plays rows and entries denote winnings of Player I. What is the value of each game?

(a) $\begin{pmatrix} 8 & 3 & 8 \\ 6 & 5 & 4 \\ -2 & 4 & 1 \end{pmatrix}$

(d) $\begin{pmatrix} 4 & -5 & 5 \\ -6 & 3 & 3 \\ 2 & -6 & 3 \end{pmatrix}$

(b) $\begin{pmatrix} 2 & 1 & 0 & 6 \\ 3 & -2 & 1 & 2 \end{pmatrix}$

(e) $\begin{pmatrix} 1 & 3 & 0 \\ 0 & -3 & 1 \\ 0 & 4 & 1 \\ -2 & 1 & 1 \end{pmatrix}$

(c) $\begin{pmatrix} 6 & -4 & 2 & -3 \\ -4 & 6 & -5 & 7 \end{pmatrix}$

(f) $\begin{pmatrix} 4 & 3 & -1 \\ 1 & 1 & 4 \\ 1 & 0 & 2 \end{pmatrix}$

2. Find optimal strategies for both players in each of the following games. What is the value of each game? Player I plays rows and the entries denote his winnings.

(a) $\begin{pmatrix} 3 & -1 & 0 \\ -2 & 1 & -1 \end{pmatrix}$

(d) $\begin{pmatrix} -5 & -4 & -3 & 2 & 3 \\ 3 & 2 & 1 & -2 & -4 \end{pmatrix}$

(b) $\begin{pmatrix} -1 & 1 \\ 5 & -3 \\ 1 & -2 \\ -2 & 5 \end{pmatrix}$

(e) $\begin{pmatrix} 6 & -4 \\ 4 & -3 \\ 1 & 0 \\ -3 & 2 \\ -5 & 4 \end{pmatrix}$

(c) $\begin{pmatrix} 3 & -2 & 2 \\ -1 & 1 & 0 \end{pmatrix}$

3. In a department store one area (A) is usually very crowded and the other area (B) is usually relatively empty. The store employs two detectives and has closed-circuit television (T) to control pilferage. The television covers A and B and the detectives can be in either area (A) or (B) or watching the television (T). The matrix below gives an estimate of the probability for the detectives to find and arrest a thief.

		Thief	
		A	B
Detectives	TT	.51	.75
	AA	.64	.36
	BB	.19	.91
	TA	.58	.60
	TB	.37	.85
	AB	.46	.76

Here TT means both detectives are at the television, TA means the first detective is at the television and the second is in area A, and so on. Find the optimal strategy for the thief and the detectives. What is the value of the game?

4. This problem is from J. D. Williams.[3] Three antibiotics A_1, A_2, and A_3, and five types of bacilli M_1, M_2, M_3, M_4, and M_5 are involved in a study of the effectiveness of antibiotics on bacilli, with A_1 having a probability .3 of destroying M_2, and so on as given below. Without knowing the proportion in which these germs are distributed during an epidemic, in what ratio should the antibiotics be mixed to have the greatest probability of being effective?

Bacilli

		M_1	M_2	M_3	M_4	M_5
	A_1	.3	.4	.5	1	0
Antibiotics	A_2	.2	.3	.6	0	1
	A_3	.1	.5	.3	.1	0

11.6
TWO-PERSON
NONZERO-SUM
GAMES

Thus far we have only been concerned with two-person games in which the winnings of Player I are equal to the losses of Player II, and vice versa; that is, we have considered only zero-sum games. In this section we shall discuss the situation in which the play can result in a gain for both players, or a loss for both players, or a gain for one not equal to the loss of the other. Such games between two players are called *two-person nonzero-sum games*.

We divide the class of two-person nonzero-sum games into two categories: (1) *cooperative games* in which preplay communication between the players can occur or preplay binding contracts are used, and (2) *noncooperative games* in which no sharing of information and no communication between the players takes place.

For two-person nonzero-sum games, we use two matrices A and B to describe the payoff for a given strategy. Here the matrix A represents the gains of Player I and B represents the gains of Player II. If Player I chooses to play row i and Player II plays column j, then the element a_{ij} in the matrix A gives the payoff to Player I and the entry b_{ij} in the matrix B gives the payoff to Player II.

11.6.1
Example

In a two-person nonzero-sum game, the matrices A and B give the payoffs of Player I and Player II, respectively,

$$\text{Player I} \qquad\qquad \text{Player II}$$

$$A = \begin{pmatrix} 2 & -1 & 3 \\ 1 & 4 & -3 \end{pmatrix} \qquad B = \begin{pmatrix} 1 & 0 & 5 \\ -2 & 6 & -3 \end{pmatrix}$$

[3] J. D. William, *La Strategie dans les actions humaines*, Dunod, Paris, 1956.

Here Player I has two strategies and Player II has three strategies. If Player I plays row one and Player II plays column three, then Player I wins 3 and Player II wins 5.

For the data given in Example 11.1.4, describe the payoff matrices A and B for each prisoner.

Before writing the matrices, let us assign values or utilities to each decision. If one confesses, although the other does not, then the one who confessed has done quite well for himself while the one who did not confess has done very poorly. Let us assign a high utility of 10 for confessing and a low utility of 0 for not confessing. If both confess, the jail terms are not as severe as when one confesses and the other does not. We assign a utility of 3 to this situation. Finally, if neither confesses, the jail terms are quite lenient for each so we assign a utility of 7 for this occurrence.

Based on this assignment of utilities for the possible situations, the payoff matrices A and B are

$$A = \begin{array}{c} \\ \text{Confess} \\ \text{Not confess} \end{array} \begin{array}{c} \text{Confess} \quad \text{Not confess} \\ \left(\begin{array}{cc} 3 & 10 \\ 0 & 7 \end{array} \right) \end{array}$$

$$B = \begin{array}{c} \\ \text{Confess} \\ \text{Not confess} \end{array} \begin{array}{c} \text{Confess} \quad \text{Not confess} \\ \left(\begin{array}{cc} 3 & 0 \\ 10 & 7 \end{array} \right) \end{array}$$

in which the entries of A are those of Prisoner I who plays rows and the entries of B are those of Prisoner II who plays columns.

At this point, we shall confine our discussion to noncooperative games. In a manner quite similar to that of Section 11.2, we can define a *saddle point* for nonzero-sum games.

In a nonzero-sum game, let A and B denote payoff matrices in which A is the payoff matrix for Player I who plays rows and B is the payoff matrix for Player II who plays columns. If each entry in the ith row of matrix A is greater than or equal to either corresponding entries in the other rows of A and if each entry in the jth column of matrix B is greater than or equal to the corresponding entries in the other columns of B, then the *saddle pair* for this game is a_{ij} and b_{ij}.

For example, in the prisoner's dilemma of Example 11.6.2, each entry in row one of matrix A exceeds the corresponding entries of row two. Thus, Player I would always choose to play row one. Also, each entry in column one of matrix B exceeds the corresponding entries in column two, so that Player II would always choose column one. (Remember that the entries in matrix B denote payoffs for Player II so that he wishes to maximize these values if he can.) Thus, row one and column one give a saddle pair for this game.

It is interesting to notice that this saddle pair (both confess) is not the *best* choice each prisoner could have made. Clearly, if neither one confesses, they (as a team) do much better. However, without cooperation and communication, the choice of confessing is *to their knowledge* the best strategy.

Just as in two-person zero-sum games, it turns out that two-person non-zero-sum games do not always possess a saddle pair. When a saddle pair exists, then a pure strategy also exists. When we try to determine an optimal strategy for two-person, nonzero-sum games, we encounter one of the more important complications of such games. For zero-sum games, we considered the notion of an expected payoff and then, in some sense, each player is found to have an optimal strategy which maximizes his expected payoff. However, this approach will not hold, in general, for nonzero-sum games. In fact, it is difficult to establish that any kind of "optimal strategy" is really optimal in a mathematical sense.

Let us now turn our attention to two-person, nonzero-sum games in which cooperation takes place.

In the prisoner's dilemma example we saw that without cooperation each prisoner finds it to his advantage to confess. In doing so each prisoner maximizes his own position while at the same time minimizing the other prisoner's position. The dilemma occurs since each prisoner thinks it to his personal disadvantage to choose the strategy that is most advantageous from a cooperative point of view. The only way for the prisoners to reach the attractive strategy of both not confessing, which is not maximal individual strategy, is through cooperation in the form of prior communication and agreement, which can somehow be enforced through means not described in the game matrix.

As a final note, the reader should not be left with the impression that the discussion here of nonzero-sum games is complete. As a matter of fact, nonzero-sum games are much too complicated to be discussed in any detail here. There are many unsolved problems in this area involving both the nature of play and possible application. The interested reader will find many game theoretical analyses of bargaining, arbitration, and fair divisions of property as well as applications to the fields of antitrust law, international law, and international relations in articles found under Additional Reading (see Kaplan, Luce, *Mathematics in the Modern World,* and Shiebik).

CHAPTER
REVIEW

Important
Terms

two-person game	mixed strategy
zero-sum game	expected payoff
matrix game	optimal strategy
payoff	dominant row
strategy	recessive column
best strategy	reduced matrix
value	two-person nonzero-sum games
fair game	cooperative games
strictly determined	noncooperative games
saddle point	saddle pair
pure strategy	

Exercises

1. Determine which of the following two-person zero-sum games are strictly determined. For those that are, find the value of the game.

a. $\begin{pmatrix} 5 & 3 \\ 2 & 2 \end{pmatrix}$

b. $\begin{pmatrix} 29 & 15 \\ 79 & 3 \end{pmatrix}$

c. $\begin{pmatrix} 50 & 75 \\ 30 & 15 \end{pmatrix}$

d. $\begin{pmatrix} 7 & 14 \\ 9 & 13 \end{pmatrix}$

e. $\begin{pmatrix} 0 & 2 & 4 \\ 4 & 6 & 10 \\ 16 & 14 & 12 \end{pmatrix}$

2. Find the value of the game

$$\begin{pmatrix} -1 & 1 \\ 1 & -1 \end{pmatrix}$$

for the strategies:

a. $P = \begin{pmatrix} \frac{1}{3} & \frac{2}{3} \end{pmatrix}$ $\quad Q = \begin{pmatrix} 1 \\ 0 \end{pmatrix}$

b. $P = (0 \quad 1)$ $\quad Q = \begin{pmatrix} \frac{1}{2} \\ \frac{1}{2} \end{pmatrix}$

c. $P = \begin{pmatrix} \frac{1}{2} & \frac{1}{2} \end{pmatrix}$ $\quad Q = \begin{pmatrix} \frac{1}{2} \\ \frac{1}{2} \end{pmatrix}$

3. Show that if a 2×2 or 2×3 matrix game has a saddle point, then either one row dominates the other or one column dominates another column.

4. Give an example to show that the result of Problem 3 is not true for 3×3 matrix games.

5. Find optimal strategies for each player in the following games. Assume Player I plays rows and entries denote winnings of Player I. What is the value of each game?

a. $\begin{pmatrix} 4 & 6 & 3 \\ 1 & 2 & 5 \end{pmatrix}$

b. $\begin{pmatrix} 1 & 6 \\ 5 & 2 \\ 7 & 4 \end{pmatrix}$

c. $\begin{pmatrix} 2 & 1 \\ 4 & 0 \\ 3 & 4 \end{pmatrix}$

d. $\begin{pmatrix} 0 & 3 & 2 \\ 4 & 2 & 3 \end{pmatrix}$

6. Consider a neighborhood in which there are only two competitive stores handling two different, but similar brands of spark plugs. In ordinary circumstances each retailer pays $0.60 for each plug and sells it for $1.00. However, the manufacturers from time to time have incentive plans in which they sell the plugs to the retailers for $0.40, provided the retailer will sell it for $0.70. Each month the retailers must decide independent of one another what the selling price for the spark plugs should be. From previous sales patterns, each retailer observes the following pattern: At the usual price, each sells 1000 plugs per month; if one retailer discounts the price and the other does not, the discount store will sell 2000 plugs each month and the other will sell only 300 plugs; if both stores discount the price, they will each sell 1300 plugs per month. Set up the game matrices for this problem. In your opinion, how should each store manager proceed?

Additional Reading

Alker, Hayward R., Jr., *Mathematics and Politics*, New York, The Macmillan Company, 1965.

Buchler, Ira, and Nutini, Hugo, *Game Theory in the Behavioral Sciences*, University of Pittsburgh Press, 1969.

Kaplan, Martin, and Katzenbach, Nicholas, *The Political Foundations of International Law*, New York, John Wiley, 1961.

Luce, R. Duncan, and Raiffa, Howard, *Games and Decisions*, New York, John Wiley, 1957.

Maki, Daniel P. and Thompson, Maynard, *Mathematical Models and Applications*, Indiana University, 1970.

Mathematics in the Modern World, readings from *Scientific American*, San Francisco, W. H. Freeman and Company, 1968, pp. 300–312.

Rapoport, A., *Strategy and Conscience*, New York, Harper and Row, 1964.

Shiebik, Martin (Ed.) *Game Theory and Related Approaches to Social Behavior*, New York, Wiley, 1964.

Shiebik, Martin, *Strategy and Market Structure*, New York, John Wiley, 1959.

Statistics Chapter 12

Statistics is the science of collecting, organizing, analyzing, and interpreting numerical facts. By making observations, statisticians obtain *data* in the form of measurements or counts. By *organization of data* we mean the presentation of collected measurements or counts in a form suitable to determine logical conclusions. Usually tables or graphs are used to represent collected data. *Analysis of data* is the process of extracting, from given measurements or counts, related and relevant information from which a summarized and comprehensible numerical description can be formulated. To obtain this we shall use concepts known as the *mean, median, range, variance,* and *standard deviation*. By *interpretation of data* we mean the art of drawing conclusions from the analysis of the data. This involves the formulation of predictions concerning a large collection of objects based on the information available from a small collection of similar objects.

In collecting data concerning varied characteristics it is often impossible or impractical to observe an entire group. Instead of examining an entire group called the *population,* a small segment is chosen, called the *sample.* It would be difficult for example, to question all cigarette smokers in order to study the effects of smoking. Therefore, appropriate samples of smokers are usually selected for questioning.

The method of selecting the sample is extremely important if we wish the results to be reliable. All members of the population under investigation should have an equal probability of being selected; otherwise a biased sample could result. For example, if it is desired to study the relationship between smoking cigarettes and lung cancer, it will not do to choose a sample of smokers who all live in the same location. The individuals chosen might have dozens of characteristics peculiar to their area, which in turn would give a false impression with regard to all smokers.

For example, suppose it is desired to study the effects of drugs on youths. If we decide to choose a sample from a group of students at a specific university or from a group of youths in a ghetto we will get a *biased sample,* since university students and ghetto youth may be heavy users of drugs. It would be more appropriate for the person conducting the study to arrange the sample so that all members of the population under investigation have an equal probability of being selected.

Samples collected in such a way that each selection is equally likely to be chosen are called *random samples.* Of course, there are many random samples that can be chosen from a population. By combining the results of more than one random sample of a population, it is possible to obtain a more accurate representation of the population.

If a sample is representative of a population, important conclusions about the population can often be inferred from analysis of the sample. The phase of statistics dealing with conditions under which such inference is valid is called *inductive statistics* or *statistical inference.* Since such inference cannot be absolutely certain, the language of probability is often used in stating conclusions. Thus, when a weatherman makes his forecast, he has studied weather data collected over a large region — and based on this study he makes his weather forecast in terms of chances. A typical forecast is "There is a 20 percent possibility for rain tomorrow."

To summarize, in statistics we are interested in four principles: gathering data or information, organizing it, analyzing it, and interpreting it.

In gathering data or in choosing a random sample it is important to
(a) describe the method for choosing the sample clearly and carefully
(b) choose the sample so that it is random, that is, so that it is dependable and not subject to personal choice or bias.

**12.1.1
Example**

Suppose television tubes on an assembly line pass an inspection and suppose it is desired to test on the average one out of four tubes. If the test is to be performed in a random fashion, how should the inspection proceed?

To remove any personal choice on the part of the inspector, he can flip two fair coins. Then whenever two tails appear (probability 1/4), the inspector can select a tube for testing.

**12.1
Exercise**

1. List some possible ways to choose random samples for the following:
   (a) A study of the spreading of a disease by rats in a certain town.
   (b) A study to determine opinion about a certain television program.
   (c) A study to detect defective radio resistors.
   (d) A study of the opinions of people toward medicare.
   (e) A study to determine opinions about an election of a United States president.

   (f) A study of the number of savings accounts per family in the United States.

   (g) A national study of the monthly budget for a family of four.

2. The following is an example of a biased sample. In the study of political party preferences, poorly dressed interviewers obtained a significantly greater proportion of answers favoring democratic party candidates in their samples than did their well dressed and wealthier looking counterparts. Give two more examples of biased samples.

3. In a study of the number of savings accounts per family, a sample of accounts totaling less than $10,000 was taken, and from the owners of these accounts the information about the total number of accounts, owned by all family members, was obtained. Criticize this sample.

4. It is customary for newsmen to sample the opinions of a few people to find out how the population at large feels about the events of the day. If a newsman questions people on a downtown street corner, is there anything wrong with such an approach?

5. In 1936 the Literary Digest conducted a poll to predict the presidential election. Based on their poll they predicted the election of Landon against Roosevelt. In the actual election Roosevelt won. The sample was taken by drawing the mailing list from the telephone directories and lists of car owners. What was wrong with the sample?

Quite often a study will result in a collection of large masses of data. If such data is to be understood and at the same time be effective it must be summarized in some manner. Two methods of presenting data are in common use. One method involves a summarized presentation of the numbers themselves according to order in a tabular form; the other involves presenting the quantitative data in pictorial form, such as by using graphs or diagrams.

**12.2
ORGANIZATION
OF DATA**

Suppose a random sample of 71 children from a group of 10,000 indicates weight measurements as shown in Figure 12.1.

**12.2.1
Example**

Weight measurements in pounds of 71 students.

69	71	71	55	52	55	58	58	58	62	67	94
82	94	95	89	89	104	93	93	58	62	67	62
94	85	92	75	75	79	75	82	94	105	115	104
105	109	94	92	89	85	85	89	95	92	105	71
72	72	79	79	85	72	79	119	89	72	72	69
79	79	69	93	85	93	79	85	85	69	79	

Figure 12.1

Certain information available from the sample becomes more evident once the data is ordered according to some scheme. If the 71 measurements are written in order of magnitude, we obtain Figure 12.2.

52	55	55	58	58	58	58	62	62	62	67	67
69	69	69	69	71	71	71	72	72	72	72	72
75	75	75	79	79	79	79	79	79	79	79	82
82	85	85	85	85	85	85	85	89	89	89	89
89	92	92	92	93	93	93	93	94	94	94	94
94	95	95	104	104	105	105	105	109	115	119	

Figure 12.2

The data in Figure 12.2 can be presented in the so called *frequency table*. This is done as follows. Tally marks are used to record the occurrence of the respective scores, then the *frequency f* with which each score occurred can be determined. In doing so, further information may become evident. See Figure 12.3.

Score	Tally	Frequency f	Score	Tally	Frequency f
119	/	1	82	//	2
115	/	1	79	〼 ///	8
109	/	1	75	///	3
105	///	3	72	〼	5
104	//	2	71	///	3
95	//	2	69	////	4
94	〼	5	67	//	2
93	////	4	62	///	3
92	///	3	58	////	4
89	〼	5	55	//	2
85	〼 //	7	52	/	1

Figure 12.3

A graph representation of the data in Figure 12.2 is called a *line chart* and is obtained in the following way. If we let the y-axis denote the frequency f and the x-axis denote the score data, we obtain the graph in Figure 12.4.

In studying data a distinction should be made as to whether the data is *discrete* or *continuous*.

12.2.1
Definition
A measurable characteristic is called a *variable.*

12.2.2
Definition
If a variable can assume any real value between certain limits, it is called a *continuous variable.* **It is called a** *discrete variable* **if it can assume only integral values.**

Examples of continuous variables are weight, height, length, time, etc. Examples of discrete variables are the number of votes a candidate gets, number of cars sold, etc.

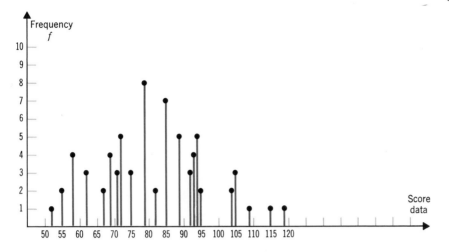

Figure 12.4

A random sample of 71 children from a group of 10,000 indicates weight measurement as shown in Figure 12.5 (this is the data of Figure 12.2, but measured more accurately).

52.30	55.61	55.71	58.01	58.41	58.51	58.91	62.33	62.50	62.71
67.13	67.23	69.51	69.67	69.80	69.82	71.34	71.65	71.83	72.15
72.22	72.41	72.59	72.67	75.11	75.71	75.82	79.03	79.06	79.09
79.15	79.28	79.32	79.51	79.62	82.32	82.61	85.09	85.13	85.25
85.31	85.41	85.51	85.58	89.21	89.32	89.49	89.61	89.78	92.41
92.63	92.89	93.05	93.19	93.28	93.91	94.17	94.28	94.31	94.52
94.71	95.32	95.51	104.31	104.71	105.21	105.37	105.71	109.34	115.71
119.38									

Figure 12.5

The data in Figure 12.5 is an example of a continuous variable, whereas the data given in Figure 12.1 is discrete. The difference lies with the accuracy of the measuring device – in this case a scale.

The data in Figure 12.5 is ordered, but it is still considered to be *raw data* in the sense that it has not yet been subjected to any kind of statistical treatment. To begin to classify our raw data two decisions have to be made:

(a) we have to decide on the *number of classes* into which the data is to be grouped.

(b) we must decide on the *range of values* each class is to cover.

In grouping any data, experience indicates that we should seldom use fewer than six classes or more than twenty. This is of course not a firm rule and there are exceptions to it.

The size of each class depends to a large extent on the nature of the data, and above all, on the actual number of items within each class. For the data in Figure 12.5, the smallest value is 52.30 and the largest value is 119.38. In order to use all of our data we shall have to cover the interval from 52.30 to 119.38.

12.2.3 **The** *range* **of a set of numbers is the difference between the largest and the smallest value in the data under consideration.**

For the weight and measurements of Example 12.2.2, the range is

$$119.38 - 52.30 = 67.08 \qquad (12.2.1)$$

We would like to present the data in Figure 12.5 in the form of a *histogram*. To do this we shall have to determine the *class intervals* and the *class limits*. The class intervals for our data will be obtained by dividing the range into intervals.

Figures 12.6 and 12.7 show the use of two different class intervals — one of size 5 and the other of size 10.

Class	Class Interval	Tally	Frequency
14	115–119.99	//	2
13	110–114.99		0
12	105–109.99	////	4
11	100–104.99	//	2
10	95– 99.99	//	2
9	90– 94.99	⅋⅋ ⅋⅋ //	12
8	85– 89.99	⅋⅋ ⅋⅋ //	12
7	80– 84.99	//	2
6	75– 79.99	⅋⅋ ⅋⅋ /	11
5	70– 74.99	⅋⅋ ///	8
4	65– 69.99	⅋⅋ /	6
3	60– 64.99	///	3
2	55– 59.99	⅋⅋ /	6
1	50– 54.99	/	1

Figure 12.6 *Class size 5.*

Class	Class Interval	Tally	Frequency
7	110–119.99	//	2
6	100–109.99	⅋⅋ /	6
5	90– 99.99	⅋⅋ ⅋⅋ ////	14
4	80– 89.99	⅋⅋ ⅋⅋ ////	14
3	70– 79.99	⅋⅋ ⅋⅋ ⅋⅋ ////	19
2	60– 69.99	⅋⅋ ////	9
1	50– 59.99	⅋⅋ //	7

Figure 12.7 *Class size 10.*

The interval given in column 2 of Figure 12.7 is called a *class interval*. Numbers such as 50–59.99 are called *class limits:* 50 is the *lower class limit* and 59.99 is the *upper class limit* for the class interval 50–59.99.

To build a histogram for the data in Figure 12.7, construct a set of rectangles having as a base the size of the class interval and as height the

frequency of occurrence of data in that particular interval. The center of the
base is the midpoint of each class interval.

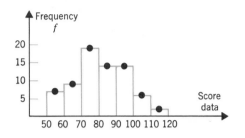

Figure 12.8

If we connect all the midpoints of the tops of the rectangles in Figure 12.8
we will obtain a line graph called a *frequency polygon* (In order not to leave
the graph hanging, we always connect it to the x-axis on both sides). See Figure 12.9.

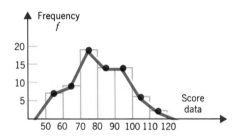

Figure 12.9

Sometimes it is more useful to learn how many cases fall below (or above)
a certain value. For the data of Figure 12.7, we may want to know how many
students had weights less than 99.99 or less than 69.99. (or how many had
weights more than 60 or more than 100). If this is the case, we can easily
convert the data in Figure 12.7 as follows:

Start at the lowest class interval (50–59.99) and note how many scores are
below the upper limit of this interval. The number is 7. So 7 appears in the
row 50–59.99 and in column 3 of Figure 12.10. Next we ask how many
scores fall below the upper limit of the next class interval (60–69.99), that is,

	Tally	f	cf
110–119.99	//	2	71
100–109.99	ℳℒ /	6	69
90– 99.99	ℳℒ ℳℒ ////	14	63
80– 89.99	ℳℒ ℳℒ ////	14	49
70– 79.99	ℳℒ ℳℒ ℳℒ ////	19	35
60– 69.99	ℳℒ ////	9	16
50– 59.99	ℳℒ //	7	7

Figure 12.10

how many scores are below 69.99? The answer is $16 = 7 + 9$. The process is continued. The last entry of the third column should agree with the total number of scores in the sample. The data in column 3 is called the *cumulative (less than) frequency* and is denoted by *cf*. See Figure 12.10.

The graph in which the *x*-axis represents class intervals and the *y*-axis cumulative frequencies is called the *cumulative* (less than) *frequency* distribution for the data in Figure 12.10. See Figure 12.11. Notice that the

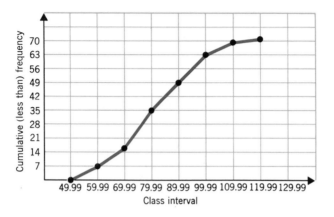

Figure 12.11

points obtained are connected by lines in order to aid interpretation of the graph.

In a similar manner, the *cumulative* (more than) *frequency* distribution can be obtained.

12.2
Exercise

1. Consider the following data.

Votes Cast	Number of Precincts
600–649	1
550–599	9
500–549	26
450–499	48
400–449	67
350–399	104
300–349	150
250–299	190
200–249	120
150–199	33
100–149	4
50–99	1
Total	750

Distribution of Cleveland Voting Precincts according to total vote cast for governor.
Source: *Ohio Election Statistics,* 1932, pp. 218–242.

With reference to this table determine the following.
(a) The lower limit of the fifth class.
(b) The upper limit of the fourth class.
(c) The class midpoint of the fifth class.
(d) The size of the fifth interval.
(e) The frequency in the third class.
(f) The class interval having the largest frequency.
(g) The number of precincts with less than 600 votes.
(h) Construct the histogram.
(i) Construct the frequency polygon.

2. The following scores were made on a 60-item test.

25	31	36	41	43	48	53
26	32	37	41	44	48	53
28	33	37	41	44	49	54
29	33	37	41	45	50	54
30	34	37	41	46	51	55
30	34	38	42	46	52	
30	35	39	42	47	52	
31	36	40	42	48	52	

(a) For the above data set up a frequency table. What is the range?
(b) Draw a line chart for this data.
(c) Draw a histogram for the data using a class interval of size 2.
(d) Draw the frequency polygon for this histogram.
(e) Find the cumulative (less than) frequency.
(f) Draw the cumulative (less than) frequency distribution.
(g) Find the cumulative (more than) frequency.
(h) Draw the cumulative (more than) frequency distribution.

3. For the frequency table in Figure 12.6,
(a) Draw a line chart.
(b) Draw a histogram.
(c) Draw the frequency polygon.
(d) Find the cumulative (less than) frequency.
(e) Draw the cumulative (less than) frequency distribution.

4. According to the *Fortune Directory,* June 15, 1967, the following are the earnings of the 50 largest commercial banks in the United States as percentage of capital funds for the year 1966.

12.2	9.9	11.2	12.5	9.8
11.5	11.8	11.1	12.3	10.1
11.4	9.2	12.8	9.8	12.6
9.9	10.2	12.6	14.4	10.9
10.2	10.3	11.6	10.2	13.1
10.4	10.9	8.4	14.6	13.4
12.3	11.4	9.2	12.8	11.0
11.2	10.9	10.1	10.9	12.9
11.2	13.2	10.2	16.0	13.6
10.9	11.4	11.6	11.7	13.0

Answer the same questions as in Problem 2, using a class interval of 0.5.

5. The following are the number of physicians per 100,000 population in 110 selected large American cities in 1962: (Source: *Statistical Abstract of the United States 1967*.)

```
131 131 113 137 127 153 123 202 131 198 218 222 112
185 134 166 245 138 111 232 224 110 146 153 169 123
169 245 157 184  78 156 230 224 212 156 132 142
141 166 190 154 137 129 152 256 171 188 161 128
176 158 145 115 132 146 185 175 131 190 136 289
165 116 198 130 108  95 211 126 204 154 185 119
119 162 116 129 153 172 148 207 161 190 165 122
194 129 176 127 192 144 169 178 140 296 149 144
105 116 100 171 155 127  91 145 218 240 136 128
```

Answer the same questions as in Problem 2, using a class interval of 10.

Measures of Central Tendency

The idea of *average* is a familiar concept to practically everyone. Quite often we hear people talk about average salary, average height, average grade, average family, and so on. If we have a set of real numbers, we can try to represent this set of values by a measure, say *average*, that is most representative of the members of the set. However, the idea of averages is so commonly used that it is not surprising that several kinds of averages have been introduced in statistics.

Averages will be called *measures of central tendency*. The three measures in common use are *arithmetic mean, median,* and *mode*.

**12.3.1
Definition**

The *arithmetic mean,* **or** *mean,* **of a set of real numbers** $x_1, x_2, \ldots, x_n$ **is denoted by** $\bar{X}$ **and is defined as**

$$X = \frac{x_1 + x_2 + \cdots + x_n}{n} \qquad (12.3.1)$$

**12.3.1
Example**

The grades of a student on eight examinations were 70, 65, 69, 85, 94, 62, 79, 100. The mean of this set of grades is

$$\bar{X} = \frac{70 + 65 + 69 + 85 + 94 + 62 + 79 + 100}{8} = 78$$

In this example $n = 8$.

An interesting fact about the mean is that the sum of deviations of each item from the mean is zero. In Example 12.3.1, the deviation of each score from the mean $\bar{X} = 78$ is $(100 - 78)$, $(94 - 78)$, $(85 - 78)$, $(79 - 78)$, $(70 - 78)$, $(69 - 78)$, $(65 - 78)$, and $(62 - 78)$.

Figure 12.12 lists each score, the mean, and the deviation from the mean. If we add up the deviations from the mean, we obtain a sum of zero.

Score	Mean	Deviation from Mean
100	78	22
94	78	16
85	78	7
79	78	1
70	78	−8
69	78	−9
65	78	−13
62	78	−16
	Sum of deviations	0

Figure 12.12

For any data, the following result is true.
The sum of the deviations from the mean is zero.
An alternative way of defining the mean is that real number for which the sum of the deviations is zero.

Another interesting fact about the mean is that if Y is any guessed or assumed mean (which may be any real number) and if we let d_j denote the deviation of each item of the data from the assumed mean, $(d_j = x_j - Y)$, then the actual mean is

$$\bar{X} = Y + \frac{d_1 + d_2 + \cdots + d_n}{n} \qquad (12.3.2)$$

Consider Example 12.3.1. We know that the actual mean is 78. Suppose we had guessed the mean to be 52. Then, using formula (12.3.2), we obtain

$$\bar{X} = 52 + \frac{\begin{aligned}(100 - 52) + (94 - 52) + (85 - 52) + (79 - 52) + (70 - 52) \\ + (69 - 52) + (55 - 52) + (62 - 52)\end{aligned}}{8}$$
$$= 52 + 26 = 78$$

which agrees with what we have already found.

The purpose of introducing (12.3.2) to find the mean is that if the numbers to be added in finding the mean are large, (12.3.2) can simplify the computation.

A method for computing the mean for grouped data given in a frequency table is illustrated here by the use of an example.

Find the mean for the grouped data given in the frequency table of Figure 12.7.

12.3.2
Example

Figure 12.13 displays the information needed to complete the example.

(a) Take the midpoint of one of the intervals as an arbitrary reference point. As far as the result is concerned *it will make no difference which interval midpoint is used.* In this example, we take as an arbitrary reference point the midpoint of the interval 80–89.99, namely 85.

(b) Set up a third column labeled as x^1. Since the interval 80–89.99 is the interval containing our reference point, a zero is placed in column 3 for this interval. The class 90–99.99 is one class interval above the interval containing the arbitrary reference point. A 1 is entered for this interval in column 3. A 2 is entered in column 3 for the class interval 100–109.99 since it is two class intervals above 80–89.99. This process continues upward until each interval has been assigned a value. We do the same thing for the intervals below the reference point, except that we use a minus sign to denote the number of intervals each class is below the one containing the reference point.

(c) Next multiply the entry in column 3 by the frequency f for that class interval and enter the product in column 4, which is labeled $f \cdot x^1$.

(d) Add the entries in column 4.

	f	x^1	$f \cdot x^1$
110–119.99	2	3	6
100–109.99	6	2	12
90– 99.99	14	1	14
80– 89.99	14	0	0
70– 79.99	19	−1	−19
60– 69.99	9	−2	−18
50– 59.99	7	−3	−21
n = 71			$\Sigma fx^1 = -26$

Figure 12.13

The mean is then computed by substituting in the following equation

$$\bar{X} = h + \frac{\Sigma fx^1}{n} \cdot i$$

in which

$h =$ arbitrary reference point
$i =$ the size of the class interval
$n =$ number of items.
Σ means to add up the entries

Using the data in Figure 12.13 we obtain

$$\bar{X} = 85 + \frac{-26}{71}(10) = 85 - 3.7 = 81.3$$

12.3.2
Definition
The *median* of a set of real numbers arranged in order of magnitude is the middle value if the number of items is odd and it is the arithmatic mean of the two middle values if the number of items is even.

12.3.3
Example
The data 2, 2, 3, 4, 5, 7, 7, 7, 11 has median 5.
The data 2, 2, 3, 3, 4, 5, 7, 7, 7, 11 has median 4.5 since

$$\frac{4+5}{2} = 4.5$$

To find the median for the grouped data in Figure 12.7 we proceed as follows. The median is that point in the data that will have 50 percent of the cases above it and 50 percent below it. Now, 50 percent of 71 cases is 35.5 cases. Hence we are interested in finding that point in the distribution with 35 cases above it and 35 below it.

We start by counting up from the bottom until we come as close to 35 cases as possible, but not exceeding it. This brings us through the interval 70–79.99. Thus, the median must lie in the interval 80–89.99. Now the median will equal the lower limit of the interval 80–89.99, namely 80, plus an *interpolation factor*. The interpolation factor is determined as follows:

(a) Count the number of entries or fractional entries needed to reach the median (in our example, the number is .5).

(b) If the frequency for the interval is f, divide the interval into f parts.

(c) The interpolation factor I is

$$I = n \cdot \frac{1}{f} \cdot i$$

where

n = number of entries needed to reach the median
f = number of entries in the interval
i = size of the interval

The median M is then given by

$$M = (\text{lower limit of interval}) + (\text{interpolation factor})$$

For the data of Figure 12.7, the median M is

$$M = 80 + 0.5 \cdot \frac{1}{14} \cdot 10 = 80.36$$

The median is sometimes called the *centile point* and is denoted by C_{50} to indicate that 50 percent of the data is below and 50 percent is above it. Similarly, we can find C_{25} or the first quartile and C_{75} or the third quartile.

Thus, for the example based on Figure 12.7, C_{25} is formed by first finding the class interval containing the tally equal to 25 percent of all the tallies. Thus, the tally corresponding to C_{25} is found in the class interval $70 - 79.99$ since

$$25 \text{ percent of } 71 = 17.75$$

and 16 tallies lie in the first two class intervals. Using the interpolation factor, we find that

$$C_{25} = 70 + (1.75) \frac{1}{19} (10) = 70 + 0.921 = 70.921$$

The *mode* of a set of real numbers arranged in order of magnitude is that value which occurs with the greatest frequency exceeding a frequency of one.

12.3.3
Definition

The mode need not exist and if it does it need not be unique. For the data in Figure 12.3, 79 is the mode (8 is the highest frequency).

12.3.4
Example

The data 2, 3, 4, 5, 7, 15 has no mode.

12.3.5
Example

The data 2, 2, 2, 3, 3, 7, 7, 7, 11, 15 has mode 2 and 7 and is called *bimodal.*
When data has been listed in a frequency table, the mode is defined as the midpoint of the interval consisting of the largest number of cases. For example, the mode for Figure 12.7 is 75 (the midpoint of the interval 70–79.99).

Among the three measures of central tendency consider so far, the most important and the one most frequently used is the mean. The reason for this is that it is easy to understand, easy to compute, and uses all the data in the collection. If two samples are chosen from the same population, the two means corresponding to the two samples will not generally differ by as much as the two medians of these samples.

The second most reliable measure is the median; it, too, is easy to understand and easy to compute. One advantage of the median over the mean is that it is independent of extreme values. Furthermore, in situations in which only the frequency of extreme values is known, it is still possible to compute the median, whereas to compute the mean is impossible.

12.3.1
Exercise

1. For data given in Problems 2, 4, and 5 in Exercise 12.2, find the mean, median, and mode.
2. For the frequency table in Figure 12.6, compute the mean, median, and mode.
3. The annual salaries of five faculty members in the Mathematics Department at a large university are $10,000, $11,000, $12,000, $12,500, $35,000. Compute the mean and median. Which measure describes the situation more realistically? If you were among the four lowest paid members, which measure would you use to describe the situation? What if you were the one making $35,000?
4. In a labor/management wage negotiation in which the laborers are the lowest paid of the workers in the company, which measure of central tendency would labor tend to use as an argument for more pay? Which would management use? Why?
5. For the data given in Problems 1, 2, 4, and 5 in Exercise 12.2, find the mean, using an assumed mean.
6. Find C_{75} and C_{40} for the frequency tables in Figure 12.6 and 12.7.
*7. In a frequency table, the score x_1 appears f_1 times, the score x_2 appears f_2 times, . . . , and the score x_n appears f_n times. Show that the mean $\bar{X}$ is given by the formula.

$$\bar{X} = \frac{x_1 \cdot f_1 + x_2 \cdot f_2 + \cdots + x_n \cdot f_n}{f_1 + f_2 + \cdots + f_n}$$

Measures of dispersion

We begin with the following example.

Consider the sets of scores:

S_1: 4, 6, 8, 10, 12, 14, 16
S_2: 4, 7, 9, 10, 11, 13, 16

Notice that the mean of S_1 and S_2 is 10 and the median of S_1 and S_2 is 10, yet the scores in each set are different and those in S_2 seem to be more closely clustered around 10 than those in S_1.

Thus we need, in addition to the measures of central tendency, a statistical measure to indicate the extent to which the scores are spread out. Such measures are called *measures of dispersion*.

The simplest measure of dispersion is the *range*. It is the difference between the largest and the lowest score. For S_1 and S_2 the range is $16 - 4 = 12$. We can see that the range is a poor measure of dispersion since it depends only on two measures but tells us nothing about the rest of the scores.

Another measure of dispersion is the *deviation from the mean*. Recall that this measure is characterized by the fact that if the deviations from the mean of each score are all added up the result is zero. Because of this, it is not widely used as a measure of dispersion.

We need, therefore, a measure that will give us an idea of how much deviation is involved without having these deviations add up to zero. By squaring each deviation from the mean, adding them, dividing by the number of scores, we obtain an average squared deviation, which is called the *variance* of the set of scores. Thus, the formula for the variance which is denoted by σ^2, is

$$\sigma^2 = \frac{(x_1 - \bar{X})^2 + (x_2 - \bar{X})^2 + \cdots + (x_n - \bar{X})^2}{n}$$

where $\bar{X}$ is the mean of the scores $x_1, x_2, \ldots, x_n$ and n is the number of scores.

In order to apply this measure in practical situations (for instance, if our data represents dollars, we cannot talk about "squared dollars") we will use the square root of the variance. This is called the *standard deviation* of a set of scores. The standard deviation is denoted by σ and is given by the formula:

$$\sigma = \sqrt{\frac{(x_1 - \bar{X})^2 + (x_2 - \bar{X})^2 + \cdots + (x_n - \bar{X})^2}{n}}$$

where $\bar{X}$ and the x_i's are defined the same way as for the variance.

For the data in Example 12.3.6, the standard deviation for S_1, is

$$\sigma = \sqrt{\frac{36 + 16 + 4 + 0 + 4 + 16 + 36}{7}} = \sqrt{\frac{112}{7}} = \sqrt{16} = 4$$

and the standard deviation for S_2 is

$$\sigma = \sqrt{\frac{36 + 9 + 1 + 0 + 1 + 9 + 36}{7}} = \sqrt{\frac{92}{7}} = \sqrt{13.14} = 3.625$$

The fact that the standard deviation of the set S_2 is less than that for the set S_1 is an indication that the scores from S_2 are more clustered around the mean than those from S_1 are.

Find the standard deviation for the data

$$100, 90, 90, 85, 80, 75, 75, 75, 70, 70, 65, 65, 60, 40, 40, 40$$

The mean is

$$\bar{X} = \frac{100 + 2 \cdot 90 + 85 + 80 + 3 \cdot 75 + 2 \cdot 70 + 2 \cdot 65 + 60 + 3 \cdot 40}{16}$$

$$= 70$$

The deviations from the mean and their square are given in Figure 12.14.

Scores x	Deviation from the Mean $x - \bar{X}$	Deviation Squared $(x - \bar{X})^2$
100	30	900
90	20	400
90	20	400
85	15	225
80	10	100
75	5	25
75	5	25
75	5	25
70	0	0
70	0	0
65	−5	25
65	−5	25
60	−10	100
40	−30	900
40	−30	900
40	−30	900
Mean = 70 $n = 16$	sum = 0	sum = 4950

Figure 12.14

The standard deviation is

$$\sigma = \sqrt{\frac{4950}{16}} = \frac{70.3}{4} = 17.6$$

Find the standard deviation for the scores

$$80, 80, 80, 80, 75, 75, 75, 75, 70, 70, 65, 65, 60, 60, 55, 55$$

Here the mean is $\bar{X} = 70$ for the 16 scores. Figure 12.15 gives the deviations from the mean and their square.

Scores	Deviation from the Mean $x - \bar{X}$	Deviation Squared $(x - \bar{X})^2$
80	10	100
80	10	100
80	10	100
80	10	100
75	5	25
75	5	25
75	5	25
75	5	25
70	0	0
70	0	0
65	−5	25
65	−5	25
60	−10	100
60	−10	100
55	−15	225
55	−15	225
Mean = 70 $n = 16$	sum = 0	sum = 1200

Figure 12.15

The standard deviation is

$$\sigma = \sqrt{\frac{1200}{16}} = \sqrt{75} = 8.7$$

These two examples show that although the samples have the same mean, 70, and the same sample size, 16, the scores in the first test deviate further from the mean than do the scores in the second test.

In general, a relatively small standard deviation indicates that the measures tend to cluster close to the mean, and a relatively high one shows that the measures are widely scattered from the mean.

To find the standard deviation for grouped data we use the following formula

$$\sigma = \sqrt{\frac{(x_1 - \bar{X})^2 f_1 + (x_2 - \bar{X})^2 f_2 + \cdots + (x_n - \bar{X})^2 f_n}{n}}$$

where $x_1, x_2, \ldots, x_n$ are the class midpoints, $f_1, f_2, \ldots, f_n$ are the respective frequencies, n is the sum of the frequencies, that is, $n = f_1 + f_2 + \cdots + f_n$, and $\bar{X}$ is the mean.

Find the standard deviation for the grouped data given in Figure 12.13. The mean for this data is

$$\bar{X} = 81.3$$

12.3.9
Example

The class midpoints are 55, 65, 75, 85, 95, 105, 115. The deviation of the mean from the class midpoints, their square, and the product of their square by their respective frequency are listed in Figure 12.16.

Class Midpoint	f_i	$x_i - \bar{X}$	$(x_i - \bar{X})^2$	$(x_i - \bar{X})^2 \cdot f_i$
115	2	33.7	1135.69	2271.38
105	6	23.7	561.69	3370.14
95	14	13.7	187.69	2627.66
85	14	3.7	13.69	191.66
75	19	−6.3	39.69	754.11
65	9	−16.3	265.69	2391.21
55	7	−26.3	691.69	4841.83
Sum	71			16447.99

Figure 12.16

The standard deviation is

$$\sigma = \sqrt{\frac{16447.99}{71}} = \sqrt{231.66} = 15.22$$

A little computation shows that the sum of the deviations of the approximate mean from the class midpoints is not exactly zero. This is because we are using only an approximation to the mean, since we cannot compute the exact mean for grouped data.

**12.3.2
Exercise**

1. Compute the standard deviation for the following data.

    4, 5, 9, 9, 10, 14, 25

2. Find the mean, mode, range, median, and standard deviation of the following sample of scores from a test in biology.

    99, 91, 83, 77, 65, 60, 40, 35, 20

3. A group of 25 applicants for admission to Midwestern University made the following scores on the quantitative part of an aptitude test.

591	570	425	472	555
490	415	479	517	570
606	614	542	607	441
502	506	603	488	460
550	551	420	590	482

    Find the mean, median, range, and standard deviation of these scores.

4. Find the standard deviation for Problems 1, 2, 4, and 5 in Exercise 12.2.
5. Find the standard deviation for the grouped data given in Figure 12.6.

Frequency polygons or frequency distributions can assume almost any shape or form, depending on the data. However, the data obtained from many experiments follows a common pattern which has been thoroughly investigated. For example, heights of people, weights of people, test scores, coin tossing, all lead to data which have the same kind of frequency distribution. This distribution is referred to as the *normal distribution* or the *bell-shaped distribution*. Because it occurs so often in practical situations, it is generally regarded as the most important distribution and is one on which much statistical theory is based.

12.4
NORMAL
DISTRIBUTION

Draw the histogram and frequency polygon for the data given in Figure 12.17.

12.4.1
Example

Class Interval	Frequency of Occurrence of Scores in the Class Interval
120.5–125.5	1
115.5–120.5	2
110.5–115.5	3
105.5–110.5	5
100.5–105.5	7
95.5–100.5	7
90.5– 95.5	5
85.5– 90.5	3
80.5– 85.5	2
75.5– 80.5	1

Figure 12.17

Figure 12.18 gives the histogram and the frequency polygon for this data and is an example of a *normal curve* or *bell-shaped curve*.

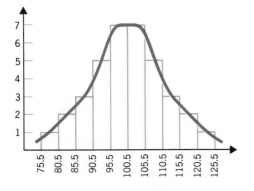

Figure 12.18

Consider an experiment in which a fair coin is tossed ten times. Find the frequency distribution for the probability of tossing a head.

The probability for obtaining exactly k heads is given by a binomial distribution $b(10, k; 1/2)$. Thus, from Table 9 in the Appendix, we obtain a distribution as given in Figure 12.19.

No. Heads	Probability $b(10,k;1/2)$
0	.0010
1	.0098
2	.0439
3	.1172
4	.2051
5	.2461
6	.2051
7	.1172
8	.0439
9	.0098
10	.0010

Figure 12.19

If we graph this frequency distribution we obtain the line chart of Figure 12.20.

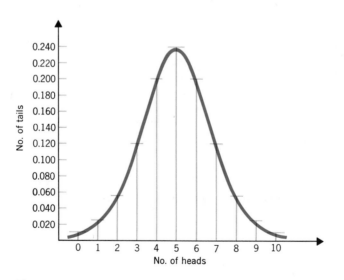

Figure 12.20

Upon connecting the tops of each line of the line chart, we obtain a *normal curve*.

This particular distribution for $n = 10$, and $p = 1/2$ is not a result of the choice of n or p. As a matter of fact, the line chart for any binomial probability $b(n, k; p)$ will give a normal curve. The student should verify this for the cases in which $n = 15$, $p = 1/3$; and $n = 8$, $p = 3/4$.

We now turn our attention to the study of normal curves. In both of the previous examples, notice that the highest part of the normal curve occurred at the mean of the distribution. It is characteristic of the normal distribution that the frequency of occurrence of events is symmetric about the mean. That is, for a normal curve, half of the area beneath the curve lies on one side of the mean and half lies on the other side. See Figure 12.21.

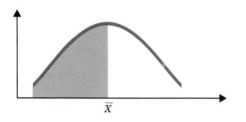

Figure 12.21

It is also important to recognize that in theory the normal curve will never touch the x-axis but will extend to infinity in either direction. Also, because of its shape, every normal distribution has its mean, median, and mode at the same point.

The standard deviation of a normal distribution plays a major role in describing the area under the normal curve. For example, it can be shown that the area under the normal curve from $\bar{X} - \sigma$ to $\bar{X} + \sigma$ is approximately 68.27 percent of the total area under the curve. The area from $\bar{X} - 2\sigma$ to $\bar{X} + 2\sigma$ is approximately 95.45 percent of the total area under the curve. The area under the normal curve between $\bar{X} - 3\sigma$ and $\bar{X} + 3\sigma$ is approximately 99.73 percent of the total area. See Figure 12.22.

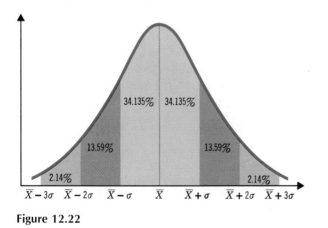

Figure 12.22

For the data in Example 12.4.1, the mean and standard deviation are

$$\bar{X} = 100.5, \qquad \sigma = 10.31$$

Knowing this, we can infer that about 68 percent of the students tested have scores between 90.19 and 110.81; about 95 percent have scores between 79.88 and 121.12; and about 99.7 percent have scores between 69.57 and 131.43.

The percent of items falling between the mean and a point determined by a fractional multiple of standard deviations can be ascertained by referring to a *normal curve table*. The use of such table will be introduced later in this chapter.

A normal distribution curve is completely determined by $\bar{X}$ and σ. Hence, different normal distributions of data with different means and standard deviations give rise to different shapes of the normal curve. Figure 12.23 indicates how the normal curve will change if the standard deviation changes. For the sake of clarity, we assume all data have mean 0. (By sliding the normal curve along the *x*-axis, it is always possible to transform the curve so that its mean is $\bar{X} = 0$).

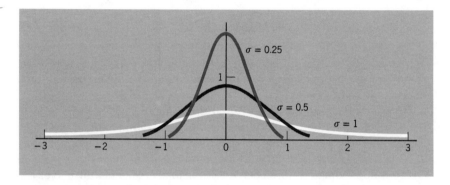

Figure 12.23

Notice that as the standard deviation increases, the normal curve flattens out.

When a normal distribution has a mean of $\bar{X} = 0$ and a standard deviation of $\sigma = 1$, its normal curve is referred to as a *standard normal curve*. Fortunately, every normal distribution can be changed to standard form. This is achieved by introducing new score data, called *Z-score*, defined as

$$Z = \frac{x - \bar{X}}{\sigma} \qquad (12.4.1)$$

where

$x =$ the old score data
$\bar{X} =$ the mean of the "old" data
$\sigma =$ the standard deviation of the "old" data

The new score data defined by (12.4.1) will always have a *zero mean* and a *unit standard deviation*. Such data are said to be expressed in *standard units* or *standard scores*. By expressing data in terms of standard units, it becomes possible to make a comparison of distributions. Furthermore, the total area under a standard normal curve is one.

A student receives a grade of 82 on a final examination in biology for which
the mean is 73 and the standard deviation is 9. In his final examination in sociology for which the mean grade is 81 and the standard deviation is 15, he receives an 89. In which examination is his relative standing higher?

In their present form, these distributions are not comparable since each has different means and, more importantly, different standard deviations. In order to compare the data, we transform the data to standard scores. For the biology data, the new score data for the student's examination score is

$$Z = \frac{82 - 73}{9} = \frac{9}{9} = 1$$

For the sociology data, the new score data for the students examination score is

$$Z = \frac{89 - 81}{15} = \frac{8}{15} = 0.533$$

This means the student's score in the biology exam is one standard unit above the mean, while his score in the sociology exam is 0.533 standard units above the mean. Hence, his *relative standing* is higher in biology.

The curve in Figure 12.23 with mean $\bar{X} = 0$ and standard deviation $\sigma = 1$ is the standard normal curve. For this curve, the areas between $Z = -1$ and 1, $Z = -2$ and 2, $Z = -3$ and 3 are equal, respectively, to 68.27 percent, 95.45 percent, and 99.73 percent of the total area under the curve, which is one. To find the areas cut off between other points, we proceed as in the following example.

Suppose, to begin with, we consider the standard normal curve illustrated in
Figure 12.24. We wish to find the proportion of the area or the proportion of cases included between the two points 0.6 and 1.86 units from the mean.

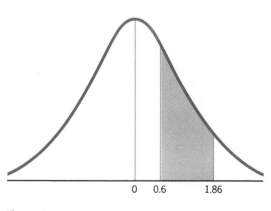

0   0.6   1.86

Figure 12.24

This problem is worked by using the normal curve table, given in Table 10 in the Appendix. We begin by checking the table to find the area of the curve cut off between the mean and a point equivalent to a standard score of 0.6 from the mean. This value appears in the second column of the table and is found to be 0.2257. Next we continue down the table in the left-hand column until we come to a standard score of 1.86. By looking in column 7, we find that 0.4686 of the area is included between the mean and this point. Then the area of the curve between these two points is the difference between the two areas, 0.4686 − 0.2257, which is 0.2429. We can then state that approximately 24.29 percent of the cases fall between 0.6 and 1.86, or *that the probability* of a score falling between these two points is about 0.2429.

In the next illustration, we shall take two points that are on different sides of the mean.

12.4.5
Example

We wish to determine what proportion of the area of the normal curve falls between a standard score of −0.39 and one of 1.86 for the standard normal curve given in Figure 12.25.

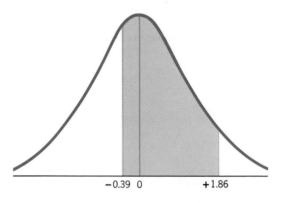

−0.39 0   +1.86

Figure 12.25

There are no values for negative standard scores in Table 10. As far as areas are concerned, because of the symmetry of normal curves, equal standard scores, whether positive or negative, give equal areas when taken from the mean. From the table we find that a standard score of −0.39 cuts off an area of 0.1517 between it and the mean. A standard score of 1.86 likewise includes 0.4686 of the area of the curve between it and the mean. The area included between both points is then equal to the sum of these two areas, 0.1517 + 0.4686, which is 0.6203. Thus, approximately 62.03 percent of the area is between −0.39 and 1.86. In other words, the probability of a score falling between these two points is about 0.6203.

12.4
Exercise

1. Draw the line chart and frequency curve for the probability of a head in an experiment in which a biased coin is tossed 15 times and the probability that a head occurs is 1/3. *Hint:* Find $b(15, k; 1/3)$ for $k = 0, 1, \ldots, 15$, by using Table 9 in the Appendix.

2. Follow the same directions as in Problem 1 for an experiment in which a biased coin is tossed 8 times and the probability that heads appears is 3/4.

3. Given a normal distribution with a mean of 13.1 and a standard deviation of 9.3, find the Z score equivalent of the following scores in the distribution:

$$7, 9, 13, 15, 29, 37, 41$$

4. Given the following standard scores or Z scores on a standard normal distribution, find the area from the mean to each score.

   (a) 0.89   (e) −0.75
   (b) 1.10   (f) −2.31
   (c) 2.50   (g) 0.80
   (d) 3.00   (h) 3.03

5. An instructor assigns grades in an examination according to the following procedure:

   A if score exceeds $\bar{X} + 1.6\sigma$
   B if score is between $\bar{X} + 0.6\sigma$ and $\bar{X} + 1.6\sigma$
   C if score is between $\bar{X} - 0.3\sigma$ and $\bar{X} + 0.6\sigma$
   D if score is between $\bar{X} - 1.4\sigma$ and $\bar{X} - 0.3\sigma$
   F if score is below $\bar{X} - 1.4\sigma$

   What percentage of each grade does this instructor give, assuming that the scores are normally distributed?

6. If the weight of 100 college students closely follows a normal distribution with a mean of 130 pounds and a standard deviation of 5.2 pounds,

   (a) How many of these students would you expect to be at least 142 pounds?
   (b) What range of weights would you expect to include the middle 70 percent of the students in this group?

7. If the average life of a certain make of clothing is 40 months with standard deviation of 7 months, what percentage of these clothes can be expected to last from 28 months to 42 months? Assume that clothing lifetime follows a normal distribution.

8. Records show that the average life expectancy of a pair of shoes is 2.2 years with a standard deviation of 1.7 years. A manufacturer guarantees that shoes lasting less than a year are replaced free. For every 1000 shoes he sells, how many shoes should he expect to replace free?

9. The attendance over a weekly period of time at a movie theater is normally distributed with a mean of 10,000 and a standard deviation of 1000 persons. Find

   (a) The number in the lowest 70 percent of the attendance figures.
   (b) The percentage of attendance figures that falls between 8500 and 11,000 persons.
   (c) The percentage of attendance figures that differs from the mean by 1500 persons or more.

10. Caryl, Mary, and Kathleen are vying for a position as secretary. Caryl, who is tested with group I gets a score of 76 on her test; Mary, who is tested with group II, gets a score of 89; and Kathleen, who is tested with Group III, gets a score of 21. If the average score for group I is 82, for group II is 93, and for group III is 24 and if the standard deviations for each group are 7, 2, and 9, respectively, which person has the highest relative standing?

11. In Mathematics 135, the average final grade is 75.0 and the standard deviation is 10.0. The professor's grade distribution shows that 15 students with grades from 68.0 to 82.0 received C's. Assuming the grades follow a normal distribution, how many students are in Mathematics 135?

*12. According to Mendel, by cross-pollinating pure lime green peas with pure lime yellow peas, hybrid seeds are obtained. From these seeds, the resulting plants yielded 25 percent green seeds How many hybrid seeds need to be planted so that there is a probability of 90 percent that at least 40 green seeds are obtained.

12.5
CHI-SQUARE
DISTRIBUTION

In studying experiments of chance, there usually exists a discrepancy between the observed frequencies of occurrence of an event and the expected frequencies. As examples of such discrepancies we look at the following experiments.

12.5.1
Example

A die is tossed 60 times. The results are listed in Figure 12.26.

Outcome							
	1	2	3	4	5	6	Total
O	11	8	12	9	11	9	60
E	10	10	10	10	10	10	60

Figure 12.26

Here O denotes the observed frequency, and E denotes the expected, theoretical, or hypothetical frequency.

12.5.2
Example
Sex ratios
in rats

A sample of 50 rats yields 38 males and 12 females. Is this sample consistent with the assumption (hypothesis) that the sex ratio in the population is $1:1$ (that is the probability of male = probability of female = 1/2)? See Figure 12.27.

	Male	Female
O	38	12
E	25	25

Figure 12.27

A coin is tossed 100 times, and the observed results are 65 heads and 35 tails. Can we assume (hypothesize) that this distribution of 65 heads and 35 tails does not differ from what we would expect by chance, that is, 50 heads and 50 tails? See Figure 12.28.

12.5.3
Example

	H	*T*
O	65	35
E	50	50

Figure 12.28

From the above three examples and from previous discussions, we see that one would like to be able to guess (hypothesize) as to how data for a given problem will be distributed, and then to accumulate and examine data to see how well the hypothesis predicted the actual pattern of data. This is called *hypothesis testing*.

The technique that we shall be using to implement such a task is called the *chi-square distribution*. This distribution will enable us to determine if a certain distribution differs from some predetermined theoretical distribution. For Examples 12.5.2 and 12.5.3, we have a distribution based on the roll of a die and the toss of a coin. We can determine whether our observed frequencies differ from the frequencies that we would expect if our distribution follows a stated theoretical distribution in the following way.

Let us return to Example 12.5.3. In this example we expect each of the outcomes to occur 1/2 of the time. That is, our hypothesis is that the coin is fair so that each face will turn up 1/2 of the time. Notice in Figure 12.28 that the sum of the observed frequencies equals the sum of the expected frequencies. Also, it is important to note that we must use all of the data; that is, if no head appears this fact must also be taken into account.

We test our hypothesis by using the measure χ^2, called *chi square*, which is obtained from the general formula

$$\chi^2 = \frac{(O_1 - E_1)^2}{E_1} + \frac{(O_2 - E_2)^2}{E_2} + \cdots + \frac{(O_n - E_n)^2}{E_n}$$

where the O_i is the ith observed frequency, E_i is the corresponding expected frequency, and n is the number of possible outcomes.

For our example χ^2 is found to be 9, since

$$\chi^2 = \frac{(65-50)^2}{50} + \frac{(35-50)^2}{50} = 9$$

The question that should be asked is whether the coin is really fair, based on the fact that $\chi^2 = 9$?

Had the results of tossing the coin corresponded exactly to the expected frequency, that is, had there been no deviation of the observed frequencies from the expected frequencies (so that instead of $O_1 = 65$ and $O_2 = 35$, we would have had $O_1 = 50$, and $O_2 = 50$) then we would have calculated χ^2 to be

$$\chi^2 = \frac{(50-50)^2}{50} + \frac{(50-50)^2}{50} = 0$$

Thus, in the case of an experiment agreeing completely with the theoretical frequencies, the measure χ^2 will equal 0. Similarly, the more the observed frequencies deviate from the theoretical, the larger the measure χ^2 will be.

12.5.4
Example

For the data given in Example 12.5.1, compute χ^2.

To find χ^2, we use Figure 12.29 and determine that for this experiment, $\chi^2 = 1.2$.

Face	O	E	$O - E$	$(O - E)^2$	$\dfrac{(O - E)^2}{E}$
1	11	10	1	1	1/10
2	8	10	-2	4	4/10
3	12	10	2	4	4/10
4	9	10	-1	1	1/10
5	11	10	1	1	1/10
6	9	10	-1	1	1/10
Total	60	60			$12/10 = 1.2$

Figure 12.29

For the above example, notice that the smallest value for χ^2 is 0. The next value for χ^2 occurs when, for example, the face 1 is observed to occur 9 times, the face 2 occurs 11 times, and the others 10 each. In this case

$$\chi^2 = \frac{(9-10)^2}{10} + \frac{(11-10)^2}{10} + \frac{(10-10)^2}{10} + \frac{(10-10)^2}{10}$$
$$+ \frac{(10-10)^2}{10} + \frac{(10-10)^2}{10} = \frac{1}{10} + \frac{1}{10} = 0.2$$

Thus, χ^2 cannot assume values between 0 and 0.2; that is, χ^2 is a discrete variable.

If an experiment, like the one mentioned above, is repeated many times, each time under the same hypothesis, and each time the measure χ^2 is calculated, we obtain a set of values for χ^2. A histogram can be drawn using these values. We can do the same for the χ^2 distribution as was done with the normal distribution when we approximated discrete data by a continuous graph. That is, even though χ^2 is a discrete variable, it is possible to find a frequency curve which is an excellent approximation to the histogram of χ^2. One such approximation to the measure χ^2 is given in Figure 12.30.

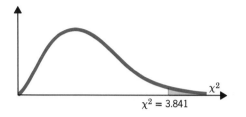

Figure 12.30

In Figure 12.30 we marked a point corresponding to $\chi^2 = 3.841$. This point divides the area under the curve into two parts. The shaded area to the right of the point contains 5 percent of the total area and the area on the left contains 95 percent of the total area. The 5 percent shaded area is called the *critical region*. Any result of χ^2 that lies in this 5 percent shaded area is said to be *significant;* otherwise it is called *not significant*. The 5 percent is called the *significance level*. The notation $\chi^2_{0.005} = 3.841$ is used to indicate that 5 percent of the possible occurrences of χ^2 lie to the right of the point.

For the data of Example 12.5.3, the computed value of χ^2 is 9. Should we reject our hypothesis that the coin is fair at a 5 percent level of significance? Since $\chi^2 = 9$ is much larger than 3.841, we *reject* our hypothesis that the coin is fair at a 5 percent level of significance. That is, we can be fairly confident (with probability .95) that these results are different from those produced by chance alone. In other words, we suspect the coin is loaded.

Table 11 in the Appendix gives various levels of significance for the measure χ^2. This table enables us to evaluate the approximate significance of the measure χ^2.

The student will notice that the first column of Table 11 is headed by the letter ν. This is the number of *degrees of freedom* which the χ^2 distribution depends on. The degree of freedom is determined as follows:

Organize the data of the experiment in tabular form, called a *contingency table* as done in Figure 12.26, 12.27, and 12.28. Then, the degree of freedom is determined by the formula

$$\nu = (r - 1)(c - 1)$$

where

$r =$ the number of rows in the contingency table
$c =$ the number of columns in the contingency table

For example 12.5.1, the degree of freedom is

$$\nu = (2 - 1)(6 - 1) = 1 \cdot 5 = 5$$

For example 12.5.2 we have

$$\nu = (2 - 1)(2 - 1) = 1 \cdot 1 = 1$$

Return to Table 11 in the Appendix. For $\nu = 4$ the value of χ^2 for a 30 percent significant level is 4.878 which means that for 4 degrees of freedom, the probability of obtaining a value of χ^2 greater than or equal to 4.878 is 0.30 (30 percent significant level).

Figure 12.31 gives the graphs that approximate very nearly the distribution χ^2 for $\nu = 1, 3, 5,$ and 15.

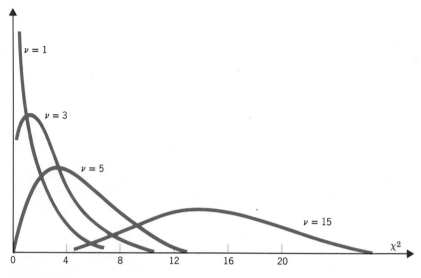

Figure 12.31

To summarize, in testing a hypothesis,
(1) find the degrees of freedom
(2) determine the value χ^2
There is evidence against the hypothesis at the p level if χ^2 exceeds the tabulated value of $\chi_p{}^2$ for the degrees of freedom determined in (1).

12.5.5
Example
Application
to Genetics

In searching for hereditary variations in the garden plant *Coleus*, Boye and Rife[1] (1938) employed self-pollination of plants which had previously been propagated vegetatively. In the latter case, no variations due to segregation are observed. With self-pollination, one case resulted in 787 plants, of which 207 bore leaves with a green-purple pattern and 580 had purple leaves. These observed frequencies are not exactly in the ratio 3:1 as is expected. Is there evidence against the hypothesis of 3:1?

First, construct the contingency table. See Figure 12.32.

	Purple	Pattern
O	580	207
E	590.25	196.75

Figure 12.32

[1] C. L. Boye, and D. C. Rife, *Jour. Heredity* **29**:55 (1938).

The expected frequency is found by noting that 3/4 of the 787 of the plants should be purple and 1/4 of the 787 plants should have a pattern. The degree of freedom is

$$\nu = (2-1)(2-1) = 1$$

Next, we compute χ^2, obtaining

$$\chi^2 = \frac{(580 - 590.25)^2}{590.25} + \frac{(207 - 196.75)^2}{196.75} = 0.712$$

Consulting Table 11 in the Appendix, we find that $\chi^2 = 0.712$ falls between levels of significance of 30 and 50 percent. This means that the observed frequencies will occur more than 30 percent of the time by chance alone when the expected ratio is $3:1$. Thus, there is no significant evidence against the hypothesis.

In an experiment to study the effect of smoking, a sample of 500 people were selected randomly, of which 300 were smokers and 200 were non-smokers. After 10 years 40 smokers and 10 nonsmokers had died. Is there evidence to substantiate the hypothesis that the death rate of smokers and non-smokers is the same?

12.5.6
Example

Figure 12.33 summarizes the information given in the problem.

	Died	Survived	Total
Smokers	40	260	300
Nonsmokers	10	190	200
Total	50	450	500

Figure 12.33

To obtain the expected frequencies we note that for the total group 50 of 500, died, that is, the probability of death is $50/500 = 0.10$, and hence the probability of survival is $1 - 0.10 = 0.90$. Under the hypothesis we assume that the probability of death for smokers and nonsmokers is the same, namely, 0.10: Similarly, the probability of survival for smokers and non-smokers is assumed the same, namely, 0.90. Using this information we can construct the contingency table. See Figure 12.34.

	Smokers Died	Nonsmokers Died	Smokers Survived	Nonsmokers Survived
O	40	10	260	190
E	$(.10)(300) = 30$	$(.10)(200) = 20$	$(.90)300 = 270$	$(.90)(200) = 180$

Figure 12.34

The measure χ^2 is

$$\chi^2 = \frac{(40-30)^2}{30} + \frac{(10-20)^2}{20} + \frac{(260-270)^2}{270} + \frac{(190-180)^2}{180}$$

$$= \frac{10}{3} + 5 + \frac{10}{27} + \frac{5}{9} = 9.26$$

For this example $\nu = 3$. This value of χ^2 lies just above a level of significance of 2 percent. This means that the hypothesis is substantiated.

It is interesting to note that most of the recent studies pertaining to cancer and smoking give the same kind of result. Thus whether smoking is or is not a cause of cancer should be the subject of further and possibly more sophisticated experimentation.

12.5
Exercise

1. Five pennies were tossed 75 times, with the following results

   5 heads 0 tails   1
   4 heads 1 tails   6
   3 heads 2 tails 15
   2 heads 3 tails 35
   1 heads 4 tails 16
   0 heads 5 tails   2

   Are the results different from what would be expected by chance?

2. A nationwide sample of 2500 college students was asked to agree or to disagree with the statement: "The drinking age should be lowered to 18 years old." The responses of the two sexes were tabulated.

	Disagree	Agree
Boys	540	710
Girls	380	870

   Is there significant evidence at the 5 percent level against the hypothesis that boys and girls are likely to give the same answer?

3. As a test for a cold vaccine, 100 subjects were inoculated, 50 with the cold vaccine and 50 with a dummy shot. The result showed that of those inoculated with the vaccine 16 came down with a cold and of those inoculated with the dummy shot, 20 came down with a cold. Is there promise here at the 5 percent level for a vaccine to cure colds?

4. In a random sample of 500 housewives, 60 percent showed a preference for Tide and 40 percent for Ivory Flakes. Is there evidence against the hypothesis at the 5 percent level that 50 percent of all housewives prefer Tide over Ivory Flakes?

5. A random sample of 1000 people of which 450 are male is taken and it is found that 40 males are color blind and 10 females are color blind. Is there evidence against the hypothesis at the 5 percent level that males and females are equally likely to be color blind?
6. A certain plant when self-pollinated produced 400 offspring, 317 of which had white flowers and 83 of which had colored flowers. Using χ^2, determine whether this segregation fits better a ratio of 3:1 or a ratio of 13:3.
7. Punnet[2] in 1923 reported the following observations to a dehybrid cross in sweet peas. If the plants are self pollinated, we should expect a ratio of 9 bright, tendril; 3 bright, acacia; 3 dull, tendril; 1 dull, acacia, which give expected frequencies of 9/16, 3/16, 3/16, and 1/16, respectively. For the observed frequencies given in Figure 12.35, is there evidence against the hypothesis of 9:3:3:1 at the 5 percent level?

Class	Observed Frequency
Bright, tendril	847
Bright, acacia	298
Dull, tendril	300
Dull, acacia	49

Figure 12.35

CHAPTER REVIEW

Important Terms

population
sample
biased sample
random sample
frequency table
line chart
variable
continuous variable
discrete variable
range
class interval
class limits
upper class limit
lower class limit
frequency polygon
cumulative (less than) frequency
cumulative (more than) frequency
measure of central tendency
mean
median
mode
deviation from the mean
centile point
standard deviation
normal distribution
normal curve, bell-shaped curve
normal curve table
standard normal curve
***Z*-score**
chi-square distribution
critical region
significance level
degrees of freedom

[2] R. C. Punnett, *Jour. Genetics* **13:**101 (1923).

Exercises 1. The following scores were made on a mathematics examination:

80	99	82	21	100	55	80	26	78	52
12	73	20	44	72	63	19	85	33	66
78	42	87	90	30	10	48	75	83	77
63	85	69	80	14	87	66	52	17	60
74	70	73	95	89	14	92	8	100	72

a. For the above data set up a frequency table. What is the range?

b. Draw a line chart for this data.

c. Draw a histogram for the data using a class interval of size 5.

d. Draw the frequency polygon for the histogram.

e. Find the cumulative (more than) frequency.

f. Find the cumulative (less than) frequency.

2. Find the mean, the median, and the mode for each of the following sets of measurements.

a. 12, 10, 8, 2, 0, 4, 10, 5, 4, 4, 8, 0

b. 195, 5, 2, 2, 2, 2, 1, 0

c. 2, 5, 5, 7, 7, 7, 9, 9, 11

3. In which of the sets in Problem 2 is the mean a poor measure of central tendency? Why?

4. Give an example of data in which the preferred measure of central tendency would be:

a. mean

b. mode

c. median

5. Give an example of two sets of scores for which the mean is the same yet their standard deviation is different.

6. Give one advantage of the standard deviation over the variance. Give an example.

7. In 7 different rounds of golf, Joe scored 74, 72, 76, 81, 77, 76, and 73. What was the standard deviation of his scores?

8. A normal distribution has a mean of 25 and a standard deviation of 5.

a. what proportion of the scores fall between 20 and 30?

b. what proportion of scores will lie above 35?

9. A set of 600 scores is normally distributed. How many scores would you expect to find:

a. between $\pm 1\sigma$ of the mean?

b. between 1σ and 3σ above the mean?

c. between $\pm(\frac{2}{3})\sigma$ of the mean?

10. The average life expectancy of a dog is 14 years with a standard deviation of about 1.25 years. Assuming that the life spans of dogs are normally distributed, approximately how many dogs will die before reaching the age of 10 years, 4 months.

11. Use Table 10 in the Appendix to calculate the area under the normal curve between:

a. $Z = -1.35$ and $Z = -2.75$

b. $Z = 1.2$ and $Z = 1.75$

12. Bob got an 89 on the mathematics final examination and a 79 on the sociology exam. In the mathematics class the average grade was 79

with a standard deviation of 5 and in the sociology class the average grade was 72 with a standard deviation of 3.5. Assuming that the grades in both subjects were normally distributed, in which class did Bob rank higher?

13. The table below summarizes religious affiliations and voting preferences.

Party	Protestants	Catholics and Jews	Total
Republicans	128	101	229
Democrats	73	164	237
Total	201	265	466

a. Compute χ^2.

b. Using this value for χ^2, state whether there is evidence against the hypothesis of no difference among religious populations with respect to political preference at the 5 percent level of significance.

Additional Reading

Neyman, Jerzy, "Statistics—Servant of All Science," *Science*, Vol. 122, No. 3166, September 1955.

Mathematics of Finance

A knowledge of interest — whether on money borrowed or on money saved — is of ultimate importance today. The old adage "Neither a lender nor a borrower be" is not true in this age of charge accounts and golden passbook savings plans. This section gives a brief introduction into the mathematics behind the various kinds of interest on the market.

Very simply, *interest* is money paid for the use of money. The total amount of money borrowed (whether by an individual from a bank in the form of a loan or by a bank from an individual in the form of a savings account) is called the *principal*. The *rate of interest* is the amount charged for the use of the principal for a given period of time (usually on a yearly or *per annum* basis). Rates of interest are generally expressed as a *percentage*.

By way of explanation, *r percent* means the ratio $r/100$. Thus,

$$5\% = \frac{5}{100} = 0.05, \qquad 10\% = \frac{10}{100} = 0.1, \qquad 100\% = \frac{100}{100} = 1$$

$$5\frac{3}{4}\% = \frac{5.75}{100} = \frac{575}{10,000} = 0.0575, \qquad 214\% = \frac{214}{100} = 2.14$$

Simple interest **is interest computed on the principal for the entire period it is borrowed.**

If \$250 is borrowed for 9 months at a simple interest rate of 8 percent per annum, what will be the interest charged?

Here, the actual period the money is borrowed for is 9 months or 3/4 of a year. Thus, the interest charged will be the product of the principal ($250) times the annual rate of interest (0.08) times the period of time held in years (3/4). Thus

$$\text{interest charged} = \$(250)(0.08)\left(\frac{3}{4}\right) = \$15$$

In general, if a principal of P dollars is borrowed at a simple interest rate r expressed as a decimal expansion, for a period of n years, the interest I charged is

$$I = P \cdot n \cdot r$$

The amount A owed at the end of a period of time is the sum of the principal and the interest. That is

$$A = P + I = P + P \cdot n \cdot r = P(1 + nr)$$

13.1.2 Example Find the interest and amount if $500 is borrowed for 4 months at a simple interest rate of 10 percent per annum.

Here, the interest I is

$$I = (\$500)\left(\frac{4}{12}\right)(0.10) = \$16.67$$

The amount A due after the 4-month period is

$$A = P + I = \$500.00 + \$16.67 = \$516.67$$

13.1.3 Example A man deposits $5000 in a bank that pays 5 percent per annum every six months. The man will withdraw $500 from his principal plus any interest accrued at each six-month period. How much total interest can he expect to receive?

Here the bank is borrowing $5000 at 5 percent interest and will pay off its debt in 10 equal installments of $500 each every six months. The interest the bank will pay for the first six-month period is

$$I = \$5000\left(\frac{1}{2}\right)(0.05) = \$125$$

For the second six-month period, the principal is $4500. The interest is

$$I = (4500)\left(\frac{1}{2}\right)(0.05) = \$112.50$$

Continuing this way, we have

$$I = (4000)\left(\frac{1}{2}\right)(0.05) = \$100.00$$

. . . .

$$I = (1500) \left(\frac{1}{2}\right) (0.05) = \$37.50$$

$$I = (1000) \left(\frac{1}{2}\right) (0.05) = \$25.00$$

$$I = (500) \left(\frac{1}{2}\right) (0.05) = \$12.50$$

The total interest paid by the bank (received by the man) is

$$125.00 + 112.50 + 100.00 + \cdots + 37.50 + 25.00 + 12.50$$
$$= 12.50 + (12.50)(2) + (12.50)(3) + \cdots + (12.50)(10)$$
$$= (12.50)(1 + 2 + 3 + \cdots + 10)$$
$$= (12.50) \frac{(10)(11)}{2} = \$687.50$$

A trick used in this example and worth knowing is that the sum of the first n positive integers is $n(n + 1)/2$. That is,

$$1 + 2 + 3 + \cdots + n = \frac{n(n + 1)}{2}$$

If the interest due at the end of a unit payment period is added to the principal so that the interest computed for this next unit payment period is based on this new principal amount (old principal plus interest), then the interest is said to have been *compounded*. That is, *compound interest* is simply interest paid on previously earned interest.

Quite often the term *effective rate of interest* is used. This is the equivalent annual rate of interest due to compounding. When interest is compounded annually, there is no difference between the per annum rate and the effective rate; however, when interest is compounded more than once a year, the effective rate always exceeds the per annum rate. The following example illustrates this distinction.

A bank pays 5 percent per annum compounded quarterly. If $200 is placed in a savings account and the quarterly interest is left in the account, how much money is in the account after one year? What is the effective rate of interest?

**13.1.4
Example**

Here, at the first quarter (3 months), the interest earned is

$$I = (\$200) \left(\frac{1}{4}\right) (0.05) = \$2.50$$

The new principal is $P + I = 202.50$. The interest on this principal at the second quarter is

$$I = (202.50) \left(\frac{1}{4}\right) (0.05) = \$2.53$$

The interest at the third quarter on the principal of $205.03 ($202.50 + $2.53) is

$$I = (205.03) \left(\frac{1}{4}\right) (0.05) = \$2.56$$

The interest for the fourth quarter is

$$I = (207.59)\left(\frac{1}{4}\right)(0.05) = \$2.59$$

Thus, after one year, the total in the savings account is $210.18.

To find out what the effective rate of interest rate is, we use the formula $I = P \cdot n \cdot r$. The total interest paid for the one year period is $10.18 on a principal of $200. Thus

$$\$10.18 = (200)(1)(r)$$

Solving for r, we obtain

$$r = 0.0509$$

The effective rate of interest is thus 5.09 percent.

Let us develop a formula for computing the amount when interest is compounded. Suppose the principal is P, the rate of interest per payment period is r (in decimal form), n is the number of payment periods, and A_n is the amount accrued after n payment periods. Then, for the first payment period,

$$A_1 = P + Pr = P(1 + r)$$

For the second payment period, and subsequent ones,

$$A_2 = A_1 + A_1 r = A_1(1 + r) = P(1 + r)(1 + r) = P(1 + r)^2$$
$$A_3 = A_2 + A_2 r = A_2(1 + r) = P(1 + r)^3$$
$$\vdots$$
$$A_n = A_{n-1} + A_{n-1} r = A_{n-1}(1 + r) = P(1 + r)^n$$

The amount A_n accrued on a principal P after n payment periods at r interest (r in decimal form) per payment period is

$$\boxed{A_n = P(1 + r)^n} \tag{13.1.1}$$

Table 1 in the Appendix gives values for $(1 + r)^n$ for typical rates of interest and number of payment periods.

In the compound interest formula (13.1.1), n is the total number of payment periods, while r = per annum rate ÷ number of annual payments.

13.1.5 Example If $300 is invested at 6 percent interest per annum paid (a) yearly (b) semi-annually (c) quarterly (d) daily, what is the value after 4 years?

For this problem, $P = \$300$. The values of n and r vary depending on how often the interest is paid.

(a) Here $P = 300$, $n = 4$, $r = 0.06$. Now, we want to find A_4. Thus, using Table 1 in the Appendix, we obtain

$$A_4 = \$300(1 + 0.06)^4 = (\$300)(1.262477) = 378.74$$

(b) Here, $P = \$300$, $n = 8$ (4 semi-annual payments), and $r = .03$

$(0.06 \div 2)$. We want to find A_8. Now

$$A_8 = \$300(1 + 0.03)^8 = (\$300)(1.26677) = \$380.03$$

(c) Here, $P = \$300$, $n = 16$ (4 quarterly payments), and $r = 0.015$ $(0.06 \div 4)$. We want to find A_{16}. Now

$$A_{16} = \$300(1 + 0.015)^{16} = (\$300)(1.268986) = \$380.70$$

(d) Here $P = \$300$, $n = (365)(4) = 1460$, and $r = 0.06/365 = 0.000165$. For A_{1460} we use a calculator and find

$$A_{1460} = \$300(1 + 0.000165)^{1460} = \$381.37$$

It is worth noting that although the difference between a bank paying interest yearly versus quarterly is fairly substantial, the difference between quarterly compounding and daily compounding is quite insignificant.

For computing the number of payment periods of a loan, we can use the *ordinary interest year* (based on a 360-day year) or the *exact interest year* (based on a 365-day year). In the former, each month has 30 days; in the latter, the exact number of days of the loan is used. In most problems, it will make no difference which measure of time is used; when there is an ambiguity, we shall stipulate what interest year should be used.

The compound interest formula for the amount A_n accrued on a principal P after n payment periods at r interest (r in decimal form) is

$$A_n = P(1 + r)^n$$

If we solve for P in the above formula, we obtain

$$\boxed{P = A_n(1 + r)^{-n}}$$

In this formula, P is called the *present value* of A_n dollars due at the end of n interest periods at a rate of r per interest period. In other words, P is the amount that must be invested for n interest periods at a rate r per interest period in order to accumulate A_n dollars.

Table 2 in the Appendix gives values for $(1 + r)^{-n}$ for typical rates of interest and number of payment periods.

The compound interest formula and the present value formula can be used to solve many different kinds of problems. The examples below illustrate some of these applications.

How much money should be invested at 6 percent per annum so that after 4 years the amount will be $1000 when the interest is compounded (a) annually (b) quarterly (c) daily (always use exact interest year for daily compounding)?

13.1.6
Example

In this problem, we want to find the principal P if we know the amount after 4 years, namely, $1000. Thus, we want the present value of $1000.

(a) Here, $n = 4$, $r = 0.06$, and $A_4 = \$1000$. Now, using Table 2 in the Appendix, we have

$$P = \$1000(1.06)^{-4} = \$1000(0.792094) = \$792.09$$

(b) Here, $n = 16$, $r = 0.015(0.06 \div 4)$, $A_{16} = \$1000$.

Again

$$\$1000 = P(1 + 0.015)^{16}$$
$$P = \$1000(1.015)^{-16} = \$1000(0.788031) = \$788.03$$

(c) Here, $n = 365 \cdot 4 = 1460$, $r = 0.06/365 = 0.000165$ and $A_{1460} = \$1000$. Then

$$\$1000 = P(1 + 0.000165)^{1460}$$
$$P = \$1000(1.000165)^{-1460} = \$786.64$$

13.1.7 Example What annual rate of interest compounded quarterly should one obtain if he wants to double his investment in five years?

Here, if P is the principal, then $A = 2P$ and $n = 4 \cdot 5 = 20$. We want to find r in the equation

$$2P = P(1 + r)^{20}$$
$$2 = (1 + r)^{20}$$
$$1 + r = \sqrt[20]{2}$$

Using Table 4 in the Appendix, we obtain

$$r = \sqrt[20]{2} - 1 = 1.035265 - 1 = 0.035265$$

The annual rate of interest needed to double principal in five years is $4r = 0.141060 = 14.1$ percent.

For the following two examples, a knowledge of logarithms is needed.

13.1.8 Example At 8 percent interest compounded quarterly, how long will it take for a principal to double in value?

In this problem, let P denote the principal. The amount A will then be $2P$. For $r = 0.08/4 = 0.02$, we need to find n in the equation

$$2P = P(1 + 0.02)^n$$
$$2 = (1 + 0.02)^n$$

Using Table 3 in the Appendix, we obtain

$$n = \log_{1.02} 2 = \frac{\log_{10} 2}{\log_{10} 1.02} = \frac{0.3010}{0.0086} = 35$$

Thus, since payments are made quarterly, principal invested at 8 percent compounded quarterly will double in $n/4 = 8.75$ years.

13.1:9 Example How long will it take a principal to double at 16 percent compounded quarterly?

Again, we want to find n in the equation

$$2P = P(1 + 0.04)^n$$
$$2 = (1 + 0.04)^n$$
$$n = \frac{\log_{10} 2}{\log_{10} 1.04} = 17.7$$

Thus, principal will double in $17.7/4 = 4.425$ years if invested at 16 percent compounded quarterly.

Notice from the results of the above two examples that if the interest rate is doubled, the time necessary to double the principal is not halved.

1. Find the interest I and amount A for the following loans
   (a) $420 for 3 months at 6 percent simple interest.
   (b) $6000 for 5 months at 7 percent simple interest.
   (c) $8000 for 18 months at 9 percent simple interest.
   (d) $400 for 10 years at 5 percent simple interest.
   (e) $60 for 2 years 3 months at 5 3/4 percent simple interest.
2. Find the principal P for the following simple interest cases.
   (a) The amount A is $230 at 4 percent at the end of 6 months.
   (b) The amount A is $189.98 at 3 1/2 percent at the end of 18 months.
   (c) The amount A is $183.68 at 8 percent at the end of 2 years, 4 months.
3. Find the amount A accrued for each of the following investments. What is the total interest earned on each investment?
   (a) $250 for 3 years at 6 percent per annum compounded
       (1) semi-annually   (2) quarterly
   (b) $3250 for 2 years 6 months at 6 percent per annum compounded
       (1) semi-annually   (2) quarterly
   (c) $4270 for 5 years 6 months at 8 percent per annum compounded
       (1) semi-annually   (2) quarterly
   (d) $60 for 18 months at 12 percent per annum compounded
       (1) semi-annually   (2) quarterly   (3) monthly
4. What is the effective rate of interest for a rate of 6 percent per annum compounded
   (1) semi-annually   (2) quarterly   (3) monthly?
5. Find the present value of the following:
   (a) The amount is $300 at the end of 3 years at 4 percent per annum compounded
       (1) annually   (2) semi-annually   (3) quarterly
   (b) The amount is $1000 at the end of 2 years at 6 percent per annum compounded
       (1) annually   (2) semi-annually   (3) quarterly
   (c) The amount is $150 at the end of 18 months at 18 percent per annum compounded
       (1) quarterly   (2) monthly
   (d) The amount is $300 at the end of 9 months at 18 percent per annum compounded
       (1) quarterly   (2) monthly
6. A man wants to borrow money for 3 months at 6 percent per annum interest payable in advance. How much should he borrow if he needs $250 immediately?

7. Easy Money Finance Company lends $500 to a man and requires him to repay in $27.50 per month installments of which $25 is for principal and $2.50 is for interest. What is the total amount of money paid to the finance company and what is the rate of interest?

8. Mr. Graff needs to borrow $300 for two years. Which of the following loans should he take: (a) 4.1 percent simple interest or (b) 4 percent per annum compounded semi-annually?

9. What rate of interest compounded semi-annually is needed to double an investment in 5 years?

10. If after two years, a $1000 investment is worth $2000, what is the annual rate of interest?

11. What rate of interest compounded quarterly is needed to double an investment in 4 years?

12. How long does it take for an investment to double at
   (a) 12 percent compounded quarterly?
   (b) 4 percent compounded quarterly?

13. Answer Problem 12 if the investment is to triple in value.

13.2
ANNUITY

An *annuity* is a sequence of equal periodic payments. When the payments are made at the same time the interest is credited, the annuity is termed *ordinary*. We shall only concern ourselves with *ordinary annuities* in this section.

One common example of an ordinary annuity is a life insurance policy—such as 20 payment life. In this example, 20 equal payments or premiums are paid on an annual basis with a fixed interest paid on the anniversary date of the policy. Of course, the *payment period* could have been semi-annual, quarterly, or even monthly instead of yearly. The *term* of the annuity need not be 20 years, but could be any fixed length of time.

13.2.1
Definition

The *amount of an annuity* **is the sum of all payments made plus all interest accumulated.**

13.2.1
Example

Find the amount of an annuity after 5 payments in which the payment is $100 paid on an annual basis at an interest of 5 percent per annum.

After 5 payments, the first $100 payment will have accumulated interest compounded at 5 percent for 4 years. Its value A_1 after 4 years is

$$A_1 = \$100(1 + 0.05)^4 = \$100(1.215506) = \$121.55$$

The second payment of $100, made 1 year after the first payment, will accumulate interest compounded at 5 percent for 3 years. Its value A_2 at the end of the fifth payment is

$$A_2 = \$100(1 + 0.05)^3 = \$100(1.157625) = \$115.76$$

Similarly, the third, fourth, and fifth payments will have the values

$$A_3 = \$100(1 + 0.05)^2 = \$100(1.10250) = \$110.25$$
$$A_4 = \$100(1 + 0.05)^1 = \$100(1.05) = \$105.00$$
$$A_5 = \$100$$

The amount of the annuity after five payments is

$$A_1 + A_2 + A_3 + A_4 + A_5 = \$121.55 + \$115.76$$
$$+ \$110.25 + \$105.00 + \$100.00 = \$552.56$$

To develop a formula for the amount of an annuity, suppose $1.00 is the payment for an annuity whose interest is r percent per payment period (in decimal form) and whose term is n payment periods. The first payment will accumulate the value A_1 compounded over $n - 1$ periods at r percent per payment of an annuity whose interest is r per payment period (in decimal form) and whose term is n payment periods. The second payment will accumulate the value A_2 compounded over $n - 2$ periods at r percent per payment period, and so on. Then

$$A_1 = \$1(1 + r)^{n-1}, \qquad A_2 = \$1(1 + r)^{n-2}, \ldots, A_n = \$1(1 + r)^0 = \$1$$

The total amount of the annuity, after n payment periods denoted by $s_{\overline{n}|r}$,[1] is

$$s_{\overline{n}|r} = A_1 + \cdots + A_n = (1 + r)^{n-1} + (1 + r)^{n-2} + \cdots + (1 + r) + 1$$

$$= [1 + (1 + r) + \cdots + (1 + r)^{n-1}]$$

$$= \frac{[1 + (1 + r) + \cdots + (1 + r)^{n-1}][1 - (1 + r)]}{1 - (1 + r)}$$

$$= \frac{[1 - (1 + r)^n]}{-r} = \frac{[(1 + r)^n - 1]}{r}$$

Thus, if P represents the payment in dollars made at each payment period for an annuity at r percent interest per payment period, the amount A of the annuity after n payment periods is

$$\boxed{A = \$P \cdot s_{\overline{n}|r}}$$

Some values for $s_{\overline{n}|r}$ are found in Table 5 in the Appendix.

Find the amount of an annuity of $100 per year at 5 percent after 5 payments.
    Here $P = \$100$ and $s_{\overline{5}|0.05} = 5.525631$. Thus, the amount A is

$$A = P \cdot s_{\overline{5}|0.05} = \$100(5.525631) = \$552.56$$

13.2.2
Example

Mary decides to put aside $100 every 3 months in a savings account that pays 5 percent quarterly. After making 7 deposits, how much money does Mary have?

13.2.3
Example

[1] $s_{\overline{n}|r}$ is sometimes read as "s angle n at r."

This is an annuity problem in which $P = \$100$. To find the amount after 7 payments, we need to look up in Table 5 the value of $s_{\overline{7}|0.0125}$. Now, $s_{\overline{7}|0.0125} = 7.268037$. Thus, the amount A of money after seven deposits is

$$A = P \cdot s_{\overline{7}|0.0125} = \$100(7.268037) = \$726.80$$

**13.2.4
Example**

To save for his son's college education, Mr. Graff decides to put aside every 6 months an amount of $50 in a time-deposit bank account paying 6 percent interest semi-annually. If he begins this savings program when his son is 6 months old, how much will he have saved by the time his son is 18 years old?

When his son is 18 years old, Mr. Graff will have made his 36th payment. The rate per payment period is 0.03. The principal P is $50 and $s_{\overline{36}|0.03} = 63.275942$. The amount A saved is

$$A = 50 \cdot s_{\overline{36}|}0.03 = \$50(63.275942) = \$3163.80$$

**13.2.2
Definition**

The *present value* of an annuity is the sum of the present values of the payments.

Thus the present value of an annuity is the amount of money needed now so that if it is invested at r percent, n equal payments can be withdrawn without any money left over.

**13.2.5
Example**

Compute the present value of an annuity of $100 per year at 5 percent after 5 payments.

After the first payment, the present value V_2 is

$$V_1 = \$100(1 + 0.05)^{-1} = \$100(0.952381) = \$95.24$$

After the second payment, the present value V_2 for the second payment is

$$V_2 = \$100(1 + 0.05)^{-2} = \$100(0.907029) = \$90.70$$

Similarly

$$V_3 = \$100(1 + 0.05)^{-3} = \$100(0.0863838) = \$86.38$$
$$V_4 = \$100(1 + 0.05)^{-4} = \$100(0.822702) = \$82.27$$
$$V_5 = \$100(1 + 0.05)^{-5} = \$100(0.783526) = \$78.35$$

The present value V after 5 payments is

$$V = V_1 + V_2 + V_3 + V_4 + V_5 = \$95.24 + \$90.70$$
$$+ \$86.38 + \$82.27 + \$78.35 = \$432.94$$

Thus, a man needs $432.94 now invested at 5 percent per annum in order to withdraw $100 per year for the next 5 years.

Figure 13.1 illustrates the results of Example 13.2.5.

To develop a formula for present values, suppose $1.00 is the payment for an annuity whose interest rate is r percent per payment period (in decimal

Payment	Present Value
1st	$100(1.05)^{-1} = \$95.24$
2nd	$100(1.05)^{-2} = \$90.70$
3rd	$100(1.05)^{-3} = \$86.38$
4th	$100(1.05)^{-4} = \$82.27$
5th	$100(1.05)^{-5} = \$78.35$
Total	$432.94

Figure 13.1

form) and whose term is n payment periods. Then the present value V_1 of the first payment is

$$V_1 = (1 + r)^{-1}$$

The present value V_2 for the second payment is

$$V_2 = (1 + r)^{-2}$$

The present value V_n for the nth payment is

$$V_n = (1 + r)^{-n}$$

The total present value $a_{\overline{n}|r}$[2] of the annuity is

$$a_{\overline{n}|r} = V_1 + \cdots + V_n = (1 + r)^{-1} + \cdots + (1 + r)^{-n}$$
$$= (1 + r)^{-n}[1 + (1 + r) + \cdots + (1 + r)^{n-1}]$$
$$= \frac{1 - (1 + r)^n}{1 - (1 + r)}(1 + r)^{-n} = \frac{(1 + r)^n - 1}{r(1 + r)^n}$$

Thus, if P represents the payment made in dollars, the present value V of the annuity at a rate r per payment period for n payment periods is

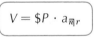

$$V = \$P \cdot a_{\overline{n}|r}$$

Some values for $a_{\overline{n}|r}$ are found in Table 6 in the Appendix.

Find the present value of an annuity of $100 per year at 5 percent after 5 payments.

13.2.6
Example

   Here, $P = \$100$ and $a_{\overline{5}|0.05} = 4.329477$. Then the present value V is

$$V = \$100 a_{\overline{5}|0.05} = \$100(4.329477) = \$432.95$$

A man agrees to pay $150 per month for 30 months to pay off a used car loan. If the interest of 18 percent per annum is charged monthly, how much did the car originally cost? How much interest was paid?

13.2.7
Example

---

[2] $a_{\overline{n}|r}$ is sometimes read as "a angle n at r."

This is the same as asking for the present value V of an annuity of $150 per month at 18 percent for 30 months. The original cost of the car is

$$V = \$150a_{\overline{30}|0.015} = \$150(24.015838)$$
$$= \$3602.38$$

The total payment is $(\$150)(30) = \$4500$. Thus the interest paid is

$$\$4500 - \$3602.38 = \$897.62$$

1. Find the amount and present value of the following annuities.
   (a) $1500 after 15 years at 6 percent compounded annually.
   (b) $600 after 10 years at 8 percent compounded semi-annually.
   (c) $9000 after 6 years at 12 percent compounded quarterly.
   (d) $10,000 after 8 years at 6 percent compounded quarterly.
   (e) $400 after 5 years at 12 percent compounded semi-annually.

2. Find the payment for the following annuities to obtain a present value of
   (a) $1000 after 5 years at 6 percent annually
   (b) $2000 after 3 years at 12 percent semi-annually
   (c) $6000 after 5 years at 10 percent semi-annually
   (d) $1500 after 4 years at 12 percent quarterly
   (e) $4000 after 12 years at 8 percent quarterly

3. For the data of Problem 2, what payments are needed to obtain these sums as the amount of the annuity?

4. Mike each month deposits $10 in a special account paying 1/2 percent per month interest. How much is in Mike's account after 5 years?

5. How much should Mr. Graff put aside every quarter at 8 percent (paid quarterly) for his son's college education if he anticipates needing a total of $20,000 in 15 years?

6. Do Problem 5 if the rate of interest is 6 percent paid quarterly.

7. A man at age 65 can expect to live for 15 years. If he can invest at 6 percent per annum compounded quarterly, how much does he need now to guarantee himself $250 every three months for the next 15 years?

8. A woman at age 65 can expect to live for 19 years. If she can invest at 6 percent per annum compounded quarterly, how much does she need now to guarantee herself $200 every three months for the next 19 years?

A loan with a fixed rate of interest is said to be *amortized* if both principal and interest are paid by a sequence of equal payments made over equal periods of time.

When a loan of V dollars is amortized at a particular rate r of interest per payment period over n payment periods, the question is what is the payment P? In other words, in amortization problems, we want to find the amount of payment P which after n payment periods at r percent interest per payment period gives us a present value equal to the amount of the loan. Thus, we need to find P in

$$V = P \cdot a_{\overline{n}|r}$$

Since we are interested in P, we can solve for P obtaining

$$P = V \cdot \frac{1}{a_{\overline{n}|r}}$$

In the Appendix, Table 7 gives typical values for $1/a_{\overline{n}|r}$.

What monthly payment is necessary to pay off a loan of $800 at 18 percent per annum in two years? In three years?

13.3.1
Example

For the two-year loan, $V = \$800$, $n = 24$, $r = 0.015$. Now, the monthly payment P is

$$P = \$800 \left(\frac{1}{a_{\overline{24}|0.015}} \right) = \$800(0.049924) = \$39.94$$

For the three-year loan, $V = \$800$, $n = 36$, $r = 0.015$
The monthly payment P is

$$P = \$800 \left(\frac{1}{a_{\overline{36}|0.015}} \right) = \$800(0.036152) = \$28.92$$

For the two-year loan, the total amount paid out is $(\$39.94)(24) = \$958.56$; for the three-year loan, the total amount paid out is $(\$26.92)(36) = \$969.12$. It should be clear that the longer the term of a debt, the more it costs the borrower to pay off the loan.

Mr. and Mrs. Corey have just purchased a $35,000 house and have made a down payment of $10,000. They can amortize the balance ($25,000) at 9 percent for 7 years. What are the monthly payments? What is their total interest payment? After 3 years, what equity do they have in their house?

13.3.2
Example

The monthly payment V needed to pay off the loan of $25,000 at 9 percent for 7 years is

$$V = \$25,000 \left(\frac{1}{a_{\overline{84}|0.0075}} \right)$$
$$= \$25,000(0.016089) = \$402.23$$

The total paid out for the loan is

$$(\$402.23)(84) = \$33,787.32$$

Thus, the interest on this loan amounted to $8,787.32.
After three years, (36 months), the present value of the loan is

$$(\$402.23) \cdot a_{\overline{48}|0.0075} = (\$402.23)(40.184780)$$
$$= \$16,163.52$$

Thus, the equity after three years is

$$\$25,000 - \$16,163.52 = \$8836.48$$

13.3.3
Example

When Mr. Nicholson died, he left an inheritance of $15,000 for his family to be paid to them over a ten-year period in equal amounts at the end of each year. If the $15,000 is invested at 6 percent what is the annual payout to the family?

This example asks what annual payment is needed at 6 percent for 10 years to give a total of $15,000. That is, we can think of the $15,000 as a loan amortized at 6 percent for 10 years. The payment needed to pay off the loan is the yearly amount Mr. Nicholson's family will receive. Thus, the yearly payout P is

$$P = (\$15,000)\left(\frac{1}{a_{\overline{10}|0.06}}\right) = (\$15,000)(0.135868)$$

$$= \$2038.02$$

Quite often, a person with a debt decides to accumulate sufficient funds to pay off his debt by agreeing to set aside enough money each month (or quarter or year) so that when the debt becomes payable the money set aside each month plus the interest earned equals the debt. The kind of fund created by such a plan is called a *sinking fund.* Companies use sinking funds to accumulate capital for the purpose of purchasing new equipment.

We shall limit our discussion of sinking funds to those in which equal payments are made at equal time intervals. Usually, too, the debtor agrees to pay interest on his debt as a separate item so that the amount necessary in a sinking fund need only equal the amount he originally borrows.

13.3.4
Example

A man borrows $3000 and agrees to pay interest quarterly at an annual rate of 8 percent. At the same time, he sets up a sinking fund in order to repay the loan at the end of 5 years. If the sinking fund earns interest at the rate of 6 percent compounded semi-annually, find the size of each semi-annual sinking fund deposit. Construct a table showing the growth of the sinking fund.

The quarterly interest payments due on the debt are

$$\$3000(0.02) = \$60$$

The size of the sinking deposit is calculated by using the formula

$$A = P s_{\overline{n}|r}$$

in which A represents the amount to be saved, and P is the payment. Thus

$$P = \$3000 \, \frac{1}{s_{\overline{n}|r}}$$

where $n = 10$ and $r = 0.03$. Values for $\dfrac{1}{s_{\overline{n}|r}}$ are found in Table 8 of the Appendix. Thus

$$P = \$3000\,\frac{1}{s_{\overline{10}|0.03}}$$
$$= \$3000(0.087231)$$
$$= \$261.69$$

Thus, semi-annual sinking fund payments of $261.69 are needed.
The growth of the sinking fund is given in Figure 13.2.

Payment	Interest	Sinking Fund Deposit	Total
0	—	—	—
1	—0—	261.69	261.69
2	7.85	261.69	531.23
3	15.94	261.69	808.86
4	24.27	261.69	1094.82
5	32.84	261.69	1389.35
6	41.68	261.69	1692.72
7	50.78	261.69	2005.19
8	60.16	261.69	2327.04
9	69.81	261.69	2658.54
10	79.76	261.69	2999.99

Figure 13.2

A gold mine is expected to yield an annual net return of $20,000 for the next 10 years, after which it will be worthless. An investor wants an annual return on his investment of 8 percent. If he can establish a sinking fund earning 5 percent annually, how much should he be willing to pay for the mine?   **13.3.5 Example**

Let P denote the purchase price. Then $0.08P$ represents an 8 percent return on investment. The quantity $P1/s_{\overline{10}|0.05}$ represents the annual payment into the sinking fund needed to obtain the amount P in 10 years. The investor should be willing to pay an amount P so that

$$0.08P + P\,\frac{1}{s_{\overline{10}|0.05}} = \$20,000$$
$$0.08P + 0.079505P = \$20,000$$
$$0.159505P = \$20,000$$
$$P = \$125,388 \text{ (rounded off to nearest dollar)}$$

13.3 Exercise

1. What quarterly payment is needed to pay off a loan of $10,000 amortized after 10 years at 8 percent?
2. What monthly payment is needed to pay off a loan of $500 amortized at 1 1/2 percent per month for 2 years?

3. For the data of Example 13.3.2, what is Mr. and Mrs. Corey's equity after 4 years? After 6 years?

4. For Example 13.3.2, if Mr. and Mrs. Corey amortize their $25,000 loan at 6 percent for 8 years, what is their monthly payment?

5. In Example 13.3.3, if Mr. Nicholson left $15,000 to be paid over 20 years in equal yearly payments and if this amount were invested at 8 percent, what would the annual payout be?

6. A man has a sum of $30,000 that he invests at 8 percent quarterly. What equal quarterly payments can he receive over a 10-year period? Over a 20-year period?

7. A company establishes a sinking fund to provide for the payment of $100,000 debt, maturing in 4 years. Contributions to the fund are to be made at the end of every 6 months. Find the amount of each semiannual deposit if interest is at 8 percent compounded semi-annually. Construct a sinking fund schedule.

8. A state has $5,000,000 worth of toll-way bonds that are due in 20 years. A sinking fund is established to pay off the debt. If the state can earn 5 percent annually on its money, what is the annual sinking fund deposit needed?

9. An investor wishes to know the amount he should pay for an oil well expected to yield an annual return of $30,000 for the next 30 years, after which the well will be dry. Find the amount he should pay to yield him a 10 percent annual return if a sinking fund earns 6 percent annually.

CHAPTER REVIEW		
Important Terms	interest	compound interest formula
	simple interest	annuity
	compound interest	ordinary annuity
	principal	payment period
	rate of interest	amount of annuity
	per annum	present value of annuity
	amount	amortization
	effective annual rate of interest	equity
	present value	sinking fund

Exercises

1. Find the interest (I) and amount (A) if $400 is borrowed for 9 months at 12 percent simple interest.

2. Dan borrows $500 at 9 percent per annum simple interest for 1 year 2 months. What is the interest charged and what is the amount of the loan?

3. Find the amount of an investment of $100 after 2 years 3 months at 8 percent compounded quarterly.

4. Mike places $200 in a savings account that pays 5 percent per annum compounded quarterly. How much is in his account after 9 months?

5. Find the effective annual rate of interest for 8 percent compounded quarterly.

6. What rate of interest compounded annually should one obtain if he wants to double his investment in 10 years?

7. A car dealer offers Mike the choice of two loans:
   a. $3000 for 3 years at 18 percent per annum simple interest;
   b. $3000 for 3 years at 16 percent per annum compounded quarterly.
   Which loan costs Mike least?

8. a. What annual rate of interest compounded quarterly is needed to double an investment in 5 years?
   b. A bank pays 4 percent per annum compounded quarterly. How much should I invest now so that 2 years from now I will have $100.00 in the account?

9. Katy wants to buy a bicycle that costs $75 and will purchase it in 6 months. How much should she put in her savings account for this if she can get 6 percent per annum compounded monthly?

10. What annual rate of interest will double an investment in 6 years if the investment is placed in an account that receives interest compounded semiannually?

11. Mike decides he needs $500.00 6 years from now to buy a cheap car. If he can invest at 6 percent compounded quarterly, how much should he save every three months to buy the car?

12. Mr. and Mrs. Corey are newlyweds and want to purchase a home, but need a down payment of $10,000. If they want to buy their home in two years, how much should they save each month in their savings account that pays 6 percent per annum compounded monthly?

13. Mr. and Mrs. Corey have just purchased a $40,000 home and made a 25 percent down payment. The balance can be amortized at 9 percent for 8 years and 4 months. What are the monthly payments? How much interest will be paid? What is their equity after 2 years?

14. Mike has just purchased a used car on time and will make equal payments of $50 per month for 18 months at 12 percent per annum charged monthly. How much did the car actually cost?

15. An inheritance of $25,000 is to be paid on equal amounts over a 5-year period at the end of each year. If the $25,000 can be invested at 8 percent per annum, what is the annual payment?

16. A mortgage of $25,000 is to be amortized at 9 percent per annum for 8 years. What are the monthly payments?

17. A state has $8,000,000 worth construction bonds that are due in 25 years. What annual sinking fund deposit is needed if the state can earn 6 percent per annum on its money?

18. How much should Mr. Graff pay for a gold mine expected to yield an annual return of $20,000 that has a life expectancy of 20 years, if he wants to have a 15 percent annual return on his investment and he can set up a sinking fund that earns 7 percent a year?

19. Mr. Doody at age 70 is expected to live for 12 years. If he can invest at 8 percent per annum compounded quarterly, how much does he need now to guarantee himself every three months $300 for the next 12 years?

20. An oil well is expected to yield an annual net return of $25,000 for the next 15 years, after which it will run dry. An investor wants a return on his investment of 10 percent. He can establish a sinking fund earning 7 percent annually. How much should he pay for the oil well?

Additional Reading

Kemeny, J., Schleifer, A., Snell, J., and Thompson, G., *Finite Mathematics with Business Applications*, Englewood, N. J.: Prentice-Hall, Inc., 1962.

Mouzon, E., and Rees, P., *Mathematics of Finance,* Boston: Ginn and Company, 1952.

Simpson, T., Pirenian, Z. and Crenshaw, B., *Mathematics of Finance,* Englewood, N. J.: Prentice-Hall, Inc., 1951.

Tabor, O., *Mathematics of Finance,* Cambridge, Mass.: Addison-Wesley Press, Inc., 1952.

Tables Appendix

Table 1

$(1 + r)^n$

r = rate of interest per payment period; n = number of payment periods

n	¼%	½%	¾%	1%	1¼%
1	1.002500	1.005000	1.007500	1.010000	1.012500
2	1.005006	1.010025	1.015056	1.020100	1.025156
3	1.007519	1.015075	1.022669	1.030301	1.037971
4	1.010038	1.020151	1.030339	1.040604	1.050945
5	1.012563	1.025251	1.038067	1.051010	1.064082
6	1.015094	1.030378	1.045852	1.061520	1.077383
7	1.017632	1.035529	1.053696	1.072135	1.090850
8	1.020176	1.040707	1.061599	1.082857	1.104486
9	1.022726	1.045911	1.069561	1.093685	1.118292
10	1.025283	1.051140	1.077583	1.104622	1.132271
11	1.027846	1.056396	1.085664	1.115668	1.146424
12	1.030416	1.061678	1.093807	1.126825	1.160755
13	1.032992	1.066986	1.102010	1.138093	1.175264
14	1.035574	1.072321	1.110276	1.149474	1.189955
15	1.038163	1.077683	1.118603	1.160969	1.204829
16	1.040759	1.083071	1.126992	1.172579	1.219890
17	1.043361	1.088487	1.135445	1.184304	1.235138
18	1.045969	1.093929	1.143960	1.196147	1.250577
19	1.048584	1.099399	1.152540	1.208109	1.266210
20	1.051205	1.104896	1.161184	1.220190	1.282037
21	1.053833	1.110420	1.169893	1.232392	1.298063
22	1.056468	1.115972	1.178667	1.244716	1.314288
23	1.059109	1.121552	1.187507	1.257163	1.330717
24	1.061757	1.127160	1.196414	1.269735	1.347351
25	1.064411	1.132796	1.205387	1.282432	1.364193
26	1.067072	1.138460	1.214427	1.295256	1.381245
27	1.069740	1.144152	1.223535	1.308209	1.398511
28	1.072414	1.149873	1.232712	1.321291	1.415992
29	1.075096	1.155622	1.241957	1.334504	1.433692
30	1.077783	1.161400	1.251272	1.347849	1.451613
31	1.080478	1.167207	1.260656	1.361327	1.469758
32	1.083179	1.173043	1.270111	1.374941	1.488130
33	1.085887	1.178908	1.279637	1.388690	1.506732
34	1.088602	1.184803	1.289234	1.402577	1.525566
35	1.091323	1.190727	1.298904	1.416603	1.544636
36	1.094051	1.196681	1.308645	1.430769	1.563944
37	1.096786	1.202664	1.318460	1.445076	1.583493
38	1.099528	1.208677	1.328349	1.459527	1.603287
39	1.102277	1.214721	1.338311	1.474122	1.623328
40	1.105033	1.220794	1.348349	1.488864	1.643619
41	1.107796	1.226898	1.358461	1.503752	1.664165
42	1.110565	1.233033	1.368650	1.518790	1.684967
43	1.113341	1.239198	1.378915	1.533978	1.706029
44	1.116125	1.245394	1.389256	1.549318	1.727354
45	1.118915	1.251621	1.399676	1.564811	1.748946
46	1.121712	1.257879	1.410173	1.580459	1.770808
47	1.124517	1.264168	1.420750	1.596263	1.792943
48	1.127328	1.270489	1.431405	1.612226	1.815355
49	1.130146	1.276842	1.442141	1.628348	1.838047
50	1.132972	1.283226	1.452957	1.644632	1.861022

n	¼%	½%	¾%	1%	1¼%
51	1.135804	1.289642	1.463854	1.661078	1.884285
52	1.138644	1.296090	1.474833	1.677688	1.907839
53	1.141490	1.302571	1.485894	1.694466	1.931687
54	1.144344	1.309083	1.497038	1.711410	1.955833
55	1.147205	1.315629	1.508266	1.728525	1.980281
56	1.150073	1.322207	1.519578	1.745810	2.005034
57	1.152948	1.328818	1.530975	1.763268	2.030097
58	1.155830	1.335462	1.542457	1.780901	2.055473
59	1.158720	1.342139	1.554026	1.798710	2.081167
60	1.161617	1.348850	1.565681	1.816697	2.107181
61	1.164521	1.355594	1.577424	1.834864	2.133521
62	1.167432	1.362372	1.589254	1.853212	2.160190
63	1.170351	1.369184	1.601174	1.871744	2.187192
64	1.173277	1.376030	1.613182	1.890462	2.214532
65	1.176210	1.382910	1.625281	1.909366	2.242214
66	1.179150	1.389825	1.637471	1.928460	2.270242
67	1.182098	1.396774	1.649752	1.947745	2.298620
68	1.185053	1.403758	1.662125	1.967222	2.327352
69	1.188016	1.410777	1.674591	1.986894	2.356444
70	1.190986	1.417831	1.687151	2.006763	2.385900
71	1.193963	1.424920	1.699804	2.026831	2.415724
72	1.196948	1.432044	1.712553	2.047099	2.445920
73	1.199941	1.439205	1.725397	2.067570	2.476494
74	1.202941	1.446401	1.738337	2.088246	2.507450
75	1.205948	1.453633	1.751375	2.109128	2.538793
76	1.208963	1.460901	1.764510	2.130220	2.570528
77	1.211985	1.468205	1.777744	2.151522	2.602660
78	1.215015	1.475546	1.791077	2.173037	2.635193
79	1.218053	1.482924	1.804510	2.194767	2.668133
80	1.221098	1.490339	1.818044	2.216715	2.701485
81	1.224151	1.497790	1.831679	2.238882	2.735253
82	1.227211	1.505279	1.845417	2.261271	2.769444
83	1.230279	1.512806	1.859257	2.283884	2.804062
84	1.233355	1.520370	1.873202	2.306723	2.839113
85	1.236438	1.527972	1.887251	2.329790	2.874602
86	1.239529	1.535611	1.901405	2.353088	2.910534
87	1.242628	1.543289	1.915666	2.376619	2.946916
88	1.245735	1.551006	1.930033	2.400385	2.983752
89	1.248849	1.558761	1.944509	2.424389	3.021049
90	1.251971	1.566555	1.959092	2.448633	3.058812
91	1.255101	1.574387	1.973786	2.473119	3.097048
92	1.258239	1.582259	1.988589	2.497850	3.135761
93	1.261384	1.590171	2.003503	2.522829	3.174958
94	1.264538	1.598122	2.018530	2.548057	3.214645
95	1.267699	1.606112	2.033669	2.573537	3.254828
96	1.270868	1.614143	2.048921	2.599273	3.295513
97	1.274046	1.622213	2.064288	2.625266	3.336707
98	1.277231	1.630325	2.079770	2.651518	3.378416
99	1.280424	1.638476	2.095368	2.678033	3.420646
100	1.283625	1.646669	2.111084	2.704814	3.463404

Table 1 (continued)

n	1½%	1¾%	2%	2½%	3%
1	1.015000	1.017500	1.020000	1.025000	1.030000
2	1.030225	1.035306	1.040400	1.050625	1.060900
3	1.045678	1.053424	1.061208	1.076891	1.092727
4	1.061364	1.071859	1.082432	1.103813	1.125509
5	1.077284	1.090617	1.104081	1.131408	1.159274
6	1.093443	1.109702	1.126162	1.159693	1.194052
7	1.109845	1.129122	1.148686	1.188686	1.229874
8	1.126493	1.148882	1.171659	1.218403	1.266770
9	1.143390	1.168987	1.195093	1.248863	1.304773
10	1.160541	1.189444	1.218994	1.280085	1.343916
11	1.177949	1.210260	1.243374	1.312087	1.384234
12	1.195618	1.231439	1.268242	1.344889	1.425761
13	1.213552	1.252989	1.293607	1.378511	1.468534
14	1.231756	1.274917	1.319479	1.412974	1.512590
15	1.250232	1.297228	1.345868	1.448298	1.557967
16	1.268986	1.319929	1.372786	1.484506	1.604706
17	1.288020	1.343028	1.400241	1.521618	1.652848
18	1.307341	1.366531	1.428246	1.559659	1.702433
19	1.326951	1.390445	1.456811	1.598650	1.753506
20	1.346855	1.414778	1.485947	1.638616	1.806111
21	1.367058	1.439537	1.515666	1.679582	1.860295
22	1.387564	1.464729	1.545980	1.721571	1.916103
23	1.408377	1.490361	1.576899	1.764611	1.973586
24	1.429503	1.516443	1.608437	1.808726	2.032794
25	1.450945	1.542981	1.640606	1.853944	2.093778
26	1.472710	1.569983	1.673418	1.900293	2.156591
27	1.494800	1.597457	1.706886	1.947800	2.221289
28	1.517222	1.625413	1.741024	1.996495	2.287928
29	1.539981	1.653858	1.775845	2.046407	2.356565
30	1.563080	1.682800	1.811362	2.097568	2.427262
31	1.586526	1.712249	1.847589	2.150007	2.500080
32	1.610324	1.742213	1.884541	2.203757	2.575083
33	1.634479	1.772702	1.922231	2.258851	2.652335
34	1.658996	1.803724	1.960676	2.315322	2.731905
35	1.683881	1.835290	1.999889	2.373205	2.813862
36	1.709140	1.867407	2.039887	2.432535	2.898278
37	1.734777	1.900087	2.080685	2.493349	2.985227
38	1.760798	1.933338	2.122299	2.555682	3.074783
39	1.787210	1.967172	2.164745	2.619574	3.167027
40	1.814018	2.001597	2.208040	2.685064	3.262038
41	1.841229	2.036625	2.252200	2.752190	3.359899
42	1.868847	2.072266	2.297244	2.820995	3.460696
43	1.896880	2.108531	2.343189	2.891520	3.564517
44	1.925333	2.145333	2.390053	2.963808	3.671452
45	1.954213	2.182975	2.437854	3.037902	3.781596
46	1.983526	2.221177	2.486611	3.113851	3.895044
47	2.013279	2.260048	2.536343	3.191697	4.011895
48	2.043478	2.299599	2.587070	3.271489	4.132252
49	2.074130	2.339842	2.638812	3.353277	4.256219
50	2.105242	2.380789	2.691588	3.437109	4.381906
51	2.136821	2.422453	2.745420	3.523036	4.515423
52	2.168873	2.464846	2.800328	3.611112	4.650886
53	2.201406	2.507980	2.856335	3.701390	4.790412
54	2.234428	2.551870	2.913461	3.793925	4.934125
55	2.267944	2.596528	2.971731	3.888773	5.082148
56	2.301963	2.641967	3.031165	3.985992	5.234613
57	2.336493	2.688201	3.091788	4.085642	5.391651
58	2.371540	2.735245	3.153624	4.187783	5.553401
59	2.407113	2.783112	3.216697	4.292478	5.720003
60	2.443220	2.831816	3.281031	4.399790	5.891603
61	2.479868	2.881373	3.346651	4.509784	6.068351
62	2.517066	2.931797	3.413584	4.622529	6.250402
63	2.554822	2.983103	3.481856	4.738092	6.437914
64	2.593144	3.035308	3.551493	4.856544	6.631051
65	2.632042	3.088426	3.622523	4.977958	6.829982
66	2.671522	3.142473	3.694973	5.102407	7.034882
67	2.711595	3.197466	3.768873	5.229967	7.245928
68	2.752269	3.253422	3.844250	5.360716	7.463306
69	2.793553	3.310357	3.921135	5.494734	7.687205
70	2.835456	3.368288	3.999558	5.632103	7.917822
71	2.877988	3.427233	4.079549	5.772905	8.155356
72	2.921158	3.487210	4.161140	5.917228	8.400017
73	2.964975	3.548236	4.244363	6.065158	8.652017
74	3.009450	3.610330	4.329250	6.216787	8.911578
75	3.054592	3.673511	4.415835	6.372207	9.178925
76	3.100411	3.737797	4.504152	6.531512	9.454293
77	3.146917	3.803209	4.594235	6.694800	9.737922
78	3.194120	3.869765	4.686120	6.862170	10.030060
79	3.242032	3.937486	4.779842	7.033724	10.330961
80	3.290663	4.006392	4.875439	7.209567	10.640890
81	3.340023	4.076504	4.972948	7.389806	10.960117
82	3.390123	4.147842	5.072407	7.574552	11.288920
83	3.440975	4.220430	5.173855	7.763915	11.627588
84	3.492590	4.294287	5.277332	7.958013	11.976416
85	3.544978	4.369437	5.382878	8.156964	12.335708
86	3.598153	4.445902	5.490536	8.360888	12.705779
87	3.652125	4.523706	5.600347	8.569910	13.086953
88	3.706907	4.602870	5.712354	8.784158	13.479561
89	3.762511	4.683421	5.826601	9.003762	13.883948
90	3.818948	4.765380	5.943133	9.228856	14.300466
91	3.876233	4.848775	6.061995	9.459577	14.729480
92	3.934376	4.933628	6.183235	9.696066	15.171365
93	3.993392	5.019967	6.306900	9.938468	15.626506
94	4.053293	5.107816	6.433038	10.186930	16.095301
95	4.114092	5.197203	6.561699	10.441603	16.578160
96	4.175804	5.288154	6.692933	10.702643	17.075505
97	4.238441	5.380697	6.826791	10.970209	17.587770
98	4.302017	5.474859	6.963327	11.244464	18.115403
99	4.366547	5.570669	7.102594	11.525576	18.658865
100	4.432046	5.668156	7.244645	11.813715	19.218631

Table 1 (continued)

n	3½%	4%	4½%	5%	5½%
1	1.035000	1.040000	1.045000	1.050000	1.055000
2	1.071225	1.081600	1.092025	1.102500	1.113025
3	1.108718	1.124864	1.141166	1.157625	1.174241
4	1.147523	1.169859	1.192519	1.215506	1.238825
5	1.187686	1.216653	1.246182	1.276282	1.306960
6	1.229225	1.265319	1.302260	1.340096	1.378843
7	1.272279	1.315932	1.360862	1.407100	1.454679
8	1.316809	1.368569	1.422101	1.477455	1.534687
9	1.362897	1.423321	1.486095	1.551328	1.619094
10	1.410599	1.480244	1.552969	1.628895	1.708144
11	1.459970	1.539454	1.622853	1.710339	1.802092
12	1.511069	1.601032	1.695881	1.795856	1.901207
13	1.563956	1.665073	1.772196	1.885649	2.005774
14	1.618695	1.731676	1.851945	1.979932	2.116091
15	1.675349	1.800943	1.935282	2.078928	2.232476
16	1.733986	1.872981	2.022370	2.182875	2.355263
17	1.794676	1.947900	2.113377	2.292018	2.484802
18	1.857489	2.025816	2.208479	2.406619	2.621466
19	1.922501	2.106849	2.307860	2.526950	2.765647
20	1.989789	2.191123	2.411714	2.653298	2.917757
21	2.059431	2.278768	2.520241	2.785963	3.078234
22	2.131512	2.369919	2.633652	2.925261	3.247537
23	2.206114	2.464715	2.752166	3.071524	3.426152
24	2.283328	2.563304	2.876014	3.225100	3.614590
25	2.363245	2.665836	3.005434	3.386355	3.813392
26	2.445959	2.772470	3.140679	3.555673	4.023125
27	2.531567	2.883368	3.282010	3.733456	4.244401
28	2.620172	2.998703	3.429700	3.920129	4.477843
29	2.711878	3.118651	3.584037	4.116136	4.724124
30	2.806794	3.243397	3.745318	4.321942	4.983951
31	2.905031	3.373133	3.913857	4.538039	5.258068
32	3.006708	3.508059	4.089981	4.764941	5.547262
33	3.111942	3.648381	4.274030	5.003188	5.852362
34	3.220860	3.794316	4.466362	5.253348	6.174242
35	3.333590	3.946089	4.667348	5.516015	6.513825
36	3.450266	4.103932	4.877376	5.791816	6.872085
37	3.571025	4.268090	5.096861	6.081407	7.250050
38	3.696011	4.438813	5.326119	6.385477	7.648803
39	3.825372	4.616366	5.565899	6.704751	8.069487
40	3.959260	4.801020	5.816365	7.039989	8.513309
41	4.097834	4.993061	6.078101	7.391988	8.981541
42	4.241258	5.192784	6.351616	7.761587	9.475525
43	4.389702	5.400495	6.637438	8.149667	9.996679
44	4.543341	5.616515	6.936123	8.557150	10.546496
45	4.702358	5.841175	7.248048	8.985008	11.126521
46	4.866941	6.074822	7.574420	9.434258	11.738554
47	5.037284	6.317815	7.915269	9.905727	12.384132
48	5.213589	6.570528	8.271456	10.401269	13.065260
49	5.396064	6.833349	8.643671	10.921333	13.783849
50	5.584927	7.106683	9.032636	11.467400	14.541961

n	3½%	4%	4½%	5%	5½%
51	5.780399	7.390950	9.439105	12.040770	15.341768
52	5.982713	7.686588	9.863865	12.642808	16.185566
53	6.192108	7.994052	10.307739	13.274948	17.075772
54	6.408832	8.313814	10.771587	13.938696	18.014939
55	6.633141	8.646306	11.256308	14.635631	19.005761
56	6.865301	8.992221	11.762842	15.367412	20.051079
57	7.105586	9.351910	12.292170	16.135783	21.153887
58	7.354282	9.725986	12.845318	16.942572	22.317351
59	7.611682	10.115026	13.423357	17.789700	23.544805
60	7.878091	10.519627	14.027408	18.679185	24.839769
61	8.153824	10.940412	14.658641	19.613145	26.205957
62	8.439207	11.378028	15.318280	20.593802	27.647284
63	8.734580	11.833149	16.007603	21.623492	29.167885
64	9.040290	12.306475	16.727945	22.704667	30.772118
65	9.356700	12.798734	17.480703	23.839900	32.464585
66	9.684185	13.310684	18.267334	25.031895	34.250137
67	10.023131	13.843111	19.089364	26.283490	36.133895
68	10.373941	14.396835	19.948386	27.597664	38.121259
69	10.737029	14.972709	20.846063	28.977547	40.217928
70	11.112825	15.571617	21.784136	30.426425	42.429914
71	11.501773	16.194482	22.764422	31.947746	44.763559
72	11.904336	16.842261	23.788821	33.545133	47.225555
73	12.320987	17.515951	24.859318	35.222390	49.822961
74	12.752222	18.216589	25.977987	36.983509	52.563223
75	13.198550	18.945253	27.146997	38.832685	55.454201
76	13.660499	19.703063	28.368611	40.774319	58.504182
77	14.138616	20.491186	29.645199	42.813035	61.721911
78	14.633468	21.310833	30.979233	44.953687	65.116617
79	15.145639	22.163266	32.373298	47.201371	68.698030
80	15.675736	23.049797	33.830097	49.561440	72.476422
81	16.224387	23.971789	35.352451	52.039512	76.462625
82	16.792241	24.930660	36.943312	54.641487	80.668069
83	17.379969	25.927887	38.605761	57.373561	85.104813
84	17.988268	26.965002	40.343020	60.242239	89.785578
85	18.617852	28.043602	42.158456	63.254351	94.723785
86	19.269482	29.165346	44.055586	66.417069	99.933593
87	19.943914	30.331960	46.038086	69.737922	105.429940
88	20.641951	31.545238	48.109802	73.224818	111.228587
89	21.364420	32.807048	50.274743	76.886059	117.346159
90	22.112174	34.119330	52.537106	80.730362	123.800198
91	22.886100	35.484103	54.901276	84.766880	130.609209
92	23.687114	36.903467	57.371833	89.005224	137.792715
93	24.516163	38.379606	59.953566	92.455486	145.371314
94	25.374229	39.914790	62.651470	98.128260	151.366736
95	26.262327	41.511381	65.470793	103.034673	161.801907
96	27.181508	43.171836	68.416978	108.186406	170.701011
97	28.132861	44.898710	71.495742	113.595727	180.089567
98	29.117511	46.694658	74.713051	119.275513	189.994493
99	30.136624	48.562444	78.075138	125.239289	200.444190
100	31.191405	50.504942	81.588519	131.501253	211.468620

Table 1 (continued)

n	6%	6½%	7%	7½%	8%
1	1.060000	1.065000	1.070000	1.075000	1.080000
2	1.123600	1.134225	1.144900	1.155625	1.166400
3	1.191016	1.207950	1.225043	1.242297	1.259712
4	1.262477	1.286466	1.310796	1.335469	1.360489
5	1.338226	1.370087	1.402552	1.435629	1.469328
6	1.418519	1.459142	1.500730	1.543302	1.586874
7	1.503630	1.553987	1.605781	1.659045	1.713824
8	1.593848	1.654996	1.718186	1.783478	1.850930
9	1.689479	1.762570	1.838459	1.917239	1.999005
10	1.790848	1.877137	1.967151	2.061032	2.158925
11	1.898299	1.999151	2.104852	2.215609	2.331639
12	2.012196	2.129096	2.252191	2.381780	2.518170
13	2.132928	2.267487	2.409845	2.560413	2.719624
14	2.260904	2.414874	2.578534	2.752444	2.937194
15	2.396558	2.571841	2.759032	2.958877	3.172169
16	2.540352	2.739011	2.952164	3.180793	3.425943
17	2.692773	2.917046	3.158815	3.419353	3.700018
18	2.854339	3.106654	3.379932	3.675804	3.996019
19	3.025599	3.308587	3.616527	3.951489	4.315701
20	3.207135	3.523645	3.869684	4.247851	4.660957
21	3.399564	3.752682	4.140562	4.566440	5.033834
22	3.603537	3.996606	4.430402	4.908923	5.436540
23	3.819750	4.256386	4.740530	5.277092	5.871464
24	4.048935	4.533051	5.072367	5.672874	6.341181
25	4.291871	4.827433	5.427433	6.098340	6.848475
26	4.549383	5.141500	5.807353	6.555715	7.396353
27	4.822346	5.475697	6.213867	7.047394	7.980061
28	5.111687	5.831617	6.648838	7.575948	8.627106
29	5.418388	6.210672	7.114257	8.144144	9.317275
30	5.743491	6.614366	7.612255	8.754955	10.062657
31	6.088101	7.044300	8.145113	9.411577	10.867669
32	6.453387	7.502179	8.715271	10.117445	11.737083
33	6.840590	7.989821	9.325340	10.876253	12.676049
34	7.251025	8.509160	9.978113	11.691972	13.690133
35	7.686087	9.062255	10.676581	12.568870	14.785344
36	8.147252	9.651301	11.423942	13.511535	15.968171
37	8.636087	10.278636	12.223618	14.524901	17.245625
38	9.154252	10.946747	13.079271	15.614268	18.625275
39	9.703507	11.658286	13.994820	16.785338	20.115297
40	10.285718	12.416075	14.974457	18.044239	21.724521
41	10.902861	13.223119	16.022669	19.397557	23.462483
42	11.557032	14.082622	17.144256	20.852373	25.339481
43	12.250454	14.997993	18.344354	22.416301	27.366640
44	12.985482	15.972862	19.628459	24.097524	29.555971
45	13.764610	17.011098	21.002451	25.904838	31.920449
46	14.590487	18.116820	22.472622	27.847701	34.474084
47	15.465916	19.294413	24.045706	29.936278	37.232011
48	16.393871	20.548550	25.728905	32.181498	40.210572
49	17.377504	21.884205	27.529929	34.595112	43.427418
50	18.420154	23.306679	29.457024	37.189745	46.901611
51	19.525363	24.821613	31.519016	39.978976	50.653740
52	20.696885	26.435018	33.725346	42.977399	54.706039
53	21.938698	28.153294	36.086121	46.200704	59.082522
54	23.255020	29.983258	38.612149	49.665757	63.809124
55	24.650321	31.932170	41.315000	53.390689	68.913854
56	26.129340	34.007761	44.207049	57.394990	74.426962
57	27.697100	36.218265	47.301543	61.699614	80.381119
58	29.358926	38.572452	50.612651	66.327086	86.811608
59	31.120462	41.079662	54.155536	71.301617	93.756537
60	32.987690	43.749840	57.946424	76.649238	101.257060
61	34.966951	46.593579	62.002673	82.397931	109.357625
62	37.064948	49.622162	66.342861	88.577776	118.106234
63	39.288865	52.847603	70.986861	95.221109	127.554733
64	41.646198	56.282697	75.955941	102.362692	137.759112
65	44.144970	59.941072	81.272857	110.039894	148.779841
66	46.793668	63.837242	86.961957	118.292886	160.682228
67	49.601288	67.986662	93.049294	127.164852	173.536806
68	52.577365	72.405796	99.562744	136.702216	187.415750
69	55.732007	77.112172	106.532136	146.954882	202.413330
70	59.075928	82.124464	113.989385	157.976498	218.606396
71	62.620483	87.462554	121.968642	169.824735	236.094908
72	66.377712	93.147620	130.506447	182.561591	254.982500
73	70.360375	99.202215	139.641898	196.253710	275.381101
74	74.581997	105.650359	149.416831	210.972738	297.411588
75	79.056917	112.517632	159.876009	226.795693	321.204515
76	83.800332	119.831279	171.067330	243.805370	346.900876
77	88.828352	127.620312	183.042042	262.090773	374.652946
78	94.158053	135.915632	195.854985	281.747581	404.625181
79	99.807536	144.750148	209.564834	302.878649	436.995196
80	105.795988	154.158908	224.234372	325.594547	471.954811
81	112.143748	164.179237	239.930778	350.014138	509.711196
82	118.872372	174.850887	256.725932	376.265199	550.488090
83	126.004715	186.216194	274.696748	404.485088	594.527138
84	133.564997	198.320247	293.925519	434.821470	642.089308
85	141.578897	211.211063	314.500305	467.433080	693.456453
86	150.073631	224.939782	336.515326	502.490560	748.932968
87	159.078049	239.560868	360.071399	540.177352	808.847606
88	168.622731	255.132325	385.276396	580.690654	873.555413
89	178.740095	271.715926	412.245744	624.242453	943.439846
90	189.464501	289.377461	441.102946	671.060636	1018.915031
91	200.832371	308.186996	471.980152	721.390183	1100.428236
92	212.882312	328.219151	505.018761	775.494447	1188.462491
93	225.655252	349.553396	540.370075	833.656529	1283.539492
94	239.194566	372.274366	578.195979	896.180769	1386.222649
95	253.546240	396.472200	618.669698	963.394325	1497.120463
96	258.759014	422.242893	661.976577	1035.648900	1616.890095
97	284.844555	449.688681	708.314935	1113.322566	1746.241303
98	301.977628	478.918445	757.896980	1196.821759	1885.940604
99	320.096286	510.048144	810.949769	1286.583390	2036.815854
100	329.302062	543.201275	867.716251	1383.077144	2199.761119

Table 2

$(1 + r)^{-n}$

r = rate of interest per payment period; n = number of payment periods

n	$\frac{1}{4}\%$	$\frac{1}{2}\%$	$\frac{3}{4}\%$	1%	$1\frac{1}{4}\%$
1	0.997506	0.995025	0.992556	0.990099	0.987654
2	0.995019	0.990075	0.985167	0.980296	0.975461
3	0.992537	0.985149	0.977833	0.970590	0.963418
4	0.990062	0.980248	0.970554	0.960980	0.951524
5	0.987593	0.975371	0.963329	0.951466	0.939777
6	0.985130	0.970518	0.956158	0.942045	0.928175
7	0.982674	0.965690	0.949040	0.932718	0.916716
8	0.980223	0.960885	0.941975	0.923483	0.905398
9	0.977779	0.956105	0.934963	0.914340	0.894221
10	0.975340	0.951348	0.928003	0.905287	0.883181
11	0.972908	0.946615	0.921095	0.896324	0.872277
12	0.970482	0.941905	0.914238	0.887449	0.861509
13	0.968062	0.937219	0.907432	0.878663	0.850873
14	0.965648	0.932556	0.900677	0.869963	0.840368
15	0.963240	0.927917	0.893973	0.861349	0.829993
16	0.960837	0.923300	0.887318	0.852821	0.819746
17	0.958441	0.918707	0.880712	0.844377	0.809626
18	0.956051	0.914136	0.874156	0.836017	0.799631
19	0.953667	0.909588	0.867649	0.827740	0.789759
20	0.951289	0.905063	0.861190	0.819544	0.780009
21	0.948917	0.900560	0.854779	0.811430	0.770379
22	0.946550	0.896080	0.848416	0.803396	0.760868
23	0.944190	0.891622	0.842100	0.795442	0.751475
24	0.941835	0.887186	0.835831	0.787566	0.742197
25	0.939486	0.882772	0.829609	0.779768	0.733034
26	0.937144	0.878380	0.823434	0.772048	0.723984
27	0.934806	0.874010	0.817304	0.764404	0.715046
28	0.932475	0.869662	0.811220	0.756836	0.706219
29	0.930150	0.865335	0.805181	0.749342	0.697500
30	0.927830	0.861030	0.799187	0.741923	0.688889
31	0.925517	0.856746	0.793238	0.734577	0.680384
32	0.923209	0.852484	0.787333	0.727304	0.671984
33	0.920906	0.848242	0.781472	0.720103	0.663688
34	0.918610	0.844022	0.775654	0.712973	0.655494
35	0.916319	0.839823	0.769880	0.705914	0.647402
36	0.914034	0.835645	0.764149	0.698925	0.639409
37	0.911754	0.831487	0.758461	0.692005	0.631515
38	0.909481	0.827351	0.752814	0.685153	0.623719
39	0.907213	0.823235	0.747210	0.678370	0.616019
40	0.904950	0.819139	0.741648	0.671653	0.608413
41	0.902694	0.815064	0.736127	0.665003	0.600902
42	0.900443	0.811008	0.730647	0.658419	0.593484
43	0.898197	0.806974	0.725208	0.651900	0.586157
44	0.895957	0.802959	0.719810	0.645445	0.578920
45	0.893723	0.798964	0.714451	0.639055	0.571773
46	0.891494	0.794989	0.709133	0.632728	0.564714
47	0.889271	0.791034	0.703854	0.626463	0.557742
48	0.887053	0.787098	0.698614	0.620260	0.550857
49	0.884841	0.783182	0.693414	0.614119	0.544056
50	0.882635	0.779286	0.688252	0.608039	0.537339

n	$\frac{1}{4}\%$	$\frac{1}{2}\%$	$\frac{3}{4}\%$	1%	$1\frac{1}{4}\%$
51	0.880434	0.775409	0.683128	0.602019	0.530705
52	0.878238	0.771551	0.678043	0.596058	0.524153
53	0.876048	0.767713	0.672995	0.590157	0.517682
54	0.873863	0.763893	0.667986	0.584313	0.511291
55	0.871684	0.760093	0.663013	0.578528	0.504979
56	0.869510	0.756311	0.658077	0.572800	0.498745
57	0.867342	0.752548	0.653179	0.567129	0.492587
58	0.865179	0.748804	0.648316	0.561514	0.486506
59	0.863021	0.745079	0.643490	0.555954	0.480500
60	0.860869	0.741372	0.638700	0.550450	0.474568
61	0.858722	0.737684	0.633945	0.545000	0.468709
62	0.856581	0.734014	0.629226	0.539604	0.462922
63	0.854445	0.730362	0.624542	0.534261	0.457207
64	0.852314	0.726728	0.619893	0.528971	0.451563
65	0.850189	0.723113	0.615278	0.523734	0.445988
66	0.848068	0.719515	0.610698	0.518548	0.440482
67	0.845953	0.715935	0.606152	0.513414	0.435044
68	0.843844	0.712374	0.601639	0.508331	0.429673
69	0.841740	0.708829	0.597161	0.503298	0.424368
70	0.839640	0.705303	0.592715	0.498315	0.419129
71	0.837547	0.701794	0.588303	0.493381	0.413955
72	0.835458	0.698302	0.583924	0.488496	0.408844
73	0.833374	0.694828	0.579577	0.483660	0.403797
74	0.831296	0.691371	0.575262	0.478871	0.398811
75	0.829233	0.687932	0.570980	0.474130	0.393888
76	0.827155	0.684509	0.566730	0.469435	0.389025
77	0.825093	0.681104	0.562511	0.464787	0.384222
78	0.823035	0.677715	0.558323	0.460185	0.379479
79	0.820983	0.674343	0.554167	0.455629	0.374794
80	0.818935	0.670988	0.550042	0.451118	0.370167
81	0.816893	0.667650	0.545947	0.446651	0.365597
82	0.814856	0.664329	0.541883	0.442229	0.361083
83	0.812824	0.661023	0.537849	0.437851	0.356625
84	0.810797	0.657735	0.533845	0.433515	0.352223
85	0.808775	0.654462	0.529871	0.429223	0.347874
86	0.806758	0.651206	0.525927	0.424974	0.343580
87	0.804746	0.647967	0.522012	0.420766	0.339338
88	0.802739	0.644743	0.518126	0.416600	0.335148
89	0.800737	0.641535	0.514269	0.412475	0.331011
90	0.798741	0.638343	0.510440	0.408391	0.326924
91	0.796749	0.635168	0.506641	0.404348	0.322888
92	0.794762	0.632008	0.502869	0.400344	0.318902
93	0.792780	0.628863	0.499126	0.396380	0.314965
94	0.790803	0.625735	0.495410	0.392456	0.311076
95	0.788831	0.622622	0.491722	0.388570	0.307236
96	0.786864	0.619524	0.488062	0.384723	0.303443
97	0.784901	0.616442	0.484429	0.380914	0.299697
98	0.782944	0.613375	0.480822	0.377142	0.295997
99	0.780991	0.610323	0.477243	0.373408	0.292342
100	0.779044	0.607287	0.473690	0.369711	0.288733

Table 2 (continued)

n	1½%	1¾%	2%	2½%	3%	n	1½%	1¾%	2%	2½%	3%
1	0.985222	0.982801	0.980392	0.975610	0.970874	51	0.467985	0.412805	0.364243	0.283846	0.221463
2	0.970662	0.965898	0.961169	0.951814	0.942596	52	0.461069	0.405705	0.357101	0.276923	0.215013
3	0.956317	0.949285	0.942322	0.928599	0.915142	53	0.454255	0.398727	0.350099	0.270169	0.208750
4	0.942184	0.932959	0.923845	0.905951	0.888487	54	0.447542	0.391869	0.343234	0.263579	0.202670
5	0.928260	0.916913	0.905731	0.883854	0.862609	55	0.440928	0.385130	0.336504	0.257151	0.196767
6	0.914542	0.901143	0.887971	0.862297	0.837484	56	0.434412	0.378506	0.329906	0.250879	0.191036
7	0.901027	0.885644	0.870560	0.841265	0.813092	57	0.427992	0.371996	0.323437	0.244760	0.185472
8	0.887711	0.870412	0.853490	0.820747	0.789409	58	0.421667	0.365598	0.317095	0.238790	0.180070
9	0.874592	0.855441	0.836755	0.800728	0.766417	59	0.415435	0.359310	0.310878	0.232966	0.174825
10	0.861667	0.840729	0.820348	0.781198	0.744094	60	0.409296	0.353130	0.304782	0.227284	0.169733
11	0.848933	0.826269	0.804263	0.762145	0.722421	61	0.403247	0.347057	0.298806	0.221740	0.164789
12	0.836387	0.812058	0.788493	0.743556	0.701380	62	0.397288	0.341088	0.292947	0.216332	0.159990
13	0.824027	0.798091	0.773033	0.725420	0.680951	63	0.391417	0.335221	0.287203	0.211055	0.155330
14	0.811849	0.784365	0.757875	0.707727	0.661118	64	0.385632	0.329456	0.281572	0.205908	0.150806
15	0.799852	0.770875	0.743015	0.690466	0.641862	65	0.379933	0.323790	0.276051	0.200886	0.146413
16	0.788031	0.757616	0.728446	0.673625	0.623167	66	0.374318	0.318221	0.270638	0.195986	0.142149
17	0.776385	0.744586	0.714163	0.657195	0.605016	67	0.368787	0.312748	0.265331	0.191206	0.138009
18	0.764912	0.731780	0.700159	0.641166	0.587395	68	0.363337	0.307369	0.260129	0.186542	0.133989
19	0.753607	0.719194	0.686431	0.625528	0.570286	69	0.357967	0.302082	0.255028	0.181992	0.130086
20	0.742470	0.706825	0.672971	0.610271	0.553676	70	0.352677	0.296887	0.250028	0.177554	0.126297
21	0.731498	0.694668	0.659776	0.595386	0.537549	71	0.347465	0.291781	0.245125	0.173223	0.122619
22	0.720688	0.682720	0.646839	0.580865	0.521893	72	0.342330	0.286762	0.240319	0.168998	0.119047
23	0.710037	0.670978	0.634156	0.566697	0.506692	73	0.337271	0.281830	0.235607	0.164876	0.115580
24	0.699544	0.659438	0.621722	0.552875	0.491934	74	0.332287	0.276983	0.230987	0.160855	0.112214
25	0.689206	0.648096	0.609531	0.539391	0.477606	75	0.327376	0.272219	0.226458	0.156931	0.108945
26	0.679021	0.636950	0.597579	0.526235	0.463695	76	0.322538	0.267537	0.222017	0.153104	0.105772
27	0.668986	0.625995	0.585862	0.513400	0.450189	77	0.317771	0.262936	0.217664	0.149370	0.102691
28	0.659099	0.615228	0.574375	0.500878	0.437077	78	0.313075	0.258414	0.213396	0.145776	0.099700
29	0.649359	0.604647	0.563112	0.488661	0.424346	79	0.308449	0.253969	0.209212	0.142172	0.096796
30	0.639762	0.594248	0.552071	0.476743	0.411987	80	0.303890	0.249601	0.205110	0.138705	0.093977
31	0.630308	0.584027	0.541246	0.465115	0.399987	81	0.299399	0.245308	0.201088	0.135322	0.091240
32	0.620993	0.573982	0.530633	0.453771	0.388337	82	0.294975	0.241089	0.197145	0.132021	0.088582
33	0.611816	0.564111	0.520229	0.442703	0.377026	83	0.290615	0.236943	0.193279	0.128801	0.086002
34	0.602774	0.554408	0.510028	0.431905	0.366045	84	0.286321	0.232868	0.189490	0.125660	0.083497
35	0.593866	0.544873	0.500028	0.421371	0.355383	85	0.282089	0.228862	0.185774	0.122595	0.081065
36	0.585090	0.535502	0.490223	0.411094	0.345032	86	0.277920	0.224926	0.182132	0.119605	0.078704
37	0.576443	0.526292	0.480611	0.401067	0.334983	87	0.273813	0.221058	0.178560	0.116687	0.076412
38	0.567924	0.517240	0.471187	0.391285	0.325226	88	0.269767	0.217256	0.175059	0.113841	0.074186
39	0.559531	0.508344	0.461948	0.381741	0.315754	89	0.265780	0.213519	0.171627	0.111065	0.072026
40	0.551262	0.499601	0.452890	0.372431	0.306557	90	0.261852	0.209847	0.168261	0.108356	0.069928
41	0.543116	0.491008	0.444010	0.363347	0.297628	91	0.257982	0.206238	0.164962	0.105713	0.067891
42	0.535089	0.482563	0.435304	0.354485	0.288959	92	0.254170	0.202691	0.161728	0.103135	0.065914
43	0.527182	0.474264	0.426769	0.345839	0.280543	93	0.250414	0.199205	0.158557	0.100619	0.063994
44	0.519391	0.466107	0.418401	0.337404	0.272372	94	0.246713	0.195778	0.155448	0.098165	0.062130
45	0.511715	0.458090	0.410197	0.329174	0.264439	95	0.243067	0.192411	0.152400	0.095771	0.060320
46	0.504153	0.450212	0.402154	0.321146	0.256737	96	0.239475	0.189102	0.149411	0.093435	0.058563
47	0.496702	0.442469	0.394268	0.313313	0.249259	97	0.235936	0.185850	0.146482	0.091156	0.056858
48	0.489362	0.434858	0.386538	0.305671	0.241999	98	0.232449	0.182653	0.143610	0.088933	0.055202
49	0.482130	0.427379	0.378958	0.298216	0.234950	99	0.229014	0.179512	0.140794	0.086764	0.053594
50	0.475005	0.420029	0.371528	0.290942	0.228107	100	0.225629	0.176424	0.138033	0.084647	0.052033

Table 2 (continued)

n	3½%	4%	4½%	5%	5½%
1	0.966184	0.961538	0.956938	0.952381	0.947867
2	0.933511	0.924556	0.915730	0.907029	0.898452
3	0.901943	0.888996	0.876297	0.863838	0.851614
4	0.871442	0.854804	0.838561	0.822702	0.807217
5	0.841973	0.821927	0.802451	0.783526	0.765134
6	0.813501	0.790315	0.767896	0.746215	0.725246
7	0.785991	0.759918	0.734828	0.710681	0.687437
8	0.759412	0.730690	0.703185	0.676839	0.651599
9	0.733731	0.702587	0.672904	0.644609	0.617629
10	0.708919	0.675564	0.643928	0.613913	0.585431
11	0.684946	0.649581	0.616199	0.584679	0.554911
12	0.661783	0.624597	0.589664	0.556837	0.525982
13	0.639404	0.600574	0.564272	0.530321	0.498561
14	0.617782	0.577475	0.539973	0.505068	0.472569
15	0.596891	0.555265	0.516720	0.481017	0.447933
16	0.576706	0.533908	0.494469	0.458112	0.424581
17	0.557204	0.513373	0.473176	0.436297	0.402447
18	0.538361	0.493628	0.452800	0.415521	0.381466
19	0.520156	0.474642	0.433302	0.395734	0.361579
20	0.502566	0.456387	0.414643	0.376889	0.342729
21	0.485571	0.438834	0.396787	0.358942	0.324862
22	0.469151	0.421955	0.379701	0.341850	0.307926
23	0.453286	0.405726	0.363350	0.325571	0.291873
24	0.437957	0.390121	0.347703	0.310068	0.276657
25	0.423147	0.375117	0.332731	0.295303	0.262234
26	0.408838	0.360689	0.318402	0.281241	0.248563
27	0.395012	0.346817	0.304691	0.267848	0.235605
28	0.381654	0.333477	0.291571	0.255094	0.223322
29	0.368748	0.320651	0.279015	0.242946	0.211679
30	0.356278	0.308319	0.267000	0.231377	0.200644
31	0.344230	0.296460	0.255502	0.220359	0.190184
32	0.332590	0.285058	0.244500	0.209866	0.180269
33	0.321343	0.274094	0.233971	0.199873	0.170871
34	0.310476	0.263552	0.223896	0.190355	0.161963
35	0.299977	0.253415	0.214254	0.181290	0.153520
36	0.289833	0.243669	0.205028	0.172657	0.145516
37	0.280032	0.234297	0.196199	0.164436	0.137930
38	0.270562	0.225285	0.187750	0.156605	0.130739
39	0.261413	0.216621	0.179665	0.149148	0.123924
40	0.252572	0.208289	0.171929	0.142046	0.117463
41	0.244031	0.200278	0.164525	0.135282	0.111339
42	0.235779	0.192575	0.157440	0.128840	0.105535
43	0.227806	0.185168	0.150661	0.122704	0.100033
44	0.220102	0.178046	0.144173	0.116861	0.094818
45	0.212659	0.171198	0.137964	0.111297	0.089875
46	0.205468	0.164614	0.132023	0.105997	0.085190
47	0.198520	0.158283	0.126338	0.100949	0.080748
48	0.191806	0.152195	0.120898	0.096142	0.076539
49	0.185320	0.146341	0.115692	0.091564	0.072549
50	0.179053	0.140713	0.110710	0.087204	0.068767

n	3½%	4%	4½%	5%	5½%
51	0.172998	0.135301	0.105942	0.083051	0.065182
52	0.167148	0.130097	0.101380	0.079096	0.061783
53	0.161496	0.125093	0.097014	0.075330	0.058563
54	0.156035	0.120282	0.092837	0.071743	0.055509
55	0.150758	0.115656	0.088839	0.068326	0.052616
56	0.145660	0.111207	0.085013	0.065073	0.049873
57	0.140734	0.106930	0.081353	0.061974	0.047273
58	0.135975	0.102817	0.077849	0.059023	0.044808
59	0.131377	0.098863	0.074497	0.056212	0.042472
60	0.126934	0.095060	0.071289	0.053536	0.040258
61	0.122642	0.091404	0.068219	0.050986	0.038159
62	0.118495	0.087889	0.065281	0.048558	0.036170
63	0.114487	0.084508	0.062470	0.046246	0.034284
64	0.110616	0.081258	0.059780	0.044044	0.032497
65	0.106875	0.078133	0.057206	0.041946	0.030803
66	0.103261	0.075128	0.054743	0.039949	0.029197
67	0.099769	0.072238	0.052385	0.038047	0.027675
68	0.096395	0.069460	0.050129	0.036235	0.026232
69	0.093136	0.066788	0.047971	0.034509	0.024865
70	0.089986	0.064219	0.045905	0.032866	0.023568
71	0.086943	0.061749	0.043928	0.031301	0.022340
72	0.084003	0.059374	0.042037	0.029811	0.021175
73	0.081162	0.057091	0.040226	0.028391	0.020071
74	0.078418	0.054895	0.038494	0.027039	0.019025
75	0.075766	0.052784	0.036836	0.025752	0.018033
76	0.073204	0.050754	0.035250	0.024525	0.017093
77	0.070728	0.048801	0.033732	0.023357	0.016202
78	0.068337	0.046924	0.032280	0.022245	0.015357
79	0.066026	0.045120	0.030890	0.021186	0.014556
80	0.063793	0.043384	0.029559	0.020177	0.013798
81	0.061636	0.041716	0.028287	0.019216	0.013078
82	0.059551	0.040111	0.027068	0.018301	0.012396
83	0.057538	0.038569	0.025903	0.017430	0.011750
84	0.055592	0.037085	0.024787	0.016600	0.011138
85	0.053712	0.035659	0.023720	0.015809	0.010557
86	0.051896	0.034287	0.022699	0.015056	0.010007
87	0.050141	0.032969	0.021721	0.014339	0.009485
88	0.048445	0.031701	0.020786	0.013657	0.008990
89	0.046807	0.030481	0.019891	0.013006	0.008522
90	0.045224	0.029309	0.019034	0.012387	0.008078
91	0.043695	0.028182	0.018215	0.011797	0.007656
92	0.042217	0.027098	0.017430	0.011235	0.007257
93	0.040789	0.026056	0.016680	0.010700	0.006879
94	0.039410	0.025053	0.015961	0.010191	0.006520
95	0.038077	0.024090	0.015274	0.009705	0.006180
96	0.036790	0.023163	0.014616	0.009243	0.005858
97	0.035546	0.022272	0.013987	0.008803	0.005553
98	0.034344	0.021416	0.013385	0.008384	0.005263
99	0.033182	0.020592	0.012808	0.007985	0.004989
100	0.032060	0.019800	0.012257	0.007604	0.004729

Table 2 (continued)

n	6%	6½%	7%	7½%	8%
1	0.943396	0.938967	0.934579	0.930233	0.925926
2	0.889996	0.881659	0.873439	0.865333	0.857339
3	0.839619	0.827849	0.816298	0.804961	0.793832
4	0.792094	0.777323	0.762895	0.748801	0.735030
5	0.747258	0.729881	0.712986	0.696559	0.680583
6	0.704961	0.685334	0.666342	0.647962	0.630170
7	0.665057	0.643506	0.622750	0.602755	0.583490
8	0.627412	0.604231	0.582009	0.560702	0.540269
9	0.591898	0.567353	0.543934	0.521583	0.500249
10	0.558395	0.532726	0.508349	0.485194	0.463193
11	0.526788	0.500212	0.475093	0.451343	0.428883
12	0.496969	0.469683	0.444012	0.419854	0.397114
13	0.468839	0.441017	0.414964	0.390562	0.367698
14	0.442301	0.414100	0.387817	0.363313	0.340461
15	0.417265	0.388827	0.362446	0.337966	0.315242
16	0.393646	0.365095	0.338735	0.314487	0.291890
17	0.371364	0.342813	0.316574	0.292453	0.270269
18	0.350344	0.321890	0.295864	0.272049	0.250249
19	0.330513	0.302244	0.276508	0.253069	0.231712
20	0.311805	0.283797	0.258419	0.235413	0.214548
21	0.294155	0.266476	0.241513	0.218989	0.198656
22	0.277505	0.250212	0.225713	0.203711	0.183941
23	0.261797	0.234941	0.210947	0.189498	0.170315
24	0.246979	0.220602	0.197147	0.176277	0.157699
25	0.232999	0.207138	0.184249	0.163979	0.146018
26	0.219810	0.194496	0.172195	0.152539	0.135202
27	0.207368	0.182625	0.160930	0.141896	0.125187
28	0.195630	0.171479	0.150402	0.131997	0.115914
29	0.184557	0.161013	0.140563	0.122788	0.107328
30	0.174110	0.151186	0.131367	0.114221	0.099377
31	0.164255	0.141959	0.122773	0.106252	0.092016
32	0.154957	0.133295	0.114741	0.098839	0.085200
33	0.146186	0.125159	0.107235	0.091943	0.078889
34	0.137912	0.117520	0.100219	0.085529	0.073045
35	0.130105	0.110348	0.093663	0.079562	0.067635
36	0.122741	0.103613	0.087535	0.074011	0.062625
37	0.115793	0.097289	0.081809	0.068847	0.057986
38	0.109239	0.091351	0.076457	0.064044	0.053690
39	0.103056	0.085776	0.071455	0.059576	0.049713
40	0.097222	0.080541	0.066780	0.055419	0.046031
41	0.091719	0.075625	0.062412	0.051553	0.042621
42	0.086527	0.071010	0.058329	0.047956	0.039464
43	0.081630	0.066676	0.054513	0.044610	0.036541
44	0.077009	0.062606	0.050946	0.041498	0.033834
45	0.072650	0.058785	0.047613	0.038603	0.031328
46	0.068538	0.055197	0.044499	0.035910	0.029007
47	0.064658	0.051828	0.041587	0.033404	0.026859
48	0.060998	0.048665	0.038867	0.031074	0.024869
49	0.057546	0.045695	0.036324	0.028906	0.023027
50	0.054288	0.042906	0.033948	0.026889	0.021321

n	6%	6½%	7%	7½%	8%
51	0.051215	0.040287	0.031727	0.025013	0.019742
52	0.048316	0.037829	0.029651	0.023268	0.018280
53	0.045582	0.035520	0.027711	0.021645	0.016925
54	0.043001	0.033352	0.025899	0.020135	0.015672
55	0.040567	0.031316	0.024204	0.018730	0.014511
56	0.038271	0.029405	0.022621	0.017423	0.013436
57	0.036105	0.027610	0.021141	0.016208	0.012441
58	0.034061	0.025925	0.019758	0.015077	0.011519
59	0.032133	0.024343	0.018465	0.014025	0.010666
60	0.030314	0.022857	0.017257	0.013046	0.009876
61	0.028598	0.021462	0.016128	0.012136	0.009144
62	0.026980	0.020152	0.015073	0.011290	0.008467
63	0.025453	0.018922	0.014087	0.010502	0.007840
64	0.024012	0.017767	0.013166	0.009769	0.007259
65	0.022653	0.016683	0.012304	0.009088	0.006721
66	0.021370	0.015665	0.011499	0.008454	0.006223
67	0.020161	0.014709	0.010747	0.007864	0.005762
68	0.019020	0.013811	0.010044	0.007315	0.005336
69	0.017943	0.012968	0.009387	0.006805	0.004940
70	0.016927	0.012177	0.008773	0.006330	0.004574
71	0.015969	0.011433	0.008199	0.005888	0.004236
72	0.015065	0.010736	0.007662	0.005478	0.003922
73	0.014213	0.010080	0.007161	0.005095	0.003631
74	0.013408	0.009465	0.006693	0.004740	0.003362
75	0.012649	0.008887	0.006255	0.004409	0.003113
76	0.011933	0.008345	0.005846	0.004102	0.002883
77	0.011258	0.007836	0.005463	0.003815	0.002669
78	0.010620	0.007358	0.005106	0.003549	0.002471
79	0.010019	0.006908	0.004772	0.003302	0.002288
80	0.009452	0.006487	0.004460	0.003071	0.002119
81	0.008917	0.006091	0.004168	0.002857	0.001962
82	0.008412	0.005719	0.003895	0.002658	0.001817
83	0.007936	0.005370	0.003640	0.002472	0.001682
84	0.007487	0.005042	0.003402	0.002300	0.001557
85	0.007063	0.004735	0.003180	0.002139	0.001442
86	0.006663	0.004446	0.002972	0.001990	0.001335
87	0.006286	0.004174	0.002777	0.001851	0.001236
88	0.005930	0.003920	0.002596	0.001722	0.001145
89	0.005595	0.003680	0.002426	0.001602	0.001060
90	0.005278	0.003456	0.002267	0.001490	0.000981
91	0.004979	0.003245	0.002119	0.001386	0.000909
92	0.004697	0.003047	0.001980	0.001289	0.000841
93	0.004432	0.002861	0.001851	0.001200	0.000779
94	0.004181	0.002686	0.001730	0.001116	0.000721
95	0.003944	0.002522	0.001616	0.001038	0.000668
96	0.003721	0.002368	0.001511	0.000966	0.000618
97	0.003510	0.002224	0.001412	0.000898	0.000573
98	0.003312	0.002088	0.001319	0.000836	0.000530
99	0.003124	0.001961	0.001233	0.000777	0.000491
100	0.002947	0.001841	0.001152	0.000723	0.000455

Table 3
$\log_{10} N$

N	0	1	2	3	4	5	6	7	8	9
1.0	0.0000	0043	0086	0128	0170	0212	0253	0294	0334	0374
1.1	0.0414	0453	0492	0531	0569	0607	0645	0682	0719	0755
1.2	0.0792	0828	0864	0899	0934	0969	1004	1038	1072	1106
1.3	0.1139	1173	1206	1239	1271	1303	1335	1367	1399	1430
1.4	0.1461	1492	1523	1553	1584	1614	1644	1673	1703	1732
1.5	0.1761	1790	1818	1847	1875	1903	1931	1959	1987	2014
1.6	0.2041	2068	2095	2122	2148	2175	2201	2227	2253	2279
1.7	0.2304	2330	2355	2380	2405	2430	2455	2480	2504	2529
1.8	0.2553	2577	2601	2625	2648	2672	2695	2718	2742	2765
1.9	0.2788	2810	2833	2856	2878	2900	2923	2945	2967	2989
2.0	0.3010	3032	3054	3075	3096	3118	3139	3160	3181	3201
2.1	0.3222	3243	3263	3284	3304	3324	3345	3365	3385	3404
2.2	0.3424	3444	3464	3483	3502	3522	3541	3560	3579	3598
2.3	0.3617	3636	3655	3674	3692	3711	3729	3747	3766	3784
2.4	0.3802	3820	3838	3856	3874	3892	3909	3927	3945	3962
2.5	0.3979	3997	4014	4031	4048	4065	4082	4099	4116	4133
2.6	0.4150	4166	4183	4200	4216	4232	4249	4265	4281	4298
2.7	0.4314	4330	4346	4362	4378	4393	4409	4425	4440	4456
2.8	0.4472	4487	4502	4518	4533	4548	4564	4579	4594	4609
2.9	0.4624	4639	4654	4669	4683	4698	4713	4728	4742	4757
3.0	0.4771	4786	4800	4814	4829	4843	4857	4871	4886	4900
3.1	0.4914	4928	4942	4955	4969	4983	4997	5011	5024	5038
3.2	0.5051	5065	5079	5092	5105	5119	5132	5145	5159	5172
3.3	0.5185	5198	5211	5224	5237	5250	5263	5276	5289	5302
3.4	0.5315	5328	5340	5353	5366	5378	5391	5403	5416	5428
3.5	0.5441	5453	5465	5478	5490	5502	5514	5527	5539	5551
3.6	0.5563	5575	5587	5599	5611	5623	5635	5647	5658	5670
3.7	0.5682	5694	5705	5717	5729	5740	5752	5763	5775	5786
3.8	0.5798	5809	5821	5832	5843	5855	5866	5877	5888	5899
3.9	0.5911	5922	5933	5944	5955	5966	5977	5988	5999	6010
4.0	0.6021	6031	6042	6053	6064	6075	6085	6096	6107	6117
4.1	0.6128	6138	6149	6160	6170	6180	6191	6201	6212	6222
4.2	0.6232	6243	6253	6263	6274	6284	6294	6304	6314	6325
4.3	0.6335	6345	6355	6365	6375	6385	6395	6405	6415	6425
4.4	0.6435	6444	6454	6464		6484	6493	6503	6513	6522
4.5	0.6532	6542	6551	6561	6571	6580	6590	6599	6609	6618
4.6	0.6628	6637	6646	6656	6665	6675	6684	6693	6702	6712
4.7	0.6721	6730	6739	6749	6758	6767	6776	6785	6794	6803
4.8	0.6812	6821	6830	6839	6848	6857	6866	6875	6884	6893
4.9	0.6902	6911	6920	6928	6937	6946	6955	6964	6972	6981
5.0	0.6990	6998	7007	7016	7024	7033	7042	7050	7059	7067
5.1	0.7076	7084	7093	7101	7110	7118	7126	7135	7143	7152
5.2	0.7160	7168	7177	7185	7193	7202	7210	7218	7226	7235
5.3	0.7243	7251	7259	7267	7275	7284	7292	7300	7308	7316
5.4	0.7324	7332	7340	7348	7356	7364	7372	7380	7388	7396
5.5	0.7404	7412	7419	7427	7435	7443	7451	7459	7466	7474
5.6	0.7482	7490	7497	7505	7513	7520	7528	7536	7543	7551
5.7	0.7559	7566	7574	7582	7589	7597	7604	7612	7619	7627
5.8	0.7634	7642	7649	7657	7664	7672	7679	7686	7694	7701
5.9	0.7709	7716	7723	7731	7738	7745	7752	7760	7767	7774
6.0	0.7782	7789	7796	7803	7810	7818	7825	7832	7839	7846
N	0	1	2	3	4	5	6	7	8	9

Table 3 continued

N	0	1	2	3	4	5	6	7	8	9
6.0	0.7782	7789	7796	7803	7810	7818	7825	7832	7839	7846
6.1	0.7853	7860	7868	7875	7882	7889	7896	7903	7910	7917
6.2	0.7924	7931	7938	7945	7952	7959	7966	7973	7980	7987
6.3	0.7993	8000	8007	8014	8021	8028	8035	8041	8048	8055
6.4	0.8062	8069	8075	8082	8089	8096	8102	8109	8116	8122
6.5	0.8129	8136	8142	8149	8156	8162	8169	8176	8182	8189
6.6	0.8195	8202	8209	8215	8222	8228	8235	8241	8248	8254
6.7	0.8261	8267	8274	8280	8287	8293	9299	9306	8312	8319
6.8	0.8325	8331	8338	8344	8351	8357	8363	8370	8376	8382
6.9	0.8388	8395	8401	8407	8414	8420	8426	8432	8439	8445
7.0	0.8451	8457	8463	8470	8476	8482	8488	8494	8500	8506
7.1	0.8513	8519	8525	8531	8537	8543	8549	8555	8561	8567
7.2	0.8573	8579	8585	8591	8597	8603	8609	8615	8621	8627
7.3	0.8633	8639	8645	8651	8657	8663	8669	8675	8681	8686
7.4	0.8692	8698	8704	8710	8716	8722	8727	8733	8739	8745
7.5	0.8751	8756	8762	8768	8774	8779	8785	8791	8797	8802
7.6	0.8808	8814	8820	8825	8831	8837	8842	8848	8854	8859
7.7	0.8865	8871	8876	8882	8887	8893	8899	8904	8910	8915
7.8	0.8921	8927	8932	8938	8943	8949	8954	8960	8965	8971
7.9	0.8976	8982	8987	8993	8998	9004	9009	9015	9020	9025
8.0	0.9031	9036	9042	9047	9053	9058	9063	9069	9074	9079
8.1	0.9085	9090	9096	9101	9106	9112	9117	9122	9128	9133
8.2	0.9138	9143	9149	9154	9159	9165	9170	9175	9180	9186
8.3	0.9191	9196	9201	9206	9212	9217	9222	9227	9232	9238
8.4	0.9243	9248	9253	9258	9263	9269	9274	9279	9284	9289
8.5	0.9294	9299	9304	9309	9315	9320	9325	9330	9335	9340
8.6	0.9345	9350	9355	9360	9365	9370	9375	9380	9386	9390
8.7	0.9395	9400	9405	9410	9415	9420	9425	9430	9435	9440
8.8	0.9445	9450	9455	9460	9465	9469	9474	9479	9484	9489
8.9	0.9494	9499	9504	9509	9513	9518	9523	9528	9533	9538
9.0	0.9542	9547	9552	9557	9562	9566	9571	9576	9581	9586
9.1	0.9590	9595	9600	9605	9609	9614	9619	9624	9628	9633
9.2	0.9638	9643	9647	9652	9657	9661	9666	9671	9675	9680
9.3	0.9685	9689	9694	9699	9703	9708	9713	9717	9722	9727
9.4	0.9731	9736	9741	9745	9750	9754	9759	9763	9768	9773
9.5	0.9777	9782	9786	9791	9795	9800	9805	9809	9814	9818
9.6	0.9823	9827	9832	9836	9841	9845	9850	9854	9859	9863
9.7	0.9868	9872	9877	9881	9886	9890	9894	9899	9903	9908
9.8	0.9912	9917	9921	9926	9930	9934	9939	9943	9948	9952
9.9	0.9956	9961	9965	9969	9974	9978	9983	9987	9991	9996
N	0	1	2	3	4	5	6	7	8	9

Table 4

n	$\sqrt[n]{2}$
2	1.414213
3	1.259921
4	1.189207
5	1.148698
6	1.122462
7	1.104090
8	1.090508
9	1.080060
10	1.071773
11	1.065041
12	1.059463
13	1.054766
14	1.050757
15	1.047294
16	1.044274
17	1.041616
18	1.039259
19	1.037155
20	1.035265

Table 5

$s_{\overline{n}|r}$

r = interest rate per payment period; n = number of payment periods

n	¼%	½%	¾%	1%	1¼%
1	1.000000	1.000000	1.000000	1.000000	1.000000
2	2.002499	2.005000	2.007500	2.010000	2.012500
3	3.007505	3.015025	3.022556	3.030100	3.037656
4	4.015023	4.030100	4.045225	4.060401	4.075627
5	5.025060	5.050251	5.075564	5.101005	5.126572
6	6.037623	6.075502	6.113631	6.152015	6.190654
7	7.052717	7.105880	7.159483	7.213535	7.268037
8	8.070347	8.141409	8.213179	8.285670	8.358888
9	9.090523	9.182116	9.274778	9.368527	9.463374
10	10.113249	10.228027	10.344339	10.462212	10.581666
11	11.138532	11.279167	11.421921	11.566834	11.713936
12	12.166377	12.335563	12.507586	12.682502	12.860361
13	13.196793	13.397241	13.601393	13.809327	14.021115
14	14.229784	14.464227	14.703403	14.947421	15.196379
15	15.265359	15.536549	15.813679	16.096895	16.386334
16	16.303521	16.614231	16.932281	17.257864	17.591163
17	17.344280	17.697302	18.059273	18.430442	18.811052
18	18.387640	18.785789	19.194717	19.614747	20.046190
19	19.433609	19.879718	20.338678	20.810894	21.296767
20	20.482192	20.979116	21.491218	22.019003	22.562977
21	21.533398	22.084012	22.652402	23.239193	23.845014
22	22.587230	23.194432	23.822295	24.471585	25.143077
23	23.643699	24.310404	25.000962	25.716301	26.457365
24	24.702807	25.431957	26.188469	26.973463	27.788082
25	25.764564	26.559116	27.384883	28.243198	29.135433
26	26.828975	27.691912	28.590269	29.525630	30.499626
27	27.896046	28.830372	29.804696	30.820886	31.880871
28	28.965785	29.974524	31.028231	32.129095	33.279382
29	30.038200	31.124396	32.260943	33.450386	34.695374
30	31.113295	32.280018	33.502900	34.784890	36.129066
31	32.191078	33.441419	34.754172	36.132739	37.580679
32	33.271555	34.608626	36.014828	37.494066	39.050438
33	34.354734	35.781669	37.284939	38.869006	40.538568
34	35.440620	36.960577	38.564576	40.257696	42.045300
35	36.529221	38.145380	39.853810	41.660273	43.570866
36	37.620543	39.336107	41.152714	43.076876	45.115502
37	38.714594	40.532788	42.461359	44.507645	46.679446
38	39.811380	41.735452	43.779819	45.992721	48.262939
39	40.910909	42.944129	45.108168	47.412248	49.866225
40	42.013185	44.158850	46.446479	48.886371	51.489553
41	43.118218	45.379644	47.794828	50.375234	53.133172
42	44.226012	46.606543	49.153289	51.878987	54.797337
43	45.336577	47.839575	50.521938	53.397776	56.482304
44	46.449918	49.078773	51.900853	54.931754	58.188332
45	47.566043	50.324167	53.290109	56.481072	59.915686
46	48.684957	51.575788	54.689785	58.045882	61.664632
47	49.806669	52.833667	56.099958	59.626341	63.435440
48	50.931185	54.097835	57.520707	61.222604	65.228383
49	52.058514	55.368324	58.952113	62.834830	67.043738
50	53.188659	56.645166	60.384253	64.463178	68.881786

n	¼%	½%	¾%	1%	1¼%
51	54.321630	57.928392	61.847210	66.107810	70.742806
52	55.457433	59.218034	63.311064	67.768888	72.627092
53	56.596077	60.514125	64.785897	69.446577	74.534930
54	57.737566	61.816695	66.271791	71.141043	76.466616
55	58.881910	63.125778	67.768830	72.852453	78.422449
56	60.029113	64.441408	69.277096	74.580977	80.402730
57	61.179186	65.763614	70.796674	76.326787	82.407764
58	62.332134	67.092433	72.327649	78.090055	84.437861
59	63.487963	68.427895	73.870107	79.870956	86.493334
60	64.646682	69.770034	75.424132	81.669665	88.574500
61	65.808299	71.118885	76.989813	83.486361	90.681681
62	66.972818	72.474479	78.567236	85.321225	92.815202
63	68.140251	73.836852	80.156491	87.174437	94.975392
64	69.310600	75.206036	81.757665	89.046181	97.162584
65	70.483877	76.582066	83.370847	90.936643	99.377116
66	71.660086	77.964977	84.996128	92.846010	101.619330
67	72.839236	79.354802	86.633599	94.779970	103.889572
68	74.021333	80.751576	88.283351	96.722214	106.188191
69	75.206386	82.155334	89.945476	98.689436	108.515543
70	76.394402	83.566111	91.620067	100.676380	110.871988
71	77.585387	84.983941	93.307217	102.683094	113.257887
72	78.779350	86.408861	95.007022	104.709924	115.673611
73	79.976298	87.840905	96.719574	106.757024	118.119531
74	81.176238	89.280110	98.444971	100.824594	120.596025
75	82.379178	90.726511	100.183308	110.912840	123.103475
76	83.585124	92.180143	101.934683	113.021968	125.642268
77	84.794088	93.641044	103.699193	115.152188	128.212797
78	86.006071	95.109249	105.476936	117.303709	130.815456
79	87.221088	96.584796	107.268014	119.476747	133.450649
80	88.439139	98.067720	109.072523	121.671514	136.118782
81	89.660237	99.558058	110.890567	123.888229	138.820267
82	90.884387	101.055849	112.722246	126.127111	141.555520
83	92.111597	102.561128	114.567663	128.388382	144.324964
84	93.341875	104.073934	116.426920	130.672266	147.129026
85	94.575230	105.594304	118.300123	132.978988	149.968138
86	95.811667	107.122275	120.187373	135.308778	152.842740
87	97.051197	108.657887	122.088778	137.661866	155.753274
88	98.293823	110.201176	124.004444	140.038484	158.700190
89	99.539557	111.752182	125.934477	142.438869	161.683942
90	100.788406	113.310943	127.878986	144.863258	164.704991
91	102.040376	114.877498	129.838078	147.311890	167.763803
92	103.295475	116.451885	131.811864	149.785009	170.860850
93	104.553715	118.034145	133.800453	152.282859	173.996611
94	105.815098	119.624315	135.803956	154.805687	177.171568
95	107.079636	121.222438	137.822486	157.353744	180.386213
96	108.347334	122.828550	139.856154	159.927281	183.641040
97	109.618202	124.442693	141.905075	162.526554	186.936553
98	110.892247	126.064906	143.969368	165.151819	190.273260
99	112.169477	127.695231	146.049133	167.803338	193.651675
100	113.449899	129.333707	148.144501	170.481370	197.072322

Table 5 (continued)

n	1½%	1¾%	2%	2½%	3%	n	1½%	1¾%	2%	2½%	3%
1	1.000000	1.000000	1.000000	1.000000	1.000000	51	75.788070	81.283009	87.270984	100.921451	117.180769
2	2.015000	2.017500	2.020000	2.025000	2.030000	52	77.924891	83.705461	90.016403	104.444487	121.696192
3	3.045225	3.052806	3.060400	3.075625	3.090900	53	80.093765	86.170307	92.816731	108.055599	126.347078
4	4.090903	4.106230	4.121608	4.152515	4.183627	54	82.295171	88.678287	95.673065	111.756989	131.137490
5	5.152267	5.178089	5.204040	5.256328	5.309136	55	84.529599	91.230157	98.586527	115.550914	136.071615
6	6.229551	6.268706	6.308121	6.387737	6.468410	56	86.797543	93.826684	101.558257	119.439686	141.153763
7	7.322994	7.378408	7.434283	7.547430	7.662462	57	89.099506	96.468651	104.589422	123.425679	146.388376
8	8.432839	8.507530	8.582969	8.736116	8.892336	58	91.435998	99.156852	107.681210	127.511320	151.780027
9	9.559332	9.656412	9.754628	9.954518	10.159106	59	93.807539	101.892097	110.834834	131.699103	157.333428
10	10.702722	10.825399	10.949720	11.203381	11.463879	60	96.214651	104.675209	114.051531	135.991581	163.053431
11	11.863262	12.014844	12.168715	12.483466	12.807795	61	98.657871	107.507025	117.332562	140.391370	168.945034
12	13.041211	13.225103	13.412089	13.795552	14.192029	62	101.137739	110.388398	120.679212	144.901154	175.013384
13	14.236830	14.456542	14.680331	15.140441	15.617790	63	103.654805	113.320195	124.092797	149.523683	181.263786
14	15.450382	15.709532	15.973937	16.518952	17.086324	64	106.209628	116.303298	127.574652	154.261775	187.701699
15	16.682138	16.984449	17.293416	17.931926	18.598913	65	108.802772	119.338605	131.126145	159.118319	194.332750
16	17.932370	18.281676	18.639284	19.380224	20.156881	66	111.434813	122.427031	134.748668	164.096277	201.162733
17	19.201355	19.601606	20.012070	20.864730	21.761587	67	114.106336	125.569504	138.443642	169.198684	208.197614
18	20.489376	20.944634	21.412311	22.386348	23.414435	68	116.817937	128.766970	142.212514	174.428650	215.443543
19	21.796716	22.311165	22.840558	23.946006	25.116868	69	119.570200	132.020392	146.056764	179.789366	222.906849
20	23.123667	23.701610	24.297369	25.544656	26.870374	70	122.363753	135.330748	149.977899	185.284100	230.594054
21	24.470522	25.116388	25.783316	27.183273	28.676485	71	125.199209	138.699037	153.977457	190.916203	238.511875
22	25.837580	26.555925	27.298982	28.862855	30.536780	72	128.077197	142.126269	158.057006	196.689107	246.667232
23	27.225143	28.020654	28.844962	30.584426	32.452883	73	130.998355	145.613479	162.218146	202.606335	255.067249
24	28.633521	29.511015	30.421861	32.349036	34.426469	74	133.963330	149.161715	166.462508	208.671493	263.719266
25	30.063024	31.027458	32.030298	34.157762	36.459263	75	136.972780	152.772045	170.791759	214.888280	272.630844
26	31.513969	32.570438	33.670904	36.011706	38.553041	76	140.027372	156.445555	175.207593	221.260487	281.809769
27	32.986678	34.140421	35.344322	37.911999	40.709632	77	143.127783	160.183352	179.711746	227.791999	291.264062
28	34.481478	35.737878	37.051208	39.859799	42.930921	78	146.274699	163.986561	184.305980	234.486799	301.001983
29	35.998701	37.363291	38.792232	41.856294	45.218849	79	149.468820	167.856326	188.992100	241.348968	311.032043
30	37.538681	39.017148	40.568077	43.902701	47.575414	80	152.710852	171.793811	193.771941	248.382692	321.363004
31	39.101761	40.699948	42.379438	46.000268	50.002677	81	156.001515	175.800202	198.647380	255.592259	332.003894
32	40.688288	42.412197	44.227027	48.150275	52.502757	82	159.341538	179.876706	203.620327	262.982065	342.964010
33	42.298612	44.154411	46.111568	50.354032	55.077840	83	162.731661	184.024548	208.692734	270.556617	354.252930
34	43.933091	45.927113	48.033799	52.612883	57.730175	84	166.172636	188.244977	213.866588	278.320532	365.880518
35	45.592088	47.730837	49.994475	54.928205	60.462060	85	169.665225	192.539264	219.143920	286.278545	377.856933
36	47.275969	49.566127	51.994365	57.301409	63.275942	86	173.210204	196.908701	224.526798	294.435508	390.192641
37	48.985109	51.433534	54.034251	59.733945	66.174221	87	176.808356	201.354604	230.017333	302.796396	402.898420
38	50.719886	53.333621	56.114936	62.227293	69.159447	88	180.460482	205.878308	235.617680	311.366305	415.985373
39	52.480683	55.266959	58.237235	64.782976	72.234231	89	184.167389	210.481179	241.330033	320.150463	429.464934
40	54.267894	57.234131	60.401979	67.402550	75.401258	90	187.929900	215.164599	247.156633	329.154224	443.348881
41	56.081912	59.235728	62.610019	70.087614	78.663295	91	191.748848	219.929980	253.099766	338.383079	457.649348
42	57.923141	61.272353	64.862219	72.839804	82.023194	92	195.625081	224.778753	259.161761	347.842656	472.378828
43	59.791988	63.344619	67.159464	75.660799	85.483890	93	199.559458	229.712382	265.344996	357.538722	487.550192
44	61.688868	65.453150	69.502653	78.552318	89.048406	94	203.552865	234.732348	271.651895	367.477190	503.176698
45	63.614201	67.598580	71.892706	81.516126	92.719858	95	207.606142	239.840165	278.084933	377.664119	519.271998
46	65.568414	69.781555	74.330560	84.554030	96.501454	96	211.720234	245.037367	284.646631	388.105722	535.850158
47	67.551940	72.002732	76.817171	87.667880	100.396498	97	215.896038	250.325521	291.339564	398.808365	552.925662
48	69.565219	74.262780	79.353514	90.859577	104.408392	98	220.134478	255.706217	298.166354	409.778573	570.513433
49	71.608698	76.562378	81.940584	94.131066	108.540644	99	224.436456	261.181070	305.129682	421.023038	588.628835
50	73.682828	78.902220	84.579396	97.484343	112.796863	100	228.803043	266.751744	312.232215	432.548612	607.287700

Table 5 (continued)

n	3½%	4%	4½%	5%	5½%
1	1.000000	1.000000	1.000000	1.000000	1.000000
2	2.035000	2.040000	2.045000	2.050000	2.055000
3	3.106225	3.121600	3.137025	3.152500	3.168025
4	4.214943	4.246464	4.278191	4.310125	4.342266
5	5.362466	5.416322	5.470710	5.525631	5.581091
6	6.550152	6.632975	6.716892	6.801913	6.888051
7	7.779407	7.898294	8.019152	8.142008	8.266894
8	9.051687	9.214226	9.380014	9.549109	9.721573
9	10.368496	10.582795	10.802114	11.026564	11.256259
10	11.731393	12.006107	12.288209	12.577892	12.875354
11	13.141992	13.486351	13.841179	14.206787	14.583498
12	14.601961	15.025805	15.464032	15.917126	16.385590
13	16.113030	16.626837	17.159913	17.712983	18.286798
14	17.676986	18.291911	18.932110	19.598632	20.292572
15	19.295680	20.023587	20.784054	21.578563	22.408663
16	20.971029	21.824530	22.719337	23.657492	24.641139
17	22.705015	23.697511	24.741707	25.840366	26.996402
18	24.499691	25.645412	26.855084	28.132384	29.481204
19	26.357180	27.671228	29.063563	30.539004	32.102670
20	28.279681	29.778077	31.371423	33.065954	34.868317
21	30.269470	31.969200	33.783137	35.719251	37.786075
22	32.328901	34.247887	36.303378	38.505214	40.864309
23	34.460413	36.617887	38.937030	41.430475	44.111846
24	36.666527	39.082602	41.689197	44.501998	47.537997
25	38.949855	41.645906	44.565906	47.727098	51.152587
26	41.313100	44.311742	47.570645	51.113453	54.965979
27	43.759059	47.084212	50.711324	54.669126	58.989108
28	46.290626	49.967580	53.993334	58.402582	63.233509
29	48.910798	52.966284	57.423034	62.322711	67.711352
30	51.622675	56.084935	61.007070	66.438846	72.435476
31	54.429469	59.328332	64.752388	70.760789	77.419427
32	57.334500	62.701465	68.666246	75.298828	82.677496
33	60.341208	66.209524	72.756227	80.063770	88.224758
34	63.453150	69.857905	77.030257	85.066958	94.077119
35	66.674010	73.652221	81.496619	90.320306	100.251361
36	70.007600	77.598309	86.163966	95.836321	106.765186
37	73.457866	81.702242	91.041345	101.628137	113.637271
38	77.028891	85.970331	96.138206	107.709544	120.887320
39	80.724903	90.409144	101.464425	114.095021	128.536123
40	84.550274	95.025510	107.030324	120.799772	136.605610
41	88.509534	99.826530	112.846689	127.839761	145.118918
42	92.607367	104.819591	118.924790	135.231749	154.100458
43	96.848625	110.012375	125.276405	142.993336	163.575984
44	101.238326	115.412870	131.913843	151.143003	173.572663
45	105.781668	121.029384	138.849966	159.700153	184.119159
46	110.484026	126.870560	146.098215	168.685160	195.245712
47	115.350967	132.945382	153.672635	178.119419	206.984226
48	120.388251	139.263197	161.587903	188.025389	219.368358
49	125.601839	145.833724	169.859359	198.426659	232.433618
50	130.997904	152.667073	178.503030	209.347992	246.217467

5½%	5%	4½%	4%	3½%	n
260.759427	220.815391	187.535667	159.773756	136.582830	51
276.101198	232.856160	196.974772	167.164706	142.363229	52
292.286761	245.498969	206.838636	174.851294	148.345942	53
309.362533	258.773917	217.146375	182.845345	154.538050	54
327.377472	272.712612	227.917962	191.159159	160.946882	55
346.383232	287.348243	239.174270	199.805525	167.580022	56
366.434311	302.715655	250.937112	208.797746	174.445322	57
387.588197	318.851437	263.229282	218.149655	181.550909	58
409.905548	335.794010	276.074601	227.875641	188.905191	59
433.450352	353.583710	289.497957	237.990667	196.516872	60
458.290121	372.262896	303.525365	248.510293	204.394962	61
484.496077	391.876039	318.184607	259.450704	212.548786	62
512.143361	412.469841	333.502287	270.828732	220.987993	63
541.311246	434.093334	349.509890	282.661881	229.722573	64
572.083364	456.798000	366.237835	294.968356	238.762862	65
604.547948	480.637899	383.718538	307.767089	248.119562	66
638.798088	505.669795	401.985872	321.077773	257.803747	67
674.931979	531.953284	421.075236	334.920883	267.826878	68
713.053237	559.550949	441.023622	349.317718	278.200818	69
753.271165	588.528495	461.869685	364.290426	288.937846	70
795.701079	618.954919	483.653821	379.862043	300.050671	71
840.464637	650.902666	506.418243	396.056524	311.552444	72
887.690192	684.447799	530.207064	412.898785	323.456779	73
937.513151	719.670188	555.066382	430.414735	335.777766	74
990.076374	756.653697	581.044370	448.631325	348.529988	75
1045.530574	795.486382	608.191366	467.576577	361.728537	76
1104.034758	836.260701	636.559978	487.279640	375.389035	77
1165.756665	879.073734	666.205177	507.770825	389.527651	78
1230.873281	924.027421	697.184410	529.081656	404.161119	79
1299.571310	971.228793	729.557709	551.244922	419.306757	80
1372.047730	1020.790232	763.387806	574.294718	434.982494	81
1448.510354	1072.829742	798.740257	598.266505	451.206880	82
1529.178424	1127.471228	835.683570	623.197166	467.999121	83
1614.283236	1184.844790	874.289330	649.125051	485.379090	84
1704.068810	1245.087029	914.632349	676.090053	503.367357	85
1798.792593	1308.341380	956.790805	704.133654	521.985214	86
1898.726187	1374.758448	1000.846391	733.299000	541.254696	87
2004.156123	1444.496370	1046.884479	763.630957	561.198610	88
2115.384712	1517.721189	1094.994280	795.176195	581.840561	89
2232.730868	1594.607245	1145.269024	827.983241	603.204980	90
2356.531064	1675.337609	1197.806130	862.102572	625.317154	91
2487.140272	1760.104489	1252.707404	897.586673	648.203253	92
2624.932984	1849.109716	1310.079238	934.490139	671.890367	93
2770.304297	1942.565195	1370.032805	972.869744	696.406529	94
2923.671030	2040.693453	1432.684283	1012.784531	721.780759	95
3085.472935	2143.728127	1498.155074	1054.265909	748.043082	96
3256.263509	2251.914536	1566.572051	1097.467747	775.224590	97
3436.263509	2365.510255	1638.067795	1142.366453	808.357450	98
3626.257999	2484.785771	1712.780848	1189.061112	832.474961	99
3826.702184	2610.025058	1790.855984	1237.623554	862.611582	100

Table 5 (continued)

n	6%	6½%	7%	7½%	8%
1	1.000000	1.000000	1.000000	1.000000	1.000000
2	2.060000	2.065000	2.070000	2.075000	2.080000
3	3.183600	3.199225	3.214900	3.230625	3.246400
4	4.374616	4.407175	4.439943	4.472922	4.506112
5	5.637093	5.693641	5.750739	5.808391	5.866601
6	6.975318	7.063728	7.153291	7.244020	7.335929
7	8.393838	8.522870	8.654021	8.787322	8.922803
8	9.897468	10.076857	10.259802	10.446371	10.636628
9	11.491316	11.731852	11.977989	12.229849	12.487558
10	13.180795	13.494423	13.816448	14.147087	14.486562
11	14.971642	15.371560	15.783599	16.208119	16.645487
12	16.869941	17.370711	17.888451	18.423728	18.977126
13	18.882137	19.499808	20.140643	20.805507	21.495296
14	21.015066	21.767295	22.550487	23.365920	24.214920
15	23.275970	24.182169	25.129022	26.118364	27.152114
16	25.672528	26.754010	27.888053	29.077242	30.324283
17	28.212879	29.493021	30.840217	32.258035	33.750225
18	30.905652	32.410067	33.999032	35.677387	37.450244
19	33.759991	35.516722	37.378964	39.353191	41.446263
20	36.785591	38.825309	40.995491	43.304681	45.761964
21	39.992726	42.348954	44.865176	47.552532	50.422921
22	43.392289	46.101636	49.005738	52.118972	55.456754
23	46.995827	50.098242	53.436140	57.027894	60.893295
24	50.815576	54.354628	58.176669	62.304987	66.764758
25	54.864511	58.887679	63.249036	67.977861	73.105939
26	59.156381	63.715378	68.676469	74.076200	79.954414
27	63.705764	68.856877	74.483821	80.631915	87.350767
28	68.528110	74.332575	80.697689	87.679309	95.338828
29	73.639797	80.164192	87.346527	95.255257	103.965934
30	79.058184	86.374864	94.460783	103.399401	113.283209
31	84.801676	92.989230	102.073039	112.154356	123.345866
32	90.889776	100.033530	110.218151	121.565933	134.213535
33	97.343163	107.535710	118.933422	131.683377	145.950617
34	104.183752	115.525531	128.258761	142.559631	158.626667
35	111.434777	124.034001	138.236874	154.251603	172.316800
36	119.120864	133.096946	148.913455	166.820473	187.102144
37	127.268116	142.748247	160.337397	180.332008	203.070315
38	135.904202	153.026883	172.561014	194.856909	220.315940
39	145.058455	163.973630	185.640285	210.471177	238.941216
40	154.761961	175.631916	199.635105	227.256515	259.056512
41	165.047679	188.047991	214.609562	245.300754	280.781033
42	175.950540	201.271110	230.632231	264.698310	304.243515
43	187.507572	215.353732	247.776488	285.550683	329.582997
44	199.758026	230.351775	266.120841	307.966984	356.949636
45	212.743508	246.324588	285.749300	332.064508	386.505607
46	226.508118	263.335686	306.751749	357.969346	418.426055
47	241.098605	281.452255	329.224373	385.817046	452.900140
48	256.564521	300.746919	353.270078	415.753325	490.132150
49	272.958392	321.295468	378.998984	447.934824	530.342722
50	290.335895	343.179673	406.528912	482.529936	573.770138

8%	7½%	7%	6½%	6%	n
620.671751	519.719680	435.985936	366.486352	308.756049	51
671.325489	559.698656	467.504951	391.307965	328.281411	52
726.031528	602.676055	501.230297	417.742982	348.978296	53
785.114049	648.876758	537.316416	445.896276	370.916993	54
848.923175	698.542515	575.928566	475.879534	394.172013	55
917.837026	751.933203	617.243564	507.811705	418.822333	56
992.263989	809.328194	661.450614	541.819465	444.951673	57
1072.645104	871.027808	708.752155	578.037730	472.648773	58
1159.456715	937.354893	759.364807	616.610182	502.007700	59
1253.213249	1008.656509	813.520340	657.689845	533.128160	60
1354.470310	1085.305746	871.466765	701.439684	566.115851	61
1463.827931	1167.703671	933.469437	748.033264	601.082800	62
1581.934169	1256.281450	999.812300	797.655426	638.147769	63
1709.488897	1351.502560	1070.799156	850.503029	677.436635	64
1847.248009	1453.865253	1146.755097	906.785726	719.082833	65
1996.027847	1563.905145	1228.027951	966.726798	763.227802	66
2156.710075	1682.198029	1314.989908	1030.564038	810.021470	67
2330.246878	1809.362883	1408.039199	1098.550703	859.622755	68
2517.666628	1946.065099	1507.601942	1170.956497	912.200122	69
2720.079956	2093.019979	1614.134075	1248.068670	967.932127	70
2938.686356	2250.996476	1728.123464	1330.193133	1027.008055	71
3174.781254	2420.821210	1850.092102	1417.655689	1089.628537	72
3429.763757	2603.382801	1980.598549	1510.803308	1156.006250	73
3705.144851	2799.636508	2120.240443	1610.005523	1226.366622	74
4002.556443	3010.609246	2269.657275	1715.655881	1300.948621	75
4323.760948	3237.404937	2429.533280	1828.173516	1380.005534	76
4670.661830	3481.210308	2600.600607	1948.004794	1463.805867	77
5045.314764	3743.301081	2783.642642	2075.625104	1552.634216	78
5449.939954	4025.048657	2979.497633	2211.540734	1646.792271	79
5886.935134	4327.927299	3189.062458	2356.290888	1746.599804	80
6358.889949	4653.521842	3413.296833	2510.449792	1852.395794	81
6868.601137	5003.535984	3653.227602	2674.629030	1964.539537	82
7419.089235	5379.801177	3909.953540	2848.479914	2083.411913	83
8013.616357	5784.286270	4184.650276	3035.696113	2209.416623	84
8655.705661	6219.107736	4478.575796	3234.616355	2342.981621	85
9349.162105	6686.540805	4793.076093	3445.227421	2484.560511	86
10098.095077	7189.031364	5129.591424	3670.167201	2634.634147	87
10906.942661	7729.208723	5489.662807	3909.662807	2793.712188	88
11780.498081	8309.899372	5874.939210	4164.860403	2962.334920	89
12723.937900	8934.141819	6287.184940	4436.576330	3141.075010	90
13742.852951	9605.202449	6728.287887	4725.953783	3330.539515	91
14843.281143	10326.592628	7200.268024	5034.140785	3531.371874	92
16031.743671	11102.087059	7705.286788	5362.359933	3744.254194	93
17315.283134	11935.743587	8245.656841	5711.913330	3969.909436	94
18701.505798	12831.924335	8823.852836	6084.187692	4209.104005	95
20198.626205	13795.318672	9442.522521	6480.659896	4462.650238	96
21815.516296	14830.967571	10104.499080	6902.902790	4731.409255	97
23561.757575	15944.290138	10812.814002	7352.591470	5016.293804	98
25447.698181	17141.111877	11570.710987	7831.509906	5318.271438	99
27484.514007	18427.695266	12381.660732	8341.558067	5638.567708	100

Table 6

$a_{\overline{n}|r}$

r = interest rate per payment period; n = number of payment periods

n	¼%	½%	¾%	1%	1¼%
1	0.997506	0.995025	0.992556	0.990099	0.987654
2	1.992524	1.985099	1.977723	1.970395	1.963115
3	2.985061	2.970248	2.955556	2.940985	2.926534
4	3.975123	3.950496	3.926439	3.901965	3.878058
5	4.962716	4.925867	4.889439	4.853431	4.817835
6	5.947846	5.896385	5.845597	5.795476	5.746010
7	6.930519	6.862074	6.794637	6.728194	6.662725
8	7.910741	7.822960	7.736613	7.651677	7.568124
9	8.888520	8.779064	8.671576	8.566017	8.462344
10	9.863860	9.730412	9.599525	9.471304	9.345525
11	10.836767	10.677027	10.520674	10.367628	10.217803
12	11.807249	11.618933	11.434912	11.255077	11.079311
13	12.775310	12.556152	12.342345	12.133740	11.930184
14	13.740957	13.488708	13.243022	13.003702	12.770552
15	14.704197	14.416626	14.136994	13.865052	13.600545
16	15.665033	15.339926	15.024312	14.717873	14.420291
17	16.623475	16.258633	15.905024	15.562251	15.229918
18	17.579525	17.172769	16.779180	16.398268	16.029548
19	18.533192	18.082357	17.646829	17.226008	16.819307
20	19.484480	18.987420	18.508019	18.045552	17.599315
21	20.433396	19.887980	19.362798	18.856982	18.369694
22	21.379946	20.784060	20.211214	19.660379	19.130562
23	22.324136	21.675682	21.053314	20.455820	19.882036
24	23.265970	22.562867	21.889145	21.243386	20.624233
25	24.205456	23.445639	22.718754	22.023155	21.357268
26	25.142599	24.324190	23.542188	22.795203	22.081252
27	26.077405	25.198029	24.359492	23.559607	22.796298
28	27.009879	26.067691	25.170711	24.316442	23.502517
29	27.940030	26.933025	25.975892	25.065784	24.200016
30	28.867859	27.794055	26.775079	25.807707	24.888905
31	29.793376	28.650802	27.568317	26.542284	25.569289
32	30.716584	29.503285	28.355649	27.269588	26.241273
33	31.637490	30.351527	29.137121	27.989691	26.904961
34	32.556099	31.195550	29.912755	28.702665	27.560455
35	33.472417	32.035373	30.682655	29.408579	28.207857
36	34.386451	32.871018	31.446804	30.107504	28.847266
37	35.298205	33.702505	32.205264	30.799509	29.478781
38	36.207685	34.529856	32.958079	31.484662	30.102500
39	37.114898	35.353091	33.705289	32.163032	30.718518
40	38.019848	36.172230	34.446937	32.834685	31.326932
41	38.922541	36.987293	35.183064	33.499688	31.927834
42	39.822983	37.798302	35.913711	34.158107	32.521317
43	40.721180	38.605275	36.638919	34.810007	33.107474
44	41.617136	39.408234	37.358729	35.455472	33.686394
45	42.510859	40.207198	38.073180	36.094507	34.258167
46	43.402353	41.002187	38.782312	36.727235	34.822881
47	44.291624	41.793221	39.486166	37.353698	35.380623
48	45.178676	42.580320	40.184780	37.973958	35.931479
49	46.063518	43.363502	40.878194	38.588077	36.475535
50	46.946152	44.142788	41.566445	39.196116	37.012874

n	¼%	½%	¾%	1%	1¼%
51	47.826585	44.918198	42.249573	39.798135	37.543579
52	48.704822	45.689749	42.927616	40.394193	38.067733
53	49.580870	46.457462	43.600612	40.984349	38.585415
54	50.454732	47.221355	44.268597	41.568663	39.096706
55	51.326417	47.981447	44.931610	42.147191	39.601685
56	52.195926	48.737759	45.589687	42.719991	40.100430
57	53.063268	49.490307	46.242866	43.287120	40.593017
58	53.928446	50.239112	46.891182	43.848633	41.079523
59	54.791466	50.984191	47.534672	44.404587	41.560023
60	55.652335	51.725563	48.173372	44.955037	42.034590
61	56.511058	52.463247	48.807317	45.500037	42.503290
62	57.367637	53.197261	49.436542	46.039640	42.966221
63	58.222083	53.927623	50.061085	46.573901	43.423428
64	59.074396	54.654351	50.680977	47.102872	43.874991
65	59.924584	55.377464	51.296255	47.626606	44.320978
66	60.772652	56.096979	51.906953	48.145155	44.761460
67	61.618605	56.812914	52.513105	48.658569	45.196504
68	62.462449	57.525288	53.114744	49.166900	45.626177
69	63.304188	58.234117	53.711905	49.670198	46.050545
70	64.143828	58.939420	54.304620	50.168513	46.469674
71	64.981375	59.641214	54.892923	50.661894	46.883629
72	65.816832	60.339517	55.476847	51.150390	47.292473
73	66.650206	61.034345	56.056424	51.634049	47.696269
74	67.481502	61.725716	56.631686	52.112920	48.095081
75	68.310725	62.413648	57.202666	52.587050	48.488969
76	69.137879	63.098157	57.769395	53.056485	48.877994
77	69.962972	63.779261	58.331906	53.521272	49.262216
78	70.786006	64.456976	58.890229	53.981457	49.641695
79	71.606989	65.131320	59.444396	54.437087	50.016488
80	72.425923	65.802308	59.994438	54.888205	50.386655
81	73.242816	66.469958	60.540385	55.334856	50.752252
82	74.057672	67.134287	61.082268	55.777085	51.113335
83	74.870495	67.795311	61.620117	56.214936	51.469961
84	75.681291	68.453045	62.153962	56.648451	51.822184
85	76.490066	69.107508	62.683834	57.077674	52.170058
86	77.296823	69.758714	63.209760	57.502648	52.513637
87	78.101570	70.406681	63.731772	57.923414	52.852975
88	78.904308	71.051424	64.249898	58.340014	53.188124
89	79.705045	71.692959	64.764167	58.752489	53.519134
90	80.503785	72.331303	65.274607	59.160880	53.846059
91	81.300533	72.966470	65.781248	59.565228	54.168947
92	82.095294	73.598478	66.284117	59.965572	54.487849
93	82.888075	74.227341	66.783242	60.361952	54.802813
94	83.678877	74.853076	67.278652	60.754408	55.113890
95	84.467708	75.475697	67.770375	61.142978	55.421126
96	85.254571	76.095221	68.258436	61.527701	55.724569
97	86.039472	76.711663	68.742865	61.908615	56.024265
98	86.822415	77.325038	69.223687	62.285758	56.320262
99	87.603406	77.935361	69.700930	62.659166	56.612604
100	88.382449	78.542648	70.174620	63.028877	56.901338

Table 6 (continued)

3%	2½%	2%	1¾%	1½%	n
25.951227	28.646157	31.787848	33.554013	35.467673	51
26.166240	28.923080	32.144949	33.959718	35.928742	52
26.374990	29.193249	32.495048	34.358445	36.382997	53
26.577660	29.456828	32.838282	34.750315	36.830539	54
26.774427	29.713979	33.174787	35.135445	37.271467	55
26.965464	29.964857	33.504693	35.513950	37.705879	56
27.150935	30.209617	33.828130	35.885946	38.133871	57
27.331005	30.448407	34.145226	36.251544	38.555537	58
27.505830	30.681372	34.456104	36.610854	38.970973	59
27.675564	30.908656	34.760886	36.963985	39.380269	60
27.840353	31.130396	35.059692	37.311041	39.783516	61
28.000343	31.346728	35.352639	37.652129	40.180804	62
28.155672	31.557783	35.639842	37.987351	40.572221	63
28.306478	31.763691	35.921414	38.316806	40.957853	64
28.452891	31.964577	36.197465	38.640596	41.337786	65
28.595040	32.160562	36.468103	38.958817	41.712105	66
28.733049	32.351768	36.733434	39.271564	42.080891	67
28.867038	32.538311	36.993563	39.578933	42.444228	68
28.997124	32.720303	37.248591	39.881015	42.802195	69
29.123421	32.897857	37.498619	40.177902	43.154872	70
29.246040	33.071080	37.743744	40.469682	43.502337	71
29.365087	33.240078	37.984062	40.756445	43.844667	72
29.480667	33.404954	38.219669	41.038275	44.181938	73
29.592881	33.565809	38.450656	41.315258	44.514224	74
29.701826	33.722740	38.677114	41.587477	44.841600	75
29.807598	33.875844	38.899131	41.855014	45.164138	76
29.910290	34.025214	39.116795	42.117950	45.481910	77
30.009990	34.170940	39.330191	42.376364	45.794985	78
30.106786	34.313112	39.539403	42.630333	46.103433	79
30.200763	34.451817	39.744513	42.879934	46.407323	80
30.292003	34.587138	39.945601	43.125242	46.706723	81
30.380586	34.719159	40.142746	43.366331	47.001697	82
30.466588	34.847960	40.336025	43.603274	47.292313	83
30.550085	34.973620	40.525515	43.836142	47.578633	84
30.631151	35.096214	40.711289	44.065004	47.860722	85
30.709855	35.215819	40.893421	44.289930	48.138643	86
30.786267	35.332506	41.071981	44.510988	48.412456	87
30.860454	35.446348	41.247040	44.728244	48.682242	88
30.932479	35.557412	41.418667	44.941763	48.948002	89
31.002407	35.665768	41.586929	45.151610	49.209854	90
31.070298	35.771481	41.751891	45.357847	49.467837	91
31.136212	35.874616	41.913618	45.560538	49.722007	92
31.200206	35.975235	42.072175	45.759742	49.972421	93
31.262336	36.073400	42.227622	45.955521	50.219134	94
31.322656	36.169171	42.380022	46.147932	50.462201	95
31.381219	36.262605	42.529433	46.337034	50.701675	96
31.438077	36.353761	42.675915	46.522883	50.937611	97
31.493279	36.442694	42.819524	46.705357	51.170060	98
31.546872	36.529458	42.960318	46.885048	51.399074	99
31.598905	36.614105	43.098351	47.061472	51.624704	100

n	1½%	1¾%	2%	2½%	3%
1	0.985222	0.982801	0.980392	0.975610	0.970874
2	1.955883	1.948699	1.941561	1.927424	1.913470
3	2.912200	2.897984	2.883883	2.856024	2.828611
4	3.854385	3.830942	3.807729	3.761974	3.717098
5	4.782645	4.747855	4.713459	4.645828	4.579707
6	5.697187	5.648997	5.601431	5.508125	5.417191
7	6.598214	6.534641	6.471991	6.349390	6.230283
8	7.485925	7.405053	7.325481	7.170137	7.019692
9	8.360517	8.260494	8.162236	7.970865	7.786109
10	9.222184	9.101223	8.982585	8.752064	8.530203
11	10.071118	9.927492	9.786848	9.514208	9.252624
12	10.907505	10.739549	10.575341	10.257764	9.954004
13	11.731532	11.537641	11.348373	10.983185	10.634955
14	12.543381	12.322005	12.106248	11.690912	11.296073
15	13.343233	13.092880	12.849263	12.381377	11.937935
16	14.131264	13.850496	13.577709	13.055002	12.561102
17	14.907649	14.595082	14.291871	13.712197	13.166118
18	15.672561	15.326862	14.992031	14.353363	13.753513
19	16.426168	16.046056	15.678462	14.978891	14.323799
20	17.168639	16.752881	16.351433	15.589162	14.877475
21	17.900137	17.447549	17.011209	16.184548	15.415024
22	18.620824	18.130269	17.658048	16.765413	15.936916
23	19.330861	18.801247	18.292204	17.332110	16.443608
24	20.030405	19.460685	18.913925	17.884985	16.935542
25	20.719611	20.108781	19.523456	18.424376	17.413147
26	21.398632	20.745731	20.121035	18.950901	17.876842
27	22.067617	21.371726	20.706897	19.464010	18.327031
28	22.726717	21.986954	21.281272	19.964888	18.764108
29	23.376076	22.591601	21.844384	20.453549	19.188454
30	24.015838	23.185849	22.396455	20.930292	19.600441
31	24.646146	23.769876	22.937701	21.395407	20.000428
32	25.267139	24.343858	23.468334	21.849177	20.388765
33	25.878954	24.907969	23.988563	22.291880	20.765792
34	26.481728	25.462377	24.498591	22.723786	21.131836
35	27.075595	26.007250	24.998619	23.145157	21.487220
36	27.660684	26.542752	25.488842	23.556251	21.832252
37	28.237127	27.069044	25.969453	23.957318	22.167235
38	28.805052	27.586284	26.440640	24.348603	22.492461
39	29.364583	28.094628	26.902588	24.730344	22.808215
40	29.915845	28.594229	27.355478	25.102775	23.114772
41	30.458961	29.085237	27.799489	25.466121	23.412400
42	30.994050	29.567801	28.234703	25.820606	23.701359
43	31.521232	30.042064	28.661562	26.166445	23.981902
44	32.040622	30.508171	29.079962	26.503849	24.254274
45	32.552337	30.966262	29.490159	26.833023	24.518712
46	33.056490	31.416473	29.892313	27.154169	24.775449
47	33.553192	31.858942	30.286581	27.467482	25.024708
48	34.042554	32.293800	30.673119	27.773153	25.266706
49	34.524683	32.721180	31.052077	28.071369	25.501657
50	34.999688	33.141209	31.423605	28.362311	25.729764

Table 6 (continued)

n	3½%	4%	4½%	5%	5½%
1	0.966184	0.961538	0.956938	0.952381	0.947867
2	1.899694	1.886095	1.872668	1.859410	1.846320
3	2.801637	2.775091	2.748964	2.723248	2.697933
4	3.673079	3.629895	3.587526	3.545950	3.505150
5	4.515052	4.451822	4.389977	4.329477	4.270284
6	5.328553	5.242137	5.157873	5.075692	4.995530
7	6.114544	6.002055	5.892701	5.786373	5.682967
8	6.873955	6.732745	6.595886	6.463213	6.334566
9	7.607686	7.435331	7.268791	7.107822	6.952195
10	8.316605	8.110896	7.912718	7.721735	7.537626
11	9.001551	8.760477	8.528917	8.306414	8.092536
12	9.663334	9.385074	9.118581	8.863252	8.618518
13	10.302738	9.985648	9.682852	9.393573	9.117078
14	10.920520	10.563123	10.222825	9.898641	9.589648
15	11.517411	11.118387	10.739658	10.379658	10.037581
16	12.094117	11.652295	11.234015	10.837770	10.462162
17	12.651320	12.165669	11.707191	11.274066	10.864608
18	13.189682	12.659297	12.159992	11.689587	11.246074
19	13.709837	13.133939	12.593264	12.085321	11.607653
20	14.212403	13.590326	13.007937	12.462210	11.950382
21	14.697974	14.029160	13.404724	12.821153	12.275244
22	15.167125	14.451115	13.784425	13.163003	12.583170
23	15.620410	14.856841	14.147775	13.488574	12.875042
24	16.058367	15.246963	14.495478	13.798642	13.151699
25	16.481514	15.622080	14.828209	14.093945	13.413933
26	16.890352	15.982769	15.146611	14.375185	13.662495
27	17.285364	16.329585	15.451303	14.643034	13.898100
28	17.667019	16.663063	15.742874	14.898127	14.121422
29	18.035767	16.983714	16.021889	15.141074	14.333101
30	18.392045	17.292033	16.288889	15.372451	14.533745
31	18.736276	17.588493	16.544391	15.592810	14.723929
32	19.068865	17.873551	16.788891	15.802677	14.904198
33	19.390208	18.147645	17.022862	16.002549	15.075069
34	19.700684	18.411197	17.246758	16.192904	15.237033
35	20.000661	18.664613	17.461012	16.374194	15.390552
36	20.290494	18.908282	17.666041	16.546852	15.536068
37	20.570525	19.142579	17.862240	16.711287	15.673998
38	20.841087	19.367864	18.049990	16.867893	15.804738
39	21.102500	19.584485	18.229656	17.017041	15.928662
40	21.355072	19.792774	18.401584	17.159086	16.046125
41	21.599103	19.993052	18.566110	17.294368	16.157464
42	21.834883	20.185627	18.723550	17.423208	16.262999
43	22.062688	20.370795	18.874210	17.545912	16.363032
44	22.282791	20.548841	19.018383	17.662773	16.457851
45	22.495450	20.720040	19.156347	17.774070	16.547756
46	22.700918	20.884653	19.288371	17.880066	16.632915
47	22.899438	21.042936	19.414709	17.981016	16.713664
48	23.091244	21.195131	19.535607	18.077158	16.790203
49	23.276564	21.341472	19.651298	18.168722	16.862751
50	23.455618	21.482184	19.762008	18.255925	16.931518

n	3½%	4%	4½%	5%	5½%
51	23.628616	21.617485	19.867950	18.338977	16.996699
52	23.795764	21.747582	19.969330	18.418073	17.058483
53	23.957764	21.872675	20.066345	18.493403	17.117045
54	24.113295	21.992966	20.159182	18.565146	17.172555
55	24.264053	22.108612	20.248021	18.633472	17.225170
56	24.409713	22.219819	20.333034	18.698545	17.275043
57	24.550447	22.326749	20.414387	18.760519	17.322316
58	24.686423	22.429567	20.492236	18.819542	17.367124
59	24.817800	22.528429	20.566733	18.875754	17.409596
60	24.944734	22.623490	20.638022	18.929290	17.449854
61	25.067376	22.714894	20.706241	18.980276	17.488013
62	25.185870	22.802783	20.771523	19.028834	17.524183
63	25.300358	22.887291	20.833993	19.075080	17.558468
64	25.410974	22.968549	20.893773	19.119124	17.590965
65	25.517849	23.046682	20.950979	19.161070	17.621767
66	25.621110	23.121809	21.005722	19.201019	17.650964
67	25.720879	23.194048	21.058107	19.239066	17.678639
68	25.817275	23.263507	21.108236	19.275301	17.704871
69	25.910410	23.330295	21.156207	19.309810	17.729736
70	26.000397	23.394515	21.202112	19.342677	17.753304
71	26.087340	23.456264	21.246040	19.373987	17.775644
72	26.171343	23.515639	21.288077	19.403788	17.796819
73	26.252505	23.572730	21.328303	19.432179	17.816890
74	26.330923	23.627625	21.366797	19.459218	17.835914
75	26.406699	23.680408	21.403634	19.484970	17.853947
76	26.479892	23.731162	21.438884	19.509495	17.871040
77	26.550621	23.779963	21.472616	19.532853	17.887242
78	26.618957	23.826888	21.504896	19.555098	17.902599
79	26.684983	23.872007	21.535785	19.576283	17.917155
80	26.748776	23.915392	21.565345	19.596460	17.930953
81	26.810411	23.957107	21.593632	19.615677	17.944031
82	26.869962	23.997219	21.620700	19.633978	17.956428
83	26.927500	24.035787	21.646603	19.651407	17.968178
84	26.983092	24.072872	21.671390	19.668007	17.979316
85	27.036804	24.108531	21.695110	19.683816	17.989873
86	27.088699	24.142818	21.717809	19.698873	17.999879
87	27.138840	24.175787	21.739530	19.713212	18.009364
88	27.187285	24.207487	21.760316	19.726869	18.018355
89	27.234092	24.237969	21.780207	19.739875	18.026876
90	27.279316	24.267278	21.799241	19.752262	18.034954
91	27.323010	24.295459	21.817455	19.764059	18.042610
92	27.365227	24.322557	21.834885	19.775294	18.049868
93	27.406017	24.348612	21.851565	19.785994	18.056747
94	27.445427	24.373666	21.867526	19.796185	18.063267
95	27.483504	24.397756	21.882800	19.805891	18.069447
96	27.520294	24.420919	21.897417	19.815134	18.075306
97	27.555839	24.443191	21.911403	19.823937	18.080858
98	27.590183	24.464607	21.924788	19.832321	18.086122
99	27.623365	24.485199	21.937596	19.840306	18.091111
100	27.655525	24.504999	21.949853	19.847910	18.095839

Table 6 (continued)

n	6%	6½%	7%	7½%	8%
1	0.943396	0.938967	0.934579	0.930233	0.925926
2	1.833393	1.820626	1.808018	1.795565	1.783265
3	2.673012	2.648475	2.624316	2.600526	2.577097
4	3.465106	3.425799	3.387211	3.349326	3.312127
5	4.212364	4.155679	4.100197	4.045885	3.992710
6	4.917324	4.841014	4.766540	4.693846	4.622880
7	5.582381	5.484520	5.389289	5.296601	5.206370
8	6.209794	6.088751	5.971298	5.857304	5.746639
9	6.801692	6.656104	6.515232	6.378887	6.246888
10	7.360087	7.188830	7.023581	6.864081	6.710081
11	7.886875	7.689042	7.498674	7.315424	7.138964
12	8.383844	8.158725	7.942686	7.735278	7.536078
13	8.852683	8.599742	8.357651	8.125840	7.903776
14	9.294984	9.013842	8.745468	8.489154	8.244237
15	9.712249	9.402669	9.107914	8.827120	8.559479
16	10.105895	9.767764	9.446649	9.141507	8.851369
17	10.477260	10.110577	9.763223	9.433960	9.121638
18	10.827603	10.432466	10.059087	9.706009	9.371887
19	11.158116	10.734710	10.335595	9.959078	9.603599
20	11.469921	11.018507	10.594014	10.194491	9.818147
21	11.764077	11.284983	10.835527	10.413480	10.016803
22	12.041582	11.535196	11.061240	10.617191	10.200744
23	12.303379	11.770137	11.272187	10.806689	10.371059
24	12.550357	11.990739	11.469334	10.982967	10.528758
25	12.783356	12.197877	11.653583	11.146946	10.674776
26	13.003166	12.392373	11.825779	11.299485	10.809978
27	13.210534	12.574998	11.986709	11.441381	10.935165
28	13.406164	12.746477	12.137111	11.573378	11.051078
29	13.590721	12.907490	12.277674	11.696165	11.158406
30	13.764831	13.058676	12.409041	11.810386	11.257783
31	13.929086	13.200635	12.531814	11.916638	11.349799
32	14.084043	13.333929	12.646555	12.015478	11.434999
33	14.230230	13.459089	12.753790	12.107421	11.513888
34	14.368141	13.576609	12.854009	12.192950	11.586934
35	14.498246	13.686957	12.947672	12.272511	11.654568
36	14.620987	13.790570	13.035208	12.346522	11.717193
37	14.736780	13.887859	13.117017	12.415370	11.775179
38	14.846019	13.979210	13.193473	12.479414	11.828869
39	14.949075	14.064986	13.264928	12.538989	11.878582
40	15.046297	14.145527	13.331709	12.594409	11.924613
41	15.138016	14.221152	13.394120	12.645962	11.967235
42	15.224543	14.292162	13.452449	12.693918	12.006699
43	15.306173	14.358837	13.506962	12.738528	12.043240
44	15.383182	14.421443	13.557908	12.780026	12.077074
45	15.455832	14.480228	13.605522	12.818629	12.108401
46	15.524370	14.535426	13.650020	12.854539	12.137409
47	15.589028	14.587254	13.691608	12.887943	12.164267
48	15.650027	14.635919	13.730474	12.919017	12.189137
49	15.707572	14.681615	13.766799	12.947922	12.212163
50	15.761861	14.724521	13.800746	12.974812	12.233485
51	15.813076	14.764808	13.832473	12.999825	12.253224
52	15.861393	14.802637	13.862124	13.023093	12.271506
53	15.906974	14.838157	13.889836	13.044737	12.288432
54	15.949976	14.871509	13.915735	13.064872	12.304103
55	15.990543	14.902825	13.939939	13.083602	12.318614
56	16.028814	14.932230	13.962560	13.101025	12.332050
57	16.064919	14.959840	13.983701	13.117233	12.344491
58	16.098980	14.985766	14.003459	13.132309	12.356010
59	16.131113	15.010109	14.021924	13.146334	12.366676
60	16.161428	15.032966	14.039181	13.159381	12.376552
61	16.190026	15.054428	14.055309	13.171517	12.385696
62	16.217006	15.074580	14.070383	13.182807	12.394163
63	16.242458	15.093503	14.084470	13.193308	12.402003
64	16.266470	15.111270	14.097635	13.203078	12.409262
65	16.289123	15.127953	14.109940	13.212165	12.415983
66	16.310493	15.143618	14.121439	13.220619	12.422207
67	16.330654	15.158327	14.132186	13.228483	12.427969
68	16.349673	15.172138	14.142230	13.235798	12.433305
69	16.367617	15.185106	14.151617	13.242603	12.438245
70	16.384543	15.197282	14.160389	13.248933	12.442820
71	16.400544	15.208716	14.168588	13.254821	12.447005
72	16.415578	15.219452	14.176251	13.260299	12.450977
73	16.429791	15.229532	14.183412	13.265394	12.454608
74	16.443199	15.238997	14.190105	13.270134	12.457971
75	16.455848	15.247885	14.196359	13.274543	12.461084
76	16.467781	15.256230	14.202205	13.278645	12.463967
77	16.479039	15.264065	14.207668	13.282460	12.466636
78	16.489659	15.271423	14.212774	13.286010	12.469107
79	16.499679	15.278331	14.217546	13.289311	12.471396
80	16.509131	15.284818	14.222005	13.292383	12.473514
81	16.518048	15.290909	14.226173	13.295240	12.475476
82	16.526460	15.296628	14.230069	13.297897	12.477293
83	16.534396	15.301998	14.233709	13.300370	12.478975
84	16.541883	15.307041	14.237111	13.302669	12.480532
85	16.548947	15.311775	14.240291	13.304809	12.481974
86	16.555610	15.316221	14.243262	13.306799	12.483310
87	16.561896	15.320395	14.246040	13.308650	12.484546
88	16.567827	15.324315	14.248635	13.310372	12.485691
89	16.573421	15.327995	14.251061	13.311974	12.486751
90	16.578699	15.331451	14.253328	13.313464	12.487732
91	16.583679	15.334696	14.255447	13.314851	12.488641
92	16.588376	15.337742	14.257427	13.316140	12.489482
93	16.592808	15.340603	14.259277	13.317340	12.490261
94	16.596988	15.343289	14.261007	13.318455	12.490983
95	16.600932	15.345812	14.262623	13.319493	12.491651
96	16.604653	15.348180	14.264134	13.320459	12.492269
97	16.608163	15.350404	14.265546	13.321357	12.492842
98	16.611475	15.352492	14.266865	13.322193	12.493372
99	16.614599	15.354452	14.268098	13.322970	12.493863
100	16.617546	15.356293	14.269251	13.323693	12.494318

Table 7

$$\frac{1}{a_{\overline{n}|r}}$$

r = interest rate per payment period; n = number of payment periods

n	$\tfrac{1}{4}\%$	$\tfrac{1}{2}\%$	$\tfrac{3}{4}\%$	1%	$1\tfrac{1}{4}\%$
1	1.002500	1.005000	1.007500	1.010000	1.012500
2	0.501876	0.503753	0.505632	0.507512	0.509394
3	0.335002	0.336672	0.338346	0.340022	0.341701
4	0.251565	0.253133	0.254705	0.256281	0.257861
5	0.201503	0.203010	0.204522	0.206040	0.207562
6	0.168128	0.169595	0.171069	0.172548	0.174034
7	0.144289	0.145729	0.147175	0.148628	0.150089
8	0.126410	0.127829	0.129256	0.130690	0.132133
9	0.112505	0.113907	0.115319	0.116740	0.118171
10	0.101380	0.102771	0.104171	0.105582	0.107003
11	0.092278	0.093659	0.095051	0.096454	0.097868
12	0.084694	0.086066	0.087451	0.088849	0.090258
13	0.078276	0.079642	0.081022	0.082415	0.083821
14	0.072775	0.074136	0.075511	0.076901	0.078305
15	0.068008	0.069364	0.070736	0.072124	0.073526
16	0.063836	0.065189	0.066559	0.067945	0.069347
17	0.060156	0.061506	0.062873	0.064258	0.065660
18	0.056884	0.058232	0.059598	0.060982	0.062385
19	0.053957	0.055303	0.056667	0.058052	0.059455
20	0.051323	0.052666	0.054031	0.055415	0.056820
21	0.048939	0.050282	0.051645	0.053031	0.054437
22	0.046773	0.048114	0.049477	0.050864	0.052272
23	0.044795	0.046135	0.047498	0.048886	0.050297
24	0.042981	0.044321	0.045685	0.047073	0.048487
25	0.041313	0.042652	0.044016	0.045407	0.046822
26	0.039773	0.041112	0.042487	0.043869	0.045287
27	0.038347	0.039686	0.041052	0.042446	0.043867
28	0.037023	0.038362	0.039729	0.041124	0.042549
29	0.035791	0.037129	0.038497	0.039895	0.041322
30	0.034641	0.035979	0.037348	0.038748	0.040179
31	0.033565	0.034903	0.036274	0.037676	0.039109
32	0.032556	0.033895	0.035266	0.036671	0.038108
33	0.031608	0.032947	0.034320	0.035727	0.037168
34	0.030716	0.032056	0.033431	0.034840	0.036284
35	0.029875	0.031215	0.032592	0.034004	0.035451
36	0.029081	0.030422	0.031800	0.033214	0.034665
37	0.028330	0.029671	0.031051	0.032468	0.033923
38	0.027618	0.028960	0.030342	0.031761	0.033220
39	0.026943	0.028286	0.029669	0.031092	0.032554
40	0.026302	0.027646	0.029030	0.030456	0.031921
41	0.025692	0.027036	0.028423	0.029851	0.031321
42	0.025111	0.026456	0.027845	0.029276	0.030749
43	0.024557	0.025903	0.027293	0.028727	0.030205
44	0.024029	0.025375	0.026768	0.028204	0.029686
45	0.023523	0.024871	0.026265	0.027705	0.029190
46	0.023040	0.024389	0.025785	0.027228	0.028717
47	0.022578	0.023927	0.025325	0.126771	0.028264
48	0.022134	0.023485	0.024885	0.026334	0.027831
49	0.021709	0.023061	0.024463	0.025915	0.027416
50	0.021301	0.022654	0.024058	0.025513	0.027018

n	$\tfrac{1}{4}\%$	$\tfrac{1}{2}\%$	$\tfrac{3}{4}\%$	1%	$1\tfrac{1}{4}\%$
51	0.020909	0.022263	0.023669	0.025127	0.026636
52	0.020532	0.021887	0.023295	0.024756	0.026269
53	0.020169	0.021525	0.022935	0.024400	0.025917
54	0.019820	0.021177	0.022589	0.024057	0.025578
55	0.019483	0.020841	0.022256	0.023726	0.025251
56	0.019159	0.020518	0.021935	0.023408	0.024937
57	0.018845	0.020206	0.021625	0.023102	0.024635
58	0.018543	0.019905	0.021326	0.022806	0.024343
59	0.018251	0.019614	0.021037	0.022520	0.024062
60	0.017969	0.019333	0.020758	0.022244	0.023790
61	0.017696	0.019061	0.020489	0.021978	0.023528
62	0.017431	0.018798	0.020228	0.021720	0.023274
63	0.017176	0.018543	0.019976	0.021471	0.023029
64	0.016928	0.018297	0.019731	0.021230	0.022792
65	0.016688	0.018058	0.019495	0.020997	0.022563
66	0.016455	0.017826	0.019265	0.020771	0.022341
67	0.016229	0.017602	0.019043	0.020551	0.022126
68	0.016010	0.017384	0.018827	0.020339	0.021917
69	0.015797	0.017172	0.018618	0.020133	0.021715
70	0.015590	0.016967	0.018415	0.019933	0.021519
71	0.015389	0.016767	0.018217	0.019739	0.021329
72	0.015194	0.016573	0.018026	0.019550	0.021145
73	0.015004	0.016384	0.017839	0.019367	0.020966
74	0.014819	0.016201	0.017658	0.019189	0.020792
75	0.014639	0.016022	0.017482	0.019016	0.020623
76	0.014464	0.015848	0.017310	0.018848	0.020459
77	0.014293	0.015679	0.017143	0.018684	0.020300
78	0.014127	0.015514	0.016981	0.018525	0.020144
79	0.013965	0.015354	0.016822	0.018370	0.019993
80	0.013807	0.015197	0.016668	0.018219	0.019847
81	0.013653	0.015044	0.016518	0.018072	0.019704
82	0.013503	0.014896	0.016371	0.017929	0.019564
83	0.013356	0.014750	0.016228	0.017789	0.019429
84	0.013213	0.014609	0.016089	0.017653	0.019297
85	0.013074	0.014470	0.015953	0.017520	0.019168
86	0.012937	0.014335	0.015820	0.017391	0.019043
87	0.012804	0.014203	0.015691	0.017264	0.018920
88	0.012674	0.014074	0.015564	0.017141	0.018801
89	0.012546	0.013948	0.015441	0.017021	0.018685
90	0.012422	0.013825	0.015320	0.016903	0.018571
91	0.012300	0.013705	0.015202	0.016788	0.018461
92	0.012181	0.013587	0.015087	0.016676	0.018353
93	0.012064	0.013472	0.014974	0.016567	0.018247
94	0.011950	0.013360	0.014864	0.016460	0.018144
95	0.011839	0.013249	0.014756	0.016355	0.018044
96	0.011730	0.013141	0.014650	0.016253	0.017945
97	0.011623	0.013036	0.014547	0.016153	0.017849
98	0.011518	0.012932	0.014446	0.016055	0.017756
99	0.011415	0.012831	0.014347	0.015959	0.017664
100	0.011314	0.012732	0.014250	0.015866	0.017574

Table 7 (continued)

n	1½%	1¾%	2%	2½%	3%
1	1.015000	1.017500	1.020000	1.025000	1.030000
2	0.511278	0.513163	0.515050	0.518827	0.522611
3	0.343383	0.345067	0.346755	0.350137	0.353530
4	0.259445	0.261032	0.262624	0.265818	0.269027
5	0.209089	0.210621	0.212158	0.215247	0.218355
6	0.175525	0.177023	0.178526	0.181550	0.184598
7	0.151556	0.153031	0.154512	0.157495	0.160506
8	0.133584	0.135043	0.136510	0.139467	0.142456
9	0.119610	0.121058	0.122515	0.125457	0.128434
10	0.108434	0.109875	0.111327	0.114259	0.117231
11	0.099294	0.100730	0.102178	0.105106	0.108077
12	0.091680	0.093114	0.094560	0.097487	0.100462
13	0.085240	0.086673	0.088118	0.091048	0.094030
14	0.079723	0.081156	0.082602	0.085537	0.088526
15	0.074944	0.076377	0.077825	0.080766	0.083767
16	0.070765	0.072200	0.073650	0.076599	0.079611
17	0.067080	0.068516	0.069970	0.072928	0.075953
18	0.063806	0.065245	0.066702	0.069670	0.072709
19	0.060878	0.062321	0.063782	0.066761	0.069814
20	0.058246	0.059691	9.061157	0.064147	0.067216
21	0.055865	0.057315	0.058785	0.061787	0.064872
22	0.053703	0.055156	0.056631	0.059647	0.062747
23	0.051731	0.053188	0.054668	0.057696	0.060814
24	0.049924	0.051386	0.052871	0.055913	0.059047
25	0.048263	0.049730	0.051220	0.054276	0.057428
26	0.046732	0.048203	0.049699	0.052769	0.055938
27	0.045315	0.046791	0.048293	0.051377	0.054564
28	0.044001	0.045488	0.046990	0.050088	0.053293
29	0.042779	0.044264	0.045778	0.048891	0.052115
30	0.041639	0.043130	0.044650	0.047778	0.051019
31	0.040574	0.042070	0.043596	0.046739	0.049999
32	0.039577	0.041078	0.042611	0.045768	0.049047
33	0.038641	0.040148	0.041687	0.044859	0.048156
34	0.037762	0.039274	0.040819	0.044007	0.047322
35	0.036934	0.038451	0.040002	0.043206	0.046539
36	0.036152	0.037675	0.039233	0.042452	0.045804
37	0.035414	0.036943	0.038507	0.041741	0.045112
38	0.034716	0.036250	0.037821	0.041070	0.044459
39	0.034055	0.035594	0.037171	0.040436	0.043844
40	0.033427	0.034972	0.036556	0.039836	0.043262
41	0.032831	0.034382	0.035972	0.039268	0.042712
42	0.032264	0.033821	0.035417	0.038729	0.042192
43	0.031725	0.033287	0.034890	0.038217	0.041698
44	0.031210	0.032778	0.034388	0.037730	0.041230
45	0.030720	0.032293	0.033910	0.037268	0.040785
46	0.030251	0.031830	0.033453	0.036827	0.040363
47	0.029803	0.031388	0.033018	0.036407	0.039961
48	0.029375	0.030966	0.032602	0.036006	0.039578
49	0.028965	0.030561	0.032204	0.035623	0.039213
50	0.028572	0.030174	0.031823	0.035258	0.038865

n	1½%	1¾%	2%	2½%	3%
51	0.028195	0.029803	0.031459	0.034909	0.038534
52	0.027833	0.029447	0.031109	0.034574	0.038217
53	0.027485	0.029105	0.030774	0.034254	0.037915
54	0.027151	0.028777	0.030452	0.033948	0.037626
55	0.026830	0.028461	0.030143	0.033654	0.037349
56	0.026521	0.028158	0.029847	0.033372	0.037084
57	0.026223	0.027866	0.029561	0.033102	0.036831
58	0.025937	0.027585	0.029287	0.032842	0.036588
59	0.025660	0.027314	0.029022	0.032593	0.036356
60	0.025393	0.027053	0.028768	0.032353	0.036133
61	0.025136	0.026802	0.028523	0.032123	0.035919
62	0.024888	0.026559	0.028286	0.031901	0.035714
63	0.024647	0.026325	0.028058	0.031688	0.035517
64	0.024415	0.026098	0.027839	0.031482	0.035328
65	0.024191	0.025880	0.027626	0.031285	0.035146
66	0.023974	0.025668	0.027421	0.031094	0.034971
67	0.023764	0.025464	0.027223	0.030910	0.034803
68	0.023560	0.025266	0.027032	0.030733	0.034642
69	0.023363	0.025075	0.026847	0.030562	0.034486
70	0.023172	0.024889	0.026668	0.030397	0.034337
71	0.022987	0.024710	0.026494	0.030238	0.034193
72	0.022808	0.024536	0.026327	0.030084	0.034054
73	0.022634	0.024367	0.026165	0.029936	0.033921
74	0.022465	0.024204	0.026007	0.029792	0.033792
75	0.022301	0.024046	0.025855	0.029654	0.033668
76	0.022141	0.023892	0.025708	0.029520	0.033548
77	0.021987	0.023743	0.025564	0.029390	0.033433
78	0.021836	0.023598	0.025426	0.029265	0.033322
79	0.021690	0.023457	0.025291	0.029143	0.033215
80	0.021548	0.023321	0.025161	0.029026	0.033112
81	0.021410	0.023188	0.025034	0.028912	0.033012
82	0.021276	0.023059	0.024911	0.028803	0.032916
83	0.021145	0.022934	0.024792	0.028696	0.032823
84	0.021018	0.022812	0.024676	0.028593	0.032733
85	0.020894	0.022694	0.024563	0.028493	0.032647
86	0.020773	0.022578	0.024454	0.028396	0.032563
87	0.020656	0.022466	0.024347	0.028303	0.032482
88	0.020541	0.022357	0.024244	0.028212	0.032404
89	0.020430	0.022251	0.024144	0.028124	0.032328
90	0.020321	0.022148	0.024046	0.028038	0.032256
91	0.020215	0.022047	0.023951	0.027955	0.032185
92	0.020112	0.021949	0.023859	0.027875	0.032117
93	0.020011	0.021853	0.023769	0.027797	0.032051
94	0.019913	0.021760	0.023681	0.027721	0.031987
95	0.019817	0.021669	0.023596	0.027648	0.031926
96	0.019723	0.021581	0.023513	0.027577	0.031866
97	0.019632	0.021495	0.023432	0.027507	0.031809
98	0.019543	0.021411	0.023354	0.027440	0.031753
99	0.019456	0.021329	0.023277	0.027375	0.031699
100	0.019371	0.021249	0.023203	0.927312	0.931647

Table 7 (continued)

n	$3\frac{1}{2}\%$	4%	$4\frac{1}{2}\%$	5%	$5\frac{1}{2}\%$
1	1.035000	1.040000	1.045000	1.050000	1.055000
2	0.526401	0.530196	0.533998	0.537805	0.541618
3	0.356934	0.360349	0.363773	0.367209	0.370654
4	0.272251	0.275490	0.278744	0.282012	0.285294
5	0.221481	0.224627	0.227792	0.230975	0.234176
6	0.187668	0.190762	0.193878	0.197017	0.200179
7	0.163544	0.166610	0.169701	0.172820	0.175964
8	0.145477	0.148528	0.151610	0.154722	0.157864
9	0.131446	0.134493	0.137574	0.140690	0.143839
10	0.120241	0.123291	0.126379	0.129505	0.132668
11	0.111092	0.114149	0.117248	0.120389	0.123571
12	0.103484	0.106552	0.109666	0.112825	0.116029
13	0.097062	0.100144	0.103275	0.106456	0.109684
14	0.091571	0.094669	0.097820	0.101024	0.104279
15	0.086825	0.089941	0.093114	0.096342	0.099626
16	0.082685	0.085820	0.089015	0.092270	0.095583
17	0.079043	0.082199	0.085418	0.088699	0.092042
18	0.075817	0.078993	0.082237	0.085546	0.088920
19	0.072940	0.076139	0.079407	0.082745	0.086150
20	0.070361	0.073582	0.076876	0.080243	0.083679
21	0.068037	0.071280	0.074601	0.077996	0.081465
22	0.065932	0.069199	0.072546	0.075971	0.079471
23	0.064019	0.067309	0.070682	0.074137	0.077670
24	0.062273	0.065587	0.068987	0.072471	0.076036
25	0.060674	0.064012	0.067439	0.070952	0.074549
26	0.059205	0.062567	0.066021	0.069564	0.073193
27	0.057852	0.061239	0.064719	0.068292	0.071952
28	0.056603	0.060013	0.063521	0.067123	0.070814
29	0.055445	0.058880	0.062415	0.066046	0.069769
30	0.054371	0.057830	0.061392	0.065051	0.068805
31	0.053372	0.056855	0.060443	0.064132	0.067917
32	0.052442	0.055949	0.059563	0.063280	0.067095
33	0.051572	0.055104	0.058745	0.062490	0.066335
34	0.050760	0.054315	0.057982	0.061755	0.065630
35	0.049998	0.053577	0.057270	0.061072	0.064975
36	0.049284	0.052887	0.056606	0.060434	0.064366
37	0.048613	0.052240	0.055984	0.059840	0.063800
38	0.047982	0.051632	0.055402	0.059284	0.063272
39	0.047388	0.051061	0.054856	0.058765	0.062780
40	0.046827	0.050523	0.054343	0.058278	0.062320
41	0.046298	0.050017	0.053862	0.057822	0.061891
42	0.045798	0.049540	0.053409	0.057395	0.061489
43	0.045325	0.049090	0.052982	0.056993	0.061113
44	0.044878	0.048665	0.052581	0.056616	0.060761
45	0.044453	0.048262	0.052202	0.056262	0.060431
46	0.044051	0.047882	0.051845	0.055928	0.060122
47	0.043669	0.047522	0.051507	0.055614	0.059831
48	0.043306	0.047181	0.051189	0.055318	0.059559
49	0.042962	0.046857	0.050887	0.055040	0.059302
50	0.042634	0.046550	0.050602	0.054777	0.059061
51	0.042322	0.046259	0.050332	0.054529	0.058835
52	0.042024	0.045982	0.050077	0.054294	0.058622
53	0.041741	0.045719	0.049835	0.054073	0.058421
54	0.041471	0.045469	0.049605	0.053864	0.058232
55	0.041213	0.045231	0.049388	0.053667	0.058055
56	0.040967	0.045005	0.049181	0.053480	0.057887
57	0.040732	0.044789	0.048985	0.053303	0.057729
58	0.040508	0.044584	0.048799	0.053136	0.057580
59	0.040294	0.044388	0.048622	0.052978	0.057440
60	0.040089	0.044202	0.048454	0.052828	0.057307
61	0.039892	0.044024	0.048295	0.052686	0.057182
62	0.039705	0.043854	0.048143	0.052552	0.057064
63	0.039525	0.043692	0.047998	0.052424	0.056953
64	0.039353	0.043538	0.047861	0.052304	0.056847
65	0.039188	0.043390	0.047730	0.052189	0.056748
66	0.039030	0.043249	0.047606	0.052081	0.056654
67	0.038879	0.043115	0.047488	0.051978	0.056565
68	0.038734	0.042986	0.047375	0.051880	0.056482
69	0.038595	0.042863	0.047267	0.051787	0.056402
70	0.038461	0.042745	0.047165	0.051699	0.056328
71	0.038333	0.042633	0.047068	0.051616	0.056257
72	0.038210	0.042525	0.046975	0.051536	0.056190
73	0.038092	0.042422	0.046886	0.051461	0.056127
74	0.037978	0.042323	0.046802	0.051390	0.056067
75	0.037869	0.042229	0.046721	0.051322	0.056010
76	0.037765	0.042139	0.046644	0.051257	0.055956
77	0.037664	0.042052	0.046571	0.051196	0.055906
78	0.037567	0.041969	0.046501	0.051138	0.055858
79	0.037474	0.041890	0.046434	0.051082	0.055812
80	0.037385	0.041814	0.046371	0.051030	0.055769
81	0.037299	0.041741	0.046310	0.050980	0.055729
82	0.037216	0.041671	0.046252	0.050932	0.055690
83	0.037137	0.041605	0.046197	0.050887	0.055654
84	0.037060	0.041541	0.046144	0.050844	0.055619
85	0.036987	0.041479	0.046093	0.050803	0.055587
86	0.036916	0.041420	0.046045	0.050764	0.055556
87	0.036848	0.041364	0.045999	0.050727	0.055527
88	0.036782	0.041310	0.045955	0.050692	0.055499
89	0.036719	0.041258	0.045913	0.050659	0.055473
90	0.036658	0.041208	0.045873	0.050627	0.055448
91	0.036599	0.041160	0.045835	0.050597	0.055424
92	0.036543	0.041114	0.045798	0.050568	0.055402
93	0.036488	0.041070	0.045763	0.050541	0.055381
94	0.036436	0.041028	0.045730	0.050515	0.055361
95	0.036385	0.040987	0.045698	0.050490	0.055342
96	0.036337	0.040949	0.045667	0.050466	0.055324
97	0.036290	0.040911	0.045638	0.050444	0.055307
98	0.036245	0.040875	0.045610	0.050423	0.055291
99	0.036201	0.040841	0.045584	0.050402	0.055276
100	0.036159	0.040808	0.045558	0.050383	0.055261

Table 7 (continued)

n	6%	6½%	7%	7½%	8%
1	1.060000	1.065000	1.070000	1.075000	1.080000
2	0.545437	0.549262	0.553092	0.556928	0.560769
3	0.374110	0.377576	0.381052	0.384538	0.388034
4	0.288591	0.291903	0.295228	0.298568	0.301921
5	0.237396	0.240635	0.243891	0.247165	0.250456
6	0.203363	0.206568	0.209796	0.213045	0.216315
7	0.179135	0.182331	0.185553	0.188800	0.192072
8	0.161036	0.164237	0.167468	0.170727	0.174015
9	0.147022	0.150238	0.153486	0.156767	0.160080
10	0.135868	0.139105	0.142378	0.145686	0.149029
11	0.126793	0.130055	0.133357	0.136697	0.140076
12	0.119277	0.122568	0.125902	0.129278	0.132695
13	0.112960	0.116283	0.119651	0.123064	0.126522
14	0.107585	0.110940	0.114345	0.117797	0.121297
15	0.102963	0.106353	0.109795	0.113287	0.116830
16	0.098952	0.102378	0.105858	0.109391	0.112977
17	0.095445	0.098906	0.102425	0.106000	0.109629
18	0.092357	0.095855	0.099413	0.103029	0.106702
19	0.089621	0.093156	0.096753	0.100411	0.104128
20	0.087185	0.090756	0.094393	0.098092	0.101852
21	0.085005	0.088613	0.092289	0.096029	0.099832
22	0.083046	0.086691	0.090406	0.094187	0.098032
23	0.081278	0.084961	0.088714	0.092535	0.096422
24	0.079679	0.083398	0.087189	0.091050	0.094978
25	0.078227	0.081981	0.085811	0.089711	0.093679
26	0.076904	0.080695	0.084561	0.088500	0.092507
27	0.075697	0.079523	0.083426	0.087402	0.091448
28	0.074593	0.078453	0.082392	0.086405	0.090489
29	0.073580	0.077474	0.081449	0.085498	0.089619
30	0.072649	0.076577	0.080586	0.084671	0.088827
31	0.071792	0.075754	0.079797	0.083916	0.088107
32	0.071002	0.074997	0.079073	0.083226	0.087451
33	0.070273	0.074299	0.078408	0.082594	0.086852
34	0.069598	0.073656	0.077797	0.082015	0.086304
35	0.068974	0.073062	0.077234	0.081483	0.085803
36	0.068395	0.072513	0.076715	0.080994	0.085345
37	0.067857	0.072005	0.076237	0.080545	0.084924
38	0.067358	0.071535	0.075795	0.080132	0.084539
39	0.066894	0.071099	0.075387	0.079751	0.084185
40	0.066462	0.070694	0.075009	0.079400	0.083860
41	0.066059	0.070318	0.074660	0.079077	0.083561
42	0.065683	0.069968	0.074336	0.078778	0.083287
43	0.065333	0.069644	0.074036	0.078502	0.083034
44	0.065006	0.069341	0.073758	0.078247	0.082802
45	0.064700	0.069060	0.073500	0.078011	0.082587
46	0.064415	0.068797	0.073260	0.077794	0.082390
47	0.064148	0.068553	0.073037	0.077592	0.082208
48	0.063898	0.068325	0.072831	0.077405	0.082040
49	0.063664	0.068112	0.072639	0.077232	0.081886
50	0.063444	0.067914	0.072460	0.077072	0.081743

n	6%	6½%	7%	7½%	8%
51	0.063239	0.067729	0.072294	0.076924	0.081611
52	0.063046	0.067556	0.072139	0.076787	0.081490
53	0.062866	0.067394	0.071995	0.076659	0.081377
54	0.062696	0.067243	0.071861	0.076541	0.081274
55	0.062537	0.067101	0.071736	0.076432	0.081178
56	0.062388	0.066969	0.071620	0.076330	0.081090
57	0.062247	0.066846	0.071512	0.076236	0.081008
58	0.062116	0.066730	0.071411	0.076148	0.080932
59	0.061992	0.066622	0.071317	0.076067	0.080862
60	0.061876	0.066520	0.071229	0.075991	0.080798
61	0.061766	0.066426	0.071147	0.075921	0.080738
62	0.061664	0.066337	0.071071	0.075856	0.080683
63	0.061567	0.066254	0.071000	0.075796	0.080632
64	0.061476	0.066176	0.070934	0.075740	0.080585
65	0.061391	0.066103	0.070872	0.075688	0.080541
66	0.061310	0.066034	0.070814	0.075639	0.080501
67	0.061235	0.065970	0.070760	0.075594	0.080464
68	0.061163	0.065910	0.070710	0.075553	0.080429
69	0.061096	0.065854	0.070663	0.075514	0.080397
70	0.061033	0.065801	0.070620	0.075478	0.080368
71	0.060974	0.065752	0.070579	0.075444	0.080340
72	0.060918	0.065705	0.070541	0.075413	0.080315
73	0.060865	0.065662	0.070505	0.075384	0.080292
74	0.060815	0.065621	0.070472	0.075357	0.080270
75	0.060769	0.065583	0.070441	0.075332	0.080250
76	0.060725	0.065547	0.070412	0.075304	0.080231
77	0.060683	0.065513	0.070385	0.075287	0.082214
78	0.060644	0.065482	0.070359	0.075267	0.080198
79	0.060607	0.065452	0.070336	0.075248	0.080183
80	0.060573	0.065424	0.070314	0.075231	0.080170
81	0.060540	0.065398	0.070293	0.075215	0.080157
82	0.060509	0.065374	0.070274	0.075200	0.080146
83	0.060480	0.065351	0.070256	0.075186	0.080135
84	0.060453	0.065329	0.070239	0.075173	0.080125
85	0.060427	0.065309	0.070223	0.075161	0.080116
86	0.060402	0.065290	0.070209	0.075150	0.080107
87	0.060380	0.065272	0.070195	0.075139	0.080099
88	0.060358	0.065256	0.070182	0.075129	0.080092
89	0.060338	0.065240	0.070170	0.075120	0.080085
90	0.060318	0.065225	0.070159	0.075112	0.080079
91	0.060300	0.065212	0.070149	0.075104	0.080073
92	0.060283	0.065199	0.070139	0.075097	0.080067
93	0.060267	0.065186	0.070130	0.075090	0.080062
94	0.060252	0.065175	0.070121	0.075084	0.080058
95	0.060238	0.065164	0.070113	0.075078	0.080053
96	0.060224	0.065154	0.070106	0.075072	0.080050
97	0.060211	0.065145	0.070097	0.075067	0.080046
98	0.060199	0.065136	0.070092	0.075063	0.080042
99	0.060188	0.065128	0.070086	0.075058	0.080039
100	0.060177	0.065120	0.070081	0.075054	0.080036

Table 8

$$\frac{1}{s_{\overline{n}|r}}$$

r = interest rate per payment period; n = number of payment periods

n	$\tfrac{1}{4}\%$	$\tfrac{1}{2}\%$	$\tfrac{3}{4}\%$	1%	$1\tfrac{1}{4}\%$
1	1.000000	1.000000	1.000000	1.000000	1.000000
2	0.499376	0.498753	0.498132	0.497512	0.496894
3	0.332502	0.331672	0.330846	0.330022	0.329201
4	0.249065	0.248133	0.247205	0.246281	0.245361
5	0.199003	0.198010	0.197022	0.196040	0.195062
6	0.165628	0.164595	0.163569	0.162548	0.161534
7	0.141789	0.140729	0.139675	0.138628	0.137589
8	0.123910	0.122829	0.121756	0.120690	0.119633
9	0.110005	0.108907	0.107819	0.106740	0.105671
10	0.098880	0.097771	0.096671	0.095582	0.094503
11	0.089778	0.088659	0.087551	0.086454	0.085368
12	0.082194	0.081066	0.079951	0.078849	0.077758
13	0.075776	0.074642	0.073522	0.072415	0.071321
14	0.070275	0.069136	0.068011	0.066901	0.065805
15	0.065508	0.064364	0.063236	0.062124	0.061026
16	0.061336	0.060189	0.059059	0.057945	0.056847
17	0.057656	0.056506	0.055373	0.054258	0.053160
18	0.054384	0.053232	0.052098	0.050982	0.049885
19	0.051457	0.050303	0.049167	0.048052	0.046955
20	0.048823	0.047666	0.046531	0.045415	0.044320
21	0.046439	0.045282	0.044145	0.043031	0.041937
22	0.044273	0.043114	0.041977	0.040864	0.039772
23	0.042295	0.041135	0.039998	0.038886	0.037797
24	0.040481	0.039321	0.038185	0.037073	0.035987
25	0.038813	0.037652	0.036516	0.035407	0.034322
26	0.037273	0.036112	0.034977	0.033869	0.032787
27	0.035847	0.034686	0.033552	0.032446	0.031367
28	0.034523	0.033362	0.032229	0.031124	0.030049
29	0.033291	0.032129	0.030997	0.029895	0.028822
30	0.032141	0.030979	0.029848	0.028748	0.027679
31	0.031065	0.029903	0.028774	0.027676	0.026609
32	0.030056	0.028895	0.027766	0.026671	0.025608
33	0.029108	0.027947	0.026820	0.025727	0.024668
34	0.028216	0.027056	0.025931	0.024840	0.023784
35	0.027375	0.026215	0.025092	0.024004	0.022951
36	0.026581	0.025422	0.024300	0.023214	0.022165
37	0.025830	0.024671	0.023551	0.022468	0.021423
38	0.025118	0.023960	0.022842	0.021761	0.020720
39	0.024443	0.023286	0.022169	0.021092	0.020054
40	0.023802	0.022646	0.021530	0.020456	0.019421
41	0.023192	0.022036	0.020923	0.019851	0.018821
42	0.022611	0.021456	0.020345	0.019276	0.018249
43	0.022057	0.020903	0.019793	0.018727	0.017705
44	0.021529	0.020375	0.019268	0.018204	0.017186
45	0.021023	0.019871	0.018765	0.017705	0.016690
46	0.020540	0.019389	0.018285	0.017228	0.016217
47	0.020078	0.018927	0.017825	0.016771	0.015764
48	0.019634	0.018485	0.017385	0.016334	0.015331
49	0.019209	0.018061	0.016963	0.015915	0.014916
50	0.018801	0.017654	0.016558	0.015513	0.014518
51	0.018409	0.017263	0.016169	0.015127	0.014136
52	0.018032	0.016887	0.015795	0.014756	0.013769
53	0.017669	0.016525	0.015435	0.014400	0.013417
54	0.017320	0.016177	0.015089	0.014057	0.013078
55	0.016983	0.015841	0.014756	0.013726	0.012751
56	0.016659	0.015518	0.014435	0.013408	0.012437
57	0.016345	0.015206	0.014125	0.013102	0.012135
58	0.016043	0.014905	0.013826	0.012806	0.011843
59	0.015751	0.014614	0.013537	0.012520	0.011562
60	0.015469	0.014333	0.013258	0.012244	0.011290
61	0.015196	0.014061	0.012989	0.011978	0.011028
62	0.014931	0.013798	0.012728	0.011720	0.010774
63	0.014676	0.013543	0.012476	0.011471	0.010529
64	0.014428	0.013297	0.012231	0.011230	0.010292
65	0.014188	0.013058	0.011995	0.010997	0.010063
66	0.013955	0.012826	0.011765	0.010771	0.009841
67	0.013729	0.012602	0.011543	0.010551	0.009626
68	0.013510	0.012384	0.011327	0.010339	0.009417
69	0.013297	0.012172	0.011118	0.010133	0.009215
70	0.013090	0.011967	0.010915	0.009933	0.009019
71	0.012889	0.011767	0.010717	0.009739	0.008829
72	0.012694	0.011573	0.010526	0.009550	0.008645
73	0.012504	0.011384	0.010339	0.009367	0.008466
74	0.012319	0.011201	0.010158	0.009189	0.008292
75	0.012139	0.011022	0.009982	0.009016	0.008123
76	0.011964	0.010848	0.009810	0.008848	0.007959
77	0.011793	0.010679	0.009643	0.008684	0.007800
78	0.011627	0.010514	0.009481	0.008525	0.007644
79	0.011465	0.010354	0.009322	0.008370	0.007493
80	0.011307	0.010197	0.009168	0.008219	0.007347
81	0.011153	0.010044	0.009018	0.008072	0.007204
82	0.011003	0.009896	0.008871	0.007929	0.007064
83	0.010856	0.009750	0.008728	0.007789	0.006929
84	0.010713	0.009609	0.008589	0.007653	0.006797
85	0.010574	0.009470	0.008453	0.007520	0.006668
86	0.010437	0.009335	0.008320	0.007391	0.006543
87	0.010304	0.009203	0.008191	0.007264	0.006420
88	0.010174	0.009074	0.008064	0.007141	0.006301
89	0.010046	0.008948	0.007941	0.007021	0.006185
90	0.009922	0.008825	0.007820	0.006903	0.006071
91	0.009800	0.008705	0.007702	0.006788	0.005961
92	0.009681	0.008587	0.007587	0.006676	0.005853
93	0.009564	0.008472	0.007474	0.006567	0.005747
94	0.009450	0.008360	0.007364	0.006460	0.005644
95	0.009339	0.008249	0.007256	0.006355	0.005544
96	0.009230	0.008141	0.007150	0.006253	0.005445
97	0.009123	0.008036	0.007047	0.006153	0.005349
98	0.009018	0.007932	0.006946	0.006055	0.005256
99	0.008915	0.007831	0.006847	0.005959	0.005164
100	0.008814	0.007732	0.006750	0.005866	0.005074

Table 8 (continued)

n	1½%	1¾%	2%	2½%	3%
1	1.000000	1.000000	1.000000	1.000000	1.000000
2	0.496278	0.495663	0.495050	0.493827	0.492611
3	0.328383	0.327567	0.326755	0.325137	0.323530
4	0.244445	0.243532	0.242624	0.240818	0.239027
5	0.194089	0.193121	0.192158	0.190247	0.188355
6	0.160525	0.159523	0.158526	0.156550	0.154598
7	0.136556	0.135531	0.134512	0.132495	0.130506
8	0.118584	0.117543	0.116510	0.114467	0.112456
9	0.104610	0.103558	0.102515	0.100457	0.098434
10	0.093434	0.092375	0.091327	0.089259	0.087231
11	0.084294	0.083230	0.082178	0.080106	0.078077
12	0.076680	0.075614	0.074560	0.072487	0.070462
13	0.070240	0.069173	0.068118	0.066048	0.064030
14	0.064723	0.063656	0.062602	0.060537	0.058526
15	0.059944	0.058877	0.057825	0.055766	0.053767
16	0.055765	0.054700	0.053650	0.051599	0.049611
17	0.052080	0.051016	0.049970	0.047928	0.045953
18	0.048806	0.047745	0.046702	0.044670	0.042709
19	0.045878	0.044821	0.043782	0.041761	0.039814
20	0.043246	0.042191	0.041157	0.039147	0.037216
21	0.040865	0.039815	0.038785	0.036787	0.034872
22	0.038703	0.037656	0.036631	0.034647	0.032747
23	0.036731	0.035688	0.034668	0.032696	0.030814
24	0.034924	0.033886	0.032871	0.030913	0.029047
25	0.033263	0.032230	0.031220	0.029276	0.027428
26	0.031732	0.030703	0.029699	0.027769	0.025938
27	0.030315	0.029291	0.028293	0.026377	0.024564
28	0.029001	0.027982	0.026990	0.025088	0.023293
29	0.027779	0.026764	0.025778	0.023891	0.022115
30	0.026639	0.025630	0.024650	0.022788	0.021019
31	0.025574	0.024570	0.023596	0.021739	0.019999
32	0.024577	0.023578	0.022611	0.020768	0.019047
33	0.023641	0.022648	0.021687	0.019859	0.018156
34	0.022762	0.021774	0.020819	0.019007	0.017322
35	0.021934	0.020951	0.020002	0.018206	0.016539
36	0.021152	0.020175	0.019233	0.017452	0.015804
37	0.020414	0.019443	0.018507	0.016741	0.015112
38	0.019716	0.018750	0.017821	0.016070	0.014459
39	0.019055	0.018094	0.017171	0.015436	0.013844
40	0.018427	0.017472	0.016556	0.014836	0.013262
41	0.017831	0.016882	0.015972	0.014268	0.012712
42	0.017264	0.016321	0.015417	0.013729	0.012192
43	0.016725	0.015787	0.014890	0.013217	0.011698
44	0.016210	0.015278	0.014388	0.012730	0.011230
45	0.015720	0.014793	0.013910	0.012268	0.010785
46	0.015251	0.014330	0.013453	0.011827	0.010363
47	0.014803	0.013888	0.013018	0.011407	0.009961
48	0.014375	0.013466	0.012602	0.011006	0.009578
49	0.013965	0.013061	0.012204	0.010623	0.009213
50	0.013572	0.012674	0.011823	0.010258	0.008865

n	1½%	1¾%	2%	2½%	3%
51	0.013195	0.012303	0.011459	0.009909	0.008534
52	0.012833	0.011947	0.011109	0.009574	0.008217
53	0.012485	0.011605	0.010774	0.009254	0.007915
54	0.012151	0.011277	0.010452	0.008948	0.007626
55	0.011830	0.010961	0.010143	0.008654	0.007349
56	0.011521	0.010658	0.009847	0.008372	0.007084
57	0.011223	0.010366	0.009561	0.008102	0.006831
58	0.010937	0.010085	0.009287	0.007842	0.006588
59	0.010660	0.009814	0.009022	0.007593	0.006356
60	0.010393	0.009553	0.008768	0.007353	0.006133
61	0.010136	0.009302	0.008523	0.007123	0.005919
62	0.009888	0.009059	0.008286	0.006901	0.005714
63	0.009647	0.008825	0.008058	0.006688	0.005517
64	0.009415	0.008598	0.007839	0.006482	0.005328
65	0.009191	0.008380	0.007626	0.006285	0.005146
66	0.008974	0.008168	0.007421	0.006094	0.004971
67	0.008764	0.007964	0.007223	0.005910	0.004803
68	0.008560	0.007766	0.007032	0.005733	0.004642
69	0.008363	0.007575	0.006847	0.005562	0.004486
70	0.008172	0.007389	0.006668	0.005397	0.004337
71	0.007987	0.007210	0.006494	0.005238	0.004193
72	0.007808	0.007036	0.006327	0.005084	0.004054
73	0.007634	0.006867	0.006165	0.004936	0.003921
74	0.007465	0.006704	0.006007	0.004792	0.003792
75	0.007301	0.006546	0.005855	0.004654	0.003668
76	0.007141	0.006392	0.005708	0.004520	0.003548
77	0.006987	0.006243	0.005564	0.004390	0.003433
78	0.006836	0.006098	0.005426	0.004265	0.003322
79	0.006690	0.005957	0.005291	0.004143	0.003215
80	0.006548	0.005821	0.005161	0.004026	0.003112
81	0.006410	0.005688	0.005034	0.003912	0.003012
82	0.006276	0.005559	0.004911	0.003803	0.002916
83	0.006145	0.005434	0.004792	0.003696	0.002823
84	0.006018	0.005312	0.004676	0.003593	0.002733
85	0.005894	0.005194	0.004563	0.003493	0.002647
86	0.005773	0.005078	0.004454	0.003396	0.002563
87	0.005656	0.004966	0.004347	0.003303	0.002482
88	0.005541	0.004857	0.004244	0.003212	0.002404
89	0.005430	0.004751	0.004144	0.003124	0.002328
90	0.005321	0.004648	0.004046	0.003038	0.002256
91	0.005215	0.004547	0.003951	0.002955	0.002185
92	0.005112	0.004449	0.003859	0.002875	0.002117
93	0.005011	0.004353	0.003769	0.002797	0.002051
94	0.004913	0.004260	0.003681	0.002721	0.001987
95	0.004817	0.004169	0.003596	0.002648	0.001926
96	0.004723	0.004081	0.003513	0.002577	0.001866
97	0.004632	0.003995	0.003432	0.002507	0.001809
98	0.004543	0.003911	0.003354	0.002440	0.001753
99	0.004456	0.003829	0.003277	0.002375	0.001699
100	0.004371	0.003749	0.003203	0.002312	0.001647

Table 8 (continued)

n	3½%	4%	4½%	5%	5½%
1	1.000000	1.000000	1.000000	1.000000	1.000000
2	0.491401	0.490196	0.488998	0.487805	0.486618
3	0.321934	0.320349	0.318773	0.317209	0.315654
4	0.237251	0.235490	0.233744	0.232012	0.230294
5	0.186481	0.184627	0.182792	0.180975	0.179176
6	0.152668	0.150762	0.148878	0.147017	0.145179
7	0.128544	0.126610	0.124701	0.122820	0.120964
8	0.110477	0.108528	0.106610	0.104722	0.102864
9	0.096446	0.094493	0.092574	0.090690	0.088839
10	0.085241	0.083291	0.081379	0.079505	0.077668
11	0.076092	0.074149	0.072248	0.070389	0.068571
12	0.068484	0.066552	0.064666	0.062825	0.061029
13	0.062062	0.060144	0.058275	0.056456	0.054684
14	0.056571	0.054669	0.052820	0.051024	0.049279
15	0.051825	0.049941	0.048114	0.046342	0.044626
16	0.047685	0.045820	0.044015	0.042270	0.040583
17	0.044043	0.042199	0.040418	0.038699	0.037042
18	0.040817	0.038993	0.037237	0.035546	0.033920
19	0.037940	0.036139	0.034407	0.032745	0.031150
20	0.035361	0.033582	0.031876	0.030243	0.028679
21	0.033037	0.031280	0.029601	0.027996	0.026465
22	0.030932	0.029199	0.027546	0.025971	0.024471
23	0.029019	0.027309	0.025682	0.024137	0.022670
24	0.027273	0.025587	0.023987	0.022471	0.021036
25	0.025674	0.024012	0.022439	0.020952	0.019549
26	0.024205	0.022567	0.021021	0.019564	0.018193
27	0.022852	0.021239	0.019719	0.018292	0.016952
28	0.021603	0.020013	0.018521	0.017123	0.015814
29	0.020445	0.018880	0.017415	0.016046	0.014769
30	0.019371	0.017830	0.016392	0.015051	0.013805
31	0.018372	0.016855	0.015443	0.014132	0.012917
32	0.017442	0.015949	0.014563	0.013280	0.012095
33	0.016572	0.015104	0.013745	0.012490	0.011335
34	0.015760	0.014315	0.012982	0.011755	0.010630
35	0.014998	0.013577	0.012270	0.011072	0.009975
36	0.014284	0.012887	0.011606	0.010434	0.009366
37	0.013613	0.012240	0.010984	0.009840	0.008800
38	0.012982	0.011632	0.010402	0.009284	0.008272
39	0.012388	0.011061	0.009856	0.008765	0.007780
40	0.011827	0.010523	0.009343	0.008278	0.007320
41	0.011298	0.010017	0.008862	0.007822	0.006891
42	0.010798	0.009540	0.008409	0.007395	0.006489
43	0.010325	0.009090	0.007982	0.006993	0.006113
44	0.009878	0.008665	0.007581	0.006616	0.005761
45	0.009453	0.008262	0.007202	0.006262	0.005431
46	0.009051	0.007882	0.006845	0.005928	0.005122
47	0.008669	0.007522	0.006507	0.005614	0.004831
48	0.008306	0.007181	0.006189	0.005318	0.004559
49	0.007962	0.006857	0.005887	0.005040	0.004302
50	0.007634	0.006550	0.005602	0.004777	0.004061

n	3½%	4%	4½%	5%	5½%
51	0.007322	0.006259	0.005332	0.004529	0.003835
52	0.007024	0.005982	0.005077	0.004294	0.003622
53	0.006741	0.005719	0.004835	0.004073	0.003421
54	0.006471	0.005469	0.004605	0.003864	0.003232
55	0.006213	0.005231	0.004388	0.003667	0.003055
56	0.005967	0.005005	0.004181	0.003480	0.002887
57	0.005732	0.004789	0.003985	0.003303	0.002729
58	0.005508	0.004584	0.003799	0.003136	0.002580
59	0.005294	0.004388	0.003622	0.002978	0.002440
60	0.005089	0.004202	0.003454	0.002828	0.002307
61	0.004892	0.004024	0.003295	0.002686	0.002182
62	0.004705	0.003854	0.003143	0.002552	0.002064
63	0.004525	0.003692	0.002998	0.002424	0.001953
64	0.004353	0.003538	0.002861	0.002304	0.001847
65	0.004188	0.003390	0.002730	0.002189	0.001748
66	0.004030	0.003249	0.002606	0.002081	0.001654
67	0.003879	0.003115	0.002488	0.001978	0.001565
68	0.003734	0.002986	0.002375	0.001880	0.001482
69	0.003595	0.002863	0.002267	0.001787	0.001402
70	0.003461	0.002745	0.002165	0.001699	0.001328
71	0.003333	0.002633	0.002068	0.001616	0.001257
72	0.003210	0.002525	0.001975	0.001536	0.001190
73	0.003092	0.002422	0.001886	0.001461	0.001127
74	0.002978	0.002323	0.001802	0.001390	0.001067
75	0.002869	0.002229	0.001721	0.001322	0.001010
76	0.002765	0.002139	0.001644	0.001257	0.000956
77	0.002664	0.002052	0.001571	0.001196	0.000906
78	0.002567	0.001969	0.001501	0.001138	0.000858
79	0.002474	0.001890	0.001434	0.001082	0.000812
80	0.002385	0.001814	0.001371	0.001030	0.000769
81	0.002299	0.001741	0.001310	0.000980	0.000729
82	0.002216	0.001671	0.001252	0.000932	0.000690
83	0.002137	0.001605	0.001197	0.000887	0.000654
84	0.002060	0.001541	0.001144	0.000844	0.000619
85	0.001987	0.001479	0.001093	0.000803	0.000587
86	0.001916	0.001420	0.001045	0.000764	0.000556
87	0.001848	0.001364	0.000999	0.000727	0.000527
88	0.001782	0.001310	0.000955	0.000692	0.000499
89	0.001719	0.001258	0.000913	0.000659	0.000473
90	0.001658	0.001208	0.000873	0.000627	0.000448
91	0.001599	0.001160	0.000835	0.000597	0.000424
92	0.001543	0.001114	0.000798	0.000568	0.000402
93	0.001488	0.001070	0.000763	0.000541	0.000381
94	0.001436	0.001028	0.000730	0.000515	0.000361
95	0.001385	0.000987	0.000698	0.000490	0.000342
96	0.001337	0.000949	0.000667	0.000466	0.000324
97	0.001290	0.000911	0.000638	0.000444	0.000307
98	0.001245	0.000875	0.000610	0.000423	0.000291
99	0.001201	0.000841	0.000584	0.000402	0.000276
100	0.001159	0.000808	0.000558	0.000383	0.000261

Table 8 (continued)

n	6%	6½%	7%	7½%	8%
1	1.000000	1.000000	1.000000	1.000000	1.000000
2	0.485437	0.484262	0.483092	0.481928	0.480769
3	0.314110	0.312576	0.311052	0.309538	0.308034
4	0.228591	0.226903	0.225228	0.223568	0.221921
5	0.177396	0.175635	0.173891	0.172165	0.170456
6	0.143363	0.141568	0.139796	0.138045	0.136315
7	0.119135	0.117331	0.115553	0.113800	0.112072
8	0.101036	0.099237	0.097468	0.095727	0.094015
9	0.087022	0.085238	0.083486	0.081767	0.080080
10	0.075868	0.074105	0.072378	0.070686	0.069029
11	0.066793	0.065055	0.063357	0.061697	0.060076
12	0.059277	0.057568	0.055902	0.054278	0.052695
13	0.052960	0.051283	0.049651	0.048064	0.046522
14	0.047585	0.045940	0.044345	0.042797	0.041297
15	0.042963	0.041353	0.039795	0.038287	0.036830
16	0.038952	0.037378	0.035858	0.034391	0.032977
17	0.035445	0.033906	0.032425	0.031000	0.029629
18	0.032357	0.030855	0.029413	0.028029	0.026702
19	0.029621	0.028156	0.026753	0.025411	0.024128
20	0.027185	0.025756	0.024393	0.023092	0.021852
21	0.025005	0.023613	0.022289	0.021029	0.019832
22	0.023046	0.021691	0.020406	0.019187	0.018032
23	0.021278	0.019961	0.018714	0.017535	0.016422
24	0.019679	0.018398	0.017189	0.016050	0.014978
25	0.018227	0.016981	0.015811	0.014711	0.013679
26	0.016904	0.015695	0.014561	0.013500	0.012507
27	0.015697	0.014523	0.013426	0.012402	0.011448
28	0.014593	0.013453	0.012392	0.011405	0.010489
29	0.013580	0.012474	0.011449	0.010498	0.009619
30	0.012649	0.011577	0.010586	0.009671	0.008827
31	0.011792	0.010754	0.009797	0.008916	0.008107
32	0.011002	0.009997	0.009073	0.008226	0.007451
33	0.010273	0.009299	0.008408	0.007594	0.006852
34	0.009598	0.008656	0.007797	0.007015	0.006304
35	0.008974	0.008062	0.007234	0.006483	0.005803
36	0.008395	0.007513	0.006715	0.005994	0.005345
37	0.007857	0.007005	0.006237	0.005545	0.004924
38	0.007358	0.006535	0.005795	0.005132	0.004539
39	0.006894	0.006099	0.005387	0.004751	0.004185
40	0.006462	0.005694	0.005009	0.004400	0.003860
41	0.006059	0.005318	0.004660	0.004077	0.003561
42	0.005683	0.004968	0.004336	0.003778	0.003287
43	0.005333	0.004644	0.004036	0.003502	0.003034
44	0.005006	0.004341	0.003758	0.003247	0.002802
45	0.004700	0.004060	0.003500	0.003011	0.002587
46	0.004415	0.003797	0.003260	0.002794	0.002390
47	0.004148	0.003553	0.003037	0.002592	0.002208
48	0.003898	0.003325	0.002831	0.002405	0.002040
49	0.003664	0.003112	0.002639	0.002232	0.001886
50	0.003444	0.002914	0.002460	0.002072	0.001743

n	6%	6½%	7%	7½%	8%
51	0.003239	0.002729	0.002294	0.001924	0.001611
52	0.003046	0.002556	0.002139	0.001787	0.001490
53	0.002866	0.002394	0.001995	0.001659	0.001377
54	0.002696	0.002243	0.001861	0.001541	0.001274
55	0.002537	0.002101	0.001736	0.001432	0.001178
56	0.002388	0.001969	0.001620	0.001330	0.001090
57	0.002247	0.001846	0.001512	0.001236	0.001008
58	0.002116	0.001730	0.001411	0.001148	0.000932
59	0.001992	0.001622	0.001317	0.001067	0.000862
60	0.001876	0.001520	0.001229	0.000991	0.000798
61	0.001766	0.001426	0.001147	0.000921	0.000738
62	0.001664	0.001337	0.001071	0.000856	0.000683
63	0.001567	0.001254	0.001000	0.000796	0.000632
64	0.001476	0.001176	0.000934	0.000740	0.000585
65	0.001391	0.001103	0.000872	0.000688	0.000541
66	0.001310	0.001034	0.000814	0.000639	0.000501
67	0.001235	0.000970	0.000760	0.000594	0.000464
68	0.001163	0.000910	0.000710	0.000553	0.000429
69	0.001096	0.000854	0.000663	0.000514	0.000397
70	0.001033	0.000801	0.000620	0.000478	0.000368
71	0.000974	0.000752	0.000579	0.000444	0.000340
72	0.000918	0.000705	0.000541	0.000413	0.000315
73	0.000865	0.000662	0.000505	0.000384	0.000292
74	0.000815	0.000621	0.000472	0.000357	0.000270
75	0.000769	0.000583	0.000441	0.000332	0.000250
76	0.000725	0.000547	0.000412	0.000309	0.000231
77	0.000683	0.000513	0.000385	0.000287	0.000214
78	0.000644	0.000482	0.000359	0.000267	0.000198
79	0.000607	0.000452	0.000336	0.000248	0.000183
80	0.000573	0.000424	0.000314	0.000231	0.000170
81	0.000540	0.000398	0.000293	0.000215	0.000157
82	0.000509	0.000374	0.000274	0.000200	0.000146
83	0.000480	0.000351	0.000256	0.000186	0.000135
84	0.000453	0.000329	0.000239	0.000173	0.000125
85	0.000427	0.000309	0.000223	0.000161	0.000116
86	0.000402	0.000290	0.000209	0.000150	0.000107
87	0.000380	0.000272	0.000195	0.000139	0.000099
88	0.000358	0.000256	0.000182	0.000129	0.000092
89	0.000338	0.000240	0.000170	0.000120	0.000085
90	0.000318	0.000225	0.000159	0.000112	0.000079
91	0.000300	0.000212	0.000149	0.000104	0.000073
92	0.000283	0.000199	0.000139	0.000097	0.000067
93	0.000267	0.000186	0.000130	0.000090	0.000062
94	0.000252	0.000175	0.000121	0.000084	0.000058
95	0.000238	0.000164	0.000113	0.000078	0.000053
96	0.000224	0.000154	0.000106	0.000072	0.000050
97	0.000211	0.000145	0.000099	0.000067	0.000046
98	0.000199	0.000136	0.000092	0.000063	0.000042
99	0.000188	0.000128	0.000086	0.000058	0.000039
100	0.000177	0.000120	0.000081	0.000054	0.000036

Table 9
Binomial Probabilities $b(n,k;p)$

n	k	.05	.10	.15	.20	.25	.30	.35	.40	.45	.50
1	0	.9500	.9000	.8500	.8000	.7500	.7000	.6500	.6000	.5500	.5000
	1	.0500	.1000	.1500	.2000	.2500	.3000	.3500	.4000	.4500	.5000
2	0	.9025	.8100	.7225	.6400	.5625	.4900	.4225	.3600	.3025	.2500
	1	.0950	.1800	.2550	.3200	.3750	.4200	.4550	.4800	.4950	.5000
	2	.0025	.0100	.0225	.0400	.0625	.0900	.1225	.1600	.2025	.2500
3	0	.8574	.7290	.6141	.5120	.4219	.3430	.2746	.2160	.1664	.1250
	1	.1354	.2430	.3251	.3840	.4219	.4410	.4436	.4320	.4084	.3750
	2	.0071	.0270	.0574	.0960	.1406	.1890	.2389	.2880	.3341	.3750
	3	.0001	.0010	.0034	.0080	.0156	.0270	.0429	.0640	.0911	.1250
4	0	.8145	.6561	.5220	.4096	.3164	.2401	.1785	.1296	.0915	.0625
	1	.1715	.2916	.3685	.4096	.4219	.4116	.3845	.3456	.2995	.2500
	2	.0135	.0486	.0975	.1536	.2109	.2646	.3105	.3456	.3675	.3750
	3	.0005	.0036	.0115	.0256	.0469	.0756	.1115	.1536	.2005	.2500
	4	.0000	.0001	.0005	.0016	.0039	.0081	.0150	.0256	.0410	.0625
5	0	.7738	.5905	.4437	.3277	.2373	.1681	.1160	.0778	.0503	.0312
	1	.2036	.3280	.3915	.4096	.3955	.3602	.3124	.2592	.2059	.1562
	2	.0214	.0729	.1382	.2048	.2637	.3087	.3364	.3456	.3369	.3125
	3	.0011	.0081	.0244	.0512	.0879	.1323	.1811	.2304	.2757	.3125
	4	.0000	.0004	.0022	.0064	.0146	.0284	.0488	.0768	.1128	.1562
	5	.0000	.0000	.0001	.0003	.0010	.0024	.0053	.0102	.0185	.0312
6	0	.7351	.5314	.3771	.2621	.1780	.1176	.0754	.0467	.0277	.0156
	1	.2321	.3543	.3993	.3932	.3560	.3025	.2437	.1866	.1359	.0938
	2	.0305	.0984	.1762	.2458	.2966	.3241	.3280	.3110	.2780	.2344
	3	.0021	.0146	.0415	.0819	.1318	.1852	.2355	.2765	.3032	.3125
	4	.0001	.0012	.0055	.0154	.0330	.0595	.0951	.1382	.1861	.2344
	5	.0000	.0001	.0004	.0015	.0044	.0102	.0205	.0369	.0609	.0938
	6	.0000	.0000	.0000	.0001	.0002	.0007	.0018	.0041	.0083	.0156
7	0	.6983	.4783	.3206	.2097	.1335	.0824	.0490	.0280	.0152	.0078
	1	.2573	.3720	.3960	.3670	.3115	.2471	.1848	.1306	.0872	.0547
	2	.0406	.1240	.2097	.2753	.3115	.3177	.2985	.2613	.2140	.1641
	3	.0036	.0230	.0617	.1147	.1730	.2269	.2679	.2903	.2918	.2734
	4	.0002	.0026	.0109	.0287	.0577	.0972	.1442	.1935	.2388	.2734
	5	.0000	.0002	.0012	.0043	.0115	.0250	.0466	.0774	.1172	.1641
	6	.0000	.0000	.0001	.0004	.0013	.0036	.0084	.0172	.0320	.0547
	7	.0000	.0000	.0000	.0000	.0001	.0002	.0006	.0016	.0037	.0078
8	0	.6634	.4305	.2725	.1678	.1001	.0576	.0319	.0168	.0084	.0039
	1	.2793	.3826	.3847	.3355	.2670	.1977	.1373	.0896	.0548	.0312
	2	.0515	.1488	.2376	.2936	.3115	.2965	.2587	.2090	.1569	.1094
	3	.0054	.0331	.0839	.1468	.2076	.2541	.2786	.2787	.2568	.2188
	4	.0004	.0046	.0185	.0459	.0865	.1361	.1875	.2322	.2627	.2734
	5	.0000	.0004	.0026	.0092	.0231	.0467	.0808	.1239	.1719	.2188
	6	.0000	.0000	.0002	.0011	.0038	.0100	.0217	.0413	.0703	.1094
	7	.0000	.0000	.0000	.0001	.0004	.0012	.0033	.0079	.0164	.0312
	8	.0000	.0000	.0000	.0000	.0000	.0001	.0002	.0007	.0017	.0039

Table 9 (continued)

n	k	.05	.10	.15	.20	.25	.30	.35	.40	.45	.50
9	0	.6302	.3874	.2316	.1342	.0751	.0404	.0207	.0101	.0046	.0020
	1	.2985	.3874	.3679	.3020	.2253	.1556	.1004	.0605	.0339	.0176
	2	.0629	.1722	.2597	.3020	.3003	.2668	.2162	.1612	.1110	.0703
	3	.0077	.0446	.1069	.1762	.2336	.2668	.2716	.2508	.2119	.1641
	4	.0006	.0074	.0283	.0661	.1168	.1715	.2194	.2508	.2600	.2461
	5	.0000	.0008	.0050	.0165	.0389	.0735	.1181	.1672	.2128	.2461
	6	.0000	.0001	.0006	.0028	.0087	.0210	.0424	.0743	.1160	.1641
	7	.0000	.0000	.0000	.0003	.0012	.0039	.0098	.0212	.0407	.0703
	8	.0000	.0000	.0000	.0000	.0001	.0004	.0013	.0035	.0083	.0176
	9	.0000	.0000	.0000	.0000	.0000	.0000	.0001	.0003	.0008	.0020
10	0	.5987	.3487	.1969	.1074	.0563	.0282	.0135	.0060	.0025	.0010
	1	.3151	.3874	.3474	.2684	.1877	.1211	.0725	.0403	.0207	.0098
	2	.0746	.1937	.2759	.3020	.2816	.2335	.1757	.1209	.0763	.0439
	3	.0105	.0574	.1298	.2013	.2503	.2668	.2522	.2150	.1665	.1172
	4	.0010	.0112	.0401	.0881	.1460	.2001	.2377	.2508	.2384	.2051
	5	.0001	.0015	.0085	.0264	.0584	.1029	.1536	.2007	.2340	.2461
	6	.0000	.0001	.0012	.0055	.0162	.0368	.0689	.1115	.1596	.2051
	7	.0000	.0000	.0001	.0008	.0031	.0090	.0212	.0425	.0746	.1172
	8	.0000	.0000	.0000	.0001	.0004	.0014	.0043	.0106	.0229	.0439
	9	.0000	.0000	.0000	.0000	.0000	.0001	.0005	.0016	.0042	.0098
	10	.0000	.0000	.0000	.0000	.0000	.0000	.0000	.0001	.0003	.0010
11	0	.5688	.3138	.1673	.0859	.0422	.0198	.0088	.0036	.0014	.0005
	1	.3293	.3835	.3248	.2362	.1549	.0932	.0518	.0266	.0125	.0054
	2	.0867	.2131	.2866	.2953	.2581	.1998	.1395	.0887	.0513	.0269
	3	.0137	.0710	.1517	.2215	.2581	.2568	.2254	.1774	.1259	.0806
	4	.0014	.0158	.0536	.1107	.1721	.2201	.2428	.2365	.2060	.1611
	5	.0001	.0025	.0132	.0388	.0803	.1321	.1830	.2207	.2360	.2256
	6	.0000	.0003	.0023	.0097	.0268	.0566	.0985	.1471	.1931	.2256
	7	.0000	.0000	.0003	.0017	.0064	.0173	.0379	.0701	.1128	.1611
	8	.0000	.0000	.0000	.0002	.0011	.0037	.0102	.0234	.0462	.0806
	9	.0000	.0000	.0000	.0000	.0001	.0005	.0018	.0052	.0126	.0269
	10	.0000	.0000	.0000	.0000	.0000	.0000	.0002	.0007	.0021	.0054
	11	.0000	.0000	.0000	.0000	.0000	.0000	.0000	.0000	.0002	.0005
12	0	.5404	.2824	.1422	.0687	.0317	.0138	.0057	.0022	.0008	.0002
	1	.3413	.3766	.3012	.2062	.1267	.0712	.0368	.0174	.0075	.0029
	2	.0988	.2301	.2924	.2835	.2323	.1678	.1088	.0639	.0339	.0161
	3	.0173	.0852	.1720	.2362	.2581	.2397	.1954	.1419	.0923	.0537
	4	.0021	.0213	.0683	.1329	.1936	.2311	.2367	.2128	.1700	.1208
	5	.0002	.0038	.0193	.0532	.1032	.1585	.2039	.2270	.2225	.1934
	6	.0000	.0005	.0040	.0155	.0401	.0792	.1281	.1766	.2124	.2256
	7	.0000	.0000	.0006	.0033	.0115	.0291	.0591	.1009	.1489	.1934
	8	.0000	.0000	.0001	.0005	.0024	.0078	.0199	.0420	.0762	.1208
	9	.0000	.0000	.0000	.0001	.0004	.0015	.0048	.0125	.0277	.0537
	10	.0000	.0000	.0000	.0000	.0000	.0002	.0008	.0025	.0068	.0161
	11	.0000	.0000	.0000	.0000	.0000	.0000	.0001	.0003	.0010	.0029
	12	.0000	.0000	.0000	.0000	.0000	.0000	.0000	.0000	.0001	.0002

Table 9 (continued)

n	k	.05	.10	.15	.20	.25	.30	.35	.40	.45	.50
13	0	.5133	.2542	.1209	.0550	.0238	.0097	.0037	.0013	.0004	.0001
	1	.3512	.3672	.2774	.1787	.1029	.0540	.0259	.0113	.0045	.0016
	2	.1109	.2448	.2937	.2680	.2059	.1388	.0836	.0453	.0220	.0095
	3	.0214	.0997	.1900	.2457	.2517	.2181	.1651	.1107	.0660	.0349
	4	.0028	.0277	.0838	.1535	.2097	.2337	.2222	.1845	.1350	.0873
	5	.0003	.0055	.0266	.0691	.1258	.1803	.2154	.2214	.1989	.1571
	6	.0000	.0008	.0063	.0230	.0559	.1030	.1546	.1968	.2169	.2095
	7	.0000	.0001	.0011	.0058	.0186	.0442	.0833	.1312	.1775	.2095
	8	.0000	.0000	.0001	.0011	.0047	.0142	.0336	.0656	.1089	.1571
	9	.0000	.0000	.0000	.0001	.0009	.0034	.0101	.0243	.0495	.0873
	10	.0000	.0000	.0000	.0000	.0001	.0006	.0022	.0065	.0162	.0349
	11	.0000	.0000	.0000	.0000	.0000	.0001	.0003	.0012	.0036	.0095
	12	.0000	.0000	.0000	.0000	.0000	.0000	.0000	.0001	.0005	.0016
	13	.0000	.0000	.0000	.0000	.0000	.0000	.0000	.0000	.0000	.0001
14	0	.4877	.2288	.1028	.0440	.0178	.0068	.0024	.0008	.0002	.0001
	1	.3593	.3559	.2539	.1539	.0832	.0407	.0181	.0073	.0027	.0009
	2	.1229	.2570	.2912	.2501	.1802	.1134	.0634	.0317	.0141	.0056
	3	.0259	.1142	.2056	.2501	.2402	.1943	.1366	.0845	.0462	.0222
	4	.0037	.0349	.0998	.1720	.2202	.2290	.2022	.1549	.1040	.0611
	5	.0004	.0078	.0352	.0860	.1468	.1963	.2178	.2066	.1701	.1222
	6	.0000	.0013	.0093	.0322	.0734	.1262	.1759	.2066	.2088	.1833
	7	.0000	.0002	.0019	.0092	.0280	.0618	.1082	.1574	.1952	.2095
	8	.0000	.0000	.0003	.0020	.0082	.0232	.0510	.0918	.1398	.1833
	9	.0000	.0000	.0000	.0003	.0018	.0066	.0183	.0408	.0762	.1222
	10	.0000	.0000	.0000	.0000	.0003	.0014	.0049	.0136	.0312	.0611
	11	.0000	.0000	.0000	.0000	.0000	.0002	.0010	.0033	.0093	.0222
	12	.0000	.0000	.0000	.0000	.0000	.0000	.0001	.0005	.0019	.0056
	13	.0000	.0000	.0000	.0000	.0000	.0000	.0000	.0001	.0002	.0009
	14	.0000	.0000	.0000	.0000	.0000	.0000	.0000	.0000	.0000	.0001
15	0	.4633	.2059	.0874	.0352	.0134	.0047	.0016	.0005	.0001	.0000
	1	.3658	.3432	.2312	.1329	.0668	.0305	.0126	.0047	.0016	.0005
	2	.1348	.2669	.2856	.2309	.1559	.0916	.0476	.0219	.0090	.0032
	3	.0307	.1285	.2184	.2501	.2252	.1700	.1110	.0634	.0318	.0139
	4	.0049	.0428	.1156	.1876	.2252	.2186	.1792	.1268	.0780	.0417
	5	.0006	.0105	.0449	.1032	.1651	.2061	.2123	.1859	.1404	.0916
	6	.0000	.0019	.0132	.0430	.0917	.1472	.1906	.2066	.1914	.1527
	7	.0000	.0003	.0030	.0138	.0393	.0811	.1319	.1771	.2013	.1964
	8	.0000	.0000	.0005	.0035	.0131	.0348	.0710	.1181	.1647	.1964
	9	.0000	.0000	.0001	.0007	.0034	.0116	.0298	.0612	.1048	.1527
	10	.0000	.0000	.0000	.0001	.0007	.0030	.0096	.0245	.0515	.0916
	11	.0000	.0000	.0000	.0000	.0001	.0006	.0024	.0074	.0191	.0417
	12	.0000	.0000	.0000	.0000	.0000	.0001	.0004	.0016	.0052	.0139
	13	.0000	.0000	.0000	.0000	.0000	.0000	.0001	.0003	.0010	.0032
	14	.0000	.0000	.0000	.0000	.0000	.0000	.0000	.0000	.0001	.0005
	15	.0000	.0000	.0000	.0000	.0000	.0000	.0000	.0000	.0000	.0000

Table 9 (continued)

n	k	.05	.10	.15	.20	.25	.30	.35	.40	.45	.50
16	0	.4401	.1853	.0743	.0281	.0100	.0033	.0010	.0003	.0001	.0000
	1	.3706	.3294	.2097	.1126	.0535	.0228	.0087	.0030	.0009	.0002
	2	.1463	.2745	.2775	.2111	.1336	.0732	.0353	.0150	.0056	.0018
	3	.0359	.1423	.2285	.2463	.2079	.1465	.0888	.0468	.0215	.0085
	4	.0061	.0514	.1311	.2001	.2252	.2040	.1553	.1014	.0572	.0278
	5	.0008	.0137	.0555	.1201	.1802	.2099	.2008	.1623	.1123	.0667
	6	.0001	.0028	.0180	.0550	.1101	.1649	.1982	.1983	.1684	.1222
	7	.0000	.0004	.0045	.0197	.0524	.1010	.1524	.1889	.1969	.1746
	8	.0000	.0001	.0009	.0055	.0197	.0487	.0923	.1417	.1812	.1964
	9	.0000	.0000	.0001	.0012	.0058	.0185	.0442	.0840	.1318	.1746
	10	.0000	.0000	.0000	.0002	.0014	.0056	.0167	.0392	.0755	.1222
	11	.0000	.0000	.0000	.0000	.0002	.0013	.0049	.0142	.0337	.0667
	12	.0000	.0000	.0000	.0000	.0000	.0002	.0011	.0040	.0115	.0278
	13	.0000	.0000	.0000	.0000	.0000	.0000	.0002	.0008	.0029	.0085
	14	.0000	.0000	.0000	.0000	.0000	.0000	.0000	.0001	.0005	.0018
	15	.0000	.0000	.0000	.0000	.0000	.0000	.0000	.0000	.0001	.0002
	16	.0000	.0000	.0000	.0000	.0000	.0000	.0000	.0000	.0000	.0000
17	0	.4181	.1668	.0631	.0225	.0075	.0023	.0007	.0002	.0000	.0000
	1	.3741	.3150	.1893	.0957	.0426	.0169	.0060	.0019	.0005	.0001
	2	.1575	.2800	.2673	.1914	.1136	.0581	.0260	.0102	.0035	.0010
	3	.0415	.1556	.2359	.2393	.1893	.1245	.0701	.0341	.0144	.0052
	4	.0076	.0605	.1457	.2093	.2209	.1868	.1320	.0796	.0411	.0182
	5	.0010	.0175	.0668	.1361	.1914	.2081	.1849	.1379	.0875	.0472
	6	.0001	.0039	.0236	.0680	.1276	.1784	.1991	.1839	.1432	.0944
	7	.0000	.0007	.0065	.0267	.0668	.1201	.1685	.1927	.1841	.1484
	8	.0000	.0001	.0014	.0084	.0279	.0644	.1134	.1606	.1883	.1855
	9	.0000	.0000	.0003	.0021	.0093	.0276	.0611	.1070	.1540	.1855
	10	.0000	.0000	.0000	.0004	.0025	.0095	.0263	.0571	.1008	.1484
	11	.0000	.0000	.0000	.0001	.0005	.0026	.0090	.0242	.0525	.0944
	12	.0000	.0000	.0000	.0000	.0001	.0006	.0024	.0081	.0215	.0472
	13	.0000	.0000	.0000	.0000	.0000	.0001	.0005	.0021	.0068	.0182
	14	.0000	.0000	.0000	.0000	.0000	.0000	.0001	.0004	.0016	.0052
	15	.0000	.0000	.0000	.0000	.0000	.0000	.0000	.0001	.0003	.0010
	16	.0000	.0000	.0000	.0000	.0000	.0000	.0000	.0000	.0000	.0001
	17	.0000	.0000	.0000	.0000	.0000	.0000	.0000	.0000	.0000	.0000
18	0	.3972	.1501	.0536	.0180	.0056	.0016	.0004	.0001	.0000	.0000
	1	.3763	.3002	.1704	.0811	.0338	.0126	.0042	.0012	.0003	.0001
	2	.1683	.2835	.2556	.1723	.0958	.0458	.0190	.0069	.0022	.0006
	3	.0473	.1680	.2406	.2297	.1704	.1046	.0547	.0246	.0095	.0031
	4	.0093	.0700	.1592	.2153	.2130	.1681	.1104	.0614	.0291	.0117
	5	.0014	.0218	.0787	.1507	.1988	.2017	.1664	.1146	.0666	.0327
	6	.0002	.0052	.0301	.0816	.1436	.1873	.1941	.1655	.1181	.0708
	7	.0000	.0010	.0091	.0350	.0820	.1376	.1792	.1892	.1657	.1214
	8	.0000	.0002	.0022	.0120	.0376	.0811	.1327	.1734	.1864	.1669
	9	.0000	.0000	.0004	.0033	.0139	.0386	.0794	.1284	.1694	.1855
	10	.0000	.0000	.0001	.0008	.0042	.0149	.0385	.0771	.1248	.1669
	11	.0000	.0000	.0000	.0001	.0010	.0046	.0151	.0374	.0742	.1214
	12	.0000	.0000	.0000	.0000	.0002	.0012	.0047	.0145	.0354	.0708
	13	.0000	.0000	.0000	.0000	.0000	.0002	.0012	.0045	.0134	.0327
	14	.0000	.0000	.0000	.0000	.0000	.0000	.0002	.0011	.0039	.0117
	15	.0000	.0000	.0000	.0000	.0000	.0000	.0000	.0002	.0009	.0031
	16	.0000	.0000	.0000	.0000	.0000	.0000	.0000	.0000	.0001	.0006
	17	.0000	.0000	.0000	.0000	.0000	.0000	.0000	.0000	.0000	.0001
	18	.0000	.0000	.0000	.0000	.0000	.0000	.0000	.0000	.0000	.0000

Table 9 (continued)

n	k	.05	.10	.15	.20	.25	.30	.35	.40	.45	.50
19	0	.3774	.1351	.0456	.0144	.0042	.0011	.0003	.0001	.0000	.0000
	1	.3774	.2852	.1529	.0685	.0268	.0093	.0029	.0008	.0002	.0000
	2	.1787	.2852	.2428	.1540	.0803	.0358	.0138	.0046	.0013	.0003
	3	.0533	.1796	.2428	.2182	.1517	.0869	.0422	.0175	.0062	.0018
	4	.0112	.0798	.1714	.2182	.2023	.1491	.0909	.0467	.0203	.0074
	5	.0018	.0266	.0907	.1636	.2023	.1916	.1468	.0933	.0497	.0222
	6	.0002	.0069	.0374	.0955	.1574	.1916	.1844	.1451	.0949	.1518
	7	.0000	.0014	.0122	.0443	.0974	.1525	.1844	.1797	.1443	.0961
	8	.0000	.0002	.0032	.0166	.0487	.0981	.1489	.1797	.1771	.1442
	9	.0000	.0000	.0007	.0051	.0198	.0514	.0980	.1464	.1771	.1762
	10	.0000	.0000	.0001	.0013	.0066	.0220	.0528	.0976	.1449	.1762
	11	.0000	.0000	.0000	.0003	.0018	.0077	.0233	.0532	.0970	.1442
	12	.0000	.0000	.0000	.0000	.0004	.0022	.0083	.0237	.0529	.0961
	13	.0000	.0000	.0000	.0000	.0001	.0005	.0024	.0085	.0233	.0518
	14	.0000	.0000	.0000	.0000	.0000	.0001	.0006	.0024	.0082	.0222
	15	.0000	.0000	.0000	.0000	.0000	.0000	.0001	.0005	.0022	.0074
	16	.0000	.0000	.0000	.0000	.0000	.0000	.0000	.0001	.0005	.0018
	17	.0000	.0000	.0000	.0000	.0000	.0000	.0000	.0000	.0001	.0003
	18	.0000	.0000	.0000	.0000	.0000	.0000	.0000	.0000	.0000	.0000
	19	.0000	.0000	.0000	.0000	.0000	.0000	.0000	.0000	.0000	.0000
20	0	.3585	.1216	.0388	.0115	.0032	.0008	.0002	.0000	.0000	.0000
	1	.3774	.2702	.1368	.0576	.0211	.0068	.0020	.0005	.0001	.0000
	2	.1887	.2852	.2293	.1369	.0669	.0278	.0100	.0031	.0008	.0002
	3	.0596	.1901	.2428	.2054	.1339	.0716	.0323	.0123	.0040	.0011
	4	.0133	.0898	.1821	.2182	.1897	.1304	.0738	.0350	.0139	.0046
	5	.0022	.0319	.1028	.1746	.2023	.1789	.1272	.0746	.0365	.0148
	6	.0003	.0089	.0454	.1091	.1686	.1916	.1712	.1244	.0746	.0370
	7	.0000	.0020	.0160	.0545	.1124	.1643	.1844	.1659	.1221	.0739
	8	.0000	.0004	.0046	.0222	.0609	.1144	.1614	.1797	.1623	.1201
	9	.0000	.0001	.0011	.0074	.0271	.0654	.1158	.1597	.1771	.1602
	10	.0000	.0000	.0002	.0020	.0099	.0308	.0686	.1171	.1593	.1762
	11	.0000	.0000	.0000	.0005	.0030	.0120	.0336	.0710	.1185	.1602
	12	.0000	.0000	.0000	.0001	.0008	.0039	.1036	.0355	.0727	.1201
	13	.0000	.0000	.0000	.0000	.0002	.0010	.0045	.0146	.0366	.0739
	14	.0000	.0000	.0000	.0000	.0000	.0002	.0012	.0049	.0150	.0370
	15	.0000	.0000	.0000	.0000	.0000	.0000	.0003	.0013	.0049	.0148
	16	.0000	.0000	.0000	.0000	.0000	.0000	.0000	.0003	.0013	.0046
	17	.0000	.0000	.0000	.0000	.0000	.0000	.0000	.0000	.0002	.0011
	18	.0000	.0000	.0000	.0000	.0000	.0000	.0000	.0000	.0000	.0002
	19	.0000	.0000	.0000	.0000	.0000	.0000	.0000	.0000	.0000	.0000
	20	.0000	.0000	.0000	.0000	.0000	.0000	.0000	.0000	.0000	.0000

Table 10
Normal Curve Table
$Z = Z - score$

An entry in the table is the proportion under the curve between $Z = 0$ and a positive value of Z. Areas for negative values of Z are obtained by symmetry.

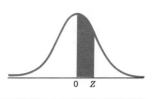

Z	0.00	0.01	0.02	0.03	0.04	0.05	0.06	0.07	0.08	0.09
0.0	0.0000	0.0040	0.0080	0.0120	0.0160	0.0199	0.0239	0.0279	0.0319	0.0359
0.1	0.0398	0.0438	0.0478	0.0517	0.0557	0.0596	0.0636	0.0675	0.0714	0.0753
0.2	0.0793	0.0832	0.0871	0.0910	0.0948	0.0987	0.1026	0.1064	0.1103	0.1141
0.3	0.1179	0.1217	0.1255	0.1293	0.1331	0.1368	0.1406	0.1443	0.1480	0.1517
0.4	0.1554	0.1591	0.1628	0.1664	0.1700	0.1736	0.1772	0.1808	0.1844	0.1879
0.5	0.1915	0.1950	0.1985	0.2019	0.2054	0.2088	0.2123	0.2157	0.2190	0.2224
0.6	0.2257	0.2291	0.2324	0.2357	0.2389	0.2422	0.2454	0.2486	0.2517	0.2549
0.7	0.2580	0.2611	0.2642	0.2673	0.2703	0.2734	0.2764	0.2794	0.2823	0.2852
0.8	0.2881	0.2910	0.2939	0.2967	0.2995	0.3023	0.3051	0.3078	0.3106	0.3133
0.9	0.3159	0.3186	0.3212	0.3238	0.3264	0.3289	0.3315	0.3340	0.3365	0.3389
1.0	0.3413	0.3438	0.3461	0.3485	0.3508	0.3531	0.3554	0.3577	0.3599	0.3621
1.1	0.3642	0.3665	0.3686	0.3708	0.3729	0.3749	0.3770	0.3790	0.3810	0.3830
1.2	0.3849	0.3869	0.3888	0.3907	0.3925	0.3944	0.3962	0.3980	0.3997	0.4015
1.3	0.4032	0.4049	0.4066	0.4082	0.4099	0.4115	0.4131	0.4147	0.4162	0.4177
1.4	0.4192	0.4207	0.4222	0.4236	0.4251	0.4265	0.4279	0.4292	0.4306	0.4319
1.5	0.4332	0.4345	0.4357	0.4370	0.4382	0.4394	0.4406	0.4418	0.4429	0.4441
1.6	0.4452	0.4463	0.4474	0.4484	0.4495	0.4505	0.4515	0.4525	0.4535	0.4545
1.7	0.4554	0.4564	0.4573	0.4582	0.4591	0.4599	0.4608	0.4616	0.4625	0.4633
1.8	0.4641	0.4649	0.4656	0.4664	0.4671	0.4678	0.4686	0.4693	0.4699	0.4706
1.9	0.4713	0.4719	0.4726	0.4732	0.4738	0.4744	0.4750	0.4756	0.4761	0.4767
2.0	0.4772	0.4778	0.4783	0.4788	0.4793	0.4798	0.4803	0.4808	0.4812	0.4817
2.1	0.4821	0.4826	0.4830	0.4834	0.4838	0.4842	0.4846	0.4850	0.4854	0.4857
2.2	0.4861	0.4864	0.4868	0.4871	0.4875	0.4878	0.4881	0.4884	0.4887	0.4890
2.3	0.4893	0.4896	0.4898	0.4901	0.4904	0.4906	0.4909	0.4911	0.4913	0.4916
2.4	0.4918	0.4920	0.4922	0.4925	0.4927	0.4929	0.4931	0.4932	0.4934	0.4936
2.5	0.4938	0.4940	0.4941	0.4943	0.4945	0.4946	0.4948	0.4949	0.4951	0.4952
2.6	0.4953	0.4955	0.4956	0.4957	0.4959	0.4960	0.4961	0.4962	0.4963	0.4964
2.7	0.4965	0.4966	0.4967	0.4968	0.4969	0.4970	0.4971	0.4972	0.4973	0.4974
2.8	0.4974	0.4975	0.4976	0.4977	0.4977	0.4978	0.4979	0.4979	0.4980	0.4981
2.9	0.4981	0.4982	0.4982	0.4983	0.4984	0.4984	0.4985	0.4985	0.4986	0.4986
3.0	0.4987	0.4987	0.4987	0.4988	0.4988	0.4989	0.4989	0.4989	0.4990	0.4990

Table 11
χ² Distribution

Degree of freedom ν	$p = 0.99$	0.98	0.95	0.90	0.80	0.70	0.50	0.30	0.20	0.10	0.05	0.02	0.01
1	0.000157	0.000628	0.00393	0.0158	0.0642	0.148	0.455	1.074	1.642	2.706	3.841	5.412	6.635
2	0.0201	0.0404	0.103	0.211	0.446	0.713	1.386	2.408	3.219	4.605	5.991	7.824	9.210
3	0.115	0.185	0.352	0.584	1.005	1.424	2.366	3.665	4.642	6.251	7.815	9.837	11.341
4	0.297	0.429	0.711	1.064	1.649	2.195	3.357	4.878	5.989	7.779	9.488	11.668	13.277
5	0.554	0.752	1.145	1.610	2.343	3.000	4.351	6.064	7.289	9.236	11.070	13.388	15.086
6	0.872	1.134	1.635	2.204	3.070	3.828	5.348	7.231	8.558	10.645	12.592	15.033	16.812
7	1.239	1.564	2.167	2.833	3.822	4.671	6.346	8.383	9.803	12.017	14.067	16.622	18.475
8	1.646	2.032	2.733	3.490	4.594	5.527	7.344	9.524	11.030	13.362	15.507	18.168	20.090
9	2.088	2.532	3.325	4.168	5.380	6.393	8.343	10.656	12.242	14.684	16.919	19.679	21.666
10	2.558	3.059	3.940	4.865	6.179	7.267	9.342	11.781	13.442	15.987	18.307	21.161	23.209
11	3.053	3.609	4.575	5.578	6.989	8.148	10.341	12.899	14.631	17.275	19.675	22.618	24.725
12	3.571	4.178	6.226	6.304	7.807	9.034	11.340	14.011	15.812	18.549	21.026	24.054	26.217
13	4.107	4.765	5.892	7.042	8.634	9.926	12.340	15.119	16.985	19.812	22.362	25.472	27.688
14	4.660	5.368	6.571	7.790	9.467	10.821	13.339	16.222	18.151	21.064	23.685	26.873	29.141
15	5.229	5.985	7.261	8.547	10.307	11.721	14.339	17.322	19.311	22.307	24.996	28.259	30.578
16	5.812	6.614	7.962	9.312	11.152	12.624	15.338	18.418	20.465	23.542	26.296	29.633	32.000
17	6.408	7.255	8.672	10.085	12.002	13.531	16.338	19.511	21.615	24.769	27.587	30.995	33.409
18	7.015	7.906	9.390	10.865	12.857	14.440	17.338	20.601	22.760	25.989	28.869	32.346	34.805
19	7.633	8.567	10.117	11.651	13.716	15.352	18.338	21.689	23.900	27.204	30.144	33.687	36.191
20	8.260	9.237	10.851	12.443	14.578	16.266	19.337	22.775	25.038	28.412	31.410	35.020	37.566
21	8.897	9.915	11.591	13.240	15.445	17.182	20.337	23.858	26.171	29.615	32.671	36.343	38.932
22	9.542	10.600	12.338	14.041	16.314	18.101	21.337	24.939	27.301	30.813	33.924	37.659	40.289
23	10.196	11.293	13.091	14.848	17.187	19.021	22.337	26.018	28.429	32.007	35.172	38.968	41.638
24	10.856	11.992	13.848	15.659	18.062	19.943	23.337	27.096	29.553	33.196	36.415	40.270	42.980
25	11.524	12.697	14.611	16.473	18.940	20.867	24.337	28.172	30.675	34.382	37.652	41.566	44.314
26	12.198	13.409	15.379	17.292	19.820	21.792	25.336	29.246	31.795	35.563	38.885	42.856	45.642
27	12.879	14.125	16.151	18.114	20.703	22.719	26.336	30.319	32.912	36.741	40.113	44.140	46.963
28	13.565	14.847	16.928	18.939	21.588	23.647	27.336	31.391	34.027	37.916	41.337	45.419	48.278
29	14.256	15.574	17.708	19.768	22.475	24.577	28.336	32.461	35.139	39.087	42.557	46.693	49.588
30	14.953	16.306	18.493	20.599	23.364	25.508	29.336	33.530	36.250	40.256	43.773	47.962	50.892

A Short Review of Number Systems and Their Properties Appendix

The numbers we use for listing objects or counting objects, such as the number of members of the House of Representatives or the number of committees that can be formed from a group of five people, are called *counting numbers* or *whole numbers*. In set notation, the counting numbers can be enumerated as

$$W = \{0, 1, 2, 3, 4, \ldots\}$$

However, the set W of whole numbers will not suffice for many applications. For example, if your checking account has a balance of $24.00 in it and you write a check for $30.00, how will you represent the balance in your account (without reverting to red ink)? If the temperature during the day is 15°F and that night the temperature falls by 24°F, what is the new outside temperature? How is it represented?

Of course, what we are saying is that we need some new numbers, the *negative numbers,* to aid us in representing situations like those described above. In accounting circles, a debit or money owed is generally represented by placing parentheses around the debt. In the checking account example, the balance would be listed as ($6.00). Usually, though, a dash (—) before a number is used to denote that it is negative. Thus, we could say that the temperature outside in the example above was "minus 9" or "9° below zero" and we would write this temperature as −9°F.

The numbers we use to represent situations such as those given above are called *integers*. In set notation, the *set of integers* is

$$J = \{0, 1, -1, 2, -2, 3, -3, \ldots\}$$

The whole numbers 0, 1, 2, . . . form a subset of the set of integers as do the negative (whole) numbers $-1, -2, -3, \ldots$.

Even with the set J of integers, we run into difficulties in some applications. For example, can we use an integer to answer the question what part of a dollar is 49 cents? Or, can we use an integer to represent the length of a city lot if when we use a foot-long ruler, we end up with the length more than 125 feet and less than 126 feet?

The answer to both these questions is no! We need to invent new numbers to handle such situations. This new set of numbers is called the *set R of rational numbers*.

For example, to answer what part of a dollar is 49 cents, we can say 49/100. Rational numbers are written as *ratios of integers*. For a rational number a/b, the integer a is called the *numerator,* and the integer b, which cannot be zero, is called the denominator.

However, in some situations, even a rational number will not accurately describe the situations. For example, if one has an isosceles right triangle in which the two equal sides are 1 foot long, can the length of the third side be expressed as a rational number? See Figure A.1.

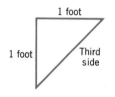

1 foot

1 foot   Third side

Figure A.1

The Greeks were the first to learn that no matter what two circles are used, the ratio of circumference to diameter of one is always the same as the ratio of circumference to diameter of the second. Can this common value be represented by a rational number? See Figure A.2.

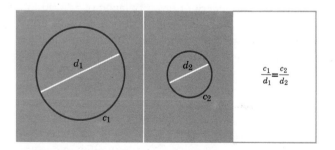

$$\frac{c_1}{d_1} = \frac{c_2}{d_2}$$

Figure A.2

As might be expected, the answer to both these questions is no. For the first question, we all know by the Pythagorean Theorem that the length of the third side is $\sqrt{2}$. However, $\sqrt{2}$ is *not* a rational number — it is not the ratio of two integers. The well-known symbol assigned to the ratio of circumference to diameter of a circle is π, which also cannot be expressed as the ratio of two integers. Such numbers as $\sqrt{2}$, π, $\sqrt[3]{5}$ are called *irrational numbers*.

If we form the union of the set of irrational numbers with the set of rational numbers, we obtain the *set of real numbers*.

In order to represent real numbers, we use what is commonly referred to as a *decimal expansion*. For example, the decimal expansions of the rational numbers 3/4, 5/2, 2/3, are

$$\frac{3}{4} = .75, \qquad \frac{5}{2} = 2.5, \qquad \frac{2}{3} = .666 \ldots$$

The decimal expansion of rational numbers are always of two types: (1) terminating or ending (eg. 3/4, 5/2) and (2) repeating (eg. 2/3, 1/7). The decimal expansion of an irrational number never terminates and never repeats. Thus

$$\sqrt{2} = 1.414 \ldots \qquad \pi = 3.14159 \ldots$$

That is, if the decimal expansion of a real number repeats or terminates, the real number is rational; if the decimal expansion neither repeats nor terminates, the real number is irrational.

As an aid to your review of real numbers and their properties, several of the more important concepts involving rules and notation are listed below.

1. *Reflexive property of equality*
   $a = a$ for any real number a
2. *Symmetric property of equality*
   if $a = b$, then $b = a$ for any real numbers a, b
3. *Transitive property of equality*
   if $a = b$ and if $b = c$, then $a = c$ for all real numbers a, b, c
4. *Commutative Laws*
   (a) $a + b = b + a$ (b) $a \cdot b = b \cdot a$ for all real numbers a, b
5. *Associative laws*
   (a) $a + b + c = (a + b) + c = a + (b + c)$ for all real numbers a, b, c
   (b) $a \cdot b \cdot c = (a \cdot b) \cdot c = a \cdot (b \cdot c)$ for all real numbers a, b, c
6. *Distributive Laws*
   $a \cdot (b + c) = (a \cdot b) + (a \cdot c)$ for all real numbers a, b, c
7. *Properties of Zero*
   (a) $a + 0 = a$ (b) $a \cdot 0 = 0$ for any real number a
8. *Property of One*
   $a \cdot 1 = a$ for any real number a
9. *Properties of Inverses*
   (a) $a + (-a) = 0$ for any real number a
   (b) $a \cdot \dfrac{1}{a} = 1$ for any real number a, except 0
10. *Arithmetic of Ratios*
    (a) $\dfrac{a}{b} = a \cdot \dfrac{1}{b}$
    (b) $\dfrac{a}{b} + \dfrac{c}{d} = \dfrac{ad + bc}{bd}$, $b \neq 0$, $d \neq 0$

(c) $\dfrac{a}{b} \cdot \dfrac{c}{d} = \dfrac{ac}{bd}$ $b \neq 0, d \neq 0$

(d) $\dfrac{a}{b} \div \dfrac{c}{d} = \dfrac{a}{b} \cdot \dfrac{d}{c} = \dfrac{ad}{bc}$ $b \neq 0, c \neq 0, d \neq 0$

11. *Rules for Division*

$0 \div a = 0$ $\dfrac{0}{a} = 0$ for any real number a, except 0

$a \div 0$ $\dfrac{a}{0}$ is undefined for any real number a

$a \div a = 1$ for any real number a, except 0

12. *Rules of Signs*

   (a) $a \cdot (-b) = -(ab)$

   (b) $(-a) \cdot b = -(ab)$ for any real numbers a, b

   (c) $(-a) \cdot (-b) = ab$

13. *Agreements; notations*

   (a) In $a \cdot b + c$, we agree to multiply *first*, and then *add*.

   (b) A mixed number $3\dfrac{5}{8}$ means $3 + \dfrac{5}{8}$

14. *Exponents*

   (a) For $n \geqq 0$ a whole number and a any real number,

   $a^0 = 1$

   $a^1 = a$

   $a^2 = a \cdot a$

   .

   .

   .

   $a^n = \underbrace{a \cdot a \cdot \cdot \cdot a}_{n \text{ times}}$

   (b) For $n < 0$ a negative whole number and $a \neq 0$ any real number,

   $a^{-1} = \dfrac{1}{a}$

   $a^{-2} = \dfrac{1}{a^2}$

   $\cdot \ \cdot \ \cdot \ \cdot \ \cdot$

   $a^{-n} = \dfrac{1}{a^n}$

A.1
Exercise

1. Perform the indicated operation.

   (a) $5 \cdot (-3) + 2$

   (b) $6 - 3 \cdot 4$

   (c) $(-5) \cdot (6 - 2)$

   (d) $-3 - 4 - 5$

   (e) $\dfrac{2}{3} + \dfrac{6}{7}$

   (f) $\dfrac{5}{2} + \dfrac{2}{3}$

(g) $\dfrac{3-2}{4-2}$

(h) $2\dfrac{1}{2}+3\dfrac{3}{8}$

(i) $4\dfrac{7}{8}+3\dfrac{3}{4}$

(j) $\dfrac{4}{3}+\dfrac{2}{3}$

(k) $-\dfrac{4}{3}\cdot\dfrac{6}{8}$

(l) $7+3-\dfrac{1}{3}\cdot\dfrac{30}{10}$

(m) $\left(\dfrac{2}{3}-5\right)\cdot\dfrac{9}{8}$

2. Find the solution x of
   (a) $2x+5=7$
   (b) $x+6=2$
   (c) $6-x=0$
   (d) $6+x=0$
   (e) $3\cdot(2-x)=0$
   (f) $5x-8=-9$
   (g) $(x+2)(-3)=5$

   (h) $\dfrac{3x-5}{x+2}=1$

   (i) $\dfrac{x}{3}+\dfrac{2x}{4}=\dfrac{5}{12}$

   (j) $ax+b=0$

   (k) $\dfrac{x}{a}+\dfrac{x}{b}=\dfrac{a+b}{ab}$
   (l) $3x-2=14$
   (m) $4x-7=-5-2x$

3. Find x in the following problems

   (a) $x=3^2$ (i) $x^3=8$
   (b) $x=3^{-2}$ (j) $x^4=256$
   (c) $x=4^4$ (k) $x^5=-32$
   (d) $x=(\sqrt{2})^4$ (l) $x^3=-27$
   (e) $x=(-3)^2$ (m) $2^x=4^4$
   (f) $x=(-3)^3$ (n) $10^x=1000$
   (g) $2^x=4$ (o) $4^x=4^5$
   (h) $3^x=81$ (p) $(2x)^5=32$

Now that we have at least an intuitive idea of what a real number is and what some of the properties of real numbers are, we can discuss an important feature of real numbers.

The set of real numbers can be divided into three subsets, that are nonempty and disjoint. These subsets are (1) the set of *positive* real numbers, (2) the set with just 0 as a member, (3) the set of *negative* real numbers. It is important to realize that every real number belongs to one and only one of them.

Some positive real numbers are

$$\frac{2}{3}, 5, \sqrt{2}, \pi, 5\frac{1}{2}, 1, 6.327$$

Some negative real numbers are

$$-\frac{3}{2}, -6, -\frac{1}{2}, -2, -5.219$$

Properties of the positive real numbers follow.

1. The sum of two positive real numbers is a positive real number.
2. The product of two positive real numbers is a positive real number.

Some properties of negative real numbers follow.

1. The sum of two negative real numbers is a negative real number.
2. The product of two negative real numbers is a positive real number.

Before we begin a study of inequalities, we shall discuss the *real line*. This review will help us understand some of the properties of inequalities studied in this textbook.

A real line L can be described as a collection of points P so that each point P can be matched with exactly one real number x. The real number x is called the *coordinate x* of the point P.

Let us see how this matching of points P and real numbers x takes place.

Consider a line L. Pick a point O on L. Call this point the *origin O*. Suppose we agree to associate to this point O, the real number $x = 0$. See Figure A.3.

Figure A.3

Pick another point U, different from the origin O, on L. Let $x = 1$ be associated with the point U. Figure A.4 depicts this situation in which we agree to pick U to the right of O.

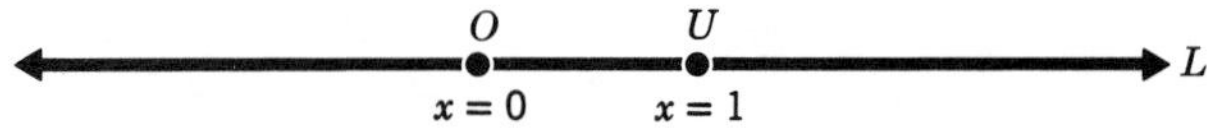

Figure A.4

The distance from O to U is called the *scale*; it may be one inch, or one mile. Now, with this scale established, we can associate real numbers x to points on *L*. We agree to abide by the usual convention that points to the *right* of the origin *O* will be associated with *positive* real numbers and those to the *left* of *O* to *negative* real numbers. The real number *x* associated to the point *P* is called the *coordinate of P*.

For example, the coordinate of the origin *O* is zero; the coordinate of *U* is one. Thus, we can represent the real line by Figure A.5.

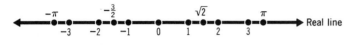

Figure A.5

With these properties in mind, we are ready to discuss the *arithmetic of inequalities.*

Let *a*, *b* be any real numbers. We shall say that *a is less than b* **or that** *b is greater than a,* **written as**

A.1
Definition

$$a < b \quad \textbf{or} \quad b > a$$

if and only of the difference $b - a$ **is a positive real number.**

For example, $2 < 7$, since $7 - 2 = 5$ is positive. Also, $6 > 3$, since $6 - 3 = 3$ is positive. On the real line, a real number *a* is *less than* a number *b*, when *a* is to the *left* of *b*.

Let *a*, *b* be real numbers. We shall say that *a is less than or equal to b* **or that** *b is greater than or equal to a,* **written as**

A.2
Definition

$$a \leqq b \quad \textbf{or} \quad b \geqq a$$

if and only if the difference $b - a$ **is either positive or zero.**

For example, $3 \leqq 8$ since $8 - 3 = 5$ is positive. Also, $4 \geqq 4$ since $4 - 4 = 0$ is zero.

It is easy to see that

$$a \text{ is positive if and only if } a > 0$$
$$a \text{ is negative if and only if } a < 0$$

When it becomes necessary to solve equations, we solve them by certain manipulations. Every time a manipulation is used, it is used subject to the laws or properties of real numbers. For example, when we solve

$$2x - 3 = 6$$

we first add 3 to both members obtaining

$$2x = 9$$

Then we multiply by 1/2 to get

$$x = \frac{9}{2}$$

Now to solve *inequalities* (expressions which involve $<$, $\leqq$, $\geqq$, or $>$), we attack the problem in much the same way. However, as will be seen, some of the laws for inequalities are different than those for equalities. The laws of inequalities are

1. *Addition Law*
   If $a \leqq b$, then $a + c \leqq b + c$
   (That is, addition will not affect the sense or direction of the inequality)
2. *Multiplication Law*
   (a) If $a \leqq b$ and $c > 0$, then $ac \leqq bc$
   (b) If $a \leqq b$ and $c < 0$, then $ac \geqq bc$
   (When multiplying an inequality, the sense or direction of the inequality remains the same if we multiply by a positive number; it is reversed if we multiply by a negative number).
3. *Division Law*
   (a) If $0 < a$, then $1/a > 0$
   (That is, the reciprocal of a positive number is positive.)
   (b) If a, b are positive and if $a < b$, then $1/a > 1/b$

A.1
Example

Examples of the above laws are

1. $2 < 3$, then $2 + 5 < 3 + 5$ or $7 < 8$
2. (a) If $2 < 3$ and $6 > 0$, then $2 \cdot 6 < 3 \cdot 6$ or $12 < 18$
   (b) If $2 < 3$ and $-4 < 0$, then $2(-4) > 3(-4)$ or $-8 > -12$
3. (a) If $3 > 0$, so is $1/3 > 0$
   (b) If $2 < 3$, then $1/3 < 1/2$

With these laws in mind, we can solve some inequality problems. Those values of an unknown x that make the inequality a true statement are members of the *solution set* of the inequality.

A.2
Example

Find all real numbers x for which

$$2x + 3 \leqq 6$$

To solve the inequality, treat it as if it were an equality, but remember that some of the laws are different. Then, if we add -3 to both members, we have

$$(2x + 3) + (-3) \leqq 6 + (-3)$$

$$2x \leqq 3$$

Now we multiply both members by 1/2, which is positive. Since $1/2 > 0$, the direction of the inequality will remain the same. Thus

$$\frac{1}{2}(2x) \leqq \frac{1}{2}(3)$$

$$x \leqq \frac{3}{2}$$

The solution set X is

$$X = \left\{ x \mid x \leq \frac{3}{2} \right\}$$

The graph of this solution set is given in Figure A.6.

Figure A.6

Find the solution set of

A.3
Example

$$-3x - 2 \leq 6$$

Again, we proceed as we would for an equality. Adding 2 to both members, we obtain

$$-3x \leq 8$$

Now we multiply by $-1/3$. Since $-1/3 < 0$, this manipulation will reverse the inequalities. Thus

$$\left(-\frac{1}{3} \right)(-3x) \geq \left(-\frac{1}{3} \right)(8)$$

$$x \geq -\frac{8}{3}$$

The solution set X is

$$X = \left\{ x \mid x \geq -\frac{8}{3} \right\}$$

The graph of the solution is given in Figure A.7.

Figure A.7

Find and graph the solution set X of the following

A.2
Exercise

1. $3x + 5 = 2$
2. $3x + 5 \geq 2$
3. $-3x + 5 \leq 2$
4. $6x - 3 \geq 8x + 5$
5. $14x - 12x + 16 \leq 3x - 2$
6. $4 - 5x \geq 3$
7. $8 - 2x \leq 5x - 6$

Answers to
Selected Problems

1. a, b, e, g are propositions.
2. **c** I am not buying stocks and bonds.
   e Someone wants to buy my house.
   g All people have a car.
   h Jones is not permitted not to see that all votes are not counted.
3. **a** John is an economics major or a sociology major.
   b John is an economics major or else he is a sociology major but not both.
   e John is not an economics major or he is not a sociology major.
   f It is not the case that John is not an economics major.

2.

p	q	$\sim p$	$\sim q$	$\sim p \lor \sim q$
T	T	F	F	F
T	F	F	T	T
F	T	T	F	T
F	F	T	T	T

5.

p	q	$\sim p$	$\sim p \land q$	$\sim(\sim p \land q)$
T	T	F	F	T
T	F	F	F	T
F	T	T	T	F
F	F	T	F	T

6.

p	q	$\sim p$	$\sim q$	$p \vee \sim q$	$(p \vee \sim q) \wedge \sim p$
T	T	F	F	T	F
T	F	F	T	T	F
F	T	T	F	F	F
F	F	T	T	T	T

8.

p	q	$\sim p$	$\sim q$	$p \vee \sim q$	$q \wedge \sim p$	$(p \vee \sim q) \wedge (q \wedge \sim p)$
T	T	F	F	T	F	F
T	F	F	T	T	F	F
F	T	T	F	F	T	F
F	F	T	T	T	F	F

11.

p	q	$\sim q$	$p \vee q$	$p \wedge \sim q$	$(p \vee q) \wedge (p \wedge \sim q)$
T	T	F	F	F	F
T	F	T	T	T	T
F	T	F	T	F	F
F	F	T	F	F	F

14.

p	q	r	$p \wedge q$	$p \wedge r$	$(p \wedge q) \vee (p \wedge r)$
T	T	T	T	T	T
T	T	F	T	F	T
T	F	T	F	T	T
T	F	F	F	F	F
F	T	T	F	F	F
F	T	F	F	F	F
F	F	T	F	F	F
F	F	F	F	F	F

15.

p	q	r	$\sim q$	$p \wedge \sim q$	$(p \wedge \sim q) \vee r$
T	T	T	F	F	T
T	T	F	F	F	F
T	F	T	T	T	F
T	F	F	T	T	T
F	T	T	F	F	T
F	T	F	F	F	F
F	F	T	T	F	T
F	F	F	T	F	F

1.3.2
Exercise

1. **c**

p	q	r	$p \wedge q$	$(p \wedge q) \wedge r$	$q \wedge r$	$p \wedge (q \wedge r)$	$(p \vee q)$
T	T	T	T	T	T	T	T
T	T	F	T	F	F	F	T
T	F	T	F	F	F	F	T
T	F	F	F	F	F	F	T
F	T	T	F	F	T	F	T
F	T	F	F	F	F	F	T
F	F	T	F	F	F	F	F
F	F	F	F	F	F	F	F
1	2	3	4	5	6	7	8

$(p \lor q) \lor r$	$q \lor r$	$p \lor (q \lor r)$
T	T	T
T	T	T
T	T	T
T	F	T
T	T	T
T	T	T
T	T	T
F	F	F
9	10	11

Columns 5 and 7 are the same so that $(p \land q) \land r \equiv p \land (q \land r)$.
Columns 9 and 11 are the same so that $(p \lor q) \lor r \equiv p \lor (q \lor r)$.

e

p	q	$p \lor q$	$p \land q$	$p \land (p \lor q)$	$p \lor (p \land q)$
T	T	T	T	T	T
T	F	T	F	T	T
F	T	T	F	F	F
F	F	F	F	F	F
1	2	3	4	5	6

Columns 1 and 5 are the same so that $p \equiv p \land (p \lor q)$.
Columns 1 and 6 are the same so that $p \equiv p \lor (p \land q)$.

2. a

p	q	$\sim q$	$\sim q \lor q$	$p \land (\sim q \lor q)$
T	T	F	T	T
T	F	T	T	T
F	T	F	T	F
F	F	T	T	F
1	2	3	4	5

Columns 1 and 5 are the same; thus $p \equiv p \land (\sim q \lor q)$.

3. c

p	q	$\sim p$	$\sim q$	$p \land q$	$\sim p \land \sim q$	$(p \land q) \lor (\sim p \land \sim q)$
T	T	F	F	T	F	T
T	F	F	T	F	F	F
F	T	T	F	F	F	F
F	F	T	T	F	T	T

$\{(p \land q) \lor (\sim p \land \sim q)\} \land p$
T
F
F
F

d

p	q	r	$\sim p$	$\sim q$	$\sim p \land \sim q \land r$	$p \land q \land r$
T	T	T	F	F	F	T
T	T	F	F	F	F	F
T	F	T	F	T	F	F
T	F	F	F	T	F	F
F	T	T	T	F	F	F
F	T	F	T	F	F	F
F	F	T	T	T	T	F
F	F	F	T	T	F	F

$$
\begin{array}{|c|}
\hline
(\sim p \wedge \sim q \wedge r) \vee (p \wedge q \wedge r) \\
T \\
F \\
F \\
F \\
F \\
F \\
T \\
F \\
\hline
\end{array}
$$

4. **b** "Smith is an ex-convict and Smith is rehabilitated" is equivalent to "Smith is rehabilitated and Smith is an ex-convict." "Smith is an ex-convict or Smith is rehabilitated" is equivalent to "Smith is rehabilitated or Smith is an ex-convict."

1.4
Exercise

	Implication	*Converse*	*Contrapositive*	*Inverse*
1. **a**	$\sim p \Rightarrow q$	$q \Rightarrow \sim p$	$\sim q \Rightarrow p$	$p \Rightarrow \sim q$
c	$\sim q \Rightarrow \sim p$	$\sim p \Rightarrow \sim q$	$p \Rightarrow q$	$q \Rightarrow p$

3. *Converse:* It is cloudy if it is raining.
Contrapositive: It is not cloudy if it is not raining.
Inverse: It is not raining if it is not cloudy.

6. *Converse:* A necessary condition for clouds is that it be raining.
Contrapositive: A necessary condition for no clouds is that it not be raining.
Inverse: A necessary condition for no rain is that it not be cloudy.

7. *Converse:* A sufficient condition for clouds is that it be raining.
Contrapositive: A sufficient condition for no clouds is that it not be raining.
Inverse: A sufficient condition for no rain is that it not be cloudy.

9. **a** If Jack studies psychology, then Mary studies sociology.

1.5
Exercise

1. **e**

p	q	$\sim p$	$\sim p \Rightarrow q$
T	T	F	T
T	F	F	T
F	T	T	T
F	F	T	F

f

p	q	$p \vee q$	$(p \vee q) \Rightarrow p$
T	T	T	T
T	F	T	T
F	T	T	F
F	F	F	T

i

p	q	$p \Rightarrow q$	$p \wedge (p \Rightarrow q)$
T	T	T	T
T	F	F	F
F	T	T	F
F	F	T	F

2. **b**

p	q	$p \vee q$	$p \wedge (p \vee q)$	$p \wedge (p \vee q) \Leftrightarrow p$
T	T	T	T	T
T	F	T	T	T
F	T	T	F	T
F	F	F	F	T

3. **a** $p \Rightarrow q$

   b $\sim p \wedge \sim q$

1. Let p and q be the statements, p: it is raining, q: John is going to school. Then,

$$p \Rightarrow \sim q, \qquad q \text{ are true.}$$

Prove: $\sim p$ is true.
Direct: $p \Rightarrow \sim q$ is true.
   Also its contrapositive $q \Rightarrow \sim p$ is true, q is true.
   Thus $\sim p$ is true by the Law of Detachment.
Indirect: Assume $\sim p$ is false.
   Then p is true. $p \Rightarrow \sim q$ is true.
   Thus $\sim q$ is true by the Law of Detachment.
   But q is true and we have a contradiction.
   The assumption is false and $\sim p$ is true.

3. Let p, q and r be the statements, p: Smith is elected president, q: Kuntz is elected secretary, r: Brown is elected treasurer. Then,

$$p \Rightarrow q, \qquad q \Rightarrow \sim r, \qquad p \text{ are true.}$$

Prove: $\sim r$ is true.
Direct: $p \Rightarrow q$ and $q \Rightarrow \sim r$ are true.
   So $p \Rightarrow \sim r$ is true by the Law of Syllogisms. p is true.
   Thus $\sim r$ is true by the Law of Detachment.
Indirect: Assume $\sim r$ is false.
   Then r is true. $p \Rightarrow q$ is true. $q \Rightarrow \sim r$ is true.
   So $p \Rightarrow \sim r$ is true by the Law of Syllogisms.
   $r \Rightarrow \sim p$, its contrapositive, is true.
   Thus $\sim p$ is true by the Law of Detachment,
   but p is true and we have a contradiction.
   The assumption is false and $\sim r$ is true.

1. Current flows from A to B in the following circuits in those cases in which the final value is C.

b

p	q	$\sim p$	$\sim q$	$\sim p \wedge \sim q$	$p \vee (\sim p \wedge \sim q)$
C	C	O	O	O	C
C	O	O	C	O	C
O	C	C	O	O	O
O	O	C	C	C	C

$p \wedge [p \vee (\sim p \wedge \sim q)] \wedge q$
C
O
O
O

d	p	q	$p \wedge q$	$\sim p \wedge q$	$p \wedge \sim q$	$(p \wedge q) \vee (\sim p \wedge q) \vee (p \wedge \sim q)$
	C	C	C	O	O	C
	C	O	O	O	C	C
	O	C	O	C	O	C
	O	O	O	O	O	O

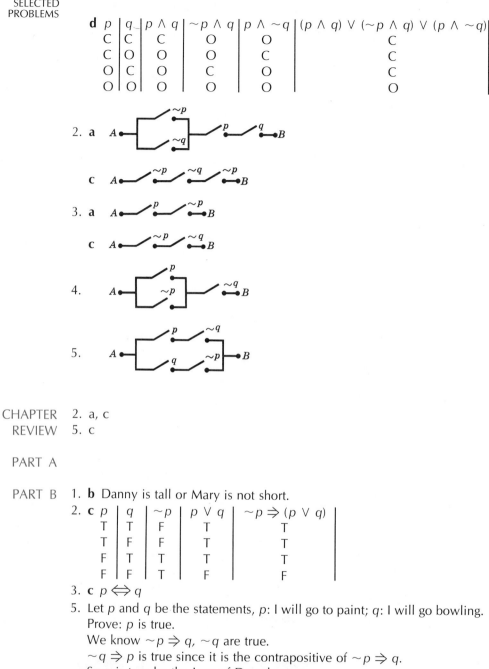

2. **a**

  c

3. **a**

  c

4.

5.

CHAPTER   2. a, c
REVIEW   5. c

PART A

PART B   1. **b** Danny is tall or Mary is not short.

2. **c**

p	q	$\sim p$	$p \vee q$	$\sim p \Rightarrow (p \vee q)$
T	T	F	T	T
T	F	F	T	T
F	T	T	T	T
F	F	T	F	F

3. **c** $p \Leftrightarrow q$

5. Let p and q be the statements, p: I will go to paint; q: I will go bowling.
Prove: p is true.
We know $\sim p \Rightarrow q$, $\sim q$ are true.
$\sim q \Rightarrow p$ is true since it is the contrapositive of $\sim p \Rightarrow q$.
So p is true by the Law of Detachment.

7.

p	q	$\sim q$	$\sim p \vee q$	$p \Rightarrow q$
T	T	F	T	T
T	F	F	F	F
F	T	T	T	T
F	F	T	T	T
1	2	3	4	5

Since columns 4 and 5 are the same, $\sim p \vee q \equiv p \Rightarrow q$.

1. $A = \{6, 7, 8, 9\}$ $A = \{x | 6 \leq x \leq 9 \text{ and } x \text{ is a digit}\}$
5. $\notin$
7. $\notin$
9. $R = \{x | x \text{ is a rational number}\}$ or $P = \{x | x \text{ is a prime integer}\}$.
10. Any random selection such as $S = \{1, 1/2, \sqrt{2}, \pi, -5, 6\}$.

1. $\supset, \supseteq$
3. $\sim$
6. none of these
9. $\sim, =, \subseteq, \supseteq$
12. For a set with n elements, there are 2^n subsets.
    a $\{a, b, c, d\}, \{a, b, c\}, \{a, c, d\}, \{a, b, d\}, \{b, c, d\}, \{a, b\} \{a, c\},$
      $\{a, d\}, \{b, c\}, \{b, d\} \{c, d\}, \{a\}, \{b\}, \{c\}, \{d\} \varnothing$
13. $C \subseteq A, C \subseteq B, A \supseteq C, B \supseteq C$

1. **a** A **c** U **d** A
2. **c** $A - B = \{0, 1, 7\}$ **d** $\overline{A - B} = \{2, 3, 4, 5, 6, 8, 9\}$
    e $\overline{A} - \overline{B} = \{2, 3, 4, 6, 8, 9\} - \{0, 1, 4, 6, 7, 9\} = \{2, 3, 8\}$
    g $(C - A) \cap \overline{A} = \{6, 9\} \cap \{2, 3, 4, 6, 8, 9\} = \{6, 9\}$
3. **a** $\overline{A} - \overline{C} = \{1, 2, 4\} - \{1, 5\} = \{2, 4\}$
    e $\overline{A} - C = \{1, 2, 3, 4\}$
    f $\overline{A \cup B} = \overline{\{1, 2, 3, 5\}} = \{4\}$
4. **a** $A \cap E = \{x | x \text{ is a customer of IBM and is a member of the Board of Directors of IBM}\}$
    c $B \cap D = \{x | x \text{ is a secretary employed by IBM and is a stockholder of IBM}\}$

5. **a**

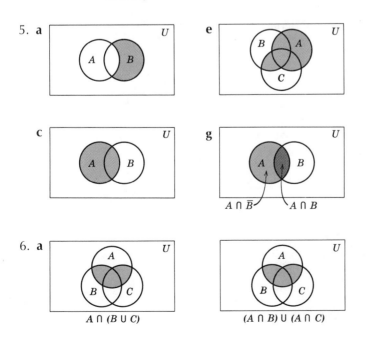

e

c

g

$A \cap \overline{B}$ $A \cap B$

6. **a**

$A \cap (B \cup C)$

$(A \cap B) \cup (A \cap C)$

e

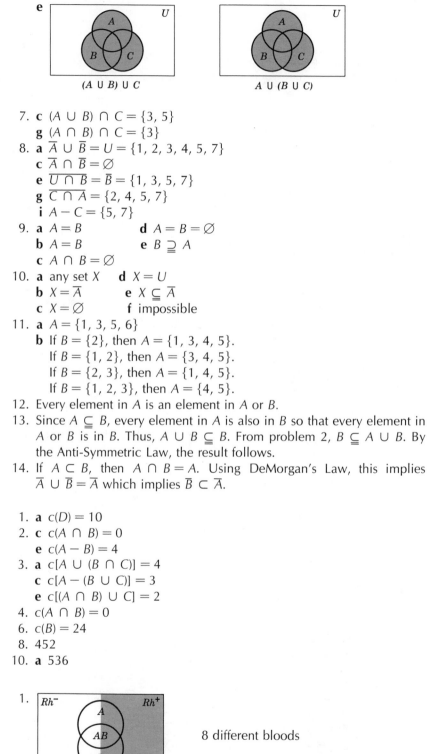

$(A \cup B) \cup C$ $A \cup (B \cup C)$

7. **c** $(A \cup B) \cap C = \{3, 5\}$
   g $(A \cap B) \cap C = \{3\}$
8. **a** $\overline{A} \cup \overline{B} = U = \{1, 2, 3, 4, 5, 7\}$
   c $\overline{A} \cap \overline{B} = \varnothing$
   e $\overline{U \cap B} = \overline{B} = \{1, 3, 5, 7\}$
   g $\overline{C \cap A} = \{2, 4, 5, 7\}$
   i $A - C = \{5, 7\}$
9. **a** $A = B$ **d** $A = B = \varnothing$
   b $A = B$ **e** $B \supseteq A$
   c $A \cap B = \varnothing$
10. **a** any set X **d** $X = U$
    b $X = \overline{A}$ **e** $X \subseteq \overline{A}$
    c $X = \varnothing$ **f** impossible
11. **a** $A = \{1, 3, 5, 6\}$
    b If $B = \{2\}$, then $A = \{1, 3, 4, 5\}$.
    If $B = \{1, 2\}$, then $A = \{3, 4, 5\}$.
    If $B = \{2, 3\}$, then $A = \{1, 4, 5\}$.
    If $B = \{1, 2, 3\}$, then $A = \{4, 5\}$.
12. Every element in A is an element in A or B.
13. Since $A \subseteq B$, every element in A is also in B so that every element in A or B is in B. Thus, $A \cup B \subseteq B$. From problem 2, $B \subseteq A \cup B$. By the Anti-Symmetric Law, the result follows.
14. If $A \subseteq B$, then $A \cap B = A$. Using DeMorgan's Law, this implies $\overline{A} \cup \overline{B} = \overline{A}$ which implies $\overline{B} \subset \overline{A}$.

2.5
Exercise

1. **a** $c(D) = 10$
2. **c** $c(A \cap B) = 0$
   e $c(A - B) = 4$
3. **a** $c[A \cup (B \cap C)] = 4$
   c $c[A - (B \cup C)] = 3$
   e $c[(A \cap B) \cup C] = 2$
4. $c(A \cap B) = 0$
6. $c(B) = 24$
8. 452
10. **a** 536

2.6
Exercise

1.

8 different bloods

2.

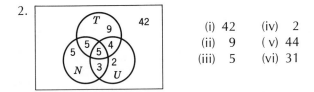

(i) 42   (iv)   2
(ii) 9   (v) 44
(iii) 5   (vi) 31

5.

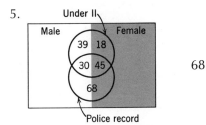

68

1. **a** $P(6, 4) = 6 \cdot 5 \cdot 4 \cdot 3 = 360$
   e $P(8, 7) = 8 \cdot 7 \cdot 6 \cdot 5 \cdot 4 \cdot 3 \cdot 2 = 40{,}320$
   f $P(6, 6) = 6! = 720$
2. **a** $C(6, 4) = 15$ **d** $C(5, 4) = 5$
   b $C(7, 2) = 21$
3. **a** $x = 5$ **c** $x = 2$
   b $x = 5$ **d** $x = 3$ or $x = 4$
4. **a** $C(x,y) = \dfrac{P(x,y)}{y!}$ $5 = \dfrac{120}{y!}$ $y! = 24$ $y = 4, x = 5$

   b $35 = \dfrac{210}{y!}$ $y! = 6$ $y = 3, x = 7$
11. $(3)\,(2)\,(4) = 24$
12. $(3)\,(6) = 18$
13. $\dfrac{8!}{2!2!} = \dfrac{8 \cdot 7 \cdot 6 \cdot 5 \cdot 4 \cdot 3 \cdot 2}{2 \cdot 2} = 10{,}080$
14. **a** $P(4, 2) = 4 \cdot 3 = 12$
    b $C(4, 2) = 6$
15. $C(6, 2) = 15$
16. $\dbinom{2}{1}\dbinom{3}{2}\dbinom{7}{2} = 2 \cdot 3 \cdot 21 = 126$
17. $\dbinom{3}{1}\dbinom{2}{1}\dbinom{5}{2} = 3 \cdot 2 \cdot 10 = 60$
18. $\dbinom{1352}{641}\dbinom{711}{234}\dbinom{477}{477}$
19. $C(17, 4) = 2210$
20. $\dbinom{52}{13}$
21. $4^{10} \cdot 2^{15} = 2^{35}$
22. **a** $(31)(31) = 961$
    b $P(31, 2) = (31)(30) = 930$
    c $C(31, 2) = (31)(15) = 465$
23. $\dfrac{100!}{22!13!10!5!16!17!17!}$

2.7
Exercise

24. $\dbinom{10}{3}\dbinom{7}{3}\dbinom{4}{4}$

CHAPTER
REVIEW

PART A

2. c, d
4. g
6. a
8. c, d
10. e
12. b
14. g
16. b

PART B

3. $A = \{1, 2, 3\}$, $A = \{1, 2\}$, $A = \{1, 3\}$, $A = \{1\}$

6.

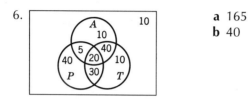

a 165
b 40

8. **a** $P(6, 3) = 6 \cdot 5 \cdot 4 = 120$

   b $C(6, 3) = \dfrac{120}{3} = 40$

9. Let A, B, C, D, E be the five people and let $X = AB$ be the ones that can't stand each other. There are 5! ways of arranging A, B, C, D, E and 4! ways to rearrange X, C, D, E. But A and B are next to each other in $2 \cdot 4!$ ways since neither $X = AB$ nor $X = BA$ are desirable. Thus, in all, the number of ways is

$$5! - 2 \cdot 4! = 3 \cdot 4! = 72$$

10. $\dbinom{16}{4}\dbinom{10}{3}$

11. One path from A to B is $R\ R\ R\ R\ R\ R\ U\ U\ U\ U\ U\ U$. All paths from A to B are exactly 12 moves of which exactly 6 are to the right (R). Thus, in all, there are $\dbinom{12}{6}$ paths from A to B.

PART C

1. By the Fundamental Principle of Counting, the number of ways is $5 \cdot 6 \cdot 8 = 240$.

2. We can buy a selection of 3 "single-novel" books or a selection of 1 "double-novel" book and 1 "single-novel" book. The first can be done in $6 \cdot 3 \cdot 4$ ways and the second in $5 \cdot 4 + 7 \cdot 6$ ways. It follows that the total numbers of ways is

$$6 \cdot 3 \cdot 4 + 5 \cdot 4 + 7 \cdot 6 = 134$$

3. The number of chances is

$$100 + 100 \cdot 99 + 100 \cdot 99 \cdot 98$$

4. Consider the number of ways of obtaining the team consisting of 1 boy and 3 girls. The boy can be chosen in $C(3, 1) = 3$ ways and the three girls in $C(5, 3) = 10$ ways. By the Fundamental Principle of Counting, such a team can be made in $3 \cdot 10 = 30$ ways.

5. There are 5! ways of ordering the speakers. A will precede B the same number of times that B precedes A so 1/2 of the arrangements must be eliminated. Therefore we have $\dfrac{5!}{2} = \dfrac{5 \cdot 4 \cdot 3 \cdot 2 \cdot 1}{2} = 60$ ways of ordering the speakers.

6. Let $AB = X$ then we have X, C, D, E to order. We have $4! = 4 \cdot 3 \cdot 2 \cdot 1 = 24$ ways to order the speakers.

7. There are $26 \cdot 10^4$ licenses with one letter and $26^2 \cdot 10^4$ licenses with two letters. Thus, there are at most $26 \cdot 10^4 + 26^2 \cdot 10^4$ different licenses.

1. **a** $S = \{TTTTT, TTTTH, TTTHT, TTTHH, TTHTT, TTHTH, TTHHT,$ CHAPTER 3
   $TTHHH, THTTT, THTTH, THTHT, THTHH, THHTT, THHTH,$
   $THHHT, THHHH, HTTTT, HTTTH, HTTHT, HTTHH, HTHTT,$ 3.2
   $HTHTH, HTHHT, HTHHH, HHTTT, HHTTH, HHTHT, HHTHH,$ Exercise
   $HHHTT, HHHTH, HHHHT, HHHHH\}$, 32

   b $S = \{H, TH, TTH, TTTH, \ldots\}$, infinite

   c S is the same as in problem 1a.

   e $S = \{(1, 1), (1, 2), (1, 3), (1, 4), (1, 5), (2, 1), (2, 2), (2, 3), (2, 4),$
   $(2, 5), (3, 1), (3, 2), (3, 3), (3, 4), (3, 5), (4, 1), (4, 2), (4, 3), (4, 4),$
   $(4, 5), (5, 1), (5, 2), (5, 3), (5, 4), (5, 5)\}$, 25

   $S = \{(1, 1, H), (1, 1, T), (1, 2, H), (1, 2, T), (1, 3, H), (1, 3, T), (1, 4, H),$
   $(1, 4, T), (1, 5, H), (1, 5, T), (1, 6, H), (1, 6, T), (2, 1, H), (2, 1, T),$
   $(2, 2, H), (2, 2, T), (2, 3, H), (2, 3, T), (2, 4, H), (2, 4, T), (2, 5, H),$
   $(2, 5, T), (2, 6, H), (2, 6, T), (3, 1, H), (3, 1, T), (3, 2, H), (3, 2, T),$
   $(3, 3, H), (3, 3, T), (3, 4, H), (3, 4, T), (3, 5, H), (3, 5, T), (3, 6, H),$
   $(3, 6, T), (4, 1, H), (4, 1, T), (4, 2, H), (4, 2, T), (4, 3, H), (4, 3, T),$
   $(4, 4, H), (4, 4, T), (4, 5, H), (4, 5, T), (4, 6, H), (4, 6, T), (5, 1, H),$
   $(5, 1, T), (5, 2, H), (5, 2, T), (5, 3, H), (5, 3, T), (5, 4, H), (5, 4, T),$
   $(5, 5, H), (5, 5, T), (5, 6, H), (5, 6, T), (6, 1, H), (6, 1, T), (6, 2, H),$
   $(6, 2, T), (6, 3, H), (6, 3, T), (6, 4, H), (6, 4, T), (6, 5, H), (6, 5, T),$
   $(6, 6, H), (6, 6, T)\}$
   $6 \cdot 6 \cdot 2 = 72.$

2. **a** $\dbinom{52}{5} = 2{,}598{,}960$

   b $\dbinom{11}{5} = 462$

3. The model is the sample space S and the probability assignment.
   (1a) One assignment is $P(\text{each simple event}) = 1/32$.
   Another assignment is $P(HHHHH) = 1$; $P(\text{other simple events}) = 0$.
   Other assignments are possible.

4. $S = \{[(H), (Gabcd)], [(Ha), (Gbcd)], [(Hb), (Gacd)], [(Hc), (Gabd)],$
   $[(Hd), (Gabc)], [(Hab), (Gcd)], [(Hac), (Gbd)], [(Had), (Gbc)],$

[(Hbc), (Gad)], [(Hbd), (Gac)], [(Hcd), (Gab)], [(Habc), (Gd)], [(Habd), (Gc)], [(Hacd), (Gb)], [(Hbcd), (Ga)], [(Habcd), (G)]}

Peace: {[(Hab), (Gcd)], [(Hac), (Gbd)], [(Had), (Gbc)], [(Hbc), (Gad)], [(Hbd), (Gac)], [(Hcd), (Gab)]}

6. **a** Let

$$x = P(\{e_1\}).$$

Since

$$P(\{e_1\}) + \cdots + P(\{e_7\}) = 1,$$
$$x + x + 1/2x + 1/4x + 1/4x + x + 1/2x = 1$$
$$9/2x = 1 \qquad x = 2/9$$
$$P(\{e_1\}) = 2/9 \qquad P(\{e_7\}) = 1/9$$
$$P(\{e_2\}) = 2/9$$
$$P(\{e_3\}) = 1/9$$
$$P(\{e_4\}) = 1/18$$
$$P(\{e_5\}) = 1/18$$
$$P(\{e_6\}) = 2/9$$

8. **a** $S = \{1, 2, 3, 4, 5, 6\}$

Let

$$x = P(\{1\})$$

Then,

$$x + 2x + 3x + 4x + 5x + 6x = 1$$
$$21x = 1 \qquad x = 1/21$$
$$P(\{1\}) = 1/21 \qquad P(\{4\}) = 4/21$$
$$P(\{2\}) = 2/21 \qquad P(\{5\}) = 5/21$$
$$P(\{3\}) = 1/7 \qquad P(\{6\}) = 2/7$$

9. **a** The number on the red die is three times the number on the green die.

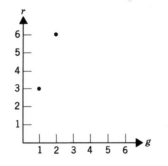

9. **c** The number on the red die is smaller or the same as the number on the green die.

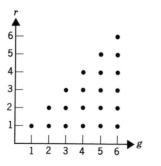

10. **b**

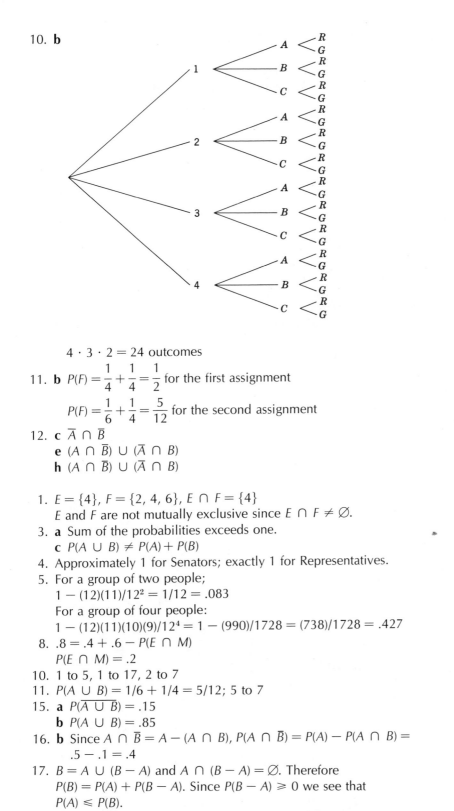

$4 \cdot 3 \cdot 2 = 24$ outcomes

11. **b** $P(F) = \dfrac{1}{4} + \dfrac{1}{4} = \dfrac{1}{2}$ for the first assignment

$P(F) = \dfrac{1}{6} + \dfrac{1}{4} = \dfrac{5}{12}$ for the second assignment

12. **c** $\bar{A} \cap \bar{B}$

e $(A \cap \bar{B}) \cup (\bar{A} \cap B)$

h $(A \cap \bar{B}) \cup (\bar{A} \cap B)$

1. $E = \{4\}$, $F = \{2, 4, 6\}$, $E \cap F = \{4\}$

E and F are not mutually exclusive since $E \cap F \neq \varnothing$.

3. **a** Sum of the probabilities exceeds one.

c $P(A \cup B) \neq P(A) + P(B)$

4. Approximately 1 for Senators; exactly 1 for Representatives.

5. For a group of two people;

$1 - (12)(11)/12^2 = 1/12 = .083$

For a group of four people:

$1 - (12)(11)(10)(9)/12^4 = 1 - (990)/1728 = (738)/1728 = .427$

8. $.8 = .4 + .6 - P(E \cap M)$

$P(E \cap M) = .2$

10. 1 to 5, 1 to 17, 2 to 7

11. $P(A \cup B) = 1/6 + 1/4 = 5/12$; 5 to 7

15. **a** $P(\overline{A \cup B}) = .15$

b $P(A \cup B) = .85$

16. **b** Since $A \cap \bar{B} = A - (A \cap B)$, $P(A \cap \bar{B}) = P(A) - P(A \cap B) = .5 - .1 = .4$

17. $B = A \cup (B - A)$ and $A \cap (B - A) = \varnothing$. Therefore $P(B) = P(A) + P(B - A)$. Since $P(B - A) \geq 0$ we see that $P(A) \leq P(B)$.

18. $P(A \cup B \cup C) = P(A \cup B) + P(C) - P[(A \cup B) \cap C]$

3.3
Exercise

$$= P(A) + P(B) - P(A \cap B) + P(C) - P[(A \cup B) \cap C]$$
$$= P(A) + P(B) + P(C) - P(A \cap B)$$
$$- P[(A \cap C) \cup (B \cap C)]$$
$$= P(A) + P(B) + P(C) - P(A \cap B) - P(A \cap C)$$
$$- P(B \cap C) + P[(A \cap C) \cap (B \cap C)]$$
$$= P(A) + P(B) + P(C) - P(A \cap B) - P(A \cap C)$$
$$- P(B \cap C) + P(A \cap B \cap C)$$

3.4
Exercise

1. 1/18, 1/12, 1/18
3. 1/4, 1/2
5. 2/9
6. **a** 7/15   **c** 2/5
7. $A \cap B = \{(1, 2), (1, 4), (1, 6), (2, 1), (4, 1), (6, 1)\}$
   $P(A \cap B) = 1/6$
   $A \cup \bar{B} = \{(1, 1), (1, 2), (1, 3), (1, 4), (1, 5), (1, 6), (2, 1), (3, 1), (4, 1),$
   $\qquad\qquad (5, 1), (6, 1), (2, 3), (2, 5), (3, 2), (5, 2), (3, 4), (3, 6), (4, 3),$
   $\qquad\qquad (6, 3), (4, 5), (5, 4), (5, 6), (6, 5)\}$
   $P(A \cup B) = 23/36$
   $A \cap \bar{B} = \{(2, 3), (2, 5), (3, 2), (5, 2), (3, 4), (3, 6), (4, 3), (6, 3), (4, 5),$
   $\qquad\qquad (5, 4), (5, 6), (6, 5)\}$
   $P(A \cap \bar{B}) = 1/3$
8. **b** $.20 + .24 + .31 = .75$

9.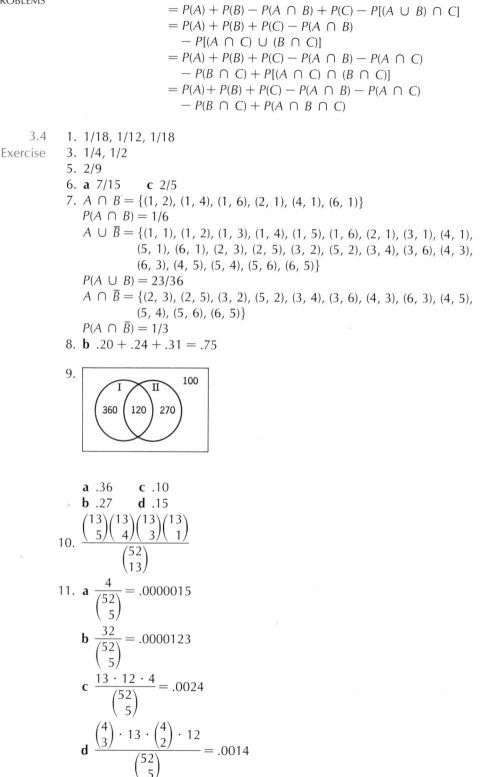

   a .36   **c** .10
   b .27   **d** .15

10. $\dfrac{\dbinom{13}{5}\dbinom{13}{4}\dbinom{13}{3}\dbinom{13}{1}}{\dbinom{52}{13}}$

11. **a** $\dfrac{4}{\dbinom{52}{5}} = .0000015$

    b $\dfrac{32}{\dbinom{52}{5}} = .0000123$

    c $\dfrac{13 \cdot 12 \cdot 4}{\dbinom{52}{5}} = .0024$

    d $\dfrac{\dbinom{4}{3} \cdot 13 \cdot \dbinom{4}{2} \cdot 12}{\dbinom{52}{5}} = .0014$

e $.0020 + .0039 + .0014 + .00024 + .0000123 + .0000015 = .0076$

2. $S = \{H, TH, TTH, TTTH, TTTT\}$
   $P(\{H\}) = 1/4$
   $P(\{TH\}) = 3/4 \cdot 1/4 = 3/16$

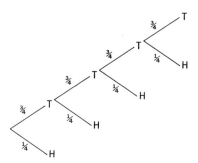

   $P(\{TTH\}) = 3/4 \cdot 3/4 \cdot 1/4 = 9/64$
   $P(\{TTTH\}) = 3/4 \cdot 3/4 \cdot 3/4 \cdot 1/4 = 27/256$
   $P(\{TTTT\}) = 3/4 \cdot 3/4 \cdot 3/4 \cdot 3/4 = 81/256$
   $E = 1 \cdot 1/4 + 2 \cdot 3/16 + 3 \cdot 9/64 + 4 \cdot 27/256 + 4 \cdot 81/256$
   $= 175/64 = 2.73$ tosses

4. $E = 1 \cdot 1/6 + 2 \cdot 1/6 + 3 \cdot 1/6 + 4 \cdot 1/6 + 5 \cdot 1/6 + 6 \cdot 1/6$
   $= 21/6 = \$3.50$

6. $E = 30 \cdot 1/2 = 15$ right answers
   Score is 0.

8. $E_1 = 15,000 \cdot 2/3 - 3,000 \cdot 1/3 = 10,000 - 1,000 = 9,000$
   $E_2 = 20,000 \cdot 1/3 - 6,000 \cdot 2/3 = 6,667 - 2,000 = 4,667$
   Location 1

9. $E = 1 \cdot \dfrac{\binom{3}{1} \cdot \binom{9}{4}}{\binom{12}{5}} + 2 \cdot \dfrac{\binom{3}{2} \cdot \binom{9}{3}}{\binom{12}{5}} + 3 \cdot \dfrac{\binom{3}{3} \cdot \binom{9}{2}}{\binom{12}{5}} = 1.25$

10. $E_1 = m_1 p_1 + m_2 p_2 + \cdots + m_n p_n$.
    Multiplying each value by c we get:
    $E_2 = cm_1 p_1 + cm_2 p_2 + \cdots + cm_n p_n$
    $= c[m_1 p_1 + m_2 p_2 + \cdots + m_n p_n] = c \cdot E_1$
    Thus we can see that the expected value of the new experiment, E_2, is c times the original expected value E_1.
    Add to each outcome used in figuring E_1 the constant k. The new expected value is:
    $E_3 = (m_1 + k)p_1 + (m_2 + k)p_2 + \cdots + (m_n + k)p_n$
    $= m_1 p_1 + kp_1 + m_2 p_2 + kp_2 + \cdots + m_n p_n + kp_n$
    $= m_1 p_1 + m_2 p_2 + \cdots + m_n p_n + kp_1 + kp_2 + \cdots kp_n$
    $= E_1 + k(p_1 + p_2 + \cdots + p_n)$
    Since $p_1 + p_2 + \cdots + p_n = 1$ we get
    $E_3 = E_1 + k$
    Thus we see that the expected value of the new experiment, E_3, is the expected value of the original experiment, E_1, plus k.

2. $M = \{\text{males}\}$, $F = \{\text{females}\}$, $C = \{\text{people with cancer}\}$
Assume 200 people: 100M, 100F

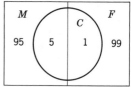

a $P(M|C) = \dfrac{P(M \cap C)}{P(C)} = \dfrac{5/200}{6/200} = \dfrac{5}{6}$

b $P(F|C) = 1 - P(M|C) = 1 - 5/6 = 1/6$

3. $A = \{\text{students with an A average}\}$ $P(A) = .24$
$R = \{\text{students who attended private schools}\}$ $P(R) = .40$
$U = \{\text{students who attended public schools}\}$ $P(U) = .60$
$P(A|R) = .30$

$$P(R|A) = \frac{P(R \cap A)}{P(A)} = \frac{P(A|R) \cdot P(R)}{P(A)} = \frac{(.4)(.3)}{.24} = \frac{1}{2}$$

Venn diagram solution: Assume 100 people

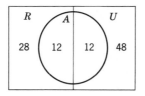

$$P(R|A) = \frac{P(R \cap A)}{P(A)} = \frac{.12}{.24} = \frac{1}{2}$$

4. $P(\{0 \text{ children}\}) = .25$ $G = \{\text{at least one child}\}$
$P(\{1 \text{ child}\}) = .25$ $P(G) = 1 - .25 = .75$
$P(\{2 \text{ children}\}) = .18$ $H = \{\text{more than 2 children}\}$
$P(\{3 \text{ children}\}) = .16$ $P(H) = .16 + .08 + .08 = .32$
$P(\{4 \text{ children}\}) = .08$
$P(\{5 + \text{children}\}) = .08$ $P(H|G) = \dfrac{P(H \cap G)}{P(G)} = \dfrac{P(H)}{P(G)} = \dfrac{32}{75}$

6. $M = \{\text{men}\}$, $W = \{\text{women}\}$, $U = \{\text{under 160 lbs.}\}$
Assume 200 people

$P(W|U) = \dfrac{P(W \cap U)}{P(U)} = \dfrac{70/200}{105/200}$

$= 70/105 = 2/3$

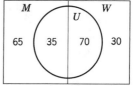

7. $M = \{\text{couples where man votes}\}$
$W = \{\text{couples where woman votes}\}$
$P(M) = .5$
$P(W) = .6$
$P(W|M) = .9$

a $P(M \cap W) = P(M) \cdot P(W|M) = (.5)(.9) = .45$

b $P(M|M \cup W) = \dfrac{P(M \cap (M \cup W))}{P(M \cup W)} = \dfrac{P(M)}{P(M) + P(W) - P(M \cap W)}$

$= \dfrac{.50}{.50 + .60 - .45} = \dfrac{.50}{.65} = \dfrac{10}{13} = .77$

10. $R = \{\text{Republicans}\}$, $D = \{\text{Democrats}\}$
$V = \{\text{People who voted Democratic}\}$
$P(R) = 3/4$, $P(D) = 1/4$, $P(V) = 5/9$

$$P(V) = P(V \cap R) + P(V \cap D)$$
$$5/9 = P(V \cap R) + 1/4$$
$$P(V \cap R) = 5/9 - 1/4 = 11/36$$

$$P(R|V) = \frac{P(R \cap V)}{P(V)} = \frac{\frac{11}{36}}{\frac{5}{9}} = \frac{11}{20} = .55$$

3.7
Exercise

1. $P(A \cap B) = P(A) + P(B) - P(A \cap B)$
   $P(A \cap B) = P(A) \cdot P(B)$ since A, B are independent
   $P(A \cup B) = P(A) + P(B) - P(A) \cdot P(B)$
   $$\frac{1}{3} = \frac{1}{4} + P(B) - \frac{1}{4} \cdot P(B)$$
   $$\frac{1}{9} = P(B)$$

2. $S = \{RRR, RRL, RLR, LRR, RLL, LRL, RLL, LLL\}$
   $E = \{RRL, LRR\} \qquad F = \{LLL\}$
   $E \cap F = \emptyset, P(E \cap F) = 0$
   $P(E) = 1/4, P(F) = 1/8, P(E) \cdot P(F) = 1/32$
   $P(E \cap F) \neq P(E) \cdot P(F)$
   E and F are not independent.

4. $S = \{BB, BG, GB, GG\}$
   $E = \{BG, GB, GG\} \qquad P(E) = 3/4$
   $F = \{BG, GB\} \qquad P(F) = 1/2$
   $E \cap E = \{BG, GB\} \qquad P(E \cap F) = 1/2$
   $$P(E) \cdot P(F) = \frac{3}{4} \cdot \frac{1}{2} = \frac{3}{8} \neq \frac{1}{2} = P(E \cap F)$$
   E and F are not independent.

7. $P(A \cap B) = P(\{2\}) = 1/4$
   $$P(A) \cdot P(B) = \frac{1}{2} \cdot \frac{1}{2} = \frac{1}{4}$$
   $P(A \cap B) = P(A) \cdot P(B)$
   $P(A \cap C) = P(\{1\}) = 1/4$
   $$P(A) \cdot P(C) = \frac{1}{2} \cdot \frac{1}{2} = \frac{1}{4}$$
   $P(A \cap C) = P(A) \cdot P(C)$
   $P(B \cap C) = P(\{3\}) = 1/4$
   $$P(B) \cdot P(C) = \frac{1}{2} \cdot \frac{1}{2} = \frac{1}{4}$$
   $P(B \cap C) = P(B) \cdot P(C)$

9. $P(E) = .70 \qquad P(F) = .60$
   $P(\bar{E}) = .30 \qquad P(\bar{F}) = .40$
   a $P(E \cap F) = .52$
   $P(E) \cdot P(F) = (.70) \cdot (.30) = .21$
   E and F are *not* independent.

11. $P(E) \cdot P(F) = P(E \cap F)$
    $P(\bar{E}) = 1 - P(E) \qquad P(\bar{F}) = 1 - P(F)$

$$P(\bar{E}) \cdot P(\bar{F}) = (1 - P(E)) \cdot (1 - P(F))$$
$$= 1 - P(E) - P(F) + P(E) \cdot P(F)$$
$$= 1 - [P(E) + P(F) - P(E \cap F)]$$
$$= 1 - P(E \cup F)$$
$$= P(\overline{E \cup F}) = P(\bar{E} \cap \bar{F}) \text{ by DeMorgan's Law}$$

13. $P(E) = 1/6$, $P(F) = 1/6$, $P(G) = 1/6$
$P(E \cap F) = 1/36$, $P(E \cap G) = 1/36$
$P(F \cap G) = 1/36$

$$P(E) \cdot P(F) = \frac{1}{6} \cdot \frac{1}{6} = \frac{1}{36} = P(E \cap F)$$

$$P(E) \cdot P(G) = \frac{1}{6} \cdot \frac{1}{6} = \frac{1}{36} = P(E \cap G)$$

$$P(F) \cdot P(G) = \frac{1}{6} \cdot \frac{1}{6} = \frac{1}{36} = P(F \cap G)$$

$$P(E \cap F \cap G) = 0$$

$$P(E) \cdot P(F) \cdot P(G) = \frac{1}{6} \cdot \frac{1}{6} \cdot \frac{1}{6} = \frac{1}{216}$$

$P(E \cap F \cap G) \neq P(E) \cdot P(F) \cdot P(G)$ therefore E, F, and G are not independent.

14. **a** E: at least one ace
F: no ace
$P(E) = 1 - P(F) = 1 - .4823 = .5177$
b G: at least one pair of aces
H: no pairs of aces
$P(G) = 1 - P(H) = 1 - .512 = .488$

15. *Note:* This problem requires the use of information from the section on Bernoulli trials (3.9).
a A: The test for a pooled sample of 30 people will be positive.
$$P(A) = 1 - b(30, 0; p)$$
$$= 1 - \frac{30!}{0!30!} p^0 (1 - p)^{30}$$
$$= 1 - (1 - p)^{30}$$

3.8
Exercise

2. E: item is defective
A_1: item is from machine I
A_2: item is from machine II
A_3: item is from machine III
$$P(A_1|E) = \frac{(0.2)(.4)}{(.02)(.4) + (.04)(.5) + (.01)(.1)} = \frac{8}{29}$$
$$P(A_2|E) = \frac{(.04)(.5)}{.029} = \frac{20}{29}$$
$$P(A_3|E) = \frac{(.01)(.1)}{.029} = \frac{1}{29}$$

4. $$P(A_1|E) = \frac{(.05)(.98)}{(.05)(.98) + (.95)(.15)} = \frac{.049}{.049 + .1425} = .256$$

5. $$P(U_1|E) = \frac{P(E|U_1)}{P(E|U_1) + P(E|U_2) + P(E|U_3)}$$
$$= \frac{5/14}{5/14 + 1/4 + 7/16} = \frac{.357}{.357 + .25 + .437} = .342$$

$$P(U_{II}|E) = \frac{P(E|U_{II})}{1.044} = \frac{.25}{1.044} = .239$$

$$P(U_{III}|E) = \frac{P(E|U_{III})}{1.044} = \frac{.437}{1.044} = .419$$

6. A: a person has cholera
   B: test is positive

$$P(A|B) = \frac{P(B|A)P(A)}{P(B|A) \cdot P(A) + P(B|\bar{A}) \cdot P(\bar{A})}$$

$$= \frac{(.90)(.11)}{(.90)(.11) + (.3)(.89)} = .27$$

7. $P(I) = .67 \qquad P(D|I) = .02 \qquad$ (a priori)
   $P(II) = .33 \qquad P(D|II) = .01$

$$P(I|D) = \frac{P(D|I)P(I)}{P(D|I)P(I) + P(D|II)P(II)}$$

$$= \frac{(.02)(.67)}{(.02)(.67) + (.33)(.01)} = .80 \qquad$$ (a posteriori)

9. $R =$ soil is rock
   $C =$ soil is clay
   $S =$ soil is sand
   $A =$ test is positive
   $P(R) = .53 \qquad P(A|R) = .35$
   $P(C) = .21 \qquad P(A|C) = .48$
   $P(S) = .26 \qquad P(A|S) = .75$

$$P(R|A) = \frac{P(R) \cdot P(A|R)}{P(R) \cdot P(A|R) + P(C) \cdot P(A|C) + P(S) \cdot P(A|S)}$$

$$= \frac{(.53)(.35)}{(.53)(.35) + (.21)(.48) + (.26)(.75)} = .39$$

$$P(C|A) = \frac{P(C) \cdot P(A|C)}{P(A)} = \frac{.1008}{.4813} = .21$$

$$P(S|A) = \frac{P(S) \cdot P(A|S)}{P(A)} = \frac{.1950}{.4813} = .41$$

10. $P(A_j|E) = \dfrac{P(A_j \cap E)}{P(E)} = \dfrac{P(A_j \cap E)}{P(A_1 \cap E) + P(A_2 \cap E) + \cdots + P(A_n \cap E)}$

$$= \frac{P(A_j)P(E|A_j)}{P(A_1) \cdot P(E|A_1) + P(A_2)P(E|A_2) + \cdots + P(A_n) \cdot P(E|A_n)}$$

1. $b\left(5, 2; \dfrac{1}{6}\right) = \dbinom{5}{2}\left(\dfrac{1}{6}\right)^2\left(\dfrac{5}{6}\right)^3 = \dfrac{5!}{2!3!} \cdot \dfrac{1}{36} \cdot \dfrac{125}{216} = .16$

2. **a** $b\left(6, 2; \dfrac{1}{2}\right) = .2344$

   b E: exactly two heads are obtained
   F: at least one head is obtained
   G: no heads are obtained

$$P(E|F) = \frac{P(E \cap F)}{P(F)} = \frac{P(E)}{1 - P(G)} = \frac{\dfrac{15}{64}}{1 - \dfrac{1}{64}} = \frac{\dfrac{15}{64}}{\dfrac{63}{64}} = \frac{15}{63} = .24$$

4. **a**

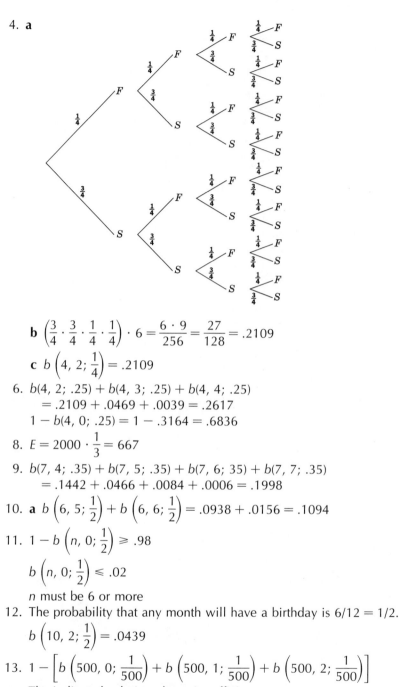

b $\left(\dfrac{3}{4} \cdot \dfrac{3}{4} \cdot \dfrac{1}{4} \cdot \dfrac{1}{4}\right) \cdot 6 = \dfrac{6 \cdot 9}{256} = \dfrac{27}{128} = .2109$

c $b\left(4, 2; \dfrac{1}{4}\right) = .2109$

6. $b(4, 2; .25) + b(4, 3; .25) + b(4, 4; .25)$
$= .2109 + .0469 + .0039 = .2617$
$1 - b(4, 0; .25) = 1 - .3164 = .6836$

8. $E = 2000 \cdot \dfrac{1}{3} = 667$

9. $b(7, 4; .35) + b(7, 5; .35) + b(7, 6; 35) + b(7, 7; .35)$
$= .1442 + .0466 + .0084 + .0006 = .1998$

10. **a** $b\left(6, 5; \dfrac{1}{2}\right) + b\left(6, 6; \dfrac{1}{2}\right) = .0938 + .0156 = .1094$

11. $1 - b\left(n, 0; \dfrac{1}{2}\right) \geq .98$

$b\left(n, 0; \dfrac{1}{2}\right) \leq .02$

n must be 6 or more

12. The probability that any month will have a birthday is $6/12 = 1/2$.

$b\left(10, 2; \dfrac{1}{2}\right) = .0439$

13. $1 - \left[b\left(500, 0; \dfrac{1}{500}\right) + b\left(500, 1; \dfrac{1}{500}\right) + b\left(500, 2; \dfrac{1}{500}\right)\right]$

The indicated solution above is sufficient.
For the interested student, the answer is 0.08.

14. Investigate the binomial for $n = 5, 6, 7$, $x = 1, 2, 3$, and $p = 1/3$.
When $n = 5$ there is a dual maximum for 1 or 2 successes.
When $n = 6$ there is a singular maximum at 2 successes.
When $n = 7$ there is a singular maximum at 2 successes. We are look-
ing for the smallest n that has a singular maximum at 2 successes.
Thus $n = 6$.

16. $\dfrac{9}{10} \cdot \dfrac{8}{9} \cdot \dfrac{7}{8} \cdot \dfrac{6}{7} \cdot \dfrac{1}{6} = \dfrac{1}{10}$

17. $\dfrac{P(8,\ 5)}{8^5} = \dfrac{\dfrac{8!}{3!}}{8^5} = \dfrac{8 \cdot 7 \cdot 6 \cdot 5 \cdot 4}{8^5} = \dfrac{840}{8^4} = \dfrac{840}{4096} = .205$

1. $S = \{BB,\ GB,\ BG,\ GG\}$

2. **a** $S = \{HHH,\ HHT,\ HTH,\ HTT,\ THH,\ THT,\ TTH,\ TTT\}$
   Let E be a simple event in S, $P(E) = 1/8$.
   b (i) 1/2, (ii) 1/2, (iii) 3/4, (iv) 7/8, (v) 1/2, (vi) 1/8

4. There are 16 different paths he might take each with probability 1/16.
   Four paths lead to station G. The probability of ending at G is $4 \cdot 1/16 = 4/16 = 1/4$.

5. **a** No.
   b $(0, 0, 0)$ has the highest probability; $(1, 1, 1)$ has the lowest probability.
   c $F = \{(0, 1, 2), (0, 2, 1), (1, 2, 0), (1, 0, 2), (2, 0, 1), (2, 1, 0)\}$
   Each simple event in F has probability 12/512.
   $$P(F) = 6\ \frac{12}{512} = \frac{72}{512} = \frac{9}{64}$$

8.

Envelope	Possible arrangements of letters					
E_1	1	1	2	2	3	3
E_2	2	3	1	3	1	2
E_3	3	2	3	1	2	1

Four out of the six possible ways of mailing the letters are such that at least one letter gets to the correct person; therefore the probability is $4/6 = 2/3$.

12. $\{HH,\ HT,\ TH,\ TT\}$
    $P\{HH\} = 1/16,\ P\{HT\} = 3/16,\ P\{TH\} = 3/16$
    $P\{TT\} = 9/16$
    $E = \{HH,\ HT\} \qquad P(E) = 1/4$
    $F = \{HT,\ TT\} \qquad P(F) = 3/4$
    $E \cap F = \{HT\} \qquad P(E \cap F) = 3/16$
    $$P(E) \cdot P(F) = \frac{1}{4} \cdot \frac{3}{4} = 3/16$$
    $P(E \cap F) = P(E) \cdot P(F)$
    E and F are independent.

16. C: have cancer
    D: test detects cancer
    $P(C) = .018$
    $P(C) = .982$

$P(D|C) = .85$

$P(D|\overline{C}) = .08$

$P(C|D) = \dfrac{P(D|C) \cdot P(C)}{P(D|C) \cdot P(C) + P(D|\overline{C}) \cdot P(\overline{C})}$

$= \dfrac{(.85)(.018)}{(.85) \cdot (.018) + (.08) \cdot (.982)}$

$= \dfrac{.0153}{.0153 + .07856} = \dfrac{.0153}{.09386} = .163$

17. $E = 1/6 \cdot (.80) + 1/3(.30) + 1/2(.10)$

$\quad = 8/60 + 6/60 + 3/60 = 17/60 = \$.28$

The game is not fair to the player.

22. $1 - b\left(5, 0; \dfrac{1}{3}\right) = 1 - \dbinom{5}{0}\left(\dfrac{1}{3}\right)^0\left(\dfrac{2}{3}\right)^5 = 1 - \left(\dfrac{2}{3}\right)^5$

$= 1 - \dfrac{32}{243} = \dfrac{211}{243} = .868$

CHAPTER 4

4.1

Exercise

1. **a** $f(-2) = 2(-2) + 1 = -3$

   c $f(12) = 2(12) + 1 = 25$

2. **b** $f(h) = 2(h)^3 + 1 = 2h^3 + 1$

   c $f(h + 1) = 2(h + 1)^3 + 1 = 2(h^3 + 3h^2 + 3h + 1) + 1$

   $\qquad = 2h^3 + 6h^2 + 6h + 3$

3. **a** $f(-2, 3) = (-2)^2 3 + (-2) = 1$

   c $f(x + 1, 0) = (x + 1)^2(0) + (x + 1) = x + 1$

4. $128 = 16t^2,\ 8 = t^2,\ 2\sqrt{2} = t,\ t = 2.8$ seconds

5. Smallest number of stages   Largest number of stages

   $m(a) = 1 \cdot 2 + 2 \cdot 3 = 8$ $m(a) = 1 \cdot 2 + 2 \cdot 2 + 3 \cdot 1 = 9$

   $m(b) = 1 \cdot 1 = 1$ $m(b) = 1 \cdot 1 = 1$

   $m(c) = 1 \cdot 2 = 2$ $m(c) = 1 \cdot 1 + 2 \cdot 1 = 3$

   $m(d) = 0$ $m(d) = 0$

   $m(e) = 1 \cdot 1 = 1$ $m(e) = 1 \cdot 1 = 1$

   $m(f) = 0$ $m(f) = 0$

8. N_0 is the original number of cells; t is time in seconds.

   $f(t) = 2^{t/5} \cdot N_0$

   $f(120) = 2^{120/5} \cdot 1000 = 2^{24} \cdot 1000$

   $f(3600) = 2^{3600/5} \cdot 1000 = 2^{720} \cdot 1000$

10. W_0 is the original amount.

   a $\dfrac{W_0}{4} = \left(\dfrac{1}{2}\right)^{t/8} \cdot W_0$ **b** $f(28) = \left(\dfrac{1}{2}\right)^{28/8} \cdot W_0$

   $\dfrac{1}{4} = \left(\dfrac{1}{2}\right)^{t/8}$ $= \left(\dfrac{1}{2}\right)^{7/2} \cdot W_0$

   $\left(\dfrac{1}{2}\right)^2 = \left(\dfrac{1}{2}\right)^{t/8}$ $= \dfrac{1}{8} \cdot \left(\dfrac{1}{2}\right)^{1/2} \cdot W_0$

   $2 = t/8$ $= \dfrac{1}{8} \cdot \dfrac{\sqrt{2}}{2} \cdot W_0$

   $t = 16$ years $= \dfrac{\sqrt{2}}{16} W_0$

   $= .088 W_0$

   c It would never disappear completely.

2. $A = (4, 2)$ $E = (-2, -3)$
    $B = (6, 2)$ $F = (3, -2)$
    $C = (5, 3)$ $G = (6, -2)$
    $D = (-2, 1)$ $H = (5, 0)$

3. **a** $\dfrac{f_2 - a_2}{f_1 - a_1} = \dfrac{-2 - 2}{3 - 4} = \dfrac{-4}{-1} = 4$

4. **a** 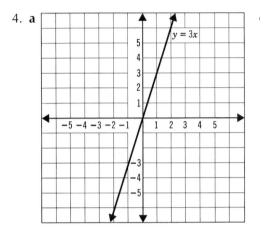 **c**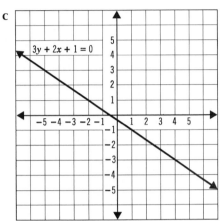

5.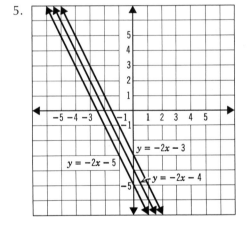

1. **b** $\dfrac{1 - (-6)}{1 - 5} = \dfrac{7}{-4} = \dfrac{-7}{4}$

   d $\dfrac{-3 - 0}{4 - 0} = \dfrac{-3}{4}$

   f $\dfrac{-2 - (-2)}{-3 - 6} = \dfrac{0}{-9} = 0$

2. **b** $\dfrac{y - 1}{x - 1} = \dfrac{-7}{4}$

     $4y - 4 = -7x + 7$
     $4y + 7x - 11 = 0$

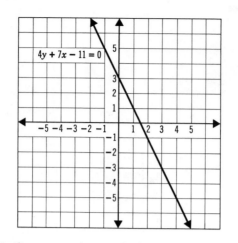

2. **f** $y = -2$

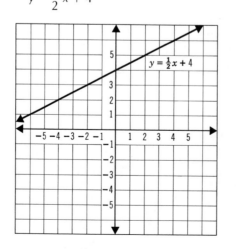

3. **a** $\dfrac{y-3}{x+2} = \dfrac{1}{2}$

$2y - 6 = x + 2$

$y = \dfrac{1}{2}x + 4$

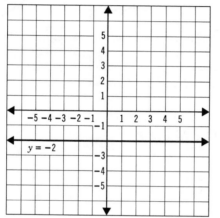

3. **f** $\dfrac{y - 0}{x - \dfrac{1}{2}} = 3$

$y = 3x - \dfrac{3}{2}$

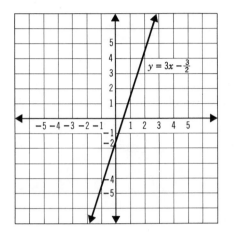

4. **a** $y = x - 3$

x	0	.1	$-1/2$	6	3.2	5	-3
y	-3	-2.9	-3.5	3	.2	2	-6

5.

	Slope	y-intercept
a	3/2	-3
c	$-2/5$	2
d	undefined	none

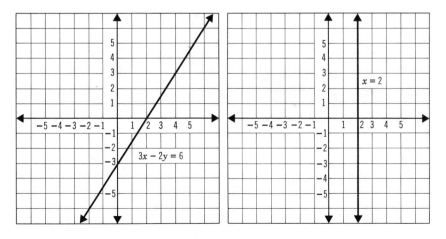

6. **a, b**

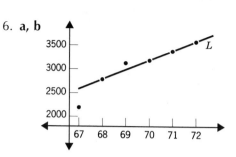

6. **c** (using only the last two digits of the date)
Use the points (70, 3200) and (71, 3400).

$$\frac{y - 3200}{x - 70} = \frac{3400 - 3200}{71 - 70}$$

$$y - 3200 = (x - 70)200$$

$$y - 3200 = 200x - 14000$$

$$y = 200x - 10800$$

d $y = 200 \cdot 72 - 10800 = 14400 - 10800 = 3600$

5.3
Exercise

1. **a** $L:\ 2x - 3y + 6 = 0$ $\quad\quad M:\ 4x - 6y + 7 = 0$

$$-3y = -2x - 6 \quad\quad\quad\quad -6y = -4x - 7$$

$$y = 2/3x + 2 \quad\quad\quad\quad\quad y = 2/3x + 7/6$$

L and M are parallel.

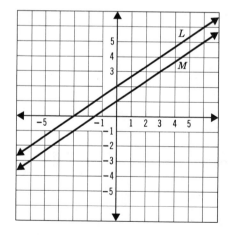

1. **b** $L:\ -2x + 3y + 6 = 0$ $\quad\quad M:\ 4x - 6y - 12 = 0$

$$3y = 2x - 6 \quad\quad\quad\quad\quad -6y = -4x + 12$$

$$y = 2/3x - 2 \quad\quad\quad\quad\quad\quad y = 2/3x - 2$$

L and M are identical.

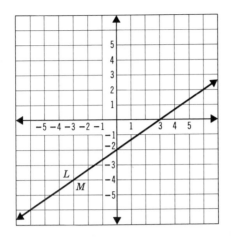

1. c L: $3x - 3y + 10 = 0$ M: $x + y - 2 = 0$
$-3y = -3x - 10$ $y = -x + 2$
$y = x + 10/3$
$x_0 + 10/3 = -x_0 + 2$
$2x_0 = -4/3$
$x_0 = -2/3$
$y_0 = 2/3 + 2 = 8/3$
L and M intersect at $(-2/3, 8/3)$.

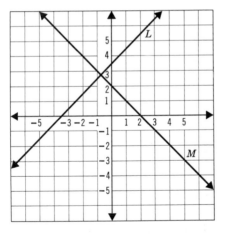

2. a L: $3x - 2y - 5 = 0$ M: $x + 3y - 9 = 0$
$-2y = -3x + 5$ $3y = -x + 9$
$y = 3/2x - 5/2$ $y = -1/3x + 3$
$3/2x_0 - 5/2 = -1/3x_0 + 3$
$9x_0 - 15 = -2x_0 + 18$
$11x_0 = 33$
$x_0 = 3$
$y_0 = -1/3 \cdot 3 + 3 = -1 + 3 = 2$
N: $3x - y - 7 = 0$
$3 \cdot 3 - 2 - 7 = 9 - 9 = 0$
L, M, and N are concurrent at $(3, 2)$.

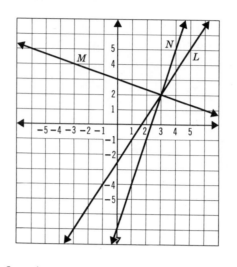

2. **c** L: $x - y + 2 = 0$ M: $x - y + 3 = 0$
$\quad\quad -y = -x - 2$ $\quad\quad\quad -y = -x - 3$
$\quad\quad\quad y = x + 2$ $\quad\quad\quad\quad y = x + 3$

L and M are parallel, hence the three lines are not concurrent.

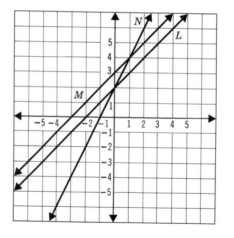

4. $x =$ amount in AAA bonds; $y =$ amount in Savings and Loan
$y = \$50{,}000 - x$ and $.09x + .07y = 4000$
$(.09)x + (.07)(50{,}000 - x) = 4{,}000$
$\quad (.09)x + 3{,}500 - (.07)x = 4{,}000$
$(.02)x = 500$
$\quad\quad x = \dfrac{500}{.02} = 25{,}000$
$x = 25{,}000$ in AAA bonds
$y = 25{,}000$ in the Savings and Loan

6. $x =$ lbs. of cashews; $y =$ lbs. of pecans
$y = 60 - x$ and $1.5x + 1.8y + 40(.8) = 1.25(100)$
$x(1.5) + (60 - x)(1.8) + (40)(.8) = 125$
$(1.5)x - (1.8)x = -15$
$\quad\quad .3x = 15$

$x = 50$ lbs. of cashews

$y = 10$ lbs. of pecans

8. $x =$ amount of $.75/lb. coffee; $y =$ amount of $1.00/lb. coffee.

$y = 100 - x$ and $.75x + y = .9(100)$

$(.75)x + (100 - x) = (.90)(100)$

$$10 = .25x$$

$$40 = x$$

$x = 40$ lbs. of $.75/lb. coffee

$y = 60$ lbs. of $1.00/lb. coffee

10. $x =$ amount at 8%, $y =$ amount at 18%

$y = 10,000 - x$ and $.08x + .18y = 1000$

$(.08)x + (.18)(10,000 - x) = 1,000$

$$800 = .1x$$

$$8,000 = x$$

$x = \$8,000$ at 8%

$y = \$2,000$ at 18%

12. $x =$ total distance

$y =$ speed

$1/3x = y \cdot 1$

$$x = 3y$$

$$\frac{x}{2} + 18 = 2y$$

$$\frac{3y}{2} + 18 = 2y$$

$$3y + 36 = 4y$$

$$36 = y$$

$$x = 3 \cdot 36 = 108$$

Distance is 108 miles.

Speed is 36 mph.

Time is 3 hrs.

5.4
Exercise

1. **a** $C = \$10x + \$600$, $A = \$30x$

$$10x + 600 = 30x$$

$$600 = 20x$$

$$30 = x$$

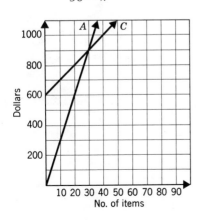

2. $C = \$0.75x + 300$, $A = \$1 \cdot x$
$$0.75x + 300 = x$$
$$300 = .25x$$
$$1{,}200 = x$$

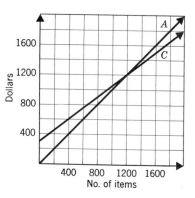

4. $S = 0.7p + 0.4$, $D = -0.5p + 1.6$
$$0.7p + 0.4 = -0.5p + 1.6$$
$$7p + 4 = -5p + 16$$
$$12p = 12$$
$$p = \$1$$
$$S = 0.7 \cdot 1 + 0.4 = 1.1$$

The coordinates of the point of intersection are (market price, quantity demanded).

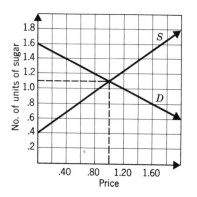

5.5
Exercise

1. **a**   1. **c**

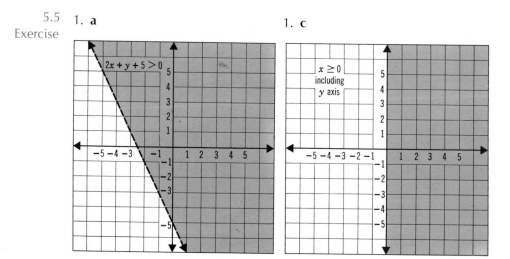

1. **e**

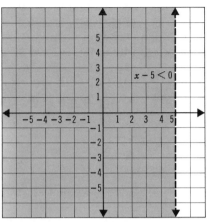

2. **b**

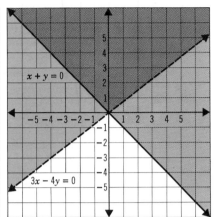

2. **e**

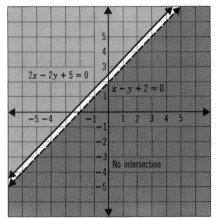

2. **g**

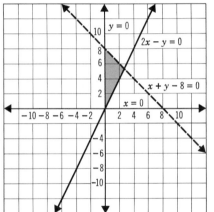

2. **k**

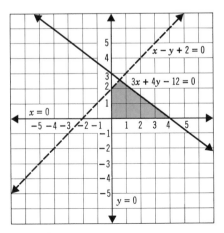

$$y_0 = -2\left(\frac{10}{3}\right) + 10 = \frac{-20}{3} + \frac{30}{3} = \frac{10}{3}$$

The point of intersection is $\left(\frac{10}{3}, \frac{10}{3}\right)$.

This clearly minimizes the objective function $f = x + y$.

$$f = x + y = \frac{10}{3} + \frac{10}{3} = \frac{20}{3}$$

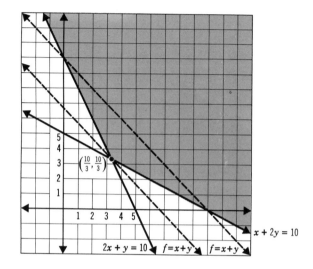

3. The vertices are $\left(\frac{10}{3}, \frac{10}{3}\right)$, (0, 10), (10, 0).

The value of f at (10/3, 10/3) is $f = 10/3 - 10/3 = 0$.
The value of f at (0, 10) is $f = 0 - 10 = -10$.
The value of f at (10,0) is $f = 10 - 0 = 10$, and is the maximum.

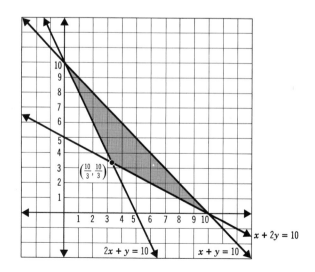

5. $2x + 3y = 12,$ $3x + y = 12$

$3y = -2x + 12$ $y = -3x + 12$

$y = -2/3x + 4$

$-2/3x_0 + 4 = -3x_0 + 12$

$-2x_0 + 12 = -9x_0 + 36$

$7x_0 = 24$

$x_0 = 24/7$

$y_0 = -2/3 \left(\dfrac{24}{7}\right) + 4 = \dfrac{-16}{7} + \dfrac{28}{7} = \dfrac{12}{7}$

The vertices are: $(0, 0)$, $(0, 4)$, $(4, 0)$, $(24/7, 12/7)$.

Testing these in the function $f = 5x + 7y$ we get:

$f = 5 \cdot 0 + 7 \cdot 0 = 0$

$f = 5 \cdot 0 + 7 \cdot 4 = 28$

$f = 5 \cdot 4 + 7 \cdot 0 = 20$

$f = 5 \cdot \dfrac{24}{7} + 7 \cdot \dfrac{12}{7} = \dfrac{120}{7} + \dfrac{84}{7} = \dfrac{204}{7} = 29 \ 1/7$

Thus we see that the maximum for f is $29 \ 1/7$ and the minimum is 0.

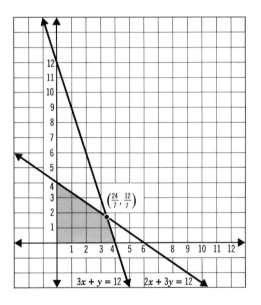

7. The vertices are: $(0, 2)$, $(0, 8)$, $(2, 0)$, $(4, 0)$, $(2, 6)$.

Testing these in the function $f = 5x + 7y$ we get:

$f = 5 \cdot 0 + 7 \cdot 2 = 14$

$f = 5 \cdot 0 + 7 \cdot 8 = 56$

$f = 5 \cdot 2 + 7 \cdot 0 = 10$

$f = 5 \cdot 4 + 7 \cdot 0 = 20$

$f = 5 \cdot 2 + 7 \cdot 6 = 52$

The maximum is 56 at $(0, 8)$.

The minimum is 10 at $(2, 0)$.

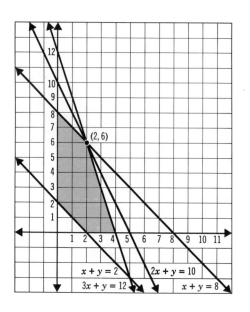

9. The vertices are: $(0, 0)$, $(0, 4)$, $(4, 0)$, $(24/7, 12/7)$.
Testing these in the function $f = 5x - 7y$ we get:
$f = 5 \cdot 0 - 7 \cdot 0 = 0$
$f = 5 \cdot 0 - 7 \cdot 4 = -28$
$f = 5 \cdot 4 - 7 \cdot 0 = 20$
$f = 5\left(\dfrac{24}{7}\right) - 7\left(\dfrac{12}{7}\right) = \dfrac{120}{7} - \dfrac{84}{7} = \dfrac{36}{7} = 5\ 1/7$
The maximum is 20 at $(4, 0)$.
The minimum is -28 at $(0, 4)$.

11. The vertices are: $(0, 2)$, $(0, 8)$, $(2, 0)$, $(4, 0)$, $(2, 6)$.
Testing these in the function $f = 5x - 7y$ we get:
$f = 5 \cdot 0 - 7 \cdot 2 = -14$
$f = 5 \cdot 0 - 7 \cdot 8 = -56$
$f = 5 \cdot 2 - 7 \cdot 0 = 10$
$f = 5 \cdot 4 - 7 \cdot 0 = 20$
$f = 5 \cdot 2 - 7 \cdot 6 = -32$
Maximum is 20 at $(4, 0)$.
Minimum is -56 at $(0, 8)$.

14. $x =$ number of units of F_1.
$y =$ number of units of F_2.
The problem is to minimize
$\quad C = (\$0.05)x + (\$0.03)y$
Subject to
$\quad x \geqq 0,\ y \geqq 0$
$\quad 2x + y \geqq 400$
$\quad x + 2y \geqq 500$
$\quad 2x + 4y \geqq 1{,}000 \text{ or } x + 2y \geqq 500$
The vertices are: $(0, 400)$, $(500, 0)$, $(100, 200)$.
$C_1 = (\$0.05) \cdot 0 + (\$0.03) \cdot 400 = \$12.00$
$C_2 = (\$0.05) \cdot 500 + (\$0.03) \cdot 0 = \$25.00$

$C_3 = (\$0.05) \cdot 100 + (\$0.03) \cdot 200 = \$5.00 + \$6.00 = \$11.00$

The minimum cost is $110.00 for 100 units of F_1 and 200 units of F_2.

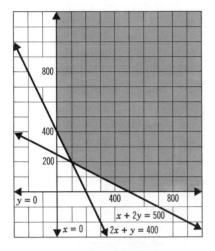

15. x = ounces of supplement I

y = ounces of supplement II

The problem is to minimize

$C = (\$0.03) \cdot x + \$(0.04) \cdot y$

Subject to

$x \geqq 0, y \geqq 0$

$5x + 25y \geqq 50$ or $x + 5y \geqq 10$

$25x + 10y \geqq 100$ or $5x + 2y \geqq 20$

$10x + 10y \geqq 60$ or $x + y \geqq 6$

$35x + 20y \geqq 180$ or $7x + 4y \geqq 36$

The vertices are: (0, 10), (10, 0), (5, 1), (4, 2), (4/3, 20/3).

$C_1 = (\$0.03) \cdot 0 + (\$0.04) \cdot 10 = \$0.40$

$C_2 = (\$0.03) \cdot 10 + (\$0.04) \cdot 0 = \$0.30$

$C_3 = (\$0.03) \cdot 5 + (\$0.04) \cdot 1 = \$0.15 + \$0.04 = \$0.19$

$C_4 = (\$0.03) \cdot 4 + (\$0.04) \cdot 2 = \$0.12 + \$0.08 + \$0.20$

$C_5 = (\$0.03) \cdot 4/3 + (\$0.04) \cdot 20/3 \doteq \$0.04 + \$0.27 + \$0.31$

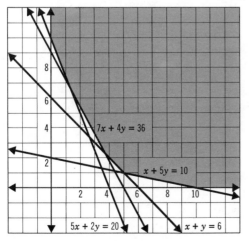

He should add 5 ounces of Supplement I and 1 ounce of Supplement II to each 100 ounces of feed.

18. $x =$ acres of crop A

$y =$ acres of crop B

The problem is to maximize

$P = \$40 \cdot x + \$120 \cdot y$

Subject to

$x \geq 0, y \geq 0$

$\$10x + \$40y \leq \$1,100$ or $x + 4y \leq 110$

$2x + 3y \leq 160$

See graph following.

The vertices are: $(0, 0)$, $(0, 55/2)$, $(80, 0)$, $(62, 12)$.

$P_1 = \$40 \cdot 0 + \$120 \cdot 0 = \$0$

$P_2 = \$40 \cdot 0 + \$120 \cdot 55/2 = \$3,300$

$P_3 = \$40 \cdot 80 + \$120 \cdot 0 = \$3,200$

$P_4 = \$40 \cdot 62 + \$120 \cdot 12 = \$2,480 + \$1,440 = \$3,920$

62 acres of crop A should be planted and 12 acres of crop B should be planted; 74 acres of land are used leaving 26 acres idle.

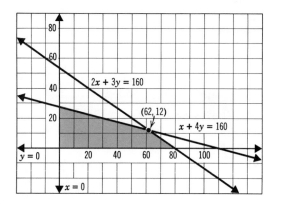

19. $f = 2x + y + 3z$

L_1: $x + 2y + Z \leq 25$

L_2: $3x + 2y + 3Z \leq 30$

L_3: $x \geq 0$

L_4: $y \geq 0$

L_5: $Z \geq 0$

a L_1, L_2, L_3 give: $x_0 = 0$

$2y + Z = 25 \qquad 2y + 3Z = 30$

$-Z_0 + 25 = -3Z_0 + 30$

$2Z_0 = 5$

$Z_0 = 5/2$

$2y_0 + 5/2 = 25$

$y_0 = \dfrac{-5}{4} + \dfrac{25}{2} = \dfrac{-5 + 50}{4} = \dfrac{45}{4} \qquad (0, 45/4, 5/2)$

b L_1, L_2, L_4 give: $y_0 = 0$

$x + Z = 25, \; 3x + 3Z = 30$

$$x + Z = 10$$

No solution

c L_1, L_2, L_5 give: $Z_0 = 0$

$x + 2y = 25$, $3x + 2y = 30$

$x_0 - 25 = 3x_0 - 30$

$$5 = 2x_0$$

$$5/2 = x_0$$

$5/2 + 2y_0 = 25$

$$y_0 = \frac{-5}{4} + \frac{25}{2} = \frac{-5}{4} + \frac{50}{4} = \frac{45}{4}$$

(5/2), 45/4, 0)

d L_1, L_3, L_4 give: $x_0 = 0$, $y_0 = 0$, $Z_0 = 25$

but (0, 0, 25) does not satisfy L_2.

e L_1, L_3, L_5 give: $x_0 = 0$, $Z_0 = 0$

$2y_0 = 25$

$y_0 = 25/2$

(0, 25/2, 0)

f L_1, L_4, L_5 give: $y_0 = 0$, $Z_0 = 0$, $x_0 = 25$

(25, 0, 0) does not satisfy L_2.

g L_2, L_3, L_4 give: $x_0 = 0$, $y_0 = 0$

$3Z_0 = 30$

$Z_0 = 10$ (0, 0, 10)

h L_2, L_3, L_5 give: $x_0 = 0$, $Z_0 = 0$

$2y_0 = 30$

$y_0 = 15$ (0, 15, 0) does not satisfy L_1.

i L_2, L_4, L_5 give: $y_0 = 0$, $Z_0 = 0$

$3x_0 = 30$

$x_0 = 10$ (10, 0, 0)

j L_3, L_4, L_5 give: (0, 0, 0)

The points in the set of feasible solutions are: (0, 45/4, 5/2),
(5/2, 45/4, 0), (0, 25/2, 0), (0, 0, 10), (10, 0, 0), (0, 0, 0).

$f_1 = 2 \cdot 0 + 45/4 + 3 \cdot 5/2 = 75/4 = 18\ 3/4$

$f_2 = 2 \cdot 5/2 + 45/4 + 3 \cdot 0 = 65/4 = 16\ 1/4$

$f_3 = 2 \cdot 0 + 25/2 + 3 \cdot 0 = 25/2 = 12\ 1/2$

$f_4 = 2 \cdot 0 + 0 + 3 \cdot 10 = 30$

$f_5 = 2 \cdot 10 + 0 + 3 \cdot 0 = 20$

$f_6 = 2 \cdot 0 + 0 + 3 \cdot 0 = 0$

The maximum is $f = 30$ at (0, 0, 10).

1. a $f = 15x + 20y$

The vertices are: (0, 0), (0, 3), (4, 0).

$f_1 = 15 \cdot 0 + 20 \cdot 0 = 0$

$f_2 = 15 \cdot 0 + 20 \cdot 3 = 60$

$f_3 = 15 \cdot 4 + 20 \cdot 0 = 60$

Maximum is 60 at any point on the line $3x + 4y = 12$ between (0, 3)
and (4, 0). Minimum is 0 at (0, 0).

CHAPTER
REVIEW

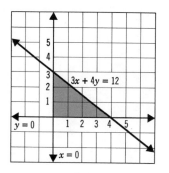

c $f = 15x + 20y$
The vertices are: (0, 0), (0, 9), (4, 5), (6, 0).
$f_1 = 15 \cdot 0 + 20 \cdot 0 = 0$
$f_2 = 15 \cdot 0 + 20 \cdot 9 = 180$
$f_3 = 15 \cdot 4 + 20 \cdot 5 = 160$
$f_4 = 15 \cdot 9 + 20 \cdot 0 = 80$
Maximum is 180 at (0, 9). Minimum is 0 at (0, 0).

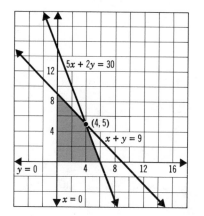

2. **a** $f = 15x - 20y$
The vertices are: (0, 0), (0, 3), (4, 0).
$f_1 = 15 \cdot 0 - 20 \cdot 0 = 0$
$f_2 = 15 \cdot 0 - 20 \cdot 3 = -60$
$f_3 = 15 \cdot 4 - 20 \cdot 0 = 60$
Maximum is 60 at (4, 0). Minimum is −60 at (0, 3).
c $f = 15x - 20y$
The vertices are: (0, 0), (0, 9), (4, 5), (6, 0).
$f_1 = 15 \cdot 0 - 20 \cdot 0 = 0$
$f_2 = 15 \cdot 0 - 20 \cdot 9 = -180$
$f_3 = 15 \cdot 4 - 20 \cdot 5 = -40$
$f_4 = 15 \cdot 6 - 20 \cdot 0 = 90$
Maximum is 90 at (6, 0). Minimum is −180 at (0, 9).

3. $x =$ pounds of food A
$y =$ pounds of food B
$C =$ cost of the foods per month
$C = \$1.30x + \$0.80y$

$x \geqq 0, y \geqq 0$

$5x + 2y \geqq 60$

$3x + 2y \geqq 45$

$4x + 1y \geqq 30$

The vertices are (0, 30), (15/2, 45/4), (15, 0).

$C_1 = \$1.30 \cdot 0 + \$0.80 \cdot 30 = \$24.00$

$C_2 = \$1.30 \cdot \dfrac{15}{2} + \$0.80 \cdot \dfrac{45}{4} = \$18.75$

$C_3 = \$1.30 \cdot 15 + \$0.80 \cdot 0 = \$19.50$

She should buy 7 1/2 pounds of A and 11 1/4 pounds of B.

1. **a** 2×3

   c 1×3 **f** 1×1

3.

$$
\begin{array}{c}
\\
\text{gum} \\
\text{ice cream} \\
\text{jelly beans} \\
\text{candy bars}
\end{array}
\begin{array}{ccc}
\text{Katy} & \text{Mike} & \text{Danny} \\
\left(\begin{array}{ccc}
5 & 2 & 1 \\
2 & 0 & 1 \\
10 & 15 & 0 \\
0 & 2 & 4
\end{array}\right)
\end{array}
\quad \text{or}
$$

$$
\begin{array}{c}
\\
\text{Katy} \\
\text{Mike} \\
\text{Danny}
\end{array}
\begin{array}{cccc}
\text{gum} & \text{ice cream} & \text{jelly beans} & \text{candy bars} \\
\left(\begin{array}{cccc}
5 & 2 & 10 & 0 \\
2 & 0 & 15 & 2 \\
1 & 1 & 0 & 4
\end{array}\right)
\end{array}
$$

5. $A = \begin{pmatrix} x+y & 2 \\ 4 & 0 \end{pmatrix}$ $B = \begin{pmatrix} 6 & x-y \\ 4 & Z \end{pmatrix};$

$x + y = 6 \qquad x - y = 2 \qquad z = 0$

$\quad 2x = 8 \qquad\quad x = 4 \qquad y = 2$

$A = \begin{pmatrix} 6 & 2 \\ 4 & 0 \end{pmatrix} = B$

1. **a** $\begin{pmatrix} 2 & -1/2 & -1/3 \\ 6 & 4 & 2/3 \end{pmatrix} + \begin{pmatrix} -2 & 6 & 0 \\ 3 & -1 & 2/3 \end{pmatrix} = \begin{pmatrix} 0 & 11/2 & -1/3 \\ 9 & 3 & 4/3 \end{pmatrix}$

   d $\begin{pmatrix} 2 & -1/2 & -1/3 \\ 6 & 4 & 2/3 \end{pmatrix} - \begin{pmatrix} -2 & 6 & 0 \\ 3 & -1 & 2/3 \end{pmatrix} = \begin{pmatrix} 4 & -13/2 & -1/3 \\ 3 & 5 & 0 \end{pmatrix}$

2. $2 + x = 6; \qquad x = 4$

   $3 + y = -8; \qquad y = -11$

   $-4 + Z = 2 \qquad Z = 6$

1. **a** $\begin{pmatrix} 1 & -1 & 1 \\ 2 & 0 & 1 \\ 3 & -1 & 1 \end{pmatrix} \begin{pmatrix} 1 & 2 \\ -1 & 1 \\ 1 & 3 \end{pmatrix} = \begin{pmatrix} 3 & 4 \\ 3 & 7 \\ 5 & 8 \end{pmatrix}$

3. $\begin{pmatrix} a & b \\ c & d \end{pmatrix} \begin{pmatrix} 0 & 1 \\ 2 & -1 \end{pmatrix} = \begin{pmatrix} 2 & 1 \\ -1 & 0 \end{pmatrix}$ $\begin{array}{ll} 2b = 2; & b = 1 \\ a - b = 1; & a = 2 \\ 2d = -1; & d = -1/2 \\ c - d = 0; & c = -1/2 \end{array}$

7. $\begin{pmatrix} 2 \\ 1 \\ 0 \end{pmatrix} + \begin{pmatrix} a_1 \\ a_2 \\ a_3 \end{pmatrix} = \begin{pmatrix} 2 \\ -1 \\ 3 \end{pmatrix}$ $\quad \begin{aligned} 2 + a_1 &= 2; \quad a_1 = 0 \\ 1 + a_2 &= -1; \; a_2 = -2 \\ 0 + a_3 &= 3; \quad a_3 = 3 \end{aligned}$

9. $\begin{pmatrix} a & b \\ c & d \end{pmatrix} \begin{pmatrix} 1 & 1 \\ -1 & 1 \end{pmatrix} = \begin{pmatrix} 1 & 1 \\ -1 & 1 \end{pmatrix} \begin{pmatrix} a & b \\ c & d \end{pmatrix}$; $\left. \begin{aligned} a - b &= a + c \\ a + b &= b + d \\ c - d &= -a + c \\ c + d &= -b + d \end{aligned} \right\}$ $\begin{aligned} a &= d \\ c &= -b \end{aligned}$

13. $A \cdot A = \begin{pmatrix} a & 1-a \\ 1+a & -a \end{pmatrix} \begin{pmatrix} a & 1-a \\ 1+a & -a \end{pmatrix}$

$= \begin{pmatrix} a^2 + (1-a^2) & a(1-a) - a(1-a) \\ a(1+a) - a(1+a) & (1-a^2) + a^2 \end{pmatrix} = \begin{pmatrix} 1 & 0 \\ 0 & 1 \end{pmatrix}$

$= I_2$

14. $(x_1 \quad x_2) \begin{pmatrix} 1/2 & 1/2 \\ 1/4 & 3/4 \end{pmatrix} = (x_1 \quad x_2)$ $\quad \begin{aligned} 1/2 x_1 + 1/4 x_2 &= x_1 \\ 1/2 x_1 + 3/4 x_2 &= x_2 \end{aligned}$'

18.

	Mike	Danny
pants	6	2
shirts	8	5
jackets	2	3

matrix $= \begin{pmatrix} 6 & 2 \\ 8 & 5 \\ 2 & 3 \end{pmatrix}$;

$(5 \quad 3 \quad 9) \begin{pmatrix} 6 & 2 \\ 8 & 5 \\ 2 & 3 \end{pmatrix} = (72 \quad 52)$

Mike spent $72.00. Danny spent $52.00.

**7.4
Exercise**

1. **a** $\begin{pmatrix} 3 & 2 & 1 \\ 2 & 1 & 0 \end{pmatrix} \approx \begin{pmatrix} 1 & 2 & 3 \\ 0 & 1 & 2 \end{pmatrix}$ $\qquad$ Interchange columns 1 and 3.

2. **a** $\begin{pmatrix} 1 & 2 & 3 & 8 \\ 0 & 5 & -2 & 1 \\ -2 & 0 & -3 & 4 \\ 2 & 2 & 2 & 2 \end{pmatrix} \approx \begin{pmatrix} 1 & 2 & 3 & 8 \\ 0 & 5 & -2 & 1 \\ 0 & 4 & 3 & 20 \\ 0 & -2 & -4 & -14 \end{pmatrix}$

$\approx \begin{pmatrix} 1 & 0 & 0 & 0 \\ 0 & 5 & -2 & 1 \\ 0 & 4 & 3 & 20 \\ 0 & -2 & -4 & -14 \end{pmatrix}$

$\approx \begin{pmatrix} 1 & 0 & 0 & 0 \\ 0 & 1 & -2 & 5 \\ 0 & 20 & 3 & 4 \\ 0 & -14 & -4 & -2 \end{pmatrix}$

$\approx \begin{pmatrix} 1 & 0 & 0 & 0 \\ 0 & 1 & -2 & 5 \\ 0 & 0 & 43 & -96 \\ 0 & 0 & -32 & 68 \end{pmatrix}$

$\approx \begin{pmatrix} 1 & 0 & 0 & 0 \\ 0 & 1 & 0 & 0 \\ 0 & 0 & 43 & -96 \\ 0 & 0 & -32 & 68 \end{pmatrix}$

$$\approx \begin{pmatrix} 1 & 0 & 0 & 0 \\ 0 & 1 & 0 & 0 \\ 0 & 0 & 11 & -28 \\ 0 & 0 & -32 & 88 \end{pmatrix}$$

$$\approx \begin{pmatrix} 1 & 0 & 0 & 0 \\ 0 & 1 & 0 & 0 \\ 0 & 0 & 1 & -7 \\ 0 & 0 & -32/11 & 22 \end{pmatrix}$$

$$\approx \begin{pmatrix} 1 & 0 & 0 & 0 \\ 0 & 1 & 0 & 0 \\ 0 & 0 & 1 & -7 \\ 0 & 0 & 0 & 22 + 7 \cdot 32/11 \end{pmatrix}$$

$$\approx \begin{pmatrix} 1 & 0 & 0 & 0 \\ 0 & 1 & 0 & 0 \\ 0 & 0 & 1 & 0 \\ 0 & 0 & 0 & 466/11 \end{pmatrix}$$

$$\approx \begin{pmatrix} 1 & 0 & 0 & 0 \\ 0 & 1 & 0 & 0 \\ 0 & 0 & 1 & 0 \\ 0 & 0 & 0 & 1 \end{pmatrix} \quad \text{rank is four}$$

7.5
Exercise

1. **a** coefficient matrix $A = \begin{pmatrix} 2 & 3 & -1 \\ 1 & 1 & 1 \\ 0 & 2 & -1 \end{pmatrix}$

augmented matrix $A|B = \begin{pmatrix} 2 & 3 & -1 & 8 \\ 1 & 1 & 1 & 7 \\ 0 & 2 & -1 & 3 \end{pmatrix}$

rank $A = 3$; rank $A|B = 3$; number of unknowns $= 3$
The set of solution is unique.

$$A|B = \begin{pmatrix} 2 & 3 & -1 & 8 \\ 1 & 1 & 1 & 7 \\ 0 & 2 & -1 & 3 \end{pmatrix}$$

$$\approx \begin{pmatrix} 1 & 1 & 1 & 7 \\ 0 & 2 & -1 & 3 \\ 2 & 3 & -1 & 8 \end{pmatrix}$$

$$\approx \begin{pmatrix} 1 & 1 & 1 & 7 \\ 0 & 2 & -1 & 3 \\ 0 & 1 & -3 & -6 \end{pmatrix}$$

$$\approx \begin{pmatrix} 1 & 1 & 1 & 7 \\ 0 & 1 & -1/2 & 3/2 \\ 0 & 1 & -3 & -6 \end{pmatrix}$$

$$\approx \begin{pmatrix} 1 & 0 & 3/2 & 11/2 \\ 0 & 1 & -1/2 & 3/2 \\ 0 & 0 & -5/2 & -15/2 \end{pmatrix}$$

$$\approx \begin{pmatrix} 1 & 0 & 3/2 & | & 11/2 \\ 0 & 1 & -1/2 & | & 3/2 \\ 0 & 0 & 1 & | & 3 \end{pmatrix}$$

$$\approx \begin{pmatrix} 1 & 0 & 0 & | & 1 \\ 0 & 1 & 0 & | & 3 \\ 0 & 0 & 1 & | & 3 \end{pmatrix}$$

Solution is $x_1 = 1$, $x_2 = 3$, $x_3 = 3$.

3. **a** $\begin{pmatrix} 0 & 0 & 1 & | & 1 & 0 & 0 \\ 0 & 1 & 0 & | & 0 & 1 & 0 \\ 1 & 0 & 0 & | & 0 & 0 & 1 \end{pmatrix} \approx \begin{pmatrix} 1 & 0 & 0 & | & 0 & 0 & 1 \\ 0 & 1 & 0 & | & 0 & 1 & 0 \\ 0 & 0 & 1 & | & 1 & 0 & 0 \end{pmatrix}$

$$A^{-1} = \begin{pmatrix} 0 & 0 & 1 \\ 0 & 1 & 0 \\ 1 & 0 & 0 \end{pmatrix}$$

c $\begin{pmatrix} 2 & 3 & -1 & | & 1 & 0 & 0 \\ 1 & 1 & 1 & | & 0 & 1 & 0 \\ 0 & 2 & -1 & | & 0 & 0 & 1 \end{pmatrix} \approx \begin{pmatrix} 1 & 0 & 0 & | & 3/5 & -1/5 & -4/5 \\ 0 & 1 & 0 & | & -1/5 & 2/5 & 3/5 \\ 0 & 0 & 1 & | & -2/5 & 4/5 & 1/5 \end{pmatrix}$

6. $\begin{pmatrix} 1 & 2 & | & 1 & 0 \\ 3 & 4 & | & 0 & 1 \end{pmatrix} \approx \begin{pmatrix} 1 & 0 & | & -2 & 1 \\ 0 & 1 & | & 3/2 & -1/2 \end{pmatrix}$

$$\therefore \begin{pmatrix} -2 & 1 \\ 3/2 & -1/2 \end{pmatrix} \cdot \begin{pmatrix} 1 & 2 \\ 3 & 4 \end{pmatrix} \cdot A = \begin{pmatrix} -2 & 1 \\ 3/2 & -1/2 \end{pmatrix} \cdot \begin{pmatrix} 9 & 1 \\ 0 & 7 \end{pmatrix}$$

$$I_2 \cdot A = A = \begin{pmatrix} -18 & 5 \\ 27/2 & -2 \end{pmatrix}$$

10. $I_2 - A = \begin{pmatrix} 0 & -2 \\ -7 & -8 \end{pmatrix}$

$$\begin{pmatrix} 0 & -2 & | & 1 & 0 \\ -7 & -8 & | & 0 & 1 \end{pmatrix} \approx \begin{pmatrix} 1 & 0 & | & 4/7 & -1/7 \\ 0 & 1 & | & -1/2 & 0 \end{pmatrix}$$

$$(I_2 - A)^{-1} = \begin{pmatrix} 4/7 & -1/7 \\ -1/2 & 0 \end{pmatrix}$$

**7.6.1
Exercise**

1. **a** MEET ME AT THE CASBAH
   a 41 23 70 45 41 23 62 41 64 36 19 11 59 39
   7 4 94 60
   b 13 69 −21 20 98 −35 1 150 18 8 44 −13 1
   32 0 1 141 24

2. **a** $A^{-1} = \begin{pmatrix} 2 & -3 \\ -1 & 2 \end{pmatrix}$

$$A^{-1} \cdot \begin{pmatrix} 51 \\ 30 \end{pmatrix} = \begin{pmatrix} 12 \\ 9 \end{pmatrix} = \begin{matrix} L \\ I \end{matrix}$$

$$A^{-1} \cdot \begin{pmatrix} 27 \\ 16 \end{pmatrix} = \begin{pmatrix} 6 \\ 5 \end{pmatrix} = \begin{matrix} F \\ E \end{matrix}$$

$$A^{-1} \cdot \begin{pmatrix} 75 \\ 47 \end{pmatrix} = \begin{pmatrix} 9 \\ 19 \end{pmatrix} = \begin{matrix} I \\ S \end{matrix}$$

$$A^{-1} \cdot \begin{pmatrix} 19 \\ 10 \end{pmatrix} = \begin{pmatrix} 8 \\ 1 \end{pmatrix} = \begin{matrix} H \\ A \end{matrix}$$

$$A^{-1} \cdot \begin{pmatrix} 48 \\ 26 \end{pmatrix} = \begin{pmatrix} 18 \\ 4 \end{pmatrix} = \begin{matrix} R \\ D \end{matrix}$$

LIFE IS HARD

3. $(t_1 \quad t_2) \begin{pmatrix} 1/4 & 3/4 \\ 2/3 & 1/3 \end{pmatrix} = (t_1 \quad t_2), \; t_1 + t_2 = 1$

$1/4t_1 + 2/3t_2 = t_1; \; 3/4t_1 + 1/3t_2 = t_2$

$3/4t_1 = 2/3t_2 \quad \text{or} \quad 9t_1 = 8t_2$

$$t_1 + t_2 = 1$$
$$8/9t_2 + t_2 = 1$$
$$17/9t_2 = 1$$
$$t_2 = 9/17, \; t_1 = 8/17$$

6. coefficient matrix $A = \begin{pmatrix} 2 & -1 & 1 \\ 1 & 1 & -1 \\ 3 & -1 & 1 \end{pmatrix}$

augmented matrix $A|B = \begin{pmatrix} 2 & -1 & 1 & | & 1 \\ 1 & 1 & -1 & | & 2 \\ 3 & -1 & 1 & | & 0 \end{pmatrix}$

rank $A = 2$; rank $A|B = 3$; number of unknowns $= 3$
This system has no solution.

1. **a** $\begin{pmatrix} 6 & -2 & 1 \\ 4 & 3 & ③ \end{pmatrix} \overset{①}{\Rightarrow} \begin{pmatrix} 6 \cdot 3 - 4 \cdot 1 & -2 \cdot 3 - 3 & 1 \\ & 4 & 3 & 3 \end{pmatrix}$

$= \begin{pmatrix} 14 & -9 & 1 \\ 4 & 3 & 2 \end{pmatrix} \overset{②}{\Rightarrow} \begin{pmatrix} 14 & -9 & 1 \\ -4 & -3 & 3 \end{pmatrix} \overset{③}{\Rightarrow} \begin{pmatrix} 14 & -9 & 1 \\ -4 & -3 & 1 \end{pmatrix}$

$\overset{④}{\Rightarrow} \begin{pmatrix} 14/3 & -3 & 1/3 \\ -4/3 & -1 & 1/3 \end{pmatrix}$

c $\begin{pmatrix} -3 & -1 \\ -2 & ⊖1 \\ 4 & 2 \end{pmatrix} \overset{①}{\Rightarrow} \begin{pmatrix} (-3)(-1) - (-1)(-2) & -1 \\ -2 & -1 \\ 4(-1) - (2)(-2) & 2 \end{pmatrix}$

$= \begin{pmatrix} 1 & -1 \\ -2 & -1 \\ 0 & 2 \end{pmatrix} \overset{②}{\Rightarrow} \begin{pmatrix} 1 & -1 \\ 2 & -1 \\ 0 & 2 \end{pmatrix} \overset{③}{\Rightarrow} \begin{pmatrix} 1 & -1 \\ 2 & 1 \\ 0 & 2 \end{pmatrix} \overset{④}{\Rightarrow} \begin{pmatrix} -1 & 1 \\ -2 & -1 \\ 0 & -2 \end{pmatrix}$

2. $x = 3 - 2u + 4v$
   $y = 6 - u + v$ interchange v and y

$\begin{matrix} & 1 & u & v \\ x & \begin{pmatrix} 3 & -2 & 4 \\ 6 & -1 & ① \end{pmatrix} \end{matrix} \overset{①}{\Rightarrow} \begin{pmatrix} 3 \cdot 1 - 6 \cdot 4 & -2 \cdot 1 - (-1)4 & 4 \\ 6 & -1 & 1 \end{pmatrix}$

$= \begin{pmatrix} -21 & 2 & 4 \\ 6 & -1 & 1 \end{pmatrix} \overset{②}{\Rightarrow} \begin{pmatrix} -21 & 2 & 4 \\ -6 & 1 & 1 \end{pmatrix}$

$$
\begin{array}{c}
\quad\quad 1 \quad\ u \quad y \\
\begin{array}{c} x \\ v \end{array}
\begin{pmatrix} -21 & 2 & 4 \\ -6 & 1 & 1 \end{pmatrix}
\end{array}
\quad \text{gives} \quad
\begin{array}{l}
x = -21 + 2u + 4y \\
v = -6 + u + y
\end{array}
$$

8.2

Exercise

1. $f = x + 5y$

$$2x + y + u = 10 \rightarrow u = 10 - 2x - y$$
$$x + 2y + v = 10 \rightarrow v = 10 - x - 2y$$

$$
\begin{array}{c}
\quad\quad 1 \quad\ x \quad\ y \\
\begin{array}{c} f \\ u \\ v \end{array}
\begin{pmatrix} 0 & 1 & 5 \\ 10 & -2 & -1 \\ 10 & -1 & -2 \end{pmatrix}
\end{array}
\quad
\begin{array}{l}
u = 10 - y,\ x = 0 \\
v = 10 - 2y,\ x = 0 \\
y = 10 \text{ or } y = 5, \text{ pick } y = 5 \text{ since} \\
y = 10 \text{ would make } v \text{ negative.}
\end{array}
$$

Interchange v and y so -2 is the pivot element.

$$
\begin{pmatrix} 0 & 1 & 5 \\ 10 & -2 & -1 \\ 10 & -1 & \boxed{-2} \end{pmatrix}
$$

$$
\overset{①}{\rightarrow}
\begin{pmatrix}
-5 \cdot 10 & 1(-2) - (-1)5 & 5 \\
(-2)10 - 10(-1) & (-2)(-2) - (-1)(-1) & -1 \\
10 & -1 & -2
\end{pmatrix}
$$

$$
=
\begin{pmatrix} -50 & 3 & 5 \\ -10 & 3 & -1 \\ 10 & -1 & -2 \end{pmatrix}
\overset{②}{\rightarrow}
\begin{pmatrix} -50 & 3 & 5 \\ -10 & 3 & -1 \\ -10 & 1 & -2 \end{pmatrix}
$$

$$
\overset{③}{\rightarrow}
\begin{pmatrix} -50 & 3 & 5 \\ -10 & 3 & -1 \\ -10 & 1 & 1 \end{pmatrix}
\overset{④}{\rightarrow}
\begin{pmatrix} 25 & -3/2 & -5/2 \\ 5 & -3/2 & 1/2 \\ 5 & -1/2 & -1/2 \end{pmatrix}
\quad \text{Max at } f = 25
$$

2. $f = 5x + 7y$

$$2x + y + u = 12 \rightarrow u = 12 - 2x - y$$
$$x + 3y + v = 12 \rightarrow v = 12 - x - 3y$$

$$
\begin{array}{c}
\quad\quad 1 \quad\ x \quad\ y \\
\begin{array}{c} f \\ u \\ v \end{array}
\begin{pmatrix} 0 & 5 & 7 \\ 12 & -2 & -1 \\ 12 & -1 & -3 \end{pmatrix}
\end{array}
\quad
\begin{array}{l}
u = 12 - y,\ x = 0 \\
v = 12 - 3y,\ x = 0 \\
y = 12 \text{ or } y = 4, \text{ pick } y = 4 \text{ since} \\
y = 12 \text{ would make } v \text{ negative.}
\end{array}
$$

Interchange v and y so -3 is the pivot element.

$$
\begin{pmatrix} 0 & 5 & 7 \\ 12 & -2 & -1 \\ 12 & -1 & \boxed{-3} \end{pmatrix}
$$

$$
\overset{①}{\rightarrow}
\begin{pmatrix}
-12 \cdot 7 & 5(-3) - (-1)7 & 7 \\
(-3)12 - (-1)12 & (-2)(-3) - (-1)(-1) & -1 \\
12 & -1 & -3
\end{pmatrix}
$$

$$
=
\begin{pmatrix} -84 & -8 & 7 \\ -24 & 5 & -1 \\ 12 & -1 & -3 \end{pmatrix}
\overset{②}{\rightarrow}
\begin{pmatrix} -84 & -8 & 7 \\ -24 & 5 & -1 \\ -12 & 1 & -3 \end{pmatrix}
$$

$$
\overset{③}{\rightarrow}
\begin{pmatrix} -84 & -8 & 7 \\ -24 & 5 & -1 \\ -12 & 1 & 1 \end{pmatrix}
\overset{④}{\rightarrow}
\begin{pmatrix} 28 & 8/3 & -7/3 \\ 8 & -5/3 & 1/3 \\ 4 & -1/3 & -1/3 \end{pmatrix}
$$

$$\begin{array}{cccc} & 1 & x & v \\ f & \begin{pmatrix} 28 & 8/3 & -7/3 \\ 8 & -5/3 & 1/3 \\ 4 & -1/3 & -1/3 \end{pmatrix} \\ u & \\ y & \end{array}$$

$u = 8 - 5/3\,x,\ v = 0$
$y = 4 - 1/3\,x,\ v = 0$
$x = 24/5$ or $x = 12$, pick $x = 24/5$ since
$x = 12$ makes u negative.

Interchange x and u so $-5/3$ is the pivot element.

$$\begin{pmatrix} 28 & 8/3 & -7/3 \\ 8 & \boxed{-5/3} & 1/3 \\ 4 & -1/3 & -1/3 \end{pmatrix}$$

$$\overset{①}{\to} \begin{pmatrix} 28(-5/3) - (8/3)8 & 8/3 & (-7/3)(-5/3) - (8/3)(1/3) \\ 8 & -5/3 & 1/3 \\ 4(-5/3) - (-1/3)8 & -1/3 & (-1/3)(-5/3) - (1/3)(-1/3) \end{pmatrix}$$

$$= \begin{pmatrix} -204/3 & 8/3 & 3 \\ 8 & -5/3 & 1/3 \\ -4 & -1/3 & 2/3 \end{pmatrix} \overset{②}{\to} \begin{pmatrix} -204/3 & 8/3 & 3 \\ -8 & -5/3 & -1/3 \\ -4 & -1/3 & 2/3 \end{pmatrix}$$

$$\overset{③}{\to} \begin{pmatrix} -204/3 & 8/3 & 3 \\ -8 & 1 & -1/3 \\ -4 & -1/3 & 2/3 \end{pmatrix} \overset{④}{\to} \begin{pmatrix} 204/5 & -8/5 & -9/5 \\ 24/5 & -3/5 & 1/5 \\ 12/5 & 1/5 & -2/5 \end{pmatrix}$$

Max at $f = 204/5$

3. $f = 5x + 7y$

$x + y + u = 8 \to u = 8 - x - y$
$2x + y + v = 10 \to v = 10 - 2x - y$
$3x + y + w = 12 \to w = 12 - 3x - y$

$$\begin{array}{cccc} & 1 & x & y \\ f & \begin{pmatrix} 0 & 5 & 7 \\ 8 & -1 & -1 \\ 10 & -2 & -1 \\ 12 & -3 & -1 \end{pmatrix} \\ u & \\ v & \\ w & \end{array}$$

$u = 8 - y,\ x = 0$
$v = 10 - y,\ x = 0$
$w = 12 - y,\ x = 0$
$y = 8,\ y = 10,\ y = 12$, pick $y = 8$, since 10 or
12 makes u negative.

Interchange u and y using -1 as pivot element.

$$\begin{pmatrix} 0 & 5 & 7 \\ 8 & -1 & \boxed{-1} \\ 10 & -2 & -1 \\ 12 & -3 & -1 \end{pmatrix}$$

$$\overset{①}{\to} \begin{pmatrix} 0(-1) - 7 \cdot 8 & 5(-1) - 7(-1) & 7 \\ 8 & -1 & -1 \\ 10(-1) - 8(-1) & (-2)(-1) - (-1)(-1) & -1 \\ 12(-1) - 8(-1) & (-3)(-1) - (-1)(-1) & -1 \end{pmatrix}$$

$$= \begin{pmatrix} -56 & 2 & 7 \\ 8 & -1 & -1 \\ -2 & 1 & -1 \\ -4 & 2 & -1 \end{pmatrix} \overset{②}{\to} \begin{pmatrix} -56 & 2 & 7 \\ -8 & 1 & -1 \\ -2 & 1 & -1 \\ -4 & 2 & -1 \end{pmatrix}$$

$$\overset{③}{\to} \begin{pmatrix} -56 & 2 & 7 \\ -8 & 1 & 1 \\ -2 & 1 & -1 \\ -4 & 2 & -1 \end{pmatrix} \overset{④}{\to} \begin{pmatrix} 56 & -2 & -7 \\ 8 & -1 & -1 \\ 2 & -1 & 1 \\ 4 & -2 & 1 \end{pmatrix}$$

Max at $f = 56$

8.3 Exercise

1. Minimize $f = 6x + 3y \to$ Maximize $-f = -6x - 3y$
   subject to $x + y \geqslant 4$, $3x + 4y \geqslant 12$
          $x + y = 4 + u$, $3x + 4y = 12 + v$
          $u = -4 + x + y$, $v = -12 + 3x + 4y$

   Solve the first equation for y.

   $y = 4 - x + u$
   $v = -12 + 3x + 4(4 - x + u)$
      $= 4 - x + 4u$
   $-f = -6x - 3(4 - x + u)$
       $= -6x - 12 + 3x - 3u$
       $= -12 - 3x - 3u$

   Since all the entries in the $-f$ row of the matrix will be negative, the maximum will be at $-f = -12$ so that the minimum will be at $f = 12$.

4. Minimize $f = 2x + 3y \to$ Maximize $-f = -2x - 3y$
   subject to $x + y \geqslant 3$, $2x + 3y \geqslant 6$
          $x + y = 3 + u$, $2x + 3y = 6 + v$
          $u = x + y - 3$ $v = 2x + 3y - 6$

   Solve for y.

   $y = 3 - x + u$
   $v = 2x + 3(3 - x + u) - 6$
      $= 3 - x + 3u$
   $-f = -2x - 3(3 - x + u)$
       $= -9 + x - 3u$

$$\begin{array}{cc} & \begin{array}{ccc} 1 & x & u \end{array} \\ \begin{array}{c} -f \\ y \\ v \end{array} & \begin{pmatrix} -9 & 1 & -3 \\ 3 & -1 & 1 \\ 3 & -1 & 3 \end{pmatrix} \end{array} \qquad \begin{array}{l} y = 3 - x, \; u = 0 \\ v = 3 - x, \; u = 0 \\ x = 3 \end{array}$$

x may be interchanged for y or v.

$$\begin{pmatrix} -9 & 1 & -3 \\ 3 & -1 & 1 \\ 3 & \boxed{-1} & 3 \end{pmatrix}$$

$$\overset{①}{\to} \begin{pmatrix} (-9)(-1) - 1 \cdot 3 & 1 & (-3)(-1) - 1 \cdot 3 \\ 3(-1) - 3(-1) & -1 & 1(-1) - 3(-1) \\ 3 & -1 & 3 \end{pmatrix}$$

$$= \begin{pmatrix} 6 & 1 & 0 \\ 0 & -1 & 2 \\ 3 & -1 & 3 \end{pmatrix} \overset{②}{\to} \begin{pmatrix} 6 & 1 & 0 \\ 0 & -1 & 2 \\ -3 & -1 & -3 \end{pmatrix} \overset{③}{\to} \begin{pmatrix} 6 & 1 & 0 \\ 0 & -1 & 2 \\ -3 & 1 & -3 \end{pmatrix}$$

$$\overset{④}{\to} \begin{pmatrix} -6 & -1 & 0 \\ 0 & 1 & -2 \\ 3 & -1 & 3 \end{pmatrix} \qquad \begin{array}{l} \text{Maximum for } -f \text{ at } -6. \\ \text{Minimum for } f \text{ at } 6. \end{array}$$

7. Minimize $f = 1 + 2x + 3y + 4z \rightarrow$ Maximize $-f = -1 - 2x - 3y - 4z$

$$u = 2 + 3x - 2y + 2z$$

subject to: $v = -2 + x + 2y + z$

$$w = -6 + 2x + 3y$$

Solve w for x.

$x = 3 - 3/2y + 1/2w$

$u = 2 + 3(3 - 3/2y + 1/2w) - 2y + 2z$

$\quad = 11 - 13/2y + 2z + 3/2w$

$v = -2 + 3 - 3/2y + 1/2w + 2y + z$

$\quad = 1 + 1/2y + z + 1/2w$

$-f = -1 - 2(3 - 3/2y + 1/2w) - 3y - 4z$

$\quad = -7 - 4z - w$

Since all the entries in the $-f$ row of the matrix will be nonpositive, the maximum will be at $-f = -7$ so that the minimum will be at $f = 7$.

1. $x_1 =$ units of Food I

$x_2 =$ units of Food II

$x_3 =$ units of Food III

Minimize Cost $\quad C = 2x_1 + x_2 + 3x_3$

$$2x_1 + 3x_2 + 4x_3 \geq 20$$

subject to:

$$4x_1 + 2x_2 + 2x_3 \geq 15$$

or Maximize $\quad -C = -2x_1 - x_2 - 3x_3$

$$u = -20 + 2x_1 + 3x_2 + 4x_3$$

$$v = -15 + 4x_1 + 2x_2 + 2x_3$$

Solve u for x_1

$$x_1 = 10 - 3/2x_2 - 2x_3 + 1/2u$$

$$v = -15 + 4(10 - 3/2x_2 - 2x_3 + 1/2u)$$

$$+ 2x_2 + 2x_3$$

$$= 25 - 4x_2 - 6x_3 + 2u$$

$$-C = -2(10 - 3/2x_2 - 2x_3 + 1/2u) - x_2 - 3x_3$$

$$= -20 + 2x_2 + x_3 - u$$

$$\begin{array}{cccc} & 1 & x_2 & x_3 & u \\ -C & \begin{pmatrix} -20 & 2 & 1 & -1 \\ x_1 & 10 & -3/2 & -2 & 1/2 \\ v & 25 & -4 & -6 & 2 \end{pmatrix} \end{array}$$

$x_1 = 10 - 3/2x_2,\ x_3 = u = 0$

$v = 25 - 4x_2,\quad x_3 = u = 0$

$x_2 = 20/3$ or $x_2 = 25/4$, pick $25/4$

Interchange v and x_2 using -4 as pivot element.

$$\begin{pmatrix} -20 & 2 & 1 & -1 \\ 10 & -3/2 & -2 & 1/2 \\ 25 & \boxed{-4} & -6 & 2 \end{pmatrix} \xrightarrow{\text{①}} \begin{pmatrix} 30 & 2 & 8 & 0 \\ -5/2 & -3/2 & -1 & 1 \\ 25 & -4 & -6 & 2 \end{pmatrix}$$

$$\xrightarrow{\text{②}} \begin{pmatrix} 30 & 2 & 8 & 0 \\ -5/2 & -3/2 & -1 & 1 \\ -25 & -4 & 6 & -2 \end{pmatrix} \xrightarrow{\text{③}} \begin{pmatrix} 30 & 2 & 8 & 0 \\ -5/2 & -3/2 & -1 & 1 \\ -25 & 1 & 6 & -2 \end{pmatrix}$$

$$\xrightarrow{\text{④}} \begin{pmatrix} -15/2 & -1/2 & -2 & 0 \\ 5/8 & 3/8 & 1/4 & -1/4 \\ 25/4 & -1/4 & -3/2 & 1/2 \end{pmatrix}$$

Maximum for $-C$ is $-C = -15/2$

Minimum for C is $C = 15/2$

CHAPTER 9   1. **a** dominance or clique

b perfect communication, business communication or clique

9.1   2. **a**
Exercise

$$\begin{array}{c} \\ A \\ B \\ C \\ D \\ E \\ F \end{array} \begin{array}{cccccc} A & B & C & D & E & F \\ \begin{pmatrix} 0 & 0 & 1 & 1 & 0 & 1 \\ 0 & 0 & 1 & 0 & 1 & 1 \\ 0 & 0 & 0 & 0 & 0 & 0 \\ 0 & 0 & 0 & 0 & 0 & 1 \\ 0 & 0 & 0 & 0 & 0 & 0 \\ 0 & 0 & 0 & 0 & 1 & 0 \end{pmatrix} \end{array}$$

clique

c

$$\begin{array}{c} \\ A \\ B \\ C \end{array} \begin{array}{ccc} A & B & C \\ \begin{pmatrix} 0 & 1 & 1 \\ 0 & 0 & 1 \\ 0 & 0 & 0 \end{pmatrix} \end{array}$$

dominance or clique

9.2   1. **a** Cannot be interpreted as dominance matrix.
Exercise

d Can be interpreted as dominance matrix.

$$M^2 = \begin{pmatrix} 0 & 0 & 0 \\ 1 & 0 & 0 \\ 0 & 0 & 0 \end{pmatrix}$$

A dominates no one in one or two stages; B dominates A in two ways in one or two stages and C in one way in one or two stages; C dominates A in no ways and B in one way in one or two stages.

4.

$$M = \begin{array}{c} A \\ B \\ C \\ D \end{array} \begin{array}{cccc} A & B & C & D \\ \begin{pmatrix} 0 & 1 & 1 & 0 \\ 0 & 0 & 0 & 1 \\ 0 & 1 & 0 & 0 \\ 1 & 0 & 1 & 0 \end{pmatrix} \end{array}$$

$$M^2 = \begin{pmatrix} 0 & 1 & 0 & 1 \\ 1 & 0 & 1 & 0 \\ 0 & 0 & 0 & 1 \\ 0 & 2 & 1 & 0 \end{pmatrix}$$

A dominates 4 in one or two stages; B dominates 3; and C dominates 2.

5. Team B should be declared the winner since B dominates or has won the most in one or two stages.

9.3   1. **a** Cannot be interpreted as a perfect communication matrix.
Exercise   2.

$$M = \begin{array}{c} A \\ B \\ C \end{array} \begin{array}{ccc} A & B & C \\ \begin{pmatrix} 0 & 2 & 2 \\ 2 & 0 & 2 \\ 2 & 2 & 0 \end{pmatrix} \end{array}$$

$$M^2 = \begin{pmatrix} 8 & 4 & 4 \\ 4 & 8 & 4 \\ 4 & 4 & 8 \end{pmatrix}$$

M^2 gives the number of lines connecting two cities passing through exactly one other city.

4. $\begin{array}{ccc} & K & M & D \end{array}$

$M = \begin{array}{c} K \\ M \\ D \end{array} \begin{pmatrix} 0 & 1 & 1 \\ 0 & 0 & 1 \\ 1 & 1 & 0 \end{pmatrix}$

$M^2 = \begin{pmatrix} 1 & 1 & 1 \\ 1 & 1 & 0 \\ 0 & 1 & 2 \end{pmatrix}$

Katy can communicate with Mike through no other or one other person in 2 ways; Mike has 1 way of getting feedback.

1. **a** $\begin{array}{cccc} & A & B & C & D \end{array}$

$\begin{array}{c} A \\ B \\ C \\ D \end{array} \begin{pmatrix} 0 & 1 & 1 & 1 \\ 1 & 0 & 1 & 0 \\ 1 & 1 & 0 & 1 \\ 1 & 0 & 1 & 0 \end{pmatrix}$

9.4
Exercise

   b no
   c none of them
5. *B* and *E* are liaison officials
6. yes

4. $\begin{array}{cccc} & A & B & C & D \end{array}$

$M = \begin{array}{c} A \\ B \\ C \\ D \end{array} \begin{pmatrix} 0 & 2 & 1 & 1 \\ 2 & 0 & 1 & 1 \\ 1 & 1 & 0 & 0 \\ 1 & 1 & 0 & 0 \end{pmatrix}$

CHAPTER
REVIEW

City *A* can communicate with city *B* through one other city in 2 ways. This is the entry in row *A*, column *B* of M^2.
5. There are none.
6.

$A = \begin{pmatrix} 1 & 0 & 2 & 2 & 0 \\ 2 & 2 & 0 & 1 & 0 \\ 3 & 2 & 1 & 0 & 1 \\ 4 & 0 & 0 & 1 & 0 \end{pmatrix}$

1. *a, b, d, f, g* are stochastic matrices.

CHAPTER 10

3. $A^{(2)} = A^{(0)}P^2 = (1/2 \quad 0 \quad 1/2 \quad 0) \begin{pmatrix} 1/3 & 2/9 & 2/9 & 2/9 \\ 2/9 & 1/3 & 2/9 & 2/9 \\ 2/9 & 2/9 & 1/3 & 2/9 \\ 2/9 & 2/9 & 2/9 & 1/3 \end{pmatrix}$

10.1
Exercise

$= (5/18 \quad 2/9 \quad 5/18 \quad 2/9)$

4. $A^{(5)} = A^{(0)}P^5 = (.7 \quad .3) \begin{pmatrix} .7017 & .2983 \\ .0426 & .9574 \end{pmatrix}$

$= (.5040 \quad .4960)$

7. Consider the professor's behavior as an experiment with two outcomes. Each depends only on the outcome of the previous experiment so we have a Markov Chain.

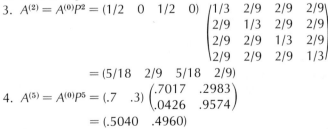

$\begin{array}{c} \\ \text{walk} \\ \text{drive} \end{array} \begin{array}{cc} \text{walk} & \text{drive} \end{array} \\ \begin{pmatrix} 1/2 & 1/2 \\ 1 & 0 \end{pmatrix}$

10.2 Exercise

1. **a** $\begin{pmatrix} 1/2 & 1/2 \\ 1 & 0 \end{pmatrix}^2 = \begin{pmatrix} 3/4 & 1/4 \\ 1/2 & 1/2 \end{pmatrix}$ regular

b $\begin{pmatrix} 1/2 & 1/2 \\ 0 & 1 \end{pmatrix}^2 = \begin{pmatrix} 1/4 & 3/4 \\ 0 & 1 \end{pmatrix}$

The 0 will perpetuate itself so the matrix is not regular.

4. The transition matrix is:

$$\begin{array}{cccc} & A & B & C \\ A & 0 & 1 & 0 \\ B & 3/4 & 0 & 1/4 \\ C & 3/4 & 1/4 & 0 \end{array}$$

$(x \quad y \quad z)\begin{pmatrix} 0 & 1 & 0 \\ 3/4 & 0 & 1/4 \\ 3/4 & 1/4 & 0 \end{pmatrix} = (3/4y + 3/4z \quad x + 1/4z \quad 1/4y)$

$= (x \quad y \quad z)$

$3/4y + 3/4z = x, \ x + 1/4z = y, \ 1/4y = z, \ x + y + z = 1$

$3y + 3z = 4x \qquad 4x + z = 4y, \ y = 4z$

$15z = 4x, \ y = 4z$

$\therefore x + y + z = 1 \Rightarrow 15z + 16z + 4z = 4$ or $35z = 4$ or $z = 4/35$

$x = 15/4z = 15/4 \cdot 4/35 = 3/7$

$y = 4z = 16/35$

She buys A 3/7 of the time

B 16/35 of the time and

C 4/25 of the time in the long run.

10.3 Exercise

1. **a** nonabsorbing **d** nonabsorbing
b absorbing **e** absorbing
c nonabsorbing

10.4 Exercise

1.

$(x \quad y \quad z) \cdot \begin{pmatrix} 1/2 & 1/2 & 0 \\ 1/4 & 1/2 & 1/4 \\ 0 & 1/2 & 1/2 \end{pmatrix}$

$= (1/2x + 1/4y \quad 1/2x + 1/2y + 1/2z \quad 1/4y + 1/2z) = (x \quad y \quad z)$

$x = 1/2x + 1/4y \Rightarrow 1/2x = 1/4y \Rightarrow x = 1/2y$

$y = 1/2x + 1/2y + 1/2z \Rightarrow y = x + z$

$z = 1/4y + 1/2z \Rightarrow 1/2z = 1/4y \Rightarrow z = 1/2y$

$(x \quad y \quad z) = (1/2y \quad y \quad 1/2y)$

$1/2y + y + 1/2y = 1$

$2y = 1$

$y = 1/2$

$(x \quad y \quad z) = (1/4 \quad 1/2 \quad 1/4)$

CHAPTER REVIEW

1. **a** $(x \quad y)\begin{pmatrix} 1/4 & 3/4 \\ 1/2 & 1/2 \end{pmatrix} = (1/4x + 1/2y \quad 3/4x + 1/2y) = (x \quad y)$

$x = 1/4x + 1/2y$

$3/4x = 1/2y$

$x = 2/3y$

$(x \quad y) = (2/3y \quad y)$

$2/3y + y = 1$

$$5/3y = 1$$
$$y = 3/5$$
$$(x \quad y) = (2/5 \quad 3/5)$$

6. The transition matrix is

	Fat Son	Skinny Son
Fat Father	.7	.3
Skinny Father	.6	.4

$$P^2 = \begin{pmatrix} .67 & .33 \\ .66 & .34 \end{pmatrix}$$

The probability is .67. The long run distribution is (2/3   1/3).
No.

1. Let positive numbers denote Tami's winnings and negative numbers denote Laura's winnings.

CHAPTER 11

Laura

$$\text{Tami} \begin{array}{c} \text{I} \\ \text{II} \end{array} \begin{pmatrix} -10 & 10 \\ 10 & -10 \end{pmatrix} \quad \text{entries are in cents.}$$

4. **a** strictly determined, value is -1 **f** strictly determined, value is 0
   b strictly determined, value is 2   **g** strictly determined, value is 0
   c not strictly determined   **h** not strictly determined
   d not strictly determined   **i** strictly determined, value is 2
   e not strictly determined

1. $P = (.3 \quad .7)$

$$Q = \begin{pmatrix} .4 \\ .6 \end{pmatrix}$$

$$E = (.3 \quad .7) \begin{pmatrix} 6 & 0 \\ -2 & 3 \end{pmatrix} \begin{pmatrix} .4 \\ .6 \end{pmatrix} = (.4 \quad 2.1) \begin{pmatrix} .4 \\ .6 \end{pmatrix}$$
$$= .16 + 1.26 = 1.42$$

2. **a** $E = (1/2 \quad 1/2) \begin{pmatrix} 4 & 0 \\ 2 & 3 \end{pmatrix} \begin{pmatrix} 1/2 \\ 1/2 \end{pmatrix} = (3 \quad 3/2) \begin{pmatrix} 1/2 \\ 1/2 \end{pmatrix}$
   $$= 3/2 + 3/4 = 9/4$$

3. **a** $E = (2/3 \quad 1/3) \begin{pmatrix} 4 & 0 \\ -3 & 6 \end{pmatrix} \begin{pmatrix} 1/3 \\ 2/3 \end{pmatrix} = (5/3 \quad 2) \begin{pmatrix} 1/3 \\ 2/3 \end{pmatrix}$
   $$= 5/9 + 4/3 = 17/9$$

1. **a** $\begin{pmatrix} 1 & 2 \\ 4 & 1 \end{pmatrix}$ $p_1 = \dfrac{1-4}{1+1-2-4} = -3/-4 = 3/4$

$$p_2 = \frac{1-2}{1+1-2-4} = -1/-4 = 1/4$$
$$q_1 = \frac{1-2}{1+1-2-4} = -1/-4 = 1/4$$
$$q_2 = \frac{1-4}{1+1-2-4} = -3/-4 = 3/4$$
$$V = (3/4 \quad 1/4) \begin{pmatrix} 1 & 2 \\ 4 & 1 \end{pmatrix} \begin{pmatrix} 1/4 \\ 3/4 \end{pmatrix} = (7/4 \quad 7/4) \begin{pmatrix} 1/4 \\ 3/4 \end{pmatrix} = 28/16$$

b $\begin{pmatrix} -3 & 2 \\ 1 & 0 \end{pmatrix}$ $p_1 = \dfrac{0-1}{-3+0-2-1} = -1/-6 = 1/6$

$$p_2 = \frac{-3-2}{-6} = -5/-6 = 5/6$$

$$q_1 = \frac{0-2}{-6} = 2/6 = 1/3$$

$$q_2 = \frac{-3-1}{-6} = -4/-6 = 2/3$$

$$V = (1/6 \quad 5/6) \begin{pmatrix} -3 & 2 \\ 1 & 0 \end{pmatrix}\begin{pmatrix} 1/3 \\ 2/3 \end{pmatrix} = (1/3 \quad 1/3) \begin{pmatrix} 1/3 \\ 2/3 \end{pmatrix} = 1/3$$

c $\begin{pmatrix} 2 & -1 \\ -1 & 4 \end{pmatrix}$ $p_1 = \dfrac{4-(-1)}{2+4+1+1} = 5/8$

$$p_2 = \frac{2+1}{8} = 3/8$$

$$q_1 = \frac{4+1}{8} = 5/8$$

$$q_2 = \frac{2+1}{8} = 3/8$$

$$V = (5/8 \quad 3/8) \begin{pmatrix} 2 & -1 \\ -1 & 4 \end{pmatrix}\begin{pmatrix} 5/8 \\ 3/8 \end{pmatrix} = (7/8 \quad 7/8) \begin{pmatrix} 5/8 \\ 3/8 \end{pmatrix} = 7/8$$

2. $\begin{pmatrix} 4 & -1 \\ 0 & 3 \end{pmatrix}$ $p_1 = \dfrac{3-0}{4+3+1} = 3/8$

$$p_2 = \frac{4+1}{8} = 5/8$$

$$q_1 = \frac{3+1}{8} = 1/2$$

$$q_2 = \frac{4}{8} = 1/2$$

$$V = (3/8 \quad 5/8) \begin{pmatrix} 4 & -1 \\ 0 & 3 \end{pmatrix}\begin{pmatrix} 1/2 \\ 1/2 \end{pmatrix} = (3/2 \quad 3/2) \begin{pmatrix} 1/2 \\ 1/2 \end{pmatrix} = 1.5$$

The game favors the Democrats.

11.5
Exercise

1. **a** $\begin{pmatrix} 8 & 3 & 8 \\ 6 & 5 & 4 \\ -2 & 4 & 1 \end{pmatrix}$ row three is dominated by row two, the reduced matrix is:

$\begin{pmatrix} 8 & 3 & 8 \\ 6 & 5 & 4 \end{pmatrix}$ column 1 is dominated by column two, the reduced matrix is:

$\begin{pmatrix} 3 & 8 \\ 5 & 4 \end{pmatrix}$ $p_1 = \dfrac{4-5}{3+4-8-5} = -1/-6 = 1/6$

$$p_2 = \frac{3-8}{-6} = -5/-6 = 5/6$$

$$q_1 = \frac{4-8}{-6} = -4/-6 = 2/3$$

$$q_2 = \frac{3-5}{-6} = -2/-6 = 1/3$$

$$V = (1/6 \quad 5/6) \begin{pmatrix} 3 & 8 \\ 5 & 4 \end{pmatrix}\begin{pmatrix} 2/3 \\ 1/3 \end{pmatrix} = (14/3 \quad 14/3) \begin{pmatrix} 2/3 \\ 1/3 \end{pmatrix} = 14/3$$

b $\begin{pmatrix} 2 & 1 & 0 & 6 \\ 3 & -2 & 1 & 2 \end{pmatrix}$ column three dominates columns one and four; the reduced matrix is:

$$\begin{pmatrix} 1 & 0 \\ -2 & 1 \end{pmatrix} \quad p_1 = \frac{1+2}{1+1+2} = 3/4$$

$$p_2 = 1/4$$

$$q_1 = 1/4$$

$$q_2 = \frac{1+2}{4} = 3/4$$

$$V = (3/4 \quad 1/4) \begin{pmatrix} 1 & 0 \\ -2 & 1 \end{pmatrix} \begin{pmatrix} 1/4 \\ 3/4 \end{pmatrix} = (1/4 \quad 1/4) \begin{pmatrix} 1/4 \\ 3/4 \end{pmatrix} = 1/4$$

c $\begin{pmatrix} 6 & -4 & 2 & -3 \\ -4 & 6 & -5 & 7 \end{pmatrix}$ Column three dominates column one
Column two dominates column four; the
reduced matrix is:

$$\begin{pmatrix} -4 & 2 \\ 6 & -5 \end{pmatrix} \quad p_1 = \frac{-5-6}{-4-5-2-6} = 11/17$$

$$p_2 = \frac{-4-2}{-17} = 6/17$$

$$q_1 = \frac{-5-2}{-17} = \frac{7}{17}$$

$$q_2 = \frac{-4-6}{-17} = 10/17$$

$$V = (11/7 \quad 6/17) \begin{pmatrix} -4 & 2 \\ 6 & -5 \end{pmatrix} \begin{pmatrix} 7/17 \\ 10/17 \end{pmatrix} = (-8/17 \quad -8/17) \begin{pmatrix} 7/17 \\ 10/17 \end{pmatrix}$$

$$= -136/289$$

d $\begin{pmatrix} 4 & -5 & 5 \\ -6 & 3 & 3 \\ 2 & -6 & 3 \end{pmatrix}$ row one dominates row three, the reduced matrix
is:

$$\begin{pmatrix} 4 & -5 & 5 \\ -6 & 3 & 3 \end{pmatrix}$$ column two dominates column three, the reduced
matrix is:

$$\begin{pmatrix} 4 & -5 \\ -6 & 3 \end{pmatrix} \quad p_1 = \frac{3+6}{4+3+5+6} = 9/18 = 1/2$$

$$p_2 = \frac{4+5}{18} = 9/18 = 1/2$$

$$q_1 = \frac{3+5}{18} = 8/18 = 4/9$$

$$q_2 = \frac{4+6}{18} = 10/18 = 5/9$$

$$V = (1/2 \quad 1/2) \begin{pmatrix} 4 & -5 \\ -6 & 3 \end{pmatrix} \begin{pmatrix} 4/9 \\ 5/9 \end{pmatrix} = (-1 \quad -1) \begin{pmatrix} 4/9 \\ 5/9 \end{pmatrix} = -1$$

1. **a** strictly determined, value is 3.
   b strictly determined, value is 15.
   c strictly determined, value is 50.

2. **a** $V = (1/3 \quad 2/3) \begin{pmatrix} -1 & 1 \\ 1 & -1 \end{pmatrix} \begin{pmatrix} 1 \\ 0 \end{pmatrix} = (1/3 \quad -1/3) \begin{pmatrix} 1 \\ 0 \end{pmatrix} = 1/3$

   b $V = (0 \quad 1) \begin{pmatrix} -1 & 1 \\ 1 & -1 \end{pmatrix} \begin{pmatrix} 1/2 \\ 1/2 \end{pmatrix} = (1 \quad -1) \begin{pmatrix} 1/2 \\ 1/2 \end{pmatrix} = 0$

5. **a** $\begin{pmatrix} 4 & 6 & 3 \\ 1 & 2 & 5 \end{pmatrix}$ Column one dominates column two, the reduced
matrix is:

CHAPTER
REVIEW

$$\begin{pmatrix} 4 & 3 \\ 1 & 5 \end{pmatrix} \quad p_1 = \frac{5-1}{4+5-3-1} = 4/5$$

$$p_2 = \frac{4-3}{5} = 1/5$$

$$q_1 = \frac{5-3}{5} = 2/5$$

$$q_2 = \frac{4-1}{5} = 3/5$$

$$V = (4/5 \quad 1/5) \begin{pmatrix} 4 & 3 \\ 1 & 5 \end{pmatrix} \begin{pmatrix} 2/5 \\ 3/5 \end{pmatrix} = (17/5 \quad 17/5) \begin{pmatrix} 2/5 \\ 3/5 \end{pmatrix} = 17/5$$

CHAPTER 12

**12.1
Exercise**

1. **a** A study of the spreading of a disease by rats in a certain town. The data should be gathered from all areas or sections of the town.
   f A study of the number of savings accounts per family in the U.S. The data should be gathered from all different kinds of banks.
   g A national study of the monthly budget for a family of four. The study should be made from families with different incomes.
2. Biased Samples:
   a Asking a group of children if they like candy.
3. This sample is biased since the study was made from accounts totaling less than $10,000.
5. In 1936 not very many people had telephones or owned cars, so the sample was biased.

**12.2
Exercise**

1. **a** the lower limit of 5th class is *250*
   b the upper limit of 4th class is *249*
   e the frequency in the 3rd class is *33*
2. **a** Frequency Table

Score	Tally	Frequency	Score	Tally	Frequency
55	/	1	40	/	1
54	//	2	39	/	1
53	//	2	38	/	1
52	///	3	37	////	4
51	/	1	36	//	2
50	/	1	35	/	1
49	/	1	34	//	2
48	///	3	33	//	2
47	/	1	32	/	1
46	//	2	31	//	2
45	/	1	30	///	3
44	//	2	29	/	1
43	/	1	28	/	1
42	///	3	26	/	1
41	̷̷̷̷̷	5	25	/	1

range is *30*

1. #2 mean is *40.81*
   median is *41*
   mode is *41*
2. mean is *81.87*
   median is *81.25*
   two modes are *92.5* and *87.5*
3. mean is *$16,000*
   median is *$12,000*
   The *median* describes the situation more realistically.
6. For Figure 12.6
   40% of 71 = 28.4
   28.4 − 24 = 4.4

   $C_{40} = 75 + (4.4) \dfrac{1}{11} (5) = 75$

   $C_{40} = 75 + 2 = 77$
   75% of 71 = 53.25
   53.25 − 49 = 4.25

   $C_{70} = 90 + (4.25) \dfrac{1}{12} (5) =$

   $C_{70} = 90 + 1.77 = 91.77$

12.3.1
Exercise

1. $\bar{x} = \dfrac{4 + 5 + 9 + 9 + 10 + 14 + 25}{7}$

   $\bar{x} = 10.86$

x	$x - \bar{x}$	$(x - \bar{x})^2$
4	− 6.86	47.0596
5	− 5.86	34.3396
9	− 1.86	3.4596
9	− 1.86	3.4596
10	− .86	.7396
14	3.14	9.8596
25	14.14	199.9396
		298.8572

   $\sigma = \sqrt{\dfrac{298.8572}{7}} = \sqrt{42.6939} = 6.53$

2. mean is *63.33*
   median is *65*
   no mode
   range is *79*
   $\bar{x} = 63.33$

   $\sigma = \sqrt{\dfrac{5850.0001}{9}} = \sqrt{650} = 25.5$

3. $Z = \dfrac{7 - 13.1}{9.3} = -.6559$ $\qquad Z = \dfrac{29 - 13.1}{9.3} = 1.7097$

12.3.2
Exercise

12.4
Exercise

4. **a** .89 → *.3133* **d** 3.00 → *.4987* **f** −2.31 → *.4896*
5. A → *5.48%*
   B → *21.95%*
   C → *34.36%*
   D → *30.13%*
   F → *8.08%*

6. **a** $\dfrac{142 - 130}{5.2} = 2.31$ **b** $124.59 - 135.41$

$.5000 - .4896 = .0104 = 1.04\%$

10. C: $z = \dfrac{76 - 82}{7} = -.86$

   M: $z = \dfrac{89 - 93}{2} = -2$

   K: $z = \dfrac{21 - 24}{9} = -.33$

Kathleen has the highest relative standing.

12.5 Exercise

1.

	5H/0T	4H/1T	3H/2T	2H/3T	1H/4T	0H/5T	Total
O	1	6	15	35	16	2	75
E	2.34	11.72	23.44	23.44	11.72	2.34	75

$\nu = 5$

$\chi^2 = \dfrac{(1 - 2.34)^2}{2.34} + \dfrac{(6 - 11.72)^2}{11.72} + \dfrac{(15 - 23.44)^2}{23.44}$

$\quad + \dfrac{(35 - 23.44)^2}{23.44} + \dfrac{(16 - 11.72)^2}{11.72} + \dfrac{(2 - 2.34)^2}{2.34}$

$\quad = .77 + 2.79 + 3.04 + 5.70 + 1.56 + .05$

$\quad = 13.91$

Yes: this result occurs about 2% of the time due to chance alone.

4.

	Tide	Ivory	Total
O	300	200	500
E	250	250	500

$\nu = 1$

$\chi^2 = \dfrac{(300 - 250)^2}{250} + \dfrac{(200 - 250)^2}{250} = 20$

Probability is less than .1% that this could occur by chance alone so there is evidence against the hypothesis.

CHAPTER REVIEW

2. **a** Mean $= 5.58$; Median $= 4.5$; Mode $= 4$

7.

	x'	$(x')^2$
81	5.43	29.48
77	1.43	2.04
76	.43	.18
76	.43	.18
74	−1.57	2.46
73	−2.57	6.60
72	−3.57	12.74
		53.68

Mean $= 75.57$

$\Sigma(x')^2 = 53.68$

$\sigma = \dfrac{53.68}{7} = 7.67$

10. $Z = \dfrac{-14 + 10.33}{1.25} = -2.93$

About .17% will die before 10 years, 4 months.

12. Mathematics: $Z = \dfrac{89 - 79}{5} = 2$

Sociology: $Z = \dfrac{79 - 72}{3.5} = 2$

Bob ranked the same in both classes.

1. **a** $I = Prt = (\$420)(.06)\left(\dfrac{1}{4}\right) = \$6.30; \ A = P + I = \$426.30.$

   d $I = (\$400)(.05)(10) = \$200; \ A = \$600.$

2. **a** $A = P + PI = P(1 + rt); \ P = \dfrac{A}{(1 + rt)}$

   c $P = \dfrac{\$183.68}{(1 + .1867)} = \$154.78$

3. **b** (1) $A = P(1 + r)^n = (\$3250)(1 + .03)^5$
   $= (3250)(1.159274) = \$3,767.64$
   $I = A - P = 3,767.64 - 3,250 = \$517.64$

   (2) $A = P(1 + r)^n = (\$3250)(1 + .015)^{10}$
   $= (3250)(1.160541) = \$3,771.76$
   $I = A - P = 3,771.76 - 3250 = \$521.76$

4. (1) Use a principal of $100.00 or $1000.00.
   $A = (\$100)(1 + .03)^2 = \$106.09$ effective rate is 6.09%

5. **d** (1) $P = A_n(1 + r)^{-n} = (300)(1 + .045)^{-3}$
   $= (300)(.876297) = \$262.89$

   (2) $P = A^n(1 + r)^{-n} = (300)(1 + .015)^{-9}$
   $= (300)(.874592) = \$262.38$

7. $A = P + I$
   $I = Prt$

   $50 = 500 \left(\dfrac{20}{12}\right) r$

   $12 = 200r$

   $r = \dfrac{12}{200}$

   $r = 6\%$

9. $2P = P(1 + r)^{10}$
   $2 = (1 + r)^{10}$
   $\sqrt[10]{2} = 1 + r$
   $1.071773 = 1 + r$
   $.071773 = r$
   $1.43546 = 2r$
   rate of interest $= 14.35\%$

12. **a** $2P = P(1 + .03)^n$
   $2 = (1.03)^n$

   $n = \log_{1.03} 2 = \dfrac{\log_{10} 2}{\log_{10} 1.03} = \dfrac{.3010}{.0128} = 23.51$ quarterly periods

   $= 5.87$ years

13.2
Exercise

1. **a** $A = P \cdot s_{\overline{n}|r} = 1500 \cdot s_{\overline{15}|.06} = (1500)(23.275970)$
   $= 34{,}913.96$
   $V = P \cdot a_{\overline{n}|r} = 1500a_{\overline{15}|.06} = (1500)(9.712249)$
   $= 14{,}568.37.$

2. **c** $V = P \cdot a_{\overline{n}|r}; \ P = V\left(\dfrac{1}{a_{\overline{n}|r}}\right) = \dfrac{6000}{a_{\overline{10}|.05}}$
   $= (6000)(.129505) = 777.03.$

4. $A = P \cdot s_{\overline{n}|r} = 10s_{\overline{60}|.005} = (10)(69.770034) = 697.70.$

8. $V = P \cdot a_{\overline{n}|r} = 200a_{\overline{76}|.015} = (200)(45.164138) = 9032.83$

13.3
Exercise

1. $P = A\left(\dfrac{1}{a_{\overline{n}|r}}\right) = 10{,}000\left(\dfrac{1}{a_{\overline{40}|.02}}\right) = (10{,}000)(.036556)$

3. **a** Equity after 4 years $= 25{,}000 - [(402.23)(a_{\overline{36}|.0075})]$
   $= 25{,}000 - [(402.23)(31.446804)]$
   $= 25{,}000 - 12{,}648.85 = 12{,}351.15.$

   b Equity after 6 years $= 25{,}000 - [(402.23)(a_{\overline{12}|.0075})]$
   $= 25{,}000 - [(402.23)(11.434912)]$
   $= 25{,}000 - 4599.46 = 20{,}400.54.$

6. $P = (30{,}000)\left(\dfrac{1}{a_{\overline{40}|.02}}\right) = (30{,}000)(.036556)$
   $= 1{,}096.68$ over 10 years
   $P = (30{,}000)\left(\dfrac{1}{a_{\overline{80}|.02}}\right) = (30{,}000)(.025161)$
   $= 754.83$ over 20 years.

8. $P = (5{,}000{,}000)\left(\dfrac{1}{s_{\overline{20}|.05}}\right) = (5{,}000{,}000)(.030243)$
   $= 151{,}215.00$

CHAPTER
REVIEW

3. $A = P(1 + r)^n = 100(1.02)^9 = 100(1.195093)$
   $= \$119.51$

6. $2P = P(1 + r)^{10}$
   $2 = (1 + r)^{10}$
   $\sqrt[10]{2} - 1 = r$
   $.071773 = r$
   $r = 7.18\%$

7. **a** $I = Prt = (3000)(3)(.18) = \$1620.00$
   b $A = P(1 + r)^n = (3000)(1.04)^{12} = (3000)(1.601032)$
   $= \$4803.09 \quad 4803.09 - 3000 = 1803.09 = I$
   The simple interest loan costs least.

9. $P = A(1 + r)^{-n} = 75(1 + .005)^{-6} = 75(.970518)$

11. $P = A\left(\dfrac{1}{s_{\overline{n}|r}}\right) = 500\left(\dfrac{1}{s_{\overline{24}|.015}}\right) = 500(.034924) = 17.46$

14. $V = Pa_{\overline{n}|r} = 50 \cdot a_{\overline{18}|.01} = 50(16.398268) = 819.91$

15. $P = V\left(\dfrac{1}{a_{\overline{n}|r}}\right) = 25{,}000\left(\dfrac{1}{a_{\overline{5}|.08}}\right) = (25{,}000)(.250456) = 6261.40$

20. $.1x + x\left(\dfrac{1}{s_{\overline{15}|.07}}\right) = 25{,}000$
    $.1x + x(.039795) = 25{,}000$
    $x(.139795) = 25{,}000$
    $x = 178{,}833.29$

Index

Economics Today

THE MICRO VIEW

1999–2000 EDITION

THE ADDISON-WESLEY SERIES IN ECONOMICS

Economics Today

THE MICRO VIEW   1999-2000 EDITION

R O G E R   L E R O Y   M I L L E R

INSTITUTE FOR UNIVERSITY STUDIES, ARLINGTON, TEXAS

 **ADDISON-WESLEY**

An imprint of Addison Wesley Longman, Inc.

Reading, Massachusetts • Menlo Park, California • New York • Harlow, England
Don Mills, Ontario • Sydney • Mexico City • Madrid • Amsterdam

Executive Editor: Denise Clinton
Senior Editor: Andrea Shaw
Developmental Editor: Mary Draper
Supplements Editor: Deb Kiernan
Senior Production Supervisor: Nancy Fenton
Marketing Manager: Amy Cronin
Senior Project Manager: Melissa Honig
Designer: Regina Hagen
Cover illustration: Photomosaic™ ©1997 Robert Silvers, www.photomosaic.com
Art Studio: ElectraGraphics, Inc.
Photo Researcher: Billie Porter
Print Buyer: Sheila Spinney
Media Buyer: Sue Ward
Composition: WestWords, Inc.
Printer and Binder: R.R. Donnelley & Sons Company
Cover Printer: Coral Graphic Services, Inc.

Library of Congress Cataloging-in-Publication Data

Miller, Roger LeRoy.
    Economics today: the micro view / Roger LeRoy Miller. — 10th ed.
       p.   cm. — (The Addison-Wesley series in economics)
    Includes index.
    ISBN 0-201-36013-6
    1. Microeconomics. 2. Economics. I. Title. II. Series.
  HB171.5.M642   1998
338.5—dc21   98-22981
                                                          CIP

ISBN 0-201-36013-6
12345678910—DOW—0201009998

To Victor and Max

*Learning about life is a slow
process. Don't be too impatient!*

R.L.M.

CONTENTS IN BRIEF

IN THIS VOLUME, CHAPTER 6 IS FOLLOWED BY CHAPTER 19.

CONTENTS IN DETAIL

IN THIS VOLUME, CHAPTER 6 IS FOLLOWED BY CHAPTER 19.

The 1999–2000 Edition of *Economics Today, The Micro View* presents economic principles within the context of sweeping changes occurring in the economic landscape. These changes, including the "wiring" of the economy, have prompted me to revise this market-leading textbook in two years instead of the usual three. Alongside changes in the economy are the dramatic new approaches to teaching and learning introductory economics. The 1999–2000 Edition responds to these changes with significant revisions to the text and supplements.

In the textbook you will find all new contemporary issues presented in a hallmark feature, Issues and Applications, at the start and end of each chapter. Because economic problems are being influenced by today's "wired world," I have also added new Cyberspace Examples throughout the text and a new Chapter 35, "Cybernomics." In addition, every chart, table, and graph has been revised to reflect the most recent data available.

This new edition also responds to the latest teaching methods to enhance your lectures and aid student learning. Many of you have been asking for PowerPoint slides. Accompanying this text is a comprehensive, dynamic PowerPoint Lecture Presentation system of key terms and concepts and animated graphs from the text. In addition, the 1999–2000 Edition is accompanied by a rich variety of economic experiments to involve students in testing economic theory.

To explore economic theory and real-world applications, students will receive the Economics in Action, 1999–2000 Edition, CD-ROM with every purchase of a text. This interactive software uses dynamic graphs, sound effects, and step-by-step tutorials to guide students in their understanding of economic concepts.

In addition, Internet exercises and a Web site (**www.econtoday.com**) featuring practice quizzes will get students on line to test and expand their knowledge.

I am grateful for the extensive feedback received from reviewers, focus groups, and students, which continues to shape and enhance *Economics Today, The Micro View*. You may reach me at **www.econtoday.com** to share your feedback and suggestions for improving the text and supplements package.

Roger LeRoy Miller

ACKNOWLEDGMENTS

I feel that I am one of the luckiest textbook writers around, for I get the benefit of continuous feedback from professors who use *Economics Today, The Micro View.* I am grateful for the constructive criticisms that you continue to send me. Below I list those of you who generously offered your time to participate in the reviewing process for this edition. Please accept my sincere appreciation.

Mohammed Akacem, Metropolitan State College
John Allen, Texas A&M University
Ann AlYasiri, University of Wisconsin, Platteville
Abraham Bertisch, Nassua Community College
Steffany Ellis, University of Michigan–Dearborne
Sandy Evans, St. John's River Community College
Arthur Friedberg, Mohawk Valley Community College

Edward Greenberg, Washington University
Nick Grunt, Tarrant City Junior College
Kwabena Gyimah-Brempong, University of Southern Florida
Grover A. Howard, Rio Hondo College
Mark Jensen, Southern Illinois University
Faik Koray, Louisiana State University
Akbar Marvasti, University of Houston–Downtown
Michael Metzger, University of Central Oklahoma
Margaret Moore, Franklin University
Randy Parker, East Carolina University

Norm Paul, San Jacinto College
Mannie Poen, Houston Community College
Henry Ryder, Gloucester County College
David Schorow, Richland College
Columbus Stephens, Brevard Community College
Kay Unger, University of Montana
Mark Wilkening, Blinn Community College
Pete Wyman, Spokane Falls Community College
Paul Zarembka, SUNY Buffalo

Those who reviewed previous editions:

Esmond Adams
John Adams
John R. Aidem
M. C. Alderfer
Leslie J. Anderson
Fatima W. Antar
Aliakbar Ataiifar
Leonard Atencio
Glen W. Atkinson
Thomas R. Atkinson
James Q. Aylesworth
Charlie Ballard
Maurice B. Ballabon
G. Jeffrey Barbour
Daniel Barszcz
Robin L. Bartlett
Kari Battaglia
Robert Becker
Charles Beem
Glen Beeson
Charles Berry
Scott Bloom
M. L. Bodnar
Mary Bone
Karl Bonnhi
Thomas W. Bonsor
John M. Booth
Wesley F. Booth
Thomas Borcherding
Tom Boston
Barry Boyer
Maryanna Boynton
Ronald Brandolini
Fenton L. Broadhead
Elba Brown

William Brown
Michael Bull
Maureen Burton
Ralph T. Byrns
Conrad P. Caligaris
Kevin Carey
Dancy R. Carr
Doris Cash
Thomas H. Cate
Richard J. Cebula
Richard Chapman
Young Back Choi
Carol Cies
Joy L. Clark
Gary Clayton
Marsha Clayton
Warren L. Coats
Ed Coen
Pat Conroy
James Cox
Stephen R. Cox
Eleanor D. Craig
Joanna Cruse
John P. Cullity
Thomas Curtis
Andrew J. Dane
Mahmoud Davoudi
Edward Dennis
Carol Dimamro
William Dougherty
Barry Duman
Diane Dumont
Floyd Durham
G. B. Duwaji
James A. Dyal

Ishita Edwards
Robert P. Edwards
Alan E. Ellis
Mike Ellis
Frank Emerson
Zaki Eusufzai
John L. Ewing-Smith
Frank Falero
Frank Fato
Grant Ferguson
David Fletcher
James Foley
John Foreman
Ralph G. Fowler
Arthur Friedberg
Peter Frost
E. Gabriel
Steve Gardner
Peter C. Garlick
Alexander Garvin
Joe Garwood
J. P. Gilbert
Otis Gilley
Frank Glesber
Jack Goddard
Allen C. Goodman
Richard J. Gosselin
Gary Greene
Nicholas Grunt
William Gunther
Demos Hadjiyanis
Martin D. Haney
Mehdi Haririan
Ray Harvey
E. L. Hazlett

Sanford B. Helman
John Hensel
Robert Herman
Gus W. Herring
Charles Hill
John M. Hill
Morton Hirsch
Benjamin Hitchner
R. Bradley Hoppes
James Horner
Grover Howard
Nancy Howe-Ford
R. Jack Inch
Christopher Inya
Tomotaka Ishimine
E. E. Jarvis
Parvis Jenab
S. D. Jevremovic
J. Paul Jewell
Frederick Johnson
David Jones
Lamar B. Jones
Paul A. Joray
Daniel A. Joseph
Craig Justice
Septimus Kai Kai
Devajyoti Kataky
Timothy R. Keely
Ziad Keilany
Norman F. Keiser
Randall G. Kesselring
E. D. Key
M. Barbara Killen
Bruce Kimzey
Philip G. King

Terrence Kinal
E. R. Kittrell
David Klingman
Charles Knapp
Jerry Knarr
Janet Koscianski
Peter Kressler
Michael Kupilik
Larry Landrum
Margaret Landman
Keith Langford
Anthony T. Lee
George Lieu
Stephen E. Lile
Lawrence W. Lovick
Warren T. Matthews
Robert McAuliffe
Howard J. McBride
Bruce McClung
John McDowell
E. S. McKuskey
James L. McLain
John L. Madden
Mary Lou Madden
Glen Marston
John M. Martin
Paul J. Mascotti
James D. Mason
Paul M. Mason
Tom Mathew
Warren Matthews
G. Hartley Mellish
Mike Melvin
Dan C. Messerschmidt

Herbert C. Milikien
Joel C. Millonzi
Glenn Milner
Thomas Molloy
Margaret D. Moore
William E. Morgan
Stephen Morrell
Irving Morrissett
James W. Moser
Martin F. Murray
George L. Nagy
Jerome Neadly
James E. Needham
Claron Nelson
Douglas Nettleton
Gerald T. O'Boyle
Lucian T. Orlowski
Diane S. Osborne
Jan Palmer
Gerald Parker
Randall E. Parker
Raymond A. Pepin
Martin M. Perline
Timothy Perri
Jerry Petr
Maurice Pfannesteil
James Phillips
Raymond J. Phillips
I. James Pickl
Dennis Placone
William L. Polvent
Reneé Prim
Robert W. Pulsinelli
Rod D. Raehsler
Kambriz Raffiee

Sandra Rahman
John Rapp
Gautam
    Raychaudhuri
Ron Reddall
Mitchell Redlo
Charles Reichhelu
Robert S. Rippey
Ray C. Roberts
Richard Romano
Duane Rosa
Richard Rosenberg
Larry Ross
Barbara Ross-Pfeiffer
Philip Rothman

John Roufagalas
Patricia Sanderson
Thomas N. Schaap
William A. Schaeffer
William Schaniel
David Schauer
A. C. Schlenker
Scott J. Schroeder
William Scott
Dan Segebarth
Robert Sexton
Augustus Shackelford
Richard Sherman Jr.
Liang-rong Shiau
David Shorow

Vishwa Shukla
R. J. Sidwell
David E. Sisk
Alden Smith
Howard F. Smith
Lynn A. Smith
Phil Smith
Steve Smith
William Doyle Smith
Lee Spector
George Spiva
Richard L. Sprinkle
Herbert F. Steeper
William Stine
Allen D. Stone

Osman Suliman
J. M. Sullivan
Rebecca Summary
Joseph L. Swaffar
Frank D. Taylor
Daniel Teferra
Gary Theige
Robert P. Thomas
Deborah Thorsen
Richard Trieff
George Troxler
William T. Trulove
William N. Trumbull
Arianne K. Turner
John Vahaly

Jim VanBeek
Lee J. Van Scyoc
Roy Van Til
Robert F. Wallace
Henry C. Wallich
Milledge Weathers
Robert G. Welch
Terence West
Wylie Whalthall
Everett E. White
Michael D. White
Mark A. Wilkening
Raburn M. Williams
James Willis
George Wilson

Travis Wilson
Ken Woodward
Peter R. Wyman
Whitney Yamamura
Donald Yankovic
Alex Yguado
Alex A. Yguado
Paul Young
Shik Young
Mohammed Zaheer
Ed Zajicek
William J. Zimmer Jr.

No author alone can complete a new large-scale revision of a textbook. I was helped by a hard-working group of people, from start to finish. My editor at Addison Wesley, Denise Clinton, provided assistance in all aspects of this project. My developmental editor, Mary Draper, helped me make many important decisions about the direction of this revision. She also managed many of the new supplements and the revisions of old. Deborah Kiernan saw to the production details for each and every print supplement, as did Melissa Honig for all of the multimedia supplements, including the major task of getting the CD-ROM out on time and without errors. My production editor, Nancy Fenton, probably spent more time talking, faxing, and e-mailing me than she would have preferred, but the results are certainly worth all of her efforts, I believe. My long-time copy editor, Bruce Emmer, came through again and made my prose as smooth as possible. To the above-mentioned Addison-Wesley team members and all of the others who have helped me, I thank you and look forward to working with you again.

Many of my colleagues worked with me intimately in redoing or providing new important supplements. Dan Benjamin updated the *Internet Activities* as well as added ones for each of the 35 new *Issues and Applications*. David VanHoose worked tirelessly on the new interactive CD-ROM and finished it on time in the face of time-consuming technical issues. Andy Dane again made masterful changes in the *Instructor's Manual* and the *Lecture Outlines with Transparency Masters*. Steve Smith, Jeff Caldwell, and Mark Mitchell came up with an incredibly useful PowerPoint presentation system for this edition. Randall Parker worked tirelessly on new test questions and revisions of old. Denise Hazlett provided a state-of-the-art active learning guide to go along with this edition. To these professors I extend a special note of appreciation.

As always, I wish to thank Sue Jasin of K&M Consulting for her expert manuscript preparation as well as camera-ready copy for some of the supplements.

Keeping with the cyberage, and because I always enjoy reading suggestions about what to do in future editions, you and your students can contact me directly via my Web site at: **www.econtoday.com**

Roger LeRoy Miller

ECONOMIC PRINCIPLES IN PRACTICE

Chapter-Opening Issues.   Each Chapter-Opening Issue motivates student interest in the key chapter concepts with student-friendly examples.

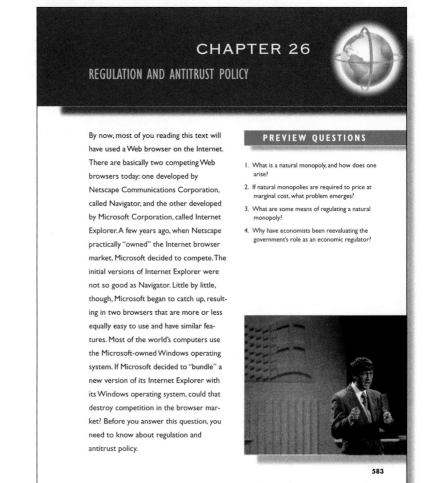

CHAPTER 26

REGULATION AND ANTITRUST POLICY

By now, most of you reading this text will have used a Web browser on the Internet. There are basically two competing Web browsers today: one developed by Netscape Communications Corporation, called Navigator, and the other developed by Microsoft Corporation, called Internet Explorer. A few years ago, when Netscape practically "owned" the Internet browser market, Microsoft decided to compete. The initial versions of Internet Explorer were not so good as Navigator. Little by little, though, Microsoft began to catch up, resulting in two browsers that are more or less equally easy to use and have similar features. Most of the world's computers use the Microsoft-owned Windows operating system. If Microsoft decided to "bundle" a new version of its Internet Explorer with its Windows operating system, could that destroy competition in the browser market? Before you answer this question, you need to know about regulation and antitrust policy.

PREVIEW QUESTIONS

1. What is a natural monopoly, and how does one arise?
2. If natural monopolies are required to price at marginal cost, what problem emerges?
3. What are some means of regulating a natural monopoly?
4. Why have economists been reevaluating the government's role as an economic regulator?

583

Issues and Applications.   Each Issues and Applications feature is linked to the Chapter-Opening Issue and is designed to encourage students to apply economic concepts and think critically about those concepts. Each begins with the concepts being applied and is followed by several critical thinking questions that may be used to prompt in-class discussion. You will find suggested answers to the critical thinking questions in the Instructor's Manual.

Microsoft CEO Bill Gates has had to defend himself in recent years against federal charges of attempting to monopolize the Internet browser market. Is it possible for any one company to have a monopoly in electronic commerce?

ISSUES AND APPLICATIONS

The Justice Department Goes After Microsoft Again

CONCEPTS APPLIED:
COMPETITION, MONOPOLY, MARKET POWER, ANTITRUST LAW

 Visit www.econtoday.com for an Internet Activity that expands your understanding of these concepts.

Microsoft has been engaged in a head-to-head battle for dominance in the Internet browser market. As

stated that the Justice Department has to look to the future. In other words, the Justice Depart-

Thinking Critically About the Media. Thinking Critically About the Media offers a twist on typical news reporting and encourages students to think critically about what they hear reported in the news. These boxed features also keep students abreast of recent news-making issues. See page 48.

Policy Examples. Many of the economic discussions presented by the media involve important policy issues. In the 1999–2000 Edition, students are exposed to important policy questions on both the domestic and international fronts in over 30 Policy Examples.

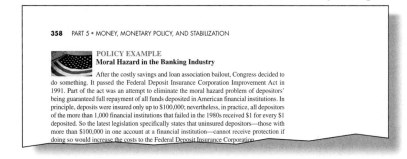

358 PART 5 • MONEY, MONETARY POLICY, AND STABILIZATION

POLICY EXAMPLE
Moral Hazard in the Banking Industry

After the costly savings and loan association bailout, Congress decided to do something. It passed the Federal Deposit Insurance Corporation Improvement Act in 1991. Part of the act was an attempt to eliminate the moral hazard problem of depositors' being guaranteed full repayment of all funds deposited in American financial institutions. In principle, deposits were insured only up to $100,000; nevertheless, in practice, all depositors of the more than 1,000 financial institutions that failed in the 1980s received $1 for every $1 deposited. So the latest legislation specifically states that uninsured depositors—those with more than $100,000 in one account at a financial institution—cannot receive protection if doing so would increase the costs to the Federal Deposit Insurance Corporation.

A World Of Global Examples. Over 50 international examples emphasize today's global economy.

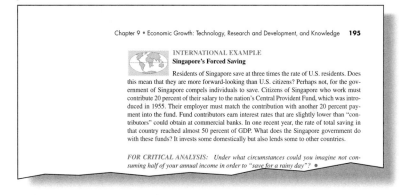

Chapter 9 • Economic Growth: Technology, Research and Development, and Knowledge **195**

INTERNATIONAL EXAMPLE
Singapore's Forced Saving

Residents of Singapore save at three times the rate of U.S. residents. Does this mean that they are more forward-looking than U.S. citizens? Perhaps not, for the government of Singapore compels individuals to save. Citizens of Singapore who work must contribute 20 percent of their salary to the nation's Central Provident Fund, which was introduced in 1955. Their employer must match the contribution with another 20 percent payment into the fund. Fund contributors earn interest rates that are slightly lower than "contributors" could obtain at commercial banks. In one recent year, the rate of total saving in that country reached almost 50 percent of GDP. What does the Singapore government do with these funds? It invests some domestically but also lends some to other countries.

FOR CRITICAL ANALYSIS: *Under what circumstances could you imagine not consuming half of your annual income in order to "save for a rainy day"?* ●

Examples Closer to Home. More than 50 thought-provoking and relevant examples highlight U.S. current events and demonstrate economic principles.

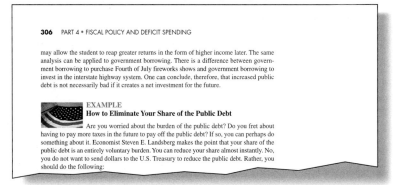

306 PART 4 • FISCAL POLICY AND DEFICIT SPENDING

may allow the student to reap greater returns in the form of higher income later. The same analysis can be applied to government borrowing. There is a difference between government borrowing to purchase Fourth of July fireworks shows and government borrowing to invest in the interstate highway system. One can conclude, therefore, that increased public debt is not necessarily bad if it creates a net investment for the future.

EXAMPLE
How to Eliminate Your Share of the Public Debt

Are you worried about the burden of the public debt? Do you fret about having to pay more taxes in the future to pay off the public debt? If so, you can perhaps do something about it. Economist Steven E. Landsberg makes the point that your share of the public debt is an entirely voluntary burden. You can reduce your share almost instantly. No, you do not want to send dollars to the U.S. Treasury to reduce the public debt. Rather, you should do the following:

ALL NEW! Issues and Applications. Continuing a hallmark tradition, the 1999–2000 Edition of *Economics Today* includes 35 new Issues and Applications features, one at the end of each chapter. These features encourage students to apply economic concepts and to think critically about how they apply those concepts in everyday life. Each is supported by new suggested Internet Activities that will permit students to continue their exploration.

NEW! Full Chapter on Cybernomics. How do technological innovations change economic theory? The new Chapter 35, beginning on page 775, explores how the Information Age affects our study of economics.

NEW! Internet Activities. In every chapter, students have the option of going online to build research skills and reinforce their understanding of economics concepts. The Internet Activities were written by Daniel K. Benjamin of Clemson University. When you see this icon in the margin of the text, go to **www.econtoday.com** to gain more insights into related issues.

Exercise 7.2
Visit www.econtoday.com for more about the CPI.

NEW! Cyberspace Examples. Today's "wired" students learn and benefit from advances in technology. New Cyberspace Examples demonstrate the significant impact of technology on our economic choices.

---

334 PART 5 • MONEY, MONETARY POLICY, AND STABILIZATION

7. *The Fed regulates the money supply.* Perhaps the Fed's most important task is its ability to regulate the nation's money supply. To understand how the Fed manages the money supply, we must examine more closely its reserve-holding function and the way in which depository institutions aid in expansion and contraction of the money supply. We will do this in Chapter 16.

FORCED INTO ELECTRONIC BANKING BY THE GOVERNMENT

The federal government is making cyberbanking, or at least a small part of it, a reality for millions of Americans. In an attempt to save on transaction costs, it is trying to force all recipients of federal funds to receive payments electronically, rather than by paper checks. For example, it is attempting to force military contractors who receive millions of dollars, as well as Social Security recipients who receive only thousands of dollars, to have those deposits made directly into their bank accounts. The goal is to eliminate all paper checks, at an estimated savings of over $500 million during the period 1999 to 2004.

Consider that the federal government makes over 850 million individual payments a year. Until recently, about half were made with paper checks, which cost 42 cents each to process, compared to electronic direct deposits, which cost only 2 cents. To achieve some of these savings, the federal government is turning to the E-Pay network of Visa U.S.A. Companies that receive federal payments must install software that they obtain from Visa. When many companies have the same software, they will surely start settling private trans-

The 1999–2000 Edition of *Economics Today* highlights the dramatic changes technology has made to the economic landscape. Fresh, new examples throughout the chapters bring relevance to the changing world of economics.

Current Data. Every chart, table, and graph in the book has been updated to reflect the most recent data available.

NEW! www.econtoday.com. The *Economics Today* web site provides on-line access to innovative teaching and learning tools.

- The Weekly Student Quiz tests students' understanding of key concepts. After completing each multiple-choice quiz, students quickly receive quiz results and are guided to appropriate sections of the text if they need further study.
- The Practice Exam is designed to test students' readiness for a midterm or final exam. The Practice Exam offers immediate test results and suggestions for students on how to improve their grades.
- Nearly 100 Internet Activities, organized by chapter and referenced with an icon in the margins of the text, will build students' research skills and reinforce key concepts. The Internet Activities can be accessed from the PowerPoint Lecture Presentations for in-class or group discussion.
- Ask the Author gives professors and students immediate access to Roger L. Miller to ask questions and give feedback on the text or supplements.
- All the URLs from Interacting with the Internet are kept current and organized by chapter.

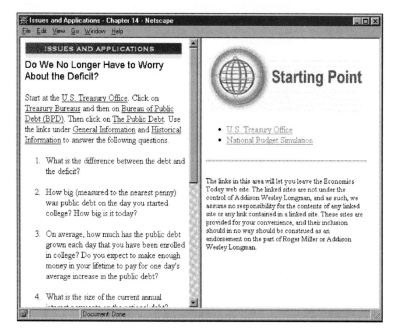

NEW! **Economics in Action 1999–2000 CD-ROM.** This interactive tutorial software has been developed by Michael Parkin and Robin Bade of the University of Western Ontario and adapted by David VanHoose of the University of Alabama for use with *Economics Today.* Already used by thousands of introductory economics students, Economics in Action uses dynamic graphs, sound effects, and step-by-step tutorials to guide students in their discovery of relationships between economic theory and real-world applications.

- Graphs from the textbook are re-created for more in-depth exploration and analysis.
- Economic data are presented in shifting curves and dynamic graphical output.
- Detailed, customizable quizzes help students prepare for exams and test their knowledge.

PEDAGOGY WITH PURPOSE

The 1999–2000 Edition of *Economics Today, The Micro View* is loaded with time-tested pedagody that helps students apply what they learn.

For Critical Analysis. At the end of each example, students are asked to "think like economists" and answer the "For Critical Analysis" questions. The answers to all questions are found in the Instructor's Manual. See page 53.

Did You Know That...? Each chapter starts with a provocative question to engage students and lead them into the content of the chapter.

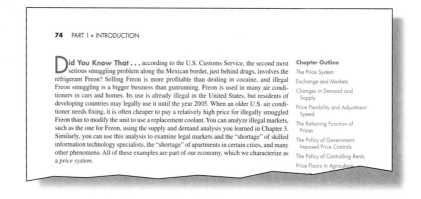

Preview Questions. On the first page of each chapter, several questions are posed and then fully answered at the end of the chapter. See page 733.

Graphs. Articulate and precise, the four-color graphs illustrate key concepts.

Key Terms. Key terms are printed in bold type and defined in the margin of the text the first time they appear.

Concepts in Brief. At the end of each major section, Concepts in Brief summarizes the main points of the section to reinforce and test learning.

Chapter Summary. Every chapter ends with a concise but thorough summary of the important ideas of the chapter.

Problems. A variety of problems support each chapter, and answers for all odd-numbered problems are provided at the back of the textbook.

EXPANSIVE, INNOVATIVE TEACHING/LEARNING PACKAGE

FOR THE INSTRUCTOR

NEW! **Instructor's Resource Disk (IRD) with PowerPoint Lecture Presentation.** The PowerPoint Lecture Presentation is available for Windows 95 and Macintosh computers—all on one IRD. The Power-Point Lecture Presentation was developed by Jeff Caldwell, Steve Smith, and Mark Mitchell of Rose State College. With nearly 100 slides per chapter, the PowerPoint Lecture Presentation animates graphs from the text; outlines key terms, concepts, and figures; and provides direct links to **www.econtoday.com** for in-class Internet Activities. The IRD also includes the Instructor's Manual in a Word file.

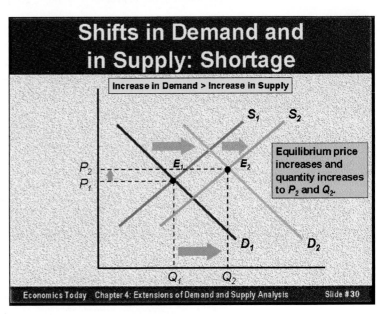

NEW! **Economic Experiments in the Classroom.** These economic experiments were developed by Denise Hazlett of Whitman College to involve students in actively testing economic theory. In addition to providing a variety of micro and macro experiments, this new supplement offers step-by-step guidelines for successfully running experiments in the classroom.

NEW! **www.econtoday.com.** The *Economics Today* Web site provides on-line access to innovative teaching and learning tools. The Weekly Student Quiz and Practice Midterm Exams test students' understanding of key concepts and directs them to appropriate sections of the text for further study. Students and professors have instant access to the author to share feedback, offer suggestions, and ask questions. Internet Activities, organized by chapter, are designed to build student research skills and reinforce key concepts.

Pocket Guide to Economics Today for Printed and Electronic Supplements. This pocket guide is designed to coordinate the extensive teaching/learning package that accompanies the 1999–2000 Edition of *Economics Today*. For each chapter heading, the author has organized a list of print and electronic ancillaries with page references to help organize lectures, develop class assignments, and prepare examinations.

Instructor's Manual. Prepared by Andrew J. Dane of Angelo State University, the Instructor's Manual provides the following instructor materials, three-hole-punched for easy insertion into the Instructor's Binder.

- Chapter overviews, objectives, and outlines
- Points to emphasize for those who wish to stress theory
- Answers to Issues and Applications critical thinking questions
- Further questions for class discussion
- Answers to even-numbered end-of-chapter problems
- Detailed step-by-step analysis of end-of-chapter problems
- Annotated answers to selected Student Learning Questions
- Selected references

The 1999–2000 Edition is at the forefront of teac
with a broad spectrum of support, from traditi
materials to the latest integrated classroom technologies.

Lecture Outlines with Transparency Masters. Prepared by Andrew J. Dane of Angelo State University, this lecture system features more than 500 pages of lecture outlines and text illustrations, including numerous tables taken from the text. Its pages can be made into transparencies or handouts to assist student note taking.

Four-color Overhead Transparencies. One hundred of the most important tables and graphs from the textbook are reproduced as full-color transparency acetates. Many contain multiple overlays.

Test Bank One. This test bank provides over 3,000 multiple-choice questions with answers. It has been developed by Susan G. Mason. The questions have been extensively classroom-tested for a number of years. Randall Parker of East Carolina University enhanced each of the three test banks with questions that cover the new Cybernomics chapter.

Test Bank Two. John Lunn of Hope College developed Test Bank Two, which includes over 3,000 multiple-choice questions. These questions have been class-tested by many professors, including Clark G. Ross, coauthor of the National Competency Test for economics majors for the Educational Testing Service in Princeton, New Jersey.

Short Essay Test Bank. As an alternative to the multiple-choice questions presented in the Test Banks One and Two, this completely separate test bank, developed by John Lunn of Hope College, provides short-answer essay questions.

NEW! Computerized Test Banks. The test banks are also available in Test Generator Software (TestGen-EQ with QuizMaster-EQ). Fully networkable, this software is available for Windows and Macintosh. TestGen-EQ's friendly graphical interface enables instructors to easily view, edit, and add questions; transfer questions to tests; and print tests in a variety of fonts and forms. Search and sort features let the instructor quickly locate questions and arrange them in a preferred order. QuizMaster-EQ automatically grades the exams, stores results on disk, and allows the instructor to view or print a variety of reports. Ask your publisher's representative for information about our test preparation service.

Economic Video Series. A series of micro and macro videotapes are available based on the award-winning MacNeil/Lehrer business reports. Each segment is reported by Paul Solman, MacNeil/Lehrer's special business correspondent.

The macroeconomics videotapes include

- Numbers Crunching
- Balance Act
- Productivity: Man or Machine
- Boom or Bust
- Budget Scoring
- The S&L Crisis: In Irreverent History
- Making Sense of the Sanctum
- European Currency Crisis
- Steering the Course
- What's the Dollar Worth: The Pros and Cons of Devaluation

The microeconomics videotapes include

- Trade-Off: NAFTA
- Heated Up
- Second Look: Prices and Profits
- Taxing or Energizing?
- Beer Wars?
- Special Delivery: Attempt to Unionize Bicycle Messengers in New York
- Factory Fight
- Tax Cutters: Report on Middle Income Americans
- A Fish Story

Additional Homework Problems.   For each chapter of the text, more than 20 additional homework problems are provided for homework or in-class assignments in two separate and distinct sets of reproducible homework assignments, Set A and Set B. Many problems involve working with graphs. Written by Eirik Evenhouse and Siobhan Reilly, both of Vanderbilt University, each homework problem is accompanied by suggested answers and is three-hole-punched for insertion into the Instructor's Binder.

Regional Case Studies for the East Coast, Texas, and California.   Additional case studies, available in either East Coast, Texas, or California versions, can be used for in-class team exercises or for additional homework assignments.

NEW! Student Study Notes for PowerPoint Lecture Presentation. Developed by Jeff Caldwell of Rose State College, the Student Study Notes provide students with an individualized note-taking and study device designed to be used in conjunction with the PowerPoint Lecture Presentation.

Study Guide. Available in micro, macro, and complete versions, the Study Guide has been written by the author and includes the following sections:

- Putting the chapter into perspective
- Learning objectives
- Chapter outlines
- Key terms
- Key concepts
- Completion questions
- True-or-false questions
- Multiple-choice questions
- Problems
- Matching questions
- Further notes on working with graphs
- Case studies
- Glossary of terms defined exactly as in the textbook
- Answers to problems and questions

Your Economic Life. This free booklet is provided with every purchase of *Economics Today*. It is a student guide to economics' practical applications. In this guide, the author takes students through practical problems in the world today to help them see the application of economics to everyday life and to help them analyze economic news.

ET Computer-Assisted Instruction. Prepared by Daniel K. Benjamin of Clemson University, this free student software presents additional problems and learning modules for nearly all chapters in the text. The software contains interactive problems and computer-assisted instruction as indicated by the following icon in each chapter. Check out **www.econtoday.com** for more details.

Economics Today

The Micro View

1999–2000 EDITION

PART 1

INTRODUCTION

CHAPTER 1

THE NATURE OF ECONOMICS

Woody Allen once said, "Money is better than poverty, if only for financial reasons." Yet who has not heard or even said that "money cannot buy happiness"? Such a statement seems to pose problems for the study of economics. As you will see, economics does deal with people's quest for money or, more correctly, for wealth. Is it possible to study economics even if "money doesn't buy happiness"? You will find out as you read about the nature of economics in this introductory chapter.

PREVIEW QUESTIONS

1. What is the difference between microeconomics and macroeconomics?
2. What role does rational self-interest play in economic analysis?
3. Why is the study of economics a science?
4. What is the difference between positive and normative economics?

Did You Know That . . . since 1989, the number of fax machines in U.S. offices and homes has increased by over 10,000 percent? During the same time period, the number of bike messengers in downtown New York City *decreased* by over 65 percent. The world around us is definitely changing. Much of that change is due to the dramatically falling cost of communications and information technology. By 2002, the computers inside video games will cost only about $100 yet will have 50 times the processing power that a $10 million IBM mainframe had in 1975. Not surprisingly, since the start of the 1990s, American firms have been spending more on communications equipment and computers than on new construction and heavy machinery.

Cyberspace, the Internet, the World Wide Web—call it what you want, but your next home (if not your current one) will almost certainly have an address on it. The percentage of U.S. households that have at least one telephone is close to 100 percent, and those that have video game players is over 50 percent. Over 42 percent of homes have personal computers, and more than half of those machines are set up to receive and access information via phone lines. Your decisions about such things as when and what type of computer to buy, whether to accept a collect call from a friend traveling in Europe, and how much time you should invest in learning to use the latest Web browser involve an untold number of variables: where you live, the work your parents do, what your friends think, and so on. But, as you will see, there are economic underpinnings for nearly all the decisions you make.

THE POWER OF ECONOMIC ANALYSIS

Knowing that an economic problem exists every time you make a decision is not enough. You also have to develop a framework that will allow you to analyze solutions to each economic problem—whether you are trying to decide how much to study, which courses to take, whether to finish school, or whether America should send troops abroad or raise tariffs. The framework that you will learn in this text is based on the *economic way of thinking.*

This framework gives you power—the power to reach informed conclusions about what is happening in the world. You can, of course, live your life without the power of economic analysis as part of your analytical framework. Indeed, most people do. But economists believe that economic analysis can help you make better decisions concerning your career, your education, financing your home, and other important areas. In the business world, the power of economic analysis can help you increase your competitive edge as an employee or as the owner of a business. As a voter, for the rest of your life you will be asked to make judgments about policies that are advocated by a particular political party. Many of these policies will deal with questions related to international economics, such as whether the U.S. government should encourage or discourage immigration, prevent foreigners from investing in domestic TV stations and newspapers, or restrict other countries from selling their goods here. Finally, just as taking an art, music, or literature appreciation class increases the pleasure you receive when you view paintings, listen to concerts, or read novels, taking an economics course will increase your understanding when watching the news on TV or reading the newspaper.

DEFINING ECONOMICS

What is economics exactly? Some cynics have defined *economics* as "common sense made difficult." But common sense, by definition, should be within everyone's grasp. You will encounter in the following pages numerous examples that show that economics is, in fact, pure and simple common sense.

Economics
The study of how people allocate their limited resources to satisfy their unlimited wants.

Economics is part of the social sciences and as such seeks explanations of real events. All social sciences analyze human behavior, as opposed to the physical sciences, which generally analyze the behavior of electrons, atoms, and other nonhuman phenomena.

> **Economics is the study of how people allocate their limited resources in an attempt to satisfy their unlimited wants. As such, economics is the study of how people make choices.**

To understand this definition fully, two other words need explaining: *resources* and *wants*. **Resources** are things that have value and, more specifically, are used to produce things that satisfy people's wants. **Wants** are all of the things that people would consume if they had unlimited income.

Resources
Things used to produce other things to satisfy people's wants.

Wants
What people would buy if their incomes were unlimited.

Whenever an individual, a business, or a nation faces alternatives, a choice must be made, and economics helps us study how those choices are made. For example, you have to choose how to spend your limited income. You also have to choose how to spend your limited time. You may have to choose how much of your company's limited funds to spend on advertising and how much to spend on new-product research. In economics, we examine situations in which individuals choose how to do things, when to do things, and with whom to do them. Ultimately, the purpose of economics is to explain choices.

MICROECONOMICS VERSUS MACROECONOMICS

Economics is typically divided into two types of analysis: **microeconomics** and **macroeconomics.**

Microeconomics
The study of decision making undertaken by individuals (or households) and by firms.

> **Microeconomics is the part of economic analysis that studies decision making undertaken by individuals (or households) and by firms. It is like looking through a microscope to focus on the small parts of our economy.**

> **Macroeconomics is the part of economic analysis that studies the behavior of the economy as a whole. It deals with economywide phenomena such as changes in unemployment, the general price level, and national income.**

Macroeconomics
The study of the behavior of the economy as a whole, including such economywide phenomena as changes in unemployment, the general price level, and national income.

Microeconomic analysis, for example, is concerned with the effects of changes in the price of gasoline relative to that of other energy sources. It examines the effects of new taxes on a specific product or industry. If price controls were reinstituted in the United States, how individual firms and consumers would react to them would be in the realm of microeconomics. The raising of wages by an effective union strike would also be analyzed using the tools of microeconomics.

By contrast, issues such as the rate of inflation, the amount of economywide unemployment, and the yearly growth in the output of goods and services in the nation all fall into the realm of macroeconomic analysis. In other words, macroeconomics deals with **aggregates,** or totals—such as total output in an economy.

Aggregates
Total amounts or quantities; aggregate demand, for example, is total planned expenditures throughout a nation.

Be aware, however, of the blending of microeconomics and macroeconomics in modern economic theory. Modern economists are increasingly using microeconomic analysis—the study of decision making by individuals and by firms—as the basis of macroeconomic analysis. They do this because even though in macroeconomic analysis aggregates are being examined, those aggregates are made up of individuals and firms.

THE ECONOMIC PERSON: RATIONAL SELF-INTEREST

Exercise 1.1
Visit www.econtoday.com for more about the national economy.

Economists assume that individuals act *as if* motivated by self-interest and respond predictably to opportunities for gain. This central insight of economics was first clearly articulated by Adam Smith in 1776. Smith wrote in his most famous book, *An Inquiry into the*

Nature and Causes of the Wealth of Nations, that "it is not from the benevolence of the butcher, the brewer, or the baker that we expect our dinner, but from their regard to their own interest." Otherwise stated, the typical person about whom economists make behavioral predictions is assumed to look out for his or her own self-interest in a rational manner. Because monetary benefits and costs of actions are often the most easily measured, economists most often make behavioral predictions about individuals' responses to ways to increase their wealth, measured in money terms. Let's see if we can apply the theory of rational self-interest to explain an anomaly concerning the makeup of the U.S. population.

Exercise 1.2
Visit www.econtoday.com
for more about your home state.

EXAMPLE
The Increasing Native American Population

Look at Figure 1-1. You see that the proportion of Native Americans increased quite dramatically from 1970 to 1990. Can we use Adam Smith's ideas to understand why so many Native Americans have decided to rejoin their tribes? Perhaps. Consider the benefits of being a member of the Mdewakanton *(bday-WAH-kan-toon),* a tribe of about 100 that runs a casino in which in a recent year gamblers wagered over $500 million. Each member of the tribe received over $400,000. There is now a clear economic reason for Native Americans to return home. Over 200 of the nation's 544 tribes have introduced gambling of some sort, and almost half of those have big-time casinos. Reservations are grossing almost $6 billion a year from gaming. Tribe members sometimes get direct payments and others get the benefits of better health care, subsidized mortgages, and jobs. Self-identified Native Americans increased in number by 137 percent between 1970 and 1990.

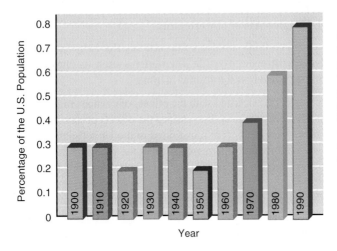

FIGURE 1-1

Native American Population of the United States, 1900–1990
The percentage of the U.S. population identifying itself as Native American has increased substantially in recent decades. Is there an economic explanation for this demographic trend?

FOR CRITICAL ANALYSIS: What nonmonetary reasons are there for Native Americans to rejoin their tribes? ●

The Rationality Assumption

The **rationality assumption** of economics, simply stated, is as follows:

We assume that individuals do not intentionally make decisions that would leave them worse off.

Rationality assumption
The assumption that people do not intentionally make decisions that would leave them worse off.

The distinction here is between what people may think—the realm of psychology and psychiatry and perhaps sociology—and what they do. Economics does *not* involve itself in analyzing individual or group thought processes. Economics looks at what people actually do in life with their limited resources. It does little good to criticize the rationality assumption by stating, "Nobody thinks that way" or "I never think that way" or "How unrealistic! That's as irrational as anyone can get!"

Take the example of driving. When you consider passing another car on a two-lane highway with oncoming traffic, you have to make very quick decisions: You must estimate the speed of the car that you are going to pass, the speed of the oncoming cars, the distance between your car and the oncoming cars, and your car's potential rate of acceleration. If we were to apply a model to your behavior, we would use the laws of calculus. In actual fact, you and most other drivers in such a situation do not actually think of using the laws of calculus, but to predict your behavior, we could make the prediction *as if* you understood the laws of calculus.

In any event, when you observe behavior around you, what may seem irrational often has its basis in the rationality assumption, as you can see by the following example.

EXAMPLE
When It Is Rational *Not* to Learn New Technology

The standard young person's view of older people (particularly one's parents) is that they're reluctant to learn new things. The saying "You can't teach an old dog new tricks" seems to apply. Young people, in contrast, seem eager to learn about new technology—mastering computers and multimedia, playing interactive games, surfing the Internet. But there is a rational reason for older people's reduced willingness to learn new technologies. If you are 20 years old and learn a new skill, you will be able to gain returns from your investment in learning over the course of many decades. If you are 60, however, and invest the same amount of time and effort learning the same skill, you will almost certainly not be able to reap those returns for as long a time period. Hence it is perfectly rational for "old dogs" not to want to learn new tricks.

FOR CRITICAL ANALYSIS: Some older people do learn to use new technologies as they emerge. What might explain this behavior? ●

Responding to Incentives

If it can be assumed that individuals never intentionally make decisions that would leave them worse off, then almost by definition they will respond to different incentives. We define **incentives** as the potential rewards available if a particular activity is undertaken. Indeed, much of human behavior can be explained in terms of how individuals respond to changing incentives over time.

Incentives
Rewards for engaging in a particular activity.

Schoolchildren are motivated to do better by a variety of incentive systems, ranging from gold stars and certificates of achievement when they are young to better grades with accompanying promises of a "better life" as they get older. There are, of course, negative incentives that affect our behavior, too. Children who disrupt the class are given after-school detention or sent to the vice principal for other punishment.

Implicitly, people react to changing incentives after they have done some sort of rough comparison of the costs and benefits of various courses of action. In fact, making rational choices invariably involves balancing costs and benefits.

The linked concepts of incentive and costs and benefits can be used to explain seeming anomalies in the world around us.

INTERNATIONAL EXAMPLE
Why Are There So Few Whiplash Complaints in Lithuania?

Rear-end car collisions occur about as frequently in the country of Lithuania as they do in the rest of the world. Curiously, chronic whiplash, or whiplash syndrome, appears to be unknown there. In the United States, auto accident victims commonly complain of whiplash, sometimes years after the accidents. In Norway, which has a population of only 4.2 million, over 70,000 people currently claim chronic disability because of whiplash.

What accounts for such differences in whiplash rate across countries? One answer relates to the potential payoff to auto accident victims from claiming such injuries. In Lithuania, personal injury insurance is virtually nonexistent. As a result, no money can be won from an insurance company because of a diagnosis of whiplash. By contrast, in Norway, in the United States, and elsewhere, significant financial settlements can be obtained through such claims.

FOR CRITICAL ANALYSIS: Does the fact that there are few reported claims of whiplash in Lithuania necessarily mean that headaches and lingering neck pains after being rear-ended do not occur in that country? ●

Defining Self-Interest

Self-interest does not always mean increasing one's wealth measured in dollars and cents. We assume that individuals seek many goals, not just increased wealth measured in monetary terms. Thus the self-interest part of our economic-person assumption includes goals relating to prestige, friendship, love, power, helping others, creating works of art, and many other matters. We can also think in terms of enlightened self-interest whereby individuals, in the pursuit of what makes them better off, also achieve the betterment of others around them. In brief, individuals are assumed to want the right to further their goals by making decisions about how things around them are used. The head of a charitable organization usually will not turn down an additional contribution, because accepting it lets that person control how that money is used, even if it is always for other people's benefit.

Otherwise stated, charitable acts are not ruled out by self-interest. Giving gifts to relatives can be considered a form of charity that is nonetheless in the self-interest of the giver. But how efficient is such gift giving?

EXAMPLE
The Perceived Value of Gifts

Every holiday season, aunts, uncles, grandparents, mothers, and fathers give gifts to their college-aged loved ones. Joel Waldfogel, an economist at Yale University, surveyed several thousand college students after Christmas to find out the value of holiday gifts. He found that compact discs and outerwear (coats and jackets) had a perceived intrinsic value about equal to their actual cash equivalent. By the time he got down the list to socks, underwear, and cosmetics, the students' valuation was only about 85 percent of the cash value of the gift. He found out that aunts, uncles, and grandparents gave the "worst" gifts and friends, siblings, and parents gave the "best."

FOR CRITICAL ANALYSIS: What argument could you use against the idea of substituting cash or gift certificates for physical gifts? ●

CONCEPTS IN BRIEF

- Economics is a social science that involves the study of how individuals choose among alternatives to satisfy their wants, which are what people would buy if their incomes were unlimited.

- Microeconomics, the study of the decision-making processes of individuals (or households) and firms, and macroeconomics, the study of the performance of the economy as a whole, are the two main branches into which the study of economics is divided.

- In economics, we assume that people do not intentionally make decisions that will leave them worse off. This is known as the rationality assumption.

- Self-interest is not confined to material well-being but also involves any action that makes a person feel better off, such as having more friends, love, power, affection, or providing more help to others.

ECONOMICS AS A SCIENCE

Models, or theories
Simplified representations of the real world used as the basis for predictions or explanations.

Economics is a social science that makes use of the same kinds of methods used in other sciences, such as biology, physics, and chemistry. Similar to these other sciences, economics uses models, or theories. Economic **models, or theories,** are simplified representations of the real world that we use to help us understand, explain, and predict economic phenomena in the real world. There are, of course, differences between sciences. The social sciences—especially economics—make little use of laboratory methods in which changes in variables can be explained under controlled conditions. Rather, social scientists, and especially economists, usually have to examine what has already happened in the real world in order to test their models, or theories.

Models and Realism

At the outset it must be emphasized that no model in *any* science, and therefore no economic model, is complete in the sense that it captures *every* detail or interrelationship that exists. Indeed, a model, by definition, is an abstraction from reality. It is conceptually impossible to construct a perfectly complete realistic model. For example, in physics we cannot account for every molecule and its position and certainly not for every atom and subparticle. Not only is such a model impossibly expensive to build, but working with it would be impossibly complex.

The nature of scientific model building is such that the model should capture only the *essential* relationships that are sufficient to analyze the particular problem or answer the particular question with which we are concerned. *An economic model cannot be faulted as unrealistic simply because it does not represent every detail of the real world.* A map of a city that shows only major streets is not necessarily unrealistic if, in fact, all you need to know is how to pass through the city using major streets. As long as a model is realistic in terms of shedding light on the *central* issue at hand or forces at work, it may be useful.

A map is the quintessential model. It is always a simplified representation. It is always unrealistic. But it is also useful in making (refutable) predictions about the world. If the model—the map—predicts that when you take Campus Avenue to the north, you always run into the campus, that is a (refutable) prediction. If our goal is to explain observed behavior, the simplicity or complexity of the model we use is irrelevant. If a simple model can explain observed behavior in repeated settings just as well as a complex one, the simple model has some value and is probably easier to use.

Assumptions

Every model, or theory, must be based on a set of assumptions. Assumptions define the set of circumstances in which our model is most likely to be applicable. When scientists predicted that sailing ships would fall off the edge of the earth, they used the *assumption* that the earth was flat. Columbus did not accept the implications of such a model. He assumed that the world was round. The real-world test of his own model refuted the flat-earth model. Indirectly, then, it was a test of the assumption of the flat-earth model.

EXAMPLE
Getting Directions

Assumptions are a shorthand for reality. Imagine that you have decided to drive from your home in San Diego to downtown San Francisco. Because you have never driven this route, you decide to get directions from the local office of the Automobile Association of America (AAA).

When you ask for directions, the travel planner could give you a set of detailed maps that shows each city through which you will travel—Oceanside, San Clemente, Irvine, Anaheim, Los Angeles, Bakersfield, Modesto, and so on—and then, opening each map, show you exactly how the freeway threads through each of these cities. You would get a nearly complete description of reality because the AAA travel planner will not have used many simplifying assumptions. It is more likely, however, that the travel planner will simply say, "Get on Interstate 5 going north. Stay on it for about 500 miles. Follow the signs for San Francisco. After crossing the toll bridge, take any exit marked 'Downtown.'" By omitting all of the trivial details, the travel planner has told you all that you really need and want to know. The models you will be using in this text are similar to the simplified directions on how to drive from San Diego to San Francisco—they focus on what is relevant to the problem at hand and omit what is not.

FOR CRITICAL ANALYSIS: *In what way do small talk and gossip represent the use of simplifying assumptions?* ●

The *Ceteris Paribus* Assumption: All Other Things Being Equal. Everything in the world seems to relate in some way to everything else in the world. It would be impossible to isolate the effects of changes in one variable on another variable if we always had to worry about the many other variables that might also enter the analysis. As in other sciences, economics uses the **ceteris paribus assumption.** *Ceteris paribus* means "other things constant" or "other things equal."

Consider an example taken from economics. One of the most important determinants of how much of a particular product a family buys is how expensive that product is relative to other products. We know that in addition to relative prices, other factors influence decisions about making purchases. Some of them have to do with income, others with tastes, and yet others with custom and religious beliefs. Whatever these other factors are, we hold them constant when we look at the relationship between changes in prices and changes in how much of a given product people will purchase.

Ceteris paribus [KAY-ter-us PEAR-uh-bus] assumption
The assumption that nothing changes except the factor or factors being studied.

Deciding on the Usefulness of a Model

We generally do not attempt to determine the usefulness, or "goodness," of a model merely by evaluating how realistic its assumptions are. Rather, we consider a model good if it yields usable predictions and implications for the real world. In other words, can we use the model to predict what will happen in the world around us? Does the model provide useful implications of how things happen in our world?

Once we have determined that the model does predict real-world phenomena, the scientific approach to the analysis of the world around us requires that we consider evidence. Evidence is used to test the usefulness of a model. This is why we call economics an **empirical** science, *empirical* meaning that evidence (data) is looked at to see whether we are right. Economists are often engaged in empirically testing their models.

Consider two competing models for the way students act when doing complicated probability problems to choose the best gambles. One model predicts that, based on the assumption of rational self-interest, students who are paid more money for better performance will in fact perform better on average during the experiment. A competing model might be that students whose last names start with the letters *A* through *L* will do better than students with last names starting with *M* through *Z,* irrespective of how much they are paid. The model that consistently predicts more accurately is the model that we would normally choose. In this example, the "alphabet" model did not work well: The first letter of the last name of the students who actually did the experiment at UCLA was irrelevant in predicting how well they would perform the mathematical calculations necessary to choose the correct gambles. On average, students who received higher cash payments for better gambles did choose a higher percentage of better gambles. Thus the model based on rational self-interest predicted well.

Models of Behavior, Not Thought Processes

Take special note of the fact that economists' models do not relate to the way people *think;* they relate to the way people *act,* to what they do in life with their limited resources. Models tend to generalize human behavior. Normally, the economist does not attempt to predict how people will think about a particular topic, such as a higher price of oil products, accelerated inflation, or higher taxes. Rather, the task at hand is to predict how people will act, which may be quite different from what they say they will do (much to the consternation of poll takers and market researchers). The people involved in examining thought processes are psychologists and psychiatrists, not typically economists.

EXAMPLE
Incentives Work for Pigeons and Rats, Too

Researchers at Texas A&M University did a series of experiments with pigeons and rats. They allowed them to "purchase" food and drink by pushing various levers. The "price" was the number of times a lever had to be pushed. A piece of cheese required 10 pushes, a drop of root beer only one. The "incomes" that the animals were given equaled a certain number of total pushes per day. Once the income was used up, the levers did not work. The researchers discovered that when the price of cheese went down, the animals purchased more cheese. Similarly, they found that when the price of root beer was increased, the animals purchased less root beer. These are exactly the predictions that we make about human behavior.

FOR CRITICAL ANALYSIS: "People respond to incentives." Is this assumption also usable in the animal world? •

Empirical
Relying on real-world data in evaluating the usefulness of a model.

POSITIVE VERSUS NORMATIVE ECONOMICS

Economics uses *positive analysis,* a value-free approach to inquiry. No subjective or moral judgments enter into the analysis. Positive analysis relates to statements such as "If A, then B." For example, "If the price of gasoline goes up relative to all other prices, then the amount of it that people will buy will fall." That is a positive economic statement. It is a statement of *what is.* It is not a statement of anyone's value judgment or subjective feelings. For many problems analyzed in the hard sciences such as physics and chemistry, the analyses are considered to be virtually value-free. After all, how can someone's values enter into a theory of molecular behavior? But economists face a different problem. They deal with the behavior of individuals, not molecules. That makes it more difficult to stick to what we consider to be value-free or **positive economics** without reference to our feelings.

When our values are interjected into the analysis, we enter the realm of **normative economics,** involving *normative analysis.* A positive economic statement is "If the price of gas rises, people will buy less." If we add to that analysis the statement "so we should not allow the price to go up," we have entered the realm of normative economics—we have expressed a value judgment. In fact, any time you see the word *should,* you will know that values are entering into the discussion. Just remember that positive statements are concerned with *what is,* whereas normative statements are concerned with *what ought to be.*

Each of us has a desire for different things. That means that we have different values. When we express a value judgment, we are simply saying what we prefer, like, or desire. Because individual values are diverse, we expect—and indeed observe—people expressing widely varying value judgments about how the world ought to be.

Positive economics
Analysis that is strictly limited to making either purely descriptive statements or scientific predictions; for example, "If A, then B." A statement of *what is.*

Normative economics
Analysis involving value judgments about economic policies; relates to whether things are good or bad. A statement of *what ought to be.*

A Warning: Recognize Normative Analysis

It is easy to define positive economics. It is quite another matter to catch all unlabeled normative statements in a textbook such as this one (or any other), even though an author goes over the manuscript many times before it is printed. Therefore, do not get the impression that a textbook author will be able to keep all personal values out of the book. They will slip through. In fact, the very choice of which topics to include in an introductory textbook involves normative economics. There is no value-free, or objective, way to decide which topics to use in a textbook. The author's values ultimately make a difference when choices have to be made. But from your own standpoint, you might want to be able to recognize when you are engaging in normative as opposed to positive economic analysis. Reading this text will help equip you for that task.

CONCEPTS IN BRIEF

- A model, or theory, uses assumptions and is by nature a simplification of the real world. The usefulness of a model can be evaluated by bringing empirical evidence to bear on its predictions.

- Models are not necessarily deficient simply because they are unrealistic and use simplifying assumptions, for every model in every science requires simplification compared to the real world.

- Most models use the *ceteris paribus* assumption, that all other things are held constant, or equal.

- Positive economics is value-free and relates to statements that can be refuted, such as "If A, then B." Normative economics involves people's values, and normative statements typically contain the word *should.*

The very rich often buy expensive "toys," such as this Rolls-Royce. But do such goods bring happiness?

CONCEPTS APPLIED:

RATIONAL SELF-INTEREST, THE RATIONALITY ASSUMPTION, INCENTIVES, MODELS, REALISM

Visit www.econtoday.com for an Internet Activity that expands your understanding of these concepts.

One of the major criticisms of economics is that it seems to posit that more money (wealth) is better than less. In other words, economic theory appears to assume that people act in such a way as to make higher and higher incomes. People are assumed always to act so as to maximize their incomes, even if "money cannot buy happiness." A recent study in the *Journal of Personality and Social Psychology* presents evidence to support the notion that seeking ever-higher wealth does not lead to any greater level of happiness.

What Researchers Have Found

The researchers of this study randomly selected 100 of America's wealthiest individuals identified as such in popular business magazines. Each wealthy American in the study filled out a detailed inquiry, which included the question "How do you feel about how happy you are?" to which the answer choices ranged from "delighted" to "terrible." The same questionnaire was given to a randomly selected set of individuals who were not rich. The average happiness score for the rich was only slightly above the nonrich. Indeed, one-third of the superrich scored below the average group.

The conclusion the researchers reached was that an increase in income is like a martini: It induces optimism and raises the spirits, but only temporarily. The researchers argued that only recent life events (occurring within the past three months) have any influence on one's feelings of subjective well-being.

International Confirmation

The researchers discovered that international data confirmed their findings. Only residents of the poorest countries (India and Bangladesh) had below-average happi-

ness ratings. Happiness in all the others appeared about the same. Moreover, neither U.S. nor Japanese residents showed any rising trend in reported subjective well-being over the past few decades despite rising average household incomes.

But Asking Gets You Nowhere

Do the research results summarized here contradict the methodology we use in economics? Hardly. Economics is a science of *revealed* preferences. We find out virtually no useful information by asking people to rate their happiness on a scale of 1 to 10. We assume that people act rationally. In other words, they will not knowingly do things that make them worse off. We can predict that given the choice between a lower-paying job and an otherwise identical yet higher-paying job, people will choose the latter. We make no assumptions about their thought processes.

One Can Always Become Poorer

Finally, if indeed income does not buy happiness, the rich and the very rich always have an option—they can dispose of their wealth at any time. No one is forced to keep wealth. Because we rarely see individuals routinely giving away all of their wealth, we can infer that higher income is preferred to lower income.

FOR CRITICAL ANALYSIS

1. Even if you choose not to spend income that you earn on yourself, what other options do you have?
2. Are we making a value judgment when we assume that an individual prefers higher income over lower income?

CHAPTER SUMMARY

1. Economics as a social science is the study of how individuals make choices to satisfy wants. Wants are defined as what people would buy if their incomes were unlimited.

2. Economics is usually divided into microeconomic analysis, which is the study of individual decision making by households and firms, and macroeconomics, which is the study of nationwide phenomena, such as inflation and unemployment.

3. The rationality assumption is that individuals never intentionally make decisions that would leave them worse off.

4. We use models, or theories, to explain and predict behavior. Models, or theories, are never completely realistic because by definition they are simplifica-

tions using assumptions that are not directly testable. The usefulness of a theory, or model, is determined not by the realism of its assumptions but by how well it predicts real-world phenomena.

5. An important simplifying assumption is that all other things are held equal, or constant. This is sometimes known as the *ceteris paribus* assumption.

6. No model in economics relates to individuals' thought processes; all models relate to what people do, not to what they think or say they will do.

7. Much economic analysis involves positive economics; that is, it is value-free. Whenever statements embodying values are made, we enter the realm of normative economics, or how individuals and groups think things ought to be.

DISCUSSION OF PREVIEW QUESTIONS

1. What is the difference between microeconomics and macroeconomics?

Microeconomics is concerned with the choice-making processes of individuals, households, and firms, whereas macroeconomics focuses on the performance of the economy as a whole.

2. What role does rational self-interest play in economic analysis?

Rational self-interest is the assumption that individuals behave in a reasonable (rational) way in making choices to further their interests. In other words, we assume that individuals' actions are motivated primarily by their self-interest, keeping in mind that self-interest can relate to monetary and nonmonetary objectives, such as love, prestige, and helping others.

3. Why is the study of economics a science?

Economics is a science in that it uses models, or theories, that are simplified representations of the real world to analyze and make predictions about the real world. These predictions are then subjected to empirical tests in which real-world data are used to decide whether or not to reject the predictions.

4. What is the difference between positive and normative economics?

Positive economics deals with *what is,* whereas normative economics deals with *what ought to be.* Positive economic statements are of the "if . . . then" variety; they are descriptive and predictive and are not related to what "should" happen. Normative economics, by contrast, is concerned with what ought to be and is intimately tied to value judgments.

PROBLEMS

(Answers to the odd-numbered problems appear at the back of the book.)

1-1. Construct four separate models to predict the probability that a person will die within the next five

years. Include only one determining factor in each of your models.

1-2. Does it matter whether all of a model's assumptions are "realistic"? Why or why not?

1-3. Give a refutable implication (one that can be disproved by evidence from the real world) for each of the following models:

a. The accident rate of drivers is inversely related to their age.
b. The rate of inflation is directly related to the rate of change in the nation's money supply.
c. The wages of professional basketball players are directly related to their high school grade point averages.
d. The rate at which bank employees are promoted is inversely related to their frequency of absenteeism.

1-4. Is gambling an example of rational or irrational behavior? What is the difference between gambling and insurance?

1-5. Over the past 20 years, first-class mail rates have more than tripled, while prices of long-distance phone calls, televisions, and sound systems have decreased. Over a similar period, it has been reported that there has been a steady decline in the ability of high school graduates to communicate effectively in writing. Do you feel that this increase in the relative price of written communi-cation (first-class mail rates) is related to the alleged decline in writing ability? If so, what do you feel is the direction of causation? Which is causing which?

1-6. If there is no way to test a theory with real-world data, can we determine if it is a good theory? Why is empirical evidence used to validate a theory?

1-7. Identify which of the following statements use positive economic analysis and which use normative economic analysis.

a. The government should not regulate the banking system because recent problems have demonstrated that it does not know what it is doing.
b. The elimination of barriers to the free movement of individuals across European borders has caused wages to become more equal in many industries.
c. Paying members of Congress more provides them with less incentive to commit wrongful acts.
d. We need more restrictions on companies that pollute because air pollution is destroying our way of life.

COMPUTER-ASSISTED INSTRUCTION

Key elements of the scientific way of thinking are illustrated by applying them to everyday situations.

Complete problem and answer appear on disk.

INTERACTING WITH THE INTERNET

The Internet is a worldwide network of computers; it includes the computer on which you will do the exercises in this book. Three types of computers are involved: servers, routers, and clients. Servers are the machines that contain and dispense the information you are looking for. Routers direct your request to the correct server and make sure the information gets back to you. The computer on which you are working is the client, because it (and you) are being served by the other two types of machines.

The information available on the Internet is staggering in both volume and variety—not to mention the speed with which it changes, appearing and disappearing in a manner that even the White Rabbit would find astonishing. Just a few years ago, most of the information moving on the Internet was scientific and of interest chiefly to academics and members of the military and defense community. Increasingly, however, the Internet is being transformed into a combination giant shopping mall, meeting hall, publishing frontier, and entertainment center. It also has some sites that offer vast amounts of information about the economy, the environment, and the world—indeed information about almost any question you can ask. It is in search of information such as this that we will be headed in this book.

Searching Through the Internet

Besides sending and receiving electronic mail (e-mail), the most common usage of the Internet is searching for and retrieving information. This is done through a variety of Internet *browsers*.

The most popular Internet browsers are Netscape Navigator and Microsoft Explorer. By using one of these browsers, you can also access numerous *search engines*, which help you find the information you want if you do not know the exact address. Some search engines are Yahoo!, WebCrawler, HotBot, Lycos, Infoseek, and Excite.

Addresses

Each site on the Internet has an address. Many of the ones that you access will have somewhere in the address the letters *edu* or *gov*, indicating educational institutions or government organizations, respectively. All addresses that start with *www* indicate that they are part of the World Wide Web. This means that the site has the capacity to display photographs, animated icons, and elaborate graphics, in addition to routine text. Today, many sites dispense with the *www* and can be reached without this prefix.

In any event, successful navigation requires that you type the correct address into your browser. These addresses are called *uniform resource locators* (URLs). Although most URLs start with *http://* (which stands for *hypertext transfer protocol*), the latest browsers allow you to omit these initials.

Getting Started

If you want to "surf" (browse) economics resources immediately, use your browser to go directly to Resources for Economists by typing in

http://econwpa.wustl.edu/EconFAQ/EconFAQ.html

You can also access the World Wide Web Resources for Economics at WebEc at

netec.wustl.edu/WebEc.html

In URLs in this text, we will dispense with *http://* before the actual address.
By the way, if you want to look up some jokes about economists, go to

netec.wustl.edu/JokEc.html

Happy surfing!

CHAPTER 2

SCARCITY AND THE WORLD OF TRADE-OFFS

What seems to be the scarcest thing around? For a lot of people, it is time. You can be the richest person on earth and still not have "enough time." When you are driving, you are ordinarily aware of time—how long it takes for you to get to your destination. When traffic lanes are congested, you lose time. And that time is valuable to you. Why? Because you could be doing something else instead of sitting in your car waiting for traffic to clear. In this chapter, you will learn about how to put a value on that time.

PREVIEW QUESTIONS

1. Do affluent people face the problem of scarcity?
2. Fresh air may be consumed at no charge, but is it free of cost to society?
3. Why does the scarcity problem force individuals to consider opportunity costs?
4. Can a "free" college education ever be truly free?

Did You Know That . . . Chris Van Horn, president of CVK Group in Washington, D.C., grosses over $200,000 a year for having people wait in line? Adam Goldin loves working as a "line waiter" because he gets paid for "doing nothing." His job is to arrive early in the morning on Capitol Hill to hold places for lobbyists who must attend congressional hearings. Van Horn charges his more than 100 lobbyists and law firm clients $27 an hour and pays his part-time line waiters like Mr. Goldin $10 an hour. For example, when Congress was going to hold hearings for the proposed 1997 tax cut, $10-an-hour professional standees arrived to hold places for $300-an-hour lobbyists who would not show up until hours later. After all, lobbyists do not have an unlimited amount of time. Their time is scarce. It is worth more than what they are charged to "save" it.

SCARCITY

Whenever individuals or communities cannot obtain everything they desire simultaneously, choices occur. Choices occur because of *scarcity*. **Scarcity** is the most basic concept in all of economics. Scarcity means that we do not and cannot have enough income or wealth to satisfy our *every* desire. Scarcity exists because human wants always exceed what can be produced with the limited resources and time that nature makes available.

What Scarcity Is Not

Scarcity is not a shortage. After a hurricane hits and cuts off supplies to a community, TV newscasts often show people standing in line to get minimum amounts of cooking fuel and food. A news commentator might say that the line is caused by the "scarcity" of these products. But cooking fuel and food are always scarce—we cannot obtain all that we want at a zero price. Therefore, do not confuse the concept of scarcity, which is general and all-encompassing, with the concept of shortages as evidenced by people waiting in line to obtain a particular product.

Scarcity is not the same thing as poverty. Scarcity occurs among the poor and among the rich. Even the richest person on earth faces scarcity because available time is limited. Low income levels do not create more scarcity. High income levels do not create less scarcity.

Scarcity is a fact of life, like gravity. And just as physicists did not invent gravity, economists did not invent scarcity—it existed well before the first economist ever lived. It exists even when we are not using all of our resources.

Scarcity and Resources

The scarcity concept arises from the fact that resources are insufficient to satisfy our every desire. Resources are the inputs used in the production of the things that we want. **Production** can be defined as virtually any activity that results in the conversion of resources into products that can be used in consumption. Production includes delivering things from one part of the country to another. It includes taking ice from an ice tray to put it in your soft-drink glass. The resources used in production are called *factors of production*, and some economists use the terms *resources* and *factors of production* interchangeably. The total quantity of all resources that an economy has at any one time determines what that economy can produce.

Factors of production can be classified in many ways. Here is one such classification:

1. **Land. Land** encompasses all the nonhuman gifts of nature, including timber, water, fish, minerals, and the original fertility of land. It is often called the *natural resource*.

Chapter Outline

Scarcity

Wants and Needs

Scarcity, Choice, and Opportunity Cost

The World of Trade-Offs

The Choices Society Faces

Economic Growth and the Production Possibilities Curve

The Trade-off Between the Present and the Future

Specialization and Greater Productivity

The Division of Labor

Comparative Advantage and Trade Among Nations

Scarcity
A situation in which the ingredients for producing the things that people desire are insufficient to satisfy all wants.

Production
Any activity that results in the conversion of resources into products that can be used in consumption.

Land
The natural resources that are available from nature. Land as a resource includes location, original fertility and mineral deposits, topography, climate, water, and vegetation.

Labor
Productive contributions of humans who work, involving both mental and physical activities.

Physical capital
All manufactured resources, including buildings, equipment, machines, and improvements to land that is used for production.

Human capital
The accumulated training and education of workers.

Entrepreneurship
The factor of production involving human resources that perform the functions of raising capital, organizing, managing, assembling other factors of production, and making basic business policy decisions. The entrepreneur is a risk taker.

2. **Labor. Labor** is the human resource, which includes all productive contributions made by individuals who work, such as steelworkers, ballet dancers, and professional baseball players.
3. **Physical capital. Physical capital** consists of the factories and equipment used in production. It also includes improvements to natural resources, such as irrigation ditches.
4. **Human capital. Human capital** is the economic characterization of the education and training of workers. How much the nation produces depends not only on how many hours people work but also on how productive they are, and that, in turn, depends in part on education and training. To become more educated, individuals have to devote time and resources, just as a business has to devote resources if it wants to increase its physical capital. Whenever a worker's skills increase, human capital has been improved.
5. **Entrepreneurship.** The factor of production known as **entrepreneurship** (actually a subdivision of labor) involves human resources that perform the functions of organizing, managing, and assembling the other factors of production to make business ventures. Entrepreneurship also encompasses taking risks that involve the possibility of losing large sums of wealth on new ventures. It includes new methods of doing common things and generally experimenting with any type of new thinking that could lead to making more money income. Without entrepreneurship, virtually no business organization could operate.

Goods Versus Economic Goods

Goods
All things from which individuals derive satisfaction or happiness.

Economic goods
Goods that are scarce, for which the quantity demanded exceeds the quantity supplied at a zero price.

Goods are defined as all things from which individuals derive satisfaction or happiness. Goods therefore include air to breathe and the beauty of a sunset as well as food, cars, and CD players.

Economic goods are a subset of all goods—they are goods derived from scarce resources about which we must constantly make decisions regarding their best use. By definition, the desired quantity of an economic good exceeds the amount that is directly available at a zero price. Virtually every example we use in economics concerns economic goods—cars, CD players, computers, socks, baseball bats, and corn. Weeds are a good example of *bads*—goods for which the desired quantity is much *less* than what nature provides at a zero price.

Services
Mental or physical labor or help purchased by consumers. Examples are the assistance of doctors, lawyers, dentists, repair personnel, housecleaners, educators, retailers, and wholesalers; things purchased or used by consumers that do not have physical characteristics.

Sometimes you will see references to "goods and services." **Services** are tasks that are performed for someone else, such as laundry, cleaning, hospital care, restaurant meal preparation, car polishing, psychological counseling, and teaching. One way of looking at services is thinking of them as *intangible goods.*

WANTS AND NEEDS

Wants are not the same as needs. Indeed, from the economist's point of view, the term *needs* is objectively undefinable. When someone says, "I need some new clothes," there is no way to know whether that person is stating a vague wish, a want, or a life-saving necessity. If the individual making the statement were dying of exposure in a northern country during the winter, we might argue that indeed the person does need clothes—perhaps not new ones, but at least some articles of warm clothing. Typically, however, the term *need* is used very casually in most conversations. What people mean, usually, is that they want something that they do not currently have.

Humans have unlimited wants. Just imagine if every single material want that you might have were satisfied. You can have all of the clothes, cars, houses, CDs, tickets to concerts, and other things that you want. Does that mean that nothing else could add to your total level of happiness? Probably not, because you might think of new goods and services that you could obtain, particularly as they came to market. You would also still be lacking in fulfilling all of your wants for compassion, friendship, love, affection, prestige, musical abilities, sports abilities, and so on.

In reality, every individual has competing wants but cannot satisfy all of them, given limited resources. This is the reality of scarcity. Each person must therefore make choices. Whenever a choice is made to do or buy something, something else that is also desired is not done or not purchased. In other words, in a world of scarcity, every want that ends up being satisfied causes one or more other wants to remain unsatisfied or to be forfeited.

CONCEPTS IN BRIEF

- Scarcity exists because human wants always exceed what can be produced with the limited resources and time that nature makes available.

- We use scarce resources, such as land, labor, physical and human capital, and entrepreneurship, to produce economic goods—goods that are desired but are not directly obtainable from nature to the extent demanded or desired at a zero price.

- Wants are unlimited; they include all material desires and all nonmaterial desires, such as love, affection, power, and prestige.

- The concept of need is difficult to define objectively for every person; consequently, we simply consider that every person's wants are unlimited. In a world of scarcity, satisfaction of one want necessarily means nonsatisfaction of one or more other wants.

SCARCITY, CHOICE, AND OPPORTUNITY COST

The natural fact of scarcity implies that we must make choices. One of the most important results of this fact is that every choice made (or not made, for that matter) means that some opportunity had to be sacrificed. Every choice involves giving up another opportunity to do or use something else.

Consider a practical example. Every choice you make to study one more hour of economics requires that you give up the opportunity to do any of the following activities: study more of another subject, listen to music, sleep, browse at a local store, read a novel, or work out at the gym. Many more opportunities are forgone also if you choose to study economics an additional hour.

Because there were so many alternatives from which to choose, how could you determine the value of what you gave up to engage in that extra hour of studying economics? First of all, no one else can tell you the answer because only you can *subjectively* put a value on the alternatives forgone. Only you know what is the value of another hour of sleep or of an hour looking for the latest CDs. That means that only you can determine the highest-valued, next-best alternative that you had to sacrifice in order to study economics one more hour. It is you who come up with the *subjective* estimate of the expected value of the next-best alternative.

The value of the next-best alternative is called **opportunity cost.** The opportunity cost of any action is the value of what is given up—the next-highest-ranked alternative—

Opportunity cost
The highest-valued, next-best alternative that must be sacrificed to attain something or to satisfy a want.

because a choice was made. When you study one more hour, there may be many alternatives available for the use of that hour, but assume that you can do only one thing in that hour—your next-highest-ranked alternative. What is important is the choice that you would have made if you hadn't studied one more hour. Your opportunity cost is the *next-highest-ranked* alternative, not *all* alternatives.

In economics, cost is always a forgone opportunity.

One way to think about opportunity cost is to understand that when you choose to do something, you lose. What you lose is being able to engage in your next-highest-valued alternative. The cost of your choice is what you lose, which is by definition your next-highest-valued alternative. This is your opportunity cost.

Let's consider opportunity cost in cyberspace—on the Web, and particularly for Web browsers such as Navigator and Explorer and search engines such as Yahoo! and Excite.

AD SPACE AND PLACEMENT DECISIONS ON THE WEB

When you access the Internet, your home page is typically either your Internet service provider's page, Netscape's or Explorer's home page, or a search engine's home page. Each time you access the Net, you see advertising—banners, buttons, keywords, cobranded ads, or other promotions or links. Some of the biggest advertisers on the Web are Microsoft, Toyota, General Motors, Disney, IBM, AT&T, and American Express. All in all, these advertisers will spend almost $100 million on the Web in the year 2001. The owner of any Web page that carries an ad faces an opportunity cost. For example, the opening page of the Yahoo! search engine is considered "prime real estate" because so many people see it every day. But there is relatively little space on the screen. Thus Yahoo! faces an opportunity cost. Any space that it uses to promote its own services and products, it cannot sell it to, say, IBM or Microsoft. And if it fills up too much of the screen with ads, some users will switch to a less cluttered search engine. Thus there is an opportunity cost for literally every square centimeter on a Web page.

FOR CRITICAL ANALYSIS: How does a Web home page owner decide how to use the "real estate"? •

THE WORLD OF TRADE-OFFS

Whenever you engage in any activity using any resource, even time, you are *trading off* the use of that resource for one or more alternative uses. The value of the trade-off is represented by the opportunity cost. The opportunity cost of studying economics has already been mentioned—it is the value of the next-best alternative. When you think of any alternative, you are thinking of trade-offs.

Let's consider a hypothetical example of a one-for-one trade-off between the results of spending time studying economics and accounting. For the sake of this argument, we will assume that additional time studying either economics or accounting will lead to a higher grade in the subject studied more. One of the best ways to examine this trade-off is with a graph. (If you would like a refresher on graphical techniques, study Appendix A at the end of this chapter before going on.)

Exercise 2.1
Visit www.econtoday.com
for more about shopping trade-offs.

Graphical Analysis

In Figure 2-1, the expected grade in accounting is measured on the vertical axis of the graph, and the expected grade in economics is measured on the horizontal axis. We simplify the world and assume that you have a maximum of 10 hours per week to spend studying these two subjects and that if you spend all 10 hours on economics, you will get an A in the course. You will, however, fail accounting. Conversely, if you spend all of your 10 hours studying accounting, you will get an A in that subject, but you will flunk economics. Here the trade-off is a special case: one-to-one. A one-to-one trade-off means that the opportunity cost of receiving one grade higher in economics (for example, improving from a C to a B) is one grade lower in accounting (falling from a C to a D).

The Production Possibilities Curve (PPC)

The graph in Figure 2-1 illustrates the relationship between the possible results that can be produced in each of two activities, depending on how much time you choose to devote to each activity. This graph shows a representation of a **production possibilities curve (PPC).**

Consider that you are producing a grade in economics when you study economics and a grade in accounting when you study accounting. Then the graph in Figure 2-1 can be related to the production possibilities you face. The line that goes from A on one axis to A on the other axis therefore becomes a production possibilities curve. It is defined as the maximum quantity of one good or service that can be produced, given that a specific quantity of another is produced. It is a curve that shows the possibilities available for increasing the output of one good or service by reducing the amount of another. In the example in Figure 2-1, your time for studying was limited to 10 hours per week. The two possible outputs were grades in accounting and grades in economics. The particular production possibilities curve presented in Figure 2-1 is a graphical representation of the opportunity cost of studying one more hour in one subject. It is a *straight-line production possibilities curve,* which is a special case. (The more general case will be discussed next.) If you decide to be at point *x* in Figure 2-1, 5 hours of study time will be spent on accounting and 5 hours will be spent on economics. The expected grade in each course will be a C. If you are more interested in getting a B in economics, you will go to point *y* on the production possibilities curve, spending only 2.5 hours on accounting but 7.5 hours on economics. Your expected grade in accounting will then drop from a C to a D.

Exercise 2.2

Visit www.econtoday.com for more about trade-offs concerning cars.

Production possibilities curve (PPC)

A curve representing all possible combinations of total output that could be produced assuming (1) a fixed amount of productive resources of a given quality and (2) the efficient use of those resources.

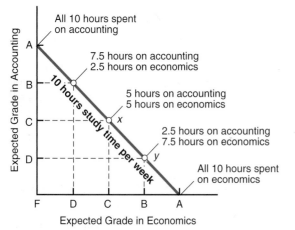

FIGURE 2-1

Production Possibilities Curve for Grades in Accounting and Economics (Trade-offs)

We assume that only 10 hours can be spent per week on studying. If the student is at point *x*, equal time (5 hours a week) is spent on both courses and equal grades of C will be received. If a higher grade in economics is desired, the student may go to point *y*, thereby receiving a B in economics but a D in accounting. At point *y*, 2.5 hours are spent on accounting and 7.5 hours on economics.

Note that these trade-offs between expected grades in accounting and economics are the result of *holding constant* total study time as well as all other factors that might influence a student's ability to learn, such as computerized study aids. Quite clearly, if you wished to spend more total time studying, it would be possible to have higher grades in both economics and accounting. In that case, however, we would no longer be on the specific production possibilities curve illustrated in Figure 2-1. We would have to draw a new curve, farther to the right, to show the greater total study time and a different set of possible trade-offs.

CONCEPTS IN BRIEF

- Scarcity requires us to choose. When we choose, we lose the next-highest-valued alternative.
- Cost is always a forgone opportunity.
- Another way to look at opportunity cost is the trade-off that occurs when one activity is undertaken rather than the next-best alternative activity.
- A production possibilities curve (PPC) graphically shows the trade-off that occurs when more of one output is obtained at the sacrifice of another. The PPC is a graphical representation of, among other things, opportunity cost.

THE CHOICES SOCIETY FACES

The straight-line production possibilities curve presented in Figure 2-1 can be generalized to demonstrate the related concepts of scarcity, choice, and trade-offs that our entire nation faces. As you will see, the production possibilities curve is a simple but powerful economic model because it can demonstrate these related concepts. The example we will use is the choice between the production of M-16 semiautomatic rifles and CD-ROM players. We assume for the moment that these are the only two goods that can be produced in the nation. Panel (a) of Figure 2-2 on page 24 gives the various combinations of M-16s and CD-ROM players that are possible. If all resources are devoted to M-16 production, 10 billion per year can be produced. If all resources are devoted to CD-ROM player production, 12 billion per year can be produced. In between are various possible combinations. These combinations are plotted as points A, B, C, D, E, F, and G in panel (b) of Figure 2-2. If these points are connected with a smooth curve, the nation's production possibilities curve is shown, demonstrating the trade-off between the production of M-16 semiautomatic rifles and CD-ROM players. These trade-offs occur *on* the production possibilities curve.

Notice the major difference in the shape of the production possibilities curves in Figures 2-1 and 2-2. In Figure 2-1, there is a one-to-one trade-off between grades in economics and in accounting. In Figure 2-2, the trade-off between CD-ROM production and M-16 production is not constant, and therefore the production possibilities curve is a *bowed* line. To understand why the production possibilities curve for a society is typically bowed outward, you must understand the assumptions underlying the PPC.

Assumptions Underlying the Production Possibilities Curve

When we draw the curve that is shown in Figure 2-2, we make the following assumptions:

1. That resources are fully employed
2. That we are looking at production over a specific time period—for example, one year

Panel (a)

Combination	M-16 Rifles (billions of units per year)	CD-ROM Players (billions of units per year)
A	10.0	0
B	9.6	2
C	9.0	4
D	8.0	6
E	6.6	8
F	4.5	10
G	0	12

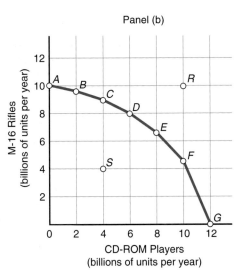

Panel (b)

FIGURE 2-2

Society's Trade-off Between M-16 Rifles and CD-ROM Players
Both the production of M-16 semiautomatic rifles and the production of CD-ROM players are measured in billions of units per year. The various combinations are given in panel (a) and plotted in panel (b). Connecting the points *A–G* with a relatively smooth line gives the society's production possibilities curve for M-16 rifles and CD-ROM players. Point *R* lies outside the production possibilities curve and is therefore unattainable at the point in time for which the graph is drawn. Point *S* lies inside the production possibilities curve and therefore represents an inefficient use of available resources.

3. That the resource inputs, in both quantity and quality, used to produce M-16 rifles or CD-ROM players are fixed over this time period
4. That technology does not change over this time period

Technology is defined as society's pool of applied knowledge concerning how goods and services can be produced by managers, workers, engineers, scientists, and craftspeople, using land and capital. You can think of technology as the formula (or recipe) used to combine factors of production. (When better formulas are developed, more production can be obtained from the same amount of resources.) The level of technology sets the limit on the amount and types of goods and services that we can derive from any given amount of resources. The production possibilities curve is drawn under the assumption that we use the best technology that we currently have available and that this technology doesn't change over the time period under study.

Technology
Society's pool of applied knowledge concerning how goods and services can be produced.

Being off the Production Possibilities Curve

Look again at panel (b) of Figure 2-2. Point *R* lies *outside* the production possibilities curve and is *impossible* to achieve during the time period assumed. By definition, the production possibilities curve indicates the *maximum* quantity of one good given some quantity of the other.

It is possible, however, to be at point *S* in Figure 2-2. That point lies beneath the production possibilities curve. If the nation is at point *S*, it means that its resources are not being fully utilized. This occurs, for example, during periods of unemployment. Point *S* and all such points within the production possibilities curve are always attainable but usually not desirable.

Efficiency

The production possibilities curve can be used to define the notion of efficiency. Whenever the economy is operating on the PPC, at points such as *A, B, C,* or *D,* we say that its production is efficient. Points such as *S* in Figure 2-2, which lie beneath the production possibilities curve, are said to represent production situations that are not efficient.

Efficiency can mean many things to many people. Even within economics, there are different types of efficiency. Here we are discussing efficiency in production, or productive efficiency. An economy is productively efficient whenever it is producing the maximum output with given technology and resources.

A simple commonsense definition of efficiency is getting the most out of what we have as an economy. Clearly, we are not getting the most that we have if we are at point *S* in panel (b) of Figure 2-2. We can move from point *S* to, say, point *C*, thereby increasing the total quantity of M-16s produced without any decrease in the total quantity of CD-ROM players produced. We can move from point *S* to point *E,* for example, and have both more M-16s and more CD-ROM players. Point *S* is called an **inefficient point,** which is defined as any point below the production possibilities curve.

The concept of economic efficiency relates to how goods are distributed among different individuals and entities. An efficient economy is one in which people who value specific goods relatively the most end up with those goods. If you own a vintage electric Fender guitar, but I value it more than you, I can buy it from you. Such trading benefits you and me mutually. In the process, the economy becomes more efficient. The maximum efficiency an economy can reach is when all such mutual benefits through trade have been exhausted.

The Law of Increasing Relative Cost

In the example in Figure 2-1, the trade-off between a grade in accounting and a grade in economics is one-to-one. The trade-off ratio was fixed. That is to say, the production possibilities curve was a straight line. The curve in Figure 2-2 is a more general case. We have re-created the curve in Figure 2-2 as Figure 2-3. Each combination, *A* through *G,* of M-16s and CD-ROM players is represented on the production possibilities curve. Starting with the production of zero CD-ROM players, the nation can produce 10 billion units of M-16s with its available resources and technology. When we increase production of CD-ROM players from zero to 2 billion units per year, the nation has to give up in M-16s that first vertical arrow, *Aa.* From panel (a) of Figure 2-2 you can see that this is .4 billion M-16s a

Efficiency
The case in which a given level of inputs is used to produce the maximum output possible. Alternatively, the situation in which a given output is produced at minimum cost.

Inefficient point
Any point below the production possibilities curve at which resources are being used inefficiently.

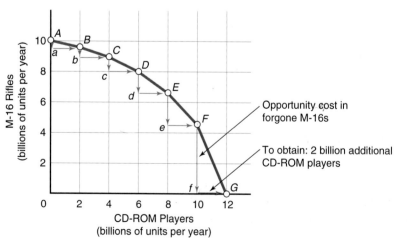

FIGURE 2-3
The Law of Increasing Relative Cost
Consider equal increments of CD-ROM player production, as measured on the horizontal axis. All of the horizontal arrows—*aB, bC,* and so on—are of equal length (2 billion units). The opportunity cost of going from 10 billion CD-ROM players per year to 12 billion *(Ff)* is much greater than going from zero units to 2 billion units *(Aa).* The opportunity cost of each additional equal increase in CD-ROM production rises.

year (10.0 billion − 9.6 billion). Again, if we increase production of CD-ROM players by 2 billion units per year, we go from *B* to *C*. In order to do so, the nation has to give up the vertical distance *Bb,* or .6 billion M-16s a year. By the time we go from 10 billion to 12 billion CD-ROM players, to obtain that 2 billion unit increase, we have to forgo the vertical distance *Ff,* or 4.5 billion M-16s. In other words, we see an increase in the opportunity cost of the last 2 billion units of CD-ROM players—4.5 billion M-16s—compared to an equivalent increase in CD-ROM players when we started with none being produced at all—.4 billion M-16s.

What we are observing is called the **law of increasing relative cost.** When society takes more resources and applies them to the production of any specific good, the opportunity cost increases for each additional unit produced. The reason that, as a nation, we face the law of increasing relative cost (which causes the production possibilities curve to bow outward) is that certain resources are better suited for producing some goods than they are for other goods. Resources are generally not *perfectly* adaptable for alternative uses. When increasing the output of a particular good, producers must use less efficient resources than those already used in order to produce the additional output. Hence the cost of producing the additional units increases. With respect to our hypothetical example here, at first the electronic technicians in the armed services would shift over to producing CD-ROM players. After a while, though, janitors and army cooks would be asked to help. Clearly, they would be less effective in making CD-ROM players.

As a rule of thumb, *the more specialized the resources, the more bowed the production possibilities curve.* At the other extreme, if all resources are equally suitable for CD-ROM player production or M-16 production, the curves in Figures 2-2 and 2-3 would approach the straight line shown in our first example in Figure 2-1.

Law of increasing relative cost
The observation that the opportunity cost of additional units of a good generally increases as society attempts to produce more of that good. This accounts for the bowed-out shape of the production possibilities curve.

CONCEPTS IN BRIEF

- Trade-offs are represented graphically by a production possibilities curve showing the maximum quantity of one good or service that can be produced, given a specific quantity of another, from a given set of resources over a specified period of time—for example, one year.
- A PPC is drawn holding the quantity and quality of all resources fixed over the time period under study.
- Points outside the production possibilities curve are unattainable; points inside are attainable but represent an inefficient use or underuse of available resources.
- Because many resources are better suited for certain productive tasks than for others, society's production possibilities curve is bowed outward, following the law of increasing relative cost.

ECONOMIC GROWTH AND THE PRODUCTION POSSIBILITIES CURVE

Over any particular time period, a society cannot be outside the production possibilities curve. Over time, however, it is possible to have more of everything. This occurs through economic growth (why economic growth occurs will be discussed in a later chapter). Figure 2-4 shows the production possibilities curve for M-16 rifles and CD-ROM players shifting outward. The two additional curves shown represent new choices open to an economy that has experienced economic growth. Such economic growth occurs because of

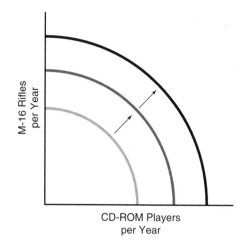

FIGURE 2-4

Economic Growth Allows for More of Everything

If the nation experiences economic growth, the production possibilities curve between M-16 rifles and CD-ROM players will move out, as is shown. This takes time, however, and it does not occur automatically. This means, therefore, that we can have more M-16s and more CD-ROM players only after a period of time during which we have experienced economic growth.

many things, including increases in the number of workers and productive investment in equipment.

Scarcity still exists, however, no matter how much economic growth there is. At any point in time, we will always be on some production possibilities curve; thus we will always face trade-offs. The more we want of one thing, the less we can have of others.

If a nation experiences economic growth, the production possibilities curve between M-16 rifles and CD-ROM players will move outward, as is shown in Figure 2-4. This takes time and does not occur automatically. One reason it will occur involves the choice about how much to consume today.

THE TRADE-OFF BETWEEN THE PRESENT AND THE FUTURE

Consumption
The use of goods and services for personal satisfaction.

The production possibilities curve and economic growth can be used to examine the trade-off between present **consumption** and future consumption. When we consume today, we are using up what we call consumption or consumer goods—food and clothes, for example. And we have already defined physical capital as the manufactured goods, such as machines and factories, used to make other goods and services.

Why We Make Capital Goods

Why would we be willing to use productive resources to make things—capital goods—that we cannot consume directly? For one thing, capital goods enable us to produce larger quantities of consumer goods or to produce them less expensively than we otherwise could. Before fish are "produced" for the market, equipment such as fishing boats, nets, and poles are produced first. Imagine how expensive it would be to obtain fish for market without using these capital goods. Catching fish with one's hands is not an easy task. The price per fish would be very high if capital goods weren't used.

Forgoing Current Consumption

Whenever we use productive resources to make capital goods, we are implicitly forgoing current consumption. We are waiting for some time in the future to consume the fruits that will be reaped from the use of capital goods. In effect, when we forgo current consumption to invest in capital goods, we are engaging in an economic activity that is forward-looking—we do not get instant utility or satisfaction from our activity. Indeed, if we were to produce only consumer goods now and no capital goods, our capacity to produce consumer goods in the future would suffer. Here we see a trade-off situation.

The Trade-off Between Consumption Goods and Capital Goods

To have more consumer goods in the future, we must accept fewer consumer goods today. In other words, an opportunity cost is involved here. Every time we make a choice for more goods today, we incur an opportunity cost of fewer goods tomorrow, and every time we make a choice of more goods in the future, we incur an opportunity cost of fewer goods today. With the resources that we don't use to produce consumer goods for today, we invest in capital goods that will produce more consumer goods for us later. The trade-off is shown in Figure 2-5. On the left in panel (a), you can see this trade-off depicted as a production possibilities curve between capital goods and consumption goods.

Assume that we are willing to give up $1 trillion worth of consumption today. We will be at point A in the left-hand diagram of panel (a). This will allow the economy to grow. We will have more future consumption because we invested in more capital goods today. In the right-hand diagram of panel (a), we see two goods represented, food and recreation. The production possibilities curve will move outward if we collectively decide to restrict consumption each year and invest in capital goods.

In panel (b), we show the results of our willingness to forgo more current consumption. We move to point C, where we have many fewer consumer goods today but produce a lot

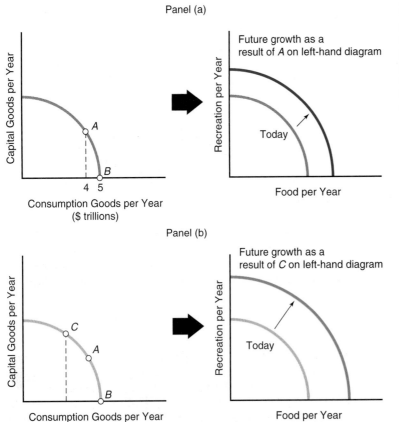

Panel (a)

FIGURE 2-5

Capital Goods and Growth

In panel (a), the nation chooses not to consume $1 trillion, so it invests that amount in capital goods. In panel (b), it chooses even more capital goods. The PPC moves even more to the right on the right-hand diagram in panel (b) as a result.

more capital goods. This leads to more future growth in this simplified model, and thus the production possibilities curve in the right-hand side of panel (b) shifts outward more than it did in the right-hand side of panel (a).

In other words, the more we give up today, the more we can have tomorrow, provided, of course, that the capital goods are productive in future periods and that society desires the consumer goods produced by this additional capital.

INTERNATIONAL EXAMPLE
Consumption Versus Capital Goods in the United States and Japan

The trade-off represented in Figure 2-5 on the production possibilities curve of capital versus consumption goods can be observed in real life when we compare different countries. The Japanese, for example, have chosen to devote more than twice the amount of resources each year to the production of capital goods than we have in the United States. Not surprisingly, the Japanese have until recently experienced economic growth at a much higher rate than the United States has. In effect, then, Japan is represented by panel (b) in Figure 2-5—choosing more capital goods—and America by panel (a)—choosing fewer capital goods.

FOR CRITICAL ANALYSIS: Does this analysis apply to the trade-off between consumption and human capital for you as an individual? If so, how? ●

CONCEPTS IN BRIEF

- The use of capital requires using productive resources to produce capital goods that will later be used to produce consumer goods.

- A trade-off is involved between current consumption and capital goods or, alternatively, between current consumption and future consumption because the more we invest in capital goods today, the greater the amount of consumer goods we can produce in the future and the smaller the amount of consumer goods we can produce today.

SPECIALIZATION AND GREATER PRODUCTIVITY

Specialization
The division of productive activities among persons and regions so that no one individual or one area is totally self-sufficient. An individual may specialize, for example, in law or medicine. A nation may specialize in the production of coffee, computers, or cameras.

Specialization involves working at a relatively well-defined, limited endeavor, such as accounting or teaching. It involves a division of labor among different individuals and regions. Most individuals, in fact, do specialize. For example, you could change the oil in your car if you wanted to. Typically, though, you take your car to a garage and let the mechanic change the oil. You benefit by letting the garage mechanic specialize in changing the oil and in doing other repairs on your car. The specialist will get the job finished sooner than you could and has the proper equipment to make the job go more smoothly. Specialization usually leads to greater productivity, not only for each individual but also for the nation.

Absolute Advantage

Absolute advantage
The ability to produce a good or service at an "absolutely" lower cost, usually measured in units of labor or resource input required to produce one unit of the good or service.

Specialization occurs because different individuals and different nations have different skills. Sometimes it seems that some individuals are better at doing everything than anyone else. A president of a large company might be able to type better than any of the typists, file better than any of the file clerks, and wash windows better than any of the window washers. The president has an **absolute advantage** in all of these endeavors—he uses fewer labor hours for each task than anyone else in the company. The president does not, however, spend his time doing those other activities. Why not? Because he is being paid the most for undertaking the president's managerial duties. The president specializes in one particular task in spite of having an absolute advantage in all tasks. Indeed, absolute advantage is irrelevant in predicting how he uses his time; only *comparative advantage* matters.

Comparative Advantage

Comparative advantage is the ability to perform an activity at the lowest opportunity cost. You have a comparative advantage in one activity whenever you have the lowest opportunity cost of performing that activity. Comparative advantage is always a *relative* concept. You may be able to change the oil in your car; you might even be able to change it faster than the local mechanic. But if the opportunity cost you face by changing the oil exceeds the mechanic's opportunity cost, the mechanic has a comparative advantage in changing the oil. The mechanic faces a lower opportunity cost for that activity.

Comparative advantage
The ability to produce a good or service at a lower opportunity cost compared to other producers.

You may be convinced that everybody can do everything better than you. In this extreme situation, do you still have a comparative advantage? The answer is yes. What you need to do to discover your comparative advantage is to find a job in which your *disadvantage* relative to others is the smallest. You do not have to be a mathematical genius to figure this out. The market tells you very clearly by offering you the highest income for the job for which you have the smallest disadvantage compared to others. Stated differently, to find your comparative advantage no matter how much better everybody else can do the jobs that you want to do, you simply find which job maximizes your income.

The coaches of sports teams are constantly faced with determining each player's comparative advantage. Babe Ruth was originally one of the best pitchers in professional baseball when he played for the Boston Red Sox. After he was traded to the New York Yankees, the owner and the coach decided to make him an outfielder, even though he was a better pitcher than anyone else on the team roster. They wanted "The Babe" to concentrate on his hitting. Good pitchers do not bring in as many fans as home-run kings. Babe Ruth's comparative advantage was clearly in hitting homers rather than practicing and developing his pitching game.

Scarcity, Self-Interest, and Specialization

In Chapter 1, you learned about the assumption of rational self-interest. To repeat, for the purposes of our analyses we assume that individuals are rational in that they will do what is in their own self-interest. They will not consciously carry out actions that will make them worse off. In this chapter, you learned that scarcity requires people to make choices. We assume that they make choices based on their self-interest. When they make these choices, they attempt to maximize benefits net of opportunity cost. In so doing, individuals choose their comparative advantage and end up specializing. Ultimately, when people specialize, they increase the money income they make and therefore become richer. When all individuals and businesses specialize simultaneously, the gains are seen in greater material well-being. With any given set of resources, specialization will result in higher output.

INTERNATIONAL EXAMPLE
Why Foreign Graduate Students Specialize When Studying in the United States

Specialization is evident in the fields of endeavor that foreign students choose when they come to the United States for graduate studies. Consider the following statistics: More than

60 percent of U.S. doctorates in engineering and 55 percent of those in mathematics, computer science, and the physical sciences are earned by foreign-born students. Yet foreign nationals are awarded relatively few advanced degrees in business, law, or medicine. The reason has nothing to do with intelligence or giftedness; it is simply that many more of the best American students choose schools in these professional fields rather than ones offering science and engineering programs.

Why does this specialization occur? For American students, the greatest returns for about the same effort come from business, law, and medicine. In contrast, foreign-born graduate students face fewer language and cultural obstacles (and hence better job prospects) if they choose technical subjects.

When students from foreign countries come to American graduate schools to obtain their Ph.D. degrees, more than 70 percent of them remain in the United States after graduation, thereby augmenting America's supply of engineers and scientists. Such specialization has helped the United States maintain its leadership in both the technoscientific and sociocultural areas.

FOR CRITICAL ANALYSIS: What type of capital do foreign-born students bring with them to the United States? ●

THE DIVISION OF LABOR

Division of labor
The segregation of a resource into different specific tasks; for example, one automobile worker puts on bumpers, another doors, and so on.

In any firm that includes specialized human and nonhuman resources, there is a **division of labor** among those resources. The best-known example of all time comes from one of the earliest and perhaps most famous economists, Adam Smith, who in *The Wealth of Nations* (1776) illustrated the benefits of a division of labor in the making of pins, as depicted in the following example:

> One man draws out the wire, another straightens it, a third cuts it, a fourth points it, a fifth grinds it at the top for receiving the head; to make the head requires two or three distinct operations; to put it on is a peculiar business, to whiten the pins is another; it is even a trade by itself to put them into the paper.

Making pins this way allowed 10 workers without very much skill to make almost 48,000 pins "of a middling size" in a day. One worker, toiling alone, could have made perhaps 20 pins a day; therefore, 10 workers could have produced 200. Division of labor allowed for an increase in the daily output of the pin factory from 200 to 48,000! (Smith did not attribute all of the gain to the division of labor according to talent but credited also the use of machinery and the fact that less time was spent shifting from task to task.)

What we are discussing here involves a division of the resource called labor into different kinds of labor. The different kinds of labor are organized in such a way as to increase the amount of output possible from the fixed resources available. We can therefore talk about an organized division of labor within a firm leading to increased output.

COMPARATIVE ADVANTAGE AND TRADE AMONG NATIONS

Though most of our analysis of absolute advantage, comparative advantage, and specialization has dealt with individuals, it is equally applicable to nations. First consider the United States. The Plains states have a comparative advantage in the production of grains and other agricultural goods. The states to the north and east tend to specialize in industrialized production, such as automobiles. Not surprisingly, grains are shipped from the

Plains states to the northern states, and automobiles are shipped in the reverse direction. Such specialization and trade allow for higher incomes and standards of living. If both the Plains states and the northern states were politically defined as separate nations, the same analysis would still hold, but we would call it international trade. Indeed, Europe is comparable to the United States in area and population, but instead of one nation, Europe has 15. What in America we call *interstate* trade, in Europe they call *international* trade. There is no difference, however, in the economic results—both yield greater economic efficiency and higher average incomes.

Political problems that do not normally arise within a particular nation often do between nations. For example, if California avocado growers develop a cheaper method than growers in southern Florida to produce a tastier avocado, the Florida growers will lose out. They cannot do much about the situation except try to lower their own costs of production or improve their product. If avocado growers in Mexico, however, develop a cheaper method to produce better-tasting avocados, both California and Florida growers can (and likely will) try to raise political barriers that will prevent Mexican avocado growers from freely selling their product in America. U.S. avocado growers will use such arguments as "unfair" competition and loss of American jobs. In so doing, they are only partly right: Avocado-growing jobs may decline in America, but jobs will not necessarily decline overall. If the argument of U.S. avocado growers had any validity, every time a region in the United States developed a better way to produce a product manufactured somewhere else in the country, employment in America would decline. That has never happened and never will.

When nations specialize where they have a comparative advantage and then trade with the rest of the world, the average standard of living in the world rises. In effect, international trade allows the world to move from inside the global production possibilities curve toward the curve itself, thereby improving worldwide economic efficiency.

> ## THINKING CRITICALLY ABOUT THE MEDIA
>
> ### International Trade
>
> If you watch enough news on TV or frequently read the popular press, you get a distinct impression that international trade is somehow different from trade within our borders. At any given time, the United States is either at economic war with Japan or other countries in Asia or we are fighting with the European Union over whether American films should be allowed to dominate cinema offerings there. International economics is just like any other type of economics; trade is just another economic activity. Indeed, one can think of international trade as a production process that transforms goods that we sell to other countries (exports) into what we buy from other countries (imports). International trade is a mutually beneficial exchange that occurs across political borders. If you imagine a world that was just one country, trade would still exist worldwide, but it would not be called international trade.

CONCEPTS IN BRIEF

- With a given set of resources, specialization results in higher output; in other words, there are gains to specialization in terms of greater material well-being.

- Individuals and nations specialize in their areas of comparative advantage in order to reap the gains of specialization.

- Comparative advantages are found by determining which activities have the lowest opportunity cost—that is, which activities yield the highest return for the time and resources used.

- A division of labor occurs when different workers are assigned different tasks. Together, the workers produce a desired product.

When you're stuck in traffic, you pay an opportunity cost. How is this driver reducing that cost?

CONCEPTS APPLIED:
SCARCITY, OPPORTUNITY COST, TRADE-OFFS

Visit www.econtoday.com for an Internet Activity that expands your understanding of these concepts.

"Time is money." Translated into the economic terminology you have learned in this chapter, time represents an opportunity cost. Highway planners ignored this reality for many years. Then they started to add high-occupancy vehicle lanes, sometimes called carpool lanes or diamond lanes. At rush hour, only cars carrying at least two (or in some places three) passengers can use this special fast lane.

Using a carpool lane imposes a cost on the driver. The driver has to arrange for there to be a passenger in the car (we will ignore the cheaters who have tried to get away with putting lifelike dummies in the passenger seat). The benefit, of course, is saving time by avoiding the more congested normal lanes on freeways and expressways. The rational driver is assumed, therefore, to compare the opportunity cost of time saved with the "cost" of picking up someone with whom to carpool. The opportunity cost is the highest-valued use of the time saved. It may be measured by extra pay for working more, which may be a proxy for the value of extra time spent with one's family, going to the gym, and the like.

Direct Payments for Using Fast Lanes— an Alternative

Some people may value their time highly yet be unwilling always to try to find a carpooler with whom to drive to work. Some of these individuals would be willing to pay for the ability to drive in less congested lanes on freeways and expressways.

In San Diego, California, highway planners decided to let drivers do just that. The experiment started in December 1996 and continues to this day. In the first seven hours, 500 express passes were sold at $50 per month each. The price

has now been increased to $70 per month. As the process becomes more popular, officials plan to raise the price even higher. By March 1997, over $70,000 had been collected. That money was destined to be used to build a new bus route along the Interstate 15 corridor.

By the time you read this, overhead antennas should have been installed to deduct tolls electronically from a coaster-sized transponder inside each car. That way, motorists can pay on a trip-by-trip basis rather than by the month.

Did Fast Lanes Become "Lexus Lanes"?

At the beginning of the San Diego experiment, critics argued that the fast lanes would simply become "Lexus lanes," meaning that well-to-do drivers would be the only ones purchasing the right to use those fast lanes without carrying additional passengers. That has turned out to be inaccurate. Certainly drivers of luxury cars have purchased the rights to drive those lanes, but so have owners of plain old Fords, Chevrolets, and Toyotas. A priori, we cannot be certain how individuals value their time. While in general those with higher earning abilities face a higher opportunity cost of time, many with lower earnings place a high value on free time in order to engage in, say, sports, theater, meditation, or movies. Those lower-income individuals may be willing to sacrifice a relatively larger percentage of their incomes to drive in the fast lanes because of the high value they place on time.

But Is It Fair?

The first thought that comes to some people's minds when they see lone drivers in the fast lane is that it "isn't fair." Why should people, just because they paid for the right, be able to drive in the fast lane? The issue of fairness cannot be answered by economics. Remember that economics is a positive science.

We can point out, though, that for virtually all goods and services, people who are willing to pay more generally get more in both quantity and quality. Is it fair that people who are willing to pay a relatively high price for hothouse-grown strawberries in the middle of winter get to buy them? Is it fair that people who are willing to pay a higher price for luxury cars get to buy them? Is it fair that people who want to pay higher prices for more sophisticated five-channel surround-sound home theater systems get to buy them? Economists cannot answer such questions. Suffice it to say that all of us make choices all the time about how to use our limited incomes. No value judgment can be reached about the choices other individuals make.

Montana's Answer to Reducing Driving Time

Montana, a relatively unpopulated state, has chosen another way to reduce driving time. It changed its speed limit to whatever is "reasonable and prudent." Some 85 percent of traffic now moves at around 74 miles an hour. Driving speeds tend to be higher where there are long stretches of straight, flat road. For interstate truckers, who are generally paid 23 to 25 cents a mile, the higher highway speeds translate directly into increased pay. On these roads, truckers can specifically estimate the opportunity cost of time. For example, a trucker paid 25 cents per mile for a 480-mile trip would earn $120. At 60 miles an hour, the trip would take eight hours, yielding an hourly wage of $15. But the same trip made at 80 miles an hour would take six hours, and the trucker's wage would jump to $20 an hour. Is it any wonder that long-distance truckers favor higher speed limits . . . or none at all?

FOR CRITICAL ANALYSIS

1. What is the relationship between paying a fee for fast lane use and giving a tip to maître d' to be seated more quickly at a crowded restaurant? Does the question of fairness enter into either of these practices?
2. Many bridges in major cities are extremely congested at rush hour. How could traffic planners reduce such congestion?
3. Under what circumstances would relatively poor individuals be willing to pay to drive in fast lanes?
4. How do potential purchasers of express lane passes determine whether the pass is worth the money they have to pay each month?

CHAPTER SUMMARY

1. All societies at all times face the universal problem of scarcity because we cannot obtain everything we want from nature without sacrifice. Thus scarcity and poverty are not synonymous. Even the richest persons face scarcity because they also have to make choices among alternatives.
2. The resources we use to produce desired goods and services can be classified into land, labor, physical and human capital, and entrepreneurship.
3. Goods are all things from which individuals derive satisfaction. Economic goods are those for which the desired quantity exceeds the amount that is directly available from nature at a zero price. The goods that we want are not necessarily those that we need. The term *need* is undefinable in economics, whereas humans have unlimited *wants*, which are defined as the goods and services on which we place a positive value.

4. We measure the cost of anything by what has to be given up in order to have it. This cost is called opportunity cost.

5. The trade-offs we face as individuals and those we face as a society can be represented graphically by a production possibilities curve (PPC). This curve shows the maximum quantity of one good or service that can be produced, given a specific quantity of another, from a given set of resources over a specified period of time, usually one year.

6. Because resources are specialized, production possibilities curves bow outward. This means that each additional increment of one good can be obtained only by giving up more and more of the other goods. This is called the law of increasing relative cost.

7. It is impossible to be outside the production possibilities curve, but we can be inside it. When we are, we are in a situation of unemployment, inefficiently organized resources, or some combination of the two.

8. There is a trade-off between consumption goods and capital goods. The more resources we devote to capital goods, the more consumption goods we can normally have in the future (and less currently). This is because more capital goods allow the economy to grow, thereby moving the production possibilities curve outward.

9. One finds one's comparative advantage by looking at the activity that has the lowest opportunity cost. That is, one's comparative advantage lies in the activity that generates the highest income. By specializing in one's comparative advantage, one is assured of reaping the gains of specialization.

10. Division of labor occurs when workers are assigned different tasks.

DISCUSSION OF PREVIEW QUESTIONS

1. **Do affluent people face the problem of scarcity?**

   Scarcity is a relative concept and exists because wants are great relative to the means of satisfying those wants (wealth or income). Even though affluent people have relatively and absolutely high levels of income or wealth, they nevertheless typically want more than they can have (in luxury goods, power, prestige, and so on).

2. **Fresh air may be consumed at no charge, but is it free of cost to society?**

   Individuals are not charged a price for the use of air. Yet truly fresh air is not free to society. If a good were free to society, every person would be able to use all that he or she wanted to use; no one would have to sacrifice anything in order to use that good, and people would not have to compete for it. In the United States, different groups compete for air; for example, environmentalists and concerned citizens compete with automobile drivers and factories for clean air.

3. **Why does the scarcity problem force people to consider opportunity costs?**

   Individuals have limited incomes; as a consequence, an expenditure on an automobile necessarily precludes expenditures on other goods and services. The same is true for society, which also faces the scarcity problem; if society allocates specific resources to the production of a steel mill, those same resources cannot be allocated elsewhere. Because resources are limited, society is forced to decide how to allocate its available resources; scarcity means that the cost of allocating resources to produce specific goods is ultimately assessed in terms of other goods that are necessarily sacrificed. Because there are millions of ways in which the resources allocated to a steel mill might otherwise be allocated, one is forced to consider the *highest-valued* alternative. We define the opportunity cost of a good as its highest-valued alternative; the opportunity cost of the steel mill to society is the highest-valued output that those same resources could otherwise have produced.

4. **Can a "free" college education ever be truly free?**

   Suppose that you were given a college education without having to pay any fees whatsoever. You could say that you were receiving a free education. But someone is paying for your education because you are using scarce resources—buildings, professors' time, electricity for lighting, etc. The opportunity cost of your education is certainly not zero, so in that sense it is not free. Furthermore, by going to college, you are giving up the ability to earn income during that time period. Therefore, there is an opportunity cost to your attending classes and studying. You can approximate that opportunity cost by estimating what your current after-tax income would be if you were working instead of going to school.

PROBLEMS

(Answers to the odd-numbered problems appear at the back of the book.)

2-1. The following sets of numbers represent hypothetical production possibilities for a nation in 1998. Plot these points on graph paper.

Butter	Guns
4	0
3	1.6
2	2.4
1	2.8
0	3.0

Does the law of increasing relative cost seem to hold? Why? On the same graph, plot and draw the production possibilities curve that will represent 10 percent economic growth.

2-2. There are 150,000 conscripts (draftees) in the French army, each paid $2,000 a year. The average salary of each conscript prior to military service was $18,500 per year. What does it cost for conscripts in France each year?

2-3. Answer the questions using the following information.

Employee	Daily Work Effort	Production
Ann Jones	4 hours	8 jackets
	4 hours	12 ties
Ned Lopez	4 hours	8 jackets
	4 hours	12 ties
Total daily output		16 jackets
		24 ties

a. Who has an absolute advantage in jacket production?
b. Who has a comparative advantage in tie production?
c. Will Jones and Lopez specialize?
d. If they specialize, what will total output equal?

2-4. Two countries, Workland and Playland, have similar populations and identical production possibilities curves but different preferences. The production possibilities combinations are as follows:

Point	Capital Goods	Consumption Goods
A	0	20
B	1	19
C	2	17
D	3	14
E	4	10
F	5	5
G	7	0

Playland is located at point *B* on the PPC, and Workland is located at point *E*. Assume that this situation continues into the future and that all other things remain the same.

a. What is Workland's opportunity cost of capital goods in terms of consumption goods?
b. What is Playland's opportunity cost of capital goods in terms of consumption goods?
c. How would the PPCs of Workland and Playland be expected to compare to each other 50 years in the future?

2-5. Which of the following are part of the opportunity cost of going to a football game in town instead of watching it on TV at home? Explain why.

a. The expense of lunch in a restaurant prior to the football game.

b. The value of one hour of sleep lost because of a traffic jam after the game.

c. The expense of a babysitter for your children if they are too young to go to a football game.

2-6. Assume that your economics and English exams are scheduled for the same day. How would you determine how much time you should spend study-ing for each exam? Does the grade you are cur-rently receiving in each course affect your deci-sion? Why or why not?

2-7. Some people argue that air is not an economic good. If you agree with this statement, explain why. If you disagree, explain why. (Hint: Is all air the same?)

COMPUTER-ASSISTED INSTRUCTION

If you are given a production possibilities table, can you calculate the opportunity cost of successive units of one good in terms of forgone units of the other? By requiring specific calculations, the concept of opportunity cost is revealed.

Complete problem and answer appear on disk.

INTERACTING WITH THE INTERNET

What Happens When You Are Lost in Cyberspace?

All of the Internet addresses that you will find in this text were active at the time of publication. Beware, though: The saying "Here today, gone tomorrow" is especially true with reference to Inter-net sites.

If an address does not work, the first thing you should do is check the spelling, punctuation, and capitalization of your URL to make sure it corresponds exactly to what is printed in the book. Your Internet browser may still tell you that it is "unable to locate the server" or that "the server does not have DNS entry." Don't despair; even if a particular link or page no longer exists, there might be something of value hidden somewhere.

The trick is to start "trimming" the URL, one slash at a time. If your first destination is not found, click on the URL shown in your browser and delete all of the information to the right of the forward slash that is farthest to the right. Then press Enter and see where you go. If you still cannot find what you want, trim back to the next forward slash, and so forth. Eventually, you will get to the home page and can restart your investigation. (A temporary problem you might encounter at any time and for any location is the message "This server is not responding" or the like. This simply means that there is a temporary problem with the server you are trying to access; another attempt later in the day or the next day will probably be successful.)

Let's say you wanted to get information on the economic status of the United States. You might go to the Federal Reserve Board's "Beige Book" at the following Web site:

www.bog.frb.fed.us/fomc/bb/current/

You could start trimming this URL by deleting *current/*. Then if that did not work, you would delete *bb/*. And if that did not work, you would delete *fomc/*. You would end up at the home page of the Fed-eral Reserve Board.

APPENDIX A

READING AND WORKING WITH GRAPHS

A graph is a visual representation of the relationship between variables. In this appendix, we'll stick to just two variables: an **independent variable,** which can change in value freely, and a **dependent variable,** which changes only as a result of changes in the value of the independent variable. For example, if nothing else is changing in your life, your weight depends on the amount of food you eat. Food is the independent variable and weight the dependent variable.

A table is a list of numerical values showing the relationship between two (or more) variables. Any table can be converted into a graph, which is a visual representation of that list. Once you understand how a table can be converted to a graph, you will understand what graphs are and how to construct and use them.

Consider a practical example. A conservationist may try to convince you that driving at lower highway speeds will help you conserve gas. Table A-1 shows the relationship between speed—the independent variable—and the distance you can go on a gallon of gas at that speed—the dependent variable. This table does show a pattern of sorts. As the data in the first column get larger in value, the data in the second column get smaller.

Now let's take a look at the different ways in which variables can be related.

DIRECT AND INVERSE RELATIONSHIPS

Two variables can be related in different ways, some simple, others more complex. For example, a person's weight and height are often related. If we measured the height and weight of thousands of people, we would surely find that taller people tend to weigh more than shorter people. That is, we would discover that there is a **direct relationship** between height and weight. By this we simply mean that an *increase* in one variable is usually associated with an *increase* in the related variable. This can easily be seen in panel (a) of Figure A-1.

Let's look at another simple way in which two variables can be related. Much evidence indicates that as the price of a specific commodity rises, the amount purchased decreases—there is an **inverse relationship** between the variable's price per unit and quantity purchased. A table listing the data for this relationship would indicate that for higher and higher prices, smaller and smaller quantities would be purchased. We see this relationship in panel (b) of Figure A-1.

Independent variable
A variable whose value is determined independently of, or outside, the equation under study.

Dependent variable
A variable whose value changes according to changes in the value of one or more independent variables.

TABLE A-1

Gas Mileage as a Function of Driving Speed

Miles per Hour	Miles per Gallon
45	25
50	24
55	23
60	21
65	19
70	16
75	13

Direct relationship
A relationship between two variables that is positive, meaning that an increase in one variable is associated with an increase in the other and a decrease in one variable is associated with a decrease in the other.

Inverse relationship
A relationship between two variables that is negative, meaning that an increase in one variable is associated with a decrease in the other and a decrease in one variable is associated with an increase in the other.

FIGURE A-1

Relationships

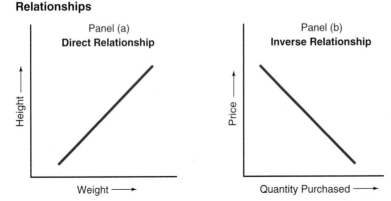

Panel (a) Direct Relationship — Height (vertical axis), Weight (horizontal axis)

Panel (b) Inverse Relationship — Price (vertical axis), Quantity Purchased (horizontal axis)

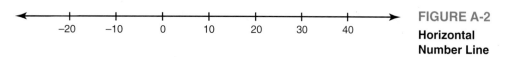

FIGURE A-2

Horizontal Number Line

CONSTRUCTING A GRAPH

Let us now examine how to construct a graph to illustrate a relationship between two variables.

A Number Line

Number line

A line that can be divided into segments of equal length, each associated with a number.

The first step is to become familiar with what is called a **number line.** One is shown in Figure A-2. There are two things that you should know about it.

1. The points on the line divide the line into equal segments.
2. The numbers associated with the points on the line increase in value from left to right; saying it the other way around, the numbers decrease in value from right to left. However you say it, what we're describing is formally called an *ordered set of points.*

On the number line, we have shown the line segments—that is, the distance from 0 to 10 or the distance between 30 and 40. They all appear to be equal and, indeed, are equal to $\frac{1}{2}$ inch. When we use a distance to represent a quantity, such as barrels of oil, graphically, we are *scaling* the number line. In the example shown, the distance between 0 and 10 might represent 10 barrels of oil, or the distance from 0 to 40 might represent 40 barrels. Of course, the scale may differ on different number lines. For example, a distance of 1 inch could represent 10 units on one number line but 5,000 units on another. Notice that on our number line, points to the left of 0 correspond to negative numbers and points to the right of 0 correspond to positive numbers.

Of course, we can also construct a vertical number line. Consider the one in Figure A-3. As we move up this vertical number line, the numbers increase in value; conversely, as we descend, they decrease in value. Below 0 the numbers are negative, and above 0 the numbers are positive. And as on the horizontal number line, all the line segments are equal. This line is divided into segments such that the distance between -2 and -1 is the same as the distance between 0 and 1.

Combining Vertical and Horizontal Number Lines

By drawing the horizontal and vertical lines on the same sheet of paper, we are able to express the relationships between variables graphically. We do this in Figure A-4.

FIGURE A-3

Vertical Number Line

FIGURE A-4

A Set of Coordinate Axes

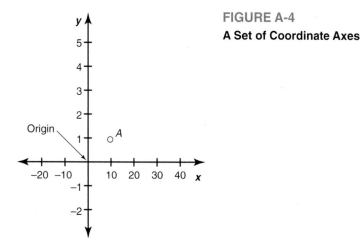

We draw them (1) so that they intersect at each other's 0 point and (2) so that they are perpendicular to each other. The result is a set of coordinate axes, where each line is called an *axis.* When we have two axes, they span a plane.

For one number line, you need only one number to specify any point on the line; equivalently, when you see a point on the line, you know that it represents one number or one value. With a coordinate value system, you need two numbers to specify a single point in the plane; when you see a single point on a graph, you know that it represents two numbers or two values.

The basic things that you should know about a coordinate number system are that the vertical number line is referred to as the **y axis,** the horizontal number line is referred to as the **x axis,** and the point of intersection of the two lines is referred to as the **origin.**

Any point such as *A* in Figure A-4 represents two numbers—a value of *x* and a value of *y.* But we know more than that; we also know that point *A* represents a positive value of *y* because it is above the *x* axis, and we know that it represents a positive value of *x* because it is to the right of the *y* axis.

Point *A* represents a "paired observation" of the variables *x* and *y;* in particular, in Figure A-4, *A* represents an observation of the pair of values $x = 10$ and $y = 1$. Every point in the coordinate system corresponds to a paired observation of *x* and *y,* which can be simply written (x, y)—the *x* value is always specified first, then the *y* value. When we give the values associated with the position of point *A* in the coordinate number system, we are in effect giving the coordinates of that point. *A*'s coordinates are $x = 10$, $y = 1$, or $(10, 1)$.

GRAPHING NUMBERS IN A TABLE

Consider Table A-2. Column 1 shows different prices for T-shirts, and column 2 gives the number of T-shirts purchased per week at these prices. Notice the pattern of these numbers. As the price of T-shirts falls, the number of T-shirts purchased per week increases. Therefore, an inverse relationship exists between these two variables, and as soon as we represent it on a graph, you will be able to see the relationship. We can graph this relationship using a coordinate number system—a vertical and horizontal number line for each of these two variables. Such a graph is shown in panel (b) of Figure A-5.

y axis
The vertical axis in a graph.

x axis
The horizontal axis in a graph.

Origin
The intersection of the *y* axis and the *x* axis in a graph.

TABLE A-2
T-Shirts Purchased

(1) Price of T-Shirts	(2) Number of T-Shirts Purchased per Week
$10	20
9	30
8	40
7	50
6	60
5	70

FIGURE A-5

Graphing the Relationship Between T-Shirts Purchased and Price

Panel (a)

Price per T-Shirt	T-Shirts Purchased per Week	Point on Graph
$10	20	I (20, 10)
9	30	J (30, 9)
8	40	K (40, 8)
7	50	L (50, 7)
6	60	M (60, 6)
5	70	N (70, 5)

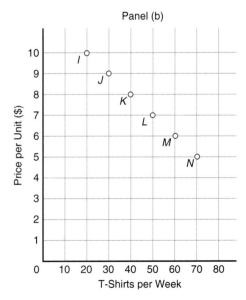

Panel (b)

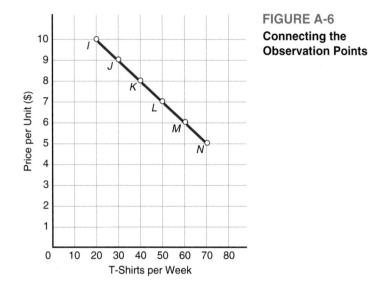

FIGURE A-6

Connecting the Observation Points

In economics, it is conventional to put dollar values on the *y* axis. We therefore construct a vertical number line for price and a horizontal number line, the *x* axis, for quantity of T-shirts purchased per week. The resulting coordinate system allows the plotting of each of the paired observation points; in panel (a), we repeat Table A-2, with a column added expressing these points in paired-data (*x, y*) form. For example, point *J* is the paired observation (30, 9). It indicates that when the price of a T-shirt is $9, 30 will be purchased per week.

If it were possible to sell parts of a T-shirt ($\frac{1}{2}$ or $\frac{1}{20}$ of a shirt), we would have observations at every possible price. That is, we would be able to connect our paired observations, represented as lettered points. Let's assume that we can make T-shirts perfectly divisible. We would then have a line that connects these points, as shown in the graph in Figure A-6.

In short, we have now represented the data from the table in the form of a graph. Note that an inverse relationship between two variables shows up on a graph as a line or curve that slopes *downward* from left to right. (You might as well get used to the idea that economists call a straight line a "curve" even though it may not curve at all. Much of economists' data turn out to be curves, so they refer to everything represented graphically, even straight lines, as curves.)

THE SLOPE OF A LINE (A LINEAR CURVE)

An important property of a curve represented on a graph is its *slope*. Consider Figure A-7 on page 42, which represents the quantities of shoes per week that a seller is willing to offer at different prices. Note that in panel (a) of Figure A-7, as in Figure A-5, we have expressed the coordinates of the points in parentheses in paired-data form.

Slope

The change in the *y* value divided by the corresponding change in the *x* value of a curve; the "incline" of the curve.

The **slope** of a line is defined as the change in the *y* values divided by the corresponding change in the *x* values as we move along the line. Let's move from point *E* to point *D* in panel (b) of Figure A-7. As we move, we note that the change in the *y* values, which is the change in price, is +$20, because we have moved from a price of $20 to a price of $40 per pair. As we move from *E* to *D*, the change in the *x* values is +80; the number of pairs of shoes willingly offered per week rises from 80 to 160 pairs. The slope calculated as a change in the *y* values divided by the change in the *x* values is therefore

$$\frac{20}{80} = \frac{1}{4}$$

FIGURE A-7

A Positively Sloped Curve

Panel (a)

Price per Pair	Pairs of Shoes Offered per Week	Point on Graph
$100	400	A (400, 100)
80	320	B (320, 80)
60	240	C (240, 60)
40	160	D (160, 40)
20	80	E (80, 20)

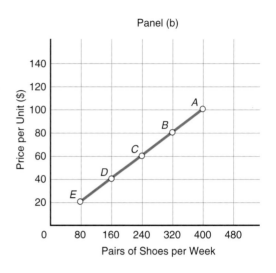

Panel (b)

It may be helpful for you to think of slope as a "rise" (movement in the vertical direction) over a "run" (movement in the horizontal direction). We show this abstractly in Figure A-8. The slope is measured by the amount of rise divided by the amount of run. In the example in Figure A-8, and of course in Figure A-7, the amount of rise is positive and so is the amount of run. That's because it's a direct relationship. We show an inverse relationship in Figure A-9. The slope is still equal to the rise divided by the run, but in this case the rise and the run have opposite signs because the curve slopes downward. That means that the slope will have to be negative and that we are dealing with an inverse relationship.

Now let's calculate the slope for a different part of the curve in panel (b) of Figure A-7. We will find the slope as we move from point *B* to point *A*. Again, we note that the slope, or rise over run, from *B* to *A* equals

$$\frac{20}{80} = \frac{1}{4}$$

A specific property of a straight line is that its slope is the same between any two points; in other words, the slope is constant at all points on a straight line in a graph.

We conclude that for our example in Figure A-7, the relationship between the price of a pair of shoes and the number of pairs of shoes willingly offered per week is *linear,* which simply means "in a straight line," and our calculations indicate a constant slope. Moreover, we calculate a direct relationship between these two variables, which turns out to be an

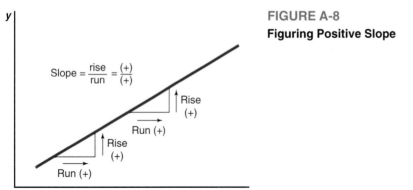

FIGURE A-8

Figuring Positive Slope

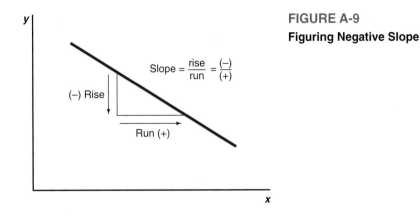

FIGURE A-9
Figuring Negative Slope

upward-sloping (from left to right) curve. Upward-sloping curves have positive slopes—in this case, it is $+\frac{1}{4}$.

We know that an inverse relationship between two variables shows up as a downward-sloping curve—rise over run will be a negative slope because the rise and run have opposite signs as shown in Figure A-9. When we see a negative slope, we know that increases in one variable are associated with decreases in the other. Therefore, we say that downward-sloping curves have negative slopes. Can you verify that the slope of the graph representing the relationship between T-shirt prices and the quantity of T-shirts purchased per week in Figure A-6 is $-\frac{1}{10}$?

Slopes of Nonlinear Curves

The graph presented in Figure A-10 indicates a *nonlinear* relationship between two variables, total profits and output per unit of time. Inspection of this graph indicates that at first, increases in output lead to increases in total profits; that is, total profits rise as output increases. But beyond some output level, further increases in output cause decreases in total profits.

Can you see how this curve rises at first, reaches a peak at point *C*, and then falls? This curve relating total profits to output levels appears mountain-shaped.

Considering that this curve is nonlinear (it is obviously not a straight line), should we expect a constant slope when we compute changes in *y* divided by corresponding changes in *x* in moving from one point to another? A quick inspection, even without specific numbers, should lead us to conclude that the slopes of lines joining different points in this curve, such as between *A* and *B, B* and *C,* or *C* and *D,* will *not* be the same. The curve slopes upward (in a positive direction) for some values and downward (in a negative direction) for

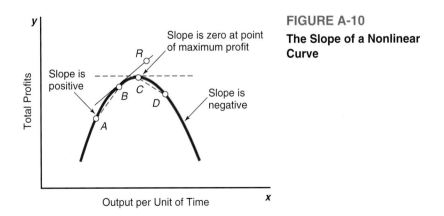

FIGURE A-10

The Slope of a Nonlinear Curve

other values. In fact, the slope of the line between any two points on this curve will be different from the slope of the line between any two other points. Each slope will be different as we move along the curve.

Instead of using a line between two points to discuss slope, mathematicians and economists prefer to discuss the slope *at a particular point*. The slope at a point on the curve, such as point *B* in the graph in Figure A-10, is the slope of a line *tangent* to that point. A tangent line is a straight line that touches a curve at only one point. For example, it might be helpful to think of the tangent at *B* as the straight line that just "kisses" the curve at point *B*.

To calculate the slope of a tangent line, you need to have some additional information besides the two values of the point of tangency. For example, in Figure A-10, if we knew that the point *R* also lay on the tangent line and we knew the two values of that point, we could calculate the slope of the tangent line. We could calculate rise over run between points *B* and *R*, and the result would be the slope of the line tangent to the one point *B* on the curve.

APPENDIX SUMMARY

1. Direct relationships involve a dependent variable changing in the same direction as the change in the independent variable.
2. Inverse relationships involve the dependent variable changing in the opposite direction of the change in the independent variable.
3. When we draw a graph showing the relationship between two economic variables, we are holding all other things constant (the Latin term for which is *ceteris paribus*).
4. We obtain a set of coordinates by putting vertical and horizontal number lines together. The vertical line is called the *y* axis; the horizontal line, the *x* axis.

5. The slope of any linear (straight-line) curve is the change in the *y* values divided by the corresponding change in the *x* values as we move along the line. Otherwise stated, the slope is calculated as the amount of rise over the amount of run, where rise is movement in the vertical direction and run is movement in the horizontal direction.
6. The slope of a nonlinear curve changes; it is positive when the curve is rising and negative when the curve is falling. At a maximum or minimum point, the slope of the nonlinear curve is zero.

PROBLEMS

(The answer to Problem A-1 appears at the back of the book.)

A-1. Complete the schedule and plot the following function:

$y = 3x$

y	x
	4
	3
	2
	1
	0
	−1
	−2
	−3
	−4

A-2. Complete the schedule and plot the following function:

$y = x^2$

y	x
	4
	3
	2
	1
	0
	−1
	−2
	−3
	−4

CHAPTER 3

DEMAND AND SUPPLY

Auctions have been around for centuries. Farmers first used auctions to sell their grains to people who would use the grains to make flour and other food products. Today, some of the best-publicized auctions involve fine art at Sotheby's and Christie's. In addition to the normal auction scene, however, a whole new revolution in auctioneering is taking place. Hundreds, if not thousands, of auctions are taking place on the Internet as you read this sentence. To understand better how auctions work, whether on-line or elsewhere, you will need the tools of supply and demand analysis.

PREVIEW QUESTIONS

1. Why are relative prices important in understanding the law of demand?

2. How can we distinguish between a change in *demand* and a change in *quantity demanded*?

3. Why is there normally a direct relationship between price and quantity supplied (other things being equal)?

4. Why will the market clearing price occur at the intersection of the supply and demand curves rather than at a higher or lower price?

Did You Know That . . . more than 60 million people currently own portable cellular phones? This is a huge jump from the mere 200,000 who owned them in 1985. Since 1992, two out of every three new telephone numbers have been assigned to cellular phones. There are several reasons for the growth of cellular phones, not the least being the dramatic reduction in both price and size due to improved and cheaper computer chips that go into making them. There is something else at work, though. It has to do with crime. In a recent survey, 46 percent of new cellular phone users said that personal safety was the main reason they bought a portable phone. In Florida, for example, most cellular phone companies allow users simply to dial *FHP to reach the Florida Highway Patrol. The rush to cellular phones is worldwide. Over the past decade, sales have grown by nearly 50 percent every year outside the United States.

We could attempt to explain the phenomenon by saying that more people like to use portable phones. But that explanation is neither satisfying nor entirely accurate. If we use the economist's primary set of tools, *demand and supply,* we will have a better understanding of the cellular phone explosion, as well as many other phenomena in our world. Demand and supply are two ways of categorizing the influences on the price of goods that you buy and the quantities available. As such, demand and supply form the basis of virtually all economic analysis of the world around us.

As you will see throughout this text, the operation of the forces of demand and supply take place in *markets*. A **market** is an abstract concept referring to all the arrangements individuals have for exchanging with one another. Goods and services are sold in markets, such as the automobile market, the health market, and the compact disc market. Workers offer their services in the labor market. Companies, or firms, buy workers' labor services in the labor market. Firms also buy other inputs in order to produce the goods and services that you buy as a consumer. Firms purchase machines, buildings, and land. These markets are in operation at all times. One of the most important activities in these markets is the setting of the prices of all of the inputs and outputs that are bought and sold in our complicated economy. To understand the determination of prices, you first need to look at the law of demand.

Market
All of the arrangements that individuals have for exchanging with one another. Thus we can speak of the labor market, the automobile market, and the credit market.

THE LAW OF DEMAND

Demand has a special meaning in economics. It refers to the quantities of specific goods or services that individuals, taken singly or as a group, will purchase at various possible prices, other things being constant. We can therefore talk about the demand for microprocessor chips, French fries, compact disc players, children, and criminal activities.

Associated with the concept of demand is the **law of demand,** which can be stated as follows:

> **When the price of a good goes up, people buy less of it, other things being equal. When the price of a good goes down, people buy more of it, other things being equal.**

The law of demand tells us that the quantity demanded of any commodity is inversely related to its price, other things being equal. In an inverse relationship, one variable moves up in value when the other moves down. The law of demand states that a change in price causes a change in the quantity demanded in the *opposite* direction.

Notice that we tacked onto the end of the law of demand the statement "other things being equal." We referred to this in Chapter 1 as the *ceteris paribus* assumption. It means, for example, that when we predict that people will buy fewer DVD (digital videodisc) play-

Demand
A schedule of how much of a good or service people will purchase at any price during a specified time period, other things being constant.

Law of demand
The observation that there is a negative, or inverse, relationship between the price of any good or service and the quantity demanded, holding other factors constant.

ers if their price goes up, we are holding constant the price of all other goods in the economy as well as people's incomes. Implicitly, therefore, if we are assuming that no other prices change when we examine the price behavior of DVD players, we are looking at the *relative* price of DVD players.

The law of demand is supported by millions of observations of people's behavior in the marketplace. Theoretically, it can be derived from an economic model based on rational behavior, as was discussed in Chapter 1. Basically, if nothing else changes and the price of a good falls, the lower price induces us to buy more over a certain period of time because we can enjoy additional net gains that were unavailable at the higher price. For the most part, if you examine your own behavior, you will see that it generally follows the law of demand.

Relative Prices Versus Money Prices

Relative price
The price of one commodity divided by the price of another commodity; the number of units of one commodity that must be sacrificed to purchase one unit of another commodity.

Money price
The price that we observe today, expressed in today's dollars. Also called the *absolute, nominal,* or *current price.*

The **relative price** of any commodity is its price in terms of another commodity. The price that you pay in dollars and cents for any good or service at any point in time is called its **money price.** Consider an example that you might hear quite often around parents and grandparents. "When I bought my first new car, it cost only fifteen hundred dollars." The implication, of course, is that the price of cars today is outrageously high because the average new car might cost $19,000. But that is not an accurate comparison. What was the price of the average house during that same year? Perhaps it was only $12,000. By comparison, then, given that houses today average about $145,000, the price of a new car today doesn't sound so far out of line, does it?

The point is that money prices during different time periods don't tell you much. You have to find out relative prices. Consider an example of the price of CDs versus cassettes from last year and this year. In Table 3-1, we show the money price of CDs and cassettes for two years during which they have both gone up. That means that we have to pay out in today's dollars and cents more for CDs and more for cassettes. If we look, though, at the relative prices of CDs and cassettes, we find that last year, CDs were twice as expensive as cassettes, whereas this year they are only $1\frac{3}{4}$ times as expensive. Conversely, if we compare cassettes to CDs, last year they cost only half as much as CDs, but today they cost about 57 percent as much. In the one-year period, while both prices have gone up in money terms, the relative price of CDs has fallen (and, equivalently, the relative price of cassettes has risen).

TABLE 3-1

Money Price Versus Relative Price
The money price of both compact discs (CDs) and cassettes has risen. But the relative price of CDs has fallen (or conversely, the relative price of cassettes has risen).

Exercise 3.1
Visit www.econtoday.com for more about currency exchange rates.

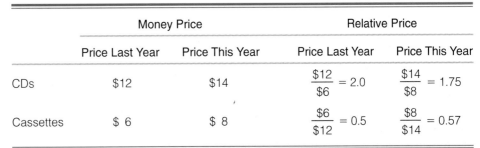

	Money Price		Relative Price	
	Price Last Year	Price This Year	Price Last Year	Price This Year
CDs	$12	$14	$\frac{\$12}{\$6} = 2.0$	$\frac{\$14}{\$8} = 1.75$
Cassettes	$ 6	$ 8	$\frac{\$6}{\$12} = 0.5$	$\frac{\$8}{\$14} = 0.57$

INTERNATIONAL EXAMPLE
Cross-Border Shopping for Pharmaceuticals

Throughout the world, cross-border shopping has increased as individuals respond to changing relative prices. For example, for some Americans, it is worth an 800-mile car ride from northern California to travel to Los Algodones, Mexico. This tiny border town of 5,000 people offers prescription drugs at much lower prices than in the United States. An inhaler for asthmatics priced at $83.70 in the States costs only $15.60 in Mexico. Shoppers may legally purchase other prescription drugs at similarly low prices. So it's not surprising that between 7,000 and 10,000 Americans line up at pharmacy counters in this small Mexican town every day. A few years ago, there were 10 drugstores in Los Algodones; today there are over 30. People who purchase Prozac pay less than half the price in the United States. A bottle of ninety 10-mg tablets of Valium is priced below $10—less than one-tenth the cost north of the border.

Realizing the potential business that exists, Mexican dentists and optometrists have flocked to Los Algodones. They offer discount services as well.

FOR CRITICAL ANALYSIS: The average age of the Americans traveling to Los Algodones is over 60. Why is there a disproportionate share of senior citizens among the American clientele of Los Algodones drugstores? (Hint: What important concept did you learn in Chapter 2?) ●

THINKING CRITICALLY ABOUT THE MEDIA

The Real Price of Stamps

The press is fond of pointing out the rise in the price of a particular good, such as a stamp for first-class mail. In the 1940s, a first-class stamp cost only 3 cents, but by the mid-1990s, it had climbed to 32 cents. That is the absolute price of postage, however. What about the relative price, the price relative to the average of all other prices? The relative price of postage is actually lower today than when it reached its peak in 1975. Many other relative prices have fallen over the years, ranging from gasoline prices to the president's salary. Indeed, relatively speaking, the president's current $200,000-a-year salary is peanuts compared to what President Truman earned in 1947. In relative terms (dollars in 1947), the current president only earns about $30,000, even though in absolute terms, the current president makes more. Remember, everything is relative.

CONCEPTS IN BRIEF

- The law of demand posits an inverse relationship between the quantity demanded of a good and its price, other things being equal.
- The law of demand applies when other things, such as income and the prices of all other goods and services, are held constant.

THE DEMAND SCHEDULE

Let's take a hypothetical demand situation to see how the inverse relationship between the price and the quantity demanded looks (holding other things equal). We will consider the quantity of diskettes demanded *per year.* Without stating the *time dimension,* we could not make sense out of this demand relationship because the numbers would be different if we were talking about the quantity demanded per month or the quantity demanded per decade.

In addition to implicitly or explicitly stating a time dimension for a demand relationship, we are also implicitly referring to *constant-quality* units of the good or service in question. Prices are always expressed in constant-quality units in order to avoid the problem of comparing commodities that are in fact not truly comparable.

In panel (a) of Figure 3-1, we see that if the price were $1 per diskette, 50 of them would be bought each year by our representative individual, but if the price were $5 per diskette,

FIGURE 3-1

The Individual Demand Schedule and the Individual Demand Curve

In panel (a), we show combinations *A* through *E* of the quantities of diskettes demanded, measured in constant-quality units at prices ranging from $5 down to $1 per disk. In panel (b), we plot combinations *A* through *E* on a grid. The result is the individual demand curve for diskettes.

Panel (a)

Combination	Price per Constant-Quality Diskette	Quantity of Constant-Quality Diskettes per Year
A	$5	10
B	4	20
C	3	30
D	2	40
E	1	50

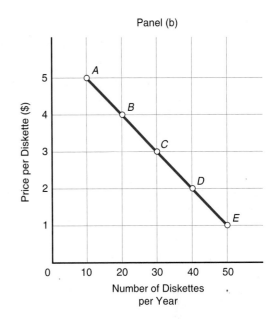

Panel (b)

only 10 diskettes would be bought each year. This reflects the law of demand. Panel (a) is also called simply demand, or a *demand schedule,* because it gives a schedule of alternative quantities demanded per year at different possible prices.

The Demand Curve

Tables expressing relationships between two variables can be represented in graphical terms. To do this, we need only construct a graph that has the price per constant-quality diskette on the vertical axis and the quantity measured in constant-quality diskettes per year on the horizontal axis. All we have to do is take combinations *A* through *E* from panel (a) of Figure 3-1 and plot those points in panel (b). Now we connect the points with a smooth line, and *voilà,* we have a **demand curve.**[1] It is downward-sloping (from left to right) to indicate the inverse relationship between the price of diskettes and the quantity demanded per year. Our presentation of demand schedules and curves applies equally well to all commodities, including toothpicks, hamburgers, textbooks, credit, and labor services. Remember, the demand curve is simply a graphical representation of the law of demand.

Demand curve
A graphical representation of the demand schedule; a negatively sloped line showing the inverse relationship between the price and the quantity demanded (other things being equal).

Individual Versus Market Demand Curves

The demand schedule shown in panel (a) of Figure 3-1 and the resulting demand curve shown in panel (b) are both given for an individual. As we shall see, the determination of price in the marketplace depends on, among other things, the **market demand** for a particular commodity. The way in which we measure a market demand schedule and derive a

Market demand
The demand of all consumers in the marketplace for a particular good or service. The summing at each price of the quantity demanded by each individual.

---

[1]Even though we call them "curves," for the purposes of exposition we often draw straight lines. In many real-world situations, demand and supply curves will in fact be lines that do curve. To connect the points in panel (b) with a line, we assume that for all prices in between the ones shown, the quantities demanded will be found along that line.

market demand curve for diskettes or any other commodity is by summing (at each price) the individual demand for all those in the market. Suppose that the market demand for diskettes consists of only two buyers: buyer 1, for whom we've already shown the demand schedule, and buyer 2, whose demand schedule is displayed in column 3 of panel (a) of Figure 3-2. Column 1 shows the price, and column 2 shows the quantity demanded by buyer 1 at each price. These data are taken directly from Figure 3-1. In column 3, we show the quantity demanded by buyer 2. Column 4 shows the total quantity demanded at each price, which is obtained by simply adding columns 2 and 3. Graphically, in panel (d) of Figure 3-2, we add the demand curves of buyer 1 [panel (b)] and buyer 2 [panel (c)] to derive the market demand curve.

There are, of course, literally tens of millions of potential consumers of diskettes. We'll simply assume that the summation of all of the consumers in the market results in a demand schedule, given in panel (a) of Figure 3-3, and a demand curve, given in panel (b). The quantity demanded is now measured in billions of units per year. Remember, panel (b) in Figure 3-3 shows the market demand curve for the millions of users of diskettes. The "market" demand curve that we derived in Figure 3-2 was undertaken assuming that there were only two buyers in the entire market. That's why the "market" demand curve for two

FIGURE 3-2

The Horizontal Summation of Two Demand Schedules

Panel (a) shows how to sum the demand schedule for one buyer with that of another buyer. In column 2 is the quantity demanded by buyer 1, taken from panel (a) of Figure 3-1. Column 4 is the sum of columns 2 and 3. We plot the demand curve for buyer 1 in panel (b) and the demand curve for buyer 2 in panel (c). When we add those two demand curves horizontally, we get the market demand curve for two buyers, shown in panel (d).

Panel (a)

(1) Price per Diskette	(2) Buyer 1 Quantity Demanded	(3) Buyer 2 Quantity Demanded	(4) = 2 + 3 Combined Quantity Demanded per Year
$5	10	10	20
4	20	20	40
3	30	40	70
2	40	50	90
1	50	60	110

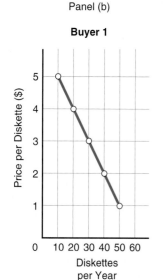

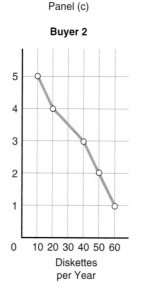

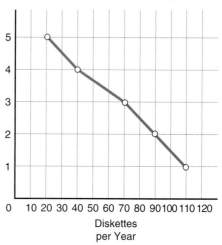

FIGURE 3-3

The Market Demand Schedule for Diskettes

In panel (a), we add up the millions of existing demand schedules for diskettes. In panel (b), we plot the quantities from panel (a) on a grid; connecting them produces the market demand curve for diskettes.

Panel (b)

Panel (a)

Price per Constant-Quality Diskette	Total Quantity Demanded of Constant-Quality Diskettes per Year (billions)
$5	2
4	4
3	6
2	8
1	10

buyers in panel (d) of Figure 3-2 is not a smooth line, whereas the true market demand curve in panel (b) of Figure 3-3 is a smooth line with no kinks.

Now consider some special aspects of the market demand curve for compact discs.

EXAMPLE
Garth Brooks, Used CDs, and the Law of Demand

A few years ago, country singer Garth Brooks tried to prevent his latest album from being sold to any chain or store that also sells used CDs. His argument was that the used-CD market deprived labels and artists of earnings. His announcement came after Wherehouse Entertainment, Inc., a 339-store retailer based in Torrance, California, started selling used CDs side by side with new releases, at half the price. Brooks, along with the distribution arms of Sony, Warner Music, Capitol-EMI, and MCA, was trying to quash the used-CD market. By so doing, it appears that none of these parties understands the law of demand.

Let's say the price of a new CD is $15. The existence of a secondary used-CD market means that to people who choose to resell their CDs for $5, the cost of a new CD is in fact only $10. Because we know that quantity demanded is inversely related to price, we know that more of a new CD will be sold at a price of $10 than of the same CD at a price of $15. Taking only this force into account, eliminating the used-CD market tends to reduce sales of new CDs.

But there is another force at work here, too. Used CDs are substitutes for new CDs. If used CDs are not available, some people who would have purchased them will instead purchase new CDs. If this second effect outweighs the incentive to buy less because of the higher effective price, then Brooks is behaving correctly in trying to suppress the used market.

FOR CRITICAL ANALYSIS: Can you apply this argument to the used-book market, in which both authors and publishers have long argued that used books are "killing them"? •

Exercise 3.2
Visit www.econtoday.com for more about purchasing CDs.

SHIFTS IN DEMAND

Assume that the federal government gives every student registered in a college, university, or technical school in the United States a personal computer that uses diskettes. The demand curve presented in panel (b) of Figure 3-3 would no longer be an accurate representation of total market demand for diskettes. What we have to do is shift the curve outward, or to the right, to represent the rise in demand. There will now be an increase in the number of diskettes demanded *at each and every possible price*. The demand curve shown in Figure 3-4 will shift from D_1 to D_2. Take any price, say, $3 per diskette. Originally, before the federal government giveaway of personal computers, the amount demanded at $3 was 6 billion diskettes per year. After the government giveaway, however, the new amount demanded at $3 is 10 billion diskettes per year. What we have seen is a shift in the demand for diskettes.

The shift can also go in the opposite direction. What if colleges uniformly outlawed the use of personal computers by any of their students? Such a regulation would cause a shift inward—to the left—of the demand curve for diskettes. In Figure 3-4, the demand curve would shift to D_3; the amount demanded would now be less at each and every possible price.

The Other Determinants of Demand

The demand curve in panel (b) of Figure 3-3 is drawn with other things held constant, specifically all of the other factors that determine how much will be bought. There are many such determinants. The major other determinants are income; tastes and preferences; the prices of related goods; expectations regarding future prices, future incomes, and future product availability; and population (market size). Let's examine each determinant more closely.

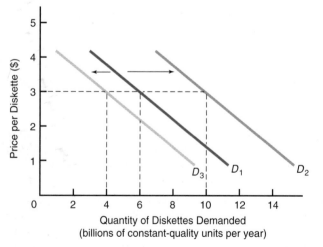

Quantity of Diskettes Demanded
(billions of constant-quality units per year)

FIGURE 3-4

A Shift in the Demand Curve
If some factor other than price changes, the only way we can show its effect is by moving the entire demand curve, say, from D_1 to D_2. We have assumed in our example that the move was precipitated by the government's giving a free personal computer to every registered college student in America. That meant that at *all* prices, a larger number of diskettes would be demanded than before. Curve D_3 represents reduced demand compared to curve D_1, caused by a law prohibiting computers on campus.

Income. For most goods, an increase in income will lead to an increase in demand. The phrase *increase in demand* always refers to a comparison between two different demand curves. Thus for most goods, an increase in income will lead to a rightward shift in the position of the demand curve from, say, D_1 to D_2 in Figure 3-4. You can avoid confusion about shifts in curves by always relating a rise in demand to a rightward shift in the demand curve and a fall in demand to a leftward shift in the demand curve. Goods for which the demand rises when income rises are called **normal goods.** Most goods, such as shoes, computers, and CDs, are "normal goods." For some goods, however, demand *falls* as income rises. These are called **inferior goods.** Beans might be an example. As households get richer, they tend to spend less and less on beans and more and more on meat. (The terms *normal* and *inferior* are merely part of the economist's terminology; no value judgments are associated with them.)

Remember, a shift to the left in the demand curve represents a fall in demand, and a shift to the right represents a rise, or increase, in demand.

Normal goods
Goods for which demand rises as income rises. Most goods are considered normal.

Inferior goods
Goods for which demand falls as income rises.

Tastes and Preferences. A change in consumer tastes in favor of a good can shift its demand curve outward to the right. When Frisbees® became the rage, the demand curve for them shifted outward to the right; when the rage died out, the demand curve shifted inward to the left. Fashions depend to a large extent on people's tastes and preferences. Economists have little to say about the determination of tastes; that is, they don't have any "good" theories of taste determination or why people buy one brand of product rather than others. Advertisers, however, have various theories that they use to try to make consumers prefer their products over those of competitors.

KIDS ARE TURNING OFF THE TV

Suppliers of children's television programs are finding out what happens when there is a shift in demand for their commodity. The average number of hours that children aged 2 to 11 spend watching television has dropped by about 20 percent since 1984.

Preteens are spending relatively more time sitting in front of a computer screen. The amount of interactive children's software, particularly on CD-ROM, is staggering today compared to what it was a few years ago. Perhaps more important, computers and TV sets hooked into the Internet now offer preteens thousands of games that can be played, some with other people anywhere in the world. A typical interactive Web game search on the Internet yields literally thousands of games. Preteens also chat with other preteens on the Net and "surf" the World Wide Web.

FOR CRITICAL ANALYSIS: What happened to the demand curve for traditional preteen TV programs? ●

Prices of Related Goods: Substitutes and Complements. Demand schedules are always drawn with the prices of all other commodities held constant. That is to say, when deriving a given demand curve, we assume that only the price of the good under study changes. For example, when we draw the demand curve for butter, we assume that the price of margarine is held constant. When we draw the demand curve for stereo speakers, we assume that the price of stereo amplifiers is held constant. When we refer to *related goods,* we are talking about goods for which demand is interdependent. If a change in the price of one good shifts the demand for another good, those two goods are related. There are two types of related goods: *substitutes* and *complements*. We can define and distinguish between substitutes and complements in terms of how the change in price of one commodity affects the demand for its related commodity.

Butter and margarine are **substitutes.** Let's assume that each originally cost $2 per pound. If the price of butter remains the same and the price of margarine falls from $2 per pound to $1 per pound, people will buy more margarine and less butter. The demand curve for butter will shift inward to the left. If, conversely, the price of margarine rises from $2 per pound to $3 per pound, people will buy more butter and less margarine. The demand curve for butter will shift outward to the right. In other words, an increase in the price of margarine will lead to an increase in the demand for butter, and an increase in the price of butter will lead to an increase in the demand for margarine. For substitutes, a price change in the substitute will cause a change in demand *in the same direction.*

For **complements,** the situation is reversed. Consider stereo speakers and stereo amplifiers. We draw the demand curve for speakers with the price of amplifiers held constant. If the price per constant-quality unit of stereo amplifiers decreases from, say, $500 to $200, that will encourage more people to purchase component stereo systems. They will now buy more speakers, at any given speaker price, than before. The demand curve for speakers will shift outward to the right. If, by contrast, the price of amplifiers increases from $200 to $500, fewer people will purchase component stereo systems. The demand curve for speakers will shift inward to the left. To summarize, a decrease in the price of amplifiers leads to an increase in the demand for speakers. An increase in the price of amplifiers leads to a decrease in the demand for speakers. Thus for complements, a price change in a product will cause a change in demand *in the opposite direction.*

Are new learning technologies complements or substitutes for college instructors? Read on.

Substitutes

Two goods are substitutes when either one can be used for consumption to satisfy a similar want—for example, coffee and tea. The more you buy of one, the less you buy of the other. For substitutes, the change in the price of one causes a shift in demand for the other in the same direction as the price change.

Complements

Two goods are complements if both are used together for consumption or enjoyment—for example, coffee and cream. The more you buy of one, the more you buy of the other. For complements, a change in the price of one causes an opposite shift in the demand for the other.

GETTING YOUR DEGREE VIA THE NET

In this class and in others, you have most likely been exposed to such instructional technologies as films, videos, and interactive CD-ROM learning systems. The future for some of you, or at least the next few generations, may be quite different. All of the instructional technology that your professor provides may be packaged in the form of on-line courses.
Many institutions of higher learning are now using the Internet to provide full instruction. It is called *distance learning* or *distributive learning*. And it is worldwide. For example, the University of Michigan, in conjunction with companies in Hong Kong, South Korea, and Europe, offers a global M.B.A. through the Internet. A professor teaches a course "live" via video and uses the software program Lotus Notes, which allows course information to be sent via the Internet. Students submit their homework assignments the same way. Duke University runs the Global Executive M.B.A. program, in which students "attend" CD-ROM video lectures, download additional video and audio materials, and receive interactive study aids, all via the Internet.

Virtually all major college publishers now have projects to develop distance learning via the Internet. In addition, a consortium of over 100 universities has put in place what is called Internet II. Internet II permits full-motion video and virtually instantaneous interactivity for participating universities. The age of fully interactive distance learning with full-motion video is not far off. Certainly, even better technology, as yet undeveloped, will speed up this process.

FOR CRITICAL ANALYSIS: What do you predict will happen to the demand curve for college professors in the future? ●

Expectations. Consumers' expectations regarding future prices, future incomes, and future availability may prompt them to buy more or less of a particular good without a change in its current money price. For example, consumers getting wind of a scheduled 100 percent price increase in diskettes next month may buy more of them today at today's prices. Today's demand curve for diskettes will shift from D_1 to D_2 in Figure 3-4 on page 52. The opposite would occur if a decrease in the price of diskettes were scheduled for next month.

Expectations of a rise in income may cause consumers to want to purchase more of everything today at today's prices. Again, such a change in expectations of higher future income will cause a shift in the demand curve from D_1 to D_2 in Figure 3-4.

Finally, expectations that goods will not be available at any price will induce consumers to stock up now, increasing current demand.

Population. An increase in the population in an economy (holding per capita income constant) often shifts the market demand outward for most products. This is because an increase in population leads to an increase in the number of buyers in the market. Conversely, a reduction in the population will shift most market demand curves inward because of the reduction in the number of buyers in the market.

Changes in Demand Versus Changes in Quantity Demanded

We have made repeated references to demand and to quantity demanded. It is important to realize that there is a difference between a *change in demand* and a *change in quantity demanded.*

Demand refers to a schedule of planned rates of purchase and depends on a great many nonprice determinants. Whenever there is a change in a nonprice determinant, there will be a change in demand—a shift in the entire demand curve to the right or to the left.

A quantity demanded is a specific quantity at a specific price, represented by a single point on a demand curve. When price changes, quantity demanded changes according to the law of demand, and there will be a movement from one point to another along the same demand curve. Look at Figure 3-5 on page 56. At a price of $3 per diskette, 6 billion diskettes per year are demanded. If the price falls to $1, quantity demanded increases to 10 billion per year. This movement occurs because the current market price for the product changes. In Figure 3-5, you can see the arrow pointing down the given demand curve D.

When you think of demand, think of the entire curve itself. Quantity demanded, in contrast, is represented by a single point on the demand curve.

A change or shift in demand causes the *entire* curve to move. The *only* thing that can cause the entire curve to move is a change in a determinant *other than its own price.*

In economic analysis, we cannot emphasize too much the following distinction that must constantly be made:

A change in a good's own price leads to a change in quantity demanded, for any given demand curve, other things held constant. This is a movement *on* the curve.

A change in any other determinant of demand leads to a change in demand. This causes a movement *of* the curve.

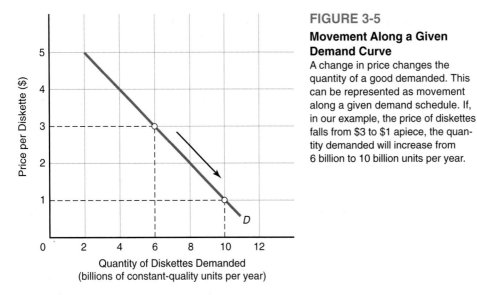

FIGURE 3-5

Movement Along a Given Demand Curve

A change in price changes the quantity of a good demanded. This can be represented as movement along a given demand schedule. If, in our example, the price of diskettes falls from $3 to $1 apiece, the quantity demanded will increase from 6 billion to 10 billion units per year.

CONCEPTS IN BRIEF

- Demand curves are drawn with determinants other than the price of the good held constant. These other determinants are (1) income; (2) tastes and preferences; (3) prices of related goods; (4) expectations about future prices, future incomes, and future availability of goods; and (5) population (number of buyers in the market). If any one of these determinants changes, the demand schedule will shift to the right or to the left.

- A change in demand comes about only because of a change in the other determinants of demand. This change in demand shifts the demand curve to the left or to the right.

- A change in the quantity demanded comes about when there is a change in the price of the good (other things held constant). Such a change in quantity demanded involves a movement along a given demand curve.

THE LAW OF SUPPLY

The other side of the basic model in economics involves the quantities of goods and services that firms will offer for sale to the market. The **supply** of any good or service is the amount that firms will offer for sale under certain conditions during a specified time period. The relationship between price and quantity supplied, called the **law of supply,** can be summarized as follows:

> **At higher prices, a larger quantity will generally be supplied than at lower prices, all other things held constant. At lower prices, a smaller quantity will generally be supplied than at higher prices, all other things held constant.**

There is generally a direct relationship between quantity supplied and price. For supply, as the price rises, the quantity supplied rises; as price falls, the quantity supplied also falls. Producers are normally willing to produce and sell more of their product at a higher price than at a lower price, other things being constant. At $5 per diskette, 3M, Sony, Maxell, Fuji, and other manufacturers would almost certainly be willing to supply a larger quantity than at $1 per unit, assuming, of course, that no other prices in the economy had changed.

Supply
A schedule showing the relationship between price and quantity supplied for a specified period of time, other things being equal.

Law of supply
The observation that the higher the price of a good, the more of that good sellers will make available over a specified time period, other things being equal.

As with the law of demand, millions of instances in the real world have given us confidence in the law of supply. On a theoretical level, the law of supply is based on a model in which producers and sellers seek to make the most gain possible from their activities. For example, as a diskette manufacturer attempts to produce more and more diskettes over the same time period, it will eventually have to hire more workers, pay overtime wages (which are higher), and overutilize its machines. Only if offered a higher price per diskette will the diskette manufacturer be willing to incur these higher costs. That is why the law of supply implies a direct relationship between price and quantity supplied.

THE SUPPLY SCHEDULE

Just as we were able to construct a demand schedule, we can construct a *supply schedule*, which is a table relating prices to the quantity supplied at each price. A supply schedule can also be referred to simply as *supply*. It is a set of planned production rates that depends on the price of the product. We show the individual supply schedule for a hypothetical producer in panel (a) of Figure 3-6. At $1 per diskette, for example, this producer will supply 20 million diskettes per year; at $5, this producer will supply 55 million diskettes per year.

The Supply Curve

Supply curve
The graphical representation of the supply schedule; a line (curve) showing the supply schedule, which generally slopes upward (has a positive slope), other things being equal.

We can convert the supply schedule in panel (a) of Figure 3-6 into a **supply curve,** just as we earlier created a demand curve in Figure 3-1. All we do is take the price-quantity combinations from panel (a) of Figure 3-6 and plot them in panel (b). We have labeled these combinations *F* through *J*. Connecting these points, we obtain an upward-sloping curve that shows the typically direct relationship between price and quantity supplied. Again, we have to remember that we are talking about quantity supplied *per year*, measured in constant-quality units.

FIGURE 3-6

The Individual Producer's Supply Schedule and Supply Curve for Diskettes

Panel (a) shows that at higher prices, a hypothetical supplier will be willing to provide a greater quantity of diskettes. We plot the various price-quantity combinations in panel (a) on the grid in panel (b). When we connect these points, we find the individual supply curve for diskettes. It is positively sloped.

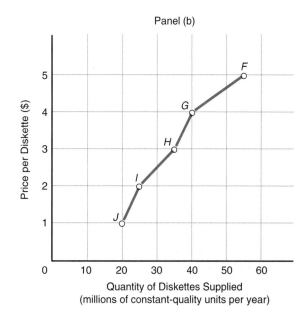

Panel (a)

Combination	Price per Constant-Quality Diskette	Quantity of Diskettes Supplied (millions of constant-quality units per year)
F	$5	55
G	4	40
H	3	35
I	2	25
J	1	20

The Market Supply Curve

Just as we had to sum the individual demand curves to get the market demand curve, we need to sum the individual producers' supply curves to get the market supply curve. Look at Figure 3-7, in which we horizontally sum two typical diskette manufacturers' supply curves. Supplier 1's data are taken from Figure 3-6; supplier 2 is added. The numbers are presented in panel (a). The graphical representation of supplier 1 is in panel (b), of supplier 2 in panel (c), and of the summation in panel (d). The result, then, is the supply curve for diskettes for suppliers 1 and 2. There are many more suppliers of diskettes, however. The total market supply schedule and total market demand curve for diskettes are represented in Figure 3-8, with the curve in panel (b) obtained by adding all of the supply curves such as those shown in panels (b) and (c) of Figure 3-7. Notice the difference between the

Panel (a)

(1) Price per Diskette	(2) Supplier 1 Quantity Supplied (millions)	(3) Supplier 2 Quantity Supplied (millions)	(4) = (2) + (3) Combined Quantity Supplied per Year (millions)
$5	55	35	90
4	40	30	70
3	35	20	55
2	25	15	40
1	20	10	30

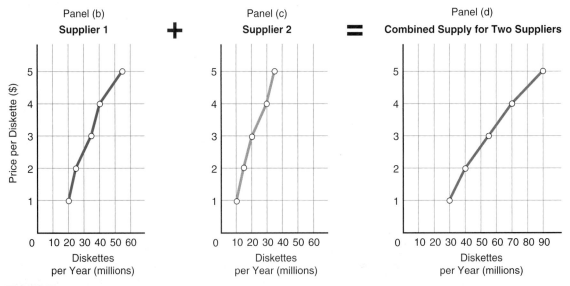

FIGURE 3-7

Horizontal Summation of Supply Curves

In panel (a), we show the data for two individual suppliers of diskettes. Adding how much each is willing to supply at different prices, we come up with the combined quantities supplied in column 4. When we plot the values in columns 2 and 3 on grids in panels (b) and (c) and add them horizontally, we obtain the combined supply curve for the two suppliers in question, shown in panel (d).

FIGURE 3-8

The Market Supply Schedule and the Market Supply Curve for Diskettes

In panel (a), we show the summation of all the individual producers' supply schedules; in panel (b), we graph the resulting supply curve. It represents the market supply curve for diskettes and is upward-sloping.

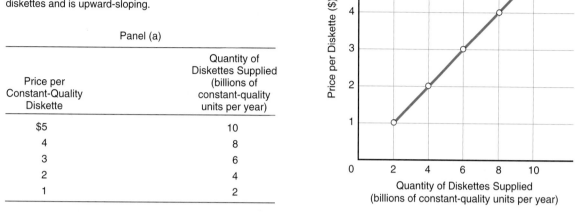

Panel (a)

Price per Constant-Quality Diskette	Quantity of Diskettes Supplied (billions of constant-quality units per year)
$5	10
4	8
3	6
2	4
1	2

Panel (b)

market supply curve with only two suppliers in Figure 3-7 and the one with a large number of suppliers—the entire true market—in panel (b) of Figure 3-8. There are no kinks in the true total market supply curve because there are so many suppliers.

Notice what happens at the market level when price changes. If the price is $3, the quantity supplied is 6 billion diskettes. If the price goes up to $4, the quantity supplied increases to 8 billion per year. If the price falls to $2, the quantity supplied decreases to 4 billion diskettes per year. Changes in quantity supplied are represented by movements along the supply curve in panel (b) of Figure 3-8.

CONCEPTS IN BRIEF

- There is normally a direct, or positive, relationship between price and quantity of a good supplied, other things held constant.
- The supply curve normally shows a direct relationship between price and quantity supplied. The market supply curve is obtained by horizontally adding individual supply curves in the market.

SHIFTS IN SUPPLY

When we looked at demand, we found out that any change in anything relevant besides the price of the good or service caused the demand curve to shift inward or outward. The same is true for the supply curve. If something relevant changes besides the price of the product or service being supplied, we will see the entire supply curve shift.

Consider an example. A new method of putting magnetic material on diskettes has been invented. It reduces the cost of producing a diskette by 50 percent. In this situation, diskette producers will supply more product at *all* prices because their cost of so doing has fallen dramatically. Competition among diskette manufacturers to produce more at each and

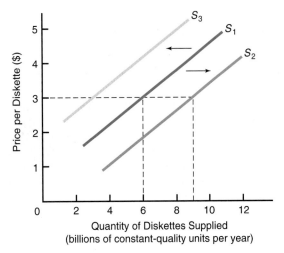

FIGURE 3-9

A Shift in the Supply Schedule
If the cost of producing diskettes were to fall dramatically, the supply schedule would shift rightward from S_1 to S_2 such that at all prices, a larger quantity would be forthcoming from suppliers. Conversely, if the cost of production rose, the supply curve would shift leftward to S_3.

every price will shift the supply schedule of diskettes outward to the right from S_1 to S_2 in Figure 3-9. At a price of $3, the quantity supplied was originally 6 billion diskettes per year, but now the quantity supplied (after the reduction in the costs of production) at $3 a diskette will be 9 billion diskettes a year. (This is similar to what has happened to the supply curve of personal computers and fax machines in recent years as computer memory chip prices have fallen.)

Consider the opposite case. If the cost of the magnetic material needed for making diskettes doubles, the supply curve in Figure 3-9 will shift from S_1 to S_3. At each and every price, the number of diskettes supplied will fall due to the increase in the price of raw materials.

The Other Determinants of Supply

When supply curves are drawn, only the price of the good in question changes, and it is assumed that other things remain constant. The other things assumed constant are the costs of resources (inputs) used to produce the product, technology and productivity, taxes and subsidies, producers' price expectations, and the number of firms in the industry. These are the major nonprice determinants of supply. If *any* of them changes, there will be a shift in the supply curve.

Cost of Inputs Used to Produce the Product. If one or more input prices fall, the supply curve will shift outward to the right; that is, more will be supplied at each and every price. The opposite will be true if one or more inputs become more expensive. For example, when we draw the supply curve of new cars, we are holding the cost of steel (and other inputs) constant. When we draw the supply curve of blue jeans, we are holding the cost of cotton fabric fixed.

Technology and Productivity. Supply curves are drawn by assuming a given technology, or "state of the art." When the available production techniques change, the supply curve will shift. For example, when a better production technique for diskettes becomes available, the supply curve will shift to the right. A larger quantity will be forthcoming at each and every price because the cost of production is lower.

INTERNATIONAL EXAMPLE
Changing Technology and the Supply of Salmon

One example of how changes in technology can shift the supply curve out to the right involves salmon. In 1980, the total worldwide catch of salmon (wild and farmed) was just over 10,000 metric tons. Since 1980, new technology has been developed in what is called aquaculture, or the farm-raising of fish and related products. Aquaculture currently generates over $30 billion in worldwide revenues and is one of the world's fastest-growing industries. Farmed salmon from Chile, Scotland, Canada, Norway, and Iceland now exceeds 240,000 metric tons a year. Thus it is not surprising that despite a depletion of many wild salmon fishing grounds and a worldwide increase in the consumer demand for salmon, the retail price of salmon today (corrected for inflation) is about 50 percent of what it was in 1980.

FOR CRITICAL ANALYSIS: What might slow down the growth in salmon farming throughout the world? •

Subsidy
A negative tax; a payment to a producer from the government, usually in the form of a cash grant.

Taxes and Subsidies. Certain taxes, such as a per-unit tax, are effectively an addition to production costs and therefore reduce the supply. If the supply curve were S_1 in Figure 3-9, a per-unit tax increase would shift it to S_3. A **subsidy** would do the opposite; it would shift the curve to S_2. Every producer would get a "gift" from the government of a few cents for each unit produced.

Price Expectations. A change in the expectation of a future relative price of a product can affect a producer's current willingness to supply, just as price expectations affect a consumer's current willingness to purchase. For example, diskette suppliers may withhold from the market part of their current supply if they anticipate higher prices in the future. The current amount supplied at each and every price will decrease.

Number of Firms in the Industry. In the short run, when firms can only change the number of employees they use, we hold the number of firms in the industry constant. In the long run, the number of firms (or the size of some existing firms) may change. If the number of firms increases, the supply curve will shift outward to the right. If the number of firms decreases, it will shift inward to the left.

Changes in Supply Versus Changes in Quantity Supplied

We cannot overstress the importance of distinguishing between a movement along the supply curve—which occurs only when the price changes for a given supply curve—and a shift in the supply curve—which occurs only with changes in other nonprice factors. A change in price always brings about a change in quantity supplied along a given supply curve. We move to a different coordinate on the existing supply curve. This is specifically called a *change in quantity supplied.* When price changes, quantity supplied changes, and there will be a movement from one point to another along the same supply curve.

When you think of *supply,* think of the entire curve itself. Quantity supplied is represented by a single point on the supply curve.

A change or shift in supply causes the entire curve to move. The *only* thing that can cause the entire curve to move is a change in a determinant *other than price*.

Consequently,

> **A change in the price leads to a change in the quantity supplied, other things being constant. This is a movement *on* the curve.**

> **A change in any other determinant of supply leads to a change in supply. This causes a movement *of* the curve.**

CONCEPTS IN BRIEF

- If the price changes, we *move along* a curve—there is a change in quantity demanded or supplied. If some other determinant changes, we *shift* a curve—there is a change in demand or supply.
- The supply curve is drawn with other things held constant. If other determinants of supply change, the supply curve will shift. The other major determinants are (1) input costs, (2) technology and productivity, (3) taxes and subsidies, (4) expectations of future relative prices, and (5) the number of firms in the industry.

PUTTING DEMAND AND SUPPLY TOGETHER

In the sections on supply and demand, we tried to confine each discussion to supply or demand only. But you have probably already realized that we can't view the world just from the supply side or just from the demand side. There is an interaction between the two. In this section, we will discuss how they interact and how that interaction determines the prices that prevail in our economy. Understanding how demand and supply interact is essential to understanding how prices are determined in our economy and other economies in which the forces of supply and demand are allowed to work.

Let's first combine the demand and supply schedules and then combine the curves.

Demand and Supply Schedules Combined

Let's place panel (a) from Figure 3-3 (the market demand schedule) and panel (a) from Figure 3-8 (the market supply schedule) together in panel (a) of Figure 3-10. Column 1 shows the price; column 2, the quantity supplied per year at any given price; and column 3, the quantity demanded. Column 4 is merely the difference between columns 2 and 3, or the difference between the quantity supplied and the quantity demanded. In column 5, we label those differences as either excess quantity supplied (a surplus) or excess quantity demanded (a shortage). For example, at a price of $1, only 2 billion diskettes would be supplied, but the quantity demanded would be 10 billion. The difference would be −8 billion, which we label excess quantity demanded (a shortage). At the other end of the scale, a price of $5 per diskette would elicit 10 billion in quantity supplied, but quantity demanded would drop to 2 billion, leaving a difference of +8 billion units, which we call excess quantity supplied (a surplus).

Panel (a)

(1) Price per Constant-Quality Diskette	(2) Quantity Supplied (diskettes per year)	(3) Quantity Demanded (diskettes per year)	(4) Difference (2) – (3) (diskettes per year)	(5) Condition
$5	10 billion	2 billion	8 billion	Excess quantity supplied (surplus)
4	8 billion	4 billion	4 billion	Excess quantity supplied (surplus)
3	6 billion	6 billion	0	Market clearing price—equilibrium (no surplus, no shortage)
2	4 billion	8 billion	–4 billion	Excess quantity demanded (shortage)
1	2 billion	10 billion	–8 billion	Excess quantity demanded (shortage)

Panel (b)

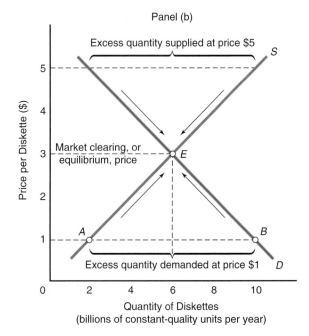

FIGURE 3-10

Putting Demand and Supply Together

In panel (a), we see that at the price of $3, the quantity supplied and the quantity demanded are
equal, resulting in neither an excess in the quantity demanded nor an excess in the quantity supplied.
We call this price the equilibrium, or market clearing, price. In panel (b), the intersection of the supply
and demand curves is at *E,* at a price of $3 per constant-quality diskette and a quantity of 6 billion per
year. At point *E,* there is neither an excess in the quantity demanded nor an excess in the quantity
supplied. At a price of $1, the quantity supplied will be only 2 billion disks per year, but the quantity
demanded will be 10 billion. The difference is excess quantity demanded at a price of $1. The price
will rise, so we will move from point *A* up the supply curve and point *B* up the demand curve to point
E. At the other extreme, $5 elicits a quantity supplied of 10 billion but a quantity demanded of only
2 billion. The difference is excess quantity supplied at a price of $5. The price will fall, so we will move
down the demand curve and the supply curve to the equilibrium price, $3 per diskette.

Now, do you notice something special about the price of $3? At that price, both the quantity supplied and the quantity demanded per year are 6 billion diskettes. The difference then is zero. There is neither excess quantity demanded (shortage) nor excess quantity supplied (surplus). Hence the price of $3 is very special. It is called the **market clearing price**—it clears the market of all excess supply or excess demand. There are no willing consumers who want to pay $3 per diskette but are turned away by sellers, and there are no willing suppliers who want to sell diskettes at $3 who cannot sell all they want at that price. Another term for the market clearing price is the **equilibrium price,** the price at which there is no tendency for change. Consumers are able to get all they want at that price, and suppliers are able to sell the amount that they want at that price.

Equilibrium

We can define **equilibrium** in general as a point from which there tends to be no movement unless demand or supply changes. Any movement away from this point will set into motion certain forces that will cause movement back to it. Therefore, equilibrium is a stable point. Any point that is not at equilibrium is unstable and cannot be maintained.

The equilibrium point occurs where the supply and demand curves intersect. The equilibrium price is given on the vertical axis directly to the left of where the supply and demand curves cross. The equilibrium quantity demanded and supplied is given on the horizontal axis directly underneath the intersection of the demand and supply curves. Equilibrium can change whenever there is a *shock.*

A shock to the supply-and-demand system can be represented by a shift in the supply curve, a shift in the demand curve, or a shift in both curves. Any shock to the system will result in a new set of supply-and-demand relationships and a new equilibrium; forces will come into play to move the system from the old price-quantity equilibrium (now a disequilibrium situation) to the new equilibrium, where the new demand and supply curves intersect.

Panel (b) in Figure 3-3 and panel (b) in Figure 3-8 are combined as panel (b) in Figure 3-10 on page 63. The only difference now is that the horizontal axis measures both the quantity supplied and the quantity demanded per year. Everything else is the same. The demand curve is labeled D, the supply curve S. We have labeled the intersection of the supply curve with the demand curve as point E, for equilibrium. That corresponds to a market clearing price of $3, at which both the quantity supplied and the quantity demanded are 6 billion units per year. There is neither excess quantity supplied nor excess quantity demanded. Point E, the equilibrium point, always occurs at the intersection of the supply and demand curves. This is the price toward which the market price will automatically tend to gravitate.

EXAMPLE
Dinosaurs and the Price of Amber

When there is a shift in either supply or demand, there is a movement toward equilibrium that usually involves a change in the equilibrium quantity and the equilibrium price. A good example is found in the market for amber, a semiprecious stone that often preserves fossil plants and animals from millions of years ago. In Figure 3-11, you see the original supply and demand curves for amber, labeled S and D_1. The equilibrium price is P_1, and the equilibrium quantity is Q_1. Then along came a book, and later a movie, called *Jurassic Park,* written by Michael Crichton. In the story, million-year-old mosquitoes that had feasted on dinosaurs were trapped in amber. Scientists were able to clone

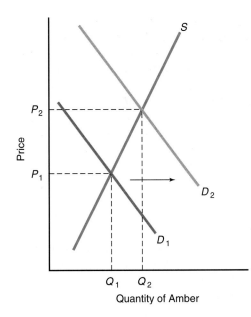

FIGURE 3-11
The Changing Price of Amber
With stable supply, a shift in the demand curve for amber from D_1 to D_2 will cause the equilibrium price of amber to rise from P_1 to P_2 and the equilibrium quantity to increase from Q_1 to Q_2.

various dinosaurs by removing the DNA from the dinosaur blood inside the mosquitoes. (The technique remains in the realm of science fiction.) The success of the book and the movie in the early 1990s made amber suddenly popular; in economic terms, the demand curve for amber shifted outward to D_2. Very quickly, the price rose to P_2 and the equilibrium quantity increased to Q_2.

FOR CRITICAL ANALYSIS: The sequel to Jurassic Park *came out in 1997. Assuming that there is no* Jurassic Park III, *what would you expect to happen to the demand curve for amber over the next few years?* ●

Shortages

The demand and supply curves depicted in Figure 3-10 represent a situation of equilibrium. But a non-market-clearing, or disequilibrium, price will put into play forces that cause the price to change toward the market clearing price at which equilibrium will again be sustained. Look again at panel (b) in Figure 3-10 on page 63. Suppose that instead of being at the market clearing price of $3 per diskette, for some reason the market price is $1 per diskette. At this price, the quantity demanded exceeds the quantity supplied, the former being 10 billion diskettes per year and the latter, 2 billion per year. We have a situation of excess quantity demanded at the price of $1. This is usually called a **shortage.** Consumers of diskettes would find that they could not buy all that they wished at $1 apiece. But forces will cause the price to rise: Competing consumers will bid up the price, and suppliers will raise the price and increase output, whether explicitly or implicitly. (Remember, some buyers would pay $5 or more rather than do without diskettes. They do not want to be left out.) We would move from points A and B toward point E. The process would stop when the price again reached $3 per diskette.

At this point, it is important to recall a distinction made in Chapter 2:

Shortages and scarcity are not the same thing.

Shortage
A situation in which quantity demanded is greater than quantity supplied at a price below the market clearing price.

A shortage is a situation in which the quantity demanded exceeds the quantity supplied at a price *below* the market clearing price. Our definition of scarcity was much more general and all-encompassing: a situation in which the resources available for producing output are insufficient to satisfy all wants. Any choice necessarily costs an opportunity, and the opportunity is lost. Hence we will always live in a world of scarcity because we must constantly make choices, but we do not necessarily have to live in a world of shortages.

Surpluses

Now let's repeat the experiment with the market price at $5 per diskette rather than at the market clearing price of $3. Clearly, the quantity supplied will exceed the quantity demanded at that price. The result will be an excess quantity supplied at $5 per unit. This excess quantity supplied is often called a **surplus.** Given the curves in panel (b) in Figure 3-10, however, there will be forces pushing the price back down toward $3 per diskette: Competing suppliers will attempt to reduce their inventories by cutting prices and reducing output, and consumers will offer to purchase more at lower prices. Suppliers will want to reduce inventories, which will be above their optimal level; that is, there will be an excess over what each seller believes to be the most profitable stock of diskettes. After all, inventories are costly to hold. But consumers may find out about such excess inventories and see the possibility of obtaining increased quantities of diskettes at a decreased price. It behooves consumers to attempt to obtain a good at a lower price, and they will therefore try to do so. If the two forces of supply and demand are unrestricted, they will bring the price back to $3 per diskette.

Surplus
A situation in which quantity supplied is greater than quantity demanded at a price above the market clearing price.

Shortages and surpluses are resolved in unfettered markets—markets in which price changes are free to occur. The forces that resolve them are those of competition: In the case of shortages, consumers competing for a limited quantity supplied drive up the price; in the case of surpluses, sellers compete for the limited quantity demanded, thus driving prices down to equilibrium. The equilibrium price is the only stable price, and all (unrestricted) market prices tend to gravitate toward it.

What happens when the price is set below the equilibrium price? Here come the scalpers.

POLICY EXAMPLE
Should Shortages in the Ticket Market Be Solved by Scalpers?

If you have ever tried to get tickets to a playoff game in sports, a popular Broadway play, or a superstar's rock concert, you know about "shortages." The standard ticket situation for a Super Bowl is shown in Figure 3-12. At the face-value price of Super Bowl tickets (P_1), the quantity demanded (Q_2) greatly exceeds the quantity supplied (Q_1). Because shortages last only so long as prices and quantities do not change, markets tend to exhibit a movement out of this disequilibrium toward equilibrium. Obviously, the quantity of Super Bowl tickets cannot change, but the price can go as high as P_2.

Enter the scalper. This colorful term is used because when you purchase a ticket that is being resold at a price that is higher than face value, the seller is skimming an extra profit off the top. Every time an event sells out, ticket prices by definition have been lower than

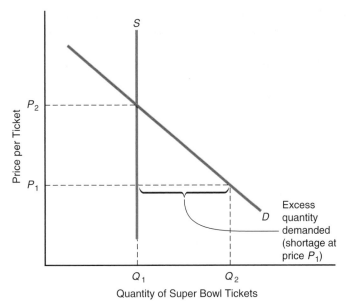

FIGURE 3-12

Shortages of Super Bowl Tickets
The quantity of tickets for any one Super Bowl is fixed at Q_1. At the price per ticket of P_1, the quantity demanded is Q_2, which is greater than Q_1. Consequently, there is an excess quantity demanded at the below–market clearing price. Prices can go as high as P_2 in the scalpers' market.

market clearing prices. Sellouts indicate that the event is very popular and that there may be people without tickets willing to buy high-priced tickets because they place a greater value on the entertainment event than the actual face value of the ticket. Without scalpers, those individuals would not be able to attend the event. In the case of the Super Bowl, various forms of scalping occur nationwide. Tickets for a seat on the 50-yard line have been sold for more than $2,000 a piece. In front of every Super Bowl arena, you can find ticket scalpers hawking their wares.

In most states, scalping is illegal. In Pennsylvania, convicted scalpers are either fined $5,000 or sentenced to two years behind bars. For an economist, such legislation seems strange. As one New York ticket broker said, "I look at scalping like working as a stockbroker, buying low and selling high. If people are willing to pay me the money, what kind of problem is that?"

FOR CRITICAL ANALYSIS: What happens to ticket scalpers who are still holding tickets after an event has started? ●

CONCEPTS IN BRIEF

- The market clearing price occurs at the intersection of the market demand curve and the market supply curve. It is also called the equilibrium price, the price from which there is no tendency to change unless there is a change in demand or supply.

- Whenever the price is greater than the equilibrium price, there is an excess quantity supplied (a surplus).

- Whenever the price is less than the equilibrium price, there is an excess quantity demanded (a shortage).

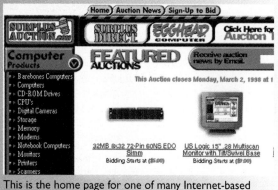

This is the home page for one of many Internet-based auction companies. How do they affect the marketplace?

On-Line Auctions: Reaching the Equilibrium Price on the Web

CONCEPTS APPLIED:
DEMAND AND SUPPLY, SHIFTS IN DEMAND AND SUPPLY, EQUILIBRIUM

Visit www.econtoday.com for an Internet Activity that expands your understanding of these concepts.

In the absence of constraints, the equilibrium price of just about anything tends toward where the demand curve intersects the supply curve. Notice the word *tends*. As with everything, reaching an equilibrium price takes time. A shift in demand or supply normally does not immediately result in a change in price to its equilibrium level. Where we see the equilibrium price determined rapidly, though, is at auctions. Certain commodities in certain quantities are offered for sale at auctions, typically to the highest bidder. The equilibrium price becomes obvious when the auctioneer pounds the gavel and says something like "Going once, going twice, gone."

Enter the Internet Auction

Nowadays, just about anything in the world can be auctioned off on the Internet. Indeed, one of the fastest-growing activities on the Internet is the on-line auction. For example, the Web-based auctioneer company OnSale, Inc., of Palo Alto, California, recently cut a deal with America Online (AOL) to be featured on its "shopping channel." That gave OnSale instant access to AOL's 12 million members.

OnSale started out as an on-line auction company for computer equipment. Visitors to OnSale's Web site can still bid on a wide range of new and refurbished computer equipment that OnSale buys from manufacturers. OnSale lists items with minimum prices. Visitors to the site post their offers over a short time period, usually two days. The highest bidder gets the product. Today OnSale also auctions off microwave ovens, Omaha steaks, and beachfront rentals, among a great many other commodities.

As of 1998, there were over 200 on-line auctions. Auction seekers can gain access by using BidFind (**www.vsn.net/af/**). This is a search engine that allows you to type in the item you would like to purchase.

BidFind will display for you a list of matches on the product or service and the names of on-line auctioneers who have it for sale. There are "hot links" (instant transfers) directly to those sites.

On-line Auctions Are Different, Though

Notice the difference between on-line auctions and traditional auctions. At a traditional auction, you have to go or send a representative who is physically present (although for fine art auctions, you can sometimes do your bidding over the phone). The auction process for each item takes only a few minutes. On the Internet, in contrast, auctions may last from a day to a week or longer.

Reverse, or Dutch, Auctions

Rather than the normal "selling to the highest bidder" type of auction, there are also so-called reverse, or Dutch, auctions on the Internet. Klik-Klok OnLine Dutch Auction (**www.klik-klok.com**) reverses the normal bidding process. Klik-Klok's gardening tools and jewelry are offered with a clock ticking and prices dropping every few seconds. Registered users who click their computer's mouse get the product at the currently displayed price.

A very successful reverse auction system has been used by Internet Liquidators, which is co-owned by America Online. Every five minutes, the prices of offered goods decline. Bidders time their move to get the best price before the goods they wish to buy sell out.

Buying and Selling Electronics Parts over the Internet

One of the fastest-growing on-line auction markets involves electronics parts. Electronics manufacturing managers routinely end up with too few or too many parts. They do not want to disclose anything about their business to rivals, however. Therefore, they need an anonymous way to auction parts. Today they use FastParts, which started in 1996. About 300 electronics firms trade their excess parts at an Internet auction that FastParts holds three times a week. Prices typically average about two-thirds of the original manufacturing cost of the parts.

Getting a Cheap Round Trip to Anywhere

Airlines often find themselves with excess inventory, just as electronics companies do. Many airlines have turned to the Internet to auction off their excess seats. They offer silent auctions and also last-minute fare deals handled via e-mail.

American Airlines was one of the first companies to start electronic auctions on a regular basis a few years ago. American Airlines usually runs its auctions for 24 to 48 hours. The company periodically posts the highest bid during each round of bidding. American also sends last-minute deals by e-mail each Wednesday, offering discounted travel on the following weekend. Table 3-2 highlights some of the auction deals that American has provided.

One airline, Cathay Pacific, has even held on-line auctions for use with its frequent-flier mileage. A typical first-class round-trip ticket normally requires 125,000 frequent-flier miles, but some lucky on-line bidders got them for 60,000 frequent-flier miles. When Cathay Pacific inaugurated its first New York–Hong Kong flights, it held an on-line auction for all 387 seats on one of its flights.

TABLE 3-2

Buying a Cheap Round-Trip Ticket on the Internet
Here you see the prices of a pair of first-class tickets obtained via different American Airlines Internet auctions compared with the estimated value of the tickets.

Route	List Price	Internet Price
Amarillo, Tex., to Seattle	$3,496	$ 895
Carlsbad, Calif., to Washington, D.C.	$4,176	$ 800
Los Angeles to New York	$2,916	$1,020
San Antonio to Miami	$2,976	$ 865
Washington, D.C., to San Diego	$4,176	$ 680

Source: American Airlines.

The Future of On-Line Auctioning

The future of on-line auctions is limited. Not everyone wants to purchase overstocked, discontinued, and reconditioned items. Even for airline flights and holiday offers, many on-line auctions attract no bids at all. Nonetheless, some people enjoy the "thrill of the chase" that an auction provides. On-line auctions have found their niche.

FOR CRITICAL ANALYSIS
1. Increased on-line security in the form of better encryption systems is being developed. How will this affect the use of on-line auctions?
2. What goods or services might never be sold on-line? Why not?

CHAPTER SUMMARY

1. The law of demand says that at higher prices, individuals will purchase less of a commodity and at lower prices, they will purchase more, other things being equal.
2. Relative prices must be distinguished from absolute, or money, prices. During periods of rising prices, almost all prices go up, but some rise faster than others.
3. All references to the laws of supply and demand refer to constant-quality units of a commodity. A time period for the analysis must also be specified.
4. The demand schedule shows the relationship between various possible prices and their respective quantities purchased per unit time period. Graphically, the demand schedule is a demand curve and is downward-sloping.

5. The determinants of demand other than price are (a) income, (b) tastes and preferences, (c) the prices of related goods, (d) expectations, and (e) population, or market, size. Whenever any of these determinants of demand changes, the demand curve shifts.

6. The supply curve is generally upward-sloping such that at higher prices, more will be forthcoming than at lower prices. At higher prices, suppliers are willing to incur the increasing costs of higher rates of production.

7. The determinants of supply other than price are (a) input costs, (b) technology and productivity, (c) taxes and subsidies, (d) price expectations, and (e) entry and exit of firms.

8. A movement along a demand or supply curve is not the same thing as a shift in the curve. A change in price causes movement along the curve. A change in any other determinant of supply or demand shifts the entire curve.

9. The demand and supply curves intersect at the equilibrium point, marking the market clearing price, where quantity demanded just equals quantity supplied. At that point, the plans of buyers and sellers mesh exactly.

10. When the price of a good is greater than its market clearing price, an excess quantity is supplied at that price; it is called a surplus. When the price is below the market clearing price, an excess quantity is demanded at that price; it is called a shortage.

DISCUSSION OF PREVIEW QUESTIONS

1. Why are relative prices important in understanding the law of demand?

People respond to changes in relative prices rather than absolute prices. If the price of CDs rises by 50 percent next year, while at the same time the prices of everything else, including your wages, also increase by 50 percent, the relative price of CDs has not changed. If nothing else has changed in your life, your normal quantity demanded of CDs will remain about the same. In a world of generally rising prices (inflation), you have to compare the price of one good with the average of all other goods in order to decide whether the relative price of that one good has gone up, gone down, or stayed the same.

2. How can we distinguish between a change in *demand* and a change in *quantity demanded*?

Use the accompanying graphs to aid you. Because demand is a curve, a change in demand is equivalent to a *shift* in the demand curve. Changes in demand result from changes in the other determinants of demand, such as income, tastes and preferences, expectations, prices of related goods, and population. A change in quantity demanded, given demand, is a movement along a demand curve and results only from a change in the price of the commodity in question.

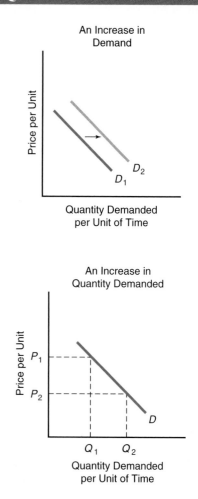

3. Why is there generally a direct relationship be-tween price and quantity supplied (other things being equal)?

In general, businesses experience increasing *extra* costs as they expand output in the short run. This means that additional units of output, which may be quite similar in physical attributes to initial units of output, actually cost the firm more to produce. Con-sequently, firms often require a higher and higher price (as an incentive) in order to produce more in the short run; this "incentive" effect implies that higher prices, other things being constant, lead to increases in quantity supplied.

4. Why will the market clearing price occur at the intersection of the supply and demand curves rather than at a higher or lower price?

Consider the accompanying graph. To demonstrate that the equilibrium price will be at P_e, we can elim-inate all other prices as possibilities. Consider a price above P_e, $8 per unit. By inspection of the graph, we can see that at that price, the quantity supplied ex-ceeds the quantity demanded for this product ($B > A$). Clearly, sellers cannot sell all they wish at $8, and they therefore find it profitable to lower price and de-crease output. In fact, this surplus situation exists at *all* prices above P_e. Sellers, competing for sales, will reduce prices if a surplus exists.

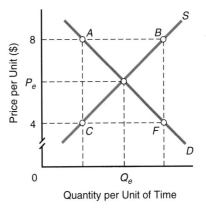

Consider a price of $4 per unit, where the quantity demanded exceeds the quantity supplied ($F > C$); a shortage of this commodity exists at a price of $4 per unit. Buyers will not be able to get all they want at that relatively low price. Because buyers are competing for this good, buyers who are willing to give up more of other goods in order to get this one will offer high-er and higher prices. By doing so, they eliminate buy-ers who are not willing to give up more of other goods. An increase in price encourages sellers to pro-duce and sell more. A shortage exists at *any* price below P_e, and therefore price will rise if it is below P_e.

At P_e, the quantity supplied equals the quantity de-manded, Q_e, and both buyers and sellers are able to re-alize their intentions. Because neither group has an in-centive to change its behavior, equilibrium exists at P_e.

PROBLEMS

(Answers to the odd-numbered problems appear at the back of the book.)

3-1. Construct a demand curve and a supply curve for skateboards, based on the data provided in the fol-lowing tables.

Price per Skateboard	Quantity Demanded per Year
$75	3 million
50	6 million
35	9 million
25	12 million
15	15 million
10	18 million

Price per Skateboard	Quantity Supplied per Year
$75	18 million
50	15 million
35	12 million
25	9 million
15	6 million
10	3 million

What is the equilibrium price? What is the equilib-rium quantity at that price?

3-2. "Drugs are obviously complementary to physicians' services." Is this statement always correct?

3-3. Five factors, other than price, that affect the demand for a good were discussed in this chapter. Place each of the following events in its proper category, and state how it would shift the demand curve in parentheses.

a. New information is disclosed that large doses of vitamin C prevent common colds. (Demand for vitamin C)

b. A drop in the price of educational interactive CD-ROMs occurs. (Demand for teachers)

c. A fall in the price of pretzels occurs. (Demand for beer)

3-4. Examine the following table, and then answer the questions.

	Price per Unit Last Year	Price per Unit Today
Heating oil	$1.00	$2.00
Natural gas	.80	3.20

What has happened to the absolute price of heating oil? Of natural gas? What has happened to the price of heating oil relative to the price of natural gas? What has happened to the relative price of heating oil? Will consumers, through time, change their relative purchases? If so, how?

3-5. Suppose that the demand for oranges remains constant but a frost occurs in Florida that could potentially destroy one-third of the orange crop. What will happen to the equilibrium price and quantity for Florida oranges?

3-6. "The demand has increased so much in response to our offering of a $75 rebate that our inventory of portable laptop computers is now running very low." What is wrong with this assertion?

3-7. Analyze the following statement: "Federal farm price supports can never achieve their goals because the above-equilibrium price floors that are established by Congress and the Department of Agriculture invariably create surpluses (quantities supplied in excess of quantities demanded), which in turn drive the price right back down toward equilibrium."

3-8. Suppose that an island economy exists in which there is no money. Suppose further that every Sunday morning, at a certain location, hog farmers and cattle ranchers gather to exchange live pigs for cows. Is this a market, and if so, what do the supply and demand diagrams use as a price? Can you imagine any problems arising at the price at which cows and pigs are exchanged?

3-9. Here is a supply and demand schedule for rain in an Amazon jungle settlement where cloud seeding or other scientific techniques can be used to coax rainfall from the skies.

Price (cruzeiros per yearly centimeter of rain)	Quantity Supplied (centimeters of rain per year)	Quantity Demanded (centimeters of rain per year)
0	200	150
10	225	125
20	250	100
30	275	75
40	300	50
50	325	25
60	350	0
70	375	0
80	400	0

What are the equilibrium price and the equilibrium quantity? Explain.

COMPUTER-ASSISTED INSTRUCTION

By examining the consequence of a specific price change, we examine the roles of the substitution effect and the income effect in producing the law of demand.

Complete problem and answer appear on disk.

CHAPTER 4

EXTENSIONS OF DEMAND AND SUPPLY ANALYSIS

They are big, they are fat, and they are smelly. But for the people who love them—who call themselves *aficionados*—they are heavenly. The commodity in question is the handrolled Cuban cigar. Recently, the prices of Cuban cigars in the United States have increased dramatically to double or triple what they were a few years ago. Even if you do not like cigar smoke, you might wonder why the prices of Cuban cigars could increase so dramatically. To understand why, you need to understand some extensions of supply and demand analysis, which are presented in this chapter. Many of them have to do with government restrictions on the market.

PREVIEW QUESTIONS

1. Does an increase in demand always lead to a rise in price?
2. Can there ever be shortages in a market with no restrictions?
3. How are goods rationed?
4. When would you expect to encounter black markets?

Did You Know That . . . according to the U.S. Customs Service, the second most serious smuggling problem along the Mexican border, just behind drugs, involves the refrigerant Freon? Selling Freon is more profitable than dealing in cocaine, and illegal Freon smuggling is a bigger business than gunrunning. Freon is used in many air conditioners in cars and homes. Its use is already illegal in the United States, but residents of developing countries may legally use it until the year 2005. When an older U.S. air conditioner needs fixing, it is often cheaper to pay a relatively high price for illegally smuggled Freon than to modify the unit to use a replacement coolant. You can analyze illegal markets, such as the one for Freon, using the supply and demand analysis you learned in Chapter 3. Similarly, you can use this analysis to examine legal markets and the "shortage" of skilled information technology specialists, the "shortage" of apartments in certain cities, and many other phenomena. All of these examples are part of our economy, which we characterize as a *price system.*

THE PRICE SYSTEM

A **price system,** otherwise known as a *market system,* is one in which relative prices are constantly changing to reflect changes in supply and demand for different commodities. The prices of those commodities are the signals to everyone within the system as to what is relatively scarce and what is relatively abundant. Indeed, it is the *signaling* aspect of the price system that provides the information to buyers and sellers about what should be bought and what should be produced. In a price system, there is a clear-cut chain of events in which any changes in demand and supply cause changes in prices that in turn affect the opportunities that businesses and individuals have for profit and personal gain. Such changes influence our use of resources.

Price system
An economic system in which relative prices are constantly changing to reflect changes in supply and demand for different commodities. The prices of those commodities are signals to everyone within the system as to what is relatively scarce and what is relatively abundant.

EXCHANGE AND MARKETS

The price system features **voluntary exchange,** acts of trading between individuals that make both parties to the trade subjectively better off. The **terms of exchange**—the prices we pay for the desired items—are determined by the interaction of the forces underlying supply and demand. In our economy, the majority of exchanges take place voluntarily in markets. A market encompasses the exchange arrangements of both buyers and sellers that underlie the forces of supply and demand. Indeed, one definition of a market is a low-cost institution for facilitating exchange. A market in essence increases incomes by helping resources move to their highest-valued uses by means of prices. Prices are the providers of information.

Voluntary exchange
An act of trading, done on a voluntary basis, in which both parties to the trade are subjectively better off after the exchange.

Terms of exchange
The terms under which trading takes place. Usually the terms of exchange are equal to the price at which a good is traded.

Transaction Costs

Individuals turn to markets because markets reduce the cost of exchanges. These costs are sometimes referred to as **transaction costs,** which are broadly defined as the costs associated with finding out exactly what is being transacted as well as the cost of enforcing contracts. If you were Robinson Crusoe and lived alone on an island, you would never incur a transaction cost. For everyone else, transaction costs are just as real as the costs of produc-

Transaction costs
All of the costs associated with exchanging, including the informational costs of finding out price and quality, service record, and durability of a product, plus the cost of contracting and enforcing that contract.

tion. High-speed large-scale computers have allowed us to reduce transaction costs by increasing our ability to process information and keep records.

Consider some simple examples of transaction costs. The supermarket reduces transaction costs relative to your having to go to numerous specialty stores to obtain the items you desire. Organized stock exchanges, such as the New York Stock Exchange, have reduced transaction costs of buying and selling stocks and bonds. In general, the more organized the market, the lower the transaction costs. One group of individuals who constantly attempt to lower transaction costs are the much maligned middlemen.

The Role of Middlemen

Exercise 4.1
Visit www.econtoday.com for more about on-line travel agencies.

As long as there are costs to bringing together buyers and sellers, there will be an incentive for intermediaries, normally called middlemen, to lower those costs. This means that middlemen specialize in lowering transaction costs. Whenever producers do not sell their products directly to the final consumer, there are, by definition, one or more middlemen involved. Farmers typically sell their output to distributors, who are usually called wholesalers, who then sell those products to supermarkets.

Recently, technology has changed the way middlemen work.

CYBERSPACE EXAMPLE   MIDDLEMEN FIND WAYS TO SURVIVE ON-LINE SHOPPING

Will the Internet eliminate intermediaries? Or will it just change the identity and activities of middlemen? Though it is true that on-line information about air travel and the on-line purchasing of tickets are shifting the demand curve for travel agents inward, such is not the case for all intermediaries. Middleman sites are popping up everywhere on the Web. People wishing to buy a car can access Auto-By-Tel Corp., which acts as an Internet intermediary to find the best price on a car. Other sites are available for buying computers, books, wine, and insurance. InsWeb Corp. has such a Web site, which allows users to compare quotes from several insurance companies. In any event, because total revenues from on-line retail shopping are projected to exceed $25 billion by 2001, electronic middlemen are certain to proliferate.

FOR CRITICAL ANALYSIS: Anybody connected to the Internet can find the same information that an Internet intermediary can. Why, then, would someone pay for the intermediary's services? •

CHANGES IN DEMAND AND SUPPLY

It is in markets that we see the results of changes in demand and supply. In certain situations, it is possible to predict what will happen to equilibrium price and equilibrium quantity when a change occurs in demand or supply. Specifically, whenever one curve is stable while the other curve shifts, we can tell what will happen to price and quantity. Consider the four possibilities in Figure 4-1 on page 76. In panel (a), the supply curve remains stable but demand increases from D_1 to D_2. Note that the result is both an increase in the market clearing price from P_1 to P_2 and an increase in the equilibrium quantity from Q_1 to Q_2.

In panel (b), there is a decrease in demand from D_1 to D_3. This results in a decrease in both the relative price of the good and the equilibrium quantity. Panels (c) and (d) show the

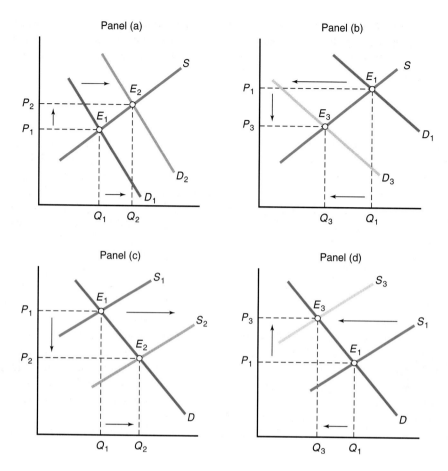

Panel (a)

Panel (b)

Panel (c)

Panel (d)

FIGURE 4-1

Shifts in Demand and in Supply: Determinate Results
In panel (a), the supply curve is stable at S. The demand curve shifts outward from D_1 to D_2. The equilibrium price and quantity rise from P_1, Q_1 to P_2, Q_2, respectively. In panel (b), again the supply curve remains stable at S. The demand curve, however, shifts inward to the left, showing a decrease in demand from D_1 to D_3. Both equilibrium price and equilibrium quantity fall. In panel (c), the demand curve now remains stable at D. The supply curve shifts from S_1 to S_2. The equilibrium price falls from P_1 to P_2. The equilibrium quantity increases, however, from Q_1 to Q_2. In panel (d), the demand curve is stable at D. Supply decreases as shown by a leftward shift of the supply curve from S_1 to S_3. The market clearing price increases from P_1 to P_3. The equilibrium quantity falls from Q_1 to Q_3.

effects of a shift in the supply curve while the demand curve is stable. In panel (c), the supply curve has shifted rightward. The relative price of the product falls; the equilibrium quantity increases. In panel (d), supply has shifted leftward—there has been a supply decrease. The product's relative price increases; the equilibrium quantity decreases.

When Both Demand and Supply Shift

The examples given in Figure 4-1 each showed a theoretically determinate outcome of a shift in either the demand curve holding the supply curve constant or the supply curve holding the demand curve constant. When both supply and demand curves change, the outcome is indeterminate for either equilibrium price or equilibrium quantity.

When both demand and supply increase, all we can be certain of is that equilibrium quantity will increase. We do not know what will happen to equilibrium price until we determine whether demand increased relative to supply (equilibrium price will rise) or supply increased relative to demand (equilibrium price will fall). The same analysis applies to decreases in both demand and supply, except that in this case equilibrium quantity falls.

We can be certain that when demand decreases and supply increases, the equilibrium price will fall, but we do not know what will happen to the equilibrium quantity unless we actually draw the new curves. If supply decreases and demand increases, we can be sure that equilibrium price will rise, but again we do not know what happens to equilibrium quantity without drawing the curves. In every situation in which both supply and demand change, you should always draw graphs to determine the resulting change in equilibrium price and quantity.

PRICE FLEXIBILITY AND ADJUSTMENT SPEED

We have used as an illustration for our analysis a market in which prices are quite flexible. Some markets are indeed like that. In others, however, price flexibility may take the form of indirect adjustments such as hidden payments or quality changes. For example, although the published price of bouquets of flowers may stay the same, the freshness of the flowers may change, meaning that the price per constant-quality unit changes. The published price of French bread might stay the same, but the quality could go up or down, thereby changing the price per constant-quality unit. There are many ways to change prices without actually changing the published price for a *nominal* unit of a product or service.

We must also consider the fact that markets do not return to equilibrium immediately. There must be an adjustment time. A shock to the economy in the form of an oil embargo, a drought, or a long strike will not be absorbed overnight. This means that even in unfettered market situations, in which there are no restrictions on changes in prices and quantities, temporary excess quantities supplied and excess quantities demanded may appear. Our analysis simply indicates what the market clearing price ultimately will be, given a demand curve and a supply curve. Nowhere in the analysis is there any indication of the speed with which a market will get to a new equilibrium if there has been a shock. The price may overshoot the equilibrium level. Remember this warning when we examine changes in demand and in supply due to changes in their nonprice determinants.

Now consider how long it takes the labor market to adjust to changes in supply and demand.

EXAMPLE
If You Are a Wired "Techie," There Is a Job for You

At the end of 1997, the Information Technology Association of America claimed that there were over 200,000 unfilled jobs available for skilled computer professionals. Those numbers did not include openings at small companies, government agencies, or nonprofit institutions. Information technology (IT) specialists are in demand because they help companies "tweak" software so that different computers can communicate with each other in what is know as a client-server network. IT specialists also create Web sites (home pages) and staff so-called help desks.

So what is happening here? Why are there so many unfilled job openings for IT specialists? One of the reasons has to do with a 43 percent drop in bachelor's degrees awarded in computer sciences during the period from 1986 to 1994. But on the demand side of the picture, by the mid-1990s, the demand curve for IT specialists had shifted outward to the right. The supply curve was unable to shift outward at the same swift pace. Consequently, even though salaries for software engineers increased more than 30 percent between 1995 and 1997, the equilibrium salary has still not been reached. There continues to be an excess quantity demanded of information technology specialists at current salaries.

You can see what might have happened using the supply and demand curves in Figure 4-2. The supply curve shift from S_1 to S_2 represents the period 1986–1994, reflecting

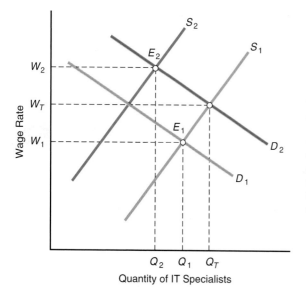

Quantity of IT Specialists

FIGURE 4-2

Rising Wages for Information Technology (IT) Specialists
Prior to the shift in supply and demand for IT specialists, the equilibrium wage rate was W_1. During the period from 1986 to 1994, the supply curve shifted to S_2. From the mid-1990s onward, the demand increased, as shown by a shift in the curve to D_2. Wages have increased somewhat to, say, W_T but not yet to the full equilibrium level of W_2. In the meantime, there is a "shortage" of skilled IT specialists at W_T.

the decrease in the number of computer science bachelor's degrees awarded. From the mid-1990s on, the demand curve has, in contrast, shifted outward from D_1 to D_2, reflecting the increase in the demand for information technology specialists. At the initial equilibrium E_1, the wage rate was W_1 and the equilibrium quantity of software engineers was Q_1. When the supply curve shifted to S_1 and the demand curve shifted to D_2, there was an excess quantity demanded at wage rate W_1. Though the wage rate has increased to, say, W_T (T for temporary), it has not yet reached the new equilibrium level at W_2. Until it gets to that level, there will continue to be an excess quantity demanded of skilled computer professionals.

FOR CRITICAL ANALYSIS: Why do you think so few university students chose to seek computer science degrees from 1986 to 1994? •

CONCEPTS IN BRIEF

• The terms of exchange in a voluntary exchange are determined by the interaction of the forces underlying demand and supply. These forces take place in markets, which tend to minimize transaction costs.

• When the demand curve shifts outward or inward with a stable supply curve, equilibrium price and quantity increase or decrease, respectively. When the supply curve shifts outward or inward given a stable demand curve, equilibrium price moves in the direction opposite of equilibrium quantity.

• When there is a shift in demand or supply, the new equilibrium price is not obtained instantaneously. Adjustment takes time.

THE RATIONING FUNCTION OF PRICES

A shortage creates a situation that forces price to rise toward a market clearing, or equilibrium, level. A surplus brings into play forces that cause price to fall toward its market clearing level. The synchronization of decisions by buyers and sellers that creates a situa-

Water "Rationing"

More and more these days, we hear about the lack of water in some city, state, or country. For seven successive years in the 1980s and 1990s, California suffered droughts and was "forced" to "ration" water. Puerto Rico suffered a drought when rainfall dropped to 35 percent below normal; residents of San Juan were subjected to water cutoffs every other day. These stories about "running out of water" always focus on the supply of water, never on the demand. The demand curve for water slopes downward, just like that for any other good or service. When the supply of strawberries increases in the summer, their prices go down; when the supply decreases, their prices go up. When the supply of water falls because of a drought, one way to ration a smaller supply is to increase the price. For some reason, politicians and media announcers reject this possibility, implying that water is different. Beware when you see the word *rationing* in the media; it typically means that the price of a good or service has not been allowed to reach equilibrium.

tion of equilibrium is called the *rationing function of prices.* Prices are indicators of relative scarcity. An equilibrium price clears the market. The plans of buyers and sellers, given the price, are not frustrated.[1] It is the free interaction of buyers and sellers that sets the price that eventually clears the market. Price, in effect, rations a commodity to demanders who are willing and able to pay the highest price. Whenever the rationing function of prices is frustrated by government-enforced price ceilings that set prices below the market clearing level, a prolonged shortage situation is not allowed to be corrected by the upward adjustment of the price.

There are other ways to ration goods. *First come, first served* is one method. *Political power* is another. *Physical force* is yet another. Cultural, religious, and physical differences have been and are used as rationing devices throughout the world.

Consider first come, first served as a rationing device. In countries that do not allow prices to reflect true relative scarcity, first come, first served has become a way of life. We call this *rationing by queues,* where *queue* means "line," as in Britain. Whoever is willing to wait in line the longest obtains meat that is being sold at less than the market clearing price. All who wait in line are paying a higher *total* price than the money price paid for the meat. Personal time has an opportunity cost. To calculate the total price of the meat, we must add up the money price plus the opportunity cost of the time spent waiting.

Lotteries are another way to ration goods. You may have been involved in a rationing-by-lottery scheme during your first year in college when you were assigned a university-provided housing unit. Sometimes for popular classes, rationing by lottery is used to fill the available number of slots.

Rationing by *coupons* has also been used, particularly during wartime. In the United States during World War II, families were allotted coupons that allowed them to purchase specified quantities of rationed goods, such as meat and gasoline. To purchase such goods, you had to pay a specified price *and* give up a coupon.

Rationing by waiting may occur in situations in which entrepreneurs are free to change prices to equate quantity demanded with quantity supplied but choose not to do so. This results in queues of potential buyers. The most obvious conclusion seems to be that the price in the market is being held below equilibrium by some noncompetitive force. That is not true, however.

The reason is that queuing may also arise when the demand characteristics of a market are subject to large or unpredictable fluctuations, and the additional costs to firms (and ultimately to consumers) of constantly changing prices or of holding sufficient inventories or providing sufficient excess capacity to cover these peak demands are greater than the costs to consumers of waiting for the good. This is the usual case of waiting in line to purchase a fast-food lunch or to purchase a movie ticket a few minutes before the next show.

---

[1]There is a difference between frustration and unhappiness. You may be unhappy because you can't buy a Rolls Royce, but if you had sufficient income, you would not be frustrated in your attempt to purchase one at the current market price. By contrast, you would be frustrated if you went to your local supermarket and could get only two cans of your favorite soft drink when you had wanted to purchase a dozen and had the necessary income.

The Essential Role of Rationing

In a world of scarcity, there is, by definition, competition for what is scarce. After all, any resources that are not scarce can be had by everyone at a zero price in as large a quantity as everyone wants, such as air to burn in internal combustion engines. Once scarcity arises, there has to be some method to ration the available resources, goods, and services. The price system is one form of rationing; the others that we mentioned are alternatives. Economists cannot say which system of rationing is best. They can, however, say that rationing via the price system leads to the most efficient use of available resources. This means that generally in a price system, further trades could not occur without making somebody worse off. In other words, in a freely functioning price system, all of the gains from mutually beneficial trade will be exhausted.

CONCEPTS IN BRIEF

- Prices in a market economy perform a rationing function because they reflect relative scarcity, allowing the market to clear. Other ways to ration goods include first come, first served; political power; physical force; lotteries; and coupons.

- Even when businesspeople can change prices, some rationing by waiting will occur. Such queuing arises when there are large unexpected changes in demand coupled with high costs of satisfying those changes immediately.

THE POLICY OF GOVERNMENT-IMPOSED PRICE CONTROLS

The rationing function of prices is often not allowed to operate when governments impose price controls. **Price controls** typically involve setting a **price ceiling**—the maximum price that may be allowed in an exchange. The world has had a long history of price ceilings applied to some goods, wages, rents, and interest rates, among other things. Occasionally a government will set a **price floor**—a minimum price below which a good or service may not be sold. These have most often been applied to wages and agricultural products. Let's consider price controls in terms of price ceilings.

Price Ceilings and Black Markets

As long as a price ceiling is below the market clearing price, imposing a price ceiling creates a shortage, as can be seen in Figure 4-3. At any price below the market clearing, or equilibrium, price of P_e, there will always be a larger quantity demanded than quantity supplied, that is, a shortage. This was discussed initially in Chapter 3. Normally, whenever a shortage exists, there is a tendency for price and output to rise to equilibrium levels. This is exactly what we pointed out when discussing shortages in the labor market. But with a price ceiling, this tendency cannot be fully realized because everyone is forbidden to trade at the equilibrium price.

Price controls
Government-mandated minimum or maximum prices that may be charged for goods and services.

Price ceiling
A legal maximum price that may be charged for a particular good or service.

Price floor
A legal minimum price below which a good or service may not be sold. Legal minimum wages are an example.

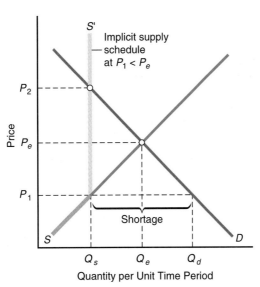

FIGURE 4-3
Black Markets
The demand curve is D. The supply curve is S. The equilibrium price is P_e. The government, however, steps in and imposes a maximum price of P_1. At that lower price, the quantity demanded will be Q_d, but the quantity supplied will only be Q_s. There is a "shortage." The implicit price (including time costs) tends to rise to P_2. If black markets arise, as they generally will, the equilibrium black market price will end up somewhere between P_2 and P_e.

Nonprice rationing devices
All methods used to ration scarce goods that are price-controlled. Whenever the price system is not allowed to work, nonprice rationing devices will evolve to ration the affected goods and services.

Black market
A market in which goods are traded at prices above their legal maximum prices or in which illegal goods are sold.

The result is fewer exchanges and **nonprice rationing devices.** In Figure 4-3, at an equilibrium price of P_e, the equilibrium quantity demanded and supplied (or traded) is Q_e. But at the price ceiling of P_1, the equilibrium quantity offered is only Q_s. What happens if there is a shortage? The most obvious nonprice rationing device to help clear the market is queuing, or long lines, which we have already discussed.

Typically, an effective price ceiling leads to a **black market.** A black market is a market in which the price-controlled good is sold at an illegally high price through various methods. For example, if the price of gasoline is controlled at lower than the market clearing price, a gas station attendant may take a cash payment on the side in order to fill up a driver's car (as happened in the 1970s in the United States during price controls on gasoline). If the price of beef is controlled at below its market clearing price, the butcher may give special service to a customer who offers the butcher great seats at an upcoming football game. Indeed, the number of ways in which the true implicit price of a price-controlled good or service can be increased is infinite, limited only by the imagination. (Black markets also occur when goods are made illegal—their legal price is set at zero.)

Whenever a nation attempts to freeze all prices, a variety of problems arise. Many of them occurred a few years ago in one African country, Sierra Leone.

INTERNATIONAL EXAMPLE
Price Controls in Sierra Leone

Lisa Walker spent a year as a Peace Corps volunteer in Sierra Leone, West Africa, and she kept a diary of her experiences. One thing she wrote about was what happened when the government imposed price controls on many common items: "For the last five days," she wrote, "nobody has sold cigarettes, kerosene, Maggi [bouillon] cubes, or rice here. . . . This is the result of the government's new order. The government says that Maggi cubes have to be sold for 30 cents, but sellers bought them for 50 cents, so when military men enter the village to enforce the government price, those with Maggis hide them. Same story for cigarettes and kerosene. The rice supplies are now hidden because of government prices. Unless one is willing to pay an outrageous price, it is impossible to buy rice in the marketplace. The only way to get rice legally is to buy it from the government. This means standing in long lines for many hours to get a rationed amount. I don't know how Sierra Leoneans are managing or how long this artificial rice shortage will last."

FOR CRITICAL ANALYSIS: How would you graphically illustrate the market for rice in Sierra Leone in the presence of price controls? •

CONCEPTS IN BRIEF

- Government policy can impose price controls in the form of price ceilings and price floors.
- An effective price ceiling is one that sets the legal price below the market clearing price and is enforced. Effective price ceilings lead to nonprice rationing devices and black markets.

THE POLICY OF CONTROLLING RENTS

Over 200 American cities and towns, including Santa Monica, Berkeley, and New York City, operate under some kind of rent control. **Rent control** is a system under which the local government tells building owners how much they can charge their tenants in rent. In the United States, rent controls date back to at least World War II. The objective of rent control is to keep rents below levels that would be observed in a freely competitive market.

Rent control
The placement of price ceilings on rents in particular cities.

The Functions of Rental Prices

In any housing market, rental prices serve three functions: (1) to promote the efficient maintenance of existing housing and stimulate the construction of new housing, (2) to allocate existing scarce housing among competing claimants, and (3) to ration the use of existing housing by current demanders.

Rent Controls and Construction. Rent controls have discouraged the construction of new rental units. Rents are the most important long-term determinant of profitability, and rent controls have artificially depressed them. Consider some examples. In a recent year in Dallas, Texas, with a 16 percent rental vacancy rate but no rent control laws, 11,000 new rental housing units were built. In the same year in San Francisco, California, only 2,000 units were built. The major difference? San Francisco has only a 1.6 percent vacancy rate but stringent rent control laws. In New York City, until a change in the law in 1997, the only rental units being built were luxury units, which were exempt from controls. In Santa Monica, California, new apartments were not being constructed at all until 1996 when that city's rent control law was softened by the state legislature. New office rental space and commercial developments have always been exempt from rent controls.

Effects on the Existing Supply of Housing. When rental rates are held below equilibrium levels, property owners cannot recover the cost of maintenance, repairs, and capital improvements through higher rents. Hence they curtail these activities. In the extreme situation, taxes, utilities, and the expenses of basic repairs exceed rental receipts. The result is abandoned buildings. Numerous buildings have been abandoned in New York City. Some owners have resorted to arson, hoping to collect the insurance on their empty buildings before the city claims them for back taxes.

In Santa Monica, the result is bizarre contrasts: Run-down rental units sit next to homes costing more than $500,000, and abandoned apartment buildings share the block with luxury car dealerships. With the new law, such an anomaly should gradually disappear.

Rationing the Current Use of Housing. Rent controls also affect the current use of housing because they restrict tenant mobility. Consider the family whose children have gone off to college. That family might want to live in a smaller apartment. But in a rent-controlled environment, there can be a substantial cost to giving up a rent-controlled unit. In most rent-controlled cities, rents can be adjusted only when a tenant leaves. That means that a move from a long-occupied rent-controlled apartment to a smaller apartment can involve a hefty rent hike. This artificial preservation of the status quo became known in New York as "housing gridlock."

Attempts at Evading Rent Controls

The distortions produced by rent controls lead to efforts by both property owners and tenants to evade the rules. This leads to the growth of expensive government bureaucracies whose job it is to make sure that rent controls aren't evaded. In New York City, property owners have had an incentive to make life unpleasant for tenants to drive them out or to evict them on the slightest pretense as the only way to raise the rent. The city has responded by making evictions extremely costly for property owners. Eviction requires a tedious and expensive judicial proceeding. Tenants, for their part, routinely try to sublet all or part of their rent-controlled apartments at fees substantially above the rent they pay to the owner. Both the city and the property owners try to prohibit subletting and typically end up in the city's housing courts—an entire judicial system developed to deal with disputes involving rent-controlled apartments. The overflow and appeals from the city's housing courts is now clogging the rest of New York's judicial system. Santa Monica has a similar rent control board. Its budget grew 500 percent in less than a decade. The property owners pay for it through a special annual assessment of more than $150 per rental unit per year.

Who Gains and Who Loses from Rent Controls?

The big losers from rent controls are clearly property owners. But there is another group of losers—low-income individuals, especially single mothers, trying to find their first apartment. Some observers now believe that rent controls have worsened the problem of homelessness in such cities as New York.

Typically, owners of rent-controlled apartments often charge "key money" before a new tenant is allowed to move in. This is a large up-front cash payment, usually illegal but demanded nonetheless—just one aspect of the black market in rent-controlled apartments. Poor individuals cannot afford a hefty key money payment, nor can they assure the owner that their rent will be on time or even paid each month. Because controlled rents are usually below market clearing levels, there is little incentive for apartment owners to take any risk on low-income-earning individuals as tenants. This is particularly true when a prospective tenant's chief source of income is a welfare check. Indeed, a large number of the litigants in the New York housing courts are welfare mothers who have missed their rent payments due to emergency expenses or delayed welfare checks. Often their appeals end in evictions and a new home in a temporary public shelter—or on the streets.

Who benefits from rent control? Ample evidence indicates that upper-income professionals benefit the most. These are the people who can use their mastery of the bureaucracy and their large network of friends and connections to exploit the rent control system. Consider that in New York, actresses Mia Farrow and Cicely Tyson live in rent-controlled apartments, paying well below market rates. So do State Senate Democratic leader Manfred Ohrenstein, the director of the Metropolitan Museum of Art, the chairman of Pathmark Stores, and writer Alistair Cooke.

The average subsidy from rent regulation in New York City has been about $345 a month for tenant households with annual incomes above $75,000 but only $176 a month for households with incomes between $10,000 and $20,000. The results of a study by the Pacific Legal Foundation concerning rent controls in Santa Monica and Berkeley are instructive. Since the institution of rent controls in those two communities, they have become more exclusive in terms of median income and average education level compared to surrounding communities. In other words, both Santa Monica and Berkeley have experienced significant declines in the populations that the legislation was intended to protect.

 INTERNATIONAL EXAMPLE
Rent Controls in Bombay

In the mid-1990s, the most expensive capital in the world with respect to rents was Bombay, India. The annual rent per square foot for *available* unleased space was estimated at about $177, compared to $45 in midtown Manhattan. In addition, most landlords insist on receiving a year's rent in advance plus an additional security deposit equal to two years' rent. For major businesses, this can add up to millions of dollars, which are usually returned, but in three to five years and without payment of any interest.

One reason why Bombay rents are so high is the existence of rent controls and other laws intended to protect tenants. These controls and restrictions have kept out real estate developers and even scared owners of rentable property from renting that property, be it commercial or residential. One rent control law makes it almost impossible for a landlord to evict a tenant or to raise rents. Tenants can obtain what is called *statutory tenancy,* which allows them and their descendents to remain without a lease in any property they currently rent. There are situations in Bombay in which renters from 50 years ago still live in the same apartment, paying approximately the same rent as they originally did. Not surprisingly, unleased rental space is hard to find and hence quite expensive.

FOR CRITICAL ANALYSIS: What effect do you think Bombay's high rents might have on foreign firms' desire to operate in that city? •

CONCEPTS IN BRIEF

- Rental prices perform three functions: (1) allocating existing scarce housing among competing claimants, (2) promoting efficient maintenance of existing houses and stimulating new housing construction, and (3) rationing the use of existing houses by current demanders.

- Effective rent controls reduce or alter the three functions of rental prices. Construction of new rental units is discouraged. Rent controls decrease spending on maintenance of existing ones and also lead to "housing gridlock."

- There are numerous ways to evade rent controls; key money is one.

PRICE FLOORS IN AGRICULTURE

Another way that government can affect markets is by imposing price floors or price supports. In the United States, price supports are most often associated with agricultural products.

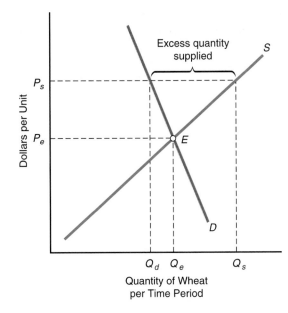

FIGURE 4-4

Agricultural Price Supports
Free market equilibrium occurs at E, with an equilibrium price of P_e and an equilibrium quantity of Q_e. When the government set a support price at P_s, the quantity demanded was Q_d, and the quantity supplied was Q_s. The difference was the surplus, which the government bought. Note that farmers' total income was from consumers ($P_s \times Q_d$) plus tax-payers [$(Q_s - Q_d) \times P_s$].

Price Supports

During the Great Depression, the federal government swung into action to help farmers. In 1933, it established a system of price supports for many agricultural products. Until recently there were price supports for wheat, feed grains, cotton, rice, soybeans, sorghum, and dairy products. The nature of the supports was quite simple: The government simply chose a *support price* for an agricultural product and then acted to ensure that the price of the product never fell below the support level. Figure 4-4 shows the market demand and supply of wheat. Without a price support program, competitive forces would yield an equilibrium price of P_e and an equilibrium quantity of Q_e. Clearly, if the government sets the support price at P_e or below, nothing will happen, because farmers can sell all they want at the market clearing price of P_e.

Until 1996, however, the government set the support price *above* P_e, at P_s. At a support price of P_s, the quantity demanded is only Q_d, but the quantity supplied is Q_s. The difference between them is called the *excess quantity supplied,* or *surplus.* As simple as this program seems, two questions arise: (1) How did the government decide on the level of the support price P_s? (2) How did it prevent market forces from pushing the actual price down to P_e?

If production exceeded the amount consumers wanted to buy at the support price, what happened to the surplus? Quite simply, the government had to buy the surplus—the difference between Q_s and Q_d—if the price support program was to work. As a practical matter, the government acquired the quantity $Q_s - Q_d$ indirectly through a government agency. The government either stored the surplus or sold it to foreign countries at a greatly reduced price (or gave it away free of charge) under the Food for Peace program.

Who Benefited from Agricultural Price Supports?

Traditionally advocated as a way to guarantee a decent wage for low-income farmers, most of the benefits of agricultural price supports were skewed toward owners of very large farms. Price supports were made on a per-bushel basis, not on a per-farm basis. Thus traditionally, the larger the farm, the bigger the benefit from agricultural price supports. In addition, *all* of the benefits from price supports ultimately accrued to *landowners* on whose land price-supported crops could grow. Except for peanuts, tobacco, and sugar, the price-support program was eliminated in 1996.

PRICE FLOORS IN THE LABOR MARKET

The **minimum wage** is the lowest hourly wage rate that firms may legally pay their workers. Proponents want higher minimum wages to ensure low-income workers a "decent" standard of living. Opponents claim that higher minimum wages cause increased unemployment, particularly among unskilled minority teenagers.

The federal minimum wage started in 1938 at 25 cents an hour, about 40 percent of the average manufacturing wage at the time. Typically, its level has stayed at about 40 to 50 percent of average manufacturing wages. It was increased to $4.25 in 1991 and may be higher by the time you read this. Many states and cities have their own minimum wage laws that sometimes exceed the federal minimum.

What happens when the government passes a floor on wages? The effects can be seen in Figure 4-5. We start off in equilibrium with the equilibrium wage rate of W_e and the equilibrium quantity of labor demanded and supplied equal to Q_e. A minimum wage, W_m, higher than W_e, is imposed. At W_m, the quantity demanded for labor is reduced to Q_d, and some workers now become unemployed. Note that the reduction in employment from Q_e to Q_d, or the distance from *B* to *A,* is less than the excess quantity of labor supplied at wage rate W_m. This excess quantity supplied is the distance between *A* and *C,* or the distance between Q_d and Q_s. The reason the reduction in employment is smaller than the excess supply of labor at the minimum wage is that the latter also includes a second component that consists of the additional workers who would like to work more hours at the new, higher minimum wage. Some workers may become unemployed as a result of the minimum wage, but others will move to sectors where minimum wage laws do not apply; wages will be pushed down in these uncovered sectors.

In the long run (a time period that is long enough to allow for adjustment by workers and firms), some of the reduction in labor demanded will result from a reduction in the number of firms, and some will result from changes in the number of workers employed by each firm. Economists estimate that a 10 percent increase in the real minimum wage decreases total employment of those affected by 1 to 2 percent.[2]

QUANTITY RESTRICTIONS

Governments can impose quantity restrictions on a market. The most obvious restriction is an outright ban on the ownership or trading of a good. It is presently illegal to buy and sell human organs. It is also currently illegal to buy and sell certain psychoactive drugs such as cocaine, heroin, and marijuana. In some states, it is illegal to start a new hospital without obtaining a license for a particular number of beds to be offered to patients. This licensing requirement effectively limits the quantity of hospital beds in some states. From 1933 to

Minimum wage
A wage floor, legislated by government, setting the lowest hourly rate that firms may legally pay workers.

Exercise 4.2
Visit www.econtoday.com for more about minimum wage.

---

[2]Because we are referring to a long-run analysis here, the reduction in labor demanded would be demonstrated by an eventual shift inward to the left of the short-run demand curve, *D,* in Figure 4-5.

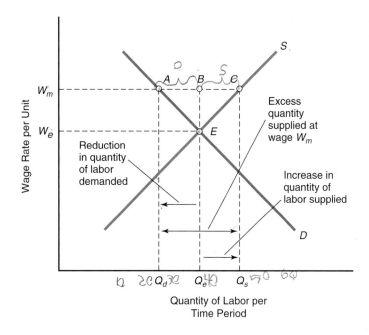

FIGURE 4-5

The Effect of Minimum Wages
The market clearing wage rate is W_e. The market clearing quantity of employment is Q_e, determined by the intersection of supply and demand at point E. A minimum wage equal to W_m is established. The quantity of labor demanded is reduced to Q_d; the reduction in employment from Q_e to Q_d is equal to the distance between B and A. That distance is smaller than the excess quantity of labor supplied at wage rate W_m. The distance between B and C is the increase in the quantity of labor supplied that results from the higher minimum wage rate.

1973, it was illegal for U.S. citizens to own gold except for manufacturing, medicinal, or jewelry purposes.

Some of the most common quantity restrictions exist in the area of international trade. The U.S. government, as well as many foreign governments, imposes import quotas on a variety of goods. An **import quota** is a supply restriction that prohibits the importation of more than a specified quantity of a particular good in a one-year period. The United States has had import quotas on tobacco, sugar, and immigrant labor. For many years, there were import quotas on oil coming into the United States. There are also "voluntary" import quotas on certain goods. Japanese automakers have agreed since 1981 "voluntarily" to restrict the amount of Japanese cars they send to the United States.

Import quota
A physical supply restriction on imports of a particular good, such as sugar. Foreign exporters are unable to sell in the United States more than the quantity specified in the import quota.

POLICY EXAMPLE
Should the Legal Quantity of Cigarettes Supplied Be Set at Zero?

Nicotine has been used as a psychoactive drug by the native people of the Americas for approximately 8,000 years. Five hundred years ago, Christopher Columbus introduced tobacco to the Europeans, who discovered that once they overcame the nausea and dizziness produced by chewing, snorting, or smoking the tobacco, they simply could not get along without it. Nicotine quickly joined alcohol and caffeine as one of the world's principal psychoactive drugs of choice.

In the century after Columbus returned from the Americas with tobacco, the use of and addiction to nicotine spread quickly around the world. There followed numerous efforts to quash what had become known as the "evil weed." In 1603, the Japanese prohibited the use of tobacco and repeatedly increased the penalties for violating the ban, which wasn't lifted until 1625. By the middle of the seventeenth century, similar bans on tobacco were in place in Bavaria, Saxony, Zurich, Turkey, and Russia, with punishments ranging from confiscation of property to execution. Even in the early twentieth century, several state governments in the United States attempted to ban the use of tobacco.

A proposed quantity restriction—outright prohibition—was in the news again a few years ago when the head of the Food and Drug Administration announced that his agency had finally determined that nicotine is addictive. He even argued that it should be classified with marijuana, heroin, and cocaine.

What can we predict if tobacco were ever completely prohibited today? Because tobacco is legal, the supply of illegal tobacco is zero. If the use of tobacco were restricted, the supply of illegal tobacco would not remain zero for long. Even if U.S. tobacco growers were forced out of business, the production of tobacco in other countries would increase to meet the demand. Consequently, the supply curve of illegal tobacco products would shift outward to the right as more foreign sources determined they wanted to enter the illegal U.S. tobacco market. The demand curve for illegal tobacco products would emerge almost immediately after the quantity restriction. The price people pay to satisfy their nicotine addiction would go up.

If you do not believe that cigarette smuggling would become big business after any type of ban on cigarettes in the United States, consider what has happened in Europe. In Germany, there are currently gang wars similar to those that occurred between rival bootleggers in the United States during Prohibition and in recent years between rival gangs selling crack cocaine. In Germany, the gangs are Vietnamese, and their stock in trade is cigarettes. They import the cigarettes illegally by buying them in Eastern European countries or at free ports, such as Rotterdam, without paying taxes or customs duties and then smuggling them into Germany. The gangs distribute the cigarettes to thousands of Vietnamese street sellers, who sell the cigarettes to German smokers for 50 to 65 percent of the normal retail price. German authorities estimate that 300 million packages of cigarettes are sold this way every year. In Italy, criminal organizations allegedly even sign "contracts" with tobacco companies to supply them directly, again without payment of taxes or customs duties. The agreements supposedly specify that the tobacco company not sell to any of the gang's competitors. All tobacco companies maintain, of course, that they do not knowingly sell to smugglers.

FOR CRITICAL ANALYSIS: What other goods or services follow the same analysis as the one presented here? •

CONCEPTS IN BRIEF

- With a price support system, the government sets a minimum price at which, say, qualifying farm products can be sold. Any farmers who cannot sell at that price can "sell" their surplus to the government. The only way a price support system can survive is for the government or some other entity to buy up the excess quantity supplied at the support price.

- When a floor is placed on wages at a rate that is above market equilibrium, the result is an excess quantity of labor supplied at that minimum wage.

- Quantity restrictions may take the form of import quotas, which are limits on the quantity of specific foreign goods that can be brought into the United States for resale purposes.

These smokers might like Cuban cigars, but imports from Cuba are illegal. Does that mean Cuban cigars can't be bought in America?

You Can Smoke a Big Cuban If You Are Willing to Pay a Big Price

CONCEPTS APPLIED:

SUPPLY, DEMAND, GOVERNMENT RESTRICTIONS, SHIFT IN SUPPLY, SHIFT IN DEMAND, EQUILIBRIUM

 Visit www.econtoday.com for an Internet Activity that expands your understanding of these concepts.

"**H**ey, mister! How would you like to buy a box of big Cubans—8 inches long?"

"How much?"

"Only $700."

"Really?"

This hypothetical conversation between a seller of big Cuban cigars and a cigar *aficionado* is only partly hypothetical. The price is about right. Compared with other cigars, big Cubans are quite expensive. The reason is not hard to find: It is illegal to import them into the United States.

The Trade Embargo

In July 1963, President John F. Kennedy imposed a trade embargo on the Cuban regime. Since then, products of Cuban origin cannot be imported legally into the United States. Cigar *aficionados* in the United States did not, however, lose their desire to smoke big Cubans overnight. Look at Figure 4-6. There you see the demand curve for Cubans. The supply curve prior to the embargo ($S_{\text{pre-embargo}}$) intersected the demand curve at price P_e. After the embargo, the supply curve for legal imports became the vertical axis (labeled S_{legal}). Because of illegal imports, the true supply curve is S_{illegal}. The equilibrium price increased to P_1.

Explaining Recent Price Increases

During the past few years, the price of illegally imported Cubans has doubled or even tripled. There are two reasons why this has occurred. For one thing, cigar demand in America is smokin'. The demand curve for premium cigars—handmade with long, not chopped, filler leaf—has been surging outward. Consolidated Cigar Holdings, Inc., the largest domestic manufacturer, started off the year 1996 with a backlog of 4.3 million

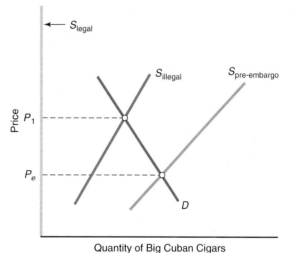

FIGURE 4-6

Cigar Prices Rise for a Reason

When the embargo was placed on Cuban goods, the supply curve for legal imports became the vertical axis. The supply curve shifted to S_{illegal}. The equilibrium price rose from P_e to P_1.

cigars. By 1997, it had 18 million on backorder. Because premium cigars use tobacco leaves aged for two to five years, increases in demand cannot be met with immediate increases in quantity supplied.

The second reason for the surge in price is that the market for Cuban cigars changed abruptly. After the collapse of the Soviet Union in 1991, Cuba was no longer able to obtain big subsidies from the Soviets. Island tobacco farmers subsequently saw their supplies of fuel, fertilizer, and even twine and boxes fall dramatically. The result was higher costs of producing cigars and a reduction in their supply. In 1990, Cuba was producing 90 million cigars per year; five years later, production had dropped to 50 million per year.

FOR CRITICAL ANALYSIS

1. According to the marketing director of Hunters & Frankau, the distributor of Cuban cigars in Britain, "The worldwide demand for these cigars is still around 100 million." What is wrong with this statement?

2. What do you think has happened to the supply of fake Cuban cigars? Why?

CHAPTER SUMMARY

1. A price system, otherwise called a market system, allows prices to respond to changes in supply and demand for different commodities. Consumers and business managers' decisions on resource use depend on what happens to prices.

2. Exchanges take place in markets. The terms of exchange—prices—are registered in markets that tend to minimize transaction costs.

3. With a stable supply curve, a rise in demand leads to an increase in equilibrium price and quantity; a decrease in demand leads to a reduction in equilibrium price and quantity. With a stable demand curve, a rise in supply leads to a decrease in equilibrium price and an increase in equilibrium quantity; a fall in supply leads to an increase in equilibrium price and a decrease in equilibrium quantity.

4. When both demand and supply shift at the same time, indeterminate results occur. We must know the direction and degree of each shift in order to predict the change in equilibrium price and quantity.

5. When there is a shift in demand or supply, it takes time for markets to adjust to the new equilibrium. During that time, there will be temporary shortages or surpluses.

6. In a market system, prices perform a rationing function—they ration scarce goods and services. Other ways of rationing include first come, first served; political power; physical force; lotteries; and coupons.

7. Government-imposed price controls can take the form of price ceilings and price floors. Effective price ceilings—ones that are set below the market clearing price and enforced—lead to nonprice rationing devices and black markets.

8. Rent controls interfere with many of the functions of rental prices. For example, effective rent controls discourage the construction of new rental units. They also encourage "housing gridlock." Landlords lose during effective rent controls. Other losers are typically low-income individuals, especially single mothers, trying to find their first apartments.

9. A price floor can take the form of a government-imposed price support for agricultural products. This creates an excess quantity supplied at the supported price. To maintain that price, the government must buy up the surplus agricultural products. A price floor can apply to wages. When the government-imposed minimum wage exceeds the equilibrium wage rate, an excess quantity of labor is supplied. The result is higher unemployment for the affected group of workers.

10. Quantity restrictions can take the form of import quotas, under which there is a limit to the quantity of the affected good that can be brought into the United States and sold.

DISCUSSION OF PREVIEW QUESTIONS

1. Does an increase in demand always lead to a rise in price?

Yes, provided that the supply curve doesn't shift also. If the supply is stable, every rise in demand will cause a shift outward to the right in the demand curve. The new equilibrium price will be higher than the old equilibrium price. If, however, the supply curve shifts at the same time, you have to know in which direction and by how much. If the supply curve shifts outward, indicating a rise in supply, the equilibrium price can rise if the shift is not as great as in demand. If the increase in supply is greater than in demand, the price can actually fall. We can be sure, though, that if demand increases and supply decreases, the equilibrium price will rise. This can be seen in the accompanying graph.

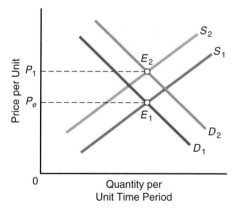

2. Can there ever be shortages in a market with no restrictions?

Yes, there can, because adjustment is never instantaneous. It takes time for the forces of supply and demand to work. In all our graphs, we draw new equilibrium points where a new supply curve meets a new demand curve. That doesn't mean that in the marketplace buyers and sellers will react immediately to a change in supply or demand. Information is not perfect. Moreover, people are often slow to adapt to higher or lower prices. Suppliers may require months or years to respond to an increase in the demand for their product. Consumers take time to respond to new information about changing relative prices.

3. How are goods rationed?

In a pure price system, prices ration goods. Prices are the indicators of relative scarcity. Prices change so that quantity demanded equals quantity supplied. In the absence of a price system, an alternative way to ration goods is first come, first served. In many systems, political power is another method. In certain cultures, physical force is a way to ration goods. Cultural, religious, and physical differences among individuals can be used as rationing devices. The fact is that given a world of scarcity, there has to be some method to ration goods. The price system is only one alternative.

4. When would you expect to encounter black markets?

Black markets occur in two situations. The first occurs whenever a good or service is made illegal by legislation. There are black markets in the United States for prostitution, gambling, and drugs. Second, there are black markets whenever a price ceiling (one type of price control) is imposed on any good or service. The price ceiling has to be below the market clearing price and enforced for a black market to exist, however. Price ceilings on rents in cities in the United States have created black markets for rental units.

PROBLEMS

(Answers to the odd-numbered problems appear at the back of the book.)

4-1. This is a graph of the supply and demand for oranges.

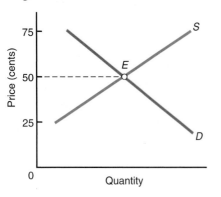

Explain the effect on this graph of each of the following events.

   a. It is discovered that oranges can cure acne.
   b. A new machine is developed that will automatically pick oranges.
   c. The government declares a price floor of 25 cents.
   d. The government declares a price floor of 75 cents.
   e. The price of grapefruits increases.
   f. Income decreases.

4-2. What might be the long-run results of price controls that maintained a good's money price below its equilibrium price? Above its equilibrium price?

4-3. Here is a demand schedule and a supply schedule for scientific hand calculators.

Price	Quantity Demanded	Quantity Supplied
$10	100,000	0
20	60,000	0
30	20,000	0
40	0	0
50	0	100,000
60	0	300,000
70	0	500,000

What are the equilibrium price and the equilibrium quantity? Explain.

4-4. This is a graph of the supply and demand for raisins.

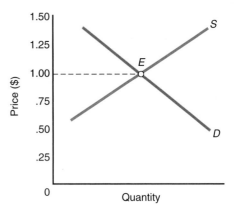

The following series of events occurs. Explain the result of the occurrence of each event.

   a. An advertising campaign for California raisins is successful.
   b. A fungus wipes out half the grape crop (used to make raisins) in California.
   c. The price of bran flakes (a complement) increases.
   d. The price of dried cranberries (a substitute) increases.
   e. The government declares a price floor of 75 cents.
   f. The government imposes and enforces a price ceiling of 75 cents.
   g. Income increases (assume that raisins are an inferior good).

4-5. Below is a demand schedule and a supply schedule for lettuce.

Price per Crate	Quantity Demanded (crates per year)	Quantity Supplied (crates per year)
$1	100 million	0 million
2	90 million	10 million
3	70 million	30 million
4	50 million	50 million
5	20 million	80 million

What are the equilibrium price and the equilibrium quantity? At a price of $2 per crate, what is the quantity demanded? The quantity supplied? What is this disequilibrium situation called? What is the magnitude of the disequilibrium, expressed in terms of quantities? Now answer the same questions for a price of $5 per crate.

4-6. What is wrong with the following assertion? "The demand has increased so much in response to our offering of a $500 rebate that our inventory of cars is now running very low."

4-7. Rent control is a price ceiling. There are also legislated price floors. Assume that the equilibrium price for oranges is 10 cents each. Draw the supply and demand diagram to show the effect of a government-imposed price floor, or minimum price, of 15 cents per orange. Be sure to label any shortages or surpluses that result. Then show the effect of a price floor of 5 cents per orange.

COMPUTER-ASSISTED INSTRUCTION

A set of price ceiling and price floor situations is presented. You are asked to predict different outcomes for each situation in both the short and the long run.

Complete problem and answer appear on disk.

INTERACTING WITH THE INTERNET

If you enter "price controls" in the Yahoo! search engine, you will be directed to more than 6,000 Web sites. (Put the phrase in quotation marks so that the entire phrase is used in the search procedure.) You will find articles on all types of price controls, ranging from those on health care to those on gasoline and agricultural products.

Here's a hint: If you use the Yahoo! search engine, at the end of the of the list of the first 20 sites found, you will see the heading "Other Search Engines." Click on one of them, such as Lycos, Hot-Bot, or Excite, and you will get a variation on Yahoo!'s search of the subject requested.

CHAPTER 5

THE PUBLIC SECTOR

After Congress got through completing the tax legislation of 1997—touted as the "great middle-class tax reduction"—the average American family was to see its taxes decline by all of $70 per year. The new legislation will actually cause some households that apply for new tax credits for children to be worse off! Nonetheless, two groups of individuals are now definitely better off—tax attorneys and accountants. The federal income tax is currently so complicated that more and more households feel that they must turn to professionals to calculate the taxes they owe. Is there an alternative way for government to raise revenues? Before you can answer that question, you must learn some details about the public sector in America.

Did You Know That . . . the average American works from January 1 through May 7 each year to pay for all local, state, and federal taxes? The average New York resident works approximately three weeks longer to pay for all of the taxes owed each year. Looked at another way, the average American in a typical eight-hour day works about 2 hours and 42 minutes to pay for government at all levels. Every citizen, including children, averages about $8,000 a year in taxes of all kinds. The total amount paid exceeds $2 trillion. What is a trillion dollars? It is a million times a million. Thus it would take more than 2 million millionaires to have as much money as is spent each year by government. So we cannot ignore the presence of government in our society. Government exists, at a minimum, to take care of what the price system does not do well.

WHAT A PRICE SYSTEM CAN AND CANNOT DO

Throughout the book so far, we have alluded to the benefits of a price system. High on the list is economic efficiency. In its most ideal form, a price system allows resources to move from lower-valued uses to higher-valued uses through voluntary exchange. The supreme point of economic efficiency occurs when all mutually advantageous trades have taken place. In a price system, consumers are sovereign; that is to say, they have the individual freedom to decide what they wish to purchase. Politicians and even business managers do not ultimately decide what is produced; consumers decide. Some proponents of the price system argue that this is its most important characteristic. A market organization of economic activity generally prevents one person from interfering with another in respect to most of his or her activities. Competition among sellers protects consumers from coercion by one seller, and sellers are protected from coercion by one consumer because other consumers are available.

Sometimes the price system does not generate these results, with too few or too many resources going to specific economic activities. Such situations are called **market failures.** Market failures prevent the price system from attaining economic efficiency and individual freedom, as well as other social goals. Market failures offer one of the strongest arguments in favor of certain economic functions of government, which we now examine.

Market failure
A situation in which an unrestrained market economy leads to too few or too many resources going to a specific economic activity.

CORRECTING FOR EXTERNALITIES

In a pure market system, competition generates economic efficiency only when individuals know the true opportunity cost of their actions. In some circumstances, the price that someone actually pays for a resource, good, or service is higher or lower than the opportunity cost that all of society pays for that same resource, good, or service.

Consider a hypothetical world in which there is no government regulation against pollution. You are living in a town that until now has had clean air. A steel mill moves into town. It produces steel and has paid for the inputs—land, labor, capital, and entrepreneurship. The price it charges for the steel reflects, in this example, only the costs that the steel mill incurred. In the course of production, however, the mill gets one input—clean air—by simply taking it. This is indeed an input because in the making of steel, the furnaces emit smoke. The steel mill doesn't have to pay the cost of using the clean air; rather, it is the people in the community who pay that cost in the form of dirtier clothes, dirtier cars and houses, and more respiratory illnesses. The effect is similar to what would happen if the steel mill could take coal or oil or workers' services free. There has been an **externality,** an external cost. Some of the costs associated with the production of the steel have "spilled over" to affect **third parties,** parties other than the buyer and the seller of the steel.

Externality
A consequence of an economic activity that spills over to affect third parties. Pollution is an externality.

Third parties
Parties who are not directly involved in a given activity or transaction.

External Costs in Graphical Form

Look at panel (a) in Figure 5-1. Here we show the demand curve for steel to be D. The supply curve is S_1. The supply curve includes only the costs that the firms have to pay. The equilibrium, or market clearing, situation will occur at quantity Q_1. Let us take into account the fact that there are externalities—the external costs that you and your neighbors pay in the form of dirtier clothes, cars, and houses and increased respiratory disease due to the air pollution emitted from the steel mill; we also assume that all other suppliers of steel use clean air without having to pay for it. Let's include these external costs in our graph to find out what the full cost of steel production really is. This is equivalent to saying that the price of an input used in steel production increased. Recall from Chapter 3 that an increase in input prices shifts the supply curve. Thus in panel (a) of the figure, the supply curve shifts from S_1 to S_2; the external costs equal the vertical distance between A and E_1. If the external costs were somehow taken into account, the equilibrium quantity would fall to Q_2 and the price would rise to P_2. Equilibrium would shift from E to E_1. If the price does not account for external costs, third parties bear those costs—represented by the distance between A and E_1—in the form of dirtier clothes, houses, and cars and increased respiratory illnesses.

External Benefits in Graphical Form

Externalities can also be positive. To demonstrate external benefits in graphical form, we will use the example of inoculations against communicable disease. In panel (b) of Figure

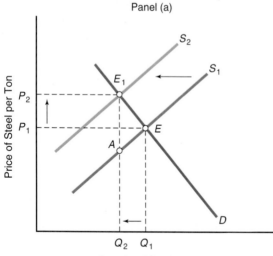

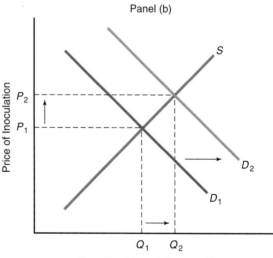

FIGURE 5-1

External Costs and Benefits

In panel (a), we show a situation in which the production of steel generates external costs. If the steel mills ignore pollution, at equilibrium the quantity of steel will be Q_1. If the mills had to pay for the additional cost borne by nearby residents that is caused by the steel mill's production, the supply curve would shift the vertical distance A–E_1, to S_2. If consumers were forced to pay a price that reflected the spillover costs, the quantity demanded would fall to Q_2. In panel (b), we show the situation in which inoculations against communicable diseases generate external benefits to those individuals who may not be inoculated but who will benefit because epidemics will not occur. If each individual ignores the external benefit of inoculations, the market clearing quantity will be Q_1. If external benefits are taken into account by purchasers of inoculations, however, the demand curve would shift to D_2. The new equilibrium quantity would be Q_2 and the price would be higher, P_2.

5-1, we show the demand curve as D_1 (without taking account of any external benefits) and the supply curve as S. The equilibrium price is P_1, and the equilibrium quantity is Q_1. We assume, however, that inoculations against communicable diseases generate external benefits to individuals who may not be inoculated but will benefit nevertheless because epidemics will not break out. If such external benefits were taken into account, the demand curve would shift from D_1 to D_2. The new equilibrium quantity would be Q_2, and the new equilibrium price would be P_2. With no corrective action, this society is not devoting enough resources to inoculations against communicable diseases.

When there are external costs, the market will tend to *overallocate* resources to the production of the good or service in question, for those goods or services will be deceptively low-priced. With the example of steel, too much will be produced because the steel mill owners and managers are not required to take account of the external cost that steel production is imposing on the rest of society. In essence, the full cost of production is unknown to the owners and managers, so the price they charge the public for steel is lower than it would be otherwise. And of course, the lower price means that buyers are willing and able to buy more. More steel is produced and consumed than is socially optimal.

When there are external benefits, the market *underallocates* resources to the production of that good or service because the good or service is relatively too expensive (because the demand is relatively too low). In a market system, too many of the goods that generate external costs are produced and too few of the goods that generate external benefits are produced.

How the Government Corrects Negative Externalities

The government can in theory correct externality situations in a variety of ways in all cases that warrant such action. In the case of negative externalities, at least two avenues are open to the government: special taxes and legislative regulation or prohibition.

Effluent fee
A charge to a polluter that gives the right to discharge into the air or water a certain amount of pollution. Also called a *pollution tax.*

Special Taxes. In our example of the steel mill, the externality problem originates from the fact that the air as a waste disposal place is costless to the firm but not to society. The government could make the steel mill pay a tax for dumping its pollutants into the air. The government could attempt to tax the steel mill commensurate with the cost to third parties from smoke in the air. This, in effect, would be a pollution tax or an **effluent fee.** The ultimate effect would be to reduce the supply of steel and raise the price to consumers, ideally making the price equal to the full cost of production to society.

Regulation. To correct a negative externality arising from steel production, the government could specify a maximum allowable rate of pollution. This action would require that the steel mill install pollution abatement equipment within its facilities, that it reduce its rate of output, or some combination of the two. Note that the government's job would not be that simple, for it still would have to determine the level of pollution and then actually measure its output from steel production in order to enforce such regulation.

How the Government Corrects Positive Externalities

What can the government do when the production of one good spills *benefits* over to third parties? It has several policy options: financing the production of the good or producing the good itself, subsidies (negative taxes), and regulation.

Government Financing and Production. If the positive externalities seem extremely large, the government has the option of financing the desired additional production facilities so that the "right" amount of the good will be produced. Again consider inoculations against communicable diseases. The government could—and often does—finance campaigns to inoculate the population. It could (and does) even produce and operate centers for inoculation in which such inoculations would be free.

Subsidies. A subsidy is a negative tax; it is a payment made either to a business or to a consumer when the business produces or the consumer buys a good or a service. In the case of inoculations against communicable diseases, the government could subsidize everyone who obtains an inoculation by directly reimbursing those inoculated or by making payments to private firms that provide inoculations. If you are attending a state university, taxpayers are helping to pay the cost of providing your education; you are being subsidized by as much as 80 percent of the total cost. Subsidies reduce the net price to consumers, thereby causing a larger quantity to be demanded.

Regulation. In some cases involving positive externalities, the government can require by law that a certain action be undertaken by individuals in the society. For example, regulations require that all school-age children be inoculated before entering public and private schools. Some people believe that a basic school education itself generates positive externalities. Perhaps as a result of this belief, we have regulations—laws—that require all school-age children to be enrolled in a public or private school.

CONCEPTS IN BRIEF

- External costs lead to an overallocation of resources to the specific economic activity. Two possible ways of correcting these spillovers are taxation and regulation.

- External benefits result in an underallocation of resources to the specific activity. Three possible government corrections are financing the production of the activity, subsidizing private firms or consumers to engage in the activity, and regulation.

THE OTHER ECONOMIC FUNCTIONS OF GOVERNMENT

Besides compensating for externalities, the government performs many other functions that affect the way in which exchange is carried out in the economy. In contrast, the political functions of government have to do with deciding how income should be redistributed among households and selecting which goods and services have special merits and should therefore be treated differently. The economic and political functions of government can and do overlap.

Let's look at four more economic functions of government.

Providing a Legal System

The courts and the police may not at first seem like economic functions of government (although judges and police personnel must be paid). Their activities nonetheless have important consequences on economic activities in any country. You and I enter into contracts constantly, whether they be oral or written, expressed or implied. When we believe that we have been wronged, we seek redress of our grievances within our legal institutions. Moreover, consider the legal system that is necessary for the smooth functioning of our system. Our system has defined quite explicitly the legal status of businesses, the rights of private ownership, and a method for the enforcement of contracts. All relationships among consumers and businesses are governed by the legal rules of the game. We might consider the government in its judicial function, then, as the referee when there are disputes in the economic arena.

Much of our legal system is involved with defining and protecting *property rights*. **Property rights** are the rights of an owner to use and to exchange his or her property. One might say that property rights are really the rules of our economic game. When property rights are well defined, owners of property have an incentive to use that property efficiently. Any mistakes in their decision about the use of property have negative consequences that the owners suffer. Furthermore, when property rights are well defined, owners of property have an incentive to maintain that property so that if those owners ever desire to sell it, it will fetch a better price.

Establishing and maintaining an independent constitutional judiciary, a familiar activity in the United States, is relatively new to Central and Eastern European countries.

Property rights
The rights of an owner to use and to exchange property.

INTERNATIONAL EXAMPLE
Post-Communist Rule of Law

Prior to the collapse of the Soviet empire, Central and Eastern European nations did not have an independent constitutional judiciary. Today that has changed. As a result, there is more of an institutional climate favorable for both domestic and foreign businesses.

The new constitutional frameworks in Central and Eastern European countries are based in large part on the U.S. Constitution. They emphasize the doctrines of separation of powers and checks and balances. They even allow for the courts to have the power of judicial review. (In the United States, this power allows the courts to declare laws unconstitutional.) A good case in point is Hungary. There, legislators passed laws providing for restitution of nationalized land to pre-Communist owners. The court ruled that such laws were retroactive and thus invalid. The Hungarian court further stated that the only basis for returning land to former owners was through the transition to a market economy.

Bulgaria's constitutional court has consistently angered politicians. The court curbed government efforts to control radio and television. In Poland, the constitutional court voided a law passed by Parliament that would have lowered pensions of former state employees. This legal decision alone created a government obligation to pay almost $3 billion in compensation to almost 10 million Poles. This forced the government to sell bonds to pay for those pensions.

The trend toward highly independent court systems continues throughout Central and Eastern Europe.

FOR CRITICAL ANALYSIS: Why would an independent constitutional judiciary be important to someone who wished to invest in a new business in a Central or Eastern European country? ●

Promoting Competition

Antitrust legislation
Laws that restrict the formation of monopolies and regulate certain anticompetitive business practices.

Monopoly
A firm that has great control over the price of a good. In the extreme case, a monopoly is the only seller of a good or service.

Many people believe that the only way to attain economic efficiency is through competition. One of the roles of government is to serve as the protector of a competitive economic system. Congress and the various state governments have passed **antitrust legislation.** Such legislation makes illegal certain (but not all) economic activities that might, in legal terms, restrain trade—that is, prevent free competition among actual and potential rival firms in the marketplace. The avowed aim of antitrust legislation is to reduce the power of **monopolies**—firms that have great control over the price of the goods they sell. A large number of antitrust laws have been passed that prohibit specific anticompetitive business behavior. Both the Antitrust Division of the Department of Justice and the Federal Trade Commission attempt to enforce these antitrust laws. Various state judicial agencies also expend efforts at maintaining competition.

Providing Public Goods

The goods used in our examples up to this point have been **private goods.** When I eat a cheeseburger, you cannot eat the same one. So you and I are rivals for that cheeseburger, just as much as rivals for the title of world champion are. When I use a CD-ROM player, you cannot use the same player. When I use the services of an auto mechanic, that person cannot work at the same time for you. That is the distinguishing feature of private goods—their use is exclusive to the people who purchase or rent them. The **principle of rival consumption** applies to all private goods by definition. Rival consumption is easy to understand. With private goods, either you use them or I use them.

There is an entire class of goods that are not private goods. These are called **public goods.** The principle of rival consumption does not apply to them. That is, they can be consumed *jointly* by many individuals simultaneously. National defense, police protection, and the legal system, for example, are public goods. If you partake of them, you do not necessarily take away from anyone else's share of those goods.

Characteristics of Public Goods. Several distinguishing characteristics of public goods set them apart from all other goods.[1]

1. **Public goods are often indivisible.** You can't buy or sell $5 worth of our ability to annihilate the world with bombs. Public goods cannot usually be produced or sold very easily in small units.

2. **Public goods can be used by more and more people at no additional cost.** Once money has been spent on national defense, the defense protection you receive does not reduce the amount of protection bestowed on anyone else. The opportunity cost of your receiving national defense once it is in place is zero.

3. **Additional users of public goods do not deprive others of any of the services of the goods.** If you turn on your television set, your neighbors don't get weaker reception because of your action.

4. **It is difficult to design a collection system for a public good on the basis of how much individuals use it.** It is nearly impossible to determine how much any person uses or values national defense. No one can be denied the benefits of national defense for failing to pay for that public good. This is often called the **exclusion principle.**

One of the problems of public goods is that the private sector has a difficult, if not impossible, time in providing them. There is little or no incentive for individuals in the private sector to offer public goods because it is so difficult to make a profit in so doing. Consequently, a true public good must necessarily be provided by government.

INTERNATIONAL EXAMPLE
Are Lighthouses a Public Good?

One of the most common examples of a public good is a lighthouse. Arguably, it satisfies all the criteria listed in points 1 through 4. In one instance, however, a lighthouse was not a public good in that a collection system was devised and enforced on the basis of how much individuals used it. In the thirteenth century, the city of Aigues-Mortes, a French southern port, erected a tower, called the King's Tower, designed to assert

Private goods
Goods that can be consumed by only one individual at a time. Private goods are subject to the principle of rival consumption.

Principle of rival consumption
The recognition that individuals are rivals in consuming private goods because one person's consumption reduces the amount available for others to consume.

Public goods
Goods to which the principle of rival consumption does not apply; they can be jointly consumed by many individuals simultaneously at no additional cost and with no reduction in quality or quantity.

Exclusion principle
The principle that no one can be excluded from the benefits of a public good, even if that person hasn't paid for it.

---

[1]Sometimes the distinction is made between pure public goods, which have all the characteristics we have described here, and quasi- or near-public goods, which do not. The major feature of near-public goods is that they are jointly consumed, even though nonpaying customers can be, and often are, excluded—for example, movies, football games, and concerts.

the will and power of Louis IX (Saint Louis). The 105-foot tower served as a lighthouse for ships. More important, it served as a lookout so that ships sailing on the open sea, but in its view, did not escape paying for use of the lighthouse. Those payments were then used for the construction of the city walls.

FOR CRITICAL ANALYSIS: Explain how a lighthouse satisfies the characteristics of public goods described in points 1, 2, and 3. ●

Free-rider problem
A problem that arises when individuals presume that others will pay for public goods so that, individually, they can escape paying for their portion without causing a reduction in production.

Free Riders. The nature of public goods leads to the **free-rider problem,** a situation in which some individuals take advantage of the fact that others will take on the burden of paying for public goods such as national defense. Free riders will argue that they receive no value from such government services as national defense and therefore really should not pay for it. Suppose that citizens were taxed directly in proportion to how much they tell an interviewer that they value national defense. Some people will probably tell interviewers that they are unwilling to pay for national defense because they don't want any of it—it is of no value to them. Many of us may end up being free riders when we assume that others will pay for the desired public good. We may all want to be free riders if we believe that someone else will provide the commodity in question that we actually value.

The free-rider problem is a definite problem among nations with respect to the international burden of defense and how it should be shared. A country may choose to belong to a multilateral defense organization, such as the North American Treaty Organization (NATO), but then consistently attempt not to contribute funds to the organization. The nation knows it would be defended by others in NATO if it were attacked but would rather not pay for such defense. In short, it seeks a "free ride."

Ensuring Economywide Stability

The government attempts to stabilize the economy by smoothing out the ups and downs in overall business activity. Our economy sometimes faces the problems of unemployment and rising prices. The government, especially the federal government, has made an attempt to solve these problems by trying to stabilize the economy. The notion that the federal government should undertake actions to stabilize business activity is a relatively new idea in the United States, encouraged by high unemployment rates during the Great Depression of the 1930s and subsequent theories about possible ways by which government could reduce unemployment. In 1946, the government passed the Employment Act, a landmark law concerning government responsibility for economic performance. It established three goals for government accountability: full employment, price stability, and economic growth. These goals have provided the justification for many government economic programs during the post–World War II period.

CONCEPTS IN BRIEF

- The economic activities of government include (1) correcting for externalities, (2) providing a judicial system, (3) promoting competition, (4) producing public goods, and (5) ensuring economywide stability.

- Public goods can be consumed jointly. The principle of rival consumption does not apply as it does with private goods.

- Public goods have the following characteristics: (1) They are indivisible; (2) once they are produced, there is no opportunity cost when additional consumers use them; (3) your use of a public good does not deprive others of its simultaneous use; and (4) consumers cannot conveniently be charged on the basis of use.

THE POLITICAL FUNCTIONS OF GOVERNMENT

At least two areas of government are in the realm of political, or normative, functions rather than that of the economic ones discussed in the first part of this chapter. These two areas are (1) the regulation and/or provision of merit and demerit goods and (2) income redistribution.

Merit and Demerit Goods

Certain goods are considered to have special merit. A **merit good** is defined as any good that the political process has deemed socially desirable. (Note that nothing inherent in any particular good makes it a merit good. It is a matter of who chooses.) Some examples of merit goods in our society are museums, ballets, plays, and concerts. In these areas, the government's role is the provision of merit goods to the people in society who would not otherwise purchase them at market clearing prices or who would not purchase an amount of them judged to be sufficient. This provision may take the form of government production and distribution of merit goods. It can also take the form of reimbursement for payment on merit goods or subsidies to producers or consumers for part of the cost of merit goods. Governments do indeed subsidize such merit goods as concerts, ballets, museums, and plays. In most cases, such merit goods would rarely be so numerous without subsidization.

Demerit goods are the opposite of merit goods. They are goods that, through the political process, are deemed socially undesirable. Heroin, cigarettes, gambling, and cocaine are examples. The government exercises its role in the area of demerit goods by taxing, regulating, or prohibiting their manufacture, sale, and use. Governments justify the relatively high taxes on alcohol and tobacco by declaring them demerit goods. The best-known example of governmental exercise of power in this area is the stance against certain psychoactive drugs. Most psychoactives (except nicotine, caffeine, and alcohol) are either expressly prohibited, as is the case for heroin, cocaine, and opium, or heavily regulated, as in the case of prescription psychoactives.

Merit good
A good that has been deemed socially desirable through the political process. Museums are an example.

Demerit good
A good that has been deemed socially undesirable through the political process. Heroin is an example.

Income Redistribution

Another relatively recent political function of government has been the explicit redistribution of income. This redistribution uses two systems: the progressive income tax (described later in this chapter) and *transfer payments*. **Transfer payments** are payments made to individuals for which in return no services or goods are concurrently rendered. The three key money transfer payments in our system are welfare, Social Security, and unemployment insurance benefits. Income redistribution also includes a large amount of income **transfers in kind,** as opposed to money transfers. Some income transfers in kind are food stamps, Medicare and Medicaid, government health care services, and low-cost public housing.

The government has also engaged in other activities as a form of redistribution of income. For example, the provision of public education is at least in part an attempt to redistribute income by making sure that the very poor have access to education.

Transfer payments
Money payments made by governments to individuals for which in return no services or goods are concurrently rendered. Examples are welfare, Social Security, and unemployment insurance benefits.

Transfers in kind
Payments that are in the form of actual goods and services, such as food stamps, low-cost public housing, and medical care, and for which in return no goods or services are rendered concurrently.

CONCEPTS IN BRIEF

- Political, or normative, activities of the government include the provision and regulation of merit and demerit goods and income redistribution.

- Merit and demerit goods do not have any inherent characteristics that qualify them as such; rather, collectively, through the political process, we make judgments about which goods and services are "good" for society and which are "bad."

• Income redistribution can be carried out by a system of progressive taxation, coupled with transfer payments, which can be made in money or in kind, such as food stamps and Medicare.

PAYING FOR THE PUBLIC SECTOR

Jean-Baptiste Colbert, the seventeenth-century French finance minister, said the art of taxation was in "plucking the goose so as to obtain the largest amount of feathers with the least possible amount of hissing." In the United States, governments have designed a variety of methods of plucking the private-sector goose. To analyze any tax system, we must first understand the distinction between marginal tax rates and average tax rates.

Marginal and Average Tax Rates

If somebody says, "I pay 28 percent in taxes," you cannot really tell what that person means unless you know if he or she is referring to average taxes paid or the tax rate on the last dollars earned. The latter concept has to do with the **marginal tax rate.**[2]

The marginal tax rate is expressed as follows:

$$\text{Marginal tax rate} = \frac{\text{change in taxes due}}{\text{change in taxable income}}$$

It is important to understand that the marginal tax rate applies only to the income in the highest **tax bracket** reached, where a tax bracket is defined as a specified level of taxable income to which a specific and unique marginal tax rate is applied.

The marginal tax rate is not the same thing as the **average tax rate,** which is defined as follows:

$$\text{Average tax rate} = \frac{\text{total taxes due}}{\text{total taxable income}}$$

Taxation Systems

No matter how governments raise revenues—from income taxes, sales taxes, or other taxes—all of those taxes can fit into one of three types of taxation systems—proportional, progressive, and regressive, expressing a relationship between the percentage tax, or tax rate, paid and income. To determine whether a tax system is proportional, progressive, or regressive, we simply ask the question, What is the relationship between the average tax rate and the marginal tax rate?

Proportional Taxation. **Proportional taxation** means that regardless of an individual's income, his or her taxes comprise exactly the same proportion. In terms of marginal versus average tax rates, in a proportional taxation system, the marginal tax rate is always equal to the average tax rate. If every dollar is taxed at 20 percent, then the average tax rate is 20 percent, as is the marginal tax rate.

A proportional tax system is also called a *flat-rate tax.* Taxpayers at all income levels end up paying the same *percentage* of their income in taxes. If the proportional tax rate were 20 percent, an individual with an income of $10,000 would pay $2,000 in taxes, while an individual making $100,000 would pay $20,000, the identical 20 percent rate being levied on both.

Marginal tax rate
The change in the tax payment divided by the change in income, or the percentage of additional dollars that must be paid in taxes. The marginal tax rate is applied to the highest tax bracket of taxable income reached.

Tax bracket
A specified interval of income to which a specific and unique marginal tax rate is applied.

Average tax rate
The total tax payment divided by total income. It is the proportion of total income paid in taxes.

Proportional taxation
A tax system in which regardless of an individual's income, the tax bill comprises exactly the same proportion. Also called a *flat-rate tax.*

[2]The word *marginal* means "incremental" (or "decremental") here.

Progressive Taxation. Under **progressive taxation,** as a person's taxable income increases, the percentage of income paid in taxes increases. In terms of marginal versus average tax rates, in a progressive system, the marginal tax rate is above the average tax rate. If you are taxed 5 percent on the first $10,000 you make, 10 percent on the next $10,000 you make, and 30 percent on the last $10,000 you make, you face a progressive income tax system. Your marginal tax rate is always above your average tax rate.

Progressive taxation
A tax system in which as income increases, a higher percentage of the additional income is taxed. The marginal tax rate exceeds the average tax rate as income rises.

EXAMPLE
The Most Progressive Tax System of All: College Financial Aid

Strangely enough, it is not a government agency that imposes the most progressive tax system in the United States but rather colleges and universities. Through their financial aid programs, they severely punish parents who earn progressively more income during the years that their children are attending college and receiving financial aid. Starting at very low annual parents' income, most college financial aid departments begin reducing financial aid as parents' incomes rise. This constitutes an implicit additional marginal income tax. In Figure 5-2, you see that federal marginal tax rates start at zero, rise to 19 percent, and then rise again to 32 percent at about $60,000. When one adds the effective impact of the reduction in financial aid for parents in these different tax brackets, the actual marginal tax rate reaches as high as 79 percent. This is because the effective marginal tax rate of losing financial aid as income rises is between 22 and 47 percent, all added on top of local, state, and federal income taxes.

FOR CRITICAL ANALYSIS: What effect do you think this system of college financial aid has on parents' incentive to earn more income while their children are in college? ●

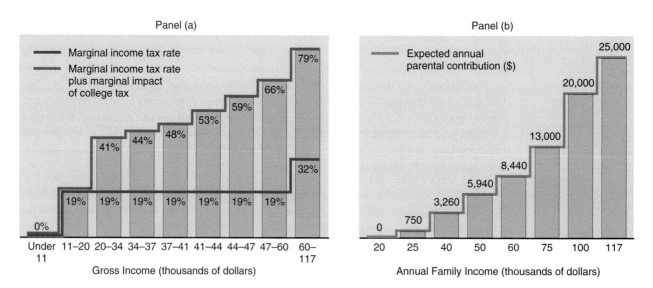

FIGURE 5-2

College Financial Aid and High Implicit Marginal Income Tax Rates for Parents
Because most college and university financial aid officers decrease aid to students whose families earn more, parents of college-enrolled children face relatively high implicit marginal income tax rates. At an income of $60,000 the actual rate faced is almost 80 percent.
Source: Data from *Forbes,* January 17, 1994, p. 74.

Regressive taxation
A tax system in which as more dollars are earned, the percentage of tax paid on them falls. The marginal tax rate is less than the average tax rate as income rises.

Regressive Taxation. With **regressive taxation,** a smaller percentage of taxable income is taken in taxes as taxable income increases. The marginal rate is *below* the average rate. As income increases, the marginal tax rate falls, and so does the average tax rate. The U.S. Social Security tax is regressive. Once the legislative maximum taxable wage base is reached, no further Social Security taxes are paid. Consider a simplified hypothetical example: Every dollar up to $50,000 is taxed at 10 percent. After $50,000 there is no Social Security tax. Someone making $100,000 still pays only $5,000 in Social Security taxes. That person's average Social Security tax is 5 percent. The person making $50,000, by contrast, effectively pays 10 percent. The person making $1 million faces an average Social Security tax rate of only .5 percent in our simplified example.

CONCEPTS IN BRIEF

- Marginal tax rates are applied to marginal tax brackets, defined as spreads of income over which the tax rate is constant.

- Tax systems can be proportional, progressive, or regressive, depending on whether the marginal tax rate is the same as, greater than, or less than the average tax rate as income rises.

THE MOST IMPORTANT FEDERAL TAXES

The federal government imposes income taxes on both individuals and corporations and collects Social Security taxes and a variety of other taxes.

The Federal Personal Income Tax

The most important tax in the U.S. economy is the federal personal income tax, which accounts for about 46 percent of all federal revenues. All American citizens, resident aliens, and most others who earn income in the United States are required to pay federal income taxes on all taxable income. The rates that are paid rise up to a specified amount, depending on marital status, and then fall, as can be seen in Table 5-1. Marginal income tax rates at the federal level have varied from as low as 1 percent after the passage of the Sixteenth Amendment to as high as 94 percent (reached in 1944). There were 14 separate tax brackets prior to the Tax Reform Act of 1986, which reduced the number to three. Advocates of a more progressive income tax system in the United States argue that such a system redistributes income from the rich to the poor, taxes people according to their ability to pay, and

TABLE 5-1

Federal Marginal Income Tax Rates
These rates became effective in 1998. The highest rate includes a 10 percent surcharge on taxable income above $278,450.

Single Persons		Married Couples	
Marginal Tax Bracket	Marginal Tax Rate	Marginal Tax Bracket	Marginal Tax Rate
$0–$25,350	15%	$0–$42,350	15%
$25,351–$61,400	28%	$42,351–$102,300	28%
$61,401–$128,100	31%	$102,301–$155,950	31%
$128,101–$278,450	36%	$155,951–$278,450	36%
$278,451 and up	39.6%	$278,451 and up	39.6%

Source: U.S. Department of the Treasury.

taxes people according to the benefits they receive from government. Although there is much controversy over the redistributional nature of our progressive tax system, there is no strong evidence that in fact the tax system has never done much income redistribution in this country. Currently, about 85 percent of all Americans, rich or poor, pay roughly the same proportion of their income in federal income taxes.

The Treatment of Capital Gains

The difference between the buying and selling price of an asset, such as a share of stock or a plot of land, is called a **capital gain** if it is a profit and a **capital loss** if it is not. As of 1998, there were several capital gains tax rates.

Capital gains are not always real. If you pay $100,000 for a house in one year and sell it for 50 percent more 10 years later, your nominal capital gain is $50,000. But what if, during those 10 years, there had been inflation such that average prices had also gone up by 50 percent? Your *real* capital gain would be zero. But you still have to pay taxes on that $50,000. To counter this problem, many economists have argued that capital gains should be indexed to the rate of inflation. This is exactly what is done with the marginal tax brackets in the federal income tax code. Tax brackets for the purposes of calculating marginal tax rates each year are expanded at the rate of inflation, or the rate at which the average of all prices is rising. So if the rate of inflation is 10 percent, each tax bracket is moved up by 10 percent. The same concept could be applied to capital gains. Thus far, Congress has refused to enact such a measure.

Capital gain
The positive difference between the purchase price and the sale price of an asset. If a share of stock is bought for $5 and then sold for $15, the capital gain is $10.

Capital loss
The negative difference between the purchase price and the sale price of an asset.

The Corporate Income Tax

Corporate income taxes account for about 12 percent of all federal taxes collected and almost 8 percent of all state and local taxes collected. Corporations are generally taxed on the difference between their total revenues (or receipts) and their expenses. The federal corporate income tax structure is given in Table 5-2.

Double Taxation. Because individual stockholders must pay taxes on the dividends they receive, paid out of *after-tax* profits by the corporation, corporate profits are taxed twice. If you receive $1,000 in dividends, you have to declare them as income, and you must pay taxes at your marginal tax rate. Before the corporation was able to pay you those dividends, it had to pay taxes on all its profits, including any that it put back into the company or did not distribute in the form of dividends. Eventually the new investment made possible by those **retained earnings**—profits not given out to stockholders—along with borrowed funds will be reflected in the increased value of the stock in that company. When you sell your stock in that company, you will have to pay taxes on the difference between

Retained earnings
Earnings that a corporation saves, or retains, for investment in other productive activities; earnings that are not distributed to stockholders.

Corporate Taxable Income	Corporate Tax Rate
$0–$50,000	15%
$50,001–$75,000	25%
$75,001–$10,000,000	34%
$10,000,000 and up	35%

Source: Internal Revenue Service.

TABLE 5-2

Federal Corporate Income Tax Schedule
The rates were in effect through 1999.

what you paid for the stock and what you sold it for. In both cases, dividends and retained earnings (corporate profits) are taxed twice.

Who Really Pays the Corporate Income Tax? Corporations can exist only as long as consumers buy their products, employees make their goods, stockholders (owners) buy their shares, and bondholders buy their bonds. Corporations per se do not do anything. We must ask, then, who really pays the tax on corporate income. This is a question of **tax incidence.** (The question of tax incidence applies to all taxes, including sales taxes and Social Security taxes.) There remains considerable debate about the incidence of corporate taxation. Some economists say that corporations pass their tax burdens on to consumers by charging higher prices. Other economists believe that it is the stockholders who bear most of the tax. Still others believe that employees pay at least part of the tax by receiving lower wages than they would otherwise. Because the debate is not yet settled, we will not hazard a guess here as to what the correct conclusion should be. Suffice it to say that you should be cautious when you advocate increasing corporation income taxes. You may be the one who ultimately ends up paying the increase, at least in part, if you own shares in a corporation, buy its products, or work for it.

Tax incidence
The distribution of tax burdens among various groups in society.

CONCEPTS IN BRIEF

- Because corporations must first pay an income tax on most earnings, the personal income tax shareholders pay on dividends received (or realized capital gains) constitutes double taxation.
- The corporate income tax is paid by one or more of the following groups: stockholder-owners, consumers of corporate-produced products, and employees in corporations.

Social Security and Unemployment Taxes

An increasing percentage of federal tax receipts is accounted for each year by taxes (other than income taxes) levied on payrolls. These taxes are for Social Security, retirement, survivors' disability, and old-age medical benefits (Medicare). As of 1998, the Social Security tax was imposed on earnings up to $68,400 at a rate of 6.2 percent on employers and 6.2 percent on employees. That is, the employer matches your "contribution" to Social Security. (The employer's contribution is really paid, at least in part, in the form of a reduced wage rate paid to employees.) A Medicare tax is imposed on all wage earnings at a combined rate of 2.9 percent. These taxes and the base on which they are levied will rise in the next decade. Social Security taxes came into existence when the Federal Insurance Contributions Act (FICA) was passed in 1935.

There is also a federal unemployment tax, which obviously has something to do with unemployment insurance. This tax rate is .8 percent on the first $7,000 of annual wages of each employee who earns more than $1,500. Only the employer makes the tax payment. This tax covers the costs of the unemployment insurance system and the costs of employment services. In addition to this federal tax, some states with an unemployment system impose an additional tax of up to about 3 percent, depending on the past record of the particular employer. An employer who frequently lays off workers will have a slightly higher state unemployment tax rate than an employer who never lays off workers.

It has been argued that Social Security is a system in which current workers subsidize already retired workers. It is also argued that the system is not an insurance system because Social Security benefits are legislated by Congress; they are not part of the original Federal Insurance Contributions Act. Therefore, future generations may decide that they do not want to give large Social Security benefits to retired workers. Even if workers had paid large amounts into Social Security, they could conceivably be denied the benefits of a Social Security retirement income.

INTERNATIONAL EXAMPLE
Chile's Privatized Social Security System

Since 1981, Chile has gradually transformed its government-sponsored social security system into a private pension plan. Entrants into the labor force have been required to contribute 10 percent of their gross monthly earnings to private pension fund accounts that they own outright. During this time period, and even today, virtually anyone still in the public social security system can decide to leave it. Those who choose to leave the public system are given a type of bond that is deposited in their new private pension account to be redeemed at retirement. Fully 94 percent of Chile's labor force is enrolled in 20 competing private pension plans.

FOR CRITICAL ANALYSIS: Under what circumstances might American workers choose to "opt out" of the current federal Social Security system if they were offered the same options as Chilean workers? ●

SPENDING, GOVERNMENT SIZE, AND TAX RECEIPTS

The size of the public sector can be measured in many different ways. One way is to count the number of public employees. Another is to look at total government outlays. Government outlays include all of its expenditures on employees, rent, electricity, and the like. In addition, total government outlays include transfer payments, such as welfare and Social Security. In Figure 5-3, you see that government outlays prior to

THINKING CRITICALLY ABOUT THE MEDIA

Social Security

Countless articles have been written about the problem with the Social Security system in America. They all make reference to the employer and employee "contributions" to the Social Security trust fund. One gets the impression that Social Security payments by employees go into a special government account and that employees do not pay for their employers' "contribution" to this account. Both concepts are not merely flawed but grossly misleading. Though there may be an official Social Security trust fund in the accounts of the U.S. government, "contributing" employees simply have no legal claim on the assets of that trust fund. Indeed, they are just commingled with the rest of government taxes collected and spent every year. Social Security "contributions" are not contributions at all; they are merely taxes paid to the federal government. The so-called employer contribution, which matches the employee payments, is not in fact paid for by employers but rather by employees because of the lower wages that they are paid. Anybody who quits a job and becomes self-employed finds this out when the time comes to pay one's self-employment taxes (Social Security "contributions"), which effectively double the payments previously being made as an employee.

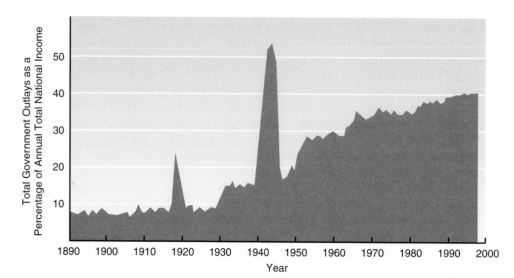

FIGURE 5-3

Total Government Outlays over Time
Here you see that total government outlays (federal, state, and local combined) remained small until the 1930s, except during World War I. Since World War II, government outlays have not fallen back to their historical average.

Sources: Facts and Figures on Government Finance and Economic Indicators, various issues.

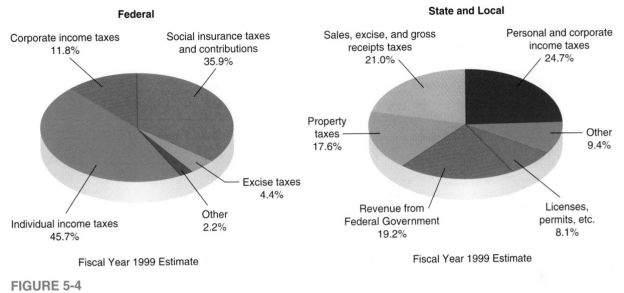

FIGURE 5-4

Sources of Government Tax Receipts

Over 80 percent of federal revenues come from income and Social Security taxes, whereas state government revenues are spread more evenly across sources, with less emphasis on taxes based on individual income.

Source: U.S. Department of Commerce, Bureau of Economic Analysis.

World War I did not exceed 10 percent of annual national income. There was a spike during World War I, a general increase during the Great Depression, and then a huge spike during World War II. Contrary to previous postwar periods, since World War II government outlays as a percentage of total national income have not gradually fallen but rather have risen fairly regularly.

Government Receipts

The main revenue raiser for all levels of government is taxes. We show in the two pie diagrams in Figure 5-4 the percentage of receipts from various taxes obtained by the federal government and by state and local governments.

The Federal Government. The largest source of receipts for the federal government is the individual income tax. It accounts for 45.7 percent of all federal revenues. After that come social insurance taxes and contributions (Social Security), which account for 35.9 percent of total revenues. Next come corporate income taxes and then a number of other items, such as taxes on imported goods and excise taxes on such things as gasoline and alcoholic beverages.

State and Local Governments. As can be seen in Figure 5-4, there is quite a bit of difference between the origin of receipts for state and local governments and for the federal government. Personal and corporate income taxes account for only 24.7 percent of total state and local revenues. There are even a number of states that collect no personal income tax. The largest sources of state and local receipts (other than from the federal government) are personal and corporate income taxes, sales taxes, and property taxes.

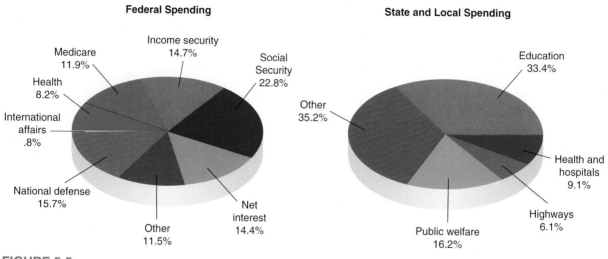

FIGURE 5-5

Federal Government Spending Compared to State and Local Spending

The federal government's spending habits are quite different from those of the states and cities. On the left you can see that the categories of most importance in the federal budget are defense, income security, and Social Security, which make up 53.2 percent. The most important category at the state and local level is education, which makes up 33.4 percent. "Other" includes expenditures in such areas as waste treatment, garbage collection, mosquito abatement, and the judicial system.

Sources: Budget of the United States Government; Government Finances.

Comparing Federal with State and Local Spending. A typical federal government budget is given in Figure 5-5. The largest three categories are defense, income security, and Social Security, which together constitute 53.2 percent of the total federal budget.

The makeup of state and local expenditures is quite different. Education is the biggest category, accounting for 33.4 percent of all expenditures.

CONCEPTS IN BRIEF

- Total government outlays including transfers have continued to grow since World War II and now account for about 40 percent of yearly total national output.

- Government spending at the federal level is different from that at the state and local levels. At the federal level, defense, income security, and Social Security account for about 53 percent of the federal budget. At the state and local levels, education comprises 33 percent of all expenditures.

Every year, Americans spend time worth about $70 billion figuring out their taxes. Many also pay tax specialists. Why is calculating taxes so difficult?

Scrap the Income Tax—Switch to a National Sales Tax

CONCEPTS APPLIED:
MARGINAL TAX RATE, FEDERAL INCOME TAX, INCENTIVES, OPPORTUNITY COST

Visit www.econtoday.com for an Internet Activity that expands your understanding of these concepts.

When Congress got done with the Tax Act of 1997, it made 824 changes to the 3,570-page Internal Revenue Code. Previously, there was one long-term capital gains rate. Now there are four rates (or even more, depending on how you count). One part of the law allows a $400 to $500 child credit. The only problem is that many taxpayers will have to use the so-called alternative minimum tax tables. As a consequence, if they try to reduce their normal taxes owed with child credits, they will find that they actually owe *more* because their taxes under the alternative minimum tax will be higher.

So 45 days after the 1997 Tax Act was signed, Congress started working on a "technical corrections" tax act. When you make 824 tax code changes, you cannot get all of them right, can you?

The Cost of the Current Federal Income Tax System

Because our tax system is so complicated, individuals who fill in their own tax returns must spend many hours doing so. These hours have an opportunity cost. Economist Joel Slemrod has estimated that this opportunity cost is currently about $70 billion a year. In addition, the amount of resources devoted to tax lawyers and accountants probably adds another $70 billion a year. Yet another cost to society of our tax code derives from the fact that it alters individual and business behavior. People respond to incentives. When marginal tax rates are relatively high, some individuals will change their behavior to avoid those high marginal rates. In particular, at high marginal income tax rates, some individuals will work less, retire earlier, not take on a second job, enter the labor market later, and so on. With respect to saving, if the income from saving is taxed at a relatively high marginal rate, some people will be induced to save less than they would otherwise.

The Federal Income Tax, Then and Now

Although the United States first enacted an income tax in 1861 to help pay for the Civil War, it was not until the Sixteenth Amendment was ratified in 1913 that the modern federal income tax came into being. Then, however, very few Americans had to pay it. Look at Table 5-3. It shows the tax rates imposed on various income brackets in 1913 and those same brackets expressed in 1998 dollars. A 1 percent tax rate would be in effect on incomes up to around $300,000. The highest rate, 7 percent, would take effect on incomes over $7.5 million measured in 1998 dollars. Obviously, that is not the situation today—look again at Table 5-1.

Clearly, the federal income tax system as initiated in 1913 was a quite different animal than it is today. If you go back to Table 5-1, you will see that current tax rates are considerably higher than they were in 1913, and they affect virtually all Americans. (Note also that inflation-adjusted federal expenditures increased more than 13,000 percent between 1913 and 1998.)

A National Sales Tax—A Viable Alternative?

Every few years, there is public debate on "simplifying" the federal income tax system. Numerous suggestions have been made, including a "flat tax." But not everyone who wants to change our complicated system agrees that a flat tax is the best alternative. Some critics want to scrap the federal income tax completely. They point out that even when tax rates were simplified in 1986, Congress and the president gradually made them more and more complicated. Thus even if we were to legislate a "flat" income tax rate, it would not last very long, according to these critics.

111

Tax Rate	Income Level in 1913	Income Level in 1998 Dollars	TABLE 5-3
1%	Up to $20,000	Up to $298,507	**1913 U.S. Income Tax Rates and Brackets**
2%	$20,000–$50,000	$298,507–746,269	
3%	$50,000–$75,000	$746,269–$1,119,403	
4%	$75,000–$100,000	$1,119,403–$1,492,537	
5%	$100,000–$250,000	$1,492,537–$3,731,343	
6%	$250,000–$500,000	$3,731,343–$7,462,687	
7%	Over $500,000	Over $7,462,687	

Source: *U.S. Department of the Treasury*

What they want to see put in place is a national sales tax. This is not just pie-in-the-sky theorizing—proposed legislation was actually introduced in 1996. Some politicians take it seriously. Proponents of a national sales tax want it to replace the personal income tax, the corporate income tax, and estate and gift taxes.

The Proposed Rate

Proponents of a national sales tax argue that it could replace all of the above-mentioned federal taxes using a rate of 15 percent on all *final* purchases of goods and services at the retail level. Many poor people would effectively be exempt from the taxes, however, because there would be a universal rebate for every household up to the poverty level of around $20,000 for a family of four. That would mean that the first $20,000 of consumption each year for a family of four would be tax-free. In addition, the federal government would reimburse states and retailers for the cost of collecting the national sales tax.

Adios IRS

Obviously, the replacement of a current complicated federal tax system with a simple national sales tax could mean the abolition or dramatic downsizing of the Internal Revenue Service. The states would bear the primary responsibility for administering the national sales tax. Thus most Americans would be freed from the scrutiny of the IRS. More than 100 million Americans who file personal tax returns would no longer have to file them. The number of tax returns filed would fall by as much as 80 percent.

Businesses would find their paperwork burden reduced dramatically. Business-to-business purchases would be exempt from the tax because it would apply only to final purchases of goods and services from retailers. Retailers would have to determine which sales they made to consumers, but they already do that in most states in order to remit state sales taxes.

An Increased Reward for Saving

Because a national sales tax would be assessed only on final purchases of goods and services, individuals would be rewarded more for saving. They would pay no tax on the income they put into savings or on the earnings of those savings. According to some economists, this would increase the rate of saving in America and be beneficial to the economy. Proponents of the national sales tax even argue that because the economy would grow so much faster under the new system, the national sales tax rate could drop from 15 percent to 12 or even 10 percent over time.

Not Universally Favored

To be sure, some groups in society would be hurt by a switch from our current federal tax system to a national sales tax. Tax and estate attorneys, as well as accountants, would find dramatic reductions in their incomes. The employees of the Internal Revenue Service would have to look for other work. Tax preparation companies such as H&R Block would suffer large reductions in revenues.

Another group would be hurt by the switch to a national sales tax: current members of Congress. Even if the national sales tax generated exactly the same amount of government revenues for Congress to spend, members of that body will have lost an effective means of raising campaign reelection funds. Currently, many members of Congress receive campaign contributions from individuals and lobbyists who wish to obtain special exemptions from the income tax system. The abolition of the current system would eliminate this source of campaign contributions.

FOR CRITICAL ANALYSIS

1. What types of businesses would most easily be able—albeit illegally—to evade a national sales tax?
2. How would you calculate whether to fill out your own tax returns or to pay a consulting firm such as H&R Block to do them?

CHAPTER SUMMARY

1. Government can correct external costs through taxation, legislation, and prohibition. It can correct external benefits through financing or production of a good or service, subsidies, and regulation.

2. Government provides a legal system in which the rights of private ownership, the enforcement of contracts, and the legal status of businesses are provided. In other words, government sets the legal rules of the game and enforces them.

3. Public goods, once produced, can be consumed jointly by additional individuals at zero opportunity cost.

4. If users of public goods know that they will be taxed on the basis of their expressed valuation of those public goods, their expressed valuation will be low. They expect to get a free ride.

5. Merit goods (chosen as such, collectively, through the political process) may not be purchased at all or not in sufficient quantities at market clearing prices. Therefore, government subsidizes or provides such merit goods at a subsidized or zero price to specified classes of consumers.

6. When it is collectively decided that something is a demerit good, government taxes, regulates, or prohibits the manufacture, sale, and use of that good.

7. Marginal tax rates are those paid on the last dollars of income, whereas average taxes rates are determined by the proportion of income paid in income taxes.

8. With a proportional income tax system, marginal rates are constant. With a regressive system, they go down as income rises, and with a progressive system, they go up as income rises.

9. Total government outlays including transfers have continued to grow since World War II and now account for about 40 percent of yearly total national output.

10. Government spending at the federal level is different from that at the state and local levels. Defense, income security, and Social Security account for about 55 percent of the federal budget.

DISCUSSION OF PREVIEW QUESTIONS

1. **What problems will you encounter if you refuse to pay a portion of your income tax because you oppose national defense spending?**

   You must share in national defense collectively with the rest of the country. Unlike private goods, national defense is a public good and must be consumed collectively. You receive national defense benefits whether you choose to or not; the exclusion principle does not work for public goods, such as national defense. The government could make the exclusion principle work better by deporting you to foreign shores if you don't wish to pay for national defense. This is typically not done. If you were allowed to forgo taxes allocated to national defense, the IRS would be swamped with similar requests. Everyone would have an incentive to claim no benefits from national defense (whether true or not) because it must be consumed collectively. So, if you refuse, you may go to jail.

2. **Will you benefit from many so-called tax loopholes when you first start working?**

   Probably not, for you will not be making enough income to put you into the highest marginal income tax bracket. Tax loopholes are more beneficial the more they save you in taxes. At low incomes, your marginal tax rate is low, so each dollar in tax saved because of your use of a tax loophole yields you very little additional after-tax income. If you're in the 15 percent marginal tax bracket, you only benefit by 15 cents for every dollar in tax loopholes you find. Compare this to the benefit for someone in the 39.6 percent marginal tax bracket.

3. **In what ways do regressive, proportional, and progressive tax structures differ?**

   Under a regressive tax structure, the average tax rate (the percentage of income paid in taxes) falls as income rises. The marginal tax rate is below the average tax rate. Proportional tax structures are those in which the average tax rate remains constant as income rises; the marginal tax rate equals the average tax rate. Under a progressive tax structure, the average tax rate rises as income rises; the marginal tax rate is above the average tax rate. Our federal personal income tax system is an example of a progressive system.

4. Who pays the corporate income tax?
Ultimately, only people can be taxed. As a consequence, corporate taxes are ultimately paid by people: corporate owners (in the form of reduced dividends and less stock appreciation for stockholders), consumers of corporate products (in the form of higher prices for goods), and/or employees working for corporations (in the form of lower wages).

PROBLEMS

(Answers to the odd-numbered problems appear at the back of the book.)

5-1. Consider the following system of taxation, which has been labeled *degressive*. The first $5,000 of income is not taxed. After that, all income is assessed at 20 percent (a proportional system). What is the marginal tax rate on $3,000 of taxable income? $10,000? $100,000? What is the average tax rate on $3,000? $10,000? $100,000? What is the maximum average tax rate?

5-2. You are offered two possible bonds to buy as part of your investing program. One is a corporate bond yielding 9 percent. The other is a tax-exempt municipal bond yielding only 6 percent. Assuming that you are certain you will be paid your interest and principal on these two bonds, what marginal tax bracket must you be in to decide in favor of the tax-exempt bond?

5-3. Consider the following tax structure:

Income Bracket	Marginal Tax Rate
$0–$1,500	0%
$1,501–$2,000	14%
$2,001–$3,000	20%

Mr. Smith has an income of $2,500 per annum. Calculate his tax bill for the year. What is his average tax rate? His highest marginal tax rate?

5-4. Assume that Social Security tax payments on wages are 7.65 percent of wages, on wages up to $51,300. No *further* Social Security payments are made on earnings above this figure. Calculate the *average* Social Security tax rate for annual wages of (a) $4,000, (b) $51,300, (c) $56,000, (d) $100,000. Is this Social Security system a progressive, proportional, or regressive tax structure?

5-5. Briefly, what factors could be included as part of the requirements for a "good" tax structure?

5-6. What is meant by the expression "market failure"?

5-7. Is local police protection a public good? Explain.

5-8. TV signals have characteristics of public goods, yet TV stations and commercial networks are private businesses. Analyze this situation.

5-9. Assume that you live in a relatively small suburban neighborhood called Parkwood. The Parkwood Homeowners' Association collects money from homeowners to pay for upkeep of the surrounding stone wall, lighting at the entrances to Parkwood, and mowing the lawn around the perimeter of the area. Each year you are asked to donate $50. No one forces you to do it. There are 100 homeowners in Parkwood.

  a. What percentage of the total yearly revenue of the homeowners' association will you account for?

b. At what level of participation will the absence of your $50 contribution make a difference?

c. If you do not contribute your $50, are you really receiving a totally free ride?

5-10. Assume that the only textile firm that exists has created a negative externality by polluting a nearby stream with the wastes associated with production. Assume further that the government can measure the external costs to the community with accuracy and charges the firm for its pollution, based on the social cost of pollution per unit of textile output. Show how such a charge will lead to a higher selling price for textiles and a reduction in the equilibrium quantity of textiles.

5-11. Label two columns on your paper "Private Goods" and "Public Goods." List each of the following under the heading that describes it better.

a. Sandwich
b. Public television
c. Cable television
d. National defense
e. Shirt
f. Elementary education
g. College education
h. Health clinic flu shots
i. Opera
j. Museum
k. Automobile

COMPUTER-ASSISTED INSTRUCTION

The decisions made by people in the government (bureaucrats) and people in the private sector often differ because of the different constraints they face. We show the impact of this on innovation in the ethical drug industry.

Complete problem and answer appear on disk.

INTERACTING WITH THE INTERNET

To get information on the federal budget, go to

www.access.gpo.gov/su_docs/budget/index.html

If you would like more information about Social Security, go to

www.ssa.gov/

There you can find hypothetical personal earnings and benefits estimate statements as well as facts and figures on the Social Security system. A history of Social Security can also be found there. To get the latest information on taxes, go to the Internal Revenue Service's site at

www.irs.ustreas.gov/cover.html

Today you are studying economics and many other subjects. By the time you finish your studies, you will probably have made a decision about what type of work to seek. When you look for your first job (or a better one after completing your degree), you and only you decide which job you will take. Imagine a world in which, just before graduation, someone else—a government official—tells you what job you will have and where you will live to do that job. That is exactly the world in which college and university students in the People's Republic of China have lived for decades. The job assignment system is changing, though. Before you read about the implications of the changes, you need to understand how resource use is determined in a market economy such as that of the United States.

PREVIEW QUESTIONS

1. Why does the scarcity problem force all societies to answer the questions *what, how,* and *for whom?*

2. How can economies be classified?

3. Why do we say that *all* economies are mixed economies?

4. What are the "three *P*s" of pure capitalism?

Economic system
The institutional means through
which resources are used to
satisfy human wants.

Resource allocation
The assignment of resources to
specific uses by determining
what will be produced, how it
will be produced, and for whom
it will be produced.

Did You Know That . . . there used to be a country called the Soviet Union whose chief of state in 1960 took off his shoe at the United Nations and pounded it on the desk while shouting, "We will bury you"? That person was Nikita Khrushchev; he died in 1971. It took quite a few more years for his country to die, but die it did. The Soviet Union is no more. The 74-year experiment in trying to run an economy without using the price, or market, system will go down in history as one of the greatest social and economic failures of all time. Just because the Soviet Union dissolved itself at the end of 1991 does not mean that the entire world economy automatically became like that of the United States. In particular, the 15 republics of the former Soviet Union, the Soviet "satellite" countries of Eastern Europe, and other nations, including China, are what we call *economies in transition.*

At any point in time, every nation has its own **economic system,** which can be defined as the institutional means through which resources are used to satisfy human wants. No matter what institutional means—marketplace or government—a nation chooses to use, three basic economic questions must always be answered.

THE THREE BASIC ECONOMIC QUESTIONS

In every nation, no matter what the form of government, what the type of economic system, who is running the government, or how poor or rich it is, three basic economic questions must be answered. They concern the problem of **resource allocation,** which is simply how resources are to be allocated. As such, resource allocation answers the three basic economic questions of *what, how,* and *for whom* goods and services will be produced.

1. *What and how much will be produced?* Literally billions of different things could be produced with society's scarce resources. Some mechanism must exist that causes some things to be produced and others to remain as either inventors' pipe dreams or individuals' unfulfilled desires.
2. *How will it be produced?* There are many ways to produce a desired item. It is possible to use more labor and less capital or vice versa. It is possible to use more unskilled labor and fewer units of skilled labor. Somehow, in some way, a decision must be made as to the particular mix of inputs, the way they should be organized, and how they are brought together at a particular place.
3. *For whom will it be produced?* Once a commodity is produced, who should get it? In a market economy, individuals and businesses purchase commodities with money income. The question then is what mechanism there is to distribute income, which then determines how commodities are distributed throughout the economy.

THE PRICE SYSTEM AND HOW IT ANSWERS
THE THREE ECONOMIC QUESTIONS

As explained in Chapter 4, a price (or market) system is an economic system in which (relative) prices are constantly changing to reflect changes in supply and demand for different commodities. In addition, the prices of those commodities are the signals to everyone within the system as to what is relatively scarce and what is relatively abundant. Indeed, it is the *signaling* aspect of the price system that provides the information to buyers and sellers about what should be bought and what should be produced. The price system, which is characteristic of a market economy, is only one possible way to organize society.

What and How Much Will Be Produced?

In a price system, the interaction of demand and supply for each good determines what and how much to produce. Note, however, that if the highest price that consumers are willing to pay is less than the lowest cost at which a good can be produced, output will be zero. That doesn't mean that the price system has failed. Today consumers do not purchase their own private space shuttles. The demand is not high enough in relation to the supply to create a market. But it may be someday.

How Will It Be Produced?

The question of how output will be produced in a price system relates to the efficient use of scarce inputs. Consider the possibility of using only two types of resources, capital and labor. A firm may have the options given in Table 6-1. It can use various combinations of labor and capital to produce the same amount of output. Two hypothetical combinations are given in the table. How, then, is it decided which combination should be used? In the price system, the **least-cost combination** (technique B in our example) will in fact be chosen because it maximizes profits. We assume that the owners of business firms act as if they are maximizing profits. Recall from Chapter 1 that we assume that individuals act *as if* they are rational.

Least-cost combination
The level of input use that produces a given level of output at minimum cost.

In a price system, competition *forces* firms to use least-cost production techniques. Any firm that fails to employ the least costly technique will find that other firms can undercut its price. In other words, other firms that choose the least-cost production technique will be able to offer the product at a lower price and still make a profit. This lower price will induce consumers to shift purchases from the higher-priced firm to the lower-priced firm. Inefficient firms will be forced out of business.

For Whom Will It Be Produced?

This last question that every economic system must answer involves who gets what. In a market system, the choice about what is purchased is made by individuals, but that choice is determined by the ability to pay. Who gets what is determined by the distribution of money income.

Determination of Money Income. In a price system, a consumer's ability to pay for consumer products is based on the size of that consumer's money income. That in turn depends on the quantities, qualities, and types of the various human and nonhuman resources that the individual owns and supplies to the marketplace. It also depends on the prices, or payments, for those resources. When you are selling your human resources as labor

---

TABLE 6-1

Production Costs for 100 Units of Product X

Technique A or B can be used to produce the same output. Obviously, B will be used because its total cost is less than A's. Using production technique B will generate a $2 savings for every 100 units produced.

		A		B	
Inputs	Input Unit Price	Production Technique A (input units)	Cost	Production Technique B (input units)	Cost
Labor	$10	5	$50	4	$40
Capital	8	4	32	5	40
Total cost of 100 units			82		80

services, your money income is based on the wages you can earn in the labor market. If you own nonhuman resources—physical capital and land, for example—the level of interest and rents that you are paid for your physical capital and land will clearly influence the size of your money income and thus your ability to buy consumer products.

Which Consumers Get What? In a price system, the distribution of finished products to consumers is based on consumers' ability and willingness to pay the market price for the product. If the market price of compact discs is $9, consumers who are able and willing to pay that price will get those CDs. All others won't.

Here we are talking about the *rationing* function of market prices in a price system. Rather than have a central political figure or agency decide which consumers will get which goods, those consumers who are willing and able to pay the market price obtain the goods. That is to say, relative prices ration the available resources, goods, and services at any point in time among those who place the highest value on those items. If scarcity didn't exist, we would not need any system to ration available resources, goods, and services. All of us could have all of everything that we wanted without taking away from what anyone else obtained.

CONCEPTS IN BRIEF

- Any economic system must answer three questions: (1) *What* will be produced? (2) *How* will it be produced? (3) *For whom* will it be produced?

- In a price system, supply and demand determine the prices at which exchanges take place.

- In a price system, firms choose the least-cost combination use of inputs to produce any given output. Competition forces firms to do so.

- In a price system, who gets what is determined by consumers' money income and choices about how to use that money income.

TODAY'S INCREASINGLY ALL-CAPITALIST WORLD

Not long ago, textbooks presented a range of economic systems, usually capitalism, socialism, and communism. **Communism** was intended as a system in which the state disappeared and individuals contributed to the economy according to their productivity and received income according to their needs. Under **socialism,** the state owned a major share of productive resources except labor. **Capitalism** has been defined as a system under which individuals hold government-protected private property rights to all goods, including those used in production, and their own labor.

Pure Capitalism in Theory

In its purest theoretical form, market capitalism, or pure capitalism, has the following attributes:

1. Private property rights exist and are upheld by the judicial system.
2. Prices are allowed to seek their own level as determined by the forces of supply and demand. In this sense, pure capitalism is a price system.
3. Resources, including human labor, are free to move in and out of industries and geographic locations. The movement of resources follows the lure of profits—higher expected profits create an incentive for more resources to go where those profits might occur.

Communism
In its purest form, an economic system in which the state has disappeared and individuals contribute to the economy according to their productivity and are given income according to their needs.

Socialism
An economic system in which the state owns the major share of productive resources except labor. Socialism also usually involves the redistribution of income.

Capitalism
An economic system in which individuals own productive resources; these individuals can use the resources in whatever manner they choose, subject to common protective legal restrictions.

4. Risk takers are rewarded by higher profits, but those whose risks turn out to be bad business decisions suffer the consequences directly in terms of reduced wealth.

5. Decisions about what and how much should be produced, how it should be produced, and for whom it should be produced are left to the market. In a pure market capitalist system, all decisions are decentralized and made by individuals in a process of *spontaneous coordination* throughout the economy.

One way to remember the attributes of pure capitalism is by thinking of the three *P*s: prices, profits, and private property.

The role of government is limited to provision of certain public goods, such as defense, police protection, and a legal framework within which property rights and contracts are enforced.

Pure capitalism has also been called a **laissez-faire** system. The French term means "leave [it] alone" or "let [it] be." A pure capitalist system is one in which the government lets the economic actors in the economy make their own decisions without government constraints.

Laissez-faire
French for "leave [it] alone"; applied to an economic system in which the government minimizes its interference with the economy.

The Importance of Incentives

Though it is doubtful that full-blown communism ever really existed or could survive in a whole economy, various forms of socialism, in which the state owned important parts of the economy, have existed. Indeed, one can argue that the most important distinguishing feature between capitalist countries and everywhere else is the lack of private property rights. Economics predicts that, for example, when an apartment building is owned by no one (that is, owned by the "state"), there is less incentive for anyone to take care of it. This analysis has predicted well with respect to public housing in the United States. Just imagine an entire country for which all housing is public housing. That is what the former Soviet Union was like. (Note that we are not passing judgment on a system that has few private property rights. Rather, we are simply pointing out the predictions that economists can make with respect to how individuals treat such property.)

We pointed out in Chapter 4 that in a world of scarcity, resources must always be rationed. In economic systems in which prices were not allowed to be the rationing device, other methods had to be used. In the former Soviet Union, rationing by queuing (waiting) was one of the most prevalent. Some economists estimated that the average Russian spent as many hours a week waiting in lines as the average American spends watching television.

Today one might say that the collapse of communism has left the world with one system only, the **mixed economy,** in which decisions about how resources are used are made partly by the private sector and partly by the public sector—capitalism with government. Figure 6-1 represents the size of government relative to annual national output. You can see that even among the traditional capitalist countries of the world, there are great variations. These can be regarded as the different faces of capitalism.

Exercise 6.1
Visit www.econtoday.com
for more about alternative systems.

Mixed economy
An economic system in which decisions about how resources should be used are made partly by the private sector and partly by the government, or the public sector.

CONCEPTS IN BRIEF

- Communism is an economic system in which, in theory, individuals would produce according to their abilities and consume according to their needs. Under socialism, the state owns most major capital goods and attempts to redistribute income.

- Pure capitalism allows for the spontaneous coordination of millions of individuals by allowing the free play of the three *P*s—prices, profits, and property rights. Often, pure capitalism is called a laissez-faire system.

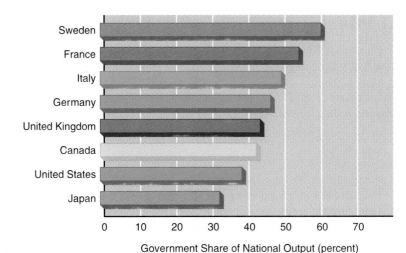

FIGURE 6-1

Percentage of National Yearly Output Accounted for by Government in Various Countries

Even among countries that have embraced capitalism for a long time, government plays an important, but widely different, role. It constitutes over 60 percent of the economy in Sweden, but less than 40 percent in the United States.

- Incentives matter in any economic system; therefore, in countries that have had few or unenforced property rights, individuals lacked the incentives to take care of most property that wasn't theirs.

- Most economies today can be viewed as mixed in that they combine private decisions and government controls.

THE DIFFERENT FACES OF CAPITALISM

The world is left with a single economic system that, thanks to the diversity of human cultures, has a variety of faces. Table 6-2 presents one way to categorize today's economic systems.

TABLE 6-2

Four Faces of Capitalism

Type of Capitalism	Examples	Characteristics	Problem Areas
Consumer	Canada, United States, New Zealand, Australia, United Kingdom	Borders are relatively open; focus is on profit maximization and laissez-faire.	Low saving and investment rates; income inequality
Producer	Japan, France, Germany	Production is emphasized over consumption; employment is a major policy issue; state controls a relatively large part of the economy.	Consumer dissatisfaction; potential slow future growth rates; inertia within the economy
Family	Indonesia, Malaysia, Thailand, Taiwan	Extended clans dominate business and capital flows.	Lack of modern corporate organizations; lack of money markets
Frontier	Russia, China, Ukraine, Romania, Albania	Many government enterprises pursue for-profit activities; new entrepreneurs emerge every day.	Difficulty of crossing borders; rising criminal activity

Source: Based, in part, on "21st Century Capitalism," *Business Week,* February 23, 1995, p. 19.

THE TRANSITIONAL PHASE: FRONTIER CAPITALISM

Frontier capitalism describes economies in transition from state ownership and control of most of the factors of production to a system of private property rights in which the price system is used to answer the basic economic questions. Table 6-3 presents theoretical stages in the development of frontier capitalism. Two aspects appear to be the most important: developing the legal system and selling off state-owned businesses.

Development of the Legal System

In the United States and many other countries, we take a well-established legal system as a given. That does not imply the total absence of a legal system in countries where we are now seeing frontier capitalism. To be sure, the former Soviet Union had a legal system, but virtually none of it had to do with economic transactions, which were carried out by state dictates. Individuals could not own the factors of production, and therefore, by definition, there were no legal disputes over property rights involving them. Consequently, the legal system in the former Soviet Union and its Eastern European satellites consisted of many volumes of criminal codes—laws against robbery, murder, rape, and theft as well as so-called economic crimes.

Enter the new world of private property rights and unfettered exchange of those rights among buyers and sellers. Now what happens when a buyer claims that a seller breached a particular agreement? In the United States, lawyers, courts, and the Uniform Commercial Code can be used to settle the dispute. Yet until recently in the frontier economies of the former Soviet Union, there was nothing even vaguely comparable. The rule of law in the United States and Great Britain has developed over hundreds of years; we cannot expect that in countries in transition toward full capitalism, an entire body of law and procedure can be developed overnight.

Privatization

The transition toward capitalism requires that the government lessen its role in the economy. This transition involves what has become known as *privatization.* **Privatization** is the transfer of ownership or responsibility for businesses run by the government, so-called *state enterprises,* to individuals and companies in the private sector. Even in capitalist countries, the government has owned and run various parts of the economy. During and after World War II, it became fashionable for many European governments to "nationalize" different industries. This was particularly prevalent in the United Kingdom, where the steel industry was nationalized, for example. In the early 1980s, France nationalized the banking industry. The opposite of nationalization is privatization.

In the early 1980s, Turkey and Chile were the first capitalist countries to start carrying out mass privatization of government-owned businesses. Under Margaret Thatcher, the United Kingdom pioneered the mass privatization of state industry, including the huge road haulage company (NFC), a health care group (Amersham International), British Telecom, British Petroleum, and British Aerospace.

A country must employ some method to put government-owned businesses into the hands of the private sector; government-owned businesses are not simply given away to the first party who asks. Imagine if the U.S. government said that it wanted to sell the United States Postal Service. How would it do so? One way is to sell it outright, but there might not be any buyers who would be willing to pay to take over such a giant money-losing corporation. An alternative would involve selling shares of stock to anyone who wanted to buy

Privatization
The sale or transfer of state-owned property and businesses to the private sector, in part or in whole. Also refers to *contracting out*—letting private business take over government-provided services such as trash collection.

	Stage	Characteristics
TABLE 6-3 **How Frontier Capitalism Develops**	**I**	The central government, as the controller of all economic activities, collapses and starts to disappear. The black market, typically involving government enterprises still owned by the state, expands enormously. Many former state factory managers and other bosses become involved in criminal activities using the state's resources. Government corruption flourishes more than before.
	II	Small businesses start to flourish. Families pool funds in order to become entrepreneurs. The rules of commerce are not well understood because there is not yet a well-established commercial law system, nor are property rights well defined or protected by the state.
	III	The economy is growing, but much of its growth is not measured by government statisticians. Small financial markets, such as stock markets, begin to develop. Foreigners cautiously invest in the new stock markets. The government attempts to develop a clear set of commercial laws.
	IV	Foreign corporations are more willing to invest directly in new factories and stores. The state gets serious about selling all businesses that it owns. More resources are devoted to suppressing criminal activity. Commercial law becomes better established and better understood.

them at the stated price. This latter technique is indeed the way in which most privatizations have been carried out in established capitalist countries throughout the world over the past 15 or 20 years.

In the former Soviet Union and in Eastern Europe, alternative systems have been devised. For example, citizens, at various times, have been given vouchers granting them the right to purchase a specified number of shares in particular government-owned companies that were being sold off.

The trend in privatization versus nationalization can be seen in panel (a) of Figure 6-2 on page 124. The cumulative worldwide sales of state-owned enterprises can be seen in panel (b). In Europe, privatization will probably continue at the rate of over $50 billion a year into the next century. Privatization in Latin America will continue much longer. Finally, because privatization in the former Soviet Union and Eastern Europe has in a sense just begun, such wholesale privatization may take a long time indeed.

Political Opposition to Privatization

There is often strong political pressure to slow down or even prevent privatization of state-owned businesses. The political pressure to prevent privatization is derived from simple economics: Managers of state-owned businesses typically have had lifetime job security, better working conditions than they could obtain elsewhere, and little threat of competition. In other words, life for a manager is typically better in a state-owned firm than in that same firm once it has been privatized.

Workers in state-run firms also believe, often rightly, that their lot in life will not be quite so good if the state-owned firm is sold to the private sector. State-owned firms tend to pay their workers higher wages and give them better fringe benefits, including much better pension plans, than similar firms that are privately owned. For example, an examination of state-owned phone companies in France and Germany shows that they have two to three

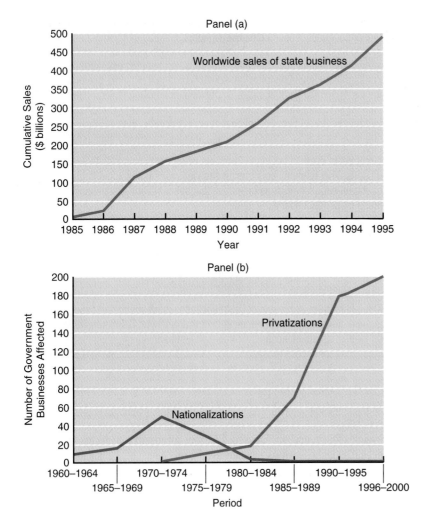

FIGURE 6-2

The Trend Toward Privatization
Privatization worldwide has been on the upswing since 1985, as shown in panel (a). Nationalizations (the opposite of privatizations) reached their peak in about 1970 as is shown in panel (b).

Source: OECD and *The Economist*, August 21, 1993, p. 19; United Nations.

times as many workers per telephone customer as the private telephone companies in the United States. This comparative overuse of labor in state-owned firms is even more obvious in the republics of the former Soviet Union and in Eastern Europe.

Economists cannot say whether privatization of state-owned firms is good or bad. Rather, economists can simply state that the rigors of a competitive market will generally cause resources to be used more efficiently after privatization occurs. In the process, however, some managers and workers may be made worse off.

Is There a Right Way to Go About the Transition?

Ever since the fall of the Berlin Wall in 1989, economists have debated whether there is a "right" way for former socialist and communist countries to move toward capitalist systems. The once-communist nations have, indeed, embarked on a social experiment in how to move toward a market economy. Basically, they have chosen two methods—a slow one and a fast one. Romania, Belarus, and Ukraine have only gradually privatized their economies, whereas the Czech Republic and, to a lesser extent, Poland and Estonia opted for a "shock treatment."

The rapid move toward a market economy, though not free of problems, has seemed to work better than the go-slow approach. The slower the transition occurs, the more the former entrenched bureaucrats in the state-owned businesses have been able to maintain their power over the use of resources. In the meantime, the state-owned businesses continue to use valuable resources inefficiently in these developing countries.

In contrast, a country like the Czech Republic used a voucher system to privatize over 2,000 state-owned enterprises. All citizens were given vouchers—legal rights evidenced on printed certificates—which could be used to purchase shares of stock in state-owned businesses. A stock market quickly developed in which shares of hundreds of companies are now traded every day. After an initial period of transition to a market economy, the Czech Republic has now achieved one of the lowest unemployment rates in Europe.

We will next examine the current situation of two of the largest countries in the world that are in the throes of frontier capitalism. Both are grappling with the problems of the transition from communism to capitalism.

CONCEPTS IN BRIEF

- Today there are four types of capitalism: consumer, producer, family, and frontier. The last begins when a centralized economy starts collapsing and black markets thrive. Eventually small businesses flourish, and then financial markets develop. Finally, foreign investment is attracted, and state-owned businesses are privatized.

- The development of a well-functioning legal system is one of the most difficult problems for an economy in the frontier capitalism stage. Such economies do not have the laws or courts to handle the new system of property right transfers.

- Privatization, or the turning over to the private sector of state-owned and state-run businesses, is occurring all over the world in all types of economies. There is much political opposition, however, whenever managers in soon-to-be privatized businesses realize that they may face harder times in a private setting.

RUSSIA AND ITS FORMER SATELLITES, YESTERDAY AND TODAY

Russia was the largest republic in the former Soviet Union. The economic system in place was at times called communism and at other times called command socialism. There is no question that it was a command economy in which there was centralized economic leadership and planning. All economies involve planning, of course; the difference is that in capitalist societies, most of the planning is done by private businesses rather than the government. Leaders in the former Soviet Union somehow believed that its economic planners in Moscow could micromanage an economy spanning 11 time zones, involving millions and millions of consumers and producers, and affecting vast quantities of goods and services.

Imagine trying to run a single business that big! No one can. Perhaps more important, state ownership in such a large country resulted in perverse incentives throughout the economy. For example, when the government issued production quotas for glass based on the number of panes, they ended up being almost paper thin and shattering easily. When the government then changed its quotas to weight, the glass panes were so thick that they were useless. In short, former Soviet citizens responded appropriately every time central planners figured out a new way to set production quotas. In the process, untold resources were inefficiently used or completely wasted.

By the time the Soviet Union collapsed in 1991, it consisted of a society in which perhaps 1 or 2 percent of the population (the communists, privileged bureaucrats, athletes, and artists) enjoyed a nice lifestyle and the rest of the citizens were forced to scrape by. The same was true perhaps to an even greater degree in the former East Germany, Romania, Poland, Hungary, Czechoslovakia (now the Czech Republic and Slovakia), and Albania. The standard of living of the average citizen prior to the Soviet Union's breakup was at best a quarter but more realistically one-tenth of that in the United States.

Rapid Privatization

One of the most dramatic privatization movements in history has occurred in Russia. Since 1992, about 18,000 state-owned companies have been privatized. Two-thirds of Russia's economy is now in private hands, and the private sector currently accounts for more than half of Russian output. The switch to privatization was Russia's decisive step into capitalism. Although official government statistics do not show much or any economic growth, they do not reflect reality (see the accompanying Thinking Critically About the Media box). The underground economy represents at least 40 percent and perhaps 50 percent of officially measured total economic activity. The standard of living has also improved because price controls (see Chapter 4) were abandoned in 1992. Prior to 1992, shortages at the officially controlled prices were common, and many consumer goods were constantly unavailable. That is no longer true today.

Russian housing has also been privatized for the most part. Some observers argue that the privatization of virtually all businesses and housing has been one of the most remarkable achievements of the post-Soviet era.

One Major Problem: Business Wars

The quick switch to a capitalist economy has not been without problems in Russia. Because of the lack of both a well-established legal system and an adequate police force, crimes against business people have shocked much of the Western world. Indeed, some observers argue that the breakdown of law enforcement and the proliferation of private armies and protection rackets prone to ruthless gangland tactics may be a threat to this new free market economy. Sergei Concharov, head of a group of former KGB (Soviet security) troops who now runs a protection agency for Russian businesses, stated that the power of bandits is important. He puts the power of bandits as perhaps the most important governing business power today. The International Institute of Strategic Studies in London estimates that over 80 percent of Russian enterprises pay an average of 10 to 20 percent of their profits as protection money. From 1994 through 1997, almost 130 bankers were murdered. Russia's Interior Ministry contends that criminal gangs control 40,000 enterprises, 500 of which are banks.

The judiciary is surely corrupt and underpaid. Anyone in business eventually has to hire the services of a *krysha*—a "fixer." The fixer will sort out disputes. Resorting to such extralegal intermediaries is the only way to survive in a system in which the law does not count.

The massive transfer of property to private hands has led to a steady struggle for wealth made even riskier in the absence of the rule of law. The Russian economy currently has a

---

THINKING CRITICALLY ABOUT THE MEDIA

Taking Russia's Pulse

When economists and journalists discuss the transition from the centralized Soviet economy to its current market orientation, they lament the tremendous reduction in national output. Official estimates for the period 1989 to 1995, for example, claim that national output dropped by over 50 percent. True though it may be that output dropped during this time, it is not clear what the actual value of that output was to the population. Much of the reduction was in military hardware, such as missiles. How much did the average citizen lose when that output shrank? Also, fewer television sets and radios were produced during this time period—but the ones produced earlier either never worked properly or tended to explode. Steel mills have been shut down in Russia but they had been using technology that was 45 years old. Further, the official Russian state agency that measures the economy, Goskomstat, has none of the sophistication that the U.S. Department of Commerce and the Bureau of Labor Statistics have for measuring a nation's output. Even if Goskomstat had better computers and more refined techniques, it would still miss a vast off-the-books economy that won't be counted by government statisticians for years to come. All in all, Russia's 150 million people earn more and live better than what Goskomstat statistics say.

small cadre of "business barons," who are often allied with powerful politicians. These business barons frequently enter into deals with state officials that prevent free competition from occurring. Many observers of the economic scene in Russia are not particularly worried, though. They point out that because Russia has opened its borders to competitors from other countries, industrial concentration will not be a serious problem. If foreign goods are available domestically, they provide a competitive check that will prevent excessive prices or poor quality. Today one sees foreign goods in virtually all Russian stores.

The Nightmare They Call Their Tax System

A major problem preventing Russia from truly entering a modern era is its bizarre and exceedingly complex tax system. Many tax rates are so high that if enforced, they would amount to a confiscation of wealth, and that situation has led to a culture of tax evasion and a huge underground economy. The problem is so serious that the Russian government collects less than half the taxes it is owed.

Exchanging Goods for Goods In modern economies, most transactions are completed using money. When goods are instead exchanged directly for other goods, the process is called *barter* (discussed in more detail in Chapter 15). Not surprisingly, to avoid the tax collector, many industrial sales are done without using money and hence are not recorded conventionally. Figure 6-3 shows the share of barter in industrial sales in Russia from 1992 to the present. The percentage is starting to fall, but it still exceeds that in any other modern industrial economy today by a wide margin.

Is There a Solution? Clearly, one solution is to simplify the tax system. Cutting the number of different taxes from over 200 to, say, a half a dozen at much lower rates would reduce the incentive for evasion and bring the underground economy back into official statistics. A sensible and nonconfiscatory tax system would eliminate the need for private businesses to bribe government tax collectors. And more foreign investment would be drawn into Russia under a reformed system. To reduce criminal activities in that country, more resources need to be devoted to the development of a true judiciary and a noncorrupt police force.

FIGURE 6-3

The Share of Barter in Industrial Sales in Russia

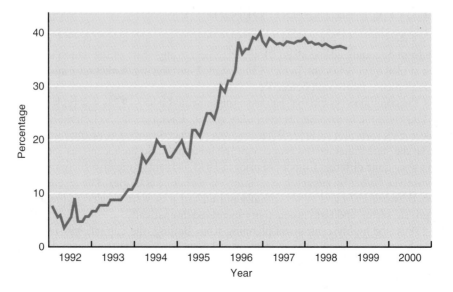

INTERNATIONAL EXAMPLE
Capitalism May Start Early in Russia

A growing number of grammar school children in Russia are learning about capitalism as part of their official school curriculum. What they learn now is quite different from what they learned under communism. The textbook they use, published in 1997, is called *Economics for Little Ones, or How Misha Became a Businessman.* The text involves an industrious bear who opens a honey, berry, and nut store. His only competitor is Winnie the Pooh's overpriced Golden Beehive Cooperative. Textbooks for older students bear such titles as *Enterprise for Everyone*, and *Tales of Queen Economy, Evil Inflation, the Magical Computer, and Their Trusty Friends.* A computer game called *100 Steps to the Market Economy* is proving to be very popular as well.

FOR CRITICAL ANALYSIS: Little teaching of capitalism occurs in grammar schools in the United States. Why would Russian educators wish to teach more about capitalism than we do in the United States? ●

CONCEPTS IN BRIEF

- Russia and its former satellite states in Eastern Europe operated under a system of command socialism with much centralized economic planning. The end result was a declining economy in which a small percentage of the population lived extremely well and the rest very poorly.

- Russia and Eastern Europe are privatizing at varying speeds, depending on the level of political opposition.

- Russia has experienced a crime wave during its transition to capitalism. One can compare this period to America's Wild West and to our period of Prohibition. As property rights and the legal system become more efficient, much of the crime associated with illegal economic activities will probably disappear.

THE PEOPLE'S REPUBLIC OF CHINA

The People's Republic of China remains the largest nation on earth and hence the largest with some form of command socialism. However, a decreasing share of the nation's activity is being guided by government. In fact, China started introducing market reforms in various sectors of the economy well before Russia did.

In 1978, the commune system that had been implemented in the 1950s was replaced by what was known as the *household responsibility system.* Each peasant household became responsible for its own plot of land. Whatever was produced in excess of the minimum obligation to the state remained the property of the household. So the incentives for peasant farmers were quite different from those prior to 1978. Peasants were also encouraged to enrich themselves further by engaging in a variety of economic activities. The results were impressive. Between 1979 and 1984, virtually millions of jobs were created in the urban and rural private sector, and farm productivity increased dramatically.

In the 1980s, the highly centralized planning from Beijing, the capital, was relaxed. Decision-making powers were given to state-owned enterprises at the local level. Indeed,

China had embarked on a gradual sell-off of state-owned enterprises so that the size of the state-run sector, which accounted for 70 percent of industrial production in the mid-1980s, dropped to less than 40 percent in 1998. The result was an increase in output. The problem with state-run factories was the **incentive structure.** Managers of those factories never had much incentive to maximize the equivalent of profits. Rather, managers of state-run factories attempted to maximize incomes and benefits for their workers because workers constituted a political constituency that was more important than the politicians at the national level.

Incentive structure
The motivational rewards and costs that individuals face in any given situation. Each economic system has its own incentive structure. The incentive structure is different under a system of private property than under a system of government-owned property, for example.

Two Decades of Economic Reform

Another major economic reform in China began in 1979, when the central government created a special economic zone in Guangdong province, bordering the then separate nation of Hong Kong. In that special zone, the three *P*s of pure capitalism—prices, profits, and private property—have now prevailed for nearly two decades. The result has been economic growth rates that have exceeded those in virtually any other part of the world. Within an area housing less than 1.5 percent of the population, Guangdong province now accounts for about 7 percent of the entire country's industrial output.

Transition Problems in Farming

Even though the Chinese central government was able to increase agricultural production dramatically when it gave peasants the household responsibility system, the agricultural sector has been lagging well behind the industrial sector in recent years. In effect, China has been undergoing an industrial revolution but not an agricultural one. One of the major problems is that peasants do not have legal title to their land. In other words, farmers cannot obtain legal property rights. As a result, the techniques used by agribusiness companies elsewhere in the world cannot be used by most of China's farmers. Peasants, in effect, have their land on loan from the state. The average size of a peasant farm is less than an acre for a family of six. It takes this family about 60 workdays to cultivate this amount of land, whereas a single American farmer can cultivate the same amount of land in about two hours.

Changes are occurring, though. At the Communist Party's 15th Congress in 1997, party leader Deng Xiaoping introduced market reforms into agriculture.

A Major Problem: The Rule of Law

As with virtually all countries experiencing frontier capitalism, China faces the perennial issue of how to establish the rule of law. When no specific property rights exist because resources are owned by "the people," the inevitable result is corruption. As with Russia, there is a sense of the Wild West in China, an atmosphere of lawlessness and unpredictability for anyone doing business. Both the government and the

THINKING CRITICALLY ABOUT THE MEDIA

268 Million Chinese Unemployed?

"China Sees 268 Million Unemployed in 2000." This was the headline a few years ago, reportedly based on statements by mainland Chinese officials in the Labor Ministry. Imagine that—the number of unemployed in China equaling the entire population of men, women, and children in the United States! A frightening prospect, no doubt, but also pure nonsense. Such a large number of unemployed presupposes that there is no way for them to find jobs of any sort. As China shifts toward a market economy, however, many of the unemployed will be able to find jobs in businesses that the current Chinese leadership cannot even conceive of today. That is what happens in a country in transition toward market capitalism. Of course, during the transition, there will be social and human costs associated with higher-than-normal unemployment rates, but that is statistically a temporary blip, not a long-term trend.

army continue to seek bribes and other favors because those two institutions still control many of the resources and influence the way business is conducted in China.

Only very slowly is China becoming a nation of laws, rather than of men and women. Otherwise stated, only gradually is the institution of a strong legal system being built up in China. The notion of property rights is slow to take in a nation where the communist dogma has denied their legitimacy. A good example is the state-supported bootleg compact disc factories that were first shut down because of international pressure and then reopened a few years ago. That American singers and musicians are being denied royalties seems not to bother some mainland Chinese government officials.

Exercise 6.2
Visit www.econtoday.com for more about the Chinese economy.

INTERNATIONAL EXAMPLE
The Rule of Law Is Still Precarious in China

In Imperial China, Mandarins were members of any of the nine ranks of high public officials. They exercised absolute and arbitrary powers. They often acted unpredictably. Apparently that is still how the final arbiters of what is legal today—Communist Party officials—still behave. In China, according to American-trained Chinese lawyers, there is not yet any true rule of law. In legal disputes, references to laws typically lead nowhere. An official may simply say, "It may be the law, but it is not our policy." Judges are normally under the control of local businesspersons. Consider the following: If a person from province A sues a business in province B, the case is handled in the court of province B. The local court's professional expenses, wages, and welfare benefits all depend on the local tax administration. Consequently, the local court will rarely defend the rights of an outside party. Also, the Chinese Supreme Court will hear only criminal cases; economic cases have no true "court of last resort" as they do in the United States. There is not even an unbiased intermediate court system for businesses from different provinces to use.

Foreign investors try to avoid China's court system altogether. They know that judges serve the needs of local Communist Party leaders and that many judges are former military officers who lack legal experience. So to safeguard their own interests, most non-Chinese businesses now insist on clauses in their contracts that provide for at least one foreign arbitrator.

FOR CRITICAL ANALYSIS: Which groups in China would be against the rule of law, and why? ●

The Slow Pace of Privatization

Virtually all state-run companies in China have provided cradle-to-grave social welfare benefits to their workers. The process of privatization, which started gradually years ago, first requires that these companies slowly eliminate many of these social welfare programs. Such programs are one of the reasons why over 50 percent of state-run enterprises are losing money every year. You can see from Figure 6-4 which state-run industrial enterprises are most prevalent. It clearly will be many years before the Chinese government is completely (if ever) out of the petroleum and tobacco businesses. But as Figure 6-5 shows, a growing percentage of firms are escaping from state control.

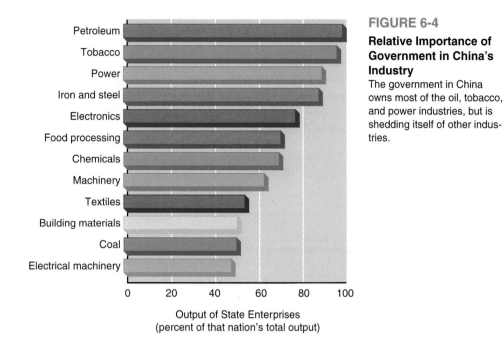

FIGURE 6-4

Relative Importance of Government in China's Industry
The government in China owns most of the oil, tobacco, and power industries, but is shedding itself of other industries.

The trend toward privatization in China is inevitably leading to labor dislocations. As state-run enterprises become privatized, new technology will be introduced that will require fewer labor hours per unit of output. Workers have been and will continue to be laid off in recently privatized firms. Laid-off workers will have to seek employment elsewhere, and in the process unemployment rates will rise, at least temporarily.

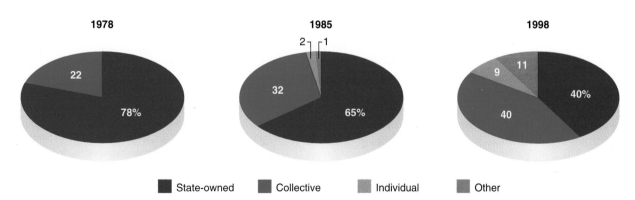

FIGURE 6-5

The Changing Face of China's Business Ownership
State ownership of all industries in China has fallen from 78 percent in 1978 to only 40 percent in 1998.

INTERNATIONAL EXAMPLE
Town- and Village-Owned Enterprises in China

In the past two decades, China's per capita income has quadrupled. According to Rudiger Dornbush of MIT, this success is due to the nation's 1.5 million town- and village-owned enterprises (TVEs). TVEs have been at the core of the Chinese economic performance. What is remarkable is that there are 7 million industrial companies in China; TVEs account for less than 20 percent.

FOR CRITICAL ANALYSIS: *In the past, who has owned and operated the other millions of industrial companies in China?* •

CONCEPTS IN BRIEF

• China started instituting market reforms in 1979 when it created special economic zones in which the three *P*s of capitalism were allowed to work. Problems remain in agriculture because peasant farmers cannot obtain property rights in land.

• The rule of law as capitalist countries know it is coming slowly to China. Government officials sometimes break contract agreements with foreign investors.

• The process of privatization started years ago but is proceeding slowly. The state still owns most of the businesses in oil, tobacco, power, and iron and steel.

FUTURE ECONOMIC POWER SHIFTS

The fact that there are so many economies in transition today is not just a momentary curiosity. It has implications for the future with respect to which nations will become economic powerhouses. Look at the three panels of Figure 6-6. You see in panel (a) that in the mid-1990s, the United States was clearly the world's largest economy. Japan and China were not even half its size. Now look at panel (b), which shows the World Bank's prediction of the largest economies in the year 2020. The leading economic powerhouse then is predicted to be China, with the United States a distant second. (These numbers reflect the total size of the economy, not how rich the average citizen is.) Japan will still be among the top three, but India and Indonesia will have expanded dramatically relative to 1995. Indeed, Asia, including India, will be a major economic power in the year 2020. These developments are reflected in panel (c) of Figure 6-6, where we show the projected shares of world output of today's industrial countries relative to today's developing countries. Realize, however, that the fact that developing Asian countries will dramatically increase the size of their economies does not mean that westerners will be worse off. Rather, the incomes of most westerners will also increase, but not as rapidly. Given that per-person incomes are generally higher in the West than in Asia, westerners will still remain rich by historical standards. The rest of the world is simply catching up with us.

THINKING CRITICALLY ABOUT THE MEDIA

Rich Industrial Nations—Really?

Virtually all news commentators and research organizations continue to classify countries such as the United States, the United Kingdom, and France as the industrial economies. Such an appellation today is a misnomer. In the industrial economies of today, less than one-third of the output is from "industry." Two-thirds of the jobs in so-called industrial economies are from services—doctors, lawyers, computer programmers, and Internet facilitators. Indeed, it might be more appropriate to call the richer countries *knowledge economies* because that is where the primary source of growth will lie—the storage, processing, and distribution of knowledge.

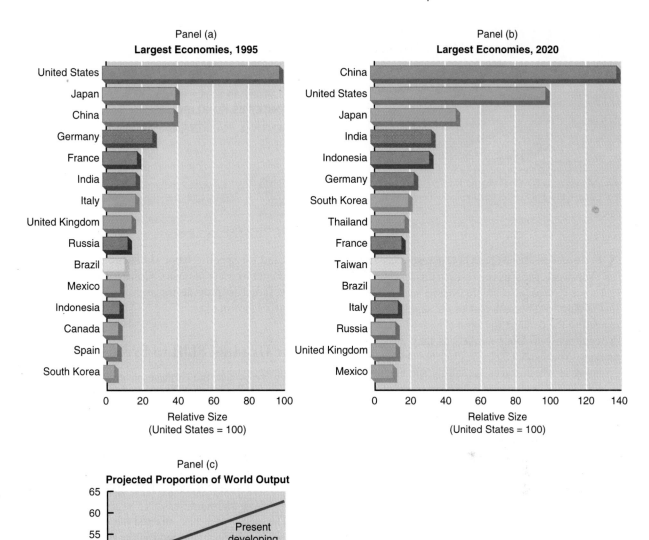

FIGURE 6-6

World Economic Powerhouses, 1995–2020

While the United States is the largest economy today, by 2020, China may be the world's greatest economic power. In any event, the share of world output from developing countries will increase steadily during that same time period.

Source: World Bank, *Global Economic Prospects.*

These mainland Chinese university students may be receiving their education free of charge. If so, a government official can tell them what job to take and where to live.

China Abandons Its Job Assignment System

CONCEPTS APPLIED:
INCENTIVES, MARKETS, CAPITALISM, LAISSEZ-FAIRE

Visit www.econtoday.com for an Internet Activity that expands your understanding of these concepts.

You know firsthand about how unrestricted labor markets work. Most of you reading this text have already had some type of job or might even be working full time. In so doing, you became part of the supply of labor. You reacted to the demand for labor. The laws of supply and demand apply to labor markets as they do to all other markets. You cannot help hearing about sectors in the economy in which wages are falling and unemployment is high, just as you cannot help hearing about sectors in which wages are rising and unemployment is low—such as telecommunications, software, engineering, and multimedia. No central planner in the United States has ever decided how many college graduates will go into any particular occupation. The choice has been decided by each graduate.

In China, every student who was given a free education had to agree to allow a state planner to tell him or her where to work. Consequently, many graduates ended up with jobs they never wanted, and many ended up living in cities that they never would have chosen. Such state-planned decisions usually lasted a lifetime.

The Problem with Mandatory Job Assignments

Perhaps state planners were capable of predicting changes in the demand for different types of labor in the past, when virtually all industry was owned and operated by the state. Gradually, though, state-owned enterprises have become a less important part of the Chinese economy (particularly because 50 percent of them run at a loss). The ever more market-oriented Chinese economy is becoming as dynamic as other market economies throughout the world. Changes in the demand for specific labor skills can no longer be well predicted by state planners. Consequently, the planners have failed to provide the right mix of job skills for today's labor market.

The Gradual Shift to Freedom of Choice

A few years ago, the Chinese government started a new system. Students who choose to pay their own way to colleges and universities can then choose an occupation and where they want to work. The tuition of $180 a year may seem small, but it represents about one-third of a Chinese citizen's annual income. To help students who choose the fee system, arrangements for student loans have been made, and many students have been able to borrow money from their families.

The new system has attracted the best students in the major cities of Shanghai and Beijing. They know that after graduation, they will easily find relatively high-paying jobs, particularly with foreign-owned companies and joint ventures, which tend to concentrate in China's largest cities. Of the more than 900,000 students who graduated in 1998, only 20,000 paid for their schooling—but that is twice as many as the year before, and their numbers continue to rise.

FOR CRITICAL ANALYSIS

1. So far, relatively few students in the less developed parts of China have chosen to pay for their own studies. Why do you think that they are less interested in the new system?
2. What were the benefits, if any, of the old-style, centrally planned job assignment system in China?

CHAPTER SUMMARY

1. The price system answers the resource allocation and distribution questions relating to what and how much will be produced, how it will be produced, and for whom it will be produced. The question of what to produce is answered by the value people place on a good—the highest price they are willing to pay for it. How goods are produced is determined by competition, which inevitably results in least-cost production techniques. Finally, goods and services are distributed to the individuals who are willing and able to pay for them. This answers the question about for whom goods are produced.

2. Pure capitalism can be defined by the three *P*s: prices, profits, and private property.

3. Communism is an economic system in which, theoretically, individuals would produce according to their abilities and consume according to their needs. Under socialism, the state owns most major capital goods and attempts to redistribute income. Most economies today can be viewed as mixed in that they rely on a combination of private decisions and government controls.

4. Incentives matter in any economic system; consequently, in countries that have had few or unenforced property rights, individuals lacked the incentives to take care of property that wasn't theirs.

5. Today there are four types of capitalism: consumer, producer, family, and frontier. The last emerges when a centralized economy starts collapsing and black markets thrive. Eventually, small businesses flourish and financial markets develop. Finally, foreign investment is attracted, and state-owned businesses are privatized.

6. The development of a well-functioning legal system is one of the most difficult problems for an economy in the frontier capitalism stage. Such economies do not have the laws or courts to handle property right protection and transfers.

7. Privatization, or turning over state-owned or state-run businesses to the private sector is occurring all over the world in all types of economies. There is much political opposition, however, whenever managers in soon-to-be-privatized businesses realize that they may face harder times in a private setting.

8. Russia and its former satellite states in Eastern Europe operated under a system of command socialism with much centralized economic planning. The end result was a declining economy in which a small percentage of the population lived extremely well and the rest very poorly.

9. Russia has experienced a crime wave during its transition to capitalism. One can compare this period to America's Wild West and to our period of Prohibition. As property rights and the legal system become more efficient, much of the crime associated with illegal economic activities probably will disappear.

10. China started instituting true market reforms in 1979, when it created special economic zones in which the three *P*s of capitalism—prices, profits, and private property—were allowed to work. Problems remain in agriculture because peasant farmers cannot obtain property rights to land.

11. The process of privatization in China started years ago but is proceeding slowly. The state still owns most of the businesses in oil, tobacco, power, and iron and steel.

12. The United States and Japan will remain economic powerhouses, but China could take the lead over the next 25 years. Other Asian countries, including Indonesia, India, Taiwan, South Korea, and Thailand, will become economically much stronger than they are today.

DISCUSSION OF PREVIEW QUESTIONS

1. **Why does the scarcity problem force all societies to answer the questions *what, how,* and *for whom?***
Scarcity exists for a society because people want more than their resources will allow them to have.

Society must decide *what* to produce because of scarcity. But if wants are severely restricted and resources are relatively superabundant, the question of *what* to produce is trivial—society simply produces *everything* that everyone wants. Superabundant resources relative to restricted wants also make the question of *how* to produce trivial. If scarcity doesn't exist, superabundant resources can be combined in *any* manner; waste and efficiency have no meaning without scarcity. Similarly, without scarcity, *for whom* is meaningless; *all* people can consume *all* they want.

2. How can economies be classified?

All societies must resolve the three fundamental economic problems: what, how, and for whom? One way to classify economies is according to the manner in which they answer these questions. In particular, we can classify them according to the degree to which *individuals* privately are allowed to make these decisions. Under pure command socialism, practically all economic decisions are made by a central authority; under pure capitalism, practically all economic decisions are made by private individuals pursuing their own economic self-interest.

3. Why do we say that *all* economies are mixed economies?

No economy in the real world is purely capitalistic. Resource allocation decisions in all economies are made by some combination of private individuals and governments. Even under an idealized capitalistic economy, important roles are played by the government; it is generally agreed that government is required for some income redistribution, national defense, protection of property rights, and so on.

4. What are the "three *P*s" of pure capitalism?

They are prices, profits, and property rights. In a pure capitalist economic system, prices are allowed to change when supply or demand changes. Prices are the signals to all about the relative scarcity of different resources. Profits are not constrained. When profits are relatively great in an industry, more resources flow to it. The converse is also true. Finally, property rights exist and are supported by the legal system.

PROBLEMS

(Answers to the odd-numbered problems appear at the back of the book.)

6-1. Suppose that you are an economic planner and you have been told by your country's political leaders that they want to increase automobile production by 10 percent over last year. What other industries will be affected by this decision?

6-2. Some argue that prices and profits automatically follow from well-established property rights. Explain how this might occur.

6-3. A business has found that it makes the most profits when it produces $172 worth of output of a particular product. It can choose from three possible techniques, A, B, and C, to produce the desired level of output. The table gives the amount of inputs these techniques use along with each input price.

 a. Which technique will the firm choose, and why?
 b. What would the firm's maximum profit be?
 c. If the price of labor increases to $4 per unit, which technique will be chosen, and why? What will happen to profits?

| | | Production Technique | | |
| | Input Unit Price | A (units) | B (units) | C (units) |
Input				
Land	$10	7	4	1
Labor	2	6	7	18
Capital	15	2	6	3
Entrepreneurship	8	1	3	2

6-4. Answer the questions on the basis of the accompanying graph.

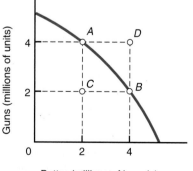

Butter (millions of barrels)

a. A switch to a decentralized, more market-oriented economy might do what to the production possibilities curve, and why?

b. What point on the graph represents an economy with unemployment?

6-5. The table gives the production techniques and input prices for 100 units of product X.

| Input | Input Unit Price | Production Technique | | |
		A (units)	B (units)	C (units)
Labor	$10	6	5	4
Capital	8	5	6	7

a. In a market system, which techniques will be used to produce 100 units of product X?

b. If the market price of a unit of X is $1, which technique will lead to the greatest profit?

c. The output of X is still $1, but the price of labor and capital changes so that labor is $8 and capital is $10. Which production technique will be used?

d. Using the information in (c), what is the potential profit of producing 100 units of X?

6-6. The table gives the production techniques and input prices for one unit of product Y.

| Input | Input Unit Price | Production Technique | | |
		A (units)	B (units)	C (units)
Labor	$10	1	3	2
Capital	5	2	2	4
Land	4	3	1	1

a. If the market price of a unit of product Y is $50, which technique generates the greatest potential profit?

b. If input unit prices change so that labor is $10, capital is $10, and land is $10, which technique will be chosen?

c. Assuming that the unit cost of each input is $10 and the price of a unit of Y is $50, which technique generates the greatest profit?

COMPUTER-ASSISTED INSTRUCTION

The role of prices in communicating information and allocating goods and services are illustrated by examining the ongoing transformation of the economies of Russia and China.

Complete problem and answer appear on disk.

INTERACTING WITH THE INTERNET

Extensive information on Eastern European economic conditions, with an emphasis on financial matters, can be found (for a fee) at

www.securities.com/

You can obtain general information on the countries studied in this chapter as well as other countries in the CIA's *World Fact Book*, which you can access at

www.odci.gov/cia/publications/pubs.html

You can also access the *Handbook of International Economic Statistics* for the latest year. Information on different countries' economic and trade policies can be found at

gopher://gopher.umsl.edu/11/library/govdocs/crpt

A very nice guide with extensive links to trade, economic, and business information for Eastern Europe and the former Soviet Union can be obtained from REESweb: Russian and East European

Studies, sponsored by the University Center for Russian and East European Studies of the University of Pittsburgh. It is located at

www.pitt.edu/~cjp/Econ/econind.html

If you would like to find out what is happening in the 15 member nations of the European Union (EU), you can access the European Commission's extensive Web site at

www.europa.eu.int

There you will start at the *Europa* home page for the European Union. Click on *Welcome*, then *News*, then *Eurostat* to obtain a menu of keywords from which you can choose.

You can get information about China from China's home page at

www.ihep.ac.cn/china.html

To find Internet resources on the economics of doing business in Russia and the other nations of the former Soviet Union, go to

dylee.keel.econ.ship.edu/INTNTL/INTDEV/Russia.htm

A great page of links on the economy of China can be found at

www.mindspring.com/~gsecondi/china.html

PART 6

DIMENSIONS OF MICROECONOMICS

The chapters in this book were extracted from the hardbound one-volume edition of *Economics Today.* In previous editions, the hardbound text and the macroeconomics and microeconomics paperbound texts were all numbered individually. Instructors and students who were using different versions of the book (or the software or other supplements) were forced to consult a conversion chart to find their place. Instead, the chapters in all three volumes of this edition are numbered the same—even if there are lapses in sequence—in order to avoid confusion and make the books as easy to use as possible.

CHAPTER 19

CONSUMER CHOICE

"One person's meat is another person's poison." That familiar saying can be translated into economic terms as follows: The utility, or satisfaction, that some other individual derives from consuming a good or service cannot be measured by how *you* value that particular good or service. Consider the satisfaction that smokers derive from the act of inhaling smoke that includes tars and nicotine. Such an activity is, in the long run, harmful to most people who engage in it. Nonetheless, smoking continues. But the government has decided to "do something about it." It has tentatively assessed tobacco companies billions of dollars in fines. Many states have raised taxes on cigarettes. What group of Americans will be most affected by a higher price for cigarettes? Before we answer that question, we want to consider the theory of consumer choice.

PREVIEW QUESTIONS

1. What is the law of diminishing marginal utility?
2. How does a consumer maximize total utility?
3. What happens to consumer optimum when price changes?
4. How can the law of diminishing marginal utility account for the law of demand?

THIS IS AN ALCOHOL AND DRUG FREE PROJECT

VIOLATORS BE DISMI

Did You Know That . . . in a typical year, an American family spends about 15 percent of its income on food and about the same on housing? Within individual families, however, these relative percentages may be quite different. Some families devote much higher percentages of their income to housing than others. What determines how much each family spends on different items in their budget? One explanation is simply tastes—the values that family members place on different items on which they can spend their income. The saying "You can't argue with tastes" suggests that different individuals have different preferences for how to allocate their limited incomes. Although there is no real theory of what determines people's tastes, we can examine some of the behavior that underlies how consumers react to changes in the prices of the goods and services that they purchase. Recall from Chapter 3 that people generally purchase less at higher prices than at lower prices. This is called the law of demand.

Because the law of demand is important, its derivation is useful because it allows us to arrange the relevant variables, such as price, income, and tastes, in such a way as to understand the real world better and even perhaps generate predictions about it. One way of deriving the law of demand involves an analysis of the logic of consumer choice in a world of limited resources. In this chapter, therefore, we discuss what is called *utility analysis.*

UTILITY THEORY

When you buy something, you do so because of the satisfaction you expect to receive from having and using that good. For everything that you like to have, the more you have of it, the higher the level of satisfaction you receive. Another term that can be used for satisfaction is **utility,** or want-satisfying power. This property is common to all goods that are desired. The concept of utility is purely subjective, however. There is no way that you or I can measure the amount of utility that a consumer might be able to obtain from a particular good, for utility does not imply "useful" or "utilitarian" or "practical." For this reason, there can be no accurate scientific assessment of the utility that someone might receive by consuming a frozen dinner or a movie relative to the utility that another person might receive from that same good or service. Nevertheless, we can infer whether a person receives more utility from consuming one good versus another by that person's behavior. For example, if an individual buys more coffee than tea (when both tea and coffee are priced equally), we are able to say that the individual receives more utility from consuming coffee than from consuming tea.

The utility that individuals receive from consuming a good depends on their tastes and preferences. These tastes and preferences are normally assumed to be given and stable for a given individual. An individual's tastes determine how much utility that individual derives from consuming a good, and this in turn determines how that individual allocates his or her income. People spend a greater proportion of their incomes on goods they like. But we cannot explain why tastes are different between individuals. For example, we cannot explain why some people like yogurt but others do not.

We can analyze in terms of utility the way consumers decide what to buy, just as physicists have analyzed some of their problems in terms of what they call force. No physicist has ever seen a unit of force, and no economist has ever seen a unit of utility. In both cases, however, these concepts have proved useful for analysis.

Throughout this chapter, we will be discussing **utility analysis,** which is the analysis of consumer decision making based on utility maximization.

Utility
The want-satisfying power of a good or service.

Utility analysis
The analysis of consumer decision making based on utility maximization.

Utility and Utils

Economists once believed that utility could be measured. In fact, there is a philosophical school of thought based on utility theory called *utilitarianism,* developed by the English philosopher Jeremy Bentham (1748–1832). Bentham held that society should seek the greatest happiness for the greatest number. He sought to apply an arithmetic formula for measuring happiness. He and his followers developed the notion of measurable utility and invented the **util** to measure it. For the moment, we will also assume that we can measure satisfaction using this representative unit. Our assumption will allow us to quantify the way we examine consumer behavior.[1] Thus the first chocolate bar that you eat might yield you 4 utils of satisfaction; the first peanut cluster, 6 utils; and so on. Today, no one really believes that we can actually measure utils, but the ideas forthcoming from such analysis will prove useful in our understanding of the way in which consumers choose among alternatives.

Util
A representative unit by which utility is measured.

Total and Marginal Utility

Consider the satisfaction, or utility, that you receive each time that you rent and watch a video on your VCR. To make the example straightforward, let's say that there are hundreds of videos to choose from each year and that each of them is of the same quality. Let's say that you normally rent one video per week. You could, of course, rent two, or three, or four per week. Presumably, each time you rent another video per week, you will get additional satisfaction, or utility. The question, though, that we must ask is, given that you are already renting one per week, will the next one rented that week give you the same amount of additional utility?

That additional, or incremental, utility is called **marginal utility,** where *marginal,* as before, means "incremental" or "additional." (Marginal changes also refer to decreases, in which cases we talk about *decremental* changes.) The concept of marginality is important in economics because we make decisions at the margin. At any particular point, we compare additional (marginal) benefits with additional (marginal) costs.

Marginal utility
The change in total utility due to a one-unit change in the quantity of a good or service consumed.

Applying Marginal Analysis to Utility

The specific example presented in Figure 19-1 on page 416 will clarify the distinction between total utility and marginal utility. The table in panel (a) shows the total utility and the marginal utility of watching videos each week. Marginal utility is the difference between total utility derived from one level of consumption and total utility derived from another level of consumption. A simple formula for marginal utility is this:

$$\text{Marginal utility} = \frac{\text{change in total utility}}{\text{change in number of units consumed}}$$

In our example, when a person has already watched two videos in one week and then watches another, total utility increases from 16 utils to 19. Therefore, the marginal utility (of watching one more video after already having watched two in one week) is equal to 3 utils.

---

[1]What follows is typically called *cardinal utility analysis* by economists. It requires cardinal measurement. Numbers such as 1, 2, and 3 are cardinals. We know that 2 is exactly twice as many as 1 and that 3 is exactly three times as many as 1. You will see in Appendix E at the end of this chapter a type of consumer behavior analysis that requires only *ordinal* measurement of utility, meaning ranked or ordered. *First, second,* and *third* are ordinal numbers; nothing can be said about their exact size relationships. We can only talk about their importance relative to each other. Temperature, for example, is an ordinal ranking. One hundred degrees Celsius is not twice as warm as 50 degrees Celsius. All we can say is that 100 degrees Celsius is warmer than 50 degrees Celsius.

Panel (a)

(1) Number of Videos Watched per Week	(2) Total Utility (utils per week)	(3) Marginal Utility (utils per week)
0	0	
		10 (10 − 0)
1	10	
		6 (16 − 10)
2	16	
		3 (19 − 16)
3	19	
		1 (20 − 19)
4	20	
		0 (20 − 20)
5	20	
		−2 (18 − 20)
6	18	

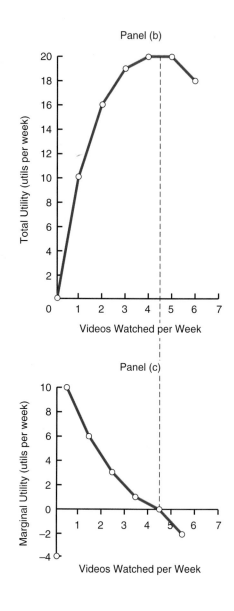

FIGURE 19-1

Total and Marginal Utility of Watching Videos

If we were able to assign specific values to the utility derived from watching videos each week, we could obtain a marginal utility schedule similar in pattern to the one shown in panel (a). In column 1 is the number of videos watched per week; in column 2, the total utility derived from each quantity; and in column 3, the marginal utility derived from each additional quantity, which is defined as the change in total utility due to a change of one unit of watching videos per week. Total utility from panel (a) is plotted in panel (b). Marginal utility is plotted in panel (c), where you see that it reaches zero where total utility hits its maximum at between 4 and 5 units.

GRAPHIC ANALYSIS

We can transfer the information in panel (a) onto a graph, as we do in panels (b) and (c) of Figure 19-1. Total utility, which is represented in column 2 of panel (a), is transferred to panel (b).

Total utility continues to rise until four videos are watched per week. This measure of utility remains at 20 utils through the fifth video, and at the sixth video per week it falls to 18 utils; we assume that at some quantity consumed per unit time period, boredom sets in. This is shown in panel (b).

Marginal Utility

Exercise 19.1
Visit www.econtoday.com for more about chocolate's marginal utility.

If you look carefully at panels (b) and (c) of Figure 19-1, the notion of marginal utility becomes very clear. In economics, the term *marginal* always refers to a change in the total. The marginal utility of watching three videos per week instead of two videos per week is the increment in total utility and is equal to 3 utils per week. All of the points in panel (c) are taken from column 3 of the table in panel (a). Notice that marginal utility falls throughout the graph. A special point occurs after four videos are watched per week because the total utility curve in panel (b) is unchanged after the consumption of the fourth video. That means that the consumer receives no additional (marginal) utility from watching the fifth video. This is shown in panel (c) as *zero* marginal utility. After that point, marginal utility becomes negative.

In our example, when marginal utility becomes negative, it means that the consumer is fed up with watching videos and would require some form of compensation to watch any more. When marginal utility is negative, an additional unit consumed actually lowers total utility by becoming a nuisance. Rarely does a consumer face a situation of negative marginal utility. Whenever this point is reached, goods become in effect "bads." A rational consumer will stop consuming at the point at which marginal utility becomes negative, even if the good is free.

> **CONCEPTS IN BRIEF**
>
> • Utility is defined as want-satisfying power; it is a power common to all desired goods and services.
>
> • We arbitrarily measure utility in units called utils.
>
> • It is important to distinguish between total utility and marginal utility. Total utility is the total satisfaction derived from the consumption of a given quantity of a good or service. Marginal utility is the *change* in total utility due to a one-unit change in the consumption of the good or service.

Diminishing marginal utility
The principle that as more of any good or service is consumed, its extra benefit declines. Otherwise stated, increases in total utility from the consumption of a good or service become smaller and smaller as more is consumed during a given time period.

DIMINISHING MARGINAL UTILITY

Notice that in panel (c) of Figure 19-1, marginal utility is continuously declining. This property has been named the principle of **diminishing marginal utility.** There is no way that we can prove diminishing marginal utility; nonetheless, economists and others have for years believed strongly in the notion. Diminishing marginal utility has even been called a law. This supposed law concerns a psychological, or subjective, utility that you receive as you consume more and more of a particular good. Stated formally, the law is as follows:

> As an individual consumes more of a particular commodity, the total level of utility, or satisfaction, derived from that consumption usually increases. Eventually, however, the *rate* at which it increases diminishes as more is consumed.

Take a hungry individual at a dinner table. The first serving is greatly appreciated, and the individual derives a substantial amount of utility from it. The second serving does not have quite as much impact as the first one, and the third serving is likely to be even less satisfying. This individual experiences diminishing marginal utility of food until he or she stops eating, and this is true for most people. All-you-can-eat restaurants count on this fact; a second helping of ribs may provide some marginal utility, but the third helping would have only a little or even negative marginal utility. The fall in the marginal utility of other goods is even more dramatic.

Consider for a moment the opposite possibility—increasing marginal utility. Under such a situation, the marginal utility after consuming, say, one hamburger would increase. The second hamburger would be more valuable to you, and the third would be even more valuable yet. If increasing marginal utility existed, each of us would consume only one good or service! Rather than observing that "variety is the spice of life," we would see that monotony in consumption was preferred. We do not observe this, and therefore we have great confidence in the concept of diminishing marginal utility.

Consider an example that may affect you or someone you know—having a birthday on or within a few days of December 25. Even if you receive exactly the same number of presents that you would have if your birthday were six months later, your total level of utility, or satisfaction, from your presents will be lower. Why? Because of diminishing marginal utility. Let's say that your relatives and friends all give you compact discs. The total utility you receive from, say, 20 CDs on December 25 is less than if you received 10 in December and 10 on your birthday several months later.

EXAMPLE
Newspaper Vending Machines Versus Candy Vending Machines

Have you ever noticed that newspaper vending machines nearly everywhere in the United States allow you to put in the correct change, lift up the door, and take as many newspapers as you want? Contrast this type of vending machine with candy machines. They are completely locked at all times. You must designate the candy that you wish, normally by using some type of keypad. The candy then drops down to a place where you reach to retrieve it but from which you cannot grab any other candy. The difference between these two types of vending machines is explained by diminishing marginal utility. Newspaper companies dispense newspapers from coin-operated boxes that allow dishonest people to take more copies than they pay for. What would a dishonest person do with more than one copy of a newspaper, however? The marginal utility of a second newspaper is normally zero. The benefit of storing excessive newspapers is usually nil because yesterday's news has no value. But the same analysis does not hold for candy. The marginal utility of a second candy bar is certainly less than the first, but it is normally not zero. Moreover, one can store candy for relatively long periods of time at relatively low cost. Consequently, food vending machine companies have to worry about dishonest users of their machines and must make their machines much more theftproof than newspaper companies do.

FOR CRITICAL ANALYSIS: Can you think of a circumstance under which a substantial number of newspaper purchasers might be inclined to take more than one newspaper out of a vending machine? ●

OPTIMIZING CONSUMPTION CHOICES

Every consumer has a limited income. Choices must be made. When a consumer has made all of his or her choices about what to buy and in what quantities, and when the total level of satisfaction, or utility, from that set of choices is as great as it can be, we say that the consumer has *optimized.* When the consumer has attained an optimum consumption set of goods and services, we say that he or she has reached **consumer optimum.**[2]

Consumer optimum
A choice of a set of goods and services that maximizes the level of satisfaction for each consumer, subject to limited income.

Consider a simple two-good example. The consumer has to choose between spending income on the rental of videos at $5 each and on purchasing deluxe hamburgers at $3 each. Let's say that the last dollar spent on hamburgers yields 3 utils of utility but the last dollar spent on video rentals yields 10 utils. Wouldn't this consumer increase total utility if some dollars were taken away from hamburger consumption and allocated to video rentals? The answer is yes. Given diminishing marginal utility, more dollars spent on video rentals will reduce marginal utility per last dollar spent, whereas fewer dollars spent on hamburger consumption will increase marginal utility per last dollar spent. The optimum—where total utility is maximized—might occur when the satisfaction per last dollar spent on both hamburgers and video rentals per week is equal for the two goods. Thus the amount of goods consumed depends on the prices of the goods, the income of the consumers, and the marginal utility derived from each good.

Table 19-1 presents information on utility derived from consuming various quantities of videos and hamburgers. Columns 4 and 8 show the marginal utility per dollar spent on

TABLE 19-1
Total and Marginal Utility from Consuming Videos and Hamburgers on an Income of $26

(1) Videos per Period	(2) Total Utility of Videos per Period (utils)	(3) Marginal Utility (utils) MU_v	(4) Marginal Utility per Dollar Spent (MU_v/P_v) (price = $5)	(5) Hamburgers per Period	(6) Total Utility of Hamburgers per Period (utils)	(7) Marginal Utility (utils) MU_h	(8) Marginal Utility per Dollar Spent (MU_h/P_h) (price = $3)
0	0.0	—	—	0	0	—	—
1	50.0	50.0	10.0	1	25	25	8.3
2	95.0	45.0	9.0	2	47	22	7.3
3	135.0	40.0	8.0	3	65	18	6.0
4	171.5	36.5	7.3	4	80	15	5.0
5	200.0	28.5	5.7	5	89	9	3.0

[2]Optimization typically refers to individual decision-making processes. When we deal with many individuals interacting in the marketplace, we talk in terms of an equilibrium in the marketplace. Generally speaking, equilibrium is a property of markets rather than of individual decision making.

videos and hamburgers, respectively. If the prices of both goods are zero, individuals will consume each as long as their respective marginal utility is positive (at least five units of each and probably much more). It is also true that a consumer with infinite income will continue consuming goods until the marginal utility of each is equal to zero. When the price is zero or the consumer's income is infinite, there is no effective constraint on consumption.

Consumer optimum is attained when the marginal utility of the last dollar spent on each good yields the same utility and income is completely exhausted. The individual's income is $26. From columns 4 and 8 of Table 19-1, maximum equal marginal utilities occur at the consumption level of four videos and two hamburgers (the marginal utility per dollar spent equals 7.3). Notice that the marginal utility per dollar spent for both goods is also (approximately) equal at the consumption level of three videos and one hamburger, but here total income is not completely exhausted. Likewise, the marginal utility per dollar spent is (approximately) equal at five videos and three hamburgers, but the expenditures necessary for that level of consumption exceed the individual's income.

Table 19-2 shows the steps taken to arrive at consumer optimum. The first video would yield a marginal utility per dollar of 10, while the first hamburger would yield a marginal utility of only 8.3 per dollar. Because it yields the higher marginal utility per dollar, the video is purchased. This leaves $21 of income. The second video yields a higher marginal utility per dollar (9, versus 8.3 for hamburgers), so it is also purchased, leaving an unspent income of $16. At the third purchase, the first hamburger now yields a higher marginal utility per dollar than the next video (8.3 versus 8), so the first hamburger is purchased. This leaves income of $13 to spend. The process continues until all income is exhausted and the marginal utility per dollar spent is equal for both goods.

To restate, consumer optimum requires the following:

A consumer's money income should be allocated so that the last dollar spent on each good purchased yields the same amount of marginal utility (when all income is spent).

Exercise 19.2
Visit www.econtoday.com for more about making choices.

TABLE 19-2

Steps to Consumer Optimum

In each purchase situation described here, the consumer always purchases the good with the higher marginal utility per dollar spent (MU/P). For example, at the time of the third purchase, the marginal utility per last dollar spent on videos is 8, but it is 8.3 for hamburgers, and $16 of income remains, so the next purchase will be a hamburger. Here $P_v = \$5$ and $P_h = \$3$.

	Choices					
	Videos		Hamburgers			
Purchase	Unit	(MU_v/P_v)	Unit	$(MU_h/(P_h)$	Buying Decision	Remaining Income
1	First	10.0	First	8.3	First video	$26 − $5 = $21
2	Second	9.0	First	8.3	Second video	$21 − $5 = $16
3	Third	8.0	First	8.3	First hamburger	$16 − $3 = $13
4	Third	8.0	Second	7.3	Third video	$13 − $5 = $ 8
5	Fourth	7.3	Second	7.3	Fourth video and	$ 8 − $5 = $ 3
					second hamburger	$ 3 − $3 = $ 0

A Little Math

We can state the rule of consumer optimum in algebraic terms by examining the ratio of marginal utilities and prices of individual products. This is sometimes called the *rule of equal marginal utilities per dollar spent* on a basket of goods. The rule simply states that a consumer maximizes personal satisfaction when allocating money income in such a way that the last dollars spent on good A, good B, good C, and so on, yield equal amounts of marginal utility. Marginal utility (*MU*) from good A is indicated by *MU* of good A. For good B, it is *MU* of good B. Our algebraic formulation of this rule, therefore, becomes

$$\frac{MU \text{ of good A}}{\text{price of good A}} = \frac{MU \text{ of good B}}{\text{price of good B}} = \cdots = \frac{MU \text{ of good Z}}{\text{price of good Z}}$$

The letters A, B, . . . , Z indicate the various goods and services that the consumer might purchase.

We know, then, that the marginal utility of good A divided by the price of good A must equal the marginal utility of any other good divided by its price in order for the consumer to maximize utility. Note, though, that the application of the rule of equal marginal utility per dollar spent is not an explicit or conscious act on the part of consumers. Rather, this is a model of consumer optimum.

HOW A PRICE CHANGE AFFECTS CONSUMER OPTIMUM

Consumption decisions are summarized in the law of demand, which states that the amount purchased is inversely related to price. We can now see why by using the law of diminishing marginal utility.

Purchase decisions are made such that the value of the marginal utility of the last unit purchased and consumed is just equal to the price that had to be paid. No consumer will, when optimizing, buy 10 units of a good per unit time period when the personal valuation placed on the tenth unit is less than the price of the tenth unit.

If we start out at consumer optimum and then observe a price decrease, we can predict that consumers will respond to the price decrease by consuming more. Why? Because before the price change, the marginal utility of the last unit was about equal to the price paid for the last unit. Now, with a lower price, it is possible to consume more than before and still not have the marginal utility be less than the price, because the price has fallen. If the law of diminishing marginal utility holds, the purchase and consumption of additional units will cause marginal utility to fall. Eventually it will fall to the point at which it is equal to the price of the final good consumed. The limit to this increase in consumption is given by the law of diminishing marginal utility. At some point, the marginal utility of an additional unit will be less than what the person would have to give up (price) for that additional unit, and the person will stop buying.

A hypothetical demand curve for video rentals per week for a typical consumer is presented in Figure 19-2 on page 422. At a rental price of $5 per video, the marginal utility of the last video rented per week is MU_1. At a rental price of $4 per video per week, the marginal utility is represented by MU_2. Because of the law of diminishing marginal utility—with the consumption of more videos, the marginal utility of the last unit of these additional videos is lower—MU_2 must be less than MU_1. What has happened is that at a lower price, the number of video rentals per week increased from two to three; marginal utility must have fallen. At a higher consumption rate, the marginal utility falls to meet the lower price for video rentals per week.

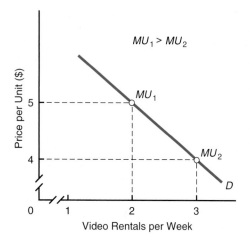

The Substitution Effect

What is happening as the price of video rental falls is that consumers are substituting the now relatively cheaper video rentals for other goods and services, such as restaurant meals and live concerts. We call this the **substitution effect** of a change in price of a good because it occurs when consumers substitute relatively cheaper goods for relatively more expensive ones.

We assume that people desire a variety of goods and pursue a variety of goals. That means that few, if any, goods are irreplaceable in meeting demand. We are generally able to substitute one product for another to satisfy demand. This is commonly referred to as the **principle of substitution.**

Let's assume now that there are several goods, not exactly the same, and perhaps even very different from one another, but all serving basically the same purpose. If the relative price of one particular good falls, we will most likely substitute in favor of the lower-priced good and against the other similar goods that we might have been purchasing. Conversely, if the price of that good rises relative to the price of the other similar goods, we will substitute in favor of them and not buy as much of the now higher-priced good.

If the price of some item that you purchase goes down while your money income and all other prices stay the same, your ability to purchase goods goes up. That is to say that your effective **purchasing power** is increased, even though your money income has stayed the same. If you purchase 20 gallons of gas a week at $1.20 per gallon, your total outlay for gas is $24. If the price goes down by 50 percent, to 60 cents a gallon, you would have to spend only $12 a week to purchase the same number of gallons of gas. If your money income and the prices of other goods remain the same, it would be possible for you to continue purchasing 20 gallons of gas a week *and* to purchase more of other goods. You will feel richer and will indeed probably purchase more of a number of goods, including perhaps even more gasoline.

The converse will also be true. When the price of one good you are purchasing goes up, without any other change in prices or income, the purchasing power of your income will drop. You will have to reduce your purchases of either the now higher-priced good or other goods (or a combination).

In general, this **real-income effect** is usually quite small. After all, unless we consider broad categories, such as housing or food, a change in the price of one particular item that

Substitution effect
The tendency of people to substitute cheaper commodities for more expensive commodities.

Principle of substitution
The principle that consumers and producers shift away from goods and resources that become relatively higher priced in favor of goods and resources that are now relatively lower priced.

Purchasing power
The value of money for buying goods and services. If your money income stays the same but the price of one good that you are buying goes up, your effective purchasing power falls and vice versa.

Real-income effect
The change in people's purchasing power that occurs when, other things being constant, the price of one good that they purchase changes. When that price goes up, real income, or purchasing power, falls, and when that price goes down, real income increases.

we purchase will have a relatively small effect on our total purchasing power. Thus we expect the substitution effect usually to be more important than the real-income effect in causing us to purchase more of goods that have become cheaper and less of goods that have become more expensive.

THE DEMAND CURVE REVISITED

Linking the "law" of diminishing marginal utility and the rule of equal marginal utilities per dollar gives us a negative relationship between the quantity demanded of a good or service and its price. As the relative price of video rentals goes up, for example, the quantity demanded will fall; and as the relative price of video rentals goes down, the quantity demanded will rise. Figure 19-2 shows this demand curve for video rentals. As the price of video rentals falls, the consumer can maximize total utility only by renting more videos, and vice versa. In other words, the relationship between price and quantity desired is simply a downward-sloping demand curve. Note, though, that this downward-sloping demand curve (the law of demand) is derived under the assumption of constant tastes and incomes. You must remember that we are keeping these important determining variables constant when we simply look at the relationship between price and quantity demanded.

Marginal Utility, Total Utility, and the Diamond-Water Paradox

Even though water is essential to life and diamonds are not, water is cheap and diamonds are dear. The economist Adam Smith in 1776 called this the "diamond-water paradox." The paradox is easily understood when we make the distinction between total utility and marginal utility. The total utility of water greatly exceeds the total utility derived from diamonds. What determines the price, though, is what happens on the margin. We have relatively few diamonds, so the marginal utility of the last diamond consumed is high. The opposite is true for water. Total utility does not determine what people are willing to pay for a unit of a particular commodity; marginal utility does. Look at the situation graphically in Figure 19-3. We show the demand curve for diamonds, labeled $D_{diamonds}$. The demand curve for water is labeled D_{water}. We plot quantity in terms of kilograms per unit time

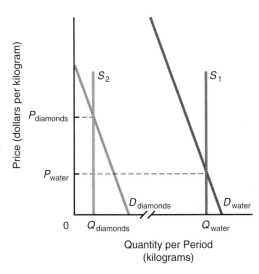

FIGURE 19-3

The Diamond-Water Paradox

We pick kilograms as a common unit of measurement for both water and diamonds. To demonstrate that the demand and supply of water is immense, we have put a break in the horizontal quantity axis. Although the demand for water is much greater than the demand for diamonds, the marginal valuation of water is given by the marginal value placed on the last unit of water consumed. To find that, we must know the supply of water, which is given as S_1. At that supply, the price of water is P_{water}. But the supply for diamonds is given by S_2. At that supply, the price of diamonds is $P_{diamonds}$. The total valuation that consumers place on water is tremendous relative to the total valuation consumers place on diamonds. What is important for price determination, however, is the marginal valuation, or the marginal utility received.

period on the horizontal axis. On the vertical axis we plot price in dollars per kilogram. We use kilograms as our common unit of measurement for water and for diamonds. We could just as well have used gallons, acre-feet, or liters.

Notice that the demand for water is many, many times the demand for diamonds (even though we really don't show this in the diagram). We draw the supply curve of water as S_1 at a quantity of Q_{water}. The supply curve for diamonds is given as S_2 at quantity $Q_{diamonds}$. At the intersection of the supply curve of water with the demand curve of water, the price per kilogram is P_{water}. The intersection of the supply curve of diamonds with the demand curve of diamonds is at $P_{diamonds}$. Notice that $P_{diamonds}$ exceeds P_{water}. Diamonds sell at a higher price than water.

Exercise 19.3
Visit www.econtoday.com for more about paying for nature.

INTERNATIONAL EXAMPLE
The World of Water in Saudi Arabia

The diamond-water paradox deals with the situation in which water, although necessary for life, may be much cheaper than some luxury item. In Saudi Arabia, as you might expect, the contrary can be true. A liter of water costs five times as much as a liter of gasoline, whereas a pair of custom-made British wool dress pants only costs $20. These relative prices are quite different from what we are used to seeing in America. Water costs next to nothing, a liter of gas about 40 cents, and custom-made wool pants at least $200. To understand what has happened in Saudi Arabia, simply substitute gasoline for water and water for diamonds in Figure 19-3.

FOR CRITICAL ANALYSIS: List some of the effects on human behavior that such a high relative price of water would cause. ●

CONCEPTS IN BRIEF

- The law of diminishing marginal utility tells us that each successive marginal unit of a good consumed adds less extra utility.

- Each consumer with a limited income must make a choice about the basket of commodities to purchase; economic theory assumes that the consumer chooses the basket of commodities that yields optimum consumption. The consumer maximizes total utility by equating the marginal utility of the last dollar spent on one good with the marginal utility per last dollar spent on all other goods. That is the state of consumer optimum.

- To remain in consumer optimum, a price decrease requires an increase in consumption; a price increase requires a decrease in consumption.

- Each change in price has a substitution effect and a real-income effect. When price falls, the consumer substitutes in favor of the relatively cheaper good. When price falls, the consumer's real purchasing power increases, causing the consumer to purchase more of most goods. The opposite would occur when price increases. Assuming that the law of diminishing marginal utility holds, the demand curve must slope downward.

Despite the evidence on the negative effects of smoking, many Americans continue to smoke. Those who earn the lowest incomes smoke disproportionately more than those in higher income brackets. Consequently, who will bear the greatest burden of a significant increase in the price per pack of cigarettes?

Increased Cigarette Prices: Who Is Hit Hardest?

CONCEPTS APPLIED:

UTILITY, MARGINAL UTILITY, DEMAND, REVEALED PREFERENCES

 Visit www.econtoday.com for an Internet Activity that expands your understanding of these concepts.

There is little doubt that smoking leads to shortness of breath, emphysema, lung cancer, early death, and increased emotional pain to relatives of affected victims. But so far, at least for individuals over 18, smoking is a legal activity. Consequently, tobacco companies may sell cigarettes to any willing adult. For many decades, most people have known that smoking is harmful—as early as the 1920s, cigarettes were being referred to as "coffin nails." In any event, lawsuits against tobacco companies filed by sick smokers or their surviving relatives consistently failed in court. Enter the state governments. They decided to sue the tobacco companies on the basis of how much their Medicaid expenses increased from having to treat sick smokers. Rather than fight, the tobacco companies reached an agreement with the state governments. That agreement called for billions of dollars in "reparations" to be paid to various state governments each year.

Taxes, Too

Various state governments have imposed higher cigarette taxes in order to discourage smoking. As can be expected, the taxes are lowest in the tobacco-producing states. As can also be expected, cigarettes have been smuggled from low-tax states, such as Virginia, to high-tax states, such as New York.

The Effect of Higher Cigarette Prices

The tens and eventually hundreds of billions of dollars that the tobacco companies will pay out for any settlement will lead to higher cigarette prices. Which group of individuals is affected the most by higher cigarette prices? Look at Figure 19-4. The shaded area of the graph indicates the proportion of individuals in each income bracket who smoke. Poor individuals' revealed preferences show that they receive higher marginal utility from

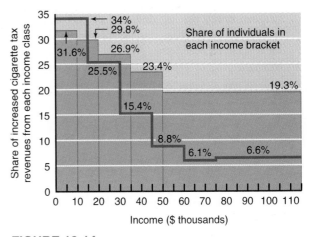

FIGURE 19-14

Who Will Pay the Higher Cigarette Prices

Lower-income earners smoke proportionately more than higher-income earners and will pay a disproportionately higher share of any tax on cigarettes.

Source: National Center for Health Statistics.

smoking than higher-income individuals. Whereas almost 32 percent of Americans earning $10,000 or less smoke, only about 19 percent of those earning above $50,000 smoke.

Now consider what will happen following a multibillion-dollar payment from tobacco companies to the government. The Tax Foundation in Washington, D.C., calculated that over a third of those dollars will be paid by 22 percent of Americans earning $15,000 or less. About 60 percent will be paid by the 45 percent of Americans earning below $30,000, as can be seen in the "stepladder" curve in the figure.

1. If states save money because smokers die early, does that necessarily mean that we should subsidize smoking?

2. Why aren't cigarette smokers effectively fighting against higher cigarette taxes?

CHAPTER SUMMARY

1. As an individual consumes more of a particular commodity, the total level of utility, or satisfaction, derived from that consumption increases. However, the *rate* at which it increases diminishes as more is consumed. This is known as the law of diminishing marginal utility.

2. An individual reaches consumer optimum when the marginal utility per last dollar spent on each commodity consumed is equal to the marginal utility per dollar spent on every other good.

3. When the price of a particular commodity goes up, to get back into an optimum position, the consumer must reduce consumption of the now relatively more expensive commodity. As this consumer moves back up the marginal utility curve, marginal utility increases. A change in price has both a substitution effect and a real-income effect. As the price goes down, for example, the consumer substitutes in favor of the cheaper good, and also as the price goes down, real purchasing power increases, causing a general increase in consumer purchases of most goods and services.

4. It is possible to derive a downward-sloping demand curve by using the principle of diminishing marginal utility.

DISCUSSION OF PREVIEW QUESTIONS

1. **What is the law of diminishing marginal utility?**
   The law of diminishing marginal utility states that as an individual consumes more and more units of a commodity per unit of time, eventually the extra benefit derived from consuming successive units will fall. Thus the fourth hamburger consumed in an eight-hour period yields less satisfaction than the third, and the third less than the second. The law is quite general and holds for almost any commodity.

2. **How does a consumer maximize total utility?**
   This question deals with the maximization of utility derived not from the consumption of one commodity but from the consumption of all commodities that the individual wants, subject to an income constraint. The rule is that maximization of total utility requires that the last dollar spent on each commodity consumed by the individual have the same marginal utility. Stated differently, the consumer should purchase goods and services up to the point where the consumer's marginal utilities per dollar (marginal utility divided by price) for all commodities are equated and all income is spent (or saved for future spending). For example, assume that you are about to spend all of your income but discover that the marginal utility per dollar's worth for bread will be 10 utils and the marginal utility per dollar's worth of milk will be 30 utils. This means that the last dollar you are going to spend on bread will increase your total utility by 10, whereas the last dollar you are going to spend on milk will increase your total utility by 30. By spending one dollar more on milk and one dollar less on bread, you raise your total utility by about 20 utils, while your total dollar expenditures remain constant. This reallocation causes the marginal utility per dollar's worth of milk to fall and the marginal utility per dollar's worth of bread to rise. To maximize total utility, you will continue to buy more or less of each commodity until the marginal utilities per dollar's worth of all goods you consume are equated.

3. **What happens to consumer optimum when price changes?**
   Assume that you have reached an optimum: The marginal utilities per dollar's worth for all the goods you purchase are equated. Assume that the last dollar spent on each of the commodities you purchase increases your total utility by 20 utils. Now suppose that the price of bread falls while all other prices remain constant. Because the price of bread has fallen, the last dollar spent on bread now has a higher marginal utility. This is true because at a lower price

for bread, a $1 bill can purchase a greater quantity of bread. This means that marginal utility per dollar's worth of bread now *exceeds* 20 utils, whereas the marginal utility per dollar's worth of each of the other goods you purchase still equals 20 utils. In short, you are no longer optimizing; your old pattern of expenditures does not maximize your total utility. You can now increase your total utility by purchasing more bread. Note that a reduction in the price of bread (other things held constant) leads to your purchasing more bread per unit of time.

4. How can the law of diminishing marginal utility account for the law of demand?

When a consumer is optimizing, total utility is maximized. An increase in expenditures on any specific commodity will necessarily lead to a reduction in expenditure on another commodity and a reduction in overall total utility. Why? Because of the law of diminishing marginal utility. For example, suppose that you are maximizing your overall total utility and that the marginal utility per dollar's worth of each commodity you purchase is 20 utils. Suppose that you experiment and spend another dollar on bread—and therefore spend one dollar less on milk. Your total utility must fall because you will receive less than 20 utils for the next dollar's worth of bread, and you lose 20 utils by spending a dollar less on milk. Thus, on net balance, you lose utility. We can see intuitively, then, that because you get less and less additional benefit from consuming more and more bread (or any other commodity), the price of bread (or any other commodity) *must fall* before you will voluntarily purchase more of it. That is how diminishing marginal utility helps explain the law of demand.

PROBLEMS

(Answers to the odd-numbered problems appear at the back of the book.)

19-1. Suppose that you are standing in the checkout line of a grocery store. You have 5 pounds of oranges and three ears of corn. A pound of oranges costs 30 cents; so does an ear of corn. You have $2.40 to spend. You are satisfied that you have reached the highest level of satisfaction, or total utility. Your sister comes along and tries to convince you that you have to put some of the corn back and replace it with oranges. From what you know about utility analysis, how would you explain this disagreement?

19-2. To increase marginal utility, the consumer must decrease consumption (other things being constant). This sounds paradoxical. Why is it a correct statement nonetheless?

19-3. Assume that Alice Warfield's marginal utility is 100 utils for the last hamburger she consumed. If the price of hamburgers is $1 apiece, what is Warfield's marginal utility per dollar's worth of hamburger? What is her marginal utility per dollar's worth if the price is 50 cents per hamburger? If the price is $2? How do we calculate marginal utility per dollar's worth of specific commodities?

19-4. A fall in the price of one good leads to more of that good being consumed, other things remaining constant. How might this increase in consumption be broken down?

19-5. Consider the accompanying table. Following the optimizing rule, how much of each good will be consumed?

Quantity of Good A	Marginal Utility of Good A	Price of Good A	Quantity of Good B	Marginal Utility of Good B	Price of Good B
100	15	$4.51	9	7	$1.69
101	12	4.51	10	5	1.69
102	8	4.51	11	3	1.69
103	6	4.51	12	2	1.69

19-6. If total utility is increasing as more is consumed, what is happening to marginal utility?

19-7. Yesterday you were consuming four eggs and two strips of bacon. Today you are consuming three eggs and three strips of bacon. Your tastes did not change overnight. What might have caused this change? Are you better or worse off?

19-8. The marginal utility of X is five times the marginal utility of Y, but the price of X is only four times the price of Y. How can this disequilibrium be remedied?

19-9. Look at the accompanying table; then answer the questions that follow.

Quantity of X Consumed	Total Utility (utils)
0	0
1	20
2	50
3	70
4	80

a. What is the marginal utility of consuming the first unit of X?

b. What is the marginal utility of consuming the fourth unit of X?

c. When does marginal utility start to diminish?

COMPUTER-ASSISTED INSTRUCTION

The consumer is optimizing when $MU_a/P_a = MU_b/P_b = \cdots = MU_z/P_z$. What does it mean if $MU_a/P_a > MU_b/P_b$? If $MU_a/P_a < MU_b/P_b$? How is a consumer likely to react to such inequalities? Why will the consumer's total utility increase on buying more or less of each good if an inequality exists? Specific calculations shed light on these questions.

Complete problem and answer appear on disk.

APPENDIX E

MORE ADVANCED CONSUMER CHOICE THEORY

It is possible to analyze consumer choice verbally, as we did for the most part in Chapter 19. The theory of diminishing marginal utility can be fairly well accepted on intuitive grounds and by introspection. If we want to be more formal and perhaps more elegant in our theorizing, however, we can translate our discussion into a graphic analysis with what we call indifference curves and the budget constraint. Here we discuss these terms and their relationship and demonstrate consumer equilibrium in geometric form.

ON BEING INDIFFERENT

What does it mean to be indifferent? It usually means that you don't care one way or the other about something—you are equally disposed to either of two alternatives. With this interpretation in mind, we will turn to two choices, video rentals and restaurant meals. In panel (a) of Figure E-1, we show several combinations of video rentals and restaurant meals per week that a representative consumer considers equally satisfactory. That is to say, for each combination, A, B, C, and D, this consumer will have exactly the same level of total utility.

The simple numerical example that we have used happens to concern video rentals and restaurant meals per week. This example is used to illustrate general features of indifference curves and related analytical tools that are necessary for deriving the demand curve. Obviously, we could have used any two commodities. Just remember that we are using a *specific* example to illustrate a *general* analysis.

We can plot these combinations graphically in panel (b) of Figure E-1, with restaurant meals per week on the horizontal axis and video rentals per week on the vertical axis. These are our consumer's indifference combinations—the consumer finds each combination as acceptable as the others. When we connect these combinations with a smooth curve, we obtain what is called the consumer's **indifference curve.** Along the indifference curve, every combination of the two goods in question yields the same level of satisfaction. Every point along the

Indifference curve
A curve composed of a set of consumption alternatives, each of which yields the same total amount of satisfaction.

FIGURE E-1

Combinations That Yield Equal Levels of Satisfaction
A, B, C, and D represent combinations of video rentals and restaurant meals per week that give an equal level of satisfaction to this consumer. In other words, the consumer is indifferent among these four combinations.

Panel (a)

Combination	Video Rentals per Week	Restaurant Meals per Week
A	1	7
B	2	4
C	3	2
D	4	1

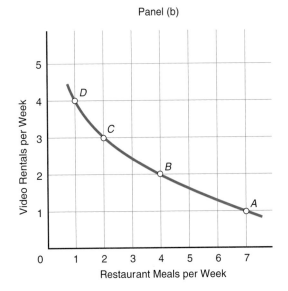

Panel (b)

429

indifference curve is equally desirable to the consumer. For example, four video rentals per week and one restaurant meal per week will give our representative consumer exactly the same total satisfaction as two video rentals per week and four restaurant meals per week.

PROPERTIES OF INDIFFERENCE CURVES

Indifference curves have special properties relating to their slope and shape.

Downward Slope

The indifference curve shown in panel (b) of Figure E-1 slopes downward; that is, it has a negative slope. Now consider Figure E-2. Here we show two points, *A* and *B*. Point *A* represents four video rentals per week and two restaurant meals per week. Point *B* represents five video rentals per week and six restaurant meals per week. Clearly, *B* is always preferred to *A* because *B* represents more of everything. If *B* is always preferred to *A*, it is impossible for points *A* and *B* to be on the same indifference curve because the definition of the indifference curve is a set of combinations of two goods that are equally preferred.

Curvature

The indifference curve that we have drawn in panel (b) of Figure E-1 is special. Notice that it is curved. Why didn't we just draw a straight line, as we have usually done for a demand curve? To find out why we don't posit straight-line indifference curves, consider the implications. We show such a straight-line indifference curve in Figure E-3. Start at point *A*. The consumer has no restaurant meals and five video rentals per week. Now the consumer wishes to go to point *B*. He or she is willing to give up only one video rental in order to get one restaurant meal. Now let's assume that the consumer is at point *C*, consuming one video rental and four restaurant meals per week. If the consumer wants to go to point *D*, he or she is again willing to give up one video rental in order to get one more restaurant meal per week.

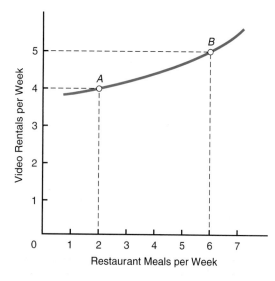

FIGURE E-2

Indifference Curves: Impossibility of an Upward Slope

Point *B* represents a consumption of more video rentals per week and more restaurant meals per week than point *A*. *B* is always preferred to *A*. Therefore, *A* and *B* cannot be on the same indifference curve, which is positively sloped, because an indifference curve shows *equally preferred* combinations of the two goods.

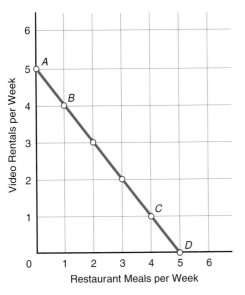

Implications of a Straight-Line Indifference Curve

If the indifference curve is a straight line, the consumer will be willing to give up the same number of video rentals (one for one in this simple example) to get one more restaurant meal per week, whether the consumer has no restaurant meals or a lot of restaurant meals per week. For example, the consumer at point *A* has five video rentals and no restaurant meals per week. He or she is willing to give up one video rental in order to get one restaurant meal per week. At point *C*, however, the consumer has only one video rental and four restaurant meals per week. Because of the straight-line indifference curve, this consumer is willing to give up the last video rental in order to get one more restaurant meal per week, even though he or she already has four.

In other words, no matter how many videos the consumer rents, he or she is willing to give up one video rental to get one restaurant meal per week—which does not seem plausible. Doesn't it make sense to hypothesize that the more videos the consumer rents per week, the less he or she will value an *additional* video rental? Presumably, when the consumer has five video rentals and no restaurant meals per week, he or she should be willing to give up more than one video rental in order to get one restaurant meal. Therefore, a straight-line indifference curve as shown in Figure E-3 no longer seems plausible.

In mathematical jargon, an indifference curve is convex with respect to the origin. Let's look at this in panel (a) of Figure E-1. Starting with combination *A*, the consumer has one video rental but seven restaurant meals per week. To remain indifferent, the consumer would have to be willing to give up three restaurant meals to obtain one more video rental (as shown in combination *B*). However, to go from combination *C* to combination *D*, notice that the consumer would have to be willing to give up only one restaurant meal for an additional video rental per week. The quantity of the substitute considered acceptable changes as the rate of consumption of the original item changes.

Consequently the indifference curve in panel (b) of Figure E-1 will be convex when viewed from the origin.

THE MARGINAL RATE OF SUBSTITUTION

Instead of using marginal utility, we can talk in terms of the marginal rate of substitution between restaurant meals and video rentals per week. We can formally define the consumer's marginal rate of substitution as follows:

> **The marginal rate of substitution is equal to the change in the quantity of one good that just offsets a one-unit change in the consumption of another good, such that total satisfaction remains constant.**

We can see numerically what happens to the marginal rate of substitution in our example if we rearrange panel (a) of Figure E-1 into Table E-1. Here we show restaurant meals

(1) Combination	(2) Restaurant Meals Per Week	(3) Video Rentals Per Week	(4) Marginal Rate of Substitution of Restaurant Meals for Video Rentals
A	7	1	
			3:1
B	4	2	
			2:1
C	2	3	
			1:1
D	1	4	

TABLE E-1

Calculating the Marginal Rate of Substitution

As we move from combination A to combination B, we are still on the same indifference curve. To stay on that curve, the number of restaurant meals decreases by three and the number of video rentals increases by one. The marginal rate of substitution is 3:1. A three-unit decrease in restaurant meals requires an increase in one video rental to leave the consumer's total utility unaltered.

in the second column and video rentals in the third. Now we ask the question, What change in the consumption of video rentals per week will just compensate for a three-unit change in the consumption of restaurant meals per week and leave the consumer's total utility constant? The movement from A to B increases video rental consumption by one. Here the marginal rate of substitution is 3:1—a three-unit decrease in restaurant meals requires an increase of one video rental to leave the consumer's total utility unaltered. Thus the consumer values the three restaurant meals as the equivalent of one video rental. We do this for the rest of the table and find that as restaurant meals decrease further, the marginal rate of substitution goes from 3:1 to 1:1. The marginal rate of substitution of restaurant meals for video rentals per week falls as the consumer obtains more video rentals. That is, the consumer values successive units of video rentals less and less in terms of restaurant meals. The first video rental is valued at three restaurant meals; the last (fourth) video rental is valued at only one restaurant meal. The fact that the marginal rate of substitution falls is sometimes called the *law of substitution*.

In geometric language, the slope of the consumer's indifference curve (actually, the negative of the slope) measures the consumer's marginal rate of substitution. Notice that this marginal rate of substitution is purely subjective or psychological.

THE INDIFFERENCE MAP

Let's now consider the possibility of having both more video rentals *and* more restaurant meals per week. When we do this, we can no longer stay on the same indifference curve that we drew in Figure E-1. That indifference curve was drawn for equally satisfying combinations of video rentals and restaurant meals per week. If the individual can now attain more of both, a new indifference curve will have to be drawn, above and to the right of the one shown in panel (b) of Figure E-1. Alternatively, if the individual faces the possibility of having less of both video rentals and restaurant meals per week, an indifference curve will have to be drawn below and to the left of the one in panel (b) of Figure E-1. We can map out a whole set of indifference curves corresponding to these possibilities.

Figure E-4 shows three possible indifference curves. Indifference curves that are higher than others necessarily imply that for every given quantity of one good, more of the other good can be obtained on a higher indifference curve. Looked at another way, if one goes from curve I_1 to I_2, it is possible to consume the same number of restaurant meals *and* be able to rent more videos per week. This is shown as a movement from point A to point B in Figure E-4. We could do it the other way. When we move from a lower to a higher indif-

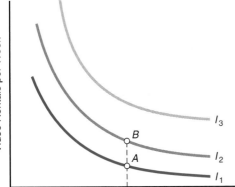

FIGURE E-4

A Set of Indifference Curves

An infinite number of indifference curves can be drawn. We show three possible ones. Realize that a higher indifference curve represents the possibility of higher rates of consumption of both goods. Hence a higher indifference curve is preferred to a lower one because more is preferred to less. Look at points A and B. Point B represents more video rentals than point A; therefore, bundles on indifference curve I_2 have to be preferred over bundles on I_1 because the number of restaurant meals per week is the same at points A and B.

ference curve, it is possible to rent the same number of videos *and* to consume more restaurant meals per week. Thus the higher a consumer is on the indifference map, the greater that consumer's total level of satisfaction.

THE BUDGET CONSTRAINT

Budget Constraint

All of the possible combinations of goods that can be purchased (at fixed prices) with a specific budget.

Our problem here is to find out how to maximize consumer satisfaction. To do so, we must consult not only our *preferences*—given by indifference curves—but also our *market opportunities*—given by our available income and prices, called our **budget constraint.** We might want more of everything, but for any given budget constraint, we have to make choices, or trade-offs, among possible goods. Everyone has a budget constraint; that is, everyone faces a limited consumption potential. How do we show this graphically? We must find the prices of the goods in question and determine the maximum consumption of each allowed by our budget. For example, let's assume that videos rent for $10 apiece and restaurant meals cost $20. Let's also assume that our representative consumer has a total budget of $60 per week. What is the maximum number of videos the consumer can rent? Six. And the maximum number of restaurant meals per week he or she can consume? Three. So now, as shown in Figure E-5, we have two points on our budget line, which is sometimes called the *consumption possibilities curve.* These anchor points of the budget line are obtained by dividing money income by the price of each product. The first point is at b on the vertical axis; the second, at b' on the horizontal axis. The budget line is linear because prices are given.

Any combination along line bb' is possible; in fact, any combination in the colored area is possible. We will assume, however, that the individual consumer completely uses up the available budget, and we will consider as possible only those points along bb'.

Slope of the Budget Constraint

The budget constraint is a line that slopes downward from left to right. The slope of that line has a special meaning. Look carefully at the budget line in Figure E-5. Remember from our discussion of graphs in Appendix A that we measure a negative slope by the ratio of the fall in Y over the run in X. In this case, Y is video rentals per week and X is restaurant meals per week. In Figure E-5, the fall in Y is -2 video rentals per week (a drop from 4 to 2) for a run in X of one restaurant meal per week (an increase from 1 to 2); therefore, the slope of

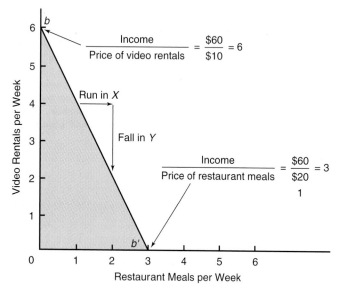

FIGURE E-5

The Budget Constraint

The line *bb'* represents this individual's budget constraint. Assuming that video rentals cost $10 each, restaurant meals cost $20 each, and the individual has a budget of $60 per week, a maximum of six video rentals or three restaurant meals can be bought each week. These two extreme points are connected to form the budget constraint. All combinations within the colored area and on the budget constraint line are feasible.

the budget constraint is −2/1, or −2. This slope of the budget constraint represents the rate of exchange between video rentals and restaurant meals; it is the realistic rate of exchange, given their prices.

Now we are ready to determine how the consumer achieves the optimum consumption rate.

CONSUMER OPTIMUM REVISITED

Consumers will try to attain the highest level of total utility possible, given their budget constraints. How can this be shown graphically? We draw a set of indifference curves similar to those in Figure E-4, and we bring in reality—the budget constraint *bb'*. Both are drawn in Figure E-6. Because a higher level of total satisfaction is represented by a higher indifference curve, we know that the consumer will strive to be on the highest indifference

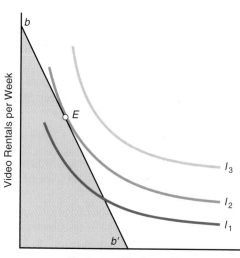

FIGURE E-6

Consumer Optimum

A consumer reaches an optimum when he or she ends up on the highest indifference curve possible, given a limited budget. This occurs at the tangency between an indifference curve and the budget constraint. In this diagram, the tangency is at *E*.

curve possible. However, the consumer cannot get to indifference curve I_3 because the budget will be exhausted before any combination of video rentals and restaurant meals represented on indifference curve I_3 is attained. This consumer can maximize total utility, subject to the budget constraint, only by being at point E on indifference curve I_2 because here the consumer's income is just being exhausted. Mathematically, point E is called the tangency point of the curve I_2 to the straight line bb'.

Consumer optimum is achieved when the marginal rate of substitution (which is subjective) is just equal to the feasible, or realistic, rate of exchange between video rentals and restaurant meals. This realistic rate is the ratio of the two prices of the goods involved. It is represented by the absolute value of the slope of the budget constraint. At point E, the point of tangency between indifference curve I_2 and budget constraint bb', the rate at which the consumer wishes to substitute video rentals for restaurant meals (the numerical value of slope of the indifference curve) is just equal to the rate at which the consumer *can* substitute video rentals for restaurant meals (the slope of the budget line).

EFFECTS OF CHANGES IN INCOME

A change in income will shift the budget constraint bb' in Figure E-6. Consider only increases in income and no changes in price. The budget constraint will shift outward. Each new budget line will be parallel to the original one because we are not allowing a change in the relative prices of video rentals and restaurant meals. We would now like to find out how an individual consumer responds to successive increases in income when relative prices remain constant. We do this in Figure E-7. We start out with an income that is represented by a budget line bb'. Consumer optimum is at point E, where the consumer attains the highest indifference curve I_1, given the budget constraint bb'. Now we let income increase. This is shown by a shift outward in the budget line to cc'. The consumer attains a new optimum at point E'. That is where a higher indifference curve, I_2, is reached. Again, the consumer's income is increased so that the new budget line is dd'. The new optimum now moves to E''. This is where indifference curve I_3 is reached. If we connect the three consumer optimum points, E, E', and E'', we have what is called an income-consumption curve. The **income-consumption curve** shows the optimum consumption points that would occur if income

Income-consumption curve
The set of optimum consumption points that would occur if income were increased, relative prices remaining constant.

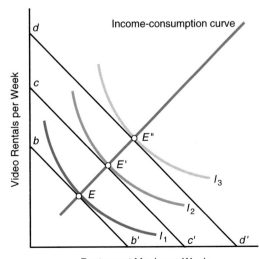

Restaurant Meals per Week

FIGURE E-7

Income-Consumption Curve
We start off with income sufficient to yield budget constraint bb'. The highest attainable indifference curve is I_1, which is just tangent to bb' at E. Next we increase income. The budget line moves outward to cc', which is parallel to bb'. The new highest indifference curve is I_2, which is just tangent to cc' at E'. We increase income again, which is represented by a shift in the budget line to dd'. The new tangency point of the highest indifference curve, I_3, with dd', is at point E''. When we connect these three points, we obtain the income-consumption curve.

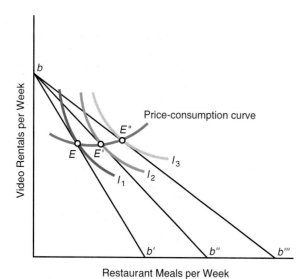

FIGURE E-8

Price-Consumption Curve

As we lower the price of restaurant meals, income measured in terms of restaurant meals per week increases. We show this by rotating the budget constraint from *bb'* to *bb''* and finally to *bb'''*. We then find the highest indifference curve that is attainable for each successive budget constraint. For budget constraint *bb'*, the highest indifference curve is I_1, which is tangent to *bb'* at point *E*. We do this for the next two budget constraints. When we connect the optimum points, *E, E'*, and *E''*, we derive the price-consumption curve, which shows the combinations of the two commodities that a consumer will purchase when money income and the price of one commodity remain constant while the other commodity's price changes.

for that consumer were increased continuously, holding the prices of video rentals and restaurant meals constant.

THE PRICE-CONSUMPTION CURVE

In Figure E-8, we hold money income and the price of video rentals constant while we lower the price of restaurant meals. As we keep lowering the price of restaurant meals, the quantity of meals that could be purchased if all income were spent on restaurant meals increases; thus the extreme points for the budget constraint keep moving outward to the right as the price of restaurant meals falls. In other words, the budget line rotates outward from *bb'* to *bb''* and *bb'''*. Each time the price of restaurant meals falls, a new budget line is formed. There has to be a new optimum point. We find it by locating on each new budget line the highest attainable indifference curve. This is shown at points *E, E'*, and *E''*. We see that as price decreases for restaurant meals, the consumer purchases more restaurant meals per week. We call the line connecting points *E, E'*, and *E''* the **price-consumption curve.** It connects the tangency points of the budget constraints and indifference curves, thus showing the amounts of two goods that a consumer will buy when money income and the price of one commodity are held constant while the price of the remaining good changes.

DERIVING THE DEMAND CURVE

We are now in a position to derive the demand curve using indifference curve analysis. In panel (a) of Figure E-9, we show what happens when the price of restaurant meals decreases, holding both the price of video rentals and income constant. If the price of restaurant meals decreases, the budget line rotates from *bb'* to *bb''*. The two optimum points are given by the tangency at the highest indifference curve that just touches those two budget lines. This is at *E* and *E'*. But those two points give us two price-quantity pairs. At point *E,* the price of restaurant meals is $20; the quantity demanded is 2. Thus we have one point that we can transfer to panel (b) of Figure E-9. At point *E'*, we have another price-quantity pair. The price has fallen to $10; the quantity demanded has increased to 5. We therefore transfer this other point to panel (b). When we connect these two points (and all the others in between), we derive the demand curve for restaurant meals; it slopes downward.

Price-consumption curve

The set of consumer optimum combinations of two goods that the consumer would choose as the price of one good changes, while money income and the price of the other good remain constant.

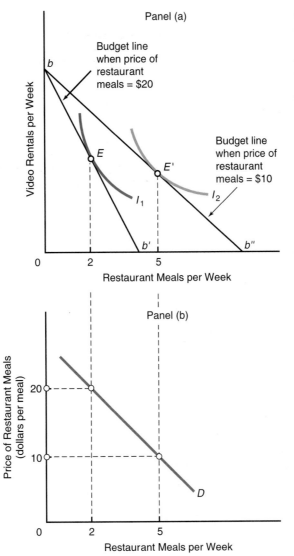

FIGURE E-9

Deriving the Demand Curve

In panel (a), we show the effects of a decrease in the price of restaurant meals from $20 to $10. At $20, the highest indifference curve touches the budget line *bb'* at point *E*. The quantity of restaurant meals consumed is two. We transfer this combination—price, $20; quantity demanded, 2—down to panel (b). Next we decrease the price of restaurant meals to $10. This generates a new budget line, or constraint, which is *bb''*. Consumer optimum is now at *E'*. The optimum quantity of restaurant meals demanded at a price of $10 is five. We transfer this point—price, $10; quantity demanded, 5—down to panel (b). When we connect these two points, we have a demand curve, *D*, for restaurant meals.

APPENDIX SUMMARY

1. Along an indifference curve, the consumer experiences equal levels of satisfaction. That is to say, along any indifference curve, every combination of the two goods in question yields exactly the same level of satisfaction.
2. Indifference curves usually slope downward and are usually convex to the origin.
3. To measure the marginal rate of substitution, we find out how much of one good has to be given up in order to allow the consumer to consume one more unit of the other good while still remaining on the same indifference curve. The marginal rate of substitution falls as one moves down an indifference curve.
4. Indifference curves represent preferences. A budget constraint represents opportunities—how much can be purchased with a given level of income. Consumer optimum is obtained when the highest indifference curve is just tangent to the budget constraint line; at

that point, the consumer reaches the highest feasible indifference curve.

5. When income increases, the budget constraint shifts outward to the right, parallel to the previous budget constraint line.

6. As income increases, the consumer optimum moves up to higher and higher indifference curves. When

we connect those points with a line, we derive the income-consumption curve.

7. As the price of one good decreases, the budget line rotates. When we connect the tangency points of the highest indifference curves to these new budget lines, we derive the price-consumption curve.

PROBLEMS

(Answers to the odd-numbered problems appear at the back of the book.)

E-1. Suppose that a consumer prefers *A* to *B* and *B* to *C* but insists that she also prefers *C* to *A*. Explain the logical problem here.

E-2. Suppose that you are indifferent among the following three combinations of food (*f*) and drink (*d*): 1*f* and 10*d*, 2*f* and 7*d*, 3*f* and 2*d*. Calculate the marginal rate of substitution in consumption between the two goods. Does the substitution of the third *f* imply a greater sacrifice of *d* than the second did?

E-3. Construct a budget line from the following information: nominal income of $100 per week; price of beef, P_b, $2 per pound; price of shelter, P_s, $20 per week; all income is spent on beef and shelter. Suppose that your money income remains constant, the price of beef doubles to $4 per pound, and the price of housing falls to $10 per week. Draw the new budget line. Are you now better off or worse off? What do you need to know before deciding?

E-4. Given the following three combinations of goods, $A = 3x + 4y$, $B = 4x + 6y$, and $C = 5x + 4y$, answer the following questions:

   a. Is any one bundle preferred to the other two?
   b. Could a consumer possibly find *B* and *C* to be equally acceptable? How about *A* and *C*?

E-5. Calculate the marginal rate of substitution of burritos for yogurt for the following consumer's indifference schedule:

Servings of Yogurt per Week	Burritos per Week
10	1
6	2
3	3
1	4

E-6. Assume that you are consuming only yogurt (*Y*) and gymnasium exercise (*G*). Each serving of yogurt costs $4, and each visit to the gym costs $8. Given your food and exercise budget, you consume 15 servings of yogurt and five visits to the gym each week. One day, the price of yogurt falls to $3 per serving and the price of gym visits increases to $10. Now you buy 20 servings of yogurt and four gym visits per week.

   a. Draw the old and new budget constraints, and show the two equilibrium bundles of yogurt servings and visits to the gym.
   b. What is your weekly budget for food and exercise?

E-7. Explain why each of the following statements is or is not consistent with our assumptions about consumer preferences.

   a. I can't decide whether to go abroad this summer or to stay at home.
   b. That is mine. You cannot have it. There is nothing you can do to make me change my mind.
   c. I love hot pretzels with mustard at football games. If I had my way, I would never stop eating them.

Europeans living in major cities have used subways most of their lives, whereas most Americans have never used the subway. The reason, of course, is that few subway systems exist in America. The city with the most extensive subway system is New York. The New York City subway has rarely been known for its cleanliness or safety. Transit authorities in that city did, however, make a concerted effort to clean it up as well as to make it safer. Subway ridership reached its highest level in 21 years in November 1995. The very next month, however, ridership fell by nearly 4 million, compared to December a year earlier. What happened in New York City? To understand this issue, you need to know more about how people respond to changing prices.

PREVIEW QUESTIONS

1. How is total revenue related to the price elasticity of demand?
2. What are the determinants of the price elasticity of demand?
3. What is the income elasticity of demand?
4. What is the price elasticity of supply?

Did You Know That . . . the government predicted it would raise $6 million per year in new revenues from a new 10 percent luxury tax on private airplane and yacht sales a few years ago, but it actually collected only $53,000? How can that be? The answer lies in understanding the relationship between the quantities that people demand at lower prices relative to the quantities that people demand at higher prices. The year during which the 10 percent luxury tax was imposed also saw expensive new yacht sales fall to almost nothing. Clearly, even rich people respond to rising prices, which in this case were caused by a new government tax.

It is not only the government that has to worry about how individuals respond to rising prices; it is perhaps even more important that all businesses take into account consumer response to changing prices. If McDonald's lowers its prices by 10 percent, will fast-food consumers respond by buying so many more Big Macs that the company's revenues will rise? At the other end of the spectrum, can Rolls Royce dealers "get away" with a 2 percent increase in prices? Otherwise stated, will Rolls Royce purchasers respond so little to the relatively small increase in price that the total revenues received for Rolls Royce sales will not fall and may actually rise? The only way to answer these questions is to know how responsive people in the real world will be to changes in prices. Economists have a special name for price responsiveness—*elasticity,* which is the subject of this chapter.

PRICE ELASTICITY

To begin to understand what elasticity is all about, just keep in mind that it means "responsiveness" or "stretchiness." Here we are concerned with the price elasticity of demand and the price elasticity of supply. We wish to know the extent to which a change in the price of, say, petroleum products will cause the quantity demanded and the quantity supplied to change, other things held constant. Let's restrict our discussion at first to the demand side.

Price Elasticity of Demand

We will formally define the **price elasticity of demand,** which we will label E_p, as follows:

$$E_p = \frac{\text{percentage change in quantity demanded}}{\text{percentage change in price}}$$

Price elasticity of demand (E_p)
The responsiveness of the quantity demanded of a commodity to changes in its price; defined as the percentage change in quantity demanded divided by the percentage change in price.

What will price elasticity of demand tell us? It will tell us the relative amount by which the quantity demanded will change in response to a change in the price of a particular good.

Consider an example in which a 10 percent rise in the price of oil leads to a reduction in quantity demanded of only 1 percent. Putting these numbers into the formula, we find that the price elasticity of demand for oil in this case equals the percentage change in quantity demanded divided by the percentage change in price, or

$$E_p = \frac{-1\%}{+10\%} = -.1$$

An elasticity of $-.1$ means that a 1 percent *increase* in the price would lead to a mere .1 percent *decrease* in the quantity demanded. If you were now told, in contrast, that the price elasticity of demand for oil was -1, you would know that a 1 percent increase in the price of oil would lead to a 1 percent decrease in the quantity demanded.

Relative Quantities Only. Notice that in our elasticity formula, we talk about *percentage* changes in quantity demanded divided by *percentage* changes in price. We are therefore not interested in the absolute changes, only in relative amounts. This means that it doesn't matter if we measure price changes in terms of cents, dollars, or hundreds of dollars. It also doesn't matter whether we measure quantity changes in ounces, grams, or pounds. The percentage change will be independent of the units chosen.

POLICY EXAMPLE
How Will a $1.50-per-Pack Tax Affect Your Smoking?

As part of his "war on tobacco," President Clinton announced a centerpiece $1.50-per-pack tax increase for cigarettes. He declared that he wanted to cut youth smoking in half by the year 2005. One researcher at the University of Illinois, Professor Frank Chaloup, had already estimated the price responsiveness of teens to cigarette price increases: a 10 percent increase in the price of cigarettes causes a 6.7 percent decrease in the number of teens who smoke. So a $1.50 tax hike, which would increase the average nationwide price of a pack of cigarettes by 80 percent, should lead to a reduction of more than 50 percent in teen smoking.

FOR CRITICAL ANALYSIS: When Canada increased tobacco taxes by more than 250 percent, bootlegging from abroad—especially the United States—became a serious problem. What does Canada's experience tell us about the proposed $1.50-per-pack increase in the U.S. tax on cigarettes? ●

Always Negative. The law of demand states that quantity demanded is *inversely* related to the relative price. An increase in the price of a good leads to a decrease in the quantity demanded. If a decrease in the relative price of a good should occur, the quantity demanded would increase by a certain percentage. The point is that price elasticity of demand will always be negative. By convention, *we will ignore the minus sign in our discussion from this point on.*

Basically, the greater the *absolute* price elasticity of demand (disregarding sign), the greater the demand responsiveness to relative price changes—a small change in price has a great impact on quantity demanded. The smaller the absolute price elasticity of demand, the smaller the demand responsiveness to relative price changes—a large change in price has little effect on quantity demanded.

CONCEPTS IN BRIEF

- Elasticity is a measure of the price responsiveness of the quantity demanded and quantity supplied.

- The price elasticity of demand is equal to the percentage change in quantity demanded divided by the percentage change in price.

- Price elasticity of demand is calculated in terms of percentage changes in quantity demanded and in price. Thus it is expressed as a unitless, dimensionless number.

- The law of demand states that quantity demanded and price are inversely related. Therefore, the price elasticity of demand is always negative, because an increase in price will lead to a decrease in quantity demanded and a decrease in price will lead to an increase in quantity demanded. By convention, we ignore the negative sign in discussions of the price elasticity of demand.

Calculating Elasticity

To calculate the price elasticity of demand, we have to compute percentage changes in quantity demanded and in relative price. To obtain the percentage change in quantity demanded, we divide the change in the quantity demanded by the original quantity demanded:

$$\frac{\text{Change in quantity demanded}}{\text{Original quantity demanded}}$$

To find the percentage change in price, we divide the change in price by the original price:

$$\frac{\text{Change in price}}{\text{Original price}}$$

There is an arithmetic problem, though, when we calculate percentage changes in this manner. The percentage change, say, from 2 to 3—50 percent—is not the same as the percentage change from 3 to 2—$33\frac{1}{3}$ percent. In other words, it makes a difference where you start. One way out of this dilemma is simply to use average values.

To compute the price elasticity of demand, we need to deal with the average change in quantity demanded caused by the average change in price. That means that we take the average of the two prices and the two quantities over the range we are considering and compare the change with these averages. For relatively small changes in price, the formula for computing the price elasticity of demand then becomes

$$E_p = \frac{\text{change in quantity}}{\text{sum of quantities}/2} \div \frac{\text{change in price}}{\text{sum of prices}/2}$$

We can rewrite this more simply if we do two things: (1) We can let Q_1 and Q_2 equal the two different quantities demanded before and after the price change and let P_1 and P_2 equal the two different prices. (2) Because we will be dividing a percentage by a percentage, we simply use the ratio, or the decimal form, of the percentages. Therefore,

$$E_p = \frac{\Delta Q}{(Q_1 + Q_2)/2} \div \frac{\Delta P}{(P_1 + P_2)/2}$$

where the Greek letter Δ stands for "change in."

INTERNATIONAL EXAMPLE
The Price Elasticity of Demand for Newspapers

Newspaper owners are always seeking to increase their paper's circulation, not because they want the revenue generated from the sales of the paper, but because the larger the circulation, the more the newspaper can charge for its advertising space. The source of most of a paper's revenues—and profits—comes from its advertisers.

One newspaper owner, Rupert Murdoch, ran an experiment to see how high he could boost sales of a particular newspaper by lowering its price. For one day, he lowered the price of the British daily paper *Today* from 25 pence to 10 pence. According to London's *Financial Times,* the sales of *Today* almost doubled that day, increasing the circulation from

---

THINKING CRITICALLY ABOUT THE MEDIA

"If They Doubled the Price, We'd Still Drink Coffee"

Every time there is a frost in Brazil, the price of coffee beans rises, and everyone fears a big rise in the price of coffee. Members of the media interview coffee drinkers and ask how they will respond to the higher prices. Not surprisingly, even when coffee prices soared 150 percent a few years ago, some interviewees said they had to have their cup of coffee no matter what. But if that were true for all coffee drinkers, why don't coffee prices rise as much as bean prices? If what coffee drinkers tell us were really true, their price elasticity of demand would be zero, and the retail price of coffee could skyrocket. But it never does. The truth is, interviewing coffee drinkers (or other consumers) about intentions tells us little. We need to examine the change in total market quantity demanded after an increase in price. The data make it clear: At least some people drink less coffee when the relative price goes up.

590,000 to 1.05 million copies. We can estimate the price elasticity of demand for *Today* by using the formula presented earlier (under the assumption, of course, that all other things were held constant):

$$E_p = \frac{\Delta Q}{(Q_1 + Q_2)/2} \div \frac{\Delta P}{(P_1 + P_2)/2}$$

$$= \frac{1,050,000 - 590,000}{(590,000 + 1,050,000)/2} \div \frac{25 \text{ pence} - 10 \text{ pence}}{(10 \text{ pence} + 25 \text{ pence})/2}$$

$$= \frac{460,000}{820,000} \div \frac{15 \text{ pence}}{17.5 \text{ pence}} = .66$$

The price elasticity of demand of .66 means that a 1 percent decrease in price will lead to a .66 percent increase in quantity demanded.

FOR CRITICAL ANALYSIS: Would the estimated price elasticity of the Today *newspaper have been different if we had* not *used the average-values formula? How?* •

PRICE ELASTICITY RANGES

We have names for the varying ranges of price elasticities, depending on whether a 1 percent change in price elicits more or less than a 1 percent change in the quantity demanded.

Elastic demand
A demand relationship in which a given percentage change in price will result in a larger percentage change in quantity demanded. Total expenditures and price changes are inversely related in the elastic region of the demand curve.

Unit elasticity of demand
A demand relationship in which the quantity demanded changes exactly in proportion to the change in price. Total expenditures are invariant to price changes in the unit-elastic region of the demand curve.

Inelastic demand
A demand relationship in which a given percentage change in price will result in a less than proportionate percentage change in the quantity demanded. Total expenditures and price are directly related in the inelastic region of the demand curve.

1. *Elastic demand.* We say that a good has an **elastic demand** whenever the price elasticity of demand is greater than 1. A 1 percent change in price causes a greater than a 1 percent change in the quantity demanded.
2. *Unit elasticity of demand.* In a situation of **unit elasticity of demand,** a 1 percent change in price causes a response of exactly a 1 percent change in the quantity demanded.
3. *Inelastic demand.* In a situation of **inelastic demand,** a 1 percent change in price causes a response of less than a 1 percent change in the quantity demanded. The most extreme inelastic demand is *perfectly inelastic;* no matter what the price, the quantity demanded remains the same, so the price elasticity of demand is zero.

When we say that a commodity's demand is elastic, we are indicating that consumers are relatively responsive to changes in price. When we say that a commodity's demand is inelastic, we are indicating that its consumers are relatively unresponsive to price changes. When economists say that demand is inelastic, it does not mean that quantity demanded is totally unresponsive to price changes. Remember, the law of demand suggests that there will be some responsiveness in quantity demanded to a price change. The question is how much. That's what elasticity attempts to determine.

Extreme Elasticities

There are two extremes in price elasticities of demand. One extreme represents total unresponsiveness of quantity demanded to price changes, which is referred to as

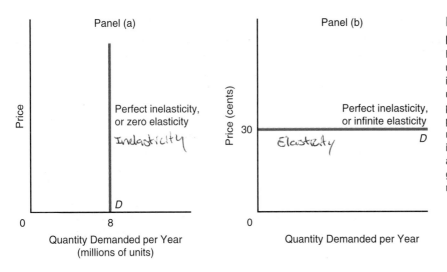

FIGURE 20-1

Extreme Price Elasticities
In panel (a), we show complete price unresponsiveness. The demand curve is vertical at the quantity of 8 million units per year. This means that the price elasticity of demand is zero. In panel (b), we show complete price responsiveness. At a price of 30 cents, in this example, consumers will demand an unlimited quantity of the particular good in question. This is a case of infinite price elasticity of demand.

perfectly inelastic demand, or zero elasticity. The other represents total responsiveness, which is referred to as, infinitely, or **perfectly elastic demand.**

We show perfect inelasticity in panel (a) of Figure 20-1. Notice that the quantity demanded per year is 8 million units, no matter what the price. Hence for any percentage price change, the quantity demanded will remain the same, and thus the change in the quantity demanded will be zero. Look back at our formula for computing elasticity. If the change in the quantity demanded is zero, the numerator is also zero, and a nonzero number divided into zero results in an answer of zero too. Hence there is perfect inelasticity. At the opposite extreme is the situation depicted in panel (b) of Figure 20-1. Here we show that at a price of 30 cents, an unlimited quantity will be demanded. At a price that is only slightly above 30 cents, no quantity will be demanded. There is complete, or infinite, responsiveness here, and hence we call the demand schedule in panel (b) infinitely elastic.

Perfectly inelastic demand
A demand that exhibits zero responsiveness to price changes; no matter what the price is, the quantity demanded remains the same.

Perfectly elastic demand
A demand that has the characteristic that even the slightest increase in price will lead to zero quantity demanded.

CONCEPTS IN BRIEF

• One extreme elasticity occurs when a demand curve is vertical. It has zero price elasticity of demand; it is completely inelastic.

• Another extreme elasticity occurs when a demand curve is horizontal. It has completely elastic demand; its price elasticity of demand is infinite.

ELASTICITY AND TOTAL REVENUES

Suppose that you are in charge of the pricing decision for a cellular telephone service company. How would you know when it is best to raise or not to raise prices? The answer depends in part on the effect of your pricing decision on total revenues, or the total receipts of your company. (The rest of the equation is, of course, your cost structure, a subject we examine in Chapter 22.) It is commonly thought that the way to increase total receipts is to increase price per unit. But is this always the case? Is it possible that a rise in price per unit

For Addicts, Price Does Not Matter?

Both the media and the commonsense definition of a drug addict is a person who has to get a fix "at any price." Consequently, numerous media stories abound about how addicts will do anything they must to get their fixes. The implication is that the price elasticity of demand by addicts for a particular drug is zero—that their demand curves are vertical. There is a problem with this analysis, though. Everyone, addicts included, faces a budget constraint. Consequently, it is impossible for anyone's demand curve to be vertical at *all* prices because he or she could not spend an amount greater than his or her budget constraint.

could lead to a decrease in total revenues? The answers to these questions depend on the price elasticity of demand.

Let's look at Figure 20-2 on page 446. In panel (a), column 1 shows the price of cellular telephone service in dollars per minute, and column 2 represents billions of minutes per year. In column 3, we multiply column 1 times column 2 to derive total revenue because total revenue is always equal to the number of units (quantity) sold times the price per unit, and in column 4, we calculate values of elasticity. Notice what happens to total revenues throughout the schedule. They rise steadily as the price rises from 10 cents to 50 cents per minute; but when the price rises further to 60 cents per minute, total revenues remain constant at $3 billion. At prices per minute higher than 60 cents, total revenues fall as price increases. Indeed, if prices are above 60 cents per minute, total revenues can be increased only by *cutting* prices, not by raising them.

Labeling Elasticity

The relationship between price and quantity on the demand schedule is given in columns 1 and 2 of panel (a) in Figure 20-2. In panel (b), the demand curve, *D,* representing that schedule is drawn. In panel (c), the total revenue curve representing the data in column 3 is drawn. Notice first the level of these curves at small quantities. The demand curve is at a maximum height, but total revenue is zero, which makes sense according to this demand schedule—at a price of $1.10 and above, no units will be purchased, and therefore total revenue will be zero. As price is lowered, we travel down the demand curve, and total revenues increase until price is 60 cents per minute, remain constant from 60 cents to 50 cents per minute, and then fall at lower unit prices. Corresponding to those three sections, demand is elastic, unit-elastic, and inelastic. Hence we have three relationships among the three types of price elasticity and total revenues.

1. *Elastic demand.* A negative relationship exists between small changes in price and changes in total revenues. That is to say, if price is lowered, total revenues will rise when the firm faces demand that is elastic, and if it raises price, total revenues will fall. Consider another example. If the price of Diet Coke were raised by 25 percent and the price of all other soft drinks remained constant, the quantity demanded of Diet Coke would probably fall dramatically. The decrease in quantity demanded due to the increase in the price of Diet Coke would lead in this example to a reduction in the total revenues of the Coca-Cola Company. Therefore, if demand is elastic, price and total revenues will move in *opposite* directions.
2. *Unit-elastic demand.* Changes in price do not change total revenues. When the firm is facing demand that is unit-elastic, if it increases price, total revenues will not change; if it decreases price, total revenues will not change either.
3. *Inelastic demand.* A positive relationship exists between changes in price and total revenues. When the firm is facing demand that is inelastic, if it raises price, total revenues will go up; if it lowers price, total revenues will fall. Consider another example. You have just invented a cure for the common cold that has been approved by the Food and Drug Administration for sale to the public. You are not sure what price you should charge, so you start out with a price of $1 per pill. You sell 20 million pills at that price over a year. The next year, you decide to raise the price by 25 percent, to $1.25. The number of pills you sell drops to 18 million per year. The price increase of 25 percent

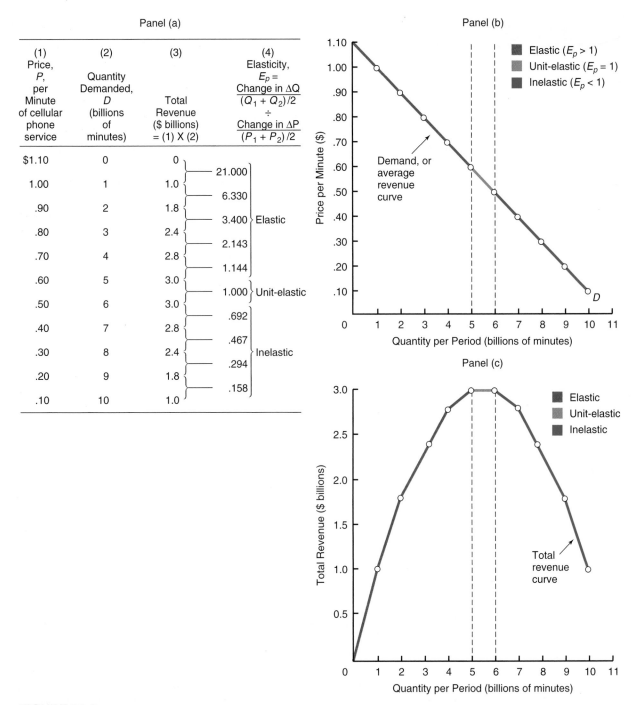

FIGURE 20-2

The Relationship Between Price Elasticity of Demand and Total Revenues for Cellular Phone Service

In panel (a), we show the elastic, unit-elastic, and inelastic sections of the demand schedule according to whether a reduction in price increases total revenues, causes them to remain constant, or causes them to decrease, respectively. In panel (b), we show these regions graphically on the demand curve. In panel (c), we show them on the total revenue curve.

has led to a 10 percent decrease in quantity demanded. Your total revenues, however, will rise to $22.5 million because of the price increase. We therefore conclude that if demand is inelastic, price and total revenues move in the *same* direction.

The elastic, unit-elastic, and inelastic areas of the demand curve are shown in Figure 20-2. For prices from $1.10 per minute of cellular phone time to 60 cents per minute, as price decreases, total revenues rise from zero to $3 billion. Demand is price-elastic. When price changes from 60 cents to 50 cents, however, total revenues remain constant at $3 billion; demand is unit-elastic. Finally, when price falls from 50 cents to 10 cents, total revenues decrease from $3 billion to $1 billion; demand is inelastic. In panels (b) and (c) of Figure 20-2, we have labeled the sections of the demand curve accordingly, and we have also shown how total revenues first rise, then remain constant, and finally fall.

The relationship between price elasticity of demand and total revenues brings together some important microeconomic concepts. Total revenues, as we have noted, are the product of price per unit times number of units sold. The law of demand states that along a given demand curve, price and quantity changes will move in opposite directions: One increases as the other decreases. Consequently, what happens to the product of price times quantity depends on which of the opposing changes exerts a greater force on total revenues. But this is just what price elasticity of demand is designed to measure—responsiveness of quantity demanded to a change in price. The relationship between price elasticity of demand and total revenues is summarized in Table 20-1.

TABLE 20-1

Relationship Between Price Elasticity of Demand and Total Revenues

Price Elasticity of Demand		Effect of Price Change on Total Revenues (TR)	
		Price Decrease	Price Increase
Inelastic	$(E_p < 1)$	TR ↓	TR ↑
Unit-elastic	$(E_p = 1)$	No change in TR	No change in TR
Elastic	$(E_p > 1)$	TR ↑	TR ↓

INTERNATIONAL EXAMPLE
A Pricing Decision at Disneyland Paris

Several years after it opened with great fanfare, the $4 billion investment in Disneyland Paris (formerly called EuroDisney) was in trouble. In an attempt to improve profits (actually, decrease losses), Disney management decided to lower prices starting in the summer of 1995. Entrance fees during peak periods (April 1 to October 1) dropped from 250 francs (about $50) to 195 francs (about $40). Was this 22 percent reduction in ticket prices a good management strategy for Disney officials? That depends in part on what happened to total revenues. As it turned out, park attendance increased by 700,000 visitors. Thus total revenues increased by more than 22 percent, indicating that the demand for Disneyland Paris is elastic in the price range between $40 to $50.

FOR CRITICAL ANALYSIS: What other factors may have affected attendance at Disneyland Paris? ●

CONCEPTS IN BRIEF

- Price elasticity of demand is related to total revenues (and total consumer expenditures).
- When demand is *elastic,* the change in price elicits a change in total revenues (and total consumer expenditures) in the direction opposite that of the price change.
- When demand is *unit-elastic,* a change in price elicits no change in total revenues (or in total consumer expenditures).
- When demand is *inelastic,* a change in price elicits a change in total revenues (and in consumer expenditures) in the same direction as the price change.

Exercise 20.1
Visit www.econtoday.com for more about food price elasticity.

DETERMINANTS OF THE PRICE ELASTICITY OF DEMAND

We have learned how to calculate the price elasticity of demand. We know that theoretically, it ranges numerically from zero, completely inelastic, to infinity, completely elastic. What we would like to do now is come up with a list of the determinants of the price elasticity of demand. The price elasticity of demand for a particular commodity at any price depends, at a minimum, on the following:

1. The existence, number, and quality of substitutes
2. The percentage of a consumer's total budget devoted to purchases of that commodity
3. The length of time allowed for adjustment to changes in the price of the commodity

Existence of Substitutes

The closer the substitutes for a particular commodity and the more substitutes there are, the greater will be its price elasticity of demand. At the limit, if there is a perfect substitute, the elasticity of demand for the commodity will be infinity. Thus even the slightest increase in the commodity's price will cause an enormous reduction in the quantity demanded: quantity demanded will fall to zero. We are really talking about two goods that the consumer believes are exactly alike and equally desirable, like dollar bills whose only difference is serial numbers. When we talk about less extreme examples, we can only speak in terms of the number and the similarity of substitutes that are available. Thus we will find that the more narrowly we define a good, the closer and greater will be the number of substitutes available. For example, the demand for a Diet Coke may be highly elastic because consumers can switch to Diet Pepsi. The demand for diet drinks in general, however, is relatively less elastic because there are fewer substitutes.

Share of Budget

We know that the greater the percentage of a total budget spent on the commodity, the greater the person's price elasticity of demand for that commodity. The demand for pepper is thought to be very inelastic merely because individuals spend so little on it relative to their total budgets. In contrast, the demand for things such as transportation and housing is thought to be far more elastic because they occupy a large part of people's budgets—changes in their prices cannot be ignored so easily without sacrificing a lot of other alternative goods that could be purchased.

Consider a numerical example. A household earns $40,000 a year. It purchases $4 of pepper per year and $4,000 of transportation services. Now consider the spending power of this family when the price of pepper and the price of transportation both go up by 100 percent. If the household buys the same amount of pepper, it will now spend $8. It will thus have to reduce other expenditures by $4. This $4 represents only .01 percent of the entire household budget. By contrast, a doubling of transportation costs requires that the family spend $8,000, or $4,000 more on transportation, if it is to purchase the same quantity. That increased expenditure on transportation of $4,000 represents 10 percent of total expenditures that must be switched from other purchases. We would therefore predict that the household will react differently to the doubling of prices for pepper than it will for transportation. It will buy almost the same amount of pepper but will spend significantly less on transportation.

Time for Adjustment

Exercise 20.2
Visit www.econtoday.com for more about demand for wine.

When the price of a commodity changes and that price change persists, more people will learn about it. Further, consumers will be better able to revise their consumption patterns the longer the time period they have to do so. And in fact, the longer the time they do take, the less costly it will be for them to engage in this revision of consumption patterns. Consider a price decrease. The longer the price decrease persists, the greater will be the number of new uses that consumers will discover for the particular commodity, and the greater will be the number of new users of that particular commodity.

It is possible to make a very strong statement about the relationship between the price elasticity of demand and the time allowed for adjustment:

> **The longer any price change persists, the greater the elasticity of demand, other things held constant. Elasticity of demand is greater in the long run than in the short run.**

Let's take an example. Suppose that the price of electricity goes up 50 percent. How do you adjust in the short run? You can turn the lights off more often, you can stop using the stereo as much as you do, and so on. Otherwise it's very difficult to cut back on your consumption of electricity. In the long run, though, you can devise methods to reduce your consumption. Instead of using electric heaters, the next time you have a house built you will install gas heaters. Instead of using an electric stove, the next time you move you will have a gas stove installed. You will purchase fluorescent bulbs because they use less electricity. The more time you have to think about it, the more ways you will find to cut your electricity consumption. We would expect, therefore, that the short-run demand curve for electricity would be relatively inelastic (in the price range around P_e), as demonstrated by D_1 in Figure 20-3 on page 450. However, the long-run demand curve may exhibit much more elasticity (in the neighborhood of P_e), as demonstrated by D_3. Indeed, we can think of an entire family of demand curves such as those depicted in that figure. The short-run demand curve is for the period when there is no time for adjustment. As more time is allowed, the demand curve goes first to D_2 and then all the way to D_3. Thus in the neighborhood of P_e, elasticity differs for each of these curves. It is greater for the less steep curves (but, slope alone does not measure elasticity for the entire curve).

How to Define the Short Run and the Long Run. We've mentioned the short run and the long run. Is the short run one week, two weeks, one month, two months? Is the long run three years, four years, five years? The answer is that there is no single answer. What we mean by the long run is the period of time necessary for consumers to make a full adjustment to a given price change, all other things held constant. In the case of the demand for electricity, the long run will be however long it takes consumers to switch over to cheaper sources of heating, to buy houses that are more energy-efficient, to purchase manufactured appliances that are more energy-efficient, and so on. The long-run elasticity of

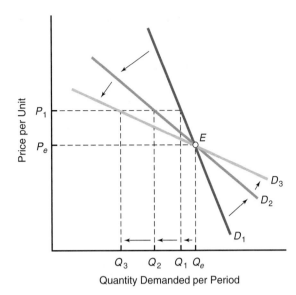

Price per Unit (vertical axis)

P_1, P_e, E, D_3, D_2, D_1

Q_3 Q_2 Q_1 Q_e

Quantity Demanded per Period

FIGURE 20-3
Short-Run and Long-Run Price Elasticity of Demand
Consider an equilibrium situation in which the market price is P_e and the quantity demanded is Q_e. Then there is a price increase to P_1. In the short run, as evidenced by the demand curve D_1, we move from equilibrium quantity demanded, Q_e, to Q_1. After more time is allowed for adjustment, the demand curve rotates at original price P_e to D_2. Quantity demanded falls again, now to Q_2. After even more time is allowed for adjustment, the demand curve rotates at price P_e to D_3. At the higher price P_1, in the long run, the quantity demanded falls all the way to Q_3.

demand for electricity therefore relates to a period of at least several years. The short run—by default—is any period less than the long run.

EXAMPLE
What Do Real-World Price Elasticities of Demand Look Like?

In Table 20-2, we present demand elasticities for selected goods. None of them is zero, and the largest is 3.8—a far cry from infinity. Remember that even though we are leaving off the negative sign, there is an inverse relationship between price and quantity demanded,

TABLE 20-2
Demand Elasticity for Selected Goods
Here are estimated demand elasticities for selected goods. All of them are negative, although we omit the minus sign. We have given some estimates of the long-run price elasticities of demand. The long run is associated with the time necessary for consumers to adjust fully to any given price change.

Category	Estimated Elasticity	
	Short Run	Long Run
Lamb	2.65	—
Bread	.15	—
Tires and related items	.8	1.2
Auto repair and related services	1.4	2.4
Radio and television repair	.5	3.8
Legitimate theater and opera	.2	.31
Motion pictures	.87	3.7
Foreign travel by U.S. residents	.1	1.8
Taxicabs	.6	—
Local public transportation	.6	1.2
Intercity bus	.2	2.2
Electricity	.1	1.8
Jewelry and watches	.4	.6

and the minus sign is understood. Also remember that these elasticities represent averages over given price ranges. Choosing different price ranges would yield different elasticity estimates for these goods.

Economists have consistently found that estimated price elasticities of demand are greater in the long run than in the short run, as seen in Table 20-2. There you see, for example, in the far-right column that the long-run price elasticity of demand for tires and related items is 1.2, whereas the estimate for the short run is .8. Throughout the table, you see that all estimates of long-run price elasticities of demand exceed their short-run counterparts.

FOR CRITICAL ANALYSIS: Explain the intuitive reasoning behind the difference between long-run and short-run price elasticity of demand. ●

CROSS PRICE ELASTICITY OF DEMAND

In Chapter 3, we discussed the effect of a change in the price of one good on the demand for a related good. We defined substitutes and complements in terms of whether a reduction in the price of one caused a decrease or an increase, respectively, in the demand for the other. If the price of compact discs is held constant, the amount of CDs demanded (at any price) will certainly be influenced by the price of a close substitute such as audiocassettes. If the price of stereo speakers is held constant, the amount of stereo speakers demanded (at any price) will certainly be affected by changes in the price of stereo amplifiers.

What we now need to do is come up with a numerical measure of the price responsiveness of demand to the prices of related goods. This is called the **cross price elasticity of demand (E_{xy}),** which is defined as the percentage change in the demand for one good (a shift in the demand curve) divided by the percentage change in the price of the related good. In equation form, the cross price elasticity of demand for good X with good Y is

$$E_{xy} = \frac{\text{percentage change in demand for good X}}{\text{percentage change in price of good Y}}$$

Cross price elasticity of demand (E_{xy})
The percentage change in the demand for one good (holding its price constant) divided by the percentage change in the price of a related good.

Alternatively, the cross price elasticity of demand for good Y with good X would use the percentage change in the demand for good Y as the numerator and the percentage change in the price of good X as the denominator.

When two goods are substitutes, the cross price elasticity of demand will be positive. For example, when the price of margarine goes up, the demand for butter will rise too as consumers shift away from the now relatively more expensive margarine to butter. A producer of margarine could benefit from a numerical estimate of the cross price elasticity of demand between butter and margarine. For example, if the price of butter went up by 10 percent and the margarine producer knew that the cross price elasticity of demand was 1, the margarine producer could estimate that the demand for margarine would also go up by 10 percent at any given price. Plans for increasing margarine production could then be made.

When two related goods are complements, the cross price elasticity of demand will be negative (and we will not disregard the minus sign). For example, when the price of stereo amplifiers goes up, the demand for stereo speakers will fall. This is because as prices of amplifiers increase, the quantity of amplifiers demanded will naturally decrease. Because amplifiers and stereo speakers are often used together, the demand for speakers is likely to fall. Any manufacturer of stereo speakers must take this into account in making production plans.

If goods are completely unrelated, their cross price elasticity of demand will be zero.

Exercise 20.3
Visit www.econtoday.com for more about cross price elasticity.

LIBRARIES VERSUS THE INTERNET

A significant portion of property taxes in the United States goes for public libraries. Some policymakers argue that there is no longer any reason to subsidize public libraries. Fewer and fewer people are using libraries. Their substitute is the Internet. Anyone can use a variety of popular search engines to find out just about anything electronically. Furthermore, encyclopedias and other information sources are available on inexpensive CD-ROMs. On-line information services are also relatively cheap. Indeed, as the price of such services has fallen, the demand for traditional library services has decreased. No one has yet calculated the exact cross price elasticity of demand for traditional library services, but we know that the decrease in usage of such libraries has been significant.

FOR CRITICAL ANALYSIS: Compare your cost of using the library with the cost of using on-line information services. ●

INCOME ELASTICITY OF DEMAND

In Chapter 3, we discussed the determinants of demand. One of those determinants was income. Briefly, we can apply our understanding of elasticity to the relationship between changes in income and changes in demand. We measure the responsiveness of quantity demanded to income changes by the **income elasticity of demand (E_i):**

Income elasticity of demand (E_i)
The percentage change in demand for any good, holding its price constant, divided by the percentage change in income; the responsiveness of demand to changes in income, holding the good's relative price constant.

$$E_i = \frac{\text{percentage change in demand}}{\text{percentage change in income}}$$

holding relative price constant.

Income elasticity of demand refers to a *horizontal shift* in the demand curve in response to changes in income, whereas price elasticity of demand refers to a movement *along* the curve in response to price changes. Thus income elasticity of demand is calculated at a given price, and price elasticity of demand is calculated at a given income.

A simple example will demonstrate how income elasticity of demand can be computed. Table 20-3 gives the relevant data. The product in question is compact discs. We assume that the price of compact discs remains constant relative to other prices. In period 1, six CDs per month are purchased. Income per month is $400. In period 2, monthly income increases to $600, and the quantity of CDs demanded per month is increased to eight. We can apply the following calculation:

$$E_i = \frac{(8 - 6)/6}{(600 - 400)/400} = \frac{1/3}{1/2} = \frac{2}{3} = .667$$

Hence measured income elasticity of demand for CDs for the individual represented in this example is .667. Note that this holds only for the move from six CDs to eight CDs purchased per month. If the situation were reversed, with income decreasing from $600 to

TABLE 20-3			
How Income Affects		Number of CDs	
Quantity of CDs	Period	Demanded per Month	Income per Month
Demanded	1	6	$400
	2	8	600

$400 per month and CDs purchased dropping from eight to six CDs per month, the calculation becomes

$$E_i = \frac{(6-8)/8}{(400-600)/600} = \frac{-2/8}{-1/3} = \frac{-1/4}{-1/3} = \frac{3}{4} = .75$$

In this case, the measured income elasticity of demand is equal to .75.

To get the same income elasticity of demand over the same range of values regardless of direction of change (increase or decrease), we can use the same formula that we used in computing the price elasticity of demand. When doing so, we have:

$$E_i = \frac{\text{change in quantity}}{\text{sum of quantities}/2} \div \frac{\text{change in income}}{\text{sum of incomes}/2}$$

You have just been introduced to three types of elasticities. Two of them—the price elasticity of demand (E_p), and income elasticity (E_i)—are the two most important factors in influencing the quantity demanded for most goods. Reasonably accurate estimates of these can go a long way toward making accurate forecasts of demand for goods or services.

EXAMPLE
Traffic Fatalities, Rising Incomes, and Alcohol Consumption

Economist Christopher Ruhm of the National Bureau of Economic Research discovered that the income elasticity of demand for alcoholic beverages is significant. He found that over a 14-year period, a $1,250 rise in real per capita personal income (expressed in 1996 dollars) increased alcoholic beverage consumption by 1.2 percent. There were also resulting increases in traffic fatalities.

FOR CRITICAL ANALYSIS: A common view is that people turn to drink in times of economic distress. What do the data tell us? •

CONCEPTS IN BRIEF

- Some determinants of price elasticity of demand are (1) the existence, number, and quality of substitutes, (2) the share of the total budget spent on the good in question, and (3) the length of time allowed for adjustment to a change in prices.
- Cross elasticity of demand measures one good's demand responsiveness to another's price changes. For substitutes, it is positive; for complements, it is negative.
- Income elasticity of demand tells you by what percentage demand will change for a particular percentage change in income.

ELASTICITY OF SUPPLY

Price elasticity of supply (E_s)
The responsiveness of the quantity supplied of a commodity to a change in its price; the percentage change in quantity supplied divided by the percentage change in price.

The **price elasticity of supply (E_s)** is defined similarly to the price elasticity of demand. Supply elasticities are generally positive; this is because at higher prices, larger quantities will generally be forthcoming from suppliers. The definition of the price elasticity of supply is as follows:

$$E_s = \frac{\text{percentage change in quantity supplied}}{\text{percentage change in price}}$$

Classifying Supply Elasticities

Just as with demand, there are different types of supply elasticities. They are similar in definition to the types of demand elasticities.

If a 1 percent increase in price elicits a greater than 1 percent increase in the quantity supplied, we say that at the particular price in question on the supply schedule, *supply is elastic.* The most extreme elastic supply is called **perfectly elastic supply**—the slightest reduction in price will cause quantity supplied to fall to zero.

If, conversely, a 1 percent increase in price elicits a less than 1 percent increase in the quantity supplied, we refer to that as an *inelastic supply.* The most extreme inelastic supply is called **perfectly inelastic supply**—no matter what the price, the quantity supplied remains the same.

If the percentage change in the quantity supplied is just equal to the percentage change in the price, we call this *unit-elastic supply.*

We show in Figure 20-4 two supply schedules, *S* and *S′.* You can tell at a glance, without reading the labels, which one is infinitely elastic and which one is perfectly inelastic. As you might expect, most supply schedules exhibit elasticities that are somewhere between zero and infinity.

Perfectly elastic supply
A supply characterized by a reduction in quantity supplied to zero when there is the slightest decrease in price.

Perfectly inelastic supply
A supply for which quantity supplied remains constant, no matter what happens to price.

Price Elasticity of Supply and Length of Time for Adjustment

We pointed out earlier that the longer the time period allowed for adjustment, the greater the price elasticity of demand. It turns out that the same proposition applies to supply. The longer the time for adjustment, the more elastic the supply curve. Consider why this is true:

1. The longer the time allowed for adjustment, the more firms are able to figure out ways to increase (or decrease) production in an industry.
2. The longer the time allowed for adjustment, the more resources can flow into (or out of) an industry through expansion (or contraction) of existing firms.

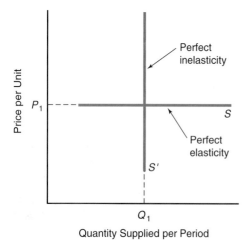

FIGURE 20-4

The Extremes in Supply Curves
Here we have drawn two extremes of supply schedules: *S* is a perfectly elastic supply curve; *S′* is a perfectly inelastic one. In the former, an unlimited quantity will be supplied at price P_1. In the latter, no matter what the price, the quantity supplied will be Q_1. An example of *S′* might be the supply curve for fresh fish on the morning the boats come in.

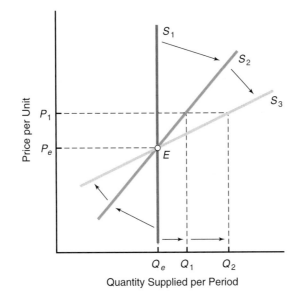

FIGURE 20-5

Short-Run and Long-Run Price Elasticity of Supply

Consider a situation in which the price is P_e and the quantity supplied is Q_e. In the immediate run, we hypothesize a vertical supply curve, S_1. With the price increase to P_1, therefore, there will be no change in the short run in quantity supplied; it will remain at Q_e. Given some time for adjustment, the supply curve will rotate to S_2. The new amount supplied will increase to Q_1. The long-run supply curve is shown by S_3. The amount supplied again increases to Q_2.

We therefore talk about short-run and long-run price elasticities of supply. The short run is defined as the time period during which full adjustment has not yet taken place. The long run is the time period during which firms have been able to adjust fully to the change in price.

Consider an increase in the price of housing. In the immediate run, when there is no time allowed for any adjustment, the amount of housing offered for rent or for sale is perfectly inelastic. However, as more time is allowed for adjustment, current owners of the housing stock can find ways to increase the amount of housing they will offer for rent from given buildings. The owner of a large house can decide, for example, to have two children move into one room so that a "new" extra bedroom can be rented out. This can also be done by the owner of a large house who decides to move into an apartment and rent each floor of the house to a separate family. Thus the quantity of housing supplied will increase. With more time, landlords will find it profitable to build new rental units.

We can show a whole set of supply curves similar to the ones we generated for demand. As Figure 20-5 shows, when nothing can be done in the immediate run, the supply curve is vertical, S_1. As more time is allowed for adjustment, the supply curve rotates to S_2 and then to S_3, becoming more elastic as it rotates.

INTERNATIONAL EXAMPLE
French Truffle Production Takes a Nosedive

Some of the best truffles in the world come from the seven *départements* (counties) in the middle of France that make up the Périgord region. Black truffles are often called "black diamonds" because they are so expensive and also because they have a faceted skin. Their official name is *Tuber melanosporum.* Ranging in size from that of a hazelnut to that of a baseball, truffles are sliced fine and used in cooking as a pungent addition to many refined dishes. Their prices range from $250 to $500 a pound wholesale to as much as $1,000 a pound retail. Yet things are not well in the French truffle industry. The Chinese have started exporting their version of truffles, considered inferior by the French but popular nonetheless in the open market. The average price for French-grown truffles in 1996 dropped by 30 percent. Many French farmers, fed up with lower prices, are simply giving up on truffles. That same year, French production decreased by 25 percent. Hence the estimated short-run price elasticity of supply was .83. (Why?)

FOR CRITICAL ANALYSIS: There is a company in the United States that will sell you trees inoculated with the truffle organism so that you can "grow your own." How will this affect the price of truffles and thus French production? ●

CONCEPTS IN BRIEF

- Price elasticity of supply is calculated by dividing the percentage change in quantity supplied by the percentage change in price.

- Usually, price elasticities of supply are positive—higher prices yield larger quantities supplied.

- Long-run supply curves are more elastic than short-run supply curves because the longer the time allowed, the more resources can flow into or out of an industry when price changes.

When New York transit authorities raised subway fares a few years ago, ridership dropped immediately. Is there a difference between short-run and long-run responses to price increases?

Mass Transit Riders Respond to Higher Prices

CONCEPTS APPLIED:

PRICE ELASTICITY OF DEMAND, LONG RUN, SHORT RUN, REAL PRICES

Visit www.econtoday.com for an Internet Activity that expands your understanding of these concepts.

Early in the 1990s, the New York City Transit Authority started to experience increased ridership. The subway system had previously suffered from a series of brutal killings and had become, according to some riders, filthy. Homeless people had taken over some seats, and the trains did not run on schedule. Roving gangs of youths terrorized riders. Graffiti was everywhere. The lighting was dim on most of the platforms, lending a sinister feeling to the waiting areas.

Ridership had started a long decline more than two decades earlier, in 1970. Then there were 1.3 billion riders a year. By 1991, ridership had dropped to 995 million. But from 1992 through 1995, subway ridership increased by 9.7 percent (with the biggest rise on weekends), due to improved service and better security, plus a growing local economy.

The Effects of a Fare Increase

In December 1995, the Transit Authority raised subway fares by 25 cents to $1.50. Ridership dropped, relative to the previous December by 4.3 percent. Let's figure out the *short-run* price elasticity of demand. The original price was $1.25, and the increase was 25 cents, or 20 percent. So using the simplest price elasticity of demand formula, the short-run price elasticity of demand for ridership on the New York subway system is

$$E_p = \frac{\text{percentage change in quantity demand}}{\text{percentage change in price}} = \frac{4.3\%}{20\%} = .215$$

Thus at the original price of $1.25, the short-run price elasticity of demand for subway ridership in New York City was inelastic.

What about the *long-run* price elasticity of demand? Historically, similar drop-offs in ridership have occurred virtually every time there has been a fare increase in the system. Most ridership drop-offs, however, were temporary. In other words, it appears that the long-run price elasticity of demand is even less than the short-run price elasticity of demand. There is a problem with this analysis, however. It ignores inflation. For the most part, fares on New York City's subway have simply kept up with inflation. That means that in the long run, the real price of using the subway in New York City has not risen by much at all, so accurately measuring the long-run elasticity of demand is not feasible.

The Bus System Is Affected Also

At the same time that subway prices rose, so did New York bus prices. An identical price increase led to an 11 percent reduction in bus riders compared to the previous December. The short-run price elasticity of demand for bus ridership turned out to be .55 (using the same simple price elasticity of demand formula).

We cannot accurately estimate the long-run price elasticity of demand without correcting all fare increases for inflation. Corrected for inflation, bus fares have not changed over the years.

FOR CRITICAL ANALYSIS

1. Assume that the 4.3 percent ridership decline for the subway system was derived using the last formula on page 442. Recalculate the short-run price elasticity of demand using the average-change formula for the price change.

2. Even though the real (inflation-corrected) price of subway fares has changed little, people react in the short run to a nominal increase in price. Why?

CHAPTER SUMMARY

1. Price elasticity of demand is a measure of the percentage change in quantity demanded relative to the percentage change in price, given income, the prices of other goods, and time. Because of the law of demand, price elasticity of demand is always negative.

2. We classify demand as *elastic* if a 1 percent change in price leads to a more than 1 percent change in quantity demanded, *unit-elastic* if it leads to exactly a 1 percent change in quantity demanded, and *inelastic* if it leads to less than a 1 percent change in quantity demanded.

3. When facing a perfectly elastic demand, the slightest increase in price leads to zero quantity demanded; when facing a perfectly inelastic demand, no matter what the price, the quantity demanded remains unchanged. Perfect inelasticity means absolutely no price responsiveness.

4. Price elasticity of demand falls as we move down a straight-line demand curve. It goes from infinity to zero. Elasticity and slope are not equivalent; for example, the slope of a straight-line curve is always constant, whereas elasticity changes as we move along a linear curve. A vertical demand curve is perfectly inelastic; a horizontal demand curve is perfectly elastic.

5. Price elasticity of demand depends on (a) the existence, number, and quality of substitutes, (b) the share of total budget accounted for by the commodity, and (c) the length of time allowed for adjustment to changes in price of the commodity.

6. Cross price elasticity of demand measures the responsiveness of the demand for one product, either a substitute or a complement, to changes in the price of another product. When the cross price elasticity of demand is negative, the two commodities under study are complements; when the cross price elasticity of demand is positive, they are substitutes.

7. Income elasticity of demand is given by the percentage change in demand divided by the percentage change in income, given relative price.

8. Price elasticity of supply is given by the percentage change in quantity supplied divided by the percentage change in price. The greater the time allowed for adjustment, the greater the price elasticity of supply.

DISCUSSION OF PREVIEW QUESTIONS

1. How is total revenue related to the price elasticity of demand?

Total revenue is defined as price times quantity demanded; because price changes lead to changes in quantity demanded, total revenue and elasticity are intimately related. If, over the price range in question, demand is inelastic, this means that buyers are relatively unresponsive to price changes. Intuitively, then, we know that if price rises and quantity demanded does not fall by much, total revenue will rise. Conversely, if price falls and quantity demanded rises only slightly, total revenue will fall. If, over the price range in question, demand is elastic, buyers will be quite responsive to price changes. We can tell intuitively that if price rises and quantity demanded falls greatly, total revenue will fall. Similarly, if price falls and quantity demanded rises greatly, total revenue will rise. Finally, if we are in the range of unit elasticity, given percentage changes in price will lead to equal percentage changes in quantity. Thus total revenue remains unaffected in the unit-elasticity range.

2. What are the determinants of the price elasticity of demand?

Three major determinants of price elasticity of demand are (a) the existence, number, and quality of substitutes, (b) the share of the total budget that the commodity represents, and (c) the length of time buyers have to react to price changes. Clearly, the more substitutes and the better they are, the greater will be the price elasticity of demand. Therefore, the price elasticity of demand rises as we consider the commodities "fruit," then "oranges," then "Sunkist oranges"; more and better substitutes exist for a specific brand of oranges than for the fruit group. Also, when a commodity takes up a small percentage of the consumer budget (other things being constant), we expect the price elasticity of demand to be lower, compared with items important to a budget. Presumably, buyers will have a greater incentive to shop around and seek substitutes for high-cost items than for low-cost items. Finally, for a given percentage change in price, quantity responsiveness (and therefore elasticity) will increase with the time period allowed for adjustment. With the passage of time, buyers are better able to find and use substitutes.

3. What is the income elasticity of demand?

Income elasticity of demand refers to the responsiveness of buyers to income changes, given relative price. Technically, income elasticity of demand is defined as the percentage change in demand divided by the percentage change in income. The resulting measure is referred to as being income-elastic, unit-elastic, or income-inelastic, depending on whether or not it is greater than, equal to, or less than 1.

4. What is the price elasticity of supply?

Price elasticity of supply refers to the responsiveness of sellers to changes in price. Technically, price elasticity of supply is defined as the percentage change in quantity supplied divided by the percentage change in price. The resulting measure can be greater than, equal to, or less than the number 1—referred to as elastic, unit-elastic, and inelastic price, respectively. The longer the adjustment time, the greater the quantity responsiveness of sellers to given price changes (and hence the greater the price elasticity of supply).

PROBLEMS

(Answers to the odd-numbered problems appear at the back of the book.)

20-1. Use the following hypothetical demand schedule for tea to answer the questions.

Quantity Demanded per Week (ounces)	Price per Ounce	Elasticity
1,000	$ 5	_____
800	10	_____
600	15	_____
400	20	_____
200	25	

a. Using the demand schedule, determine the elasticity of demand for each price change. (Example: When price changes from $5 to $10, quantity demanded changes from 1,000 to 800 ounces, so the elasticity of demand, using average values, is $\frac{1}{3}$, or .33.)

b. The data given in the demand schedule would plot as a straight-line demand curve. Why is demand more elastic the higher the price?

20-2. Calculate the price elasticity of demand for the product in the table on the next page using average values for the prices and quantities in your formula. Over the price range in question, is this demand schedule inelastic, unit-elastic, or elastic? Is total revenue greater at the lower price or the higher price?

Price per Unit	Quantity Demanded
$4	22
6	18

20-3. Calculate the income elasticity of demand for the product in the following table, using average values for incomes and quantities.

Quantity of VCRs per Year	Per Capita Annual Group Income
1,000	$15,000
2,000	20,000

a. Is the demand for this product income-elastic or income-inelastic?

b. Would you consider this commodity a luxury or a necessity?

20-4. Can any demand curve possibly be perfectly inelastic ($E_p = 0$) regardless of price? Explain.

20-5. A new mobile home park charges nothing whatsoever for water used by its inhabitants. Consumption is 100,000 gallons per month. The decision is then made to charge according to how much each mobile home owner uses, at a rate of $10 per 1,000 gallons. Consumption declines to 50,000 gallons per month. What is the difficulty here in accurately estimating the price elasticity of the demand for water by these residents?

20-6. Which of the following cross elasticities of demand would you expect to be positive and which to be negative?

a. Tennis balls and tennis racquets
b. Tennis balls and golf balls
c. Dental services and toothpaste
d. Dental services and candy
e. Liquor and ice cubes
f. Liquor and cocaine

20-7. Suppose that the price of salt rises from 15 cents to 17 cents a pound. The quantity demanded decreases from 525 pounds to 475 pounds per month, and the quantity supplied increases from 525 pounds to 600 pounds per month. (Use averages in calculating elasticities.)

a. Calculate the price elasticity of demand (E_p) for salt.

b. Is the demand for salt price-elastic or price-inelastic?

c. Calculate the elasticity of supply (E_s) for salt.

d. Is the supply for salt price-elastic or price-inelastic?

20-8. Suppose that an automobile dealer cuts his car prices by 15 percent. He then finds that his car sales revenues have increased by 10 percent.

a. What can you say about the price elasticity of demand for cars?

b. What will happen to the dealer's total revenue?

20-9. For any given relative price, would you think that the demand for canal transportation was more or less elastic in 1840 than in 1880? How about the demand for Pony Express messengers before and after the transcontinental telegraph? The demand for rail transportation before and after the Model T Ford? The demand for transatlantic cable-laying equipment before and after communications satellites? The demand for slide rules before and after introduction of the pocket-sized calculator? Why?

COMPUTER-ASSISTED INSTRUCTION

Given a (linear) demand schedule, can you demonstrate that the price elasticity of demand falls as price falls? This problem requires specific calculations of the price elasticity of demand at various prices.

Complete problem and answer appear on disk.

CHAPTER 21

THE FINANCIAL ENVIRONMENT OF BUSINESS

You have probably heard about the stock market crash of 1929, which preceded the Great Depression. You may even have heard about the stock market crash of 1987, which did not precede anything of note in the overall economy. Then there was a stock market minicrash of 1997. Do these periodic stock market crashes tell you to avoid placing your accumulated savings in the stock market? You have to do *something* with your savings. Fortunately, your choices among alternative allocations are virtually unlimited. In addition to stocks, you can invest in corporate bonds, tax-free state and municipal bonds, taxable U.S. Treasury bonds, diamonds, precious metals, real estate, art—the list is long indeed. Before you determine what is the best choice for your savings, you need to know more about the financial environment of business.

PREVIEW QUESTIONS

1. What are the main organizational forms that firms take, and what are their advantages and disadvantages?
2. What are corporations' primary sources of financial capital?
3. What are the major differences between stocks and bonds?
4. Is there a world market for U.S. government securities?

461

Did You Know That . . . every year in the United States, over 2 million new businesses are started? Although most of these involve individuals going into business for themselves, many entrepreneurs raise large sums of money from investors to get under way. These companies turn to financial markets to raise money. They seek **financial capital.**

You've been introduced to the term *physical capital* as one of the five factors of production. In that context, capital consists of the goods that do not directly satisfy human wants but are used to make other goods. *Financial capital* is the money that is made available to purchase capital goods.

Different types of businesses are able to raise financial capital in different ways. Your first step in understanding the firm's financial environment is therefore to understand the way firms are organized.

THE LEGAL ORGANIZATION OF FIRMS

We all know that firms differ from one another. Some sell frozen yogurt, others make automobiles; some advertise, some do not; some have annual sales of a few thousand dollars, others have sales in the billions of dollars. The list of differences is probably endless. Yet for all this diversity, the basic organization of *all* firms can be thought of in terms of a few simple structures, the most important of which are the proprietorship, the partnership, and the corporation.

Proprietorships

The most common form of business organization is the **proprietorship;** as shown in Table 21-1, more than 74 percent of all firms in the United States are proprietorships. Each is owned by a single individual who makes the business decisions, receives all the profits, and is legally responsible for all the debts of the firm. Although proprietorships are numerous, generally they are rather small businesses, with annual sales typically under $50,000. For this reason, even though there are more than 10 million proprietorships in the United States, they account for only about 6 percent of all business revenues.

Advantages of Proprietorships. Proprietorships offer several advantages as a form of business organization. First, they are *easy to form and to dissolve.* In the simplest case, all one must do to start a business is to start working; to dissolve the firm, one simply stops working. Even a more complicated proposition, such as starting a restaurant or a small retail shop, involves only meeting broadly defined health and zoning rules and the payment of a modest business license fee to the local government. To go out of business, one simply

Chapter Outline

The Legal Organization of Firms

Methods of Corporate Financing

The Markets for Stocks and Bonds

Global Capital Markets

Problems in Corporate Governance

Financial capital
Money used to purchase capital goods such as buildings and equipment.

Proprietorship
A business owned by one individual who makes the business decisions, receives all the profits, and is legally responsible for all the debts of the firm.

TABLE 21-1
Forms of Business Organization

Type of Firm	Percentage of U.S. Firms	Average Size (annual sales in dollars)	Percentage of Total Business Revenues
Proprietorship	74.5	47,766	5.7
Partnership	6.9	427,111	4.8
Corporation	18.6	2,979,571	89.5

Sources: U.S. Bureau of the Census; *1998 Statistical Abstract.*

locks the front door. The second advantage of the proprietorship is that *all decision-making power resides with the sole proprietor.* The owner decides what and how much will be offered for sale, what the hours of operation will be, and who will perform what tasks. No partners, shareholders, or board of directors need be consulted. The third advantage is that its *profit is taxed only once.* All profit is treated by law as the net income of the proprietor and as such is subject only to personal income taxation.

Unlimited liability

A legal concept whereby the personal assets of the owner of a firm can be seized to pay off the firm's debts.

Disadvantages of Proprietorships. The most important disadvantage of a proprietorship is that the proprietor faces **unlimited liability** *for the debts of the firm.* This means that the owner is personally responsible for all of the firm's debts. Thus the owner's personal assets—home, car, savings account, coin collection—can be subject to seizure by the firm's creditors. The second disadvantage is that it has *limited ability to raise funds,* to expand the business or even simply to help it survive bad times. Because the success of a proprietorship depends so heavily on the good judgment and hard work of but one person—the owner—many lenders are reluctant to lend large sums to a proprietorship. Thus much of the financing of proprietorships often comes from the personal funds of the owner, which helps explain why proprietorships are usually small. The third disadvantage of proprietorships is that they normally *end with the death of the proprietor.* This, of course, creates added uncertainty for prospective lenders or employees, for a freak accident or sudden illness can turn a prosperous firm into a bittersweet memory.

Partnerships

Partnership

A business owned by two or more co-owners, or partners, who share the responsibilities and the profits of the firm and are individually liable for all of the debts of the partnership.

The second important form of business organization is the **partnership.** As shown in Table 21-1, partnerships are far less numerous than proprietorships but tend to be significantly larger, with average sales about eight times greater. A partnership differs from a proprietorship chiefly in that there are two or more co-owners, called partners. They share the responsibilities of operating the firm and its profits, and they are *each* legally responsible for *all* of the debts incurred by the firm. In this sense, a partnership may be viewed as a proprietorship with more than one owner. The partners may contribute equal or different amounts of financial capital to the firm, may have widely different operating responsibilities, and may share the profits in any way they see fit. Not surprisingly, partnerships share many of the advantages and disadvantages of proprietorships.

Advantages of Partnerships. The first advantage of a partnership is that it is *easy to form.* In fact, it is almost as easy as forming a proprietorship, except that it requires two or more participants. Second, partnerships, like proprietorships, often help *reduce the costs of monitoring job performance.* This is particularly true when interpersonal skills are important for successful performance and in lines of business where, even after the fact, it is difficult to measure performance objectively. Thus attorneys and physicians often organize themselves as partnerships. Similarly, in professions such as these, a spectacular success may consist of a greatly reduced jail term for a client or greatly delayed death for a patient. In such circumstances, each partner has far more incentive to monitor his or her own work performance than he or she would as an employee, because the partner shares in the profits of the firm. A third advantage of the partnership is that it *permits more effective specialization* in occupations where, for legal or other reasons, the multiple talents required for success are unlikely to be uniform across individuals. Finally, partnerships share with proprietorships the advantage that the income of the partnership is treated as personal income and thus is subject only to personal taxation.

Exercise 21.1

Visit www.econtoday.com for more about business organizations.

Disadvantages of Partnerships. Not surprisingly, partnerships also have their disadvantages. First, the *partners each have unlimited liability.* Thus the personal assets of *each* partner are at risk due to debts incurred on behalf of the partnership by *any* of the partners. One partner's poor business judgment may impose substantial losses on all the other partners, a problem the sole proprietor need not worry about. Second, *decision making is generally more costly* in a partnership than in a proprietorship; there are more people involved in making decisions, and they may have differences of opinion that must be resolved before action is possible. Finally, *dissolution of the partnership is generally necessary* when a partner dies or voluntarily withdraws or when one or more partners wish to remove someone from the partnership. As with proprietorships, this creates potential uncertainty for creditors and employees.

Corporations

A **corporation** is a legal entity that may conduct business in its own name just as an individual does. The owners of a corporation are called *shareholders* because they own shares of the profits earned by the firm. By law, shareholders enjoy **limited liability,** which means that if the corporation incurs debts that it cannot pay, creditors have no recourse to the shareholders' personal property. As shown in Table 21-1, corporations are far less numerous than proprietorships, but because of their large size, they are responsible for over 90 percent of all business revenues in the United States. Many, such as Microsoft, IBM, AT&T, and Exxon, are so large that their annual sales are measured in billions of dollars and their names are household words.

Advantages of Corporations. The fact that corporations conduct most of the nation's business suggests that the corporation offers significant advantages as a form of business organization. Perhaps the greatest of these is that the owners of a corporation (the shareholders) enjoy *limited liability.* The liability of shareholders is limited to the value of their shares. The second advantage arises because the law treats it as a legal entity in and of itself; thus the corporation *continues to exist* even if one or more owners of the corporation cease to be owners. A third advantage of the corporation stems from the first two: Corporations are well positioned for *raising large sums of financial capital.* People are able to buy ownership shares or lend money to the corporation knowing that their liability is limited to the amount of money they invest and confident that the corporation's existence does not depend on the life of any one of the firm's owners.

Disadvantages of Corporations. The chief disadvantage of the corporation is the fact that corporate income is subject to *double taxation.* The profits of the corporation are subject first to corporate taxation. Then, if any of the after-tax profits are distributed to shareholders as **dividends,** such payments are treated as personal income to the shareholders and subject to personal taxation. The combined effect is that owners of corporations pay about twice as much in taxes on corporate income as they do on other forms of income.

A second disadvantage of the corporation is that corporations are potentially subject to problems associated with the *separation of ownership and control.* Specifically, it is commonplace for the owners (shareholders) of corporations to have little, if anything, to do with the actual management of the firm. Instead, these tasks are handled by professional managers who may have little or no ownership interest in the firm. The objective of the shareholders is presumably to maximize the value of their holdings. Unless their sole compensation is in the form of shares of stock in the corporation, however, the objective of the managers may differ from this. For example, managers may choose to have more luxurious

Corporation
A legal entity that may conduct business in its own name just as an individual does; the owners of a corporation, called shareholders, own shares of the firm's profits and enjoy the protection of limited liability.

Limited liability
A legal concept whereby the responsibility, or liability, of the owners of a corporation is limited to the value of the shares in the firm that they own.

Dividends
Portion of a corporation's profits paid to its owners (shareholders).

offices than are needed for the efficient operation of the firm. If there are costs to the shareholders in preventing such behavior, the result may be that the market value of the firm is not maximized.

In principle, such problems could arise with a partnership or a proprietorship if the owner or partners hired a manager to take care of day-to-day operations. Nevertheless, the separation of ownership and control is widely regarded as a more important problem for corporations; their attractiveness as a means of raising financial capital from many investors makes them subject to higher costs of agreement among owners with respect to penalties for managers who fail to maximize the value of the firm.

CONCEPTS IN BRIEF

- Proprietorships are the most common form of business organization, comprising more than 74 percent of all firms. Each is owned by a single individual who makes all business decisions, receives all the profits, and has unlimited liability for the firm's debts.

- Partnerships are much like proprietorships, except that two or more individuals, or partners, share the decisions and the profits of the firm. In addition, each partner has unlimited liability for the debts of the firms.

- Corporations are responsible for the largest share of business revenues. The owners, called shareholders, share in the firm's profits but normally have little responsibility for the firm's day-to-day operations. They enjoy limited liability for the debts of the firm.

METHODS OF CORPORATE FINANCING

When the Dutch East India Company was founded in 1602, it raised financial capital by selling shares of its expected future profits to investors. The investors thus became the owners of the company, and their ownership shares eventually became known as "shares of stock," or simply *stocks.* The company also issued notes of indebtedness, which involved borrowing money in return for interest on the funds, plus eventual repayment of the principal amount borrowed. In modern parlance, these notes of indebtedness are called *bonds.* As the company prospered over time, some of its revenues were used to pay lenders the interest and principal owed them; of the profits that remained, some were paid to shareholders in the form of dividends, and some were retained by the company for reinvestment in further enterprises. The methods of financing used by the Dutch East India Company nearly four centuries ago—stocks, bonds, and reinvestment—remain the principal methods of financing for today's corporations.

Share of stock
A legal claim to a share of a corporation's future profits; if it is *common stock,* it incorporates certain voting rights regarding major policy decisions of the corporation; if it is *preferred stock,* its owners are accorded preferential treatment in the payment of dividends.

A **share of stock** in a corporation is simply a legal claim to a share of the corporation's future profits. If there are 100,000 shares of stock in a company and you own 1,000 of them, you own the right to 1 percent of that company's future profits. If the stock you own is *common stock,* you also have the right to vote on major policy decisions affecting the company, such as the selection of the corporation's board of directors. Your 1,000 shares would entitle you to cast 1 percent of the votes on such issues. If the stock you own is *preferred stock,* you also own a share of the future profits of the corporation, but you do *not* have regular voting rights. You do, however, get something in return for giving up your voting rights: preferential treatment in the payment of dividends. Specifically, the owners of preferred stock generally must receive at least a certain amount of dividends in each period before the owners of common stock can receive *any* dividends.

A **bond** is a legal claim against a firm, entitling the owner of the bond to receive a fixed annual *coupon* payment, plus a lump-sum payment at the maturity date of the bond.[1] Bonds are issued in return for funds lent to the firm; the coupon payments represent interest on the amount borrowed by the firm, and the lump-sum payment at maturity of the bond generally equals the amount originally borrowed by the firm. Bonds are *not* claims to the future profits of the firm; legally, bondholders are to be paid whether the firm prospers or not. To help ensure this, bondholders generally must receive their coupon payments each year, and any principal that is due, before *any* shareholders can receive dividend payments.

You can see a comparison of stocks and bonds in Table 21-2.

Reinvestment takes place when the firm uses some of its profits to purchase new capital equipment rather than paying the money out as dividends to shareholders. Although sales of stock are an important source of financing for new firms, reinvestment and borrowing are the principal means of financing for existing firms. Indeed, reinvestment by established firms is such an important source of financing that it dominates the other two sources of corporate finance, amounting to roughly 75 percent of new financial capital for corporations in recent years. Also, small businesses, which are the source of much current growth, usually cannot rely on the stock market to raise investment funds.

Bond
A legal claim against a firm, usually entitling the owner of the bond to receive a fixed annual coupon payment, plus a lump-sum payment at the bond's maturity date. Bonds are issued in return for funds lent to the firm.

Reinvestment
Profits (or depreciation reserves) used to purchase new capital equipment.

Primary and Secondary Financial Markets

Both businesses and investors engage in financial transactions in primary and secondary financial markets.

Primary Markets. If you have ever heard of a "new issue," you are familiar with one aspect of a primary securities market. A **primary market** is one in which newly issued

Primary market
A financial market in which newly issued securities are bought and sold.

TABLE 21-2	Stocks	Bonds
The Difference Between Stocks and Bonds	1. Stocks represent ownership.	1. Bonds represent debt.
	2. Common stocks do not have a fixed dividend rate.	2. Interest on bonds must always be paid, whether or not any profit is earned.
	3. Stockholders can elect a board of directors, which controls the corporation.	3. Bondholders usually have no voice in or control over management of the corporation.
	4. Stocks do not have a maturity date; the corporation does not usually repay the stockholder.	4. Bonds have a maturity date on which the bondholder is to be repaid the face value of the bond.
	5. All corporations issue or offer to sell stocks. This is the usual definition of a corporation.	5. Corporations need not issue bonds.
	6. Stockholders have a claim against the property and income of a corporation after all creditors' claims have been met.	6. Bondholders have a claim against the property and income of a corporation that must be met before the claims of stockholders.

---

[1]Coupon payments on bonds get their name from the fact that bonds once had coupons attached to them when they were issued. Each year, the owner would clip a coupon off the bond and send it to the issuing firm in return for that year's interest on the bond.

securities are bought and sold. A company that is raising money for the first time goes to the primary market, usually to sell stocks. Corporations can also sell newly issued bonds in primary securities markets. Sometimes you may read about large corporations, such as General Motors, issuing new bonds.

Secondary market
A financial market in which previously issued securities are bought and sold.

Secondary Markets. A **secondary market** is one in which existing securities are exchanged. When you read about what happened on the stock market today, that is information about a secondary market. Secondary markets are important to primary markets because they make stocks and bonds sold in primary markets more liquid. Most of the activities of stockbrokers involve dealings for investors in secondary market transactions. The stockbroker is an intermediary (middleman) who brings together buyers and sellers of various stocks and bonds. In return for the broker's services, which include executing market exchanges for buyers and sellers, the broker receives a commission, or brokerage fee.

THE MARKETS FOR STOCKS AND BONDS

Economists often refer to the "market for wheat" or the "market for labor." For stocks and bonds, there really are markets—centralized, physical locations where exchange takes place. By far the largest and most prestigious of these are the New York Stock Exchange (NYSE) and the New York Bond Exchange, both located in New York City. Numerous other stock and bond markets, or exchanges, are located throughout the United States and in various financial capitals of the world, such as London and Tokyo. Although the exact process by which exchanges are conducted in these markets varies slightly from one to another, the process used on the NYSE is representative of the principles involved.[2]

More than 2,500 stocks are traded on the NYSE, which is sometimes called the "Big Board." Leading brokerage firms—about 600 of them—own seats on the NYSE. These seats, which are actually rights to buy and sell stocks on the floor of the Big Board, are themselves regularly exchanged. In recent years, their value has fluctuated between $350,000 and $1 million each. These prices reflect the fact that stock trades on the NYSE are ultimately handled by the firms owning these seats, and the firms earn commissions on each trade. As trading volume rises, as it did during the 1980s, the value of the seats rises.

The Theory of Efficient Markets

At any point in time, there are tens of thousands, even millions of persons looking for any bit of information that will enable them to forecast correctly the future prices of stocks. Responding to any information that seems useful, these people try to buy low and sell high. The result is that all publicly available information that might be used to forecast stock prices gets taken into account by those with access to the information and the knowledge and ability to learn from it, leaving no

---

THINKING CRITICALLY ABOUT THE MEDIA

Heard on the Street

Every weekday, along with the stock market information, the *Wall Street Journal* carries a column titled "Heard on the Street." Essentially, it consists of statements made by people involved in the stock market, most of whom comment on why the market went up or down the previous day. Similar financial stories are presented both in the printed press and on TV, all of them purportedly explaining why the market did what it did. Such analysis is, in a word, meaningless. All one has to do is choose an important event in domestic or world news and then relate it in the appropriate way to what happened to the market *yesterday*. There is no way to disprove such hypotheses. Certainly, one should never take them seriously enough to bet money on the same line of causation in the future. But if you can ever get a job explaining why the market went up or down yesterday, take it. You will be right 100 percent of the time.

---

[2]A number of stocks and bonds are traded in so-called over-the-counter (OTC) markets, which, although not physically centralized, otherwise operate in much the same way as the NYSE and so are not treated separately in this text.

forecastable profit opportunities. And because so many people are involved in this process, it occurs quite swiftly. Indeed, there is some evidence that *all* information entering the market is fully incorporated into stock prices within less than a minute of its arrival. One view of the stock market is that most public information you will obtain will prove to have little value.

The result of this process is that stock prices tend to follow a *random walk,* which is to say that the best forecast of tomorrow's price is today's price. This is called the **random walk theory.** Although large values of the random component of stock price changes are less likely than small values, nothing else about the magnitude or direction of a stock price change can be predicted. Indeed, the random component of stock prices exhibits behavior much like what would occur if you rolled two dice and subtracted 7 from the resulting score. On average, the dice will show a total of 7, so after you subtract 7, the average result will be zero. It is true that rolling a 12 or a 2 (resulting in a net score of +5 or −5) is less likely than rolling an 8 or a 6 (yielding a net score of +1 or −1). Nevertheless, positive and negative net scores are equally likely, and the expected net score is zero.

Random walk theory
The theory that there are no predictable trends in security prices that can be used to "get rich quick."

Inside Information

Isn't there any way to "beat the market"? The answer is yes—but normally only if you have **inside information** that is not available to the public. Suppose that your best friend is in charge of new product development at the country's largest software firm, Microsoft Corporation. Your friend tells you that the company's smartest programmer has just come up with major new software that millions of computer users will want to buy. No one but your friend and the programmer—and now you—is aware of this. You could indeed make money using this information by purchasing shares of Microsoft and then selling them (at a higher price) as soon as the new product is publicly announced. There is one problem: Stock trading based on inside information such as this is illegal, punishable by substantial fines and even imprisonment. So unless you happen to have a stronger than average desire for a long vacation in a federal prison, you might be better off investing in Microsoft after the new program is publicly announced.

Inside information
Information that is not available to the general public about what is happening in a corporation.

EXAMPLE
How to Read the Financial Press: Stock Prices

Table 21-3, reproduced from the *Wall Street Journal,* contains information about the stocks of four companies. Across the top of the financial page are a series of column headings. Under the heading "Stock" we find the name of the company—in the second row, for example, is Eastman Kodak, the photographic materials firm. The two columns to the left of the company's name show the highest and lowest prices at which shares of that company's stock traded during the past 52 weeks. These prices are typically quoted in dollars and eighths of dollars.

Immediately to the right of the company's name you will find the company's *symbol* on the NYSE. This symbol (omitted by some newspapers) is simply the unique identifier used by the exchange when it reports information about the stock. For example, the designation EK is used by the exchange as the unique identifier for the firm Eastman Kodak.

The last four columns of information for each firm summarize the behavior of the firm's stock price on the latest trading day. On this particular day, the highest price at which Kodak stock traded was $59.00, the lowest price was $56.5625, and the last (or closing) price at which it traded was $58.00 per share. The *net change* in the price of Kodak stock

TABLE 21-3

Reading Stock Quotes

52 Weeks		Stock	Sym	Div	Yld %	PE	Vol 100s	Hi	Lo	Close	Net Chg
Hi	Lo										
$65\frac{3}{8}$	$50\frac{3}{4}$	Eastman Chm	EMN	1.76	3.0	14	2348	$58\frac{13}{16}$	$57\frac{1}{4}$	$57\frac{3}{4}$	$-\frac{3}{4}$
$94\frac{3}{4}$	$53\frac{5}{16}$	EKodak	EK	1.76	3.0	21	22451	59	$56\frac{9}{16}$	58	. . .
$103\frac{3}{8}$	$66\frac{3}{4}$	Eaton	ETN	1.76	2.0	20	3124	$90\frac{11}{16}$	$89\frac{1}{16}$	$90\frac{1}{16}$	$-1\frac{1}{4}$
$37\frac{13}{16}$	$20\frac{7}{8}$	Eaton/Vance	EV	48f	1.3	17	271	$36\frac{1}{16}$	$35\frac{7}{8}$	$35\frac{15}{16}$	$-\frac{1}{16}$

The summary of stock market information presented on the financial pages of many newspapers reveals the following:

52 Weeks Hi/Lo: The highest and lowest prices, in dollars per share, of the stock during the previous 52 weeks.

Stock: The name of the company (frequently abbreviated).

Sym: Highly abbreviated name of the company, as it appears on the stock exchange ticker tape.

Div: Dividend paid, in dollars per share.

Yld %: Yield in percent per year; the dividend divided by the price of the stock.

PE: Price-earnings ratio; the price of the stock divided by the earnings (profits) per share of the company.

Vol 100s: Number of shares traded during the day, in hundreds of shares.

Hi: Highest price at which the stock traded that day.

Lo: Lowest price at which the stock traded that day.

Close: Last price at which the stock traded that day.

Net Chg: Net change in the stock's price from the previous day's closing price.

was zero, which means that it *closed* the day at a price per share equal to the price at which it closed the day before.

The dividend column, headed "Div," shows the annual dividend (in dollars and cents) that the company has paid over the preceding year on each share of its stock. In Kodak's case, this amounts to $1.76 a share. If the dividend is divided by the closing price of the stock ($1.76 ÷ $58.00), the result is 3.0 percent, which is shown in the yield percentage ("Yld %") column for Kodak. In a sense, the company is paying interest on the stock at a rate of about 3.0 percent. At first glance, this seems like an absurdly low amount; after all, at the time this issue of the *Wall Street Journal* was printed, ordinary checking accounts were paying about 4.0 percent. The reason people tolerate this seemingly low yield on Kodak (or any other stock) is that they expect that the price of the stock will rise over time, yielding capital gains.

The column heading "PE" stands for *price-earnings ratio*. To obtain the entries for this column, the firm's total earnings (profits) for the year are divided by the number of the firm's shares in existence to give the earnings per share. When the price of the stock is divided by the earnings per share, the result is the price-earnings ratio.

The column to the right of the PE ratio shows the total *volume* of the shares of the stock traded that day, measured in hundreds of shares.

FOR CRITICAL ANALYSIS: Is there necessarily any relationship between the net change in a stock's price and how many shares have been sold on a particular day? ●

CONCEPTS IN BRIEF

- Many economists believe that asset markets, especially the stock market, are efficient, meaning that one cannot make a higher than normal rate of return without having inside information (information that the general public does not possess).

- Stock prices normally follow a random walk, meaning that you cannot predict changes in future stock prices based on information about stock price behavior in the past.

Exercise 21.2

Visit www.econtoday.com for more about the stock market.

GLOBAL CAPITAL MARKETS

Financial institutions in the United States are tied to the rest of the world via their lending capacities. In addition, integration of all financial markets is increasing. Indeed, recent changes in world finance have been nothing short of remarkable. Distinctions among financial institutions and between financial institutions and nonfinancial institutions have blurred. As the legal barriers that have preserved such distinctions are dismantled, multinational corporations offering a wide array of financial services are becoming dominant worldwide.

Globalizing Financial Markets

The globalization of financial markets is not entirely new. U.S. banks developed worldwide branch networks in the 1960s and 1970s for loans, check clearing, and foreign exchange (currency) trading. Also in the 1970s, firms dealing in U.S. securities (stocks and bonds) expanded their operations in London (on the Eurobond market) and then into other financial centers, including Tokyo. Similarly, foreign firms invaded U.S. shores: first the banks, then securities firms. The "big four" Japanese securities firms now have offices in New York and London.

Money and capital markets today are truly international. Markets for U.S. government securities, interbank lending and borrowing, foreign exchange trading, and common stocks are now trading continuously, in vast quantities, around the clock and around the world.

The World Market for U.S. Government Debt. Trading for U.S. government securities has been described as "the world's fastest-growing 24-hour market." This market was made possible by (1) sophisticated communications and computer technology, (2) deregulation of financial markets in foreign countries to permit such trading, (3) U.S. legislation in 1984 to enable foreign investors to buy U.S. government securities tax-free, and (4) huge annual U.S. government budget deficits, which have poured a steady stream of tradable debt into the world markets.

Other Globalized Markets. Foreign exchange—the buying and selling of foreign currencies—became a 24-hour, worldwide market in the 1970s. Instruments tied to government bonds, foreign exchange, stock market indexes, and commodities (grains, metals, oil) are now traded increasingly in financial futures markets in all the world's major centers of commerce. Most financial firms are coming to the conclusion that to survive as a force in any one of the world's leading financial markets, a firm must have a significant presence in all of them. It is predicted that by the turn of the twenty-first century, between 30 and 50 financial institutions will be at the centers of world finance—New York, London, Tokyo, and Frankfurt—and they will be competing in all those markets to do business with the world's major corporations and portfolio managers. Today, major corporate borrowers throughout the world can choose to borrow from a wide variety of lenders, also located throughout the world. Borrowing on the international capital markets was estimated at $850 billion for the year 1996 for the 24 leading industrialized nations, according to the Organization for Economic Cooperation and Development (OECD).

CONCEPTS IN BRIEF

- Financial markets throughout the world have become increasingly integrated, leading to a global financial market. Interbank lending and borrowing, foreign exchange trading, and common stock sales now occur virtually 24 hours a day throughout the world.
- Many U.S. government or government-guaranteed securities trade 24 hours a day.

PROBLEMS IN CORPORATE GOVERNANCE

Many corporations issue stock to raise financial capital that they will use to fund expansion or modernization. The decision to raise capital in this way is ordinarily made not by the owners of the corporation—the holders of its stock—but by the company's managers. This **separation of ownership and control** in corporations leads to incentive problems. Managers may not act in the best interest of shareholders. Further incentive problems arise when corporations borrow money in financial markets. These corporate governance problems have to do with information that is not the same for everyone.

Asymmetric Information: The Perils of Adverse Selection and Moral Hazard

If you invest in a corporation, you give purchasing power to the managers of that corporation. Those managers have much more information about what is happening to the corporation and its future than you do. The inequality of information between the two parties is called **asymmetric information.** If asymmetric information exists before a transaction takes place, we have a circumstance of **adverse selection.** In financial markets, adverse selection occurs because borrowers who are the worst credit risks (and thus likely to yield the most adverse outcomes) are the ones most likely to seek, and perhaps to receive, loans.

Consider two firms seeking to borrow funds by selling bonds. Suppose that one of the firms, the Dynamic Corporation, is pursuing a project with a small chance of yielding large profits and a large chance of bankruptcy. The other firm, the Reliable Company, intends to invest in a project that is guaranteed to yield the competitive rate of return, thereby ensuring repayment of its debts. Because Dynamic knows the chance is high that it will go bankrupt and never have to pay its debts, it can offer a high interest rate on the bonds it issues. Unless prospective bond purchasers can distinguish perfectly between the two firms' projects, they will select the high-yielding bonds offered by Dynamic and refuse to buy the low-yielding bonds offered by Reliable. Firms like Reliable will be unable to get funding, yet lenders will lose money on firms like Dynamic. Adverse selection thus makes investors less likely to lend to anyone and more inclined to charge higher interest rates when they do lend.

Moral hazard occurs as a result of asymmetric information *after* a transaction occurs. To continue with our example of the Dynamic Corporation, once the firm has sold the bonds, it must choose among alternative strategies in executing its project. Lenders face the hazard that Dynamic may choose strategies contrary to the lenders' well-being and thus immoral from their perspective. Because bondholders are entitled to a fixed amount regardless of the firm's profits, Dynamic has an incentive to select strategies offering a small chance of high profits, thereby enabling the owners to keep the largest amount after paying

---

Separation of ownership and control

The situation that exists in corporations in which the owners (shareholders) are not the people who control the operation of the corporation (managers). The goals of these two groups are often different.

Asymmetric information

Information possessed by one side of a transaction but not the other. The side with more information will be at an advantage.

Adverse selection

The circumstance that arises in financial markets when borrowers who are the worst credit risks are the ones most likely to seek loans.

Moral hazard

A problem that occurs because of asymmetric information *after* a transaction occurs. In financial markets, a person to whom money has been lent may indulge in more risky behavior, thereby increasing the probability of default on the debt.

bondholders. Such strategies are also the riskiest—ones that make it more likely that lenders will not be repaid—so the presence of moral hazard makes lenders less likely to lend to anyone and more inclined to charge higher interest rates when they do lend.

EXAMPLE
Explaining the Success of at Least One Multibillionaire

Multibillionaires are special, and Warren Buffett is one of them. He initially invested $100 and ended up with Berkshire Hathaway, a company with businesses in insurance, candy manufacturing, and newspaper publishing, among others. The company's market value is over $20 billion, though Buffett doesn't own it all. His technique has been an attempt to eliminate the asymmetry problem that is associated with the separation of ownership and control. Buffett invests large sums of money only in businesses that he understands thoroughly. He pays special attention to what management does with excess cash that cannot be properly reinvested inside the corporation. For that is where managers can easily divert funds in ways that do not serve shareholders' best interests. One way of obtaining more information than a typical investor in the companies in which he invests, Buffett has discovered, is becoming a member of the board of directors and befriending the chief executive. He has done so in every enterprise in which he has invested heavily. As a result, he has profited handsomely from his ability to reduce information costs.

FOR CRITICAL ANALYSIS: Is it possible for the average investor to avoid the asymmetric information problem when making an investment decision? •

The Principal-Agent Problem

A type of moral hazard problem that occurs within firms is called the **principal-agent problem.** The shareholders who own a firm are referred to as *principals,* and the managers who operate the firm are the *agents* of the owners. When the managers do not own all of a firm (as is usually the case), a separation of ownership and control exists, and if the stockholders have less information about the firm's opportunities and risks than the managers do (as is also usually the case), the managers may act in their own self-interests rather than in the interests of the shareholders.

    Consider, for example, the choice between two investment projects, one of which involves an enormous amount of work but also promises high profits, while the other requires little effort and promises small returns. Because the managers must do all the work while the shareholders receive all the profits, the managers' incentives are different from those of the shareholders. In this case, the presence of moral hazard will induce the managers to choose the "good life," the easy but low-yielding project—an outcome that fails to maximize the economic value of the firm.

Solving Principal-Agent and Moral Hazard Problems

The dangers associated with asymmetric information are well known to participants in financial markets, who regularly undertake vigorous steps to minimize its costly conse-

Principal-agent problem
The conflict of interest that occurs when agents—managers of firms—pursue their own objectives to the detriment of the goals of the firms' principals, or owners.

Collateral

An asset pledged to guarantee the repayment of a loan.

Incentive-compatible contract

A loan contract under which a significant amount of the borrower's assets are at risk, providing an incentive for the borrower to look after the lender's interests.

quences. For example, research companies such as Standard & Poor's gather financial data and other information about corporations and sell the information to their subscribers. When even this is insufficient to eliminate the dangers of adverse selection, lenders often require that borrowers post **collateral**—assets that the borrower will forfeit in the event that repayment of a debt is not made. A variant of this strategy, designed to reduce moral hazard problems, is called the **incentive-compatible contract:** Lenders make sure that borrowers have a large amount of their own assets at risk so that the incentives of the borrower are compatible with the interests of the lender. Although measures such as these cannot eliminate the losses caused by asymmetric information, they reduce them below what would otherwise be the case.

EXAMPLE
Making Executives Own a Share of the Company

One way to minimize the principal-agent problem is to require that executives own stock in the companies for which they work. An increasing number of corporations are requiring directors and top management to own shares of stock. By the mid-1990s, almost 20 percent of companies surveyed by *Fortune* prepared "guidelines" specifying the amount of stock that executives must own. These include Black & Decker, Union Pacific, and US West. Usually executives are told that they must buy over a period of five years an amount ranging from one to four times their annual salaries.

Do shareholders benefit from top management's owning "a piece of the rock"? One study indicated that companies in which the chief executives had significant ownership experienced a 4 percent higher annual rate of return over a five-year period than similar companies that did not require executives to own stock.

FOR CRITICAL ANALYSIS: Is there any way you can use this information to determine in which corporations you should invest? •

CONCEPTS IN BRIEF

- When two parties to a transaction have different amounts of information, we call this asymmetric information. Whenever asymmetric information occurs before a transaction takes place, it can result in adverse selection. Adverse selection causes borrowers who are the worst credit risks to be the ones most likely to seek loans.

- When asymmetric information occurs after a transaction, this can cause moral hazard. Lenders often face the hazard that borrowers will choose more risky actions after borrowers have taken out loans.

- The separation of ownership and control in today's large corporations can give rise to the principal-agent problem, whereby the agents (managers) may have interests that differ from those of the principals (shareholders).

- Several methods exist for solving the principal-agent and moral hazard problems. They include requiring lenders to post collateral and devising incentive-compatible contracts in which borrowers have a large amount of their own assets at risk.

The stock market crashed in 1929 and again in 1987, when it lost more than 20 percent of its value in one day. Does that mean investing in stocks is too risky?

The Truth About Investing in Stocks

CONCEPTS APPLIED:

LONG RUN, SHORT RUN, INFLATION, STOCKS VERSUS BONDS, EQUITY VERSUS DEBT, RISK-INVESTED YIELDS

Visit www.econtoday.com for an Internet Activity that expands your understanding of these concepts.

The boom market during most of the 1990s seemed to indicate that stocks were the way to go. After all, anybody who invested in a broad range of stocks—through a mutual fund, for example—would have seen his or her wealth increase rather dramatically. As single years go, nothing beats the percentage rate of return that investors in the stock market obtained in 1933. During that one-year period, stocks increased in value by 54 percent! But the market has done well at other times, too. For the five-year period from 1950 to 1954, for example, the annual compounded rate of return for holding stocks was 24 percent. A $10,000 stock market investment in 1950 would have been worth almost $30,000 at the end of 1954. Consider an even longer period, 1942 to 1961. A $10,000 investment during that period would have grown to $220,542.

Sounds great, doesn't it? There is one problem with such analyses. It has to do with selectively choosing the time period. Consider that if you had invested $1,000 in the stock market at the beginning of 1931, by January 1, 1932, that $1,000 would have been worth only $570. If you had started your investing in 1929 with $10,000, twenty years later, at the end of 1948, you would have had only $18,440.

Although the 84 percent rise in the value of your savings in the last example might sound good, it brings us to two serious long-run problems. The first has to do with inflation; the other has to do with taxes.

Correcting for Inflation and Taxes

Inflation is important because it reduces the purchasing power of your savings. You need to know how much you can purchase in real terms when making historical comparisons. Figure 21-1 contains several curves. The top curve shows the long-run average total return that is *inflation-*

adjusted from 1801 until 1998. This long-run "real" rate of return turns out to be an annualized corrected rate of 6.6 percent—not bad. But when you take taxes into account, assuming that you are in the highest marginal tax bracket starting in 1913 when income taxes were introduced, your after-tax real inflation-adjusted annualized rate of return drops to 2.4 percent. So you can beat inflation by investing in the stock market in the long run, but taxes tend to beat you down.

The Demographics of U.S. Stock Market Investors

Who owns stocks in the United States? As it turns out, a considerable number of Americans own stocks, either directly or indirectly through pension plans. More than one household in four owns stocks and mutual funds shares directly. An even greater number own stocks indirectly through their pension plans. Whereas in 1962 the wealthiest 2.5 percent of U.S. households owned 75 percent of publicly traded stocks, today the wealthiest 2 percent of U.S. households hold less than 20 percent of publicly traded stocks. The median household income of shareholders of publicly traded stock is below $60,000.

What About Bonds?

In the investing world, risk and rate of return are positively correlated. Because there is so much variation in what happens to stock prices, you would expect that the rate of return for investing in the stock market has to be higher than in bonds, which are more stable. Look at the three curves in Figure 21-1 that show corporate and Treasury bonds, inflation-adjusted but before taxes; municipal bonds, inflation-adjusted (they are nontaxable); and corporate and Treasury bonds, inflation-adjusted after taxes.

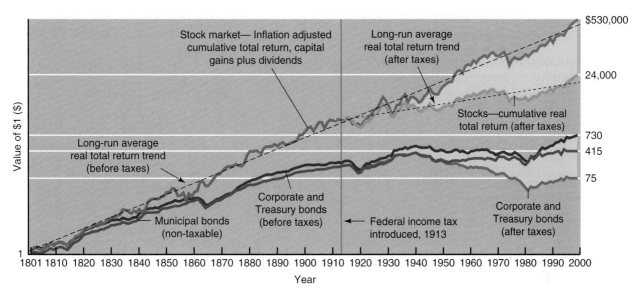

FIGURE 21-1

Stocks Are the Best Investment—but Are They Really So Good?

Stocks are clearly a better investment than any type of bonds, at least in the long run. Here you see what happened to $1 invested at the beginning of the 1800s, depending on whether it was invested in stocks or in taxable or nontaxable bonds. Almost 200 years later, that $1 would have compounded to about $530,000 (corrected for inflation) if left in the stock market, but after taking account of taxes, it would have only been about $24,000. That's still better than nontaxable bonds ($415) or taxable bonds (after taxes only $75).

Sources: Jeremy J. Siegel and author's estimates

After accounting for inflation, $1 invested in 1801 in municipal bonds would have yielded after inflation about $415 in 1998. Corporate and Treasury bonds after inflation and after taxes would have yielded only about $75. The graph shows you that in the long run, stocks are better than bonds. Moreover, for any 30-year period from 1801 to the present, stocks have outperformed bonds. And since 1926, for any 20-year holding period, stocks have outperformed bonds 98 percent of the time.

Art Is Up Too

Recent art auctions have yielded record sums for paintings by well-known artists, leading some commentators to argue that they are superior assets in which to invest. Economic theory nonetheless implies that total returns, adjusted for risk, should be about the same over the long run for all investments. Art objects include a psychic or consumption benefit from owning and viewing them. Therefore, one should expect that the real (financial) rate of return for art objects will be lower than the rate of return on financial assets.

According to economists Bruno Frey and Werner Pommerehne, this is exactly the case. They examined the auction prices of quality paintings by over 300 of the world's best-known painters for a 350-year period. They found that the real rate of return on paintings was 1.5 percent per year. During that same time period, the real rate of return on government bonds was 3 percent per year, or double the financial return on paintings. In the period since 1950, the real rate of return on paintings has increased slightly to 1.7 percent a year, but the real rate of return on bonds was higher still, at about 2.5 percent per year.

FOR CRITICAL ANALYSIS

1. The government provides for numerous types of savings programs that allow individuals to accumulate assets tax-free, only to pay taxes when they take out funds after retirement. How do such plans affect our analysis with respect to stock market returns?
2. Our analysis notwithstanding, are there some individuals who should invest mainly in bonds? Why?

CHAPTER SUMMARY

1. Proprietorships are the most common form of business organization, comprising more than 74 percent of all firms. Each is owned by a single individual who makes all business decisions, receives all the profits, and has unlimited liability for the firm's debts.
2. Partnerships are much like proprietorships, except that two or more individuals, or partners, share the decisions and the profits of the firm; each partner has unlimited liability for the debts of the firm.
3. Corporations are responsible for the largest share of business revenues. The owners, called shareholders, share in the firm's profits but normally have little responsibility for the firm's day-to-day operations. Owners of corporations enjoy limited liability for the debts of the firm.
4. When two parties to a transaction have different amounts of information, we call this asymmetric information. Whenever asymmetric information occurs be-

fore a transaction takes place, it can result in adverse selection. Adverse selection causes borrowers who are the worst credit risks to be the ones most likely to seek loans.
5. When asymmetric information occurs after a transaction, this can cause moral hazard. Lenders often face the hazard that borrowers will choose more risky actions after borrowers have taken out loans.
6. The separation of ownership and control in today's large corporation has led to the principal-agent problem, whereby the agents (managers) may have interests that differ from those of the principals (shareholders).
7. Several methods exist for solving the principal-agent and moral hazard problems, including requiring lenders to post collateral and devising incentive-compatible contracts in which borrowers have a large amount of their own assets at risk.

DISCUSSION OF PREVIEW QUESTIONS

1. What are the main organizational forms that firms take, and what are their advantages and disadvantages?

The primary organizational forms businesses take are the proprietorship, the partnership, and the corporation. The proprietorship is owned by a single person, the proprietor, who makes the business decisions, is entitled to all the profits, and is subject to unlimited liability—that is, is personally responsible for all debts incurred by the firm. The partnership differs from the proprietorship chiefly in that there are two or more owners, called partners. They share the responsibility for decision making, share the firm's profits, and individually bear unlimited liability for the firm's debts. The net income, or profits, of both proprietorships and partnerships is subject only to personal income taxes. Both types of firms legally cease to

exist when the proprietor or a partner gives up ownership or dies. The corporation differs from proprietorships and partnerships in three important dimensions. Owners of corporations enjoy limited liability; that is, their responsibility for the debts of the corporation is limited to the value of their ownership shares. In addition, the income from corporations is subject to double taxation—corporate taxation when income is earned by the corporation and personal taxation when after-tax profits are paid as dividends to the owners. Finally, corporations do not legally cease to exist due to a change of ownership or the death of an owner.

2. What are corporations' primary sources of financial capital?

The main sources of financial capital for corporations are stocks, bonds, and reinvestment of profits. Stocks are ownership shares, promising a share of profits, sold to investors. Common stocks also embody voting rights regarding the major decisions of the firm; preferred stocks typically have no voting rights but enjoy priority status in the payment of dividends. Bonds are notes of indebtedness, issued in return for the loan of money. They typically promise to pay interest in the form of annual coupon payments, plus repayment of the original principal amount upon maturity. Bondholders are generally promised payment before any payment of dividends to shareholders, and for this reason bonds are less risky than stocks. Reinvestment involves the purchase of assets by the firm, using retained profits or depreciation reserves it has set aside for this purpose. No new stocks or bonds are issued in the course of reinvestment, although its value is fully reflected in the price of existing shares of stock.

3. **What are the major differences between stocks and bonds?**

Stocks represent ownership in a corporation. They are called equity capital. Bonds represent the debt of a corporation. They are part of the debt capital of a corporation. Bond owners normally receive a fixed interest payment on a regular basis, whereas owners of stock are not normally guaranteed any dividends. If a corporation goes out of business, bondholders have first priority on whatever value still exists in the entity. Owners of stock get whatever is left over. Finally, if the corporation is very successful, owners of stock can reap the increases in the market value of their shares of stock. In contrast, the market value of corporate bonds is not so closely tied to the profits of a corporation but is rather influenced by how interest rates are changing in the economy in general.

4. **Is there a world market for U.S. government securities?**

Trading in U.S. government securities is one of the fastest-growing 24-hour markets in the world, thanks to sophisticated communications and computer technology. The deregulation of financial markets in foreign countries now permits much more of such trading. Also, since 1984, the United States has allowed foreign investors to buy U.S. government securities tax-free.

PROBLEMS

(Answers to the odd-numbered problems appear at the back of the book.)

21-1. Suppose that federal tax policy were changed to exempt the first $10,000 in dividends each year from personal taxation. How would this affect the choice of organizational form for businesses?

21-2. How would the change in corporate tax policy mentioned in Problem 21-1 affect the method of financing that corporations use?

*21-3. Consider a firm that wishes to borrow $10,000 for one year. Suppose that there is a 20 percent chance that this firm will go out of business before the end of the year (repaying none of its debts) and an 80 percent chance that it will survive and repay all of its debts. If potential lenders can earn 10 percent per year by lending to other firms that are certain to repay their debts, what rate of interest will the risky firm have to offer if it is to be able to borrow the $10,000?

21-4. Should the government guarantee junk bonds to make sure that the buyers of these bonds do not lose money? What would happen if the government did this?

*This problem is optional; albegra is required.

COMPUTER-ASSISTED INSTRUCTION

Key determinants of the prices of shares of corporate stock are illustrated using numerical problems.

Complete problem and answer appear on disk.

INTERACTING WITH THE INTERNET

An excellent tool for learning about the functioning of financial markets is the Iowa Electronic Markets. It is a registered market that runs on the Internet and is designed to teach the fundamentals of trading in financial markets. To make the learning "real," participants risk their own funds (you can invest quite small amounts). There are two types of markets: political ones, based on the outcome of elections, and financial ones. See

www.biz.uiowa.edu/iem/

One service that provides financial information, some of it free, is QuoteCom at

www.quote.com

The American Stock Exchange can be reached at

www.amex.com

The New York Stock Exchange is at

www.nyse.com

NASDAQ can be found at

www.nasdaq.com

The Chicago Mercantile Exchange is at

www.interaccess.com/cme/

And the London International Financial Futures and Options Exchange can be reached at

www.liffe.com/

Not all exchanges offer complete pricing information, but they generally do have extensive material on themselves.

For information and discussion groups, go to StockMaster at

www.stockmaster.com

You can find out more about sole proprietorship, partnerships, and corporations at the following Web site:

www.comerica.com/smallbiz/workshop/bizstruc.html

You can find out more about how the stock market works by going to

tqd.advanced.org/3088/

When you start on the EduStock welcome page, choose *Stock Market* from the menu.

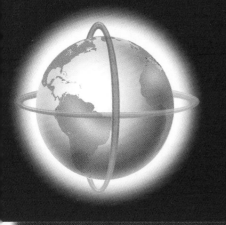

PART 7

MARKET STRUCTURE, RESOURCE ALLOCATION, AND REGULATION

CHAPTER 22

THE FIRM: COST AND OUTPUT DETERMINATION

By the time you read this, about 50 percent of American households will have access to the Internet. If you are one of them, you are connected through an Internet service provider, or ISP. There are many ISPs in America. They include AT&T, MCI, Sprint, and America Online (AOL). They also include literally thousands of smaller local companies. A few years ago, AOL followed the trend set by many smaller ISPs by declaring that instead of paying by the hour, its customers could have unlimited access to the Internet for $19.95 a month. AOL settled a class action lawsuit as a result of access problems resulting from charging a flat monthly fee pricing structure. To understand what these lawsuits are about and how people responded to a change in the pricing structure of Internet access, you need to know about the cost curves that individual businesses face.

Did You Know That . . . there are more than 25 steps in the process of manufacturing a simple lead pencil? In the production of an automobile, there are literally thousands. At each step, the manufacturer can have the job done by workers or machines or some combination of the two. The manufacturer must also figure out how much to produce each month. Should a new machine be bought that can replace 10 workers? Should more workers be hired, or should the existing workers be paid overtime? If the price of aluminum is rising, should the company try to make do with plastic? What you will learn about in this chapter is how producers can select the best combination of inputs for any given output that is desired.

Before we look at the firm's costs, we need to define a firm.

THE FIRM

We define a business, or **firm,** as follows:

> **A firm is an organization that brings together factors of production—labor, land, physical capital, human capital, and entrepreneurial skill—to produce a product or service that it hopes can be sold at a profit.**

A typical firm will have an organizational structure consisting of an entrepreneur, managers, and workers. The entrepreneur is the person who takes the risks, mainly of losing his or her personal wealth. In compensation, the entrepreneur will get any profits that are made. Recall from Chapter 2 that entrepreneurs take the initiative in combining land, labor, and capital to produce a good or a service. Entrepreneurs are the ones who innovate in the form of new production and new products. The entrepreneur also decides whom to hire to manage the firm. Some economists maintain that the true quality of an entrepreneur becomes evident with his or her selection of managers. Managers, in turn, decide who should be hired and fired and how the business generally should be set up. The workers ultimately use the other inputs to produce the products or services that are being sold by the firm. Workers and managers are paid contractual wages. They receive a specified amount of income for a specified time period. Entrepreneurs are not paid contractual wages. They receive no reward specified in advance. The entrepreneurs make profits if there are any, for profits accrue to those who are willing to take risks. (Because the entrepreneur gets only what is left over after all expenses are paid, he or she is often referred to as a *residual claimant.* The entrepreneur lays claim to the residual—whatever is left.)

Profit and Costs

Most people think of profit as the difference between the amount of revenues a business takes in and the amount it spends for wages, materials, and so on. In a bookkeeping sense, the following formula could be used:

$$\text{Accounting profits} = \text{total revenues} - \text{explicit costs}$$

where **explicit costs** are expenses that the business managers must take account of because they must actually be paid out by the firm. This definition of profit is known as **accounting profit.** It is appropriate when used by accountants to determine a firm's taxable income. Economists are more interested in how firm managers react not just to changes in explicit costs but also to changes in **implicit costs,** defined as expenses that business managers do not have to pay out of pocket but are costs to the firm nonetheless because they represent an opportunity cost. These are noncash costs—they do not involve any direct cash outlay by the firm and must therefore be measured by the alternative cost principle. That is to say,

Firm
A business organization that employs resources to produce goods or services for profit. A firm normally owns and operates at least one plant in order to produce.

Explicit costs
Costs that business managers must take account of because they must be paid; examples are wages, taxes, and rent.

Accounting profit
Total revenues minus total explicit costs.

Implicit costs
Expenses that managers do not have to pay out of pocket and hence do not normally explicitly calculate, such as the opportunity cost of factors of production that are owned; examples are owner-provided capital and owner-provided labor.

they are measured by what the resources (land, capital) currently used in producing a particular good or service could earn in other uses. Economists therefore use the full opportunity cost of all resources as the figure to subtract from revenues to obtain a definition of profit. Another definition of implicit cost is therefore the opportunity cost of using factors that a producer does not buy or hire but already owns.

Opportunity Cost of Capital

Normal rate of return
The amount that must be paid to an investor to induce investment in a business; also known as the *opportunity cost of capital.*

Opportunity cost of capital
The normal rate of return, or the available return on the next-best alternative investment. Economists consider this a cost of production, and it is included in our cost examples.

Firms enter or remain in an industry if they earn, at minimum, a **normal rate of return.** People will not invest their wealth in a business unless they obtain a positive normal (competitive) rate of return—that is, unless their invested wealth pays off. Any business wishing to attract capital must expect to pay at least the same rate of return on that capital as all other businesses (of similar risk) are willing to pay. Put another way, when a firm requires the use of a resource in producing a particular product, it must bid against alternative users of that resource. Thus the firm must offer a price that is at least as much as other users are offering to pay. For example, if individuals can invest their wealth in almost any publishing firm and get a rate of return of 10 percent per year, each firm in the publishing industry must *expect* to pay 10 percent as the normal rate of return to present and future investors. This 10 percent is a *cost to the firm,* the **opportunity cost of capital.** The opportunity cost of capital is the amount of income, or yield, that could have been earned by investing in the next-best alternative. Capital will not stay in firms or industries in which the expected rate of return falls below its opportunity cost, that is, what could be earned elsewhere. If a firm owns some capital equipment, it can either use it or lease it and earn a return. If the firm uses the equipment for production, part of the cost of using that equipment is the forgone revenue that the firm could have earned had it leased out that equipment.

Opportunity Cost of Owner-Provided Labor and Capital

Single-owner proprietorships often grossly exaggerate their profit rates because they understate the opportunity cost of the labor that the proprietor provides to the business. Here we are referring to the opportunity cost of labor. For example, you may know people who run small grocery stores. These people will sit down at the end of the year and figure out what their "profits" are. They will add up all their sales and subtract what they had to pay to other workers, what they had to pay to their suppliers, what they had to pay in taxes, and so on. The end result they will call "profit." They normally will not, however, have figured into their costs the salary that they could have made if they had worked for somebody else in a similar type of job. By working for themselves, they become residual claimants—they receive what is left after all explicit costs have been accounted for. However, part of the costs should include the salary the owner-operator could have received working for someone else.

Consider a simple example of a skilled auto mechanic working 14 hours a day at his own service station, six days a week. Compare this situation to how much he could earn as a trucking company mechanic 84 hours a week. This self-employed auto mechanic might have an opportunity cost of about $20 an hour. For his 84-hour week in his own service station, he is forfeiting $1,680. Unless his service station shows accounting profits of more than that per week, he is losing money in an economic sense.

Another way of looking at the opportunity cost of running a business is that opportunity cost consists of all explicit and implicit costs. Accountants only take account of explicit costs. Therefore, accounting profit ends up being the residual after only explicit costs are subtracted from total revenues.

This same analysis can apply to owner-provided capital, such as land or buildings. The fact that the owner owns the building or the land with which he or she operates a business does not mean that it is "free." Rather, use of the building and land still has an opportunity cost—the value of the next-best alternative use for those assets.

Accounting Profits Versus Economic Profits

The term *profits* in economics means the income that entrepreneurs earn, over and above all costs including their own opportunity cost of time, plus the opportunity cost of the capital they have invested in their business. Profits can be regarded as total revenues minus total costs—which is how accountants think of them—but we must now include *all* costs. Our definition of **economic profits** will be the following:

$$\text{Economic profits} = \text{total revenues} - \text{total opportunity cost of all inputs used}$$

or

$$\text{Economic profits} = \text{total revenues} - (\text{explicit} + \text{implicit costs})$$

Remember that implicit costs include a normal rate of return on invested capital. We show this relationship in Figure 22-1.

The Goal of the Firm: Profit Maximization

When we examined the theory of consumer demand, utility (or satisfaction) maximization by the individual provided the basis for the analysis. In the theory of the firm and production, *profit maximization* is the underlying hypothesis of our predictive theory. The goal of the firm is to maximize economic profits, and the firm is expected to try to make the positive difference between total revenues and total costs as large as it can.

Economic profits
Total revenues minus total opportunity costs of all inputs used, or the total of all implicit and explicit costs.

THINKING CRITICALLY ABOUT THE MEDIA

Profits Increase by $500 Million!

Headlines like the one on this box make great eyecatchers in a newspaper. But without any other information, being told what the *absolute* profits of some company, such as General Motors or Exxon, are is meaningless. If the total reported yearly profits of Exxon are, say, $1 billion, that can mean that Exxon is doing well or doing abysmally. If the total investment in Exxon is $10 billion, then $1 billion in reported profits represents a 10 percent rate of return. If the investment in Exxon is $50 billion, in contrast, then $1 billion in profits represents only a 2 percent rate of return on investment, which could be considered terrible. Don't be fooled by "huge profits" headlines.

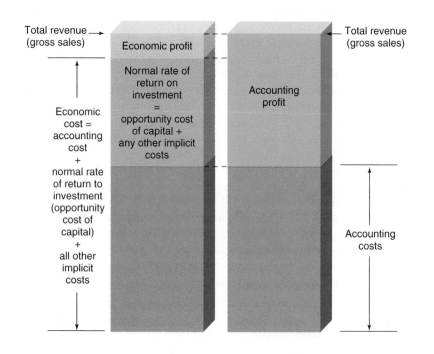

Total revenue (gross sales)
Economic profit
Normal rate of return on investment = opportunity cost of capital + any other implicit costs
Economic cost = accounting cost + normal rate of return to investment (opportunity cost of capital) + all other implicit costs

Total revenue (gross sales)
Accounting profit
Accounting costs

FIGURE 22-1

Simplified View of Economic and Accounting Profit
We see on the right column that accounting profit is the difference between total revenues and total explicit accounting costs. Conversely, we see on the left column that economic profit is equal to total revenues minus economic costs. Economic costs equal explicit accounting costs plus all implicit costs, including a normal rate of return on invested capital.

Our justification for assuming profit maximization by firms is similar to our belief in utility maximization by individuals. To obtain labor, capital, and other resources required to produce commodities, firms must first obtain financing from investors. In general, investors are indifferent about the details of how a firm uses the money they provide. They are most interested in the earnings on this money and the risk of obtaining lower returns or losing the money they have invested. Firms that can provide relatively higher risk-corrected returns will therefore have an advantage in obtaining the financing needed to continue or expand production. Over time we would expect a policy of profit maximization to become the dominant mode of behavior for firms that survive.

CONCEPTS IN BRIEF

- Accounting profits differ from economic profits. Economic profits are defined as total revenues minus total costs, where costs include the full opportunity cost of all of the factors of production plus all other implicit costs.

- Single-owner proprietorships often fail to consider the opportunity cost of the labor services provided by the owner.

- The full opportunity cost of capital invested in a business is generally not included as a cost when accounting profits are calculated. Thus accounting profits often overstate economic profits.

- We assume throughout these chapters that the goal of the firm is to maximize economic profits.

SHORT RUN VERSUS LONG RUN

In Chapter 20, we discussed short-run and long-run price elasticities of supply and demand. For consumers, the long run meant the time period during which all adjustments to a change in price could be made, and anything shorter than that was considered the short run. For suppliers, the long run was the time in which all adjustments could be made, and anything shorter than that was the short run.

Now that we are discussing firms only, we will maintain a similar distinction between the short and the long run, but we will be more specific. In the theory of the firm, the **short run** is defined as any time period that is so short that there is at least one input, such as current **plant size,** that the firm cannot alter.[1] In other words, during the short run, a firm makes do with whatever big machines and factory size it already has, no matter how much more it wants to produce because of increased demand for its product. We consider the plant and heavy equipment, the size or amount of which cannot be varied in the short run, as fixed resources. In agriculture and in some other businesses, land may be a fixed resource.

There are, of course, variable resources that the firm can alter when it wants to change its rate of production. These are called *variable inputs* or *variable factors of production.* Typically, the variable inputs of a firm are its labor and its purchases of raw materials. In the short run, in response to changes in demand, the firm can, by definition, vary only its variable inputs.

The **long run** can now be considered the period of time in which *all* inputs can be varied. Specifically, in the long run, the firm can alter its plant size. How long is the long run? That depends on each individual industry. For Wendy's or McDonald's, the long run may be four

Short run
The time period when at least one input, such as plant size, cannot be changed.

Plant size
The physical size of the factories that a firm owns and operates to produce its output. Plant size can be defined by square footage, maximum physical capacity, and other physical measures.

Long run
The time period in which all factors of production can be varied.

---

[1]There can be many short runs but only one long run. For ease of analysis, in this section we simplify the case to one short run and talk about short-run costs.

or five months, because that is the time it takes to add new franchises. For a steel company, the long run may be several years, because that's how long it takes to plan and build a new plant. An electric utility might need over a decade to build a new plant, for example.

Short run and *long run* in our discussion are in fact management planning terms that apply to decisions made by managers. The firm can operate only in the short run in the sense that decisions must be made in the present. The same analysis applies to your own behavior. You may have many long-run plans about graduate school, vacations, and the like, but you always operate in the short run—you make decisions every day about what you do every day.

THE RELATIONSHIP BETWEEN OUTPUT AND INPUTS

A firm takes numerous inputs, combines them using a technological production process, and ends up with an output. There are, of course, a great many factors of production, or inputs. We classify production inputs into two broad categories (ignoring land)—labor and capital. The relationship between output and these two inputs is as follows:

Output per time period = some function of capital and labor inputs

In simple math, the production relationship can be written $Q = f(K, L)$, where Q = output per time period, K = capital, and L = labor.

We have used the word *production* but have not defined it. **Production** is any process by which resources are transformed into goods or services. Production includes not only making things but also transporting them, retailing, repackaging them, and so on. Notice that if we know that production occurs, we do not necessarily know the value of the output. The production relationship tells nothing about the worth or value of the inputs or the output.

Production
Any activity that results in the conversion of resources into products that can be used in consumption.

INTERNATIONAL EXAMPLE
Europeans Use More Capital

Since 1970, the 15 nations of the European Union (EU) have increased their total annual output of goods and services about as much as the United States. But over this same time period, the EU has dramatically increased the amount of capital relative to the amount of labor it uses in its production processes. Business managers in the EU have substituted capital for labor much more than in the United States because the cost of labor (wages corrected for inflation) has increased by almost 60 percent in the EU but by only 15 percent in the United States.

FOR CRITICAL ANALYSIS: How does a firm decide when to buy more machines? •

The Production Function: A Numerical Example

The relationship between maximum physical output and the quantity of capital and labor used in the production process is sometimes called a **production function.** The production function is a technological relationship between inputs and output. Firms that are inefficient or wasteful in their use of capital and labor will obtain less output than the production function in theory will show. No firm can obtain more output than the production function shows, however. The production function specifies the maximum possible output that can be produced with a given amount of inputs. It also specifies the minimum amount of inputs necessary to produce a given level of output. The production function depends on the tech-

Production function
The relationship between inputs and output. A production function is a technological, not an economic, relationship.

nology available to the firm. It follows that an improvement in technology that allows the firm to produce more output with the same amount of inputs (or the same output with fewer inputs) results in a new production function.

Look at panel (a) of Figure 22-2. It shows a production function relating total output in column 2 to the quantity of labor measured in workers in column 1. When there are zero

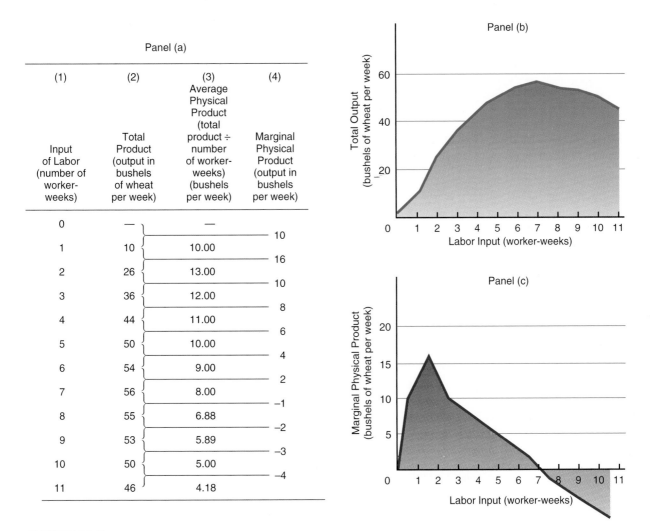

Panel (a)

(1) Input of Labor (number of worker-weeks)	(2) Total Product (output in bushels of wheat per week)	(3) Average Physical Product (total product ÷ number of worker-weeks) (bushels per week)	(4) Marginal Physical Product (output in bushels per week)
0	—	—	
			10
1	10	10.00	
			16
2	26	13.00	
			10
3	36	12.00	
			8
4	44	11.00	
			6
5	50	10.00	
			4
6	54	9.00	
			2
7	56	8.00	
			−1
8	55	6.88	
			−2
9	53	5.89	
			−3
10	50	5.00	
			−4
11	46	4.18	

FIGURE 22-2

Diminishing Returns, the Production Function, and Marginal Product: A Hypothetical Case

Marginal product is the addition to the total product that results when one additional worker is hired. Thus the marginal product of the fourth worker is eight bushels of wheat. With four workers, 44 bushels are produced, but with three workers, only 36 are produced; the difference is 8. In panel (b), we plot the numbers from columns 1 and 2 of panel (a). In panel (c), we plot the numbers from columns 1 and 4 of panel (a). When we go from 0 to 1, marginal product is 10. When we go from one worker to two workers, marginal product increases to 16. After two workers, marginal product declines, but it is still positive. Total product (output) reaches its peak at seven workers, so after seven workers marginal product is negative. When we move from seven to eight workers, marginal product becomes −1 bushel.

workers per week of input, there is no output. When there are 5 workers per week of input (given the capital stock), there is a total output of 50 bushels per week. (Ignore for the moment the rest of that panel.) Panel (b) of Figure 22-2 shows this particular hypothetical production function graphically. Note again that it relates to the short run and that it is for an individual firm.

Panel (b) shows a total physical product curve, or the maximum amount of physical output that is possible when we add successive equal-sized units of labor while holding all other inputs constant. The graph of the production function in panel (b) is not a straight line. In fact, it peaks at 7 workers per week and starts to go down. To understand why it starts to go down with an individual firm in the short run, we have to analyze in detail the **law of diminishing (marginal) returns.**

But before that, let's examine the meaning of columns 3 and 4 of panel (a) of Figure 22-2—that is, average and marginal physical product.

Average and Physical Marginal Product

The definition of **average physical product** is straightforward: It is the total product divided by the number of workers expressed in output per week. You can see in column 3 of panel (a) of Figure 22-2 that the average physical product of labor first rises and then steadily falls after two workers are hired.

Remember that *marginal* means "additional." Hence the **marginal physical product** of labor is the change in total product that occurs when a worker joins an existing production process. (The term *physical* here emphasizes the fact that we are measuring in terms of physical units of production, not in dollar terms.) It is also the *change* in total product that occurs when that worker quits or is laid off an existing production process. The marginal physical product of labor therefore refers to the *change in output caused by a one-unit change in the labor input.* (Marginal physical product is also referred to as *marginal productivity* and *marginal return.*)

DIMINISHING MARGINAL RETURNS

The concept of diminishing marginal returns—also known as diminishing marginal product—applies to many situations. If you put a seat belt across your lap, a certain amount of safety is obtained. If you add another seat belt over your shoulder, some additional safety is obtained, but less than when the first belt was secured. When you add a third seat belt over the other shoulder, the amount of *additional* safety obtained is even smaller.

The same analysis holds for firms in their use of productive inputs. When the returns from hiring more workers are diminishing, it does not necessarily mean that more workers won't be hired. In fact, workers will be hired until the returns, in terms of the *value* of the *extra* output produced, are equal to the additional wages that have to be paid for those workers to produce the extra output. Before we get into that decision-making process, let's demonstrate that diminishing returns can be represented graphically and can be used in our analysis of the firm.

Measuring Diminishing Returns

How do we measure diminishing returns? First, we limit the analysis to only one variable factor of production (or input)—let's say the factor is labor. Every other factor of produc-

Law of diminishing (marginal) returns
The observation that after some point, successive equal-sized increases in a variable factor of production, such as labor, added to fixed factors of production, will result in smaller increases in output.

Average physical product
Total product divided by the variable input.

Marginal physical product
The physical output that is due to the addition of one more unit of a variable factor of production; the change in total product occurring when a variable input is increased and all other inputs are held constant; also called *marginal productivity* or *marginal return.*

tion, such as machines, must be held constant. Only in this way can we calculate the marginal returns from using more workers and know when we reach the point of diminishing marginal returns.

The marginal productivity of labor may increase rapidly at the very beginning. A firm starts with no workers, only machines. The firm then hires one worker, who finds it difficult to get the work started. But when the firm hires more workers, each is able to *specialize,* and the marginal productivity of those additional workers may actually be greater than it was with the previous few workers. Beyond some point, however, diminishing returns must set in, *not* because new workers are less qualified, but because each worker has (on average) fewer machines with which to work (remember, all other inputs are fixed). In fact, eventually the firm will become so crowded that workers will start to get in each other's way. At that point, total production declines and marginal physical product becomes negative.

Using these ideas, we can define the law of diminishing returns as follows:

As successive equal increases in a variable factor of production are added to fixed factors of production, there will be a point beyond which the extra, or marginal, product that can be attributed to each additional unit of the variable factor of production will decline.

Note that the law of diminishing returns is a statement about the *physical* relationships between inputs and outputs that we have observed in many firms. If the law of diminishing returns were not a fairly accurate statement about the world, what would stop firms from hiring additional workers forever?

An Example of the Law of Diminishing Returns

Agriculture provides an example of the law of diminishing returns. With a fixed amount of land, fertilizer, and tractors, the addition of more farm workers eventually yields decreasing increases in output. After a while, when all the tractors are being used, additional farm workers will have to start farming manually. They obviously won't be as productive as the first farm workers who manned the tractors. The marginal physical product of an additional farm worker, given a specified amount of capital, must eventually be less than that for the previous workers.

A hypothetical set of numbers illustrating the law of diminishing marginal returns is presented in panel (a) of Figure 22-2. The numbers are presented graphically in panel (c). Marginal productivity (returns from adding more workers) first increases, then decreases, and finally becomes negative.

When one worker is hired, total output goes from 0 to 10. Thus marginal physical product is 10 bushels of wheat per week. When the second worker is hired, total product goes from 10 to 26 bushels of wheat per week. Marginal physical product therefore increases to 16 bushels of wheat per week. When a third worker is hired, total product again increases, from 26 to 36 bushels of wheat per week. This represents a marginal physical product of only 10 bushels of wheat per week. Therefore, the point of diminishing marginal returns occurs after two workers are hired.

Notice that after 7 workers per week, marginal physical product becomes negative. That means that the hiring of an eighth worker would create a situation that reduces total product. Sometimes this is called the *point of saturation,* indicating that given the amount of fixed inputs, there is no further positive use for more of the variable input. We have entered the region of negative marginal returns.

CONCEPTS IN BRIEF

- The technological relationship between output and input is called the production function. It relates output per time period to the several inputs, such as capital and labor.

- After some rate of output, the firm generally experiences diminishing marginal returns.

- The law of diminishing returns states that if all factors of production are held constant except one, equal increments in that one variable factor will eventually yield decreasing increments in output.

SHORT-RUN COSTS TO THE FIRM

You will see that costs are the extension of the production ideas just presented. Let's consider the costs the firm faces in the short run. To make this example simple, assume that there are only two factors of production, capital and labor. Our definition of the short run will be the time during which capital is fixed but labor is variable.

In the short run, a firm incurs certain types of costs. We label all costs incurred **total costs.** Then we break total costs down into total fixed costs and total variable costs, which we will explain shortly. Therefore,

> Total costs (TC) = total fixed costs (TFC) + total variable costs (TVC)

Remember that these total costs include both explicit and implicit costs, including the normal rate of return on investment.

After we have looked at the elements of total costs, we will find out how to compute average and marginal costs.

Total costs
The sum of total fixed costs and total variable costs.

Total Fixed Costs

Let's look at an ongoing business such as Compaq Computer. The decision makers in that corporate giant can look around and see big machines, thousands of parts, huge buildings, and a multitude of other components of plant and equipment that have already been bought and are in place. Compaq has to take account of the technological obsolescence of this equipment, no matter how many computers it produces. The payments on the loans taken out to buy the equipment will all be exactly the same. The opportunity costs of any land that Compaq owns will all be exactly the same. These costs are more or less the same for Compaq no matter how many computers it produces.

We also have to point out that the opportunity cost (or normal rate of return) of capital must be included along with other costs. Remember that we are dealing in the short run, during which capital is fixed. If investors in Compaq Computer have already put $100 million into a new factory addition, the opportunity cost of that capital invested is now, in essence, a *fixed cost.* Why? Because in the short run, nothing can be done about that cost; the investment has already been made. This leads us to a very straightforward definition of fixed costs: All costs that do not vary—that is, all costs that do not depend on the rate of production—are called **fixed costs.**

Let's now take as an example the fixed costs incurred by an assembler of pocket calculators. This firm's total fixed costs will equal the cost of the rent on its equipment and the insurance it has to pay. We see in panel (a) of Figure 22-3 that total fixed costs per day are $10. In panel (b), these total fixed costs are represented by the horizontal line at $10 per day. They are invariant to changes in the output of calculators per day—no matter how many are produced, fixed costs will remain at $10 per day.

Fixed costs
Costs that do not vary with output. Fixed costs include such things as rent on a building. These costs are fixed for a certain period of time; in the long run, they are variable.

Panel (a)

(1) Total Output (Q/day)	(2) Total Fixed Costs (TFC)	(3) Total Variable Costs (TVC)	(4) Total Costs (TC) (4) = (2) + (3)	(5) Average Fixed Costs (AFC) (5) = (2) ÷ (1)	(6) Average Variable Costs (AVC) (6) = (3) ÷ (1)	(7) Average Total Costs (ATC) (7) = (4) ÷ (1)	(8) Total Costs (TC) (4)	(9) Marginal Cost (MC) $(9) = \frac{\text{change in (8)}}{\text{change in (1)}}$
0	$10	$ 0	$10	—	—	—	$10	
								$5
1	10	5	15	$10.00	$5.00	$15.00	15	
								3
2	10	8	18	5.00	4.00	9.00	18	
								2
3	10	10	20	3.33	3.33	6.67	20	
								1
4	10	11	21	2.50	2.75	5.25	21	
								2
5	10	13	23	2.00	2.60	4.60	23	
								3
6	10	16	26	1.67	2.67	4.33	26	
								4
7	10	20	30	1.43	2.86	4.28	30	
								5
8	10	25	35	1.25	3.13	4.38	35	
								6
9	10	31	41	1.11	3.44	4.56	41	
								7
10	10	38	48	1.00	3.80	4.80	48	
								8
11	10	46	56	.91	4.18	5.09	56	

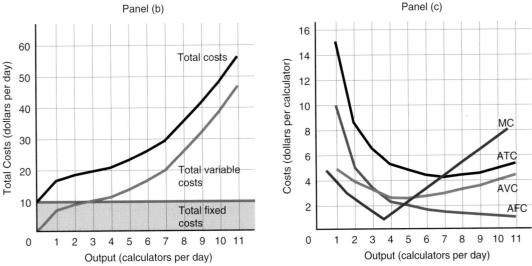

FIGURE 22-3

Cost of Production: An Example

In panel (a), the derivation of columns 4 through 9 are given in parentheses in each column heading. For example, column 6, average variable costs, is derived by dividing column 3, total variable costs, by column 1, total output per day. Note that marginal cost (MC) in panel (c) intersects average variable costs (AVC) at the latter's minimum point. Also, MC intersects average total costs (ATC) at that latter's minimum point. It is a little more difficult to see that MC equals AVC and ATC at their respective minimum points in panel (a) because we are using discrete one-unit changes. You can see, though, that the marginal cost of going from 4 units per day to 5 units per day is $2 and increases to $3 when we move to 6 units per day. Somewhere in the middle it equals AVC of $2.60, which is in fact the minimum average variable cost. The same analysis holds for ATC, which hits minimum at 7 units per day at $4.28 per unit. MC goes from $4 to $5 and just equals ATC somewhere in between.

Total Variable Costs

Total **variable costs** are costs whose magnitude varies with the rate of production. One obvious variable cost is wages. The more the firm produces, the more labor it has to hire; therefore, the more wages it has to pay. Another variable cost is parts. In the assembly of calculators, for example, microchips must be bought. The more calculators that are made, the more chips must be bought. Part of the rate of depreciation (the rate of wear and tear) on machines that are used in the assembly process can also be considered a variable cost if depreciation depends partly on how long and how intensively the machines are used. Total variable costs are given in panel (a) of Figure 22-3 in column 3. These are translated into the total variable cost curve in panel (b). Notice that the total variable cost curve lies below the total cost curve by the vertical distance of $10. This vertical distance represents, of course, total fixed costs.

Variable costs
Costs that vary with the rate of production. They include wages paid to workers and purchases of materials.

Short-Run Average Cost Curves

In panel (b) of Figure 22-3 we see total costs, total variable costs, and total fixed costs. Now we want to look at average cost. The average cost concept is one in which we are measuring cost per unit of output. It is a matter of simple arithmetic to figure the averages of these three cost concepts. We can define them as follows:

$$\text{Average total costs (ATC)} = \frac{\text{total costs (TC)}}{\text{output (}Q\text{)}}$$

$$\text{Average variable costs (AVC)} = \frac{\text{total variable costs (TVC)}}{\text{output (}Q\text{)}}$$

$$\text{Average fixed costs (AFC)} = \frac{\text{total fixed costs (TFC)}}{\text{output (}Q\text{)}}$$

Exercise 22.2
Visit www.econtoday.com for more about different costs.

The arithmetic is done in columns 5, 6, and 7 in panel (a) of Figure 22-3. The numerical results are translated into a graphical format in panel (c). Because total costs (TC) equal variable costs (TVC) plus fixed costs (TFC), the difference between average total costs (ATC) and average variable costs (AVC) will always be identical to average fixed costs (AFC). That means that average total costs and average variable costs move together as output expands.

Now let's see what we can observe about the three average cost curves in Figure 22-3.

Average Fixed Costs (AFC). **Average fixed costs** continue to fall throughout the output range. In fact, if we were to continue the diagram farther to the right, we would find that average fixed costs would get closer and closer to the horizontal axis. That is because total fixed costs remain constant. As we divide this fixed number by a larger and larger number of units of output, the resulting AFC has to become smaller and smaller. In business, this is called "spreading the overhead."

Average fixed costs
Total fixed costs divided by the number of units produced.

Average Variable Costs (AVC). We assume a particular form of the curve for **average variable costs.** The form that it takes is U-shaped: First it falls; then it starts to rise. It is possible for the AVC curve to take other shapes in the long run.

Average variable costs
Total variable costs divided by the number of units produced.

Average Total Costs (ATC). This curve has a shape similar to that of the AVC curve. However, it falls even more dramatically in the beginning and rises more slowly after it has reached a minimum point. It falls and then rises because **average total costs** are the

Average total costs
Total costs divided by the number of units produced; sometimes called *average per-unit total costs.*

summation of the AFC curve and the AVC curve. Thus when AFC and AVC are both falling, ATC must fall too. At some point, however, AVC starts to increase while AFC continues to fall. Once the increase in the AVC curve outweighs the decrease in the AFC curve, the ATC curve will start to increase and will develop its familiar U shape.

Marginal Cost

Marginal costs
The change in total costs due to a one-unit change in production rate.

We have stated repeatedly that the basis of decisions is always on the margin—movement in economics is always determined at the margin. This dictum also holds true within the firm. Firms, according to the analysis we use to predict their behavior, are very interested in their **marginal costs.** Because the term *marginal* means "additional" or "incremental" (or "decremental," too) here, marginal costs refer to costs that result from a one-unit change in the production rate. For example, if the production of 10 calculators per day costs a firm $48 and the production of 11 calculators costs it $56 per day, the marginal cost of producing the eleventh calculator per day is $8.

Marginal costs can be measured by using the formula

$$\text{Marginal cost} = \frac{\text{change in total cost}}{\text{change in output}}$$

We show the marginal costs of calculator production per day in column 9 of panel (a) in Figure 22-3, calculated according to the formula just given. In our example, we have changed output by one unit every time, so we can ignore variations in the denominator in that particular formula.

This marginal cost schedule is shown graphically in panel (c) of Figure 22-3. Just like average variable costs and average total costs, marginal costs first fall and then rise. The U shape of the marginal cost curve is a result of increasing and then diminishing marginal returns. At lower levels of output, the marginal cost curve declines. The reasoning is that as marginal physical product increases with each addition of output, the marginal cost of this last unit of output must fall. Conversely, when diminishing marginal returns set in, marginal physical product decreases (and eventually becomes negative); it follows that the marginal cost of the last unit must rise. These relationships are clearly reflected in the geometry of panels (b) and (c) of Figure 22-3.

In summary:

> **As long as marginal physical product rises, marginal cost will fall, and when marginal physical product starts to fall (after reaching the point of diminishing marginal returns), marginal cost will begin to rise.**

POLICY EXAMPLE
Can "Three Strikes" Laws Reduce Crime?

Crime and violence have been the top concern of Americans for at least a decade. At both the federal and the state level, politicians have responded with a variety of policies aimed at reducing crime. One popular new law has been labeled "three strikes and you're out." A defendant with a prior conviction for two serious or violent offenses faces mandatory life imprisonment for a third offense.

Such legislation has dramatically affected the marginal cost of violence and murder to potential criminal defendants who have already been convicted of two felonies. Here is what one career criminal, Frank Schweickert, said in a *New York Times* interview: "Before, if I was doing a robbery and getting chased by cops, I'd lay my gun down. . . . But now you are talking about a life sentence. Why isn't it worth doing whatever it takes to get away? If that meant shooting a cop, if that meant shooting a store clerk, if that meant shooting someone innocent in my way, well, they'd have gotten shot. Because what is the worst thing that could happen to me: life imprisonment? If I'm getting a murder sentence anyway, I might as well do whatever it takes to maybe get away." In other words, the "three strikes" legislation has reduced the marginal cost of murder committed while engaging in a criminal activity after two prior felony convictions to zero.

FOR CRITICAL ANALYSIS: Do criminals subject to the new legislation have to understand the concept of marginal cost in order for our theory to predict well? Explain. ●

The Relationship Between Average and Marginal Costs

Let us now examine the relationship between average costs and marginal costs. There is always a definite relationship between averages and marginals. Consider the example of 10 football players with an average weight of 200 pounds. An eleventh player is added. His weight is 250 pounds. That represents the marginal weight. What happens now to the average weight of the team? It must increase. Thus when the marginal player weighs more than the average, the average must increase. Likewise, if the marginal player weighs less than 200 pounds, the average weight will decrease.

There is a similar relationship between average variable costs and marginal costs. When marginal costs are less than average costs, the latter must fall. Conversely, when marginal costs are greater than average costs, the latter must rise. When you think about it, the relationship makes sense. The only way for average variable costs to fall is for the extra cost of the marginal unit produced to be less than the average variable cost of all the preceding units. For example, if the average variable cost for two units of production is $4.00 a unit, the only way for the average variable cost of three units to be less than that of two units is for the variable costs attributable to the last unit—the marginal cost—to be less than the average of the past units. In this particular case, if average variable cost falls to $3.33 a unit, total variable cost for the three units would be three times $3.33, or almost exactly $10.00. Total variable cost for two units is two times $4.00, or $8.00. The marginal cost is therefore $10.00 minus $8.00, or $2.00, which is less than the average variable cost of $3.33.

A similar type of computation can be carried out for rising average variable costs. The only way for average variable costs to rise is for the average variable cost of additional units to be more than that for units already produced. But the incremental cost is the marginal cost. In this particular case, the marginal costs have to be higher than the average variable costs.

There is also a relationship between marginal costs and average total costs. Remember that average total cost is equal to total cost divided by the number of units produced. Remember also that marginal cost does not include any fixed costs. Fixed costs are, by definition, fixed and cannot influence marginal costs. Our example can therefore be repeated substituting *average total cost* for *average variable cost.*

These rising and falling relationships can be seen in Figure 22-3, where MC intersects AVC and ATC at their respective minimum points.

Minimum Cost Points

At what rate of output of calculators per day does our representative firm experience the minimum average total costs? Column 7 in panel (a) of Figure 22-3 shows that the minimum average total cost is $4.28, which occurs at an output rate of seven calculators per day.

We can also find this minimum cost by finding the point in panel (c) of Figure 22-3 at which the marginal cost curve intersects the average total cost curve. This should not be surprising. When marginal cost is below average total cost, average total cost falls. When marginal cost is above average total cost, average total cost rises. At the point where average total cost is neither falling nor rising, marginal cost must then be equal to average total cost. When we represent this graphically, the marginal cost curve will intersect the average total cost curve at the latter's minimum.

The same analysis applies to the intersection of the marginal cost curve and the average variable cost curve. When are average variable costs at a minimum? According to panel (a) of Figure 22-3, average variable costs are at a minimum of $2.60 at an output rate of five calculators per day. This is where the marginal cost curve intersects the average variable cost curve in panel (c) of Figure 22-3.

CONCEPTS IN BRIEF

- Total costs equal total fixed costs plus total variable costs.
- Fixed costs are those that do not vary with the rate of production; variable costs are those that do vary with the rate of production.
- Average total costs equal total costs divided by output (ATC = TC/Q).
- Average variable costs equal total variable costs divided by output (AVC = TVC/Q).
- Average fixed costs equal total fixed costs divided by output (AFC = TFC/Q).
- Marginal cost equals the change in total cost divided by the change in output (MC = ΔTC/ΔQ).
- The marginal cost curve intersects the minimum point of the average total cost curve and the minimum point of the average variable cost curve.

THE RELATIONSHIP BETWEEN DIMINISHING MARGINAL RETURNS AND COST CURVES

There is a unique relationship between output and the shape of the various cost curves we have drawn. Let's consider specifically the relationship between marginal cost and the example of diminishing marginal physical returns in panel (a) of Figure 22-4 on page 496. It turns out that if wage rates are constant, the shape of the marginal cost curve in panel (d) of Figure 22-4 is both a reflection of and a consequence of the law of diminishing returns. Let's assume that each unit of labor can be purchased at a constant price. Further assume that labor is the only variable input. We see that as more workers are hired, marginal physical product first rises and then falls after the point at which diminishing returns are encountered. Thus the marginal cost of each extra unit of output will first fall as long as marginal physical product is rising, and then it will rise as long as marginal physical product is falling. Recall that marginal cost is defined as

$$MC = \frac{\text{change in total cost}}{\text{change in output}}$$

Because the price of labor is assumed to be constant, the change in total cost is simply the constant price of labor, W (we are increasing labor by only one unit). The change in output

		Panel (a)			
(1)	(2)	(3)	(4)	(5)	(6)
Labor Input	Total Product (number of pairs sold)	Average Physical Product (pairs per salesperson) (3) = (2) ÷ (1)	Marginal Physical Product	Average Variable Cost (5) = W ($100) ÷ (3)	Marginal Cost (6) = W ($100) ÷ (4)
0	0	—	—	—	—
1	50	50	50	$2.00	$2.00
2	110	55	60	1.80	1.70
3	180	60	70	1.70	1.40
4	240	60	60	1.70	1.70
5	290	58	50	1.70	2.00
6	330	55	40	1.80	2.50
7	360	51	30	2.00	3.30

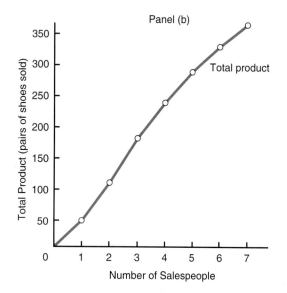

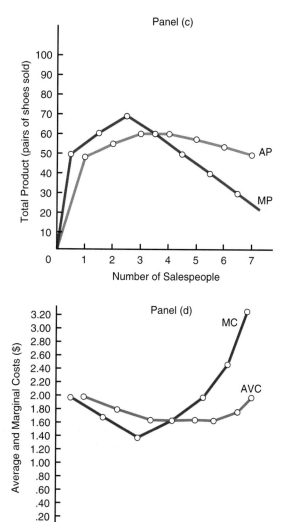

FIGURE 22-4

The Relationship Between Physical Output and Costs

As the number of salespeople increases, the total number of pairs of shoes sold rises, as shown in panels (a) and (b). In panel (c), marginal product (MP) first rises and then falls. Average product (AP) follows. The mirror image of panel (c) is shown in panel (d), in which MC and AVC first fall and then rise.

is simply the marginal physical product (MPP) of the one-unit increase in labor. Therefore, we see that

$$\text{Marginal cost} = \frac{W}{\text{MPP}}$$

This means that initially, when there are increasing returns, marginal cost falls (we are dividing W by increasingly larger numbers), and later, when diminishing returns set in and marginal physical product is falling, marginal cost must increase (we are dividing W by smaller numbers). As marginal physical product increases, marginal cost decreases, and as marginal physical product decreases, marginal cost must increase. Thus when marginal physical product reaches its maximum, marginal cost necessarily reaches its minimum. To illustrate this, let's return to Figure 22-2 on page 487 and consider specifically panel (a). Assume that a worker is paid $100 a week. When we go from zero labor input to one unit, output increases by 10 bushels of wheat. Each of those 10 bushels of wheat has a marginal cost of $10. Now the second unit of labor is hired, and it too costs $100 per week. Output increases by 16. Thus the marginal cost is $100 ÷ 16 = $6.25. We continue the experiment. We see that the next unit of labor yields only 10 additional bushels of wheat, so marginal cost starts to rise again back to $10. The following unit of labor increases marginal physical product by only 8, so marginal cost becomes $100 ÷ 8 = $12.50.

All of the foregoing can be restated in relatively straightforward terms:

> **Firms' short-run cost curves are a reflection of the law of diminishing marginal returns. Given any constant price of the variable input, marginal costs decline as long as the marginal product of the variable resource is rising. At the point at which diminishing marginal returns begin, marginal costs begin to rise as the marginal product of the variable input begins to decline.**

The result is a marginal cost curve that slopes down, hits a minimum, and then slopes up. The average total cost curve and average variable cost curve are of course affected. They will have their familiar U shape in the short run. Again, to see this, recall that

$$\text{AVC} = \frac{\text{total variable costs}}{\text{total output}}$$

As we move from zero labor input to one unit in panel (a) of Figure 22-2, output increases from zero to 10 bushels. The total variable costs are the price per worker, W ($100), times the number of workers (1). Because the average product of one worker (column 3) is 10, we can write the total product, 10, as the average product, 10, times the number of workers, 1. Thus we see that

$$\text{AVC} = \frac{\$100 \times 1}{10 \times 1} = \frac{\$100}{10} = \frac{W}{\text{AP}}$$

From column 3 in panel (a) of Figure 22-2 we see that the average product increases, reaches a maximum, and then declines. Because AVC = W/AP, average variable cost decreases as average product increases and increases as average product decreases. AVC reaches its minimum when average product reaches its maximum. Furthermore, because ATC = AVC + AFC, the average total cost curve inherits the relationship between the average variable cost and diminishing returns.

To illustrate, consider a shoe store that employs salespeople to sell shoes. Panel (a) of Figure 22-4 presents in column 2 the total number of pairs of shoes sold as the number of salespeople increases. Notice that the total product first increases at an increasing rate and later increases at a decreasing rate. This is reflected in column 4, which shows that the marginal physical product increases at first and then falls. The average physical product too first rises and then falls. The marginal and average physical products are graphed in panel (c) of Figure 22-4. Our immediate interest here is the average variable and marginal costs. Because we can define average variable cost as $100/AP (assuming that the wage paid is constant at $100), as the average product rises from 50 to 55 to 60 pairs of shoes sold, the average variable cost falls from $2.00 to $1.82 to $1.67. Conversely, as average product falls from 60 to 50, average variable cost rises from $1.67 to $2.00. Likewise, because marginal cost can also be defined as W/MPP, we see that as marginal physical product rises from 50 to 70, marginal cost falls from $2.00 to $1.43. As marginal physical product falls to 30, marginal cost rises to $3.33. These relationships are also expressed in panels (b), (c), and (d) of Figure 22-4.

LONG-RUN COST CURVES

The long run is defined as a time period during which full adjustment can be made to any change in the economic environment. Thus in the long run, *all* factors of production are variable. Long-run curves are sometimes called *planning curves,* and the long run is sometimes called the **planning horizon.** We start out our analysis of long-run cost curves by considering a single firm contemplating the construction of a single plant. The firm has three alternative plant sizes from which to choose on the planning horizon. Each particular plant size generates its own short-run average total cost curve. Now that we are talking about the difference between long-run and short-run cost curves, we will label all short-run curves with an *S* and long-run curves with an *L;* short-run average (total) costs will be labeled SAC, and long-run average cost curves will be labeled LAC.

Panel (a) of Figure 22-5 shows three short-run average cost curves for three successively larger plants. Which is the optimal size to build? That depends on the anticipated normal,

Planning horizon
The long run, during which all inputs are variable.

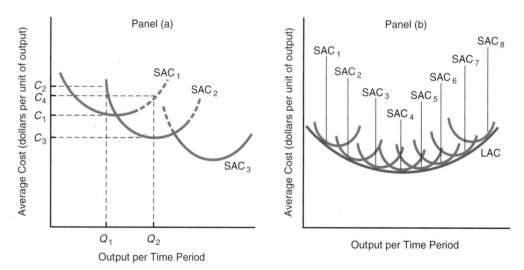

FIGURE 22-5

Preferable Plant Size and the Long-Run Average Cost Curve
If the anticipated permanent rate of output per unit time period is Q_1, the optimal plant to build would be the one corresponding to SAC$_1$ in panel (a) because average costs are lower. However, if the permanent rate of output increases to Q_2, it will be more profitable to have a plant size corresponding to SAC$_2$. Unit costs fall to C_3.

If we draw all the possible short-run average cost curves that correspond to different plant sizes and then draw the envelope (a curve tangent to each member of a set of curves) to these various curves, SAC$_1$–SAC$_8$, we obtain the long-run average cost curve, or the planning curve, as shown in panel (b).

sustained (permanent) rate of output per time period. Assume for a moment that the anticipated normal, sustained rate is Q_1. If a plant of size 1 is built, the average costs will be C_1. If a plant of size 2 is built, we see on SAC_2 that the average costs will be C_2, which is greater than C_1. Thus if the anticipated rate of output is Q_1, the appropriate plant size is the one from which SAC_1 was derived.

However, if the anticipated permanent rate of output per time period goes from Q_1 to Q_2 and a plant of size 1 had been decided on, average costs would be C_4. If a plant of size 2 had been decided on, average costs would be C_3, which is clearly less than C_4.

In choosing the appropriate plant size for a single-plant firm during the planning horizon, the firm will pick the size whose short-run average cost curve generates an average cost that is lowest for the expected rate of output.

Long-Run Average Cost Curve

Long-run average cost curve
The locus of points representing the minimum unit cost of producing any given rate of output, given current technology and resource prices.

Planning curve
The long-run average cost curve.

If we now assume that the entrepreneur faces an infinite number of choices of plant sizes in the long run, we can conceive of an infinite number of SAC curves similar to the three in panel (a) of Figure 22-5. We are not able, of course, to draw an infinite number; we have drawn quite a few, however, in panel (b) of Figure 22-5. We then draw the "envelope" to all these various short-run average cost curves. The resulting envelope is the **long-run average cost curve.** This long-run average cost curve is sometimes called the **planning curve,** for it represents the various average costs attainable at the planning stage of the firm's decision making. It represents the locus (path) of points giving the least unit cost of producing any given rate of output. Note that the LAC curve is *not* tangent to each individual SAC curve at the latter's minimum points. This is true only at the minimum point of the LAC curve. Then and only then are minimum long-run average costs equal to minimum short-run average costs.

WHY THE LONG-RUN AVERAGE COST CURVE IS U-SHAPED

Notice that the long-run average cost curve, LAC, in panel (b) of Figure 22-5 is U-shaped, similar to the U shape of the short-run average cost curve developed earlier in this chapter. The reason behind the U shape of the two curves is not the same, however. The short-run average cost curve is U-shaped because of the law of diminishing marginal returns. But the law cannot apply to the long run, because in the long run, all factors of production are variable; there is no point of diminishing marginal returns because there is no fixed factor of production. Why, then, do we see the U shape in the long-run average cost curve? The reasoning has to do with economies of scale, constant returns to scale, and diseconomies of scale. When the firm is experiencing **economies of scale,** the long-run average cost curve slopes downward—an increase in scale and production leads to a fall in unit costs. When the firm is experiencing **constant returns to scale,** the long-run average cost curve is at its minimum point, such that an increase in scale and production does not change unit costs. When the firm is experiencing **diseconomies of scale,** the long-run average cost curve slopes upward—an increase in scale and production increases unit costs. These three sections of the long-run average cost curves are broken up into panels (a), (b), and (c) in Figure 22-6 on page 500.

Economies of scale
Decreases in long-run average costs resulting from increases in output.

Constant returns to scale
No change in long-run average costs when output increases.

Diseconomies of scale
Increases in long-run average costs that occur as output increases.

Reasons for Economies of Scale

We shall examine three of the many reasons why a firm might be expected to experience economies of scale: specialization, the dimensional factor, and improved productive equipment.

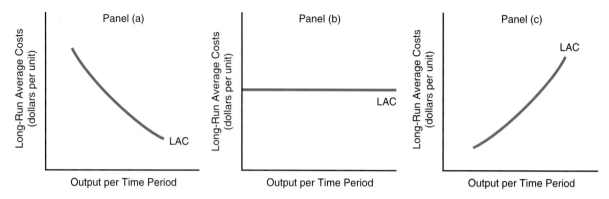

FIGURE 22-6

Economies of Scale, Constant Returns to Scale, and Diseconomies of Scale Shown with the Long-Run Average Cost Curve
Long-run average cost curves will fall when there are economies of scale, as shown in panel (a). They will be constant (flat) when the firm is experiencing constant returns to scale, as shown in panel (b). They will rise when the firm is experiencing diseconomies of scale, as shown in panel (c).

Specialization. As a firm's scale of operation increases, the opportunities for specialization in the use of resource inputs also increase. This is sometimes called *increased division of tasks* or *operations.* Gains from such division of labor or increased specialization are well known. When we consider managerial staffs, we also find that larger enterprises may be able to put together more highly specialized staffs.

Dimensional Factor. Large-scale firms often require proportionately less input per unit of output simply because certain inputs do not have to be physically doubled in order to double the output. Consider the cost of storage of oil. The cost of storage is basically related to the cost of steel that goes into building the storage container; however, the amount of steel required goes up less than in proportion to the volume (storage capacity) of the container (because the volume of a container increases more than proportionately with its surface area).

Improved Productive Equipment. The larger the scale of the enterprise, the more the firm is able to take advantage of larger-volume (output capacity) types of machinery. Small-scale operations may not be able profitably to use large-volume machines that can be more efficient per unit of output. Also, smaller firms often cannot use technologically more advanced machinery because they are unable to spread out the high cost of such sophisticated equipment over a large output.

For any of these reasons, the firm may experience economies of scale, which means that equal percentage increases in output result in a decrease in average cost. Thus output can double, but total costs will less than double; hence average cost falls. Note that the factors listed for causing economies of scale are all *internal* to the firm; they do not depend on what other firms are doing or what is happening in the economy.

DISSEMINATING IDEAS VIA THE INTERNET

Numerous economic studies have shown that the production of many goods that we consume have constant unit costs once production is under way. Otherwise stated, the production of most goods appears to look like panel (b) in Figure 22-6. Ideas, in contrast, often have exceedingly high costs for the first "unit" of knowledge. Once that first unit is produced, though, both the marginal and average costs for production of additional units is essentially zero. Numerous costs are involved in producing the ideas for new technology. Once those ideas are produced, they can be disseminated electronically on the Internet to everybody in the world at relatively small additional cost.

FOR CRITICAL ANALYSIS: Draw the appropriate long-run average cost curve for ideas. ●

Why a Firm Might Experience Diseconomies of Scale

One of the basic reasons that a firm can expect to run into diseconomies of scale is that there are limits to the efficient functioning of management. Moreover, as more workers are hired, a more than proportionate increase in managers and staff people may be needed, and this could cause increased costs per unit. This is so because larger levels of output imply successively larger *plant* size, which in turn implies successively larger *firm* size. Thus as the level of output increases, more people must be hired, and the firm gets bigger. However, as this happens, the support, supervisory, and administrative staff and the general paperwork of the firm all increase. As the layers of supervision grow, the costs of information and communication grow more than proportionately; hence the average unit cost will start to increase.

Some observers of corporate giants claim that many of them are experiencing some diseconomies of scale today. Witness the problems that General Motors and IBM had in the early 1990s. Some analysts say that the financial problems that they have experienced are at least partly a function of their size relative to their smaller, more flexible competitors, who can make decisions more quickly and then take advantage of changing market conditions more rapidly. This seems to be particularly true with IBM. It apparently adapted very slowly to the fact that the large mainframe computer business was declining as micro- and mini-computers became more and more powerful.

MINIMUM EFFICIENT SCALE

Minimum efficient scale (MES)

The lowest rate of output per unit time at which long-run average costs for a particular firm are at a minimum.

Economists and statisticians have obtained actual data on the relationship between changes in all inputs and changes in average cost. It turns out that for many industries, the long-run average cost curve does not resemble that shown in panel (b) of Figure 22-5. Rather, it more closely resembles Figure 22-7 on page 502. What you can observe there is a small portion of declining long-run average costs (economies of scale) and then a wide range of outputs over which the firm experiences relatively constant economies of scale. At the output rate when economies of scale end and constant economies of scale start, the **minimum efficient scale (MES)** for the firm is encountered. It occurs at point *A*. (The point is, of course, approximate. The more smoothly the curve declines into its flat portion, the more approximate will be our estimate of the MES.) The minimum efficient scale will always be the lowest rate of output at which long-run average costs are minimized. In any industry with a long-run average cost curve similar to the one in Figure 22-7, larger firms will have no cost-saving advantage over smaller firms as long as the smaller firms have at least obtained the minimum efficient scale at point *A*.

Among its uses, the minimum efficient scale gives us a rough measure of the degree of competition in an industry. If the MES is small relative to industry demand, the degree of competition in that industry is likely to be high because there is room for many efficiently

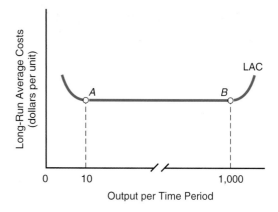

FIGURE 22-7

Minimum Efficient Scale

This long-run average cost curve reaches a minimum point at *A*. After that point, long-run average costs remain horizontal, or constant, and then rise at some later rate of output. Point *A* is called the minimum efficient scale for the firm because that is the point at which it reaches minimum costs. It is the lowest rate of output at which the average long-run costs are minimized.

sized plants. Conversely, when the MES is large relative to industry demand, the degree of competition is likely to be small because there is room for a relatively small number of efficiently sized plants or firms. Looked at another way, if it takes a very large scale of plant to obtain minimum long-run average cost, the output of just a few of these very large firms can fully satisfy total market demand. This means that there isn't room for a large number of smaller plants if maximum efficiency is to be obtained in the industry.

CONCEPTS IN BRIEF

• The long run is often called the planning horizon. The long-run average cost curve is the planning curve. It is found by drawing a line tangent to one point on a series of short-run average cost curves, each corresponding to a different plant size.

• The firm can experience economies of scale, diseconomies of scale, and constant returns to scale, all according to whether the long-run average cost curve slopes downward, slopes upward, or is horizontal (flat). Economies of scale refer to what happens to average cost when all factors of production are increased.

• We observe economies of scale for a number of reasons, among which are specialization, improved productive equipment, and the dimensional factor, because large-scale firms require proportionately less input per unit of output. The firm may experience diseconomies of scale primarily because of limits to the efficient functioning of management.

• The minimum efficient scale occurs at the lowest rate of output at which long-run average costs are minimized.

America Online, in an attempt to compete more aggressively, switched to zero-marginal-cost pricing a few years ago. What do you predict would be the effect on the quantity of AOL Internet access services demanded?

Zero Marginal Cost Pricing: The Case of Internet Access

CONCEPTS APPLIED:

FIXED COST, MARGINAL COST, FLAT-RATE PRICING, PEAK-LOAD (CONGESTION) PRICING

 Visit www.econtoday.com for an Internet Activity that expands your understanding of these concepts.

People respond to incentives. That was made astonishingly clear by the customer reaction to America Online's decision a few years ago to allow its customers unlimited access to the Internet for a flat rate of just $19.95 per month. Until then, AOL had based its access fee on the number of hours its customers spent logged on. But such marginal cost pricing had become uncompetitive and so was slated to disappear. The result could have been predicted by any student of beginning economics. Flat-rate pricing encourages more use. A flat monthly price means that once you pay the "entry fee," that fee becomes a fixed cost. The marginal cost of additional use becomes zero; all users respond accordingly.

Graphic Analysis

Figure 22-8 shows the demand curve for hours on the Internet as a function of price charged per hour. At $1 per hour, the quantity Q_1 is demanded. With the flat-rate pricing system, the price per unit is always zero after the flat-rate fee is paid. The marginal cost curve is coincident with the horizontal axis and is actually the supply curve of hours on the Internet. The quantity demanded increases dramatically to Q_2. The monthly fixed cost of $19.95 (not shown on the graph, which measures hours of Internet use per month) has no impact on Internet use. People respond to marginal costs, not sunk costs.

The Problems at AOL

With a zero marginal cost, people tend to log on and stay on much longer than in the previous metered pricing system used by AOL. Under the old system, fees were assessed by the hour after a minimum monthly threshold, typically about five hours, was reached, so many users

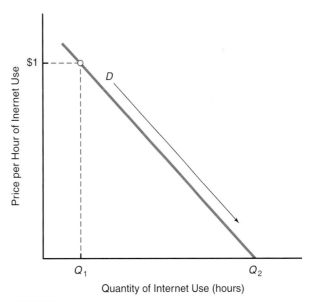

FIGURE 22-8

The Result of Eliminating Marginal Cost Pricing for Internet Use

Not surprisingly, when America Online switched its Internet access charges to a flat fee per month, the effective price for any use of the Internet became zero. Quantity demanded increased dramatically.

kept their on-line time below that minimum. Once the flat-fee pricing system went into effect, AOL's 8 million subscribers immediately began experiencing traffic jams. Many were forced to wait until the wee hours of the morning to access their e-mail and to get onto the Internet and the World Wide Web. Some could not log on for days. Many states' attorneys general brought suit against AOL for misrepresentation, fraud, and other "crimes." America Online promised to add equipment to reduce the jams. It also agreed to give rebates to dissatisfied customers.

Role of the Phone Companies

The flat-fee pricing system for Internet access would not create so much additional use if customers had to pay metered rates for local phone usage. Indeed, in Europe, there are numerous similar flat-fee Internet access pricing plans, but virtually all the phone companies in Europe charge on a per-minute basis for local phone use. Consequently, Internet customers in Europe use the Internet many fewer hours per month than customers in the United States do. In the United States, the phone companies do not usually charge for additional hours of local phone usage, so many U.S. users of the Internet, including corporations, log on and stay on. Users of popular "broadcast"-style data services, such as Pointcast, tend to leave their computers connected 24 hours a day. Yet these users pay no more than the price of a single local call and in some cases nothing at all if their local phone company charges a flat fee per month per phone line.

The ISPs' Dilemma

Most Internet service providers enroll 10 to 30 times more customers than their leased phone lines can accommodate at one time. That is fine as long as the typical customer does not spend a lot of time on-line. But when many users stay logged on, busy signals result. Then the ISP can keep its customers happy only if it leases more phone lines, but that drives costs up. To make a profit, the ISP then has to charge a higher flat rate.

Charge More for More Use?

There is a simple solution to the problem—charge a higher rate to users who log on for longer hours. Alternatively, companies can charge "premium" rates and offer premium services, such as immediate access even during peak periods. Of course, those who do not pay for the premium service may be cut off. For example, Concentric Network Corporation in Cupertino, California, has a standard $19.95-per-month plan but also a so-called consumer plan for $39.95 a month. If you pay for the premium service, you get priority access to the network. Such tiered pricing will probably grow as more and more people become heavy users of the Internet.

FOR CRITICAL ANALYSIS
1. Describe any similarities you see between restaurants that offer "all you can eat" meals for a fixed price and Internet service provider flat-rate pricing schemes.
2. Can you think of other flat-fee pricing systems that exist for goods or services that you might buy?

CHAPTER SUMMARY

1. It is important in economics to distinguish between accounting profits and economic profits. Accounting profits are equal to total revenues minus total explicit costs. Economic profits are equal to total revenues minus total opportunity costs of all factors of production.

2. The short run for the firm is defined as the period during which plant size cannot be altered. The long run is the period during which all factors of production can be varied.

3. Fixed costs are costs that cannot be altered in the short run. Fixed costs are associated with assets that the firm owns that cannot be profitably transferred to another use. Variable costs are associated with input costs that vary as the rate of output varies. Wages are a good example of a variable cost.

4. There are definitional relationships between average, total, and marginal costs:

$$ATC = \frac{TC}{Q}$$

$$AVC = \frac{TVC}{Q}$$

$$AFC = \frac{TFC}{Q}$$

$$MC = \frac{\text{change in TC}}{\text{change in } Q}$$

5. When marginal costs are less than average costs, average costs are falling. When marginal costs are greater than average costs, average costs are rising. The marginal cost curve intersects the average variable cost curve and the average total cost curve at their minimum points.

6. When we hold constant all factors of production except one, an increase in that factor will lead to a change in total physical product. That is how we derive the total physical product curve. The marginal physical product curve is derived from looking at the change in total physical product.

7. After some output rate, firms enter the region of diminishing marginal returns, or diminishing marginal physical product. In other words, after some point, each increment of the variable input will yield a smaller and smaller increment in total output.

8. Given a constant wage rate, the marginal cost curve is the mirror image of the marginal physical product curve. Thus because of the law of diminishing marginal returns, marginal costs will eventually rise.

9. We derive the long-run average cost curve by connecting a smooth line that is just tangent to all of the short-run average cost curves. This long-run average cost curve is sometimes called the planning curve.

10. It is possible for a firm to experience economies of scale, constant returns to scale, or diseconomies of scale, in which case a proportionate increase in *all* inputs will lead, respectively, to decreasing, constant, or increasing average costs. Firms may experience economies of scale because of specialization, the dimensional factor, and the ability to purchase improved productive equipment. Firms may experience diseconomies of scale because of the limitations of efficient management.

11. The long-run average cost curve will be downward-sloping, horizontal, or upward-sloping, depending on whether there are economics of scale, constant returns to scale, or diseconomies of scale.

12. Minimum efficient scale occurs at the lowest rate of output at which long-run average costs are minimized.

DISCUSSION OF PREVIEW QUESTIONS

1. How does the economist's definition of profit differ from the accountant's?

The accountant defines total profits as total revenues minus total costs; the economist defines total profits as total revenues minus total opportunity costs of all inputs used. In other words, the economist takes into account implicit as well as explicit costs; the economist's definition stresses that an opportunity cost exists for all inputs used in the production process. Specifically, the economist estimates the opportunity cost for invested capital, the owner's time, inventories on hand, and so on. Because the economist's definition of costs is more inclusive, accounting profits will exceed economic profits; economic profits exist only when all the opportunity costs are taken into account.

2. What distinguishes the long run from the short run?

The short run is defined as any time period when there is at least one factor of production that a firm cannot vary; in the long run, *all* factors of production can be varied by the firm. Because each industry is likely to be unique in its ability to vary all inputs, the long run differs from industry to industry. Presumably the long run is a lot shorter (in absolute time periods) for firms in the carpentry or plumbing industry than for firms in the automobile or steel industry. In most economic models, labor is usually assumed to be the variable input in the short run, whereas capital is considered to be fixed in the short run; this assumption is fairly descriptive of the real-world situation.

3. How does the law of diminishing marginal returns account for an *eventually* increasing marginal cost curve for a firm in the short run?

Assume that labor is the only variable factor of production. *Eventually,* the law of diminishing returns comes into play (prior to this point, specialization benefits might increase the marginal product of labor), and the marginal product of labor falls. That is, beyond the point of diminishing returns, extra laborers contribute less to total product than immediately preceding laborers do, per unit of time. In effect, this means that if output is to be increased by equal amounts (or equal "batches"), more and more labor time will be required due to its lower marginal product. Later units of output, which are physically identical to earlier units of output, embody more labor time. If wages are constant, later units, which require more worker-hours, have a higher marginal cost. We conclude that beyond the point of diminishing returns, the marginal cost of output rises for the firm in the short run. Prior to the point of diminishing returns, the marginal cost curve falls, due to rising marginal product of labor.

4. **Why is the short-run average total cost curve U-shaped?**

Average total cost (ATC) equals the sum of average fixed costs (AFC) and average variable costs (AVC); that is, ATC = AFC + AVC. The AFC curve continuously falls because it is derived by dividing a constant number (total fixed costs) by larger and larger numbers (output levels). It falls rapidly at first, then slowly. The AVC curve falls during the early output stages because the benefits of specialization cause the marginal physical product of labor to rise and the marginal cost of output to fall; beyond the point of diminishing returns, the marginal physical product of labor falls, eventually forcing marginal cost to rise above AVC, and therefore AVC rises too. As we go from zero output to higher and higher output levels per unit of time, AFC and AVC both initially fall; therefore, ATC falls too. At some point beyond the point of diminishing marginal returns, AVC rises and outweighs the now slowly falling AFC curve; the net result is that somewhere beyond the point of diminishing marginal returns, the ATC curve rises. Because the ATC curve falls at low output levels and rises at higher output levels, we describe it as U-shaped. Of course, it doesn't look exactly like a *U*, but it is close enough.

PROBLEMS

(Answers to the odd-numbered problems appear at the back of the book.)

22-1. "Now that I have paid off my van, it won't cost me anything except for the running expenses, such as gas, oil, and tune-ups, when I use it." What is wrong with this reasoning?

22-2. Examine this table.

Units of Labor (per eight-hour day)	Marginal Product of Labor (per eight-hour day)
1	2
2	4
3	6
.	.
.	.
.	.
12	20
13	10
14	5
15	3
16	2

a. Suppose that this firm wants to increase output over the short run. How much labor time is required to produce the first unit? The second and third? Do the fourth, fifth, and sixth units of output require more or less labor time than the earlier units?

b. Suppose that we have hired 11 laborers and now want to increase the short-run output in batches of 20. To produce the first batch of 20 (beyond the eleventh laborer), how many labor hours are required? What will the next batch of 20 cost, in labor hours? Do additional batches of 20 cost more or less than earlier batches (beyond the eleventh laborer)?

c. What do parts (a) and (b) imply about the relationship between the marginal product of labor and labor time embodied in equal increments of output?

22-3. Refer to the table in Problem 22-2. Assume that wage rates equal $1 per eight-hour day.

a. By hiring the twelfth unit of labor, what was the cost to the firm of this first batch of 20?

b. What was the marginal cost of output in that range? (Hint: If 20 units cost $1, what did *one* unit cost?)

c. What will the next batch of 10 cost the firm?

d. What is the marginal cost of output over that range?

e. What is happening to the marginal cost of output?

f. How are the marginal product of labor and the marginal cost of output related?

22-4. Your school's basketball team had a foul-shooting average of .800 (80 out of 100) before last night's game, during which they shot 5 for 10 at the foul line.

a. What was their marginal performance last night?

b. What happened to the team's foul-shooting average?

c. Suppose that their foul shooting in the next game is 6 for 10. What is happening to their marginal performance?

d. Now what is the team average foul-shooting percentage?

22-5. Define long-run average total cost. In light of the fact that businesses are operated day to day in the short run, of what use is the concept of long-run average total cost to the entrepreneur?

22-6. A recent college graduate turns down a $20,000-per-year job offer in order to open his own business. He borrows $150,000 to purchase equipment. Total sales during his first year are $250,000. Total labor costs for the first year are $160,000, and raw material costs are equal to $50,000. He pays $15,000 interest on the loan per year. Estimate the economic profit of this business for the first year.

22-7. Examine this table.

Output (units)	Average Fixed Cost	Total Cost
0	—	$200
5	$40	300
10	20	380
20	10	420
40	5	520

a. Find the average variable cost at each level of production.

b. What is the marginal cost of increasing output from 10 to 20 units? From 20 to 40 units?

c. Find the average total cost at each level of production.

22-8. You are given the following graph.

a. At what output level is AVC at a minimum?

b. At what output level is ATC at a minimum?

c. At what output level is MC at a minimum?

d. At what output level do the AVC and MC curves intersect?

e. At what output level do the ATC and MC curves intersect?

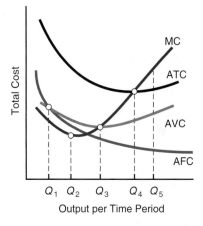

22-9. Fill in the missing values for marginal, average, and total product in the following table. Assume that capital and labor are the only two inputs in the production function and that capital is held fixed.

Units of Labor	Total Product	Marginal Product	Average Product
6	120	—	20
7	147	_____	21
8	_____	23	_____
9	_____	_____	20

COMPUTER-ASSISTED INSTRUCTION

How does the law of diminishing returns affect the marginal product of labor? When the marginal product of labor falls, why does the marginal cost of output rise? Specific calculations are required; such calculations reveal the answers to these important questions.

Complete problem and answer appear on disk.

CHAPTER 23

PERFECT COMPETITION

Few Americans today would say that competition does not exist in the U.S. marketplace. But how much competition is there really? In the world of perfect competition, which you will read about in this chapter, there are so many suppliers of a particular good or service that above-competitive profits cannot exist for long. Is that true of big corporations in this country? Or have many corporations managed to avoid serious competition? To answer this question, you need to learn about the model of perfect competition and its assumptions.

PREVIEW QUESTIONS

1. How much will a perfect competitor produce in the short run?
2. What is the perfectly competitive firm's short-run supply curve?
3. Can a perfectly competitive firm earn economic profits?
4. Why is the perfectly competitive market structure considered economically efficient?

Perfect competition
A market structure in which the decisions of individual buyers and sellers have no effect on market price.

Perfectly competitive firm
A firm that is such a small part of the total industry that it cannot affect the price of the product it sells.

Price taker
A competitive firm that must take the price of its product as given because the firm cannot influence its price.

Did You Know That . . . in the United States, there are tens of thousands of copy shops? There are also several thousand desktop publishing companies offering their services. The number of companies wanting to sell only Web site development is much smaller but growing. The number of companies offering to write software applications is somewhere in between, but that is only in the United States. Today, because of the cheapness and rapidity of modern telecommunications, much of the software code that goes in today's computer applications programs produced by American companies is written in India and elsewhere.

Competition is the word that applies to all of these situations. As used in common speech, *competition* simply means "rivalry." In perfectly competitive situations, individual buyers and sellers cannot affect the market price—it is determined by the market forces of demand and supply. In this chapter we examine what has become known as perfect competition.

CHARACTERISTICS OF A PERFECTLY COMPETITIVE MARKET STRUCTURE

We are interested in studying how a firm acting within a perfectly competitive market structure makes decisions about how much to produce. In a situation of **perfect competition,** each firm is such a small part that it cannot affect the price of the product in question. That means that each **perfectly competitive firm** in the industry is a **price taker**—the firm takes price as a given, something determined *outside* the individual firm.

This definition of a competitive firm is obviously idealized, for in one sense the individual firm *has* to set prices. How can we ever have a situation in which firms regard prices as set by forces outside their control? The answer is that even though every firm sets its own prices, a firm in a perfectly competitive situation will find that it will eventually have no customers at all if it sets its price above the competitive price. The best example is in agriculture. Although the individual farmer can set any price for a bushel of wheat, if that price doesn't coincide with the market price of a bushel of similar-quality wheat, no one will purchase the wheat at a higher price; nor would the farmer be inclined to reduce revenues by selling below the market price.

Let's examine the reasons why a firm in a perfectly competitive industry ends up being a price taker.

1. *There must be a large number of buyers and sellers.* When this is the case, no one buyer or one seller has any influence on price.
2. *The product sold by the firms in the industry must be homogeneous.* The product sold by each firm in the industry must be a perfect substitute for the product sold by each other firm. Buyers must be able to choose from a large number of sellers of a product that the buyers believe to be the same.
3. *Any firm can enter or leave the industry without serious impediments.* Firms in a competitive industry cannot be hampered in their ability to get resources or relocate resources. They move labor and capital in pursuit of profit-making opportunities to whatever business venture gives them their highest expected rate of return on their investment.
4. *Both buyers and sellers have equal information.* Consumers have to be able to find out about lower prices charged by competing firms. Firms have to be able to find out about cost-saving innovations in order to lower production costs and prices, and they have to be able to learn about profitable opportunities in other industries.

INTERNATIONAL EXAMPLE
The Global Coal Market

A good real-world example of perfect competition is the market for coal. Coal is a fossil fuel that started as luxurious vegetation growing in the swamps that covered much of the world about 300 million years ago. Today, coal is found in nearly every region of the world, although the most commercially important deposits are in Asia, Australia, Europe, and North America. Great Britain led the world in coal production until about a century ago.

Throughout the world, coal is produced in literally thousands of different mines. The purchasers of coal, such as steel mills and electric utility generating companies, constantly keep track of the prices of coal output throughout the world. If the price of coal goes up, there are literally thousands of known untapped coal deposits that can be developed. If the price of coal drops, coal mines can be closed. So the market for coal probably conforms as closely as possible to the assumptions underlining the model of perfect competition.

FOR CRITICAL ANALYSIS: There are actually several different grades of coal. Does this seriously violate assumption 2 for a perfectly competitive industry? ●

THE DEMAND CURVE OF THE PERFECT COMPETITOR

When we discussed substitutes in Chapter 20, we pointed out that the more substitutes there were and the more similar they were to the commodity in question, the greater was the price elasticity of demand. Here we assume for the perfectly competitive firm that it is producing a homogeneous commodity that has perfect substitutes. That means that if the individual firm raises its price one penny, it will lose all of its business. This, then, is how we characterize the demand schedule for a perfectly competitive firm: It is the going market price as determined by the forces of market supply and market demand—that is, where the market demand curve intersects the market supply curve. The single-firm demand curve in a perfectly competitive industry is perfectly elastic at the going market price. Remember that with a perfectly elastic demand curve, any increase in price leads to zero quantity demanded.

We show the market demand and supply curves in panel (a) of Figure 23-1. Their intersection occurs at the price of $5. The commodity in question is computer diskettes, and assume for the purposes of this exposition that all diskettes are perfect substitutes for all

Exercise 23.1
Visit www.econtoday.com for more about Wal-Mart.

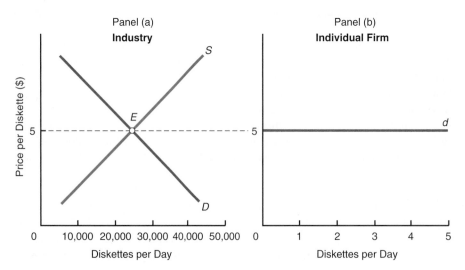

FIGURE 23-1

The Demand Curve for a Diskette Producer
At $5—where market demand, *D,* and market supply, *S,* intersect—the individual firm faces a perfectly elastic demand curve, *d.* If it raises its price even one penny, it will sell no diskettes at all. Notice the difference in the quantities of diskettes represented on the horizontal axis of panels (a) and (b).

others. At the going market price of $5 apiece, a hypothetical individual demand curve for a diskette producer who sells a very, very small part of total industry production is shown in panel (b). At the market price, this firm can sell all the output it wants. At the market price of $5 each, which is where the demand curve for the individual producer lies, consumer demand for the diskettes of that one producer is perfectly elastic. This can be seen by noting that if the firm raises its price, consumers, who are assumed to know that this supplier is charging more than other producers, will buy elsewhere, and the producer in question will have no sales at all. Thus the demand curve for that producer is perfectly elastic. We label the individual producer's demand curve *d,* whereas the *market* demand curve is always labeled *D.*

HOW MUCH SHOULD THE PERFECT COMPETITOR PRODUCE?

As we have shown, a perfect competitor has to accept the price of the product as a given. If the firm raises its price, it sells nothing; if it lowers its price, it makes less money per unit sold than it otherwise could. The firm has one decision left: How much should it produce? We will apply our model of the firm to this question to come up with an answer. We'll use the *profit-maximization model,* which assumes that firms attempt to maximize their total profits—the positive difference between total revenues and total costs.

Total Revenues

Total revenues
The price per unit times the total quantity sold.

Every firm has to consider its *total revenues,* or TR. **Total revenues** are defined as the quantity sold multiplied by the price. (They are the same as total receipts from the sale of output.) The perfect competitor must take the price as a given.

Look at Figure 23-2 on page 512. Much of the information in panel (a) comes from panel (a) of Figure 22-3, but we have added some essential columns for our analysis. Column 3 is the market price, P, of $5 per diskette, which is also equal to average revenue (AR) because

$$AR = \frac{TR}{Q} = \frac{PQ}{Q} = P$$

where Q stands for quantity. If we assume that all units sell for the same price, it becomes apparent that another name for the demand curve is the *average revenue curve* (this is true regardless of the type of market structure under consideration).

Column 4 shows the total revenues, or TR, as equal to the market price, P, times the total output in sales per day, or Q. Thus TR = PQ. We are assuming that the market supply and demand schedules intersect at a price of $5 and that this price holds for all the firm's production. We are also assuming that because our diskette maker is a small part of the market, it can sell all that it produces at that price. Thus panel (b) of Figure 23-2 shows the total revenue curve as a straight green line. For every unit of sales, total revenue is increased by $5.

Comparing Total Costs with Total Revenues

Total costs are given in column 2 of panel (a) of Figure 23-2 and plotted in panel (b). Remember, the firm's costs always include a normal rate of

---

THINKING CRITICALLY ABOUT THE MEDIA

"They" Just Raised Their Prices

The media are quick to announce price increases in industries that have big firms. In particular, there is a media fascination with oil company behavior. After all, the Exxon Corporation, headquartered in Irving, Texas, has annual sales that exceed $100 billion and profits that exceed $5 billion per year. Mobil, Texaco, Chevron, Amoco, and Shell are smaller, but their profits are still in the billions of dollars a year. The public usually sees nothing wrong with an article stating that "they decided to raise the price of gasoline." The oil market is worldwide, however. Even within the United States, Exxon accounts for only 7 percent of total oil sales. The price of oil (net of taxes) is determined by market demand and market supply, not arbitrarily by decision makers in oil companies. They are simply responding to their estimates of the intersection of world demand and supply curves.

Panel (a)

(1) Total Output and Sales per Day (Q)	(2) Total Costs (TC)*	(3) Market Price (P)	(4) Total Revenue (TR) (4) = (3) x (1)	(5) Total Profit (TR – TC) (5) = (4) – (2)	(6) Average Total Cost (ATC) (6) = (2) ÷ (1)*	(7) Average Variable Cost (AVC)*	(8) Marginal Cost (MC) (8) = Change in (2)* Change in (1)	(9) Marginal Revenue (MR) (9) = Change in (4) Change in (1)
0	$10	$5	$ 0	–$10	—	—		
							$5	$5
1	15	5	5	– 10	$15.00	$5.00		
							3	5
2	18	5	10	– 8	9.00	4.00		
							2	5
3	20	5	15	– 5	6.67	3.33		
							1	5
4	21	5	20	– 1	5.25	2.75		
							2	5
5	23	5	25	2	4.60	2.60		
							3	5
6	26	5	30	4	4.33	2.67		
							4	5
7	30	5	35	5	4.28	2.86		
							5	5
8	35	5	40	5	4.38	3.12		
							6	5
9	41	5	45	4	4.56	3.44		
							7	5
10	48	5	50	2	4.80	3.80		
							8	5
11	56	5	55	– 1	5.09	4.18		

*From Figure 22-3.

FIGURE 23-2

Profit Maximization

Profit maximization occurs where marginal revenue equals marginal cost. Panel (a) indicates that this point occurs at a rate of sales of between seven and eight diskettes per day.

In panel (b), we find maximum profits where total revenues exceed total costs by the largest amount. This occurs at a rate of production and sales per day of seven or eight diskettes.

In panel (c), the marginal cost curve, MC, intersects the marginal revenue curve at a rate of output and sales of somewhere between seven and eight diskettes per day.

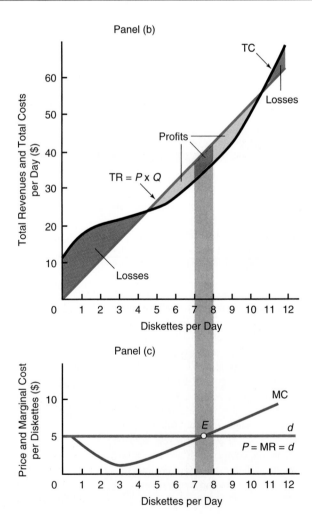

Panel (b)

Panel (c)

return on investment. So whenever we refer to total costs, we are talking not about accounting costs but about economic costs. When the total cost curve is above the total revenue curve, the firm is experiencing losses. When it is below the total revenue curve, the firm is making profits.

By comparing total costs with total revenues, we can figure out the number of diskettes the individual competitive firm should produce per day. Our analysis rests on the assumption that the firm will attempt to maximize total profits. In panel (a) of Figure 23-2, we see that total profits reach a maximum at a production rate of either seven or eight diskettes per day. We can see this graphically in panel (b) of the figure. The firm will maximize profits where the total revenue curve exceeds the total curve by the greatest amount. That occurs at a rate of output and sales of either seven or eight diskettes per day; this rate is called the **profit-maximizing rate of production.** (If output were continuously divisible or we were dealing with extremely large numbers of diskettes, we would get a unique profit-maximizing output.)

We can also find this profit-maximizing rate of production for the individual competitive firm by looking at marginal revenues and marginal costs.

Profit-maximizing rate of production
The rate of production that maximizes total profits, or the difference between total revenues and total costs; also, the rate of production at which marginal revenue equals marginal cost.

USING MARGINAL ANALYSIS TO DETERMINE THE PROFIT-MAXIMIZING RATE OF PRODUCTION

It is possible—indeed, preferred—to use marginal analysis to determine the profit-maximizing rate of production. We end up with the same results derived in a different manner, one that focuses more on where decisions are really made—on the margin. Managers examine changes in costs and relate them to changes in revenues. In fact, we almost always compare changes in cost with changes in benefits, where change is occurring at the margin, whether it be with respect to how much more or less to produce, how many more workers to hire or fire, or how much more to study or not study.

Marginal revenue represents the change in total revenues attributable to changing production by one unit of the product in question. Hence a more formal definition of marginal revenue is

$$\text{Marginal revenue} = \frac{\text{change in total revenues}}{\text{change in output}}$$

Marginal revenue
The change in total revenues resulting from a change in output (and sale) of one unit of the product in question.

In a perfectly competitive market, the marginal revenue curve is exactly equivalent to the price line or the individual firm's demand curve because the firm can sell all of its output (production) at the market price. Thus in Figure 23-1, the demand curve, *d,* for the individual producer is at a price of $5—the price line is coincident with the demand curve. But so is the marginal revenue curve, for marginal revenue in this case also equals $5.

The marginal revenue curve for our competitive diskette producer is shown as a line at $5 in panel (c) of Figure 23-2. Notice again that the marginal revenue curve is equal to the price line, which is equal to the individual firm's demand, or average revenue, curve, *d.*

When Are Profits Maximized?

Now we add the marginal cost curve, MC, taken from column 8 in panel (a) of Figure 23-2. As shown in panel (c) of that figure, the marginal cost curve first falls and then starts to rise because of the law of diminishing returns, eventually intersecting the marginal revenue curve and then rising above it. Notice that the numbers for both the marginal cost schedule, column 8 in panel (a), and the marginal revenue schedule, column 9 in panel (a), are printed *between* the rows on which the quantities appear. This indicates that we are looking at a *change* between one rate of output and the next.

In panel (c), the marginal cost curve intersects the marginal revenue curve somewhere between seven and eight diskettes per day. The firm has an incentive to produce and sell until the amount of the additional revenue received from selling one more diskette just equals the additional costs incurred for producing and selling that diskette. This is how the firm maximizes profit. Whenever marginal cost is less than marginal revenue, the firm will always make more profit by increasing production.

Now consider the possibility of producing at an output rate of 10 diskettes per day. The marginal cost curve at that output rate is higher than the marginal revenue (or d) curve. The firm would be spending more to produce that additional output than it would be receiving in revenues; it would be foolish to continue producing at this rate.

But how much should it produce? It should produce at point E, where the marginal cost curve intersects the marginal revenue curve from below.[1] The firm should continue production until the cost of increasing output by one more unit is just equal to the revenues obtainable from that extra unit. This is a fundamental rule in economics:

Profit maximization normally occurs at the rate of output at which marginal revenue equals marginal cost.

For a perfectly competitive firm, this is at the intersection of the demand schedule, d, and the marginal cost curve, MC. When MR exceeds MC, each additional unit of output adds more to total revenues than to total costs, causing losses to decrease or profits to increase. When MC is greater than MR, each unit produced adds more to total cost than to total revenues, causing profits to decrease or losses to increase. Therefore, profit maximization occurs when MC equals MR. In our particular example, our profit-maximizing, perfectly competitive diskette producer will produce at a rate of either seven or eight diskettes a day. (If we were dealing with a very large rate of output, we would come up with an exact profit-maximizing rate.)

INTERNET EXERCISE

Exercise 23.2
Visit www.econtoday.com for more about product pricing.

CONCEPTS IN BRIEF

- Four fundamental characteristics of the market in perfect competition are (1) a large number of buyers and sellers, (2) a homogeneous product, (3) unrestrained exit from and entry into the industry by other firms, and (4) good information in the hands of both buyers and sellers.

- A perfectly competitive firm is a price taker. It has no control over price and consequently has to take price as a given, but it can sell all that it wants at the going market price.

- The demand curve for a perfect competitor is a line at the going market price. The demand curve is also the perfect competitor's marginal revenue curve because marginal revenue is defined as the change in total revenue due to a one-unit change in output.

- Profit is maximized at the rate of output where the positive difference between total revenues and total costs is the greatest. This is the same level of output at which marginal revenue equals marginal cost. The perfectly competitive firm produces at an output rate at which marginal cost equals the price per unit of output, because MR ≡ P.

---

[1]The marginal cost curve, MC, also cuts the marginal revenue curve, d, from above at an output rate of less than 1 in this example. This intersection should be ignored because it is irrelevant to the firm's decisions.

SHORT-RUN PROFITS

To find what our competitive individual diskette producer is making in terms of profits in the short run, we have to add the average total cost curve to panel (c) of Figure 23-2. We take the information from column 6 in panel (a) and add it to panel (c) to get Figure 23-3. Again the profit-maximizing rate of output is between seven and eight diskettes per day. If we have production and sales of seven diskettes per day, total revenues will be $35 a day. Total costs will be $30 a day, leaving a profit of $5 a day. If the rate of output in sales is eight diskettes per day, total revenues will be $40 and total costs will be $35, again leaving a profit of $5 a day. In Figure 23-3, the lower boundary of the rectangle labeled "Profits" is determined by the intersection of the profit-maximizing quantity line represented by vertical dashes and the average total cost curve. Why? Because the ATC curve gives us the cost per unit, whereas the price ($5), represented by *d,* gives us the revenue per unit, or average revenue. The difference is profit per unit. So the height of the rectangular box representing profits equals profit per unit, the length equals the amount of units produced, and when we multiply these two quantities, we get total profits. Note, as pointed out earlier, that we are talking about *economic profits* because a normal rate of return on investment is included in the average total cost curve, ATC.

It is certainly possible, also, for the competitive firm to make short-run losses. We give an example in Figure 23-4 on page 516, where we show the firm's demand curve shifting from d_1 to d_2. The going market price has fallen from $5 to $3 per diskette because of changes in market supply or demand conditions (or both). The firm will always do the best it can by producing where marginal revenue equals marginal cost. We see in Figure 23-4 that the marginal revenue (d_2) curve is intersected (from below) by the marginal cost curve at an output rate of about $5\frac{1}{2}$ diskettes per day. The firm is clearly not making profits because average total costs at that output rate are greater than the price of $3 per diskette. The losses are shown in the shaded area. By producing where marginal revenue equals marginal cost, however, the firm is minimizing its losses; that is, losses would be greater at any other output.

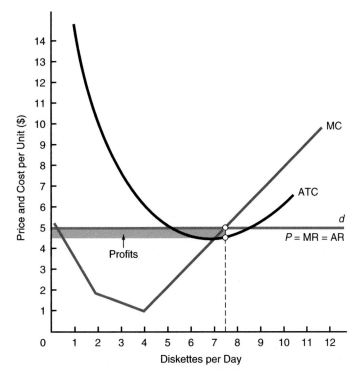

FIGURE 23-3

Measuring Total Profits

Profits are represented by the shaded area. The height of the profit rectangle is given by the difference between average total costs and price ($5), where price is also equal to average revenue. This is found by the vertical difference between the ATC curve and the price, or average revenue, line *d,* at the profit-maximizing rate of output of between seven and eight diskettes per day.

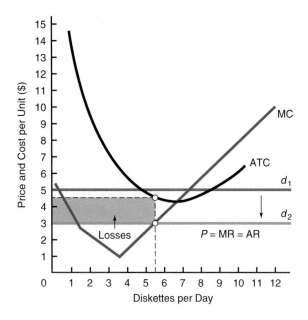

FIGURE 23-4

Minimization of Short-Run Losses

In cases in which average total costs exceed the average revenue, or price (and price is greater than or equal to average variable cost), profit maximization is equivalent to loss minimization. This again occurs where marginal cost equals marginal revenue. Losses are shown in the shaded area.

THE SHORT-RUN SHUTDOWN PRICE

In Figure 23-4, the firm is sustaining economic losses. Will it go out of business? In the long run it will, but surprisingly, in the short run the firm will not go out of business, for as long as the loss from staying in business is less than the loss from shutting down, the firm will continue to produce. A firm *goes out of business* when the owners sell its assets to someone else. A firm temporarily *shuts down* when it stops producing, but it still is in business.

Now how can we tell when the firm is sustaining economic losses in the short run and it is still worthwhile not to shut down? The firm must compare the cost of producing (while incurring losses) with the cost of closing down. The cost of staying in production in the short run is given by the total *variable* cost. Looking at the problem on a per-unit basis, as long as average variable cost (AVC) is covered by average revenues (price), the firm is better off continuing to produce. If average variable costs are exceeded even a little bit by the price of the product, staying in production produces some revenues in excess of variable costs that can be applied toward covering fixed costs.

A simple example will demonstrate this situation. The price of a product is $8, and average total costs equal $9 at an output of 100. In this example, average total costs are broken up into average variable costs of $7 and average fixed costs of $2. Total revenues, then, equal $8 × 100, or $800, and total costs equal $9 × 100, or $900. Total losses therefore equal $100. However, this does not mean that the firm will shut down. After all, if it does shut down, it still has fixed costs to pay. And in this case, because average fixed costs equal $2 at an output of 100, the fixed costs are $200. Thus the firm has losses of $100 if it continues to produce, but it has losses of $200 (the fixed costs) if it shuts down. The logic is fairly straightforward:

> **As long as the price per unit sold exceeds the average *variable* cost per unit produced, the firm will be covering at least part of the opportunity cost of the investment in the business—that is, part of its fixed costs.**

Calculating the Short-Run Break-Even Price

Look at demand curve d_1 in Figure 23-5. It just touches the minimum point of the average total cost curve, which, as you will remember, is exactly where the marginal cost curve

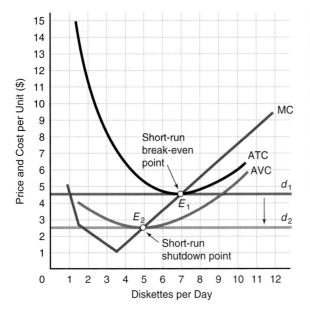

FIGURE 23-5
Short-Run Shutdown and Break-Even Prices
We can find the short-run break-even price and the short-run shut-down price by comparing price with average total costs and average variable costs. If the demand curve is d_1, profit maximization occurs at output E_1, where MC equals marginal revenue (the d curve). Because the ATC curve includes all relevant opportunity costs, point E_1 is the break-even point, and zero economic profits are being made. The firm is earning a normal rate of return. If the demand curve falls to d_2, profit maximization (loss minimization) occurs at the intersection of MC and MR (the d_2 curve), or E_2. Below this price, it does not pay for the firm to continue in operation because its average variable costs are not covered by the price of the product.

Short-run break-even price
The price at which a firm's total revenues equal its total costs. At the break-even price, the firm is just making a normal rate of return on its capital investment. (It is covering its explicit and implicit costs.)

intersects the average total cost curve. At that price, which is about $4.30, the firm will be making exactly zero short-run economic profits. That price is called the **short-run break-even price,** and point E_1 therefore occurs at the short-run break-even price for a competitive firm. It is the point at which marginal revenue, marginal cost, and average total cost are all equal (that is, at which $P = MC$ and $P = ATC$). The break-even price is the one that yields zero short-run economic profits or losses.

Calculating the Short-Run Shutdown Price

To calculate the firm's shutdown price, we must introduce the average variable cost (AVC) to our graph. In Figure 23-5, we have plotted the AVC values from column 7 in panel (a) of Figure 23-2. For the moment, consider two possible demand curves, d_1 and d_2, which are also the firm's respective marginal revenue curves. Therefore, if demand is d_1, the firm will produce at E_1, where that curve intersects the marginal cost curve. If demand falls to d_2, the firm will produce at E_2. The special feature of the hypothetical demand curve, d_2, is that it just touches the average variable cost curve at the latter's minimum point, which is also where the marginal cost curve intersects it. This price is the **short-run shutdown price.** Why? Below this price, the firm would be paying out more in variable costs than it is receiving in revenues from the sale of its product. Each unit it sold would add to its losses. Clearly, the way to avoid incurring these additional losses, if price falls below the shutdown point, is in fact to shut down operations.

Short-run shutdown price
The price that just covers average variable costs. It occurs just below the intersection of the marginal cost curve and the average variable cost curve.

The intersection of the price line, the marginal cost curve, and the average variable cost curve is labeled E_2. The resulting short-run shutdown price is valid only for the short run because, of course, in the long run the firm will not stay in business at a yield less than a normal rate of return and hence at least zero economic profits.

THE MEANING OF ZERO ECONOMIC PROFITS

The fact that we labeled point E_1 in Figure 23-5 the break-even point may have disturbed you. At point E_1, price is just equal to average total cost. If this is the case, why would a firm continue to produce if it were making no profits whatsoever? If we again make the distinction between accounting profits and economic profits, then at that price the firm has zero economic profits but positive accounting profits. Recall that accounting profits are total revenues minus total explicit costs. What is ignored in such accounting is the reward offered to investors—the opportunity cost of capital—plus all other implicit costs.

In economic analysis, the average total cost curve includes the full opportunity cost of capital. Indeed, the average total cost curve includes the opportunity cost of *all* factors of production used in the production process. At the short-run break-even price, economic profits are, by definition, zero. Accounting profits at that price are not, however, equal to zero; they are positive. Consider an example. A baseball bat manufacturer sells bats at some price. The owners of the firm have supplied all the funds in the business. They have borrowed no money from anyone else, and they explicitly pay the full opportunity cost to all factors of production, including any managerial labor that they themselves contribute to the business. Their salaries show up as a cost in the books and are equal to what they could have earned in the next-best alternative occupation. At the end of the year, the owners find that after they subtract all explicit costs from total revenues, they have earned $100,000. Let's say that their investment was $1 million. Thus the rate of return on that investment is 10 percent per year. We will assume that this turns out to be equal to the rate of return that, on average, all other baseball bat manufacturers make in the industry.

This $100,000, or 10 percent rate of return, is actually, then, a competitive, or normal, rate of return on invested capital in that industry or in other industries with similar risks. If the owners had made only $50,000, or 5 percent on their investment, they would have been able to make higher profits by leaving the industry. The 10 percent rate of return is the opportunity cost of capital. Accountants show it as a profit; economists call it a cost. We include that cost in the average total cost curve, similar to the one shown in Figure 23-5. At the short-run break-even price, average total cost, including this opportunity cost of capital, will just equal that price. The firm will be making zero economic profits but a 10 percent *accounting* rate of return.

Now we are ready to derive the firm's supply curve.

THE PERFECT COMPETITOR'S SHORT-RUN SUPPLY CURVE

What does the supply curve for the individual firm look like? Actually, we have been looking at it all along. We know that when the price of diskettes is $5, the firm will supply seven or eight of them per day. If the price falls to $3, the firm will supply five or six diskettes per day. And if the price falls below $3, the firm will shut down in the short run. Hence in Figure 23-6, the firm's supply curve is the marginal cost curve above the short-run shutdown point. This is shown as the solid part of the marginal cost curve. ***The definition, then, of the individual firm's supply curve in a competitive industry is its marginal cost curve equal to and above the point of intersection with the average variable cost curve.***

The Short-Run Industry Supply Curve

In Chapter 3, we indicated that the market supply curve was the summation of individual supply curves. At the beginning of this chapter, we drew a market supply curve in Figure 23-1. Now we want to derive more precisely a market, or industry, supply curve to reflect individual producer behavior in that industry. First we must ask, What is an industry? It is merely a collection of firms producing a particular product. Therefore, we have a way to figure out the total supply curve of any industry: We add the quantities that each firm will

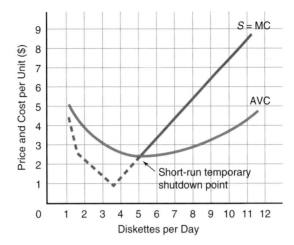

FIGURE 23-6

The Individual Firm's Short-Run Supply Curve
The individual firm's supply curve is the portion of its marginal cost curve above the minimum point on the average variable cost curve.

supply at every possible price. In other words, we sum the individual supply curves of all the competitive firms *horizontally.* The individual supply curves, as we just saw, are simply the marginal cost curves of each firm.

Consider doing this for a hypothetical world in which there are only two diskette producers in the industry, firm A and firm B. These two firms' marginal cost curves are given in panels (a) and (b) of Figure 23-7. The marginal cost curves for the two separate firms are presented as MC_A in panel (a) and MC_B in panel (b). Those two marginal cost curves are drawn only for prices above the minimum average variable cost for each respective firm. Hence we are not including any of the marginal cost curves below minimum average variable cost. In panel (a), for firm A, at price P_1, the quantity supplied would be q_{A1}. At price P_2, the quantity supplied would be q_{A2}. In panel (b), we see the two different quantities that

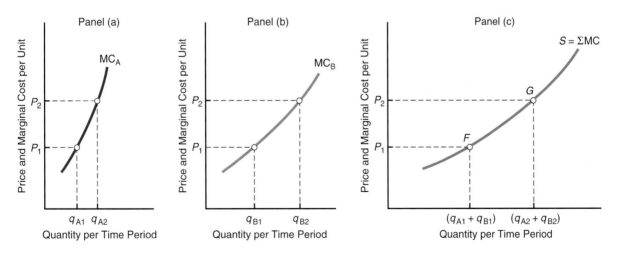

FIGURE 23-7

Deriving the Industry Supply Curve
Marginal cost curves above average minimum variable cost are presented in panels (a) and (b) for firms A and B. We horizontally sum the two quantities supplied, q_{A1} and q_{B1}, at price P_1. This gives us point F in panel (c). We do the same thing for the quantities at price P_2. This gives us point G. When we connect those points, we have the industry supply curve, S, which is the horizontal summation of the firms' marginal cost curves above their respective average minimum costs.

would be supplied by firm B corresponding to those two prices. Now for price P_1 we add horizontally the quantity of q_{A1} and q_{B1}. This gives us one point, F, for our short-run **industry supply curve,** S. We obtain the other point, G, by doing the same horizontal adding of quantities at P_2. When we connect points F and G, we obtain industry supply curve S, which is also marked ΣMC, indicating that it is the horizontal summation of the marginal cost curves (above the respective minimum average variable cost of each firm).[2] Because the law of diminishing returns makes marginal cost curves rise, the short-run supply curve of a perfectly competitive industry must be upward-sloping.

Industry supply curve
The locus of points showing the minimum prices at which given quantities will be forthcoming; also called the *market supply curve.*

Factors That Influence the Industry Supply Curve

As you have just seen, the industry supply curve is the horizontal summation of all of the individual firms' marginal cost curves above their respective minimum average variable cost points. This means that anything that affects the marginal cost curves of the firm will influence the industry supply curve. Therefore, the individual factors that will influence the supply schedule in a competitive industry can be summarized as the factors that cause the variable costs of production to change. These are factors that affect the individual marginal cost curves, such as changes in the individual firm's productivity, in factor costs (wages paid to labor, prices of raw materials, etc.), in taxes, and in anything else that would influence the individual firm's marginal cost curve.

All of these are *ceteris paribus* conditions of supply. Because they affect the position of the marginal cost curve for the individual firm, they affect the position of the industry supply curve. A change in any of these will shift the market supply curve.

CONCEPTS IN BRIEF

- Short-run average profits or average losses are determined by comparing average total costs with price (average revenue) at the profit-maximizing rate of output. In the short run, the perfectly competitive firm can make economic profits or economic losses.

- The competitive firm's short-run break-even output occurs at the minimum point on its average total cost curve, which is where the marginal cost curve intersects the average total cost curve.

- The competitive firm's short-run shutdown output is at the minimum point on its average variable cost curve, which is also where the marginal cost curve intersects the average variable cost curve. Shutdown will occur if price falls below average variable cost.

- The firm will continue production at a price that exceeds average variable costs even though the full opportunity cost of capital is not being met; at least some revenues are going toward paying fixed costs.

- At the short-run break-even price, the firm is making zero economic profits, which means that it is just making a normal rate of return in that industry.

- The firm's short-run supply curve is the portion of its marginal cost curve equal to or above minimum average variable costs. The industry short-run supply curve is a horizontal summation of the individual firms' marginal cost curves above their respective minimum average variable costs.

---

[2]The capital Greek sigma, Σ, is the symbol for summation.

FIGURE 23-8

Industry Demand and Supply Curves and the Individual Firm Demand Curve

The industry demand curve is represented by D in panel (a). The short-run industry supply curve is S and equal to ΣMC. The intersection of the demand and supply curves at E determines the equilibrium or market clearing price at P_e. The individual firm demand curve in panel (b) is set at the market clearing price determined in panel (a). If the producer has a marginal cost curve MC, this producer's individual profit-maximizing output level is at q_e. For AC_1, economic profits are zero; for AC_2, profits are negative; and for AC_3, profits are positive.

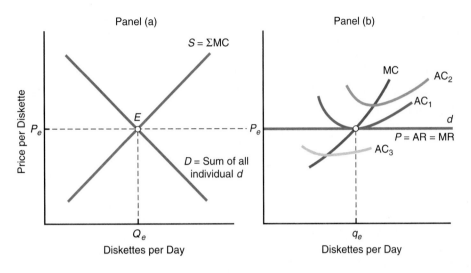

COMPETITIVE PRICE DETERMINATION

How is the market, or "going," price established in a competitive market? This price is established by the interaction of all the suppliers (firms) and all the demanders. The market demand schedule, D, in panel (a) of Figure 23-8 represents the demand schedule for the entire industry, and the supply schedule, S, represents the supply schedule for the entire industry. Price P_e is established by the forces of supply and demand at the intersection of D and the short-run industry supply curve, S. Even though each individual firm has no control or effect on the price of its product in a competitive industry, the interaction of *all* the producers and buyers determines the price at which the product will be sold. We say that the price P_e and the quantity Q_e in panel (a) of Figure 23-8 constitute the competitive solution to the pricing-quantity problem in that particular industry. It is the equilibrium where quantity demanded equals quantity supplied, and both suppliers and demanders are maximizing. The resulting individual firm demand curve, d, is shown in panel (b) of Figure 23-8 at the price P_e.

In a purely competitive industry, the individual producer takes price as a given and chooses the output level that maximizes profits. (This is also the equilibrium level of output from the producer's standpoint.) We see in panel (b) of Figure 23-8 that this is at q_e. If the producer's average costs are given by AC_1, q_e is also the short-run break-even output (see Figure 23-5); if its average costs are given by AC_2, at q_e, AC exceeds price (average revenue), and the firm is incurring losses. Alternatively, if average costs are given by AC_3, the firm will be making economic profits at q_e. In the former case, we would expect, over time, that people will cease production (exit the industry), causing supply to shift inward, whereas in the latter case, we would expect people to enter the industry to take advantage of the economic profits, thereby causing supply to shift outward. We now turn to these long-run considerations.

THE LONG-RUN INDUSTRY SITUATION: EXIT AND ENTRY

In the long run in a competitive situation, firms will be making zero economic profits. In the long run, we surmise that firms in perfect competition will tend to have average total cost curves that just touch the price (marginal revenue) curve, or individual demand curve d. How does this occur? It is through an adjustment process that depends on economic profits and losses.

Exit and Entry of Firms

Go back and look at Figures 23-3 and 23-4. The existence of either profits or losses is a signal to owners of capital both within and outside the industry. If the industry is characterized by firms showing economic profits as represented in Figure 23-3, this will signal owners of capital elsewhere in the economy that they, too, should enter this industry. If, by contrast, there are firms in the industry like the ones suffering economic losses represented in Figure 23-4, this signals resource owners outside the industry to stay out. It also signals resource owners within the industry not to reinvest and if possible to leave the industry. It is in this sense that we say that profits direct resources to their highest-valued use. In the long run, capital will flow into industries in which profitability is highest and will flow out of industries in which profitability is lowest.

The price system therefore allocates capital according to the relative expected rates of return on alternative investments. Entry restrictions will thereby hinder economic efficiency, and thus welfare, by not allowing resources to flow to their highest-valued use. Similarly, exit restrictions (such as plant closing laws) will act to trap resources (temporarily) in sectors in which their value is below that in alternative uses. Such laws will also inhibit the ability of firms to respond to changes in the domestic and international marketplace; yet to judge their desirability, we must weigh these factors against the costs to employees and local economies from such sudden economic disruptions.

Not every industry presents an immediate source of opportunity for every firm. In a brief period of time, it may be impossible for a firm that produces tractors to switch to the production of computers, even if there are very large profits to be made. Over the long run, however, we would expect to see such a change, whether or not the tractor producers want to change over to another product. In a market economy, investors supply firms in the more profitable industry with more investment funds, which they take from firms in less profitable industries. (Also, profits give existing firms internal investment funds for expansion.) Consequently, resources needed in the production of more profitable goods, such as labor, will be bid away from lower-valued opportunities. Investors and other suppliers of resources respond to market **signals** about their highest-valued opportunities.

Market adjustment to changes in demand will occur regardless of the wishes of the managers of firms in less profitable markets. They can either attempt to adjust their product line to respond to the new demands, be replaced by managers who are more responsive to new conditions, or see their firms go bankrupt as they find themselves unable to replace worn-out plant and equipment.

In addition, when we say that in a competitive long-run equilibrium situation firms will be making zero economic profits, we must realize that at a particular point in time it would be pure coincidence for a firm to be making *exactly* zero economic profits. Real-world information is not as precise as the curves we use to simplify our analysis. Things change all the time in a dynamic world, and firms, even in a very competitive situation, may for many reasons not be making exactly zero economic profits. We say that there is a *tendency* toward that equilibrium position, but firms are adjusting all the time to changes in their cost curves and in their individual demand curves.

Signals
Compact ways of conveying to economic decision makers information needed to make decisions. A true signal not only conveys information but also provides the incentive to react appropriately. Economic profits and economic losses are such signals.

EXAMPLE
Who Really Shops at Club Warehouses?

One of the most pervasive competitive innovations in retailing in the United States has been the club warehouse phenomenon. These now ubiquitous retail outlets were first developed by San Diego's Sol Price. He started the Price Club chain in 1976.

Since then, entry into the club warehouse business has been aggressive. It is dominated today by Wal-Mart-owned Sam's Club and Price Costco, the successor to the original Price Club. Smaller club warehouse chains, such as B.J.'s (a subsidiary of Waban, Inc.), dominate regional markets.

One interesting aspect of club warehouses involves who shops there and their reasons for doing so. One might assume at first glance that poorer American families would patronize club warehouses more heavily because of the their lower prices. The reality is just the opposite—the average family shopping at a club warehouse has above-average income. What accounts for that? A club warehouse stocks only a few branded goods in each product category. In essence, the club warehouse has done each customer's comparison shopping and obtained the best terms from the vendors. Individuals who have a relatively higher opportunity cost of time (usually those who make higher incomes) find this a value-added service.

FOR CRITICAL ANALYSIS: *Why do you think the club warehouse market is dominated by a few large firms?* •

Long-Run Industry Supply Curves

In panel (a) of Figure 23-8, we drew the summation of all of the portions of the individual firms' marginal cost curve above each firm's respective minimum average variable costs as the upward-sloping supply curve of the entire industry. We should be aware, however, that a relatively steep upward-sloping supply curve may be appropriate only in the short run. After all, one of the prerequisites of a competitive industry is free entry.

Long-run industry supply curve

A market supply curve showing the relationship between price and quantities forthcoming after firms have been allowed the time to enter into or exit from an industry, depending on whether there have been positive or negative economic profits.

Remember that our definition of the long run is a period of time in which adjustments can be made. The **long-run industry supply curve** is a supply curve showing the relationship between quantities supplied by the entire industry at different prices after firms have been allowed to either enter or leave the industry, depending on whether there have been positive or negative economic profits. Also, the long-run industry supply curve is drawn under the assumption that entry and exit have been completed.

The long-run industry supply curve can take one of three shapes, depending on whether input costs stay constant, increase, or decrease as the number of firms in the industry changes. In Chapter 22, we assumed that input prices remained constant to the firm regardless of the firm's rate of output. When we look at the entire industry, when all firms are expanding and new firms are entering, they may simultaneously bid up input prices.

Constant-cost industry

An industry whose total output can be increased without an increase in long-run per-unit costs; an industry whose long-run supply curve is horizontal.

Constant-Cost Industries. In principle, there are small enough industries that use such a small percentage of the total supply of inputs necessary for their production that firms can enter the industry without bidding up input prices. In such a situation, we are dealing with a **constant-cost industry.** Its long-run industry supply curve is therefore horizontal and is represented by S_L in panel (a) of Figure 23-9 on page 524.

We can work through the case in which constant costs prevail. We start out in panel (a) with demand curve D_1 and supply curve S_1. The equilibrium price is P_1. Market demand shifts rightward to D_2. In the short run, the equilibrium price rises to D_2. This generates positive economic profits for existing firms in the industry. Such economic profits induce capital to flow into the industry. The existing firms expand and/or new firms enter. The short-run supply curve shifts outward to S_2. The new intersection with the new demand curve is at E_3. The new equilibrium price is again P_1. The long-run supply curve is obtained by connecting the intersections of the corresponding pairs of demand and supply curves, E_1 and E_3. Labeled S_L, it is horizontal; its slope is zero. In a constant-cost industry, long-run

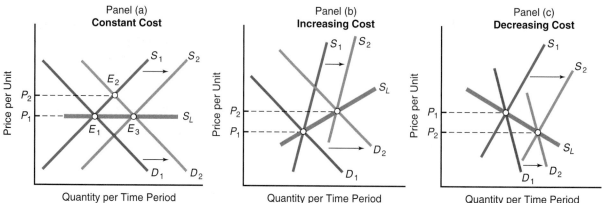

FIGURE 23-9

Constant-Cost, Increasing-Cost, and Decreasing-Cost Industries

In panel (a), we show a situation in which the demand curve shifts from D_1 to D_2. Price increases from P_1 to P_2; however, in time the short-run supply curve shifts outward because positive profits are being earned, and the equilibrium shifts from E_2 to E_3. The market clearing price is again P_1. If we connect points such as E_1 and E_3, we come up with the long-run supply curve S_L. This is a constant-cost industry. In panel (b), costs are increasing for the industry, and therefore the long-run supply curve slopes upward and long-run prices rise from P_1 to P_2. In panel (c), costs are decreasing for the industry as it expands, and therefore the long-run supply curve slopes downward such that long-run prices decline from P_1 to P_2.

---

supply is perfectly elastic. Any shift in demand is eventually met by an equal shift in supply so that the long-run price is constant at P_1.

Retail trade is often given as an example of such an industry because output can be expanded or contracted without affecting input prices. Banking is another example.

Increasing-Cost Industries. In an **increasing-cost industry,** expansion by existing firms and the addition of new firms cause the price of inputs specialized within that industry to be bid up. As costs of production rise, the ATC curve and the firms' MC curve shift upward, causing short-run supply curves (each firm's marginal cost curve) to shift upward. The result is a long-run industry supply curve that slopes upward, as represented by S_L in panel (b) of Figure 23-9. Examples are residential construction and coal mining—both use specialized inputs that cannot be obtained in ever-increasing quantities without causing their prices to rise.

Decreasing-Cost Industries. An expansion in the number of firms in an industry can lead to a reduction in input costs and a downward shift in the ATC and MC curves. When this occurs, the long-run industry supply curve will slope downward. An example is given in panel (c) of Figure 23-9. This is a **decreasing-cost industry.**

LONG-RUN EQUILIBRIUM

In the long run, the firm can change the scale of its plant, adjusting its plant size in such a way that it has no further incentive to change. It will do so until profits are maximized. Figure 23-10 shows the long-run equilibrium of the perfectly competitive firm. Given a price

Increasing-cost industry
An industry in which an increase in industry output is accompanied by an increase in long-run per-unit costs, such that the long-run industry supply curve slopes upward.

Decreasing-cost industry
An industry in which an increase in output leads to a reduction in long-run per-unit costs, such that the long-run industry supply curve slopes downward.

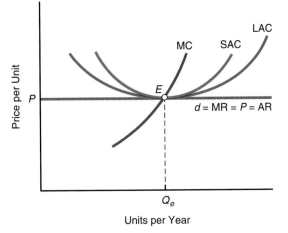

FIGURE 23-10

Long-Run Firm Competitive Equilibrium

In the long run, the firm operates where price, marginal revenue, marginal cost, short-run minimum average cost, and long-run minimum average cost are all equal. This occurs at point *E*.

of *P* and a marginal cost curve, MC, the firm produces at output Q_e. Because profits must be zero in the long run, the firm's short-run average costs (SAC) must equal *P* at Q_e, which occurs at minimum SAC. In addition, because we are in long-run equilibrium, any economies of scale must be exhausted so that we are on the minimum point of the long-run average cost curve (LAC). In other words, the long-run equilibrium position is where "everything is equal," which is at point *E* in Figure 23-10. There, *price* equals *marginal revenue* equals *marginal cost* equals *average cost* (minimum, short-run, and long-run).

Perfect Competition and Minimum Average Total Cost

Look again at Figure 23-10. In long-run equilibrium, the perfectly competitive firm finds itself producing at output rate Q_e. At that rate of output, the price is just equal to the minimum long-run average cost as well as the minimum short-run average cost. In this sense, perfect competition results in the production of goods and services using the least costly combination of resources. This is an important attribute of a perfectly competitive long-run equilibrium, particularly when we wish to compare the market structure of perfect competition with other market structures that are less than perfectly competitive. We will examine these other market structures in later chapters.

COMPETITIVE PRICING: MARGINAL COST PRICING

In a perfectly competitive industry, each firm produces where its marginal cost curve intersects its marginal revenue (*d*) curve from below. Thus perfectly competitive firms always sell their goods at a price that just equals marginal cost. This represents an optimal pricing situation because the price that consumers pay reflects the opportunity cost to society of producing the good. Recall that marginal cost is the amount that a firm must spend to purchase the additional resources needed to expand output by one unit. Given competitive markets, the amount paid for a resource will be the same in all of its alternative uses. Thus MC reflects relative resource input use; that is, if the MC of good 1 is twice the MC of good 2, one more unit of good 1 requires twice the resource input of one more unit of good 2. Because under perfect competition, price equals marginal cost, the consumer, in determining allocation of income on purchases on the basis of relative prices, is actually allocating income on the basis of relative resource input use.

Marginal Cost Pricing

The competitive firm produces up to the point at which the market price just equals the marginal cost. Herein lies the element of the optimal nature of a competitive solution. It is called **marginal cost pricing.** The competitive firm sells its product at a price that just equals the cost to society—the opportunity cost—for that is what the marginal cost curve represents. (But note here that it is the self-interest of firm owners that causes price to equal marginal social cost.) In other words, the marginal benefit to consumers, given by the price that they are willing to pay for the last unit of the good purchased, just equals the marginal cost to society of producing the last unit. (If the marginal benefit exceeds the marginal cost ($P > \text{MC}$), too little is being produced in that people value additional units more than the cost to society of producing them; if $P < \text{MC}$, the opposite is true.)

When an individual pays a price equal to the marginal cost of production, the cost to the user of that product is equal to the sacrifice or cost to society of producing that quantity of that good as opposed to more of some other good. (We are assuming that all marginal social costs are accounted for.) The competitive solution, then, is called *efficient,* in the economic sense of the word. Economic efficiency means that it is impossible to increase the output of any good without lowering the *value* of the total output produced in the economy. No juggling of resources, such as labor and capital, will result in an output that is higher in total value than the value of all of the goods and services already being produced. In an efficient situation, it is impossible to make one person better off without making someone else worse off. All resources are used in the most advantageous way possible, and society therefore enjoys an efficient allocation of productive resources. All goods and services are sold at their opportunity cost, and marginal cost pricing prevails throughout.

Marginal cost pricing
A system of pricing in which the price charged is equal to the opportunity cost to society of producing one more unit of the good or service in question. The opportunity cost is the marginal cost to society.

Market Failure

Although perfect competition does offer many desirable results, situations arise when perfectly competitive markets cannot efficiently allocate resources. Either too many or too few resources are used in the production of a good or service. These situations are instances of **market failure.** Externalities and public goods are examples. For reasons discussed in later chapters, perfectly competitive markets cannot efficiently allocate resources in these situations, and alternative allocation mechanisms are called for. Finally, the rate of innovation by perfectly competitive firms may be socially suboptimal, and the distribution of income may differ from what our normative judgment indicates. In all cases, alternative market structures, or government intervention, *may* improve the economic outcome.

Market failure
A situation in which an unrestrained market operation leads to either too few or too many resources going to a specific economic activity.

POLICY EXAMPLE
Can the Government Cure Market Failure Due to Asymmetric Information, or Are Lemons Here to Stay?

One kind of market failure may occur when assumption 4 with respect to perfect competition is violated. Specifically, if information is not the same for buyers and sellers, markets may be dominated by low-quality products. This is a situation of asymmetric information.

Lemons problem
The situation in which consumers, who do not know details about the quality of a product, are willing to pay no more than the price of a low-quality product, even if a higher-quality product at a higher price exists.

Exercise 23.3
Visit www.econtoday.com for more about lemon laws.

It has been called the **lemons problem** because cars, particularly used cars, that turn out to be "bad deals" are called lemons. The potential buyer of a used car has relatively little information about the true quality of the car—its motor, transmission, brakes, and so on. The only way the buyer can find out is to purchase the car and use it for a time. In contrast, the seller usually has much greater information about the quality of the car, for the seller has been using it for some time. The owner of the used car knows whether or not it is a lemon. In situations like this, with asymmetric information between buyer and seller, buyers typically tend to want to pay only a price that reflects the lower quality of the used car in the market, not a price that reflects the higher value of a truly good used car.

From the car seller's point of view, given that the price of used cars will tend to reflect average qualities, all of the owners of known lemons will want to put their cars up for sale. The owners of high-quality used cars will be more reluctant to do so. The logical result of this adverse selection is a disproportionate number of lemons on the used car market and consequently relatively fewer sales than would exist if information were symmetric.

So lemons will be overpriced and great-running used cars will be underpriced. Is there room for government policy to improve this market? Because the government has no better information than used-car buyers, it cannot provide any improved information. What the government has done, though, is require mileage certificates on all used cars and the disclosure of major defects and work that has been performed on them. What the market has done is use brand names both for cars and for firms that sell used cars. Additionally, used-car retailers offer extended warranties.

FOR CRITICAL ANALYSIS: If used-car dealers depend on repeat customers, is the lemons problem reduced or eliminated? •

CONCEPTS IN BRIEF

- The competitive price is determined by the intersection of the market demand curve and the market supply curve; the market supply curve is equal to the horizontal summation of the portions of the individual marginal cost curves above their respective minimum average variable costs.

- In the long run, competitive firms make zero economic profits because of entry and exit of firms into and out of the industry whenever there are industrywide economic profits or economic losses.

- A constant-cost industry will have a horizontal long-run supply curve. An increasing-cost industry will have a upward-sloping long-run supply curve. A decreasing-cost industry will have a downward-sloping long-run supply curve.

- In the long run, a competitive firm produces where price, marginal revenue, marginal cost, short-run minimum average cost, and long-run minimum average cost are all equal.

- Competitive pricing is essentially marginal cost pricing, and therefore the competitive solution is called efficient because marginal cost represents the social opportunity cost of producing one more unit of the good; when consumers face a price equal to the full opportunity cost of the product they are buying, their purchasing decisions will lead to an efficient use of available resources.

Airport waiting areas for rental-car shuttles are a microcosm of the U.S. economy. Intense competition exists at all levels and may explain why average corporate after-tax profits, as a percentage of total revenues, have fallen steadily.

Have "Greedy" Corporations Been Able to Avoid Serious Competition?

CONCEPTS APPLIED:
COMPETITION, PERFECT COMPETITION, PROFITS, ECONOMIC PROFITS

Visit www.econtoday.com for an Internet Activity that expands your understanding of these concepts.

There are plenty of politicians who believe that "greedy" corporations are keeping wages down while generating record corporate profits. Of course, we would expect to hear this argument from organized labor and even from the average employee. But this seems to be the accepted dogma from many parts of our society. When the stock market is booming, it is usually because corporations are doing well. Thus the bull market of much of the 1990s seemed to be prima facie evidence that U.S. corporations are more avaricious than ever.

The Economic Meaning of *Greed*

The word *greed* really has no analytical use in economics. Our models all assume that everyone—individuals and businesses—act *as if they were maximizing either utility or profits*. If the directors and management of corporations were not practicing profit maximization, competitive pressures would presumably force the value of their stocks to fall. The result would be takeovers by investors or other companies that were more in tune with profit maximization.

Absolute Versus Relative Profits

When judging how well corporations have done financially over time, two factors are important: past rates of inflation and the relative size of the firm. The news that corporations have earned record profits does not tell us anything about the rate of return to investment or even earnings expressed as a percentage of revenues. The absolute dollar amount of profits for large corporations is by definition much larger than it was 20 or 40 years ago, for two reasons: Corporations have much greater total revenues today, and there has been a lot of inflation. In sum, whether one corporation makes $10 million in profits and another makes $2 billion in profits tells us very little.

What the Data Show

Figure 23-11 shows profits of corporations after taxes expressed as a percentage of total revenues. During the 1990s, such after-tax profits averaged around 6 percent of revenues, compared to 8 percent in the 1970s, 9 percent in the 1960s, and more than 10 percent in the 1950s. One of the reasons the ratio of after-tax profits to total revenues has fallen is that corporations are investing more in short-lived equipment, such as computers. Even so, Figure 23-11 appears to indicate that if anything, competition has become more fierce in America's corporate world. This is probably due to deregulation in industries such as telephones, banking, airlines, and trucking. In addition, global competition is intensifying.

Are Workers Suffering?

The share of corporate revenues going to employees has remained about the same since World War II. According to the Commerce Department, in the decade of the 1990s, corporations paid out about 65 percent of revenues to employees in wages and fringe benefits. That is actually more than corporations paid out in the 1950s and 1960s. One of the reasons that workers may think, nonetheless, that they are not getting their "fair share" is that compensation has been increasingly paid out in benefits rather than in take-home pay. In the 1950s, employee benefits were 4.4 percent of corporate revenues, whereas today they are approaching 12 percent of corporate revenues.

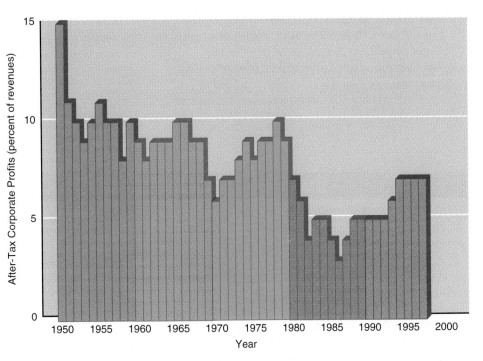

FIGURE 23-11

Declining Relative After-Tax Corporate Profits
The graph shows the ratio of corporate after-tax profits to total revenues. As you can see, this ratio is falling.

Source: U.S. Department of Commerce.

FOR CRITICAL ANALYSIS

1. What is a corporation anyway? Can such an entity be greedy?

2. How might corporate overexpansion—such as too many Borders bookstores in one city—lead to lower after-tax corporate profits as a percentage of revenues?

CHAPTER SUMMARY

1. We define a competitive situation as one in which individual firms cannot affect the price of the product they produce. This is usually when the firm is very small relative to the entire industry. A firm in a perfectly competitive situation is called a price taker; it must take price as a given.

2. The firm's total revenues will equal the price of the product times the quantity sold. Because the competitive firm can sell all it wants at the same price (the "going" price), total revenues equal the going price times the quantity the firm decides to sell.

3. The firm maximizes profits when marginal cost equals marginal revenue. The marginal revenue to the firm is represented by its own perfectly elastic demand curve. This is because marginal revenue is defined as the change in total revenues due to a change in output and sales by one unit. But the competitive firm can sell all it wants at the same price; therefore,

its marginal revenue will equal the price, which will equal its average revenue.

4. A perfectly competitive firm ends up in the long run making zero economic profits. However, it still makes a normal, or competitive, rate of return because that is the opportunity cost of capital. The competitive rate of return on investment is included in the costs as we have defined them for the firm.

5. The firm will always produce along its marginal cost curve unless the price falls below average variable costs; this would be the shutdown price. It occurs at the intersection of the average variable cost curve and the marginal cost curve. Below that price, it is not profitable to stay in production because variable costs will not be completely covered by revenues.

6. The supply curve of the firm is exactly equal to its marginal cost curve above the shutdown price. The supply curve of the industry is equal to the horizontal

summation of all the supply curves of the individual firms. This is a short-run industry supply curve, and it slopes upward.

7. The long-run supply curve will be upward-sloping, horizontal, or downward-sloping, depending on whether the industry is facing increasing, constant, or decreasing costs. The industry may have an upward-sloping long-run supply curve if it faces diseconomies of scale or increasing costs. The industry may have a downward-sloping long-run supply curve if it faces economies of scale or decreasing costs.

DISCUSSION OF PREVIEW QUESTIONS

1. How much will a perfect competitor produce in the short run?

A perfect competitor will produce at the profit-maximizing rate of output; it will maximize the positive difference between total revenues and total costs. Another way of viewing this process is through analyzing marginal revenue (MR) and marginal cost (MC). The firm can maximize total profits by producing all outputs for which MR exceeds MC. Thus if MR > MC, the firm will produce the unit in question; if MR < MC, the firm will not produce the unit in question. If MC > MR, the extra cost of producing that unit is greater than the extra revenue that the firm can earn by selling it; producing a unit for which MC > MR leads to a reduction in total profits or an increase in total losses. In short, the perfect competitor will produce up to the output rate at which MR = MC; by doing so, it will have produced all units for which MR > MC, and it will be maximizing total profits.

2. What is the perfectly competitive firm's short-run supply curve?

A supply curve indicates the various quantities per unit of time that will be offered, voluntarily, at different prices, other things being constant. Under perfect competition, price (P) equals marginal revenue (MR), and because the profit-maximizing output occurs where P = MC, it follows that any price above MC will induce more output until MC is driven up to equal that price. Thus the marginal cost curve is the firm's short-run supply schedule. We qualify this to note that because the firm has a shutdown point at the minimum average variable cost point, the technical short-run supply curve is the firm's marginal cost curve *above* the minimum average variable cost point.

3. Can a perfectly competitive firm earn economic profits?

In the short run, yes; in the long run, no. Though it is possible for a perfectly competitive firm to earn profits in the short run, our assumption of free (unfettered but not costless) entry forces us to conclude that any positive economic (abnormal) profits will be bid away. This will happen because excess profits induce entry into the industry, which amounts to an increase in industry supply. Given demand, an increase in supply will cause market price to fall, thereby shifting the individual firm's demand curve downward. This process continues until economic profits equal zero; free entry allows new entrants to compete away economic profits.

4. Why is the perfectly competitive market structure considered economically efficient?

The perfectly competitive market structure is considered economically efficient for two reasons: In the long run, economic profits are zero, and price equals marginal cost. We discuss each in turn. Profits are a signal; if economic profits are positive, the signal is that society wants *more* of this good; if economic profits are negative, this means that society wants *less* of this good; when economic profits are zero, just the "right" quantity of resources is being allocated to the production of a good. Also, the marginal cost of a good represents the social opportunity cost of producing one more unit of that good; the price of a good represents society's marginal valuation of that commodity. When price equals marginal cost, the value to society of the last unit produced (its price) is just offset by what society had to give up in order to get it (its marginal cost). Because under perfect competition, long-run economic profits equal zero and price equals marginal cost, an efficient allocation of resources exists.

PROBLEMS

(Answers to the odd-numbered problems appear at the back of the book.)

23-1. In the accompanying table, we list cost figures for a hypothetical firm. We assume that the firm is selling in a perfectly competitive market. Fill in all the blanks.

Output (units)	Fixed Cost	Average Fixed Cost (AFC)	Variable Cost	Average Variable Cost (AVC)	Total Cost	Average Total Cost (ATC)	Marginal Cost (MC)
1	$100	$_____	$40	$_____	$_____	$_____	$_____
2	100	_____	70	_____	_____	_____	_____
3	100	_____	120	_____	_____	_____	_____
4	100	_____	180	_____	_____	_____	_____
5	100	_____	250	_____	_____	_____	_____
6	100	_____	330	_____	_____	_____	_____

a. How low would the market price of its output have to go before the firm would shut down in the short run?

b. What is the price of its output at which the firm would just break even in the short run? (This is the same price below which the firm would go out of business in the long run.) What output would the firm produce at that price?

c. If the price of its output were $76, what rate of output would the firm produce, and how much profit would it earn?

23-2. Consider the accompanying graph. Then answer the questions.

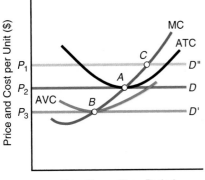

a. Which demand curve indicates that the firm is earning normal profits?

b. Which demand curve indicates that the firm is earning abnormal profits?

c. Which demand curve indicates that the firm is indifferent between shutting down and producing?

d. Which curve is the firm's supply curve?

e. Below which price will the firm shut down?

23-3. In a perfectly competitive market, what is the difference between the demand the industry faces and the demand an individual firm faces?

23-4. Why might a firm continue to produce in the short run, even though the going price is less than its average total cost?

23-5. A firm in a perfectly competitive industry has total revenue of $200,000 per year when producing 2,000 units of output per year.

a. Find the firm's average revenue.

b. Find the firm's marginal revenue.

c. Assuming that the firm is maximizing profits, what is the firm's marginal cost?

d. If the firm is at long-run equilibrium, what are its short-run average costs?

23-6. The accompanying graph is for firm J. Study it; then answer the questions.

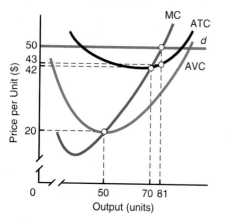

a. How many units will firm J sell in order to maximize profits?

b. What is firm J's total profit from selling the amount of output in part (a)?

c. At what price will firm J shut down in the short run?

d. If the cost curves shown represent production at the optimal long-run plant size, at what price will firm J shut down in the long run?

23-7. You have a friend who earns $25,000 a year working for a collection agency. In a savings and loan account she has $200,000 that she inherited. She is earning 6 percent per year on that money. She quits her job and buys a car wash with the $200,000. At the end of one year, she shows you her tax return. It indicates that the car wash had a pretax profit of $40,000. "What do you think about that?" she remarks. What is your answer?

COMPUTER-ASSISTED INSTRUCTION

Why do perfect competitors choose to produce at an output rate at which MR equals MC? What are the consequences for them if they fail to follow this rule?

Complete problem and answer appear on disk.

INTERACTING WITH THE INTERNET

For more information on the two largest club warehouses, go to

www.costco.com (PriceCostco)

www.samsclub.com (Sam's Club)

To investigate the international coal market, try some of the following Web addresses:

www.eia.doe.gov/historic.html

www.dri.mcgraw-hill.com/energy/eu0297.htm

www.kepl.com/coalconf/into_805.htm

CHAPTER 24

MONOPOLY

If you have traveled in the United States, you know that you are charged different prices in different cities for the same service from a taxicab. That is, the price per constant-quality unit of taxicab services differs across the United States. There is something else you might notice is different in the world of taxicabs in various cities: In some cities, you can always find a taxicab, whereas in others, it is often difficult to find one. In a competitive market with free entry and exit into the taxicab business, you would expect that the price per constant-quality unit of taxicab services would be about the same throughout the United States, as would the availability of taxicabs. Therein lies the problem—in many cities, it is not easy to enter the taxicab business. Indeed, in some cities, it is virtually impossible to start a new taxicab company unless you are willing to pay handsomely for the right to do so. To understand the motivation behind and consequences of closing a market to easy entry, you need to know about the theory of monopoly.

PREVIEW QUESTIONS

1. For the monopolist, marginal revenue is less than selling price. Why?

2. What is the profit-maximizing rate of output for the monopolist?

3. What are some common misconceptions about monopolists?

4. What is the cost to society of monopoly?

Did You Know That . . . the Central Selling Organization (CSO), a marketing group based in London, sells about 80 percent of the world's rough-cut diamonds each year, collecting handling fees of about 12 percent? The CSO is owned by South Africa's De Beers, the world's largest diamond mining company, controlled by Harry Oppenheimer. In any given year, the CSO sells between $4 and $5 billion in diamonds, making around $400 million a year in profits. It spends relatively little each year on advertising—"A diamond is forever." For all intents and purposes, there is one seller of rough-cut diamonds in the world, and you can be certain that the principal seller attempts to extract the maximum amount of profit possible under the circumstances.

Single sellers of goods and services exist all around you. The company that sells food in your school cafeteria has most probably been granted the exclusive right to do so by your college or university. The ski resort that offers you food at the top of the mountain does not allow anyone else to open a restaurant next to it. When you run a business that is the only one of its type in a particular location, you can usually charge a higher price per constant-quality unit than when there is intense competition. In this chapter you will read more about situations in which competition is restricted. We call these situations *monopoly*.

DEFINITION OF A MONOPOLIST

The word *monopoly* probably brings to mind notions of a business that gouges the consumer, sells faulty products, gets unconscionably rich, and other negative thoughts. But if we are to succeed in analyzing and predicting the behavior of noncompetitive firms, we will have to be more objective in our definition. Although most monopolies in the United States are relatively large, our definition will be equally applicable to small businesses: A **monopolist** is the *single supplier* of a good or service for which there is no close substitute.

In a monopoly market structure, the firm (the monopolist) and the industry are one and the same. Occasionally there may be a problem in identifying an industry and therefore determining if a monopoly exists. For example, should we think of aluminum and steel as separate industries, or should we define the industry in terms of basic metals? Our answer depends on the extent to which aluminum and steel can be substituted in the production of a wide range of products.

As we shall see in this chapter, a seller prefers to have a monopoly than to face competitors. In general, we think of monopoly prices as being higher than prices under perfect competition and of monopoly profits as being higher than profits under perfect competition (which are, in the long run, merely equivalent to a normal rate of return). How does a firm obtain a monopoly in an industry? Basically, there must be *barriers to entry* that enable firms to receive monopoly profits in the long run. Barriers to entry are restrictions on who can start a business or who can stay in a business.

Monopolist

A single supplier that comprises its entire industry for a good or service for which there is no close substitute.

BARRIERS TO ENTRY

For any amount of monopoly power to continue to exist in the long run, the market must be closed to entry in some way. Either legal means or certain aspects of the industry's technical or cost structure may prevent entry. We will discuss several of the barriers to entry that have allowed firms to reap monopoly profits in the long run (even if they are not pure monopolists in the technical sense).

Ownership of Resources Without Close Substitutes

Preventing a newcomer from entering an industry is often difficult. Indeed, some economists contend that no monopoly acting without government support has been able to prevent entry into the industry unless that monopoly has had the control of some essential natural resource. Consider the possibility of one firm's owning the entire supply of a raw material input that is essential to the production of a particular commodity. The exclusive ownership of such a vital resource serves as a barrier to entry until an alternative source of the raw material input is found or an alternative technology not requiring the raw material in question is developed. A good example of control over a vital input is the Aluminum Company of America (Alcoa), a firm that prior to World War II controlled the world's bauxite, the essential raw material in the production of aluminum. Such a situation is rare, though, and is ordinarily temporary.

Problems in Raising Adequate Capital

Certain industries require a large initial capital investment. The firms already in the industry can, according to some economists, obtain monopoly profits in the long run because no competitors can raise the large amount of capital needed to enter the industry. This is called the "imperfect" capital market argument employed to explain long-run, relatively high rates of return in certain industries. These industries are generally ones in which large fixed costs must be incurred merely to start production. Their fixed costs are generally for expensive machines necessary to the production process.

EXAMPLE
"Intel Inside"

Many observers of today's high-stakes high-technology world argue that the world's largest manufacturer of microprocessors, Intel, is a monopoly. They point out that to compete effectively with Intel, a potential adversary would have to invest billions of dollars. Intel provides the critical microprocessor chip that goes into the majority of the world's personal computers. Each new generation of microprocessor quickly becomes the industry standard for all IBM-compatible personal computers. Apple computers for years used a Motorola-made chip. In an attempt to fight back against Intel, Apple, Motorola, and IBM formed an alliance that did develop the Power PC microprocessor. So far, though, it has not made serious inroads into Intel's market. A few companies have attempted to clone Intel's chips, but they have not been very successful for both legal and technical reasons.

FOR CRITICAL ANALYSIS: Intel spends billions of dollars developing each new generation of microprocessor. Would it spend more or less if it had a smaller share of the microprocessor market? ●

Economies of Scale

Sometimes it is not profitable for more than one firm to exist in an industry. This is so if one firm would have to produce such a large quantity in order to realize lower unit costs that there would not be sufficient demand to warrant a second producer of the same product. Such a situation may arise because of a phenomenon we discussed in Chapter 22, economies of scale. When economies of scale exist, total costs increase less than proportionately to the increase in output. That is, proportional increases in output yield proportionately smaller

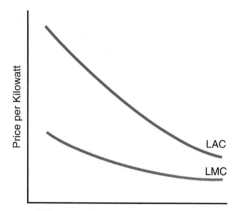

FIGURE 24-1

The Cost Curves That Might Lead to a Natural Monopoly: The Case of Electricity
Whenever long-run average costs are falling, so, too, will be long-run marginal costs. Also, long-run marginal costs (LMC) will always be below long-run average costs (LAC). A natural monopoly might arise in such a situation. The first firm to establish the low unit cost capacity would be able to take advantage of the lower average total cost curve. This firm would drive out all rivals by charging a lower price than the others could sustain at their higher average costs.

increases in total costs, and per-unit costs drop. The advantage in economies of scale lies in the fact that larger firms (with larger output) have lower costs that enable them to charge lower prices, and that drives smaller firms out of business.

When economies of scale occur over a wide range of outputs, a **natural monopoly** may develop. The natural monopoly is the firm that first takes advantage of persistent declining long-run average costs as scale increases. The natural monopolist is able to underprice its competitors and eventually force all of them out of the market.

In Figure 24-1, we have drawn a downward-sloping long-run average cost curve (LAC). Recall that when average costs are falling, marginal costs are less than average costs. We can apply the same analysis in the long run. When the long-run average cost curve (LAC) is falling, the long-run marginal cost curve (LMC) will be below the LAC.

In our example, long-run average costs are falling over such a large range of production rates that we would expect only one firm to survive in such an industry. That firm would be the natural monopolist. It would be the first one to take advantage of the decreasing average costs; that is, it would construct the large-scale facilities first. As its average costs fell, it would lower prices and get an increasingly larger share of the market. Once that firm had driven all other firms out of the industry, it would set its price to maximize profits.

Natural monopoly
A monopoly that arises from the peculiar production characteristics in an industry. It usually arises when there are large economies of scale relative to the industry's demand such that one firm can produce at a lower average cost than can be achieved by multiple firms.

Legal or Governmental Restrictions

Governments and legislatures can also erect barriers to entry. These include licenses, franchises, patents, tariffs, and specific regulations that tend to limit entry.

Licenses, Franchises, and Certificates of Convenience. In many industries, it is illegal to enter without a government license, or a "certificate of convenience and public necessity." For example, in many states you cannot form an electrical utility to compete with the electrical utility already operating in your area. You would first have to obtain a certificate of convenience and public necessity from the appropriate authority, which is usually the state's public utility commission. However, public utility commissions rarely, if ever, issue a certificate to a group of investors who want to compete directly in the same geographic area with an existing electrical utility; hence entry into the industry in a particular geographic area is prohibited, and long-run monopoly profits could conceivably be earned by the electrical utility already serving the area.

To enter interstate (and also many intrastate) markets for pipelines, television and radio broadcasting, and transmission of natural gas, to cite a few such industries, it is often necessary to obtain similar permits. Because these franchises or licenses are restricted, long-run monopoly profits might be earned by the firms already in the industry.

THE DWINDLING MONOPOLY POWER OF THE U.S. POSTAL SERVICE

In 1789, the Constitution gave Congress the power to "establish Post Offices and Post Roads." By 1792, the notion of a United States government monopoly on mail transportation was firmly established. In 1835, Congress passed definitive legislation called the Private Express Statutes to prevent any competition with the U.S. Post Office. Penalties for owners of vehicles that normally transported individuals employed as private letter carriers were spelled out. Today, the U.S. Postal Service (USPS) still maintains its monopoly on first-class mail. The USPS has always argued that because it is a natural monopoly, with large economies of scale, low-cost mail delivery is possible only with its coverage of the entire U.S. market. But entrepreneurialism and technology have eroded that argument, to the point that the concept of a USPS monopoly is losing its significance. United Parcel Service (UPS), Federal Express (FedEx), Airborne Express, DHL, and other private parcel carriers further chipped away at the USPS's monopoly. The fax machine became a player, too. And the Internet has virtually eliminated any remaining monopoly power that the USPS had, with half the businesses and households in the United States now communicating via e-mail. More than 6 billion e-mail messages are sent each year—and that's just within U.S. borders.

FOR CRITICAL ANALYSIS: In what ways might the USPS slow down the erosion of its monopoly position? ●

Patents. A patent is issued to an inventor to provide protection from having the invention copied or stolen for a period of 17 years. Suppose that engineers working for Ford Motor Company discover a way to build an engine that requires half the parts of a regular engine and weighs only half as much. If Ford is successful in obtaining a patent on this discovery, it can (in principle) prevent others from copying it. The patent holder has a monopoly. However, it is the patent holder's responsibility to defend the patent. That means that Ford—like other patent owners—must expend resources to prevent others from imitating its invention. If in fact the costs of enforcing a particular patent are greater than the benefits, the patent may not bestow any monopoly profits on its owner. The policing costs would be just too high.

Exercise 24.1
Visit www.econtoday.com for more about Coca-Cola.

EXAMPLE
Patents as Intellectual Property

A patent may bestow on its owner a monopoly for a given time period. So, too, may copyrights. Trademarks don't actually bestow monopoly power, but they do in certain cases have extreme value. Coca-Cola can exploit its trademark by licensing it for clothes and paraphernalia. So, too, can Harley-Davidson. Both of those companies have done so. Copyrights, trademarks, patents, and the like are all part of what is known as intellectual property. Songs, music, computer programs, and designs are all intellectual property. Indeed, some economists believe that the world value of intellectual property now exceeds the value of physical property, such as real estate, buildings, and equipment. Not surprisingly, in the corporate world, when a business buys another business, the acquiring company's lawyers have to worry a great deal about the acquired company's intellectual property portfolio. What intellectual property rights in terms of patents, trademarks, and copyrights does the soon-to-be-acquired company actually own?

FOR CRITICAL ANALYSIS: *Why doesn't the ownership of a well-known trademark bestow true monopoly power on its owner?* ●

Tariffs. **Tariffs** are special taxes that are imposed on certain imported goods. Tariffs have the effect of making imports relatively more expensive than their domestic counterparts so that consumers switch to the relatively cheaper domestically made products. If the tariffs are high enough, imports become overpriced, and domestic producers gain monopoly advantage as the sole suppliers. Many countries have tried this protectionist strategy by using high tariffs to shut out foreign competitors.

Tariffs
Taxes on imported goods.

Regulations. During much of the twentieth century, government regulation of the American economy has increased, especially along the dimensions of safety and quality. For example, pharmaceutical quality-control regulations enforced by the Food and Drug Administration may require that each pharmaceutical company install a $2 million computerized testing machine that requires elaborate monitoring and maintenance. Presumably, this large fixed cost can be spread over a larger number of units of output by larger firms than by smaller firms, thereby putting the smaller firms at a competitive disadvantage. It will also deter entry to the extent that the scale of operation of a potential entrant must be sufficiently large to cover the average fixed costs of the required equipment. We examine regulation in more detail in Chapter 26.

Cartels

"Being the only game in town" is preferable because such a monopoly position normally allows the monopolist to charge higher prices and make greater profits. Not surprisingly, manufacturers and sellers have often attempted to form an organization (which often is international) that acts as one. This is called a **cartel.** Cartels are an attempt by their members to earn higher than competitive profits. They set common prices and output quotas for their members. The key to the success of a cartel is keeping one member from competing against other members by expanding production and thereby lowering price. Apparently, one of the most successful international cartels ever was the Organization of Petroleum Exporting Countries (OPEC), an association of the world's largest oil-producing countries, including Saudi Arabia, which at times has accounted for a significant percentage of the world's crude oil output. OPEC effectively organized a significant cutback on the production of crude oil in the wake of the so-called Yom Kippur War in the Middle East in 1973. Within one year, the spot price of crude oil jumped from $2.12 to $7.61 per barrel on the world market. By the early 1980s, the price had risen to over $30.

Most cartels have not as much success.

Cartel
An association of producers in an industry that agree to set common prices and output quotas to prevent competition.

INTERNATIONAL EXAMPLE
"We're Just Trying to Keep the Market Stable"

The stated goal of most international cartels is keeping markets "stable." In reality, cartel members are seeking higher prices (and profits) for their product. But to achieve their aims, the producing countries have to be willing to withhold some of their production from the world market. In this way, the world price of a commodity does not fall if world production increases.

Nowhere are international cartels as prevalent as in the market for commodities. The International Coffee Organization lasted 30 years until the United States pulled out; it was succeeded by the Association of Coffee Producing Countries. Cocoa has the International Cocoa Organization. There is even an ostrich cartel called the Little Karoo Agricultural Cooperative.

The U.S. government has at times sanctioned the equivalent of a cartel. A meeting in Washington, D.C., involving executives from a dozen global aluminum producers and government officials representing the United States, the European Union, and four other nations ultimately resulted in an agreement by all those attending to reduce aluminum production. All such reductions were voluntary except by Russia. In exchange for cutting primary aluminum production by 500,000 tons over a two-year period, Russia received the promise of $250 million of U.S. taxpayers' money for equity investments. U.S. government officials claim that "the markets are still open" nonetheless.

FOR CRITICAL ANALYSIS: The price of gasoline today (corrected for inflation) is about 50 percent of what it was in 1984. What does that tell you about the long-run effectiveness of global cartels? ●

CONCEPTS IN BRIEF

- A monopolist is defined as a single seller of a product or a good for which there is no good close substitute.

- To maintain a monopoly, there must be barriers to entry. Barriers to entry include ownership of resources without close substitutes; large capital requirements in order to enter the industry; economies of scale; legally required licenses, franchises, and certificates of convenience; patents; tariffs; and safety and quality regulations.

THE DEMAND CURVE A MONOPOLIST FACES

A *pure monopolist* is the sole supplier of *one* product, good, or service. A pure monopolist faces a demand curve that is the demand curve for the entire market for that good.

The monopolist faces the industry demand curve because the monopolist is the entire industry.

Because the monopolist faces the industry demand curve, which is by definition downward-sloping, its decision-making process with respect to how much to produce is not the same as for a perfect competitor. When a monopolist changes output, it does not automatically receive the same price per unit that it did before the change.

Profits to Be Made from Increasing Production

How do firms benefit from changing production rates? What happens to price in each case? Let's first review the situation among perfect competitors.

Marginal Revenue for the Perfect Competitor. Recall that a competitive firm has a perfectly elastic demand curve. That is because the competitive firm is such a small part of the market that it cannot influence the price of its product. It is a *price taker.* If the forces of supply and demand establish that the price per constant-quality pair of shoes is $50, the individual firm can sell all the pairs of shoes it wants to produce at $50 per pair. The average revenue is $50, the price is $50, and the marginal revenue is also $50.

Let us again define marginal revenue:

Marginal revenue equals the change in total revenue due to a one-unit change in the quantity produced and sold.

In the case of a competitive industry, each time a single firm changes production by one unit, total revenue changes by the going price, and price is always the same. Marginal revenue never changes; it always equals price, or average revenue. Average revenue was defined as total revenue divided by quantity demanded, or

$$\text{Average revenue} = \frac{\text{TR}}{Q} = \frac{PQ}{Q} = P$$

Marginal Revenue for the Monopolist. What about a monopoly firm? Because a monopoly is the entire industry, the monopoly firm's demand curve is the market demand curve. The market demand curve slopes downward, just like the other demand curves that we have seen. Therefore, to sell more of a particular product, given the industry demand curve, the monopoly firm must lower the price. Thus the monopoly firm moves *down* the demand curve. If all buyers are to be charged the same price, the monopoly must lower the price on all units sold in order to sell more. It cannot just lower the price on the *last* unit sold in any given time period in order to sell a larger quantity.

Put yourself in the shoes of a monopoly ferryboat owner. You have a government-bestowed franchise, and no one can compete with you. Your ferryboat goes between two islands. If you are charging $1 per crossing, a certain quantity of your services will be demanded. Let's say that you are ferrying 100 people a day each way at that price. If you decide that you would like to ferry more individuals, you must lower your price to all individuals—you must move *down* the existing demand curve for ferrying services. To calculate the marginal revenue of your change in price, you must first calculate the total revenues you received at $1 per passenger per crossing and then calculate the total revenues you would receive at, say, 90 cents per passenger per crossing.

It is sometimes useful to compare monopoly markets with perfectly competitive markets. The only way the monopolist can increase sales is by getting consumers to spend more of their incomes on the monopolist's product and less on all other products combined. Thus the monopolist is constrained by the entire market demand curve for its product. We see this in Figure 24-2, which compares the demand curves of the perfect competitor and the monopolist.

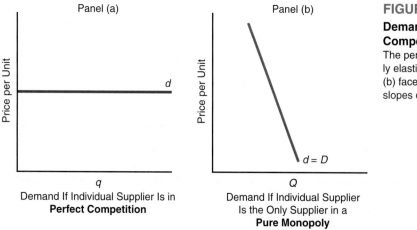

FIGURE 24-2

Demand Curves for the Perfect Competitor and the Monopolist
The perfect competitor in panel (a) faces a perfectly elastic demand curve, d. The monopolist in panel (b) faces the entire industry demand curve, which slopes downward.

Here we see the fundamental difference between the monopolist and the competitor. The competitor doesn't have to worry about lowering price to sell more. In a purely competitive situation, the competitive firm accounts for such a small part of the market that it can sell its entire output, whatever that may be, at the same price. The monopolist cannot. The more the monopolist wants to sell, the lower the price it has to charge on the last unit (and on *all* units put on the market for sale). Obviously, the extra revenues the monopolist receives from selling one more unit are going to be smaller than the extra revenues received from selling the next-to-last unit. The monopolist has to lower the price on the last unit to sell it because it is facing a downward-sloping demand curve and the only way to move down the demand curve is to lower the price on all units.

The Monopolist's Marginal Revenue: Less than Price

An essential point is that for the monopolist, marginal revenue is always less than price. To understand why, look at Figure 24-3, which shows a unit increase in sales due to a reduction in the price of a commodity from P_1 to P_2. After all, the only way that sales can increase, given a downward-sloping demand curve, is for the price to fall. Price P_2 is the price received for the last unit. Thus price P_2 times the last unit sold represents what is received from the last unit sold. That is equal to the vertical column (area A). Area A is one unit wide by P_2 high.

But price times the last unit sold is *not* the addition to *total* revenues received from selling that last unit. Why? Because price had to be reduced on all previous units sold (Q) in order to sell the larger quantity $Q + 1$. The reduction in price is represented by the vertical distance from P_1 to P_2 on the vertical axis. We must therefore subtract area B from area A to come up with the *change* in total revenues due to a one-unit increase in sales. Clearly, the change in total revenues—that is, marginal revenue—must be less than price because marginal revenue is always the difference between areas A and B in Figure 24-3. For example, if the initial price is $8 and quantity demanded is 3, to increase quantity to 4 units, it is necessary to decrease price to $7, not just for the fourth unit, but on all three previous units as well. Thus at a price of $7, marginal revenue is $7 − $3 = $4 because there is a $1 per unit price reduction on three previous units. Hence marginal revenue, $4, is less than price, $7.

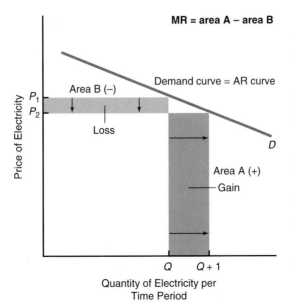

MR = area A − area B

FIGURE 24-3

Marginal Revenue: Always Less than Price

The price received for the last unit sold is equal to P_2. The revenues received from selling this last unit are equal to P_2 times one unit, or the area of the vertical column. However, if a single price is being charged for all units, total revenues do not go up by the amount of the area represented by that column. The price had to be reduced on all the previous Q units that were being sold at price P_1. Thus we must subtract area B—the rectangle between P_1 and P_2 from the origin to Q—from area A in order to derive marginal revenue. Marginal revenue is therefore always less than price.

ELASTICITY AND MONOPOLY

The monopolist faces a downward-sloping demand curve (its average revenue curve). That means that it cannot charge just *any* price with no changes in quantity (a common misconception) because, depending on the price charged, a different quantity will be demanded.

Earlier we defined a monopolist as the single seller of a well-defined good or service with no *close* substitute. This does not mean, however, that the demand curve for a monopoly is vertical or exhibits zero price elasticity of demand. (Indeed, as we shall see, the profit-maximizing monopolist will never operate in a price range in which demand is inelastic.) After all, consumers have limited incomes and alternative wants. The downward slope of a monopolist's demand curve occurs because individuals compare the marginal satisfaction they will receive to the cost of the commodity to be purchased. Take the example of telephone service. Even if miraculously there were absolutely no substitute whatsoever for telephone service, the market demand curve would still slope downward. At lower prices, people will add more phones and separate lines for different family members.

Furthermore, the demand curve for telephone service slopes downward because there are at least several *imperfect* substitutes, such as letters, telegrams, in-person conversations, and CB and VHF-FM radios. Thus even though we defined a monopolist as a single seller of a commodity with no *close* substitute, we can talk about the range of *imperfect* substitutes. The more such imperfect substitutes there are, the more elastic will be the monopolist's demand curve, all other things held constant.

CONCEPTS IN BRIEF

- The monopolist estimates its marginal revenue curve, where marginal revenue is defined as the change in total revenues due to a one-unit change in quantity sold.
- For the perfect competitor, price equals marginal revenue equals average revenue. For the monopolist, price is always greater than marginal revenue. For the monopolist, marginal revenue is always less than price because price must be reduced on all units to sell more.
- The price elasticity of demand for the monopolist depends on the number and similarity of substitutes. The more numerous and more similar the substitutes, the greater the price elasticity of demand of the monopolist's demand curve.

COSTS AND MONOPOLY PROFIT MAXIMIZATION

To find out the rate of output at which the perfect competitor would maximize profits, we had to add cost data. We will do the same thing now for the monopolist. We assume that profit maximization is the goal of the pure monopolist, just as for the perfect competitor. The perfect competitor, however, has only to decide on the profit-maximizing rate of output because price was given. The competitor is a price taker. For the pure monopolist, we must seek a profit-maximizing *price-output combination* because the monopolist is a **price searcher.** We can determine this profit-maximizing price-output combination with either of two equivalent approaches—by looking at total revenues and total costs or by looking at marginal revenues and marginal costs. We shall examine both approaches.

Price searcher
A firm that must determine the price-output combination that maximizes profit because it faces a downward-sloping demand curve.

The Total Revenues–Total Costs Approach

We show hypothetical demand (rate of output and price per unit), revenues, costs, and other data in panel (a) of Figure 24-4. In column 3, we see total revenues for our hypothetical

Panel (a)

(1) Output (units)	(2) Price per Unit	(3) Total Revenues (TR) (3) = (2) x (1)	(4) Total Costs (TC)	(5) Total Profit (5) = (3) − (4)	(6) Marginal Cost (MC)	(7) Marginal Revenue (MR)
0	$8.00	$ .00	$10.00	−$10.00		
					$4.00	$7.80
1	7.80	7.80	14.00	− 6.20		
					3.50	7.40
2	7.60	15.20	17.50	− 2.30		
					3.25	7.00
3	7.40	22.20	20.75	1.45		
					3.05	6.60
4	7.20	28.80	23.80	5.00		
					2.90	6.20
5	7.00	35.00	26.70	8.30		
					2.80	5.80
6	6.80	40.80	29.50	11.30		
					2.75	5.40
7	6.60	46.20	32.25	13.95		
					2.85	5.00
8	6.40	51.20	35.10	16.10		
					3.20	4.60
9	6.20	55.80	38.30	17.50		
					4.00	4.20
10	6.00	60.00	42.30	17.70		
					6.00	3.80
11	5.80	63.80	48.30	15.50		
					9.00	3.40
12	5.60	67.20	57.30	9.90		

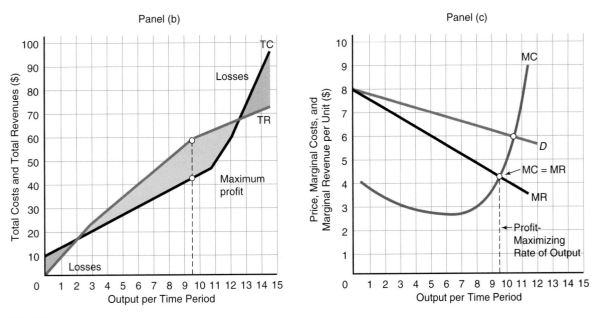

FIGURE 24-4

Monopoly Costs, Revenues, and Profits

In panel (a), we give hypothetical demand (rate of output and price per unit), revenues, costs, and other relevant data. As shown in panel (b), the monopolist maximizes profits where the positive differ-ence between TR and TC is greatest. This is at an output rate of between 9 and 10. Put another way, profit maximization occurs where marginal revenue equals marginal cost, as shown in panel (c). This is at the same output rate of between 9 and 10. (The MC curve must cut the MR curve from below.)

monopolist, and in column 4, we see total costs. We can transfer these two columns to panel (b). The only difference between the total revenue and total cost diagram in panel (b) and the one we showed for a perfect competitor in Chapter 23 is that the total revenue line is no longer straight. Rather, it curves. For any given demand curve, in order to sell more, the monopolist must lower the price. Thus, the basic difference between a monopolist and a perfect competitor has to do with the demand curve for the two types of firms. Monopoly market power is derived from facing a downward-sloping demand curve.

Profit maximization involves maximizing the positive difference between total revenues and total costs. This occurs at an output rate of between 9 and 10 units.

The Marginal Revenue–Marginal Cost Approach

Profit maximization will also occur where marginal revenue equals marginal cost. This is as true for a monopolist as it is for a perfect competitor (but the monopolist will charge a higher price). When we transfer marginal cost and marginal revenue information from columns 6 and 7 in panel (a) of Figure 24-4 to panel (c), we see that marginal revenue equals marginal cost at an output rate of between 9 and 10 units. Profit maximization occurs at the same output as in panel (b).

Why Produce Where Marginal Revenue Equals Marginal Cost? If the monopolist goes past the point where marginal revenue equals marginal cost, marginal cost will exceed marginal revenue. That is, the incremental cost of producing any more units will exceed the incremental revenue. It just wouldn't be worthwhile, as was true also in perfect competition. But if the monopolist produces less than that, it is also not making maximum profits. Look at output rate Q_1 in Figure 24-5. Here the monopolist's marginal revenue is at A, but marginal cost is at B. Marginal revenue exceeds marginal cost on the last unit sold; the profit for that *particular* unit, Q_1, is equal to the vertical difference between A

Exercise 24.2
Visit www.econtoday.com for more about new health treatments.

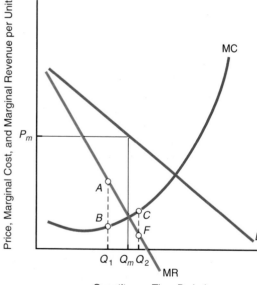

Quantity per Time Period

FIGURE 24-5

Maximizing Profits
The profit-maximizing production rate is Q_m, and the profit-maximizing price is P_m. The monopolist would be unwise to produce at the rate Q_1 because here marginal revenue would be Q_1A and marginal costs would be Q_1B. Marginal revenue exceeds marginal cost. The firm will keep producing until the point Q_m, where marginal revenue just equals marginal cost. It would be foolish to produce at the rate Q_2, for here marginal cost exceeds marginal revenue. It behooves the monopolist to cut production back to Q_m.

and *B*, or the difference between marginal revenue and marginal cost. The monopolist would be foolish to stop at output rate Q_1 because if output is expanded, marginal revenue will still exceed marginal cost, and therefore total profits will rise. In fact, the profit-maximizing monopolist will continue to expand output and sales until marginal revenue equals marginal cost, which is at output rate Q_m. The monopolist won't produce at rate Q_2 because here, as we see, marginal costs are *C* and marginal revenues are *F*. The difference between *C* and *F* represents the *reduction* in total profits from producing that additional unit. Total profits will rise as the monopolist reduces its rate of output back toward Q_m.

What Price to Charge for Output?

How does the monopolist set prices? We know the quantity is set at the point at which marginal revenue equals marginal cost. The monopolist then finds out how much can be charged—how much the market will bear—for that particular quantity, Q_m, in Figure 24-5. We know that the demand curve is defined as showing the *maximum* price for which a given quantity can be sold. That means that our monopolist knows that to sell Q_m, it can charge only P_m because that is the price at which that specific quantity, Q_m, is demanded. This price is found by drawing a vertical line from the quantity, Q_m, to the market demand curve. Where that line hits the market demand curve, the price is determined. We find that price by drawing a horizontal line from the demand curve over to the price axis; that gives us the profit-maximizing price, P_m.

In our detailed numerical example, at a profit-maximizing rate of output of a little less than 10 in Figure 24-4, the firm can charge a maximum price of about $6 and still sell all the goods produced, all at the same price.

The basic procedure for finding the profit-maximizing short-run price-quantity combination for the monopolist is first to determine the profit-maximizing rate of output, by either the total revenue–total cost method or the marginal revenue–marginal cost method, and then to determine by use of the demand curve, *D,* the maximum price that can be charged to sell that output.

Don't get the impression that just because we are able to draw an exact demand curve in Figure 24-4 and Figure 24-5, real-world monopolists have such perfect information. The process of price searching by a less than perfect competitor is just that—a process. A monopolist can only estimate the actual demand curve and therefore can only make an educated guess when it sets its profit-maximizing price. This is not a problem for the perfect competitor because price is given already by the intersection of market demand and market supply. The monopolist, in contrast, reaches the profit-maximizing output-price combination by trial and error.

CALCULATING MONOPOLY PROFIT

We have talked about the monopolist's profit, but we have yet to indicate how much profit the monopolist makes. We have actually shown total profits in column 5 of panel (a) in Figure 24-4. We can also find total profits by adding an average total cost curve to panel (c) of

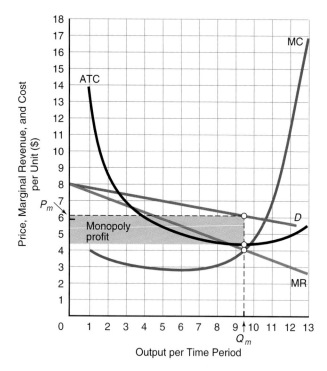

FIGURE 24-6

Monopoly Profit
We find monopoly profit by subtracting total costs from total revenues at an output rate of almost 10, labeled Q_m, which is the profit-maximizing rate of output for the monopolist. The profit-maximizing price is therefore about $6 and is labeled P_m. Monopoly profit is given by the shaded area, which is equal to total revenues (P × Q) minus total costs (ATC × Q). This diagram is similar to panel (c) of Figure 24-4, with the short-run average total cost curve (ATC) added.

that figure. We do that in Figure 24-6. When we add the average total cost curve, we find that the profit that a monopolist makes is equal to the shaded area [or total revenues minus total costs (ATC × Q)]. Given the demand curve and a uniform pricing system (i.e., all units sold at the same price), there is no way for a monopolist to make greater profits than those shown by the shaded area. The monopolist is maximizing profits where marginal cost equals marginal revenue. If the monopolist produces less than that, it will be forfeiting some profits. If the monopolist produces more than that, it will be forfeiting some profits.

The same is true of a perfect competitor. The competitor produces where marginal revenues equal marginal costs because it produces at the point where the marginal cost curve intersects the perfectly elastic firm demand curve. The perfectly elastic firm demand curve represents the marginal revenue curve for the pure competitor, for the same average revenues are obtained on all the units sold. Perfect competitors maximize profits at MR = MC, as do pure monopolists. But the perfect competitor makes no true economic profits in the long run; rather, all it makes is a normal, competitive rate of return.

In Chapter 23, we talked about companies experiencing short-run economic profits because they had, for example, invented something new. Competition, though, gradually eroded those higher than normal profits. The fact that a firm experiences higher than normal profits today does not mean that it has a monopoly forever. Try as companies may, keeping competitors away is never easy.

No Guarantee of Profits

The term *monopoly* conjures up the notion of a greedy firm ripping off the public and making exorbitant profits. However, the mere existence of a monopoly does not guarantee high

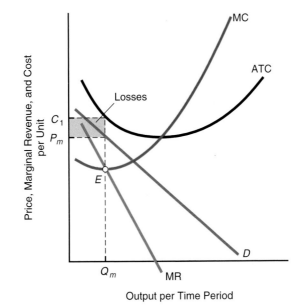

FIGURE 24-7

Monopolies: Not Always Profitable

Some monopolists face the situation shown here. The average total cost curve, ATC, is everywhere above the average revenue, or demand, curve, D. In the short run, the monopolist will produce where MC = MR at point E. Output Q_m will be sold at price P_m, but cost per unit is C_1. Losses are the shaded rectangle. Eventually, the monopolist will go out of business.

profits. Numerous monopolies have gone bankrupt. Figure 24-7 shows the monopolist's demand curve as D and the resultant marginal revenue curve as MR. It does not matter at what rate of output this particular monopolist operates; total costs cannot be covered. Look at the position of the average total cost curve. It lies everywhere above D (the average revenue curve). Thus there is no price-output combination that will allow the monopolist even to cover costs, much less earn profits. This monopolist will, in the short run, suffer economic losses as shown by the shaded area. The graph in Figure 24-7 depicts a situation for millions of typical monopolies that exist; they are called inventions. The owner of a patented invention or discovery has a pure legal monopoly, but the demand and cost curves may be such that production is not profitable. Every year at inventors' conventions, one can see many inventions that have never been put into production because they were deemed "uneconomic" by potential producers and users.

CONCEPTS IN BRIEF

- The basic difference between a monopolist and a perfect competitor is that a monopolist faces a downward-sloping demand curve, and therefore marginal revenue is less than price.

- The monopolist must choose the profit-maximizing price-output combination—the output at which marginal revenue equals marginal cost and the highest price possible as given by the demand curve for that particular output rate.

- Monopoly short-run profits are found by looking at average total costs compared to price per unit. This difference multiplied by quantity sold at that price determines monopoly profit.

- A monopolist does not necessarily earn a profit. If the average total cost curve lies entirely above the demand curve for a monopoly, production will not be profitable.

ON MAKING HIGHER PROFITS: PRICE DISCRIMINATION

In a perfectly competitive market, each buyer is charged the same price for every unit of the particular commodity (corrected for differential transportation charges). Because the product is homogeneous and we also assume full knowledge on the part of the buyers, a difference in price cannot exist. Any seller of the product who tried to charge a price higher than the going market price would find that no one would purchase it from that seller.

In this chapter we have assumed until now that the monopolist charged all consumers the same price for all units. A monopolist, however, may be able to charge different people different prices or different unit prices for successive units sought by a given buyer. When there is no cost difference, either one or a combination of these strategies is called **price discrimination.** A firm will engage in price discrimination whenever feasible to increase profits. A price-discriminating firm is able to charge some customers more than other customers.

It must be made clear at the outset that charging different prices to different people or for different units that reflect differences in the cost of service to those particular people does not amount to price discrimination. This is **price differentiation:** differences in price that reflect differences in marginal cost.

We can also say that a uniform price does not necessarily indicate an absence of price discrimination. Charging all customers the same price when production costs vary by customer is actually a case of price discrimination.

Price discrimination
Selling a given product at more than one price, with the price difference being unrelated to differences in cost.

Price differentiation
Establishing different prices for similar products to reflect differences in marginal cost in providing those commodities to different groups of buyers.

Necessary Conditions for Price Discrimination

Four conditions are necessary for price discrimination to exist:

1. The firm must face a downward-sloping demand curve.
2. The firm must be able to separate markets at a reasonable cost.
3. The buyers in the various markets must have different price elasticities of demand.
4. The firm must be able to prevent resale of the product or service.

For example, charging students a lower price than nonstudents for a movie can be done relatively easily. The cost of checking student IDs is apparently not significant. Also, it is fairly easy to make sure that students do not resell their tickets to nonstudents.

EXAMPLE
Cheaper Airfares for Some, Really Expensive Fares for Others

First-class airfares are often stunningly higher than coach class—far higher than any additional marginal cost warrants. This is a good example of price discrimination. And even in coach class, there may be fare differences of 800 percent. All coach passengers are packed in like sardines, so why the difference in price among them? The answer is again price discrimination, but this time it is based on how badly a person wants to fly. If you are a businessperson who is called to a meeting for the next day, you want to fly very badly. The fact that your company will not allow you to fly first class will not save you from having to pay, say, $2,000 to fly round-trip from Cincinnati to Los Angeles, particularly if you do not stay over on a Saturday. The Saturday stay-over requirement for low fares neatly differentiates individuals who must travel from those who have the time to stay over—people on business trips versus people on leisure trips. If you have a relatively high price elasticity of demand, you will also want to take advantage of low fares

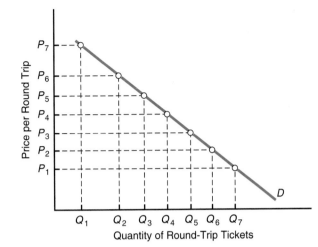

FIGURE 24-8

Toward Perfect Price Discrimination

What the airlines attempt to do by dividing any particular round-trip fare into "buckets" is to price-discriminate as finely as possible. Here we show the airlines setting seven different prices for the same round trip. Those who pay price P_7 are the ones who are the last to ask for a reservation. Those who pay price P_1 are the ones who planned furthest in advance or happened to hit it lucky when seats were added to the low-fare bucket.

that require 7 days', 14 days', or longer advance purchase. The more price-sensitive you are, the more you will pay attention to such cheap-fare requirements, and the lower will be the fare you are likely to pay.

Airlines, with sophisticated computer programs performing what is known as yield management, are also able to change prices constantly. Such programs allow them to project relatively precisely how many last-minute business travelers are going to pay full fare to get on a flight. Computerized yield management works so well because of a mathematical formula that Bell Laboratories patented in 1988. It allows rapid calculations on fare problems with thousands of variables. The airlines compare historical databases on ridership with what is happening in terms of bookings right now. A typical flight will be divided into seven fare "buckets" that may have a differential of as much as 800 percent. The yield management computers constantly adjust the number of seats available in each bucket. When advance bookings are few, more seats are added to the low-fare buckets. When advance bookings are above normal, more seats are added to the highest-fare buckets. The result is lower fares for many and much higher fares for a few. In essence, the airlines are attempting to hit every "price point" on the demand curve for airline travel, as is shown in Figure 24-8.

FOR CRITICAL ANALYSIS: Assuming that the Bell Laboratories mathematical formula had been available 20 years ago, why couldn't airlines have used it then? ●

THE SOCIAL COST OF MONOPOLIES

Let's run a little experiment. We will start with a purely competitive industry with numerous firms, each one unable to affect the price of its product. The supply curve of the industry is equal to the horizontal sum of the marginal cost curves of the individual producers above their respective minimum average variable costs. In panel (a) of Figure 24-9 on page 550, we show the market demand curve and the market supply curve in a perfectly competitive situation. The competitive price in equilibrium is equal to P_e, and the equilibrium quantity at that price is equal to Q_e. Each individual competitor faces a demand curve (not shown) that is coincident with the price line P_e. No individual supplier faces the market demand curve, D.

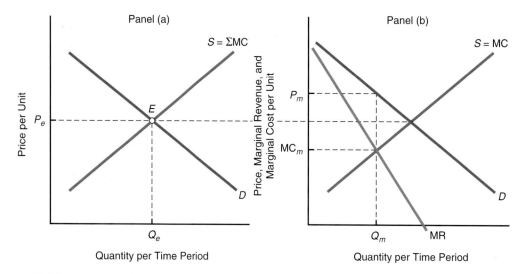

FIGURE 24-9

The Effects of Monopolizing an Industry
In panel (a), we show a competitive situation in which equilibrium is established at the intersection of D and S at point E. The equilibrium price would be P_e, and the equilibrium quantity would be Q_e. Each individual competitive producer faces a demand curve that is a horizontal line at the market clearing price, P_e. What happens if the industry is suddenly monopolized? We assume that the costs stay the same; the only thing that changes is that the monopolist now faces the entire downward-sloping demand curve. In panel (b), we draw the marginal revenue curve. Marginal cost is S because that is the horizontal summation of all the individual marginal cost curves. The monopolist therefore produces at Q_m and charges price P_m. P_m in panel (b) is higher than P_e in panel (a), and Q_m is less than Q_e. We see, then, that a monopolist charges a higher price and produces less than an industry in a competitive situation.

Now let's assume that a monopolist comes in and buys up every single competitor in the industry. In so doing, we'll assume that the monopolist does not affect any of the marginal cost curves or demand. We can therefore redraw D and S in panel (b) of Figure 24-9, exactly the same as in panel (a).

How does this monopolist decide how much to charge and how much to produce? If the monopolist is profit-maximizing, it is going to look at the marginal revenue curve and produce at the output where marginal revenue equals marginal cost. But what is the marginal cost curve in panel (b) of Figure 24-9? It is merely S because we said that S was equal to the horizontal summation of the portions of the individual marginal cost curves above each firm's respective minimum average variable cost. The monopolist therefore produces quantity Q_m and sells it at price P_m. Notice that Q_m is less than Q_e and that P_m is greater than P_e. A monopolist therefore produces a smaller quantity and sells it at a higher price. This is the reason usually given when economists criticize monopolists. Monopolists raise the price and restrict production, compared to a competitive situation. For a monopolist's product, consumers are forced to pay a price that exceeds the marginal cost of production. Resources are misallocated in such a situation—too few resources are being used in the monopolist's industry, and too many are used elsewhere.

Notice from Figure 24-9 that by setting MR = MC, the monopolist produces at a rate of output where $P > MC$ (compare P_m to MC_m). The marginal cost of a commodity (MC) represents what society had to give up in order to obtain the last unit produced. Price, by contrast, represents what buyers are willing to pay to acquire that last unit. Thus the price of a good represents society's valuation of the last unit produced. The monopoly outcome of $P > MC$ means that the value to society of the last unit produced is greater than its cost (MC); hence not enough of the good is being produced. As we have pointed out before, these differences between monopoly and competition arise not because of differences in costs but rather because of differences in the demand curves the individual firms face. The monopolist has monopoly power because it faces a downward-sloping demand curve. The individual perfect competitor faces a perfectly elastic demand curve.

Before we leave the topic of the cost to society of monopolies, we must repeat that our analysis is based on a heroic assumption. That assumption is that the monopolization of the perfectly competitive industry does not change the cost structure. If monopolization results in higher marginal cost, the cost to society is even greater. Conversely, if monopolization results in cost savings, the cost, if any, to society is less than we infer from our analysis. Indeed, we could have presented a hypothetical example in which monopolization led to such a dramatic reduction in average cost that society actually benefited. Such a situation is a possibility in industries in which economies of scale exist for a very great range of outputs.

CONCEPTS IN BRIEF

- Four conditions are necessary for price discrimination: (1) The firm must face a downward-sloping demand curve, (2) the firm must be able to distinguish markets, (3) buyers in different markets must have different price elasticities of demand, and (4) resale of the product or service must be preventable.

- A monopolist can make higher profits if it can price-discriminate. Price discrimination requires that two or more identifiable classes of buyers exist whose price elasticities of demand for the product or service are different and that these two classes of buyers can be distinguished at little cost.

- Price differentiation should not be confused with price discrimination. The former occurs when differences in price reflect differences in marginal cost.

- Monopoly results in a lower quantity being sold because the price is higher than it would be in an ideal perfectly competitive industry in which the cost curves were essentially the same as the monopolist's.

Finding a cab in New York City is not always easy. The city has severely restricted the number of licensed cabs. If you bought the right to operate a cab, would you expect to make a higher than normal rate of return on your investment?

Today's Hot Investment: A License to Operate a Taxi

CONCEPTS APPLIED:
MARKET POWER, MONOPOLY, ENTRY, COMPETITION, GOVERNMENT RESTRICTIONS

Visit www.econtoday.com for an Internet Activity that expands your understanding of these concepts.

One of the most important barriers to entry in certain markets is government restrictions. Even as it touts the importance of unfettered competition, government often supports special-interest groups by setting legal restrictions on entry. The taxicab business is one such example. Often the local government decides how many taxi "medallions" it will permit to exist. The most flagrant example of such government creation of monopoly involves New York City.

"Hey Buddy, Can You Spare $237,000?"

In a recent year, the right to operate a taxi in New York City was valued at $237,000. Why so high? Because New York City issued 11,787 licenses to operate taxis during the Great Depression—and then kept the number fixed for 60 years. Not until May 1996 did the city decide to auction off 53 new medallions. The 53 "lucky" bidders for those new medallions paid an average of $177,000. By 1998, they could have resold their licenses for $237,000. For six decades, medallions have been sold on the open market. Their price has increased about 18 percent a year, making them a better long-term investment than corporate stocks, which increased 10.9 percent per year over the same period.

Why Pay So Much for a Monopoly Right?

People who wish to buy medallions have to figure out how much they are really worth. The owner can use or lease the medallion by the day or the week. Many medal-

lion owners make their drivers supply the cars and the insurance. After all expenses are considered, a medallion owner can figure on making $20,000 to $30,000 a year. Most new purchasers of medallions take out a ten-year loan from a taxi industry credit union. The medallion is the collateral.

Does Competition Still Exist?

Because there are so few taxis relative to the population in New York City, you can expect competition to arise, even if it is illegal. Vans called *jitneys* operate illegally in many of New York's boroughs. The jitneys compete with taxis, as well as with the subway and buses. Many such vans are run by individuals who have applied for approval from the Taxi and Limousine Commission, only to be turned down by the City Council. Today, there are thousands of illegal van drivers in Brooklyn and Queens dodging the police. Many of them have banded together through a network of CB radios in order to avoid police cars.

One has to wonder about why such onerous restrictions on entry into the transportation business can last so long. The simple answer involves the "clout" that existing monopoly owners have within the political process that governs the regulation of taxicabs. (See Chapter 32 for more on special-interest groups.)

FOR CRITICAL ANALYSIS
1. Could you make a monopoly rate of return by buying a medallion?
2. What arguments might the city council use to justify refusing to license jitneys?

CHAPTER SUMMARY

1. We formally define a monopolist as the single supplier of a product or service with no close substitute. A monopolist faces the entire industry demand curve because the monopolist *is* the industry. Pure monopolists are rare.

2. A monopolist can usually remain a monopolist only if other firms are prevented from entering the industry and sharing in the monopoly profits. One barrier to entry is government restrictions. Patents are another.

3. A monopoly could arise because of firm economies of scale, which are defined as a situation in which an increase in output leads to a more than proportionate decrease in average total costs. If this were the case, average total costs would be falling as production increased. The first company to produce a great deal and take advantage of firm economies of scale could conceivably lower price and drive everyone else out of the industry. This would be a natural monopolist.

4. Health and quality regulations can be a barrier to entry because the increased fixed costs put smaller firms at a competitive disadvantage.

5. The marginal revenue that a monopolist receives is defined in the same way as the marginal revenue that a competitor receives. Nevertheless, because the monopolist faces the industry demand curve, it must lower price to increase sales, not only on the last unit sold, but also on all the preceding units. The monopolist's marginal revenue is therefore equal to the price received on the last unit sold minus the reduction in price on all the previous units times the number of previous units sold.

6. The profit-maximizing price that the monopolist charges is the maximum price that it can get away with while still selling everything produced up to the point where marginal revenue equals marginal cost.

We find this price by extending a vertical line from the intersection of the marginal revenue curve and the marginal cost curve up to the demand curve and then over to the vertical axis, which measures price.

7. Total profits are total revenues minus total costs. Total revenues are equal to the price of the product (the profit-maximizing price) times the quantity produced (the quantity found at the intersection of the marginal revenue and marginal cost curves). Total costs are equal to the quantity produced times average total costs. The difference between these total costs and total revenues is profits.

8. It can be shown that a competitive industry, if monopolized, will end up charging a higher price for its product but supplying a lower quantity of it. That is why monopolies are considered "bad" in an economic analysis. The monopolist will restrict production and increase price.

9. If a monopolist can effectively separate demanders into groups according to their demand elasticities, it can become a price-discriminating monopolist. (Resale between groups that were charged different prices must be prevented.) Price discrimination should not be confused with price differentiation, which occurs when differences in price reflect differences in marginal cost.

10. Four conditions are necessary for price discrimination to exist: (1) The firm must face a downward-sloping demand curve, (2) the firm must be able to distinguish markets, (3) buyers in different markets must have different price elasticities of demand, and (4) the firm must be able to prevent resale of the product.

11. Monopoly involves costs to society because the higher price leads to a reduction in output and consumption of the monopolized good.

DISCUSSION OF PREVIEW QUESTIONS

1. **For the monopolist, marginal revenue is less than selling price. Why?**

In the perfectly competitive model, the firm's selling price equals its marginal revenue (MR) because the firm can sell all it wants to sell at the going market price. This is not the case for the monopolist, which, as the sole supplier, faces the (downward-sloping) demand curve for the product. Thus the monopolist can sell more only by lowering price on all units sold per time period, assuming that it can't discriminate on price. Thus the monopolist's marginal revenue will equal price (which it gains from selling one more unit) *minus* the revenue that it loses from selling previously produced units at a lower price.

2. What is the profit-maximizing rate of output for the monopolist?

A monopolist will produce up to the point where marginal cost (MC) equals marginal revenue (MR). For example, if the output rate for the monopolist at which MR = MC is 80,000 units per week and MR is falling while MC is rising, any output beyond 80,000 units will have MC > MR; to produce units beyond 80,000 units will lower total profits. To produce at a rate less than 80,000 units per week would mean that not all the outputs at which MR > MC will be produced; hence total profits would not be maximized. Total profits are maximized at the output rate where MR = MC because all outputs for which MR > MC will be produced.

3. What are some common misconceptions about monopolists?

Many people think that a monopolist charges the highest price possible. This is untrue; the monopolist tries to maximize *total profits,* not price. The monopolist produces where MR = MC and *then* charges the highest price consistent with that output rate. Note that a monopolist can't charge any price *and* sell any amount; it must choose a price and have the amount

that it can sell be determined by the demand curve, or it must choose an output rate (where MR = MC) and have selling price determined by where that quantity intersects the demand curve. Another common misconception is that a monopolist must earn economic profits. This is not the case. To take an extreme example, if the monopolist's average cost curve lies above the demand curve, the monopolist will be suffering economic losses.

4. What is the cost to society of monopoly?

Because barriers to entry exist under monopoly, a monopolist could theoretically earn economic profits in the long run. Because profits are a signal that society wants more resources in that area, a misallocation of resources could exist; not enough resources flow to production of the monopolized commodity. Also, because the monopolist's selling price (P) exceeds its marginal revenue (MR) and the profit-maximizing output rate is where MR = MC (marginal cost), P > MR = MC, or simply P > MC (unlike under the perfectly competitive market structure, where P = MC). The marginal cost of the commodity reflects what society had to give up in order to get the last unit produced, and price is what buyers have to pay in order to get it. Because P > MC under monopoly, buyers must pay *more* to get this commodity than they must give up in order to get it; hence not enough of this commodity is produced. In short, under monopoly, price is higher and output is less than under perfect competition.

PROBLEMS

(Answers to the odd-numbered problems appear at the back of the book.)

24-1. Use the graph to answer the questions.

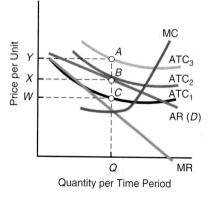
Quantity per Time Period

a. Suppose that a monopolist faces ATC_1. Define the rectangle that shows the monopolist's total costs at output rate Q. Also define the rectangle showing total revenue. Is the monopolist showing an economic loss, break-even (normal profit), or an economic profit? What is the significance of the MC = MR output?

b. Suppose that the monopolist faces ATC_2. Define the rectangle that shows the monopolist's total costs at output rate Q. Also define the rectangle showing total revenue. Is the monopolist showing an economic loss, break-even (normal profit), or an economic profit? What is the significance of the MC = MR output?

c. Suppose that the monopolist faces ATC_3. Define the rectangle that shows the monopolist's total costs at output rate Q. Also define the rectangle showing total revenue. Is the monopolist showing an economic loss, break-even (normal profit), or an economic profit? What is the significance of the MC = MR output?

24-2. Suppose that a monopolist faces the following demand schedule. Compute marginal revenue.

Price	Quantity Demanded	Marginal Revenue
$1,000	1	$_____
920	2	_____
840	3	_____
760	4	_____
680	5	_____
600	6	_____
520	7	_____
440	8	_____
350	9	_____
260	10	_____

24-3. State the necessary conditions for price discrimination. Then discuss how they might apply to the medical services of a physician.

24-4. In the text, we indicated that a monopolist will produce at the rate of output at which MR = MC and will then charge the highest price consistent with that output level. What conditions would exist if the monopolist charged a lower price? A higher price?

24-5. Summarize the relationship between price elasticity of demand and marginal revenue.

24-6. Explain why a monopolist will never set a price (and produce the corresponding output) at which the demand is price-inelastic.

24-7. Examine the revenue and cost figures for a monopoly firm in the table at the bottom of the page.

   a. Fill in the empty columns.
   b. At what rate(s) of output would the firm operate at a loss?
   c. At what rate(s) of output would the firm break even?
   d. At what rate(s) of output would the firm be maximizing its profits, and what would those profits be?

24-8. Answer the questions based on the accompanying graph for a monopolist.

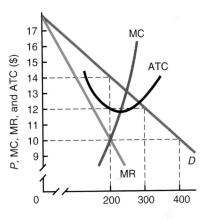

   a. If this firm is a profit maximizer, how much output will it produce?
   b. At what price will the firm sell its output?
   c. How much profit or loss will this firm realize?
   d. ATC is at its minimum at what cost per unit?

Price	Quantity Demanded	Total Revenue	Marginal Revenue	Total Cost	Marginal Cost	Profit or Loss
$20	0	$_____	$_____	$ 4	$_____	$_____
16	1	_____	_____	10	_____	_____
12	2	_____	_____	14	_____	_____
10	3	_____	_____	20	_____	_____
7	4	_____	_____	28	_____	_____
4	5	_____	_____	40	_____	_____
0	6	_____	_____	54	_____	_____

24-9. Examine this information for a monopoly product.

Price	Quantity
$10.00	1,000
8.00	2,000
6.00	3,000
4.00	4,000
2.00	5,000
.50	6,000

    a. Calculate total revenue.
    b. Calculate marginal revenue.

    c. What is the maximum output that the producer of this product would ever produce?
    d. Why would this firm never produce more than the output amount in part (c)?

24-10. Suppose that a single-price monopolist and a comparable perfectly competitive industry experience a cost increase that causes average and marginal cost curves to shift upward by 10 percent. Will the resulting increase in market price be greater or less for the monopolist than for the perfectly competitive industry?

COMPUTER-ASSISTED INSTRUCTION

Monopolists follow the rule of producing at a quantity at which MR = MC, yet the outcome differs somewhat from that under competition. Here we find out why, and we explore the consequences for the monopolist if it deviates from this rule.

Complete problem and answer appear on disk.

INTERACTING WITH THE INTERNET

Find out about the Intel Corporation at

                          www.intel.com

Visit the U.S. Postal Service at

                          www.usps.com

CHAPTER 25

MONOPOLISTIC COMPETITION, OLIGOPOLY, AND STRATEGIC BEHAVIOR

The business world is a terribly competitive place, at least for most firms. Every firm would like to be a monopoly, but few achieve that status. Most firms are in either highly competitive industries or ones that face enough competition at home and abroad to prevent them from earning higher-than-competitive rates of return in the long run. In any event, decisions made by one company may affect many other companies, including suppliers, makers of complementary items, and manufacturers of substitutes. Can business decision making be thought of as a game? Further, in today's changing business world, can cooperation be a substitute for competition? These are questions about strategic behavior, the main focus of this chapter.

PREVIEW QUESTIONS

1. What are the characteristics of the monopolistically competitive market structure?

2. How does the monopolistic competitor determine the equilibrium price-output combination?

3. How does the monopolistically competitive market structure differ from that of perfect competition?

4. What are the characteristics of the oligopolistic market structure?

557

Did You Know That . . . the so-called father of the modern department store, John Wanamaker, once said, "Half the money I spend on advertising is wasted. The trouble is, I don't know which half"? Obviously, American businesses do not know either, for they continue to advertise more each year. Total advertising expenditures amount to billions of dollars every year. The number of ads popping up on the Internet's World Wide Web shows that American businesses will leave no stone unturned in their quest to let people know about their existence, what they have to sell, how they sell it, where it can be bought, and at what price.

Advertising did not show up in our analysis of perfect competition. Nonetheless, it plays a large role in industries that cannot be described as perfectly competitive but cannot be described as pure monopolies either. A combination of consumers' preferences for variety and competition among producers has led to similar but *differentiated* products in the marketplace. This situation has been described as *monopolistic competition,* the subject of the first part of this chapter. In the second part of the chapter, we look at how firms that are neither perfect competitors nor pure monopolists make strategic decisions. Such decisions do not exist for pure monopolists, who do not have to worry about actual competitors. And clearly, perfect competitors cannot make any strategic decisions, for they must take the market price as given. We call firms that have the ability to make strategic decisions *oligopolies,* which we will define more formally later in this chapter.

MONOPOLISTIC COMPETITION

In the 1920s and 1930s, economists became increasingly aware that there were many industries for which both the perfectly competitive model and the pure monopoly model did not apply and did not seem to yield very accurate predictions. Theoretical and empirical research was instituted to develop some sort of middle ground. Two separately developed models of **monopolistic competition** resulted. At Harvard, Edward Chamberlin published *The Theory of Monopolistic Competition* in 1933. The same year, Britain's Joan Robinson published *The Economics of Imperfect Competition.* In this chapter we will outline the theory as presented by Chamberlin.

Chamberlin defined monopolistic competition as a market structure in which there is a relatively large number of producers offering similar but differentiated products. Monopolistic competition therefore has the following features:

1. Significant numbers of sellers in a highly competitive market
2. Differentiated products
3. Sales promotion and advertising
4. Easy entry of new firms in the long run

Even a cursory look at the American economy leads to the conclusion that monopolistic competition is the dominant form of market structure in the United States. Indeed, that is true of all developed economies.

Monopolistic competition
A market situation in which a large number of firms produce similar but not identical products. Entry into the industry is relatively easy.

Number of Firms

In a perfectly competitive situation, there is an extremely large number of firms; in pure monopoly, there is only one. In monopolistic competition, there is a large number of firms, but not as many as in perfect competition. This fact has several important implications for a monopolistically competitive industry.

1. *Small share of market.* With so many firms, each firm has a relatively small share of the total market. Thus it has only a very small amount of control over the market clearing price.
2. *Lack of collusion.* With so many firms, it is very difficult for all of them to get together to collude—to cooperate in setting a pure monopoly price (and output). Price rigging in a monopolistically competitive industry is virtually impossible. Also, barriers to entry are minor, and the flow of new firms into the industry makes collusive agreements less likely. The large number of firms makes the monitoring and detection of cheating very costly and extremely difficult. This difficulty is compounded by differentiated products and high rates of innovation; collusive agreements are easier for a homogeneous product than for heterogeneous ones.
3. *Independence.* Because there are so many firms, each one acts independently of the others. No firm attempts to take into account the reaction of all of its rival firms—that would be impossible with so many rivals. Rivals' reactions to output and price changes are largely ignored.

Product Differentiation

Product differentiation
The distinguishing of products by brand name, color, and other minor attributes. Product differentiation occurs in other than perfectly competitive markets in which products are, in theory, homogeneous, such as wheat or corn.

Perhaps the most important feature of the monopolistically competitive market is **product differentiation.** We can say that each individual manufacturer of a product has an absolute monopoly over its own product, which is slightly differentiated from other similar products. This means that the firm has some control over the price it charges. Unlike the perfectly competitive firm, it faces a downward-sloping demand curve.

Consider the abundance of brand names for toothpaste, soap, gasoline, vitamins, shampoo, and most other consumer goods and a great many services. We are not obliged to buy just one type of television set, just one type of jeans, or just one type of footwear. There are usually a number of similar but differentiated products from which to choose. One reason is that the greater a firm's success at product differentiation, the greater the firm's pricing options.

Each separate differentiated product has numerous similar substitutes. This clearly has an impact on the price elasticity of demand for the individual firm. Recall that one determinant of price elasticity of demand is the availability of substitutes: The greater the number of substitutes available, other things being equal, the greater the price elasticity of demand. If the consumer has a vast array of alternatives that are just about as good as the product under study, a relatively small increase in the price of that product will lead many consumers to switch to one of the many close substitutes. Thus the ability of a firm to raise the price above the price of *close* substitutes is very small. The result of this is that even though the demand curve slopes downward, it does so only slightly. In other words, it is relatively elastic (over that price range) compared to a monopolist's demand curve. In the extreme case, with perfect competition, the substitutes are perfect because we are dealing with only one particular undifferentiated product. In that case, the individual firm has a perfectly elastic demand curve.

Exercise 25.1
Visit www.econtoday.com for more about the candy market.

Ease of Entry

For any current monopolistic competitor, potential competition is always lurking in the background. The easier—that is, the less costly—entry is, the more a current monopolistic competitor must worry about losing business.

A good example of a monopolistically competitive industry is the computer software industry. Many small firms provide different programs for many applications. The fixed capital costs required to enter this industry are small; all you need are skilled programmers. In addition, there are few legal restrictions. The firms in this industry also engage in extensive advertising in over 150 computer publications.

Sales Promotion and Advertising

Monopolistic competition differs from perfect competition in that no individual firm in a perfectly competitive market will advertise. A perfectly competitive firm, by definition, can sell all that it wants to sell at the going market price anyway. Why, then, would it spend even one penny on advertising? Furthermore, by definition, the perfect competitor is selling a product that is identical to the product that all other firms in the industry are selling. Any advertisement that induces consumers to buy more of that product will, in effect, be helping all the competitors, too. A perfect competitor therefore cannot be expected to incur any advertising costs (except for all firms in an industry collectively agreeing to advertise to urge the public to buy more beef or drink more milk).

But because the monopolistic competitor has at least *some* monopoly power, advertising may result in increased profits. Advertising is used to increase demand and to differentiate one's product. How much advertising should be undertaken? It should be carried to the point at which the additional revenue from one more dollar of advertising just equals that one dollar of marginal cost.

Advertising as Signaling Behavior. Recall from Chapter 23 that signals are compact gestures or actions that convey information. For example, high profits in an industry are signals that resources should flow to that industry. Individual companies can explicitly engage in signaling behavior. They do so by establishing brand names or trademarks, and then promoting them heavily. This is a signal to prospective consumers that this is a company that plans to stay in business. Before the modern age of advertising, banks in America faced a problem of signaling their soundness. They chose to make the bank building large, imposing, and constructed out of marble and granite. Stone communicated permanence. The effect was to give the bank's customers confidence that they were not doing business with a fly-by-night operation.

When Dell Computer advertises its brand name heavily, it incurs substantial costs. The only way it can recoup those costs is by selling lots of Dell computers over a long period of time. Thus heavy advertising of its brand name is a signal to personal computer buyers that Dell is interested in each customer's repeat business.

But what about advertising that does not seem to convey any information, not even about price? What good is an advertisement for, say, Wal-Mart that simply states, "We give you value that you can count on"?

EXAMPLE
Can Advertising Lead to Efficiency?

Advertising budgets by major retailers may just seem like an added expense, not a step on the road to economic efficiency. According to research by economists Kyle Bagwell of Northwestern University and Garey Ramey of the University of California at San Diego, just the opposite is true. When retailers advertise heavily, they increase the number of shoppers that come to their store. Such increased traffic allows retailers to offer a wider selection of goods, to invest in cost-reduction technology (such as computerized inventory and satellite communications), and to exploit manufacturers' quantity discounts. Such cost reductions can help explain the success of Wal-Mart, Circuit City, and Home Depot. Consequently, Bagwell and Ramey conclude that advertising can help promote efficiency even if it provides no "hard" information. Advertising signals to consumers where they can find big-company, low-priced, high-variety stores.

FOR CRITICAL ANALYSIS: Which is true, then: "We are bigger because we are better" or "We are better because we are bigger"? ●

CONCEPTS IN BRIEF

- Monopolistic competition is a market structure that lies between pure monopoly and perfect competition.

- A monopolistically competitive market structure has (1) a large number of sellers, (2) differentiated products, (3) advertising, and (4) easy entry of firms in the long run.

- Because of the large number of firms, each has a small share of the market, making collusion difficult; the firms are independent.

PRICE AND OUTPUT FOR THE MONOPOLISTIC COMPETITOR

Now that we are aware of the assumptions underlying the monopolistic competition model, we can analyze the price and output behavior of each firm in a monopolistically competitive industry. We assume in the analysis that follows that the desired product type and quality have been chosen. We further assume that the budget and the type of promotional activity have already been chosen and do not change.

The Individual Firm's Demand and Cost Curves

Because the individual firm is not a perfect competitor, its demand curve slopes downward, as is shown in all three panels of Figure 25-1 on page 562. Hence it faces a marginal revenue curve that is also downward-sloping and below the demand curve. To find the profit-maximizing rate of output and the profit-maximizing price, we go to the output where the marginal cost curve intersects the marginal revenue curve from below. That gives us the profit-maximizing output rate. Then we draw a vertical line up to the demand curve. That gives us the price that can be charged to sell exactly that quantity produced. This is what we have done in Figure 25-1. In each panel, a marginal cost curve intersects the marginal revenue curve at E. The profit-maximizing rate of output is q_e, and the profit-maximizing price is P.

Short-Run Equilibrium

In the short run, it is possible for a monopolistic competitor to make economic profits—profits over and above the normal rate of return or beyond what is necessary to keep that firm in that industry. We show such a situation in panel (a) of Figure 25-1. The average total

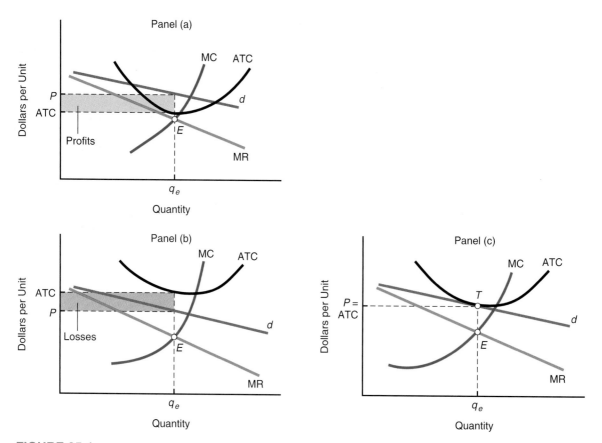

FIGURE 25-1

Short-Run and Long-Run Equilibrium with Monopolistic Competition

In panel (a), the typical monopolistic competitor is shown making economic profits. If that were the situation, there would be entry into the industry, forcing the demand curve for the individual monopolistic competitor leftward. Eventually, firms would find themselves in the situation depicted in panel (c), where zero economic profits are being made. In panel (b), the typical firm is in a monopolistically competitive industry making economic losses. If that were the case, firms would leave the industry. Each remaining firm's demand curve would shift outward to the right. Eventually, the typical firm would find itself in the situation depicted in panel (c).

cost curve is drawn in below the demand curve, *d*, at the profit-maximizing rate of output, q_e. Economic profits are shown by the shaded rectangle in that panel.

Losses in the short run are clearly also possible. They are presented in panel (b) of Figure 25-1. Here the average total cost curve lies everywhere above the individual firm's demand curve, *d*. The losses are marked as the shaded rectangle.

Just as with any market structure or any firm, in the short run it is possible to observe either economic profits or economic losses. (In the long run such is not the case with monopolistic competition, however.) In either case, the price does not equal marginal cost but rather is above it. Therefore, there is some misallocation of resources, a topic that we will discuss later in this chapter.

The Long Run: Zero Economic Profits

The long run is where the similarity between perfect competition and monopolistic competition becomes more obvious. In the long run, because so many firms produce substitutes for the product in question, any economic profits will disappear with competition. They will be reduced to zero either through entry by new firms seeing a chance to make a higher rate of return than elsewhere or by changes in product quality and advertising outlays by existing firms in the industry. (Profitable products will be imitated by other firms.) As for economic losses in the short run, they will disappear in the long run because the firms that suffer them will leave the industry. They will go into another business where the expected rate of return is at least normal. Panels (a) and (b) of Figure 25-1 therefore represent only short-run situations for a monopolistically competitive firm. In the long run, the average total cost curve will just touch the individual firm's demand curve *d* at the particular price that is profit-maximizing for that particular firm. This is shown in panel (c) of Figure 25-1.

A word of warning: This is an idealized, long-run equilibrium situation for each firm in the industry. It does not mean that even in the long run we will observe every single firm in a monopolistically competitive industry making *exactly* zero economic profits or *just* a normal rate of return. We live in a dynamic world. All we are saying is that if this model is correct, the rate of return will *tend toward* normal—economic profits will *tend toward* zero.

COMPARING PERFECT COMPETITION WITH MONOPOLISTIC COMPETITION

If both the monopolistic competitor and the perfect competitor make zero economic profits in the long run, how are they different? The answer lies in the fact that the demand curve for the individual perfect competitor is perfectly elastic. Such is not the case for the individual monopolistic competitor; its demand curve is less than perfectly elastic. This firm has some control over price. Price elasticity of demand is not infinite.

We see the two situations in Figure 25-2 on page 564. Both panels show average total costs just touching the respective demand curves at the particular price at which the firm is selling the product. Notice, however, that the perfect competitor's average total costs are at a minimum. This is not the case with the monopolistic competitor. The equilibrium rate of output is to the left of the minimum point on the average total cost curve where price is greater than marginal cost. The monopolistic competitor cannot expand output to the point of minimum costs without lowering price, and then marginal cost would exceed marginal revenue. A monopolistic competitor at profit maximization charges a price that exceeds marginal cost. In this respect it is similar to the monopolist.

It has consequently been argued that monopolistic competition involves waste because minimum average total costs are not achieved and price exceeds marginal cost. There are too many firms, each with excess capacity, producing too little output. According to critics of monopolistic competition, society's resources are being wasted.

Chamberlin had an answer to this criticism. He contended that the difference between the average cost of production for a monopolistically competitive firm in an open market and the minimum average total cost represented what he called the cost of producing

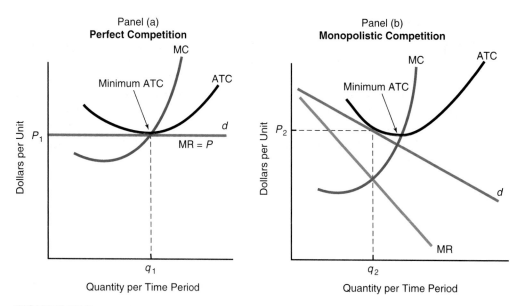

FIGURE 25-2

Comparison of the Perfect Competitor with the Monopolistic Competitor

In panel (a), the perfectly competitive firm has zero economic profits in the long run. The price is set equal to marginal cost, and the price is P_1. The firm's demand curve is just tangent to the minimum point on its average total cost curve, which means that the firm is operating at an optimum rate of production. With the monopolistically competitive firm in panel (b), there are also zero economic profits in the long run. The price is greater than marginal cost; the monopolistically competitive firm does not find itself at the minimum point on its average total cost curve. It is operating at a rate of output to the left of the minimum point on the ATC curve.

"differentness." Chamberlin did not consider this difference in cost between perfect competition and monopolistic competition a waste. In fact, he argued that it is rational for consumers to have a taste for differentiation; consumers willingly accept the resultant increased production costs in return for choice and variety of output.

CONCEPTS IN BRIEF

- In the short run, it is possible for monopolistically competitive firms to make economic profits or economic losses.

- In the long run, monopolistically competitive firms will make zero economic profits—that is, they will make a normal rate of return.

- Because the monopolistic competitor faces a downward-sloping demand curve, it does not produce at the minimum point on its average total cost curve. Hence we say that a monopolistic competitor has higher average total costs per unit than a perfect competitor would have.

- Chamberlin argued that the difference between the average cost of production for a monopolistically competitive firm and the minimum average total cost at which a competitive firm would produce is the cost of producing "differentness."

OLIGOPOLY

Oligopoly
A market situation in which there are very few sellers. Each seller knows that the other sellers will react to its changes in prices and quantities.

There is another market structure that we have yet to discuss, and it is an important one indeed. It involves a situation in which a few large firms dominate an entire industry. They are not competitive in the sense that we have used the term; they are not even monopolistically competitive. And because there are several of them, a pure monopoly does not exist. We call such a situation an **oligopoly,** which consists of a small number of interdependent sellers. Each firm in the industry knows that other firms will react to its changes in prices, quantities, and qualities. An oligopoly market structure can exist for either a homogeneous or a differentiated product.

Characteristics of Oligopoly

Oligopoly is characterized by the small number of interdependent firms that constitute the entire market.

Small Number of Firms. How many is "a small number of firms"? More than two but less than 100? The question is not easy to answer. Basically, though, oligopoly exists when a handful of firms dominate the industry enough to set prices. The top few firms in the industry account for an overwhelming percentage of total industry output.

Oligopolies usually involve three to five big companies dominating the industry. Between World War II and the 1970s, the U.S. automobile industry was dominated by three firms—General Motors, Chrysler, and Ford. Chewing-gum manufacturing and coin-operated amusement games are dominated by four large firms.

Strategic dependence
A situation in which one firm's actions with respect to price, quality, advertising, and related changes may be strategically countered by the reactions of one or more other firms in the industry. Such dependence can exist only when there are a limited number of major firms in an industry.

Interdependence. All markets and all firms are, in a sense, interdependent. But only when a few large firms dominate an industry does the question of **strategic dependence** of one on the others' actions arise. The firms must recognize that they are interdependent. Any action on the part of one firm with respect to output, price, quality, or product differentiation will cause a reaction on the part of other firms. A model of such mutual interdependence is difficult to build, but examples are not hard to find in the real world. Oligopolists in the cigarette industry, for example, are constantly reacting to each other.

Recall that in the model of perfect competition, each firm ignores the reactions of other firms because each firm is able to sell all that it wants at the going market price. At the other extreme, the pure monopolist does not have to worry about the reaction of current rivals because there are none. In an oligopolistic market structure, the managers of firms are like generals in a war: *They must attempt to predict the reaction of rival firms.* It is a strategic game.

Why Oligopoly Occurs

Why are some industries dominated by a few large firms? What causes an industry that might otherwise be competitive to tend toward oligopoly? We can provide some partial answers here.

Economies of Scale. Perhaps the strongest reason that has been offered for the existence of oligopoly is economies of scale. Recall that economies of scale are defined as a situation in which a doubling of output results in less than a doubling of total costs. When economies of scale exist, the firm's average total cost curve will slope downward as the firm produces more and more output. Average total cost can be reduced by continuing to expand the scale of operation. Smaller firms in such a situation will have a tendency to be inefficient. Their average total costs will be greater than those incurred by a large firm. Little by little, they will go out of business or be absorbed into the larger firm.

Barriers to Entry. It is possible that certain barriers to entry have prevented more competition in oligopolistic industries. They include legal barriers, such as patents, and control and ownership over critical supplies. Indeed, we can find periods in the past when firms maintained market power because they were able not only to erect a barrier to entry but also to keep it in place year after year. In principle, the chemical, electronics, and aluminum industries have been at one time or another either monopolistic or oligopolistic because of the ownership of patents and the control of strategic inputs by specific firms.

Oligopoly by Merger. Another reason that oligopolistic market structures may sometimes develop is that firms merge. A merger is the joining of two or more firms under single ownership or control. The merged firm naturally becomes larger, enjoys greater economies of scale as output increases, and may ultimately have a greater ability to control the market price for its product.

There are two types of mergers, horizontal and vertical. A **horizontal merger** involves firms selling a similar product. If two shoe manufacturing firms merge, that is a horizontal merger. If a group of firms, all producing steel, merge into one, that is also a horizontal merger. A **vertical merger** occurs when one firm merges with either a firm from which it purchases an input or a firm to which it sells its output. Vertical mergers occur, for example, when a coal-using electrical utility purchases a coal-mining firm or when a shoe manufacturer purchases retail shoe outlets. (Obviously, vertical mergers cannot create oligopoly as we have defined it.)

We have been talking about oligopoly in a theoretical manner until now. It is time to look at the actual picture of oligopolies in the United States.

Horizontal merger
The joining of firms that are producing or selling a similar product.

Vertical merger
The joining of a firm with another to which it sells an output or from which it buys an input.

Measuring Industry Concentration

As we have stated, oligopoly is a situation in which a few interdependent firms control a large part of total output in an industry. This has been called *industry concentration.* Before we show the concentration statistics in the United States, let's determine how industry concentration can be measured.

Concentration Ratio. The most popular way to compute industry concentration is to determine the percentage of total sales or production accounted for by the top four or top eight firms in an industry. This gives the four- or eight-firm **concentration ratio.** An example of an industry with 25 firms is given in Table 25-1. We can see in that table that the four largest firms account for almost 90 percent of total output in the hypothetical industry. That is an example of an oligopoly.

U.S. Concentration Ratios. Table 25-2 shows the four-firm *domestic* concentration ratios for various industries. Is there any way that we can show or determine which indus-

Concentration ratio
The percentage of all sales contributed by the leading four or leading eight firms in an industry; sometimes called the *industry concentration ratio.*

TABLE 25-1

Computing the Four-Firm Concentration Ratio

Firm	Annual Sales ($ Millions)	
1	150 ⎫	
2	100 ⎪ = 400	Total number of Firms in industry = 25
3	80 ⎪	
4	70 ⎭	
5 through 25	50	
Total	450	

Four-firm concentration ratio $= \dfrac{400}{450} = 88.9\%$

tries to classify as oligopolistic? There is no definite answer. If we arbitrarily picked a four-firm concentration ratio of 75 percent, we could indicate that tobacco products, soft drinks, breakfast cereals, and domestic motor vehicles were oligopolistic. But we would always be dealing with an arbitrary definition.

The concept of an industry is necessarily arbitrary. As a consequence, concentration ratios rise as we narrow the definition of an industry and fall as we broaden it. Thus we must be certain that we are satisfied with the measurement of the industry under study before we jump to conclusions about whether the industry is too concentrated as evidenced by a high measured concentration ratio.

Oligopoly, Efficiency, and Resource Allocation

Although oligopoly is not the dominant form of market structure in the United States, oligopolistic industries do exist. To the extent that oligopolies have market power, they lead to resource misallocations, just as monopolies do. Oligopolies charge prices that exceed marginal cost. But what about oligopolies that occur because of economies of scale? One could argue that consumers end up paying lower prices than if the industry were composed of numerous smaller firms.

TABLE 25-2

Four-Firm Domestic Concentration Ratios for Selected U.S. Industries

Industry	Percentage of Value of Total Domestic Shipments Accounted For by the Top Four Firms
Domestic motor vehicles	90
Breakfast cereals	87
Soft drinks	85
Tobacco products	82
Primary aluminum	74
Transportation equipment	52
Petroleum and coal products	30
Printing and publishing	7

Source: U.S. Bureau of the Census.

All in all, there is no definite evidence of serious resource misallocation in the United States because of oligopolies. In any event, the more U.S. firms face competition from the rest of the world, the less any current oligopoly will be able to exercise market power.

CONCEPTS IN BRIEF

- An oligopoly is a market situation in which there are a small number of interdependent sellers.

- Oligopoly may result from (1) economies of scale, (2) barriers to entry, and (3) mergers.

- Horizontal mergers involve the joining of firms selling a similar product.

- Vertical mergers involve the merging of one firm either with the supplier of an input or the purchaser of its output.

- Industry concentration can be measured by the percentage of total sales accounted for by the top four or top eight firms.

STRATEGIC BEHAVIOR AND GAME THEORY

At this point, we should be able to show oligopoly price and output determination in the way we showed it for perfect competition, pure monopoly, and monopolistic competition, but we cannot. Whenever there are relatively few firms competing in an industry, each can and does react to the price, quantity, quality, and product innovations that the others undertake. In other words, each oligopolist has a **reaction function.** Oligopolistic competitors are interdependent. Consequently, the decision makers in such firms must employ strategies. And we must be able to model their strategic behavior if we wish to predict how prices and outputs are determined in oligopolistic market structures. In general, we can think of reactions of other firms to one firm's actions as part of a *game* that is played by all firms in the industry. Not surprisingly, economists have developed **game theory** models to describe firms' rational interactions. Game theory is the analytical framework in which two or more individuals, companies, or nations compete for certain payoffs that depend on the strategy that the others employ. Poker is such a game situation because it involves a strategy of bluffing.

Some Basic Notions About Game Theory

Games can be either cooperative or noncooperative. If firms get together to collude or form a cartel, that is considered a **cooperative game.** Whenever it is too costly for firms to negotiate such collusive agreements and to enforce them, they are in a **noncooperative game** situation. Most strategic behavior in the marketplace would be described as a noncooperative game.

Games can be classified by whether the payoffs are negative, zero, or positive. A **zero-sum game** is one in which one player's losses are offset by another player's gains; at any time, sum totals are zero. If two retailers have an absolutely fixed total number of customers, the customers that one retailer wins over are exactly equal to the customers that the other retailer loses. A **negative-sum game** is one in which players as a group lose at the end of the game (although one perhaps by more than the other, and it's possible for one or more

Reaction function
The manner in which one oligopolist reacts to a change in price, output, or quality made by another oligopolist in the industry.

Game theory
A way of describing the various possible outcomes in any situation involving two or more interacting individuals when those individuals are aware of the interactive nature of their situation and plan accordingly. The plans made by these individuals are known as *game strategies.*

Cooperative game
A game in which the players explicity collude to make themselves better off. As applied to firms, it involves companies colluding in order to make higher than competitive rates of return.

Noncooperative game
A game in which the players neither negotiate nor collude in any way. As applied to firms in an industry, this is the common situation in which there are relatively few firms and each has some ability to change price.

Zero-sum game
A game in which any gains within the group are exactly offset by equal losses by the end of the game.

Negative-sum game
A game in which players as a group lose at the end of the game.

Positive-sum game
A game in which players as a group are better off at the end of the game.

Strategy
Any rule that is used to make a choice, such as "Always pick heads"; any potential choice that can be made by players in a game.

Dominant strategies
Strategies that always yield the highest benefit. Regardless of what other players do, a dominant strategy will yield the most benefit for the player using it.

Prisoners' dilemma
A famous strategic game in which two prisoners have a choice between confessing and not confessing to a crime. If neither confesses, they serve a minimum sentence. If both confess, they serve a maximum sentence. If one confesses and the other doesn't, the one who confesses goes free. The dominant strategy is always to confess.

Payoff matrix
A matrix of outcomes, or consequences, of the strategies available to the players in a game.

players to win). A **positive-sum game** is one in which players as a group end up better off. Some economists describe all voluntary exchanges as positive-sum games. After an exchange, both the buyer and the seller are better off than they were prior to the exchange.

Strategies in Noncooperative Games. Players, such as decision makers in oligopolistic firms, have to devise a **strategy**, which is defined as a rule used to make a choice. The goal of the decision maker is of course to devise a strategy that is more successful than alternative strategies. Whenever a firm's decision makers can come up with certain strategies that are generally successful no matter what actions competitors take, these are called **dominant strategies.** The dominant strategy always yields the unique best action for the decision maker no matter what action the other "players" undertake. Relatively few business decision makers over a long period of time have successfully devised dominant strategies. We know this by observation: Few firms in oligopolistic industries have maintained relatively high profits consistently over time.

EXAMPLE
The Prisoners' Dilemma

One real-world example of game theory occurs when two people involved in a bank robbery are caught. What should they do when questioned by police? The result has been called the **prisoners' dilemma.** The two suspects, Sam and Carol, are interrogated separately and given various alternatives (they cannot communicate with each other). The interrogator indicates to Sam and Carol the following:

1. If both confess to the bank robbery, they will both go to jail for five years.
2. If neither confesses, they will each be given a sentence of two years on a lesser charge.
3. If one prisoner turns state's evidence and confesses, that prisoner goes free and the other one, who did not confess, will serve 10 years on bank robbery charges.

You can see the prisoners' alternatives in the **payoff matrix** in Figure 25-3. The two possibilities for each prisoner are "confess" and "don't confess." There are four possibilities:

1. Both confess.
2. Neither confesses.
3. Sam confesses (turns state's evidence) but Carol doesn't.
4. Carol confesses (turns state's evidence) but Sam doesn't.

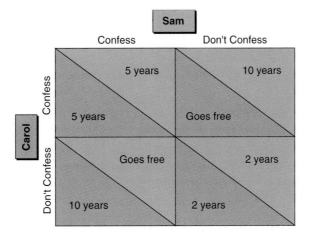

FIGURE 25-3

The Prisoners' Dilemma Payoff Matrix
Regardless of what the other prisoner does, each person is better off if he or she confesses. So confessing is the dominant strategy and each ends up behind bars for five years.

In Figure 25-3, all of Sam's possible outcomes are shown on the upper half of each rectangle, and all of Carol's possible outcomes are shown on the lower half.

By looking at the payoff matrix, you can see that if Carol confesses, Sam's best strategy is to confess also—he'll get only 5 years instead of 10. Conversely, if Sam confesses, Carol's best strategy is also to confess—she'll get 5 years instead of 10. Now let's say that Sam is being interrogated and Carol doesn't confess. Sam's best strategy is still to confess, because then he goes free instead of serving two years. Conversely, if Carol is being interrogated, her best strategy is still to confess even if Sam hasn't. She'll go free instead of serving 10 years. To confess is a dominant strategy for Sam. To confess is also a dominant strategy for Carol. The situation is exactly symmetrical. So this is the prisoners' dilemma. The prisoners know that both prisoners will be better off if neither confesses. Yet it is in each individual prisoner's interest to confess, even though the *collective* outcome of each prisoner's pursuing his or her own interest is inferior for both.

FOR CRITICAL ANALYSIS: Can you apply the prisoners' dilemma to the firms in a two-firm industry that agree to split the market? (Hint: Think about the payoff to cheating on the market-splitting agreement.) ●

Applying Game Theory to Pricing Strategies

We can apply game strategy to two firms—oligopolists—that have to decide on their pricing strategy. Each can choose either a high or a low price. Their payoff matrix is shown in Figure 25-4. If they each choose high prices, they can each make $6 million, but if they each choose low prices, they will only make $4 million each. If one sets a high price and the other a low one, the low-priced firm will make $8 million, but the high-priced firm will only make $2 million. As in the prisoners' dilemma, in the absence of collusion, they will end up choosing low prices.

Opportunistic Behavior

In the prisoners' dilemma, it was clear that cooperative behavior—both parties standing firm without admitting to anything—leads to the best outcome for both players. But each prisoner (player) stands to gain by cheating. Such action is called **opportunistic behavior.** Our daily economic activities involve the equivalent of the prisoners' dilemma all the time. We

Opportunistic behavior
Actions that ignore the possible long-run benefits of cooperation and focus solely on short-run gains.

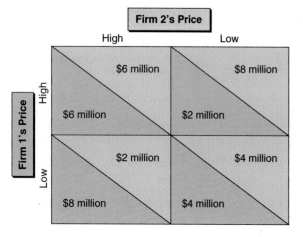

Firm 2's Price

FIGURE 25-4

Game Theory and Pricing Strategies

This payoff matrix shows that if both oligopolists choose a high price, each makes $6 million. If they both choose a low price, each makes $4 million. If one chooses a low price and the other doesn't, the low-priced firm will make $8 million. Unless they collude, however, they will end up at the low-priced solution.

could engage in opportunistic behavior. You could write a check for a purchase knowing that it is going to bounce because you have just closed that bank account. When you agree to perform a specific task for pay, you could perform your work in a substandard way. When you go to buy an item, the seller might be able to cheat you by selling you a defective item.

In short, if all of us—sellers and buyers—engaged in opportunistic behavior all of the time, we would always end up in the bottom right-hand box of the prisoners' dilemma payoff matrix in Figure 25-3. We would constantly be acting in a world of noncooperative behavior. That is not the world in which most of us live, however. Why not? Because most of us engage in *repeat transactions.* Manufacturers would like us to keep purchasing their products. Sellers would like us to keep coming back to their stores. As a seller of labor services, each of us would like to keep our jobs, get promotions, or be hired away by another firm at a higher wage rate. We engage in a **tit-for-tat strategic behavior.** In tit-for-tat strategy, manufacturers and sellers continue to guarantee their merchandise, in spite of cheating by a small percentage of consumers.

Tit-for-tat strategic behavior
In game theory, cooperation that continues so long as the other players continue to cooperate.

 INTERNATIONAL EXAMPLE
Russia's Opportunistic Behavior

Companies are not the only entities that can engage in opportunistic behavior. Nations can do so, too, particularly regarding how they act toward international agencies. A good example concerns Russia and the International Monetary Fund (IMF). The IMF routinely offers loans to developing countries. (More recently, it has offered large loans to countries that have suffered foreign exchange crises.) After Russia became an independent country at the beginning of the 1990s, it sought massive loans from the West. The West responded through the IMF, among other agencies. Typically, though, the IMF imposes a new economic "discipline" on the recipient nations. It might require, as a condition for the loan, that the recipient government reduce its rate of inflation, reduce its deficit, reduce government spending, improve its legal system, and so on. That is the tack the IMF took when it loaned Russia $10 billion. Russian officials signed the agreement promising a range of free-market reforms as well as curbs on the rate of inflation and government spending. When Russia's president, Boris Yeltsin, was up for reelection, the government flouted the agreement, but the IMF did not stop sending the money. Why? Because Western nations were desperate to have Yeltsin reelected. He and his fellow government officials acted opportunistically toward the IMF because they knew they could get away with it.

FOR CRITICAL ANALYSIS: Why might a foreign government engage in more opportunistic behavior with the IMF than it would with private lending institutions? ●

PRICE RIGIDITY AND THE KINKED DEMAND CURVE

Let's hypothesize that the decision makers in an oligopolistic firm assume that rivals will react in the following way: They will match all price decreases (in order not to be undersold) but not price increases (because they want to capture more business). There is no collusion. The implications of this reaction function are rigid prices and a kinked demand curve.

Nature of the Kinked Demand Curve

In Figure 25-5, we draw a kinked demand curve, which is implicit in the assumption that oligopolists match price decreases but not price increases. We start off at a given price of

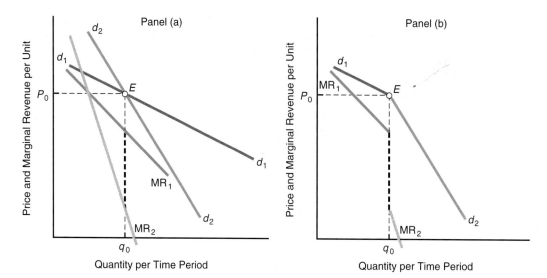

FIGURE 25-5

The Kinked Demand Curve

If the oligopolist firm assumes that rivals will not match price changes, it faces demand curve d_1d_1 and marginal revenue curve MR_1. If it assumes that rivals will match price changes, it faces demand curve d_2d_2 and marginal revenue curve MR_2. If the oligopolist believes that rivals will not react to price increases but will react to price decreases, at prices above P_0 it faces demand curve d_1d_1 and at prices below P_0 it faces the other demand curve, d_2d_2. The overall demand curve will therefore have a kink, as is seen in panel (b) at price P_0. The marginal revenue curve will have a vertical break, as shown by the dashed line in panel (b).

P_0 and assume that the quantity demanded at the price for this individual oligopolist is q_0. The starting price of P_0 is usually the stable market price. If the oligopolist assumes that rivals will not react, it faces demand curve d_1d_1 with marginal revenue curve MR_1. Conversely, if it assumes that rivals will react, it faces demand curve d_2d_2 with marginal revenue curve MR_2. More than likely, the oligopoly firm will assume that if it lowers price, rivals will react by matching that reduction to avoid losing their respective shares of the market. The oligopolist that initially lowers its price will not greatly increase its quantity demanded. So when it lowers its price, it believes that it will face demand curve d_2d_2. But if it increases price above P_0, rivals will probably not follow suit. Thus a higher price than P_0 will cause quantity demanded to decrease rapidly. The demand schedule to the left of and above point E will be relatively elastic, as represented by d_1d_1. At prices above P_0, the relevant demand curve is d_1d_1, whereas below price P_0, the relevant demand curve will be d_2d_2. Consequently, at point E there will be a *kink* in the resulting demand curve. This is shown in panel (b) of Figure 25-5, where the demand curve is labeled d_1d_2. The resulting marginal revenue curve is labeled MR_1MR_2. It has a discontinuous portion, or gap, represented by the boldfaced dashed vertical lines in both panels.

Price Rigidity

The kinked demand curve analysis may help explain why price changes might be infrequent in an oligopolistic industry without collusion. Each oligopolist can see only harm in a price change: If price is increased, the oligopolist will lose many of its customers to rivals who do not raise their prices. That is to say, the oligopolist moves up from point E along demand curve d_1 in panel (b) of Figure 25-5. However, if an oligopolist lowers its price, given that rivals will lower their prices too, its sales will not increase very much. Moving down from point E in panel (b) of Figure 25-5, we see that the demand curve is relatively inelastic. If the elasticity is less than 1, total revenues will fall rather than rise with the lowering of price. Given that the production of a larger output will increase total costs, the oligopolist's profits will fall. The lowering of price by the oligopolist might start a *price war* in which its rival firms will charge an even lower price.

The theoretical reason for price inflexibility under the kinked demand curve model has to do with the discontinuous portion of the marginal revenue curve shown in panel (b) of Figure 25-5, which we reproduce in Figure 25-6. Assume that marginal cost is represented by MC. The profit-maximizing rate of output is q_0, which can be sold at a price of P_0. Now assume that the marginal cost curve rises to MC'. What will happen to the profit-maximizing rate of output? Nothing. Both quantity and price will remain the same for this oligopolist.

Remember that the profit-maximizing rate of output is where marginal revenue equals marginal cost. The shift in the marginal cost curve to MC' does not change the profit-maximizing rate of output in Figure 25-6 because MC' still cuts the marginal revenue curve in the latter's discontinuous portion. Thus the equality between marginal revenue and marginal cost still holds at output rate q_0 even when the marginal cost curve shifts upward. What will happen when marginal costs fall to MC"? Nothing. This oligopolist will continue to produce at a rate of output q_0 and charge a price of P_0. Whenever the marginal cost curve cuts the discontinuous portion of the marginal revenue curve, fluctuations (within limits) in marginal cost will not affect output or price because the profit-maximizing condition MR = MC will hold. The result is that even when firms in an oligopolistic industry such as this experience increases or decreases in costs, their prices do not change as long as MC cuts MR in the discontinuous portion. Hence prices are seen to be rigid in oligopolistic industries if oligopolists react the way we assume they do in this model.

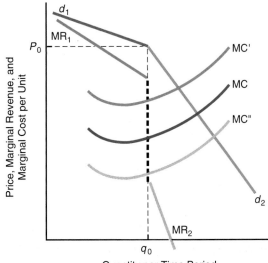

FIGURE 25-6

Changes in Cost May Not Alter the Profit-Maximizing Price and Output

As long as the marginal cost curve intersects the marginal revenue curve in the latter's discontinuous portion, the profit-maximizing price P_0 (and output q_0) will remain unchanged even with changes in MC. (However, the firm's rate of profit will change.)

Criticisms of the Kinked Demand Curve

One of the criticisms directed against the kinked demand curve is that we have no idea how the existing price, P_0, came to be. If every oligopolistic firm faced a kinked demand curve, it would not pay for it to change prices. The problem is that the kinked demand curve does not show us how demand and supply originally determine the going price of an oligopolist's product.

As far as the evidence goes, it is not encouraging. Oligopoly prices do not appear to be as rigid, particularly in the upward direction, as the kinked demand curve theory implies. During the 1970s and early 1980s, when prices in the economy were rising overall, oligopolistic producers increased their prices frequently. Evidence of price changes during the Great Depression showed that oligopolies changed prices much more frequently than monopolies.

EXAMPLE
Do Pet Products Have Nine Lives?

H. J. Heinz's Pet Products Company knows all about the kinked demand curve. It makes 9-Lives cat food. To meet increased competition (at lower prices) from Nestlé, Quaker, Grand Metropolitan, and Mars, Heinz dropped prices by over 22 percent on the wholesale price of a case of 9-Lives. Finally, it had "had enough." It decided to buck the trend by *raising* prices. The result? A disaster, because none of Heinz's four major competitors increased their prices. Heinz's market share dropped from 23 percent to 15 percent almost overnight.

FOR CRITICAL ANALYSIS: What does Heinz's experience with 9-Lives perhaps suggest about the price elasticity of demand for its product? ●

CONCEPTS IN BRIEF

- Each oligopolist has a reaction function because oligopolistic competitors are interdependent. They must therefore engage in strategic behavior. One way to model this behavior is to use game theory.

- Games can be either cooperative or noncooperative. A cartel is cooperative. When a cartel breaks down and its members start cheating, the industry becomes a noncooperative game. In a zero-sum game, one player's losses are exactly offset by another player's gains. In a negative-sum game, all players collectively lose, perhaps one more than the others. In a positive-sum game, the players as a group end up better off.

- Decision makers in oligopolistic firms must devise a strategy. A dominant strategy is one that is generally successful no matter what actions competitors take.

- The kinked demand curve oligopoly model predicts that major shifts in marginal cost will cause any change in industry price.

STRATEGIC BEHAVIOR WITH IMPLICIT COLLUSION: A MODEL OF PRICE LEADERSHIP

Price leadership
A practice in many oligopolistic industries in which the largest firm publishes its price list ahead of its competitors, who then match those announced prices. Also called *parallel pricing*.

What if oligopolists do not actually collude to raise prices and share markets but do so implicitly? There are no formal cartel arrangements and no formal meetings. Nonetheless, there is *tacit collusion*. One example of this is the model of **price leadership.**

In this model, the basic assumption is that the dominant firm, usually the biggest, sets the price and allows other firms to sell all they can at that price. The dominant firm then sells the rest. The dominant firm always makes the first move in a price leadership model. By definition, price leadership requires that one firm be the leader. Because of laws against collusion, firms in an industry cannot communicate this directly. That is why it is often natural for the largest firm to become the price leader. In the automobile industry during the period of General Motors' dominance (until the 1980s), that company was traditionally the price leader. At various times in the breakfast food industry, Kellogg was the price leader. Some observers have argued that Harvard University was the price leader among Ivy League schools. In the banking industry, various dominant banks have been price leaders in announcing changes in the prime rate, the interest rate charged on loans offered to the best credit risks. One day a large New York–based bank, such as Chase Manhattan, would announce an increase or decrease in its prime rate. Five or six hours later, all other banks would announce the same change in their prime rate.

Price Wars

Price war
A pricing campaign designed to drive competing firms out of a market by repeatedly cutting prices.

Price leadership may not always work. If the price leader ends up much better off than the firms that follow, the followers may in fact not set prices according to those set by the dominant firm. The result may be a **price war.** The dominant firm lowers its prices a little bit, but the other firms lower theirs even more. Price wars have occurred in many industries. Supermarkets within a given locale often engage in price wars, especially during holiday periods. One may offer turkeys at so much per pound on Wednesday; competing stores cut their price on turkeys on Thursday, so the first store cuts its price even more on Friday. We see price wars virtually every year in the airline industry.

EXAMPLE
Cigarette Price Wars

Price wars occur commonly between long-distance telephone companies, between airlines, and between the makers of cigarettes, soft drinks, computer disc drives, diapers, frozen dinners, and personal computer hardware and software. They do not always lead to the desired result for the company that started the price war. Consider the case of Philip Morris, which cut the price of Marlboro cigarettes by 40 cents a pack to about $1.80. Its main competitor, RJR Nabisco, matched the price cut for Camels. Philip Morris claimed victory because Marlboro's market share increased from 22.1 percent to 27.3 percent. But the domestic operating profits for both companies plummeted in the process; so, too, did the trading value of their stocks. According to business consultants Mike Marn and Robert Garda of the McKinsey Company, the reason is that most companies are unable to offset lower prices with higher volume because variable costs do not start falling until sales increase by about 20 percent. When Philip Morris cut its prices by 18 percent, unit sales increased by only 12.5 percent and profits fell by 25 percent.

FOR CRITICAL ANALYSIS: How do price wars fit into the tit-for-tat strategic behavior of game theory? ●

DETERRING ENTRY INTO AN INDUSTRY

Some economists believe that all decision making by existing firms in a stable industry involves some type of game playing. An important part of game playing does not have to do with how existing competitors might react to a decision by others. Rather, it has to do with how *potential* competitors might react. Strategic decision making requires that existing firms in an industry come up with strategies to deter entrance into that industry. One important way is, of course, to get a local, state, or federal government to restrict entry. Another way is to adopt certain pricing and investment strategies that may deter entry.

Increasing Entry Costs

One **entry deterrence strategy** is to raise the cost of entry by a new firm. The threat of a price war is one technique. To sustain a long price war, existing firms might invest in excess capacity so that they can expand output if necessary. When existing firms invest in excess capacity, they are signaling potential competitors that they will engage in a price war.

Another way that existing domestic firms can raise the entry cost of foreign firms is by getting the U.S. government to pass stringent environmental or health and safety standards. These typically raise costs more for foreign producers, often in developing countries, than for domestic producers.

> **Entry deterrence strategy**
> Any strategy undertaken by firms in an industry, either individually or together, with the intent or effect of raising the cost of entry into the industry by a new firm.

EXAMPLE
Should Hair Braiders Be Licensed?

Many service industries have raised entry costs by getting legislation passed that requires extensive training and licensing before someone can enter the industry. Physicians and lawyers are good examples. Less well known are the high entry costs imposed on individuals who wish to give therapeutic massages or trim and style hair. For example, in California, a license to style hair requires the expenditure of about $6,000 for 1,600 hours of cosmetology classes. Hairstylists in California spend about $600 million a year on classes and test administration fees.

Enter hair braiders, who are hairstylists for the African-American community. Individuals entering this business long assumed that because they use no chemicals, they would not be required to take extensive classes in the use of chemicals. But the California Barbering and Cosmetology Board has recently ruled otherwise. Given that there are about 10,000 hair braiders in America, this issue affects more than California. Currently, there are several lawsuits challenging the licensing requirement for hair braiders. Hair braiders offer a lower-cost alternative to regular beauty salons, and the latter are fighting to prevent this new competition.

FOR CRITICAL ANALYSIS: Besides currently licensed hairstylists, who else might favor required cosmetology licensing for hair braiders? ●

Limit-Pricing Strategies

If existing firms make it clear to potential competitors that the existing firms will not change their output rate after entry, this is a signal. It tells potential firms that the existing firm will simply lower its market price (moving down the firm demand curve) until it sells the same quantity as before the new entry came into the industry. The existing firms limit their price to be above competitive prices, but if there is a new entrant, the new limit price will be below the one at which the new firm can make a profit. This is called the **limit-pricing model.**

> **Limit-pricing model**
> A model that hypothesizes that a group of colluding sellers will set the highest common price that they believe they can charge without new firms seeking to enter that industry in search of relatively high profits.

Raising Customers' Switching Costs

If an existing firm can make it more costly for customers to switch from its product or service to a competitor's, the existing firm can deter entry. There are a host of ways in which existing firms can raise customers' switching costs. Makers of computer equipment have in the past produced operating systems and software that would not run on competitors' computers. Any customer wanting to change from one computer system to another faced a high switching cost.

CONCEPTS IN BRIEF

- One type of strategic behavior involving implicit collusion is price leadership. The dominant firm is assumed to set the price and then allows other firms to sell all that they want to sell at that price. Whatever is left over is sold by the dominant firm. The dominant firm always makes the first move in a price leadership model. If the nondominant firms decide to compete, they may start a price war.

- One strategic decision may be to attempt to raise the cost of entry of new firms into an industry. The threat of a price war is one technique. Another is to lobby the federal government to pass stringent environmental or health and safety standards in an attempt to keep out foreign competition.

- If existing firms limit prices to a level above competitive prices before entry but are willing to reduce it, this is called a limit-pricing model.

- Another way to raise the cost to new firms is to make it more costly for customers to switch from one product or service to a competitor's.

COMPARING MARKET STRUCTURES

Now that we have looked at perfect competition, pure monopoly, monopolistic competition, and oligopoly, we are in a position to compare the attributes of these four different market structures. We do this in summary form in Table 25-3, in which we compare the number of sellers, their ability to set price, and whether product differentiation exists, and we give some examples of each of the four market structures.

TABLE 25-3
Comparing Market Structures

Market Structure	Number of Sellers	Unrestricted Entry and Exit	Ability to Set Price	Long-Run Economic Profits Possible	Product Differentiation	Nonprice Competition	Examples
Perfect competition	Numerous	Yes	None	No	None	None	Agriculture, coal
Monopolistic competition	Many	Yes	Some	No	Considerable	Yes	Toothpaste, toilet paper, soap, retail trade
Oligopoly	Few	Partial	Some	Yes	Frequent	Yes	Cigarettes, steel
Pure monopoly	One	No (for entry)	Considerable	Yes	None (product is unique)	Yes	Electric company, local telephone company

The makers of Nintendo tried to make themselves indispensable by restricting software developers to only five games. How much bargaining power did developers have?

In the Game of Business, Does Cooperation Make Sense?

CONCEPTS APPLIED:
COMPETITION, STRATEGIC BEHAVIOR, OPPORTUNISTIC BEHAVIOR, COMPLEMENTS, GAME THEORY

Visit www.econtoday.com for an Internet Activity that expands your understanding of these concepts.

"It's a dog-eat-dog world." "If you can't take the heat, don't get close to the fire." The clichés that relate to the business world are myriad. Most of them are based on the need to compete fiercely, albeit ethically and legally, to get ahead or at least to avoid bankruptcy. To many of today's students of business administration and management, such language seems out of place, anachronistic. The budding manager of today learns about teamwork, strategic alliances, working in tandem with suppliers, and building trust and loyalty. An increasingly common approach in the business world today is the desire to create a "win-win" situation. In such a world, business feuds are considered detrimental for everyone.

Game Theory's Brainchild

Until game theory came along, most economists and business management theorists assumed that firms could behave as they wished without taking the actions of their rivals into account. This is probably still true for the perfect competitor and the pure monopolist. (Although even a pure monopolist has to worry about *potential* competition if it earns very high monopoly profits that are obvious to outsiders.)

As you learned in this chapter, game theory requires the players to consider a strategy based on what they think other players are planning to do. So the game theory view of management is that decision makers must always make predictions about rivals' reactive behavior.

Number of Players Affects Outcomes

In any type of strategic competition, the number of players can affect the outcome. Competition against only one other company is not the same as competition against 15 other companies. For example, when Holland Sweetener Company tried to break NutraSweet's monopoly in the American artificial sweetener market, this competitive foray ended up benefiting Coca-Cola and Pepsi. Holland did not get those two companies' contracts for sweetener. Instead, Coca-Cola and Pepsi used the threat of competition from Holland Sweetener to force NutraSweet to lower its prices—and then they stayed with NutraSweet.

The reverse of this situation occurred a few years ago when American Express wanted to purchase health care coverage for its workers. It organized a group of large companies, which also wanted lower-cost health care for their workforces, to ask jointly for bids from various health care providers. Looking at all the participating companies together, the contract was so huge that the competing health care providers got into a bidding war and ended up offering health care at a very low price.

Toward an Alternative Theory: "Coopetition"

According to Professors Adam Brandenburger of Harvard Business School and Barry Nalebuff of Yale School of Management, the blending of cooperation and competition—"coopetition"—is the best way for a firm's decision makers to maximize profits. These theorists argue that the time to cooperate is when the market is growing. Further, they say that in any market, it is important to cooperate with firms that produce products that are complementary to your own. Microsoft—a software producer—and Intel—a chip producer—have learned the benefit of cooperation.

Playing Hardball Works, Too

Sometimes, not allowing cooperation at all may be the best course of action for a company. When Nintendo was expanding in the video game business, it focused on one particular strategically competitive tactic. It restricted software developers to making only five games each. It then shipped fewer games to its retailers than they asked for. Finally, it did much of its development in-house. Under those circumstances, its suppliers and its retailers had little bargaining power. Not many companies find themselves in a position to pursue this strategy, though.

But Playing Hardball Can Also Backfire

Staying tough doesn't always work. Just ask the shareholders of Apple Computer, Inc. Apple developed an intuitive, user-friendly operating system many years ago. Its main competitor was Microsoft's MS-DOS system, which most novices could not use easily. Apple and Microsoft chose two separate strategies, and the results were quite different.

Apple did not open up its operating system's architecture so that clones could be made. Thus anyone who wanted the easier-to-use Macintosh computer with its simple operating system had to buy a computer manufactured by Apple. Apple's profit margins were relatively high, so initially it made lots of money.

Microsoft opened up its MS-DOS architecture to everyone to use. Clones of the industry-standard IBM PC were developed and eventually became much cheaper than Apple's Macintosh computers. As a result, little by little, Apple lost market share. The world is now dominated by the Microsoft operating system, whereas the easier-to-use Mac operating system is dying out in the marketplace.

FOR CRITICAL ANALYSIS

1. The McKenzie consulting firm is offering practice sessions in game theory to the decision makers from large corporations. Which firms are more likely to send their executives to such practice sessions?
2. Today Apple's computers are competitively priced with all others. Why may it be too late anyway?

CHAPTER SUMMARY

1. Numerous market situations lie between the extremes of pure competition and pure monopoly. Monopolistic competition and oligopoly are two of these situations.

2. Monopolistic competition is a theory developed by Edward Chamberlin of Harvard University in 1933. It refers to a market composed of specific product groups in which the different companies involved have slight monopoly powers because each has a product slightly different from the others. Examples of product groups might include the toothpaste and soap industries. The monopolistic competitor ends up with zero economic profits because there is free entry into the industry. However, according to Chamberlin, the monopolistic competitor does not produce where

price equals marginal costs and therefore does not produce at the minimum point on the average total cost curve.

3. Advertising occurs in industries in which the firms are not pure price takers. The basic goal of advertisers is to increase demand for their product.

4. In the short run, it is possible for a monopolistic competitor to make economic profits or economic losses. In the long run, monopolistic competitors make zero economic profits (that is, they make just the normal rate of return).

5. When we compare monopolistic competition with perfect competition, we find that the monopolistic competitor does not produce where average total costs are at a minimum, whereas the perfect competitor does.

6. Oligopoly is a market situation in which there are just a few firms. Each firm knows that its rivals will react to a change in price. Oligopolies are usually defined as industries in which the four-firm concentration ratio is relatively high.

7. Oligopolies are characterized by relatively high barriers to entry, interdependence, product differentiation, and growth through merger.

8. Each oligopolist has a reaction function because oligopolistic competitors are interdependent and must therefore engage in strategic behavior. One way to model this behavior is to use game theory.

9. Games can be either cooperative or noncooperative. A cartel is cooperative. When a cartel breaks down and its members start cheating, the industry becomes a noncooperative game. In a zero-sum game, one player's losses are exactly offset by another player's gains. In a negative-sum game, players as a group lose, perhaps one more than the others. In a positive-sum game, players as a group end up better off.

10. The kinked demand curve oligopoly model indicates that prices will be relatively rigid unless demand or cost conditions change substantially.

11. Price leadership is strategic behavior that involves implicit collusion. The dominant firm is assumed to set the price and then allows other firms to sell all that they want to sell at that price. Whatever is left over is sold by the dominant firm. The dominant firm always makes the first move. If the nondominant firms decide to compete, they may start a price war.

12. One strategic decision may be to attempt to raise the cost of entry of new firms into an industry. The threat of a price war is one technique. Another is to lobby the federal government to pass stringent environmental or health and safety standards in an attempt to keep out foreign competition. A third is to make it more costly for customers to switch from one product or service to a competitor's.

DISCUSSION OF PREVIEW QUESTIONS

1. What are the characteristics of the monopolistically competitive market structure?

The monopolistically competitive market structure lies between the extremes of monopoly and perfect competition, but closer to the latter. Under monopolistic competition, there are a large number of sellers, each with a small market share, acting independently of one another, producing a differentiated product. This product differentiation is advertised; advertising emphasizes product differences or, on occasion, "creates" differences.

2. How does the monopolistic competitor determine the equilibrium price-output combination?

The monopolistic competitor has some control over price; it faces a downward-sloping demand curve. The monopolistic competitor must lower price in order to increase sales; the marginal revenue curve for the monopolistic competitor is therefore downward-sloping. In equilibrium, the profit-maximizing rate of output will therefore be where the upward-sloping (increasing) marginal cost curve intersects the downward-sloping (decreasing) marginal revenue curve. The output rate being thus established, price is set at the corresponding market clearing level. Any other output rate would lead to a reduction in total profits.

3. How does the monopolistically competitive market structure differ from that of perfect competition?

Like the perfect competitor, the monopolistic competitor acts independently of its competitors and is able to earn economic profits only in the short run; competition from entrants eliminates long-run economic profits under both market structures. Yet an important difference exists in the two models: The perfect competitor faces a perfectly elastic demand curve, whereas the monopolistic competitor faces a downward-sloping demand curve. Because economic profits must equal zero in the long run, the demand (average revenue) curve must be tangent to the average total cost (ATC) curve in both models. Under perfect competition, a perfectly elastic demand curve can only be tangent to a U-shaped ATC curve at the latter's minimum point (where its slope is zero). Under monopolistic competition, the demand curve must be tangent to the firm's ATC somewhere to the *left* of the ATC's minimum point. Thus under perfect competition, long-run equilibrium will be at minimum ATC, whereas under monopolistic competition, long-run equilibrium will be at a higher ATC—and at a lower output rate.

4. What are the characteristics of the oligopolistic market structure?

Like the monopolistically competitive market structure, oligopoly lies between the extremes of perfect competition and monopoly. However, oligopoly is closer to being unique; under oligopoly, a small number of firms dominate the market, and the firms cannot act independently. An oligopolist must take into account the reactions of its rivals when it sets policy; this interdependence makes the oligopoly model unique. It also makes the price-output decision a complex one for the oligopolists—and hence for economists who analyze this market structure. It is believed that oligopolies emerge because great economies of scale, in conjunction with a limited market demand, allow the few largest to drive out competitors. Also, oligopolies may arise because of barriers to entry and mergers.

PROBLEMS

(Answers to the odd-numbered problems appear at the back of the book.)

25-1. Suppose that you own a monopolistically competitive firm that sells automobile tune-ups at a price of $25 each. You are currently selling 100 per week. As the owner-operator, you initiate an ad campaign on a local AM radio station. You promise to smooth out any ill-running car at a price of $25. The result is that you end up tuning 140 cars per week. What is the "marginal revenue" of this ad campaign? What additional information do you need to determine whether your profits have risen?

25-2. The graph depicts long-run equilibrium for a monopolistic competitor.

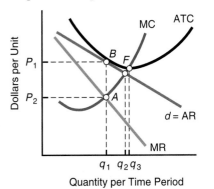

Quantity per Time Period

a. Which output rate represents equilibrium?
b. Which price represents equilibrium?
c. Which labeled point indicates that economic profits are zero?
d. Which labeled point indicates minimum ATC?
e. Is ATC at the equilibrium output rate above or at minimum ATC?
f. Is the equilibrium price greater than, less than, or equal to the marginal cost of producing at the equilibrium output rate?

25-3. The table indicates some information for industry A.

Firm	Annual Sales ($ millions)
1	200
2	150
3	100
4	75
5 through 30	300

a. What is the four-firm concentration ratio for this industry (with just 30 firms)?
b. Assume that industry A is the steel industry. What would happen to the concentration index if we redefined industry A as the cold rolled-steel industry? As the metals industry?

25-4. Explain how, in the long run, any economic profits will be eliminated in a monopolistically competitive industry.

25-5. Explain why an oligopolist's demand curve might be kinked.

25-6. The table on the following page gives some cost and demand data for an oligopolistic industry. There are five firms. Assume that each one faces the same long-run total cost curve and that each firm knows that any change in price will be matched by all other firms in the industry.

a. Fill in the blanks.
b. What will the profit-maximizing rate of output be for each firm?
c. What price will be charged for this output?
d. What will the profits be for each of the five firms?

Price	Quantity Demanded	Total Revenue	Marginal Revenue	Quantity Demanded ÷ Number of Firms	Total Revenue ÷ Number of Firms	Marginal Revenue ÷ Number of Firms	Individual Firm Quantity Supplied	Long-Run Total Costs	Long-Run Marginal Costs
$20	5	$_____	$_____	_____	_____	_____	1	$20	$_____
18	10	_____	_____	_____	_____	_____	2	30	_____
16	15	_____	_____	_____	_____	_____	3	36	_____
14	20	_____	_____	_____	_____	_____	4	44	_____
12	25	_____	_____	_____	_____	_____	5	60	_____

25-7. Suppose that you run a movie theater. At your price of $5 per person, you sell 5,000 tickets per week. Without changing your price, you initiate a $1,000-per-week advertising campaign. Assuming that all your nonadvertising costs are totally unrelated to the number of weekly viewers you have, how much additional revenue must you generate to justify continuation of the ad campaign? How many more customers would this require?

25-8. Study the accompanying graph for a firm in an oligopolistic industry.

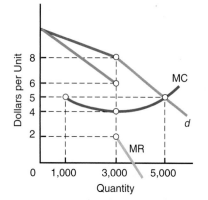

a. How much will this oligopolistic firm produce?
b. At what price will the firm sell this output?
c. How much can marginal cost vary without causing a change in price?

25-9. There are only two firms in an industry. They collude to share the market equally. They jointly set a monopoly price and split the quantity demanded at that price. Here are their options.

a. They continue to collude (no cheating) and make $10 million each in profits.
b. One firm cheats on the agreement, but the other firm doesn't. The firm that cheats makes $12 million a year in profit, whereas the firm that doesn't cheat makes $7 million in profit.
c. They both cheat and each one makes $6 million a year in profit.

Construct a payoff matrix for these two firms. How does this situation relate to the prisoners' dilemma?

COMPUTER-ASSISTED INSTRUCTION

Given a table with relevant information, can you determine an industry's four-firm concentration ratio? Does this ratio overstate or understate the true concentration of that industry? Specific calculations reveal some interesting answers about the usefulness of concentration ratios.

Complete problem and answer appear on disk.

CHAPTER 26

REGULATION AND ANTITRUST POLICY

By now, most of you reading this text will have used a Web browser on the Internet. There are basically two competing Web browsers today: one developed by Netscape Communications Corporation, called Navigator, and the other developed by Microsoft Corporation, called Internet Explorer. A few years ago, when Netscape practically "owned" the Internet browser market, Microsoft decided to compete. The initial versions of Internet Explorer were not so good as Navigator. Little by little, though, Microsoft began to catch up, resulting in two browsers that are more or less equally easy to use and have similar features. Most of the world's computers use the Microsoft-owned Windows operating system. If Microsoft decided to "bundle" a new version of its Internet Explorer with its Windows operating system, could that destroy competition in the browser market? Before you answer this question, you need to know about regulation and antitrust policy.

PREVIEW QUESTIONS

1. What is a natural monopoly, and how does one arise?

2. If natural monopolies are required to price at marginal cost, what problem emerges?

3. What are some means of regulating a natural monopoly?

4. Why have economists been reevaluating the government's role as an economic regulator?

Did You Know That . . . each year about 70,000 pages of new or modified federal regulations are published? These regulations, found in the *Federal Register,* cover virtually every aspect of the way business can be conducted, products can be built, and services can be offered. In addition, every state and municipality publishes regulations relating to worker safety, restaurant cleanliness, and the number of lights needed in each room in a daycare center. There is no question about it, American business activities are highly regulated. Consequently, how regulators should act to increase economic efficiency and how they actually act are important topics for understanding our economy today. In addition to regulation, the government has one additional weapon to use in its attempts to prevent restraints of trade. It is called antitrust law, and it is the subject of the later part of this chapter.

Let's look first at how government might best regulate a single firm that has obtained a monopoly because of constantly falling long-run average costs, a situation known as a natural monopoly.

NATURAL MONOPOLIES REVISITED

You will recall from our discussion of natural monopolies in Chapter 24 that whenever a single firm has the ability to produce all of the industry's output at a lower per-unit cost than other firms attempting to produce less than total industry output, a natural monopoly arises. Natural gas and electric utilities are examples. Long-run average costs for those firms typically fall as output increases. In a natural monopoly, economies of large-scale production dominate, leading to a single-firm industry.

The Pricing and Output Decision of the Natural Monopolist

A monopolist (like any other firm) will set the output rate where marginal revenue is equal to marginal cost. We draw the market demand curve, *D,* and the revenue curve, MR, in panel (a) of Figure 26-1. The intersection of the marginal revenue curve and the marginal cost curve is at point *A.* The monopolist would therefore produce quantity Q_m and charge a price of P_m.

What do we know about a monopolist's solution to the price-quantity question? When compared to a competitive situation, we know that consumers end up paying more for the product, and consequently they purchase less of it than they would purchase under competition. The monopoly solution is economically inefficient from society's point of view; the price charged for the product is higher than the opportunity cost to society, and consequently there is a misallocation of resources. That is, the price does not equal the true marginal cost of producing the good because the true marginal cost is at the intersection *A,* not price P_m.

Regulating the Natural Monopolist

Assume that the government wants the natural monopolist to produce at an output at which price equals marginal cost, so that the value of the satisfaction that individuals receive from the marginal unit purchased is just equal to the marginal cost to society. Where is that solution in panel (b) of Figure 26-1? It is at the intersection of the marginal cost curve and the demand curve, point *B.* Recall how we derived the competitive industry supply curve. We

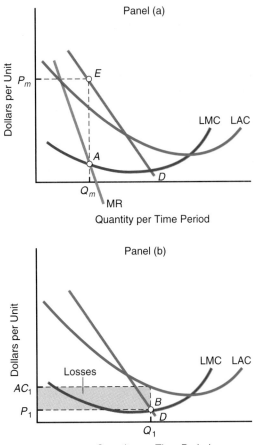

Panel (a)

Panel (b)

FIGURE 26-1

Profit Maximization and Regulation Through Marginal Cost Pricing
The profit-maximizing natural monopolist here would produce at the point in panel (a) where marginal costs equal marginal revenue—that is, at point A, which gives the quantity of production Q_m. The price charged would be P_m. If a regulatory commission attempted to regulate natural monopolies so that price equaled long-run marginal cost, the commission would make the monopolist set production at the point where the marginal cost curve intersects the demand schedule. This is shown in panel (b). The quantity produced would be Q_1, and the price would be P_1. However, average costs at Q_1 are equal to AC_1. Losses would ensue, equal to the shaded area. It would be self-defeating for a regulatory commission to force a natural monopolist to produce at an output rate at which $MC = P$ without subsidizing some of its costs because losses would eventually drive the natural monopolist out of business.

looked at all of the upward-sloping portions of actual and potential firms' marginal c curves above their respective average variable costs. We then summed all of these port of the firms' supply curves; that gave us the industry supply curve. We assume that a latory commission forces the natural monopolist to engage in marginal cost pricir hence to produce at quantity Q_1 and to sell the product at price P_1. How large monopolist's profits be? Profits, of course, are the *positive* difference between t enues and total costs. In this case, total revenues equal P_1 times Q_1, and total co average costs times the number of units produced. At Q_1, average cost is equ Average costs are higher than the price that the regulatory commission forces monopolist to charge. Profits turn out to be losses and are equal to the shaded (b) of Figure 26-1. Thus regulation that forces a natural monopolist to produc if it were in a competitive situation would also force that monopolist into n or losses. Obviously, the monopolist would rather go out of business than be regulation.

As a practical matter, then, regulators can't force a natural monopolist ginal cost pricing. Consequently, regulation of natural monopolies has o of allowing the regulated natural monopolist to set price where LAC i (b) of Figure 26-1. This is called *average cost pricing*. Average cost i ulators deem a "fair" rate of return on investment.

POLICY EXAMPLE
Are Electric Utilities Still Natural Monopolies?

When we discussed natural monopolies, we used a few examples. Panel (a) of Figure 26-1 seems to apply to electric utilities quite well. Technology is changing that situation, however. Efficient high-voltage transmission lines now exist. This means that the market for electricity generation can transcend local and even national boundaries. There is no longer any reason to restrict entry or to regulate prices in electricity generation.

Competition in the electric utility market has already started in California. The Department of Energy predicted that the average retail price of electricity will fall by 6 to 22 percent in the next couple of years and by perhaps 28 percent by the year 2010. Such numbers are consistent with what occurred after competition was allowed in the sale of natural gas, interstate long-distance telephone services, airline travel, and railroad shipping. Some economists feel that price reductions will actually be much greater than this because of increased innovation in the industry.

Initially, competition in the electric utility market has proved to be somewhat confusing for retail customers. For example, nearly 200 companies registered to sell electricity in the newly competitive California market. Confusion such as this is likely in other states that are also allowing electricity competition, including Massachusetts, Maine, Pennsylvania, Illinois, Michigan, New Jersey, and Rhode Island.

FOR CRITICAL ANALYSIS: Is there really any true natural monopoly left in the world? ●

CONCEPTS IN BRIEF

- A natural monopoly arises when one firm can produce all of an industry's output at a lower per-unit cost than other firms.

- The first firm to take advantage of the declining long-run average cost curve can undercut the prices of all other sellers, forcing them out of business, thereby obtaining a natural monopoly.

- A natural monopolist allowed to maximize profit will set quantity where marginal revenue equals long-run marginal cost. Price is determined from the demand curve at that quantity.

- A natural monopolist that is forced to set price equal to long-run marginal cost will sustain losses.

Exercise 26.1
Visit www.econtoday.com for more about post offices.

REGULATION

The U.S. government began regulating social and economic activity early in the nation's history, but the amount of government regulation has increased in the twentieth century. There are three types of government regulation:

- Regulation of natural monopolies
- Regulation of inherently competitive industries
- Regulation for public welfare across all industries, or so-called social regulation

For example, various state commissions regulate the rates and quality of service of electric power companies, which are considered natural monopolies. Trucking and interstate moving companies are inherently competitive industries but have nonetheless been made subject to government regulation in the past. And federal and state governments impose occupational, health, and safety rules on a wide variety of employers.

Objectives of Economic Regulation

Economic regulation is typically intended to control the prices that regulated enterprises are allowed to charge. Various public utility commissions throughout the United States regulate the rates (prices) of electrical utility companies and some telephone operating companies. This has usually been called rate regulation. The goal of rate regulation has, in principle, been the prevention of both monopoly profits and predatory competition.

Cost-of-service regulation
Regulation based on allowing prices to reflect only the actual cost of production and no monopoly profits.

Rate-of-return regulation
Regulation that seeks to keep the rate of return in the industry at a competitive level by not allowing excessive prices to be charged.

Two traditional methods of rate regulation have involved cost-of-service regulation and rate-of-return regulation. A regulatory commission using **cost-of-service regulation** allows the regulated companies to charge only prices that reflect the actual average cost of providing the services to the customer. In a somewhat similar vein, regulatory commissions using the **rate-of-return regulation** method allow regulated companies to set prices that ensure a normal, or competitive, rate of return on the investment in the business. We implied these two types of regulation when discussing panel (b) of Figure 26-1. If the long-run average cost curve in that figure includes a competitive rate of return on investment, regulating the price at AC_1 is an example of rate-of-return regulation.

A major problem with regulating monopolies concerns the quality of the service or product involved. Consider the many facets of telephone service: getting a dial tone, hearing other voices clearly, getting the operator to answer quickly, having out-of-order telephone lines repaired rapidly, putting through a long-distance call quickly and efficiently—the list goes on and on. But regulation of a telephone company usually dealt with the prices charged for telephone service. Of course, regulators were concerned with the quality of service, but how could that be measured? Indeed, it cannot be measured very easily. Therefore, it is extremely difficult for any type of regulation to be successful in regulating the *price per constant-quality unit*. Certainly, it is possible to regulate the price per unit, but we don't really know that the quality remains unchanged when the price is not allowed to rise "enough." Thus if regulation doesn't allow prices to rise, quality of service may be lowered, thereby raising the price per constant-quality unit.

POLICY EXAMPLE
Is There Any Reason Left to Regulate Phone Companies?

Long-distance phone service has been deregulated. Today, there may no longer be any rationale to regulate *any* type of phone service. Competition literally can be global in scope. Cellular phones can compete effectively with traditional wired telephone systems. Also, local telephone companies could be deregulated by simply allowing competitors access to each local grid if they pay a license fee for its use. Local telephone service could then be offered at unregulated but competitive rates. Also, given that it will soon be possible for electric companies to transmit phone and Internet communications through their grids, there truly will be no reason to regulate local phone service.

FOR CRITICAL ANALYSIS: Can the natural monopoly argument continue to apply to phone companies when cellular systems are available? ●

Social Regulation

As mentioned, social regulation reflects concern for public welfare across all industries. In other words, regulation is focused on the impact of production on the environment and society, the working conditions under which goods and services are produced, and sometimes the physical attributes of goods. The aim is a better quality of life for all through a less polluted environment, better working conditions, and safer and better products. For example, the Food and Drug Administration (FDA) attempts to protect against impure and unsafe foods, drugs, cosmetics, and other potentially hazardous products; the Consumer Product Safety Commission (CPSC) specifies minimum standards for consumer products in an attempt to reduce "unreasonable" risks of injury; the Environmental Protection Agency (EPA) watches over the amount of pollutants released into the environment; the Occupational Safety and Health Administration (OSHA) attempts to protect workers against work-related injuries and illnesses; and the Equal Employment Opportunity Commission (EEOC) seeks to provide fair access to jobs.

Table 26-1 lists some major federal regulatory agencies and their areas of concern. Although most people agree with the idea behind such social regulation, many disagree on whether we have too much regulation—whether it costs us more than the benefits we receive. Some contend that the costs that firms incur in abiding by regulations run into the hundreds of billions of dollars per year. The result is higher production costs, which are then passed on to consumers. Also, the resources invested in complying with regulatory measures could be invested in other uses. Furthermore, extensive regulation may have an anticompetitive effect because it may represent a relatively greater burden for smaller firms than for larger ones.

But the *potential* benefits of more social regulation are many. For example, the water we drink in some cities is known to be contaminated with cancer-causing chemicals; air pollution from emissions and toxic wastes from production processes cause many illnesses. Some contaminated areas have been cleaned up, but many other problem areas remain.

The benefits of social regulation may not be easy to measure and may accrue to society for a long time. Furthermore, it is difficult to put a dollar value on safer working conditions

TABLE 26-1

Some Federal Regulatory Agencies

Agency	Jurisdiction	Date Formed	Major Regulatory Functions
Federal Communications Commission (FCC)	Product markets	1934	Regulates broadcasting, telephone, and other communication services.
Federal Trade Commission (FTC)	Product Markets	1914	Responsible for preventing businesses from engaging in unfair trade practices and in monopolistic actions, as well as protecting consumer rights.
Equal Employment Opportunity Commission (EEOC)	Labor markets	1964	Investigates complaints of discrimination based on race, religion, sex, or age in hiring, promotion, firing, wages, testing, and all other conditions of employment.
Securities and Exchange Commission (SEC)	Financial markets	1934	Regulates all public securities markets to promote full disclosure.
Environmental Protection Agency (EPA)	Environment	1970	Develops and enforces environmental standards for air, water, toxic waste, and noise.
Occupational Safety and Health Administration (OSHA)	Health and safety	1970	Regulates workplace safety and health conditions.

and a cleaner environment. In any case, the debate goes on. However, it should be pointed out that the controversy is generally not about whether we should have social regulation but about when and how it is being done and whether we take *all* of the costs and benefits into account. For example, is regulation best carried out by federal, state, or local authorities? Is a specific regulation economically justified through a complete cost-benefit analysis?

Creative Response and Feedback Effects: Results of Regulation

Creative response
Behavior on the part of a firm that allows it to comply with the letter of the law but violate the spirit, significantly lessening the law's effects.

Regulated firms commonly try to avoid the effects of regulation whenever they can. In other words, the firms engage in **creative response,** which is a response to a regulation that conforms to the letter of the law but undermines its spirit. Take state laws requiring male-female pay-equity: The wages of women must be on a par with those paid to males who are performing the same tasks. Employers that pay the same wages to both males and females are clearly not in violation of the law. However, wages are only one component of total employee compensation. Another component is fringe benefits, such as on-the-job training. Because on-the-job training is difficult to observe from outside the firm, employers could offer less on-the-job training to women and still not be in technical violation of pay-equity laws. This unobservable difference would mean that males were able to acquire skills that could raise their future income even though current wages among males and females were equal, in compliance with the law.

Individuals have a type of creative response that has been labeled a *feedback effect.* Regulation may alter individuals' behavior after the regulation has been put into effect. If regulation requires fluoridated water, then parents know that their children's teeth have significant protection against tooth decay. Consequently, the feedback effect on parents' behavior is that they may be less concerned about how many sweets their children eat.

EXAMPLE
The Effectiveness of Auto Safety Regulation

A good example of the feedback effect has to do with automotive safety regulation. Since the 1960s, the federal government has required automobile manufacturers to make cars increasingly safer. Some of the earlier requirements involved nonprotruding door handles, collapsible steering columns, and shatterproof glass. More recent requirements involve I-beams in the doors, better seat belts, and airbags. The desired result was fewer injuries and deaths for drivers involved in accidents. According to economist Sam Peltzman, however, due to the feedback effect, drivers have gradually started driving more recklessly. Automobiles with more safety features have been involved in a disproportionate number of accidents.

FOR CRITICAL ANALYSIS: The feedback effect has also been called the law of unintended consequences. Why? ●

EXPLAINING REGULATORS' BEHAVIOR

Regulation has usually been defended by contending that government regulatory agencies are needed to correct market imperfections. We are dealing with a nonmarket situation because regulators are paid by the government and their decisions are not determined or constrained by the market. A number of theories have been put forward to describe the behavior of regulators. These theories can help us understand how regulation has often harmed consumers through higher prices and less choice and benefited producers through higher profits and fewer competitive forces. Two of the best-known theories of regulatory behavior are the *capture hypothesis* and the *share-the-gains, share-the-pains theory.*

The Capture Hypothesis

It has been observed that with the passage of time, regulators often end up adopting the views of the regulated. According to the **capture hypothesis,**[1] no matter what the reason for a regulatory agency's having been set up, it will eventually be captured by the special interests of the industry that is being regulated. Consider the reasons.

Who knows best about the industry that is being regulated? The people already in the industry. Who, then, will be asked to regulate the industry? Again, people who have been in the industry. And people who used to be in the industry have allegiances and friendships with others in the industry.

Also consider that whenever regulatory hearings are held, the affected consumer groups will have much less information about the industry than the people already in the industry, the producers. Additionally, the cost to any one consumer to show up at a regulatory hearing to express concern about a change in the rate structure will certainly exceed any perceived benefit that that consumer could obtain from going to the rate-making hearing.

Because they have little incentive to do so, consumers and taxpayers will not be well organized, nor will they be greatly concerned with regulatory actions. But the special interests of the industry are going to be well organized and well defined. Political entrepreneurs within the regulatory agency see little payoff in supporting the views of consumers and taxpayers anyway. After all, few consumers understand the benefits deriving from regulatory agency actions. Moreover, how much could a consumer directly benefit someone who works in an agency? Regulators have the most incentive to support the position of a well-organized special-interest group within the industry that is being regulated.

"Share the Gains, Share the Pains"

A somewhat different view of regulators' behavior is given in the **share-the-gains, share-the-pains theory.**[2] This theory looks at the specific aims of the regulators. It posits that a regulator simply wants to continue in the job. To do so, the regulator must obtain the approval of both the legislators who established and oversee the regulatory agency and the industry that is being regulated. A third group that must be taken into account is, of course, the customers of the industry.

Under the capture hypothesis, only the special interests of the industry being regulated had to be taken into account by the regulators. The share-the-gains, share-the-pains model contends that such a position is too risky because customers who are really hurt by improper regulation will complain to legislators, who might fire the regulators. Thus each regulator has to attach some weight to these three separate groups. What happens if there is an abrupt increase in fuel costs for electrical utilities? The capture theory would predict that regulators would relatively quickly allow for a rate increase in order to maintain the profits of the industry. The share-the-gains, share-the-pains theory, however, would predict that there will be an adjustment in rates, but not as quickly or as completely as the capture theory would predict. The regulatory agency is not completely captured by the industry; it has to take account of legislators and consumers.

Capture hypothesis
A theory of regulatory behavior that predicts that the regulators will eventually be captured by the special interests of the industry being regulated.

Share-the-gains, share-the-pains theory
A theory of regulatory behavior in which the regulators must take account of the demands of three groups: legislators, who established and who oversee the regulatory agency; members of the regulated industry; and consumers of the regulated industry's products or services.

---

[1]See George Stigler, *The Citizen and the State: Essays on Regulation* (Chicago: University of Chicago Press, 1975).

[2]See Sam Peltzman, "Towards a More General Theory of Regulation," *Journal of Law and Economics,* 19 (1976), pp. 211–240.

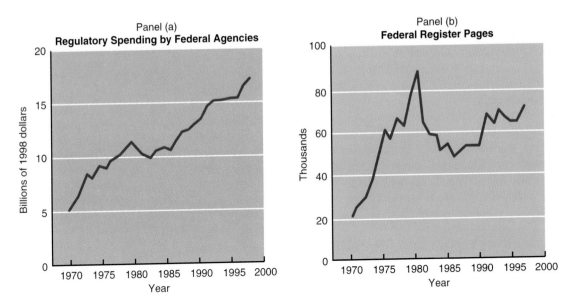

FIGURE 26-2

Regulation on the Rise

In panel (a), federal government regulatory spending is shown to exceed $16 billion per year today. State and local spending is not shown. In panel (b), the number of pages in the *Federal Register* per year has been rising since about 1990.

Sources: Institute for University Studies; *Federal Register,* various issues.

THE COSTS OF REGULATION

There is no truly accurate way to measure the costs of regulation. Panel (a) of Figure 26-2 shows regulatory spending in 1998 dollars. Except in the years 1981–1985, regulatory spending by federal agencies has increased. This is consistent with what has happened to the number of pages in the *Federal Register,* which publishes all the new federal regulatory rules; you can see that in panel (b). But actual direct costs to taxpayers are only a small part of the overall cost of regulation. Pharmaceutical-manufacturing safety standards raise the price of drugs. Automobile safety standards raise the price of cars. Environmental controls on manufacturing raise the price of manufactured goods. All of these increased prices add to the cost of regulation. According to economist Thomas Hopkins at the Rochester Institute of Technology, the economic cost of environmental and safety regulation exceeds $200 billion a year. When he adds the cost of all other kinds of regulations, he comes up with a grand total of over $600 billion a year, or about 8 percent of each year's total income in this country. Not surprisingly, the increasing cost of regulation on occasion has brought about cries for deregulation.

DEREGULATION

Deregulation
The elimination or phasing out of regulations on economic activity.

Regulation increased substantially during the 1970s. By the end of that decade, numerous proposals for **deregulation**—the removal of old regulations—had been made. Most deregulation proposals and actions since then have been aimed at industries in which price competition and entry competition by new firms continued to be thwarted by the regulators. The Air Deregulation Act of 1978 eliminated the Civil Aeronautics Board and allowed comptetition among the airlines themselves to control fares and routes flown. In 1980, the Interstate Commerce Commission's power over interstate trucking rates and routes was virtually eliminated, and the same occurred for buses in 1982. Savings account interest rates were deregulated in 1980. Railroad pricing was made more flexible during the same year.

Even prior to this spate of deregulatory acts by Congress, the Federal Communications Commission (FCC) had started in 1972 to deregulate the television broadcast industry. The result has been an increased number of channels, more direct satellite broadcasting, and more cable television transmissions. (Further deregulation occurred in 1996.) In 1975, the Securities and Exchange Commission (SEC) deregulated brokerage fees charged by brokers on the New York Stock Exchange.

Short-Run Versus Long-Run Effects of Deregulation

The short-run effects of deregulation are not the same as the long-run effects. In the short run, a regulated industry that becomes deregulated may experience numerous temporary adjustments. One is the inevitable shakeout of higher-cost producers with the concomitant removal of excess monopoly profits. Another is the sometimes dramatic displacement of workers who have labored long and hard in the formerly regulated industry. The level of service for some consumers may fall; for example, after the deregulation of the telephone industry, some aspects of telephone service decreased in quality. When airlines were deregulated, service to some small cities was eliminated or became more expensive. The power of unions in the formerly regulated industry may decrease. And bankruptcies may cause disruptions, particularly in the local economy where the headquarters of the formerly regulated firm are located.

Proponents of deregulation, or at least of less regulation, contend that there are long-run, permanent benefits. These include lower prices that are closer to marginal cost. Furthermore, fewer monopoly profits are made in the deregulated industry. Such proponents argue that deregulation has had positive *net* benefits.

Deregulation and Contestable Markets

A major argument in favor of deregulation is that when government-imposed barriers to entry are removed, competition will cause firms to enter markets that previously had only a few firms with market power due to those entry barriers. Potential competitors will become actual competitors, and prices will fall toward a competitive level. Recently, this argument has been bolstered by a relatively new model of efficient firm behavior that predicts competitive prices in spite of a lack of a large number of firms. This model is called the **theory of contestable markets.** Under the theory of contestable markets, most of the outcomes predicted by the theory of perfect competition will occur in certain industries with relatively few firms. Specifically, where the theory of contestable markets is applicable, the few firms may still produce the output at which price equals marginal cost in both the short run and the long run. These firms will receive zero economic profits in the long run.

Unconstrained and Relatively Costless Entry and Exit. For a market to be perfectly contestable, firms must be able to enter and leave the industry easily. Freedom of entry and exit implies an absence of nonprice constraints and of serious fixed costs associated with a potential competitor's decision to enter a contestable market. Such an absence of impor-

---

Exercise 26.2
Visit www.econtoday.com for more about deregulation.

Theory of contestable markets
A hypothesis concerning pricing behavior that holds that even though there are only a few firms in an industry, they are forced to price their products more or less competitively because of the ease of entry by outsiders. The key aspect of a contestable market is relatively costless entry into and exit from the industry.

tant fixed costs results if the firm need buy no specific durable inputs in order to enter, if it uses up all such inputs it does purchase, or if all of its specific durable inputs are salable upon exit without any losses beyond those normally incurred from depreciation. The important issue is whether or not a potential entrant can easily get his or her investment out at any time in the future.

The mathematical model of perfect contestability is complex, but the underlying logic is straightforward. As long as conditions for free entry prevail, any excess profits, or any inefficiencies on the part of incumbent firms, will serve as an inducement for potential entrants to enter. By entering, new firms can temporarily profit at no risk to themselves from the less than competitive situation in the industry. Once competitive conditions are again restored, these firms will leave the industry just as quickly.

Benefits of Contestable Markets. Contestable markets have several desirable characteristics. One has to do with profits. Profits that exceed the opportunity cost of capital will not exist in the long run because of freedom of entry, just as in a perfectly competitive industry. The elimination of "excess" profits can occur even with only a couple of firms in an industry. The threat of entry will cause them to expand output to eliminate excess profit.

Also, firms that have cost curves that are higher than those of the most efficient firms will find that they cannot compete. These firms will be replaced by entrants whose cost curves are consistent with the most efficient technology. In other words, in contestable markets, there will be no cost inefficiencies in the long run.

Rethinking Regulation Using Cost-Benefit Analysis

Rather than considering deregulation as the only solution to "too much" regulation, some economists argue that regulation should simply be put to a cost-benefit test. Specifically, the cost of existing and proposed regulations should be compared to the benefits. Unless it can be demonstrated that regulations generate net positive benefits (benefits greater than costs), such regulations should not be in effect.

CONCEPTS IN BRIEF

- It is difficult to regulate the price per constant-quality unit because it is difficult to measure all dimensions of quality.
- The capture hypothesis holds that regulatory agencies will eventually be captured by special interests of the industry. This is because consumers are a diffuse group who individually are not affected greatly by regulation, whereas industry groups are well focused and know that large amounts of potential profits are at stake and depend on the outcome of regulatory proceedings.
- In the share-the-gains, share-the-pains theory of regulation, regulators must take account of the interests of three groups: the industry, legislators, and consumers.
- The 1970s and 1980s were periods of deregulation during which formerly regulated industries became much more competitive. The short-run effects of deregulation in some industries were numerous bankruptcies and disrupted service. The long-run results in many deregulated industries included better service, more variety, and lower costs. One argument in favor of deregulation involves the theory of contestable markets—if entry and exit are relatively costless, the number of firms in an industry is irrelevant in terms of determining whether consumers pay competitive prices.

ANTITRUST POLICY

It is the expressed aim of our government to foster competition in the economy. To this end, numerous attempts have been made to legislate against business practices that seemingly destroy the competitive nature of the system. This is the general idea behind antitrust legislation: If the courts can prevent collusion among sellers of a product, monopoly prices will not result; there will be no restriction of output if the members of an industry are not allowed to join together in restraint of trade. Remember that the competitive solution to the price-quantity problem is one in which the price of the item produced is equal to its marginal social opportunity cost. Also, no *economic* profits are made in the long run.

The Sherman Antitrust Act of 1890

The Sherman Antitrust Act was passed in 1890. It was the first attempt by the federal government to control the growth of monopoly in the United States. The most important provisions of that act are as follows:

Section 1: Every contract, combination in the form of trust or otherwise, or conspiracy, in restraint of trade or commerce among the several states, or with foreign nations, is hereby declared to be illegal.

Section 2: Every person who shall monopolize, or attempt to monopolize, or combine or conspire with any other person or persons to monopolize any part of the trade or commerce . . . shall be guilty of a misdemeanor.[3]

Notice how vague this act really is. No definition is given for the terms *restraint of trade* or *monopolization*. Despite this vagueness, however, the act was used to prosecute the infamous Standard Oil trust of New Jersey. Standard Oil of New Jersey was charged with violations of Sections 1 and 2 of the Sherman Antitrust Act. This was in 1906, when Standard Oil controlled over 80 percent of the nation's oil-refining capacity. Among other things, Standard Oil was accused of both predatory price cutting to drive rivals out of business and obtaining preferential price treatment from the railroads for transporting Standard Oil products, thus allowing Standard to sell at lower prices.

Standard Oil was convicted in a district court. The company then appealed to the Supreme Court, which ruled that Standard's control of and power over the oil market created "a *prima facie* presumption of intent and purpose to maintain dominancy . . . not as a result from normal methods of industrial development, but by means of combination." Here the word *combination* meant taking over other businesses and obtaining preferential price treatment from railroads. The Supreme Court forced Standard Oil of New Jersey to break up into many smaller companies.

The Clayton Act of 1914

The Sherman Act was so vague that in 1914 a new law was passed to sharpen its antitrust provisions. This law was called the Clayton Act. It prohibited or limited a number of very specific business practices, which again were felt to be "unreasonable" attempts at restraining trade or commerce. Section 2 of that act made it illegal to "discriminate in price between different purchasers" except in cases in which the differences are due to actual dif-

---

[3] This is now a felony.

ferences in selling or transportation costs. Section 3 stated that producers cannot sell goods "on the condition, agreement or understanding that the . . . purchaser thereof shall not use or deal in the goods . . . of a competitor or competitors of the seller." And Section 7 provided that corporations cannot hold stock in another company if the effect "may be to substantially lessen competition."

The Federal Trade Commission Act of 1914 and Its 1938 Amendment

Exercise 26.3
Visit www.econtoday.com for more about the FTC.

The Federal Trade Commission Act was designed to stipulate acceptable competitive behavior. In particular, it was supposed to prevent cutthroat pricing—excessively aggressive competition, which would tend to eliminate too many competitors. One of the basic features of the act was the creation of the Federal Trade Commission (FTC), charged with the power to investigate unfair competitive practices. The FTC can do this on its own or at the request of firms that feel they have been wronged. It can issue cease and desist orders where "unfair methods of competition in commerce" are discovered. In 1938, the Wheeler-Lea Act amended the 1914 act. The amendment expressly prohibits "unfair or deceptive acts or practices in commerce." Pursuant to that act, the FTC engages in what it sees as a battle against false or misleading advertising, as well as the misrepresentation of goods and services for sale in the marketplace.

The Robinson-Patman Act of 1936

In 1936, Section 2 of the Clayton Act was amended by the Robinson-Patman Act. The Robinson-Patman Act was aimed at preventing producers from driving out smaller competitors by means of selected discriminatory price cuts. The act has often been referred to as the "Chain Store Act" because it was meant to protect *independent* retailers and wholesalers from "unfair discrimination" by chain stores.

The act was the natural outgrowth of increasing competition that independents faced when chain stores and mass distributors started to develop after World War I. The essential provisions of the act are as follows:

1. It was made illegal to pay brokerage fees unless an independent broker was employed.
2. It was made illegal to offer concessions, such as discounts, free advertising, or promotional allowances, to one buyer of a firm's product if the firm did not offer the same concessions to all buyers of that product.
3. Other forms of discrimination, such as quantity discounts, were also made illegal whenever they "substantially" lessened competition.
4. It was made illegal to charge lower prices in one location than in another or to sell at "unreasonably low prices" if such marketing techniques were designed to "destroy competition or eliminate a competitor."

POLICY EXAMPLE
Should Wal-Mart Be Forced to Raise Prices?

The issue of predatory pricing gained national prominence when three independent pharmacies filed suit against Wal-Mart in an Arkansas court. Independent retailers in small towns across the country have long accused Wal-Mart of selling goods below cost to drive them out of business. The three pharmacies that brought suit against

Wal-Mart claimed that it was engaging in predatory pricing by selling as many as 200 items below cost at its store in Conway, Arkansas. Wal-Mart responded that it makes its pricing decisions based on how much competition it faces: more competition, lower prices. Wal-Mart attorneys pointed out that when Wal-Mart entered the Conway business area, there were 12 pharmacies, all of which remain in existence today, plus two new ones. The number of pharmacists in the county increased from 38 to 58.

A local judge found Wal-Mart guilty; on appeal, Wal-Mart prevailed.

FOR CRITICAL ANALYSIS: Supermarkets routinely advertise "loss leaders" such as turkeys at Thanksgiving that are priced below cost. Is there any difference between spending on loss leaders and simply spending more on traditional types of advertising? ●

Exemptions from Antitrust Laws

Numerous laws exempt the following industries and business practices from antitrust legislation:

1. All labor unions
2. Public utilities—electric, gas, and telephone companies
3. Professional baseball
4. Cooperative activities among American exporters
5. Hospitals
6. Public transit and water systems
7. Suppliers of military equipment
8. Joint publishing arrangement in a single city by two or more newspapers

THE ENFORCEMENT OF ANTITRUST LAWS

Most antitrust enforcement today is based on the Sherman Act. The Supreme Court has defined the offense of **monopolization** as involving the following elements: "(1) the possession of monopoly power in the relevant market and (2) the willful acquisition or maintenance of that power, as distinguished from growth or development as a consequence of a superior product, business acumen, or historical accident."

Monopolization
The possession of monopoly power in the relevant market and the willful acquisition or maintenance of that power, as distinguished from growth or development as a consequence of a superior product, business acumen, or historical accident.

Monopoly Power and the Relevant Market

The Sherman Act does not define monopoly. Monopoly clearly is not a single entity. Also, monopoly is not a function of size alone. For example, a "mom and pop" grocery store located in an isolated desert town is a monopolist in at least one sense.

It is difficult to define and measure market power precisely. As a workable proxy, courts often look to the firm's percentage share of the "relevant market." This is the so-called **market share test.** A firm is generally considered to have monopoly power if its share of the relevant market is 70 percent or more. This is not an absolute dictum, however. It is only a loose rule of thumb; in some cases, a smaller share may be held to constitute monopoly power.

The relevant market consists of two elements: a relevant product market and a relevant geographic market. What should the relevant product market include? It must include all products produced by different firms that have identical attributes, such as sugar. Yet products that are not identical may sometimes be substituted for one another. Coffee may be substituted for tea, for example. In defining the relevant product market, the key issue is the degree of interchangeability between products. If one product is a sufficient substitute for another, the two products are considered to be part of the same product market.

Market share test
The percentage of a market that a particular firm controls, used as the primary measure of monopoly power.

The second component of the relevant market is the geographic boundaries of the market. For products that are sold nationwide, the geographic boundaries of the market encompass the entire United States. If a producer and its competitors sell in only a limited area (one in which customers have no access to other sources of the product), the geographic market is limited to that area. A national firm may thus compete in several distinct areas and have monopoly power in one area but not in another.

POLICY EXAMPLE
Should the FTC Be Allowed to Redefine the Relevant Market?

Recently, the FTC prevented the merger of Office Depot and Staples, both office supply superstore chains. To understand why the FTC opposed this proposed merger, let's consider the definition of a market. If it is office products, then firms sell such products in the following ways: (1) over the Internet, (2) via fax, (3) over the phone from different supply companies, (4) through salespeople from different suppliers who come directly to businesses, even very small ones, (5) from Wal-Mart and other general retail companies, (6) from small office supply retailers, (7) from club warehouses, such as PriceCostco, and (8) from office supply superstores. The total share of the national market for office supplies garnered by the superstores Staples and Office Depot accounts for between 4 and 5 percent.

The FTC, unable to stop the merger on the basis of a reasonable definition of the relevant market, developed a new definition—the sale of office supplies at office supply superstores! In other words, the FTC defined the market so that Office Depot and Staples would account for almost 100 percent of that market. Nowhere in the literature of antitrust does one find a definition of a market that depends on the way in which firms actually sell a good or service. The FTC nonetheless decided that Office Depot and Staples were not selling office supplies but rather a service called "one-stop shopping for office supplies." This is a strange definition coming from the Federal Trade Commission, an agency that purchases office supplies from 105 different vendors. There is also another problem, and it deals with what Office Depot and Staples actually sell. Office supplies account for about 40 percent of these two stores' sales. The other 60 percent includes cellular phones, computers, computer supplies, and furniture. They have no monopoly power in the sale of such items.

Perhaps the most important argument against the FTC's new definition of the relevant market has to do with e-commerce, the sale of goods over the Internet. Businesses, more than any other group of buyers, are using the Internet to make purchases. It is hard to imagine that Office Depot and Staples, as a merged company, could raise prices in a market in which price quotes are available at almost no cost at the click of a mouse.

FOR CRITICAL ANALYSIS: Why do you imagine that the FTC decided to change the normal definition of the relevant market? •

CONCEPTS IN BRIEF

- The first national antitrust law was the Sherman Antitrust Act, passed in 1890, which made illegal every contract and combination in the form of a trust in restraint of trade.

- The Clayton Act made price discrimination and interlocking directorates illegal.

- The Federal Trade Commission Act of 1914 established the Federal Trade Commission. The Wheeler-Lea Act of 1938 amended the 1914 act to prohibit "unfair or deceptive acts or practices in commerce."

- The Robinson-Patman Act of 1936 was aimed at preventing large producers from driving out small competitors by means of selective discriminatory price cuts.

Microsoft CEO Bill Gates has had to defend himself in recent years against federal charges of attempting to monopolize the Internet browser market. Is it possible for any one company to have a monopoly in electronic commerce?

The Justice Department Goes After Microsoft Again

CONCEPTS APPLIED:

COMPETITION, MONOPOLY, MARKET POWER, ANTITRUST LAW

Visit www.econtoday.com for an Internet Activity that expands your understanding of these concepts.

Microsoft has been engaged in a head-to-head battle for dominance in the Internet browser market. As mentioned in the opening page of this chapter, its main competitor is Netscape Communications, which owns Navigator.

The Microsoft Plan

Microsoft was going to "bundle" the latest version of its browser, Internet Explorer, with the latest version of its industry-leading Windows operating system and with any future improvements to that system. What Microsoft was proposing to do was consistent with what has been observed in the software industry for years. Microsoft, Apple, IBM, Sun, Novell, and others have little by little included more features in each operating system they have offered. These included graphical user interface, type fonts, file compression features, networking, memory management, and other niceties.

Justice Says No

The Justice Department decided that Microsoft should unbundle its Internet browser program from its operating system. The court stated that "Microsoft's 'unfettered liberty' to impose its idea of what has been 'integrated' into its operating system stops at least at the point at which it would violate established antitrust law." The idea, of course, is that because Microsoft's dominant Windows operating system is in more than 80 percent of the world's computers, Microsoft can force computer manufacturers to whom it licenses that system to incorporate Microsoft's Internet Explorer Web browser.

Unlike monopolies, in the software and computer industry in general, prices have been falling for everything, including all Microsoft products. When one Justice Department official had this fact pointed out to him, he

stated that the Justice Department has to look to the future. In other words, the Justice Department believes that it can predict what will happen in the computer industry, and that is why it is trying to prevent Microsoft from bundling Internet Explorer with Windows.

Is the Justice Department Being Consistent?

While the Justice Department does not want Windows to include browsing capabilities, many of Microsoft's competitors are doing the equivalent. They are incorporating basic operating system services, such as the ability to print files and to run applications, into their own browsers, making them a type of operating system. If Microsoft's competitors can integrate an operating system into their browsers, why can't Microsoft integrate a browser into its operating system?

Could Microsoft Control Electronic Commerce?

An additional issue concerns electronic commerce. If Microsoft's Internet Explorer browser becomes the dominant one in the marketplace, could Microsoft then be able to monopolize travel, real estate, and banking services on the Internet? Perhaps not, for a browser is only a window; it's not the view. On the World Wide Web, the *content* is what people are after; how they get to that content is immaterial. Soon there will be hundreds of thousands of content providers on the Web selling travel, banking, and other services.

FOR CRITICAL ANALYSIS

1. How valid is the Justice Department's argument about looking to the future?
2. Why do most of the nation's computers use the Microsoft operating system today?

CHAPTER SUMMARY

1. Regulation may be applied to a natural monopoly, which arises when, for example, the average total cost curve falls over a very large range of production rates. In such a situation, only one firm can survive. It will be the firm that can expand production and sales faster than the others to take advantage of the falling average total costs. If regulation seeks to force the natural monopolist to produce at the point where the marginal cost curve (supply curve in the competitive case) intersects the demand curve, the natural monopolist will incur losses, because when average total costs are falling, marginal costs are below average total costs. The regulators face a dilemma.

2. There are several ways of regulating monopolies, the most common ones being on a cost-of-service basis or a rate-of-return basis. Under cost-of-service regulation, the regulated monopolies are allowed to charge prices that reflect only reasonable costs. Under rate-of-return regulation, the regulated monopolies are allowed to set rates so as to make a competitive rate of return for the equity shareholders. Supposedly, no monopoly profits can therefore be earned.

3. The capture hypothesis predicts that because of the diffuse interests of consumers as compared to the well-focused interests of industry members, regulators will eventually be captured by those whom they regulate.

4. The share-the-gains, share-the-pains theory predicts that regulators must take account not only of the desires of members of the industry but also of the wishes of legislators and consumers.

5. The 1970s and 1980s were periods of deregulation during which formerly regulated industries became much more competitive. The short-run effects of deregulation in some industries were numerous bankruptcies and disrupted service. The long-run results in many deregulated industries included better service, more variety, and lower costs.

6. One argument in favor of deregulation involves the theory of contestable markets—if entry and exit are relatively costless, the number of firms in an industry is irrelevant in terms of determining whether consumers pay competitive prices.

7. Some economists argue that all actual and proposed regulation be subject to strict cost-benefit analysis.

8. Antitrust legislation is designed to obviate the need for regulation. The major antitrust acts are the Sherman, Clayton, and Robinson-Patman acts.

DISCUSSION OF PREVIEW QUESTIONS

1. What is a natural monopoly, and how does one arise?

A natural monopoly is a situation in which the long-run average cost curve falls persistently as output expands. Thus the natural monopolist is a firm that by expanding is able to charge a price lower than its competitors can, thereby eliminating them. A natural monopolist arises due to tremendous economies of scale; expanding output causes ATC to fall.

2. If natural monopolies are required to price at marginal cost, what problem emerges?

We have noted in earlier chapters that efficiency requires that people pay the marginal cost for a good or a service. If regulators grant a firm monopoly privileges (recognizing it as a natural monopoly and regulating it to keep it in line) but force it to price at its marginal cost of production, a problem emerges. Because long-run ATC is persistently falling, it follows that long-run marginal cost must be below long-run ATC. Forcing a firm to charge a price equal to marginal cost implies that average revenue = price = marginal cost < average total cost (AR = P = MC < ATC). It follows that AR < ATC, and therefore the regulated natural monopolist would experience *negative* economic profits. In that case, it would shut down unless subsidized. In short, forcing a regulated natural monopolist to price at marginal cost may be socially beneficial, but such a policy requires that the natural monopolist be subsidized to cover the resulting economic losses to the firm.

3. **What are some means of regulating a natural monopoly?**

Two important means of regulating a natural monopoly are cost of service and rate of return. Cost-of-service regulation aims at requiring a natural monopolist to price at levels that would result from a more competitive situation. In effect, the natural monopolist is required to charge the average cost of providing the service in question, thereby ensuring zero economic profits. The rate-of-return form of regulation in effect allows a natural monopolist to price at rates that permit it an *overall* "normal" rate of return, because the natural monopolist will remain in operation only if it earns at least a normal return on invested capital.

4. **Why have economists been reevaluating the government's role as an economic regulator?**

Presumably, regulation is an attempt to prevent monopoly abuses and to simulate a competitive market structure where one would not otherwise exist. Yet much academic research indicates that this is not the case; regulated industries apparently behave more like monopolies than the overall manufacturing sector does. Some analysts have claimed that the regulated firms sooner or later "capture" the regulatory agencies; before long, regulated industries have the protection and sanction of the regulatory bodies! Hence many economists favor deregulation—at least of the older variety of regulation, as existed in the airline, interstate transport, and communications industries. The consensus is less clear regarding regulation by the newer agencies such as the Environmental Protection Agency (EPA) and the Occupational Safety and Health Administration (OSHA).

PROBLEMS

(Answers to the odd-numbered problems appear at the back of the book.)

26-1. The accompanying graph depicts a situation for a monopolist.

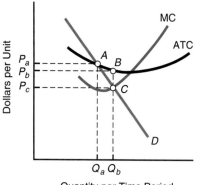

Quantity per Time Period

a. If this monopolist were required to price at marginal cost, what would the quantity and price be?

b. What rectangle would indicate total economic losses if this monopolist were required to price at marginal cost?

26-2. "The elimination of all tariffs would dissipate more monopoly power than any other single government action." What do tariffs (taxes on imported goods only) have to do with monopoly power?

26-3. Assume that you are in charge of enforcing the Occupational Safety and Health Act. If you are not constrained to consider the costs of new regulations that increase worker health and safety, what *will* constrain your behavior, if anything? If you now must consider the costs of your new rules, how might you go about your job?

26-4. Would you expect to find more or less corruption of government officials in a regulatory agency that auctioned off "certificates of convenience" or in one that rationed them according to nonfinancial criteria? Why?

26-5. Why is the right of free entry insufficient to prevent sustained economic profits within a natural monopoly?

26-6. Suppose that you own the only natural mineral spring spa in your state. Why would we *not* expect to see the state government regulating the price you charge?

26-7. "Philosophically, I am vehemently opposed to government interference in the marketplace. As the owner of a liquor store, however, I can tell you that deregulation will be bad for the citizenry. You would not want a liquor store on every corner, would you?" Why would you predict that a liquor store owner would defend regulation of the liquor industry in this way?

26-8. The federal government brought an antitrust suit against IBM in 1982. Eventually the case was dismissed as being "without merit." In the beginning of the 1990s, IBM layed off thousands of its workers. What has happened since the time IBM was being prosecuted as a monopoly and today, when it is suffering hard financial times?

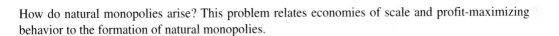

COMPUTER-ASSISTED INSTRUCTION

How do natural monopolies arise? This problem relates economies of scale and profit-maximizing behavior to the formation of natural monopolies.

INTERACTING WITH THE INTERNET

You can find the Federal Trade Commission (FTC) at

www.ftc.gov

To see what the antitrust division of the Department of Justice is doing, go to

www.usdoj.gov/atr/atr.htm

Find out what the Securities and Exchange Commission does by accessing it at

www.sec.gov

The Federal Communications Commission (FCC) home page is at

www.fcc.gov

PART 8

PRODUCTIVE FACTORS, POVERTY, THE ENVIRONMENT, AND INTEREST GROUPS

CHAPTER 27

LABOR DEMAND AND SUPPLY

One of the reasons that you are pursuing higher education is to increase your value to potential employers. Consequently, you can expect to be paid a higher salary than you would if you had only a high school diploma. President Clinton has said that "we are living in a world where what you earn is a function of what you learn." Historical data seem to reflect this view. Since the end of the 1970s, the wage premium that college graduates have enjoyed relative to other workers increased from 34 percent to over 50 percent. Some labor market researchers believe, however, that the wage differential will decline in the future. They point out that newly developed training software may reduce the value of a college education in the future. Before you can take a position on this issue, you need to understand the basic model of labor demand and supply.

PREVIEW QUESTIONS

1. When hiring labor, what general rule will be followed by employers who wish to maximize profits?
2. What is the profit-maximizing rate of employment for a perfectly competitive firm?
3. What is the profit-maximizing rate of employment for an imperfectly competitive firm?
4. How is an industry wage rate determined?

Did You Know That . . . the top 350 executives in America's biggest corporations are compensated, on the average, $2.5 million each, or about 60 times more than the median family income of a little over $40,000? Recently, the head of the Travelers Group, Sanford Weill, was paid almost $100 million in one year. You, in contrast, as a typical college student will probably make between $25,000 and $50,000 a year, or approximately one two-thousandth of Weill's annual salary. To comprehend why firms pay different employees such vastly different salaries, you must understand how the laws of demand and supply apply to labor.

A firm's demand for inputs can be studied in much the same manner as we studied the demand for output in different market situations. Again, various market situations will be examined. Our analysis will always end with the same commonsense conclusion: A firm will hire employees up to the point beyond which it isn't profitable to hire any more. It will hire employees to the point at which the marginal benefit of hiring a worker will just equal the marginal cost. Basically, in every profit-maximizing situation, it is most profitable to carry out an activity up to the point at which the marginal benefit equals the marginal cost. Remembering that guideline will help you in analyzing decision making at the firm level. We will start our analysis under the assumption that the market for input factors is perfectly competitive. We will further assume that the output market is perfectly competitive. This provides a benchmark against which to compare other situations in which labor markets or product markets are not perfectly competitive.

COMPETITION IN THE PRODUCT MARKET

Let's take as our example a compact disc (CD) manufacturing firm that is in competition with many companies selling the same kind of product. Assume that the laborers hired by our CD manufacturing firm do not need any special skills. This firm sells its product in a perfectly competitive market. A CD manufacturer also buys labor (its variable input) in a perfectly competitive market. A firm that hires labor under perfectly competitive conditions hires only a minuscule proportion of all the workers who are potentially available to the firm. By "potentially available" we mean all the workers in a given geographic area who possess the skills demanded by our perfect competitor. In such a market, it is always possible for the individual firm to pick up extra workers without having to offer a higher wage. Thus the supply of labor to the firm is perfectly elastic—that is, represented by a horizontal line at the going wage rate established by the forces of supply and demand in the entire labor market. The firm is a price taker in the labor market.

MARGINAL PHYSICAL PRODUCT

Look at panel (a) of Figure 27-1. In column 1, we show the number of workers per week that the firm can hire. In column 2, we show total physical product (TPP) per week, the total *physical* production that different quantities of the labor input (in combination with a fixed amount of other inputs) will generate in a week's time. In column 3, we show the additional output gained when a CD manufacturing company adds workers to its existing manufacturing facility. This column, the **marginal physical product (MPP) of labor,** represents the extra (additional) output attributed to employing additional units of the variable input factor. If this firm adds a seventh worker, the MPP is 118. The law of diminishing marginal returns predicts that additional units of a variable factor will, after some point, cause the MPP to decline, other things being held constant.

Marginal physical product (MPP) of labor

The change in output resulting from the addition of one more worker. The MPP of the worker equals the change in total output accounted for by hiring the worker, holding all other factors of production constant.

FIGURE 27-1

Marginal Revenue Product

In panel (a), column 4 shows marginal revenue product (MRP), which is the amount of additional revenue the firm receives for the sale of that additional output. Marginal revenue product is simply the amount of money the additional worker brings in—the combination of that worker's contribution to production and the revenue that that production will bring to the firm. For this perfectly competitive firm, marginal revenue is equal to the price of the product, or $6 per unit. At a weekly wage of $498, the profit-maximizing employer will pay for only 12 workers because then the marginal revenue product is just equal to the wage rate or weekly salary.

Panel (a)

(1) Labor Input (workers per week)	(2) Total Physical Product (TPP) CDs per Week	(3) Marginal Physical Product (MPP) CDs per Week	(4) Marginal Revenue (MR = P = $6 net) x MPP = Marginal Revenue Product (MRP) ($ per additional worker)	(5) Wage Rate ($ per week) = Marginal Factor Cost (MFC) = Change in Total Costs / Change in Labor
6	882			
		118	$708	$498
7	1,000			
		111	666	498
8	1,111			
		104	624	498
9	1,215			
		97	582	498
10	1,312			
		90	540	498
11	1,402			
		83	498	498
12	1,485			
		76	456	498
13	1,561			

In panel (b), we find the number of workers the firm will want to hire by observing the wage rate that is established by the forces of supply and demand in the entire labor market. We show that this employer is hiring labor in a perfectly competitive labor market and therefore faces a perfectly elastic supply curve represented by *s* at $498 per week. As in all other situations, we basically have a supply and demand model; in this example, the demand curve is represented by MRP, and the supply curve is *s*. Equilibrium occurs at their intersection.

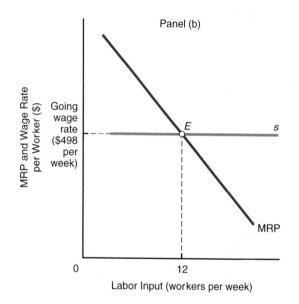

Why the Decline in MPP?

We are assuming all other nonlabor factors of production are held constant. So if our CD manufacturing firm wants to add one more worker to its production line, it has to crowd all the existing workers a little closer together because it does not increase its capital stock (the production equipment). Therefore, as we add more workers, each one has a smaller and smaller fraction of the available capital stock with which to work. If one worker uses one machine, adding another worker usually won't double the output because the machine can run only so fast and for so many hours per day. In other words, MPP declines because of the law of diminishing marginal returns.

Marginal Revenue Product

We now need to translate into a dollar value the physical product that results from hiring an additional worker. This is done by multiplying the marginal physical product by the marginal revenue of the firm. Because our CD firm is selling its product in a perfectly competitive market, marginal revenue is equal to the price of the product. If the seventh worker's MPP is 118 and the marginal revenue is $6 per CD, the **marginal revenue product (MRP)** is $708 (118 × $6). The MRP is shown in column 4 of panel (a) of Figure 27-1. *The marginal revenue product represents the worker's contribution to the firm's total revenues.*

When a firm operates in a competitive product market, the marginal physical product times the product price is also sometimes referred to as the *value of marginal product (VMP)*. Because price and marginal revenue are the same for a perfectly competitive firm, the VMP is also the MRP.

In column 5 of panel (a) of Figure 27-1, we show the wage rate, or *marginal factor cost,* of each worker. The marginal cost of workers is the extra cost incurred in employing that factor of production. We call that cost the **marginal factor cost (MFC).** Otherwise stated,

$$\text{Marginal factor cost} \equiv \frac{\text{change in total cost}}{\text{change in amount of resource used}}$$

Because each worker is paid the same competitively determined wage of $498 per week, the MFC is the same for all workers. And because the firm is buying labor in a perfectly competitive labor market, the wage rate of $498 per week really represents the firm's supply curve of labor. That curve is perfectly elastic because the firm can purchase all labor at the same wage rate, considering that it is a minuscule part of the entire labor-purchasing market. (Recall the definition of perfect competition.) We show this perfectly elastic supply curve as *s* in panel (b) of Figure 27-1.

Marginal revenue product (MRP)
The marginal physical product (MPP) times marginal revenue. The MRP gives the additional revenue obtained from a one-unit change in labor input.

Marginal factor cost (MFC)
The cost of using an additional unit of an input. For example, if a firm can hire all the workers i wants at the going wage rate, the marginal factor cost of labo is the wage rate.

EXAMPLE
Does Attractiveness Lead to Higher Marginal Revenue Product?

Economist Daniel Hamermesh of the University of Texas (Austin) and Jeff Biddle of Michigan State University discovered that "plain-looking" people earn 5 to 10 percent less than people of "average" looks, who in turn earn 5 percent less than those who are considered "good-looking." Surprisingly, their research showed that the "looks effect" on wages was greater for men than for women. This wage differential related to appearance is not, contrary to popular belief, evident only in modeling, acting, or working directly with the public. Looks seem to account for higher earnings in jobs such as bricklaying, factory work, and telemarketing.

According to Hamermesh and Biddle, part of the wage differential may be created by the fact that attractiveness leads to higher marginal revenue product. More attractive individuals may have higher self-esteem, which in turn causes them to be more productive on the job.

FOR CRITICAL ANALYSIS: What are some of the other possible reasons that more attractive people tend to earn more? •

General Rule for Hiring

Virtually every optimizing rule in economics involves comparing marginal benefits with marginal cost. The general rule, therefore, for the hiring decision of a firm is this:

> **The firm hires workers up to the point at which the additional cost associated with hiring the last worker is equal to the additional revenue generated by that worker.**

In a perfectly competitive situation, this is the point at which the wage rate just equals the marginal revenue product. If the firm hired more workers, the additional wages would not be covered by additional increases in total revenue. If the firm hired fewer workers, it would be forfeiting the contributions that those workers could make to total profits.

Therefore, referring to columns 4 and 5 in panel (a) of Figure 27-1, we see that this firm would certainly employ the seventh worker, because the MRP is $708 while the MFC is only $498. The firm would continue to employ workers up to the point at which MFC = MRP because as workers are added, they contribute more to revenue than to cost.

The MRP Curve: Demand for Labor

We can also use panel (b) of Figure 27-1 to find how many workers our firm should hire. First, we draw a straight line across from the going wage rate, which is determined by demand and supply in the labor market. The straight line is labeled *s* to indicate that it is the supply curve of labor for the *individual* firm purchasing labor in a perfectly competitive labor market. That firm can purchase all the labor it wants of equal quality at $498 per worker. This perfectly elastic supply curve, *s*, intersects the marginal revenue product curve at 12 workers per week. At the intersection, *E,* the wage rate is equal to the marginal revenue product. Equilibrium for the firm is obtained when the firm's demand curve for labor, which turns out to be its MRP curve, intersects the firm's supply curve for labor, shown as *s*. The firm in our example would not hire the thirteenth worker, who will add only $456 to revenue but $498 to cost. If the price of labor should fall to, say, $456 per worker, it would become profitable for the firm to hire an additional worker; there is an increase in the quantity of labor demanded as the wage decreases.

DERIVED DEMAND

Derived demand
Input factor demand derived from demand for the final product being produced.

We have identified an individual firm's demand for labor curve as its MRP curve. Under conditions of perfect competition in both product and labor markets, MRP is determined by multiplying MPP times the product's price. This suggests that the demand for labor is a **derived demand.** That is to say that our CD firm does not want to purchase the services of labor just for the services themselves. Factors of production are rented or purchased not because they give any intrinsic satisfaction to the firms' owners but because they can be used to manufacture output that is expected to be sold for profit.

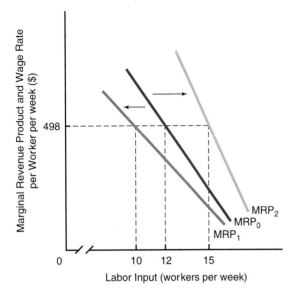

FIGURE 27-2

Demand for Labor, a Derived Demand

The demand for labor is derived from the demand for the final product being produced. Therefore, the marginal revenue product curve will shift whenever the price of the product changes. If we start with the marginal revenue product curve MRP at the going wage rate of $498 per week, 12 workers will be hired. If the price of CDs goes down, the marginal product curve will shift to MRP_1, and the number of workers hired will fall to 10. If the price of CDs goes up, the marginal revenue product curve will shift to MRP_2, and the number of workers hired will increase to 15.

We know that an increase in the market demand for a given product raises the product's price (all other things held constant), which in turn increases the marginal revenue product, or demand for the resource. Figure 27-2 illustrates the effective role played by changes in product demand in a perfectly competitive product market. The MRP curve shifts whenever there is a change in the price of the final product that the workers are making. If, for example, the market price of CDs goes down, the MRP curve will shift downward to the left from MRP_0 to MRP_1. We know that $MRP \equiv MPP \times MR$. If marginal revenue (here the output price) falls, so, too, does the demand for labor; at the same going wage rate, the firm will hire fewer workers. This is because at various levels of labor use, the marginal revenue product of labor falls so that at the initial equilibrium, the price of labor (here the MFC) becomes greater than MRP. Thus the firm would reduce the number of workers hired. Conversely, if the marginal revenue (output price) rises, the demand for labor will also rise, and the firm will want to hire more workers at each and every possible wage rate.

We just pointed out that $MRP \equiv MPP \times MR$. Clearly, then, a change in marginal productivity, or in the marginal physical product of labor, will shift the MRP curve. If the marginal productivity of labor decreases, the MRP curve, or demand curve, for labor will shift inward to the left. Again, this is because at every quantity of labor used, the MRP will be lower. A lower quantity of labor will be demanded at every possible wage rate.

THE MARKET DEMAND FOR LABOR

The downward-sloping portion of each individual firm's marginal revenue product curve is also its demand curve for the one variable factor of production—in our example, labor. When we go to the entire market for a particular type of labor in a particular industry, we find that quantity of labor demanded will vary as the wage rate changes. Given that the market demand curve for labor is made up of the individual firm demand curve for labor, we can safely assume that the market demand curve for labor will look like D in panel (b) of Figure 27-3: It will slope downward. That market demand curve for labor in the CD industry shows the quantities of labor demanded by all of the firms in the industry at various wage rates.

It is important to note that the market demand curve for labor is not a simple horizontal summation of the labor demand curves of all individual firms. Remember that the demand

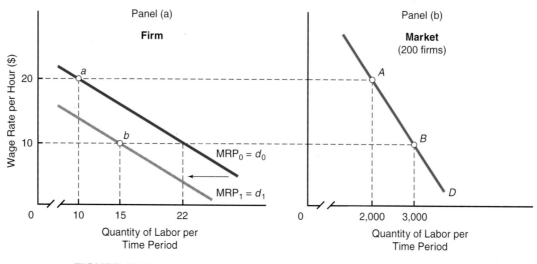

FIGURE 27-3

Derivation of the Market Demand Curve for Labor

The market demand curve for labor is not simply the horizontal summation of each individual firm's demand curve for labor. If wage rates fall from $20 to $10, all 200 firms will increase employment and therefore output, causing the price of the product to fall. This causes the marginal revenue product curve of each firm to shift inward, as from d_0 to d_1 in panel (a). The resulting market demand curve, D, in panel (b) is therefore less elastic than it would be if output price remained constant.

for labor is a derived demand. Even if we hold labor productivity constant, the demand for labor still depends on both the wage rate and the price of the final output. Assume that we start at a wage rate of $20 per hour and employment level 10 in panel (a) of Figure 27-3. If we sum all such employment levels—point a in panel (a)—across 200 firms, we get a market quantity demanded of 2,000—point A in panel (b)—at the wage rate of $20. A decrease in the wage rate to $10 per hour induces individual firms' employment level to increase toward a quantity demanded of 22. As all 200 firms simultaneously increase employment, however, there is a shift in the product supply curve such that output increases. Hence the price of the product must fall. The fall in the output price in turn causes a downward shift of each firm's MRP curve (d_0) to MRP_1 (d_1) in panel (a). Thus each firm's employment of labor increases to 15 rather than to 22 at the wage rate of $10 per hour. A summation of all such 200 employment levels gives us 3,000—point B—in panel (b).

DETERMINANTS OF DEMAND ELASTICITY FOR INPUTS

Just as we were able to discuss the price elasticity of demand for different commodities in Chapter 20, we can discuss the price elasticity of demand for inputs. The price elasticity of demand for labor is defined in a manner similar to the price elasticity of demand for goods: the percentage change in quantity demanded divided by the percentage change in the price of labor. When the numerical value of this ratio is less than 1, it is inelastic; when it is 1, unit-elastic; and when it is greater than 1, elastic.

There are four principal determinants of the price elasticity of demand for an input. The price elasticity of demand for a variable input will be greater:

1. The greater the price elasticity of demand for the final product
2. The easier it is for a particular variable input to be substituted for by other inputs

3. The larger the proportion of total costs accounted for by a particular variable input
4. The longer the time period being considered

Consider some examples. An individual radish farmer faces an extremely elastic demand for radishes, given the existence of many competing radish growers. If the farmer's laborers tried to obtain a significant wage increase, the farmer couldn't pass on the resultant higher costs to radish buyers. So any wage increase to the individual radish farmer would lead to a large reduction in the quantity of labor demanded.

Clearly, the easier it is for a producer to switch to using another factor of production, the more responsive that producer will be to an increase in an input's price. If plastic and aluminum can easily be substituted in the production of, say, car bumpers, then a price rise in aluminum will cause automakers to reduce greatly their quantity of aluminum demanded.

When a particular input's costs account for a very large share of total costs, any increase in that input's price will affect total costs relatively more. If labor costs are 80 percent of total costs, a company will cut back on employment more aggressively than if labor costs were only 8 percent of total costs, for any given wage increase.

Finally, over longer periods, firms have more time to figure out ways to economize on the use of inputs whose prices have gone up. Furthermore, over time, technological change will allow for easier substitution in favor of relatively cheaper inputs and against inputs whose prices went up. At first, a pay raise obtained by a strong telephone company union may not result in many layoffs, but over time, the telephone company will use new technology to replace many of the now more expensive workers.

CONCEPTS IN BRIEF

- The change in total output due to a one-unit change in one variable input, holding all other inputs constant, is called the marginal physical product (MPP). When we multiply marginal physical product times marginal revenue, we obtain the marginal revenue product (MRP).

- A firm will hire workers up to the point at which the additional cost of hiring one more worker is equal to the additional revenues generated. For the individual firm, therefore, its MRP of labor curve is also its demand for labor curve.

- The demand for labor is a derived demand, derived from the demand for final output. Therefore, if the price of final output changes, this will cause a shift in the MRP curve (which is also the firm's demand for labor curve).

- Input price elasticity of demand depends on final product elasticity, the ease of other input substitution, the relative importance of the input's cost in total costs, and the time allowed for adjustment.

WAGE DETERMINATION

Having developed the demand curve for labor (and all other variable inputs) in a particular industry, let's turn to the labor supply curve. By adding supply to the analysis, we can come up with the equilibrium wage rate that workers earn in an industry. We can think in terms of a supply curve for labor that slopes upward in a particular industry. At higher wage rates, more workers will want to enter that particular industry. The individual firm, however, does not face the entire *market* supply curve. Rather, in a perfectly competitive case, the indi-

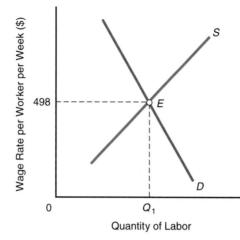

FIGURE 27-4

The Equilibrium Wage Rate and the CD Industry

The industry demand curve for labor is *D*. We put in a hypothetical upward-sloping labor supply curve for the CD industry, *S*. The intersection is at point *E*, giving an equilibrium wage rate of $498 per week and an equilibrium quantity of labor demanded of Q_1. At a price above $498 per week, there will be an excess quantity of workers supplied. At a price below $498 per week, there will be an excess quantity of workers demanded.

vidual firm is such a small part of the market that it can hire all the workers that it wants at the going wage rate. We say, therefore, that the industry faces an upward-sloping supply curve but that the individual *firm* faces a perfectly elastic supply curve for labor.

The demand curve for labor in the CD industry is *D* in Figure 27-4, and the supply curve of labor is *S*. The equilibrium wage rate of $498 a week is established at the intersection of the two curves. The quantity of workers both supplied and demanded at that rate is Q_1. If for some reason the wage rate fell to $400 a week, in our hypothetical example, there would be an excess number of workers demanded at that wage rate. Conversely, if the wage rate rose to $600 a week, there would be an excess quantity of workers supplied at that wage rate.

We have just found the equilibrium wage rate for the entire CD industry. The individual firm must take that equilibrium wage rate as given in the competitive model used here because the individual firm is a very small part of the total demand for labor. Thus each firm purchasing labor in a perfectly competitive market can purchase all of the input it wants at the going market price.

Exercise 27.1
Visit www.econtoday.com for more about labor markets.

POLICY EXAMPLE

Should the Minimum Wage Be Raised to Help Young People?

The equilibrium wage rate model shown in Figure 27-4 does not apply when the government sets a minimum wage rate below which employers are not allowed to pay workers and workers are not allowed to offer their services. Recall from Chapter 4 that in general, a minimum wage (if set above equilibrium) creates an excess quantity of labor supplied (a surplus) at that legal minimum. Thus young people probably would not be helped by an increase in minimum wages. Look at Figure 27-5 on page 614. There you see the unemployment rate for young people ages 16 to 19. As the minimum wage was raised starting in 1990, so did the rate of unemployment increase for young people. It started falling again only around 1992. Why? In part because what is important is the real, inflation-corrected minimum wage rate. In real terms, the minimum wage dropped to its lowest point in 45 years in 1989. Then it rose until 1992 and started falling again, exactly coincident with the reduction in the unemployment rate for young people. So to answer the policy question, raising the minimum wage probably would not help young people as a group, although it might help some young people who retain their jobs at the higher wage rate.

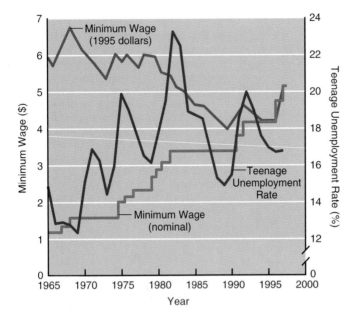

FIGURE 27-5

Teenage Unemployment and the Real Minimum Wage

Although the nominal minimum wage trends up, the real (inflation-corrected) minimum wage reached its peak in the late 1960s. The teenage unemployment rate is closely correlated with changes in the *real* minimum wage.

Source: U.S. Department of Labor, Bureau of Labor Statistics.

FOR CRITICAL ANALYSIS: Why are young people most affected by changes in the minimum wage? (Hint: Which workers have the lowest MRP?) ●

ALTERNATIVE THEORIES OF WAGE DETERMINATION: EFFICIENCY WAGES AND INSIDERS VERSUS OUTSIDERS

The relatively straightforward analysis of the supply and demand of labor just presented may not fully explain the equilibrium level of wages under certain circumstances. There are two important alternative theories of wage determination that may apply to at least some parts of the economy. We analyze those two theories now.

Efficiency Wages

Let's say that in the CD industry, employers can hire as many workers as they want at the equilibrium weekly wage rate of $498. Associated with that weekly wage rate is a specified amount of employment in each firm. Within each firm, though, there is turnover. Some workers quit to go on to other jobs. Turnover costs are significant. Workers have to be trained. What if a firm, even though it could hire workers at $498 a week, offered employment at $600 a week? Several things might occur. First, current employees would have less desire to look elsewhere to find better jobs. There would be less turnover. Second, those workers who applied for openings might be of higher quality, being attracted by the higher wage rate. Third, workers on the job might actually become more productive because they do not want to lose their jobs. They know that alternative competitive wages are $498 a week.

The higher-than-competitive wage rates offered by such a firm have been designated **efficiency wages.** The underlying assumption is that firms operate more efficiently if they pay their workers a higher wage rate.

Insiders and Outsiders

A related view of the labor market involves the notion of insiders within a firm. The insiders are those current employees who have the "inside track" and can maintain their posi-

Exercise 27.2
Visit www.econtoday.com for more about minimum wages.

Efficiency wages
Wages set above competitive levels to increase labor productivity and profits by enhancing the efficiency of the firm through lower turnover, ease of attracting higher-quality workers, and better efforts by workers.

tions because the firm would have to incur costs to replace them. These employee insiders are therefore able to exercise some control over the terms under which new employees (outsiders) are hired by the firm. They keep other potential workers out by not allowing them to offer themselves for work at a lower real wage rate than that being earned by the insiders. As pointed out earlier, the costs of hiring and firing workers are significant. Indeed, the cost of firing one worker may sometimes be relatively high: termination wages, retraining payments, and litigation if the worker believes termination was unjustified. All such costs might contribute to the development of insider-dominated labor markets. They contain significant barriers to entry by outsiders.

So the **insider-outsider theory** predicts that wages may remain higher than the standard supply and demand model would predict even though outsiders are willing to work at lower real wages.

Insider-outsider theory
A theory of labor markets in which workers who are already employed have an influence on wage bargaining in such a way that outsiders who are willing to work for lower real wages cannot get a job.

EXAMPLE
Competing for the Boss's Job

Although efficiency wage theory and the insider-outsider theory may explain wages that are somewhat above a competitive level, they have a harder time explaining really big differences in wages within a firm's management structure. CEOs tend to make many times more than vice-presidents do. Senior vice-presidents often make double what a regular vice-president makes. According to one theory, corporations create these big salary differentials, *not* in an attempt to reward the recipients, but rather to create a structure of powerful incentives to get people in the organization to work harder. Pay is based on *relative* performance, relative to one's peers within the management organization. The pay of a vice-president is not what motivates that vice-president; it is the pay of the CEO, to whose job the vice-president aspires. Economists Edward Lazer of Stanford University and Sherwin Rosen of the University of Chicago call this concept *tournament theory.* They argue that vice-presidents and others under them are involved in a series of tournaments. The winner of each tournament moves up to the next higher level. All aspire to the highest level, that of the CEO.

FOR CRITICAL ANALYSIS: If luck plays an unusually large role in a vice-president's rise to the top, will the pay differential between vice-presidents and the CEO have to be relatively large or small compared to a situation in which luck is not important? •

SHIFTS IN THE MARKET DEMAND FOR AND SUPPLY OF LABOR

Just as we discussed shifts in the supply curve and the demand curve for various products in Chapter 3, we can discuss the effects of shifts in supply and demand in labor markets.

Reasons for Labor Demand Curve Shifts

Many factors can cause the demand curve for labor to shift. We have already discussed a number of them. Clearly, because the demand for labor or any other variable input is a derived demand, the labor demand curve will shift if there is a shift in the demand for the final product. There are two other important determinants of the position of the demand curve for labor: changes in labor's productivity and changes in the price of related factors of production (substitutes and complements).

Changes in Demand for Final Product. The demand for labor or any other variable input is derived from the demand for the final product. The marginal revenue product is equal to marginal physical product times marginal revenue. Therefore, any change in the price of the final product will change MRP. This happened when we derived the market demand for labor. The general rule of thumb is as follows:

> **A change in the demand for the final product that labor (or any other variable input) is producing will shift the market demand curve for labor in the same direction.**

Changes in Labor Productivity. The second part of the MRP equation is MPP, which relates to labor productivity. We can surmise, then, that, other things being equal,

> **A change in labor productivity will shift the market labor demand curve in the same direction.**

Labor productivity can increase because labor has more capital or land to work with, because of technological improvements, or because labor's quality has improved. Such considerations explain why the real standard of living of workers in the United States is higher than in most countries. American workers generally work with a larger capital stock, have more natural resources, are in better physical condition, and are better trained than workers in many countries. Hence the demand for labor in America is, other things held constant, greater. Conversely, labor is relatively scarcer in the United States than it is in many other countries. One result of relatively greater demand and relatively smaller supply is a relatively higher wage rate.

EXAMPLE
Does It Pay to Go to College?

One way to increase labor productivity is to increase skill level. One way to do that, of course, is to go to college. Is there a big payoff? According to a recent study of identical twins carried out by economists Orley Ashenfelter and Alan Krueger, the answer is a resounding yes. They studied the earning patterns of more than 250 identical twins. In this manner, they were able to hold constant heredity, early home life, and so on. They focused on differences in the number of years of schooling. They discovered that each additional year of schooling increased wages almost 16 percent. Four years of college yielded a 67 percent increase in monthly wages compared to no college.

Some economists believe that a college degree is part of **labor market signaling.** Employers do not have much information about the future productivity of job applicants. Typically, the only way to find out is to observe someone working. Employers attempt to reduce the number of bad choices that they might make by using a job applicant's amount of higher education as a signal. According to the labor market signaling theory, even if higher education does not change productivity, it acts as an effective signal of greater individual abilities.

Labor market signaling
The process by which a potential worker's acquisition of credentials, such as a degree, is used by the employer to predict future productivity.

FOR CRITICAL ANALYSIS: Why does studying identical twins' earnings hold constant many of the factors that can determine differences in wages? ●

Change in the Price of Related Factors. Labor is not the only resource used. Some resources are substitutes and some are complements. If we hold output constant, we have the following general rule:

> **A change in the price of a substitute input will cause the demand for labor to change in the same direction. This is typically called the *substitution effect*.**

Note, however, that if the cost of production falls sufficiently, the firm will find it more profitable to produce and sell a larger output. If this so-called *output effect* is great enough, it will override the substitution effect just mentioned, and the firm will end up employing not only more of the relatively cheaper variable input but also more labor. This is exactly what happened for many years in the American automobile industry. Auto companies employed more machinery (capital), but employment continued to increase in spite of rising wage rates. The reason: Markets were expanding and the marginal physical productivity of labor was rising faster than its wage rate.

With respect to complements, we are referring to inputs that must be used jointly. Assume now that capital and labor are complementary. In general, we predict the following:

A change in the price of a complementary input will cause the demand for labor to change in the opposite direction.

If the cost of machines goes up but they must be used with labor, fewer machines will be purchased and therefore fewer workers will be used.

Determinants of the Supply of Labor

Exercise 27.3
Visit www.econtoday.com for more about immigration.

There are a number of reasons why labor supply curves will shift in a particular industry. For example, if wage rates for factory workers in the CD industry remain constant while wages for factory workers in the computer industry go up dramatically, the supply curve of factory workers in the CD industry will shift inward to the left as these workers shift to the computer industry.

Changes in working conditions in an industry can also affect its labor supply curve. If employers in the CD industry discover a new production technique that makes working conditions much more pleasant, the supply curve of labor to the CD industry will shift outward to the right.

Job flexibility also determines the position of the labor supply curve. For example, in an industry in which workers are allowed more flexibility, such as the ability to work at home via computer, the workers are likely to work more hours. That is to say, their supply curve will shift outward to the right. Some industries in which firms offer *job sharing*, particularly to people raising families, have found that the supply curve of labor has shifted outward to the right.

CONCEPTS IN BRIEF

- The individual competitive firm faces a perfectly elastic supply curve—it can buy all the labor it wants at the going market wage rate. The industry supply curve of labor slopes upward.

- By plotting an industrywide supply curve for labor and an industrywide demand curve for labor on the same coordinate system, we obtain the equilibrium wage rate in this industry.

- Efficiency wage theory predicts that wages paid above market wages may lead to high productivity because of lower turnover rates and better work effort by existing workers.

- The labor demand curve can shift because (1) the demand for the final product shifts, (2) labor productivity changes, or (3) the price of a related (substitute or complementary) factor of production changes.

MONOPOLY IN THE PRODUCT MARKET

So far we've considered only a perfectly competitive situation, both in selling the final product and in buying factors of production. We will continue our assumption that the firm purchases its factors of production in a perfectly competitive factor market. Now, however, we will assume that the firm sells its product in an *imperfectly* competitive output market. In other words, we are considering the output market structures of monopoly, oligopoly, and monopolistic competition. In all such cases, the firm, be it a monopolist, an oligopolist, or a monopolistic competitor, faces a downward-sloping demand curve for its product. Throughout the rest of this chapter, we will simply refer to a monopoly output situation for ease of analysis. The analysis holds for all industry structures that are less than perfectly competitive. In any event, the fact that our firm now faces a downward-sloping demand curve for its product means that if it wants to sell more of its product (at a uniform price), it has to lower the price, *not just on the last unit, but on all preceding units.* The *marginal revenue* received from selling an additional unit is continuously falling (and is less than price) as the firm attempts to sell more and more. This is certainly different from our earlier discussions in this chapter in which the firm could sell all it wanted at a constant price. Why? Because the firm we discussed until now was a perfect competitor.

Constructing the Monopolist's Input Demand Curve

In reconstructing our demand schedule for an input, we must account for the facts that (1) the marginal *physical* product falls because of the law of diminishing returns as more workers are added and (2) the price (and marginal revenue) received for the product sold also falls as more is produced and sold. That is, for the monopolist, we have to account for both the diminishing marginal physical product and the diminishing marginal revenue. Marginal revenue is always less than price for the monopolist. The marginal revenue curve is always below the downward-sloping demand curve.

Marginal revenue for the perfect competitor is equal to the price of the product because all units can be sold at the going market price. In our CD example, we assumed that the perfect competitor could sell all it wanted at $6 per compact disc. A one-unit change in sales always led to a $6 change in total revenues. Hence marginal revenue was always equal to $6 for that perfect competitor.

The monopolist, however, cannot simply calculate marginal revenue by looking at the price of the product. To sell the additional output from an additional unit of input, the monopolist has to cut prices on all previous units of output. As output is increasing, then, marginal revenue is falling. The underlying concept is, of course, the same for both the perfect competitor and the monopolist. We are asking exactly the same question in both cases: When an additional worker is hired, what is the benefit? In either case, the benefit is obviously the change in total revenues due to the one-unit change in the variable input, labor. In our discussion of the perfect competitor, we were able simply to look at the marginal physical product and multiply it by the *constant* per-unit price of the product because the price of the product never changed (for the perfect competitor, $P = \text{MR}$).

A single monopolist ends up hiring fewer workers than all of the competitive firms added together. To see this, we must calculate the marginal revenue product for the monopolist. To make it simple, we will look at it as simply the change in total revenues due to a one-unit change in the labor input for a monopolist. This is what we do in panel (a) of Figure 27-6, which shows the change in total revenues. Column 6, headed "Marginal Revenue

Panel (a)

(1)	(2)	(3)	(4)	(5)	(6)
	Total Physical Product (TPP)	Marginal Physical Product (MPP)	Price of Product	Total Revenue (TR)	Marginal Revenue Product (MRP_m)
Labor Input (workers per week)	CDs per week	CDs per week	(P)	$= (2) \times (4)$	$= \dfrac{\text{Change in (5)}}{\text{Change in (1)}}$
7	1,000		$8.00	$ 8,000.00	
		111			$665.80
8	1,111		7.80	8,665.80	
		104			568.20
9	1,215		7.60	9,234.00	
		97			474.80
10	1,312		7.40	9,708.80	
		90			385.60
11	1,402		7.20	10,094.40	
		83			300.60
12	1,485		7.00	10,395.00	
		76			219.80
13	1,561		6.80	10,614.80	

FIGURE 27-6

A Monopolist's Marginal Revenue Product

The monopolist hires just enough workers to make marginal revenue product equal to the going wage rate. If the going wage rate is $498 per week, as shown by the labor supply curve, *s*, the monopolist would want to hire between 9 and 10 workers per week. That is the profit-maximizing amount of labor. The MRP curve for the perfect competitor from Figure 27-1 is also plotted (MRP_c). The monopolist's MRP curve will always be less elastic than it would be if marginal revenue were constant.

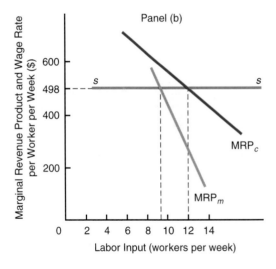

Product," gives the monopolistic firm a quantitative notion of how profitable additional workers and additional production actually are. The marginal revenue product curve for this monopolist has been plotted in panel (b) of the figure. To emphasize the steeper slope of the monopolist's MRP curve, MRP_m, the MRP curve for the perfect competitor in Figure 27-1, labeled MRP_c, has been plotted on the same graph.

Why does MRP_m represent the monopolist's input demand curve? As always, our profit-maximizing monopolist will continue to hire labor as long as additional profits result. Profits are made as long as the additional cost of more workers is outweighed by the additional revenues made from selling the output of those workers. When the wage rate equals these additional revenues, the monopolist stops hiring. That is, it stops hiring when the wage rate is equal to the marginal revenue product because additional workers would add more to cost than to revenue.

Why the Monopolist Hires Fewer Workers

Because we have used the same numbers as in Figure 27-1, we can see that the monopolist hires fewer worker-weeks than the perfect competitor. That is to say, if we could magically change the CD industry in our example from one in which there is perfect competition in the output market to one in which there is monopoly in the output market, the amount of employment would fall. Why? Because the monopolist must take account of the declining product price that must be charged in order to sell a larger number of CDs. Remember that every firm hires up to the point at which marginal benefit equals marginal cost. The marginal benefit to the monopolist of hiring an additional worker is not simply the additional output times the price of the product. Rather, the monopolist faces a reduction in the price charged on all units sold in order to be able to sell more. So the monopolist ends up hiring fewer workers than all of the perfect competitors taken together, assuming that all other factors remain the same for the two hypothetical examples. But this should not come as a surprise. In considering product markets, by implication we saw that a monopolized CD industry would produce less output than a competitive one. Therefore, the monopolized CD industry would want fewer workers.

OTHER FACTORS OF PRODUCTION

The analysis in this chapter has been given in terms of the demand for the variable input labor. The same analysis holds for any other variable factor input. We could have talked about the demand for fertilizer or the demand for the services of tractors by a farmer instead of the demand for labor and reached the same conclusions. The entrepreneur will hire or buy any variable input up to the point at which its price equals the marginal revenue product.

A further question remains: How much of each variable factor should the firm use when all the variable factors are combined to produce the product? We can answer this question by looking at either the profit-maximizing side of the question or the cost-minimizing side.[1]

Profit Maximization Revisited

If a firm wants to maximize profits, how much of each factor should be hired (or bought)? As we just saw, the firm will never hire a factor of production unless the marginal benefit from hiring that factor is at least equal to the marginal cost. What is the marginal benefit? As we have pointed out several times, the marginal benefit is the change in total revenues due to a one-unit change in use of the variable input. What is the marginal cost? In the case of a firm buying in a competitive market, it is the price of the variable factor—the wage rate if we are referring to labor.

---

[1]Many economic problems involving maximization of profit or other economic variables have *duals,* or precise restatements, in terms of *minimization* rather than maximization. The problem "How do we maximize our output, given fixed resources?" for example, is the dual of the problem "How do we minimize our cost, given fixed output?" Noneconomists sometimes confuse their discussions of economic issues by mistakenly believing that a problem and its dual are two problems rather than one. Asking, for example, "How can we maximize our profits while minimizing our costs?" makes about as much sense as asking, "How can we cross the street while getting to the other side?"

Capital Substitution Threatens Jobs

Every time there is an improvement in capital productivity, the media figure out ways to discuss the resultant loss of employment because of capital substitution. In the absence of restrictions in the labor market, though, capital substitution simply means that in a particular firm or industry, more capital is used and less labor. There are two additional factors to consider: (1) What about the workers used to make the additional capital? Won't there be increases in employment in the capital-producing industries? (2) The economy is not just machines versus workers. Even though the number of employees in manufacturing in the United States has dropped because of capital substitution, the number of employees in service industries, such as software programming, has greatly increased. The U.S. economy has added over 50 million jobs since 1970 despite machines having replaced many workers.

The profit-maximizing combination of resources for the firm will be where, in a perfectly competitive situation,

$$\text{MRP of labor} = \text{price of labor (wage rate)}$$
$$\text{MRP of land} = \text{price of land (rental rate per unit)}$$
$$\text{MRP of capital} = \text{price of capital (cost per unit of service)}$$

Alternatively, we can express this profit-maximizing rule as

$$\frac{\text{MRP of labor}}{\text{Price of labor}} = \frac{\text{MRP of land}}{\text{price of land}} = \frac{\text{MRP of capital}}{\text{price of capital}}$$

The marginal revenue product of each of a firm's resources must be exactly equal to its price. If the MRP of labor were \$20 and its price were only \$15, the firm would be underemploying labor.

Cost Minimization

From the cost minimization point of view, how can the firm minimize its total costs for a given output? Assume that you are an entrepreneur attempting to minimize costs. Consider a hypothetical situation in which if you spend \$1 more on labor, you would get 20 more units of output, but if you spend \$1 more on machines, you would get only 10 more units of output. What would you want to do in such a situation? Most likely you would wish to hire more workers or sell off some of your machines, for you are not getting as much output per last dollar spent on machines as you are per last dollar spent on labor. You would want to employ factors of production so that the marginal products per last dollar spent on each are equal. Thus the least-cost, or cost minimization, rule will be as follows:

To minimize total costs for a particular rate of production, the firm will hire factors of production up to the point at which the marginal physical product per last dollar spent on each factor of production is equalized.

That is,

$$\frac{\text{MPP of labor}}{\text{Price of labor (wage rate)}} = \frac{\text{MPP of capital}}{\text{price of capital (cost per unit of service)}} = \frac{\text{MPP of land}}{\text{price of land (rental rate per unit)}}$$

All we are saying here is that the profit-maximizing firm will always use *all* resources in such combinations that cost will be minimized for any given output rate. This is commonly called the *least-cost combination of resources*. There is an exact relationship between the profit-maximizing combination of resources and the least-cost combination of resources. In other words, either rule can be used to yield the same cost-minimizing rate of use of each variable resource.[2]

---

[2]This can be proved as follows: Profit maximization requires that the price of every input must equal that input's marginal revenue product (the general case). Let i be the input. Then $P_i = \text{MRP}_i$. But MRP_i is equal to marginal revenue times marginal physical product of the input. Therefore, $P_i = \text{MR} \times \text{MPP}_i$. If we divide both sides by MPP_i, we get $P_i/\text{MPP}_i = \text{MR}$. If we take the reciprocal, we obtain $\text{MPP}_i/P_i = 1/\text{MR}$. That is another way of stating our cost minimization rule.

INTERNATIONAL EXAMPLE
Why Are European Businesses Using More Robots and Fewer Workers than U.S. Businesses?

What a strange world we live in, you might say. European countries are experiencing the highest levels of unemployment since the Great Depression. Typical unemployment rates exceed 10 percent throughout the European Union; they are near 13 percent in France and Italy and well over 15 percent in Spain. Compare this with the below 5 percent unemployment rate in the United States, and you can tell that Europe is in trouble. One would expect, therefore, that European firms could easily replace capital with labor and that there would be general pressure toward lower wages. The opposite has occurred. For example, in Germany, department stores use robots in shoe storerooms to seek out the shoes that a salesperson wants. In Denmark, milk warehouses have gone robotic. All in all, the market for automated systems in Europe has grown by more than 10 percent a year, a much greater rate than in the United States. The reason is that businesses in Europe have figured out that it is cheaper to use robots than people. In Germany, an industrial robot costs about $10 an hour to operate. An industrial worker may cost as much as $37 an hour. And while compensation to workers has continued to rise in Germany and elsewhere since the early 1990s, the operating costs of robots have fallen.

There are many reasons why wages remain so high in spite of massive unemployment in Europe. First of all, minimum wages there may be as much as 50 percent higher than in the United States. And social security contributions that employers have to pay for each worker often equal or even exceed the wages that the worker takes home. In addition, a firm must pay significant severance penalties if it fires a worker. Finally, many workers will not take low-paying jobs in some European countries because they are actually better off receiving unemployment and welfare benefits.

FOR CRITICAL ANALYSIS: Why have robots not taken over many jobs in the United States? •

CONCEPTS IN BRIEF

- When a firm sells its output in a monopoly market, marginal revenue is less than price.

- Just as the MRP is the perfectly competitive firm's input demand curve, the MRP is also the monopolist's demand curve.

- For a less than perfectly competitive firm, the profit-maximizing combination of factors will occur where each factor is used up to the point where its MRP is equal to its unit price.

- To minimize total costs for a given output, the profit-maximizing firm will hire each factor of production up to the point where the marginal physical product per last dollar spent on each factor is equal to the marginal physical product per last dollar spent on each of the other factors of production.

This worker is being taught how to use a computerized training program which will reduce her learning time by a significant amount. Who may be hurt by such software?

Software May Be Reducing the Skill Levels Required for Many White-Collar Jobs

CONCEPTS APPLIED:

INPUT SUBSTITUTES, DEMAND FOR LABOR, VALUE OF MARGINAL PRODUCT, DERIVED DEMAND

Visit www.econtoday.com for an Internet Activity that expands your understanding of these concepts.

Let's say that you are a high school graduate but have not yet completed college. You answer a help-wanted ad from a local large corporation. When you interview for the job, the prospective employer does not ask you about any previous experience. Rather, the manager simply asks whether you would like a job selling a very complicated product. You say that you would love it, but you do not have any special training. The interviewer responds that you do not need it, for the company has a computerized training program that will teach you everything you need to know. You might end up making a lot more income than you ever thought you would.

Training Software: The Key to Expanding Job Opportunities

The scenario just outlined is not so far-fetched. In the early 1990s, a new type of software, known as electronic performance support systems, or EPSS, was developed. What sets this software apart is that it can automate many job-related mental skills as well as provide quick instructions to help users make human judgments that are still necessary for many jobs.

EPSS software was first used in blue-collar jobs. Chrysler mechanics use it to diagnose car troubles. Another use for EPSS software is in clerical jobs. Avis Rental Car Company's agents use it for navigating through paperwork and pricing decisions for leasing cars. Another field that is now making extensive use of EPSS software is the travel industry. Much of the specialized knowledge that travel agents have always had to learn in order to make plane reservations by computer is now irrelevant. All they need to use is the EPSS-based program.

Reduced Training Time and Fewer Needed Skills

In essence, the new EPSS software reduces the skill levels needed for many jobs. In addition, it reduces training time. A good example is the securities industry. The National Association of Securities Dealers (NASD) has reduced the training time required to conduct an audit of a securities firm. If you have ever used some of the household finance software, such as Quicken, produced by Intuit, you have an idea of how EPSS programs can make a difficult task seem simple. The program uses step-by-step instructions on the information and procedures that are needed to perform a securities firm audit. The results? Whereas it used to take 30 months to train a fully competent securities firm auditor, it now takes about 12.

A Boon to Less Skilled Workers

Clearly, if the new software can train someone with little experience, more highly trained workers have a smaller advantage than before. Lexus Car Company, for example, provides interactive training both in the technical features of its cars and in techniques for selling them. It has not shied away from hiring individuals with no previous sales or automobile experience, for it has found that the EPSS program it uses can make them into quality salespeople in short order.

The Rand Corporation of Santa Monica, California, has even developed an EPSS program to train some of the high-priced consultants who work for the big accounting firms, such as Price Waterhouse. Once this program is completed, it will offer all Price Waterhouse consultants—

experienced or not—information on companies and markets. This information typically takes years for an individual consultant to develop.

Smaller Premium for Experience

A possible result of EPSS systems is a reduction in the wage differentials that experienced workers currently earn. If a junior worker can obtain all the information quickly that the experienced worker has taken years to acquire, the experienced worker will not be significantly more valuable to the firm. If pay is a function of performance, the newly hired employee may quickly catch up with "old hands."

Increased Substitution of Software for Labor

While the computer revolution increases the use of labor in one sector of the economy, at the same time it may reduce employment in other sectors. In particular, accounting software (capital) is replacing certified public accountants (labor) at an increasing rate. Accounting software has become more widespread, less costly, easier to use, and more sophisticated during the past several years. Nonetheless, the number of certified accountants has risen virtually every year since 1970. Given stable demand, we might predict that the relative salaries of CPAs should therefore fall in the future (all other things held constant).

The same analysis holds for attorneys. Legal software has proliferated, become more sophisticated yet easier to use, and dropped in price. Consequently, paralegals are now able to do many of the jobs that lawyers used to do. Not surprisingly, the paralegal profession is expanding rapidly, while the growth in the number of attorneys is starting to slow down.

FOR CRITICAL ANALYSIS

1. Computers have been around for a long time, so why has it taken so long for EPSS systems to be developed?
2. What do you predict will happen to the so-called higher education premium over the next decade?

CHAPTER SUMMARY

1. In a competitive situation in which the firm is a very small part of the entire product and labor market, the firm will want to hire workers up to the point at which the marginal revenue product just equals the going wage rate.
2. The marginal revenue product curve for the individual competitive firm is the input demand curve. The competitive firm hires up to the point at which the wage rate equals the MRP.
3. The summation of all the MRP curves does not equal the market demand curve for labor. The market demand curve for labor is less elastic than the sum of the MRP curves because as more workers are hired,

output is increased and the price of the product must fall, lowering the MRP.
4. The demand for labor is derived from the demand for the product produced.
5. The elasticity of demand for an input is a function of several determinants, including the elasticity of demand for the final product. Moreover, the price elasticity of demand for a variable input will usually be larger in the long run than it is in the short run because there is time for adjustment.
6. The firm buying labor in a perfectly competitive labor market faces a perfectly elastic supply curve at the going wage rate because the firm can hire all it

wants at that wage rate. The industry supply curve of labor slopes upward.

7. Efficiency wage theory predicts that wages paid above market wages may lead to high productivity because of lower turnover rates and better work effort by existing workers.

8. The demand curve for labor will shift if (a) the demand for final product shifts, (b) labor productivity changes, or (c) the price of a substitute or a complementary factor of production changes.

9. The MRP curve is also the monopolist's input demand curve. Because marginal revenue is less than the price of the product for a monopolist, the monopolist's input demand curve is steeper.

10. A firm minimizes total costs by equating the ratio of marginal physical product of labor divided by the price of labor with the ratio of marginal physical product of machines to the price of capital with all other such ratios for all the different factors of production. This is the mirror of profit maximization.

DISCUSSION OF PREVIEW QUESTIONS

1. **When hiring labor, what general rule will be followed by employers who wish to maximize profits?**

   Employers who wish to maximize total profits will hire labor (or any other factor of production) up to the point at which the marginal cost of doing so equals the marginal benefit, MB. In that way, they will have used up all instances in which the marginal benefit of hiring labor exceeds the marginal cost, MC, of hiring labor. If MB > MC, they will hire more labor; if MB < MC, they will hire less; when MB = MC, they will be maximizing total profits.

2. **What is the profit-maximizing rate of employment for a perfectly competitive firm?**

   The perfectly competitive firm will accept prevailing wage rates; it can hire as much labor as it wishes at the going rate. It follows that the MC of hiring labor to the perfectly competitive firm is a constant that is equal to the prevailing wage rate; $MC = W$, where W is the market wage rate. The MB of hiring labor is the value of the marginal product of an additional unit of labor. The perfectly competitive firm will maximize total profits by hiring labor up to the point at which it drives the MRP down to equal the constant wage rate: $MRP = W$. This is also how the firm minimizes costs for a given output.

3. **What is the profit-maximizing rate of employment for an imperfectly competitive firm?**

   For an imperfectly competitive firm, $P > MR$. Thus in the short run the marginal benefit of hiring addi-

   tional units of labor falls for two reasons: (a) The law of diminishing returns causes marginal physical product to diminish, and (b) to increase sales, price must fall—on previously produced units as well as the new one. Thus the MB of hiring labor equals the *marginal revenue* times the marginal physical product of labor: $MB = MRP = MR \times MPP$.

   By assumption, the imperfectly competitive firm is a competitor in the input markets, so in hiring labor it (like the perfect competitor) faces a constant marginal cost equal to the going wage rate; $MC = W$ for the imperfectly competitive firm too. What about the profit-maximizing rate of employment for the imperfectly competitive firm? It hires up to the point at which it drives down the marginal revenue product of labor ($MRP = MR \times MPP$) until it equals the going wage rate; $MRP = W$ is the equilibrium condition in this model.

4. **How is an industry wage rate determined?**

   Wage rates are a price; they are the price of labor. As such, wage rates are determined like all prices, by the forces of supply and demand. The market, or industry, wage rate will be determined by the point of intersection of the industry supply of labor curve and the industry demand for labor curve. At the point of intersection, the quantity of labor supplied equals the quantity of labor demanded, and equilibrium exists; both buyers and sellers are able to realize their intentions.

PROBLEMS

(Answers to the odd-numbered problems appear at the back of the book.)

27-1. Assume that the product in the table is sold by a perfectly competitive firm for $2 per unit.

    a. Use the information in the table to derive a demand schedule for labor.

    b. What is the most that this firm would be willing to pay each worker if five workers were hired?

    c. If the going salary for this quality labor is $200 per week, how many workers will be hired?

Quantity of Labor	Total Product per Week	MPP	MRP
1	250	_____	$ _____
2	450	_____	_____
3	600	_____	_____
4	700	_____	_____
5	750	_____	_____
6	750	_____	_____

27-2. The table presents some production function data for a firm in which the only variable input is capital; the labor input is fixed. First fill in the other columns. What quantity of capital will the firm use if the price of capital is $90 per machine-week? If the price of capital is $300 per machine-week, what quantity of capital will the firm use? Explain.

27-3. The accompanying graph indicates labor supply and demand in the construction industry.

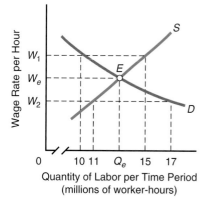

    a. When wage rates are W_1 per hour, how many worker-hours do workers intend to offer per unit?

    b. How much do businesses intend to buy at this wage rate?

    c. Which group can realize its intentions, and which can't?

    d. What forces will be set in motion at wage rate W_1, given a free market for labor?

27-4. Using the graph in Problem 27-3, answer the following questions.

    a. At wage rate W_2, how many worker-hours do workers intend to offer?

Quantity of Capital (machine-weeks)	Total Product per Week	Marginal Product of Capital per Week	Marginal Revenue (product price) per Unit	Marginal Revenue Product per Week
0	0 _____	_____	$10	$ _____
1	25 _____	_____	10	_____
2	45 _____	_____	10	_____
3	60 _____	_____	10	_____
4	70 _____	_____	10	_____
5	75 _____	_____	10	_____

b. At W_2, how many worker-hours do businesses intend to purchase?

c. Which group can realize its intentions, and which can't?

d. What forces will be set in motion at W_2 if a free market for labor exists in this industry?

e. What will the equilibrium wage rate be?

27-5. The price elasticity of demand for the final output product directly affects the elasticity of demand for the input factor. Why?

27-6. Suppose that you are seeking to maximize output for a given outlay. If the marginal physical product of input x is 10 and that of input y is 20, and the prices of the two inputs are $3 and $7, respectively, how should you alter your input mix in order to increase output and profit?

27-7. Suppose that you are a monopolist and labor is the only variable input you employ. You are currently producing 150 units of output and selling them for $20 apiece. You are considering the possibility of hiring an additional full-time employee. You estimate that daily output would increase to 160 units if you hired this additional person and that you would be able to sell all of those units at a price of $19 each. What is the MRP of labor (per worker-day)? Assuming that you take the price of labor as a given, what is the maximum daily wage that would make it in your interest to hire this additional employee?

27-8. When there is only one variable input, how does a monopoly seller's demand for that input differ from that of a perfectly competitive seller?

27-9. Assume that you have graduated from college. You decide to look for a job rather than go for further schooling. Indicate how the following criteria might affect the salary that you will receive and the type of job you may end up taking after you graduate.

a. You want to stay near your family, so you do not consider moving out of your immediate geographic area to find a job.

b. You look only for jobs that allow you to apply the knowledge and skills you have learned in your college major.

c. You now live in the city but decide that you will only work in a rural area.

COMPUTER-ASSISTED INSTRUCTION

We explore the foundations of the demand for and the supply of labor, along the way demonstrating the consequences of the minimum wage.

Complete problem and answer appear on disk.

INTERACTING WITH THE INTERNET

For more information on the minimum wage, go to

www.dol.gov/dol/esa/public/minwage/q-a.htm

You can access the minimum wage hotline at

www.dir.ca.gov/DIR/Labor_law/DLSE/Rights/Minimum_Wage.html

CHAPTER 28

UNIONS AND LABOR MARKET MONOPOLY POWER

The average worker in America does not belong to a labor union. Indeed, as you will read in this chapter, labor unions have been losing much of their importance in the U.S. labor market. Nonetheless, some labor unions still have enough clout to bring at least part of the American economy to a halt. This is exactly what happened a few years ago when the Teamsters union called for a strike of its workers against United Parcel Service (UPS). That strike was a success, according to many commentators. Was it in fact a successful strike? And if so, did its success portend the revival of the American labor movement? Before you answer these questions, you need to know about monopoly power in the market for labor.

PREVIEW QUESTIONS

1. What are the major types of unions?
2. What do unions seek to maximize?
3. Do unions help workers?
4. What is a monopsonist, and how does one determine its profit-maximizing employment rate?

Labor unions
Worker organizations that seek to secure economic improvements for their members; they also seek to improve the safety, health, and other benefits (such as job security) of their members.

Craft unions
Labor unions composed of workers who engage in a particular trade or skill, such as baking, carpentry, or plumbing.

Collective bargaining
Bargaining between the management of a company or of a group of companies and the management of a union or a group of unions for the purpose of setting a mutually agreeable contract on wages, fringe benefits, and working conditions for all employees in all the unions involved.

Did You Know That . . . in 1971, some 2.5 million workers were involved in strikes, but in the past few years, fewer than 250,000 have been involved? More than 12 times the number of workdays were lost to strikes in the 1950s than are lost to them today. The labor landscape has been changing in the United States. That does not mean that concerted activity on the part of groups of workers is insignificant in our economy, though. Some workers are able to earn more than they would in a competitive labor market because they have obtained a type of monopoly power. These are members of effective **labor unions,** workers' organizations that seek to secure economic improvements for their members. In forming unions, a certain monopoly element enters into the supply of labor equation. That is because we can no longer talk about a perfectly competitive labor supply situation when active and effective unions bargain as a single entity with management. The entire supply of a particular group of workers is controlled by a single source. Later in the chapter, we will examine the converse—a single employer who is the sole user of a particular group of workers.

THE AMERICAN LABOR MOVEMENT

The American labor movement started with local **craft unions.** These were groups of workers in individual trades, such as shoemaking, printing, or baking. Initially, in the United States, laborers struggled for the right to band together to bargain as a unit. In the years between the Civil War and the Great Depression (1861–1930s), the Knights of Labor, an organized group of both skilled and unskilled workers, demanded an eight-hour workday, equal pay for women and men, and the replacement of free enterprise with the socialist system. In 1886, a dissident group from the Knights of Labor formed the American Federation of Labor (AFL) under the leadership of Samuel Gompers. Until World War I, the government supported business's opposition to unions by offering the use of police personnel to break strikes. During World War I, the image of the unions improved and membership increased to more than 5 million. But after the war, the government decided to stop protecting labor's right to organize. Membership began to fall.

Then came the Great Depression. Franklin Roosevelt's National Industrial Recovery Act of 1933 gave labor the federal right to bargain collectively, but that act was declared unconstitutional. The 1935 National Labor Relations Act (NLRA), otherwise known as the Wagner Act, took its place. The NLRA guaranteed workers the right to start unions, to engage in **collective bargaining** (bargaining between management and representatives of all union members), and to be members in any union that was started.

INTERNATIONAL EXAMPLE
European Merchant Guilds, the Original Craft Unions

The origin of today's modern craft unions is found in a type of association that flourished in continental Europe and England during the Middle Ages. Around the eleventh century, merchants started traveling from market to market in a caravan to protect themselves from bandits. The members of the caravan elected a leader whose rules they pledged to obey. The name of such a caravan was *Gilde* in the Germanic countries of Europe. When the members of the caravan returned home, they frequently stayed in close association. They soon found it beneficial to seek exclusive rights to a particular trade from a feudal lord or, later, from the city government itself. Soon merchant guilds obtained a monopoly over an industry and its related commerce in a city. It supervised the crafts and the wholesale and retail selling of commodities manufactured in that city. Nonmember merchants were not allowed to sell goods at retail and were subject to many restrictions from which members of the guild were exempt.

FOR CRITICAL ANALYSIS: *Analyze the medieval guild in terms of the insider-outsider theory presented in Chapter 27.* •

Industrial Unions

In 1938, the Congress of Industrial Organizations (CIO) was formed by John L. Lewis, the president of the United Mine Workers. Prior to the formation of the CIO, most labor organizations were craft unions. The CIO was composed of **industrial unions** such as the Knights of Labor—unions with membership from an entire industry such as steel or automobiles. In 1955, the CIO and the AFL merged. Organized labor's failure to grow at a continuing rapid rate caused leadership in both associations to seek the merger.

Three important industrial unions declared in the summer of 1995 that they, too, planned to merge. By the beginning of the twenty-first century, the United Auto Workers, the United Steelworkers of America, and the International Association of Machinists will have formed a single industrial union with nearly 2 million members.

Congressional Control over Labor Unions

Since the Great Depression, Congress has occasionally altered the relationship between labor and management through significant legislation. One of the most important pieces of legislation was the Taft-Hartley Act of 1947 (the Labor Management Relations Act). Among other things, it allows individual states to pass their own **right-to-work laws.** A right-to-work law makes it illegal for union membership to be a requirement for continued employment in any establishment.

More specifically, the act makes a **closed shop** illegal; a closed shop requires union membership before employment can be obtained. A **union shop,** however, is legal; a union shop does not require membership as a prerequisite for employment, but it can, and usually does, require that workers join the union after a specified amount of time on the job. (Even a union shop is illegal in states with right-to-work laws.)

Jurisdictional disputes, sympathy strikes, and secondary boycotts are made illegal by this act as well. A **jurisdictional dispute** involves two or more unions fighting (and striking) over which should have control in a particular jurisdiction. For example, should a carpenter working for a steel manufacturer be part of the steelworkers' union or the carpenters' union? A **sympathy strike** occurs when one union strikes in sympathy with another union's cause or strike. For example, if the retail clerks' union in an area is striking grocery stores, Teamsters may refuse to deliver products to those stores in sympathy with the retail clerks' demands for higher wages or better working conditions. A **secondary boycott** is the boycotting of a company that deals with a struck company. For example, if union workers strike a baking company, the boycotting of grocery stores that continue to sell that company's products is a secondary boycott. The secondary boycott brings pressure on third parties to force them to stop dealing with an employer who is being struck.

In general, the Taft-Hartley Act outlawed unfair labor practices of unions, such as make-work rules and forcing unwilling workers to join a particular union. Perhaps the most famous aspect of the Taft-Hartley Act is its provision that the president can obtain a court

Exercise 28.1
Visit www.econtoday.com for more about the AFL–CIO.

Industrial unions
Labor unions that consist of workers from a particular industry, such as automobile manufacturing or steel manufacturing.

Right-to-work laws
Laws that make it illegal to require union membership as a condition of continuing employment in a particular firm.

Closed shop
A business enterprise in which employees must belong to the union before they can be hired and must remain in the union after they are hired.

Union shop
A business enterprise that allows the hiring of nonunion members, conditional on their joining the union by some specified date after employment begins.

Jurisdictional dispute
A dispute involving two or more unions over which should have control of a particular jurisdiction, such as a particular craft or skill or a particular firm or industry.

Sympathy strike
A strike by a union in sympathy with another union's strike or cause.

Secondary boycott
A boycott of companies or products sold by companies that are dealing with a company being struck.

Exercise 28.2

Visit www.econtoday.com for more about the labor movement.

injunction that will stop a strike for an 80-day cooling-off period if the strike is expected to imperil the nation's safety or health.

The Current Status of Labor Unions

If you look at Figure 28-1, you can see that organized labor's heyday occurred from the 1940s through the 1970s. Since then, union membership has fallen almost every year. Currently, it is hovering around 15 percent of the civilian labor force. If you remove labor unions in the public sector—federal, state, and local government workers—private sector union membership in the United States is only about 11 percent of the civilian labor force.

Part of the explanation for the decline in union membership has to do with the shift away from manufacturing. Unions were always strongest in so-called blue-collar jobs. In 1948, workers in goods-producing industries, transportation, and utilities constituted 51.2 percent of private nonagricultural employment. Today that number is only 25 percent. Manufacturing jobs account for only 16 percent of all employment. In addition, persistent illegal immigration has weakened the power of unions. Much of the unskilled and typically nonunionized work in the United States is done by foreign-born workers, some of whom are undocumented. They are unlikely targets for union organizers.

FIGURE 28-1

Decline in Union Membership

Numerically, union membership in the United States has increased dramatically since the 1930s, but as a percentage of the labor force, union membership peaked around 1960 and has been falling ever since. Most recently, the absolute number of union members has also diminished.

Sources: L. Davis et al., *American Economic Growth* (New York: HarperCollins, 1972), p. 220; U.S. Department of Labor, Bureau of Labor Statistics. 1996 data estimated.

The deregulation of certain industries has also led to a decline in unionism. More intense competition in formally regulated industries, such as the airlines, has led to a movement toward nonunionized labor. Finally, increased labor force participation by women has led to a decline in union importance. Women have traditionally been less inclined to join unions than their male counterparts.

 INTERNATIONAL EXAMPLE
Europe's Management-Labor Councils

Unionization rates are much higher in the European Union (EU) than in the United States, averaging 48 percent. Perhaps more important, most EU countries have institutionalized the concept of *management-labor councils*. In Germany, legislation dating back to the early 1950s created such councils, requiring that management and labor reach decisions jointly and unanimously. German management-labor councils use up a significant amount of management time. At H. C. Asmussen, a small German distilling company with 300 workers, there are five work councils, some of which meet weekly.

On a pan-European basis, an EU directive has forced 1,500 of the European Union's largest companies to set up Europe-wide worker-management consultative committees. In the United States, no such legislation exists, although there is a management desire to create more "quality circles" (to improve quality and to reduce costs) that involve workers and management. These are often used as a threat to unions or even a substitute for them. In fact, some American unions have succeeded in getting the federal government, through the National Labor Relations Board, to disband such quality circles.

FOR CRITICAL ANALYSIS: Why do you think American unions might be against quality circles involving management and workers? ●

CONCEPTS IN BRIEF

- The American Federation of Labor (AFL), composed of craft unions, was formed in 1886 under the leadership of Samuel Gompers. Membership increased until after World War I, at which time the government temporarily stopped protecting labor's right to organize.

- During the Great Depression, legislation was passed that allowed for collective bargaining. The National Labor Relations Act of 1935 guaranteed workers the right to start unions. The Congress of Industrial Organizations (CIO), composed of industrial unions, was formed during the Great Depression.

UNIONS AND COLLECTIVE BARGAINING CONTRACTS

Unions can be regarded as setters of minimum wages. Through collective bargaining, unions establish minimum wages below which no individual worker can offer his or her services. Each year, collective bargaining contracts covering wages as well as working conditions and fringe benefits for about 8 million workers are negotiated. Union negotiators act as agents for all members of the bargaining unit. They bargain with management about the provisions of a labor contract. Once union representatives believe that they have an acceptable collective contract, they will submit it to a vote of the union members. If approved by the members, the contract sets wage rates, maximum workdays, working conditions, fringe benefits, and other matters, usually for the next two or three years. Typically, collective bargaining contracts between management and the union apply also to nonunion members who are employed by the firm or the industry.

Strike: The Ultimate Bargaining Tool

Whenever union-management negotiations break down, union negotiators may turn to their ultimate bargaining tool, the threat or the reality of a strike. The first recorded strike in U.S. history occurred shortly after the Revolutionary War, when Philadelphia printers walked out in 1786 over a demand for a weekly minimum wage of $6. Strikes make headlines, but in only 4 percent of all labor-management disputes does a strike occur before the contract is signed. In the other 96 percent of cases, contracts are signed without much public fanfare.

The purpose of a strike is to impose costs on recalcitrant management to force its acceptance of the union's proposed contract terms. Strikes disrupt production and interfere with a company's or an industry's ability to sell goods and services. The strike works both ways, though. Workers draw no wages while on strike (they may be partly compensated out of union strike funds). Striking union workers may also be eligible to draw state unemployment benefits.

The impact of a strike is closely related to the ability of striking unions to prevent non-striking (and perhaps nonunion) employees from continuing to work for the targeted company or industry. Therefore, steps are usually taken to prevent others from working for the employer. **Strikebreakers** can effectively destroy whatever bargaining power rests behind a strike. Numerous methods have been used to prevent strikebreakers from breaking strikes. Violence has been known to erupt, almost always in connection with attempts to prevent strikebreaking.

Strikebreakers
Temporary or permanent workers hired by a company to replace union members who are striking.

EXAMPLE
Strikes in Professional Sports

Twice in the past two decades, professional baseball players have gone on strike. In 1994, virtually the entire season was lost. At the start of the following season, professional baseball team owners hired replacement players at much lower salaries. The same action was taken by professional football team owners during the NFL strike in 1987. For three games, substitute football players, alongside regular team players who "crossed the picket line," courageously attempted to play professional football. The results were not quite what fans were used to seeing—and therein lies the rub. Compare this situation with one in which a shoemaking factory suffers a strike. Strikebreakers (substitute "players") can learn the strikers' jobs relatively quickly; the skills involved are not too difficult. But in professional sports, it is hard, if not impossible, to duplicate the skills of the best players. Therefore, professional league players are not so easily replaced. Moreover, current professional sports management cannot figure out ways to automate sports as, say, the telephone industry has done in order to weaken the power of unions in that industry.

FOR CRITICAL ANALYSIS: Who benefited from the strikes in professional football and professional baseball? •

UNION GOALS

We have already pointed out that one of the goals of unions is to set minimum wages. In many situations, any wage rate set higher than a competitive market clearing wage rate will reduce total employment in that market. This can be seen in Figure 28-2. We have a competitive market for labor. The market demand curve is D, and the market supply curve is S. The market clearing wage rate will be W_e; the equilibrium quantity of labor will be Q_e. If the union establishes by collective bargaining a minimum wage rate that exceeds W_e, an excess quantity of labor will be supplied (assuming no change in the labor demand schedule). If the minimum wage established by union collective bargaining is W_U, the quantity supplied would be Q_S; the quantity demanded would be Q_D. The difference is the excess quantity supplied, or surplus. Hence the following point becomes clear:

> One of the major roles of a union that establishes a wage rate above the market clearing wage rate is to ration available jobs among the excess number of workers who wish to work in unionized industries.

Note also that the surplus of labor is equivalent to a shortage of jobs at wage rates above equilibrium.

The union may use a system of seniority, a lengthening of the apprenticeship period to discourage potential members from joining, and other such rationing methods. This has the effect of shifting the supply of labor curve to the left in order to support the higher wage, W_U.

There is a trade-off here that any union's leadership must face: Higher wages inevitably mean a reduction in total employment, as more persons are seeking a smaller number of positions. (Moreover, at higher wages, more workers will seek to enter the industry, thereby adding to the surplus that occurs because of the union contract.) Facing higher wages, management may replace part of the workforce with machinery.

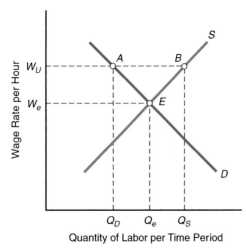

FIGURE 28-2

Unions Must Ration Jobs
If the union succeeds in obtaining wage rate W_U, the quantity of labor demanded will be Q_D, but the quantity of labor supplied will be Q_S. The union must ration a limited number of jobs to a greater number of workers; the surplus of labor is equivalent to a shortage of jobs at that wage rate.

Union Strategies

If we view unions as monopoly sellers of a service, we can identify three different wage and employment strategies that they use: ensuring employment for all members of the union, maximizing aggregate income workers, and maximizing wage rates for some workers.

Employing All Members in the Union. Assume that the union has Q_1 workers. If it faces a labor demand curve such as D in Figure 28-3, the only way it can "sell" all of those workers' services is to accept a wage rate of W_1. This is similar to any other demand curve. The demand curve tells the maximum price that can be charged to sell any particular quantity of a good or service. Here the service happens to be labor.

Maximizing Member Income. If the union is interested in maximizing the gross income of its members, it will normally want a smaller membership than Q_1—namely, Q_2 workers, all employed and paid a wage rate of W_2. The aggregate income to all members of the union is represented by the wages of only the ones who work. Total income earned by union members is maximized where the price elasticity of demand is numerically equal to 1. That occurs where marginal revenue equals zero. In Figure 28-3, marginal revenue equals zero at a quantity of labor Q_2. So we know that if the union obtains a wage rate equal to W_2, and therefore Q_2 workers are demanded, the total income to the union membership will be maximized. In other words, $Q_2 \times W_2$ (the shaded area) will be greater than any other combination of wage rates and quantities of union workers demanded. It is, for example, greater than $Q_1 \times W_1$. Note that in this situation, if the union started out with Q_1 members, there would be $Q_1 - Q_2$ members out of *union* work at the wage rate W_2. (Those out of union work either remain unemployed or go to other industries, which has a depressing effect on wages in nonunion industries due to the increase in supply of nonunion workers there.)

Maximizing Wage Rates for Certain Workers. Assume that the union wants to maximize the wage rates for some of its workers—perhaps those with the most seniority. If it wanted to keep a quantity of Q_3 workers employed, it would seek to obtain a wage rate of W_3. This would require deciding which workers should be unemployed and which workers should work and for how long each week or each year they should be employed.

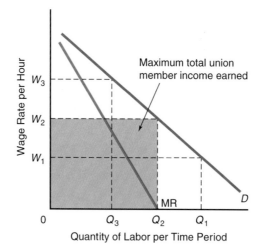

FIGURE 28-3

What Do Unions Maximize?
Assume that the union wants to employ all its Q_1 members. It will attempt to get wage rate W_1. If the union wants to maximize total wage receipts (income), it will do so at wage rate W_2, where the elasticity of the demand for labor is equal to 1. (The shaded area represents the maximum total income that the union would earn at W_2.) If the union wants to maximize the wage rate for a given number of workers, say, Q_3, it will set the wage rate at W_3.

Limiting Entry over Time

One way to raise wage rates without specifically setting wages is for unions to limit the size of their membership to the size of their employed workforce when the union was first organized. No workers are put out of work at the time the union is formed. Over time, as the demand for labor in the industry increases, there is no net increase in union membership, so larger wage increases are obtained than would otherwise be the case. We see this in Figure 28-4. Union members freeze entry into their union, thereby obtaining a wage rate of $16 per hour instead of allowing a wage rate of $15 per hour with no restriction on labor supply.

Altering the Demand for Union Labor

Another way in which unions can increase wages is to shift the demand curve for labor outward to the right. This approach compares favorably with the supply restriction approach because it increases both wage rates and employment level. The demand for union labor can be increased by increasing worker productivity, increasing the demand for union-made goods, and decreasing the demand for non-union-made goods.

Increasing Worker Productivity.   Supporters of unions have argued that unions provide a good system of industrial jurisprudence. The presence of unions may induce workers to feel that they are working in fair and just circumstances. If so, they work harder, increasing labor productivity. Productivity is also increased when unions resolve differences and reduce conflicts between workers and management, thereby providing a smoother administrative environment.

Increasing Demand for Union-Made Goods.   Because the demand for labor is a derived demand, a rise in the demand for products produced by union labor will increase the demand for union labor itself. One way in which unions attempt to increase the demand for union labor–produced products is by advertising "Look for the union label."

Decreasing the Demand for Non-Union-Made Goods.   When the demand for goods that are competing with (or are substitutes for) union-made goods is reduced, consumers

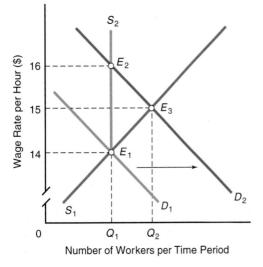

FIGURE 28-4

Restricting Supply over Time
When the union was formed, it didn't affect wage rates or employment, which remained at $14 and Q_1 (the equilibrium wage rate and quantity). However, as demand increased— that is, as the demand schedule shifted outward to D_2 from D_1—the union restricted membership to its original level of Q_1. The new supply curve is S_1S_2, which intersects D_2 at E_2, or at a wage rate of $16. Without the union, equilibrium would be at E_3 with a wage rate of $15 and employment of Q_2.

shift to union-made goods, increasing the demand. A good example is when various unions campaign against imports; restrictions on imported cars are supported by the United Auto Workers as strongly as the Textile Workers Unions support restrictions on imported textile goods. The result is greater demand for goods "made in the USA," which in turn presumably increases the demand for American union (and nonunion) labor.

HAVE UNIONS RAISED WAGES?

We have seen that unions are able to raise the wages of their members if they are successful at limiting the supply of labor in a particular industry. They are also able to raise wages above what wages would otherwise be to the extent that they can shift the demand for union labor outward to the right. This can be done using the methods we have just discussed, including collective bargaining agreements that require specified workers for any given job—for example, by requiring a pilot, a copilot, and an engineer in the cockpit of a jet airplane even if an engineer is not needed on short flights. Economists have done extensive research to determine the actual increase in union wages relative to nonunion wages. They have found that in certain industries, such as construction, and in certain occupations, such as commercial airline pilot, the union wage differential can be 50 percent or more. That is to say, unions have been able in some industries and occupations to raise wage rates 50 percent or more above what they would be in the absence of unions.

In addition, the union wage differential appears to increase during recessions. This is because unions often, through collective bargaining, have longer-term contracts than nonunion workers so that they do not have to renegotiate wage rates, even when overall demand in the economy falls.

On average, unions appear to be able to raise the wage rates of their members relative to nonunion members by 10 to 20 percent. Note, though, that when unions increase wages beyond what productivity increases would permit, some union members will be laid off. A redistribution of income from low- to high-seniority union workers is not equivalent to higher wages for *all* union members.

CAN UNIONS INCREASE PRODUCTIVITY?

A traditional view of union behavior is that unions decrease productivity by artificially shifting the demand curve for union labor outward through excessive staffing and make-work requirements. For example, some economists have traditionally felt that unions tend to bargain for excessive use of workers, as when requiring an engineer on all flights. This is referred to as **featherbedding.** Many painters' unions, for example, resisted the use of paint sprayers and required that their members use only brushes. They even specified the maximum width of the brush. Moreover, whenever a union strikes, productivity drops, and this reduction in productivity in one sector of the economy can spill over into other sectors.

This traditional view against unions has recently been countered by a view that unions can actually increase productivity. The new labor economists contend that unions act as a collective voice for their members. In the absence of a collective voice, any dissatisfied worker either simply remains at a job and works in a disgruntled manner or quits. But unions, as a collective voice, can listen to worker grievances on an individual basis and then apply pressure on the employer to change working conditions and other things. The individual worker does not run the risk of being singled out by the employer and harassed. Also, the individual worker doesn't have to spend time trying to convince the employer that some change in the working arrangement should be made. Given that unions provide this

Featherbedding
Any practice that forces employers to use more labor than they would otherwise or to use existing labor in an inefficient manner.

collective voice, worker turnover in unionized industries should be less, and this should contribute to productivity. Indeed, there is strong evidence that worker turnover is reduced when unions are present. Of course, this evidence may also be consistent with the fact that wage rates are so attractive to union members that they will not quit unless working conditions become truly intolerable.

THE BENEFITS OF LABOR UNIONS

It should by now be clear that there are two opposing views about unions. One portrays them as monopolies whose main effect is to raise the wage rate of high-seniority members at the expense of low-seniority members. The other contends that they can increase labor productivity through a variety of means. Harvard economists Richard B. Freeman and James L. Medoff argue that the truth is somewhere in between. They came up with the following conclusions:

1. Unionism probably raises social efficiency, thereby contradicting the traditional monopoly interpretation of what unions do. Even though unionism reduces employment in the unionized sector, it does permit labor to develop and implement workplace practices that are more valuable to workers. In some settings, unionism is associated with increased productivity.
2. Unions appear to reduce wage inequality.
3. Unions seem to reduce profits.
4. Internally, unions provide a political voice for all workers, and unions have been effective in promoting general social legislation.
5. Unions tend to increase the stability of the workforce by providing services, such as arbitration proceedings and grievance procedures.

Freeman and Medoff take a positive view of unionism. But their critics point out that they may have overlooked the fact that many of the benefits that unions provide do not require that unions engage in restrictive labor practices, such as the closed shop. Unions could still do positive things for workers without restricting the labor market.

CONCEPTS IN BRIEF

- When unions raise wage rates above market clearing prices, they face the problem of rationing a restricted number of jobs to a more than willing supply of workers.

- Unions may pursue any one of three goals: (1) to employ all members in the union, (2) to maximize total income of the union's workers, or (3) to maximize wages for certain, usually high-seniority, workers.

- Unions can increase the wage rate of members by engaging in practices that shift the union labor supply curve inward or shift the demand curve for union labor outward (or both).

- Some economists believe that unions can increase productivity by acting as a collective voice for their members, thereby freeing members from the task of convincing their employers that some change in working arrangements should be made. Unions may reduce turnover, thus improving productivity.

MONOPSONY: A BUYER'S MONOPOLY

Let's assume that a firm is a perfect competitor in the product market. The firm cannot alter the price of the product it sells, and it faces a perfectly elastic demand curve for its product. We also assume that the firm is the only buyer of a particular input. Although this situation may not occur often, it is useful to consider. Let's think in terms of a factory town, like those dominated by textile mills or in the mining industry. One company not only hires the workers but also owns the businesses in the community, owns the apartments that workers live in, and hires the clerks, waiters, and all other personnel. This buyer of labor is called a **monopsonist,** the single buyer.

Monopsonist
A single buyer.

What does an upward-sloping supply curve mean to a monopsonist in terms of the costs of hiring extra workers? It means that if the monopsonist wants to hire more workers, it has to offer higher wages. Our monopsonist firm cannot hire all the labor it wants at the going wage rate. If it wants to hire more workers, it has to raise wage rates, including the wage of all its current workers (assuming a non-wage-discriminating monopsonist). It therefore has to take account of these increased costs when deciding how many more workers to hire.

EXAMPLE
Monopsony in College Sports

How many times have you read stories about colleges and universities violating National Collegiate Athletic Association (NCAA) rules? If you keep up with the sports press, these stories about alleged violations occur every year. About 600 four-year colleges and universities belong to the NCAA, which controls more than 20 sports. In effect, the NCAA operates an intercollegiate cartel that is dominated by universities that operate big-time athletic programs. It operates as a cartel with monopsony (and monopoly) power in four ways:

1. It regulates the number of student athletes that universities can recruit.
2. It often fixes the prices that the university charges for tickets to important intercollegiate sporting events.
3. It sets the prices (wages) and the conditions under which the universities can recruit these student athletes.
4. It enforces its regulations and rules with sanctions and penalties.

The NCAA rules and regulations expressly prohibit bidding for college athletes in an overt manner. Rather, the NCAA requires that all athletes be paid the same for tuition, fees, room, board, and books. Moreover, the NCAA limits the number of athletic scholarships that can be given by a particular university. These rules are ostensibly to prevent the richest universities from "hiring" the best student athletes.

Not surprisingly, from the very beginning of the NCAA, individual universities and colleges have attempted to cheat on the rules in order to attract better athletes. The original agreement among the colleges was to pay no wages. Almost immediately after this agreement was put into effect, colleges switched to offering athletic scholarships, jobs, free room and board, travel expenses, and other enticements. It was not unusual for athletes to be paid $10 an hour to rake leaves when the going wage rate for such work was only $5 an hour. Finally, the NCAA had to agree to permit wages up to a certain amount per year.

If all universities had to offer exactly the same money wages and fringe benefits, the academically less distinguished colleges in metropolitan areas (with a large potential number of ticket-buying fans) would have the most inducement to violate the NCAA agreements (to compensate for the lower market value of their degrees). They would figure out all sorts of techniques to get the best student athletes. Indeed, such schools have in fact cheated more than other universities and colleges, and their violations have been detected and punished with a greater relative frequency than those of other colleges and universities.

FOR CRITICAL ANALYSIS: College and university administrators argue that the NCAA rules are necessary to "keep business out of higher education." How can one argue that college athletics is related to academics? ●

Exercise 28.3
Visit www.econtoday.com for more about sports stars.

Marginal Factor Cost

The monopsonist faces an upward-sloping supply curve of the input in question because as the only buyer, it faces the entire market supply curve. Each time the monopsonist buyer of labor, for example, wishes to hire more workers, it must raise wage rates. Thus the marginal cost of another unit of labor is rising. In fact, the marginal cost of increasing its workforce will always be greater than the wage rate. This is because in the situation in which the monopsonist pays the same wage rate to everyone in order to obtain another unit of labor, the higher wage rate has to be offered not only to the last worker but also to all its other workers. We call the additional cost to the monopsonist of hiring one more worker the marginal factor cost (MFC).

The marginal factor cost for the last worker is therefore his or her wages plus the increase in the wages of all other existing workers. As we pointed out in Chapter 27, marginal factor cost is equal to the change in total variable cost due to a one-unit change in the one variable factor of production—in this case, labor. In Chapter 27, marginal factor cost was simply the competitive wage rate because the employer could hire all workers at the same wage rate.

Derivation of a Marginal Factor Cost Curve

Panel (a) of Figure 28-5 shows the quantity of labor purchased, the wage rate per hour, the total cost of the quantity of labor purchased per hour, and the marginal factor cost per hour for the additional labor bought.

We translate the columns from panel (a) to the graph in panel (b) of the figure. We show the supply curve as *S*, which is taken from columns 1 and 2. (Note that this is the same as the *average* factor cost curve; hence you can view Figure 28-5 as showing the relationship between average factor cost and marginal factor cost.) The marginal factor cost curve (MFC) is taken from columns 1 and 4. The MFC curve must be above the supply curve whenever the supply curve is upward-sloping. If the supply curve is upward-sloping, the firm must pay a higher wage rate in order to attract a larger amount of labor. This higher wage rate must be paid to all workers; thus the increase in total costs due to an increase in the labor input will exceed the wage rate. Note that in a perfectly competitive input market, the supply curve is perfectly elastic and the marginal factor cost curve is identical to the supply curve.

Employment and Wages Under Monopsony

To determine the number of workers that a monopsonist desires to hire, we compare the marginal benefit to the marginal cost of each hiring decision. The marginal cost is the mar-

Panel (a)

(1) Quantity of Labor Supplied to Management	(2) Required Hourly Wage Rate	(3) Total Wage Bill (3) = (1) x (2)	(4) Marginal Factor Cost (MFC) = $\dfrac{\text{Change in (3)}}{\text{Change in (1)}}$
0	—	—	
			$1.00
1	$1.00	$1.00	
			3.00
2	2.00	4.00	
			3.20
3	2.40	7.20	
			4.00
4	2.80	11.20	
			6.80
5	3.60	18.00	
			7.20
6	4.20	25.20	

FIGURE 28-5

Derivation of a Marginal Factor Cost Curve

The supply curve, *S,* in panel (b) is taken from columns 1 and 2 of panel (a). The marginal factor cost curve (MFC) is taken from columns 1 and 4. It is the increase in the total wage bill resulting from a one-unit increase in labor input.

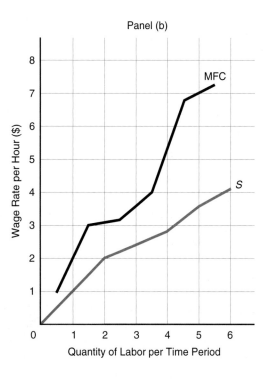

Panel (b)

ginal factor cost curve, and the marginal benefit is the marginal revenue product curve. In Figure 28-6 on page 642, we assume competition in the output market and monopsony in the input market. A monopsonist finds its profit-maximizing quantity of labor demanded at *E,* where the marginal revenue product is just equal to the marginal factor cost.

How much is the firm going to pay these workers? In a nonmonopsonistic situation it would face a given wage rate in the labor market, but because it is a monopsonist, it faces the entire supply curve, *S.*

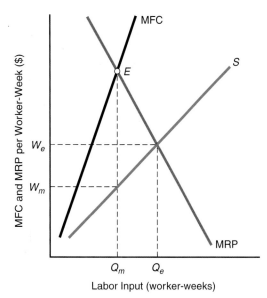

FIGURE 28-6

Marginal Factor Cost Curve for a Monopsonist

The monopsonist firm looks at a marginal cost curve, MFC, that slopes upward and is above its labor supply curve, *S*. The marginal benefit of hiring additional workers is given by the firm's MRP curve. The intersection of MFC with MRP, at point *E*, determines the number of workers hired. The firm hires Q_m workers but has to pay them only W_m in order to attract them. Compare this with the competitive solution, in which the wage rate would have to be W_e and the quantity of labor would be Q_e.

A monopsonist faces an *upward-sloping* supply curve for labor. Firms do not usually face the market supply curve; most firms can hire all the workers they want at the going wage rate and thus usually face a perfectly elastic supply curve for each factor of production. The market supply curve, however, slopes upward.

The monopsonist therefore sets the wage rate so that it will get exactly the quantity, Q_m, supplied to it by its "captive" labor force. We find that wage rate is W_m. There is no reason to pay the workers any more than W_m because at that wage rate, the firm can get exactly the quantity it wants. The actual quantity used is established at the intersection of the marginal factor cost curve and the marginal revenue product curve for labor—that is, at the point at which the marginal revenue from expanding employment just equals the marginal cost of doing so.

Notice that the profit-maximizing wage rate paid to workers (W_m) is lower than the marginal revenue product. That is to say that workers are paid a wage that is less than their contribution to the monopsonist's revenues. This is sometimes referred to as **monopsonistic exploitation** of labor. The monopsonist is able to do this because each individual worker has little power in bargaining for a higher wage. The organization of workers into a union, though, creates a monopoly supplier of labor, which gives the union some power to bargain for higher wages.

What happens when a monopsonist meets a monopolist? This is the situation called **bilateral monopoly,** defined as a market structure in which a single buyer faces a single seller. An example is a state education employer facing a single teachers' union in the labor market. Another example is a professional players' union facing an organized group of team owners. Such bilateral monopoly situations have indeed occurred in professional baseball and football. To analyze bilateral monopoly, we would have to look at the interaction of both sides, buyer and seller. The price outcome turns out to be indeterminate.

Monopsonistic exploitation
Exploitation due to monopsony power. It leads to a price for the variable input that is less than its marginal revenue product. Monopsonistic exploitation is the difference between marginal revenue product and the wage rate.

Bilateral monopoly
A market structure consisting of a monopolist and a monopsonist.

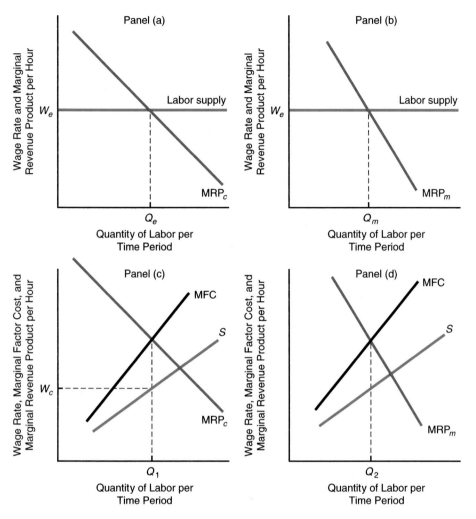

FIGURE 28-7

Summary of Pricing and Employment Under Various Market Conditions

In panel (a), the firm operates in perfect competition in both input and output markets. It purchases labor up to the point where the going rate W_e is equal to MRP_c. It hires quantity Q_e of labor. In panel (b), the firm is a perfect competitor in the input market but has a monopoly in the output market. It purchases labor up to the point where W_e is equal to MRP_m. It hires a smaller quantity of labor, Q_m, than in panel (a). In panel (c), the firm is a monopsonist in the input market and a perfect competitor in the output market. It hires labor up to the point where $\text{MFC} = \text{MRP}_c$. It will hire quantity Q_1 and pay wage rate W_c. Panel (d) shows bilateral monopoly. The wage outcome is indeterminate.

We have studied the pricing of labor in various situations, including perfect competition in both the output and input markets and monopoly in both the output and input markets. Figure 28-7 shows four possible situations graphically.

CONCEPTS IN BRIEF

- A monopsonist is a single buyer. The monopsonist faces an upward-sloping supply curve of labor.

- Because the monopsonist faces an upward-sloping supply curve of labor, the marginal factor cost of increasing the labor input by one unit is greater than the wage rate. Thus the marginal factor cost curve always lies above the supply curve.

- A monopsonist will hire workers up to the point at which marginal factor cost equals marginal revenue product. Then the monopsonist will find what minimal wage is necessary to attract that number of workers. This is taken from the supply curve.

This UPS striker went back to work after the Teamsters Union won its desired contract. In spite of this labor victory, union membership continues to fall in the United States.

LOCAL 804
AFFILIATED WITH THE
INTERNATIONAL BROTHERHOOD
OF TEAMSTERS

Are We Seeing a Rebirth of the American Labor Movement?

CONCEPTS APPLIED:

MONOPOLY, STRIKES, LABOR UNIONS, PRODUCTIVITY, UNION STRATEGIES

Visit www.econtoday.com for an Internet Activity that expands your understanding of these concepts.

Y ou have seen in this chapter that the percentage of the labor force that is unionized has been in steady decline. Figure 28-8 shows that the number of labor strikes since World War II reached its peak in about 1953 and peaked twice again in the late 1960s and mid-1970s but has been declining ever since. The decline in the number of strikes mirrors the decline in private-sector membership in labor unions.

The Teamsters Enter the Fray

In 1997, the Teamsters struck United Parcel Service of America, Inc. (UPS). For a painful several weeks, mail-order companies, college book publishers, and hundreds of thousands of other firms scrambled to replace UPS shipments with an alternative. Federal Express and Airborne Express in particular gained handsomely from the Teamsters strike against UPS. UPS ultimately settled with the union. That settlement was declared a victory for the Teamsters as well as for organized labor. But was it really a victory?

What the UPS Drivers Really Won

A complete analysis of the UPS strike requires examining the average worker's lost income and comparing it with

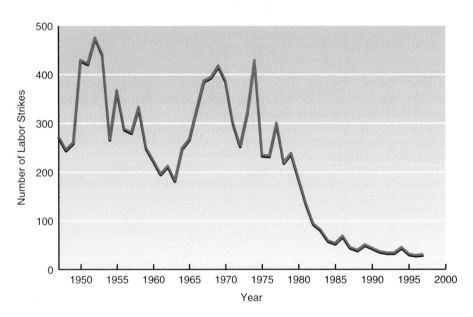

FIGURE 28-8

The Declining Number of Labor Strikes
Since about 1974, the number of labor walkouts each year has declined steadily. The power of unions seems to be on the wane.
Source: U.S. Bureau of Labor Statistics.

the present value of future wage increases. The Economic Policy Foundation estimated that the lost income for a typical UPS worker was about $1,850. The foundation calculated that it would take the average full-time UPS employee five years to come out ahead, compared to where he or she would have been had the union accepted the company's last offer before the strike. Further, the average part-time worker may earn *less* income over the life of the contract than if the union had accepted the company's final offer.

Why Strikes That Seem Irrational May Not Be So

It appears as if few strikes really earn very much for workers. It also appears that UPS may not have gained very much by holding out. Indeed, according to Professor David Lipsky of Cornell University, few strikes are ever justified on a financial basis for either side. So are they irrational? Not necessarily, for strikes might be necessary on occasion to establish bargaining credibility for future contract negotiations. After all, if a company knew that its workers' union would never strike, it would continue to make smaller and smaller offers for future contracts. If a union knew that a company would always cave in to avoid a strike, it would ask for larger and larger compensation increases in future contract demands.

Was UPS the Right Company to Strike?

One wonders if perhaps the UPS strike was not really in the best interest of members of the Teamsters union. Before the strike, UPS was already paying its full-time employees almost twice the national average wage rate. Its almost completely unskilled part-time workers were earning an average of $11 an hour with a full range of benefits. Indeed, UPS is one of the few companies (Starbucks is another) that provides full benefits to part-time workers. Part-time workers, because of fixed medical insurance and other fringe benefits, are actually a relatively expensive source of labor for UPS. UPS uses so many part-timers because it needs temporary employment during certain times of the year, such as Christmas.

It also needs thousands of workers for only a few hours each day when its planes arrive at and depart from its hubs. A majority of part-time workers at UPS are homemakers and college students who do not want to work full time.

Will the Teamsters' Victory Hurt Industrial Workers?

The Teamsters have long been at odds with other parts of organized labor. The Teamsters are basically transport workers. Transportation costs, such as trucking and railroads, are an additional cost of production, raising the price of the product to consumers and reducing quantity demanded. Hence higher wages for transportation workers typically lead to lower wages for industrial workers. Thus the Teamsters have always been on the outs with the rest of labor. Any victory that the Teamsters had in the UPS strike will be felt, perhaps not obviously, by workers in manufacturing. The products they make now will cost more to be shipped.

The Public Support for Strikers Is Growing

During the UPS strike, the public was squarely behind the striking workers. According to a Gallup poll at the time, 55 percent of the public was in favor of the workers. An examination of polls going back 60 years shows that public opinion about strikers was often far more negative. In the late 1930s, the public was sympathetic to strikers only about 33 percent of the time. Since the late 1980s, however, strikers have routinely received support from over 50 percent of Americans polled. For example, when Eastern Airlines' workers went out on strike in 1989, a Gallup poll received responses favoring the strikers from 57 percent of the people questioned.

FOR CRITICAL ANALYSIS
1. Former Secretary of Labor Robert Reich, after hearing of the Teamsters' victory in the UPS strike, hailed it as a "watershed" event in union history. What do you think he meant?
2. Is it ever possible for a strike to benefit both parties?

CHAPTER SUMMARY

1. The American labor movement started with local craft unions but was very small until the twentieth century. Important organizations in the history of labor in the United States are the Knights of Labor, the American Federation of Labor, and the Congress of Industrial Organizations.

2. The Great Depression facilitated passage of the National Industrial Recovery Act. This act established the right of labor to bargain collectively. It was later supplanted by the Wagner Act.

3. Unions raise union wage rates relative to nonunion wages. The union wage differential increases during recessions because of the longer-term nature of union collective bargaining contracts.

4. Because unions act as a collective voice for individual employees, they may increase productivity by reducing the time that employees spend trying to alter unproductive working arrangements. Unions may also increase productivity by reducing turnover.

5. Monopsony is a situation in which there is only one buyer of a particular input. The single buyer faces an upward-sloping supply curve and must therefore pay higher wage rates to attract additional workers. The single buyer faces a marginal factor cost curve that is upward-sloping and above the supply curve. The buyer hires workers up to the point at which the marginal revenue product equals the marginal factor cost. Then the labor buyer will find out how low a wage rate can be paid to get that many workers.

6. When a single buyer faces a single seller, a situation of bilateral monopsony exists.

DISCUSSION OF PREVIEW QUESTIONS

1. What are the major types of unions?

The earliest, and one of the most important forms today, is the craft union, which is an organization of skilled laborers. Another major type is the industrial union, in which all or most laborers in an industry, such as the steelworkers or mineworkers, unite.

2. What do unions seek to maximize?

Unions do not have unlimited power; in the United States, the rules that have evolved declare that unions can set wage rates *or* the number of laborers who will be employed, but not both. Consequently, a trade-off exists for union leaders: If they maximize wages, some members will become unemployed; if they maximize employment, wages will be relatively low. Union leaders often decide to maximize wages for a given number of workers—presumably the higher-seniority workers. Each union reaches its own decision as to how to resolve the trade-off.

3. Do unions help workers?

If unions are to be considered effective, they must increase real wage rates *above* productivity increas-es; after all, market forces will increase real wage rates at the rate of productivity change. Yet if real wage rates are increased more rapidly than the rate of productivity increases, unions will cause reduced employment; hence some laborers will be helped (those who retain their jobs at above-productivity wage levels), and some will be hurt (those who lose their jobs). The evidence is that unions are neither a necessary nor a sufficient condition for high real wages. Wages in the United States were relatively high before the U.S. labor movement. Moreover, labor's overall share of national income has not changed significantly since the 1930s, although *union* labor's share may have increased relative to nonunion labor's share.

4. What is a monopsonist, and how does one determine its profit-maximizing employment rate?

A monopsonist is a single buyer. A monopsonist hires labor up to the point at which the marginal benefit of doing so equals the marginal cost of doing so. The marginal benefit of hiring labor is labor's marginal revenue product: MB = MRP of labor. The marginal cost of hiring labor must reflect the fact that the monopsonist faces the industry labor supply schedule; hence the monopsonist must increase wage rates in order to hire more labor. Of course, it must increase wage rates for all the labor that it hires, not just the marginal laborer. Thus the MC of hiring labor for a monopsonist (the marginal factor cost, MFC)

will be greater than the wage rate. Since the profit-maximizing employment rate is generally where MB = MC, the monopsonist will hire labor up to the point where MRP = MFC. It then pays the lowest wage rate required to attract that quantity of labor. This wage rate will be below the MRP of labor.

PROBLEMS

(Answers to the odd-numbered problems appear at the back of the book.)

28-1. The accompanying graph indicates a monopsonistic firm that is also a perfect competitor in the product market.

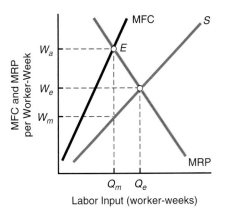

Labor Input (worker-weeks)

a. What does MRP stand for?
b. Which is the supply of labor curve?
c. How many laborers will this firm voluntarily hire?
d. Given the profit-maximizing employment rate, what is the lowest wage rate that this firm can offer to get this quantity of labor?

28-2. Does a perfectly competitive firm have to worry about the impact of its own demand for labor on the going wage rate?

28-3. Give examples of perfectly competitive sellers having monopsony power in the input market.

28-4. Suppose that you operate a firm that sells its output in a perfectly competitive market. However, you are the only employer in your island economy. You are currently employing 10 full-time employees at a wage rate of $50 per person per day, and you are producing 100 units of output per day. Labor is your only variable input. The market price of your output is $8 per unit. You estimate that daily output would rise to 108 units per day if you increased your workforce to 11 people. To attract the eleventh worker, you would have to pay a wage rate of $52 to all employees. Should you expand your workforce?

28-5. Imagine yourself managing a plant that is a monopsony buyer of its sole input and is also the monopoly seller of its output. You are currently employing 30 people, producing 20 units of output per day, and selling them for $100 apiece. Your current wage rate is $60 per day. You estimate that you would have to raise your wage scale for all workers to $61 per day in order to attract one more person to your firm. The 31 employees would be able to produce 21 units of output per day, which you would be able to sell at $99.50 apiece. Should you hire the thirty-first employee?

28-6. If a union, in its collective bargaining, sets a wage rate that maximizes total union members' income, will all union members be employed? Explain your answer.

28-7. Why will a union never want to bargain collectively for a wage rate that would exist with perfect competition in the labor market?

28-8. "The states that have right-to-work laws deprive workers from enjoying the full benefits of unions." What arguments can be used to support this statement? To deny its validity?

28-9. The marginal factor cost curve faced by a firm buying an input in a perfectly competitive market is identical to its supply curve for that input. Why is this not true for a monopsonist? Explain your answer.

COMPUTER-ASSISTED INSTRUCTION

How does the behavior of monopsonists differ from the behavior of competitive purchasers of labor? What are the consequences of these differences?

Complete problem and answer appear on disk.

INTERACTING WITH THE INTERNET

The AFL-CIO has a substantial amount of material on the organization and issues important to it at

www.aflcio.org/

You can learn about the World Federation of Labor at

www.cmt-wcl.org/

If you want to read about the activities of one of our most effective monopsonies, go to

www.ncaa.org/

CHAPTER 29

RENT, INTEREST, AND PROFITS

We all continually make decisions in which we compare a cost today with the resulting future benefit. If you choose to jog on a regular basis, there is a cost involved: You give up doing some alternative that may be more pleasurable but has only immediate benefits, such reading a novel. You choose to jog regularly because of the long-term benefit—you will look and feel better or your risk of heart disease might decrease. The same type of calculation applies to many other activities, such as going to the gym regularly. For some people, though, no matter how hard they work out, run, or diet, they still have high cholesterol. There are drugs that can reduce these people's cholesterol levels. Health-maintenance organizations (HMOs) thus face an important policy decision: Should they provide such people with cholesterol-lowering drugs to reduce the probability of heart disease? Before you can understand how such a policy question must be analyzed, you need to learn about interest and present value, as well as rent and profits.

PREVIEW QUESTIONS

1. What is rent?
2. What is interest?
3. What is the economic function of interest rates?
4. What is the economic function of profits?

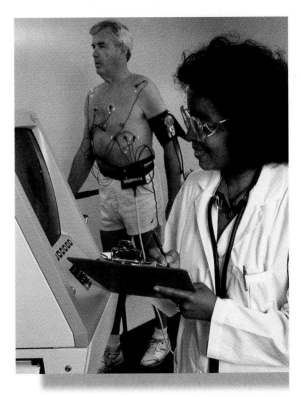

Did You Know That . . . in America, presumably one of the most industrialized countries in the world today, compensation for labor services makes up over 70 percent of national income every year? But what about the other 30 percent? It consists of compensation to the owners of the other factors of production that you read about in Part 1: land, capital, and entrepreneurship. Somebody owns the real estate downtown for which the monthly commercial rents are higher for one square foot than you might pay to rent a whole apartment. Land, obviously, is a factor of production, and it has a market clearing price. Businesses also have to use capital. Compensation for that capital is interest, and it, too, has a market clearing level. Finally, some of you may have entrepreneurial ability that you offer to the marketplace. Your compensation is called profit. In this chapter you will also learn about the sources and functions of profit.

RENT

When you hear the term *rent,* you are accustomed to having it mean the payment made to property owners for the use of land or apartments. The term *rent* has a different meaning in economics. **Economic rent** is payment to the owner of a resource in excess of its opportunity cost—the payment that would be necessary to call forth production of that amount of the resource. Economists originally used the term *rent* to designate payment for the use of land. What was thought to be important about land was that its supply is completely inelastic. Hence the supply curve for land is a vertical line; no matter what the prevailing market price for land, the quantity supplied will remain the same.

Economic rent
A payment for the use of any resource over and above its opportunity cost.

Determining Land Rent

The concept of economic rent is associated with the British economist David Ricardo (1772–1823). He looked at two plots of land on which grain was growing, one of which happened to be more fertile than the other. The owners of these two plots sold the grain that came from their land, but the one who owned the more fertile land grew more grain and therefore made more profits. According to Ricardo, the owner of the fertile land was receiving economic rents that were due not to the landowner's hard work or ingenuity but rather to an accident of nature. Ricardo asked his readers to imagine another scenario, that of walking up a hill that starts out flat with no rocks and then becomes steeper and rockier. The value of the land falls as one walks up the hill. If a different person owns the top of the hill than the bottom, the highland owner will receive very little in payment from, say, a farmer who wants to cultivate land for wheat production.

Here is how Ricardo analyzed economic rent for land. He first simplified his model by assuming that all land is equally productive. Then Ricardo assumed that the quantity of land in a country is *fixed.* Graphically, then, in terms of supply and demand, we draw the supply curve of land vertically (zero price elasticity). In Figure 29-1, the supply curve of land is represented by S. If the demand curve is D_1, it intersects the supply curve, S, at price P_1. The entire amount of revenues obtained, $P_1 \times Q_1$, is labeled "Economic rent." If the demand for land increased to D_2, the equilibrium price would rise to P_2. Additions to economic rent are labeled "More economic rent." Notice that the quantity of land remains insensitive to the change in price. Another way of stating this is that the supply curve is perfectly inelastic.

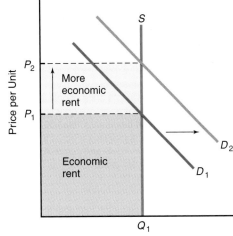

FIGURE 29-1

Economic Rent

If indeed the supply curve of land were completely price-inelastic in the long run, it would be depicted by S. At the quantity in existence, Q_1, any and all revenues are economic rent. If demand is D_1, the price will be P_1; if demand is D_2, price will rise to P_2. Economic rent would be $P_1 \times Q_1$ and $P_2 \times Q_1$, respectively.

ECONOMIC RENT TO LABOR

Land and natural resources are not the only factors of production to which the analysis of economic rent can be applied. In fact, the analysis is probably more often applicable to labor. Here is a list of people who provide different labor services, some of whom probably receive large amounts of economic rent:

Professional sports superstars
Rock stars
Movie stars
World-class models
Successful inventors and innovators
World-famous opera stars

Just apply the definition of economic rent to the phenomenal earnings that these people make. They would undoubtedly work for much, much less than they earn. Therefore, much of their earnings constitutes economic rent (but not all, as we shall see). Economic rent occurs because specific resources cannot be replicated exactly. No one can duplicate today's most highly paid entertainment figures, and therefore they receive economic rent.

Economic Rent and the Allocation of Resources

If an extremely highly paid movie star would make the same number of movies at half his or her current annual earnings, does that mean that 50 percent of his or her income is unnecessary? To answer the question, consider first why the superstar gets such a high income. The answer can be found in Figure 29-1. Substitute *entertainment activities of the superstars* for the word *land.* The high "price" received by the superstar is due to the demand for his or her services. If Kevin Costner announces that he will work for a measly $1 million a movie and do two movies a year, how is he going to know which production

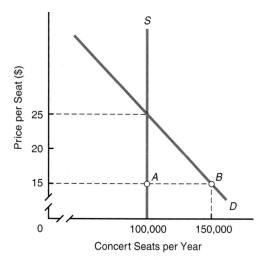

FIGURE 29-2

The Allocative Function of Rent
If the performer agrees to give five concerts a year "at any price" and there are 20,000 seats in each concert hall, the supply curve of concerts, *S*, is vertical at 100,000 seats per year. The demand curve is given by *D*. The performer wants a price of only $15 to be charged. At that price, the quantity of seats demanded per year is 150,000. The excess quantity demanded is equal to the horizontal distance between points *A* and *B*, or 50,000 seats per year.

company values his services the most highly? Costner and other movie stars let the market decide where their resources should be used. In this sense, we can say the following:

Economic rent allocates resources to their highest-valued use.

Otherwise stated, economic rent directs resources to the people who can most efficiently use them.

A common counterexample involves rock stars who claim that their tickets are over-priced. Consequently, they agree to perform, say, five concerts with all tickets being sold at the same price, $15. Assume that a star performs these concerts in halls with 20,000 seats. A total of 100,000 individuals per year will be able to see this particular performer. This is represented by point *A* in Figure 29-2. By assumption, this performer is still receiving some economic rent because we are assuming that the supply curve of concerts is vertical at 100,000 seats per year. At a price per ticket of $15, however, the annual quantity of seats demanded will be 150,000, represented by point *B*. The difference between points *A* and *B* is the excess quantity of tickets demanded at the below-market-clearing price of $15 a seat. The *additional* economic rent that could be earned by this performer by charging the clear-ing price of $25 per seat in this graph would serve as the rationing device that would make the quantity demanded equal to the quantity supplied.

In such situations, which are fairly common, part of the economic rent that could have been earned is dissipated—it is captured, for example, by radio station owners in the form of promotional gains when they are allowed to give away a certain number of tickets on the air (even if they have to pay $15 per ticket) because the tickets are worth $25. Ticket hold-ers who resell tickets at higher prices ("scalpers") also capture part of the rent. Conceiv-ably, at 100,000 seats per year, this performer could charge the market clearing price of $25 per ticket and give away to charity the portion of the economic rent ($10 per ticket) that would be dissipated. In such a manner, the performer could make sure that the recipients of the rent are worthy in his or her own esteem.

EXAMPLE
Do Entertainment Superstars Make Super Economic Rents?

Superstars certainly do well financially. Table 29-1 shows the earnings of selected individuals in the entertainment industry as estimated by *Forbes* magazine. Earn-ings are totaled for a two-year period. How much of these earnings can be called economic

TABLE 29-1
Superstar Earnings

Name	Occupation	Earnings (two years, millions of dollars)
Steven Spielberg	Director, producer, studio owner	313
George Lucas	Producer	241
Oprah Winfrey	Talk show host	201
Michael Crichton	Writer, producer	102
The Beatles	Rock group	98
Jerry Seinfeld	Actor, comedian	94
David Copperfield	Magician	85
Stephen King	Writer	84
Tom Cruise	Actor	82
Arnold Schwarzenegger	Actor	74

Source: Forbes, 1998.

rent? The question is not easy to answer, for an entertainment newcomer would almost certainly work for much less than he or she earns—thereby making high economic rents. The same cannot necessarily be said for entertainers who have been raking in millions for years. They probably have very high accumulated wealth and also a more jaded outlook about their work. It is therefore not clear how much they would work if they were not offered those huge sums of money.

FOR CRITICAL ANALYSIS: Even if some superstar entertainers would work for less, what forces cause them to make so much income anyway? ●

Taxing Away Economic Rent

Some people have argued in favor of imposing high taxes on economic rent. For example, drug companies that have developed *successful* patented drugs make large amounts of economic rent during the life of the patent. That is to say, the marginal cost of production is much less than the price charged. If the government taxed this economic rent completely, those successful drugs already on the market would in fact stay on the market. But there would be long-run consequences. Drug companies would invest fewer resources in discovering new successful drugs. So economic rent is typically a *short-run* phenomenon. In the long run, it constitutes a source of reward for risk taking in society. This is true not only in the drug business but also in entertainment and professional sports.

> **CONCEPTS IN BRIEF**
>
> • Economic rent is defined as payment for a factor of production that is completely inelastic in supply. It is payment for a resource over and above what is necessary to keep that resource in existence at its current level in the long run.
>
> • Economic rent serves an allocative function by guiding available supply to the most efficient use.

Interest
The payment for current rather than future command over resources; the cost of obtaining credit. Also, the return paid to owners of capital.

INTEREST

The term **interest** is used to mean two different things: (1) the price paid by debtors to creditors for the use of loanable funds and (2) the market return earned by (nonfinancial) capital as a factor of production. Owners of capital, whether directly or indirectly, obtain interest income. Often businesses go to credit markets to obtain so-called money capital in order to invest in physical capital from which they hope to make a satisfactory return. In other words, in our complicated society, the production of capital goods often occurs because of the existence of credit markets in which borrowing and lending take place. For the moment, we will look only at the credit market.

Interest and Credit

When you obtain credit, you actually obtain money to have command over resources today. We can say, then, that interest is the payment for current rather than future command over resources. Thus interest is the payment for obtaining credit. If you borrow $100 from me, you have command over $100 worth of goods and services today. I no longer have that command. You promise to pay me back $100 plus interest at some future date. The interest that you pay is usually expressed as a percentage of the total loan calculated on an annual basis. If at the end of one year you pay me back $110, the annual interest is $10 ÷ $100, or 10 percent. When you go out into the marketplace to obtain credit, you will find that the interest rate charged differs greatly. A loan to buy a house (a mortgage) may cost you 7 to 10 percent annual interest. An installment loan to buy an automobile may cost you 9 to 14 percent annual interest. The federal government, when it wishes to obtain credit (issues U.S. Treasury securities), may have to pay only 3 to 8 percent annual interest. Variations in the rate of annual interest that must be paid for credit depend on the following factors.

1. *Length of loan.* In some (but not all) cases, the longer the loan will be outstanding, other things being equal, the greater will be the interest rate charged.
2. *Risk.* The greater the risk of nonrepayment of the loan, other things being equal, the greater the interest rate charged. Risk is assessed on the basis of the creditworthiness of the borrower and whether the borrower provides collateral for the loan. Collateral consists of any asset that will automatically become the property of the lender should the borrower fail to comply with the loan agreement.
3. *Handling charges.* It takes resources to set up a loan. Papers have to be filled out and filed, credit references have to be checked, collateral has to be examined, and so on. The larger the amount of the loan, the smaller the handling (or administrative) charges as a percentage of the total loan. Therefore, we would predict that, other things being equal, the larger the loan, the lower the interest rate.

What Determines Interest Rates?

The overall level of interest rates can be described as the price paid for loanable funds. As with all commodities, price is determined by the interaction of supply and demand. Let's first look at the supply of loanable funds and then at the demand for them.

The Supply of Loanable Funds. The supply of loanable funds (credit available) depends on individuals' willingness to save.[1] When you save, you exchange rights to current consumption for rights to future consumption. The more current consumption you give up, the more valuable is a marginal unit of present consumption in comparison with future consumption.

Recall from our discussion of diminishing marginal utility that the more of something you have, the less you value an additional unit. Conversely, the less of something you have, the more you value an additional unit. Thus when you give up current consumption of a

---

[1]Actually, the supply of loanable funds also depends on business and government saving and on the behavior of the monetary authorities and the banking system. For simplicity of discussion, we ignore these components here.

good—that is, have less of it—you value an additional unit more. The more you save today, the more utility you attach to your last unit of today's consumption. So to be induced to save more—to consume less—you have to be offered a bigger and bigger reward to match the marginal utility of current consumption you will give up by saving. Because of this, if society wants to induce people to save more, it must offer a higher rate of interest. Hence we expect that the supply curve of loanable funds will slope upward. At higher rates of interest, savers will be willing to offer more current consumption to borrowers, other things being constant.[2] When the income of individuals increases or when there is a change in individual preferences toward more saving, the supply curve of loanable funds will shift outward to the right, and vice versa.

The Demand for Loanable Funds. There are three major sources of the demand for loanable funds:

1. Households that want loanable funds for the purchase of services and nondurable goods, as well as consumer durables such as automobiles and homes
2. Businesses that want loanable funds to make investments
3. Governments that want loanable funds, usually to cover deficits—the excess of government spending over tax revenues

We will ignore the government's demand for loanable funds and consider only consumers and businesses.

Loans are taken out both by consumers and by businesses. It is useful for us to separate the motives underlying the demand for loans by these two groups of individuals. We will therefore treat consumption loans and investment loans separately. In the discussion that follows, we will assume that there is no inflation—that is, that there is no persistent increase in the overall level of prices.

Consumer Demand for Loanable Funds. In general, consumers demand loanable funds because they tend to prefer earlier consumption to later consumption. That is to say, people subjectively value goods obtained immediately more than the same goods of the same quality obtained later on. Consider that sometimes an individual household's present income falls below the average income level expected over a lifetime. Individuals may go to the credit market to borrow whenever they perceive a temporary dip in their current income—assuming that they expect their income to go back to normal later on. Furthermore, by borrowing, they can spread out purchases more evenly during their lifetimes. In so doing, they're able to increase their lifetime total utility.

Consumers' demand for loanable funds will be inversely related to the cost of borrowing—the rate of interest. Why? For the same reason that all demand curves slope downward: A higher rate of interest means a higher cost of borrowing, and a higher cost of borrowing must be weighed against alternative uses of limited income. At higher costs of borrowing, consumers will forgo current consumption.

POLICY EXAMPLE
Should Rent-to-Own Stores Be Regulated?

A growing number of consumers are implicitly borrowing money by dealing with rent-to-own stores that offer them television sets and refrigerators for low weekly payments. At the end of a very long period, they end up owning the item. For example, a consumer can rent a television for $12 a week and at the end of 91 weeks will own it.

---

[2]A complete discussion would include the income effect: At higher interest rates, households receive a higher yield on savings, permitting them to save less to achieve any given target.

Some investigators claim that because the TV is worth only $125 new, consumers are paying over 300 percent annual interest. The U.S. Public Interest Research Group found many cases in which refrigerators with a cash price of $350 ended up costing $1,172 to a customer buying them from a rent-to-own store. Pennsylvania passed legislation to put in an 18 percent cap on the implicit annual interest rate. Because the number of rent-to-own stores nationwide has increased from 3,000 in 1983 to almost 9,000 today, empirically we know that a consumer demand exists for their services. Typically, the people who use them do not qualify for normal consumer credit. That is why they end up paying such implicitly high interest rates.

FOR CRITICAL ANALYSIS: What do you think happened to the growth in rent-to-own stores after the Pennsylvania legislation was passed? ●

Business Demand for Loanable Funds. Businesses demand loanable funds to make investments that they believe will increase productivity or profit. Whenever a business believes that by making an investment, it can increase revenues (net of other costs) by more than the cost of capital, it will make the investment. Businesses compare the interest rate they must pay in the loanable funds market with the interest rate they think they can earn by investing. This comparison helps them decide whether to invest.

In any event, we hypothesize that the demand curve for loanable funds by firms for investment purposes will be negatively sloped. At higher interest rates, fewer investment projects will make economic sense to businesses because the cost of capital (loanable funds) will exceed the net revenues derivable from the capital investment. Conversely, at lower rates of interest, more investment projects will be undertaken because the cost of capital will be less than the expected rate of return on the capital investment.

The Equilibrium Rate of Interest

When we add together the demand for loanable funds by households and businesses (and government in more complex models), we obtain a demand curve for loanable funds, as given in Figure 29-3. The supply curve is S. The equilibrium rate of interest is i_e.

Exercise 29.1
Visit www.econtoday.com for more about interest rates.

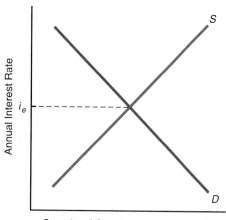

FIGURE 29-3

The Supply of and Demand for Loanable Funds

We draw D as the demand curve for all loanable funds by households and businesses (and governments). It slopes downward. S is the supply curve of credit, or loanable funds. It slopes upward. The intersection of S and D gives the equilibrium rate of interest at i_e.

INTERNATIONAL EXAMPLE
One Consequence of Privatizing Italian Banks: Loan Sharking

Until 1994, almost all Italian banks were government-owned, and loans usually were decided on political grounds. When the Italian government got out of some of the banking business, though, the newly privatized bank loan officers lacked the skills and experience necessary to judge whether a potential borrower was a good or a bad credit risk. Consequently, during this interim period after privatization, many small businesspersons in Italy were turned away when they sought loans. Bank loan officers steered them to "loan sharks." Many such lenders operate in violation of Italian law and end up charging borrowers 300 to 500 percent per year, well above the posted "equilibrium" interest rate at the nation's biggest banks.

FOR CRITICAL ANALYSIS: Who typically ends up agreeing to the high interest rates charged by loan sharks? ●

Real Versus Nominal Interest Rates

Nominal rate of interest
The market rate of interest expressed in today's dollars.

We have been assuming that there is no inflation. In a world of inflation—a persistent rise in an average of all prices—the **nominal rate of interest** will be higher than it would be in a world with no inflation. Basically, nominal, or market, rates of interest rise to take account of the anticipated rate of inflation. If, for example, there is no inflation and no inflation is expected, the nominal rate of interest might be 5 percent for home mortgages. If the rate of inflation goes to 10 percent a year and stays there, everybody will anticipate that inflation rate. The nominal rate of interest will rise to about 15 percent to take account of the anticipated rate of inflation. If the interest rate did not rise to 15 percent, the interest earned at 5 percent would be worth less in the future because inflation would have eroded its purchasing power. We can therefore say that the nominal, or market, rate of interest is approximately equal to the real rate of interest plus the anticipated rate of inflation, or

$$i_n = i_r + \text{anticipated rate of inflation}$$

Real rate of interest
The nominal rate of interest minus the anticipated rate of inflation.

where i_n equals the nominal rate of interest and i_r equals the real rate of interest. In short, you can expect to see high nominal rates of interest in periods of high or rising inflation rates. The **real rate of interest** may not necessarily be high, though. We must first correct the nominal rate of interest for the anticipated rate of inflation before determining whether the real interest rate is in fact higher than normal.

The Allocative Role of Interest

Back in Chapters 4 and 6, we talked about the price system and the role that prices play in the allocation of resources. Interest is a price that allocates loanable funds (credit) to consumers and to businesses. Within the business sector, interest allocates loanable funds to different firms and therefore to different investment projects. Investment, or capital, projects with rates of return higher than the market rate of interest in the credit market will be undertaken, given an unrestricted market for loanable funds. For example, if the expected rate of return on the purchase of a new factory in some industry is 15 percent and loanable funds can be acquired for 11 percent, the investment project may proceed. If, however, that same project had an expected rate of return of only 9 percent, it would not be undertaken. In sum, the interest rate allocates loanable funds to industries whose investments yield the highest returns—where resources will be the most productive.

It is important to realize that the interest rate performs the function of allocating money capital (loanable funds) and that this ultimately allocates real physical capital to various firms for investment projects.

Interest Rates and Present Value

Businesses make investments in which they often incur large costs today but don't make any profits until some time in the future. Somehow they have to be able to compare their investment cost today with a stream of future profits. How can they relate present cost to future benefits?

Interest rates are used to link the present with the future. After all, if you have to pay $110 at the end of the year when you borrow $100, that 10 percent interest rate gives you a measure of the premium on the earlier availability of goods and services. If you want to have things today, you have to pay the 10 percent interest rate in order to have current purchasing power.

The question could be put this way: What is the present value (the value today) of $110 that you could receive one year from now? That depends on the market rate of interest, or the rate of interest that you could earn in some appropriate savings institution, such as in a savings account. To make the arithmetic simple, let's assume that the rate of interest is 10 percent. Now you can figure out the **present value** of $110 to be received one year from now. You figure it out by asking the question, How much money must I put aside today at the market interest rate of 10 percent to receive $110 one year from now? Mathematically, we represent this equation as

$$(1 + .1)PV_1 = \$110$$

where PV_1 is the sum that you must set aside now.

Let's solve this simple equation to obtain PV_1:

$$PV_1 = \frac{\$110}{1.1} = \$100$$

That is to say, $100 will accumulate to $110 at the end of one year with a market rate of interest of 10 percent. Thus the present value of $110 one year from now, using a rate of interest of 10 percent, is $100. The formula for present value of any sums to be received one year from now thus becomes

$$PV_1 = \frac{FV_1}{1 + i}$$

where

PV_1 = present value of a sum one year hence
FV_1 = future sum of money paid or received one year hence
i = market rate of interest

Present Values for More Distant Periods. The present-value formula for figuring out today's worth of dollars to be received at a future date can now easily be seen. How much would have to be put in the same savings account today to have $110 two years from now if the account pays a rate of 10 percent per year compounded annually?

After one year, the sum that would have to be set aside, which we will call PV_2, would have grown to $PV_2 \times 1.1$. This amount during the second year would increase to $PV_2 \times 1.1 \times 1.1$, or $PV_2 \times (1.1)^2$. To find the PV_2 that would grow to $110 over two years, let

$$PV_2 \times (1.1)^2 = \$110$$

Present value
The value of a future amount expressed in today's dollars; the most that someone would pay today to receive a certain sum at some point in the future.

TABLE 29-2

Present Value of a Future Dollar

This table shows how much a dollar received at the end of a certain number of years in the future is worth today. For example, at 5 percent a year, a dollar to be received 20 years in the future is worth 37.7 cents; if received in 50 years, it isn't even worth a dime today. To find out how much $10,000 would be worth a certain number of years from now, just multiply the figures in the table by 10,000. For example, $10,000 received at the end of 10 years discounted at a 5 percent rate of interest would have a present value of $6,140.

	Compounded Annual Interest Rate				
Year	3%	5%	8%	10%	20%
1	.971	.952	.926	.909	.833
2	.943	.907	.857	.826	.694
3	.915	.864	.794	.751	.578
4	.889	.823	.735	.683	.482
5	.863	.784	.681	.620	.402
6	.838	.746	.630	.564	.335
7	.813	.711	.583	.513	.279
8	.789	.677	.540	.466	.233
9	.766	.645	.500	.424	.194
10	.744	.614	.463	.385	.162
15	.642	.481	.315	.239	.0649
20	.554	.377	.215	.148	.0261
25	.478	.295	.146	.0923	.0105
30	.412	.231	.0994	.0573	.00421
40	.307	.142	.0460	.0221	.000680
50	.228	.087	.0213	.00852	.000109

and solve for PV_2:

$$PV_2 = \frac{\$110}{(1.1)^2} = \$90.91$$

Thus the present value of $110 to be paid or received two years hence, discounted at an interest rate of 10 percent per year compounded annually, is equal to $90.91. In other words, $90.91 put into a savings account yielding 10 percent per year compounded interest would accumulate to $110 in two years.

The General Formula for Discounting. The general formula for **discounting** becomes

$$PV_t = \frac{FV_t}{(1+i)^t}$$

where t refers to the number of periods in the future the money is to be paid or received.

Table 29-2 gives the present value of $1 to be received in future years at various interest rates. The interest rate used to derive the present value is called the **rate of discount.**

Discounting
The method by which the present value of a future sum or a future stream of sums is obtained.

Rate of discount
The rate of interest used to discount future sums back to present value.

POLICY EXAMPLE
Should the "Pre-Death" Business Be Regulated?

Many Americans with terminal illnesses have life insurance policies which they would like to sell in order to use the proceeds while they are alive. To satisfy this demand, viatical ("provisions for a journey") companies make a present value calculation to determine how much they will pay to the person who is going to die. A terminally ill person with a life insurance policy may have an expected life of, say, four years. If the life insurance policy is sold to a viatical business, the latter must estimate the present value of receiving the payoff from the life insurance policy in four years. The company also has to determine an appropriate discount rate. The viatical business, which started around 1988, has enjoyed profits of around 20 percent a year. Cries in favor of state regulation of the business are now heard virtually everywhere. After all, dying people may be too willing to sell their life insurance policies at a low price because they do not have enough information. Already, state insurance commissioners have agreed that terminally ill patients with six months to live should be paid at least 80 percent of the face value of their policies.

FOR CRITICAL ANALYSIS: What alternatives do terminally ill life insurance policy holders have? (Hint: How could they use the policy as collateral?) ●

CONCEPTS IN BRIEF

- Interest is the price paid for the use of capital. It is also the cost of obtaining credit. In the credit market, the rate of interest paid depends on the length of the loan, the risk, and the handling charges, among other things.

- The interest rate is determined by the intersection of the supply curve of credit, or loanable funds, and the demand curve for credit, or loanable funds. The major sources for the demand for loanable funds are households, businesses, and governments.

- Nominal, or market, interest rates include a factor to take account of the anticipated rate of inflation. Therefore, during periods of high anticipated inflation, nominal interest rates will be relatively high.

- Payments received or costs incurred in the future are worth less than those received or incurred today. The present value of any future sum is lower the farther it occurs in the future and the greater the discount rate used.

Exercise 29.2
Visit www.econtoday.com for more about the lottery.

PROFITS

In Chapter 2, we identified entrepreneurship, or entrepreneurial talent, as a factor of production. Profit is the reward that this factor earns. You may recall that entrepreneurship involves engaging in the risk of starting new businesses. In a sense, then, nothing can be produced without an input of entrepreneurial skills.

Until now, we have been able to talk about the demand for and supply of labor, land, and capital. We can't talk as easily about the demand for and supply of entrepreneurship. For one thing, we have no way to quantify entrepreneurship. What measure should we use? We do know that entrepreneurship exists. We cannot, however, easily present a supply and demand analysis to show the market clearing price per unit of entrepreneurship. We must use a different approach, focusing on the reward for entrepreneurship—profit. First we will determine what profit is *not*. Then we will examine the sources of true, or economic, profit. Finally, we will look at the functions of profits in a market system.

Distinguishing Between Economic Profit and Business, or Accounting, Profit

In our discussion of rent, we had to make a distinction between the common notions of rent and the economist's concept of economic rent. We must do the same thing when we refer to profit. We always have to distinguish between **economic profit** and **accounting profit.** The accountant calculates profit for a business as the difference between total explicit revenues and total explicit costs. Consider an extreme example. You are given a large farm as part of your inheritance. All of the land, fertilizer, seed, machinery, and tools has been fully paid for by your deceased relative. You take over the farm and work on it diligently with

Economic profit
The difference between total revenues and the opportunity cost of all factors of production.

Accounting profit
Total revenues minus total explicit costs.

half a dozen workers. At the end of the year, you sell the output for $1 million. Your accountant then subtracts your actual ("explicit") expenses, mainly the wages you paid.

The difference is called profit, but it is not economic profit. Why? Because no accounting was taken of the *implicit* costs of using the land, seed, tools, and machinery. The only explicit cost considered was the workers' wages. But as long as the land could be rented out, the seed could be sold, and the tools and machinery could be leased, there was an opportunity cost to using them. To derive the economic profit that you might have earned last year from the farm, you must subtract from total revenues the full opportunity cost of all factors of production used (which will include both implicit and explicit costs).

In summary, then, accounting profit is used mainly to define taxable income and, as such, may include some returns to both the owner's labor and capital. Economic profit, by contrast, represents a return over and above the opportunity cost of all resources (including a normal return on the owner's entrepreneurial abilities).

When viewed in this light, it is possible for economic profit to be negative, even if accounting profit is positive. Turning to our farming example again, what if the opportunity cost of using all of the resources turned out to be $1.1 million? The economic profit would have been −$100,000. You would have suffered economic losses.

In sum, the businessperson's accounting definition and the economist's economic definition of profit usually do not coincide. Economic profit is a residual. It is whatever remains after all economic, or opportunity, costs have been taken into account.

Explanations of Economic Profit

Alternative explanations of profit are numerous. Let us examine a few of them: restrictions on entry, innovation, and reward for bearing uninsurable risks.

Restrictions on Entry.
We pointed out in Chapter 24 that monopoly profits—a special form of economic profits—are possible when there are barriers to entry, and these profits are often called monopoly rents by economists. Entry restrictions exist in many industries, including taxicabs, cable television franchises, and prescription drugs and eyeglasses. Basically, monopoly profits are built into the value of the business that owns the particular right to have the monopoly.

Innovation.
A number of economists have maintained that economic profits are created by innovation, which is defined as the creation of a new organizational strategy, a new marketing strategy, or a new product. This source of economic profit was popularized by Harvard economics professor Joseph Schumpeter (1883–1950). The innovator creates new economic profit opportunities through innovation. The successful innovator obtains a temporary monopoly position, garnering temporary economic profits. When other firms catch up, those temporary economic profits disappear.

Reward for Bearing Uninsurable Risks

There are risks in life, including those involved in any business venture. Many of these risks can be insured, however. You can insure against the risk of losing your house to fire, flood, hurricane, or earthquake. You can do the same if you own a business. You can insure against the risk of theft also. Insurance companies are willing to sell you such insurance because they can predict relatively accurately what percentage of a class of insured assets will suffer losses each year. They charge each insured person or business enough to pay for those fully anticipated losses and to make a normal rate of return.

But there are risks that cannot be insured. If you and a group of your friends get together and pool your resources to start a new business, no amount of statistical calculations can accurately predict whether your business will still be running a year from now or 10 years from now. Consequently, you can't, when you start your business, buy insurance against losing money, bad management, miscalculations about the size of the market, aggressive competition by big corporations, and the like. Entrepreneurs therefore incur uninsurable risks. According to a theory of profits advanced by economist Frank H. Knight (1885–1973), this is the origin of economic profit.

The Function of Economic Profit

In a market economy, the expectation of profits induces firms to discover new products, new production techniques, and new marketing techniques—literally all the new ways to make higher profits. Profits in this sense spur innovation and investment.

Profits also cause resources to move from lower-valued to higher-valued uses. Prices and sales are dictated by the consumer. If the demand curve is close to the origin, there will be few sales and few profits, if any. The lack of profits therefore means that there is insufficient demand to cover the opportunity cost of production. In the quest for higher profits, businesses will take resources out of areas in which either accounting losses or lower than normal rates of return are being made and put them into areas in which there is an expectation of higher profits. The profit reward is an inducement for an industry to expand when demand and supply conditions warrant it. Conversely, the existence of economic losses indicates that resources in the particular industry are not valued as highly as they might be elsewhere. These resources therefore move out of that industry, or at least no further resources are invested in it. Therefore, resources follow the businessperson's quest for higher profits. Profits allocate resources, just as wages and interest do.

CONCEPTS IN BRIEF

- Profit is the reward for entrepreneurial talent, a factor of production.

- It is necessary to distinguish between accounting profit and economic profit. Accounting profit is measured by the difference between total revenues and all explicit costs. Economic profit is measured by the difference between total revenues and the total of all opportunity costs of all factors of production.

- Theories of why profits exist include restriction on entry, innovation, and payment to entrepreneurs for taking uninsurable risks.

- The function of profits in a market economy is to allocate scarce resources. Resources will flow to wherever profits are highest.

Should HMOs Provide Cholesterol-Reducing Drugs?

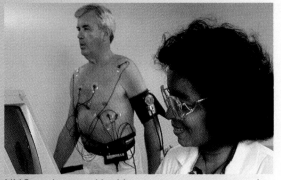

HMOs and managed health care organizations must make choices about how much to spend on preventive care. Why can't HMOs simply "spend whatever they need" to prevent illness and premature death?

CONCEPTS APPLIED:

COSTS, BENEFITS, PRESENT VALUE, SCARCITY, TRADE-OFFS, OPPORTUNITY COST

Visit www.econtoday.com for an Internet Activity that expands your understanding of these concepts.

Individuals with higher-than-average cholesterol have an increased risk of heart disease. Reduction in fatty foods, alcohol, and nicotine, plus increased exercise, can help most individuals reduce their cholesterol levels. Some individuals can do all of these things and still be plagued with high cholesterol.

Cholesterol-Reducing Drugs

There are cholesterol-lowering compounds called statins. These drugs appear to be effective in helping to prevent heart disease, but they are expensive. A typical 50-year-old male with high cholesterol would require about $700 of these drugs per year for the rest of his life. That ends up being a significant outlay for just one HMO patient. And if you add up all of the potential recipients of such heart-disease-reducing drugs, the tab would come to billions of dollars per year.

Present Value and the Cost-Benefit Analysis

HMOs have to make a decision by looking at the present value of a stream of costs that starts today, versus the present value of an anticipated benefit—less heart disease and fewer hospital and medical expenses—at some time in the future. The issue then becomes at what point the

financial burden—the present value of higher current costs—outweighs the expected gain—the present value of reduced future costs. Should HMOs target only high-risk individuals with such medications? Or should they extend such medications to other individuals? Heart disease is the costliest health problem by a large margin: a million Americans die annually from coronary artery disease. Some 800,000 patients a year undergo bypass surgery or other surgical procedures to reopen blocked arteries. The American Heart Association estimates that we are spending over 12 percent of our total yearly health care bill on heart disease.

Statins seem to be a natural for HMOs to reduce astronomical health care costs. Nonetheless, surveys show that only one-fourth of high-risk individuals are taking these drugs. One of the problems is that it takes at least two years of statin use in an HMO before the savings from prevented medical procedures start to show up. But HMOs face an annual member turnover of 15 percent or more. Some HMOs do not want to invest in expensive statins only to have such patients leave the HMO before it realizes the economic benefits.

FOR CRITICAL ANALYSIS

1. What are the ethical issues involved in prescribing preventive drugs for people at risk of heart disease?
2. How should HMOs decide these issues?

CHAPTER SUMMARY

1. Resources that have a fixed supply are paid what is called economic rent. We therefore define economic rent as the payment over and above what is necessary to keep a resource of constant quality and quantity in supply at its current level.

2. Resource owners (including labor owners) of factors with inelastic supply earn economic rent because competition among potential users of those resources bids up the price offered.

663

3. Interest can be defined as the payment for command over resources today rather than in the future. Interest is typically seen as the payment for credit, but it can also be considered the payment for the use of capital. Interest charged depends on length of loan, risk, and handling charges.

4. The equilibrium rate of interest is determined by the intersection of the demand for credit, or loanable funds, and the supply of credit, or loanable funds.

5. The nominal rate of interest includes a factor that takes account of the anticipated rate of inflation. In periods of high anticipated inflation, nominal, or

market, interest rates will be high. Real interest rates may not actually be higher, however, because they are defined as the nominal rate of interest minus the anticipated rate of inflation.

6. The present value of any sum in the future is less than that same sum today. Present value decreases as the sum is paid or obtained further and further in the future and as the rate of discount increases.

7. Frank Knight believed that profit was a payment to entrepreneurs for undertaking risks that are uninsurable. Other reasons why profit exists include restrictions on entry and reward for innovation.

DISCUSSION OF PREVIEW QUESTIONS

1. What is rent?

Rent is payment for the use of land. Economists have long played with the notion that land is completely inelastic in supply, although this is a debatable issue and depends on various definitions. Modern economists now refer to a payment to any factor of production that is in excess of opportunity cost as economic rent. For instance, from society's point of view, the total supply of land is fixed. Also, athletes and entertainers presumably earn economic rent: Beyond some "normal" income, the opportunity cost to superstars of performing is zero; hence "abnormal" income is not necessary to induce them to perform. Note that we usually discuss positively sloped supply schedules indicating that higher relative prices are necessary to induce increased quantity supplied. This is not the case with economic rent.

2. What is interest?

On the most obvious level, interest is a payment for the use of money. On another level, interest can be considered payment for obtaining credit; by borrowing, people (consumers or businesses) obtain command over resources now rather than in the future. Those who wish to make purchases now instead of later are allowed to do so even if they do not currently earn purchasing power. They do so by borrowing, and interest is the price they must pay for the privilege of making expenditures now instead of later.

3. What is the economic function of interest rates?

Interest rates are the price of credit, and like all prices, interest rates play an allocative role. That is, interest is a rationing device. We have said that interest is the price of credit; this credit is allocated to the house-

holds and businesses that are willing to pay the highest price (interest rate). Such is the rationing function of credit. On a more fundamental level, we can see that something other than scarce loanable funds is allocated. After all, businesses don't borrow money simply for the privilege of paying interest! The key to understanding what *physical* resources are being allocated is to follow the money: On what do businesses spend this borrowed money? The answer is for the most part, capital goods. Thus the interest rate plays the crucial role of allocating scarce capital goods; the firms that are willing to pay the highest interest rates will be the ones that will be able to purchase the most scarce capital goods. Firms putting capital to the most profitable uses will be able to pay the highest interest rates (and be most acceptable to lenders) and will therefore receive disproportionately greater quantities of new capital. Interest rates help bring about this capital rationing scheme in a market economy.

4. What is the economic function of profits?

Profit is the return on entrepreneurial talent or the price paid to risk takers. Profits also play a rationing role in society. Profits (in conjunction with interest rates) perform the all-important function of deciding which industries (and which firms within an industry) expand and which are forced to contract. Profitable firms can reinvest profits (and offer to pay higher interest rates), while unprofitable firms are forced to contract or go bankrupt. In short, businesses' quests for profits assure that scarce resources flow from less profitable to more profitable uses; profits help society decide which firms are to expand and which are to contract.

PROBLEMS

(Answers to the odd-numbered problems appear at the back of the book.)

29-1. "All revenues obtained by the Italian government from Renaissance art museums are economic rent." Is this statement true or false, and why?

29-2. Some people argue that the extraordinary earnings of entertainment and sports superstars are not economic rent at all but merely the cost of ensuring that a steady stream of would-be stars and starlets continues to flow into the sports and entertainment fields. How would the argument go?

29-3. "If employers paid marginal revenue product (MRP) to each of their inputs, there would be no profits left over." Is this statement true or false, and why?

29-4. The accompanying graph shows the supply of and demand for land. The vertical axis is the price per year received by landowners for permitting the land to be used by farmers.

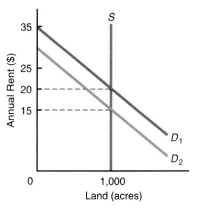

a. Assume that the demand curve for land is D_1. How much economic rent is received by landowners?
b. Now assume that the demand curve for land falls to D_2. How much economic rent is received now?

29-5. The graph shows the demand for and supply of loanable funds.

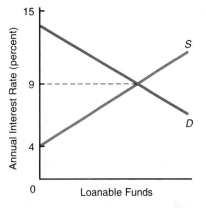

a. What is the equilibrium interest rate?
b. If the supply of loanable funds decreases, what will happen to the equilibrium interest rate?
c. If anticipated inflation is 4 percent for the year, what is the real equilibrium interest rate?

29-6. Make a list of risks that you might face in your life that you believe are insurable. Now make a list of risks that you believe are uninsurable. What is the general distinction between these lists?

29-7. Why do you think that the interest rate you have to pay on an automobile loan is greater than what you have to pay for a loan on a house? Why is the interest rate charged for a loan to purchase a used car usually more than for a loan to purchase a new car?

29-8. At the beginning of the 1980s, virtually all interest rates were much higher than they are in the 1990s. What do you think the major difference is between these two periods that might have caused interest rates to fall so dramatically?

29-9. Assume that everybody has perfect information about all events in the future. What would you expect to happen to economic profits in such a world?

COMPUTER-ASSISTED INSTRUCTION

We explore the many implications of the fact that differently dated goods are fundamentally different commodities.

Complete problem and answer appear on disk.

CHAPTER 30

INCOME, POVERTY, AND HEALTH CARE

You have heard of the baby boom generation, the millions of Americans born after
World War II, between 1946 and 1964. You
may be the offspring of baby boomer parents. The baby boom generation represents
a time bomb for all taxpayers. In the next
30 years, the number of Americans aged
65 and over will double. Today they number
about 35 million; by 2030, they will be
68 million. Over the same period, the population aged 20 to 64 will increase by only
about 20 percent. Therein lies the problem:
You, as a member of that working-age population, will probably be expected to pay an
increasingly large share in taxes to cover
baby boomers' Social Security and Medicare
benefits. To understand more about Social
Security and Medicare, you need to learn
about the issues of income distribution,
poverty, and health care.

PREVIEW QUESTIONS

1. What is a Lorenz curve, and what does it
   measure?

2. What has been happening to the distribution of
   income in the United States?

3. What is the difference between income and
   wealth?

4. Why do people earn different incomes?

Distribution of income
The way income is allocated
among the population.

Did You Know That . . . the most recent Internal Revenue Service (IRS) survey indicates that if your household makes about $75,000 or more in a one-year period, it is in the top 10 percent of income tax filers? If your income exceeds $95,000, you are in the top 5 percent of income earners, and if it exceeds $200,000, you are in the top 1 percent. Yet at the same time, there are more than 34 million people officially defined as living below the poverty line. Why do some people earn more income than others? Why is the **distribution of income** the way it is? Economists have devised various theories to explain this distribution. We will present some of these theories in this chapter. We will also present some of the more obvious institutional reasons why income is not distributed equally in the United States as well as what can be done about health care.

INCOME

Income provides each of us with the means of consuming and saving. Income can be derived from a payment for labor services or a payment for ownership of one of the other factors of production besides labor—land, physical capital, human capital, and entrepreneurship. In addition, individuals obtain spendable income from gifts and government transfers. (Some individuals also obtain income by stealing, but we will not treat this matter here.) Right now, let us examine how money income is distributed across classes of income earners within the United States.

Lorenz curve
A geometric representation of
the distribution of income. A
Lorenz curve that is perfectly
straight represents complete
income equality. The more
bowed a Lorenz curve, the
more unequally income is
distributed.

Measuring Income Distribution: The Lorenz Curve

We can represent the distribution of money income graphically with what is known as the **Lorenz curve,** named after a U.S.-born statistician, Max Otto Lorenz, who proposed it in 1905. The Lorenz curve shows what portion of total money income is accounted for by different proportions of the nation's households. Look at Figure 30-1. On the horizontal axis,

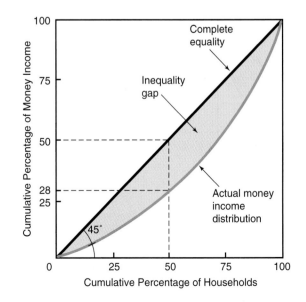

FIGURE 30-1

The Lorenz Curve
The horizontal axis measures the cumulative percentage of households from 0 to 100 percent. The vertical axis measures the cumulative percentage of money income from 0 to 100. A straight line at a 45-degree angle cuts the box in half and represents a line of complete income equality, along which 25 percent of the families get 25 percent of the money income, 50 percent get 50 percent, and so on. The Lorenz curve, showing actual money income distribution, is not a straight line but rather a curved line as shown. The difference between complete money income equality and the Lorenz curve is the inequality gap.

we measure the *cumulative* percentage of households, lowest-income households first. Starting at the left corner, there are zero households; at the right corner, we have 100 percent of households; and in the middle, we have 50 percent of households. The vertical axis represents the cumulative percentage of money income. The 45-degree line represents complete equality: 50 percent of the households obtain 50 percent of total income, 60 percent of the households obtain 60 percent of total income, and so on. Of course, in no real-world situation is there such complete equality of income; no actual Lorenz curve would be a straight line. Rather, it would be some curved line, like the one labeled "Actual money income distribution" in Figure 30-1. For example, the bottom 50 percent of households in the United States receive about 28 percent of total money income.

In Figure 30-2, we again show the actual money income distribution Lorenz curve, and we also compare it to the distribution of money income in 1929. Since that year, the Lorenz curve has become less bowed; that is, it has moved closer to the line of complete equality.

Criticisms of the Lorenz Curve. In recent years, economists have placed less and less emphasis on the shape of the Lorenz curve as an indication of the degree of income inequality in a country. There are five basic reasons why the Lorenz curve has been criticized:

1. The Lorenz curve is typically presented in terms of the distribution of *money* income only. It does not include **income in kind,** such as government-provided food stamps, education, or housing aid, and goods or services produced and consumed in the home or on the farm.
2. The Lorenz curve does not account for differences in the size of households or the number of wage earners they contain.
3. It does not account for age differences. Even if all families in the United States had exactly the same *lifetime* incomes, chances are that young families would have lower incomes, middle-aged families would have relatively high incomes, and retired families would have low incomes. Because the Lorenz curve is drawn at a moment in time, it could never tell us anything about the inequality of *lifetime* income.
4. The Lorenz curve ordinarily reflects money income *before* taxes.
5. It does not measure unreported income from the underground economy, a substantial source of income for some individuals.

Exercise 30.1
Visit www.econtoday.com for more about U.S. residents.

Income in kind
Income received in the form of goods and services, such as housing or medical care; to be contrasted with money income, which is simply income in dollars, or general purchasing power, that can be used to buy *any* goods and services.

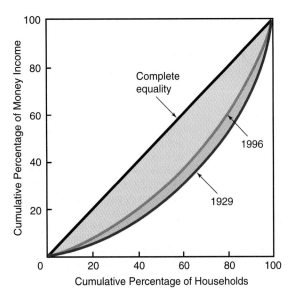

FIGURE 30-2

Lorenz Curves of Income Distribution, 1929 and 1996
Since 1929, the Lorenz curve has moved slightly inward toward the straight line of perfect income equality.
Source: U.S. Department of Commerce.

TABLE 30-1

Percentage Share of Money Income for Households Before Direct Taxes

Income Group	1996	1973	1960	1947
Lowest fifth	4.5	5.5	4.8	5.1
Second fifth	10.5	11.9	12.2	11.8
Third fifth	17.1	17.5	17.8	16.7
Fourth fifth	24.1	24.0	24.0	23.2
Highest fifth	43.9	41.1	41.3	43.3

Source: U.S. Bureau of the Census.
Note: Figures may not sum to 100 percent due to rounding.

Income Distribution in the United States

We could talk about the percentage of income earners within specific income classes—those earning between $20,001 and $30,000 per year, those earning between $30,001 and $40,000 per year, and so on. The problem with this type of analysis is that we live in a growing economy. Income, with some exceptions, is going up all the time. If we wish to make comparisons of the relative share of total income going to different income classes, we cannot look at specific amounts of money income. Instead, we talk about a distribution of income over five groups. Then we can talk about how much the bottom fifth (or quintile) makes compared with the top fifth, and so on. In Table 30-1, we see the percentage share of income for households before direct taxes. The table groups households according to whether they are in the lowest 20 percent of the income distribution, the second lowest 20 percent, and so on. We see that in 1996, the lowest 20 percent had a combined money income of 4.5 percent of the total money income of the entire population. This is a little less than the lowest 20 percent had at the end of World War II. Accordingly, the conclusion has been drawn that there have been only slight changes in the distribution of money income. Indeed, considering that the definition of money income used by the U.S. Bureau of the Census includes only wage and salary income, income from self-employment, interest and dividends, and such government transfer payments as Social Security and unemployment compensation, we have to agree that the distribution of money income has not changed. *Money* income, however, understates *total* income for individuals who receive in-kind transfers from the government in the form of food stamps, public housing, education, and so on. In particular, since World War II, the share of total income—money income plus in-kind benefits—going to the bottom 20 percent of households has probably more than doubled.

 INTERNATIONAL EXAMPLE
Relative Income Inequality Throughout the Richest Countries

The United States wins again—it has, according to the World Bank, the greatest amount of income inequality of any of the major industrialized countries. Look at Figure 30-3 on page 670. There you see the ratio of income of the richest 20 percent of households to the poorest 20 percent of households. Should something be done about such income inequality?

Public attitudes toward the government's role in reducing income inequality differ dramatically in the United States and elsewhere. Whereas fewer than 30 percent of Americans believe that government should reduce income differentials, between 60 and 80 percent of Britons, Germans, Italians, and Austrians believe it is the government's job.

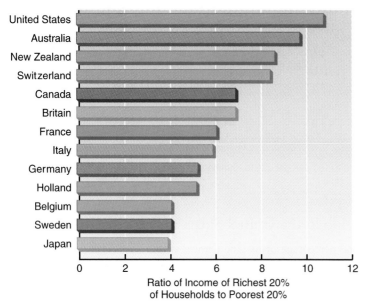

FIGURE 30-3

Relative Income Inequality in the World
The United States has greater income inequality than other developed countries.

Source: World Bank.

FOR CRITICAL ANALYSIS: Does it matter whether the same families stay in the lowest fifth of income earners over time? Otherwise stated, do we need to know anything about mobility across income groups? ●

The Distribution of Wealth

We have been referring to the distribution of income in the United States. We must realize that income—a flow—can be viewed as a return on wealth (both human and nonhuman)—a stock. A discussion of the distribution of income in the United States is not the same thing as a discussion of the distribution of wealth. A complete concept of wealth would include tangible objects, such as buildings, machinery, land, cars, and houses—nonhuman wealth—as well as people who have skills, knowledge, initiative, talents, and so on—human wealth. The total of human and nonhuman wealth in the United States makes up our nation's capital stock. (Note that the terms *wealth* and *capital* are often used only with reference to nonhuman wealth.) The capital stock consists of anything that can generate utility to individuals in the future. A fresh ripe tomato is not part of our capital stock. It has to be eaten before it turns rotten, and once it has been eaten, it can no longer generate satisfaction.

Figure 30-4 shows that the richest 10 percent of U.S. households hold about two-thirds of all wealth. The problem with those data, gathered by the Federal Reserve System, is that they do not include many important assets. The first of these is workers' claims on private pension plans, which equal at least $4 trillion according to economist Lawrence B. Lindsey. If you add the value of these pensions, household wealth increases by almost a quarter, meaning that the majority of U.S. house-

---

THINKING CRITICALLY ABOUT THE MEDIA

Increasing Income Inequality and Working Spouses

The media have been having a field day pointing out that the United States has the greatest income inequality in the industrialized world. Underlying the statistics, though, is a little-known fact: Income inequality is measured with respect to *households*. No distinction is made between one- and two-earner households. If two $80,000-a-year lawyers marry, their household income is now $160,000, and they have moved into a higher income group. Not surprisingly, most single tax returns show smaller earnings than joint returns of married couples. In 1969, some 48 percent of working-age married couples had two earners; today that figure is 72 percent. Consequently, part of the reported increase in income inequality in the United States is simply due to an increase in the number of working spouses.

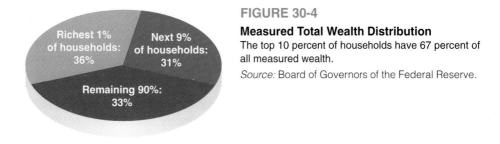

FIGURE 30-4

Measured Total Wealth Distribution

The top 10 percent of households have 67 percent of all measured wealth.

Source: Board of Governors of the Federal Reserve.

holds belong to the middle class. Also omitted is future Social Security liabilities, estimated at about $13 trillion. Again, most of this is "owned" by the middle class.

 EXAMPLE

Are We Running to Stay in Place?

There are a lot of statistics around that can show that the typical working person in the United States has not experienced an increase in standard of living since 1970. If we correct take-home wages for inflation, that is an accurate statement. Indeed, the secretary of labor has frequently announced that real wages have actually *fallen* since 1973. There are at least two problems with such statements, though. The first concerns total compensation. Compensation of workers does not consist solely of wages. Whereas in 1970, nonsalary benefits (medical care, insurance, pension payments, and so on) amounted to 24 percent of wages, they now come to around 40 percent. Second, even if after-tax real wages have not increased, the typical American household is at least 20 percent better off than in 1970. Why? Because more households have a second breadwinner. Furthermore, fewer babies are being born, so expenses per household are lower.

One other piece of data is telling: Virtually every measure of consumption per capita is growing, year in and year out. Consequently, the majority of Americans continue to experience increases in their standard of living as measured by their actual purchases of goods and services.

FOR CRITICAL ANALYSIS: Why might an individual be most concerned about total compensation? •

CONCEPTS IN BRIEF

- The Lorenz curve graphically represents the distribution of income. If it is a straight line, there is complete equality of income. The more it is bowed, the more inequality of income exists.

- The distribution of wealth is not the same as the distribution of income. Wealth includes assets such as houses, stocks, and bonds. Although the apparent distribution of wealth seems to be more concentrated at the top, the data used are not very accurate, and most summary statistics fail to take account of workers' claims on private and public pensions, which are substantial.

DETERMINANTS OF INCOME DIFFERENCES

We know that there are income differences—that is not in dispute. A more important question is why these differences in income occur, for if we know why income differences occur, perhaps we can change public policy, particularly with respect to helping people in the lowest income classes climb the income ladder. What is more, if we know the reasons for income differences, we can ascertain whether any of these determinants have changed over time. We will look at four income difference determinants: age, marginal productivity, inheritance, and discrimination.

Age

Age turns out to be a determinant of income because with age comes, usually, more education, more training, and more experience. It is not surprising that within every class of income earners, there seem to be regular cycles of earning behavior. Most individuals earn more when they are middle-aged than when they are younger or older. We call this the **age-earnings cycle.**

The Age-Earnings Cycle. Every occupation has its own age-earnings cycle, and every individual will probably experience some variation from the average. Nonetheless, we can characterize the typical age-earnings cycle graphically in Figure 30-5. Here we see that at age 18, income is relatively low. Income gradually rises until it peaks at about age 50. Then it falls until retirement, when it becomes zero (that is, currently earned income becomes zero, although retirement payments may then commence). The reason for such a regular cycle in earnings is fairly straightforward.

   When individuals start working at a young age, they typically have no work-related experience. Their ability to produce is less than that of more seasoned workers—that is, their productivity is lower. As they become older, they obtain more training and accumulate more experience. Their productivity rises, and they are therefore paid more. They also generally start to work longer hours. As the age of 50 approaches, the productivity of individual workers usually peaks. So, too, do the number of hours per week that are worked. After this peak in the age-earnings cycle, the detrimental effects of aging—decreases in stamina, strength, reaction time, and the like—usually outweigh any increases in training

Age-earnings cycle
The regular earnings profile of an individual throughout his or her lifetime. The age-earnings cycle usually starts with a low income, builds gradually to a peak at around age 50, and then gradually curves down until it approaches zero at retirement.

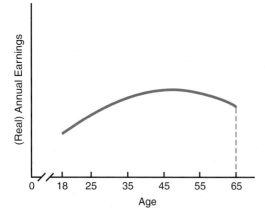

FIGURE 30-5

Typical Age-Earnings Profile
Within every class of income earners there is usually a typical age-earnings profile. Earnings are lowest when starting work at age 18, reach their peak at around age 50, and then taper off until retirement around age 65, when they become zero for most people. The rise in earnings up to age 50 is usually due to increased experience, longer working hours, and better training and schooling. (We abstract from economywide productivity changes that would shift the entire curve upward.)

or experience. Also, hours worked usually start to fall for older people. Finally, as a person reaches retirement, both productivity and hours worked diminish rather drastically.

Note that general increases in overall productivity for the entire workforce will result in an upward shift in the typical age-earnings profile given in Figure 30-5. Thus even at the end of the age-earnings cycle, when just about to retire, the worker would not receive a really low wage compared with the starting wage 45 years earlier. The wage would be higher due to factors that contribute to rising real wages for everyone, regardless of the stage in the age-earnings cycle.

Now we have some idea why specific individuals earn different incomes at different times in their lives, but we have yet to explain why different people are paid different amounts of money for their labor. One way to explain this is to recall the marginal productivity theory developed in Chapter 27.

Marginal Productivity

When trying to determine how many workers a firm would hire, we had to construct a marginal revenue product curve. We found that as more workers were hired, the marginal revenue product fell due to diminishing marginal returns. If the forces of demand and supply established a certain wage rate, workers would be hired until their marginal physical product times marginal revenue was equal to the going wage rate. Then the hiring would stop. This analysis suggests what workers can expect to be paid in the labor market: They can each expect to be paid their marginal revenue product (assuming that there are low-cost information flows and that the labor and product markets are competitive).

In a competitive situation, with mobility of labor resources (at least on the margin), workers who are being paid less than their marginal revenue product will be bid away to better employment opportunities. Either they will seek better employment themselves, or other employers will offer them a slightly higher wage rate. This process will continue until each worker is being paid his or her marginal revenue product.

You may balk at the suggestion that people are paid their marginal revenue product because you may personally know individuals whose MRP is more or less than what they are being paid. Such a situation may, in fact, exist because we do not live in a world of perfect information or in a world with perfectly competitive input and output markets. Employers cannot always seek out the most productive employees available. It takes resources to research the past records of potential employees, their training, their education, and their abilities. Nonetheless, competition creates a tendency toward equality of wages and MRP.

Determinants of Marginal Productivity.

If we accept marginal revenue product theory, we have a way to find out how people can earn higher incomes. If they can increase the value of their marginal physical product, they can expect to be paid more. Some of the determinants of marginal physical product are talent, education, experience, and training. Most of these are means by which marginal physical product can be increased. Let's examine them in greater detail.

Talent. This factor is the easiest to explain but difficult to acquire if you don't have it. Innate abilities and attributes can be very strong, if not overwhelming, determinants of a person's potential productivity. Strength, coordination, and mental alertness are facets of nonacquired human capital and thus have some bearing on the ability to earn income.

Someone who is extremely tall has a better chance of being a basketball player than someone who is short. A person born with a superior talent for abstract thinking has a better chance of making a relatively higher income as a mathematician or a physicist than someone who is not born with that talent.

Experience.   Additional experience at particular tasks is another way to increase productivity. Experience can be linked to the well-known *learning curve* that applies when the same task is done over and over. The worker repeating a task becomes more efficient: The worker can do the same task in less time or in the same amount of time but better. Take an example of a person going to work on an automobile assembly line. At first she is able to fasten only three bolts every two minutes. Then the worker becomes more adept and can fasten four bolts in the same time plus insert a rubber guard on the bumper. After a few more weeks, another task can be added. Experience allows this individual to improve her productivity. The more effectively people learn to do something, the quicker they can do it and the more efficient they are. Hence we would expect experience to lead to higher productivity. And we would expect people with more experience to be paid more than those with less experience. More experience, however, does not guarantee a higher wage rate. The *demand* for a person's services must also exist. Spending a long time to become a first-rate archer in modern society would probably add very little to a person's income. Experience has value only if the output is demanded by society.

Training.   Training is similar to experience but is more formal. Much of a person's increased productivity is due to on-the-job training. Many companies have training programs for new workers. On-the-job training is perhaps responsible for as much of an increase in productivity as is formal education beyond grade school.

EXAMPLE
Economists, Aging, and Productivity

Do the actions of professional economists fit the model that predicts a decrease in productivity after some peak at around age 50? Yes, according to University of Texas economist Daniel Hamermesh. One measure of productivity of economics professors is the number of articles they publish in professional journals. Whereas the over-50 economists constitute 30 percent of the profession, they contribute a mere 6 percent of the articles published in leading economics journals. Whereas 56 percent of economists between ages 36 and 50 submit articles on a regular basis, only 14 percent of economists over 50 do so.

FOR CRITICAL ANALYSIS: Why should we predict that an economist closer to retirement will submit fewer professional journal articles for publication than a younger economist? ●

Investment in Human Capital.   Investment in human capital is just like investment in any other thing. If you invest in yourself by going to college, rather than going to work after high school and earning more current income, you will presumably be rewarded in the future with a higher income or a more interesting job (or both). This is exactly the motivation that underlies the decision of many college-bound students to obtain a formal higher education. Undoubtedly there would be students going to school even if the rate of return on formal education were zero or negative. But we do expect that the higher the rate of return on investing in ourselves, the more such investment there will be. U.S. Labor Department data demonstrate conclusively that, on average, high school graduates make more than grade school graduates and that college graduates make more than high school graduates. The estimated annual income of a full-time worker with four years of college in the late-1990s was about $55,000. That person's high school counterpart was estimated to earn only $31,000, which gives a "college premium" of about 57 percent. Generally, the rate of return on investment in human capital is on a par with the rate of return on investment in other areas.

To figure out the rate of return on an investment in a college education, we first have to figure out the marginal costs of going to school. The main cost is not what you have to pay for books, fees, and tuition but rather the income you forgo. *The main cost of education is the income forgone—the opportunity cost of not working.* In addition, the direct expenses of college must be paid for. Not all students forgo all income during their college years. Many work part time. Taking account of those who work part time and those who are supported by state tuition grants and other scholarships, the average rate of return on going to college is somewhere between 8 and 12 percent. This is not a bad rate. Of course, this type of computation does leave out all the consumption benefits you get from attending college. Also omitted from the calculations is the change in personality after going to college. You undoubtedly come out a different person. Most people who go through college feel that they have improved themselves both culturally and intellectually in addition to having increased their potential marginal revenue product so that they can make more income. How do we measure the benefit from expanding our horizons and our desire to experience different things in life? This is not easy to measure, and such nonmoney benefits from investing in human capital are not included in normal calculations.

Inheritance

It is not unusual to inherit cash, jewelry, stocks, bonds, homes, or other real estate. Yet only about 10 percent of income inequality in the United States can be traced to differences in wealth that was inherited. If for some reason the government confiscated all property that had been inherited, there would be very little measured change in the distribution of income in the United States. In any event, at both federal and state levels of taxation, substantial inheritance taxes are levied on the estates of relatively wealthy deceased Americans (although there are some legally valid ways to avoid certain estate taxes).

Discrimination

Economic discrimination occurs whenever workers with the same marginal revenue product receive unequal pay due to some noneconomic factor such as their race, sex, or age. Alternatively, it occurs when there is unequal access to labor markets. It is possible—and indeed quite obvious—that discrimination affects the distribution of income. Certain groups in our society are not paid wages at rates comparable to those received by other groups, even when we correct for productivity. Differences in income remain between whites and nonwhites and between men and women. For example, the median income of black families is about 60 percent that of white families. The median wage rate of women is about 70 percent that of men. Some people argue that all of these differences are due to discrimination against nonwhites and against women. We cannot simply accept *any* differences in income as due to discrimination, though. What we need to do is discover why differences in income between groups exist and then determine if factors other than discrimination in the labor market can explain them. The unexplained part of income differences can rightfully be considered the result of discrimination.

Access to Education. African Americans and other minorities have faced discrimination in the acquisition of human capital. The amount and quality of schooling offered black Americans has generally been inferior to that offered whites. Even if minorities attend school as long as whites, their scholastic achievement can be lower because they are typically allotted fewer school resources than their white counterparts. Nonwhite urban individuals are more likely to live in lower-income areas, which have fewer resources to allocate to education due to the lower tax base. One study showed that nonwhite urban males receive between 23 and 27 percent less income than white urban males because of lower-quality education. This would mean that even if employment discrimination were substantially reduced, we would still expect to see a difference between white and nonwhite income because of the low quality of schooling received by the nonwhites and the resulting lower level of productivity. We say, therefore, that among other things, African Americans and certain other minority groups, such as Hispanics, suffer from too small an investment in human capital. Even when this difference in human capital is taken into account, however, there still appears to be an income differential that cannot be explained. The unexplained income differential between whites and blacks is often attributed to discrimination in the labor market. Because no better explanation is offered, we will stick with the notion that discrimination in the labor market does indeed exist.

THINKING CRITICALLY ABOUT THE MEDIA

Bad News—and Plenty of It

The media seem addicted to bad news, particularly with respect to the income and job gains of minorities and women. The reality is somewhat better, however. While it is still true that college-educated African-American males earn only 72 percent of what their white counterparts earn, 28 percent have executive, or administrative, or managerial jobs versus 30 percent of non-Hispanic whites. While it is still true that first-generation Hispanic immigrants have relatively low incomes, second-generation Mexican Americans earn almost identical wages to similarly educated non-Hispanic whites. Although women still earn less than men, in one generation they have gone from only low-level jobs to making up 40 percent of medical and law students, administrators, managers, executives, and Ph.D. candidates. Today, women make up almost 60 percent of public officials in America. Of course, the most elite jobs—senior managers in the top Fortune 500 companies—are still male-dominated. Consequently, many women are starting their own businesses.

The race and gender employment situation is not all roses, but it may not be as bad as the media tell us it is.

The Doctrine of Comparable Worth. Discrimination against women can occur because of barriers to entry in higher-paying occupations and because of discrimination in the acquisition of human capital, just as has occurred for African Americans. Consider the distribution of highest-paying and lowest-paying occupations. The lowest-paying jobs are dominated by females, both white and nonwhite. For example, the proportion of women in secretarial, clerical, janitorial, and food service jobs ranges from 70 percent (food service) to 97 percent (secretarial). Proponents of the **comparable-worth doctrine** feel that female secretaries, janitors, and food service workers should be making salaries comparable to those of male truck drivers or construction workers, assuming that the levels of skill and responsibility in these jobs are comparable. These advocates also believe that a comparable-worth policy would benefit the economy overall. They contend that adjusting the wages of workers in female-dominated jobs upward would create a move toward more efficient and less discriminatory labor markets.

Comparable-worth doctrine
The belief that women should receive the same wages as men if the levels of skill and responsibility in their jobs are equivalent.

THEORIES OF DESIRED INCOME DISTRIBUTION

We have talked about the factors affecting the distribution of income, but we have not yet mentioned the normative issue of how income *ought* to be distributed. This, of course, requires a value judgment. We are talking about the problem of economic justice. We can never completely resolve this problem because there are always going to be conflicting values. It is impossible to give all people what each thinks is just. Nonetheless, two particular normative standards for the distribution of income have been popular with economists. These are income distribution based on productivity and income distribution based on equality.

Productivity

The *productivity standard* for the distribution of income can be stated simply as "To each according to what he or she produces." This is also called the *contributive standard* because it is based on the principle of rewarding according to the contribution to society's total output. It is also sometimes referred to as the *merit standard* and is one of the oldest concepts of justice. People are rewarded according to merit, and merit is judged by one's ability to produce what is considered useful by society.

However, just as any standard is a value judgment, so is the productivity standard. It is rooted in the capitalist ethic and has been attacked vigorously by some economists and philosophers, including Karl Marx, who felt that people should be rewarded according to need and not according to productivity.

We measure a person's productive contribution in a capitalist system by the market value of that person's output. We have already referred to this as the marginal revenue product theory of wage determination.

Do not immediately jump to the conclusion that in a world of income distribution determined by productivity, society will necessarily allow the aged, the infirm, and the disabled to die of starvation because they are unproductive. In the United States today, the productivity standard is mixed with a standard based on people's "needs" so that the aged, the disabled, the involuntarily unemployed, the very young, and other unproductive (in the market sense of the word) members of the economy are provided for through private and public transfers.

Equality

The *egalitarian principle* of income distribution is simply "To each exactly the same." Everyone would have exactly the same amount of income. This criterion of income distribution has been debated as far back as biblical times. This system of income distribution has been considered equitable, meaning that presumably everybody is dealt with fairly and equally. There are problems, however, with an income distribution that is completely equal.

Some jobs are more unpleasant or more dangerous than others. Should the people undertaking these jobs be paid exactly the same as everyone else? Indeed, under an equal distribution of income, what incentive would there be for individuals to take risky, hazardous, or unpleasant jobs at all? What about overtime? Who would be willing to work overtime without additional pay? There is another problem: If everyone earned the same income, what incentive would there be for individuals to invest in their own human capital—a costly and time-consuming process?

Just consider the incentive structure within a corporation. Recall from Chapter 27 that much of the pay differential between, say, the CEO and all of the vice-presidents is meant to create competition among the vice-presidents for the CEO's job. The result is higher productivity. If all incomes were the same, much of this competition would disappear, and productivity would fall.

There is some evidence that differences in income lead to higher rates of economic growth. Future generations are therefore made better off. Elimination of income differences may reduce the rate of economic growth and cause future generations to be poorer than they otherwise might have been.

CONCEPTS IN BRIEF

- Most people follow an age-earnings cycle in which they earn relatively small incomes when they first start working, increase their incomes until about age 50, and then slowly experience a decrease in their real incomes as they approach retirement.

- If we accept the marginal revenue product theory of wages, workers can expect to be paid their marginal revenue product. However, full adjustment is never obtained, so some workers may be paid more or less than their MRP.

- Marginal physical productivity depends on talent, education, experience, and training.

- Going to school and receiving on-the-job training can be considered an investment in human capital. The main cost of education is the opportunity cost of not working.

- Discrimination is most easily observed in various groups' access to high-paying jobs and to quality education. Minorities and women are disproportionately underrepresented in high-paying jobs. Also, minorities sometimes do not receive access to higher education of the same quality offered to majority-group members.

- Proponents of the comparable-worth doctrine contend that disparate jobs can be compared by examining efforts, skill, and educational training and that wages should therefore be paid on the basis of this comparable worth.

- Two normative standards for income distribution are income distribution based on productivity and income distribution based on equality.

POVERTY AND ATTEMPTS TO ELIMINATE IT

Throughout the history of the world, mass poverty has been accepted as inevitable. However, this nation and others, particularly in the Western world, have sustained enough economic growth in the past several hundred years so that *mass* poverty can no longer be said to be a problem for these fortunate countries. As a matter of fact, the residual of poverty in the United States strikes us as bizarre, an anomaly. How can there still be so much poverty in a nation of such abundance? Having talked about the determinants of the distribution of income, we now have at least some ideas of why some people are destined to remain low-income earners throughout their lives.

There are methods of transferring income from the relatively well-to-do to the relatively poor, and as a nation we have been using them for a long time. Today, we have a vast array of welfare programs set up for the purpose of redistributing income. However, we know that these programs have not been entirely successful. Are there alternatives to our

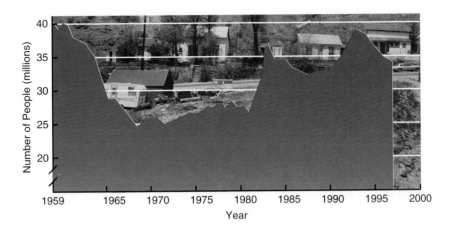

FIGURE 30-6
Official Number of Poor in the United States
The number of individuals classified as poor fell steadily from 1959 through 1969. From 1970 to 1981, the number stayed about the same. It then increased during the 1981–1982 recession, dropped off for a while, and rose in the early 1990s and then leveled off.
Source: U.S. Department of Labor.

current welfare system? Is there a better method of helping the poor? Before we answer these questions, let's look at the concept of poverty in more detail and at the characteristics of the poor. Figure 30-6 shows that those classified as poor fell steadily from 1959 to 1969, then leveled off until the recession of 1981–1982. The number started to rise dramatically, fell back during the late 1980s, rose again after the recession in the early 1990s, and has been falling slowly since then.

INTERNATIONAL EXAMPLE
Poverty Rates in the European Union

For years, politicians throughout much of the European Union have proclaimed their unwillingness to adopt the more laissez-faire, "let the chips fall where they may" economic model that prevails in the United States. They are convinced that the result is too much poverty. But they were shocked to discover in an article published in the newspaper *Le Monde* in 1997 that the poverty rate for the European Union was more than 17 percent—fully 57 million people out of a population of 330 million. Whereas the poverty rate in the United States has hovered between 13 and 15 percent of the population since the 1970s, the rate in Europe has increased over the same period from 10 percent to the current 17 percent. One-third of the officially poor in the European Union work, one-third are retired, and one-third are unemployed.

FOR CRITICAL ANALYSIS: What problems might there be in comparing poverty rates across nations? ●

Defining Poverty

The threshold income level, which is used to determine who falls into the poverty category, was originally based on the cost of a nutritionally adequate food plan designed by the U.S. Department of Agriculture for emergency or temporary use. The threshold was determined by multiplying the food plan cost by 3 on the assumption that food expenses comprise approximately one-third of a poor family's income. Annual revisions of the threshold level were based only on price changes in the food budget. In 1969, a federal interagency committee looked at the calculations of the threshold and decided to set new standards, with adjustments made on the basis of changes in the Consumer Price Index. For example, in 1996, the official poverty level for an urban family of four was around $16,000. It goes up each year to reflect whatever inflation has occurred.

Absolute Poverty

Because the low-income threshold is an absolute measure, we know that if it never changes in real terms, we will reduce poverty even if we do nothing. How can that be? The reasoning is straightforward. Real incomes in the United States have been growing at a compounded annual rate of almost 2 percent per capita for at least the past century and at about 2.5 percent since World War II. If we define the poverty line at a specific real level, more and more individuals will make incomes that exceed that poverty line. Thus in absolute terms, we will eliminate poverty (assuming continued per capita growth and no change in income distribution).

Relative Poverty

Be careful with this analysis, however. Poverty has generally been defined in relative terms; that is, it is defined in terms of the income levels of individuals or families relative to the rest of the population. As long as the distribution of income is not perfectly equal, there will always be some people who make less income than others, even if their relatively low income is high by historical standards. Thus in a relative sense, the problem of poverty will always exist, although it can be reduced. In any given year, for example, the absolute poverty level *officially* decided on by the U.S. government is far above the average income in many countries in the world.

Transfer Payments as Income

The official poverty level is based on pretax income, including cash but not in-kind subsidies—food stamps, housing vouchers, and the like. If we correct poverty levels for such benefits, the percentage of the population that is below the poverty line drops dramatically. Some economists argue that the way the official poverty level is calculated makes no sense in a nation that redistributed over $850 billion in cash and noncash transfers in 1998.

Furthermore, some of the nation's official poor partake in the informal, or underground, sectors of the economy without reporting their income from these sources. And some of the officially defined poor obtain benefits from owning their own home (40 percent of all poor households do own their own homes). Look at Figure 30-7 for two different views of what has happened to the relative position of this nation's poor. The graph shows the ratio of the top fifth of the nation's households to the bottom fifth of the nation's households. If we look only at measured income, it appears that the poor are getting relatively poorer compared to the rich (the top line). If we compare household spending (consumption), a different picture emerges. The nation's poorest households are in fact holding their own.

Attacks on Poverty: Major Income Maintenance Programs

There are a variety of income maintenance programs designed to help the poor. We examine a few of them here.

Social Security. For the retired, the unemployed, and the disabled, social insurance programs provide income payments in prescribed situations. The best known is Social Secu-

Exercise 30.2
Visit www.econtoday.com for more about poverty.

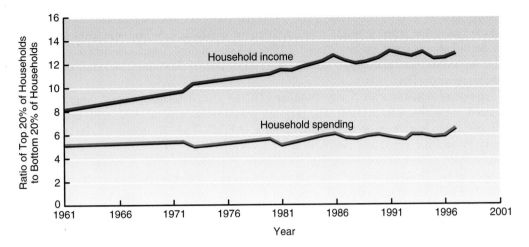

FIGURE 30-7

Relative Poverty: Comparing Household Incomes and Household Spending
This graph shows, on the vertical axis, the ratio of the top 20 percent of income-earning households
to the bottom 20 percent. If measured household income is used, there appears to be increasing
income inequality, particularly during the early to mid-1980s. If we look at household *spending*,
though, inequality appears to remain constant.
Sources: U.S. Bureau of Labor Statistics; U.S. Bureau of the Census.

rity, which includes what has been called old-age, survivors', and disability insurance
(OASDI). This is essentially a program of compulsory saving financed from compulsory
payroll taxes levied on both employers and employees. Workers pay for Social Security
while working and receive the benefits after retirement. The benefit payments are usually
made to people who have reached retirement age. When the insured worker dies, benefits
accrue to the survivors, including widows and children. Special benefits provide for disabled workers. Over 90 percent of all employed persons in the United States are covered
by OASDI. Social Security was originally designed as a social insurance program that
workers paid for themselves and under which they received benefits that varied with the
size of past contributions. Today, it is simply an intergenerational income transfer that is
only vaguely related to past earnings. It transfers income from Americans who work—the
young through the middle-aged—to those who do not work—older retired persons.

In 1998, more than 49 million people were receiving OASDI checks averaging about
$729 a month. Benefit payments from OASDI redistribute income to some degree. How-
ever, benefit payments are not based on recipient need. Participants' contributions give
them the right to benefits even if they would be financially secure without them. Social
Security is not really an insurance program because people are not guaranteed that the benefits they receive will be in line with the contributions they have made. It is not a personal
savings account. The benefits are legislated by Congress. In the future, Congress may not
be as sympathetic toward older people as it is today. It could (and probably will have to)
legislate for lower real levels of benefits instead of higher ones.

**Supplemental Security Income (SSI) and Temporary Assistance to Needy Fami-
lies (TANF).** Many people who are poor but do not qualify for Social Security benefits
are assisted through other programs. The federally financed and administered Supplemental Security Income (SSI) program was instituted in 1974. The purpose of SSI is to

establish a nationwide minimum income for the aged, the blind, and the disabled. SSI has become one of the fastest-growing transfer programs in America. Whereas in 1974 less than $8 billion was spent, the prediction for 1999 is $35.4 billion. Americans currently eligible for SSI include children and individuals claiming mental disabilities, including drug addicts and alcoholics.

Temporary Assistance to Needy Families (TANF) is a state-administered program, financed in part by federal grants. The program provides aid to families in need. TANF replaced Aid to Families with Dependant Children (AFDC). TANF is intended to be temporary. Projected expenditures for TANF are $21.4 billion in 1999.

Food Stamps.   Food stamps are government-issued coupons that can be used to purchase food. The food stamp program was started in 1964, seemingly, in retrospect, mainly to shore up the nation's agricultural sector by increasing demand for food through retail channels. In 1964, some 367,000 Americans were receiving food stamps. In 1998, the estimate is over 28 million recipients. The annual cost has jumped from $860,000 to more than $30 billion. In 1998, almost one in every nine citizens (including children) was using food stamps. The food stamp program has become a major part of the welfare system in the United States. The program has also become a method of promoting better nutrition among the poor.

The Earned Income Tax Credit Program (EITC).   In 1975, the EITC was created to provide rebates of Social Security taxes to low-income workers. Over one-fifth of all tax returns claim an earned-income tax credit. In some states, such as Mississippi, as well as the District of Columbia, nearly half of all families are eligible for EITC. The program works as follows: Households with a reported income of less than $25,300 (exclusive of welfare payments) receive EITC benefits up to $2,528. There is a catch, though. Those with earnings between $8,425 and $11,000 get a flat $2,528. But families earning between $11,000 and $25,300 get penalized 17.68 cents for every dollar they earn above $11,000. This constitutes a punitive tax. Thus the EITC discourages work by a low- or moderate-income earner more than it rewards work. In particular, it discourages low-income earners from taking on a second job. The General Accounting Office estimates that hours worked by working wives in EITC-beneficiary households have consequently decreased by 10 percent. The average EITC recipient works 1,300 hours compared to a normal work year of 2,000 hours.

No Apparent Reduction in Poverty Rates

In spite of the numerous programs in existence and the hundreds of billions of dollars transferred to the poor, the officially defined rate of poverty in the United States has shown no long-run tendency to decline. From 1945 until the early 1970s, the percentage of Americans in poverty fell steadily every year. It reached a low of around 11 percent in 1973, shot back up beyond 15 percent in 1983, fell steadily to 13.1 percent in 1990, and has stayed about that ever since. Why this has happened is a real puzzlement. Since the War on Poverty was launched under President Lyndon B. Johnson in 1965, nearly $4 trillion has been transferred to the poor, and yet more Americans are poor today than ever before. The Welfare Reform Act of 1996 put limits on people's use of welfare. The goal is now to get people off welfare and onto "workfare."

CONCEPTS IN BRIEF

- If poverty is defined in absolute terms, economic growth eventually decreases the number of officially defined poor. If poverty is defined relatively, however, we will never eliminate it.

- Major attacks on poverty have been social insurance programs in the form of Social Security, Supplemental Security Income, Aid to Families with Dependent Children, the earned-income tax credit, and food stamps.

- Although the relative lot of the poor measured by household income seems to have worsened, household spending by the bottom 20 percent of households compared to the top 20 percentile has shown little change since the 1960s.

Exercise 30.3
Visit www.econtoday.com for more about health insurance.

HEALTH CARE

It may seem strange to be reading about health care in a chapter on the distribution of income and poverty. Yet health care is in fact intimately related to those two topics. For example, sometimes people become poor because they do not have adequate health insurance (or have none at all), fall ill, and deplete all of their wealth on care. Moreover, sometimes individuals remain in certain jobs simply because their employer's health care package seems so good that they are afraid to change jobs and risk not being covered by health care insurance in the process. Finally, as you will see, much of the cause of the increased health care spending in America can be attributed to a change in the incentives that Americans face.

America's Health Care Situation

Spending for health care is estimated to account for 13 percent of the total annual income created in the U.S. economy. You can see from Figure 30-8 that in 1965, about 6 percent of annual income was spent on health care, but that percentage has been increasing ever since. Per capita spending on health care is greater in the United States than anywhere else in the world today. On a per capita basis, we spend more than twice as much as citizens of Luxembourg,

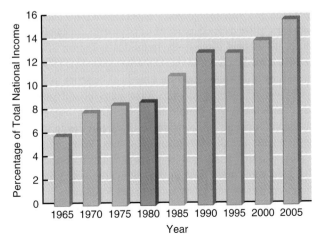

FIGURE 30-8

Percentage of Total National Income Spent on Health Care in the United States
Sources: U.S. Department of Commerce; U.S. Department of Health and Human Services; Deloitte and Touche LLP; VHA, Inc.

Austria, Australia, Japan, and Denmark. We spend almost three times as much on a per capita basis as citizens of Spain and Ireland.

Why Have Health Care Costs Risen So Much? There are numerous explanations for why health care costs have risen so much. At least one has to do with changing demographics: The U.S. population is getting older.

The Age–Health Care Expenditure Equation. The top 5 percent of health care users incur over 50 percent of all health costs. The bottom 70 percent of health care users account for only 10 percent of health care expenditures. Not surprisingly, the elderly make up most of the top users of health care services. Nursing home expenditures are made primarily by people older than 70. The use of hospitals is also dominated by the aged.

The U.S. population is aging steadily. More than 12 percent of the current 265 million Americans are over 65. It is estimated that by the year 2035, senior citizens will comprise about 22 percent of our population. This aging population stimulates the demand for health care. The elderly consume more than four times the per capita health care services that the rest of the population uses. In short, whatever the demand for health care services is today, it is likely to be considerably higher in the future as the U.S. population ages.

New Technologies. Another reason that health care costs have risen so dramatically is high technology. A CT (computerized tomography) scanner costs around $1 million. An MRI (magnetic resonance imaging) scanner can cost over $2 million. A PET (positron emission tomography) scanner costs around $4 million. All of these machines became increasingly available in the 1980s and 1990s and are desired throughout the country. Typical fees for procedures using them range from $300 to $500 for a CT scan to as high as $2,000 for a PET scan. The development of new technologies that help physicians and hospitals prolong human life is an ongoing process in an ever-advancing industry. New procedures at even higher prices can be expected in the future.

Third-Party Financing. Currently, government spending on health care constitutes over 40 percent of total health care spending (of which the *federal* government pays about 70 percent). Private insurance accounts for a little over 35 percent of payments for health care. The remainder—less than 20 percent—is paid directly by individuals. Figure 30-9 shows the change in the payment scheme for medical care in the United States since 1930. Medicare and Medicaid are the main sources of hospital and other medical benefits to 35 million Americans, most of whom are over 65. Medicaid—the joint state-federal program—provides long-term health care, particularly for people living in nursing homes. Medicare, Medicaid, and private insurance companies are considered **third parties** in the medical care equation. Caregivers and patients are the two primary parties. When third parties step in to pay for medical care, the quantity demanded for those services increases. For example, when Medicare and Medicaid went into effect in the 1960s, the volume of federal government–reimbursed medical services increased by more than 65 percent.

The availability of third-party payments for costly medical care has generated increases in the availability of hospital beds. Between 1974 and 1998, the number of hospital beds increased by over 50 percent. Present occupancy rates are only around 65 percent.

> **THINKING CRITICALLY ABOUT THE MEDIA**
>
> **The Difference Between Medical Care Expenditures and Medical Care Costs**
>
> For years, the media, as well as politicians around the country, have repeatedly decried rising medical care expenditures in the United States. In reality, the actual *cost* of being cured for a particular disease has been falling since 1900. Medical care expenditures have increased because medical progress now allows us to cure—sometimes at a very high price—more and more diseases and disorders. Back when these maladies were considered incurable, no effort was made to cure them and little was spent on treatment. That is why health care costs seemed so much lower then.

Third parties
Parties who are not directly involved in a given activity or transaction. For example, in the relationship between caregivers and patients, fees may be paid by third parties (insurance companies, government).

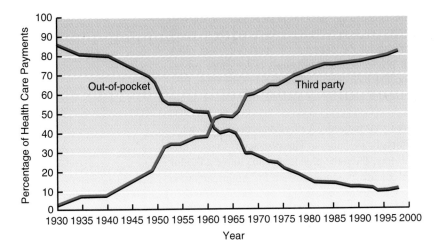

FIGURE 30-9

Third Party Versus Out-of-Pocket Health Care Payments

Out-of-pocket payments for health care services have been falling steadily since the 1930s. In contrast, third-party payments for health care have risen to the point that they account for over 80 percent of all such outlays today.

Sources: Health Care Financing Administration; U.S. Department of Health and Human Services.

Price, Quantity Demanded, and the Question of Moral Hazard. While some people may think that the demand for health care is insensitive to price changes, theory clearly indicates otherwise. Look at Figure 30-10. There you see a hypothetical demand curve for health care services. To the extent that third parties—whether government or private insurance—pay for health care, the out-of-pocket cost, or net price, to the individual will drop. In an extreme example, all medical expenses are paid for by third parties so that the price is zero in Figure 30-10 and the quantity demanded is many times what it would be at a higher price.

One of the issues here has to do with the problem of moral hazard. Consider two individuals with two different health insurance policies. The first policy pays for all medical expenses, but in the second the individual has to pay the first $1,000 a year (this amount is known as the *deductible*). Will the behavior of the two individuals be different? Generally, the answer is yes. The individual with no deductible may be more likely to seek treatment for health problems after they develop rather than try to avoid them and will generally expect medical attention on a more regular basis. In contrast, the individual who faces the first $1,000 of medical expenses each year will tend to engage in more wellness activities and will be less inclined to seek medical care for minor problems. The moral hazard here is that the individual with the zero deductible for medical care expenses may engage in a lifestyle that is less healthful than will the individual with the $1,000 deductible.

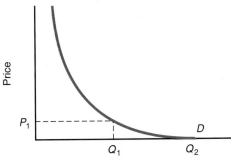

FIGURE 30-10

The Demand for Health Care Services

At price P_1, the quantity of health care services demanded per year would hypothetically be Q_1. If the price falls to zero (third-party payment with zero deductible), the quantity demanded expands to Q_2.

Quantity of Health Care Services per Year

Moral Hazard as It Affects Physicians and Hospitals. The issue of moral hazard also has a direct effect on the behavior of physicians and hospital administrators. Due to third-party payments, patients rarely have to worry about the expense of operations and other medical procedures. As a consequence, both physicians and hospitals order more procedures. Physicians are typically reimbursed on the basis of medical procedures; thus they have no financial interest in trying to keep hospital costs down. Indeed, many have an incentive to raise costs.

Such actions are most evident with terminally ill patients. A physician may order a CT scan and other costly procedures for a terminally ill patient. The physician knows that Medicare or some other type of insurance will pay. Then the physician can charge a fee for analyzing the CT scan. Fully 30 percent of Medicare expenditures are for Americans who are in the last six months of their lives.

Rising Medicare expenditures are one of the most serious problems facing the federal government today. The number of beneficiaries has increased from 19.1 million in 1966 (first year of operation) to an estimated 40 million in 1996. Figure 30-11 shows that federal spending on Medicare has been growing at over 10 percent a year, adjusted for inflation.

Is National Health Insurance the Answer?

Proponents of a national health care system believe that the current system relies too heavily on private insurers. They argue in favor of a Canadian-style system. In Canada, the government sets the fees that are paid to each doctor for seeing a patient and prohibits private practice. The Canadian government also imposes a cap on the incomes that any doctor can receive in a given year. The Canadian federal government provides a specified amount of funding to hospitals, leaving it to them to decide how to allocate the funds. If we were to follow the Canadian model, the average American would receive fewer health services than at present. Hospital stays would be longer, but there would be fewer tests and procedures. Today, there is no discernible difference in infant mortality or life expectancy between the United States and Canada. If we switched to using the Canadian health care system model, we would hence not expect to see any change in those two statistics.

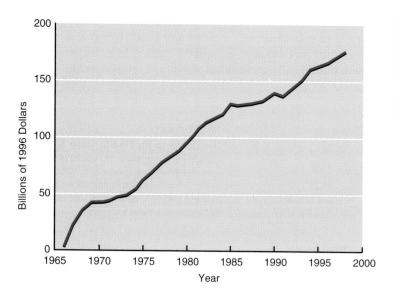

FIGURE 30-11

Federal Medicare Spending

Federal spending on Medicare has increased about 10 percent a year, after adjusting for inflation, since its inception in 1966.

Sources: Economic Report of the President; U.S. Bureau of Labor Statistics.

Alternatives to a national health care policy involve some type of national health insurance, perhaps offered only to people who qualify on the basis of low annual income. A number of politicians have offered variations on such a program. The over 20 million Americans who have no health insurance at some time during each year would certainly benefit. The share of annual national income that goes to health care expenditures would rise, however. Also, the federal budget deficit might increase by another $30 billion to $50 billion (or more) per year to pay for the program.

INTERNATIONAL EXAMPLE
Deterioration in the United Kingdom's National Health Care System

Many countries now have single-payer health care systems that in essence offer "free" universal health care. The United Kingdom's National Health Care Services (NHS) has been in existence since 1948. Once touted as one of the world's best national health care systems, both the system and the services it offers have deteriorated dramatically. In 1948, there were 10 hospital beds for every 1,000 people; today there are only 5 per 1,000. Since 1948, about 50 percent of that nation's hospitals have closed for "efficiency" reasons. The UK now has a lower hospital bed supply than any other Western European country except Portugal and Spain. Even its two most prestigious teaching hospitals are scheduled to close.

Because hospital bed space is limited, currently more than 1 million British subjects are on a waiting list for hospital admission. Many others who need medical care are not on the list because they are so discouraged by the long wait that they simply choose not to seek medical treatment. In some London hospitals, it is common for patients to wait more than 12 hours to see a doctor.

Despite all of the hospital closings and the decline in medical personnel, employment by the National Health Care system has skyrocketed. In 1948, there were .73 staff for each hospital bed; today there are 3.1. The additional staff do not deal directly with the treatment of patients, though. Rather they have become part of the NHS bureaucracy, which requires that a department or committee be established for every new area of medicine or research that develops. The NHS consists of a bureaucratic network unknown in the decentralized system in the United States.

FOR CRITICAL ANALYSIS: Why have so many hospitals been closed in the United Kingdom? •

Countering the Moral Hazard Problem: A Medical Savings Account

Medical savings accounts (MSAs)
A tax-exempt health care account to which individuals would pay into on a regular basis and from which medical care expenses could be paid.

As an alternative to completely changing the American health care industry, Congress has legislated an experiment in **medical savings accounts (MSAs).** Employers with 50 or fewer employees, as well as the self-employed and the uninsured, can set up a tax-free MSA. Eligible employees can make an annual tax-deductible contribution to an MSA up to a maximum of $2,250 for an individual and $4,500 for family. Money in the MSA accumulates tax-free, and distributions of MSA funds for medical expenses are also exempt. Any funds remaining in an MSA after an individual reaches age 65 can be withdrawn tax-free. Under current legislation, up to 750,000 employees can take advantage of the demonstration MSA program. The benefits can be impressive. A single person depositing $1,462.50 each year with no withdrawals will have $409,000 in the account after 40 years.

Combating Moral Hazard. A major benefit of an MSA is that the moral hazard problem is reduced. Individuals ultimately pay for their own minor medical expenses. They do not have the incentive to seek medical care as frequently for minor problems. In addition, they have an incentive to engage in wellness activities. Finally, for those using an MSA, the physician-patient relationship remains intact, for third parties (insurance companies or the government) do not intervene in paying or monitoring medical expenses. Patients with MSAs will not allow physicians to routinely order expensive tests for every minor ache or pain because they get to keep any money saved in the MSA.

Critics' Responses. Some critics argue that because individuals get to keep whatever they don't spend from their MSAs, they will forgo necessary visits to medical care facilities and may develop more serious medical problems as a consequence. Other critics argue that MSAs will sabotage managed care plans. Under managed care plans, deductibles are either reduced or eliminated completely. In exchange, managed health care plan participants are extremely limited in physician choice. Just the opposite would occur with MSAs—high deductibles and unlimited choice of physicians.

CYBERMEDICINE MAY REDUCE FUTURE MEDICAL COSTS

Cybermedicine, which is sometimes called *telemedicine*, involves using the Internet to send detailed digital X-rays, EKGs, and biopsy samples—reduced to computer data—to experts around the world. The use of the Internet to reach medical experts may eventually reduce medical costs. Individuals with rare diseases and medical problems will no longer have to travel to visit different experts. HMOs and managed care plans will be able to obtain second and third opinions about proposed surgery at minimal cost. Further, the Internet may eventually reduce the cost per constant-quality unit of medical care by spreading modern medical methods worldwide at a relatively low cost. Hundreds or thousands of doctors will be able to witness the latest in surgical and other procedures. Already, Massachusetts General Hospital, the Cleveland Clinic Foundation, Duke University Medical Center, and Johns Hopkins School of Medicine have formed a cybermedicine consortium called World-Care Limited in Cambridge, Massachusetts. Its goal is to spread modern medical techniques worldwide.

FOR CRITICAL ANALYSIS: Under what circumstances might cybermedicine actually increase the amount a nation's residents spend on medical care? ●

CONCEPTS IN BRIEF

- Health care costs have risen because (1) our population has been getting older and the elderly use more health care services, (2) new technologies and medicine cost more, and (3) third-party financing—private and government-sponsored health insurance—reduces the incentive for individuals to reduce their spending on health care services.

- National health insurance has been proposed as an answer to our current problems, but it does little to alter the reasons why health care costs continue to rise.

- An alternative to a national health care program might be medical savings accounts, which allow individuals to set aside money that is tax exempt, to be used only for medical care. Whatever is left over becomes a type of retirement account.

The percentage of the U.S. population over age 65 is growing so fast that Medicare expenditures threaten to become a major impediment to a balanced federal budget.

Should You Worry About Possible Medicare Bankruptcy?

CONCEPTS APPLIED:

DEMAND, MORAL HAZARD, MEDICARE, THIRD-PARTY PAYMENTS

Visit www.econtoday.com for an Internet Activity that expands your understanding of these concepts.

The major way in which retirees' medical care is paid is through the federal government program called Medicare. During the program's first full year of operation in 1967, it cost a mere $2.5 billion (or about $11 billion in 1998 dollars). Medicare outlays have increased to an estimated $198 billion in 1998. Part of this increase in Medicare spending has been due to the increase in the population of Americans over 65 years old. Part has been due, as you read in the chapter, to more expensive medical technology. Another part results from the increase in the quantity of medical care demanded due to the dramatic reduction in the price that Medicare-covered patients must actually pay directly for medical services. There is a moral hazard issue here also. When the federal government pays for all medical care, some retired people do not engage in as many "wellness" activities as they would if they had to pay at least part of their initial medical payments each time they were sick.

Does It Matter If the Medicare Trust Fund Goes Bankrupt?

As Figure 30-12 shows, the Medicare Hospital Trust Fund is projected to go bankrupt sometime after the turn of the century. The fund's assets reached their peak in 1995 at $137 billion. Under current legislation, Medicare's hospital insurance is running deficits every year. This will continue. Currently, about 3.9 taxpayers support each beneficiary of Medicare's hospital insurance, but by the year 2030, there will be just 2.3 taxpayers per beneficiary. The baby boomers' Medicare hospital insurance benefits cannot possibly be paid out of the revenues raised at current Medicare tax rates.

Actually, though, Medicare's supposed bankruptcy is not really the issue, just as Social Security's supposed potential bankruptcy is not a real issue. Within the federal government itself, trust funds mean nothing in real terms. Medicare and Social Security taxes are not specifically earmarked or kept in separate accounts. In the federal government's budget, a dollar spent is simply a dollar spent, no matter where it is spent. Likewise, a dollar of revenue is just a dollar of revenue, no matter what kind of tax it comes from. The Medicare issue is simply this: What percentage of total federal government spending is going to go to pay for the medical expenses of the nation's retired population? On the funding side, the issue is, How much more can the federal government raise tax rates to cover increased Medicare (and Social Security) spending without "killing the goose that laid the golden egg"? Specifically, if Medicare spending continues to increase, how will it be paid for, and what will be the effect?

Congress Keeps Adding to Medicare Expenses

On the one hand, Congress has attempted to reduce Medicare expenses by pressuring medical care providers to keep their costs down. On the other hand, Congress continues to expand procedures covered by Medicare and the population that is eligible. For example, each year, Congress seems to add new benefits, most recently for mammograms, osteoporosis, and education in self-testing for diabetics. Also, Medicare payments to HMOs serving rural areas recently were increased. Under the Clinton administration, "kiddy care" was added (but not as part of Medicare per se). Finally, the Clinton administration proposed adding certain individuals who were not retired to the Medicare health insurance system, albeit for a monthly charge that most experts agree will not cover the additional expenses.

When all is said and done, however, these issues are swamped by the sheer size of the baby boom generation

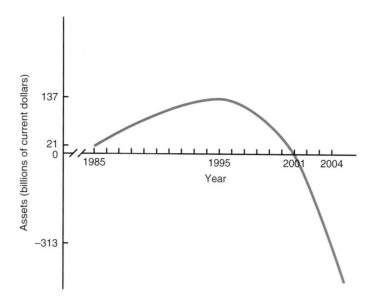

FIGURE 30-12

Rising Medicare Expenses Lead to a Depleted Medicare and Hospital Insurance Trust Fund
If current Medicare taxes stay the same, the Medicare Hospital Insurance Trust Fund will be depleted in the next few years and will accumulate deficits for years thereafter.

Source: Social Security Administration; Trustees of the Federal Hospital Insurance Trust Fund.

that is about to retire. This country is going to have an increasingly large post-65 population. The difference between current Medicare taxes and Medicare's hospital insurance payments—deficits—are projected to explode even before the baby boomers retire: $70 billion in 2003, almost $100 billion in 2005, and $115 billion in 2006. (The Federal Hospital Insurance Trust Fund trustees predict even greater deficits.)

The Bias in Medicare Spending

There is a strong bias in Medicare spending toward individuals in the last year of life. Nearly one-third of Medicare expenditures go to these individuals. Consequently, some critics of Medicare spending argue that longevity at any price should no longer be allowed. In other words, if as a society we wish to continue to provide medical insurance to retirees through the federal government, perhaps the government should limit its expenditures to only quality-enhancing medical care rather than longevity-enhancing medical care, at least for those over, say, some specific age such as 75. Britain, for example, does not allow kidney dialysis for people over a certain age. There are also restrictions on organ transplants for older people. In the United States there are none.

FOR CRITICAL ANALYSIS

1. "Life is priceless." How would the application of this philosophy change current medical spending in the United States?
2. Can you think of a way to reduce the moral hazard problem as it relates to Medicare health insurance? (Hint: Most eligible retirees pay almost nothing for most medical procedures.)

CHAPTER SUMMARY

1. We can represent the distribution of income graphically with a Lorenz curve. The extent to which the line is bowed from a straight line shows how unequal the distribution of income is.

2. The distribution of pretax money income in the United States has remained fairly constant since World War II. The lowest fifth of income earners still receive only about 5 percent of total pretax money

income, while the top fifth of income earners receive about 40 percent.

3. The distribution of wealth is not the same as the distribution of income. Wealth includes assets such as houses, stocks, and bonds. Though the apparent distribution of wealth seems to be more concentrated at the top, the data used are not very accurate, nor do most summary statistics take account of workers' claims on private and public pensions.

4. Most individuals face a particular age-earnings cycle. Earnings are lowest when starting out to work at age 18 to 24. They gradually rise and peak at about age 50, then fall until retirement age. They go up usually because of increased experience, increased training, and longer working hours.

5. The marginal productivity theory of the distribution of income indicates that workers can expect to be paid their marginal revenue product. The marginal physical product is determined largely by talent, education, experience, and training.

6. Discrimination is usually defined as a situation in which a certain group is paid a lower wage than other groups for the same work. It also exists in hiring and promotions.

7. One way to invest in your own human capital is to go to college. The investment usually pays off; the rate of return is somewhere between 8 and 12 percent.

8. A definition of poverty made in relative terms means that there will always be poor in our society because the distribution of income will never be exactly equal.

9. The major income maintenance programs are Social Security (OASDI), Aid to Families with Dependent Children (AFDC), Supplemental Security Income (SSI), and the Earned Income Tax Credit Program (EITC).

10. The costs of medical care have risen because the U.S. population has been getting older and the elderly use more health care services, new technologies and medicine cost more, and third-party financing (health insurance) lessens the incentive to reduce spending on health care services.

DISCUSSION OF PREVIEW QUESTIONS

1. **What is a Lorenz curve, and what does it measure?**
   A Lorenz curve indicates the portion of total money income accounted for by given proportions of a nation's households. It is a measure of income inequality that can be found by plotting the cumulative percentage of money income on the y axis and the percentage of households on the x axis. Two major problems with using the Lorenz curve to measure income equality are that it typically does not take into account income in kind, such as food stamps and housing aid, and that it does not account for differences in household size (and effort) or age. Adjustments for these would undoubtedly reduce the degree of measured income inequality in the United States.

2. **What has been happening to the distribution of income in the United States?**
   Since World War II, the distribution of *money* income has not changed significantly, but the distribution of

total income—which includes in-kind government transfers—has changed a great deal. Since the 1960s, *total* income inequality has been reduced significantly. The fact that more (total) income equality has been achieved in the United States in recent years is of tremendous importance, yet few people seem to be aware of this fact.

3. **What is the difference between income and wealth?**
   Income is a *flow* concept and as such is measured per unit of time; we usually state that a person's income is X dollars *per year.* Wealth is a *stock* concept; as such, it is measured at a given point in time. We usually say that a person's wealth is $200,000 or $1 million. If people save out of a given income, it is possible for their wealth to be rising while their income is constant. Technically, a person's wealth may be defined as the value of his or her assets (human and

nonhuman) minus his or her liabilities (wealth being equivalent to net worth) at some point in time.

4. Why do people earn different incomes?

The major theory to account for income differentials in market economies is the marginal productivity theory. This theory says that laborers (as well as other resources) tend to be paid the value of their marginal revenue product. Laborers who are paid less than their MRP will go to other employers who will gladly pay them more (it will be profitable for them to do

so); laborers who are being paid more than their MRP may well lose their jobs (at least in the private sector). Thus productivity differences due to age, talent (intelligence, aptitudes, coordination), experience, and training can account for income differences. Of course, imperfect markets can potentially lead to income differences, at a given productivity, due to exploitation and discrimination. Income differences can also be accounted for by differences in nonhuman wealth—individuals can earn income on their property holdings.

PROBLEMS

(Answers to the odd-numbered problems appear at the back of the book.)

30-1. It is often observed that black Americans, on average, earn less than whites. What are some possible reasons for these differences?

30-2. The accompanying graph shows Lorenz curves for two countries.

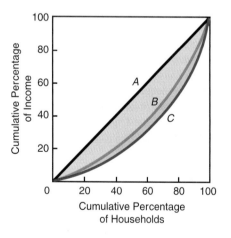

a. Which line indicates complete equality of income?
b. Which line indicates the most income inequality?
c. One country's "income inequality" is described by line *B*. Suppose that this country's income is to be adjusted for age and other variables such

that income on the *y* axis reflects *lifetime* income instead of income in a given year. Would the new, adjusted Lorenz curve move inward toward *A* or outward toward *C?*

30-3. What are two common normative standards of income distribution?

30-4. What does it mean when we say that some welfare recipients face a 120 percent marginal tax rate if they choose to go to work?

30-5. How might a program that truly made every household's income equal affect economy efficiency?

30-6. "Universal access" to health insurance has been a rallying cry for some people who wish to reform our current system. Under universal access, anyone who applies for insurance must be given it at the same rate that everybody else is paying. What might be some of the problems with such a system? (Hint: Would individuals want to join health insurance plans immediately or wait until they are sick with some long-term illness?)

30-7. What incentives do hospitals face when the federal and state governments pay for patients' health care? What incentives do government bureaucrats who work in the health care area face? What incentives do patients face when the government pays for their health care?

COMPUTER-ASSISTED INSTRUCTION

Many people believe that there is too much income inequality in the United States—that is, that the rich earn too much and the poor earn too little. This problem shows that the normal method of measuring income inequality is biased; it overstates true income inequality.

Complete problem and answer appear on disk.

INTERACTING WITH THE INTERNET

An excellent source for all sorts of statistics on the United States is the Census Bureau's site at

www.census.gov/

The holdings are quite extensive, so it may take a bit of effort to find what you want. Material includes the *Statistical Abstract of the United States,* providing details from the 1990 census, and the *County and City Data Book,* offering material on poverty. For nonmacroeconomic statistical material on the United States, you should check here first.

The Department of Health and Human Services is located at

www.os.dhhs.gov/

There you can find a number of links to its various agencies (such as the National Center for Health Statistics) and information about their programs.

For all the newest information on Medical Savings Accounts (MSAs) coming from Capitol Hill, go to

www.msanews.com/caphill.html

For general information and a whole lot more about Medicare, you can go to

www.hcfa.gov/medicare/medicare.htm

The Social Security Administration has its own Web page at

www.ssa.gov/

CHAPTER 31

ENVIRONMENTAL ECONOMICS

Recently, the founder of the CNN, Ted Turner, donated $1 billion (actually $100 million a year for ten years—he understands present value) to the United Nations. The purpose of the contribution was to help the UN fight global warming. Soon after the public announcement of the donation, Turner addressed a group of journalists on a summer day. He came into the room sweating. His first words were, "It's damn hot out there." The implication was that the extreme heat that day was a result of global warming. Is Turner right? If so, what is the best way to tackle the problem on a global scale? To answer these questions, you must learn about environmental economics. You will be looking at the costs and benefits of every action, including those already undertaken and those proposed to solve any problem of global dimension.

PREVIEW QUESTIONS

1. What is a negative externality?
2. How can poorly defined property rights create negative externalities?
3. If property rights are poorly defined, *must* negative externalities arise?
4. What is the optimal quantity of pollution?

Did You Know That . . . plants pollute? That's right, plants generate toxins as nature's attempt at protecting them from being eaten. Many of these toxins are known carcinogens. There are, for example, more known carcinogens in that cup of coffee you drink than in all of the pesticide residue on food that you consume in one year. Brussel sprouts, broccoli, mushrooms, potatoes, parsnips, and pears all contain natural carcinogens. When you think of pollution, nonetheless, you are probably thinking of smelly, foul, ugly air emanating from smokestacks across America, oil spills fouling pristine waters and killing wildlife, and other natural resources being ruined. Today, the American public, in general, appears to be willing to pay more to keep the environment "in good shape." But what does that mean?

As you might expect, after having read the previous chapters in this textbook, the economic way of thinking about the environment has a lot to do with costs. But of course your view of how to clean up the environment has a lot to do with costs also. Are you willing to give up driving your car in order to have a cleaner environment? Or would you pay $4 for a gallon of gas to help clean up the environment? In a phrase, how much of your current standard of living are you willing to give up to help the environment? The economic way of looking at ecological issues is often viewed as antienvironmental. But this is not so. Economists want to help citizens and policymakers opt for informed policies that have the maximum possible *net* benefits (benefits minus costs). As you will see, every decision in favor of "the environment" involves a trade-off.

PRIVATE VERSUS SOCIAL COSTS

Human actions often give rise to unwanted side effects—the destruction of our environment is one. Human actions generate pollutants that go into the air and the water. The question that is often asked is, Why can individuals and businesses continue to create pollution without necessarily paying directly for the negative consequences?

Until now, we've been dealing with situations in which the costs of an individual's actions are borne directly by the individual. When a business has to pay wages to workers, it knows exactly what its labor costs are. When it has to buy materials or build a plant, it knows quite well what these will cost. An individual who has to pay for car repairs or a theater ticket knows exactly what the cost will be. These costs are what we term *private costs*. **Private costs** are borne solely by the individuals who incur them. They are *internal* in the sense that the firm or household must explicitly take account of them.

Private costs
Costs borne solely by the individuals who incur them. Also called *internal costs*.

What about a situation in which a business dumps the waste products from its production process into a nearby river or in which an individual litters a public park or beach? Obviously, a cost is involved in these actions. When the firm pollutes the water, people downstream suffer the consequences. They may not want to swim in or drink the polluted water. They may also be unable to catch as many fish as before because of the pollution. In the case of littering, the people who come along after our litterer has cluttered the park or the beach are the ones who bear the costs. The cost of these actions is borne by people other than those who commit the actions. The creator of the cost is not the sole bearer. The costs are not internalized by the individual or firm; they are external. When we add *external* costs to *internal*, or private, costs, we get **social costs.** Pollution problems—indeed, all problems pertaining to the environment—may be viewed as situations in which social costs exceed private costs. Because some economic participants don't pay the full social costs of their actions but rather only the smaller private costs, their actions are socially "unacceptable." In such situations in which there is a divergence between social and private costs, we

Social costs
The full costs borne by society whenever a resource use occurs. Social costs can be measured by adding private, or internal, costs to external costs.

therefore see "too much" steel production, automobile driving, and beach littering, to pick only a few of the many possible examples.

The Costs of Polluted Air

Why is the air in cities so polluted from automobile exhaust fumes? When automobile drivers step into their cars, they bear only the private costs of driving. That is, they must pay for the gas, maintenance, depreciation, and insurance on their automobiles. However, they cause an additional cost, that of air pollution, which they are not forced to take account of when they make the decision to drive. Air pollution is a cost because it causes harm to individuals—burning eyes, respiratory ailments, and dirtier clothes, cars, and buildings. The air pollution created by automobile exhaust is a cost that individual operators of automobiles do not yet bear directly. The social cost of driving includes all the private costs plus at least the cost of air pollution, which society bears. Decisions made only on the basis of private costs lead to too much automobile driving or, alternatively, to too little money spent on the reduction of automobile pollution for a given amount of driving. Clean air is a scarce resource used by automobile drivers free of charge. They will use more of it than they would if they had to pay the full social costs.

EXTERNALITIES

When a private cost differs from a social cost, we say that there is an **externality** because individual decision makers are not paying (internalizing) all the costs. (We briefly covered this topic in Chapter 5.) Some of these costs remain external to the decision-making process. Remember that the full cost of using a scarce resource is borne one way or another by all who live in the society. That is, society must pay the full opportunity cost of any activity that uses scarce resources. The individual decision maker is the firm or the customer, and external costs and benefits will not enter into that individual's or firm's decision-making processes.

We might want to view the problem as it is presented in Figure 31-1. Here we have the market demand curve, *D,* for the product X and the supply curve, *S*₁, for product X. The

Externality
A situation in which a private cost diverges from a social cost; a situation in which the costs of an action are not fully borne by the two parties engaged in exchange or by an individual engaging in a scarce-resource-using activity. (Also applies to benefits.)

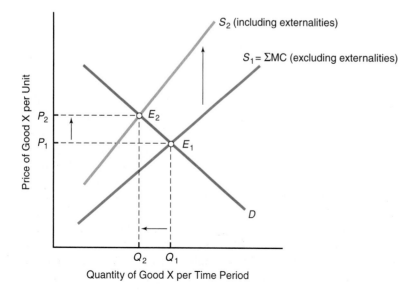

FIGURE 31-1

Reckoning with Full Social Costs
The supply curve, S_1, is equal to the horizontal summation (Σ) of the individual marginal cost curves above the respective minimum average variable costs of all the firms producing good X. These individual marginal cost curves include only internal, or private, costs. If the external costs were included and added to the private costs, we would have social costs. The supply curve would shift upward to S_2. In the uncorrected situation, the equilibrium price would be P_1 and the equilibrium quantity would be Q_1. In the corrected situation, the equilibrium price would rise to P_2 and the equilibrium quantity would fall to Q_2.

supply curve, S_1, includes only internal, or private, costs. The intersection of the demand and supply curves as drawn will be at price P_1 and quantity Q_1 (at E_1). However, we will assume that the production of good X involves externalities that the private firms did not take into account. Those externalities could be air pollution, water pollution, scenery destruction, or anything of that nature.

We know that the social costs of producing product X exceed the private costs. We show this by drawing curve S_2. It is above the original supply curve S_1 because it includes the full social costs of producing the product. If firms could be made to bear these costs, the price would be P_2 and the quantity Q_2 (at E_2). The inclusion of external costs in the decision-making process leads to a higher-priced product and a decline in quantity produced. Thus we see that when social costs are not being fully borne by the creators of those costs, the quantity produced is "excessive," because the price is too low.

CORRECTING FOR EXTERNALITIES

We can see here an easy method for reducing pollution and environmental degradation. Somehow the signals in the economy must be changed so that decision makers will take into account *all* the costs of their actions. In the case of automobile pollution, we might want to devise some method by which motorists are taxed according to the amount of pollution they cause. In the case of a firm, we might want to devise a system whereby businesses are taxed according to the amount of pollution for which they are responsible. In this manner, they would have an incentive to install pollution abatement equipment.

The Polluters' Choice

Facing an additional cost of polluting, firms will be induced to (1) install pollution abatement equipment or otherwise change production techniques so as to reduce the amount of pollution, (2) reduce pollution-causing activity, or (3) simply pay the price to pollute. The relative costs and benefits of each option for each polluter will determine which one or combination will be chosen. Allowing the choice is the efficient way to decide who pollutes and who doesn't. In principle, each polluter faces the full social cost of its actions and makes a production decision accordingly.

Is a Uniform Tax Appropriate?

It may not be appropriate to levy a *uniform* tax according to physical quantities of pollution. After all, we're talking about social costs. Such costs are not necessarily the same everywhere in the United States for the same action.

Essentially, we must establish the amount of the *economic damages* rather than the amount of the physical pollution. A polluting electrical plant in New York City will cause much more damage than the same plant in Remote, Montana. There are already innumerable demands on the air in New York City, so the pollution from smokestacks will not be cleansed away naturally. Millions of people will breathe the polluted air and thereby incur the costs of sore throats, sickness, emphysema, and even early death. Buildings will become dirtier faster because of the pollution, as will cars and clothes. A given quantity of pollution will cause more harm in concentrated urban environments than it will in less dense rural environments. If we were to establish some form of taxation to align private costs with social costs and to force people to internalize externalities, we would somehow have to come up with a measure of *economic* costs instead of *physical* quantities. But the tax, in any event, would fall on the private sector and modify private-sector economic agents' behavior. Therefore, because the economic cost for the same physical quantity of pollution would be different in different locations according to population density, the natural formation of mountains and rivers, and so forth, so-called optimal taxes on pollution would vary from location to location. (Nonetheless, a uniform tax might make sense when administrative costs, particularly the cost of ascertaining the actual economic costs, are relatively high.)

POLICY EXAMPLE
Should Car Antitheft Devices Be Subsidized?

Externalities exist for many activities. Consider the theft of automobiles. About 1.5 million cars are stolen in the United States every year. If you own an expensive car, you run a risk of having it stolen when you park on the street. Enter an antitheft device called Lojack, first used in 1986. A tiny transmitter is hidden in each Lojack-equipped car. When a car is stolen, in any of 20 major cities, the police can turn on the transmitter. About 95 percent of Lojack-equipped stolen cars are recovered and sustain less damage than other recovered stolen cars. Researchers Ian Ayres and S. D. Levitt of the National Bureau of Economic Research estimate that positive externalities are worth 15 times more than the benefit received by the Lojack-equipped car owner—when there are lots of Lojacks in the area, thieves leave the area, meaning that they don't steal non-Lojack-equipped cars either. One auto theft is eliminated annually for every three Lojacks installed in central cities.

FOR CRITICAL ANALYSIS: Who might want to subsidize Lojacks? •

CONCEPTS IN BRIEF

- Private costs are costs that are borne directly by consumers and producers when they engage in any resource-using activity.

- Social costs are private costs plus any other costs that are external to the decision maker. For example, the social costs of driving include all the private costs plus any pollution and congestion caused.

- When private costs differ from social costs, externalities exist because individual decision makers are not internalizing all the costs that society is bearing.

- When social costs exceed private costs, we say that there are externalities.

POLLUTION

The term *pollution* is used quite loosely and can refer to a variety of by-products of any activity. Industrial pollution involves mainly air and water but can also include noise and such concepts as aesthetic pollution, as when a landscape is altered in a negative way. For the most part, we will be analyzing the most common forms, air and water pollution.

When asked how much pollution there should be in the economy, many people will respond, "None." But if we ask those same people how much starvation or deprivation of consumer products should exist in the economy, many will again say, "None." Growing and distributing food or producing consumer products creates pollution, however. In effect, therefore, there is no correct answer to how much pollution should be in an economy because when we ask how much pollution there *should* be, we are entering the realm of normative economics. We are asking people to express values. There is no way to disprove somebody's value system scientifically. One way we can approach a discussion of the "correct" amount of pollution would be to set up the same type of marginal analysis we used in our discussion of a firm's employment and output decisions. That is to say, we should pursue measures to reduce pollution only up to the point at which the marginal benefit from further reduction equals the marginal cost of further reduction.

Look at Figure 31-2. On the horizontal axis, we show the degree of cleanliness of the air. A vertical line is drawn at 100 percent cleanliness—the air cannot become any cleaner. Consider the benefits of obtaining a greater degree of air cleanliness. These benefits are represented by the marginal benefit curve, which slopes downward because of the law of diminishing marginal utility.

When the air is very dirty, the marginal benefit from air that is a little cleaner appears to be relatively high, as shown on the vertical axis. As the air becomes cleaner and cleaner, however, the marginal benefit of a little bit more air cleanliness falls.

Consider the marginal cost of pollution abatement—that is, the marginal cost of obtaining cleaner air. In the 1960s, automobiles had no pollution abatement devices. Eliminating only 20 percent of the pollutants emitted by internal-combustion engines entailed a relatively small cost per unit of pollution removed. The cost of eliminating the next 20 percent rose, though. Finally, as we now get to the upper limits of removal of pollutants from the emissions of internal-combustion engines, we find that the elimination of one more percentage point of the amount of pollutants becomes astronomically expensive. To go from 97 percent cleanliness to 98 percent cleanliness involves a marginal cost that is many times greater than going from 10 percent cleanliness to 11 percent cleanliness.

It is realistic, therefore, to draw the marginal cost of pollution abatement as an upward-sloping curve, as shown in Figure 31-2. (The marginal cost curve slopes up because of the law of diminishing returns.)

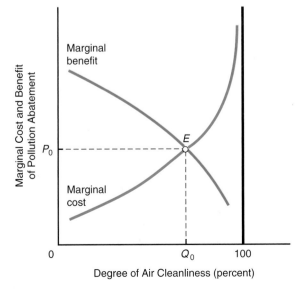

FIGURE 31-2

The Optimal Quantity of Air Pollution

As we attempt to get a greater degree of air cleanliness, the marginal cost rises until even the slightest attempt at increasing air cleanliness leads to a very high marginal cost, as can be seen at the upper right of the graph. Conversely, the marginal benefit curve slopes downward: The more pure air we have, the less we value an additional unit of pure air. Marginal cost and marginal benefit intersect at point E. The optimal degree of air cleanliness is something less than 100 percent at Q_0. The price that we should pay for the last unit of air cleanup is no greater than P_0, for that is where marginal cost equals marginal benefit.

The Optimal Quantity of Pollution

The **optimal quantity of pollution** is defined as the level of pollution at which the marginal benefit equals the marginal cost of obtaining clean air. This occurs at the intersection of the marginal benefit curve and the marginal cost curve in Figure 31-2, at point *E*, which is analytically exactly the same as for every other economic activity. If we increased pollution control by one more unit greater than Q_0, the marginal cost of that small increase in the degree of air cleanliness would be greater than the marginal benefit to society.

As is usually the case in economic analysis, the optimal quantity of just about anything occurs when marginal cost equals marginal benefit. That is, the optimal quantity of pollution occurs at the point at which the marginal cost of reducing (or abating) pollution is just equal to the marginal benefit of doing so. The marginal cost of pollution abatement rises as more and more abatement is achieved (as the environment becomes cleaner and cleaner, the *extra* cost of cleansing rises). The state of technology is such that early units of pollution abatement are easily achieved (at low cost), but attaining higher and higher levels of environmental quality becomes progressively more difficult (as the extra cost rises to prohibitive levels). At the same time, the marginal benefits of a cleaner and cleaner environment fall; the marginal benefit of pollution abatement declines as the concept of a cleaner and cleaner environment moves from human life-support requirements to recreation to beauty to a perfectly pure environment. The point at which the increasing marginal cost of pollution abatement equals the decreasing marginal benefit of pollution abatement defines the (theoretical) optimal quantity of pollution.

Recognizing that the optimal quantity of pollution is not zero becomes easier when we realize that it takes scarce resources to reduce pollution. It follows that a trade-off exists between producing a cleaner environment and producing other goods and services. In that sense, nature's ability to cleanse itself is a resource that can be analyzed like any other resource, and a cleaner environment must take its place with other societal wants.

Optimal quantity of pollution
The level of pollution for which the marginal benefit of one additional unit of clean air just equals the marginal cost of that additional unit of clean air.

Exercise 31.1
Visit www.econtoday.com for more about environmental protection.

CONCEPTS IN BRIEF

- The marginal cost of cleaning up the environment rises as we get closer to 100 percent cleanliness. Indeed, it rises at an increasing rate.

- The marginal benefit of environmental cleanliness falls as we have more of it.

- The optimal quantity of pollution is the quantity at which the marginal cost of cleanup equals the marginal benefit of cleanup.

- Pollution abatement is a trade-off. We trade off goods and services for cleaner air and water, and vice versa.

COMMON PROPERTY

In most cases, you do not have **private property rights**—exclusive ownership rights—to the air surrounding you, nor does anyone else. Air is a **common property**—nonexclusive—resource. Therein lies the crux of the problem. When no one owns a particular resource, no one has any incentive (conscience aside) to consider misuse of that resource. If one person decides not to pollute the air, there normally will be no significant effect on the total level of pollution. If one person decides not to pollute the ocean, there will still be approximately the same amount of ocean pollution—provided, of course, that the individual was previously responsible for only a small part of the total amount of ocean pollution.

Private property rights
Exclusive rights of ownership that allow the use, transfer, and exchange of property.

Common property
Property that is owned by everyone and therefore by no one. Air and water are examples of common property resources.

Basically, pollution occurs where we have poorly defined private property rights, as in air and common bodies of water. We do not, for example, have a visual pollution problem in people's attics. That is their own property, which they choose to keep as clean as they want, given their preferences for cleanliness as weighed against the costs of keeping the attic neat and tidy.

Where private property rights exist, individuals have legal recourse to any damages sustained through the misuse of their property. When private property rights are well defined, the use of property—that is, the use of resources—will generally involve contracting between the owners of those resources. If you own land, you might contract with another person who wants to use your land for raising cows. The contract would most likely be written in the form of a lease agreement.

INTERNATIONAL POLICY EXAMPLE
Dead Dogs in the Hills of Italy

Each September, about 110 miles north of Rome, a truffle hunt breaks out across 1,000 square miles of public land. Some 1,833 licensed "hunters" try their luck at finding truffles (a rare and hence expensive edible fungus), which grow wild on the buried roots of various trees. Truffle hunters use trained dogs to sniff out the hidden treasure. Each year, some of those dogs do not survive the truffle-hunting season. They are poisoned by bits of meat laced with strychnine—placed there by other truffle hunters seeking to reduce competition. In a recent year, more than 50 dogs died this way. The number of dogs poisoned turns out to be directly related to the market price of white Italian truffles. Several years ago, owing to a dry summer, the truffle crop dropped in half, the market price skyrocketed—and the number of dogs poisoned doubled from the previous year. Clearly, if the public land on which the truffles grow were not common property, the situation would be different.

FOR CRITICAL ANALYSIS: Assume that you owned all of the land in which Italian truffles grew. What system would you use for harvesting each year's crop? •

Voluntary Agreements and Transactions Costs

Is it possible for externalities to be internalized via voluntary agreement? Take a simple example. You live in a house with a nice view of a lake. The family living below you plants a tree. The tree grows so tall that it eventually starts to cut off your view. In most cities, no one has property rights to views; therefore, you cannot usually go to court to obtain relief. You do have the option of contracting with your neighbor, however.

Voluntary Agreements: Contracting. You have the option of paying your neighbors (contracting) to cut back the tree. You could start out with an offer of a small amount and keep going up until your neighbors agree or until you reach your limit. Your limit will equal the value you place on having an unobstructed view of the lake. Your neighbors will be willing if the payment is at least equal to the reduction in their intrinsic property value due to a stunted tree. Your offering the payment makes your neighbors aware of the social cost of their actions. The social cost here is equal to the care of the tree plus the cost suffered by you from an impeded view of the lake.

In essence, then, your offer of money income to your neighbors indicates to them that there is an opportunity cost to their actions. If they don't comply, they forfeit the money that you are offering them. The point here is that *opportunity cost always exists, whoever has property rights.* Therefore, we would expect under some circumstances that voluntary contracting will occur to internalize externalities.[1] The question is, When will voluntary agreements occur?

Transaction Costs. One major condition for the outcome just outlined above is that the **transaction costs**—all costs associated with making and enforcing agreements—must be low relative to the expected benefits of reaching an agreement. (We already looked at this topic briefly in Chapter 4.) If we expand our example to a much larger one such as air pollution, the transaction costs of numerous homeowners trying to reach agreements with the individuals and companies that create the pollution are relatively high. Consequently, we don't expect voluntary contracting to be an effective way to internalize the externality of air pollution.

Transaction costs
All costs associated with making, reaching, and enforcing agreements.

Changing Property Rights

In considering the problem of property rights, we can approach it by assuming that initially in a society, many property rights and many resources are not defined. But this situation does not cause a problem so long as no one cares to use the resources for which there are no property rights or so long as enough of these resources are available that people can have as much as they want at a zero price. Only when and if a use is found for a resource or the supply of a resource is inadequate at a zero price does a problem develop. The problem requires that something be done about deciding property rights. If not, the resource will be wasted and possibly even destroyed. Property rights can be assigned to individuals who will then assert control; or they may be assigned to government, which can maintain and preserve the resource, charge for its use, or implement some other rationing device. What we have seen with common property such as air and water is that governments have indeed attempted to take over the control of those resources so that they cannot be wasted or destroyed.

Another way of viewing the pollution problem is to argue that property rights are "sacred" and that there are property rights in every resource that exists. We can then say that each individual does not have the right to act on anything that is not his or her property. Hence no individual has the right to pollute because that amounts to using property that the individual does not specifically own.

Clearly, we must fill the gap between private costs and true social costs in situations in which we have to make up somehow for the fact that property rights are not well defined or assigned. There are three ways to fill this gap: taxation, subsidization, and regulation. Government is involved in all three. Unfortunately, government does not have perfect information and may not pick the appropriate tax, subsidy, or type of regulation. We also have to consider cases in which taxes are hard to enforce or subsidies are difficult to give out to "worthy" recipients. In such cases, outright prohibition of the polluting activity may be the optimal solution to a particular pollution problem. For example, if it is difficult to monitor the level of a particular type of pollution that even in small quantities can cause severe environmental damage, outright prohibition of such pollution may be the only alternative.

---

[1]This analysis is known as the *Coase theorem,* named after its originator, Ronald Coase, who demonstrated that negative or positive externalities do not necessarily require government intervention in situations in which property rights are defined and enforceable and transaction costs are relatively low.

Are There Alternatives to Pollution-Causing Resource Use?

Some people cannot understand why, if pollution is bad, we still use pollution-causing resources such as coal and oil to generate electricity. Why don't we forgo the use of such polluting resources and opt for one that apparently is pollution free, such as solar energy? Contrary to some people's beliefs, there is no nationwide or worldwide conspiracy to prevent us from shifting to solar power. The plain fact is that the cost of generating solar power in most circumstances is much higher than generating that same power through conventional means. We do not yet have the technology that allows us the luxury of driving solar-powered cars. Moreover, with current technology, the solar panels necessary to generate the electricity for the average town would cover massive sections of the countryside, and the manufacturing of those solar panels would itself generate pollution.

WILD SPECIES, COMMON PROPERTY, AND TRADE-OFFS

One of the most distressing common property problems concerns endangered species, usually in the wild. No one is too concerned about the quantity of dogs, cats, cattle, sheep, and horses. The reason is that virtually all of those species are private property. Spotted owls, bighorn mountain sheep, condors, and the like are typically common property. No one has a vested interest in making sure that they perpetuate in good health.

The federal government passed the Endangered Species Act in an attempt to prevent species from dying out. Initially, few individuals were affected by the rulings of the Interior Department with respect to which species were listed as endangered. Eventually, however, as more and more species were put on the endangered list, a trade-off became apparent. Nationwide, the trade-off was brought to the public's attention when the spotted owl was declared an endangered species in the Pacific Northwest. Ultimately, thousands of logging jobs were lost when the courts upheld the ban on logging in the areas presumed to be the spotted owl's natural habitat. Then another small bird, the marbled murrelet, was found in an ancient forest, causing the Pacific Lumber Company to cut back its logging practices. In 1995, the U.S. Supreme Court ruled that the federal government did have the right to regulate activities on private land in order to save endangered species.

The issues are not straightforward. Today, the earth has only .02 percent of all of the species that have ever lived. Every year, 1,000 to 3,000 new species are discovered and classified. Estimates of how many species are actually dying out vary from a high of 50,000 a year to a low of one every four years.

INTERNATIONAL POLICY EXAMPLE
Should Trading in Rhinoceros Horns Be Allowed?

Since 1977, the United Nations has banned international trade in rhino horns in order to save the species from extinction. The price for the illegal product has increased, and the amount of poaching of this once common species in Africa has skyrocketed—to the point that 90 percent of the world's rhinos have been lost. Some African countries have asked for the right to trade in rhino parts. They argue that they want to transfer ownership of rhinos to various tribes, which will then have an incentive to prevent poaching and to allow the rhino population to increase. The U.S. Humane Society and the U.S. Fish and Wildlife Service both continue to oppose the legalization of international trading in rhino products.

FOR CRITICAL ANALYSIS: Explain why protection of a species may require international trading in that species. ●

CONCEPTS IN BRIEF

- A common property resource is one that no one owns—or, otherwise stated, that everyone owns.

- Common property exists when property rights are indefinite or nonexistent.

- When no property rights exist, pollution occurs because no one individual or firm has a sufficient economic incentive to care for the common property in question, be it air, water, or scenery.

- Private costs will not equal social costs when common property is at issue unless only a few individuals are involved and they are able to contract among themselves.

RECYCLING

As part of the overall ecology movement, there has been a major push to save scarce resources via recycling. **Recycling** involves reusing paper products, plastics, glass, and metals rather than putting them into solid waste dumps. Many cities have instituted mandatory recycling programs.

The benefits of recycling are straightforward. Fewer *natural* resources are used. But some economists argue that recycling does not necessarily save *total* resources. For example, recycling paper products may not necessarily save trees, according to A. Clark Wiseman, an economist for Resources for the Future in Washington, D.C. He argues that an increase in paper recycling will eventually lead to a reduction in the demand for virgin paper and thus for trees. Because most trees are planted specifically to produce paper, a reduction in the demand for trees will mean that certain land now used to grow trees will be put to other uses. The end result may be smaller rather than larger forests, a result that is probably not desired in the long run.

Recycling
The reuse of raw materials derived from manufactured products.

Recycling's Invisible Costs

The recycling of paper can also pollute. Used paper has ink on it that has to be removed during the recycling process. According to the National Wildlife Federation, the product of 100 tons of deinked (bleached) fiber generates 40 tons of sludge. This sludge has to be disposed of, usually in a landfill. A lot of recycled paper companies, however, are beginning to produce unbleached paper. In general, recycling does create waste that has to be disposed of.

There is also an issue involved in the use of resources. Recycling requires human effort. The labor resources involved in recycling are often many times more costly than the potential savings in scarce resources not used. That means that net resource use, counting all resources, may sometimes be greater with recycling than without it.

Exercise 31.2
Visit www.econtoday.com for more about recycling.

Landfills

One of the arguments in favor of recycling is to avoid a solid waste "crisis." Some people believe that we are running out of solid waste dump sites in the United States. This is perhaps true in and near major cities, and indeed the most populated areas of the country might ultimately benefit from recycling programs. In the rest of the United States, however, the data do not seem to indicate that we are running out of solid waste landfill sites. Throughout the United States, the disposal price per ton of city garbage has actually fallen. Prices vary, of course, for the 180 million tons of trash generated each year. In San Jose, California, it costs $10 a ton to dump, whereas in Morris County, New Jersey, it costs $131 a ton.

Currently, municipal governments can do three things with solid waste: burn it, bury it, or recycle it. The amount of solid waste dumped in landfills is dropping, even as total trash output rises. Consider, though, that the total garbage output of the United States for the entire twenty-first century could be put in a 30-square-mile landfill that is only 1,000 feet deep. Recycling to reduce solid waste disposal may end up costing society more resources simply because putting such waste into a landfill may be a less costly alternative.

INTERNATIONAL POLICY EXAMPLE
Can Citizens Recycle Too Much? The Case of Germany

Recycling is popular throughout the European Union, but the Germans have raised it to an art form. Germany has a law requiring that manufacturers or retailers take back their packaging or ensure that 80 percent of it is collected rather than thrown away. What is collected must be recycled or reused. The law covers about 40 percent of the country's garbage. The problem is that German consumers responded more enthusiastically than anticipated: So much plastic packaging has been collected that German recyclers do not have the capacity to use it all. Consequently, Germany has been exporting its recyclable waste to neighboring Belgium, France, and the Netherlands. France threatened to curb its imports of German recyclable trash. Belgium even argued in front of the European Parliament that Germany was engaging in unfair competition. In the meantime, the company in charge of recycling Germany's trash, Duales System Deutschland, is losing hundreds of millions of dollars a year. Considering that it costs $2,000 a ton to recycle plastic and that the price of petroleum (the main ingredient in plastic) is relatively low, the future of recycling in Germany does not look bright.

FOR CRITICAL ANALYSIS: How is it possible to recycle "too much"? ●

Should We Save Scarce Resources?

Periodically, the call for recycling focuses on the necessity of saving scarce resources because "we are running out." There is little evidence to back up this claim because virtually every natural resource has fallen in price (corrected for inflation) over the past several decades. In 1980, economist Julian Simon made a $1,000 bet with well-known environmentalist Paul Erlich. Simon bet $200 per resource that any five natural resources that Erlich picked would decline in price (corrected for inflation) by the end of the 1980s. Simon won. (When Simon asked Erlich to renew the bet for $20,000 for the 1990s, Erlich declined.) During the 1980s, the price of virtually every natural resource fell (corrected for inflation), and so did the price of every agricultural commodity. The same was true for every forest product. Though few people remember the dire

---

THINKING CRITICALLY ABOUT THE MEDIA

We Are Running Out of Everything!

It is going to be a world with no more oil, natural gas, copper, or zinc. At least that is the impression one gets these days from the media. In reality, as Yale University economist William Nordhaus has discovered, the real (inflation-corrected) prices for most nonrenewable resources have fallen over the past 125 years. Real energy prices have dropped an average of 1.6 percent per year; major mineral prices have dropped 1.3 to 2.9 percent a year; even the price of land has dropped .8 percent per year. Unless supply and demand analysis is no longer valid, those numbers indicate that the supply of nonrenewable resources is increasing faster than the demand.

predictions of the 1970s, many noneconomists throughout the world argued at that time that the world's oil reserves were vanishing. If this were true, the pretax, inflation-corrected price of gasoline would not be the same today as it was in the late 1940s (which it is).

In spite of predictions in the early 1980s by World Watch Institute president Lester Brown, real food prices did not rise. Indeed, the real price of food fell by more than 30 percent for the major agricultural commodities during the 1980s. A casual knowledge of supply and demand tells you that since demand for food did not decrease, supply must have increased faster than demand.

With respect to the forests, at least in the United States and Western Europe, there are more forests today than there were 100 years ago. In this country, the major problems of deforestation seem to be on land owned by the United States Forest Service for which private timber companies are paid almost $1 billion a year in subsidies to cut down trees.

EXAMPLE
Predicting Doom Sells Books

Since 1798, when Thomas Malthus wrote a pamphlet describing how population would outstrip the food supply, predictors of doom have made fortunes in the book market. In 1865, Stanley Jevons sold many copies of a book that predicted that Britain would run out of coal. Booklets were published by the U.S. Bureau of Mines in 1914 predicting that America would run out of oil by 1924. The U.S. Department of the Interior in 1939 and again in 1951 warned that Americans would run out of oil in 13 years. In 1972, the Club of Rome published a best-selling book, *Limits to Growth.* It predicted that we would run out of oil by the year 2000. In 1973, the World Watch Institute reiterated Malthus's prediction that the population would outstrip food production. Around that same time, such books as *The Population Bomb* became best-sellers, making predictions not too dissimilar to Malthus's.

On the environmental front, disaster has been predicted for hundreds of years, also. For example, the United Nations predicted in 1984 that the desert was claiming 50 million acres of land every year. Since that time, there has been no net advance of the desert at all. In 1992, Al Gore said that deforestation was occurring in the Amazon at a rate of 200 million acres a year. He was off by a factor of eight, but nobody seemed to mind.

The fact is, doom sells. Dispassionate economic analysis does not. After all, one can find numerous economists in the 1970s who predicted abundant food (which we have), cheap oil (corrected for inflation, oil sells for the price it did right after World War II), and copious minerals (virtually all real prices have fallen). The press tends to ignore such people even today.

FOR CRITICAL ANALYSIS: Why do you think predictions of doom sell so well but level-headed analyses do not? •

CONCEPTS IN BRIEF

- Recycling involves reusing paper, glass, and other materials rather than putting them into solid waste dumps. Recycling does have a cost both in the resources used for recycling and in the pollution created during recycling, such as the sludge from deinking paper for reuse.

- Landfills are an alternative to recycling. Expansion of these solid waste disposal sites is outpacing demand increases.

- Resources may not be getting scarcer. The inflation-corrected price of most resources has been falling for decades.

Ted Turner meets with UN Secretary General Kofi Annan before announcing to the General Assembly his donation of $1 billion to be used exclusively to help fight global warming. What can the UN do with such funds?

The Real Issues Behind Global Warming

CONCEPTS APPLIED:

COSTS, BENEFITS, PRESENT VALUE, EXTERNALITIES

Visit www.econtoday.com for an Internet Activity that expands your understanding of these concepts.

Less than two decades ago, newsmagazines ran several years of articles on the "coming ice age." But today, we're worried about global warming—governments are ready to take drastic action to reduce so-called greenhouse gases, the cost of which may be in the trillions of dollars. The reality is that the earth has been experiencing a warming trend for the past 10,000 to 15,000 years—since the last ice age. Warm periods have alternated with ice ages for at least 2 million years; warming periods may last as long as 400,000 years.

Each year, humans release 6 billion tons of industrial carbon dioxide into the atmosphere. In contrast, 700 billion tons are released from geologic and biologic processes over which humans have no control. The latest major scientific study produced by the Intergovernmental Panel on Climate Change from the United Nations states that "none of the studies . . . have shown clear evidence that we can attribute the observed climate changes to the specific cause of increases in greenhouse gases." Nonetheless, President Clinton stated that "it is no longer a threat, but now a fact, that global warming is for real."

Looking at Costs and Benefits

Clearly, scientific debate continues on the issue of global warming. Let's look at the economics. If there is global warming and we do nothing, there are costs and benefits. If we do something, such as reduce greenhouse gases resulting from human activities, there are also costs and benefits. What are they?

Let's assume that the earth will warm by 2 degrees Celsius over the next century (that is far less, in fact, than what has actually occurred during various periods in the geologic past). There will be winners and losers. Much of the warming will be felt at night at higher latitudes, thereby extending growing seasons. The energy differential between polar and equatorial regions will decrease. On the cost side, some coastal areas may be affected by rising sea levels and warmer coastal waters, and some island populations may suffer.

Thus there are also costs and benefits for any policy to curtail global warming. Representatives of more than 100 countries who attended the Global Warming Summit in Kyoto, Japan, in December 1997 pledged that their nations would reduce greenhouse gases. Such a pledge, if carried out, may slow global warming, but it will carry a heavy price. Just in the United States, for example, reducing greenhouse gases to their 1990 levels would represent a loss to the economy of between 3 and 4 percent of total annual output—hundreds of billions of dollars. This would result from shutting down many electricity-generating and steelmaking plants that use coal.

FOR CRITICAL ANALYSIS

1. Any international treaty to reduce greenhouse gases must be approved by the Senate. Which groups in America will fight the hardest against approving such a treaty?
2. What are the arguments in favor of "doing something" about global warming, even if we are uncertain about its existence or severity?

CHAPTER SUMMARY

1. In some situations, there are social costs that do not equal private costs—that is, there are costs to society that exceed the cost to the individual. These costs may include air and water pollution, for which private individuals do not have to pay. Society, however, does bear the costs of these externalities. Few individuals or firms voluntarily consider social costs.

2. One way to analyze the problem of pollution is to look at it as an externality. Individual decision makers do not take account of the negative externalities they impose on the rest of society. In such a situation, they produce "too much" pollution and "too many" polluting goods.

3. It might be possible to ameliorate the situation by imposing a tax on polluters. The tax, however, should be dependent on the extent of the economic damages created rather than on the physical quantity of pollution. This tax will therefore be different for the same level of physical pollution in different parts of the country because the economic damage differs, depending on location, population density, and other factors.

4. The optimal quantity of pollution is the quantity at which the marginal cost of cleanup equals the mar-

ginal benefit of cleanup. Pollution abatement is a trade-off. We trade off goods and services for cleaner air and water, and vice versa.

5. Another way of looking at the externality problem is to realize that it involves the lack of definite property rights. No one owns common property resources such as air and water, and therefore no one takes account of the long-run pernicious effects of excessive pollution.

6. There are alternatives to pollution-causing resource use—for example, solar energy. We do not use solar energy because it is too expensive relative to conventional alternatives and because the creation of solar panels would generate pollution.

7. Recycling involves reusing paper, glass, and other materials rather than putting them into solid waste dumps. Recycling does have a cost both in the resources used for recycling and in the pollution created during recycling. Landfills are an alternative to recycling. These solid waste disposal sites are being expanded faster than the demand for them.

8. Resources may not be getting scarcer. The inflation-corrected price of most resources has been falling for decades.

DISCUSSION OF PREVIEW QUESTIONS

1. What is a negative externality?

A negative externality exists if the social costs exceed the private costs of some activity; if parties not involved in that activity are adversely affected, negative externalities are said to exist. Pollution is an example of a negative externality; for example, transactions between automobile producers and users impose costs in the form of pollution on people who neither produce nor consume the autos.

2. How can poorly defined property rights create negative externalities?

Nature's ability to cleanse itself can be considered a scarce resource, and as such, it behooves society to use this resource efficiently. However, if everyone owns natural resources, in effect *no one* owns them. Consequently, people will use natural resources, for good or for ill, as though they were free. Of course, excessive use of natural resources eventually impairs

nature's ability to cleanse itself; enter the concept of pollution (an accumulation of unwanted matter). Now the marginal cost to *private* polluters is still zero (or nearly zero), whereas the cost to society of using this (now scarce) resource is positive. In short, third parties are adversely affected when pollution results from the production and consumption of goods that lead to waste, which creates pollution.

3. If property rights are poorly defined, *must* negative externalities arise?

No. If contracting costs are small and enforcement is relatively easy, voluntary contracts will arise and the full opportunity costs of actions will be accounted for. That is, when transaction costs are small, private and social costs will converge, as the parties affected contract with the parties creating the additional costs, and externalities will disappear. What is interesting is that regardless of how property rights are assigned, resources will be allocated in the same way. Of course, the specific assignment of property rights does affect the distribution of wealth, even though resource allocation is independent of the specific property right assignment; what is important for efficient resource allocation is that *someone* have property rights. It should be noted that, unfortunately, the main externalities, such as air and water pollution, are very complex, contracting costs are very high, and enforcement is difficult. As a consequence, free market solutions are not likely to emerge—indeed, they have not.

4. What is the optimal quantity of pollution?
The optimal quantity of pollution cannot be zero because at 100 percent cleanliness, the marginal cost

of pollution abatement would greatly exceed the marginal benefit. We would have too much pollution abatement; we would be using resources in a socially suboptimal manner. That means that the resources being used in pollution abatement would have a higher value elsewhere in society.

We live in a world of scarce resources. If the value we receive from spending one more dollar on cleaning up the environment is less than the value we would receive by spending that dollar on something else—such as cancer research—we are not allocating our resources efficiently if we still choose to spend that dollar on pollution abatement.

PROBLEMS

(Answers to the odd-numbered problems appear at the back of the book.)

31-1. Construct a typical supply and demand graph. Show the initial equilibrium price and quantity. Assume that the good causes negative externalities to third parties (persons not involved in the transactions). Revise the graph to compensate for that fact. How does the revised situation compare with the original?

31-2. Construct a second supply and demand graph for any product. Show the equilibrium price and quantity. Assuming that the good generates external benefits, modify the diagram to allow for them. Show the new equilibrium price and quantity. How does the revised situation compare with the original?

31-3. Suppose that polluters are to be charged by government agencies for the privilege of polluting.
    a. How should the price be set?
    b. Which firms will treat waste, and which will pay to pollute?
    c. Is it possible that some firms will be forced to close down because they now have to pay to pollute? Why might this result be good?
    d. If producers are charged to pollute, they will pass this cost on to buyers in the form of higher prices. Why might this be good?

31-4. Why has the free market not developed contractual arrangements to eliminate excess air pollution in major U.S. cities?

31-5. What is the problem with common property resources?

31-6. The accompanying graph shows external costs arising from the production of good Y.

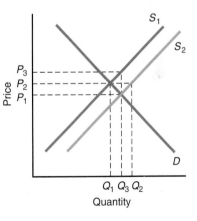

    a. Which curve includes only the private costs of producing good Y?
    b. Which supply curve includes the external costs of producing good Y?
    c. How much of good Y is produced and at what price?
    d. Who bears the cost of producing the amount of good Y in part (c)?
    e. If external costs are included, how much of good Y should be produced, and at what price should it be sold?

31-7. The table shows the costs and benefits of removing air pollution.

Annual Units of Pollution	Annual Total Air Pollution Damage	Annual Total Costs of Air Pollution Reduction
0	$ 0	$410
1	30	260
2	70	160
3	150	80
4	270	20
5	430	0

a. Find the marginal benefits of pollution reduction.
b. Find the marginal costs of pollution reduction.
c. Assume that society is currently allowing 5 units of air pollution per year. If pollution is reduced to 3 units, what is the net gain or loss to society?
d. Suppose that all air pollution is eliminated. What would be the net gain or loss to society?
e. If air pollution were regulated efficiently, how many units of air pollution would be allowed each year?

31-8. Examine this marginal cost and marginal benefit schedule for air cleanliness:

Quantity (%)	Marginal Benefit	Marginal Cost
0	$50,000	$ 5,000
20	45,000	10,000
40	35,000	15,000
60	25,000	25,000
80	10,000	40,000
100	0	∞

a. Graph the marginal benefit and marginal cost curves.
b. What is the optimal degree of air cleanliness?
c. How much will the optimal amount of air cleanliness cost?
d. What is the optimal amount of air pollution?
e. Would we want a level of zero pollution? Why or why not?

31-9. Explain why it is possible to have too little pollution. What might government do to cause private individuals and businesses to generate too little pollution?

COMPUTER-ASSISTED INSTRUCTION

Environmental problems almost always involve externalities. You are asked to examine some of them in this exercise.

Complete problem and answer appear on disk.

INTERACTING WITH THE INTERNET

The Environmental Protection Agency (EPA) is located at

www.epa.gov/

It has general information about the agency and material on its programs, initiatives, rules, regulations, and legislation. It also has "Citizen Information," which describes the role individuals can play in environmental issues. An organization that takes an economist's view toward environmental issues is Resources for the Future at

www.rff.org/

So does the Political Economy Research Center (PERC) at

www.perc.org/

CHAPTER 32

PUBLIC CHOICE: The Economics of Interest Groups

During congressional hearings about Internal Revenue Service (IRS) abuse of American taxpayers, the public became privy to some shocking horror stories. Many infuriated politicians played on public outrage by calling for both the IRS and the current tax code to be abolished. In their place would be a simple tax system, such as a flat tax or a national sales tax. Gone would be the complex Internal Revenue Code and the unpardonable sins that the IRS visits on American taxpayers every year. Could a government agency such as the IRS really be abolished? Could we have a system that allowed most Americans to fill out a postcard or a simple electronic form? Before you try to answer these questions, you need to understand how interest groups operate in our system. This involves learning more about the theory of public choice.

PREVIEW QUESTIONS

1. What is the essence of the public-choice model?

2. Why can private choice indicate intensity of wants but public choice cannot?

3. How can logrolling enable legislators to indicate the intensity of their wants?

4. When do distributional coalitions emerge?

Did You Know That . . . more than 1,200 organizations whose names begin with the word *National* are listed in the Washington, D.C., telephone directory? Another 600 begin with the word *American* or *Americans*. At least 10,000 separate groups exist for the purpose of influencing government policies, and an estimated 80,000 persons are engaged in lobbying in the nation's capital at this very instant. Perhaps without realizing it, you have been introduced to a number of important **interest groups** in the last few chapters: unions, health care professionals, medical insurance companies, poverty workers, and environmentalists. What these diverse groups have in common is that they often seek to influence government legislation and change the flow of resources in our economy.

Another interest group that has had great success in influencing government is agriculture, to which you were first introduced in Chapter 4. Throughout this chapter, we will use agriculture as a key example to explain the economics of interest groups. This analysis can be subsumed under what economists call the *theory of public choice*.

COLLECTIVE DECISION MAKING: THE THEORY OF PUBLIC CHOICE

The public sector has a vast influence on the American economy. Yet the economic model used until now has applied only to the behavior of the private sector—firms and households. Such a model does not adequately explain the behavior of the public sector. We shall attempt to do so now.

Governments consist of individuals. No government actually thinks and acts; rather, government actions are the result of decision making by individuals in their roles as elected representatives, appointed officials, and salaried bureaucrats. Therefore, to understand how government works, we must examine the incentives for the people in government as well as those who would like to be in government—avowed candidates or would-be candidates for elective or appointed positions—and special-interest lobbyists attempting to get government to do something. At issue is the analysis of **collective decision making.** Collective decision making involves the actions of voters, politicians, political parties, interest groups, and many other groups and individuals. The analysis of collective decision making is usually called the **theory of public choice.** It has been given this name because it involves hypotheses about how choices are made in the public sector, as opposed to the private sector. The foundation of public-choice theory is the assumption that individuals will act within the political process to maximize their *individual* (not collective) well-being. In that sense, the theory is similar to our analysis of the market economy, in which we also assume that individuals are motivated by self-interest.

To understand public-choice theory, it is necessary to point out other similarities between the private market sector and the public, or government, sector; then we will look at the differences.

Similarities in Market and Public-Sector Decision Making

In addition to the similar assumption of self-interest being the motivating force in both sectors, there are other similarities.

Scarcity.   At any given moment, the amount of resources is fixed. This means that for the private and the public sectors combined, there is a scarcity constraint. Everything that is

Interest group
Any group that seeks to cause government to change spending in a way that will benefit the group's members or to undertake any other action that will improve their lot. Also called a *special-interest group.*

Collective decision making
How voters, politicians, and other interested parties act and how these actions influence nonmarket decisions.

Theory of public choice
The study of collective decision making.

spent by all levels of government, plus everything that is spent by the private sector, must add up to the total income available at any point in time. Hence every government action has an opportunity cost, just as in the market sector.

Competition. Although we typically think of competition as a private market phenomenon, it is also present in collective action. Given the scarcity constraint government also faces, bureaucrats, appointed officials, and elected representatives will always be in competition for available government funds. Furthermore, the individuals within any government agency or institution will act as individuals do in the private sector: They will try to obtain higher wages, better working conditions, and higher job-level classifications. They will compete and act in their own, not society's, interest.

Similarity of Individuals. Contrary to popular belief, there are not two types of individuals, those who work in the private sector and those who work in the public sector; rather, individuals working in similar positions can be considered similar. The difference, as we shall see, is that the individuals in government face a different **incentive structure** than those in the private sector. For example, the costs and benefits of being efficient or inefficient differ when one goes from the private to the public sector.

One approach to predicting government bureaucratic behavior is to ask what incentives bureaucrats face. Take the United States Postal Service as an example. The bureaucrats running that government corporation are human beings with IQs not dissimilar to those possessed by workers in similar positions at Microsoft or American Airlines. Yet the Postal Service does not function like either of these companies. The difference can be explained, at least in part, in terms of the incentives provided for managers in the two types of institutions. When the bureaucratic managers and workers at Microsoft make incorrect decisions, work slowly, produce shoddy products, and are generally "inefficient," the profitability of the company declines. The owners—millions of shareholders—express their displeasure by selling some of their shares of company stock. The market value, as tracked on the stock exchange, falls. But what about the U.S. Postal Service? If a manager, a worker, or a bureaucrat in the Postal Service gives shoddy service, there is no straightforward mechanism by which the organization's owners—the taxpayers—can express their dissatisfaction. Despite the Postal Service's status as a "government corporation," taxpayers as shareholders do not really own shares of stock in the organization that they can sell.

The key, then, to understanding purported inefficiency in the government bureaucracy is not found in an examination of people and personalities but rather in an examination of incentives and institutional arrangements.

Differences Between Market and Collective Decision Making

There are probably more dissimilarities between the market sector and the public sector than there are similarities.

Government Goods at Zero Price. The majority of goods that governments produce are furnished to the ultimate consumers without direct money charge. **Government,** or **political, goods** can be either private goods or public goods. The fact that they are furnished to the ultimate consumer free of charge does *not* mean that the cost to society of those goods is zero, however; it only means that the price *charged* is zero. The full opportunity cost to society is the value of the resources used in the production of goods produced and provided by the government.

Incentive structure
The system of rewards and punishments individuals face with respect to their own actions.

Government, or political, goods
Goods (and services) provided by the public sector; they can be either private or public goods.

For example, none of us pays directly for each unit of consumption of defense or police protection. Rather, we pay for all these things indirectly through the taxes that support our governments—federal, state, and local. This special feature of government can be looked at in a different way. There is no longer a one-to-one relationship between the consumption of a government-provided good and the payment for that good. Consumers who pay taxes collectively pay for every political good, but the individual consumer may not be able to see the relationship between the taxes that he or she pays and the consumption of the good. Indeed, most taxpayers will find that their tax bill is the same whether or not they consume, or even like, government-provided goods.

Use of Force. All governments are able to engage in the legal use of force in their regulation of economic affairs. For example, governments can exercise the use of *expropriation,* which means that if you refuse to pay your taxes, your bank account and other assets may be seized by the Internal Revenue Service. In fact, you have no choice in the matter of paying taxes to governments. Collectively, we decide the total size of government through the political process, but individually we cannot determine how much service we pay for just for ourselves during any one year.

Voting Versus Spending. In the private market sector, a dollar voting system is in effect. This dollar voting system is not equivalent to the voting system in the public sector. There are, at minimum, three differences:

1. In a political system, one person gets one vote, whereas in the market system, the dollars one spends count as votes.
2. The political system is run by **majority rule,** whereas the market system is run by **proportional rule.**
3. The spending of dollars can indicate intensity of want, whereas because of the all-or-nothing nature of political voting, a vote cannot.

Majority rule
A collective decision-making system in which group decisions are made on the basis of 50.1 percent of the vote. In other words, whatever more than half of the electorate votes for, the entire electorate has to accept.

Proportional rule
A decision-making system in which actions are based on the proportion of the "votes" cast and are in proportion to them. In a market system, if 10 percent of the "dollar votes" are cast for blue cars, 10 percent of the output will be blue cars.

Ultimately, the main distinction between political votes and dollar votes here is that political outcomes may differ from economic outcomes. Remember that economic efficiency is a situation in which, given the prevailing distribution of income, consumers get the economic goods they want. There is no corresponding situation using political voting. Thus we can never assume that a political voting process will lead to the same decisions that a dollar voting process will lead to in the marketplace.

Indeed, consider the dilemma every voter faces. Usually a voter is not asked to decide on a single issue (although this happens); rather, a voter is asked to choose among candidates who present a large number of issues and state a position on each of them. Just consider the average U.S. senator who has to vote on several thousand different issues during a six-year term. When you vote for that senator, you are voting for a person who must make thousands of decisions during the next six years.

Political Participants: The Iron Triangle

In the private marketplace, we often focus on the behavior of the three key group participants: consumers, employees, and owners of businesses. In the political marketplace, these three groups correspond to constituents, bureaucrats, and members of Congress. As an example, let's consider the three groups that are involved in the agricultural industry. The principal constituents (consumers of Department of Agriculture subsidies and rules) are, of

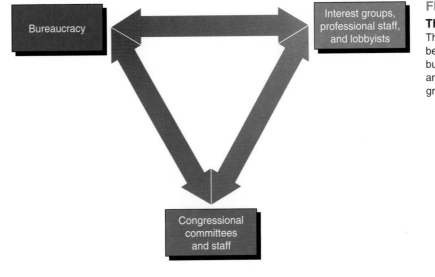

FIGURE 32-1
The Iron Triangle
The "iron triangle" is an alliance of mutual benefit among some unit within the bureaucracy, its interest or client group, and committees or subcommittees of Congress and their staff members.

course, the various interest groups that farmers have set up. These include the American Farm Bureau Federation, the National Cattlemen's Association, the National Milk Producers' Association, the Corn Growers' Association, and the Citrus Growers' Association.

The bureaucrats are within the Department of Agriculture, consisting of over 110,000 individuals who work directly for the federal government and many thousands more who work as contractors, subcontractors, or consultants to the department.

Finally, members of Congress in essence act as venture capitalists who provide the funding (via taxation) for agricultural spending programs and give overall directions to them. Within Congress, there are two major congressional committees concerned with agriculture: the House Committee on Agriculture and the Senate Committee on Agriculture, Nutrition, and Forestry. Each has seven subcommittees.

The relationship among these three groups has been said to form an "iron triangle," as shown in Figure 32-1.

EXAMPLE
Taking Over the Farm Bureaucracy

From 1933 until 1997, farmer-elected, farmer-member county committees, along with local employees of the Agricultural Department, both ran and received subsidies from the federal government. According to the Environmental Working Group in Washington, D.C., over 20 percent of county employees of the Agricultural Department received direct payments from the department as part of the farm program (to which you were first introduced in Chapter 4 using the example of price supports). The average member of the farmer-elected county committees received almost $40,000 a year, while county employees of the Agricultural Department received about $52,000 a year. As one example, county employees in agricultural department offices in Iowa during one 10-year period received $32 million in payments from the federal government, more than those in any other state.

FOR CRITICAL ANALYSIS: The way farm subsidies were given out has been compared to permitting welfare recipients to form neighborhood committees and run their own welfare programs, deciding how much each person should get every year. Is this analogy fair? ●

CONCEPTS IN BRIEF

- The theory of public choice analyzes how collective decision making is carried out in the public sector. It uses economic analysis to evaluate the operation of democratic government and assumes the self-interest of all political participants.

- Both the market sector and the public sector face scarcity, feature competition, and contain similar individuals.

- Collective decision making differs from market decision making in that many government, or political, goods are provided at zero price, collective action may involve the use of force, and political voting may lead to different results than dollar voting.

- The "iron triangle" of political participants is made up of constituents, bureaucrats, and members of Congress.

THE ECONOMICS OF INTEREST GROUPS: CONCENTRATION OF BENEFITS AND DISPERSION OF COSTS

At the heart of how interest groups influence government in our democratic system is who benefits and who pays for government actions. By definition, interest groups represent relatively well defined groups of individuals or businesses that know what is in their own best interest. Whenever an interest group can obtain more government funding for its activities, its members experience increases in economic welfare. Taxpayers, in contrast, may end up *individually* paying very little for the concentrated benefits that go to the interest group. Thus the costs for many government actions are dispersed among all potential voters.

INTERNET EXERCISE

Exercise 32.1
Visit www.econtoday.com for more about interest groups.

Distributional Coalitions

Concentrated groups in our democratic society succeed in transferring income to themselves from everybody else through what is known as **distributional coalitions.** These coalitions are small groups that gain much individually at the expense of many individuals who lose much collectively, but little individually, from the special privileges granted members of the coalition. Most collective action—action designed to influence public officials—takes place in small homogeneous groups rather than large diverse groups. Normally, individuals with a common interest will not voluntarily combine and act to further their common interest unless each individual has an incentive to participate in such collective action. Members of distributional coalitions have an incentive to act collectively to induce the median *legislator* to vote in a way that is not consistent with the interests of the median *constituent.*

Distributional coalitions
Associations such as cartels, unions, and cooperatives that are formed to gain special government privileges in order to redistribute wealth by taking small amounts from each of many people and giving large amounts to each of only a few.

EXAMPLE
Why Dairy Farmers Have Been Subsidized So Much

One clear-cut, tightly knit, homogeneous small group of individuals is dairy farmers. An examination of how much dairy farmers benefited in one state, Florida, is illustrative. In a recent year, Florida dairy farmers received $40.3 million in price support payments. Almost 100 percent went to 177 farmers. Each received an average payment in one year of $226,700. In the extreme, if the cost of these payments were borne solely by the residents of Florida, each resident in the state would pay $3.35. How much effort will the residents of Florida make—in other words, what is the value of the resources that they will spend—so as *not* to pay that $3.35 a year? At best they would pay $3.34. At worst, they would pay nothing—why should they take the effort? The 177 Florida dairy farmers, however, each have a great incentive to ensure that their payments from the federal government continue. The residents of the state have no incentive to try to stop these payments.

FOR CRITICAL ANALYSIS: There is a lobbying group aimed at helping the general public. It is called Common Cause. How much success do you think Common Cause can have? ●

Logrolling

Logrolling

The practice of exchanging political favors by elected representatives. Typically, one elected official agrees to vote for the policy of another official in exchange for the vote of the latter in favor of the former's desired policy.

Sometimes even lobbying or well-placed campaign contributions are not sufficient to get the programs that distributional coalitions want. In such cases, **logrolling** has been an effective tool. This practice involves an exchange of votes among legislators: Representative A votes for a program that benefits representative B's constituents in return for B's vote on a program that benefits A's constituents. One official may want the continuation of an army base in his hometown while another may want a new dam to be built in her home state, and so it goes. You vote for my army base, and I'll vote for your dam.

One of the major benefits of logrolling is that it allows an elected representative to demonstrate his or her *intensity* of preference, which presumably reflects the intensity of preferences of the constituents. For example, if a representative knows that it is extremely important for his constituents to keep the army base in his hometown, he may be willing to vote for a larger number of pet projects of other representatives to make sure that his pet project is passed. The problem, of course, is that typically—and our example fits perfectly—elected representatives care about geographic representation. *We have a geographically based political system.* The legislator has an incentive to represent local interests in the national legislature (Congress). The broader national issues typically suffer. National legislation becomes the vehicle for local support. The result is what is often known as "pork barrel" legislation that benefits very specific local areas.

 EXAMPLE
Logrolling with Food Stamps

A classic example of logrolling as a device to facilitate the redistribution of wealth is found in government programs for "feeding the hungry." Legislators from rural farming regions and lawmakers representing low-income urban areas have forged an effective alliance to promote subsidized food distribution to the poor. Urban legislators get cheap food for their constituents, and rural legislators obtained a convenient means of disposing of the surpluses that were generated by past agricultural price supports.

Supporters of subsidized food distribution have been particularly successful in promoting and expanding the food stamp program. Indeed, according to the U.S. Senate Committee on Agriculture, the program "has been used in legislative strategy to entice urban legislators who might not otherwise support costly farm price support programs to do so in exchange for rural support for the food stamp program." This process began with the Food Stamp Act of 1964, which laid the foundation for the present-day system. In 1968, the timing of food stamp legislation was tied to the legislative cycle of the farm bill—presumably to facilitate enforcement of logrolling deals made between rural and urban legislators. In 1970, federal expenditures on food stamps were doubled, then doubled again in 1971. By this time, legislating against hunger had become a favorite activity in Congress, spurred by the rural-urban coalition of farm representatives and legislators from low-income districts.

FOR CRITICAL ANALYSIS: Why do legislators end up supporting welfare transfers in kind rather than in cash? Would recipients prefer cash or in-kind benefits? ●

CONCEPTS IN BRIEF

- Distributional coalitions, which are associations such as unions and farmers' cooperatives, are formed to gain special government privileges for their members. The members of these coalitions tend to gain a great deal individually, at the expense of the many, who lose much collectively but little individually.

- Logrolling is the exchange of votes among elected representatives, such as occurs when farm representatives agree to vote for food stamps for the poor in return for urban representatives' votes for farm subsidies.

THE ROLE OF BUREAUCRATS

Programs require people to operate them. This is manifested in government today in the form of well-established bureaucracies, in which **bureaucrats** (nonelected officials) work. Bureaucracies can exert great influence on matters concerning themselves—the amount of funding granted them and the activities in which they engage. In the political marketplace, well-organized bureaucracies can even influence the expression of public demand itself. In many cases, they organize the clientele (interest groups), coach that clientele on what is appropriate, and stick up for the "rights" of the clientele. Farm and welfare programs are good examples.

Bureaucrats
Nonelected government officials who are responsible for the day-to-day operation of government and the observance of its regulations and laws.

Gauging Bureaucratic Performance

It is tempting, but incorrect, to think of bureaucrats as mere "technocrats," executors of orders and channels of information, in this process. They have at least two incentives to make government programs larger and more resistant to attack than we might otherwise expect. First, society has decided that in general, government should not be run on a profit-making basis. Measures of performance other than bottom-line profits must be devised. In the private market, successful firms typically expand to serve more customers; although this growth is often incidental to the underlying profitability, the two frequently go hand in hand. In parallel, performance in government is often measured by the number of clients served, and rewards are distributed accordingly. As a result, bureaucrats have an incentive to expand the size of their clientele—not because it is more profitable (beneficial) to society but because that is how *bureaucrats'* rewards are structured.

In general, performance measures that are not based on long-run profitability are less effective at gauging true performance. This makes it potentially easier for the government bureaucrat to *appear* to perform well, collect rewards for measured performance, and then leave for greener pastures. To avoid this, a much larger proportion of the rewards given bureaucrats are valuable only as long as they continue being bureaucrats—large staffs, expensive offices, generous pensions, and the like. Instead of getting large current salaries (which can be saved for a rainy day), they get rewards that disappear if their jobs disappear. Naturally, this increases the incentives of bureaucrats to make sure that their jobs don't disappear.

Rational Ignorance

At this point you may well be wondering, How do these guys get away with it? The answer lies in *rational ignorance* on the part of voters, ignorance that is carefully cultivated by the members of distributional coalitions.

On most issues, there is little incentive for the individual voter to expend resources to determine how to vote. Moreover, the ordinary course of living provides most individuals with enough knowledge to decide whether they should invest in learning more about a given issue. For example, suppose that American voters were asked to decide if the sign marking the entrance to an obscure national park should be enlarged. Most voters would decide that the potential costs and benefits of this decision were negligible: The new sign is unlikely to be the size of the state of Rhode Island, and anybody who has even *heard* of the national park in question probably already has a pretty good idea of its location. Thus most voters would choose to remain rationally ignorant about the *exact* costs and benefits of enlarging the sign, implying that (1) many will choose not to vote at all and (2) those who do vote will simply flip a coin or cast their ballot based on some other, perhaps ideological, grounds.

Why Be Rationally Ignorant? For most political decisions, majority rule prevails. Only a coalition of voters representing slightly more than 50 percent of those who vote is needed. Whenever a vote is taken, the result is going to involve costs and benefits. Voters, then, must evaluate their share of the costs and benefits of any budgetary expenditure. Voters, however, are not perfectly informed. That is one of the crucial characteristics of the real world—information is a resource that is costly to obtain. Rational voters will, in fact, decide to remain at some level of ignorance about government programs because the benefits from obtaining more information may not be worth the cost, given each individual voter's extremely limited impact on the outcome of an election. For the same reason, voters will fail to inform themselves about taxes or other revenue sources to pay for proposed expenditures because they know that for any specific expenditure program, the cost to them individually will be small. At this point it might be useful to contrast this situation with what exists in the nonpolitical private market sector of the economy. In the private market sector, the individual chooses a mix of purchases and bears fully the direct and indirect consequences of this selection (ignoring for the moment the problem of externalities).

The Costs and Benefits of Voting. Voters' incentives to remain rationally ignorant about most issues are compounded by other factors. First, even if the *total* costs or benefits of a political decision are large, the costs or benefits to any *individual* voter are likely to be small. We saw this earlier with price support payments for Florida dairy farmers. Even though these payments cost Floridians as a group roughly $40 million, the cost to any individual in the state is unlikely to be much more than about $3.35. Because individual benefits (to non–dairy farmers) are unlikely to be much different, most Floridians will not bother to find out whether or not it is in their interest to favor price supports for milk (and the tax costs are actually spread among all Americans).

Why Not Vote the Rascals Out? Each time a legislator votes in favor of an interest group at the expense of the general public (and this happens almost all the time), it would seem that voters have an incentive to "vote the rascal out." The problem is that even if the legislator's constituents as a group suffer substantial costs due to dairy price supports, the loss suffered by any individual constituent is quite small. In the case of dairy price supports, few nonfarmer constituents are likely to vote against the legislator just because he or she voted in favor of dairy price supports. A constituent's vote on a legislative candidate depends on the entire *package* of positions adopted by the legislator; for nonfarmers, the issue of price supports is a trivial component of that package. Moreover, campaign contributions from farmers enable the legislator to inform constituents of his or her supportive votes on other issues of more importance to nonfarmers—education, perhaps, or child care. This typically more than offsets any votes lost due to the legislator's support for farm subsidies. Thus the activities of distributional coalitions (interest groups) create a gap between the self-interest of the median *legislator* and the self-interest of the median *constituent.* For this reason, farm subsidies and other special-interest legislation that might not be enacted if all citizens voted on the issue may still be enacted when only legislators vote.

THE ECONOMICS OF INTEREST GROUPS IN ACTION: MORE ON AGRICULTURE

The proportion of the U.S. population living on farms has dropped from 43.8 percent in 1880 to about 1.8 percent today. Although food is essential for life, citizens of the United States, a relatively wealthy nation, spend less than 10 percent of their incomes on food. The 1,925,000 farms in the United States are able to satisfy not only Americans' demand for food but also the demand by other countries' citizens in terms of food exports. The average farming family currently earns over $50,000 a year, of which $30,000 is from nonfarm activities. Each year, the federal government spends about $30,000 per farm on U.S. Department of Agriculture programs. You were introduced to one of those programs (phased out for the most part in 1996), price supports, in Chapter 4.

Exercise 32.2
Visit www.econtoday.com for more about agricultural subsidies.

The Economics and Politics of Price Supports

Traditionally, advocates of price supports argued that it was a method to guarantee a decent income for low-income farmers. More recently, it also was argued that the price support program helped keep small farmers in business, thus preventing agribusinesses from taking over all agricultural production. In fact, these political justifications made no economic sense.

Historically, the benefits of price support programs were skewed toward the owners of very large farms. The benefits of the price support programs were proportional to output:

Population Outgrowing Farmland

The media, without any critical comment, dutifully reported the outcome of several studies purporting to show that population is outgrowing farmland and therefore not everybody will have enough to eat in the not-too-distant future. One such report was generated by Population Action International. Another report with a similar conclusion was generated by the World Bank's Consultative Group on International Agricultural Research. Interestingly, economics was named the "dismal science" because the Reverend Thomas Malthus predicted the same thing in 1798. Just as his prediction was wildly off base, so, too, are those of the present-day Malthusians. Indeed, just the opposite has occurred: World food prices, corrected for inflation, have been following a general trend downward for the past 150 years. Because of improving technology, farm productivity has increased and continues to increase even faster than population.

Big farms with large incomes produce more output and therefore received more subsidies. The 15,000 largest farms in America account for more than 25 percent of all farm profits. The 125,000 largest farms obtain over 60 percent of all farm profits.

Price supports also failed to slow the move toward larger farms. Price support subsidies were made on a *per-bushel* basis, not on a *per-farm* basis. Thus the price support system provided no advantage to growing crops on small farms rather than large farms. If other factors make it more efficient to grow food on large farms, that is where it will be grown, whether there are price supports or not. Perhaps recognizing this, Congress responded by imposing upper limits on the total cash payment that any given farmer could receive. These limits, however, were easily and routinely avoided by the owners of large farms, who, for example, "leased" portions of their land to numerous tenants, each of whom qualified individually for the full allowable payment. Thus the limits had little practical impact.

There is one further point: *All* of the benefits derived from price support subsidies ultimately accrued to *landowners* on whose land price-supported crops could be grown. When price supports were announced and put into effect, the value of land rose to reflect the full value of the future price support subsidies. Thus the original landowners, rather than operators of farms, captured the benefit of the subsidies. Most of the benefits of the farm programs were capitalized into the value of the farmland. So much for helping the poor and the landless!

Acreage Restrictions

The politicians who introduced price supports realized that farmers would respond to higher prices with higher production and that the government would be stuck with the resulting surpluses. So from the beginning, *acreage restrictions* were imposed on farmers who participated in the price support programs. Farmers agreeing to acreage restrictions, or *acreage allotment programs,* as they are called, consented to reduce the number of acres they planted. There were no direct payments to the farmers for abiding by their acreage allotments; the program was merely the implicit entry fee for farmers who wished to take advantage of the price supports.

When the government required that land be removed from production, this caused a reduction in the supply of the crop. Nevertheless, if farmers were required to reduce the amount of land they used by, say, 20 percent, output at any given price did not fall by 20 percent because farmers withdrew their *least productive* land from use. Moreover, they figured out new ways of squeezing just a little more production from any given amount of land. They could still expand output by using other factors of production, such as fertilizer and machinery. To get any given level of output, they had to use more of these nonfixed inputs than they ordinarily would because they were not allowed to expand their usage of land. Thus the marginal cost of production was higher than it would have been in the absence of the acreage restriction.

The net effects of the acreage restrictions were thus twofold. First, crop surpluses were reduced but not eliminated. Second, the restrictions led to an inefficient use of resources, not from the standpoint of the farmers, for they produced at the lowest possible cost given the acreage restriction, but from the standpoint of society. Because the most efficient means of production (more land) was not permitted, more expensive inputs had to be used.

Target Prices and Deficiency Payments

Starting in 1973, government policy toward agriculture added a new twist: the **target price.** Target prices differed from price supports in that the government guaranteed that the farmer would *receive* at least the target price but permitted the price *paid* by consumers to fluctuate, depending on how much of the crop was produced. Instead of buying and storing commodities, the government simply sent a cash payment to farmers if the price paid by consumers was less than the target price. For example, if the target price for wheat was $4.50 per bushel and the price paid by consumers was $3.50, farmers received **deficiency payments** equal to the $1 difference multiplied by the number of bushels they sold on the open market. A deficiency payment, then, was simply another way to pay a subsidy to farmers without having the government actually purchase and store their crops.

The Freedom to Farm Act of 1996

For most crops, price supports, acreage restrictions, targets prices, and deficiency payments were eliminated in 1996. You can be sure, though, that farmers were not left out in the cold to battle the free market. Indeed, projected guaranteed federal government payments to farmers through the year 2002 actually exceed projected payments that would have occurred under the old agriculture subsidy programs. The new legislation also retains some "conservation" aspects, that is, paying some farmers to keep land as wildlife habitats. Additionally, price-support programs for sugar and peanuts were retained. So, in a nutshell, most farmers will be able to respond to worldwide market forces while at the same time receiving guaranteed subsidies for several years to come. Perhaps in the long run taxpayers and food consumers will be better off—provided of course that the old program isn't reinstituted after 2002.

Target price
A price set by the government for specific agricultural products. If the market clearing price was below the target price, a *deficiency payment,* equal to the difference between the market price and the target price, was given to farmers for each unit of the good they produce.

Deficiency payment
A direct subsidy paid to farmers equal to the amount of a crop they produced multiplied by the difference between the target price for that good and its market price.

Exercise 32.3
Visit www.econtoday.com for more about sugar prices.

CONCEPTS IN BRIEF

- Because price supports benefited farmers directly in proportion to the amount of farm goods they produce, owners of large farms received the bulk of the payments. Also, because the payments were tied to output and not farms, price supports did not help keep small farmers in business in preference to large farmers.

- The ultimate beneficiaries of price supports were the owners of farmland, for the price of this land rose whenever price supports were increased.

- Target prices were an attempt by the government to avoid the surpluses caused by price supports. The government set a target price, which it guaranteed that farmers would receive for their crops, but it allowed the market price to adjust to clear the market. If the market price was less than the target price, farmers received deficiency payments equal to the difference multiplied by the amount of the crop they produced.

- Target prices reduced surpluses, but they also made it more obvious that the government was making direct subsidy payments to farmers.

EUROPE'S AGRICULTURAL POLICY

While much of the world, including the United States, is moving away from complicated subsidy programs in agriculture, the European Union (a federation of 15 countries, sometimes called the EU) is not budging. Its Common Agricultural Policy (CAP) was developed between 1958 and 1962 and has not changed much since. It has all of the trappings of the former U.S. agricultural policy—minimum prices, government purchase of overproduction, government expenditures on storage, restrictions on cheaper foreign imports, and so on. European governments also subsidize exports of food products (which the U.S. government is still doing, too). The European Union has an annual budget of over $100 billion. About two-thirds of this budget is used up by the CAP.

The average family of four in Europe ends up paying $1,500 a year in artificially higher food prices. The average consumer pays in addition about $100 per person in taxes to subsidize farmers directly. The higher food price acts as a regressive tax, for poorer families spend a larger portion of their income on food. Remember from Chapter 5 that a regressive tax is one that in effect taxes low-income individuals at higher rates than higher-income individuals.

Other Results of Europe's Agricultural Policy

Some unseen, but important, additional results occur because of the CAP. Europe has slowly but surely reduced the amount of imports from the newly free Central European countries that are trying to liberalize their own markets. For example, currently Hungary can sell only about 6,000 tons of beef to the European Union each year. In the mid-1970s, it was allowed to sell over 100,000 tons. The EU dramatically restricts food imports from many other developing countries, thereby depriving those countries of opportunities to sell what they produce on their farms. Thus the CAP causes some of the poverty in developing countries, particularly those that rely on agricultural exports.

The environment in Europe is also affected negatively by the CAP. Artificially high agricultural prices cause many European farmers to damage the environment by destroying hedgerows and forests. They also use more chemical fertilizers. Why? Because they are paid their subsidies on the basis of their output, just like American farmers used to be. European farmers have an incentive to produce as much as they can, regardless of the consequences.

No Jobs Really Saved

Agricultural subsidies in Europe have been justified as a way of maintaining jobs in the agricultural sector. Ironically, in countries where farm subsidies are the most generous, the most agricultural jobs have been lost as a share of total employment. As a counterexample, consider New Zealand. It basically eliminated all of its farming sector's subsidies several years ago. In spite of dire predictions that the farming sector would be ruined, just the opposite has happened. On a lesser scale, the same has been true in Australia. These two low-subsidy, high-efficiency countries have done a much better job at keeping farmers at work than the European Union has.

One has to ask an important question here: If no agricultural jobs have been saved in the long run, why is there so much political support for keeping the Common Agricultural Policy alive in the European Union? The answer lies in the two words *long run*. The beneficiaries of agricultural subsidies in the EU aren't very interested in the long run. They can only see the costs to them in the short run of any reduction in their subsidies. So they have lobbied vigorously to keep the CAP in its present form. Consider that America's price support system was abandoned only after farmers were assured that over the following five years, they would receive a different set of subsidies that would leave them no worse off. Until some similar policy option occurs in the EU, its citizens will continue to pay higher prices for food.

The Estimated Benefits of Undistorted Agricultural Trade

In an open economy with undistorted agricultural trade, the industrially advanced economies would benefit—over and above the savings in reduced subsidies—to the tune of about $38 billion per year each. The major beneficiaries would be Japan, the European Union, and the United States. These numbers alone suggest that there must be pressure to open up world agricultural markets and to reduce farm subsidies. The future is not so rosy, however.

The cost of farming programs continues to be spread out among all consumers. Moreover, the cost per consumer in countries that become richer, all other things held constant, is falling. This is because food constitutes a declining share in the family budget as families get richer. Moreover, because of increases in farm productivity, the trend is toward lower (inflation-corrected) prices for food. Hence farmers can still maintain their relatively high subsidy levels while nonfarmers see food prices falling.

Perhaps more important, on the producer side, as the number of farmers decreases, the benefits of farm programs are more highly concentrated. This means that lobbying efforts become more efficient to undertake. In other words, as the number of farmers decreases, protection becomes relatively cheaper to obtain. Furthermore, the declining number of farmers and farms, particularly in the industrialized world, elicits a kind of sympathy. France is a particularly good example. Surveys continually show that the average French citizen believes that rural life would disappear without farm subsidies. And the French are apparently willing to continue paying those farm subsidies. Farm subsidies, though, in France and elsewhere, cannot stop the exodus from the farms. In France, for example, 3 percent of farmers and farmhands quit every year.

We can conclude that in spite of the pressures in an open economy to reduce farm subsidies throughout the world, they are not going to disappear overnight.

CONCEPTS IN BRIEF

- Voters may be rationally ignorant about many election issues because the cost of obtaining more information may outweigh the benefits of doing so. Distributional coalitions attempt to promote rational ignorance for their own benefit by hiding the true costs of the programs they favor.

- Bureaucrats often exert great influence on the course of policy because they are in charge of the day-to-day operation of current policy and provide much of the information needed to formulate future policy. Bureaucracies often organize their clientele, coach clients on what is appropriate, and stick up for their rights.

POLITICAL RENT SEEKING

Governments have the ability to bestow large monetary benefits on individuals and firms. Government can do this, for example, by picking one defense firm to become a monopoly supplier of a particular type of armament. In the past, the federal government has routinely given a monopoly to specific parts of the electromagnetic spectrum for radio and TV. In most states, the government makes it illegal for a competing electric company to go into business. In virtually all states, the government has made it illegal for individuals to practice law without a license, thereby restricting supply in the legal profession. The same is true for the medical profession.

In short, there are potentially large profits to be captured by getting the government to create a monopoly for you. We would expect, therefore, that individuals will expend resources to capture such profits. Indeed, an army of lawyers, business executives, and expert witnesses crowd the halls of Congress and the courtrooms, attempting to obtain government-bestowed monopolies, trying to prevent competition when a monopoly already exists, and engaging in various other endeavors that allow them to control a source of monopoly profits. Put yourself in the place of a monopolist who has been given monopoly power through some act of Congress. Let's say that you are making monopoly profits—profits over and above what you would make in a competitive industry—of $1 million per year. Wouldn't you be willing to spend a quarter of that million dollars a year on a lobbying effort to make sure that Congress does not change the law to allow competition in your industry? Indeed, you might spend considerably more than that to protect your $1 million annual monopoly profit. From a use-of-resources point of view, the resources that you spend in protecting your monopoly do not yield any true social product.

Of course, not all benefits from government action involve creating or maintaining monopolies. Rather, you have seen in this chapter that government actions can benefit industries through direct payments, such as agricultural subsidies. When interest groups make an attempt to influence and manipulate public policy for their own gain, they are engaged in what is known as **rent seeking.** This inelegant term comes from the economist's view of rent to which you were introduced in Chapter 29. Remember that economic rent is defined as the amount of payment to a resource over and above what is necessary to keep it in its current use and quality. Thus rent seeking involves individuals expending resources to capture economic rent that can be created by government actions. Part of the gains from getting government to benefit a particular interest group are therefore dissipated through rent-seeking activities. Those resources involve payments to lobbyists, lawyers, and accountants and occasionally direct bribes to politicians. Because the use of those resources is simply to obtain a *transfer* within society, we say that they are wasted and that inefficiency results. The problem is that in a democratic society, it is difficult to find a way around such inefficiencies. The First Amendment to the U.S. Constitution guarantees freedom of speech. By any measure, lobbying activities are speech.

Rent seeking

The use of resources in an attempt to get government to bestow a benefit on an interest group.

The federal agency everyone loves to hate is the IRS. The Internal Revenue Code is thousands of pages long and has become incomprehensible to the average taxpayer. Will the IRS ever be abolished?

Abolish the IRS? Don't Bet on It

CONCEPTS APPLIED:

INTEREST GROUPS, COALITIONS, SUBSIDIES, REGRESSIVE TAX

Visit www.econtoday.com for an Internet Activity that expands your understanding of these concepts.

Let there be no doubt about it, the IRS has treated some taxpayers unjustly. And the Internal Revenue Code has become more complicated than ever since the Tax Relief Act of 1997, passed by Congress and signed by President Clinton, added 832 pages to the code's existing 9,400 pages. So critics of both the IRS and the tax code have a strong argument for replacing them with a simple system of virtually no deductions and a flat tax rate or a national sales tax. Nevertheless, no such changes are likely anytime soon.

Interest Groups Guarantee Tax Complexity

The higher tax rates are, the more benefit an interest group can obtain by getting Congress to create a tax loophole. Given that the highest marginal tax rate is now around 40 percent, many interest groups have succeeded in getting Congress to create special benefits for them. This is known as the action-reaction syndrome, which arises when any government passes a law. A new tax is the action, and the reaction comes from the people who are affected by the tax, who then lobby for another action on the part of the government, and so on.

Any tax reform will create gainers and losers. Let's see who the losers might be if we switch to a simplified tax system with no deductions.

Interest Groups Who Will Fight Tax Reform

If all deductions and credits would be swept away under a tax reform, the first groups that would lobby against the

idea are churches, universities, and hospitals, for most charitable donations are tax-deductible. As an interest group, such nonprofits would defend the charitable deduction. One study predicted that without this deduction, individual giving would drop by 30 percent. Consider also the almost 70 million American homeowners. Most of them get to deduct interest payments on mortgages, as well as local property taxes, from their taxable income. The real estate industry and the mortgage industry would fight against removing these valuable deductions. Without them, housing prices might drop 10 to 15 percent.

There is also a large group of tax lawyers and accountants who would find their business vanish overnight if tax simplification were really enacted. They, too, form an interest group that might fight such reform.

Do Interest Groups Always Win?

The restaurant industry as an interest group fought against a reduction in the tax deductibility of business restaurant meals. It lost. Hence not every interest group succeeds in wooing Congress. True tax simplification, however, would involve so many interest groups that it is hard to imagine such reform ever occurring.

Consider the example of the Tax Reform Act of 1986, which initially simplified our federal tax system. Multiple marginal tax rates were reduced to just a few. The top marginal tax rate for high income earners dropped to 28 percent. But the simplified system didn't last long. So-called technical corrections started to be added almost immediately. More and higher marginal rates were added in 1990 and again in 1993. In 1997, almost a thousand more pages were added to the code. It's still safe to plan a career as a tax lawyer or accountant.

FOR CRITICAL ANALYSIS

1. What other groups would lose out if the federal tax system were greatly simplified?

2. Who would be the major beneficiaries of tax simplification? Why?

CHAPTER SUMMARY

1. Public-choice economics examines motives behind political entrepreneurs and the outcomes of political actions. Public-choice theory predicts that participants in the political marketplace, such as politicians, act so as to maximize their own self-interest rather than the public interest.

2. The market sector and the public sector both face scarcity, feature competition, and contain similar individuals. They differ in that many government, or political, goods are provided at zero price, collective action may involve the use of force, and political voting can lead to different results than dollar voting.

3. Distributional coalitions, which are associations such as unions and farmers' cooperatives, are formed to gain special government privileges for their members. The members of these coalitions tend to gain a great deal individually, at the expense of the many, who lose much collectively but little individually. Distributional coalitions have played a major role in the growth of government in the twentieth century.

4. Logrolling is the exchange of votes among elected representatives, such as occurs when farm representatives agree to vote for food stamps for the poor in return for urban representatives' votes for farm subsidies.

5. Bureaucrats often exert great influence on the course of policy because they are in charge of the day-to-day operation of current policy and provide much of the information needed to formulate future policy. Bureaucracies often organize their clientele, coach clients on what is appropriate, and stick up for their rights.

6. Voters may be rationally ignorant about many election issues because the cost of obtaining more information may outweigh the benefits of doing so. Distributional coalitions attempt to promote rational ignorance for their own benefit by hiding the costs of the programs they favor.

7. Because price supports were tied to the volume of production, richer farmers received the bulk of the subsidies that resulted from price supports. Also, because price supports were paid without regard to the size of farms, they generally did not help keep smaller farmers in business.

8. Acreage restrictions were an attempt to reduce surpluses by requiring farmers to stop cultivating part of their land in return for price support subsidies. When they participated in acreage restriction programs, farmers put aside their least productive land and increased the use of nonland inputs on the remaining land in cultivation. These practices tended to offset the surplus-reducing intent of these programs.

9. Target prices avoided surpluses by making deficiency payments to farmers to make up for the difference between the government-established target price and the market clearing price.

DISCUSSION OF PREVIEW QUESTIONS

1. What is the essence of the public-choice model?
The essence of the public-choice model is that politicians, bureaucrats, and voters will act so as to maximize *their own* self-interest (or economic well-being) rather than the community's. In other words, because such people are human, they are subject to the same

motivations and drives as the rest of us. They will usually make decisions in terms of what benefits them, not society as a whole. Such an assumption permits economists to apply economic maximization principles to voters, candidates, elected officials, and policymakers.

2. **Why can private choice indicate intensity of wants but public choice cannot?**
If Ronald loves pasta, he can freely spend a high percentage of his income on it. The fact that he does spend a high percentage of his income on pasta and a zero percentage of his income on rice indicates the intensity of his wants. He can allocate his "dollar votes" in such a way as to reveal his preferences—and maximize his utility. In a "one-person, one-vote" situation, however, Ronald has only *one* vote. He must choose among different candidates, each of whom offers a platform of many publicly provided goods. Ronald's vote "buys" both the services he wants and the services he does not want.

3. **How can logrolling enable legislators to indicate the intensity of their wants?**
Logrolling is a procedure in which legislators can trade votes. If your legislator is in an oil-producing state, she presumably has an intense desire to vote for bills that promote the interests of the oil industry. Legislators, however, also have only one vote per bill. By trading her vote on issues that she (and her constituents) are not concerned with, she can induce other legislators to vote for the pro-oil bill. Such vote trading, in effect, gives her more than one vote on this bill—and no vote on other bills.

4. **When do distributional coalitions emerge?**
Distributional coalitions emerge when it is possible for a small group to benefit hugely at the expense of a large group that pays *individually* relatively small amounts. For example, assume that 10,000 honey producers value government price supports at $100 million; assume also that the cost of the program to the rest of society is about 1 cent per person in taxes and 2 cents per pound more in the price for honey. Honey producers will find it profitable to form a distributional coalition, which will contribute to a politician's campaign for election or reelection. Taxpayers and honey consumers will not find it beneficial to form a counterforce to that distributional coalition.

PROBLEMS

(Answers to the odd-numbered problems appear at the back of the book.)

32-1. The existence of information and transactions costs has many implications in economics. What are some of these implications in the context of issues discussed in this chapter?

32-2. Suppose that a government program that subsidizes a certain group in America ends up generating $200,000 per year in additional income to each member of the group. The average income in America for a family of four is about $45,000 per year, and the official poverty line is much less than that. How could you explain the continued success of such a program? Under what circumstances might such a program be terminated?

32-3. A favorite presidential campaign theme in recent years has been to reduce the size, complexity, and bureaucratic nature of the federal government. Nonetheless, the size of the federal government, however measured, continues to increase. Use the theory of public choice to explain why.

32-4. Civics textbooks often claim that voting is one of the most precious and important responsibilities of citizens living in a democracy. Yet if it is raining hard on election day, the percentage of eligible voters that actually votes usually falls. What does this tell you about the public's view of its voting responsibility?

32-5. Term limits have been declared unconstitutional at the federal level, yet many states impose term limits on their state legislatures. Use the theory of public choice to explain how such term limits might change the relationship among the participants in the political marketplace.

32-6. Suppose that you see a distinct problem in our country that needs solving. You decide to run for office and learn everything you can about the problem so that you are an expert in how government can solve it. You don't know much else about other problems or issues. How successful might you be in your campaign to be a "niche" politician? Explain.

32-7. Some people maintain that unless farmers are subsidized, many will leave the farms, a small number of farms will take over the industry (creating an oligopolistic market structure), and prices will rise correspondingly. Currently, about 1.9 million farms are in existence in the United States, and 20 percent of these farms account for 80 percent of the value of total farm output.

   a. What is the number of farms accounting for this 80 percent of output?
   b. In light of this fact, is it likely that an oligopoly, defined as a market structure with only a few firms accounting for most production and sales, will arise in the agricultural industry in the United States?

32-8. Farmers are usually required to put aside some land to take part in government programs. The objective is for farm output to be reduced. How might this objective not be achieved?

32-9. Explain how the theory of public choice predicts the persistence of agricultural subsidies in the face of a declining farm population.

32-10. Assume that farmers are poor. What is the difference between a general income redistribution program that would give poor farmers income directly and a farming subsidy program that pays them so much per unit of farm product output?

32-11. Outline what would occur if Congress eliminated all farm subsidies tomorrow. How would these events change if Congress instead indicated that it would eliminate all farm programs in 20 years?

COMPUTER-ASSISTED INSTRUCTION

Some people contend that we have had enormous food surpluses in the United States because our farmers are so efficient that they can produce more than we can eat. If that is so, how did this situation come about? Analyzing it requires the proper interpretation of graphs. Analysis reveals that food surpluses are due not to efficiency but to government price supports above the equilibrium.

Complete problem and answer appear on disk.

INTERACTING WITH THE INTERNET

You can find out about what the U.S. Department of Agriculture is doing by going to

www.usda.gov/

You can get a complete listing of the USDA's marketing programs at

www.ams.usda.gov/progserv.htm

You may especially enjoy reading about the dairy program, which is defined as one that assists "the dairy industry by providing stability and orderliness in the dairy marketplace, while at the same time assuring the availability of an abundant supply of high-quality milk and dairy products for U.S. consumers." Go to

www.ams.usda.gov/dairy/

You can also go to the "Economic Research Service" home page to get the "official source for economic analysis and information on agriculture, food, natural resources, and rural America"

www.econ.ag.gov/

You can find out about the European Union's agricultural policy by going to

www.europa.eu.int/pol/agr/en/info.htm

You can get continuing information on the flat tax by accessing House Majority Leader Dick Armey's flat tax page at

www.flattax.house.gov/

The Senate has a flat tax page, too:

www.senate.gov/~jec/fltxrept.html

PART 9

GLOBAL ECONOMICS

CHAPTER 33

COMPARATIVE ADVANTAGE AND THE OPEN ECONOMY

When you drive in any city in the United States, you cannot help but see the evidence of international trade. The names of foreign car companies are posted at auto dealerships. Foreign cars—about 30 percent of all new cars sold in the United States—are everywhere. Moreover, when you go into an American department store, many electronic goods, branded with names that you know, come from companies in Japan or South Korea. The citizens of foreign countries are also seeing the evidence of world trade. Europeans drive some imported cars. Asians and Europeans, when they go to buy computers, will find U.S. brands, such as Apple, Compaq, Dell, Gateway, and IBM. In general, though, the average foreign consumer does not seem overwhelmed by imported American products. Nonetheless, there has been a constant stream of articles in the foreign press about how American culture is being forced on the rest of the world. How can this be happening? To understand this issue better, you must first learn about the various elements of international trade, as well as the arguments for and against free trade.

PREVIEW QUESTIONS

1. Is international trade important to the United States?

2. What is the relationship between imports and exports?

3. What is the ultimate effect of a restriction on imports?

4. What are some arguments against free trade?

733

Did **You Know That...** Boeing's latest airplane and the world's largest twin-engine jetliner, the 777, is made in Everett, Washington, but its parts come from 13 other countries, including Australia (rudder and elevators), Brazil (wingtips and dorsal fins), France (landing gears), Ireland (landing gear doors), Italy (wing outboard flaps), and Great Britain (flight computers and engines)? Japan provides 20 percent of the structure, including most of the fuselage.

The story of the Boeing 777 is repeated in the automobile industry. Parts from literally all over the world end up in cars "made in America." The running shoes you buy, the sheets you sleep on, and the clothes you put on your back are often wholly or partly produced outside the United States. Clearly, international trade today affects you whether you are aware of it or not. We are entering an age of a truly global economy. Learning about international trade is simply learning about everyday life.

THE WORLDWIDE IMPORTANCE OF INTERNATIONAL TRADE

Look at panel (a) of Figure 33-1. Since the end of World War II, world output of goods and services (world gross domestic product, or GDP) has increased almost every year until the present, when it is almost six times what it was. Look at the top line in panel (a). World trade has increased to almost 13 times what it was in 1950.

The United States figured prominently in this expansion of world trade. In panel (b) of Figure 33-1, you see imports and exports expressed as a percentage of total annual yearly

Chapter Outline

The Worldwide Importance of International Trade

Why We Trade: Comparative Advantage and Exhausting Mutual Gains from Exchange

The Relationship Between Imports and Exports

International Competitiveness

Arguments Against Free Trade

Ways to Restrict Foreign Trade

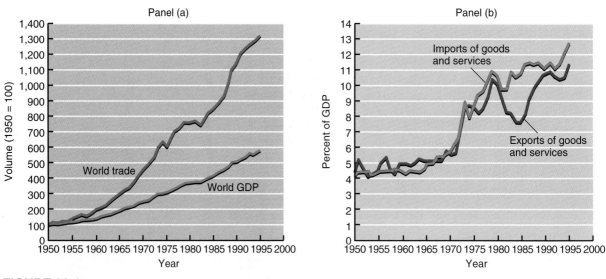

FIGURE 33-1

The Growth of World Trade

In panel (a), you can see the growth in world trade in relative terms because we use an index of 100 to represent real world trade in 1950. By the mid-1990s, that index had increased to over 1,300. At the same time, the index of world GDP (annual world income) had gone up to only around 600. World trade is clearly on the rise: Both imports and exports, expressed as a percentage of annual national income (GDP) in panel (b), have been rising.

Sources: Steven Husted and Michael Melvin, *International Economics,* 3d ed. (New York: HarperCollins, 1995), p. 11, used with permission; *International Trade;* Federal Reserve System; and U.S. Department of Commerce.

income (GDP). Whereas imports added up to barely 4 percent of annual national income in 1950, today they account for over 12 percent. International trade has definitely become more important to the economy of the United States.

INTERNATIONAL EXAMPLE
The Importance of International Trade in Various Countries

Whereas both imports and exports in the United States each account for more than 10 percent of total annual national income, in some countries the figure is much greater (see Table 33-1).

Another way to understand the worldwide importance of international trade is to look at trade flows on the world map in Figure 33-2 on page 736.

TABLE 33-1

Importance of Imports in Selected Countries

Country	Imports as a Percentage of Annual National Income
Luxembourg	95.0
Netherlands	58.0
Norway	30.0
Canada	23.5
Germany	23.0
United Kingdom	21.0
China	19.0
France	18.4
Japan	6.8

Source: International Monetary Fund.

FOR CRITICAL ANALYSIS: The yearly volume of imports in Hong Kong exceeds Hong Kong's total national income by several times. How is that possible? (Hint: Is there another reason to import a good besides wanting to consume it?) •

Exercise 33.1
Visit www.econtoday.com for more about trading with Taiwan.

WHY WE TRADE: COMPARATIVE ADVANTAGE AND EXHAUSTING MUTUAL GAINS FROM EXCHANGE

You have already been introduced to the concept of specialization and mutual gains from trade in Chapter 2. These concepts are worth repeating because they are essential to understanding why the world is better off because of more international trade. The best way to understand the gains from trade among nations is first to understand the output gains from specialization between individuals.

The Output Gains from Specialization

Suppose that a creative advertising specialist can come up with two pages of ad copy (written words) an hour or generate one computerized art rendering per hour. At the same time, a computer artist can write one page of ad copy per hour or complete one computerized art

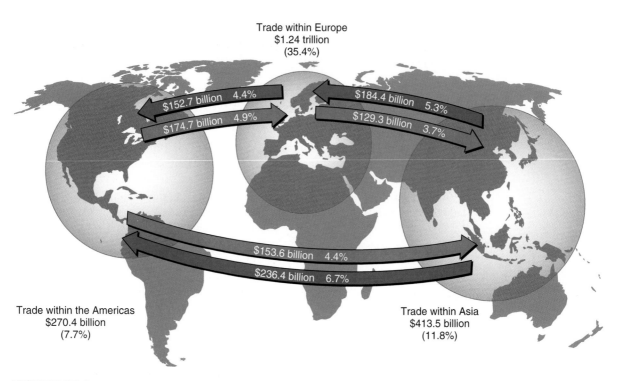

FIGURE 33-2

World Trade Flows

International merchandise trade amounts to over $3 trillion worldwide. The percentage figures show the proportion of trade flowing in the various directions.

Source: World Trade Organization (data are for 1995).

rendering per hour. Here the ad specialist can come up with more pages of ad copy per hour than the computer specialist and seemingly is just as good as the computer specialist at doing computerized art renderings. Is there any reason for the creative specialist and the computer specialist to "trade"? The answer is yes, because such trading will lead to higher output.

Consider the scenario of no trading. Assume that during each eight-hour day, the ad specialist and the computer whiz devote half of their day to writing ad copy and half to computerized art rendering. The ad specialist would create eight pages of ad copy (4 hours × 2) and four computerized art renderings (4 × 1). During that same period, the computer specialist would create four pages of ad copy (4 × 1) and four computerized art renderings (4 × 1). Each day, the combined output for the ad specialist and the computer specialist would be 12 pages of ad copy and eight computerized art renderings.

If the ad specialist specialized only in writing ad copy and the computer whiz specialized only in creating computerized art renderings, their combined output would rise to 16 pages of ad copy (8 × 2) and eight computerized art renderings (8 × 1). Overall, production would increase by four pages of ad copy per day.

The creative advertising employee has a comparative advantage in writing ad copy, and the computer specialist has a comparative advantage in doing computerized art renderings. **Comparative advantage** involves the ability to produce something at a lower opportunity cost compared to other producers, as we pointed out in Chapter 2.

Comparative advantage
The ability to produce a good or service at a lower opportunity cost compared to other producers.

TABLE 33-2
Comparative Costs of Production

Product	United States (worker-days)	France (worker-days)
Wine (1 liter)	1	1
Beer (1 liter)	1	2

Specialization Among Nations

To demonstrate the concept of comparative advantage for nations, let's take the example of France and the United States. In Table 33-2, we show the comparative costs of production of wine and beer in terms of worker-days. This is a simple two-country, two-commodity world in which we assume that labor is the only factor of production. As you can see from the table, in the United States, it takes one worker-day to produce 1 liter of wine, and the same is true for 1 liter of beer. In France, it takes one worker-day to produce 1 liter of wine but two worker-days for 1 liter of beer. In this sense, Americans appear to be just as good at producing wine as the French and actually have an **absolute advantage** in producing beer.

Absolute advantage
The ability to produce more output from given inputs of resources than other producers can.

Trade will still take place, however, which may seem paradoxical. How can trade take place if we can produce both goods at least as cheaply as the French can? Why don't we just produce both ourselves? To understand why, let's assume first that there is no trade and no specialization and that the workforce in each country consists of 200 workers. These 200 workers are divided equally in the production of wine and beer. We see in Table 33-3 that 100 liters of wine and 100 liters of beer are produced per day in the United States. In France, 100 liters of wine and 50 liters of beer are produced per day. The total daily world production in our two-country world is 200 liters of wine and 150 liters of beer.

Now the countries specialize. What can France produce more cheaply? Look at the comparative costs of production expressed in worker-days in Table 33-2. What is the cost of producing 1 liter more of wine? One worker-day. What is the cost of producing 1 liter more of beer? Two worker-days. We can say, then, that in France the opportunity cost of producing wine is less than that of producing beer. France will specialize in the activity that has the lower opportunity cost. In other words, France will specialize in its comparative advantage, which is the production of wine.

According to Table 33-4 on page 738, after specialization, the United States produces 200 liters of beer and France produces 200 liters of wine. Notice that the total world production per day has gone up from 200 liters of wine and 150 liters of beer to 200 liters of wine and 200 liters of beer per day. This was done without any increased use of resources. The gain, 50 "free" liters of beer, results from a more efficient allocation of resources worldwide. World output is greater when countries specialize in producing the goods in

TABLE 33-3
Daily World Output Before Specialization
It is assumed that 200 workers are available in each country.

Product	United States		France		
	Workers	Output (liters)	Workers	Output (liters)	World Output (liters)
Wine	100	100	100	100	200
Beer	100	100	100	50	150

	United States		France		
Product	Workers	Output (liters)	Workers	Output (liters)	World Output (liters)
Wine	—	—	200	200	200
Beer	200	200	—	—	200

TABLE 33-4

Daily World Output After Specialization

It is assumed that 200 workers are available in each country.

which they have a comparative advantage and then engage in foreign trade. Another way of looking at this is to consider the choice between two ways of producing a good. Obviously, each country would choose the less costly production process. One way of "producing" a good is to import it, so if in fact the imported good is cheaper than the domestically produced good, we will "produce" it by importing it. Not everybody, of course, is better off when free trade occurs. In our example, U.S. wine makers and French beer makers are worse off because those two *domestic* industries have disappeared.

Some people are worried that the United States (or any country, for that matter) might someday "run out of exports" because of overaggressive foreign competition. The analysis of comparative advantage tells us the contrary. No matter how much other countries compete for our business, the United States (or any other country) will always have a comparative advantage in something that it can export. In 10 or 20 years, that something may not be what we export today, but it will be exportable nonetheless because we will have a comparative advantage in producing it.

Other Benefits from International Trade: The Transmission of Ideas

Beyond the fact that comparative advantage generally results in an overall increase in the output of goods produced and consumed, there is another benefit to international trade. International trade bestows benefits on countries through the international transmission of ideas. According to economic historians, international trade has been the principal means by which new goods, services, and processes have spread around the world. For example, coffee was initially grown in Arabia near the Red Sea. Around A.D. 675, it began to be roasted and consumed as a beverage. Eventually, it was exported to other parts of the world, and the Dutch started cultivating it in their colonies during the seventeenth century and the French in the eighteenth century. The lowly potato is native to the Peruvian Andes. In the sixteenth century, it was brought to Europe by Spanish explorers. Thereafter, its cultivation and consumption spread rapidly. It became part of the American agricultural scene in the early eighteenth century.

All of the *intellectual property* that has been introduced throughout the world is a result of international trade. This includes new music, such as rock and roll in the 1950s and hip-hop and grunge in the 1990s. It includes the software applications that are common for computer users everywhere.

New processes have been transmitted through international trade. One of those involves the Japanese manufacturing innovation which emphasized redesigning the system rather than running the existing system in the best possible way. Inventories were reduced to just-in-time levels by reengineering machine setup methods. Just-in-time inventory control is now common in American factories.

Exercise 33.2
Visit www.econtoday.com for more about Korea.

INTERNATIONAL EXAMPLE
International Trade and the Alphabet

Even the alphabetic system of writing that appears to be the source of most alphabets in the world today was spread through international trade. According to some scholars, the Phoenicians, who lived on the long, narrow strip of Mediterranean coast north of Israel from the ninth century B.C. to around 300 B.C., created the first true alphabet. Presumably, they developed the alphabet to keep international trading records on their ships rather than having to take along highly trained scribes.

FOR CRITICAL ANALYSIS: *Before alphabets were used, how might have people communicated in written form?* ●

THE RELATIONSHIP BETWEEN IMPORTS AND EXPORTS

The basic proposition in understanding all of international trade is this:

In the long run, imports are paid for by exports.[1]

The reason that imports are ultimately paid for by exports is that foreigners want something in exchange for the goods that are shipped to the United States. For the most part, they want goods made in the United States. From this truism comes a remarkable corollary:

Any restriction of imports ultimately reduces exports.

This is a shocking revelation to many people who want to restrict foreign competition to protect domestic jobs. Although it is possible to protect certain U.S. jobs by restricting foreign competition, it is impossible to make *everyone* better off by imposing import restrictions. Why? Because ultimately such restrictions lead to a reduction in employment in the export industries of the nation.

Think of exports as simply another way of producing goods. International trade is merely an economic activity like all others; it is a production process that transforms exports into imports.

INTERNATIONAL EXAMPLE
The Importation of Priests into Spain

Imports affect not only goods but also services and the movement of labor. In Spain, some 3,000 priests retire each year, but barely 250 young men are ordained to replace them. Over 70 percent of the priests in Spain are now over the age of 50. The Spanish church estimates that by 2005, the number of priests will have fallen to half the 20,441 who were active in Spain in 1990. The Spanish church has had to seek young seminarians from Latin America under what it calls Operation Moses. It is currently subsidizing the travel and training of an increasing number of young Latin Americans to take over where native Spaniards have been before.

FOR CRITICAL ANALYSIS: *How might the Spanish Catholic church induce more native Spaniards to become priests?* ●

---

[1]We have to modify this rule by adding that in the short run, imports can also be paid for by the sale (or export) of real and financial assets, such as land, stocks, and bonds, or through an extension of credit from other countries.

INTERNATIONAL COMPETITIVENESS

"The United States is falling behind." "We need to stay competitive internationally." These and similar statements are often heard in government circles when the subject of international trade comes up. There are two problems with this issue. The first has to do with a simple definition. What does "global competitiveness" really mean? When one company competes against another, it is in competition. Is the United States like one big corporation, in competition with other countries? Certainly not. The standard of living in each country is almost solely a function of how well the economy functions *within that country,* not relative to other countries.

Another problem arises with respect to the real world. According to the Institute for Management Development in Lausanne, Switzerland, the United States continues to lead the pack in world competitiveness, ahead of Japan, Hong Kong, Germany, and the rest of the European Union. According to the report, America's top-class ranking is due to the rapid U.S. economic recovery from its 1990–1991 recession, widespread entrepreneurship, and a decade of economic restructuring. Other factors include America's sophisticated financial system and large investments in scientific research.

THINKING CRITICALLY ABOUT THE MEDIA

Foreigners' Productivity Improvements

With so much emphasis on America's competitiveness in the global economy, the media fail to understand a basic tenet: International trade is not a zero-sum game. If other countries in the world increase their productivity faster than in America, so be it. A more productive Germany will of course have more products to sell in the United States. At the same time, though, Germany will represent a bigger market for America's exports. In other words, a successful European or Asian economy can become successful without that success being at the expense of the United States. In fact, such successful economies are likely to help us by providing us with larger markets (and by selling us their own goods of higher quality at lower prices).

CONCEPTS IN BRIEF

- Countries can be better off materially if they specialize in producing goods for which they have a comparative advantage.

- It is important to distinguish between absolute and comparative advantage; the former refers to the ability to produce a unit of output with fewer physical units of input; the latter refers to producing output that has the lowest opportunity cost for a nation.

- Different nations will always have different comparative advantages because of differing opportunity costs due to different resource mixes.

ARGUMENTS AGAINST FREE TRADE

Numerous arguments are raised against free trade. They mainly point out the costs of trade; they do not consider the benefits or the possible alternatives for reducing the costs of free trade while still reaping benefits.

The Infant Industry Argument

A nation may feel that if a particular industry were allowed to develop domestically, it could eventually become efficient enough to compete effectively in the world market. Therefore, if some restrictions were placed on imports, domestic producers would be given the time needed to develop their efficiency to the point where they would be able to compete in the domestic market without any restrictions on imports. In graphic terminology, we would expect that if the protected industry truly does experience improvements in production techniques or technological breakthroughs toward greater efficiency in the future, the supply

Infant industry argument
The contention that tariffs should be imposed to protect from import competition an industry that is trying to get started. Presumably, after the industry becomes technologically efficient, the tariff can be lifted.

curve will shift outward to the right so that the domestic industry can produce larger quantities of each and every price. This **infant industry argument** has some merit in the short run and has been used to protect a number of industries in their infancy around the world. Such a policy can be abused, however. Often the protective import-restricting arrangements remain even after the infant has matured. If other countries can still produce more cheaply, the people who benefit from this type of situation are obviously the stockholders (and specialized factors of production that will earn economic rents) in the industry that is still being protected from world competition. The people who lose out are the consumers, who must pay a price higher than the world price for the product in question. In any event, it is very difficult to know beforehand which industries will eventually survive. In other words, we cannot predict very well the specific infant industries that should be protected. Note that when we talk about which industry "should be" protected, we are in the realm of normative economics. We are making a value judgment, a subjective statement of what *ought to be*.

EXAMPLE
An Infant Industry Blossoms Due to Protection from Foreign Imports: The Case of Marijuana

Marijuana was made illegal in the United States in the 1930s, but just as for many other outlawed drugs, a market for it remained. Until about 25 years ago, virtually all the marijuana consumed in the United States was imported. Today, earnings from the burgeoning and increasingly high-tech "pot" industry are estimated at $35 billion a year, making it the nation's biggest cash crop (compared to corn at $15 billion). Starting with President Richard Nixon in the 1970s, the federal government has in effect ended up protecting the domestic marijuana industry from imports by declaring a war on drugs. Given virtually no foreign competition, the American marijuana industry expanded and invested millions in developing both more productive and more potent seeds as well as more efficient growing technologies. Domestic marijuana growers now dominate the high end of a market in which consumers pay $300 to $500 an ounce for a reengineered home-grown product. New growing technologies allow domestic producers, using high-intensity sodium lights, carbon dioxide, and advances in genetics, to produce a kilogram of the potent sinsemilla variety every two months in a space no bigger than a phone booth.

FOR CRITICAL ANALYSIS: What has spurred domestic producers to develop highly productive indoor growing methods? ●

Countering Foreign Subsidies and Dumping

Another strong argument against unrestricted foreign trade has to do with countering other nations' subsidies to their own producers. When a foreign government subsidizes its producers, our producers claim that they cannot compete fairly with these subsidized foreigners. To the extent that such subsidies fluctuate, it can be argued that unrestricted free trade will seriously disrupt domestic producers. They will not know when foreign governments are going to subsidize their producers and when they are not. Our competing industries will be expanding and contracting too frequently.

Dumping
Selling a good or a service abroad at a price below its cost of production or below the price charged in the home market.

The phenomenon called *dumping* is also used as an argument against unrestricted trade. **Dumping** occurs when a producer sells its products abroad at a price below its cost of production or below the price that is charged in the home market. Although cries of dumping against foreign producers are often heard, they typically occur only when the foreign nation is in the throes of a serious recession. The foreign producer does not want to slow down its production at home. Because it anticipates an end to the recession and doesn't want to hold large inventories, it dumps its products abroad at prices below its costs. This does, in fact, disrupt international trade. It also creates instability in domestic production and therefore may impair commercial well-being at home.

POLICY EXAMPLE
Are America's Antidumping Laws Fair?

The International Trade Administration (ITA) is supposed to render fair and impartial judgment on American companies' dumping complaints. Its track record is far from fair, however. Over 95 percent of cases have been decided against foreign firms. When an American company wants to block foreign competition, it can go to the ITA. For example, when the American supercomputer company Cray Research lost out to a subsidiary of NEC of Japan in bidding to supply a five-year leasing contract on a weather-simulating supercomputer, it went to the ITA. It claimed that NEC was selling the weather supercomputer for about 20 percent of its cost, thereby "dumping" in the U.S. market. The ITA agreed. The U.S. government now imposes tariffs of between 173 and 454 percent on all supercomputers imported from Japan. The result is that Cray no longer faces any competition from the Japanese. During the four-week investigation of NEC, the ITA required NEC to respond to an almost 200-page questionnaire written in English.

FOR CRITICAL ANALYSIS: *Who loses because of the ITA's behavior?* ●

Protecting American Jobs

Perhaps the argument used most often against free trade is that unrestrained competition from other countries will eliminate American jobs because other countries have lower-cost labor than we do. (Less restrictive environmental standards in other countries might also lower their costs relative to ours.) This is a compelling argument, particularly for politicians from areas that might be threatened by foreign competition. For example, a representative from an area with shoe factories would certainly be upset about the possibility of constituents' losing their jobs because of competition from lower-priced shoe manufacturers in Brazil and Italy. But of course this argument against free trade is equally applicable to trade between the states.

Economists David Gould, G. L. Woodbridge, and Roy Ruffin examined the data on the relationship between increases in imports and the rate of unemployment. Their conclusion was that there is no causal link between the two. Indeed, in half the cases they studied, when imports increased, unemployment fell.

Another issue has to do with the cost of protecting American jobs by restricting international trade. The Institute for International Economics examined just the restrictions on foreign textiles and apparel goods. U.S. consumers pay $9 billion a year more to protect jobs in those industries. That comes out to $50,000 a year for each job saved in an industry in which the average job pays only $20,000 a year. Similar studies have yielded similar results: Restrictions on the imports of Japanese cars have cost $160,000 *per year* for every job saved in the auto industry. Every

---

THINKING CRITICALLY ABOUT THE MEDIA

Unfair Competition from Low-Wage Countries

Protectionists are able to get the media to carry stories about how low-wage countries are stealing American jobs. The facts are exactly the opposite. The highest-labor-cost country in the world is Germany, and it is also the largest exporter in the world. The United States, Japan, France, and the United Kingdom also have relatively high labor costs, and they, too, are some of the world's biggest exporters. If the low-wage myth were true, the United States would never be able to compete with, say, Mexican labor. Yet the reality is that the United States exports much more to Mexico than it imports. Finally, both the World Bank and the Organization for Economic Cooperation and Development have done exhaustive studies on the issue. Their conclusion is that there is no evidence that trade with low-wage countries results in large-scale job losses to industrial countries. The real competition for American manufacturing comes from high-wage countries, such as Germany and Japan.

job preserved in the glass industry has cost $200,000 each and every year. Every job preserved in the U.S. steel industry has cost an astounding $750,000 per year.

In the long run, the industries that have had the most protection—textiles, clothing, and iron and steel—have seen the most dramatic reductions in employment in the United States.

CONCEPTS IN BRIEF

- The infant industry argument against free trade contends that new industries should be protected against world competition so that they can become technologically efficient in the long run.

- Unrestricted foreign trade may allow foreign governments to subsidize exports or foreign producers to engage in dumping—selling products in other countries below their cost of production. To the extent that foreign export subsidies and dumping create more instability in domestic production, they may impair our well-being.

WAYS TO RESTRICT FOREIGN TRADE

There are many ways in which international trade can be stopped or at least stifled. These include quotas and taxes (the latter are usually called *tariffs* when applied to internationally traded items). Let's talk first about quotas.

Quotas

Quota system
A government-imposed restriction on the quantity of a specific good that another country is allowed to sell in the United States. In other words, quotas are restrictions on imports. These restrictions are usually applied to one or several specific countries.

Under the **quota system,** individual countries or groups of foreign producers are restricted to a certain amount of trade. An import quota specifies the maximum amount of a commodity that may be imported during a specified period of time. For example, the government might not allow more than 50 million barrels of foreign crude oil to enter the United States in a particular year.

Consider the example of quotas on textiles. Figure 33-3 presents the demand and the supply curves for imported textiles. In an unrestricted import market, the equilibrium quantity

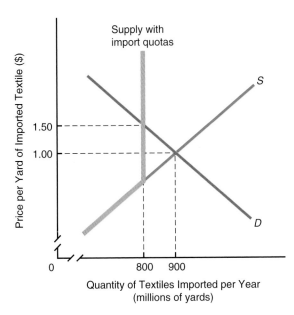

FIGURE 33-3

The Effect of Quotas on Textile Imports
Without restrictions, 900 million yards of textiles would be imported each year into the United States at the world price of $1.00 per yard. If the federal government imposes a quota of only 800 million yards, the effective supply curve becomes vertical at that quantity. It intersects the demand curve at the new equilibrium price of $1.50 per yard.

imported is 900 million yards at a price of $1 per yard (expressed in constant-quality units). When an import quota is imposed, the supply curve is no longer *S*. Rather, the supply curve becomes vertical at some amount less than the equilibrium quantity—here, 800 million yards per year. The price to the American consumer increases from $1.00 to $1.50. The domestic suppliers of textiles obviously benefit by an increase in revenues because they can now charge a higher price.

INTERNATIONAL EXAMPLE
Health Disputes in Trade: A Type of Quota

Governments, including our own, have figured out that they can impose implicit quotas on imports by claiming health concerns. Whenever a government convincingly claims that an imported product poses a health problem to its citizens, it can restrict imports of that product. The result is a benefit to domestic producers of goods that compete with the imported product.

Consider some examples. When "mad cow disease" was discovered in British cattle, the French and the rest of Europe imposed a ban on the importation of British beef. At the time of the ban, there was scant scientific evidence that the bovine disease had any effect on humans. French farmers were ecstatic at the ban. Around the same time, Russia prohibited the importation of frozen U.S. chickens. It used a vaguely worded concern about salmonella as its reason. And the ban on imports of American beef into the European Union was justified for many years over concern there that U.S. cattle farmers used hormones. In the United States, we have been able to keep out Mexican avocados because of concerns over fruit flies. California avocado growers have been the main beneficiaries.

FOR CRITICAL ANALYSIS: How do market forces tend to minimize food-related health concerns? ●

Voluntary Quotas. Quotas do not have to be explicit and defined by law. They can be "voluntary." Such a quota is called a **voluntary restraint agreement (VRA).** In the early 1980s, the United States asked Japan voluntarily to restrain its exports to the United States. The Japanese government did so, limiting itself to exporting 2.8 million Japanese automobiles. Today, there are VRAs on machine tools and textiles.

The opposite of a VRA is a **voluntary import expansion (VIE).** Under a VIE, a foreign government agrees to have its companies import more foreign goods from another country. The United States almost started a major international trade war with Japan in 1995 over just such an issue. The U.S. government wanted Japanese automobile manufacturers voluntarily to increase their imports of U.S.-made automobile parts.

Voluntary restraint agreement (VRA)
An official agreement with another country that "voluntarily" restricts the quantity of its exports to the United States.

Voluntary import expansion (VIE)
An official agreement with another country in which it agrees to import more from the United States.

Tariffs

We can analyze tariffs by using standard supply and demand diagrams. Let's use as our commodity laptop computers, some of which are made in Japan and some of which are made domestically. In panel (a) of Figure 33-4, you see the demand and supply of Japanese laptops. The equilibrium price is $1,000 per constant-quality unit, and the equilibrium quantity is 10 million per year. In panel (b), you see the same equilibrium price of $1,000, and the *domestic* equilibrium quantity is 5 million units per year.

Now a tariff of $500 is imposed on all imported Japanese laptops. The supply curve shifts upward by $500 to S_2. For purchasers of Japanese laptops, the price increases to

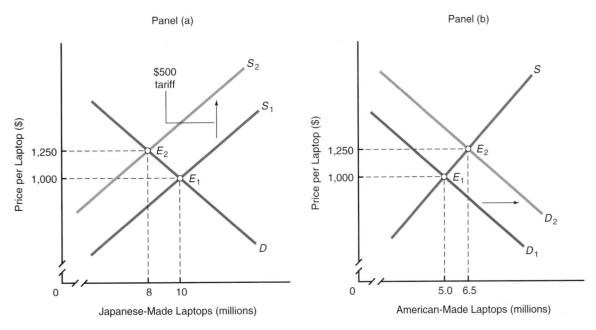

FIGURE 33-4

The Effect of a Tariff on Japanese-Made Laptop Computers
Without a tariff, the United States buys 10 million Japanese laptops per year at an average price of $1,000, as shown in panel (a). American producers sell 5 million domestically made laptops, also at $1,000 each, as shown in panel (b). A $500-per-laptop tariff will shift the Japanese import supply curve to S_2 in panel (a), so that the new equilibrium is at E_2, with price $1,250 and quantity sold reduced to 8 million per year. The demand curve for American-made laptops (for which there is no tariff) shifts to D_2 in panel (b). Sales increase to 6.5 million per year.

$1,250. The quantity demanded falls to 8 million per year. In panel (b), you see that at the higher price of imported Japanese laptops, the demand curve for American-made laptops shifts outward to the right to D_2. The equilibrium price increases to $1,250, but the equilibrium quantity increases to 6.5 million units per year. So the tariff benefits domestic laptop producers because it increases the demand for their products due to the higher price of a close substitute, Japanese laptops. This causes a redistribution of income from American consumers of laptops to American producers of laptops.

Tariffs in the United States. In Figure 33-5 on page 746, we see that tariffs on all imported goods have varied widely. The highest rates in the twentieth century occurred with the passage of the Smoot-Hawley Tariff in 1930.

POLICY EXAMPLE
Did the Smoot-Hawley Tariff Worsen the Great Depression?

By 1930, the unemployment rate had almost doubled in a year. Congress and President Hoover wanted to do something that would help stimulate U.S. production and reduce unemployment. The result was the Smoot-Hawley Tariff, which set tariff schedules for over 20,000 products, raising duties on imports by an average of 52 percent. This attempt to improve the domestic economy at the expense of foreign economies backfired. Each trading partner of the United States in turn imposed its own high tariffs, including the United Kingdom, the Netherlands, France, and Switzerland. The result was a massive reduction in international trade by an incredible 64 percent in three years. Some believe that the ensuing world Great Depression was partially caused by such tariffs.

FOR CRITICAL ANALYSIS: The Smoot-Hawley Tariff has been labeled a "beggar thy neighbor" policy. Explain why. ●

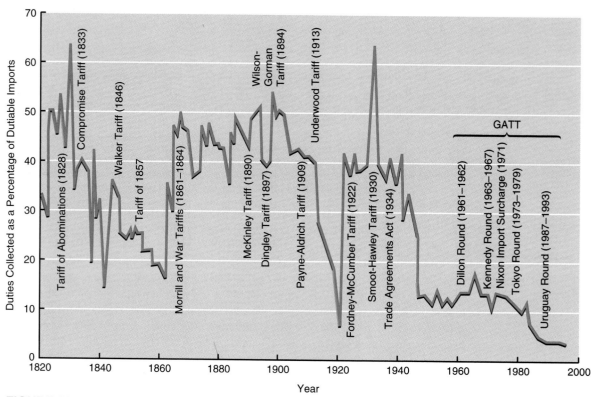

FIGURE 33-5

Tariff Rates in the United States Since 1820

Tariff rates in the United States have bounced around like a football; indeed, in Congress, tariffs are a political football. Import-competing industries prefer high tariffs. In the twentieth century, the highest tariff we have had was the Smoot-Hawley Tariff of 1930, which was almost as high as the "tariff of abominations" in 1828.

Source: U.S. Department of Commerce.

General Agreement on Tariffs and Trade (GATT)
An international agreement established in 1947 to further world trade by reducing barriers and tariffs.

Current Tariff Laws. The Trade Expansion Act of 1962 gave the president the authority to reduce tariffs by up to 50 percent. Subsequently, tariffs were reduced by about 35 percent. In 1974, the Trade Reform Act allowed the president to reduce tariffs further. In 1984, the Trade and Tariff Act resulted in the lowest tariff rates ever. All such trade agreement obligations of the United States are carried out under the auspices of the **General Agreement on Tariffs and Trade (GATT),** which was signed in 1947. Member nations of GATT account for more than 85 percent of world trade. As you can see in Figure 33-5, there have been a number of rounds of negotiations to reduce tariffs since the early 1960s. The latest round was called the Uruguay Round because that is where the meetings were held.

The World Trade Organization (WTO)

World Trade Organization (WTO)
The successor organization to GATT, it handles all trade disputes among its 132 member nations.

The Uruguay Round of the General Agreement on Tariffs and Trade (GATT) was ratified by 117 nations at the end of 1993. A year later, in a special session of Congress, the entire treaty was ratified. On January 1, 1995, the new **World Trade Organization (WTO)** replaced GATT. As of 1998, the WTO had 132 member nations, plus 32 observer governments, all but two of which have applied for membership. WTO decisions have concerned such topics as the European Union's "banana wars," in which the EU's policies were determined to favor unfairly many former European colonies in Africa, the Caribbean, and the Pacific at the expense of banana-exporting countries in Latin America. Now those former colonies no longer have a privileged position in European markets.

On a larger scale, the WTO fostered the most important and far-reaching global trade agreement ever covering financial institutions, including banks, insurers, and investment companies. The more than 100 signatories to this new treaty have legally committed themselves to giving foreigners more freedom to own and operate companies in virtually all segments of the financial services industry.

CONCEPTS IN BRIEF

- One means of restricting foreign trade is a quota system. Beneficiaries of quotas are the importers who get the quota rights and the domestic producers of the restricted good.

- Another means of restricting imports is a tariff, which is a tax on imports only. An import tariff benefits import-competing industries and harms consumers by raising prices.

- The main international institution created to improve trade among nations is the General Agreement on Tariffs and Trade (GATT). The latest round of trade talks under GATT, the Uruguay Round, led to the creation of the World Trade Organization.

今世紀最大の陰謀ミステリー。

ケヴィン・コスナー

オリヴァー・ストーン監督作品

JFK

Nowhere is American culture more pervasive than in the film industry. Although American movies account for a small share of American exports, they spread American culture worldwide.

Is American Culture More Pervasive than It Used to Be?

CONCEPTS APPLIED:

INTERNATIONAL TRADE, EXPORTS, IMPORTS, GOODS, SERVICES

Visit www.econtoday.com for an Internet Activity that expands your understanding of these concepts.

International trade, expressed as a percentage of yearly total national income in the United States, has been rising since the 1950s. This mirrors a worldwide trend—world output has been growing at an annual rate of 3.5 percent, and world trade has been growing at almost double that rate over the past 10 years.

Why Trade Has Been Growing

At least two forces having been driving the increased flows of goods and funds: (1) trade liberalization—reduced trade barriers due to such agreements as NAFTA and the WTO—and (2) rapidly falling computing and communication costs, which together have sharply reduced some of the natural barriers of time and space that separate national markets. Consider panel (a) of Figure 33-6. There you see how the price of a three-minute telephone call from New York to London in constant 1998 dollars has fallen. But this does not explain the domination of American culture worldwide.

The Export of American Services

The fact that Americans can talk more cheaply to the rest of the world and vice versa does not explain the spread of American culture. Cheaper international telephone calls are, however, indicative of a major shift in American trade. Trade involves both goods and services, and over the past two decades, the United States has been exporting a larger and larger amount of services. That accounts for much of the expansion of American culture.

Foreign tourism in the United States now amounts to about $80 billion of service exports a year. When foreign-

ers visit the United States, they are buying service exports, such as the use of hotel rooms. Obviously, the more tourists who come to the United States, the more likely that foreign residents will learn about American culture and may take some of our culture back to their home countries.

More important, the sale of intellectual property in the form of American movies and TV programs has skyrocketed. Foreign sales account for over half of our film industry's $25 billion box office revenues. Less impressive, but similar, numbers have risen in the American music business. The sale of U.S. intellectual property abroad is perhaps the single most important factor in spreading American culture.

The United States is also exporting each year more than $20 billion of the services of many of its professionals, such as engineers, architects, accountants, investment bankers, and marketing specialists. Finally, foreign students constitute over 3 percent of all U.S. college students. When they go back to their own countries, they take with them a strong dose of American culture.

Panel (b) of Figure 33-6 shows the recent trend in the export of services versus the export of goods. In the past two decades, exports of services have grown twice as rapidly as exports of goods.

FOR CRITICAL ANALYSIS

1. What are some foreign influences on American culture?
2. French law requires that 40 percent of radio and TV be of French origin. Portrayed as a law to preserve French culture, how does this restriction affect foreign trade?

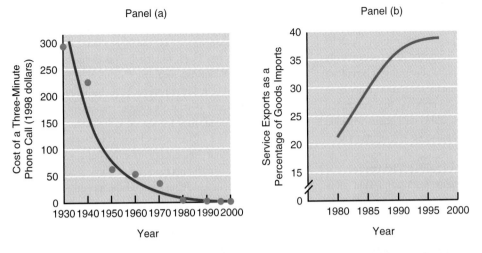

FIGURE 33-6

Cheaper International Phone Calls and the Increased Export of Services

In panel (a), you can see that the price of a three-minute call between London and New York, expressed in 1998 dollars, has fallen dramatically. In panel (b), the percentage of export services relative to goods exports has been growing steadily.

Sources: World Bank; U.S. Department of Commerce.

CHAPTER SUMMARY

1. It is important to distinguish between absolute and comparative advantage. A person or country that can do everything "better" (with higher labor productivity) than every other person or country has an absolute advantage in everything. Nevertheless, trade will still be advantageous if people will specialize in the things that they do *relatively* best, exploiting their respective comparative advantage.

2. Along with the gains, there are costs from trade. Certain industries and their employees may be hurt if trade is opened up.

3. An import quota restricts the quantity of imports coming into the country. It therefore raises the price. Consumers always lose.

4. When governments impose "voluntary" quotas, they are called voluntary restraint agreements (VRAs).

5. An import tariff raises the domestic price of foreign produced goods. It therefore allows domestic producers to raise their own prices. The result is a higher price to consumers, a lower quantity of imports, and a lower volume of international trade.

6. The main international institution created to improve trade among nations was the General Agreement on Tariffs and Trade (GATT), replaced in 1993 by the World Trade Organization (WTO).

DISCUSSION OF PREVIEW QUESTIONS

1. Is international trade important to the United States?

The direct impact of international trade on the United States, as measured by the ratio of exports to GDP, is relatively small compared with many other nations. Yet it is hard to imagine what life would be like without international trade. Initially, many prices would rise rapidly, but eventually domestic production would begin on many goods we presently import. However, consider life without imports of coffee, tea, bananas, and foreign wines, motorcycles, automobiles, televisions, VCRs, and hundreds of other goods from food and clothing to electronics—not to mention vital imports such as bauxite, chromium, cobalt, nickel, platinum, and tin.

2. What is the relationship between imports and exports?

Because foreigners eventually want real goods and services as payment for the real goods and services they export to other countries, ultimately each country pays for its imports with its exports. Hence on a worldwide basis, the value of imports must equal the value of exports.

3. What is the ultimate effect of a restriction on imports?

Because each country must pay for its imports with its exports, any restriction on imports must ultimately lead to a reduction in exports. So even though restrictions on imports because of tariffs or quotas may benefit workers and business owners in the protected domestic industry, such protection will harm workers and business owners in the export sector in general.

4. What are some arguments against free trade?

The infant industry argument maintains that new industries developing domestically need protection from foreign competitors until they are mature enough themselves to compete with foreigners, at which time protection will be removed. One problem with this argument is that it is difficult to tell when maturity has been reached, and domestic industries will fight against weaning. Moreover, this argument is hardly relevant to most U.S. industries. It is also alleged (and is true to a large extent) that free trade leads to instability for specific domestic industries as comparative advantage changes in a dynamic world. Nations that have traditionally held a comparative advantage in the production of some goods occasionally lose that advantage (while gaining others). Regional hardships are a result, and protection of domestic jobs is demanded.

PROBLEMS

(Answers to the odd-numbered problems appear at the back of the book.)

33-1. Examine the hypothetical table of worker-hours required to produce caviar and wheat in the United States and in Russia.

Product	United States	Russia
Caviar (ounce)	6 worker-hours	9 worker-hours
Wheat (bushel)	3 worker-hours	6 worker-hours

a. What is the opportunity cost to the United States of producing one ounce of caviar per time period? What is the opportunity cost to the United States of producing one bushel of wheat?

b. What is the opportunity cost to Russia of producing one ounce of caviar per time period? What is the opportunity cost to Russia of producing one bushel of wheat?

c. The United States has a comparative advantage in what? Russia has a comparative advantage in what?

33-2. Study the hypothetical table of worker-hours required to produce coffee and beans in Colombia and Turkey.

Product	Colombia	Turkey
Coffee (pound)	2 worker-hours	1 worker-hour
Beans (pound)	6 worker-hours	2 worker-hours

a. What is the opportunity cost to Colombia of producing one pound of coffee? One pound of beans?

b. What is the opportunity cost to Turkey of producing one pound of coffee? One pound of beans?

c. Colombia has a comparative advantage in what? Turkey has a comparative advantage in what?

33-3. Assume that the United States can produce *everything* with fewer labor-hours than any other country on earth. Even under this extreme assumption, why would the United States still trade with other countries?

33-4. Examine the hypothetical table of worker-hours required to produce cheese and cloth in two countries, A and B.

Product	Country A	Country B
Cheese (pound)	$\frac{2}{3}$ worker-hours	2 worker-hours
Cloth (yard)	$\frac{1}{2}$ worker-hours	1 worker-hour

a. What is the opportunity cost to country A of producing one pound of cheese? One yard of cloth?

b. What is the opportunity cost to country B of producing one pound of cheese? One yard of cloth?

c. Country A has a comparative advantage in what?

d. Country B has a comparative advantage in what?

33-5. The use of tariffs and quotas to restrict imports results in higher prices and is successful in reducing imports. In what way is using a tariff different from using a quota?

33-6. Two countries, Austral Land and Boreal Land, have the following production opportunities shown in the graphs.

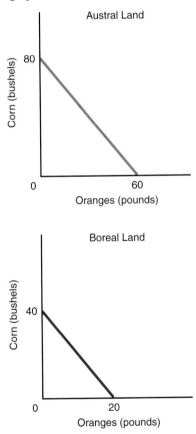

a. Who has an absolute advantage in corn? In oranges?

b. Who has a comparative advantage in corn? In oranges?

c. Should Boreal Land export at all? If so, which good should it export?

d. What is Austral Land's opportunity cost of oranges in terms of corn? What is Boreal Land's opportunity cost of corn in terms of oranges?

33-7. The accompanying graph gives the supply and demand for grapes. S and D are the United States' supply and demand curves, respectively. Assume that the world price of grapes is 50 cents per pound.

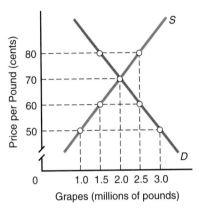

a. How many pounds are produced domestically? How many pounds are imported?

b. Suppose that the United States imposes a 10-cent-per-pound tariff. How many pounds would now be produced domestically? How many pounds would be imported? What are the U.S. government's revenues?

c. Suppose now that the government imposes a 20-cent-per-pound tariff. What price can domestic growers now receive for their grapes? How many pounds will domestic growers produce? How many pounds will be imported? What are government revenues?

33-8. If free trade is so obviously beneficial, why are there so many restrictions on international trade? (Hint: Review the theory presented in Chapter 32.)

33-9. Explain why an increase in taxes on imports (tariffs) will reduce exports.

33-10. Assume that a country with whom the United States is trading imposes restrictions on U.S.-made imports into that country. Will the United States be better off by simultaneously imposing restrictions on the other country's imports into the United States? Why or why not?

COMPUTER-ASSISTED INSTRUCTION

We show that the combination of specialization and exchange is the next best thing to a free lunch.

Complete problem and answer appear on disk.

INTERACTING WITH THE INTERNET

You can access all of the activities of the World Trade Organization (WTO) at

www.wto.org

If you are interested in the rules of international trade, go to

www.un.or.at/uncitral/

You can go to the home page of Michigan State University's Center for International Business Education and Research to access a wide variety of international business resources on the Web. Visit them at

ciber.bus.msu.edu/busres/statinfo.htm

You can get information on trade patterns in every region of the world by accessing the CIA's *World Fact Book* at

www.odci.gov/cia/publications/nsolo/wfb-all.htm

If you are interested in taking a closer look at world trade patterns, go to the World Trade Analyzer at

www.tradecompass.com/trade_analyzer/

CHAPTER 34

EXCHANGE RATES AND THE BALANCE OF PAYMENTS

In the past, if you traveled to any of the 15 countries of the European Union, you would have had to exchange dollars for each country's national currency. By the time you read this, in at least some of those 15 countries, you may have to exchange your dollars only once for a new currency called the *euro*. If all of the European Union's members agreed on a single currency, they would represent an economy 18 percent larger than that of the United States. Does this mean that the almighty dollar will lose its preeminence in world financial markets? Before you can answer such a question, you need to know more about international financial transactions and the determinants of foreign exchange rates.

PREVIEW QUESTIONS

1. What is the difference between the balance of trade and the balance of payments?
2. What is a foreign exchange rate?
3. What is a flexible exchange rate system?
4. What is the gold standard?

753

Did You Know That... every day, around the clock, over $1 trillion of foreign currencies are traded? Along with that trading come news headlines, such as "The dollar weakened today," "The dollar is clearly overvalued," "The dollar is under attack," and "Members of the Group of Seven agreed to prevent the dollar from rising." If you are confused by such newspaper headlines, join the crowd. Surprisingly, though, if you regard the dollar, the pound, the deutsche mark, the yen, and the franc as assets that are subject to the laws of supply and demand, the world of international finance can be quickly demystified. Perhaps the first step is to examine the meaning of the terms used with respect to America's international financial transactions during any one-year period.

THE BALANCE OF PAYMENTS AND INTERNATIONAL CAPITAL MOVEMENTS

Governments typically keep track of each year's economic activities by calculating the gross domestic product—the total of expenditures on all newly produced final domestic goods and services—and its components. In the world of international trade also, a summary information system has been developed. It relates to the balance of trade and the balance of payments. The **balance of trade** refers specifically to exports and imports of *goods and services* as discussed in Chapter 33. When international trade is in balance, the value of exports equals the value of imports.

The **balance of payments** is a more general concept that expresses the total of all economic transactions between two nations, usually for a period of one year. Each country's balance of payments summarizes information about that country's exports, imports, earnings by domestic residents on assets located abroad, earnings on domestic assets owned by foreign residents, international capital movements, and official transactions by central banks and governments. In essence, then, the balance of payments is a record of all the transactions between households, firms, and government of one country and the rest of the world. Any transaction that leads to a *payment* by a country's residents (or government) is a deficit item, identified by a negative sign (−) when we examine the actual numbers that might be in Table 34-1. Any transaction that leads to a *receipt* by a country's residents (or government) is a surplus item and is identified by a plus sign (+) when actual numbers are considered. Table 34-1 gives a listing of the surplus and deficit items on international accounts.

Balance of trade
The value of goods and services bought and sold in the world market.

Balance of payments
A summary record of a country's economic transactions with foreign residents and governments over a year.

TABLE 34-1

Surplus (+) and Deficit (−) Items on the International Accounts

Surplus Items (+)	Deficit Items (−)
Exports of merchandise	Imports of merchandise
Private and governmental gifts from foreigners	Private and governmental gifts to foreigners
Foreign use of domestically owned transportation	Use of foreign-owned transportation
Foreign tourists' expenditures in this country	Tourism expenditures abroad
Foreign military spending in this country	Military spending abroad
Interest and dividend receipts from foreigners	Interest and dividends paid to foreigners
Sales of domestic assets to foreigners	Purchases of foreign assets
Funds deposited in this country by foreigners	Funds placed in foreign depository institutions
Sales of gold to foreigners	Purchases of gold from foreigners
Sales of domestic currency to foreigners	Purchases of foreign currency

Accounting Identities

Accounting identities
Statements that certain numerical measurements are equal by accepted definition (for example, "assets equal liabilities plus stockholders' equity").

Accounting identities—definitions of equivalent values—exist for financial institutions and other businesses. We begin with simple accounting identities that must hold for families and then go on to describe international accounting identities.

If a family unit is spending more than its current income, such a situation necessarily implies that the family unit must be doing one of the following:

1. Drawing down its wealth. The family must reduce its money holdings, or it must sell stocks, bonds, or other assets.
2. Borrowing.
3. Receiving gifts from friends or relatives.
4. Receiving public transfers from a government, which obtained the funds by taxing others. (A transfer is a payment, in money or in goods or services, made without receiving goods or services in return.)

In effect, we can use this information to derive an identity: If a family unit is currently spending more than it is earning, it must draw on previously acquired wealth, borrow, or receive either private or public aid. Similarly, an identity exists for a family unit that is currently spending less than it is earning: It must increase its wealth by increasing its money holdings or by lending and acquiring other financial assets, or it must pay taxes or bestow gifts on others. When we consider businesses and governments, each unit in each group faces its own identities or constraints; thus, net lending by households must equal net borrowing by businesses and governments.

Even though our individual family unit's accounts must balance, in the sense that the identity discussed previously must hold, sometimes the item that brings about the balance cannot continue indefinitely. *If family expenditures exceed family income and this situation is financed by borrowing, the household may be considered to be in disequilibrium because such a situation cannot continue indefinitely.* If such a deficit is financed by drawing on previously accumulated assets, the family may also be in disequilibrium because it cannot continue indefinitely to draw on its wealth; eventually, it will become impossible for that family to continue such a lifestyle. (Of course, if the family members are retired, they may well be in equilibrium by drawing on previously acquired assets to finance current deficits; this example illustrates that it is necessary to understand circumstances fully before pronouncing an economic unit in disequilibrium.)

Individual households, businesses, and governments, as well as the entire group of households, businesses, and governments, must eventually reach equilibrium. Certain economic adjustment mechanisms have evolved to ensure equilibrium. Deficit households must eventually increase their incomes or decrease their expenditures. They will find that they have to pay higher interest rates if they wish to borrow to finance their deficits. Eventually their credit sources will dry up, and they will be forced into equilibrium. Businesses, on occasion, must lower costs and/or prices—or go bankrupt—to reach equilibrium.

When nations trade or interact, certain identities or constraints must also hold. Nations buy goods from people in other nations; they also lend to and present gifts to people in other nations. If a nation interacts with others, an accounting identity ensures a balance (but not an equilibrium, as will soon become clear). Let's look at the three categories of balance of payments transactions: current account transactions, capital account transactions, and official reserve account transactions.

Current Account Transactions

During any designated period, all payments and gifts that are related to the purchase or sale of both goods and services constitute the current account in international trade. The three major types of current account transactions are the exchange of merchandise goods, the exchange of services, and unilateral transfers.

Merchandise Trade Transactions. The largest portion of any nation's balance of payments current account is typically the importing and exporting of merchandise goods. During 1998, for example, as can be seen in lines 1 and 2 of Table 34-2, the United States exported $679.0 billion of merchandise and imported $907.3 billion. The balance of merchandise trade is defined as the difference between the value of merchandise exports and the value of merchandise imports. For 1998, the United States had a balance of merchandise trade deficit because the value of its merchandise imports exceeded the value of its merchandise exports. This deficit amounted to $228.3. billion (line 3).

Service Exports and Imports. The balance of (merchandise) trade has to do with tangible items—you can feel them, touch them, and see them. Service exports and imports have to do with invisible or intangible items that are bought and sold, such as shipping, insurance, tourist expenditures, and banking services. Also, income earned by foreigners on U.S. investments and income earned by Americans on foreign investments are part of service imports and exports. As can be seen in lines 4 and 5 of Table 34-2, in 1998, service exports were $256.7 bil-

---

THINKING CRITICALLY ABOUT THE MEDIA

Perhaps the Trade Situation Isn't So Bad After All

Virtually every month, there appears a spate of articles and TV sound bites about America's trade deficit. The official numbers may be in error, however, for they ignore the multinational nature of modern firms. American international trade figures exclude sales in other countries for subsidiaries of American-owned companies. Because of a host of other problems, some government economists believe that they are underestimating the value of U.S. exports by as much as 10 percent. Economist Paul Krugman of Stanford University agrees. When he added up the value of world exports and compared it with the value of world imports, he found that the planet Earth had a trade deficit of $100 billion! Perhaps we are trading with aliens and don't know it.

TABLE 34-2
U.S. Balance of Payments Account, 1998 Figures are Billions of Dollars.

Current Account		
(1) Exports of goods	+679.0	
(2) Imports of goods	−907.3	
(3) Balance of trade		−228.3
(4) Exports of services	+256.7	
(5) Imports of services	−175.7	
(6) Balance of services		+81.0
(7) Balance on goods and services [(3) + (6)]		−147.3
(8) Net unilateral transfers	−41.1	
(9) Balance on current account		−188.4
Capital Account		
(10) U.S. capital going abroad	−451.7	
(11) Foreign capital coming into the United States	+657.8[a]	
(12) Balance on capital account [(10) + (11)]		+206.1
(13) Balance on current account plus balance on capital account [(9) + (12)]		−17.7
(14) Official transactions		+17.7
(15) Total (balance)		$00.00

Sources: U.S. Department of Commerce, Bureau of Economic Analysis; U.S. Department of the Treasury.
[a]Includes a $54 billion statistical discrepancy, probably unaccounted capital inflows, many of which relate to the illegal drug trade.

Exercise 34.1
Visit www.econtoday.com for more
about balance of trade.

lion and service imports were $175.7 billion. Thus the balance of services was about $81.0 billion in 1998 (line 6). Exports constitute receipts or inflows into the United States and are positive; imports constitute payments abroad or outflows of money and are negative.

When we combine the balance of merchandise trade with the balance of services, we obtain a balance on goods and services equal to −$147.3 billion in 1998 (line 7).

Unilateral Transfers. Americans give gifts to relatives and others abroad. The federal government grants gifts to foreign nations. Foreigners give gifts to Americans, and some foreign governments have granted money to the U.S. government. In the current account, we see that net unilateral transfers—the total amount of gifts given by Americans minus the total amount received by Americans from abroad—came to −$41.1 billion in 1998 (line 8). The fact that there is a minus sign before the number for unilateral transfers means that Americans gave more to foreigners than foreigners gave to Americans.

Balancing the Current Account. The balance on current account tracks the value of a country's exports of goods and services (including military receipts plus income on investments abroad) and transfer payments (private and government) relative to the value of that country's import of goods and services (including military payments) and transfer payments (private and government). In 1998, it was a *negative* $188.4 billion.

If exports exceed imports, a current account surplus is said to exist; if imports exceed exports, a current account deficit is said to exist. A current account deficit means that we are importing more than we are exporting. Such a deficit must be paid for by the export of money or money equivalent, which means a capital account surplus.

Capital Account Transactions

In world markets, it is possible to buy and sell not only goods and services but also real and financial assets. This is what the capital accounts are concerned with in international transactions. Capital account transactions occur because of foreign investments—either foreigners investing in the United States or Americans investing in other countries. The purchase of shares of stock on the London stock market by an American causes an outflow of funds. The building of a Japanese automobile factory in the United States causes an inflow of funds. Any time foreigners buy U.S. government securities, that is an inflow of funds. Any time Americans buy foreign government securities, there is an outflow of funds. Loans to and from foreigners cause outflows and inflows.

Line 10 of Table 34-2 indicates that in 1998, the value of private and government capital going out of the United States was −$451.7 billion, and line 11 shows that the value of private and government capital coming into the United States (including a statistical discrepancy) was $657.8 billion. U.S. capital going abroad constitutes payments or outflows and is therefore negative. Foreign capital coming into the United States constitutes receipts or inflows and is therefore positive. Thus there was a positive net capital movement of $206.1 billion into the United States (line 12). This is also called the balance on capital account.

There is a relationship between the current account and the capital account, assuming no interventions by the central banks of nations. *The current account and the capital account must sum to zero. Stated differently, the current account deficit equals the capital account surplus. Any nation experiencing a current account deficit, such as the United States, must also be running a capital account surplus.*

POLICY EXAMPLE
Should the United States Worry About Its Continuing Trade Deficit?

Look at the current account line at the bottom of Figure 34-1. On a current account basis, the United States has been "in the red" for years. Some people believe that trade deficits are bad and should be reduced. Further, they believe that maintaining a trade deficit creates an untenable foreign debt burden for Americans. It is true that total indebtedness to foreigners increased from nothing in 1987 to almost $1 trillion in 1999. This is not surprising, for every year that we have a current account deficit, Americans must borrow more from foreigners to finance extra spending at home. The real question is, should we be worried?

The simple answer is probably not. First of all, the trade deficit enables us to increase domestic investment and consumption over and above what we could do without the trade deficit. More important, foreigners cannot invest in the United States *unless* there is a current account deficit. Look at the top line in Figure 34-1, where you see the capital account, which mirrors the current account. Most of the so-called increased net foreign debt is not really debt but rather investments in equity and in real assets that foreigners have made in the United States. They obviously believe strongly in the stability and soundness of our

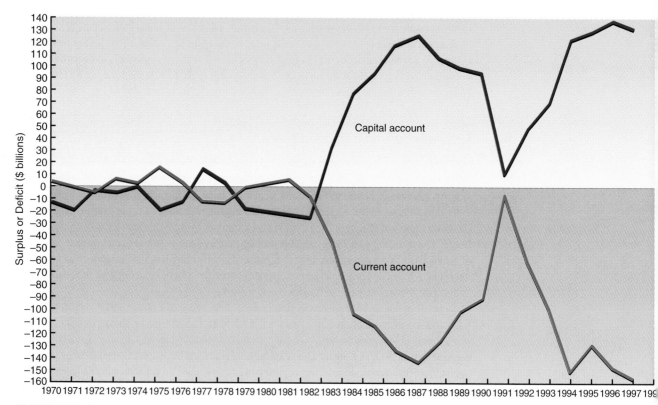

FIGURE 34-1

The Relationship Between the Current Account and the Capital Account
To some extent, the capital account is the mirror image of the current account. We can see this in the years since 1970. When the current account was in surplus, the capital account was in deficit. When the current account was in deficit, the capital account was in surplus. Indeed, virtually the only time foreigners can invest in America is when the current account is in deficit.

Sources: International Monetary Fund;: *Economic Indicators.*

economy. If we want continued foreign investment here, we have to expect continued current account deficits.

FOR CRITICAL ANALYSIS: Politicians are still worried about trade deficits. Why? ●

Official Reserve Account Transactions

The third type of balance of payments transaction concerns official reserve assets, which consist of the following:

1. Foreign currencies
2. Gold
3. **Special drawing rights (SDRs),** which are reserve assets that the International Monetary Fund created to be used by countries to settle international payment obligations
4. The reserve position in the International Monetary Fund
5. Financial assets held by an official agency, such as the U.S. Treasury Department

Special drawing rights (SDRs)
Reserve assets created by the International Monetary Fund that countries can use to settle international payments.

To consider how official reserve account transactions occur, look again at Table 34-2. The surplus in our capital account was +$206.1 billion. But the deficit in our current account was −$188.4 billion, so we had a net deficit on the combined accounts (line 13) of −$17.7 billion. In other words, the United States obtained less in foreign money in all its international transactions than it used. How is this deficiency made up? By our central bank drawing down its existing balances of foreign monies, or the +$17.7 billion in official transactions shown on line 14 in Table 34-2. You might ask why there is a plus sign on line 14. The answer is because this represents a *supply* (an inflow) of foreign exchange into our international transactions.

The balance (line 15) in Table 34-2 is zero, as it must be with double-entry bookkeeping. Our balance of payments deficit is measured by the official transactions figure on line 14. (This does not mean we are in equilibrium, though.)

What Affects the Balance of Payments?

A major factor affecting our balance of payments is our rate of inflation relative to that of our trading partners. Assume that the rate of inflation in the United States and in France is equal. All of a sudden, our inflation rate increases. The French will find that American products are becoming more expensive, and we will export fewer of them to France. Americans will find French products relatively cheaper, and we will import more. The converse will occur if our rate of inflation suddenly falls relative to that of France. All other things held constant, whenever our rate of inflation exceeds that of our trading partners, we expect to see a "worsening" of our balance of trade and payments. Conversely, when our rate of inflation is less than that of our trading partners, other things being constant, we expect to see an "improvement" in our balance of trade and payments.

Another important factor that sometimes influences our balance of payments is our relative political stability. Political instability causes *capital flight:* Owners of capital in countries anticipating or experiencing political instability will often move assets to countries that are politically stable, such as the United States. Hence our balance of payments is likely to improve whenever political instability looms in other nations in the world.

CONCEPTS IN BRIEF

- The balance of payments reflects the value of all transactions in international trade, including goods, services, financial assets, and gifts.

- The merchandise trade balance gives us the difference between exports and imports of tangible items. Merchandise trade transactions are represented by exports and imports of tangible items.

- Service exports and imports relate to the trade of intangible items, such as shipping, insurance, and tourist expenditures. They include income earned by foreigners on U.S. investments and income earned by Americans on foreign investments.

- Unilateral transfers involve international private gifts and federal government grants or gifts to foreign nations.

- When we add the balance of merchandise trade plus the balance of services and take account of net unilateral transfers, we come up with the balance on current account, which is a summary statistic taking into account the three transactions that form the current account transactions.

- There are also capital account transactions that relate to the buying and selling of financial and real assets. Foreign capital is always entering the United States, and American capital is always flowing abroad. The difference is called the balance on capital account.

- Another type of balance of payments transaction concerns the official reserve assets of individual countries, or what is often simply called official transactions. By standard accounting convention, official transactions are exactly equal to but opposite in sign to the balance of payments of the United States.

- Our balance of trade can be affected by our relative rate of inflation and by political instability elsewhere compared to the stability that exists in the United States.

DETERMINING FOREIGN EXCHANGE RATES

When you buy foreign products, such as French wine, you have dollars with which to pay the French winemaker. The French winemaker, however, cannot pay workers in dollars. The workers are French, they live in France, and they must have francs to buy goods and services in that country. There must therefore be some way of exchanging dollars for the francs that the winemaker will accept. That exchange occurs in a **foreign exchange market,** which in this case specializes in exchanging francs and dollars. (When you obtain foreign currencies at a bank or an airport currency exchange, you are participating in the foreign exchange market.)

Foreign exchange market
The market for buying and selling foreign currencies.

The particular exchange rate between francs and dollars that would prevail depends on the current demand for and supply of francs and dollars. In a sense, then, our analysis of the exchange rate between dollars and francs will be familiar, for we have used supply and demand throughout this book. If it costs you 20 cents to buy one franc, that is the **foreign exchange rate** determined by the current demand for and supply of francs in the foreign exchange market. The French person going to the foreign exchange market would need five francs to buy one dollar. (Our numbers are, of course, hypothetical.)

Foreign exchange rate
The price of one currency in terms of another.

We will continue our example in which the only two countries in the world are France and the United States. Now let's consider what determines the demand for and supply of foreign currency in the foreign exchange market.

Demand for and Supply of Foreign Currency

You wish to buy some French Bordeaux wine. To do so, you must have French francs. You go to the foreign exchange market (or your American bank). Your desire to buy the French wine therefore causes you to offer (supply) dollars to the foreign exchange market. Your demand for French francs is equivalent to your supply of American dollars to the foreign exchange market. Indeed:

> **Every U.S. transaction concerning the importation of foreign goods constitutes a supply of dollars and a demand for some foreign currency, and the opposite is true for export transactions.**

In this case, this import transaction constitutes a demand for French francs.

In our example, we will assume that only two goods are being traded, French wine and American jeans. The American demand for French wine creates a supply of dollars and a demand for francs in the foreign exchange market. Similarly, the French demand for American jeans creates a supply of francs and a demand for dollars in the foreign exchange market. In the situation of **flexible exchange rates,** the supply of and demand for dollars and francs in the foreign exchange market will determine the equilibrium foreign exchange rate. The equilibrium exchange rate will tell us how many francs a dollar can be exchanged for—that is, the dollar price of francs—or how many dollars (or fractions of a dollar) a franc can be exchanged for—the franc price of dollars.

Flexible exchange rates
Exchange rates that are allowed to fluctuate in the open market in response to changes in supply and demand. Sometimes called *floating exchange rates.*

The Equilibrium Foreign Exchange Rate

To determine the equilibrium foreign exchange rate, we have to find out what determines the demand for and supply of foreign exchange. We will ignore for the moment any speculative aspect of buying foreign exchange; that is, we assume that there are no individuals who wish to buy francs simply because they think that their price will go up in the future.

The idea of an exchange rate is no different from the idea of paying a certain price for something you want to buy. If you like coffee, you know you have to pay about 75 cents a cup. If the price went up to $2.50, you would probably buy fewer cups. If the price went down to 5 cents, you might buy more. In other words, the demand curve for cups of coffee, expressed in terms of dollars, slopes downward following the law of demand. The demand curve for francs slopes downward also, and we will see why.

Demand Schedule for French Francs. Let's think more closely about the demand schedule for francs. Let's say that it costs you 20 cents to purchase one franc; that is the exchange rate between dollars and francs. If tomorrow you had to pay 25 cents for the same franc, the exchange rate would have changed. Looking at such an increase with respect to the franc, we would say that there has been an **appreciation** in the value of the franc in the foreign exchange market. But this increase in the value of the franc means that there has been a **depreciation** in the value of the dollar in the foreign exchange market. The dollar used to buy five francs; tomorrow, the dollar will be able to buy only four francs at a price of 25 cents per franc. If the dollar price of francs rises, you will probably demand fewer francs. Why? The answer lies in looking at the reason you demand francs in the first place.

You demand francs in order to buy French wine. Your demand curve for French wine, we will assume, follows the law of demand and therefore slopes downward. If it costs you more American dollars to buy the same quantity of French wine, presumably you will not buy the same quantity; your quantity demanded will be less. We say that your demand for French francs is *derived from* your demand for French wine. In panel (a) of Figure 34-2, we present the hypothetical demand schedule for French wine in the United States by a representative wine drinker. In panel (b), we show graphically the American demand curve for French wine in terms of American dollars taken from panel (a).

Let us assume that the price per liter of French wine in France is 20 francs. Given that price, we can find the number of francs required to purchase up to 4 liters of French wine. That information is given in panel (c) of Figure 34-2. If one liter requires 20 francs, 4 liters require 80 francs. Now we have enough information to determine the derived demand curve for French francs. If one franc costs 20 cents, a bottle of wine would cost $4 (20 francs per bottle $\times$ 20 cents per franc = $4 per bottle). At $4 per bottle, the typical representative American wine drinker would, we see from panel (a) of Figure 34-2, demand 4 liters. From panel (c) we see that 80 francs would be demanded to buy the 4 liters of wine. We show this quantity demanded in panel (d). In panel (e), we draw the derived demand curve for francs. Now consider what happens if the price of francs goes up to 30 cents. A bottle of French wine costing 20 francs in France would now cost $6. From panel (a) we see that at $6 per liter, 3 liters will be imported from France into the United States by our representative domestic wine drinker. From panel (c) we see that 3 liters would require 60 francs to be purchased; thus in panels (d) and (e) we see that at a price of one franc per 30 cents, the quantity demanded will be 60 francs. We continue similar calculations all the way up to a price of 50 cents per franc. At that price a bottle of French wine costing 20 francs in France would cost $10, and our representative wine drinker would import only one bottle.

Downward-Sloping Derived Demand. As can be expected, as the price of francs falls, the quantity demanded will rise. The only difference here from the standard demand analysis developed in Chapter 3 and used throughout this text is that the demand for francs is derived from the demand for a final product—French wine in our example.

Supply of French Francs. The supply of French francs is a derived supply in that it is derived from a French person's demand for American jeans. We could go through an example similar to the one for wine to come up with a supply schedule of French francs in France. It slopes upward. Obviously, the French want dollars in order to purchase American goods. In principle, the French will be willing to supply more francs when the dollar price of francs goes up because they can then buy more American goods with the same quantity of francs; that is, the franc would be worth more in exchange for American goods than when the dollar price for francs was lower. Let's take an example. Suppose a pair of jeans in the United States costs $10. If the exchange rate is 25 cents for one franc, the French have to come up with 40 francs (= $10 at 25 cents per franc) to buy one pair of

Appreciation
An increase in the value of a currency in terms of other currencies.

Depreciation
A decrease in the value of a currency in terms of other currencies.

Panel (a)
Demand Schedule for French Wine in the United States per Week

Price per Liter	Quantity Demanded (liters)
$10	1
8	2
6	3
4	4

Panel (b)
American Demand Curve for French Wine

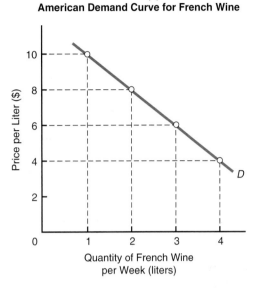

Panel (c)
Francs Required to Purchase Quantity Demanded (at P = 20 francs per liter)

Quantity Demanded	Francs Required
1	20
2	40
3	60
4	80

Panel (d)
Derived Demand Schedule for Francs in the United States with Which to Pay for Imports of Wine

Dollar Price of One Franc	Dollar Price of Wine	Quantity of Wine Demanded (liters)	Quantity of Francs Demanded per Week
$ .50	$10	1	20
.40	8	2	40
.30	6	3	60
.20	4	4	80

FIGURE 34-2

Deriving the Demand for French Francs

In panel (a), we show the demand schedule for French wine in the United States, expressed in terms of dollars per liter. In panel (b), we show the demand curve, *D*, which slopes downward. In panel (c), we show the number of francs required to purchase up to 4 liters of wine. If the price per liter of wine in France is 20 francs, we can now find the quantity of francs needed to pay for the various quantities demanded. In panel (d), we see the derived demand for francs in the United States in order to purchase the various quantities of wine given in panel (a). The resultant demand curve, D_1, is shown in panel (e). It is the American derived demand for francs.

Panel (e)
American Derived Demand for Francs

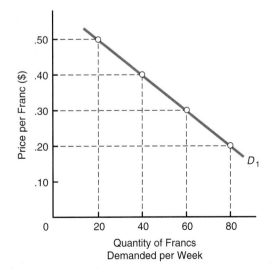

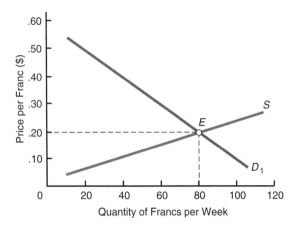

FIGURE 34-3

The Equilibrium Exchange Rate for Two Individuals
The derived demand curve for French francs is taken from panel (e) of Figure 34-2. The derived supply curve, *S,* results from the representative French purchaser of American jeans, who supplies francs to the foreign exchange market when demanding U.S. dollars in order to buy American jeans. D_1 and *S* intersect at *E.* The equilibrium exchange rate is 20 cents per franc.

jeans. If, however, the exchange rate goes up to 50 cents for one franc, the French must come up with only 20 francs (= $10 at 50 cents per franc) to buy a pair of American jeans. At a lower price (in francs) of American jeans, the French will demand a larger quantity. In other words, as the price of French francs goes up in terms of dollars, the quantity of American jeans demanded will go up, and hence the quantity of French francs supplied will go up. Therefore, the supply schedule of foreign currency (francs) will slope upward.[1]

We could easily work through a detailed numerical example to show that the supply curve of French francs slopes upward. Rather than do that, we will simply draw it as upward-sloping in Figure 34-3. In our hypothetical example, assuming that there is only one wine drinker in America and one demander of jeans in France, the equilibrium exchange rate will be set at 20 cents per franc, or 5 francs to one dollar. Let us now look at the aggregate demand for and supply of French francs. We take all demanders of French wine and all demanders of American jeans and put their demands for and supplies of francs together into one diagram. Thus we are showing an aggregate version of the demand for and supply of French francs. The horizontal axis in Figure 34-4 represents a quantity of foreign exchange—the number of francs per year. The vertical axis represents the exchange rate—the price of foreign currency (francs) expressed in dollars (per franc). Thus at the foreign currency price of 25 cents per franc, you know that it will cost you 25 cents to buy one franc. At the foreign currency price of 20 cents per franc, you know that it will cost you 20 cents to buy one franc. The equilibrium is again established at 20 cents for one franc. This equilibrium is not established because Americans like to buy francs or because the French like to buy dollars. Rather, the equilibrium exchange rate depends on how many pairs of jeans the French want and how much French wine the Americans want (given their respective incomes, their tastes, and the relative price of wine and jeans).[2]

A Shift in Demand. Assume that a successful advertising campaign by American wine importers has caused the American demand (curve) for French wine to double. Americans

---

[1]Actually, the supply schedule of foreign currency will be upward-sloping if we assume that the demand for American imported jeans on the part of the French is price-elastic. If the demand schedule for jeans is price-inelastic, the supply schedule will be negatively sloped. In the case of unit elasticity of demand, the supply schedule for francs will be a vertical line. Throughout the rest of this chapter, we will assume that demand is price-elastic. Remember that the price elasticity of demand tells us whether or not total expenditures by jeans purchasers in France will rise or fall when the French franc drops in value. In the long run, it is quite realistic to think that the price elasticity of demand for imports is numerically greater than 1 anyway.

[2]Remember that we are dealing with a two-country world in which we are considering only the exchange of American jeans and French wine. In the real world, more than just goods and services are exchanged among countries. Some Americans buy French financial assets; some French buy American financial assets. We are ignoring such transactions for the moment.

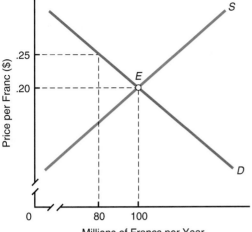

FIGURE 34-4

Aggregate Demand for and Supply of French Francs

The aggregate supply curve for French francs results from the total French demand for American jeans. The demand curve, *D*, slopes downward like most demand curves, and the supply curve, *S*, slopes upward. The foreign exchange price, or the U.S. dollar price of francs, is given on the vertical axis. The number of francs, in millions, is represented on the horizontal axis. If the foreign exchange rate is 25 cents—that is, if it takes 25 cents to buy one franc—Americans will demand 80 million francs. The equilibrium exchange rate is at the intersection of *D* and *S*. The equilibrium exchange rate is 20 cents. At this point, 100 million French francs are both demanded and supplied each year.

demand twice as much wine at all prices. Their demand curve for French wine has shifted outward to the right.

The increased demand for French wine can be translated into an increased demand for francs. All Americans clamoring for bottles of French wine will supply more dollars to the foreign exchange market while demanding more French francs to pay for the wine. Figure 34-5 presents a new demand schedule, D_2, for French francs; this demand schedule is to the right of and outward from the original demand schedule. If the French do not change their desire for American jeans, the supply schedule for French francs will remain stable. A new equilibrium will be established at a higher exchange rate. In our particular example, the new equilibrium is established at an exchange rate of 30 cents per franc. It now takes 30 cents to buy one French franc, whereas it took 20 cents before. This is translated as an increase in the price of French wine to Americans and as a decrease in the price of American jeans to the French. (Otherwise stated, there has been a decline in the foreign exchange value of the dollar.)

A Shift in Supply. We just assumed that Americans' preference for French wine had shifted. Because the demand for French francs is a derived demand by Americans for

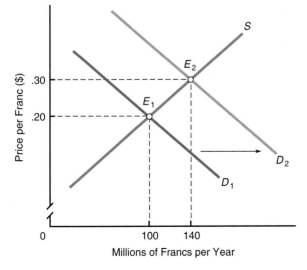

FIGURE 34-5

A Shift in the Demand Schedule

The demand schedule for French wine shifts to the right, causing the derived demand schedule for francs to shift to the right also. We have shown this as a shift from D_1 to D_2. We have assumed that the French supply schedule for francs has remained stable—that is, French demand for American jeans has remained constant. The old equilibrium foreign exchange rate was 20 cents. The new equilibrium exchange rate will be E_2; it will now cost 30 cents to buy one franc. The higher price of francs will be translated into a higher U.S. dollar price for French wine and a lower French franc price for American jeans.

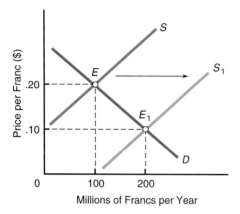

FIGURE 34-6

A Shift in the Supply of French Francs
There has been a shift in the supply curve for French francs. The new equilibrium will occur at E_1, meaning that 10 cents, rather than 20 cents, will now buy one franc. After the exchange rate adjustment, the amount of francs demanded and supplied will increase to 200 million per year.

French wine, it has caused a shift in the demand curve for francs. Alternatively, assume that the supply curve of French francs shifts outward to the right. This may occur for many reasons, the most probable one being a relative rise in the French price level. For example, if the price of all French-made clothes went up 100 percent in francs, American jeans would become relatively cheaper. That would mean that French people would want to buy more American jeans. But remember that when they want to buy more American jeans, they supply more francs to the foreign exchange market. Thus we see in Figure 34-6 that the supply curve of French francs moves from S to S_1. In the absence of restrictions—that is, in a system of flexible exchange rates—the new equilibrium exchange rate will be one franc equals 10 cents, or $1 equals 10 francs. The quantity of francs demanded and supplied will increase from 100 million per year to 200 million per year. We say, then, that in a flexible international exchange rate system, shifts in the demand for and supply of foreign currencies will cause changes in the equilibrium foreign exchange rates. Those rates will remain in effect until supply or demand shifts.

Market Determinants of Exchange Rates

The foreign exchange market is affected by many other changes in market variables in addition to changes in relative price levels, including these:

1. *Changes in real interest rates.* If the United States interest rate, corrected for people's expectations of inflation, abruptly increases relative to the rest of the world, international investors elsewhere will increase their demand for dollar-denominated assets, thereby increasing the demand for dollars in foreign exchange markets. An increased demand for dollars in foreign exchange markets, other things held constant, will cause the dollar to appreciate and other currencies to depreciate.
2. *Changes in productivity.* Whenever one country's productivity increases relative to another's, the former country will become more price competitive in world markets. The demand for its exports will increase, and so, too, will the demand for its currency.
3. *Changes in product preferences.* If Germany's citizens suddenly develop a taste for American-made automobiles, this will increase the derived demand for American dollars in foreign exchange markets.
4. *Perceptions of economic stability.* As already mentioned, if the United States looks economically and politically more stable relative to other countries, more foreigners will want to put their savings into U.S. assets than in their own domestic assets. This will increase the demand for dollars.

CONCEPTS IN BRIEF

- The foreign exchange rate is the rate at which one country's currency can be exchanged for another's.

- The demand for foreign exchange is a derived demand; it is derived from the demand for foreign goods and services (and financial assets). The supply of foreign exchange is derived from foreigners' demands for our goods and services.

- In general, the demand curve of foreign exchange slopes downward and the supply curve of foreign exchange slopes upward. The equilibrium foreign exchange rate occurs at the intersection of the demand and supply curves for a currency.

- A shift in the demand for foreign goods will result in a shift in the demand for foreign exchange. The equilibrium foreign exchange rate will change. A shift in the supply of foreign currency will also cause a change in the equilibrium exchange rate.

THE GOLD STANDARD AND THE INTERNATIONAL MONETARY FUND

The current system of more or less freely floating exchange rates is a recent development. We have had, in the past, periods of a gold standard, fixed exchange rates under the International Monetary Fund, and variants of these two.

The Gold Standard

Gold standard

An international monetary system in which nations fix their exchange rates in terms of gold. All currencies are fixed in terms of all others, and any balance of payments deficits or surpluses can be made up by shipments of gold.

Until the 1930s, many nations were on a **gold standard.** The values of their currencies were tied directly to gold.[3] Nations operating under this gold standard agreed to redeem their currencies for a fixed amount of gold at the request of any holder of that currency. Although gold was not necessarily the means of exchange for world trade, it was the unit to which all currencies under the gold standard were pegged. And because all currencies in the system were linked to gold, exchange rates between those currencies were fixed. Indeed, the gold standard has been offered as the prototype of a fixed exchange rate system. The heyday of the gold standard was from about 1870 to 1914. England had been on such a standard as far back as the 1820s.

There turns out to be a relationship between the balance of payments and changes in domestic money supplies throughout the world. Under a gold standard, the international financial market reached equilibrium through the effect of gold flows on each country's money supply. When a nation suffered a deficit in its balance of payments, more gold would flow out than in. Because the domestic money supply was based on gold, an outflow of gold to foreigners caused an automatic reduction in the domestic money supply. This caused several things to happen. Interest rates rose, thereby attracting foreign capital and improving the balance of payments. At the same time, the reduction in the money supply was equivalent to a restrictive monetary policy, which caused national output and prices to fall. Imports were discouraged and exports were encouraged, thereby again improving the balance of payments.

---

[3]This is a simplification. Most nations were on a *specie metal standard* using gold, silver, copper, and other precious metals as money. Nations operating under this standard agreed to redeem their currencies for a fixed exchange rate.

Two problems that plagued the gold standard were that no nation had control of its domestic monetary policy and that the world's commerce was at the mercy of gold discoveries.

POLICY EXAMPLE
Should We Go Back to the Gold Standard?

In the past several decades, the United States has consistently run a current account deficit. The dollar has become weaker. We have had inflation. We have had recessions. Some economists and politicians argue that we should return to the gold standard. The United States actually operated under two gold standards. From 1879 to 1933, the dollar was defined as 32.22 grains of gold, yielding a gold price of $20.671835 an ounce. During that time period, general prices more than doubled during World War I, there was a major depression in 1920–1921, and the Great Depression occurred. The second gold standard prevailed from 1933 to 1971, when the price of gold was pegged at $35 an ounce. A dollar was defined as 13.714286 grains of gold. During that time period, general prices quadrupled.

Clearly, a gold standard guarantees neither stable prices nor economic stability.

FOR CRITICAL ANALYSIS: Why does no country today operate on a gold standard? ●

Bretton Woods and the International Monetary Fund

In 1944, as World War II was ending, representatives from the world's capitalist countries met in Bretton Woods, New Hampshire, to create a new international payment system to replace the gold standard, which had collapsed during the 1930s. The Bretton Woods Agreement Act was signed on July 31, 1945, by President Harry Truman. It created a new permanent institution, the **International Monetary Fund (IMF),** to administer the agreement and to lend to member countries in balance of payments deficit. The arrangements thus provided are now called the old IMF system or the Bretton Woods system.

Each member nation was assigned an IMF contribution quota determined by its international trade volume and national income. Twenty-five percent of the quota was contributed in gold or U.S. dollars and 75 percent in its own currency. At the time, the IMF therefore consisted of a pool of gold, dollars, and other major currencies.

Member governments were then obligated to intervene to maintain the values of their currencies in foreign exchange markets within 1 percent of the declared **par value**—the officially determined value. The United States, which owned most of the world's gold stock, was similarly obligated to maintain gold prices within a 1 percent margin of the official rate of $35 an ounce. Except for a transitional arrangement permitting a one-time adjustment of up to 10 percent in par value, members could alter exchange rates thereafter only with the approval of the IMF. The agreement stated that such approval would be given only if the country's balance of payments was in *fundamental disequilibrium,* a term that has never been officially defined.

Special Drawing Rights. In 1967, the IMF created a new type of international money, *special drawing rights (SDRs)*. SDRs are exchanged only between monetary authorities (central banks). Their existence temporarily changed the IMF into a world central bank. The IMF creates SDRs the same way that the Federal Reserve can create dollars. The IMF allocates SDRs to member nations in accordance with their quotas. Currently, the SDR's

International Monetary Fund (IMF)
An institution set up to manage the international monetary system, established in 1945 under the Bretton Woods Agreement Act, which established fixed exchange rates for the world's currencies.

Par value
The legally established value of the monetary unit of one country in terms of that of another.

Exercise 34.2
Visit www.econtoday.com for more about the IMF.

value is determined by making one SDR equal to a bundle of currencies. In reality, the SDR rises or falls in terms of the dollar.

End of the Old IMF. On August 15, 1971, President Richard Nixon suspended the convertibility of the dollar into gold. On December 18, 1971, we officially devalued the dollar against the currencies of 14 major industrial nations. Finally, on March 16, 1973, the finance ministers of the European Economic Community (now the EU) announced that they would let their currencies float against the dollar, something Japan had already begun doing with its yen. Since 1973, the United States and most other trading countries have had either freely floating exchange rates or managed ("dirty") floating exchange rates.

THE DIRTY FLOAT AND MANAGED EXCHANGE RATES

Dirty float
A system between flexible and fixed exchange rates in which central banks occasionally enter foreign exchange markets to influence rates.

The United States went off the Bretton Woods system in 1973, but it has nonetheless tried to keep certain elements of that system in play. We have occasionally engaged in what is called a **dirty float,** or management of flexible exchange rates. The management of flexible exchange rates has usually come about through international policy cooperation. For example, the Group of Five (G-5) nations—France, Germany, Japan, the United Kingdom, and the United States—and the Group of Seven (G-7) nations—the G-5 nations plus Italy and Canada—have for some time shared information on their policy objectives and procedures. They do this through regular meetings between economic policy secretaries, ministers, and staff members. One of their principal objectives has been to "smooth out" foreign exchange rates. Initially, the G-5 attempted to push the value of the dollar downward to help correct U.S. trade deficits and reduce Japanese foreign trade surpluses. What the five nations agreed to do was supply dollars in foreign exchange markets. This increased supply would reduce the dollar's value.

Is it possible for these groups to "manage" foreign exchange rates? Some economists do not think so. For example, economists Michael Bordo and Anna Schwartz studied the foreign exchange intervention actions coordinated by the Federal Reserve and the U.S. Treasury for the second half of the 1980s. Besides showing that such interventions were sporadic and variable, Bordo and Schwartz came to an even more compelling conclusion: Exchange rate interventions were trivial relative to the total trading of foreign exchange on a daily basis. For example, in April 1989, total foreign exchange trading amounted to $129 billion per day, yet the American central bank purchased only $100 million in deutsche marks and yen during that entire month (and did so on a single day). For all of 1989, Fed purchases of marks and yen were only $17.7 billion, or the equivalent of less than 14 percent of the amount of an average *day's* trading in April of that year. Their conclusion is that neither the American central bank nor the central banks of the other G-7 nations can influence exchange rates in the long run.

CONCEPTS IN BRIEF

- The International Monetary Fund was developed after World War II as an institution to maintain fixed exchange rates in the world. Since 1973, however, fixed exchange rates have disappeared in most major trading countries.

- A dirty float occurs in a flexible exchange rate system whenever central banks intervene to influence exchange rates.

In May 1998, 11 of the 15 European Union members qualified to join "Euroland," in which a new currency, the euro, will replace all their individual national currencies by the year 2002.

Will the Euro Put an End to Dollar Dominance?

CONCEPTS APPLIED:

FOREIGN EXCHANGE, FOREIGN EXCHANGE RESERVES, KEY CURRENCY

Visit www.econtoday.com for an Internet Activity that expands your understanding of these concepts.

Since World War II, the U.S. dollar has been the currency of choice in international financial transactions, accounting for over 50 percent of global private financial wealth. Almost 70 percent of world trade is invoiced in dollars, as is 75 percent of international bank lending. But Figure 34-7 shows what has happened to official foreign exchange reserves throughout the world that are held in dollars. In 1973, the dollar constituted 76 percent of official reserves; today, it accounts for only 64 percent. Some analysts have predicted that the euro will weaken America by replacing the dollar as a reserve currency.

Implications of a Dollar in Less Demand

Suppose that the euro became a key currency. U.S. residents could still borrow in dollars, but perhaps they might have to pay a higher interest rate. Even if oil prices were quoted in euros instead of dollars, that would not change the real price of oil to anybody. The reality is that even if the dollar were deposed by the euro in international financial transactions, there would be no serious repercussions in the United States.

Why the Euro Probably Will Not Depose the Dollar

Consider that the dollar constitutes over 60 percent of official reserves throughout the world, yet the United States accounts for only about 23 percent of world output and one-sixth of world exports. Consider also that in the past 30 years, the dollar's value relative to the yen and the mark has dropped by about 50 percent. Nonetheless, the yen and the mark have been unable to push the dollar aside as the key international currency.

Now consider truly international markets for oil, metals, and other basic commodities. Buyers and sellers exist throughout the world. Because of the extreme distances, a single unit for commercial transactions is necessary, and it has to be one on which everyone can agree. Some economists argue that there is room for only one international "language" in financial transactions, and that language is the dollar.

Further, consider the position of the United States as the promoter and sponsor of virtually all important global

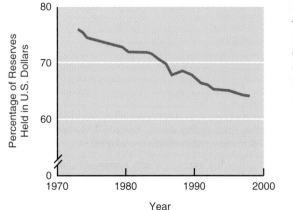

FIGURE 34-7

The Declining Share of Dollar Reserves
Central banks outside the United States now hold a smaller percentage of dollar reserves than they did 20 years ago.
Source: International Monetary Fund.

economic institutions, such as the International Monetary Fund, the World Trade Organization, and the World Bank. Moreover, consider that U.S. Treasury debt is essentially free from default. U.S. government debt serves as the reference of creditworthiness for virtually the entire international system. Thus the relative size of the U.S. economy in the world market is not the sole determinant of whether the dollar will remain the key reserve currency in the world. Equally important is that the dollar is the safest asset in the existing world economic system. At most, then, we can expect that the euro will provide an alternative to the dollar in special circumstances.

A Further Problem: Euro Vulnerability

Some U.S. economists, including Federal Reserve Chairman Alan Greenspan, have accepted that the euro will come into being, but they have serious doubts about its sustainability. Currency speculator George Soros even predicted that a single currency will bear the brunt of European anger over high unemployment rates there. The European Commission understands the vulnerability of the euro and has tried to protect it from speculative attack. In 1997, it announced that from January 1999 onward, the currencies of all its members would be expressed in euros. Until 2002, the German mark, French franc, Italian lira, and Spanish peseta will be regarded as subdivisions of a euro. These subdivisions—defined in terms of euro cents—were supposedly irrevocably fixed during 1998. What this all means is that no one can benefit by selling

lire to buy marks, for example, because they would simply be selling euros to buy euros and end up with the same quantity at the end of the transaction.

A Bigger EU Role in International Finance

In spite of doubts about the euro's long-term sustainability, European finance ministers are arguing that the European Union should take a bigger role in international finance. There is a question about how the euro zone should be represented in the Group of Seven or the International Monetary Fund because a problem that exists, at least for the next couple of years. Britain, Sweden, Denmark, and Greece have indicated that they will not immediately adopt the euro. They do not want the euro zone to have an increased say in international financial institutions such as the IMF.

If this all sounds somewhat confusing and contradictory, it has to be by its very nature. The states within the United States have had a uniform currency since 1863. The merging of 15 nations' currencies into one has never been tried. Problems are bound to arise.

FOR CRITICAL ANALYSIS

1. What might happen to the retail foreign exchange businesses throughout Europe once the euro takes hold?
2. Does it matter whether the dollar remains the key international currency?

CHAPTER SUMMARY

1. The balance of merchandise trade is defined as the value of goods bought and sold in the world market, usually during the period of one year. The balance of payments is a more inclusive concept that includes the value of all transactions in the world market.

2. Americans purchase financial assets in other countries, and foreigners purchase American financial assets, such as stocks or bonds. The buying and selling of foreign financial assets has the same effect on the balance of payments as the buying and selling of goods and services.

3. Our balance of trade and payments can be affected by our relative rate of inflation and by political instability elsewhere compared to the stability that exists in the United States.

4. Market determinants of exchange rates are changes in real interest rates (interest rates corrected for inflation), changes in productivity, changes in product preferences, and perceptions of economic stability.

5. To transact business internationally, it is necessary to convert domestic currencies into other currencies. This is done via the foreign exchange market. If we were trading with France only, French producers would want to be paid in francs because they must pay their workers in francs. American producers would want to be paid in dollars because American workers are paid in dollars.

6. An American's desire for French wine is expressed in terms of a supply of dollars, which is in turn a demand for French francs in the foreign exchange market. The opposite situation arises when the

French wish to buy American jeans. Their demand for jeans creates a demand for American dollars and a supply of French francs. We put the demand and supply schedules together to find the equilibrium foreign exchange rate. The demand schedule for foreign exchange is a derived demand—it is derived from Americans' demand for foreign products.

7. With no government intervention, a market clearing equilibrium foreign exchange rate will emerge. After a shift in demand or supply, the exchange rate will change so that it will again clear the market.

8. If Americans increase their demand for French wine, the demand curve for French wine shifts to the right. The derived demand for francs also shifts to the right. The supply schedule of francs, however, remains stable because the French demand for American jeans

has remained constant. The shifted demand schedule intersects the stable supply schedule at a higher price (the foreign exchange rate increases). This is an appreciation of the value of French francs (a depreciation of the value of the dollar against the franc).

9. In a managed exchange rate system (a "dirty float"), central banks occasionally intervene in foreign exchange markets to influence exchange rates.

10. Under a gold standard, movement of gold across countries changes domestic money supplies, causing price levels to change and to correct balance of payments imbalances.

11. In 1945, the International Monetary Fund (IMF) was created to maintain fixed exchange rates throughout the world. This system was abandoned in 1973.

DISCUSSION OF PREVIEW QUESTIONS

1. What is the difference between the balance of trade and the balance of payments?

The balance of trade is defined as the difference between the value of exports and the value of imports. If the value of exports exceeds the value of imports, a trade surplus exists; if the value of exports is less than the value of imports, a trade deficit exists; if export and import values are equal, we refer to this situation as a trade balance. The balance of payments is more general and takes into account the value of *all* international transactions. Thus the balance of payments identifies not only goods and services transactions among nations but also investments (financial and nonfinancial) and gifts (private and public). When the value of all these transactions is such that one nation is sending more to other nations than it is receiving in return, a balance of payments deficit exists. A payments surplus and payments balance are self-explanatory.

2. What is a foreign exchange rate?

We know that nations trade with one another; they buy and sell goods, make and receive financial and nonfinancial investments, and give and receive gifts. However, nations have different currencies. People who sell to, invest in, or receive gifts from the United States ultimately want their own currency so that they can use the money domestically. Similarly, U.S. residents who sell in, invest in, or receive gifts from people in other countries ultimately want U.S. dollars to spend in the United States. Because most people ultimately want to end up with their own currencies, for-

eign exchange markets have evolved to enable people to sell one currency for other currencies. A foreign exchange rate, then, is the rate at which one country's currency can be exchanged for another's. For example, the exchange rate between the United Kingdom (U.K.) and the United States might dictate that one pound sterling is equivalent to $1.50; alternately stated, the U.S. dollar is worth .667 pound sterling.

3. What is a flexible exchange rate system?

A flexible exchange rate system is an international monetary system in which foreign exchange rates are allowed to fluctuate to reflect changes in the supply of and demand for international currencies. Say that the United States and the U.K. are in payments balance at the exchange rate of one pound sterling to U.S. $1.50. The U.S. demand for sterling is derived from private and government desires to buy British goods, to invest in the U.K., or to send gifts to the British people and is *inversely* related to the number of dollars it takes to buy one pound. Conversely, the supply of sterling is derived from the U.K.'s private and governmental desires to buy U.S. goods and services, to invest in the United States, and to send gifts to U.S. residents. The supply of sterling is *directly* related to the number of dollars one pound is worth. The intersection of the supply and demand curves for sterling determines the market foreign exchange rate of dollars per pound. In a system of flexible exchange rates, shifts in the supply or demand curves will lead to changes in the foreign exchange rates between nations.

4. What is the gold standard?

The gold standard is an international monetary system in which each nation values its currency unit at a specific quantity of gold. Under such a standard, exchange rates are fixed in terms of each other. For example, the U.S. dollar was originally backed by one-twentieth of an ounce of gold, and the British valued their coins (or paper backed by gold) at one-quarter of an ounce of gold; the British monetary unit was therefore worth five times the U.S. monetary unit. The resulting exchange rate was that one pound sterling was worth $5. The gold standard was, in matters of exchange rates, similar to the fixed exchange rate system. However, payment imbalances were automatically corrected by gold flows. For instance, if the United States had a payment deficit with the U.K. (which therefore had a payment surplus with the United States), gold would flow from the United States to the U.K. The result of these gold flows (which, in effect, are equivalent to money movements) would be to raise the price level in the U.K. and lower it in the United States. This would lead to an increase in U.S. exports and a decrease in U.S. imports and a corresponding increase in British imports and decrease in British exports. Thus, in the past, the gold standard brought nations into payment balance by altering price *levels* in each country. The current system of flexible exchange rates corrects payment imbalances leaving price levels unaltered; it changes *one* price—the exchange rate.

PROBLEMS

(Answers to the odd-numbered problems appear at the back of the book.)

34-1. In the graph, what can be said about the shift from D to D_1?

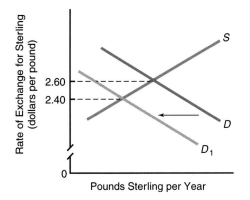

Pounds Sterling per Year

a. It could be caused by Britons demanding fewer U.S. products.
b. It is a result of increased U.S. demand for British goods.
c. It causes an appreciation of the dollar relative to the pound.
d. It causes an appreciation of the pound relative to the dollar.

34-2. If the rate of exchange between the pound and the dollar is $1.45 for one pound, and the United States then experiences severe inflation, we would expect the exchange rate (under a flexible rate system) to shift. What would be the new rate?

a. More than $1.45 for one pound
b. Less than $1.45 for one pound
c. More than one pound for $1.45
d. None of the above

34-3. The dollar, the pound sterling, and the deutsche mark are the currency units of the United States, the United Kingdom, and Germany, respectively. Suppose that these nations decide to go on a gold standard and define the value of their currencies in terms of gold as follows: $35 = 1 ounce of gold; 10 pounds sterling = 1 ounce of gold; and 100 marks = 1 ounce of gold. What would the exchange rate be between the dollar and the pound? Between the dollar and the mark? Between the mark and the pound?

34-4. Examine the following hypothetical data for U.S. international transactions, in billions of dollars.

Exports: goods, 165.8; services, 130.5
Imports: goods, −250.7; services, −99.3
Net unilateral transfers: −20.0

a. What is the balance of trade?
b. What is the balance on goods and services?
c. What is the balance on current account?

34-5. Maintenance of a fixed exchange rate system requires government intervention to keep exchange rates stable. What is the policy implication of this fact? (Hint: Think in terms of the money supply.)

34-6. Suppose that we have the following demand schedule for German beer in the United States per week:

Price per Case	Quantity Demanded (cases)
$40	2
32	4
24	6
16	8
8	10

a. If the price is 30 deutsche marks per case, how many marks are required to purchase each quantity demanded?

b. Now derive the demand schedule for marks per week in the United States to pay for German beer.

c. At a price of 80 cents per mark, how many cases of beer would be imported from Germany per week?

34-7. The accompanying graph shows the supply of and demand for pounds sterling.

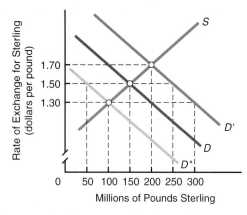

a. Assuming that the demand for sterling is represented by *D*, what is the dollar price of pounds? What is the equilibrium quantity?

b. Suppose that there is general inflation in the United States. Starting at *D*, which demand curve could represent this situation? If exchange rates are allowed to float freely, what would be the new dollar price of one pound sterling? What would be the equilibrium quantity?

c. Suppose that the inflation in part (b) occurs and the United States has the dollar price of one pound sterling fixed at $1.50. How would the Federal Reserve be able to accomplish this?

d. Now suppose that instead of inflation, there was general deflation in the United States. Which demand curve could represent this situation? How could the United States maintain a fixed price of $1.50 per pound sterling in this situation?

34-8. Which of the following will cause the yen to appreciate? Explain.

a. U.S. real incomes increase relative to Japanese real incomes.

b. It is expected that in the future the yen will depreciate relative to the dollar.

c. The U.S. inflation rate rises relative to the Japanese inflation rate.

d. The after-tax, risk-adjusted real interest rate in the United States rises relative to that in Japan.

e. U.S. tastes change in favor of Japanese-made goods.

COMPUTER-ASSISTED INSTRUCTION

Suppose that the United States and France have formed a two-country gold standard, and a balance of payments equilibrium exists. What happens if tastes change so that U.S. residents now prefer French goods more than they did previously, other things being constant? This problem shows how balance of payments equilibrium is restored under a gold standard, a specific fixed exchange rate system.

Complete problem and answer appear on disk.

INTERACTING WITH THE INTERNET

You can find out what the International Monitory Fund is doing by going to

www.imf.org

Information from the World Bank can be found easily at

www.worldbank.org

CHAPTER 35

CYBERNOMICS

In the days before inexpensive cassette recorders, record companies did not have to worry about piracy. It was simply too expensive for bootleggers to copy records. Then the cassette recorder became so cheap that bootlegged versions of popular records were common. Many people made copies for friends, not for profit. Next, with the advent of relatively cheap compact disc reproduction, bootlegged CDs started to show up worldwide. Go to any flea market in many parts of the world, and you can find CDs of live performances by well-known recording artists. These are not copies of existing CDs but rather unauthorized performance reproductions, for which the artists get paid nothing. Now the digital world has added a new twist—massive copyright violations over the Internet—and with the possibility of perfect quality. How will artists and recording companies cope with the possible onslaught of massive bootlegging? Before you tackle this issue, you need to know a little more about the impact of the Internet on our economic system.

PREVIEW QUESTIONS

1. How does technological change affect the demand for labor?

2. What is the main reason the Internet may lead to increased efficiency?

3. If different tax jurisdictions each take "their piece" of an Internet transaction, what might be the long-run result?

4. Why does the software business seem to belie the traditional law of diminishing marginal returns?

Did You Know That . . . the Internet has its origins in a 1966 U.S. Department of Defense program designed to provide a communications network for defense-related research that could survive a nuclear calamity? The program, called the Advanced Research Projects Agency Network, soon became the favorite form of communication for researchers and academics in non-defense-related fields. Then the National Science Foundation established a distributed network, which greatly increased the traffic. The current system is based on a common addressing system and communications **protocol** that was created in 1983. The world has never been the same.

In this chapter, you will explore the new world of **cybernomics**. You will find out about the growing world of electronic commerce, banking, and finance. In addition, you will find out about the changes it is bringing in the theory of the firm, monopoly, and labor markets.

A WORLD OF CONTINUOUS CHANGE

As with all technological changes, there are losers and winners. The cyberspace revolution is creating many winners and, of course, some losers. That is not new. Decades ago, when elevator control systems were automated, elevator operators lost their jobs. When optical character recognition systems were perfected, bank employees who manually sorted checks were laid off. As word processing systems have become easier to use, the demand for typing specialists has diminished. Technological change will almost always reduce the demand for traditional labor services, but at the same time it will increase the demand for new types of labor services. The fear of technological change has been around for centuries, as you can see in the following example.

INTERNATIONAL EXAMPLE
Luddites Unite Against Automated Textile Machinery

In the vicinity of Nottingham toward the end of 1811, an organized band of English craftsmen started riots with the aim of destroying the textile machines that were replacing them. The members of the band were called Luddites, named after an imaginary leader known as King Ludd. Bands of Luddites were generally masked and operated at night. They were often supported by the local townspeople—but certainly not by threatened employers. One employer, a man named Horsfall, ordered his supporters to open fire on a band of them in 1812. The Luddite movement eventually lost steam by 1817, when prosperity again reigned in England.

FOR CRITICAL ANALYSIS: What are some other technological changes that have created job losses? ●

The Age of Information

Let there be no mistake, the information age is here. What is one of the most important industries in the United States? The answer is information technology, or IT. Sales of the American computing and telecommunications industry have doubled during the 1990s, to exceed $1 trillion a year. IT is the largest American industry—ahead of food products, automotive manufacturing, and construction. The share of IT in American firms' total investment in equipment was a mere 7 percent in 1970 and is now about 45 percent. If you add software investment, current U.S. business spending on IT exceeds investment in tra-

Protocol
The data formatting system that permits computers to access each other and communicate.

Cybernomics
The application of economic analysis to human and technological activities related to the use of the Internet in all of its forms.

ditional machinery. Employment in the IT sector now accounts for around 6 million workers and is growing. The average IT worker earns wages that are about 60 to 70 percent greater than the average wage in the private sector. The American Electronics Association wants to call this the "new economy." This so-called new economy consists of high-tech companies that are generating new work practices and new challenges in public policy.

Household and Business Use of the Internet

Panel (a) of Figure 35-1 shows the rise in the percentage of households with a link to the Internet. At the beginning of the 1990s, the number was virtually zero; the estimate for the year 2005 is over 50 percent. In panel (b), you see average hours per week spent on-line per household connected to the Internet. At the beginning of the 1990s it was almost nothing, whereas today it is over eight hours per week.

For the moment, the greatest use of the Internet is electronic mail, or e-mail. U.S. businesses alone send about 10 billion e-mail messages a year, and that figure is likely to increase. The number of Internet hosts has increased from a few thousand in 1988 to about 20 million today. Worldwide, about 200 million global citizens are connected to the Net. Some estimates for the year 2030 put that number well over a billion.

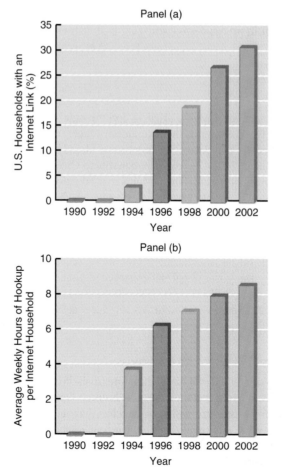

FIGURE 35-1

The Internet Invades America
Perhaps no other innovation has caught on so quickly in America. Not only are more people connecting to the Internet, but they are also using it more.

Source: Consumer Electronics Manufacturer's Association. Figures after 1998 are predictions.

EFFICIENCY, TRANSACTION COSTS, AND E-COMMERCE

In Chapter 4, you learned that individuals turn to markets because markets reduce the costs of exchange, which are called transaction costs. Remember that these are defined as the costs associated with finding out exactly what is being transacted, as well as the cost of enforcing contracts. Entrepreneurs since the beginning of time have attempted to make markets more efficient by figuring out ways to reduce transaction costs.

A big part of transaction costs is the cost of obtaining information. Buyers need information about sellers—their existence, the goods and services they offer, and the prices of those goods and services. A stroll through one's local mall may be a pastime for some, but it is a costly activity for all—time usually does not have a zero opportunity cost. The advent of mail-order shopping reduced transaction costs for many. It also introduced additional competition for retailers located in remote cities. After all, one no longer had to rely solely on the local camera store once camera ads from stores in New York City and elsewhere started appearing in nationally available print publications.

Exercise 35.1
Visit www.econtoday.com for more about e-commerce.

The Web as a Reducer of Transaction Costs

Enter the Internet and the World Wide Web. The existence of information about numerous goods and services, such as automobiles and cameras, via the Web simply means that transaction costs are being further reduced. This should make the market work more efficiently and should lead to less variation in price per constant-quality unit for any good offered for sale.

Business-to-Business E-Commerce

The first place that **e-commerce** has been extensively used is for the sale of goods between businesses. A good example is Cisco Systems, Inc., a major producer of Internet computer routers. It estimates that over 40 percent of its orders are already handled through the Internet—to the tune of about $5 billion a year. The benefits to Cisco by taking orders on-line are many: faster service for its customers, quicker production cycles, and savings on labor and printing charges. Cisco believes that it has reduced overall costs by more than $500 million a year by relying so heavily on e-commerce.

As can be expected, the first companies to take full advantage of the ease of ordering through the Internet have been those involved in information technology, particularly computers and computer parts. In any event, business-to-business Internet commerce is not highly visible, and this may explain why the government underestimated annual on-line sales for 1997 at $5 billion when they were probably closer to $25 billion. If current trends continue, e-commerce should account for almost $1 trillion of sales in the year 2002.

e-commerce
The use of the Internet in any manner that allows buyers and sellers to find each other. It can involve business selling directly to other businesses or business selling to retail customers. Both goods and services are involved in e-commerce.

"E-'Tailing"

While the growth rate in e-commerce at the retail level has been impressive, the total dollar volume is still a mere drop in the bucket compared to retail sales through normal retail outlets. An increasing proportion of Internet users are willing to purchase via the Net, but they do not do so on a regular basis. One issue that retail customers are concerned about is security. They worry that it is too easy for their credit card number to be stolen off the Net by individuals who wish to use it for fraudulent purposes. The real problem area, though, involves Internet merchants, particularly those selling software for immediate download, for these people have been the victims of cybercrimes much more than consumers who have had their credit cards "lifted" out of cyberspace.

Cybershopping Crooks. The ease of selling software over the Internet also makes it easy for cybershoppers to defraud Internet sellers of software provided on-line. Occasionally, CyberSource, the owner of the on-line retail source Software.Net, experiences more fraudulent sales than legitimate ones. Cybercrooks use someone else's credit card number to order the software. CyberSource downloads the software almost instantaneously. By the time the seller discovers the fraud, the buyer has a copy of the software and can resell it.

On-line software sellers have struck back. They have developed a computer model that looks at 150 factors to calculate the risk of fraud for any particular purchase. Any on-line company can pay 50 cents to have a pending credit card request run through the model. There is also an ever more complete name-fraud database that can be used as a reference point.

Better Encryption. Encryption systems—software systems that prevent anyone else from obtaining information provided on-line—are getting better all the time. Both Netscape's Navigator and Microsoft's Internet Explorer browsers have built-in encryption systems. On-line retailers are developing even better ones. Given the demand for a system that is totally secure, we can predict that concerns over losing a credit card number in cyberspace will virtually disappear over time. In any event, even current encryption systems are much more secure than a telephone conversation with a mail-order company operator to whom you give your credit card number in order to have goods shipped to you.

Using Intelligent Shopping Agents

Intelligent shopping agents
Computer programs that an individual or business user of the Internet can instruct to carry out a specific task, such as looking for the lowest-priced car of a particular make and model. The agent then searches the Internet (usually just the World Wide Web) and may even purchase the product when the best price has been found.

Intelligent shopping agents are software programs that search the Web to find a specific item that you specify. Using these agents saves the time you might have to spend searching all potential sites through your broswer. Suppose that you wanted to order a pair of pants. An intelligent shopping agent would ask you for essential descriptions and then go searching on the Web.

A new software program called XML—for "extensible markup language"—will assist intelligent shopping agents. Preparing a Web home page in XML makes the Web site smart enough to tell other machines what is inside in great detail. In essence, XML puts "tags" on Web pages that describe bits of information. Each group of on-line businesses—travel, stocks and bonds, and so on—will have its own set of agreed-on tags. This will allow searching intelligent shopping agents to "flip through" all of the Web sources for a particular item more easily.

Suppose that you are considering the purchase of some airline tickets in the middle of a fare price war. You are not sure how low the tickets prices are going to go. In the near future, you will be able to tell your intelligent shopping agent to keep looking for a lower fare as the airlines change prices on a daily basis. When the agent finds the best price, it can automatically order the tickets on your behalf.

The development of XML along with better intelligent shopping agents is crucial for the most efficient utilization of the Web. Currently, there are over 450,000 commercial sites selling products on-line, and the number is sure to increase rapidly. In the meantime, certain search engines, such as Excite, offer services to compare listed prices from various cyberstores for a desired product.

The Trend Away From Mass Merchandising

Electronic retailing may reverse the trend toward mass merchandising that we have seen over the past 50 years. This reversal has already taken place in the computer industry. Computer mail-order pioneer Dell does not even start the production of a computer until the customer selects all the features—size of hard drive, amount of memory, processor speed, modem speed, and so on. Over 10 percent of Dell's orders are now through the Internet. Dell asks the customer each feature it wants and gives a menu. Apple is doing the same thing on a full selection of its latest computers. Levi Strauss and Company has a customized jeans site on the Internet—a type of on-line fitting room. A similar plan has been put forth by Custom Foot, a large shoe retailer.

BUYING A CAR ON THE NET

They said it could never be done—selling cars in cyberspace. After all, the thinking went, before purchasing such an expensive item, consumers would want to "kick the tires." For most consumers, that is still true. But a growing number now use the Internet to search for the best price on exactly the car they want. And many more have discovered that the most painless way to start looking for a car is on the Net. You can go to Microsoft's CarPoint site at **www.carpoint.msn.com**. You will even find videos that display car interiors. This allows you to take a look at all your options in order to narrow your choices. You can go to Kelly Blue Book at **www.kbb.com** to get exact dealer invoice prices including destination charges. This tells you what the dealer paid for the basic car wholesale. All you have to do is add the prices of optional equipment that you want. These prices are also available at the Kelly Web site. (From the total price listed, you should deduct about 3 percent, which is what the dealer gets from the manufacturer when the car is sold—this is known as the "holdback.")

Once you know what you want, you can start shopping for the actual car via the numerous Web sites for dealers throughout the country. Some dealers are making more than 10 percent of their total sales via the Web. You can also use an on-line car-buying service that processes orders and forwards them to dealers. Detroit's Big Three—Chrysler, General Motors, and Ford—now have their own on-line selling sites.

FOR CRITICAL ANALYSIS: Car dealers argue that on-line auto shopping will destroy customer bonds. Why should this matter? ●

The Advent of the Internet Shopping Mall

Perhaps the wave of the future in Internet retail shopping is the equivalent of today's shopping mall. The biggest player in on-line shopping malls is netMarket.com. Sales for 1997 were $1.2 billion, and the company anticipates that its sales will more than double every year into the foreseeable future. The netMarket site sells everything from books and videos to cars, travel, CDs, and kitchen appliances. Within the next several years, netMarket will sell about 95 percent of the goods purchased by a typical household. The on-line firm netMarket is like a club warehouse, for it charges a $49 annual fee. In effect, though, netMarket is not a mall. Rather, it's a megastore that uses the best specialized retailers' efficiencies and discounts. Unlike the typical megastore, such as Wal-Mart or a club warehouse, such as PriceCostco, on-line megastores carry no inventory. They simply pass the orders on electronically to distributors or manufacturers, who then ship the goods from their own warehouses directly to the buyers.

Exercise 35.2
Visit www.econtoday.com for more about an e-commerce shopping mall.

Reduction in the Demand for Retail Space

If more shopping will be done over the Internet in the future, less shopping will be done in traditional retail outlets. Even in those retail outlets that exist, customization may be the order of the day because of new digital scanning and manufacturing systems. The Levi's store in Manhattan allows customers to be scanned electronically to order perfectly fitting jeans. There are a few stores where customers' feet are scanned electronically for custom-made shoes. If more consumers opt for such custom-made items, retail stores will carry much smaller inventories, keeping on hand only samples or computerized images.

The result will be a reduced demand for commercial retail space. Moreover, there will be a reduced demand for trucking to haul inventory, for electricity to light and heat retail space, and for the paper that is used for all the ordering.

CONCEPTS IN BRIEF

- Extensive use of the Web will lead to greater efficiency through a reduction in transaction costs.

- Most e-commerce is between businesses today.

- Retail business will expand as better encryption methods are used for protecting credit card numbers.

- Internet retailing requires no inventory costs for "malls" that simply send orders to other companies for fulfillment.

- If more Internet retailing occurs, the demand for traditional retail space will decrease over time.

THE INCREASING IMPORTANCE OF BRANDS

Brands have value because they indicate to potential purchasers of a branded item that a strong and successful company stands behind it. Successful companies typically have well-recognized brands—think of Microsoft, IBM, Levi's, Mercedes Benz, Sony, Nike. In the world of e-commerce, cybershoppers will increasingly look for branded items to satisfy their purchase desires. Why? Because there will be no salesperson extolling the virtues of a perhaps lower-priced but less well known item.

Brands Created on the Net

That does not rule out new brands' establishing themselves on the Net. A case in point is Amazon.com. The most successful virtual bookseller, Amazon.com didn't even exist before it went on-line. Nonetheless, it has established its brand name as a reputable place to purchase books. Amazon offers incentives to other Web site owners to link with it. If you link your Web site to Amazon, you get a 3 to 8 percent commission on each book purchase made by anyone who follows that link and buys that book from Amazon. Because Amazon orders only books that customers have agreed to buy, the return rate is less than one-quarter of 1 percent, versus 30 to 40 percent for the industry overall.

Reputation on the Web is crucial for success. Jess Bezos, CEO of the company, makes it clear: "This is the Web. If people feel mistreated by us, they don't tell five people—they tell 5,000."

SELLING CDs ON-LINE

While Amazon.com and Barnes & Noble are busily selling books on-line, the music industry has had a slower start. According to Juniper Communications, on-line music purchases represent less than a half a percent of the U.S. industry's $13 billion total sales. Some small companies are nonetheless doing well. Internet Underground Music Archive at **www.iuma.com** started in business by selling CDs of bands that were not yet under contract. Today, it carries over 1,000 bands, gets a quarter of a million "hits" (visitors to its site) a day, and is selling CDs at the rate of $1 million a day. The on-line CD purchaser gets a sample song before purchase and also typically spends less than at a regular retail CD store. Many minor artists are starting their own Web sites to publicize their works and sell them, too.

The real future in on-line CD sales will begin when Web surfers can quickly and easily download entire albums in digital quality onto blank CDs.

FOR CRITICAL ANALYSIS: Who will be affected most by the digital on-line downloading of CDs? •

Marketing and Advertising on the Net

If you are marketing a product and you have 20 potential purchasers, you can use the phone to call them. If you want to reach 20 million potential purchasers, you take out a TV ad during the Super Bowl. What do you do if you want to reach 10,000 people? Typically, you engage in direct-mail advertising, at a cost of 50 cents to $1 per person targeted. But now you've got the Internet. In principle, the Net makes it easier to reach more finely targeted audiences and to communicate with them. Consider an example. You are using the search engine InfoSeek, and you enter the keyword "airline tickets." When you do so, a banner ad for American Express's travel services will appear on top of the resulting list of potential Web sites.

The key difference between a similar-looking ad on a TV screen and one on your computer is important—you can click on the one on your computer for an instant response. For TV advertising (and space ads in newspapers and magazines, too), there is no way of really knowing how many people's behavior is truly changed. With Internet advertising, all you have to do is count the number of "click-throughs." If American Express finds out that its travel service ad on InfoSeek has only a 1 percent click-through rate, it will rethink that particular type of advertising.

The future of Internet advertising is impressive. America Online already has more "viewers" than any single cable television network and more "readers" than most popular magazines. As Internet service providers, browsers, home pages, and the like attract larger and larger audiences, the potential for more extensive advertising is dramatic. Currently, Internet advertising revenues represent only a few percent of the annual $35 billion spent on television advertising. But that proportion will change.

TAXES AND THE INTERNET

The United States has some 30,000 tax jurisdictions. In addition to the 50 states, there are thousands of municipalities as well as other taxing districts. Not surprisingly, many of these tax jurisdictions are looking covetously at e-commerce. It represents a potential boon as sales of products and services on the Internet grow. But there is a big potential problem: taxation confusion.

A single Internet transaction does not just go from one entity to another. The nature of the Internet is such that servers may be located virtually anywhere in the world, and the transaction from one end point to the other may be routed through half a dozen servers in numerous tax jurisdictions. Virtually every tax jurisdiction in the United States has different fees and regulations. If all jurisdictions started imposing their tax structures on every Internet transaction, the result would be total confusion. This chaos would inhibit firms from getting involved in electronic commerce and would slow the growth of the use of the Internet.

A bill is in Congress, a draft of the Internet Tax Freedom Act. The bill proposes a five-year moratorium on any new taxes and regulations in cyberspace. The underlying reasoning is simple: A uniform policy must be developed for on-line transactions to ward off confusion. Governors and mayors are fighting vigorously against enactment of the Internet Tax Freedom Act. They want to be able to tax Internet sales. Under current law, the Constitution has been interpreted as prohibiting the states from taxing interstate commerce. They can tax the activities only of companies that have a physical presence in the same state as the consumer. What if states argued that Internet and on-line service providers, such as America Online, are really just acting as independent agents of any company doing business on the Internet? If this interpretation were to be accepted by the courts, every company selling anything over the Internet would have a taxable telecommunications nexus in every state in the union and could owe dozens of taxes on each transaction.

Even if we assume that uniformity of taxation does not apply to transactions on the Net, the market will still punish governments that attempt to apply relatively high taxes on cybertransactions. When Tacoma, Washington, decided to subject on-line service providers to its 6 percent telecommunications tax, the companies immediately threatened to move elsewhere. The city reversed its decision.

AVOIDING TAXES BY SETTING UP OFFSHORE

If you are willing to break the law, you can set up an Internet business in a Caribbean tax haven. One such place is Anguilla. All you have to do is send your name, phone number, e-mail address, and a proposed Web address for your business to **www.offshore.com.ai**. You will have a Web site set up, and an Anguillan lawyer will register your corporation. You can open a corporate bank account with the Anguillan branch of Barclays Bank or the local National Bank of Anguilla. You can transfer the $1,500 fee using DigiCash, Inc.'s e-cash—which is untraceable. Anguilla does not impose any taxes on your venture. It does not cooperate with the U.S. Internal Revenue Service, either. You can get a corporate credit card and spend your money anywhere you want. Remember, though, that as a citizen or legal resident of the United States, you owe federal income taxes on your worldwide income. On Schedule B of your tax form 1040, there is a box to check if you have an offshore bank account. If you do not check it when you have such an account, you have committed a felony.

FOR CRITICAL ANALYSIS: What types of businesses would individuals seeking to avoid taxes most likely set up on an offshore Web site? ●

CONCEPTS IN BRIEF

- Brands can be established on the Web itself.

- The Internet allows for a better way of reaching more finely tuned groups of potential customers. It is cheaper and perhaps even more effective than traditional direct-mail marketing methods.

- Because any Internet transaction may pass through numerous jurisdictions, confusion may reign for e-commerce unless a uniform taxing policy is adopted.

E-TRADING AND CAPITAL MARKETS

Gone are the days when all stock market transactions had to be run through a licensed broker. The Internet has transformed the industry—from two angles. First, anybody can trade on-line from virtually anywhere in the world for as little as $8 a trade no matter what the size of the transaction. Second, small companies can now find financing through the Internet.

On-Line Trading

A few years ago, on-line trading seemed to be a fantasy. You had to call your broker, usually at a full-service brokerage firm, and pay hundreds or sometimes thousands of dollars in commissions, depending on the number of shares you bought or sold. Discount brokers then entered the fray. Commissions were slashed to half or less. Now on-line retail brokerage firms offer commission rates that "can't be beat." One of the first and biggest is E*Trade. You can buy or sell 200 shares of a $20 stock on-line and pay less than $15 in commissions. You can buy or sell 3,000 shares of a $10 stock and pay less than $75.

Fierce Competition

During the first half of 1998, average daily on-line financial trades increased by more than 50 percent over the previous six months. Currently, there are about 3.5 million on-line investing accounts. Forester Research, Inc., of Cambridge, Massachusetts, predicts 15 million by the year 2002.

Datek Securities, Ameritrade, and Suretrade offer a fixed-price commission. The commission prices are incredibly low compared to what people were paying just a few short years ago—in fact, none of those companies charges more than $10 a trade.

The bright future of on-line trading does not bode well for the future of regular retail securities brokers in the industry. The demand for their services should shift leftward through time.

Seeking Capital on the Web

For very small firms, it has always been difficult, if not impossible, to obtain public financing for expansion. The costs of reaching potential investors, filing with the various state and federal regulatory agencies, and dealing with all the other red tape have been just too great.

In 1996, the U.S. Small Business Administration, working with the federal Securities and Exchange Commission (SEC), helped privately financed Angel Capital Electronic Network launch its first Internet site (**ace-net.sr.unh.edu/**). The goal of this Web site is to have small business entrepreneurs provide information to investors about promising small businesses that wish to raise from $250,000 to $5 million in equity financing.

On-Line IPOs. What's more, it is now possible to go public on the Internet—to sell initial shares of stock to the public directly, as you can see in the following example.

GOING PUBLIC VIA THE NET

History was made when Spring Street Brewing Company became the first company to conduct an initial public offering (IPO) over the Internet in 1995. In March 1996, the company again made history when the SEC allowed Spring Street to trade its shares via its Web site without registering as a broker-dealer—provided that the company modified its program. Among other things, the SEC required Spring Street, which had been directly processing the funds received from buyers, to use an independent agent, such as a bank or escrow agent, to receive such funds.

FOR CRITICAL ANALYSIS: Why would the SEC give up control over public offerings? •

Advantages of Using the Web. According to the government, going public via the normal route takes about 900 hours, most of it devoted to preparing a prospectus prior to the sale of stock. It also involves hiring specialized lawyers and using an underwriter, who takes 10 percent of the IPO as a fee. The alternative is to buy a computer program called CapScape, which automates the process of compiling the offer documents. Then the shares can be sold directly to investors over the Internet.

Who will ultimately benefit from Internet IPOs? Small businesses. Who will lose? Lawyers, accountants, and financiers who specialize in raising money for small companies. The demand for their services should drop over time.

$500 MILLION OF BONDS THROUGH THE INTERNET?

One of the first major uses of the Internet in the capital market was to aid General Motors Acceptance Corporation (GMAC) in selling $500 million of bonds. It used Chicago Corporation, a regional investment bank, to get the job done. What Chicago did was unusual, though. It used a Web-based bulletin board called Direct Access Notes. Investors were able to download the prospectus for the bond offering and an interactive bond calculator. GMAC also developed a multimedia "dog and pony show" for its Web site. This allowed more investors to view the road show personally than would have otherwise. They bought bonds directly off of Chicago's Web site. Investors even participated in chat room discussions about the bond offering.

FOR CRITICAL ANALYSIS: Who benefits most from such Internet activities? •

CONCEPTS IN BRIEF

- The buying and selling of securities has become much cheaper with the advent of e-trading. Commissions are less than they used to be, and stock traders can access markets directly from their home cheaply and easily via their computers.

- The capital market for small firms may become more efficient with the new possibility of raising funds on the Internet.

THE MICRO THEORY OF BUSINESS BEHAVIOR WITH THE INTERNET ADDED

The theory of the way firms make decisions discussed in this textbook was developed well before the Internet became even a pipe dream. How has the advent of the Internet changed the theory of the firm? To understand the answers to this question we look at several areas, including pricing and cost of entry.

Pricing

In a competitive market, the perfect competitor has no control over price—the perfect competitor is a *price taker*. The market price simply equals the price at which the market demand curve intersects the market supply curve. A firm with any market power, however, is a *price setter*. The profit-maximizing price occurs at the quantity at which marginal revenue equals marginal cost, with the price being read off the market demand curve.

Marginal Cost for Software. Consider the issue of marginal cost. Once a software program is developed, the marginal cost of providing one more unit to the world via Internet transmission is very close to zero. Moreover, this marginal cost is probably constant over all of the potential demanders throughout the entire world (at least with respect to the cost incurred by the offering firm). What, then, is the correct pricing decision for a software company that can provide millions of users with its product at a virtually zero marginal cost? You will find the answer in Figure 35-2.

Such a pricing strategy cannot, however, provide revenues to compensate for the initial development costs of the program. So some software providers have come up with different ways to obtain revenues, even while "selling" their programs at a zero price. Microsoft Corporation has offered its Internet Explorer at no charge for years now. It obtains revenues from the advertising that it sells on the Explorer pages. Netscape went one step further at the beginning of 1998 and opened up its entire Navigator program free to the world. Anybody can modify Navigator now to suit a particular environment. The share of Netscape's total revenues from its Navigator browser program had already fallen to 13 percent when it made this policy change. The other 87 percent was obtained from the development of corporate intranets and the like.

Many software firms have offered their programs free of charge simply to "capture" the names of users to whom it might later sell upgraded versions. This is true, for example, of the free e-mail program Eudora. Some accounting software has also been given away free. The best-known example among game players is Doom. The first few levels of the game are given away free on the Net. Once "hooked," though, players pay extra to get to more difficult levels. Several million copies have now been sold.

No Traditional Law of Diminishing Returns. Recall from Chapter 22 the law of diminishing marginal returns. Also remember that a firm's short-run cost curves are a reflection of the law of diminishing marginal returns. When diminishing marginal returns begin, marginal cost begins to rise.

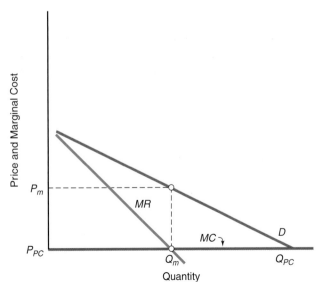

FIGURE 35-2

Pricing When Marginal Cost Equals Zero

For a monopolist, MR = MC at quantity Q_m. The monopoly price would be P_m. For a perfect competitor, MR = MC = 0, so price would be P_{PC} (=0) and quantity would be Q_{PC}.

Software production, now that the Internet exists, does not appear to follow this traditional rule. Once a program has been written, any number of copies can be sent out via the Internet at very little cost, and the cost does not increase with the number of copies. Software companies can cheaply capture a significant market share by giving away a program and then selling follow-up products (upgrades, add-ons, manuals) at higher prices.

Cost of Entry

One thing the Internet has certainly done is reduce the cost of entry, at least for companies willing to sell goods via the Internet. Amazon.com has no inventory, only an Internet site, programmers, and a small staff. Numerous CD retailers on the Internet carry no inventories. The megamalls on the Internet carry no inventories. Entry and operating costs cover simply development of the software retailing programs, paying for the server, and other relatively modest outlays.

 **YOUR BUSINESS ON THE NET FOR $25,000**

If you have an existing retail business, you can set up on the Net for an initial investment of $25,000. The offer to do so was announced by Pandesic at the beginning of 1998. For the $25,000 fee, a small to midsized company can obtain everything it needs to put its business on the Net—and do so in less than six weeks. This includes computer hardware (a server) plus software programs to handle finance, shipping, and inventory. In addition, however, once the retailer is on the Net and up and running, Pandesic takes a fee of 1 to 6 percent of monthly sales. In return, Pandesic provides all of the installation, training, upgrades, and maintenance of the system. This approach has been taken by Thin Blue Line, Inc., a small mountain-bike maker in Canada that has stormed the U.S. market via its Web site.

FOR CRITICAL ANALYSIS: To make a profit, what else must a company do besides get on the Net? ●

The Global Connection

One thing is certain: Because anybody can set up an e-commerce site from anywhere in the world, the Internet is easing entry into any retailing or wholesaling business. Moreover, foreigners can operate Internet sites just as U.S. citizens can. Thus worldwide competition is a given on the Internet. Software that can be downloaded from anywhere is a clear example.

CONCEPTS IN BRIEF

- Pricing decisions for software products that can be downloaded off of the Internet are difficult. The marginal cost becomes zero, but a product given away doesn't yield revenues to pay for its development.
- Some firms have succeeded by giving away their programs but charging for upgrades and updated versions.
- The Internet is leading to lower costs of entry, especially in retailing.

This young man is proud of his bootlegged CDs. If unauthorized copies of CDs can be downloaded easily from the Internet, how will this affect the sales of legally produced copies?

CONCEPTS APPLIED:
COPYRIGHT, INTELLECTUAL PROPERTY, MONOPOLY, LAW OF DEMAND, MARGINAL COST

Visit www.econtoday.com for an Internet Activity that expands your understanding of these concepts.

The first legal copyright protection can be found in a statute passed in Britain in 1709. Later, in 1787, the following phrase was included in the U.S. Constitution: "Congress shall have Power . . . To promote the Progress of Science and useful Arts, by securing for limited Times to Authors and Inventors the exclusive Rights to their respective Writings and Discoveries."

Currently, copyright laws are governed by the Copyright Act of 1976, as amended. No law, whether in the United States or elsewhere, has been very effective against the bootlegging of *intellectual property*—any creation whose source is a person's intellect, as opposed to physical property. The International Federation of the Phonographic Industry (IFPI) estimates that one-fifth of all sales of recorded music are of pirated copies. For CDs, that group estimates that one in three sales is pirated.

First Things First: The Law of Demand

The pirating of recorded music is widespread and worldwide. There have even been diplomatic flaps over it in China. The United States has repeatedly asked the Chinese government to close down the numerous illegal bootlegged-CD factories in that country. Recently, CD bootlegging has become a huge industry in Hong Kong.

There is a problem with the IFPI estimates, nonetheless. When estimating what legitimate CD sales would be in the absence of pirating, the IFPI assumes that pirated copies displace legitimate copies one for one, even though the pirated copies have much lower prices than legitimate copies. This assumption is a clear violation of the law of demand. In fact, there will be a larger quantity demanded at a lower price. Thus the lower-priced pirated copies of recorded music induce purchasers to buy more of them. If pirated copies did not exist, we could not predict that legal sales of CDs would simply replace them

one for one. But pirated copies do exist, inflating potential sales estimates.

This same analysis can apply to pirated copies of software. The Business Software Alliance estimates that at least half the global market for software is pirated products. That does not mean, though, that if no pirating occurred, the sales of software would double. Remember the law of demand.

Altruists on the Internet

There has been a major change in pirating with the advent of the Internet. When you purchase a bootlegged CD, the group that produced the pirated version did so to make a profit. In contrast, many Internet devotees offer downloadable copies of software and recorded music at no charge. In other words, organized profit-seeking gangs are not always involved here. Such anarchy on the Internet may have serious long-term repercussions. People invest in producing high-quality intellectual property, be it software programs or recorded music, because they expect to be paid. The more unauthorized copies of such intellectual properties that people distribute on the Internet for free, the lower the payoff to investing in the development of such property. Without ways to reduce the bootlegging of intellectual property (for one can never prevent it completely), there will certainly be a decrease in the growth of investment of people's time, effort, and creative energy in the development of software, recorded music, and other intellectual property.

How to Survive Internet Copying

It used to be that a copy of a record was of lower quality than the original. A copy of a CD on cassette has a poorer sound quality than the CD. But the same cannot be said of digital copying on the Internet. Zeros and ones copy just as well through cyberspace as they do in a sophisticated studio setup.

There are ways, though, for intellectual property owners to improve their chances of retaining direct sales of their products. They can provide more "goodies" along with legally sold CDs in the standard plastic jewel box—the words to the songs, better liner notes, perhaps contests and drawings, and so on. Software providers have already learned that by offering more useful instructional packages with legally purchased programs, they are able to encourage potential buyers to shy away from bootlegged copies.

Finally, a technological breakthrough will help recording companies track down bootleggers. It is a type of "watermarking" system imbedded in the digital information stored on a compact disc. It allows investigators to determine whether a CD was obtained legally or illegally.

Perhaps the extreme concern over the fate of recording artists in the digital Internet world is much ado about nothing. After all, when the Grateful Dead were touring, they allowed anybody to "bootleg" their live sessions. In the process, they created a cult of fans who could identify a particular concert in a particular city on a given date simply upon hearing the opening bars of a "bootlegged" CD or tape. The result was increased interest in purchasing other Grateful Dead recordings and paraphernalia.

FOR CRITICAL ANALYSIS

1. Is there any way to police the downloading of copyrighted material on the Internet?
2. Most people have at least once copied a computer program or a CD. Is this always bad for the copyright owner of such material?

CHAPTER SUMMARY

1. The twenty-first century is dawning on the age of information. The use of the Internet by businesses has mushroomed, and billions of e-mail messages are sent each year. In the home, the number of households connected to the Internet may be over 50 percent by 2005.
2. The rising use of the Internet allows for a reduction in transaction costs. Relatively inexpensive programs for searching for the lowest price on the Web will lead to less variation in the price per constant-quality unit for any given item.
3. The greatest volume of transactions on the Web is between businesses. Retailing on the Web is taking longer to establish itself, in part because of fears that credit card numbers can be stolen in cyberspace. Better encryption programs will ultimately resolve this problem.
4. Increased acceptance of Web shopping will lead to a reduction in the demand for retail space.
5. In the past, the purchase and sale of securities had to be done through a licensed retail securities broker. Today, securities transactions can be done on the Internet for relatively very low commissions per trade.
6. Capital can be raised directly through the Internet, without a costly registration process and without an expensive underwriter.
7. Pricing is a problem for software sold on the Web because once the software is produced, it can be distributed at very little cost to literally millions of potential users.
8. Because the Internet has made it easier and cheaper to go into retailing, the cost of entry has fallen. Also, foreign competition now exists that was too expensive to consider before.

DISCUSSION OF PREVIEW QUESTIONS

1. How does technological change affect the demand for labor?

Though technological change undoubtedly reduces the demand for more traditional labor services, that is never the end of the story. Individuals who provide

such services are thrown out of work, but at the same time (or perhaps after a time lag), new types of labor services are demanded. Who could have imagined 20 years ago the types of labor services now demanded for Web design, Web marketing, and the like?

2. What is the main reason the Internet may lead to increased efficiency?

The Internet can be viewed as a giant ongoing process that reduces transaction costs. The more quickly buyers can locate sellers, the more efficient our economy becomes. The more competition occurs, even from other parts of the world, the more efficient our economy becomes.

3. If different tax jurisdictions each take "their piece" of an Internet transaction, what might be the long-run result?

To enter the e-commerce world, businesses have to know what they are in for. If they can never tell when,

for example, a city government may try to tax an Internet transaction, they may be reluctant to move forward. Because Internet transactions go through many servers in many jurisdictions, too many taxes on a single transaction will hamper the growth of e-commerce.

4. Why does the software business seem to belie the traditional law of diminishing marginal returns?

Generally, after the production of an ever-increasing number of an item, its marginal cost starts to rise, due to diminishing marginal returns. For software production, an increasing number of copies can be distributed on the Internet without any significant rising marginal cost.

PROBLEMS

(The answer to Problem 35-1 appears at the back of the book.)

35-1. Imagine that you are selling a new word processing program that you have decided to give away free of charge on the Internet. How can you make a profit?

35-2. Assume that you got a great Web designer to make you a terrific-looking home page for your new business. Does this necessarily mean that you can stay in business?

INTERACTING WITH THE INTERNET

You can look at some alternative e-commerce shopping malls at

www.shopping.com

www.monacoshopping.com

www.my-world.de

You can visit the Small Business Administration on-line at

www.sbaonline.sba.gov/

You can obtain information on on-line trading of stock and bonds from numerous sources. Try some of the following:

www.dljdirect.com/

www.wallstreete.com/

www.etrade.com/

www.eschwab.com/

www.suretrade.com

www.ameritrade.com

If you want to participate in an on-line auction, you can find a long list of possible cites for many categories of products at:

www.internetauctionlist.com/

You can scan thousands of classified ads, by category, if you access:

www.classifieds2000.com/

For on-line job searching, there are many cites which offer everything from career advice to actual want ads. One of the most often used is:

www.careermosaic.com/

Try also any of the following:

www.jobbankusa.com

www.doleta.gov/programs/onet/

www.online-jobs.com/

You can learn more about e-commerce from a monthly on-line publication called *E-Business*. Go to:

www.hp.com/Ebusiness/main1.html

CHAPTER 1

1-1. A large number of possible factors might affect the probability of death, including age, occupation, diet, and current health. Thus one model would show that the older someone is, the greater is the probability of dying within the next five years; another would show that the riskier the occupation, other things being equal, the greater the probability of dying within five years; and so forth.

1-3. a. We should observe younger drivers to be more frequently involved in traffic accidents than older persons.
b. Slower monetary expansion should be associated with less inflation.
c. Professional basketball players receiving smaller salaries should be observed to have done less well in their high school studies.
d. Employees being promoted rapidly should have lower rates of absenteeism than those being promoted more slowly.

1-5. The decreasing relative attractiveness of mail communication has no doubt decreased students' demand for writing skills. Whether or not the influence has been a significant one is a subject for empirical research. As for the direction of causation, it may well be running both ways. Cheaper nonwritten forms of communication may decrease the demand for writing skills. Lower levels of writing skills probably further increase the demand for audio and video communications media.

1-7. a. Normative, involving a value judgment about what should be
b. Positive, for it is a statement of what has actually occurred
c. Positive, for it is a statement of what actually is
d. Normative, involving a value judgment about what should be

CHAPTER 2

2-1. The law of increasing relative cost does seem to hold because of the principle that some resources may be more suited to one productive use than to another. In moving from butter to guns, the economy will first transfer those resources most easily sacrificed by the butter sector, holding on to the very specialized (to butter) factors until the last. Thus different factor intensities will lead to increasing relative costs.

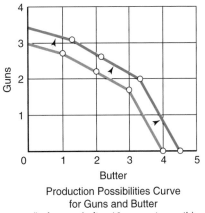

Production Possibilities Curve
for Guns and Butter
(before and after 10 percent growth)

2-3. a. Neither, because each can produce the same total number of jackets per time period (2 jackets per hour)
b. Neither, because each has the same cost of producing ties ($\frac{2}{3}$ jacket per tie)
c. No, because with equal costs of production, there are no gains from specialization
d. Output will be the same as if they did not specialize (16 jackets per day and 24 ties per day)

2-5. a. Only the extra expense of lunch in a restaurant, above what lunch at home would have cost, is part of the cost of going to the game.

b. This is part of the cost of going to the game because you would not have incurred it if you had watched the game on TV at home.

c. This is part of the cost of going to the game because you would not have incurred it if you had watched the game on TV at home.

2-7. For most people, air is probably not an economic good because most of us would not pay simply to have a larger volume of the air we are currently breathing. But for almost everyone, *clean* air is an economic good because most of us would be willing to give something up to have cleaner air.

APPENDIX A

A-1.

y	x
12	4
9	3
6	2
3	1
0	0
−3	−1
−6	−2
−9	−3
−12	−4

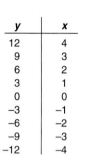

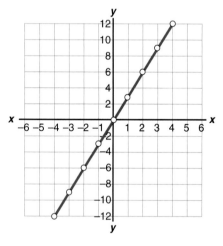

CHAPTER 3

3-1. The equilibrium price is $30. The quantity supplied and demanded is about 10.5 million skateboards per year.

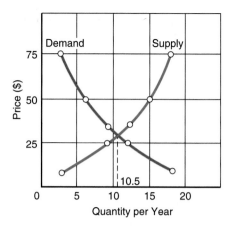

3-3. a. The demand curve for vitamin C will shift outward to the right because the product has taken on a desirable new quality.

b. The demand curve for teachers will shift inward to the left because the substitute good, the interactive educational CD-ROM, is now a lower-cost alternative. (Change in the price of a substitute)

c. The demand curve for beer will shift outward to the right because the price of a complementary good—pretzels—has decreased. Is it any wonder that tavern owners often give pretzels away? (Change in the price of a complement)

3-5. As the graph indicates, demand doesn't change, supply decreases, the equilibrium price of oranges rises, and the equilibrium quantity falls.

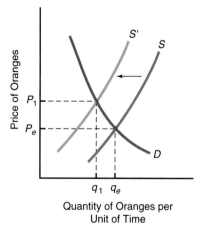

3-7. The speaker has learned well the definition of a surplus but has overlooked one point. The "surpluses" that result from the above-equilibrium minimum prices don't go begging; the excess quantities supplied are in effect purchased by the

Department of Agriculture. In that sense, they are not surpluses at all. When one includes the quantity that is demanded by the Department of Agriculture, along with the quantities being purchased by private purchasers at the support price, the quantity demanded will equal the quantity supplied, and there will be an equilibrium of sorts.

3-9. As the graph illustrates, rain consumers are not willing to pay a positive price to have nature's bounty increased. Thus the equilibrium quantity is 200 centimeters per year (the amount supplied freely by nature), and the equilibrium price is zero (the amount that consumers will pay for an additional unit, given that nature is already producing 200 centimeters per year).

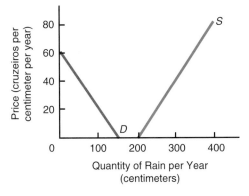

CHAPTER 4

4-1. a. The demand curve will shift to the right (increase).
   b. The supply curve will shift to the right (increase).
   c. Because the price floor, or minimum price, is below the equilibrium price of 50 cents, there will be no effect on price or quantity.
   d. Because the price floor is now greater than the equilibrium price, there will be a surplus at the new price of 75 cents.
   e. Assuming that grapefruits are a substitute for oranges, the demand curve for oranges will shift to the right (increase).
   f. Assuming that oranges are a normal good, the demand curve will shift to the left (decrease).

4-3. The "equilibrium" price is $40 per calculator, and the equilibrium quantity is zero calculators per year. This is so because at a price of $40, the quantity demanded—zero—is equal to the quantity supplied—also zero. None will be produced or bought

because the highest price that any consumer is willing to pay for even a single calculator ($30) is below the lowest price at which any producer is willing to produce even one calculator ($50).

4-5. The equilibrium price is $4 per crate, and the equilibrium quantity is 50 million crates per year. At $2 per crate, the quantity demanded is 90 million crates per year and the quantity supplied is 10. This is called a shortage, or excess quantity demanded. The excess quantity demanded is 80 million crates per year. At $5 per crate, the quantity demanded is 20 million crates per year and the quantity supplied is 80 million crates. This is called a surplus, or excess quantity supplied. The excess quantity supplied is 60 million crates per year.

4-7. As shown in the graph, if the equilibrium price of oranges is 10 cents, a price floor of 15 cents will result in a surplus equal to $Q_s - Q_d$. A price floor of 5 cents per orange will have no effect, however, because it is below the equilibrium price and thus does not prevent suppliers and demanders from doing what they want to do—produce and consume Q_e oranges at 10 cents each.

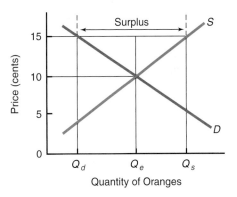

CHAPTER 5

5-1. The marginal tax rate on the first $3,000 of taxable income is 0 percent because no taxes are imposed until $5,000 is earned. The marginal rate on $10,000 is 20 percent, as it is on $100,000 and all other amounts above the $5,000 level, because for each additional dollar earned after $5,000, 20 cents will be taxed away. The average tax rate, which is the tax amount divided by the pretax income, is 0 for $3,000, 10 percent for $10,000, and 19 percent for $100,000. The average tax rate will *approach* a maximum of 20 percent as income increases. It cannot reach *exactly* 20 percent because of the untaxed $5,000 at the beginning. Such is the nature of a *degressive* tax system.

5-3. Mr. Smith pays nothing on his first $1,500 of income, 14 percent ($70) on the $500 of earnings between $1,500 and $2,000, and 20 percent ($100) on the $500 that he earns above $2,000. Thus Mr. Smith has a total tax bill of $170 on an income of $2,500; his average tax rate is 6.8 percent, and his marginal tax rate is 20 percent.

5-5. Among the ideas that have been proposed is that a good tax system should meet the requirements of equity, efficiency, and ease of administration. Equity means that each person should pay a "fair share." The efficiency requirement is that the tax system should minimize interferences with economic decisions. Ease of administration means that the tax system should not be excessively costly to administer and that it should be understandable to the taxpayer. Even though the U.S. tax system was not designed through a master plan, these ideas have had their influence on the American system.

5-7. There are both public good and private good aspects to police protection. When an officer patrols the neighborhood in a police car, criminals are deterred from burglarizing every home in the neighborhood; this is a public good aspect of police protection because the protection afforded one person is simultaneously afforded all of the neighbors. But when an officer spends time arresting the person who broke into Mr. Smith's home, that is time the officer cannot spend arresting the person who broke into Ms. Jones's home; this is the private good aspect of police protection, for when these services are provided Mr. Smith, Ms. Jones is excluded from simultaneously using those services.

5-9. a. If you give and everyone else does also, you account for 1 percent. If you are the only one who gives, you account for 100 percent. If you give nothing, you account for 0 percent, regardless of what others give.
b. In principle, your contribution matters whatever the level of participation. But as a practical matter, if participation is near 100 percent, the absence of your contribution may have little practical effect.
c. There is no free ride. If you do not make your contribution, total contributions will be lower, and the quality of the services provided will be lower.

5-11. Strictly speaking, probably all the items except national defense should go into the column labeled "Private Goods," either because residents *could* be excluded from consuming them or because one person's consumption reduces the amount available for other individuals. As a practical matter, however, there are several goods on the list (public television, elementary education, and the museum) for which full exclusion generally does not take place and/or consumption by one person reduces the amount that other persons can consume by only a small amount.

CHAPTER 6

6-1. On the supply side, all of the industries responsible for automobile inputs would have to be considered. This would include steel (and coke and coal), glass, tires (and rubber), plastics, railroads (and thus steel again), aluminum (and electricity), and manufacturers of stereos, hubcaps, and air conditioners, to name a few. On the demand side, you would have to take into account industries involving complements (such as oil, gasoline, concrete, and asphalt) and substitutes (including bicycles, motorcycles, buses, and walking shoes). Moreover, resource allocation decisions regarding labor and the other inputs, complements, and substitutes for these goods must also be made.

6-3. a. Profit equals total revenue minus total cost. Because revenue is fixed (at $172), if the firm wishes to maximize profit, this is equivalent to minimizing costs. To find total costs, simply multiply the price of each input by the amount of the input that must be used for each technique.

Costs of A = ($10)(7) + ($2)(6) + ($15)(2) + ($8)(1) = $120
Costs of B = ($10)(4) + ($2)(7) + ($15)(6) + ($8)(3) = $168
Costs of C = ($10)(1) + ($2)(18) + ($15)(3) + ($8)(2) = $107

Because C has the lowest costs, it yields the highest profits, and thus it will be used.
b. Profit equals $172 − $107 = $65.
c. Each technique's costs rise by the increase in the price of labor multiplied by the amount of labor used by that technique. Because technique A uses the least amount of labor, its costs rise the least, and it thus becomes the lowest-cost technique at $132. (The new cost of B is

$182, and the new cost of C is $143.) Hence technique A will be used, resulting in profits of $172 − $132 = $40.

6-5. a. In the market system, the techniques that yield the highest (positive) profits will be used.

b. Profit equals total revenue minus total cost. Because revenue from 100 units is fixed (at $100), if the firm wishes to maximize profit, this is equivalent to minimizing costs. To find total costs, simply multiply the price of each input by the amount of the input that must be used for each technique.

Costs of A = ($10)(6) + ($8)(5) = $100
Costs of B = ($10)(5) + ($8)(6) = $98
Costs of C = ($10)(4) + ($8)(7) = $96

Because technique C has the lowest costs, it also yields the highest profits ($100 − $96 = $4).

c. Following the same methods yields these costs: A = $98, B = $100, and C = $102. Technique A will be used because it is the most profitable.

d. The profits from using technique A to produce 100 units of X are $100 − $98 = $2.

CHAPTER 19

19-1. For you, the marginal utility of the fifth pound of oranges is equal to the marginal utility of the third ear of corn. Apparently, your sister's tastes differ from yours—for her, the marginal utilities are not equal. For her, corn's marginal utility is too low, while that of oranges is too high—that's why she wants you to get rid of some of the corn (raising its marginal utility). She would have you do this until marginal utilities, for her, were equal. If you follow her suggestions, you will end up with a market basket that maximizes *her* utility subject to the constraint of *your* income. Is it any wonder that shopping from someone else's list is a frustrating task?

19-3. Her marginal utility is 100 at $1,200 at 50 cents, and 50 at $2. To calculate marginal utility per dollar, divide marginal utility by price per unit.

19-5. Optimum satisfaction is reached when marginal utilities per dollar of both goods are equal. This occurs at 102 units of A and 11 units of B. (Marginal utility per dollar is 1.77.)

19-7. Either your income or the relative price of eggs and bacon must have changed. Without more information, you can't make any judgments about whether you are better or worse off.

19-9. a. 20
b. 10
c. With consumption of the third unit of X

APPENDIX E

E-1. The problem here is that such preferences are inconsistent (*intransitive* is the word that economists use). If this consumer's tastes really are this way, then when confronted with a choice among A, B, and C, she will be horribly confused because A is preferred to B, which is preferred to C, which is preferred to A, which is preferred to B, which is preferred to C, and so on forever. Economists generally assume that preferences are consistent (or *transitive*): If A is preferred to B and B is preferred to C, then A is preferred to C. Regardless of what people may *say* about their preferences, the assumption of transitivity seems to do quite well in predicting what people actually do.

E-3. With an income of $100 and the original prices, you could have consumed *either* 50 pounds of beef *or* 5 units of shelter *or* any linear combination shown by the budget line labeled "Original" on the graph below. With the same income but the new prices, you can now consume 25 pounds of beef or 10 units of shelter or any linear combination shown by the line labeled "New budget." Without information about your preferences, there is no way to tell whether you are better off or worse off. Draw a few indifference curves on the diagram. You will find that if you are a "shelter lover" (your indifference curves are relatively steep), the decline in the relative price of shelter will tend to make you better off. Conversely, if you are a "beef lover" (your indifference curves are relatively flat), the rise in the relative price of beef will make you worse off.

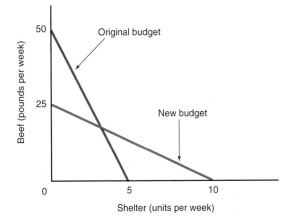

E-5. The first burrito is substituted at a rate of 10 servings of yogurt per burrito; the second burrito is substituted at a rate of 4:1; the third at a rate of 3:1; and the fourth at a rate of 2:1.

E-7. a. This person is simply indifferent between going or staying, an attitude that is perfectly consistent with our assumptions about consumer preferences.
   b. This statement denies the law of substitution and so is inconsistent with our assumptions about preferences.
   c. If we interpret "if I had my way" to mean "if I had an unlimited budget," this statement simply says that there is nonsatiation for these goods for this consumer—which is perfectly consistent with our assumptions about preferences.

CHAPTER 20

20-1. a.

Quantity Demanded per Week (ounces)	Price per Ounce	Elasticity
1,000	$ 5	
800	10	$\frac{1}{3}$, or .33
600	15	$\frac{5}{7}$, or .714
400	20	$\frac{7}{5}$, or 1.4
200	25	$\frac{9}{3}$, or 3

   b. There are several ways to explain why elasticity is greater at higher prices on a linear curve. At higher prices, a given price change will result in a smaller percentage price change. The smaller resulting denominator of the elasticity ratio leads to a larger overall ratio. Similarly, as prices rise, quantities fall, thereby implying greater percentage quantity changes for a given absolute quantity change, and a larger numerator. Alternatively, the sizes of total revenue changes first increase and then decrease as price is lowered throughout a linear demand curve, thus implying declining elasticity.

20-3. a. Using averages in the elasticity equation, the income elasticity of demand for VCRs is .6666 ÷ .2857 = 2.33. It is income-elastic.
   b. It is presumably a luxury good.

20-5. The problem is with the denominator, percentage change in P. Because the initial price was zero, any

increase in price is of infinite percentage. However, if we take the average elasticity over a segment, there will be no problem. P will become the average of P_1 (= 0) and P_2 (= 10), or $(P_1 + P_2)/2 = 5$.

20-7. a. $E_p = \dfrac{50}{(475 + 525)/2} \div \dfrac{.02}{(.15 + .17)/2} = .8$
   b. Demand is price-inelastic.
   c. $E_s = \dfrac{75}{(525 + 600)/2} \div \dfrac{.02}{(.15 + .17)/2} = 1.067$
   d. Supply is price-elastic (but only slightly so).

20-9. In each case, "before" is before the development of an acceptable substitute for the good in question, and "after" is after the development of that substitute. For example, between 1840 and 1880, the railroad emerged as a good substitute for canal transportation. In general, the better the substitutes for a good, the greater the price elasticity of demand for that good. Thus in each case we would expect the price elasticity of demand to be higher after the emergence of the substitute.

CHAPTER 21

21-1. Taxation of corporate dividend income can be thought of as a tax on the corporate form of organization. Increasing the amount of dividends exempt from taxes thus amounts to reducing taxes on dividends and hence reducing the tax on the corporate form of organization. As a result, more firms would choose to incorporate, and fewer would choose to be proprietorships or partnerships.

21-3. For simplicity, assume that potential lenders care only about the expected value of their lending decisions. If $10,000 is lent to a risk-free borrower at 10 percent interest, the borrower is certain to have ($10,000)(1 + .10) = $11,000 one year from now. If a loan is made to the risky firm, the borrower has a 20 percent chance of ending up with nothing and an 80 percent chance of repayment in full. Hence the amount the borrower expects to end up with is E = (.20)(0) + (.80)($10,000)(1 + R)$, where R is the rate of interest charged to the risky firm. We seek the value of R that makes E equal to $11,000 because that will make the lender equally well off whether lending to the risk-free borrower or to the risky borrower. Thus we solve $11,000 = 0 + ($8,000)(1 + R)$ so that at a rate of interest $R = 37.5$ percent, the risky firm will be able to borrow the $10,000.

CHAPTER 22

22-1. The opportunity cost of continuing to possess the van is being ignored. For example, if the van could be sold without much problem for $10,000 and you could earn 10 percent per year by investing that $10,000 in something else, the opportunity cost of keeping the van is $1,000 per year.

22-3. a. $1

b. 5 cents

c. $1

d. 10 cents

e. It is rising.

f. When the marginal product of labor is rising, the marginal cost of output falls; when the marginal product of labor is falling, the marginal cost of output rises.

22-5. The long-run average costs represent the points that give the least unit cost of producing any given rate of output. The concept is important when one must decide which scale of operations to adopt. Such a decision usually takes the form of deciding what size "plant" to construct.

22-7. a.

Output	AVC
0	$ 0
5	20
10	18
20	11
40	8

b. The marginal cost is $40 when increasing output from 10 to 20 units and $100 when increasing from 20 to 40.

c.

Output	ATC
0	$ 0
5	60
10	38
20	21
40	13

22-9.

Units of Labor	Total Product	Marginal Product	Average Product
6	120	—	20
7	147	27	21
8	170	23	21.25
9	180	10	20

CHAPTER 23

23-1.

Output (units)	Fixed Cost	AFC	Variable Cost	AVC	Total Cost	ATC	MC
1	$100	$100.00	$ 40	$40	$140	$140.00	$40
2	100	50.00	70	35	170	85.00	30
3	100	33.33	120	40	220	73.33	50
4	100	25.00	180	45	280	70.00	60
5	100	20.00	250	50	350	70.00	70
6	100	16.67	330	55	430	71.67	80

a. The price would have to drop below $35 before the firm would shut down in the short run.

b. $70 is the short-run break-even point for the firm. The output at this price would be 5 units per period.

c. At a price of $76, the firm would produce 5 units and earn a profit of $30 ($6 per unit over 5 units).

23-3. The industry demand curve is negatively sloped; it is relevant insofar as its interaction with the industry supply curve (ΣMC) determines the product price. The demand the individual firm faces, however, is infinitely elastic (horizontal) at the current market price.

23-5. a. $100
b. $100
c. $100
d. $100

23-7. For simplicity, assume that your friend computed her "profit" the way many small businesses do: She ignored the opportunity cost of her time and her money. Instead of operating the car wash, she could have earned $25,000 at the collection agency plus $12,000 ($200,000 × 6 percent) on her savings. Thus the opportunity cost to her of operating the car wash was $37,000. Subtracting this amount from the $40,000 yields $3,000, which is her actual profit, over and above opportunity costs. You would tell her she really isn't making such great profits.

CHAPTER 24

24-1. a. The rectangle that shows total costs under ATC_1 is $0WCQ$. Total revenue is shown by $0XBQ$.

This monopolist is in an economic profit situation. MC = MR is the output at which profit— the difference between total cost and total revenue—is maximized.
b. With ATC_2, the rectangle showing total costs is $0XBQ$. The same rectangle, $0XBQ$, gives total revenue. This monopolist is breaking even. MC = MR shows the only quantity that does not cause losses.
c. Under ATC_3, total costs are represented by rectangle $0YAQ$, total revenue by $0XBQ$. Here the monopolist is operating at an economic loss, which is minimized by producing where MC = MR.

24-3. Four conditions are necessary: (1) market power, (2) ability to separate markets at a reasonable cost, (3) differing price elasticities of demand, and (4) ability to prevent resale.

24-5. If E_p is numerically greater than 1 (elastic), marginal revenue is positive; a decrease in price will result in more total revenues. If E_p is numerically equal to 1 (unit-elastic), marginal revenue is 0; a change in price will not affect total revenues at all. If E_p is numerically less than 1 (inelastic), marginal revenue is negative; a decrease in price will result in less total revenues.

24-7. a.

Price	Quantity Demanded	Total Revenue	Marginal Revenue	Total Cost	Marginal Cost	Profit or Loss
$20	0	$ 0	—	$ 4	—	$-4
16	1	16	$ 16	10	$ 6	6
12	2	24	8	14	4	10
10	3	30	6	20	6	10
7	4	28	-2	28	8	0
4	5	20	-8	40	12	-20
0	6	0	-20	54	14	-54

b. The firm would operate at a loss if it produced 0, 5, or 6 units.

c. The firm would break even at a rate of output of 4 units.

d. The firm would maximize its profits by producing either 2 or 3 units. At either of those two outputs, it would be earning a profit of $10.

24-9. a. TR = $10,000, $16,000, $18,000, $16,000, $10,000, $3,000

b. MR = $6,000, $2,000, −$2,000, −$6,000, −$7,000

c. 3,000 units

d. A profit-maximizing firm always sets MR = MC, and at any output level greater than 3,000, MR is negative. Naturally, MC can never be negative, thus ensuring that output levels where MR is negative are impossible for a profit-maximizing firm.

CHAPTER 25

25-1. The marginal revenue of this ad campaign is $1,000. There was an addition of 40 cars per week at $25 per car. To determine whether profits have risen, we would have to know how much additional cost was incurred in the tuning of these cars, as well as the cost of the advertisement itself.

25-3. a. Approximately 64 percent ($525 million ÷ $825 million).

b. The ratio would rise as the industry is more narrowly defined and fall as it is more broadly defined. Because an "industry" is arbitrarily defined, concentration ratios may be misleading.

25-5. The kink arises from the assumptions of the model. It is assumed that if any one firm raises its price, none of the others will follow. Consequently, a maverick firm's price increase will result in a drastic decrease in its total revenue. Conversely, the model assumes that any price decrease will be matched by all rivals. For this reason, the quantity demanded will probably not increase enough to cover increased costs. And profit will probably be less. Under these assumptions, it is in no individual firm's interest to "rock the boat."

25-7. The advertising campaign must increase weekly ticket revenues by at least $1,000 per week or it will be discontinued. This will require an additional 200 movie viewers each week.

25-9. The payoff matrix looks like this:

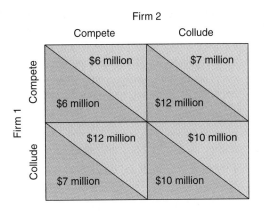

This situation parallels that of the prisoners' dilemma in that it is in the firms' *collective* interest to collude but in their *individual* interests to compete. If the possibility for collusion is a one-time-only arrangement, we have exactly the circumstances of the classic prisoners' dilemma, in which the dominant strategy is to compete, resulting in profits of $6 million for each firm. (This sounds good until you remember that each is *losing* $4 million relative to the joint maximum possible with collusion!) If this is a repeating game and if each firm can observe the behavior of its rival, it may be possible for the firms to overcome their dilemma and reach the joint maximum—for example, by employing the "tit for tat" strategy discussed in the text.

CHAPTER 26

26-1. a. Quantity produced would be Q_b, and price would be P_c.

b. Losses would equal the rectangle P_bBCP_c.

26-3. There will still be political pressure from Congress if you enforce new regulations that dramatically increase the costs and hence the prices of products. Thus you can simply do anything you feel like concerning new rules in the workplace. If you must now consider costs, you might want to estimate the impact each new rule has on the unit cost of each product affected. You would compare the total costs thus incurred because of the new rule with the estimated benefits to the community in terms of higher levels of worker safety and health.

26-5. By definition, a natural monopolist's costs are lower than those of potential entrants. Hence although other firms may be free to enter, they are unlikely to do so. The natural monopolist can thus earn economic profits equal to the difference between its costs and its potential rivals' costs.

26-7. Liquor store owners do not like to compete any more than anyone else does. Nevertheless, simply telling the truth about this distaste is unlikely to garner them much political support in favor of restricting entry into their industry. What the liquor store owners seek is an argument that what is good for them is also good for you, and many people probably find the idea of a liquor store next door distasteful.

CHAPTER 27

27-1.

Quantity of Labor	Total Product per Week	MPP	MRP
1	250	250	$500
2	450	200	400
3	600	150	300
4	700	100	200
5	750	50	100
6	750	0	0

a. Demand schedule for labor:

Weekly Wage	Laborers Demanded per Week
$500	1
400	2
300	3
200	4
100	5

b. $100 each
c. Four

27-3. a. 15 million worker-hours per time period
b. 10 million per time period
c. Buyers can get all the labor they want at W_1; laborers can't sell all they want to sell at W_1.
d. Because a surplus of labor exists, the unemployed will offer to work for less, and industry wage rates will fall toward W_e.

27-5. Suppose that the demand for the output product is highly elastic. Even a relatively small increase in the price of the input factor, which correspondingly raises the price of the output product, will cause a large decrease in the quantity of output demanded and therefore in the employment of the input.

27-7. The MRP of labor is $40 per worker-day ($3,040 less $3,000, divided by a change in labor input of one worker-day). The maximum wage that would still make it worthwhile to hire this additional employee would be $39.99 per day. If the going market wage is above that figure, you will not expand output.

27-9. Imposing limitations such as these implicitly reduces the ability of employers to compete for your services. Thus you can expect to receive a lower wage and to work in a less desirable job.

CHAPTER 28

28-1. a. Marginal revenue product
b. S
c. Q_m
d. W_m

28-3. Some examples would be Coors beer in Golden, Colorado; Bethlehem Steel in Bethlehem, Pennsylvania; Winnebago Corporation in Forest City, Iowa; and many coal-mining companies in towns in West Virginia. As long as your example is one of an employer that is dominant in its local labor market selling in fairly competitive markets, you are correct.

28-5. No, you should not. The MRP when you employ 31 people is $89.50 ($99.50 in revenue from selling the twenty-first unit, less $10 forgone in selling the first 20 units for 50 cents less than originally). The MFC is $91 ($61 to attract the twenty-first employee to your firm, plus the additional $1 per day to each of the original 20 employees). Because MFC exceeds MRP, you should not expand output.

28-7. Because the union acts in the interests of its members and the competitive wage is lower than the highest wage the union can obtain for its members.

28-9. The monopsonist's decisions about how much to purchase influence the price of the good it is buying. As a result, the marginal factor cost curve facing a monopsonist lies above the average factor cost curve (which is the supply curve of the industry producing the good being purchased by the monopsonist).

CHAPTER 29

29-1. The statement is false. Although there may be a substantial portion of rent in the revenues from these museums, we would have to assume that the museums are absolutely costless to keep in their current use in order to make the statement that *all* revenues are economic rent. The most obvious expenses of keeping the museums operating are the costs of maintenance: cleaning, lighting, and other overhead costs. But these may be minor compared to the opportunity cost involved in keeping the museum *as a museum*. The buildings might make ideal government office buildings. They may be on land that would be extremely valuable if sold on the private real estate market. If there are any such alternative uses, the value of these uses must be subtracted from the current revenues in order to arrive at the true level of economic rent. Forgoing these alternative opportunities is as much a cost of operating the museum as the monthly utility bill.

29-3. The statement is false. Because a firm utilizes an input only to the point that the input's MRP is equal to its price, and marginal product is declining, it follows that all the intramarginal (up-to-the-marginal) units are producing more value than they are being paid. This differential is used to compensate for other factor inputs. The residual, if any, would be profits.

29-5. a. 9 percent
     b. The equilibrium interest rate will increase.
     c. 5 percent

29-7. In each case, the asset that qualifies the borrower for a lower interest rate is better collateral (or security) for the lender and thus reduces both the chances of default and the lender's losses in the event that default does occur.

29-9. They would be reduced but not necessarily eliminated (because, for example, economic profits due to entry restrictions might still persist).

CHAPTER 30

30-1. Whites might invest more in human capital; blacks might receive less and lower-quality education and/or training; blacks in the workforce may, on average, be younger; discrimination may exist.

30-3. Productivity and equality.

30-5. Such a program would drastically reduce efficiency. It would eliminate individuals' incentives to maximize the economic value of resources because they would receive no reward for doing so. It would also eliminate their incentive to minimize production costs because there would be no penalty for failing to do so.

30-7. When governments pay for health care, hospitals have reduced incentives to operate efficiently because they are less likely to be penalized for being inefficient. Bureaucrats are less likely to provide the services that patients want at the lowest cost because the rewards from doing so are diminished when the government (rather than the patient) pays for the services. Finally, because the patient is not directly footing the bill, the patient has less incentive to choose wisely (that is, in a manner that equates the true marginal benefits and costs) when choosing health care.

CHAPTER 31

31-1. When the external costs are added to the supply curve (which is itself the sum of marginal costs of the industry), the total (private plus public) marginal costs of production are above the private supply schedule. At quantity Q_1 in the graph on the next page, marginal costs to society are greater than the value attached to the marginal unit. The demand curve is below the social supply curve. To bring marginal cost and marginal benefit back into line, thus promoting an economically efficient allocation of resources, quantity would have to be reduced to Q_2 and price raised to P_2.

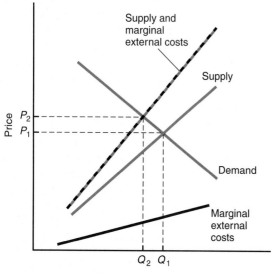

Quantity per Time Period

31-3. a. The price of polluting should be set according to the marginal economic damage imposed by polluters; this means that similar quantities of pollution will cost polluters different prices in different parts of the country; pollution will be more costly in New York City than in a small town in the Midwest.

  b. Firms that find it cheaper to treat will do so; firms that find it cheaper to pay to pollute will pollute.

  c. Yes, some firms will be forced to shut down due to increased costs; this is efficient, as the true costs to society of their operations were not paid by them and their customers; they were able to remain in business only by imposing costs on third parties.

  d. This might be good because now the people who are using the resources will be forced to pay for them instead of imposing costs on others. Those who are *not* using these products were, in effect, subsidizing lower prices to those who were. This new solution seems more fair and is certainly efficient.

31-5. Everyone owns them and nobody owns them. Consequently, there is no incentive for any user to be concerned with the future value of the resource in question. This is perhaps most clearly observable in the behavior of fishing boat owners. The goal of each boat owner is to harvest fish as long as marginal private cost is less than the going price of such fish. The opportunity cost of depleting the stock of fish does not affect the decisions of the proprietor. In light of the nonownership of the fish, any single boat operator would be foolish to behave otherwise.

31-7.

Annual Units of Pollution	a. Marginal Benefits	b. Marginal Costs
0	—	—
1	$ 30	$150
2	40	100
3	80	80
4	120	60
5	160	20

  a. The net gain is $(430 - 150) - 80 = 200$.
  b. The net gain is $430 - 410 = 20$.
  c. The optimal level is between 2 and 3 units, or where marginal benefit equals marginal cost.

31-9. The economically efficient amount of pollution occurs at a level at which the marginal costs of reducing it further would just exceed any benefits from that reduction. If pollution is reduced below this point, we would be better off with more pollution. The government might directly require firms or individuals to generate too little pollution (for example, through inappropriate environmental regulations), or it might establish pollution fees, fines, or taxes that overstate the damages done by the pollution and thus induce firms or individuals to reduce pollution too much.

CHAPTER 32

32-1. The existence of these costs implies the notion of rational ignorance, so that individuals choose not to be informed about certain issues because the cost of being informed is high relative to any benefit forthcoming from the state of the issue. This also contributes to the growth of special-interest groups because individuals have no strong economic incentive to act against them.

32-3. Legislators find themselves in a situation much like a prisoners' dilemma (see Chapter 25): They have a collective incentive to act in the best interests of society as a whole but individual incentives to act in the interests of their own constituents or other narrow special interests. The favors handed out by legislators could, in principle, come in the form of either lower taxes or higher spending. As a practical matter, it is usually easier to disguise higher spending as something socially beneficial for which the recipient is uniquely qualified. Hence spending (and thus the size of the government) tends to increase. (Clearly there is some limit to this process, for the government cannot be larger than the economy as a whole. Nevertheless, the limit does not appear to be in sight.)

32-5. Currently, lobbyists are paid to influence state legislators, the benefits of which may redound to those seeking the political favors for many years, given that often state legislators stay in office for many years. Under a system of term limits, each legislator's time in office is definitely terminated after, for example, 12 years. Thus, using the theory of public choice, we predict that fewer resources will be used to influence each legislator in those states that have term limits. The reason is that the potential payoff will last a shorter time period. More newly elected legislators will have to be influenced under term limits, so fewer resources will go toward influencing each legislator individually, all other things held constant.

32-7. a. 20 percent of 1.9 million is 380,000 farms.
b. Oligopoly seems highly unlikely in this industry in the foreseeable future—there are simply too many firms.

32-9. One of the trickiest things about handing out subsidies is that everybody wants to receive them but not everyone can receive them (at least not after netting out the taxes used to pay for them). Farmers are uniquely positioned to be the recipients of subsidies because of the natural limiting factor—farmland—that constrains their numbers.

32-11. The demand for farmland would fall, resulting in lower prices for such land and a diversion of some of it to other uses, possibly including residential neighborhoods or national parks. The demand for other farm resources—including the labor of farmers—would also fall, inducing some of these resources to move into alternative occupations as well. The price of food would fall, reducing malnutrition but also possibly increasing obesity. Imports of some crops (such as sugar) would rise sharply, while production of goods that use foodstuffs as inputs would also rise. These (and many other) effects would be greatly dampened today if the change in policy were not to take place until 20 years from now—partly because the present value of distant events is small and partly because Congress would have plenty of opportunities over 20 years to reverse itself.

CHAPTER 33

33-1. a. The opportunity cost to the United States of producing one ounce of caviar is two bushels of wheat. The six hours that were needed to make the caviar could have been used to grow two bushels. The opportunity cost of producing one bushel of wheat is $\frac{1}{2}$ ounce of caviar.
b. The opportunity cost to Russia of producing one ounce of caviar is $1\frac{1}{2}$ bushels of wheat. The opportunity cost of producing a bushel of wheat in Russia is $\frac{2}{3}$ ounce of caviar.
c. The United States has a comparative advantage in wheat because it has a lower opportunity cost in terms of caviar. Russia has a comparative advantage in caviar. Less wheat is forgone to produce an ounce of caviar in Russia.

33-3. The assumption given in the question is equivalent to the United States' having an absolute advantage in the production of all goods and services. But the basis of world trade lies in differences in *comparative* advantage. As long as other countries have a lower opportunity cost in producing some goods and services, the United States will benefit from international trade.

33-5. Tariffs yield government revenues; quotas do not.

33-7. a. One million pounds are produced and 2 million pounds are imported.
   b. With a 10-cent tariff, 1.5 million pounds would be produced and 1 million pounds would be imported. Government revenues would amount to ($2.5 million − $1.5 million) × $.10 = $100,000.
   c. With a 20-cent tariff, domestic growers can receive 70 cents per pound. They will produce 2 million pounds, and no grapes will be imported, in which case government revenues are zero.

33-9. Consider trade between the United States and Canada. The United States purchases timber from Canada, and Canada purchases computers from the United States. Ultimately, the Canadians pay for U.S.-made computers with the timber that they sell here. If the United States imposes a tax on Canadian timber and thus reduces the amount of timber that the Canadians are able to sell to the United States, the necessary result is that the Canadians will be able to buy fewer American computers. American exports of computers will decline as a result of the reduction in American imports of timber.

CHAPTER 34

34-1. The answer is (c). A declining dollar price of the pound implies an increasing pound price of the dollar—appreciation of the dollar. (a) is incorrect because an increase in demand for U.S. products would affect the supply of pounds and the demand for dollars, whereas here we are dealing with the demand for pounds. (b) explains a phenomenon that would have just the opposite result as that shown in the graph: An increased U.S. demand for British goods would lead to an increase in the demand for the pound, not a decrease as shown. (d) is incorrect because the pound depreciates.

34-3. One pound equals $3.50; $1 equals .2857 pound. One mark equals 35 cents; $1 equals 2.857 marks. One mark equals .1 pound; one pound equals 10 marks.

34-5. To maintain the exchange rate, domestic policy variables such as the money supply are also affected. Suppose that the government plans an expansive monetary policy to encourage output growth. A balance of payments deficit leads the government to buy up dollars, which in turn leads to a contraction in the domestic money supply. Therefore, in order to maintain the expansionary monetary policy, the government would have to expand the money supply in larger magnitudes than it would without the balance of payments deficits with a fixed exchange rate system.

34-7. a. The dollar price of pounds is $1.50. The equilibrium quantity is 150 million.
   b. Curve D' describes this situation. The new dollar price of pounds would be $1.70, and the equilibrium quantity would be 200 million.
   c. At a price of $1.50 per pound, 250 million pounds sterling would be demanded and only 150 million would be supplied, so the Fed would have to supply an extra 100 million to American buyers of British goods or British exporters.
   d. Curve D'' describes this situation. 150 million pounds sterling would be supplied at a price of $1.50, but only 50 million pounds would be demanded. Therefore, the Fed would have to buy up 100 million pounds sterling.

CHAPTER 35

35-1. You could do what the makers of popular game Doom did: You could offer a more complete version of your word processing program for a fee. You could use the e-mail addresses of everyone who downloaded your free program to form the basis of a new marketing campaign to sell related items, such as self-improvement CD-ROMs. You could, of course, sell everyone a new, updated version of your program every year for some low price, such as $15.

Absolute advantage The ability to produce a good or service at an "absolutely" lower cost, usually measured in units of labor or resource input required to produce one unit of the good or service. *Can also be viewed as* the ability to produce more output from given inputs of resources than other producers can.

Accounting identities Statements that certain numerical measurements are equal by accepted definition (for example, "assets equal liabilities plus stockholders' equity").

Accounting profit Total revenues minus total explicit costs.

Action time lag The time required between recognizing an economic problem and putting policy into effect. The action time lag is short for monetary policy but quite long for fiscal policy, which requires congressional approval.

Active (discretionary) policymaking All actions on the part of monetary and fiscal policymakers that are undertaken in response to or in anticipation of some change in the overall economy.

Adverse selection A problem created by asymmetric information prior to a transaction. Individuals who are the most undesirable from the other party's point of view end up being the ones who are most likely to want to engage in a particular financial transaction, such as borrowing. *Can also be viewed as* the circumstance that arises in financial markets when borrowers

who are the worst credit risks are the ones most likely to seek loans.

Age-earnings cycle The regular earnings profile of an individual throughout his or her lifetime. The age-earnings cycle usually starts with a low income, builds gradually to a peak at around age 50, and then gradually curves down until it approaches zero at retirement.

Aggregate demand The total of all planned expenditures for the entire economy.

Aggregate demand curve A curve showing planned purchase rates for all goods and services in the economy at various price levels, all other things held constant.

Aggregate demand shock

Any shock that causes the aggregate demand curve to shift inward or outward.

Aggregates Total amounts or quantities; aggregate demand, for example, is total planned expenditures throughout a nation.

Aggregate supply The total of all planned production for the entire economy.

Aggregate supply shock Any shock that causes the aggregate supply curve to shift inward or outward.

Anticipated inflation The inflation rate that we believe will occur; when it does, we are in a situation of fully anticipated inflation.

Antitrust legislation Laws that restrict the formation of monopolies and regulate certain anticompetitive business practices.

Appreciation An increase in the value of a currency in terms of other currencies.

Asset demand Holding money as a store of value instead of other assets such as certificates of deposit, corporate bonds, and stocks.

Assets Amounts owned; all items to which a business or household holds legal claim.

Asymmetric information Information possessed by one side of a transaction but not the other. The side with more information will be at an advantage.

Automatic, or built-in, stabilizers Special provisions of the tax law that cause changes in the economy without the action of Congress and the president. Examples are the progressive income tax system and unemployment compensation.

Autonomous consumption The part of consumption that is independent of (does not depend on) the level of disposable income. Changes in autonomous consumption shift the consumption function.

Average fixed costs Total fixed costs divided by the number of units produced.

Average physical product Total product divided by the variable input.

Average propensity to consume (APC)   Consumption divided by disposable income; for any given level of income, the proportion of total disposable income that is consumed.

Average propensity to save (APS)   Saving divided by disposable income; for any given level of income, the proportion of total disposable income that is saved.

Average tax rate   The total tax payment divided by total income. It is the proportion of total income paid in taxes.

Average total costs   Total costs divided by the number of units produced; sometimes called *average per-unit total costs.*

Average variable costs   Total variable costs divided by the number of units produced.

Balance of payments   A summary record of a country's economic transactions with foreign residents and governments over a year.

Balance of trade   The value of goods and services bought and sold in the world market.

Balance sheet   A statement of the assets and liabilities of any business entity, including financial institutions and the Federal Reserve System. Assets are what is owned; liabilities are what is owed.

Bank runs   Attempts by many of a bank's depositors to convert checkable and time deposits into currency out of fear for the bank's solvency.

Barter   The direct exchange of goods and services for other goods and services without the use of money.

Base year   The year that is chosen as the point of reference for comparison of prices in other years.

Bilateral monopoly   A market structure consisting of a monopolist and a monopsonist.

Black market   A market in which goods are traded at prices above their legal maximum prices or in which illegal goods are sold.

Bond   A legal claim against a firm, usually entitling the owner of the bond to receive a fixed annual coupon payment, plus a lump-sum payment at the bond's maturity date. Bonds are issued in return for funds lent to the firm.

Budget constraint   All of the possible combinations of goods that can be purchased (at fixed prices) with a specific budget.

Bureaucrats   Nonelected government officials who are responsible for the day-to-day operation of government and the observance of its regulations and laws.

Business fluctuations   The ups and downs in overall business activity, as evidenced by changes in national income, employment, and the price level.

Capital consumption allowance   Another name for depreciation, the amount that businesses would have to save in order to take care of the deterioration of machines and other equipment.

Capital gain   The positive difference between the purchase price and the sale price of an asset. If a share of stock is bought for $5 and then sold for $15, the capital gain is $10.

Capital goods   Producer durables; nonconsumable goods that firms use to make other goods.

Capitalism   An economic system in which individuals own productive resources; these individuals can use the resources in whatever manner they choose, subject to common protective legal restrictions.

Capital loss   The negative difference between the purchase price and the sale price of an asset.

Capture hypothesis   A theory of regulatory behavior that predicts that the regulators will eventually be captured by the special interests of the industry being regulated.

Cartel   An association of producers in an industry that agree to set common prices and output quotas to prevent competition.

Central bank   A banker's bank, usually an official institution that also serves as a country's treasury's bank. Central banks normally regulate commercial banks.

Certificate of deposit (CD)   A time deposit with a fixed maturity date offered by banks and other financial institutions.

Ceteris paribus **[KAY-ter-us PEAR-uh-bus] assumption**   The assumption that nothing changes except the factor or factors being studied.

Checkable deposits   Any deposits in a thrift institution or a commercial bank on which a check may be written.

Closed shop   A business enterprise in which employees must belong to the union before they can be hired and must remain in the union after they are hired.

Collateral   An asset pledged to guarantee the repayment of a loan.

Collective bargaining   Bargaining between the management of a company or of a group of companies and the management of a union or a group of unions for the purpose of setting a mutually agreeable contract on wages, fringe benefits, and working conditions for all employees in all the unions involved.

Collective decision making   How voters, politicians, and other interested parties act and how these actions influence nonmarket decisions.

Common property   Property that is owned by everyone and therefore by no one. Air and water are examples of common property resources.

Communism   In its purest form, an economic system in which the state has disappeared and individuals contribute to the economy according to their productivity and are given income according to their needs.

Comparable-worth doctrine   The belief that women should receive the same wages as men if the levels of skill and responsibility in their jobs are equivalent.

Comparative advantage The ability to produce a good or service at a lower opportunity cost compared to other producers.

Complements Two goods are complements if both are used together for consumption or enjoyment—for example, coffee and cream. The more you buy of one, the more you buy of the other. For complements, a change in the price of one causes an opposite shift in the demand for the other.

Concentration ratio The percentage of all sales contributed by the leading four or leading eight firms in an industry; sometimes called the *industry concentration ratio.*

Constant-cost industry An industry whose total output can be increased without an increase in long-run per-unit costs; an industry whose long-run supply curve is horizontal.

Constant dollars Dollars expressed in terms of real purchasing power using a particular year as the base or standard of comparison, in contrast to current dollars.

Constant returns to scale No change in long-run average costs when output increases.

Consumer optimum A choice of a set of goods and services that maximizes the level of satisfaction for each consumer, subject to limited income.

Consumer Price Index (CPI) A statistical measure of a weighted average of prices of a specified set of goods and services purchased by wage earners in urban areas.

Consumption The use of goods and services for personal satisfaction. *Can also be viewed as* spending on new goods and services out of a household's current income. Whatever is not consumed is saved. Consumption includes such things as buying food and going to a concert.

Consumption function The relationship between amount consumed and disposable income. A consumption function tells us how much people plan to consume at various levels of disposable income.

Consumption goods Goods bought by households to use up, such as food, clothing, and movies.

Contraction A business fluctuation during which the pace of national economic activity is slowing down.

Contractionary gap The gap that exists whenever the equilibrium level of real national income per year is less than the full-employment level as shown by the position of the long-run aggregate supply curve.

Cooperative game A game in which the players explicity collude to make themselves better off. As applied to firms, it involves companies colluding in order to make higher than competitive rates of return.

Corporation A legal entity that may conduct business in its own name just as an individual does; the owners of a corporation, called shareholders, own shares of the firm's profits and enjoy the protection of limited liability.

Cost-of-living adjustments (COLAs) Clauses in contracts that allow for increases in specified nominal values to take account of changes in the cost of living.

Cost-of-service regulation Regulation based on allowing prices to reflect only the actual cost of production and no monopoly profits.

Cost-push inflation Inflation caused by a continually decreasing short-run aggregate supply curve.

Craft unions Labor unions composed of workers who engage in a particular trade or skill, such as baking, carpentry, or plumbing.

Creative response Behavior on the part of a firm that allows it to comply with the letter of the law but violate the spirit, significantly lessening the law's effects.

Cross price elasticity of demand (E_{xy}) The percentage change in the demand for one good (holding its price constant) divided by the percentage change in the price of a related good.

Crowding-out effect The tendency of expansionary fiscal policy to cause a decrease in planned investment or planned consumption in the private sector; this decrease normally results from the rise in interest rates.

Crude quantity theory of money and prices The belief that changes in the money supply lead to proportional changes in the price level.

Cybernomics The application of economic analysis to human and technological activities related to the use of the Internet in all of its forms.

Cyclical unemployment Unemployment resulting from business recessions that occur when aggregate (total) demand is insufficient to create full employment.

Decreasing-cost industry An industry in which an increase in output leads to a reduction in long-run per-unit costs, such that the long-run industry supply curve slopes downward.

Deficiency payment A direct subsidy paid to farmers equal to the amount of a crop they produce multiplied by the difference between the target price for that good and its market price.

Deflation The situation in which the average of all prices of goods and services in an economy is falling.

Demand A schedule of how much of a good or service people will purchase at any price during a specified time period, other things being constant.

Demand curve A graphical representation of the demand schedule; a negatively sloped line showing the inverse relationship between the price and the quantity demanded (other things being equal).

Demand-pull inflation Inflation caused by increases in aggregate demand not matched by increases in aggregate supply.

Demerit good A good that has been deemed socially undesirable through the political process. Heroin is an example.

Dependent variable A variable whose value changes according to changes in the value of one or more independent variables.

Depository institutions Financial institutions that accept deposits from savers and lend those deposits out at interest.

Depreciation Reduction in the value of capital goods over a one-year period due to physical wear and tear and also to obsolescence; also called *capital consumption allowance. Can also be viewed as a decrease in the value of a currency in terms of other currencies.*

Depression An extremely severe recession.

Deregulation The elimination or phasing out of regulations on economic activity.

Derived demand Input factor demand derived from demand for the final product being produced.

Diminishing marginal utility The principle that as more of any good or service is consumed, its extra benefit declines. Otherwise stated, increases in total utility from the consumption of a good or service become smaller and smaller as more is consumed during a given time period.

Direct expenditure offsets
Actions on the part of the private sector in spending money that offset government fiscal policy actions. Any increase in government spending in an area that competes with the private sector will have some direct expenditure offset.

Direct relationship A relationship between two variables that is positive, meaning that an increase in one variable is associated with an increase in the other and a decrease in one variable is associated with a decrease in the other.

Dirty float A system between flexible and fixed exchange rates in which central banks occasionally enter foreign exchange markets to influence rates.

Discounting The method by which the present value of a future sum or a future stream of sums is obtained.

Discount rate The interest rate that the Federal Reserve charges for reserves that it lends to depository institutions. It is sometimes referred to as the rediscount rate or, in Canada and England, as the bank rate.

Discouraged workers Individuals who have stopped looking for a job because they are convinced that they will not find a suitable one. Typically, they become convinced after unsuccessfully searching for a job.

Diseconomies of scale Increases in long-run average costs that occur as output increases.

Disposable personal income (DPI) Personal income after personal income taxes have been paid.

Dissaving Negative saving; a situation in which spending exceeds income. Dissaving can occur when a household is able to borrow or use up existing owned assets.

Distributional coalitions Associations such as cartels, unions, and cooperatives that are formed to gain special government privileges in order to redistribute wealth by taking small amounts from each of many people and giving large amounts to each of only a few.

Distribution of income The way income is allocated among the population.

Dividends Portion of a corporation's profits paid to its owners (shareholders).

Division of labor The segregation of a resource into different specific tasks; for example, one automobile worker puts on bumpers, another doors, and so on.

Dominant strategies Strategies that always yield the highest benefit. Regardless of what other players do, a domi-nant strategy will yield the most benefit for the player using it.

Dumping Selling a good or a service abroad at a price below its cost of production or below the price charged in the home market.

Durable consumer goods Consumer goods that have a life span of more than three years.

E-commerce The use of the Internet in any manner that allows buyers and sellers to find each other. It can involve business selling directly to other businesses or business selling to retail customers. Both goods and services are involved in e-commerce.

Economic goods Goods that are scarce, for which the quantity demanded exceeds the quantity supplied at a zero price.

Economic growth Increases in per capita real GDP measured by its rate of change per year.

Economic profits Total revenues minus total opportunity costs of all inputs used, or the total of all implicit and explicit costs. *Can also be viewed as the difference between total revenues and the opportunity cost of all factors of production.*

Economic rent A payment for the use of any resource over and above its opportunity cost.

Economics The study of how people allocate their limited resources to satisfy their unlimited wants.

Economic system The institutional means through which resources are used to satisfy human wants.

Economies of scale Decreases in long-run average costs resulting from increases in output.

Effect time lag The time that elapses between the onset of policy and the results of that policy.

Efficiency The case in which a given level of inputs is used to produce the maximum output possible. Alternatively, the situation in which a given output is produced at minimum cost.

Efficiency wages Wages set above competitive levels to increase labor productivity and profits by enhancing the efficiency of the firm through lower turnover, ease of attracting higher-quality workers, and better efforts by workers.

Efficiency wage theory The hypothesis that the productivity of workers depends on the level of the real wage rate.

Effluent fee A charge to a polluter that gives the right to discharge into the air or water a certain amount of pollution. Also called a *pollution tax*.

Elastic demand A demand relationship in which a given percentage change in price will result in a larger percentage change in quantity demanded. Total expenditures are invariant to price changes in the unit's elastic portion of the demand curve.

Empirical Relying on real-world data in evaluating the usefulness of a model.

Endowments The various resources in an economy, including both physical resources and such human resources as ingenuity and management skills.

Entitlements Guaranteed benefits under a government program such as Social Security, Medicare, or Medicaid.

Entrepreneurship The factor of production involving human resources that perform the functions of raising capital, organizing, managing, assembling other factors of production, and making basic business policy decisions. The entrepreneur is a risk taker.

Entry deterrence strategy Any strategy undertaken by firms in an industry, either individually or together, with the intent or effect of raising the cost of entry into the industry by a new firm.

Equation of exchange The formula indicating that the number of monetary units times the number of times each unit is spent on final goods and services is identical to the price level times output (or nominal national income).

Equilibrium The situation when quantity supplied equals quantity demanded at a particular price.

Eurodollar deposits Deposits denominated in U.S. dollars but held in banks outside the United States, often in overseas branches of U.S. banks.

Excess reserves The difference between legal reserves and required reserves.

Exclusion principle The principle that no one can be excluded from the benefits of a public good, even if that person hasn't paid for it.

Expansion A business fluctuation in which overall business activity is rising at a more rapid rate than previously or at a more rapid rate than the overall historical trend for the nation.

Expansionary gap The gap that exists whenever the equilibrium level of real national income per year is greater than the full-employment level as shown by the position of the long-run aggregate supply curve.

Expenditure approach A way of computing national income by adding up the dollar value at current market prices of all final goods and services.

Explicit costs Costs that business managers must take account of because they must be paid; examples are wages, taxes, and rent.

Externality A consequence of an economic activity that spills over to affect third parties. Pollution is an externality. *Can also be viewed as* a situation in which a private cost diverges from a social cost; a situation in which the costs of an action are not fully borne by the two parties engaged in exchange or by an individual engaging in a scarce-resource-using activity. (Also applies to benefits.)

Featherbedding Any practice that forces employers to use more labor than they would otherwise or to use existing labor in an inefficient manner.

The Fed The Federal Reserve System; the central bank of the United States.

Federal Deposit Insurance Corporation (FDIC) A government agency that insures the deposits held in member banks; all members of the Fed and other banks that qualify can join.

Federal funds market A private market (made up mostly of banks) in which banks can borrow reserves from other banks that want to lend them. Federal funds are usually lent for overnight use.

Federal funds rate The interest rate that depository institutions pay to borrow reserves in the interbank federal funds market.

Fiduciary monetary system A system in which currency is issued by the government and its value is based uniquely on the public's faith that the currency represents command over goods and services.

Final goods and services Goods and services that are at their final stage of production and will not be transformed into yet other goods or services. For example, wheat is normally not a final good because usually it is used to make bread, which is a final good.

Financial capital Money used to purchase capital goods such as buildings and equipment.

Financial intermediaries Institutions that transfer funds between ultimate lenders (savers) and ultimate borrowers.

Financial intermediation The process by which financial institutions accept savings from businesses, households, and governments and lend the savings to other businesses, households, and governments.

Firm A business organization that employs resources to produce goods or services for profit. A firm normally owns and operates at least one plant in order to produce.

Fiscal policy The discretionary changing of government expenditures and/or taxes in order to achieve national economic goals, such as high employment with price stability.

Fixed costs Costs that do not vary with output. Fixed costs include such things as rent on a building. These costs are fixed for a certain period of time; in the long run, they are variable.

Fixed investment   Purchases by businesses of newly produced producer durables, or capital goods, such as production machinery and office equipment.

Flexible exchange rates   Exchange rates that are allowed to fluctuate in the open market in response to changes in supply and demand. Sometimes called *floating exchange rates*.

Flow   A quantity measured per unit of time; something that occurs over time, such as the income you make per week or per year or the number of individuals who are fired every month.

Foreign exchange market   The market for buying and selling foreign currencies.

Foreign exchange rate   The price of one currency in terms of another.

45-degree reference line   The line along which planned real expenditures equal real national income per year.

Fractional reserve banking   A system in which depository institutions hold reserves that are less than the amount of total deposits.

Free-rider problem   A problem that arises when individuals presume that others will pay for public goods so that, individually, they can escape paying for their portion without causing a reduction in production.

Frictional unemployment   Unemployment due to the fact that workers must search for appropriate job offers. This takes time, and so they remain temporarily ("frictionally") unemployed.

Full employment   As presented by the Council of Economic Advisers, an arbitrary level of unemployment that corresponds to "normal" friction in the labor market. In 1986, the council declared that 6.5 percent unemployment was full employment. Today, it is around 5.5 percent.

Game theory   A way of describing the various possible outcomes in any situation involving two or more interacting individuals when those individuals are aware of the interactive nature of their situation and plan accordingly.

The plans made by these individuals are known as *game strategies*.

GDP deflator   A price index measuring the changes in prices of all new goods and services produced in the economy.

General Agreement on Tariffs and Trade (GATT)   An international agreement established in 1947 to further world trade by reducing barriers and tariffs.

Gold standard   An international monetary system in which nations fix their exchange rates in terms of gold. All currencies are fixed in terms of all others, and any balance of payments deficits or surpluses can be made up by shipments of gold.

Goods   All things from which individuals derive satisfaction or happiness.

Government, or **political, goods**   Goods (and services) provided by the public sector; they can be either private or public goods.

Gross domestic income (GDI)   The sum of all income—wages, interest, rent, and profits—paid to the four factors of production.

Gross domestic product (GDP)   The total market value of all final goods and services produced by factors of production located within a nation's borders.

Gross private domestic investment   The creation of capital goods, such as factories and machines, that can yield production and hence consumption in the future. Also included in this definition are changes in business inventories and repairs made to machines or buildings.

Gross public debt   All federal government debt irrespective of who owns it.

Horizontal merger   The joining of firms that are producing or selling a similar product.

Human capital   The accumulated training and education of workers.

Hyperinflation   Extremely rapid rise of the average of all prices in an economy.

Implicit costs   Expenses that managers do not have to pay out of pocket and hence do not normally explicitly calculate, such as the opportunity cost of factors of production that are owned; examples are owner-provided capital and owner-provided labor.

Import quota   A physical supply restriction on imports of a particular good, such as sugar. Foreign exporters are unable to sell in the United States more than the quantity specified in the import quota.

Incentive-compatible contract   A loan contract under which a significant amount of the borrower's assets are at risk, providing an incentive for the borrower to look after the lender's interests.

Incentives   Rewards for engaging in a particular activity.

Incentive structure   The motivational rewards and costs that individuals face in any given situation. Each economic system has its own incentive structure. The incentive structure is different under a system of private property than under a system of government-owned property, for example. *Can also be viewed as* the system of rewards and punishments individuals face with respect to their own actions.

Income approach   A way of measuring national income by adding up all components of national income, including wages, interest, rent, and profits.

Income-consumption curve   The set of optimum consumption points that would occur if income were increased, relative prices remaining constant.

Income elasticity of demand (E_i)   The percentage change in demand for any good, holding its price constant, divided by the percentage change in income; the responsiveness of the demand to changes in income, holding the good's relative price constant.

Income in kind   Income received in the form of goods and services, such as housing or medical care; to be contrasted with money income, which is simply income in dollars, or general purchasing power, that can be used to buy *any* goods and services.

Income velocity of money The number of times per year a dollar is spent on final goods and services; equal to GDP divided by the money supply.

Increasing-cost industry An industry in which an increase in industry output is accompanied by an increase in long-run per-unit costs, such that the long-run industry supply curve slopes upward.

Independent variable A variable whose value is determined independently of, or outside, the equation under study.

Indifference curve A curve composed of a set of consumption alternatives, each of which yields the same total amount of satisfaction.

Indirect business taxes All business taxes except the tax on corporate profits. Indirect business taxes include sales and business property taxes.

Industrial unions Labor unions that consist of workers from a particular industry, such as automobile manufacturing or steel manufacturing.

Industry supply curve The locus of points showing the minimum prices at which given quantities will be forthcoming; also called the *market supply curve.*

Inefficient point Any point below the production possibilities curve at which resources are being used inefficiently.

Inelastic demand A demand relationship in which a given percentage change in price will result in a less than proportionate percentage change in the quantity demanded. Total expenditures and price are directly related in the inelastic region of the demand curve.

Infant industry argument The contention that tariffs should be imposed to protect from import competition an industry that is trying to get started. Presumably, after the industry becomes technologically efficient, the tariff can be lifted.

Inferior goods Goods for which demand falls as income rises.

Inflation The situation in which the average of all prices of goods and services in an economy is rising.

Innovation Transforming an invention into something that is useful to humans.

Inside information Information that is not available to the general public about what is happening in a corporation.

Insider-outsider theory A theory of labor markets in which workers who are already employed have an influence on wage bargaining in such a way that outsiders who are willing to work for lower real wages cannot get a job.

Intelligent shopping agents Computer programs that an individual or business user of the Internet can instruct to carry out a specific task, such as looking for the lowest-priced car of a particular make and model. The agent then searches the Internet (usually just the World Wide Web) and may even purchase the product when the best price has been found.

Interest The payment for current rather than future command over resources; the cost of obtaining credit. Also, the return paid to owners of capital.

Interest group Any group that seeks to cause government to change spending in a way that will benefit the group's members or to undertake any other action that will improve their lot. Also called a *special-interest group.*

Interest rate effect One of the reasons that the aggregate demand curve slopes down is because higher price levels indirectly increase the interest rate, which in turn causes businesses and consumers to reduce desired spending due to the higher cost of borrowing.

Intermediate goods Goods used up entirely in the production of final goods.

International Monetary Fund (IMF) An institution set up to manage the international monetary system, established in 1945 under the Bretton Woods Agreement Act, which established fixed exchange rates for the world's currencies.

Inventory investment Changes in the stocks of finished goods and goods in process, as well as changes in the raw materials that businesses keep on hand. Whenever inventories are decreasing, inventory investment is negative; whenever they are increasing, inventory investment is positive.

Inverse relationship A relationship between two variables that is negative, meaning that an increase in one variable is associated with a decrease in the other and a decrease in one variable is associated with an increase in the other.

Investment Any use of today's resources to expand tomorrow's production or consumption. *Can also be viewed as* the spending by businesses on things such as machines and buildings, which can be used to produce goods and services in the future. The investment part of total income is the portion that will be used in the process of producing goods in the future.

Job leaver An individual in the labor force who quits voluntarily.

Job loser An individual in the labor force who was employed and whose employment was involuntarily terminated or who was laid off.

Jurisdictional dispute A dispute involving two or more unions over which should have control of a particular jurisdiction, such as a particular craft or skill or a particular firm or industry.

Keynesian short-run aggregate supply curve The horizontal portion of the aggregate supply curve in which there is unemployment and unused capacity in the economy.

Labor Productive contributions of humans who work, involving both mental and physical activities.

Labor force Individuals aged 16 years or older who either have jobs or are looking and available for jobs; the number of employed plus the number of unemployed.

Labor force participation rate
The percentage of noninstitutionalized working-age individuals who are employed or seeking employment.

Labor market signaling The process by which a potential worker's acquisition of credentials, such as a degree, is used by the employer to predict future productivity.

Labor productivity Total real domestic output (real GDP) divided by the number of workers (output per worker).

Labor unions Worker organizations that seek to secure economic improvements for their members; they also seek to improve the safety, health, and other benefits (such as job security) of their members.

Laissez-faire French for "leave [it] alone"; applied to an economic system in which the government minimizes its interference with economy.

Land The natural resources that are available from nature. Land as a resource includes location, original fertility and mineral deposits, topography, climate, water, and vegetation.

Law of demand The observation that there is a negative, or inverse, relationship between the price of any good or service and the quantity demanded, holding other factors constant.

Law of diminishing (marginal) returns The observation that after some point, successive equal-sized increases in a variable factor of production, such as labor, added to fixed factors of production, will result in smaller increases in output.

Law of increasing relative cost The observation that the opportunity cost of additional units of a good generally increases as society attempts to produce more of that good. This accounts for the bowed-out shape of the production possibilities curve.

Law of supply The observation that the higher the price of a good, the more of that good sellers will make

available over a specified time period, other things being equal.

Least-cost combination The level of input use that produces a given level of output at minimum cost.

Legal reserves Reserves that depository institutions are allowed by law to claim as reserves—for example, deposits held at Federal Reserve district banks and vault cash.

Lemons problem The situation in which consumers, who do not know details about the quality of a product, are willing to pay no more than the price of a low-quality product, even if a higher-quality product at a higher price exists.

Liabilities Amounts owed; the legal claims against a business or household by nonowners.

Limited liability A legal concept whereby the responsibility, or liability, of the owners of a corporation is limited to the value of the shares in the firm that they own.

Limit-pricing model A model that hypothesizes that a group of colluding sellers will set the highest common price that they believe they can charge without new firms seeking to enter that industry in search of relatively high profits.

Liquidity The degree to which an asset can be acquired or disposed of without much danger of any intervening loss in *nominal* value and with small transaction costs. Money is the most liquid asset.

Liquidity approach A method of measuring the money supply by looking at money as a temporary store of value.

Logrolling The practice of exchanging political favors by elected representatives. Typically, one elected official agrees to vote for the policy of another official in exchange for the vote of the latter in favor of the former's desired policy.

Long run The time period in which all factors of production can be varied.

Long-run aggregate supply curve A vertical line representing real output of goods and services based on full information and after full adjustment has occurred. *Can also be viewed as* representing the real output of the economy under conditions of full employment—the full-employment level of real GDP.

Long-run average cost curve The locus of points representing the minimum unit cost of producing any given rate of output, given current technology and resource prices.

Long-run industry supply curve A market supply curve showing the relationship between price and quantities forthcoming after firms have been allowed the time to enter into or exit from an industry, depending on whether there have been positive or negative economic profits.

Lorenz curve A geometric representation of the distribution of income. A Lorenz curve that is perfectly straight represents perfect income equality. The more bowed a Lorenz curve, the more unequally income is distributed.

Lump-sum tax A tax that does not depend on income or the circumstances of the taxpayer. An example is a $1,000 tax that every family must pay, irrespective of its economic situation.

M1 The money supply, taken as the total value of currency plus checkable deposits plus traveler's checks not issued by banks.

M2 M1 plus (1) savings and small-denomination time deposits at all depository institutions, (2) overnight repurchase agreements at commercial banks, (3) overnight Eurodollars held by U.S. residents other than banks at Caribbean branches of member banks, (4) balances in retail money market mutual funds, and (5) money market deposit accounts (MMDAs).

Macroeconomics The study of the behavior of the economy as a whole, including such economywide phenomena as changes in unemployment, the general price level, and national income.

Majority rule A collective decision-making system in which group decisions are made on the basis of 50.1 percent of the vote. In other words, whatever more than half of the electorate votes for, the entire electorate has to accept.

Marginal cost pricing A system of pricing in which the price charged is equal to the opportunity cost to society of producing one more unit of the good or service in question. The opportunity cost is the marginal cost to society.

Marginal costs The change in total costs due to a one-unit change in production rate.

Marginal factor cost (MFC) The cost of using an additional unit of an input. For example, if a firm can hire all the workers it wants at the going wage rate, the marginal factor cost of labor is the wage rate.

Marginal physical product The physical output that is due to the addition of one more unit of a variable factor of production; the change in total product occurring when a variable input is increased and all other inputs are held constant; also called *marginal productivity* or *marginal return*.

Marginal physical product (MPP) of labor The change in output resulting from the addition of one more worker. The MPP of the worker equals the change in total output accounted for by hiring the worker, holding all other factors of production constant.

Marginal propensity to consume (MPC) The ratio of the change in consumption to the change in disposable income. A marginal propensity to consume of .8 tells us that an additional $100 in take-home pay will lead to an additional $80 consumed.

Marginal propensity to save (MPS) The ratio of the change in saving to the change in disposable income. A marginal propensity to save of .2 indicates that out of an additional $100 in take-home pay, $20 will be saved. Whatever is not saved is consumed. The marginal propensity to save plus the marginal propensity to save plus the marginal propensity

to consume must always equal 1, by definition.

Marginal revenue The change in total revenues resulting from a change in output (and sale) of one unit of the product in question.

Marginal revenue product (MRP) The marginal physical product (MPP) times marginal revenue. The MRP gives the additional revenue obtained from a one-unit change in labor input.

Marginal tax rate The change in the tax payment divided by the change in income, or the percentage of additional dollars that must be paid in taxes. The marginal tax rate is applied to the highest tax bracket of taxable income reached.

Marginal utility The change in total utility due to a one-unit change in the quantity of a good or service consumed.

Market All of the arrangements that individuals have for exchanging with one another. Thus we can speak of the labor market, the automobile market, and the credit market.

Market clearing, or **equilibrium, price** The price that clears the market, at which quantity demanded equals quantity supplied; the price where the demand curve intersects the supply curve.

Market demand The demand of all consumers in the marketplace for a particular good or service. The summing at each price of the quantity demanded by each individual.

Market failure A situation in which an unrestrained market economy leads to too few or too many resources going to a specific economic activity.

Market share test The percentage of a market that a particular firm controls, used as the primary measure of monopoly power.

Medical savings accounts (MSAs) A tax-exempt health care account to which individuals would pay into on a regular basis and from which medical care expenses could be paid.

Medium of exchange Any asset that sellers will accept as payment.

Merit good A good that has been deemed socially desirable through the political process. Museums are an example.

Microeconomics The study of decision making undertaken by individuals (or households) and by firms.

Minimum efficient scale (MES) The lowest rate of output per unit time at which long-run average costs for a particular firm are at a minimum.

Minimum wage A wage floor, legislated by government, setting the lowest hourly rate that firms may legally pay workers.

Mixed economy An economic system in which decisions about how resources should be used are made partly by the private sector and partly by the government, or the public sector.

Models, or **theories** Simplified representations of the real world used as the basis for predictions or explanations.

Monetarists Macroeconomists who believe that inflation is always caused by excessive monetary growth and that changes in the money supply directly affect aggregate demand both directly and indirectly.

Monetary rule A monetary policy that incorporates a rule specifying the annual rate of growth of some monetary aggregate.

Money Any medium that is universally accepted in an economy both by sellers of goods and services as payment for those goods and services and by creditors as payment for debts.

Money illusion Reacting to changes in money prices rather than relative prices. If a worker whose wages double when the price level also doubles thinks he or she is better off, the worker is suffering from money illusion.

Money market deposit accounts (MMDAs) Accounts issued by banks yielding a market rate of interest with a minimum balance requirement and a limit on transactions. They have no minimum maturity.

Money market mutual funds   Funds of investment companies that obtain funds from the public that are held in common and used to acquire short-maturity credit instruments, such as certificates of deposit and securities sold by the U.S. government.

Money multiplier   The reciprocal of the required reserve ratio, assuming no leakages into currency and no excess reserves. It is equal to 1 divided by the required reserve ratio.

Money multiplier process   The process by which an injection of new money into the banking system leads to a multiple expansion in the total money supply.

Money price   The price that we observe today, expressed in today's dollars. Also called the *absolute, nominal,* or *current price.*

Money supply   The amount of money in circulation.

Monopolist   A single supplier that comprises its entire industry for a good or service for which there is no close substitute.

Monopolistic competition   A market situation in which a large number of firms produce similar but not identical products. Entry into the industry is relatively easy.

Monopolization   The possession of monopoly power in the relevant market and the willful acquisition or maintenance of that power, as distinguished from growth or development as a consequence of a superior product, business acumen, or historical accident.

Monopoly   A firm that has great control over the price of a good. In the extreme case, a monopoly is the only seller of a good or service.

Monopsonist   A single buyer.

Monopsonistic exploitation   Exploitation due to monopsony power. It

leads to a price for the variable input that is less than its marginal revenue product. Monopsonistic exploitation is the difference between marginal revenue product and the wage rate.

Moral hazard   A situation in which, after a transaction has taken place, one of the parties to the transaction has an incentive to engage in behavior that will be undesirable from the other party's point of view. *Can also be viewed as* a problem that occurs because of asymmetric information *after* a transaction occurs. In financial markets, a person to whom money has been lent may indulge in more risky behavior, thereby increasing the probability of default on the debt.

Multiplier   The ratio of the change in the equilibrium level of real national income to the change in autonomous expenditures; the number by which a change in autonomous investment or autonomous consumption, for example, is multiplied to get the change in the equilibrium level of real national income.

National income accounting   A measurement system used to estimate national income and its components; one approach to measuring an economy's aggregate performance.

National income (NI)   The total of all factor payments to resource owners. It can be obtained by subtracting indirect business taxes from NDP.

Natural monopoly   A monopoly that arises from the peculiar production characteristics in an industry. It usually arises when there are large economies of scale relative to the industry's demand such that one firm can produce at a lower average cost than can be achieved by multiple firms.

Natural rate of unemployment   The rate of unemployment that is estimated to prevail in long-run macroeconomic equilibrium, when all workers and employers have fully adjusted to any changes in the economy.

Near monies   Assets that are almost money. They have a high degree of liq-

uidity; they can be easily converted into money without loss in value. Time deposits and short-term U.S. government securities are examples.

Negative-sum game   A game in which all players are worse off at the end of the game.

Net domestic product (NDP)   GDP minus depreciation.

Net investment   Gross private domestic investment minus an estimate of the wear and tear on the existing capital stock. Net investment therefore measures the change in capital stock over a one-year period.

Net public debt   Gross public debt minus all government interagency borrowing.

Net worth   The difference between assets and liabilities.

New classical model   A modern version of the classical model in which wages and prices are flexible, there is pure competition in all markets, and the rational expectations hypothesis is assumed to be working.

New entrant   An individual who has never held a full-time job lasting two weeks or longer but is now in the labor force.

New growth theory   A relatively modern theory of economic growth that examines the factors that determine why technology, research, innovation, and the like are undertaken and how they interact.

New Keynesian economics   Economic models based on the idea that demand creates its own supply as a result of various possible government fiscal and monetary coordination failures.

Nominal rate of interest   The market rate of interest expressed in today's dollars.

Nominal values   The values of variables such as GDP and investment expressed in current dollars, also called *money values;* measurement in terms of the actual market prices at which goods are sold.

Nonaccelerating inflation rate of unemployment (NAIRU) The rate of unemployment below which the rate of inflation tends to rise and above which the rate of inflation tends to fall.

Noncooperative game A game in which the players neither negotiate nor collude in any way. As applied to firms in an industry, this is the common situation in which there are relatively few firms and each has some ability to change price.

Nondurable consumer goods Consumer goods that are used up within three years.

Nonincome expense items The total of indirect business taxes and depreciation.

Nonprice rationing devices All methods used to ration scarce goods that are price controlled. Whenever the price system is not allowed to work, nonprice rationing devices will evolve to ration the affected goods and services.

Normal goods Goods for which demand rises as income rises. Most goods are considered normal.

Normal rate of return The amount that must be paid to an investor to induce investment in a business; also known as the *opportunity cost of capital*.

Normative economics Analysis involving value judgments about economic policies; relates to whether things are good or bad. A statement of *what ought to be*.

Number line A line that can be divided into segments of equal length, each associated with a number.

Oligopoly A market situation in which there are very few sellers. Each seller knows that the other sellers will react to its changes in prices and quantities.

Open economy effect One of the reasons that the aggregate demand curve slopes downward is because higher price levels result in foreigners' desiring to buy fewer American-made goods while Americans now desire more foreign-made

goods, thereby reducing net exports, which is equivalent to a reduction in the amount of real goods and services purchased in the United States.

Open market operations The purchase and sale of existing U.S. government securities (such as bonds) in the open private market by the Federal Reserve System.

Opportunistic behavior Actions that ignore the possible long-run benefits of cooperation and focus solely on short-run gains.

Opportunity cost The highest-valued, next-best alternative that must be sacrificed to attain something or to satisfy a want.

Opportunity cost of capital The normal rate of return, or the available return on the next-best alternative investment. Economists consider this a cost of production, and it is included in our cost examples.

Optimal quantity of pollution The level of pollution for which the marginal benefit of one additional unit of clean air just equals the marginal cost of that additional unit of clean air.

Origin The intersection of the y axis and the x axis in a graph.

Partnership A business owned by two or more co-owners, or partners, who share the responsibilities and the profits of the firm and are individually liable for all of the debts of the partnership.

Par value The legally established value of the monetary unit of one country in terms of that of another.

Passive (nondiscretionary) policy-making Policymaking that is carried out in response to a rule. It is therefore not in response to an actual or potential change in overall economic activity.

Patent A government protection that gives an inventor the exclusive right to make, use, or sell an invention for a limited period of time (currently, 17 years).

Payoff matrix A matrix of outcomes, or consequences, of the strategies available to the players in a game.

Perfect competition A market structure in which the decisions of individual buyers and sellers have no effect on market price.

Perfectly competitive firm A firm that is such a small part of the total industry that it cannot affect the price of the product it sells.

Perfectly elastic demand A demand that has the characteristic that even the slightest increase in price will lead to zero quantity demanded.

Perfectly elastic supply A supply characterized by a reduction in quantity supplied to zero when there is the slightest decrease in price.

Perfectly inelastic demand A demand that exhibits zero responsiveness to price changes; no matter what the price is, the quantity demanded remains the same.

Perfectly inelastic supply A supply for which quantity supplied remains constant, no matter what happens to price.

Personal income (PI) The amount of income that households actually receive before they pay personal income taxes.

Phillips curve A curve showing the relationship between unemployment and changes in wages or prices. It was long thought to reflect a trade-off between unemployment and inflation.

Physical capital All manufactured resources, including buildings, equipment, machines, and improvements to land that is used for production.

Planning curve The long-run average cost curve.

Planning horizon The long run, during which all inputs are variable.

Plant size The physical size of the factories that a firm owns and operates to produce its output. Plant size can be defined by square footage, maximum physical capacity, and other physical measures.

Policy irrelevance proposition   The new classical and rational expectations conclusion that policy actions have no real effects in the short run if the policy actions are anticipated and none in the long run even if the policy actions are unanticipated.

Positive economics   Analysis that is strictly limited to making either purely descriptive statements or scientific predictions; for example, "If A, then B." A statement of *what is*.

Positive-sum game   A game in which players as a group are better off at the end of the game.

Precautionary demand   Holding money to meet unplanned expenditures and emergencies.

Present value   The value of a future amount expressed in today's dollars; the most that someone would pay today to receive a certain sum at some point in the future.

Price ceiling   A legal maximum price that may be charged for a particular good or service.

Price-consumption curve   The set of consumer optimum combinations of two goods that the consumer would choose as the price of one good changes, while money income and the price of the other good remain constant.

Price controls
Government-mandated minimum or maximum prices that may be charged for goods and services.

Price differentiation   Establishing different prices for similar products to reflect differences in marginal cost in providing those commodities to different groups of buyers.

Price discrimination   Selling a given product at more than one price, with the price difference being unrelated to differences in cost.

Price elasticity of demand (E_p)
The responsiveness of the quantity de-

manded of a commodity to changes in its price; defined as the percentage change in quantity demanded divided by the percentage change in price.

Price elasticity of supply (E_s)   The responsiveness of the quantity supplied of a commodity to a change in its price; the percentage change in quantity supplied divided by the percentage change in price.

Price floor   A legal minimum price below which a good or service may not be sold. Legal minimum wages are an example.

Price index   The cost of today's market basket of goods expressed as a percentage of the cost of the same market basket during a base year.

Price leadership   A practice in many oligopolistic industries in which the largest firm publishes its price list ahead of its competitors, who then match those announced prices. Also called *parallel pricing*.

Price searcher   A firm that must determine the price-output combination that maximizes profit because it faces a downward-sloping demand curve.

Price system   An economic system in which relative prices are constantly changing to reflect changes in supply and demand for different commodities. The prices of those commodities are signals to everyone within the system as to what is relatively scarce and what is relatively abundant.

Price taker   A competitive firm that must take the price of its product as given because the firm cannot influence its price.

Price war   A pricing campaign designed to drive competing firms out of a market by repeatedly cutting prices.

Primary market   A financial market in which newly issued securities are bought and sold.

Principal-agent problem   The conflict of interest that occurs when agents—managers of firms—pursue

their own objectives to the detriment of the goals of the firms' principals, or owners.

Principle of rival consumption   The recognition that individuals are rivals in consuming private goods because one person's consumption reduces the amount available for others to consume.

Principle of substitution   The principle that consumers and producers shift away from goods and resources that become relatively higher priced in favor of goods and resources that are now relatively lower priced.

Prisoners' dilemma   A famous strategic game in which two prisoners have a choice between confessing and not confessing to a crime. If neither confesses, they serve a minimum sentence. If both confess, they serve a maximum sentence. If one confesses and the other doesn't, the one who confesses goes free. The dominant strategy is always to confess.

Private costs   Costs borne solely by the individuals who incur them. Also called *internal costs*.

Private goods   Goods that can be consumed by only one individual at a time. Private goods are subject to the principle of rival consumption.

Private property rights   Exclusive rights of ownership that allow the use, transfer, and exchange of property.

Privatization   The sale or transfer of state-owned property and businesses to the private sector, in part or in whole. Also refers to *contracting out*—letting private business take over government-provided services such as trash collection.

Producer durables, or **capital goods**   Durable goods having an expected service life of more than three years that are used by businesses to produce other goods and services.

Producer Price Index (PPI)   A statistical measure of a weighted average of prices of commodities that firms purchase from other firms.

Product differentiation The distinguishing of products by brand name, color, and other minor attributes. Product differentiation occurs in other than perfectly competitive markets in which products are, in theory, homogeneous, such as wheat or corn.

Production Any activity that results in the conversion of resources into products that can be used in consumption.

Production function The relationship between inputs and output. A production function is a technological, not an economic, relationship.

Production possibilities curve (PPC) A curve representing all possible combinations of total output that could be produced assuming (1) a fixed amount of productive resources of a given quality and (2) the efficient use of those resources.

Profit-maximizing rate of production The rate of production that maximizes total profits, or the difference between total revenues and total costs; also, the rate of production at which marginal revenue equals marginal cost.

Progressive taxation A tax system in which as income increases, a higher percentage of the additional income is taxed. The marginal tax rate exceeds the average tax rate as income rises.

Property rights The rights of an owner to use and to exchange property.

Proportional rule A decision-making system in which actions are based on the proportion of the "votes" cast and are in proportion to them. In a market system, if 10 percent of the "dollar votes" are cast for blue cars, 10 percent of the output will be blue cars.

Proportional taxation A tax system in which regardless of an individual's income, the tax bill comprises exactly the same proportion. Also called a *flat-rate tax.*

Proprietorship A business owned by one individual who makes the business decisions, receives all the profits, and is legally responsible for all the debts of the firm.

Protocol The data formatting system that permits computers to access each other and communicate.

Public debt The total value of all outstanding federal government securities.

Public goods Goods to which the principle of rival consumption does not apply; they can be jointly consumed by many individuals simultaneously at no additional cost and with no reduction in quality or quantity.

Purchasing power The value of money for buying goods and services. If your money income stays the same but the price of one good that you are buying goes up, your effective purchasing power falls, and vice versa.

Purchasing power parity Adjustment in exchange rate conversions that takes into account differences in the true cost of living across countries.

Quota system A government-imposed restriction on the quantity of a specific good that another country is allowed to sell in the United States. In other words, quotas are restrictions on imports. These restrictions are usually applied to one or several specific countries.

Random walk theory The theory there are no predictable trends in security prices that can be used to "get rich quick."

Rate of discount The rate of interest used to discount future sums back to present value.

Rate-of-return regulation Regulation that seeks to keep the rate of return in the industry at a competitive level by not allowing excessive prices to be charged.

Rational expectations hypothesis A theory stating that people combine the effects of past policy changes on important economic variables with their own judgment about the future effects of current and future policy changes.

Rationality assumption The assumption that people do not intentionally make decisions that would leave them worse off.

Reaction function The manner in which one oligopolist reacts to a change in price, output, or quality made by another oligopolist in the industry.

Real-balance effect The change in the real value of money balances when the price level changes, all other things held constant. Also called the *wealth effect.*

Real business cycle theory An extension and modification of the theories of the new classical economists of the 1970s and 1980s, in which money is neutral and only real, supply-side factors matter in influencing labor employment and real output.

Real-income effect The change in people's purchasing power that occurs when, other things being constant, the price of one good that they purchase changes. When that price goes up, real income, or purchasing power, falls, and when that price goes down, real income increases.

Real rate of interest The nominal rate of interest minus the anticipated rate of inflation.

Real values Measurement of economic values after adjustments have been made for changes in the average of prices between years.

Recession A period of time during which the rate of growth of business activity is consistently less than its long-term trend or is negative.

Recognition time lag The time required to gather information about the current state of the economy.

Recycling The reuse of raw materials derived from manufactured products.

Reentrant An individual who used to work full time but left the labor force and has now reentered it looking for a job.

Regressive taxation A tax system in which as more dollars are earned, the percentage of tax paid on them falls. The marginal tax rate is less than the average tax rate as income rises.

Reinvestment Profits (or depreciation reserves) used to purchase new capital equipment.

Relative price The price of one commodity divided by the price of another commodity; the number of units of one commodity that must be sacrificed to purchase one unit of another commodity.

Rent control The placement of price ceilings on rents in particular cities.

Rent seeking The use of resources in an attempt to get government to bestow a benefit on an interest group.

Repricing, or menu, cost of inflation The cost associated with recalculating prices and printing new price lists when there is inflation.

Repurchase agreement (REPO, or RP) An agreement made by a bank to sell Treasury or federal agency securities to its customers, coupled with an agreement to repurchase them at a price that includes accumulated interest.

Required reserve ratio The percentage of total deposits that the Fed requires depository institutions to hold in the form of vault cash or deposits with the Fed.

Required reserves The value of reserves that a depository institution must hold in the form of vault cash or deposits with the Fed.

Reserves In the U.S. Federal Reserve System, deposits held by Federal Reserve district banks for depository institutions, plus depository institutions' vault cash.

Resource allocation The assignment of resources to specific uses by determining what will be produced, how it will be produced, and for whom it will be produced.

Resources Things used to produce other things to satisfy people's wants.

Retained earnings Earnings that a corporation saves, or retains, for investment in other productive activities; earnings that are not distributed to stockholders.

Ricardian equivalence theorem The proposition that an increase in the government budget deficit has no effect on aggregate demand.

Right-to-work laws Laws that make it illegal to require union membership as a condition of continuing employment in a particular firm.

Saving The act of not consuming all of one's current income. Whatever is not consumed out of spendable income is, by definition, saved. *Saving* is an action measured over time (a flow), whereas *savings* are a stock, an accumulation resulting from the act of saving in the past.

Savings deposits Interest-earning funds that can be withdrawn at any time without payment of a penalty.

Say's law A dictum of economist J. B. Say that supply creates its own demand; producing goods and services generates the means and the willingness to purchase other goods and services.

Scarcity A situation in which the ingredients for producing the things that people desire are insufficient to satisfy all wants.

Seasonal unemployment Unemployment resulting from the seasonal pattern of work in specific industries. It is usually due to seasonal fluctuations in demand or to changing weather conditions, rendering work difficult, if not impossible, as in the agriculture, construction, and tourist industries.

Secondary boycott A boycott of companies or products sold by companies that are dealing with a company being struck.

Secondary market A financial market in which previously issued securities are bought and sold.

Separation of ownership and control The situation that exists in corporations in which the owners (shareholders) are not the people who control the operation of the corporation (managers). The goals of these two groups are often different.

Services Mental or physical labor or help purchased by consumers. Examples are the assistance of doctors, lawyers, dentists, repair personnel, housecleaners, educators, retailers, and wholesalers; things purchased or used by consumers that do not have physical characteristics.

Share of stock A legal claim to a share of a corporation's future profits; if it is *common stock,* it incorporates certain voting rights regarding major policy decisions of the corporation; if it is *preferred stock,* its owners are accorded preferential treatment in the payment of dividends.

Share-the-gains, share-the-pains theory A theory of regulatory behavior in which the regulators must take account of the demands of three groups: legislators, who established and who oversee the regulatory agency; members of the regulated industry; and consumers of the regulated industry's products or services.

Shortage A situation in which quantity demanded is greater than quantity supplied at a price below the market clearing price.

Short run The time period when at least one input, such as plant size, cannot be changed.

Short-run aggregate supply curve The relationship between aggregate supply and the price level in the short run, all other things held constant; the curve is normally positively sloped.

Short-run break-even price The price at which a firm's total revenues equal its total costs. At the break-even price, the firm is just making a normal rate of return on its capital investment. (It is covering its explicit and implicit costs.)

Short-run shutdown price The price that just covers average variable costs. It occurs just below the intersection of the marginal cost curve and the average variable cost curve.

Signals Compact ways of conveying to economic decision makers information needed to make decisions. A true signal not only conveys information but also provides the incentive to react appropriately. Economic profits and economic losses are such signals.

Slope The change in the *y* value divided by the corresponding change in the *x* value of a curve; the "incline" of the curve.

Small-menu cost theory A hypothesis that it is costly for firms to change prices in response to demand changes because of the cost of renegotiating contracts, printing price lists, and so on.

Social costs The full costs borne by society whenever a resource use occurs. Social costs can be measured by adding private, or internal, costs to external costs.

Socialism An economic system in which the state owns the major share of productive resources except labor. Socialism also usually involves the redistribution of income.

Special drawing rights (SDRs) Reserve assets created by the International Monetary Fund that countries can use to settle international payments.

Specialization The division of productive activities among persons and regions so that no one individual or one area is totally self-sufficient. An individual may specialize, for example, in law or medicine. A nation may specialize in the production of coffee, computers, or cameras.

Standard of deferred payment A property of an asset that makes it desirable for use as a means of settling debts maturing in the future; an essential property of money.

Stock The quantity of something, measured at a given point in time—for example, an inventory of goods or a bank account. Stocks are defined independently of time, although they are assessed at a point in time.

Store of value The ability to hold value over time; a necessary property of money.

Strategic dependence A situation in which one firm's actions with respect to price, quality, advertising, and related changes may be strategically countered by the reactions of one or more other firms in the industry. Such dependence can exist only when there are a limited number of major firms in an industry.

Strategy Any rule that is used to make a choice, such as "Always pick heads"; any potential choice that can be made by players in a game.

Strikebreakers Temporary or permanent workers hired by a company to replace union members who are striking.

Structural unemployment Unemployment resulting from fundamental changes in the structure of the economy. It occurs, for example, when the demand for a product falls drastically so that workers specializing in the production of that product find themselves out of work.

Subsidy A negative tax; a payment to a producer from the government, usually in the form of a cash grant.

Substitutes Two goods are substitutes when either one can be used for consumption to satisfy a similar want—for example, coffee and tea. The more you buy of one, the less you buy of the other. For substitutes, the change in the price of one causes a shift in demand for the other in the same direction as the price change.

Substitution effect The tendency of people to substitute cheaper commodities for more expensive commodities.

Supply A schedule showing the relationship between price and quantity supplied for a specified period of time, other things being equal.

Supply curve The graphical representation of the supply schedule; a line (curve) showing the supply schedule, which generally slopes upward (has a positive slope), other things being equal.

Supply-side economics The notion that creating incentives for individuals and firms to increase productivity will cause the aggregate supply curve to shift outward.

Surplus A situation in which quantity supplied is greater than quantity demanded at a price above the market clearing price.

Sympathy strike A strike by a union in sympathy with another union's strike or cause.

Target price A price set by the government for specific agricultural products. If the market clearing price is below the target price, a *deficiency payment*, equal to the difference between the market price and the target price, is given to farmers for each unit of the good they produce.

Tariffs Taxes on imported goods.

Tax bracket A specified interval of income to which a specific and unique marginal tax rate is applied.

Tax incidence The distribution of tax burdens among various groups in society.

Technology Society's pool of applied knowledge concerning how goods and services can be produced.

Terms of exchange The terms under which trading takes place. Usually the terms of exchange are equal to the price at which a good is traded.

Theory of contestable markets A hypothesis concerning pricing behavior that holds that even though there are only a few firms in an industry, they are forced to price their products more or less competitively because of the ease of entry by outsiders. The key aspect of a contestable market is relatively costless entry into and exit from the industry.

Theory of public choice The study of collective decision making.

Third parties Parties who are not directly involved in a given activity or transaction. For example, in the relationship between caregivers and patients, fees may be paid by third parties (insurance companies, government).

Thrift institutions Financial institutions that receive most of their funds from the savings of the public; they include mutual savings banks, savings and loan associations, and credit unions

Time deposit A deposit in a financial institution that requires notice of intent to withdraw or must be left for an agreed period. Withdrawal of funds prior to the end of the agreed period may result in a penalty.

Tit-for-tat strategic behavior In game theory, cooperation that continues so long as the other players continue to cooperate.

Total costs The sum of total fixed costs and total variable costs.

Total income The yearly amount earned by the nation's resources (factors of production). Total income therefore includes wages, rent, interest payments, and profits that are received, respectively, by workers, landowners, capital owners, and entrepreneurs.

Total revenues The price per unit times the total quantity sold.

Transaction costs All of the costs associated with exchanging, including the informational costs of finding out price and quality, service record, and durability of a product, plus the cost of contracting and enforcing that contract.

Transactions accounts Checking account balances in commercial banks and other types of financial institutions, such as credit unions and mutual savings banks; any accounts in financial institutions on which you can easily write checks without many restrictions.

Transactions approach A method of measuring the money supply by looking at money as a medium of exchange.

Transactions demand Holding money as a medium of exchange to make payments. The level varies directly with nominal national income.

Transfer payments Money payments made by governments to individuals for which in return no services or goods are concurrently rendered. Examples are welfare, Social Security, and unemployment insurance benefits.

Transfers in kind Payments that are in the form of actual goods and services, such as food stamps, low-cost public housing, and medical care, and for which in return no goods or services are rendered concurrently.

Traveler's checks Financial instruments purchased from a bank or a nonbanking organization and signed during purchase that can be used as cash upon a second signature by the purchaser.

Unanticipated inflation Inflation at a rate that comes as a surprise, either higher or lower than the rate anticipated.

Unemployment The total number of adults (aged 16 years or older) who are willing and able to work and who are actively looking for work but have not found a job.

Union shop A business enterprise that allows the hiring of nonunion members, conditional on their joining the union by some specified date after employment begins.

Unit elasticity of demand A demand relationship in which the quantity demanded changes exactly in proportion to the change in price. Total expenditures are invariant to price changes in the unit-elastic portion of the demand curve.

Unit of accounting A measure by which prices are expressed; the common denominator of the price system; a central property of money.

Unlimited liability A legal concept whereby the personal assets of the owner of a firm can be seized to pay off the firm's debts.

Util A representative unit by which utility is measured.

Utility The want-satisfying power of a good or service.

Utility analysis The analysis of consumer decision making based on utility maximization.

Value added The dollar value of an industry's sales minus the value of intermediate goods (for example, raw materials and parts) used in production.

Variable costs Costs that vary with the rate of production. They include wages paid to workers and purchases of materials.

Vertical merger The joining of a firm with another to which it sells an output or from which it buys an input.

Voluntary exchange An act of trading, done on a voluntary basis, in which both parties to the trade are subjectively better off after the exchange.

Voluntary import expansion (VIE) An official agreement with another country in which it agrees to import more from the United States.

Voluntary restraint agreement (VRA) An official agreement with another country that "voluntarily" restricts the quantity of its exports to the Unted States.

Wait unemployment Unemployment that is caused by wage rigidities resulting from minimum wages, unions, and other factors.

Wants What people would buy if their incomes were unlimited.

Wealth The stock of assets owned by a person, household, firm, or nation. For a household, wealth can consist of a house, cars, personal belongings, bank accounts, and cash.

World Trade Organization (WTO) The successor organization to GATT, it handles all trade disputes among its 132 member nations.

***x* axis** The horizontal axis in a graph.

***y* axis** The vertical axis in a graph.

Zero-sum game A game in which any gains within the group are exactly offset by equal losses by the end of the game.

INDEX